Ellen L. Jacobs

ANN SERANNE'S
Good Food
Without Meat

BY THE SAME AUTHOR...

The Art of Egg Cookery
Your Home Freezer
The Complete Book of Home Preserving
The Complete Book of Home Baking
Delectable Desserts
The Complete Book of Desserts
The Epicure's Companion (with John Tebbel)
The Complete Book of Home Freezing
America Cooks (Ed.)
The Pots and Pans Cookbook (with Joan Wilson)
The Best of American Cooking
Ann Seranne's Good Food & How to Cook It

With Eileen Gaden (photographer) . . .

The Blender Cookbook
The Best of Near Eastern Cookery
The Church and Club Woman's Companion
The Sandwich Book

ANN SERANNE'S
Good Food Without Meat

by Ann Seranne

William Morrow & Company, Inc.   New York   1973

Dedicated affectionately to my patient friend,
Barbara Wolferman, who had to forego many a steak dinner
during the testing of these meatless dishes

Copyright © 1973 by Ann Seranne

All rights reserved. No part of this book may be reproduced or
utilized in any form or by any means, electronic or mechanical, including photocopying, recording or by any information storage and
retrieval system, without permission in writing from the Publisher.
Inquiries should be addressed to William Morrow and Company,
Inc., 105 Madison Ave., New York, N.Y. 10016.

Printed in the United States of America.

Library of Congress Catalog Card Number 72-9563

ISBN 0-688-00159-9

1 2 3 4 5 77 76 75 74 73

Contents

Introduction

What we eat is a matter of custom and habit. As late as the fifth century B.C., the Caucasians believed that their grandfather was immortalized if he were sacrificed and eaten by his progeny, that he lived on in the off-spring who consumed his roasted flesh. It was a disgrace to allow him to die a natural death. In prehistoric times, the eating of human flesh was taken as much for granted as the eating of animal flesh. Human brains and liver were considered great delicacies, human eyes, cheeks, thighs, and buttocks were considered the choice parts, and human blood was drunk avidly at victory celebrations.

In the historical cookbook, *Cooks, Gluttons and Gourmets* by Betty Wason, the author suggests that it may have been a mystic urge that caused primitive man to eat his ancestors, but that cannibalism has had its practical rationalizations as well. An eighteenth-century cannibal chief in Brazil explained, "When I have slain an enemy, it is surely better to eat him than to let him go to waste."

Mrs. Wason relates that "In the Upper Congo, as late as the seventeenth century, living men, women, and children were bought and sold frankly as articles of food. A century later, on the island of New Britain, human meat was offered in butcher stalls along with animal flesh. Savages on the Solomon Islands fattened women for a feast just like pigs; they ranked female flesh as preferable to that of dogs because 'dogs taste of otter.'" Yet the dog had been considered a succulent dish by nations considerably more advanced in civilization and in the culinary arts. The Greeks ate dogs. Hippocrates considered dog a light and wholesome supper dish, and the Romans prepared it in much the same manner as we prepare hare today.

Have we really evolved very far from these primitive customs? The offering of Grace before the host carves the blood-rare roast beef, the suckling pig with the rosy apple in its mouth, or the plump-breasted turkey is very reminiscent of the prayer that primitive man offered up to his god during the ceremony of sacrifice.

For many years now I have found myself questioning and criticizing the meat-eating society in which we live. As a person with a growing interest in Truth and in God-man relationships, I find it very difficult to condone the slaughtering of domesticated animals for human consumption. On the other hand, as a cook and a lover of good food, I cannot imagine foregoing the pleasure of such by-products of animal husbandry as eggs, milk, cream, butter, and cheese. Yet, we can't have one without the other. To be a true vegetarian one must restrict one's eating to vegetables, fruits, nuts, and legumes and wear only man-made shoes and clothing. But in trying to practice vegetarianism either as a protest against the slaughterhouses or for reasons of religion, one becomes involved in the complications of present-day ecology. To enjoy eggs, there must be hens raised to lay them, but for every female chick born there is a cock, and one cock can service an entire henyard. For every cow born, there is likely to be a bull. Modern methods of artificial insemination make the sperm of one prize bull available to farmers across the country.

What can we do with the excess cocks and bulls? Must we put them out to pasture and feed and care for them to a ripe old age? Or do we philosophize, like the Brazilian cannibal, that it is surely better to use them to feed the human race than to let them go to waste?

Perhaps in a few hundred years we will have evolved to a higher state of consciousness and, with the help of science, can and will become a race of vegetarians who recognize that every living animal cherishes the gift of life.

The monumental advances that have taken place in the field of genetics in the past twenty years bring this dream into the realm of possibility and, according to a recent article by Dr. Braxton B. Sawyer, has caused some of our leading scientists to predict that "within the next ten years it will be possible for a woman to walk into a kind of commissary which would contain day-old embryos in frozen packets labeled to describe the sex, physical characteristics, type of temperament and IQ likely to be present in the full-grown individual. After making a selection, she could take the packet to her physician and have the embryo implanted in her uterus where it will mature for nine months like a normally conceived pregnancy."

If this is to be our brave new world, then science can conceivably enable the farmer to control the sex of his farm animals to such an extent that he can produce mainly egg-laying hens and milk-producing cows, and there will be no excess cocks or bulls to go to waste.

Meanwhile there is a surprising number of young men and women who are having serious thoughts on the subject of vegetarianism. Many have already given up eating meat and have found that they have lost nothing in the way of health, vitality, and strength. There is a rapidly increasing number of restaurants operated by young people where only vegetarian dishes are served, and theirs is good food, it is satisfying food. These young people are gravely concerned with the rapid depletion of our soil and the fact that DDT, other dangerous chemicals, and synthetic hormones are found in animal flesh. But they have spiritual concerns as well, if not downright mystical ones. A recent article in *Time* magazine quoted California's Wheeler as saying, "When carrion is consumed, people are really greedy." It went on to say that "Others maintain that food is the determining factor in the biological conditions in man that produce wars, brutality, and narrow thinking."

The youth of today are not willing to remain within the emotional or intellectual confines of the past. They are seeking the truth and they are discovering the universal law of love, which works whenever it is applied. Their God did not create creatures with the capacity to feel pain, fear, friendship, and affection to be used for food.

Whether you eat meat or don't eat meat is a personal matter. If you can justify vegetarianism in your own mind, you will find this book useful. I do not consider it a strictly vegetarian cookbook, because I have used animal by-products lavishly in the recipes. And so, until the lion lies down with the lamb, it will serve best the budget minded who find the price of good hamburger today staggering; those who wish to eat more simply, more lightly; and everyone who enjoys good honest food—meatless or not—delicious dishes made from beans, nuts, whole grains and cereals, pasta, and, of course, fruits and vegetables.

ANN SERANNE

SOUPS

Vegetable Soups

Soup can be an economical source of fine nutrition, either as an appetizer to begin a meal or as a satisfying main dish at luncheon or supper when accompanied by a hot bread and a salad.

Not all soups depend on a rich beef or chicken stock for their flavor. The wonderful raw vegetable soups of Spain—the Gazpacho-style soups, which you will find in the chapter on raw vegetables—are meatless, and the world-famous French onion soup, with its legendary restorative powers, served in the Paris markets, is frequently made with water. As a matter of fact, France has a great variety of delicate vegetable soups, hearty vegetable chowders, and unctuous bean purées which use only water or vegetable broth for the liquid. These are known as *maigre* soups, in the Lenten sense of "meatless" rather than lean, meager, or emaciated. There is nothing emaciated about the soups that follow. They are rich in the wonderful flavors that only fresh vegetables can give them. Some are actually lean, but only in calories, not in vitality; others are enriched with cream or with cream and eggs. So, it is with some truly noble soups, whose nobility lies in their simplicity, that we begin this meatless book.

POTAGE BONNE FEMME MAIGRE
(Leek, Potato, Onion, and Cabbage Soup)

Serves 6

BUY THE FRESHEST POSSIBLE

Bunch of leeks
3 medium potatoes
2 medium onions
1 small cabbage
Bunch of parsley

HAVE ON HAND	*COOKWARE*
Butter	Large soup kettle
Salt and pepper	Small skillet
Garlic	
Bread	

1. Discard the green leaves of *4 leeks.* Trim ends and wash very carefully to remove any sand. Chop the leeks. Peel and chop the *potatoes* and *onions.* Fill the tea kettle with *water* and bring to a boil.

2. In a large heavy soup kettle melt *2 tablespoons butter.* Cook the chopped vegetables in it over low heat for 3 minutes, stirring constantly. Add *8 cups boiling water* and *salt and pepper to taste.* Simmer gently for 30 minutes.

3. Meanwhile wash, core, and shred the *cabbage;* discard stems from *parsley* and chop it; peel and mince *1 clove garlic.*

4. Add cabbage, parsley, and garlic to the soup and continue to simmer for 30 minutes longer.

5. While the soup simmers, dice *2 slices of bread* and brown the cubes in *2 tablespoons butter* in a small skillet.

6. Ladle the soup into soup plates and sprinkle with croutons.

SOUP À L'OIGNON MAIGRE
(French Onion Soup)

Serves 6. Peel onions under running water and wear your sunglasses when you slice them. You won't cry.

BUY

6 large Spanish onions
Small loaf French bread

HAVE ON HAND

Garlic
Butter
Lemon
Black peppercorns

Salt
Parmesan, Gruyère, *or* Swiss cheese
Beer

COOKWARE

5-quart saucepan *or* soup kettle
Baking sheet
Individual earthenware casseroles

IN ADVANCE:

1. Peel and thinly slice the *onions*. Peel and mince *1 large clove garlic*.

2. In saucepan slowly melt *½ cup butter (1 stick)*. Add the onions and garlic and stew over medium heat for 15 minutes, or until onions are wilted and transparent but not browned, stirring often to separate onion slices into rings.

3. Add *4 cups water, juice of ½ lemon, ½ teaspoon freshly ground pepper,* and *salt to taste*. Bring to a boil, then simmer for 30 minutes. Correct seasoning. Set aside and reheat when needed.

4. Meanwhile slice the *French bread,* place on baking sheet, and toast in hot oven or under broiler until golden on both sides. Grate a *heaping bowl of cheese*.

TO FINISH AND SERVE:

5. Preheat oven to 375° F. Stir *½ cup beer* into the hot soup. Ladle onions and liquid into earthenware casseroles and set casseroles on baking sheet. Top each serving with a slice of toast, sprinkle liberally with cheese, and dot with *butter*. Bake in the hot oven for 5 minutes, or until cheese melts and becomes crusty.

6. Serve *additional cheese and crusty bread* on the side.

A MINESTRONE is nothing more than a wholesome vegetable soup to which you may add practically any vegetable you happen to have around— hence there are as many variations of it as there are cooks in Italy. But always serve minestrone with a large bowl of freshly grated Parmesan cheese and slices of hot Italian bread.

MINESTRONE DI VERDURA
(Minestrone with Greens)

Serves 6. Here is a basic recipe to which you may add peas, string beans, zucchini, parsnips, turnips, cabbage—whatever and as much as you wish.

BUY

1 pound fresh lima beans *or* peas
1 head of escarole *or* romaine
¼ pound spinach
6 small beets
8-ounce box elbow macaroni *or* small pasta tubes

HAVE ON HAND

2 stalks celery
2 small onions
1 carrot
Salt
Peppercorns
Olive oil
Dried marjoram
Parmesan cheese

COOKWARE

Large soup kettle
Small skillet

1. Shell the *lima beans or peas.* Wash and chop the *escarole or romaine* and the *spinach.* Peel and dice the *beets;* chop *2 stalks celery;* peel and chop *2 small onions* and *1 carrot.*

2. Place the lima beans, escarole, spinach, beets, and celery in a large pot. Add *1½ teaspoons salt, ¼ teaspoon freshly ground pepper,* and *enough water to cover* the vegetables. Cover pot and bring liquid to a boil. Reduce heat and simmer for 10 minutes.

3. In skillet, heat *2 tablespoons olive oil* and in it sauté the onions and carrot until onions are soft. Add to the hot vegetables, along with *¼ teaspoon marjoram,* and simmer for 30 minutes.

4. Meanwhile grate *½ cup cheese* and set aside. Cook the macaroni less than al dente, drain, and stir into soup. Simmer for 5 minutes, uncovered.

5. Serve in hot soup bowls with grated Parmesan sprinkled on top.

QUICK MINESTRONE

Serves 4 to 6

BUY

1-pound can Italian-style tomatoes with basil
1 pint tomato juice
1-pound can garbanzos *or* chick peas
Small loaf Italian bread

HAVE ON HAND	COOKWARE
Garlic	Large saucepan
Small onion	
2 stalks celery with leaves	
1 medium carrot	
Parsley	
Salad oil	
Sage	
Pepper	
Salt	
Instant rice	
Grated Parmesan cheese	

1. Peel and mince *1 clove garlic* and *1 small onion*. Slice *2 stalks celery with leaves*. Peel and chop *the carrot*. Chop *2 tablespoons parsley*.

2. In saucepan sauté garlic, onion, and celery in *2 tablespoons oil* until onion is tender.

3. Add the *tomatoes, tomato juice,* and the *carrot;* drain the *chick peas,* and add them along with *a pinch of sage, ⅛ teaspoon pepper,* and *salt to taste.*

4. Bring to a boil. Then add *½ cup instant rice* and the chopped parsley, and simmer for 5 minutes. Serve with a bowl of *grated Parmesan cheese,* and *a loaf of hot crusty Italian bread.*

VEGETARIAN BORSCHT

Serves 4 to 6

BUY

1 small cabbage
3 medium carrots
1 parsnip
3 medium beets
8-ounce can tomato purée
8-ounce container dairy sour cream
Bread

HAVE ON HAND

1 medium onion
Garlic
3 medium potatoes
Cooking oil
Bay leaves
Salt and pepper

COOKWARE

Large heavy saucepan

1. Peel and chop *1 onion*. Remove any discolored outer leaves from *cabbage;* quarter, and discard thick core. Shred cabbage. Peel the *carrots, parsnip,* and *beets* and cut into thin julienne strips. Peel *1 large clove garlic* and mince. Peel and dice the *potatoes.*

2. In heavy saucepan heat *2 tablespoons cooking oil.* Add the prepared onion, carrots, parsnip, and beets, and sauté for 5 to 8 minutes, or until onion is golden, stirring frequently. Add *6 cups water,* the garlic, *2 bay leaves,* potatoes, and the *tomato purée.* Bring liquid to a boil, season to taste with *salt and pepper,* and simmer for about 45 minutes, or until vegetables are soft. Add shredded cabbage and simmer for 15 minutes, longer.

3. Serve with hot crusty bread and top each serving with a big dollop of sour cream.

POTAGE SANTÉ
(Soup for the Health)

Serves 6. Salad greens of almost any kind may be used in this soup.

BUY

2 heads lettuce *or* romaine
1 bunch scallions
A handful fresh spinach
Bunch water cress

HAVE ON HAND

Butter
Salt and pepper
Lemon

COOKWARE

Large heavy saucepan

1. Fill the tea kettle and set to boil.

2. Wash the *lettuce or romaine.* Use only the outer leaves, reserving the hearts for salad. Shred the outer leaves. Trim, wash, and chop the *scallions.* Wash *spinach* and *water cress,* and discard any thick stems.

3. In heavy saucepan melt *2 tablespoons butter.* Add the scallions and cook over low heat, stirring constantly for 5 minutes. Add the lettuce, spinach, water cress, *6 cups boiling water,* and *salt and pepper to taste.* Simmer, uncovered, for about 30 minutes.

4. Just before serving, add *lemon juice to taste.*

VEGETABLE GUMBO

Serves 2 or 3

BUY

1 pound zucchini
Parsley
1-pound can stewed tomatoes
10-ounce package frozen okra

HAVE ON HAND

Onion
Celery
Butter
Bay leaf
Salt and pepper
Dried basil
Cayenne
Raw rice

COOKWARE

2-quart saucepan

1. Peel and mince *1 small onion*. Chop *enough celery to measure* ½ *cup*. Wash, trim, and slice the *zucchini*. Chop *2 tablespoons parsley*.

2. In saucepan melt *2 tablespoons butter* and in it sauté the onion and celery for 5 minutes. Stir in *tomatoes with the liquid* and *1 cup water*. Add *1 bay leaf, ½ teaspoon salt, or to taste, ⅛ teaspoon pepper, ½ teaspoon basil,* and *a good dash cayenne*. Bring to a boil, then simmer over low heat for 15 minutes.

3. Add *zucchini* and *2 tablespoons raw rice,* and simmer for 10 minutes. Add *okra* and parsley and cook over low heat for 10 minutes longer. Serve steaming hot.

Chowders & Bisques

Next in line are some soups which, although basically *maigre,* become a little fatter in calories with the addition of heavy cream. These are the simplest kind of creamed soups; seasoned with nothing more than salt and pepper, they allow the wonderful flavor of fresh vegetables to come through. You may add a favorite herb, fresh or dried, if you wish. Tarragon and dill are always great soup herbs, but you may prefer a little sweet marjoram or a bay leaf. Milk or a mixture of milk and cream may be substituted for the heavy cream, but the soup will not be quite so delicious.

These soups may be either chunky or smooth. If you purée the vegetables in a food mill or a blender, the soups fall into the category of vegetable bisques; if you leave the vegetables in small pieces, they are classified as vegetable chowders. Either way, garnish them with chopped parsley, chives, dill, or celery leaves.

CREAM OF CELERY SOUP

Serves 2 or 3

BUY

Head of fresh celery
8-ounce container heavy cream

HAVE ON HAND	*COOKWARE*
Onion	Saucepan
Salt and pepper	Electric blender

1. Wash and slice thinly *enough fresh celery to measure 2 cups*. Peel and mince *1 small onion*.

2. Put the vegetables in a saucepan with *2 cups water* and *salt to taste*. Bring to a boil and simmer for about 15 minutes, or until celery is tender. Set aside until ready to serve, or blend vegetables and liquid in an electric blender and return to saucepan.

3. When ready to serve, chop a *few celery leaves* for garnish. Return the soup to a simmer. Stir in the *heavy cream;* heat, stirring constantly, until steaming hot. Add *lots of freshly ground black pepper,* and serve each portion with a topping of chopped celery.

VARIATIONS: In place of the celery use any one of the following vegetables or a combination of them: sliced carrots or parsnips; chopped fresh broccoli or cauliflower; freshly shucked peas or lima beans; sliced zucchini or summer squash; peeled and diced winter squash, sweet potatoes, or white potatoes; chopped fresh mushrooms; a 10-ounce package of frozen chopped spinach or baby limas.

CURRIED CREAM OF ZUCCHINI SOUP

Serves 4

BUY

1 pound fresh young zucchini
8-ounce container heavy cream
Chives

HAVE ON HAND

Butter
Shallots *or* green onions
Garlic
Curry powder
Salt
White pepper
Milk

COOKWARE

Medium saucepan

1. Wash, trim, and slice *zucchini* thinly. Put into a saucepan with *2 tablespoons butter, 2 tablespoons minced shallots or green onions, 2 cloves garlic,* peeled and minced, *1 teaspoon curry powder, ½ teaspoon salt,* and *¼ teaspoon white pepper.* Cook over low heat for 5 minutes, shaking pan frequently.

2. Add *½ cup water* and simmer for 10 minutes, stirring occasionally.

3. Rub vegetables through a food mill or purée in blender.

4. Return to saucepan and stir in the *cream* and *1 cup milk.* Carefully reheat and serve hot, or chill and serve cold, with *chopped chives* on top.

LEEK AND POTATO SOUP

Serves 4. This is a peasant soup from France, and is always served steaming hot for supper. It was originally made with water and cream, but when it was refined by Louis Diat in America, he substituted a rich chicken stock for the water, puréed the vegetables, and served the soup cold—the result was the popular "vichyssoise."

BUY

2 large leeks
8-ounce container heavy cream
Chives

HAVE ON HAND

Medium onion
Butter
3 medium potatoes
Salt
Black peppercorns

COOKWARE

Large saucepan

1. Trim root ends from *leeks.* Cut off and discard most of the long green stems, leaving just the palest part of the green above the white part. Slit leeks lengthwise from stem end, then turn and slit once more. Rinse well, separating the leaves, under cold running water. Dry, then chop into small pieces. Peel and chop *1 medium onion.*

2. Sauté the chopped leeks and onion in *3 tablespoons butter* for 5 minutes, without letting them brown.

3. Meanwhile peel and dice *3 medium potatoes.* Add the potatoes to the onions and leeks along with *3 cups water;* bring to a boil, then simmer for 15 minutes, or until potatoes are tender. Season with *salt* and *freshly ground black pepper.* Stir in *cream* and bring just to a boil. Serve hot with *chopped chives.*

VICHYSSOISE DIAT

Serves 8

BUY

Bunch of leeks
5 medium potatoes
1 quart milk
1 pint heavy cream
Chives

HAVE ON HAND	*COOKWARE*
1 medium onion	Large heavy saucepan
Butter	
1 quart chicken broth	
(*or* use water)	
Salt	

1. Discard all of the green parts from *4 large leeks;* wash the remaining white parts thoroughly and carefully, for they are often full of sand, and slice. Peel and slice *1 medium onion.* Peel and thickly slice the *5 potatoes.*

2. In a large heavy saucepan melt *½ stick (¼ cup) butter,* and in it sauté the leeks and onion until the onion is golden. Add the potatoes and *1 quart chicken broth or water;* bring to a boil, then simmer for 35 minutes, or until potatoes are very tender. Rub soup through a strainer or food mill, or blend it 2 cups at a time in an electric blender.

3. Return the puréed soup to the saucepan and stir in *3 cups milk* and *1 cup of the cream.* Add salt to taste, and bring to a boil, then cool and once again rub through the strainer. Chill.

4. Stir in *remaining cup of cream,* and serve garnished with *chopped chives.*

BLUSHING VICHYSSOISE

Serves 6

BUY

Leeks
8-ounce container heavy cream

HAVE ON HAND	*COOKWARE*
Potatoes	Large saucepan
Carrots	
Milk	
Salt	
White pepper	

1. Peel and dice *enough potatoes to measure 2 cups*. Scrape and slice *enough carrots to measure 1¼ cups*. Trim, wash carefully, and slice the *white part of 2 leeks*.

2. Put all the vegetables in a saucepan and add *2 cups water* and *1 teaspoon salt*. Bring to a boil, then simmer for 25 minutes, or until vegetables are very tender.

3. Rub liquid and vegetables through a food mill, or purée in an electric blender. Pour into a mixing bowl. Stir in *1 cup milk, a dash of white pepper,* and the *heavy cream*. Cool, then chill.

4. Before serving, shred a *little raw carrot*. Serve the soup icy cold with a garnish of the shredded carrot on top.

QUICK CORN CHOWDER

Serves 4

BUY

1-pound can cream-style corn

HAVE ON HAND	*COOKWARE*
Onion	Saucepan
Green pepper	
Butter	
Milk *or* light cream	
Salt	
White pepper	

1. Peel and chop *enough onion to measure ½ cup*. Seed and chop *enough green pepper to measure ½ cup*.

2. In saucepan melt *2 tablespoons butter,* and in it sauté onion and green pepper over low heat for 10 minutes, or until onion is tender but not browned.

3. Add *corn, 2 cups milk or light cream,* and *salt* and *white pepper to taste*. Mix well and heat to serving temperature.

SIMPLE AND SIMPLY DELICIOUS
CREAM OF TOMATO SOUP

Serves 4

BUY

1 pint cream (light *or* heavy)
1-pound can stewed tomatoes

HAVE ON HAND   COOKWARE

Salt   2 small saucepans
Peppercorns
Parsley, chives, *or* fresh sweet basil
Dry vermouth (optional)

1. Heat *cream* in a saucepan until scalding hot.

2. In another saucepan, heat *stewed tomatoes* and season to taste with *salt* and *freshly ground black pepper.*

3. Chop 2 *tablespoons parsley, chives, or sweet basil.*

4. When ready to serve, stir the tomatoes into the hot cream. Serve with a garnish of the chopped parsley or chives or basil. *A last-minute dash of dry vermouth* will give this soup an unusual extra bit of flavor.

CREAM OF FRESH ASPARAGUS SOUP

Serves 6

BUY

1 bunch fresh asparagus (1 pound)
8-ounce container heavy cream

HAVE ON HAND	*COOKWARE*
1 medium onion	3-quart saucepan with lid
Butter	Small saucepan
Chicken broth *or* water	
Salt and pepper	
Mace	
Milk	
Lemon	

1. Snap off tough white portion of *asparagus stalks* and discard. With vegetable peeler, strip scales off stalks to remove any sand lurking beneath. Soak in cold water for 5 minutes. Drain and cut off tips. Set tips aside and cut remaining stalks into 1-inch lengths. Peel and chop *1 medium onion.*

2. In saucepan melt *2 tablespoons butter,* and in it sauté the onion for 5 minutes. Add *all the asparagus except the tips* and *2 cups chicken broth or water.* Season with *salt and pepper to taste,* and *a dash of mace.* Bring to a boil, cover, and cook over low heat for 30 minutes.

3. Meanwhile put *asparagus tips* in a small saucepan. Cover with boiling salted water and simmer for 10 minutes. Drain, reserving the *liquid,* and set aside.

4. Force cooked asparagus stalks and their liquid through a sieve, or purée a couple of cups at a time in an electric blender. Return to saucepan. Measure reserved liquid from the tips; if necessary, add *milk* to measure 2 cups. Add to soup. Stir in *1 teaspoon lemon juice.* Cool soup and then chill.

5. Just before serving, stir in the *cream* and the asparagus tips.

SPINACH SCHAV

Serves 6

BUY

10-ounce package frozen chopped spinach
Pint dairy sour cream
2 cucumbers

<table>
<tr><td>*HAVE ON HAND*</td><td>*COOKWARE*</td></tr>
</table>

HAVE ON HAND	*COOKWARE*
Salt and pepper	Saucepan
Lemon	

1. Put *spinach* into saucepan with *2 cups water* and *1 teaspoon salt* and *¼ teaspoon pepper*. Bring to a boil, then simmer for 10 minutes.

2. Remove from heat and stir in *juice of 1 lemon*. Cool and chill.

3. Stir in the *sour cream* and *2 cucumbers,* peeled, seeded, and chopped.

VEGETABLE STEW WITH CHEESE

Serves 4

BUY

1 large ripe tomato *or* 8-ounce can whole tomatoes
1 bunch parsley
Cheddar cheese, aged
1 pint heavy cream

HAVE ON HAND	*COOKWARE*
Potatoes	Saucepan with cover
1 medium onion	
Celery	
1 medium carrot	
Salt	
White peppercorns	

1. Peel and dice *enough potatoes to measure 2 cups*. Peel and dice *1 medium onion*. Wash and slice *1 large stalk celery with leaves,* and *1 medium carrot*.

2. Put all the prepared vegetables in a saucepan with *1 cup boiling water or enough to cover,* and *1 teaspoon salt*. Cut stems off bunch of *parsley;* set aside the leaves; tie the stems with string and add them to the saucepan. Cover and simmer vegetables for 15 minutes.

3. While vegetables are cooking, peel, seed, and chop the *tomato;* also chop *½ cup parsley leaves*. Shred *¼ cup cheddar cheese*. Set aside.

4. Remove parsley stems and discard. Add the parsley leaves and cheese to the soup. Add *lots of freshly ground white pepper,* and gradually stir in the *heavy cream.* Heat to serving temperature. Just before serving stir in the chopped tomato. Remove soup from heat, and let stand for 2 minutes before serving.

Soups Thickened with Flour

Another type of creamy vegetable soups is thickened with a little flour or cooked potato before the cream is added. If such soups are made with water, which allows the full flavor of fresh vegetables to come through, they are still known as *maigre.* You may, however, use part or all chicken broth—or, better still, use the cooking liquid from mild-flavored vegetables, such as peas, asparagus, carrots, string beans, and so on if the vegetable is specified in the recipe. The first recipe below takes advantage of any vegetable left over from dinner the previous day.

CREAM OF LEFTOVER-VEGETABLE SOUP

Serves 4

BUY

8-ounce container cream

HAVE ON HAND   *COOKWARE*

1 small onion   Saucepan
Butter
Flour *or* leftover potatoes
Chicken *or* vegetable broth
  (optional)

1 cup leftover cooked vegetable *or*
   a combination of leftovers
   (spinach, carrots, cauliflower,
   broccoli, Brussels sprouts, celery,
   asparagus, peas)
Celery salt
Salt
White pepper
Parsley, chives, *or* celery leaves

1. Peel and mince *1 small onion*, and sauté in *3 tablespoons butter* over low heat for about 5 minutes, or until onion is tender.

2. Stir in *3 tablespoons flour or ½ cup cooked potatoes*, then gradually stir in *1½ cups water or broth*. Add the *leftover vegetable (or vegetables)*, and *½ teaspoon celery salt*. Bring to a boil, then simmer for 10 minutes.

3. Purée the soup in a food mill, or blend 2 cups at a time in an electric blender. Return purée to saucepan, and stir in the *cream* and *salt and white pepper to taste*.

4. Chop *a little parsley, chives, or celery leaves*. Serve the soup hot or cold, sprinkling each serving with a little of the chopped garnish.

POTAGE SAINT GERMAIN

Serves 8

BUY

2 pounds unshelled fresh peas
8-ounce container heavy cream

HAVE ON HAND

Parsley
Carrot
Onion
Potato
Butter

Flour
Vegetable broth (optional)
Salt and pepper

COOKWARE

2 large saucepans
1 lid

1. Chop *2 tablespoons parsley* and set aside. Wash and shell *peas,* reserving the *pods.* Scrape and slice *1 carrot.* Peel and slice *1 onion* and *1 potato.* Put these vegetables, with the pods of the peas, into a large saucepan with *2 tablespoons butter.* Cover and braise over low heat for 10 minutes.

2. Sprinkle the vegetables with *2 tablespoons flour* and add *6 cups water or vegetable broth.* Bring liquid to a boil, then cover and cook over low heat for 10 minutes. Strain the liquid through a sieve, pressing through as much of the soft vegetables as possible into a clean saucepan. Stir in *salt and pepper to taste.* Add the peas and simmer for 8 minutes, or until peas are tender. Add the *cream* and chopped parsley.

MUSHROOM BISQUE

Serves 4. This soup is just as good if it is not blended to a purée. Just change its name to "chowder."

BUY

½ pound fresh mushrooms
8-ounce container heavy cream

HAVE ON HAND

Onion
Butter
Flour
Chicken broth (optional)
Salt
White pepper
Dry sherry
Sour cream (optional)

COOKWARE

Saucepan

1. Wash *mushrooms* and trim stem ends. Slice caps and mince stems. Peel and mince *1 medium onion.*

2. In saucepan melt *3 tablespoons butter,* and in it cook the onion over low heat until onion is tender. Add the mushrooms, and continue to

cook over low heat for 10 minutes, or until mushrooms are tender, stirring frequently.

3. Stir in *3 tablespoons flour*. Gradually stir in *2 cups water or broth, ½ teaspoon salt, or to taste,* and *¼ teaspoon white pepper.* Simmer for 30 minutes. Purée in an electric blender and return to saucepan.

4. Stir in *heavy cream* and *2 tablespoons sherry* and heat to serving temperature. Serve with a topping of *sour cream,* if desired.

CUCUMBER MINT SOUP

Serves 4. This is a cool treat for blistering summer days.

BUY

3 firm cucumbers
Bunch of fresh mint
8-ounce container heavy cream

HAVE ON HAND	*COOKWARE*
Medium onion	Saucepan with cover
Butter	
Cooking oil	
Flour	
Chicken broth (optional)	
Salt and pepper	

1. Peel *1 cucumber* and slice. Wash *a second cucumber;* this time leave on the green skin but trim the ends; slice the cucumber. Peel and slice *1 medium onion.*

2. Put all of the cucumber and onion slices in the saucepan with *2 tablespoons butter, 1 tablespoon cooking oil,* and *3 tablespoons water.* Cover and cook over low heat for 30 minutes, or until vegetables are tender.

3. Stir in *3 tablespoons flour* and *2 cups water or broth,* and *salt and white pepper to taste.* Continue stirring over moderate heat until the liquid begins to boil. Remove from heat, then rub through a strainer or food mill, or blend 2 cups at a time in an electric blender. Return soup to the saucepan.

4. Stir in ¾ *cup cream* and *1 tablespoon chopped fresh mint.* Either heat and serve, or cool, then chill, and serve on a bed of crushed ice.

5. Garnish each serving with *a little shredded cucumber* and *a sprig of mint.*

CREAM OF TOMATO SOUP

Serves 4

BUY

5 large ripe tomatoes
Small can tomato paste
1 pint heavy cream
Fresh dill

HAVE ON HAND	*COOKWARE*
Medium onion	Saucepan with cover
Garlic	
Salt and black pepper	
Flour	
Sour cream (optional)	

1. Wash *tomatoes* and peel *1 medium onion.* Slice *4 of the tomatoes* and the onion into the saucepan. Add *1 teaspoon minced garlic,* ¼ *cup cold water,* and *a sprinkling of salt and pepper.* Cover and cook over low heat for 12 minutes.

2. Remove tomato mixture from heat, then stir in *2 tablespoons tomato paste, 3 tablespoons flour,* and *1½ cups water.* Return to heat; cook, stirring, until soup comes to a boil.

3. Rub soup through a strainer or food mill, or blend 2 cups at a time in an electric blender.

4. Let the soup cool to room temperature, then stir in *1½ cups cream* and *2 tablespoons finely chopped dill.* Peel the *remaining tomato,* discard seeds, and chop the flesh. Add to the soup and chill for several hours.

5. Serve in bowls surrounded by crushed ice. Top if desired with *a dollop of sour cream,* and garnish with *a sprig of dill.*

Soups Thickened with Eggs & Cream

Here we come to a group of wonderful soups that are still creamier than the preceding ones, thickened and enriched by means of both egg yolks and cream. And we begin with my favorite of ALL soups, French sorrel soup. One of the truly great soups of the world, it is made from the common garden weed known as sour grass. Sorrel is a perennial and so easy to grow that everyone with a square yard of earth in a sunny spot should sprinkle some sorrel seeds in early spring. The plants will supply your table constantly with the sour leaves until frost and will return again the next year. I doubt that any food chemist has analyzed it for vitamins and minerals, but I'm sure that anything as good as this soup must be good for you!

CREAM OF SORREL SOUP

Serves 4. Spinach may be used in place of the sorrel leaves, and if you flavor the soup just before serving with the juice of a lemon, the flavor will come close—close and yet so far.

BUY OR HARVEST

½ pound fresh sorrel leaves (2 large handfuls)
8-ounce container heavy cream

HAVE ON HAND

Onions *or* shallots
Butter
Chicken broth (optional)

Salt
Black peppercorns
1 egg yolk

COOKWARE

Saucepan

1. Wash and pick over *sorrel leaves*. Drain well. Cut out and discard the coarse center stem from the larger leaves and shred the sorrel thinly.

2. Peel and mince *1 small onion (or 4 shallots)* and sauté in *½ stick (¼ cup) butter* for 3 or 4 minutes, or until onion is transparent. Add the shredded sorrel to the saucepan, and cook for 5 minutes, or until the sorrel is wilted, stirring frequently.

NOTE: As fall approaches and you do not want the sorrel remaining in the garden to get frostbitten, harvest it and prepare it to this point in the recipe. The wilted sorrel-and-butter mixture freezes well and will allow you to enjoy a bowlful of this fabulous soup during the winter months. Cool the sorrel mixture, spoon into freezer bags, and seal. Defrost when desired and continue . . .

3. Add *2 cups water or chicken broth, ½ teaspoon salt, some freshly ground black pepper,* and bring to a boil. Simmer for 15 minutes.

4. When ready to serve, combine the *heavy cream* with *1 egg yolk* and *½ cup of the hot soup;* gradually stir this into the remaining soup. Cook the soup over low heat for 2 minutes, stirring rapidly and being careful not to let it boil. Serve immediately.

TCHORBA
(Sour Lettuce Soup)

Serves 6. Sour soups, such as Sorrel Soup, are beloved in most countries in Europe. From Bulgaria, comes this one made with lettuce and vinegar.

BUY

2 small heads tender young lettuce
Bunch green onions
Head of garlic
8-ounce container heavy cream
Parsley

HAVE ON HAND	*COOKWARE*
Chicken *or* vegetable broth (optional)	Saucepan
Salt and pepper	
Vinegar	
2 egg yolks	

1. Wash *lettuce,* separating the leaves. Shred leaves into the saucepan. Add *6 cups broth or water* and bring to a boil.

2. Meanwhile wash and mince *6 green onions,* using as much of the green stalks as possible. Peel and mince *6 cloves garlic.* Add onions and garlic to the simmering lettuce and simmer for 10 minutes.

3. Add *1 teaspoon salt, ¼ teaspoon pepper,* and *2 tablespoons vinegar;* simmer for 5 minutes longer.

4. Just before serving combine *2 egg yolks* and *½ cup heavy cream* with *½ cup of the hot broth.*

5. Remove soup from heat and slowly stir in the egg-cream mixture.

6. Sprinkle each portion with *chopped parsley.* Serve immediately.

WHITE TURNIP SOUP

Serves 6

BUY

1 pound white turnips
1 large sweet onion
8-ounce container heavy cream
Parsley

HAVE ON HAND	*COOKWARE*
Butter	Saucepan
Vegetable broth (optional)	
Salt	
White pepper	
Bread	
2 egg yolks	

1. Put kettle of water (or enough vegetable broth for 6 cups) on heat to boil. Peel and chop the *turnips* and *sweet onion*.

2. In heavy saucepan melt *2 tablespoons butter*. Add chopped vegetables and cook, stirring constantly, for 3 minutes. Add *6 cups boiling water or vegetable broth* and *salt and white pepper to taste*. Crumble in *4 slices bread* and bring soup to a boil. Simmer over low heat for 30 minutes, or until vegetables are very tender.

3. Meanwhile chop *4 tablespoons parsley* and set aside. Rub the soup through a strainer, or blend 2 cups at a time in an electric blender, and return to saucepan. Return soup to a boil.

4. Just before serving, combine the *2 egg yolks* with the *heavy cream* and a *little of the hot soup*. Remove soup from heat and gradually stir in the egg yolk mixture. Correct seasoning with salt and pepper. Pour into soup cups. Sprinkle each serving with chopped parsley.

VARIATIONS: Use radishes or cauliflower in place of the turnips.

CHEESE SOUP

Serves 6

BUY

½ pound aged Cheddar cheese
Heavy cream

HAVE ON HAND	*COOKWARE*
Garlic	Heavy saucepan
Butter	
Flour	
Dry white wine *or* dry vermouth	
Milk	
White pepper	
Nutmeg	
2 egg yolks	

1. Shred the *cheese* and set aside. Peel and crush *1 clove garlic*.

2. In heavy saucepan melt *2 tablespoons butter.* Add garlic and cook over low heat for 3 minutes without letting the garlic brown. Discard garlic. Add *2 tablespoons flour* and stir to make a smooth paste. Cook for 2 minutes, stirring constantly.

3. Gradually stir in *½ cup dry white wine, 2½ cups milk, ⅛ teaspoon white pepper,* and *a dash of freshly grated nutmeg;* cook, stirring, until sauce is smooth and slightly thickened. Add cheese and cook over moderate heat, stirring occasionally, until cheese is melted.

4. Combine *2 egg yolks* and *½ cup heavy cream.* Stir a *little of the hot soup* into the egg mixture, then stir gradually into the soup. Cook over low heat for 2 to 3 minutes, stirring constantly, without letting soup boil. Serve immediately.

Bean Soups

No flour or potatoes are needed to thicken bean soups, for the beans themselves provide body and substance.

CURRIED LIMA BEAN SOUP

Serves 4

BUY

10-ounce package frozen baby lima beans
Bunch of green onions
8-ounce container light cream
Chives *or* parsley, for garnish

HAVE ON HAND	*COOKWARE*
Butter	Saucepan with cover
Curry powder	Food mill *or* electric blender
Salt	
White pepper	
Marjoram	
Chicken broth (optional)	
Milk	

1. In saucepan combine *lima beans, ⅓ cup sliced green onions, 2 tablespoons butter, 1 teaspoon curry powder, ½ teaspoon salt, ⅛ teaspoon white pepper, ¼ teaspoon marjoram,* and *1 cup water or chicken broth.* Bring to a boil, partially cover, and simmer for 15 minutes, or until beans are tender.

2. Press vegetables and liquid through a food mill, or purée in an electric blender. Return to saucepan and stir in *1 cup milk* and *1 cup cream.*

3. Reheat to serving temperature, or chill and serve cold. Either way, garnish each serving with *chopped chives or parsley.*

KIDNEY OR BLACK BEAN SOUP

Serves 4 to 6

BUY

1 pound dried kidney beans *or* black beans
1 large Spanish onion
Container sour cream

HAVE ON HAND	*COOKWARE*
Salt	Large heavy kettle
Coarsely cracked pepper	8-inch skillet
Bay leaves	
Garlic	
Cooking oil	
Red wine vinegar	
Water, milk, *or* light cream	

1. Wash the *beans* and put them into a large kettle with *4 quarts water.* Let them soak overnight.

2. Next day, bring beans to a boil in the same water. Add *1 table-spoon salt, 1 teaspoon coarsely cracked pepper,* and *1 bay leaf.* Simmer for 2 hours, or until beans are very tender, adding water, if necessary, to keep beans covered at all times.

3. Discard bay leaf. Rub beans and liquid through a strainer or food mill, or purée 2 cups at a time in an electric blender until smooth. You should have 6 to 7 cups thick purée, the amount depending on how rapidly the beans boiled and how much of the liquid evaporated.

4. Peel and finely chop the *large onion* and *1 large clove garlic.* Heat *½ cup cooking oil* in a skillet, and in it simmer the onion and garlic for about 10 minutes, or until onion is transparent.

5. Add onion-garlic mixture plus the pan oil to the purée. Then add *2 tablespoons red wine vinegar.* Thin with about 2 cups *water, milk, or light cream*—the amount depending on the consistency desired. Correct the seasoning with salt and pepper.

6. Heat to serving temperature. Serve with a big dollop of *sour cream* in each plate.

VARIATION: Substitute a 1-pint 7-ounce jar of cream-style schav for the water, milk, or light cream. An interesting change. Try it!

DUTCH PEA SOUP
(Snert)

Serves 6 to 8

BUY

1 pound green split peas
Bunch of leeks
1 large celery root
2 medium onions
Bunch of celery
8-ounce container heavy cream

HAVE ON HAND	*COOKWARE*
Chicken broth (optional)	Large heavy kettle
Salt	
Coarsely cracked pepper	
Butter	

1. Wash the *split peas,* and put into the kettle with *2½ quarts water or part water and part chicken broth.* Bring to a boil and simmer for 30 minutes.

2. Meanwhile discard green stalks from the *leeks,* then trim the white parts, wash thoroughly to remove any sand, and chop. Peel and chop the *celery root* and *onions.* Chop *enough celery stalks with the leaves to measure 1 cup.* Add these vegetables to the peas and liquid, along with *2 teaspoons salt* and *1 teaspoon pepper.* Simmer for 30 minutes longer, or until peas are very tender.

3. Just before serving stir in *3 tablespoons butter* and the *heavy cream.*

LENTIL SOUP

Serves 6

BUY

1-pound box lentils
8-ounce can whole tomatoes
2 medium potatoes *or* 1 large Idaho baking potato

HAVE ON HAND	*COOKWARE*
1 medium onion	Large saucepan with cover
Garlic	
2 large stalks celery with leaves	
Butter	
Salt and pepper	
Beer	

1. Wash the *lentils* thoroughly. Peel and chop *1 medium onion, 1 clove garlic,* and the *2 large stalks of celery.*

2. In saucepan stew the onion, garlic, and celery in *2 tablespoons butter* over low heat for 10 minutes, or until onion is tender.

3. Add *8 cups water,* the *tomatoes, with juice, 1½ teaspoons salt, ¼ teaspoon pepper,* and the lentils. Partially cover and cook over low heat for 2 hours.

4. Meanwhile peel and dice the *potato.* Cover with cold water and set aside.

5. Rub the soup through a strainer or food mill, or blend 2 cups at a time in an electric blender. Return to the saucepan and add *1 cup beer.* Drain the potatoes and add them to the soup. Bring soup to a boil, then simmer for 20 minutes, or until potatoes are tender. Correct seasoning and serve hot.

NAVY BEAN SOUP

Serves 6

BUY

1-pound box navy *or* pea beans
3 medium onions
2 carrots
Bunch of celery
8-ounce can stewed tomatoes
Parsley

HAVE ON HAND

Garlic
Bay leaves
Salt
Black peppercorns
1 potato

COOKWARE

Large saucepan

1. Pick over *beans,* discarding any shriveled or discolored ones. Put beans in a saucepan with *2½ quarts water* to soak overnight.

2. Next day add the *3 onions,* peeled and chopped, the *carrots,* scraped and diced, *2 cups chopped celery with leaves, 1 clove garlic,* peeled and minced, the *tomatoes, 2 bay leaves, 1 teaspoon salt,* and *a good grinding of black pepper.* Bring liquid to a boil, then simmer for 2 hours, or until beans are very tender. Discard bay leaves.

3. Peel and dice the *potato* finely. Add potato to the soup and cook for 10 minutes longer, or until potato is mushy. Add *½ cup minced parsley* and serve.

BLACK BEANS AND RICE

Serves 6

BUY

1 pound black beans (kidney beans may be substituted)

HAVE ON HAND	*COOKWARE*
Onions	Large saucepan
Celery	
Garlic	
Lemon	
Cayenne pepper	
Salt	
Coarsely ground black pepper	
Raw rice	
Dry sherry	
Parsley	

1. Wash *beans* well and soak overnight in water to cover. Next day drain *beans* and add *2 quarts cold water, 1 medium onion,* peeled and chopped, *½ cup chopped celery,* and *1 clove garlic,* peeled and minced. Bring water to a boil and simmer beans for 3 hours, or until very soft.

2. Rub beans and liquid through a strainer or food mill, or blend 2 cups at a time in an electric blender. Return bean purée to saucepan, and add *juice of 1 lemon, ¼ teaspoon cayenne pepper,* and *salt and pepper to taste.* Cook over low heat for 30 minutes, stirring occasionally.

3. Meanwhile cook *½ cup rice* according to recipe on page 191.

4. Just before serving, stir in *½ cup dry sherry.* Ladle the soup into

large soup plates; add a heaping tablespoon cooked rice to each serving, and sprinkle the rice with *minced onion and parsley*.

Fruit Soups

The Scandinavians are fond of a variety of fruit soups, which they serve either hot or cold, according to the season. Sometimes they present them as a first course, but more often as a dessert. Either way, these soups are certainly healthful, flavorful, and different—one can take advantage of fresh fruits in season or use dried fruits during winter months. For lunch on a broiling hot summer day, I prefer them (served icy cold on a bed of crushed ice) to a fruit salad. Fresh rhubarb, black cherries, fresh peaches, or apricots are excellent fruits to use. Since fruit varies in acidity, you will have to add sugar to taste, but avoid making the soups overly sweet. Use your own imagination, too, with such fruits as blueberries, raspberries, fresh plums, diced apples, or a combination of several fruits.

The first soup is a basic recipe. If raspberries are used, the soup must be strained to remove the seeds.

SWEET CHERRY SOUP

Serves 6

BUY OR PICK

1 quart sweet cherries

HAVE ON HAND

Stick cinnamon
Sugar

Cornstarch *or* instant tapioca
Lemon
Cognac *or* kirsch

COOKWARE

Large saucepan

1. Wash the *cherries,* and then pit them over the saucepan in order to collect the cherry juice. Add *1 quart boiling water,* and *1 stick cinnamon.* Simmer for 20 to 30 minutes, or until cherries are tender.

2. Stir in *sugar to taste.*

3. Combine *2 tablespoons cornstarch or instant tapioca* and *¼ cup cold water;* stir into the soup. Return to a simmer and cook, stirring, until juice is clear and thickened. Remove from heat and cool a little. Then add *juice of ½ lemon* and *2 tablespoons cognac or kirsch.* Chill and serve very cold.

SCANDINAVIAN CREAMED FRUIT SOUP

Serves 8

BUY

Box of pitted dried prunes
Box of dried apricots
1 pint light cream

HAVE ON HAND

Lemon
Salt
Sugar
Cornstarch
Sherry *or* cognac
Butter
Flour
Eggs
Vanilla extract

COOKWARE

Large heavy saucepan
Small saucepan

1. Put *1½ cups prunes* and *1½ cups apricots* into a heavy saucepan and add *2 quarts boiling water.* Let the fruit soak overnight.

2. Add to the fruit and juice the *grated rind of ½ lemon* and *a pinch of salt;* bring to a boil, then simmer for 20 minutes.

3. Combine *½ cup sugar, 2 tablespoons cornstarch,* and *½ cup sherry (or 2 tablespoons cognac),* and gradually stir this into the hot fruit mixture. Cook for about 10 minutes, stirring occasionally. Remove from heat. Cool, then pour into serving bowl and chill.

4. Meanwhile, make the cream topping: In small saucepan melt *2 tablespoons butter,* then stir in *4 tablespoons flour.* Cook, stirring, until this roux bubbles. Gradually stir in *1½ cups light cream,* and cook, stirring, until mixture is smooth and thickened. Continue to cook over low heat for 10 minutes longer, stirring occasionally.

5. Beat *2 eggs* with a *little of the hot sauce* until light, then stir into *remaining sauce.* Stir in *1 tablespoon sugar* and *1 teaspoon vanilla.* Remove from heat and pour into a small serving bowl. Chill.

6. Serve the soup and cream separately, and let each person top his portion with a big dollop of the cream.

HOT PURÉED FRUIT SOUP

Serves 6

BUY

1-pound 14-ounce can purple plums, apricots, *or* peaches, in heavy syrup
Heavy cream

HAVE ON HAND

Brown sugar
Cornstarch
Lemon
Butter
Rum
Cinnamon

COOKWARE

Large saucepan

1. Drain *fruit;* reserve *1 cup of its liquid.* Pit fruit, if necessary; then press through food mill, or blend in blender, to make a purée.

2. In saucepan combine ¼ *cup brown sugar, 1 tablespoon cornstarch,* the *cup of reserved liquid,* and *1 teaspoon lemon juice.* Bring to a boil and cook, stirring constantly, until soup is smooth and slightly thickened.

3. Stir in puréed fruit and heat to steaming.

4. Stir in *1 tablespoon butter, 2 tablespoons rum,* and ½ *cup heavy cream.* Cook, stirring, until butter melts.

5. Ladle into serving bowls, and top with *sprinkling of cinnamon.*

APPETIZERS THAT DOUBLE AS LUNCHEON DISHES

Quiches & Tarts

An appetizer can mean a dish of nuts; a platter of crisp raw vegetables; a creamy dip; a bowl of green and ripe olives and another of bright radishes; half of an avocado, cantaloupe, or papaya; or one of the many other simple foods which are discussed in the chapter on raw foods and salads. An appetizer can also be eggs with any one of a number of zesty mayonnaise sauces, or a cooked vegetable, such as an artichoke, leeks, or fresh asparagus vinaigrette, or one of those piquant vegetable combinations— the *ratatouilles, capalatinas,* or the *à la grecque* dishes—or a soup, of course, either hot or cold, or a fondue. All these have found a place in other chapters of this book.

In fact, almost any savory dish, if served in small enough quantity, can serve as an appetizer. So, rather than make this a comprehensive chapter on appetizers, I have collected here some rather special hot savories which also can double as excellent meatless luncheon dishes.

The first group includes a variety of savory custard tarts, the progenitor of which was undoubtedly the famous specialty from the French province of Lorraine; known as the *quiche Lorraine,* it consists of a hot flaky crust filled with a rich, velvety cheese custard containing bits of crisply cooked bacon or ham. A little finely chopped onion or bits of mushroom or truffles make good substitutes for the meat, even if they are not traditional. Fortunately, there are no substitutes for the fresh eggs and cream and good butter and honest cheese which go into these recipes. Rich? Yes, but the best. Just cut the slices a trifle small and serve with a water cress and Belgian endive salad, delicately flavored with lemon juice and vegetable oils, and a glass of chilled white wine.

Both the crusts and the fillings of these tarts can be made in advance, and assembled and baked when needed. Since they deserve the finest pastry that can be made, this chapter begins with how to make a flaky butter pie crust. If you want to double the quantities, go ahead. Divide the dough in two; then roll out one half, and freeze the other half for another tart another day; or line 2 pie plates—one to bake, and one to freeze.

If you have had trouble rolling out pie crust, chances are that you have not been using the indispensable canvas pastry cloth and a knit stockinette for your rolling pin. These can be saturated with flour to keep the dough from sticking without adding too much additional flour to your dough. They are inexpensive and available at most five-and-dime stores. They make pastry-making a cinch.

FLAKY PIE CRUST

For a 1-crust pie

HAVE ON HAND	COOKWARE
Flour	9-inch pie plate
Salt	
Butter	
1 egg	

THE DOUGH:

1 Into a small mixing bowl measure *1 level cup flour.* There is no need to sift it. Add *½ teaspoon salt.* Make a well in the center of the flour and into this well slice *1 stick (½ cup) butter* taken directly from the refrigerator, NOT from the freezer.

2. Separate *1 egg;* reserve the white for another use, and dump the *yolk* on top of the butter. Add *1 tablespoon cold water.*

3. With one hand, squeeze the center ingredients into a paste; then gradually knead in the flour until all ingredients are incorporated into a hard rough paste.

TO ROLL OUT:

4. Place your pastry canvas on a worktable. Dust the canvas and the stocking on your rolling pin generously with flour, rubbing it in well with the palm of your hand. With the heel of your hand, press the dough onto the floured canvas, making a circle about ½ inch thick. Now turn the dough to coat the other side with flour. Begin to roll out the dough into a thin circle. Roll from the center of the circle to the outer edge, changing the direction of the rolling pin with each roll. Turn over the circle of dough frequently, making sure that the canvas is lightly coated with flour. If your dough sticks badly, crumble it into a ball and begin again.

LINING THE PIE PLATE:

5. When the dough is rolled out as thinly as possible into a circle about 1 inch larger than your pie plate, place the floured rolling pin across the dough, but a little off center. Flip the wider side of the dough over the rolling pin. Now you're ready to transfer it to your pie plate. Hold the rolling pin at each end, with your thumbs on the dough, and slide pin and dough over the pie plate, a little off center, so that the edge of the dough under the rolling pin rests about 1 inch beyond one edge of the plate. Then flip the dough covering the rolling pin over the other side of the plate. Remove the rolling pin, and gently ease the circle of dough down into the plate, letting it cover the bottom and sides quite loosely. Pat it gently into place with your finger tips.

FLUTING THE EDGE:

6. Trim off edge of pastry with kitchen scissors, leaving ½ inch overhanging. Fold the overhanging edge under itself, thus making a double edge of the dough; press it firmly onto rim of pie plate, still keeping the dough lining the sides of the plate quite loose. Even a slight bulge just below the rim is an asset; since the dough shrinks in the baking, the bulge will keep the pastry from pulling away from the rim. Now push your left forefinger against the outer edge of the pastry rim, and pinch the inside edge of the pastry rim against the forefinger with your other thumb and forefinger. Repeat all around the rim.

7. Chill pastry until ready to bake.

TO PARTIALLY BAKE:

8. Preheat oven to 450° F. Prick bottom and sides of pie shell with tines of a fork. Bake in center of the preheated oven 8 to 10 minutes, or until pastry is set and is beginning to brown around the edges. Remove from oven to cool.

TO COMPLETELY BAKE:

Prick the shell. Bake in preheated oven for 12 to 14 minutes. Remove from oven to cool.

FOR A SEED CRUST:

When pastry is partially rolled into a circle, sprinkle each side generously with *poppy, sesame, caraway,* or *sunflower seeds,* using about *2 tablespoons* in all, then roll the seeds into the dough.

FOR AN HERB CRUST:

Add *1 tablespoon chopped fresh parsley, dill,* or *tarragon—or 1 tea-*

spoon of the dried herb—to the egg-butter mixture before kneading in the flour.

CREAM CHEESE FLAKY PASTRY

For 2 one-crust pies. Another excellent rich, flaky pie dough is made with a mixture of cream cheese and butter.

BUY

8-ounce package fresh cream cheese

HAVE ON HAND	*COOKWARE*
Butter (2 sticks)	Two 9-inch pie plates
Flour	

1. Remove the *cream cheese* and *2 sticks butter* from the refrigerator and let soften for half an hour at room temperature.

2. Slice cream cheese and butter into a mixing bowl, and beat with wooden spoon, or electric beater, until blended and fluffy.

3. Stir, or beat, in *2 level cups flour* (no need to sift), and mix until blended. Chill for at least 3 hours before rolling out and lining pie plate. Cut dough in half. Use half and freeze half, or line two plates and bake one shell and freeze the other. For fluting the edge and baking the shell, see page 50.

QUICHE AU FROMAGE

Serves 6 for lunch, 8 as an appetizer

BUY

½ pound fresh mushrooms
½ pound unprocessed Swiss or Gruyère cheese (imported is best)
1 pint cream

HAVE ON HAND	COOKWARE
Ingredients for pastry	9-inch pie plate
Butter	Skillet
6 eggs	
Dry mustard	
Salt and pepper	

IN ADVANCE:

1. Make and partially bake *a 9-inch pie shell.* Cool.

2. Wash, trim, and dry *mushrooms;* slice or dice them. Shred the *½ pound of cheese.* You should have about 2 cups. Set aside.

3. In skillet melt *2 tablespoons butter,* and in it sauté the mushrooms over moderate heat for 5 minutes, stirring frequently. Remove from heat and spread over bottom of partially baked crust. Sprinkle the mushrooms with the shredded cheese.

4. Separate *6 eggs,* reserving the whites for another use, and drop the *yolks* into a mixing bowl. Sprinkle with *½ teaspoon dry mustard* and *¼ teaspoon each salt and pepper.* Gradually beat in *1½ cups cream.*

TO BAKE:

5. Preheat oven to 350° F. Place the prepared pie plate on a baking sheet and pour in the custard. Bake in center of the preheated oven for 35 minutes, or until custard is barely set in center. Remove from the oven and let cool for 10 minutes before cutting and serving. Serve warm or at room temperature.

NOTE: Leftover quiche may be reheated in a 250° F. oven for 10 to 15 minutes. It's better warm than when served directly from the refrigerator.

LEEK AND MUSHROOM TART

Serves 6 for lunch, 8 as an appetizer

BUY

6 large leeks
½ pound fresh mushrooms
8-ounce container heavy cream

HAVE ON HAND	*COOKWARE*
Ingredients for pastry	9-inch pie plate
Salt	Saucepan
Butter	Skillet
Freshly ground black pepper	
Flour	
Grated Parmesan cheese	

IN ADVANCE:

1. Make and partially bake *a 9-inch pie shell*. Cool.

2. Trim root ends of the *leeks* and discard green leaves. Split lengthwise and wash thoroughly, then cut crosswise into 1-inch pieces. Cook in *boiling salted water to barely cover* for 20 minutes, or until almost tender. Drain, reserving *the liquid*.

3. Wash, trim, and dry *mushrooms*. Slice thinly and set aside.

4. In skillet melt *2 tablespoons butter*, and in it sauté the sliced mushrooms for about 5 minutes, stirring frequently, or until cooked. Sprinkle mushrooms with *¾ teaspoon salt* and *lots of pepper*. Sprinkle *3 tablespoons flour* over the mixture and stir well. Gradually stir in *1 cup of the reserved leek liquid* and *½ cup heavy cream*. Cook, stirring, until sauce is smooth and thickened. Stir in the leeks and set aside, partially covered.

TO BAKE:

5. Preheat oven to 350° F. Place pie shell on a baking sheet, and pour in the creamed leeks and mushrooms. Sprinkle with *¼ cup grated Parmesan cheese*. Bake in the center of the preheated oven for 20 minutes. Remove from oven and serve hot.

EGG AND SPINACH TART

Serves 6

BUY
1 pound fresh spinach
8-ounce container sour cream
8-ounce container heavy cream

HAVE ON HAND	*COOKWARE*
Ingredients for pastry	9-inch pie plate
Nutmeg	Large saucepan with cover
Whole-wheat bread	Small skillet
Parmesan cheese	
Butter	
6 eggs	

IN ADVANCE:

1. Make and partially bake *a 9-inch pie shell*. Cool.

2. Wash *spinach* and discard coarse stems and any discolored leaves. Lift spinach directly from water into a large saucepan and cook over high heat, covered, for 5 minutes, or until wilted. Drain well and chop coarsely. Spread spinach over bottom of partially baked pastry and sprinkle with *a pinch of nutmeg*.

3. Crumb *enough bread slices to measure ¾ cup*. Grate *4 tablespoons Parmesan cheese*. Melt *2 tablespoons butter*. In a small bowl toss bread, cheese, and butter together lightly. Set aside.

TO BAKE:

4. Preheat oven to 350° F. Make 6 nests in the spinach; break *1 egg* into each nest. Combine the *sour cream* and *½ cup heavy cream* and pour over the eggs and spinach. Sprinkle with the bread crumb mixture.

5. Bake in the preheated oven for 25 minutes. Serve hot.

QUICHE CIBOULE

Serves 6 for lunch, 8 as an appetizer

BUY

2 large bunches green spring onions
½ pound imported Swiss *or* Gruyère cheese (2 cups, grated)
1 pint light cream *or* half-and-half

HAVE ON HAND	*COOKWARE*
Ingredients for pastry	9-inch pie plate
Butter	Large skillet
Parmesan cheese	
4 eggs	
Salt and pepper	

IN ADVANCE:

1. Make and partially bake *a 9-inch pie shell.* Cool.

2. Wash and trim *green onions,* leaving on the tender green tops; chop *enough to measure 1 cup, firmly packed.* Sauté onions in *3 table-spoons butter* for 5 minutes, or until wilted. Spread on bottom of pie shell.

3. Shred the *Swiss or Gruyère cheese,* and grate *enough Parmesan cheese to measure ¼ cup.* Set aside.

4. Beat *4 eggs* with *¼ teaspoon each salt and pepper.* Stir in *1½ cups light cream or half-and-half* and the shredded cheese.

TO BAKE:

5. Preheat oven to 350° F. Place partially baked pie shell on a baking sheet and fill with the cheese mixture. Sprinkle with the *grated Parmesan.* Bake in the preheated oven for about 40 minutes, or until nicely browned and set.

6. Cut into wedges and serve hot or warm.

ITALIAN GREEN PEPPER TART

Serves 6 for lunch, 8 as an appetizer

BUY

3 long pale-green Italian frying peppers (¾ pound)
6 ounces mozzarella cheese
8 ounces creamed cottage cheese
8-ounce container heavy cream

HAVE ON HAND	*COOKWARE*
Ingredients for pastry	9-inch pie plate
Butter	8-inch skillet
Salt	
Coarsely cracked pepper	
Eggs	

IN ADVANCE:

1. Make and partially bake *a 9-inch pie shell.* Cool.

2. Wash *green peppers,* and discard stems and seeds. Cut into strips ½ inch wide and about 3 inches long. In 8-inch skillet, sauté the peppers in *2 tablespoons butter* for 8 minutes, or until wilted, stirring frequently.

3. With slotted spoon, spread peppers on bottom of partially baked pie shell, then sprinkle with *½ teaspoon salt* and *¼ teaspoon coarsely cracked pepper.* Dice the *mozzarella cheese* and sprinkle over the peppers.

4. Combine *3 eggs,* the *creamed cottage cheese,* and *½ cup heavy cream.* Set aside.

TO BAKE:

5. Preheat oven to 350° F. Place pie shell on baking sheet. Pour cream-cheese-egg mixture over peppers in pie shell and bake in the preheated oven for 45 minutes.

6. Cut into wedges and serve very hot.

ZUCCHINI TART

Use *¾ pound zucchini,* washed and sliced, in place of the peppers.

CAULIFLOWER TART

Serves 6 for lunch, 8 as an appetizer

BUY

¾ pound imported Swiss cheese
8-ounce container heavy cream
Medium head cauliflower

HAVE ON HAND

Ingredients for pastry
Dry bread crumbs
3 egg yolks
Milk
Salt and pepper
Butter

COOKWARE

9-inch pie plate
Saucepan

IN ADVANCE:

1. Make and partially bake *a 9-inch pastry shell*. Cool.

2. Shred the *cheese*—you should have about 3 cups. Mix the cheese with *½ cup dry bread crumbs*, the *heavy cream, 3 egg yolks, ½ cup milk, ½ teaspoon salt, and ¼ teaspoon pepper*. Set aside.

3. Wash *cauliflower* and discard leaves surrounding the head. Cut out and discard the heavy center core and break the cauliflower into bite-size flowerets. Cover with *lightly salted boiling water* and simmer for 15 minutes, or until barely tender. Drain well, then empty cauliflower into pie shell.

TO BAKE:

4. Preheat oven to 350° F. Place pie shell on baking sheet and spoon cheese mixture on top. Dot with *2 tablespoons butter*. Bake in the preheated oven for 30 minutes, or until cheese is lightly browned. Serve hot.

CABBAGE TART

Use *1 small head cabbage,* coarsely shredded (about 1 quart), in place of the cauliflower.

BROCCOLI TART

Use *1 bunch fresh broccoli* in place of the cauliflower.

BRUSSELS SPROUT TART

Use *1 quart Brussels sprouts* in place of the cauliflower.

CELERY TART

Use *1 quart coarsely diced celery* in place of the cauliflower.

Luncheon Soufflé Rolls

Another delicious appetizer—and one which doubles as a delicate luncheon dish—is a savory roll made of a soufflé mixture that is baked in a jelly roll pan and then is allowed to deflate. This fallen soufflé is then spread with a filling and rolled lengthwise like a jelly roll. It may be made early in the day and reheated before serving. Or it may be refrigerated for one to two days, and then reheated. Or you can freeze it and transfer it to the oven directly from the freezer. It will stay fresh in the freezer for several weeks. You may find the soufflé roll a bit difficult to manipulate; see page 305 for a detailed description of how to handle it easily.

The fillings may be made of eggs, cheese, vegetables, or almost any creamed seafood or poultry mixture.

SOUFFLÉ ROLL

Serves 4 for lunch, 6 to 8 as an appetizer

HAVE ON HAND	*COOKWARE*
Oil	10 x 15-inch jelly roll pan
Waxed paper	Small saucepan
Parmesan cheese	
Butter	
Flour	
Milk *or* half-and-half	
Salt and pepper	
5 eggs	

1. *Oil* the jelly roll pan, line with waxed paper, and oil the paper.

2. Preheat oven to 350° F.

3. Grate *6 tablespoons Parmesan cheese* and set aside.

4. In small saucepan melt *2 tablespoons butter*. Stir in *3 tablespoons flour*. Gradually stir in *1 cup milk or half-and-half*, and cook, stirring, until sauce is smooth and thick. Stir in *½ teaspoon salt, ¼ teaspoon pepper*, and the grated cheese. Remove from heat.

5. At intervals, break *each of the 5 eggs* carefully, emptying the *whites* into a mixing bowl, and beating *each yolk* into the sauce before adding another. Return sauce to heat; cook, stirring rapidly, for 1 minute.

6. Beat egg whites until stiff but still glossy. Beat a big spoonful of the egg whites into the yolk mixture. Now fold the egg yolk mixture gently but thoroughly into the remaining beaten whites.

7. Spread the batter onto the prepared pan evenly and well into the corners.

8. Bake in the preheated oven for exactly 15 minutes.

9. Remove soufflé from oven, cover with waxed paper, and let cool.

10. Make the desired filling; see the three recipes immediately following.

11. To ready the roll for filling, first run a knife around the edge of the pan. Flip the soufflé over onto a long sheet of waxed paper and gently remove the pan, starting at one end and working toward the other. Next, carefully remove the waxed paper from the bottom of the soufflé. You may need the help of a thin knife for, if you didn't oil the waxed paper thoroughly or fold the egg whites completely into the egg yolk mixture, you may have little spots that stick. This won't hurt the final dish at all. Just be persistent.

12. Spread the filling evenly over the soufflé. Then roll the soufflé lengthwise, using the paper underneath to help guide the roll forward. Wrap in foil, sealing the ends well.

BAKE AND SERVE or REFRIGERATE or FREEZE.

TO BAKE:

13. Preheat oven to 350° F. Place the foil-wrapped roll on a baking sheet and bake in the preheated oven for 20 minutes if freshly made or if refrigerated; for 40 to 45 minutes if frozen.

14. Unwrap, slice, and serve hot. Garnish with a dab of sour cream if desired.

CURRIED-EGG FILLING—for Soufflé Roll

HAVE ON HAND

6 eggs
Onion (preferably green scallions)
Dill weed
Dry mustard
Salt and pepper
Curry powder
Mayonnaise
Lemon

1. Hard-cook the *eggs* (page 147). Shell and cool in cold water. Drain and chop.

2. Put chopped eggs into mixing bowl. Add *2 tablespoons finely chopped onion, 1 teaspoon dill weed, ½ teaspoon dry mustard, salt to taste (about ½ teaspoon), ¼ teaspoon pepper, 1 teaspoon curry powder, 6 tablespoons mayonnaise,* and *2 teaspoons lemon juice.* Mix to a moist spread.

MUSHROOM CREAM FILLING—for Soufflé Roll

BUY

¾ pound fresh mushrooms
8-ounce container heavy *or* sour cream

HAVE ON HAND	*COOKWARE*
Medium onion	Skillet
Butter	
Flour	
Salt	
Freshly ground black pepper	

1. Wash, trim, and slice the *mushrooms*. Peel and finely chop the *onion*.

2. Sauté onion in *3 tablespoons butter* for 5 minutes, or until tender but not brown. Add mushrooms and cook over moderate heat for 5 minutes, or until tender and most of moisture is cooked away, stirring frequently. Stir in *2 tablespoons flour*. Stir in *¾ cup cream, salt to taste,* and *a good sprinkling of pepper*. Cook, stirring, until mixture is thick.

SPINACH FILLING—for Soufflé Roll

BUY

10-ounce package frozen chopped spinach
6 ounces Swiss *or* Gruyère cheese
8 ounces cream cheese *or* ricotta cheese

HAVE ON HAND

	COOKWARE
Medium onion	Skillet
Butter	
Salt and pepper	
Nutmeg	
3 eggs	

1. Thaw *spinach* and drain well. Peel and chop *1 medium onion*. Dice the *Swiss or Gruyère cheese*.

2. In skillet heat *3 tablespoons butter,* and in it sauté onion for 5 minutes, or until transparent. Add spinach, *½ teaspoon salt, some freshly ground black pepper,* and *a pinch of nutmeg*. Cook over low heat for 5 minutes, stirring frequently. Remove from heat and stir in *3 eggs*, the diced cheese, and either the *cream cheese* or *ricotta cheese*.

Egg Rolls & Blintzes

We couldn't possibly leave out recipes for Egg Rolls. The first step is making the "skins," and that's a lot of fun. The skins freeze well if you want to keep a supply on hand.

EGG-ROLL SKINS

Makes 36

HAVE ON HAND	*COOKWARE*
Flour	Small skillet *or* crêpe pan, about
4 eggs	6 inches in diameter
Salt	Deep skillet
Butter	

1. In mixing bowl combine *2 cups flour, 2 cups water, 4 eggs,* and *1 teaspoon salt* to make a thin batter.

2. Pour batter into a small pitcher and stir occasionally.

3. Heat a small skillet or crêpe pan and brush lightly with *butter.* Pour in about *2 tablespoons of the batter,* and IMMEDIATELY lift the pan up over the heat and, at the same time, tip it over the pitcher, rotating the pan so that the bottom becomes covered with a thin layer of batter and any excess drains back into the pitcher.

4. Hold the pan over moderate heat for 30 seconds, or until the thin layer of batter, or the "skin," is set, but not brown.

5. Shake out the **skin** onto a long sheet of waxed paper. Now repeat the process, but first heat the pan again thoroughly, for it is the heat of the pan that sets the batter and cooks the skin without browning it. Line up skins side by side on the waxed paper.

6. When all the skins have been cooked, place another sheet of waxed paper over them. Roll them in the papers so they will stay moist until ready to fill or freeze.

TO FREEZE THE SKINS:

Stack the cool skins with squares of waxed paper between them. Wrap in freezer paper, label, and freeze. To defrost, remove from freezer about 30 minutes before using.

TO MAKE EGG ROLLS

1. Make *desired filling;* see the two recipes immediately following.

2. Combine *1 tablespoon flour* and *2 tablespoons water.*

3. Place about *2 tablespoons of filling* on each skin. Brush edge of skin all around with the flour mixture. Fold in two sides, then roll in a small cylinder. Press the flap edge lightly against the roll in order to seal it.

4. Pour *cooking oil* to the depth of about 1 inch in a deep skillet, then heat to very hot (365° F.). Place a few egg rolls at a time in the hot oil; fry, turning once, for about 3 minutes, or until crisp and brown on all sides.

5. Drain on absorbent paper and keep warm in a 250° F. oven until ready to serve. Serve with *Chinese mustard.*

Egg-roll fillings traditionally include either seafood or meat, but here are a couple of meatless variations which make no pretense at being traditional, but are delicious. The first contains soybean curd; you can use either *tofu,* which is packed in water, or *yakidofu,* which is baked. Both types of bean curd are available in cans at Oriental grocery stores or at health-food shops.

SPINACH EGG ROLLS

Makes 18

BUY

10-ounce package frozen chopped spinach
Bunch scallions
4 large mushrooms
5-ounce can water chestnuts
Small jar preserved *or* candied ginger
8-ounce can soybean sprouts
8-ounce container cottage *or* ricotta cheese

HAVE ON HAND	COOKWARE
Soy *or* peanut oil	Skillet
Cornstarch	
Salt	
Sugar	
Soy sauce	
18 egg-roll skins	

1. Defrost *spinach* and drain in a sieve, pressing out as much of the liquid as possible. Set aside.

2. Slice *2 scallions, including tender part of the green stalks.* Wash, trim, and slice *mushrooms.* Drain and chop *water chestnuts* and *2 large pieces ginger.* Drain *soybean sprouts.*

3. In skillet heat *1 tablespoon cooking oil,* and in it sauté scallions and mushrooms for about 5 minutes, or until vegetables are tender. Stir in *1 teaspoon cornstarch, 1 teaspoon salt, ½ teaspoon sugar,* and *1 tablespoon soy sauce.* Add the spinach and bean sprouts, and cook, stirring, for 2 minutes longer. Remove from heat and stir in the *cheese,* water chestnuts, and ginger. Cool and chill.

4. Fill the *skins,* roll, and fry (page 64).

MEATLESS EGG ROLLS

Makes 24

BUY

5-ounce can water chestnuts
8-ounce can bamboo shoots
Bunch of green onions
Head of celery
8¾-ounce can soybean curd
4-ounce can mushroom stems and pieces

HAVE ON HAND

Salt
Soy sauce
2 eggs
24 egg-roll skins

1. Chop the *water chestnuts, 2 pieces bamboo shoots, 4 green onions,* and *1 cup celery.*

2. Drain the *soybean curd,* crumble into a mixing bowl, and drain again if necessary. Add the chopped vegetables, *1 teaspoon salt, 2 table-spoons soy sauce, 2 eggs,* and the can of *mushroom stems and pieces,* well drained. Mix well.

3. Fill the *24 skins,* roll, and fry (page 64).

BLINTZES

Egg-Roll Skins are used to make the popular appetizer known as blintzes, and blintzes serve also most palatably as a luncheon dish. *Makes 12.*

BUY

8-ounces cottage *or* ricotta cheese
4-ounce can shredded toasted almonds (see Note below)
8-ounce container sour cream

HAVE ON HAND	COOKWARE
2 egg yolks	Skillet
Salt	
12 egg-roll skins, fresh *or* defrosted	
1 egg (optional)	
Butter	
Sour cream	
Jam *or* jelly	

1. In mixing bowl combine the *cheese, 2 egg yolks, ¼ cup almonds,* and a *little salt to taste.*

2. Place *1 spoonful cheese mixture* in the center of *each skin.* Fold sides over and roll. Seal edge with a *little beaten egg or some remaining batter.* Chill until ready to cook.

3. Heat *¼ cup butter* in a skillet. Place blintzes in it and sauté over low heat until browned on all sides.

4. Serve hot with *sour cream* and a *little jam or jelly.*

NOTE: You can vary the flavor of this filling by omitting the almonds and substituting *2 tablespoons chopped chives or parsley.*

Crêpes & Other Savory Dishes

Crêpes are just as much fun to make as Egg-Roll Skins. The chief difference is that they are browned lightly on both sides. Crêpes to be stuffed for savory dishes contain no sugar. Otherwise they are exactly the same as those used for desserts. Freeze them the same way as for Egg-Roll Skins (page 64).

THE CRÊPES

Makes 24

HAVE ON HAND	*COOKWARE*
Butter	Small skillet *or* crêpe pan,
3 eggs	5 to 6 inches in diameter
Milk	
Flour	
Salt	
Brandy *or* cognac	

1. Melt *1 tablespoon butter* over low heat, and set aside in warm place.

2. In mixing bowl beat *3 eggs* well. Gradually beat in *1½ cups milk.* Gradually stir in *1 cup flour* and *a pinch of salt,* and continue to stir until batter is smooth. Batter should be just thick enough to coat a spoon.

3. Stir in the melted butter and *1 tablespoon brandy or cognac.* Let the batter stand for 1 to 2 hours before using it, stirring occasionally. Pour into 1-quart measuring cup or pitcher.

4. Heat the skillet until very hot. Crêpes must cook quickly or they will be tough. Put *½ teaspoon butter* in the pan, and swirl the pan to coat bottom and sides with butter.

5. As soon as the butter stops foaming and begins to turn golden brown, raise pan from heat (use pot holder), pour in *about 2 tablespoons crêpe batter,* and again swirl the pan in a circular motion to spread batter evenly and thinly over the bottom. This must be done quickly—before the batter has a chance to set.

6. Return pan to heat and cook crêpe for about 1 minute, or until set and brown on one side. Turn with a spatula and brown other side.

7. Turn crêpe out onto absorbent paper to cool. Repeat until batter is used.

8. When cool, cover the crêpes with waxed paper and roll until ready to fill.

CRÊPES AU FROMAGE

Serves 6 for lunch, 12 as an appetizer

BUY

½ pound imported Swiss *or* Gruyère cheese
8-ounce container heavy cream

HAVE ON HAND	*COOKWARE*
Ingredients for Hollandaise Sauce (page 134)	1-quart saucepan
	Oblong baking dish
Dry white wine *or* vermouth	
Cornstarch	
Milk	
12 crêpes, freshly made *or* defrosted	

IN ADVANCE:

1. Make *Hollandaise Sauce* and let cool.

2. Shred the *cheese* and put it into the saucepan with ½ *cup dry white wine.* Cook over low heat, stirring constantly, until cheese is melted and mixture is smooth.

3. Combine *2 teaspoons cornstarch* and *1 tablespoon milk.* Stir into cheese mixture and cook, stirring, until it comes to a boil. Keep warm over hot water.

4. Arrange crêpes on worktable. Spread each with *about 1½ teaspoons of the cheese mixture* and roll up like a small jelly roll. Arrange rolls side by side in a buttered oblong baking dish or lasagne pan.

TO FINISH:

5. Preheat oven to 425° F.

6. Whip ½ *cup cream* and fold into the Hollandaise Sauce.

7. Bake crêpes in the preheated oven for 8 to 10 minutes, or until bubbling hot. Remove from oven and spoon a ribbon of sauce crossways over the crêpes. Return to oven for 1 to 2 minutes, or until sauce is lightly browned.

GNOCCHI PARISIENNE

Serves 6. These delicate dumplings are another favorite appetizer, but they are also hard to top as a hot luncheon dish.

HAVE ON HAND	*COOKWARE*
Butter	2-quart saucepan
Salt	Large kettle
Cayenne pepper	2-quart au gratin *or* baking dish
Flour, all-purpose	Pastry bag and #12 pastry tube
Dry mustard	
Parmesan cheese	
4 eggs	

1. In saucepan combine *4 tablespoons butter, 1 cup water, ¼ teaspoon salt, ⅛ teaspoon cayenne pepper.* Bring slowly to a boil.

2. Meanwhile combine *1 cup all-purpose flour, ½ teaspoon dry mustard,* and *4 tablespoons grated Parmesan.*

3. When liquid is boiling rapidly, dump in flour mixture all at once, and, stirring rapidly with a wooden spoon, raise the pan a few inches above the heat; continue stirring for 30 seconds, or until the paste comes away from the sides of the saucepan and forms a rough ball in the center.

4. Beat in *4 eggs, one at a time,* beating vigorously after each addition until, after the last one, the paste is very shiny. This may be done with an electric beater if you wish.

TO COOK THE GNOCCHI:

5. Measure *4 quarts water* into the large kettle, add *1 tablespoon salt,* and bring to a boil.

6. Meanwhile spoon the paste into a pastry bag fitted with a large plain pastry tube (No. 12). When the water is boiling, reduce heat so it barely simmers. Hold the bag over the boiling water and press out the paste. As the paste is extruded, cut off 1-inch lengths with a knife, letting them drop into the simmering water. They will sink to the bottom, but as they puff and cook they will rise to the surface of the water and float. Cook the gnocchi for about 15 minutes, or until firm, constantly spooning the hot water over them so they remain moist on all sides.

7. Use a slotted spoon to lift the gnocchi out of the simmering water, and place them on paper toweling to drain.

8. Arrange them in a buttered baking dish, cover the dish with waxed paper, and refrigerate.

TO FINISH:

When needed, the gnocchi may simply be sprinkled with *hot melted butter* and *grated Parmesan cheese,* and browned and heated under the broiler. Or they may be sauced with Mornay Sauce as follows:

9. Remove gnocchi from refrigerator. Preheat oven to 350° F. Butter the au gratin dish.

10. Spread *a thin layer of Mornay Sauce* in the dish. Arrange the gnocchi in the dish, and cover with the *remaining sauce.* Bake in the preheated oven for 15 to 20 minutes, or until sauce is bubbling hot.

MORNAY SAUCE

Makes about 2½ cups

HAVE ON HAND	*COOKWARE*
Milk	Small saucepan
Bay leaves	1-quart saucepan
Onion	
Peppercorns	
Parmesan cheese	
Gruyère *or* Swiss cheese	
Butter	
Flour	
Salt	
Cayenne pepper	
Heavy cream	
Dry mustard	

1. Heat *2 cups milk* to steaming hot in small saucepan with *1 bay leaf, a slice of onion,* and a *few peppercorns.* Grate *3 tablespoons Parmesan cheese,* and shred *1 tablespoon Gruyère or Swiss cheese.* Set these items aside.

2. In a larger saucepan melt *4 tablespoons butter.* Stir in *6 tablespoons flour, ¼ teaspoon salt,* and *a dash of cayenne pepper.* When mixture begins to bubble, remove it from the heat and strain the hot milk into it. Return saucepan to heat and bring to a boil, stirring vigorously.

3. When sauce is smooth and thickened, stir in *2 tablespoons butter,* bit by bit, *½ cup heavy cream, a pinch of dry mustard,* the grated Parmesan and the shredded Gruyère or Swiss cheese. Keep sauce hot over low heat for 5 to 10 minutes.

GOUGÈRE

Slice this cheese puff for an appetizer, or for an accompaniment to soup or salad at lunchtime.

BUY

¼ pound imported Gruyère *or* Swiss cheese
Small wedge of Italian Parmesan cheese

HAVE ON HAND	*COOKWARE*
Butter	2-quart saucepan
Flour	Baking sheet
Cayenne pepper	
Dry mustard	
Salt	
5 large eggs	
Milk	

1. Shred the *Gruyère or Swiss cheese* (you will need enough for 1 cup) and grate *2 tablespoons Parmesan cheese.* Set aside.

2. Combine *1 cup (less 1 tablespoon) flour with ⅛ teaspoon cayenne, ½ teaspoon dry mustard,* and *¼ teaspoon salt.*

3. In saucepan combine *1 cup water* and *½ stick butter.* Bring to a boil over medium heat. When liquid is boiling rapidly, dump in flour mixture all at once, and stir rapidly with a wooden spoon until mixture is smooth and forms a ball in center of the pan.

4. Remove saucepan from heat, and beat in *4 of the eggs,* one at a time, beating well after each addition until a smooth, glossy paste is formed. You can do this in an electric mixer if you wish. Fold in *1 cup shredded cheese and the Parmesan.* Refrigerate paste until ready to bake.

TO BAKE:

5. Preheat oven to 375° F. Butter the baking sheet lightly, and with the tip of a finger trace on it a circle 9 inches in diameter. Spoon the paste over the perimeter of the circle, forming a ring about 2 inches wide and 1 inch high.

6. Beat *1 egg* lightly with *1 tablespoon milk,* and brush over surface of the paste.

7. Bake in the preheated oven for 45 minutes, or until well puffed and golden brown, with no tiny beads of moisture appearing on the surface. Prick the ring in several places with a cake tester or wooden pick to release the steam. Then reduce oven temperature to 300° F. and bake for 10 to 15 minutes longer.

8. Cut into wedges and serve hot.

CROSTINI

If all the preceding recipes are just too much for you, try this easy and delicious finger appetizer. It won't quite make it as a luncheon dish, but it is great served hot as an accompaniment to a salad.

HAVE ON HAND	*COOKWARE*
Sandwich bread	Large skillet
Mozzarella cheese	
Salt and pepper	
Butter	

1. Using a biscuit or cooky cutter, cut slices of *sandwich bread* into rounds about 2½ inches in diameter. Slice the *mozzarella cheese* and cut out half as many cheese rounds as you have bread rounds.

2. Place a cheese round on half of the bread slices, and sprinkle lightly with *pepper and salt*. Cover each with a second bread round, press firmly together, and chill.

3. Just before serving, sauté the crostini in *foaming butter* in a large skillet until lightly browned on both sides.

4. Keep hot in a 250° F. oven until ready to serve.

VEGETABLES—MAIN DISHES & SIDE DISHES

Vegetables for Vegetables' Sake

How does one do justice to vegetables within the confines of a single chapter? The ways to cook them, the variations and interesting combinations are endless and could fill many books, let alone just one chapter.

I can therefore touch only briefly on the wonderful world of vegetables, giving you a few favorite dishes, stews, and casseroles that are so good one can easily make an entire meal of them with crisp hot bread or homemade muffins.

Select the freshest, youngest vegetables you can buy. There are a few vegetables, such as baking potatoes, in which quality improves with size, and a few others, such as turnips, onions, and parsnips for the soup pot, in which maturity adds dignity, but, in general, the younger and fresher a vegetable is, the more succulent and flavorful. Good vegetables and salad greens are well worth the trouble it takes to seek out a reliable greengrocer who carries a large selection and keeps his produce moist and cool. They are worth many trips to country roadside stands during the growing season and the fall harvest. Once you have bought them, it is up to YOU to keep them moist and fresh in the refrigerator until you are ready to cook them.

Fresh vegetables are powerhouses of vitamins and minerals IF they are not boiled to death in massive quantities of water. To insure minimum loss of nutrients, either steam them, or cook them in the least amount of water for the least amount of time it takes to make them just fork tender.

HOW TO COOK MOST VEGETABLES
FOR BEST FLAVOR

Wash scrape, peel, trim, or otherwise prepare vegetables carefully. Leave small young vegetables whole or halve them. Slice larger vegetables or cut into thin julienne strips.

Use a heavy saucepan with a tight-fitting lid. Put the prepared vegetables into it with *2 to 3 tablespoons butter* and *an equal amount of water.* Cover tightly and steam over moderate heat, shaking the pan occasionally, for no more than 5 to 8 minutes, or until just tender.

Empty vegetables into a warm serving dish, and sprinkle with *salt and pepper* (try white pepper for a change some time). *A squeeze of lemon juice* is good on such vegetables as cabbage, spinach, cauliflower, or Brussels sprouts.

Vegetable Dinners

BASIC VEGETABLE DINNER

Serves 6. Serve with hot crusty French bread or garlic bread. Begin with the basic vegetables that are included in a New England boiled dinner: potatoes, carrots, whole onions, celery. If beets or cabbage are used, they should be cooked separately. From there you can go on to a great variety of other vegetables, depending on the best and freshest available. This dinner provides a bonus—about 2 quarts of rich vegetable broth.

BUY

Basic vegetables: potatoes, carrots, onions, celery
Leeks (if possible)
1-pound, 12-ounce can whole tomatoes
A selection of *long-cooking* vegetables, such as: yellow turnips, parsnips, celery root, Jerusalem artichokes, winter squash, pumpkin
A selection of *quick-cooking* vegetables, such as: beets, cabbage, zucchini, summer squash, peas, green beans, cauliflower, broccoli, Brussels sprouts, eggplant, kohlrabi, mushrooms, white turnips, okra
Fresh parsley, dill, tarragon, *or* chives

HAVE ON HAND	COOKWARE
Garlic	5- to 6-quart kettle
Olive oil	
Butter	
Salt	
Bay leaves	
Lemon	
Coarsely ground pepper	
Dried marjoram *or* tarragon	
Dry white wine (optional)	
Cayenne pepper	

1. Peel and coarsely chop *2 medium onions* and *1 clove garlic*. Wash and chop *3 outer stalks with leaves from a bunch of celery* and *2 leeks*.

2. In the kettle, heat *2 tablespoons each olive oil and butter* and in it sauté the prepared vegetables until lightly browned. Add *tomatoes with liquid, 1 tablespoon salt, 2 bay leaves, 1 lemon,* sliced, *½ teaspoon coarsely ground pepper, ½ teaspoon marjoram or tarragon,* and *4 quarts water (or 3 quarts water and 1 bottle dry white wine)*. Bring to a boil, then simmer for 30 minutes.

3. While broth is simmering, prepare the *long-cooking vegetables:* Peel potatoes and onions and leave them whole. Scrape carrots and leave them whole, too, or cut in half lengthwise. Cut *remaining stalks of the bunch of celery* into 6 lengthwise slices. Peel any other long-cooking vegetables and cut into large chunks. You should have about 2 quarts of cut-up vegetables in all. Add them to the simmering broth and simmer for 1 hour.

4. Meanwhile prepare the *quick-cooking vegetables,* and cut into bite-size slices or chunks.

5. When the long-cooking vegetables are almost tender, add the quick-cooking vegetables and return broth to a simmer. Correct seasoning of the broth with salt, add a *little cayenne,* and continue to simmer for 15 to 20 minutes.

6. To serve, spoon the vegetables out of the pot into a large tureen, then moisten them with a *little of the pot liquor.* Sprinkle with *chopped parsley,* or serve with *melted butter* to which is added *chopped parsley, dill, tarragon,* or *chives.*

NOTE: The remaining pot liquor makes an ideal vegetable broth. It will keep in the refrigerator for 3 or 4 days, or can be poured into containers and frozen.

HORSERADISH CREAM SAUCE

Makes 1½ cups. For a Vegetable Dinner New England style.

In saucepan melt *3 tablespoons butter.* Add *3 tablespoons flour* and cook, stirring, until mixture is blended and bubbling. Remove saucepan from heat, add *1 cup of the hot vegetable broth,* stirring vigorously. Return to heat and cook, stirring, until sauce is smooth and thick. Stir in *½ cup cream* and *fresh grated or preserved horseradish to taste (from ¼ to ½ cup).*

AÏOLI SAUCE

Makes 1 cup. For a Vegetable Dinner French style.

Peel and mash *5 or 6 large cloves garlic* and beat into *1 cup mayonnaise.* (If you have an electric blender, put garlic and mayonnaise into blender jar, stir to combine, and blend at high speed for 10 seconds.)

SKORDALIA SAUCE

Makes 2 cups. For a Vegetable Dinner Greek style.

Cook *4 large potatoes* in boiling water until very soft. Drain and mash with *8 peeled and crushed cloves garlic.* Gradually beat in *1 cup olive oil, juice of 2 lemons,* adding the olive oil and lemon juice alternately in very small amounts, stirring briskly. Season to taste with *salt and pepper,* and continue to stir in rotary motion until sauce is stiff enough to hold its shape.

VEGETABLE DINNER INDIAN STYLE

Tie in a small cloth bag *a small piece root ginger* and *1 tablespoon each coriander and fennel seeds.* Add the spice bag to the simmering broth (step 2 of Basic Vegetable Dinner), and simmer for 20 minutes. Discard spice bag before adding vegetables. When vegetable dinner is cooked, serve with:

CURRY SAUCE

Makes about 1 quart

In saucepan heat *4 tablespoons butter,* and in it sauté *1 small minced onion, 1 minced clove garlic,* and *2 tablespoons curry powder* for 2 to 3 minutes. Stir in *4 tablespoons flour.* Gradually stir in *3 cups of the hot vegetable broth* and cook, stirring, until sauce is slightly thickened. Stir in *3 tablespoons seedless raisins* and *3 tablespoons chopped pistachio nuts,* and simmer for 15 minutes, stirring frequently. Add *salt and cayenne pepper to taste,* and just before serving stir in *½ cup heavy cream.*

GHIVETCH

Serves 6. This is a traditional Romanian vegetable casserole which is baked in a moderate oven until most of the liquid has evaporated and the vegetables are tender. One does not eat it immediately, but rather allows it to cool so that the vegetables have time to blend and ripen. It is then served cold or at room temperature, or it may be reheated before serving. I hesitate to give a specific recipe for this dish, for it all depends on what vegetables are in season. In the spring, take advantage of the young fresh peas, tender new carrots and potatoes, stalks of asparagus, slim green beans. In the fall months you can use as many of the root vegetables as you can find and combine them with both hard and summer squashes, cabbage, cauliflower, and so on.

Here is just one version. Use your imagination for many others.

BUY

Selection of vegetables in season

HAVE ON HAND

4 or 5 large tomatoes, fresh or canned
Onions
Garlic
Butter
White wine *or* chicken broth
Salt and pepper
Olive *or* corn oil

COOKWARE

Heavy 4-quart casserole or clay pot
Skillet

1. Fill the large casserole or clay pot with a *large selection of vegetables,* such as: sliced *carrots* and *parsnips;* peeled and diced *potatoes; Jerusalem artichokes;* a small *eggplant,* peeled and diced; a *green pepper,* seeded and cut into strips; *half a head of cabbage or cauliflower,* cut into chunks; *a summer squash* or *a couple of zucchini,* sliced; *sliced stalks of celery or fennel,* or *a celery root,* peeled and diced; *an acorn or butternut squash,* peeled, seeded, and cut into chunks.

2. To the mixed vegetables add *4 or 5 tomatoes,* fresh or canned, cut into sections.

3. Now peel and slice *2 large onions* and *2 large cloves of garlic.*

4. In a skillet heat ½ *stick butter,* and in it sauté the onions and garlic until lightly browned. Add ½ *cup white wine and* ½ *cup water, or 1 cup chicken broth,* and *salt and pepper to taste.* Bring to a boil. Add ½ *cup olive oil or corn oil,* and bring again to a simmer. Pour the hot broth and the onions and garlic over the vegetables in the casserole.

5. Cover casserole tightly and bake in a preheated 350° F. oven for 30 to 40 minutes, or until most of the liquid has evaporated.

6. Remove from oven, and LET COOL to room temperature before serving, or before reheating.

Mixed Deep-Fried Vegetables

FRITTO MISTO

In Italy, quick-fried foods are a specialty. They may be served as a simple first course, as an accompaniment to a main dish, or as a meal in themselves. *Fritto Misto,* or mixed fry, is an impressive array of bite-size tidbits—a variety of meats, fish, cheeses, and vegetables—quickly fried to golden crispness in deep fat. It is a dish which invites you to use your imagination in selecting the plain, unusual, and exotic foods that you choose to serve. If you wish, you may certainly make the assortment strictly vegetarian by eliminating such traditional items as chicken livers, thin slices of veal, veal kidneys, sweetbreads, and so on. A *Fritto Misto* of only vegetables and cheese is a delicious simple dish.

Prepare the ingredients well in advance. This leaves only the quick cooking to be done when it is time to eat. Everything should be cut or broken into bite-size pieces. Cauliflowerets, broccoli, carrot sticks, string beans, Brussels sprouts, and other hard vegetables should be parboiled in salted water for about 5 minutes, then well-drained. Eggplant and green peppers should be cut into julienne strips; they need no precooking. Cut Camembert, Gruyère, or Swiss cheese into squares or strips.

BUY

A variety of vegetables and cheeses, and other foods if you wish

HAVE ON HAND	*COOKWARE*
Salt and pepper	Frite pan *or* deep-fat fryer
Flour	Baking sheet
Cayenne pepper	
2 eggs	
Beer or milk	
Vegetable oil	
Lemons	
Parsley	

1. Prepare the *foods to be fried* as described in introduction to recipe. Sprinkle them lightly with *salt and pepper,* cover with transparent film, and refrigerate until ready to cook.

2. In mixing bowl, combine *1½ cups flour, 1 teaspoon salt,* and *⅛ teaspoon cayenne pepper.* In another small bowl combine *2 eggs, 1 cup beer or milk,* and *2 tablespoons vegetable oil.* Stir liquid ingredients into dry ingredients to make a smooth batter. Cover and refrigerate until ready to use. Stir frequently during use.

3. To cook: Fill a frite pan or deep-fat fryer one-third full of vegetable oil. Lower the basket into the pan and heat the oil to 365° F.

4. Dip a couple of pieces of each of the foods into the batter and fry for about 2 minutes, or until golden brown. Raise the basket and let the excess oil drain off. Empty fried tidbits onto a baking sheet lined with absorbent paper, and keep warm in a low, 200° F., oven until ready to serve; or serve them to one person at a time. Garnish with *wedges of lemon* and *sprigs of parsley.*

TEMPURA

If you choose to deep fry such vegetables as sliced lotus root, *shiitake* mushrooms, snow peas, water chestnuts, bamboo shoots, and soybean curd, the method is the same as for *Fritto Misto* in the preceding recipe, but you will be leaving Italy far behind and entering the fascinating world of Japanese cuisine. Japanese *tempura* does not mean simply batter-fried butterflied shrimp; it encompasses a large assortment of edible plain and exotic tidbits, which generally do include shrimp as well as oysters and small boneless pieces of fish.

Tempura is served hot, with one or more traditional dipping sauces. These sauces include a fish stock called *dashi,* which is distilled from seaweed and dried bonito.

TEMPURA SAUCE

Combine *1 cup dashi or dashi substitute* (see following recipes), *¼ cup soy sauce,* and *¼ cup saki* (rice wine). Serve in small individual dipping bowls.

DASHI
(Japanese Fish Stock)

BUY

Small square seaweed (*kombu*)
Package dried bonito (*kanakatsuo* or *katsuobushi*)

Wash *seaweed* and put it into a saucepan with *4 cups water.* Bring water to a boil and boil for 2 minutes. Remove seaweed. Add *4 tablespoons bonito* to the rapidly boiling liquid, remove saucepan immediately from heat, and let liquid settle for 1 minute. Strain off the stock; this is dashi.

DASHI SUBSTITUTE

Combine *½ cup beef bouillon, or broth or water in which mushrooms have been simmered,* with *2 tablespoons sherry or saki, 2 tablespoons sugar,* and *¼ cup soy sauce.* Use this mixture in place of the dashi in Tempura Sauce.

SWEET AND SOUR DASHI SAUCE

In small saucepan, combine *½ cup dashi or dashi substitute, ½ cup water, 2 teaspoons soy sauce, ½ teaspoon salt, 2 tablespoons cider vinegar, and ½ teaspoon sugar.* Cook and stir over moderate heat until mixture simmers and becomes clear.

DEEP-FRIED SOY-BEAN CURD

BUY	*HAVE ON HAND*
8 ¾-ounce cans (drained weight) baked soybean curd (*yakidofu*)	1 egg white Fresh bread
Fresh ginger root	

1. Drain *bean curd.* Each can contains three ½-inch-thick slices, 4 x 2 inches. Place the curd between plates with a heavy weight on top for 1 hour to press out excess liquid, then cut each slice into 8 oblongs 2 inches long and ½ inch wide.

2. Peel the *ginger root,* wrap in transparent film, and refrigerate.

3. Crumb *2 slices white bread.* Combine *1 egg white* and *1½ tea-spoons water.*

4. Dip the pieces of bean curd into the diluted egg white, then roll in bread crumbs.

5. Fry curd in *deep oil,* heated to 365° F., for 2 minutes or until lightly browned.

6. Drain on absorbent paper, and serve hot with a spoonful of Sweet and Sour Dashi Sauce and a sprinkling of grated fresh ginger. Serve with Tempura.

Vegetables from
Artichokes to Zucchini

ARTICHOKES

One of the vegetables that many people seem to be puzzled about preparing is the artichoke, which is such a delicious vegetable served either hot or cold, as an appetizer, luncheon dish, or salad course.

Buy fresh-looking green globe artichokes with tightly closed leaves. Cut the stem off each artichoke close to the bottom to give it a steady base on which to sit. Remove a row or two of the large outer leaves, for these are tough and fibrous and have little edible meat in them. Then, with a heavy sharp knife, slice off about 1 inch from the top of the artichoke, or trim the prickly point off each leaf with kitchen scissors.

TO COOK:

Stand the artichokes on their bases in a large kettle and just cover with *cold water.* For *4 to 6 artichokes,* add *1 tablespoon salt,* the *juice of ½ lemon* and, if desired, *a cut clove of garlic.*

Bring liquid to a boil, cover kettle, then simmer over low heat for 45 minutes. When a leaf is pulled easily from the base, or a fork easily penetrates the bottom of the artichokes, they are cooked. Turn off the heat and let them rest in the hot water until ready to serve. They will keep hot for at least half an hour.

With a slotted spoon lift the artichokes, one at a time, out of the water; drain them upside down on a cake rack set into the sink. Squeeze each one gently to drain it completely before setting it upright on a serving plate. Serve hot or cold.

When artichokes are served cold, they are generally accompanied by Sauce Vinaigrette (page 127) or Garlic Mayonnaise (page 149). When served hot, they are equally good with these same sauces or with a hot butter-lemon juice sauce seasoned with salt and pepper, and, often, with finely minced garlic.

TO EAT ARTICHOKES:

Pluck off a leaf and dip into the sauce. Eat only the tender base of each leaf, scraping off the soft pulp with the teeth, until you come down to the choicest morsel, the artichoke bottom. This is covered with tiny leaves folded tightly around furry filaments known as the choke. Cut or scrape away the choke; then cut the artichoke bottom into bite-size pieces, and dip these into the sauce before enjoying each delicious bite.

ARTICHOKES BRAISED WITH VEGETABLES

Serves 4

BUY

4 globe artichokes
1 head lettuce
1 pound fresh peas *or* 2 cups canned
1 head celery
1 small head fennel
1 carrot
8 small new potatoes
1 large ripe tomato

HAVE ON HAND

Butter
Garlic
Dry white wine
Salt
Coarsely ground pepper

COOKWARE

Large heavy casserole with cover

1. Trim stems from the *artichokes,* remove 2 rows of lower outer leaves, and cut off 2 inches from tops. Separate the leaves, wash well, and scoop out the pale yellow leaves and the furry choke from center of the artichokes with a metal spoon.

2. *Butter* the casserole. Wash and shred the *lettuce,* and arrange in the bottom of the dish. Place the artichokes upright on the bed of lettuce.

3. Shell the *peas,* or drain the canned. Remove outer stalks from the *celery* (and reserve for Creamed Celery with Toasted Almonds or some

other use). Chop the heart of celery. Chop the *fennel,* scrape and slice the *carrot,* and peel the *potatoes.* Cut the *tomato* into wedges. Peel and mince *1 clove garlic.* Fill the center of the artichokes with the peas. Then surround the artichokes with the celery, fennel, carrot, potatoes, and tomato. Sprinkle with the *minced garlic.*

4. Add *1 cup dry white wine, 2 cups water, 2 teaspoons salt,* and ½ *teaspoon coarsely ground pepper.* Place casserole over heat and bring liquid to a boil. Then cover and cook over low heat for about 1 hour, or until artichokes are tender.

5. Serve one artichoke per person; surround it with some of the vegetables and moisten with some of the cooking liquid.

NOTE: Any remaining liquid makes a wonderful broth for meatless soups or casseroles.

BROCCOLI AU GRATIN

Serves 4. Other vegetables, such as white turnips, cabbage, parsnips, carrots, kohlrabi, Jerusalem artichokes, cauliflower, or Brussels sprouts, may be substituted for the broccoli.

BUY

1 bunch broccoli, about 1½ pounds
8-ounce container heavy cream

HAVE ON HAND	COOKWARE
Salt	2-quart saucepan
Milk	Shallow baking dish
Butter	Small saucepan
Flour	1½-quart saucepan
White pepper	
Parmesan cheese, grated	
Bread crumbs	

1. Discard lower tough portions of broccoli stalks, and cut stalks and flowerheads into thin slices. Put the slices into the large saucepan with *2 cups water* and ½ *teaspoon salt.* Bring liquid to a boil and simmer for

10 minutes, or until broccoli is just fork-tender. Drain well and empty broccoli into a shallow baking dish.

2. In the small saucepan heat *2 cups milk* to simmering.

3. In the medium saucepan melt *6 tablespoons butter*. Stir in *6 tablespoons flour,* and cook, stirring, until mixture bubbles. Remove saucepan from heat and let mixture cool for a moment. Then add the hot milk, all at once, and stir vigorously with a wire whisk or wooden spoon until sauce is smooth. Return to heat; cook, stirring well from bottom and sides of pan, for about 3 minutes, or until sauce is thickened. Stir in *cream, a dash of white pepper,* and about *1 teaspoon salt or to taste.* Pour sauce over broccoli.

4. Combine *2 tablespoons grated cheese* and *½ cup bread crumbs.* Sprinkle crumbs over surface of the sauce and dot with *2 tablespoons butter.* Set aside until ready to cook.

5. To bake: Preheat oven to 375° F. Bake the broccoli for 20 minutes, or until the top is crusty and golden and the sauce is bubbling.

SWEET AND SOUR RED CABBAGE

Serves 6 to 8

You need a large saucepan for this dish, for it's amazing how much shredded cabbage you'll get from one head. This does wilt considerably as it cooks. The recipe may be halved, but you might as well cook the whole head of cabbage while it is fresh, rather than reserving half of it; the cooked dish is just as good reheated for another meal.

BUY

1 crisp red cabbage, medium size
2 tart apples

HAVE ON HAND

1 medium onion
Sugar, granulated *or* brown
Cooking oil
Red wine vinegar

Caraway seeds
Salt and pepper
Dry red wine *or* water
Lemon

COOKWARE

5-quart saucepan *or* kettle, with cover

1. Remove any discolored or wilted leaves from *cabbage*. Quarter cabbage and discard white core. Shred cabbage finely. You'll have about 8 cups.

2. Chop *1 medium onion*. Peel, quarter, core, and slice the *apples*.

3. Measure *4 tablespoons sugar* and *4 tablespoons oil* into saucepan or kettle. Place over moderate heat and cook until sugar turns caramel in color. Turn heat to low, add onion and cook until onion is golden, stirring frequently.

4. Add the shredded cabbage, the sliced apples, *4 tablespoons vinegar, 1 teaspoon caraway seeds, 2 teaspoons salt, ½ teaspoon pepper,* and *1 cup dry red wine*. Bring to a boil, then cover and cook over low heat for 40 minutes, stirring occasionally.

5. Correct seasoning with *salt*. Add a *little more sugar* if cabbage is not sweet enough, and *a squeeze of lemon juice* (a good last-minute addition to many vegetables).

VITAMIN CARROTS

Serves 4. You may use this recipe for 1½ quarts of any shredded root vegetable such as parsnips, white or yellow turnips, celery root, kohlrabi, Jerusalem artichokes, and so on.

BUY

10 large fresh carrots

HAVE ON HAND

Butter
Salt
White peppercorns

COOKWARE

1½-quart casserole

1. Wash, scrape, and shred the *carrots*.

2. Preheat oven to 350° F.

3. Put the carrots into the casserole and add *1 stick butter, a sprin-kling of salt, lots of freshly ground white pepper,* and *½ cup water.*

4. Cover the casserole tightly and bake in the preheated oven for 30 minutes.

BRAISED CELERY OR BELGIAN ENDIVE

Serves 4

BUY

2 heads Pascal celery or 8 roots of Belgian endive

HAVE ON HAND	**COOKWARE**
Butter	Large heavy skillet
Salt	
Pepper	
Lemon	
Parmesan cheese	

1. Remove the coarse outer stalks of the *celery* and the large celery leaves from the top, and reserve for the soup pot. Wash the remaining head well and cut into quarters lengthwise. Or, if using *endive,* trim the root ends, and wash.

2. In skillet melt *2 tablespoons butter,* and in it arrange the stalks of celery or endive. Sprinkle with *½ teaspoon salt* and *¼ teaspoon pepper.* Add the *juice of 1 lemon* and *1 cup water.* Bring liquid to a boil, cover tightly, and cook over low heat for about 40 minutes, or until most of the moisture has cooked away.

4. Remove endive or celery to serving dish and pour over any butter and juices left in the skillet. Serve with *grated Parmesan* on the side.

CREAMED CELERY WITH TOASTED ALMONDS

Serves 6

BUY

1 head of celery
Bunch of green onions
1 container light cream
Toasted slivered almonds

HAVE ON HAND	*COOKWARE*
Butter	10-inch skillet with cover
Flour	
Milk	
Salt and pepper	
Worcestershire sauce	

1. Wash and trim the *celery* and separate into stalks. Cutting on the diagonal, thinly slice enough stalks to measure 4 cups. Wash and trim *green onions* and cut about 4, including green tops, into 1-inch diagonal pieces. They should measure about ½ cup.

2. In large skillet melt *4 tablespoons butter*. Add celery slices and toss them until coated with the melted butter; then cover and cook over low heat, stirring occasionally, for 10 minutes. Do not overcook. The celery should remain crisp.

3. Stir in the green onions, then cover and cook for 5 minutes.

4. Sprinkle the vegetables with *2 tablespoons flour*. Gradually stir in *1 cup milk,* and cook, stirring, until sauce has thickened and simmered for 1 minute.

5. Stir in *½ teaspoon salt, a good dash pepper, ½ teaspoon Worcestershire sauce,* and *½ cup light cream*. Heat to simmering.

6. Spoon into serving dish and sprinkle with *½ cup toasted almonds.*

FRESH FROM THE CORN PATCH

Whether you buy fresh corn from a local roadside stand or at your market, be sure the kernels are plump and shiny—then waste no time in getting it home and into the pot. If it is not going to be cooked immediately, dip the ears, husks and all, into cold water, wrap them in a towel, and store in the refrigerator.

Don't strip the corn of its husks until the water is boiling. And don't be like the bride who was in tears when her husband arrived home for dinner, because she had been boiling sweet corn all afternoon and couldn't get it tender. Corn should NEVER be boiled, only simmered for a brief time. Corn kernels are plump with corn milk. When the milk is boiled it will curdle and the corn is going to be tough.

CORN ON THE COB

Bring a large kettle of water to a rapid boil. Shuck *fresh ears of sweet corn* and drop them into the boiling water. This will stop the boiling. Allow the water to come back to a simmer, then turn off the heat, cover the kettle, and let the corn poach in the hot water 5 to 8 minutes. Actually, it may remain in the water longer without drastic deterioration, as the water will gradually cool.

It's quite permissible to serve one round of ears and allow the rest to remain in the hot water for second servings. It's better to keep it moist and warm than to allow it to cool and dry on the table. Serve the corn with *sweet butter* and *salt and pepper* on the side.

CORN COOKED IN CREAM

Cut *enough fresh corn kernels from the cobs to fill a small casserole. Butter* the casserole, fill with the corn, and sprinkle with a *little salt and freshly ground pepper*. Pour over *enough cream to almost cover the corn,* and top with *buttered crumbs*. Bake in a preheated 375° F. oven for 30 minutes, or until the top is browned.

VARIATION: Substitute *unpeeled yellow squash*, cut into ½-inch-thick slices, for the corn.

CORN PURÉE

Cook *fresh ears of corn* in simmering water for 5 minutes only. Plunge ears into cold water to cool them enough to make them easy to handle. Cut down through the rows of kernels with a sharp knife, splitting each kernel open. Then press out the corn purée or pulp with the back of the knife or with the side of a fork.

To *each cup of corn purée* add *2 tablespoons butter* and *salt and pepper to taste*. Cook over steaming water, stirring constantly, until purée is hot. Serve immediately.

FRESH CORN PUDDING

Serves 3 or 4

HAVE ON HAND	*COOKWARE*
2 cups corn purée (see preceding recipe)	1½-quart casserole
Butter	2-quart saucepan
Flour	
Thin cream *or* half-and-half	
Salt	
Black peppercorns	
3 egg whites	

1. Preheat oven to 375° F. *Butter* the casserole.

2. In saucepan melt *2 tablespoons butter*. Stir in *2 tablespoons flour*. Gradually stir in *1½ cups thin cream or half-and-half*, and cook, stirring, until sauce is thickened.

3. Stir in *2 cups corn purée, 1 teaspoon salt,* and *freshly ground pepper to taste.* Heat just to a simmer.

4. Beat *3 egg whites* until stiff but not dry. Fold into the corn mixture. Pour into the prepared casserole and bake in the preheated oven for 40 minutes.

EGGPLANT PARMIGIANA

Serves 4. This recipe may be doubled. Serve with salad and crusty bread.

BUY

1 medium eggplant
1 green pepper
8-ounce can tomato sauce
6- *or* 8-ounce package mozzarella cheese

HAVE ON HAND

Onion
Garlic
Flour
Salt and pepper
Olive oil
Parmesan cheese, freshly grated

COOKWARE

10 x 6 x 1½-inch baking dish
8-inch skillet

1. Peel and slice the *eggplant* ½ inch thick. One medium eggplant should give you 8 nice thick slices. Sprinkle slices with salt, stack them one on top of the other, and place a heavy weight on top for half an hour to draw out any bitter juices.

2. Meanwhile peel and chop *enough onion to measure ½ cup.* Seed and chop about *enough green pepper to make ½ cup.* Peel and mince *1 large clove garlic.* Set vegetables aside.

3. Measure *¼ cup flour, ½ teaspoon salt,* and *¼ teaspoon pepper* onto a piece of waxed paper, and mix well. Wash eggplant slices and dry between paper towels. Coat slices on both sides with the flour mixture.

4. Measure *½ cup olive oil.* Pour *2 tablespoons of this oil* into skillet, and heat to moderate temperature. Sauté the eggplant, over moderate

heat, about 2 slices at a time, until golden on both sides. Add oil to skillet as needed. Drain eggplant on absorbent paper.

5. Add *any remaining oil* to skillet, and in it sauté the onion, green pepper, and garlic over low heat for 5 minutes. Stir in *tomato sauce,* and simmer for 5 minutes. Correct seasoning with *additional salt and pepper.*

6. Spoon *half the sauce* into the baking dish, and top it with the eggplant slices. Cover with *slices of mozzarella cheese,* and spoon *remaining sauce* on top. Sprinkle with *3 tablespoons freshly grated Parmesan.* Set aside until ready to bake.

7. Preheat oven to 350° F. Bake the eggplant, uncovered, in the moderate oven for 30 minutes.

CURRIED EGGPLANT

Serves 6. Serve over cooked rice.

BUY

2 pounds eggplant
1 green *or* red sweet pepper
4 ripe tomatoes

HAVE ON HAND

Onions
Garlic
Butter
Turmeric
Powdered ginger
Dried red pepper
Salt

COOKWARE

Large heavy skillet, with cover

1. Wash and peel the *eggplant* and cut into 2-inch cubes. Peel and thinly slice *2 large onions* and *2 cloves garlic.* Wash, seed, and chop ½ *green pepper (or ½ red sweet pepper).* Peel and slice the *tomatoes.*

2. In skillet melt *4 tablespoons butter.* Add the eggplant cubes, *1 teaspoon turmeric, ½ teaspoon powdered ginger,* and *¼ teaspoon dried red pepper.* Sauté over moderate heat, stirring frequently, for 10 minutes.

3. Add onions, garlic, chopped green or red sweet pepper, and *1 cup water,* and cook over high heat until most of the water has evaporated.

4. Add the tomatoes and *salt to taste.* Mix well, cover tightly, and cook over very low heat for 15 minutes, or until vegetables are tender, shaking the skillet occasionally.

VEGETABLE BROTH WITH BRAISED LEEKS OR ZUCCHINI

Makes about 1 quart

BUY

7 large fresh leeks *or* 4 medium zucchini
1-pound can whole tomatoes *or* 6-ounce can tomato paste

HAVE ON HAND	*COOKWARE*
Onion	Heavy 10-inch skillet *or* chicken
Garlic	fryer, *or* wide top-of-the-stove cas-
Celery	serole
Carrot	
Parsley	
Butter	
Salt and pepper	
Bay leaves	
Lemon	
Thyme	
Dry white wine *or* dry vermouth (optional)	

1. Peel and coarsely chop *1 medium onion* and *1 clove garlic.* Wash and chop *2 outer stalks celery with leaves.* If you are not using zucchini, also wash and chop the *white part of 1 leek.* Scrape and chop *1 carrot,* and chop *¼ cup parsley.*

2. In the heavy pan heat *2 tablespoons butter,* and in it sauté the prepared vegetables until lightly browned. Add *entire contents of the can of tomatoes or 2 tablespoons tomato paste, 1 teaspoon salt, ¼ teaspoon pepper, 1 bay leaf, 2 slices lemon, ¼ teaspoon thyme,* and *2 quarts water or 7 cups water and 1 cup dry white wine or dry vermouth.* Bring liquid to a boil, partially cover the pan, and simmer for 40 minutes.

3. If leeks are used, discard the root ends and any withered outer leaves from the *remaining leeks*. Cut off tough green stalks, leaving the leeks no more than 6 inches long. Slit the tops of the leeks lengthwise; then wash thoroughly under cold running water, spreading leaves apart to remove any sand trapped in them. If *zucchini* are used, trim them at both ends, then slice them thickly.

4. Add the leeks or zucchini to the simmering broth, and partially cover the pan. Simmer leeks for 40 minutes; zucchini for 20 minutes.

5. Remove the leeks or zucchini, and serve hot with melted butter, or chill and serve covered with Sauce Vinaigrette (page 127).

6. Strain the broth. It will keep in the refrigerator for 4 or 5 days. Or pour into freezer containers and freeze for future use.

BREADED MUSHROOMS

Serves 4. A marvelous hot appetizer before almost any meal, or a good vegetable accompaniment to a sauced dish.

BUY

24 medium mushrooms, about 1 ounce each (1½ pounds)

HAVE ON HAND	*COOKWARE*
Salt	10-inch skillet
Pepper	
1 egg	
Flour	
Cornflake crumbs	
Butter	
Tartar sauce	

1. Wash the *mushrooms* and trim off their stems close to the caps. Reserve stems for another recipe. Drain the mushrooms, cap side up, on absorbent paper, and sprinkle lightly with *salt and pepper*.

2. Beat the *egg* in a shallow dish with *1 tablespoon water*.

3. Roll the mushrooms in *flour* to coat them evenly, then coat them evenly in the *egg mixture*. Place mushrooms on waxed paper covered with *cornflake crumbs*. Sprinkle them well with more crumbs, and turn mush-

rooms over and around to coat them heavily. Set coated mushrooms aside for 30 minutes or longer to dry.

4. When ready to cook, melt *4 tablespoons butter* in skillet. Place mushrooms in the hot butter, cap side down, and sauté over moderate heat for about 3 minutes, or until brown and crisp. Turn and continue to cook for about 3 minutes longer, or until brown and crisp on both sides.

5. Serve with *tartar sauce.*

MUSHROOMS PAPRIKASH

Serves 4

BUY

1 pound fresh mushrooms
8-ounce container sour cream

HAVE ON HAND

COOKWARE

1 small onion
Butter
Paprika (preferably Hungarian)
Salt
Cayenne pepper
Milk *or* light cream (optional)

10-inch skillet with cover

1. Clean, trim, and slice the *mushrooms.* Set aside.

2. Peel and finely chop *1 small onion,* then sauté in *4 tablespoons butter* until golden.

3. Sprinkle the onion with *1 tablespoon paprika, ½ teaspoon salt,* and *⅛ teaspoon cayenne pepper.* Add mushrooms, cover, and cook over low heat for 6 to 8 minutes.

4. Stir in the *sour cream,* bring to a boil, and turn off heat. If not ready to serve, reheat to simmering before serving. If sauce is too thick, stir in a *little milk or light cream.* Correct seasoning with *salt* and serve.

OKRA is not a popular vegetable throughout America, except in the Southern states where it is used extensively in stews, soups, and gumbos. Yet it is delicious simply boiled and served with lemon butter, or creamed, scalloped, pan-fried, or batter-fried. Okra teams naturally with tomatoes, onions, and corn.

OKRA TOMATO STEW

Serves 4

BUY

1 pound young fresh okra
3 large ripe tomatoes
Bunch of green onions
1 green pepper

HAVE ON HAND	*COOKWARE*
Salt	Large heavy skillet
Vegetable oil	
Flour	
Pepper	

1. Wash the *okra* thoroughly. Trim the stem ends, but do not cut the pods. Drop the okra into a saucepan of *boiling salted water* and boil for 10 minutes, then drain.

2. Peel and coarsely chop the *tomatoes*. Peel and chop *½ cup green onions*. Seed and chop the *green pepper*.

3. In skillet heat *2 tablespoons vegetable oil,* and in it sauté onion and green pepper for 5 minutes, or until green pepper is wilted. Stir in *1 teaspoon flour, 1 teaspoon salt,* and *¼ teaspoon pepper.* Add the tomatoes and okra, and cook over low heat for 30 minutes, stirring occasionally.

THE BEST FRIED ONION RINGS

If you decide to make these, make a lot. Store what you don't eat in freezer bags and freeze.

HAVE ON HAND	*COOKWARE*
Large sweet *or* mild onions	Heavy deep skillet *or* frite pan
Milk	
Flour	
1 quart vegetable oil	
Salt	

1. Slice *large sweet* or *mild onions* ¼ inch thick, and separate the slices into rings. Soak rings in *milk to cover* for 1 hour. Drain well and dry between sheets of absorbent paper.

2. Shake a handful of the onion rings at a time in a paper bag containing a *little flour*. Remove the onions and shake off the excess flour (a good way to do this is to place the floured rings in a colander and then shake the colander, tossing the rings, over a piece of waxed paper). Excess flour may be reused.

3. In a heavy deep skillet or frite pan, heat *1 quart of vegetable oil* to 375° F. Add a couple of handfuls of the floured onion rings at a time to the hot oil, and fry until golden brown and crisp. With a slotted spoon scoop them out onto a baking sheet lined with several thicknesses of absorbent paper to drain. Sprinkle with *salt* and keep warm in a very low oven until ready to serve.

TO HEAT FROZEN DEEP-FRIED ONION RINGS:

Empty the frozen onion rings onto a baking sheet lined with absorbent paper. Heat and crisp in a 350° F. oven for 10 minutes.

GARDEN PEAS À LA FRANÇAISE

Serves 6

BUY

2 pounds young green peas
1 head lettuce
12 small white onions

HAVE ON HAND	COOKWARE
Parsley	2-quart saucepan, with tight cover
Butter	
Thyme	
Sugar	
Salt and pepper	
Butter	

1. Shell the *peas*. Wash and shred the *lettuce*. Peel the *tiny onions*. Chop *1 tablespoon parsley*.

2. In saucepan melt *2 tablespoons butter*. Add peas, lettuce, onions, *a pinch of thyme*, the parsley, *1 teaspoon sugar*, *½ teaspoon salt*, and *¼ teaspoon pepper*.

3. Cover pan tightly, and simmer over low heat for 25 minutes, or until peas are tender, adding *a spoonful of water* from time to time if necessary.

4. Just before serving, stir in *1½ tablespoons butter*.

NIKA HAZELTON'S KARTOFFELRÖSTI

Serves 4

BUY

2 pounds potatoes

HAVE ON HAND	COOKWARE
Butter	Large saucepan
Salt	Large heavy skillet, with cover

1. In large saucepan boil *potatoes* in their jackets until tender. Cool and peel. Shred or cut potatoes into thin julienne strips.

2. In a large heavy skillet, heat *4 tablespoons butter*. Gradually add the potatoes and sprinkle with *¾ teaspoon salt*. Cook over low heat, turning frequently with a spatula, until potatoes are soft and yellow.

3. Press potatoes with the spatula into a flat cake. Sprinkle with *2 tablespoons hot water*. Cover and cook over low heat until potatoes are crusty and golden at the bottom, about 15 to 20 minutes. Shake the pan

frequently to prevent scorching and, if necessary, add a little more butter to prevent sticking.

4. Turn out, crusty side up, onto a hot serving dish. Serve immediately.

VIENNESE RAHMKARTOFFEL

Serves 4

Preheat oven to 300° F. Cook *12 new potatoes* in their jackets in *boiling water* until just fork tender. Drain, and as soon as they are cool enough to handle, peel them and cut into slices. Generously *butter* the bottom of a 1½-quart casserole. Put a layer of potatoes in the casserole and dot with *butter.* Sprinkle with *finely chopped garlic* and cover with *sour cream.* Repeat the layers until all potatoes are used. Sprinkle the top with *dry bread crumbs,* dot again with *butter,* and bake in the preheated oven for 30 minutes.

PUMPKIN should by no means be restricted to pies. There are countless other ways to cook this first cousin to the cucumber. It may be seasoned and baked, boiled in salted water, or steamed, and served with melted butter in exactly the same way as the many varieties of winter squash— the acorns, butternuts, and Hubbards. As a matter of fact, pumpkin and winter squash are interchangeable in most recipes.

The seeds of the pumpkin and the hard-skinned squash are hard and should be removed along with the fibrous tissue found in the center when the vegetable is cut.

BAKED PUMPKIN WITH WALNUTS

Serves 6. Sweet potatoes or butternut squash may be substituted for the pumpkin.

BUY

A small pumpkin

HAVE ON HAND	*COOKWARE*
Medium onion	1 large saucepan with cover
Salt	1 small saucepan
Butter	1½-quart casserole
Flour	
Light cream *or* half-and-half	
1 egg	
Orange	
Walnut meats	
Cracker crumbs	

1. Peel, seed, and thinly slice *2 pounds pumpkin* (enough slices to fill a heaping quart container). Peel and chop *1 medium onion.*

2. Put the pumpkin, onion, *1 cup water* and *1 teaspoon salt* into the large saucepan; bring to a boil, then cover and simmer for 15 minutes, or until tender. Drain and mash well with a fork or potato masher.

3. Preheat oven to 325° F. *Grease* the casserole.

4. In small saucepan melt *2 tablespoons butter.* Stir in *2 tablespoons flour.* Gradually stir in *1 cup light cream or half-and-half,* and cook, stirring constantly, until sauce is smooth and thickened. Remove from heat and stir in pumpkin, *1 egg, 1 tablespoon grated orange rind, 2 tablespoons orange juice,* and *½ cup chopped walnuts.*

5. Turn the pumpkin mixture into the prepared casserole, and sprinkle with *¼ cup fine cracker crumbs.*

6. Bake in the preheated oven for 35 minutes, or until lightly browned.

PIQUANT SPINACH

Serves 2 or 3

BUY

1½ pounds fresh spinach
8-ounce container dairy sour cream

HAVE ON HAND	COOKWARE
Salt	Large kettle with lid
Coarsely ground black pepper	
1 lemon	

1. Wash *spinach* well and discard coarse thick stems. Pick up by handfuls from sinkful of water, shake to remove excess water, and put into kettle. Cover and cook over moderate heat for 8 to 10 minutes, or until just wilted, tossing the leaves occasionally with a long two-tined fork. Remove from heat.

2. Drain spinach well, pressing out as much of the liquid as possible with the back of a spoon.

3. Cut through spinach in the kettle several times in different directions to chop it coarsely. Add *a light sprinkling of salt, a good sprinkling of coarsely ground black pepper, ½ cup sour cream,* and *1 tablespoon lemon juice.* Heat, tossing spinach with the fork until combined with the sour cream and steaming.

BAKED GLAZED SWEET POTATOES

Serves 6. These may be cooked in a skillet on top of the stove if preferred.

BUY

3 pounds sweet potatoes

HAVE ON HAND	COOKWARE
Salt	2-quart shallow baking dish
Butter	
Light brown sugar	
Corn syrup	
1 large juicy orange	

1. Peel *potatoes* and cut into thin julienne strips. Drop the strips as they are cut into *heavily salted water.* Let them soak for 1½ hours.

2. An hour before serving, melt *4 tablespoons butter* in a baking dish.

Drain and add potatoes. Sprinkle potatoes with *1 cup brown sugar, ½ cup corn syrup,* and the *grated rind and juice of 1 orange.*

3. Preheat oven to 350° F.

4. Place potatoes in the oven and bake for 35 to 50 minutes, or until glazed and tender.

WHEN VINE-RIPENED TOMATOES are in the markets, enjoy them while you can. For the purest flavor, peel and slice them thickly and serve them with nothing more than a sprinkling of coarse salt and some freshly ground pepper. Or serve them *vinaigrette* (page 127) with a touch of chopped fresh tarragon, chives, or sweet basil.

Stuffed tomatoes make excellent luncheon dishes. To serve cold: First wash the tomatoes and remove the skins. (The skins of vine-ripened tomatoes should strip off easily; if not, dip them briefly, one at a time, into a saucepan of boiling water, then slip off the skin.) Cut a thin slice from the stem end, scoop out the core and seeds, and fill the centers with your favorite salad mixture or with cooked, diced vegetables moistened with mayonnaise.

Hot stuffed tomatoes are also delicious, but are only as good as the tomatoes themselves. So don't waste your time using the pale, hot-house excuses sold in the markets during most of the cold winter months. Make the following tomato recipes only with ripe, farm-grown fruit—and fruit they are, not vegetable.

TOMATOES PORTUGAISE

Serves 6. Marvelous served with scrambled eggs.

HAVE ON HAND	*COOKWARE*
6 large ripe tomatoes	Large heavy skillet
Shallots *or* green onions	
Garlic	
Fresh parsley	
Olive oil	
Salt	
Peppercorns	

1. Peel *tomatoes* and cut in half crosswise. Squeeze gently to remove seeds and excess moisture, then chop coarsely. *Chop 2 tablespoons shallots or green onions. Peel and mince 1 large clove garlic. Chop ¼ cup parsley.*

2. In heavy skillet heat *¼ cup olive oil.* Add tomatoes and cook for 5 minutes, or until tomatoes are slightly soft. Add the shallots or green onions and the garlic, and simmer for a few minutes longer, or until most of the moisture is cooked away. Sprinkle with parsley, *salt,* and *freshly ground pepper.*

GREEN TOMATOES WITH CREAM GRAVY

Cut *green (or mostly green) tomatoes* into thick slices. Coat slices with *flour* and sprinkle with *salt and pepper.* Melt *a chunk of butter* in a large skillet, and in it sauté the tomato slices until lightly brown on one side. Sprinkle with a *little light brown sugar,* and brown them on the other side, adding *more butter* if necessary. Pour *1 cup heavy cream* over the browned tomato slices, and bring to a simmer. Remove tomato slices to serving platter, cook the cream rapidly for 2 minutes, stirring in all the nice brown bits from bottom and sides of the pan, and pour over the tomatoes.

ITALIAN STUFFED TOMATOES

Serves 4

HAVE ON HAND

4 large ripe tomatoes
Parmesan cheese
Fresh bread
1 egg
Salt and pepper
Olive oil
Garlic
Large black olives, pitted
Butter

COOKWARE

Baking pan

1. Cut a thin slice from top of *each tomato,* scoop out the seeds, and place the tomatoes upside-down on a rack to drain.

2. Preheat oven to 450° F. Grate *4 tablespoons cheese* and set aside.

3. Crumb *2 thick slices fresh bread,* and mix the crumbs with *1 egg, salt and pepper to taste, 2 tablespoons olive oil,* and *2 minced cloves garlic.*

4. Fill the center of each tomato with some of the crumb mixture, then press *1 olive* into the center of each. Arrange in baking pan. Sprinkle with cheese, dot with *butter,* and bake in the hot oven for 10 to 15 minutes.

TOMATOES PROVENÇALE

Serves 4

HAVE ON HAND	*COOKWARE*
4 large ripe tomatoes	Baking sheet
Salt and pepper	
Bread	
Garlic	
Parsley	
Butter	

1. Do NOT peel the *tomatoes.* Wash and cut in half crosswise. Arrange the halves, cut side up, on a baking sheet and sprinkle with *salt and pepper.*

2. Preheat oven to 450° F.

3. Meanwhile crumb *enough bread to make ½ cup crumbs,* then mix the crumbs with *1 clove garlic,* peeled and minced, *2 tablespoons chopped parsley,* and *4 tablespoons melted butter.*

4. Sprinkle the tomatoes with the crumb mixture, and bake them in the hot oven for 10 to 15 minutes, or until the crumbs are golden brown.

MASHED TURNIPS WITH BLACK ONIONS

Serves 4

Peel and thinly slice *2 large Spanish onions.* In a heavy skillet melt ¼ *pound (1 stick) butter.* Add the onions and let them cook over very low heat for about 1 hour, stirring frequently, until the onions are very brown. These are called "black" onions.

Meanwhile, peel *2 large rutabaga turnips.* Cut into large dice, and cook in *boiling salted water* until tender. When onions are "black," drain and mash the turnips rather coarsely. Season with *salt* and *plenty of freshly ground black pepper.* Pile the turnips into a serving dish and make a well in the center. Empty the onions into the well and serve hot.

ZUCCHINI is available during many months of the year, but in the fall, it is both abundant and inexpensive. This vegetable freezes beautifully. Simply wash and slice the slim squash, sauté the slices in butter until transparent, then drain and freeze for use in soup, stews, and casseroles all winter long.

ZUCCHINI PANCAKES

Serves 4

BUY

3 medium zucchini
Chives
Parsley

HAVE ON HAND

2 eggs
Flour
Parmesan cheese
Salt and pepper
Sour cream (optional)

COOKWARE

Griddle *or* iron skillet

1. Wash and trim the *zucchini,* and shred with a vegetable shredder. Chop *1 tablespoon each chives and parsley.* Grate *2 tablespoons Parmesan.*

2. In mixing bowl, combine *2 eggs, 3 tablespoons flour,* the grated Parmesan, the chopped chives and parsley, and *salt and pepper* to taste. Stir in the zucchini. If the batter seems to be too thin, add *another tablespoon flour.*

3. *Grease* the griddle and heat until a drop of water on it sputters and evaporates almost immediately. Drop the batter onto it by the tablespoonful and cook until the surface of the pancakes is bubbly and the underside is lightly browned. Turn and brown the other side.

4. Serve the pancakes hot, with *a dab of sour cream* on each if desired.

RAW FOODS & SALADS

Raw Food & Salads

The value of raw fruits and vegetables in daily meals can hardly be over-estimated. Besides being power plants of vitamins and minerals, they contain the cellulose or bulk needed to support the growth of essential intestinal bacteria. Some fresh raw food should be eaten at every meal. Certainly this is about the easiest and most delectable road to good health and one that never causes you to worry about your waistline.

Fresh fruit or fruit juice is a natural way to begin the day. And since we're speaking of nutrition, let's not settle for canned or bottled juices, for these are processed and their vitamin content and flavor are appreciably reduced. There is a place for these convenience juices as refreshing between-meal beverages, but not as alternatives to raw foods. Also, let's not get brainwashed by the "orange juice for breakfast" routine. Vary your breakfast fruits with ones in season, with fresh berries, plums, apricots, grapes, sweet cherries, with fresh pineapple sticks, honeydew or cantaloupe, a thick slice of fragrant watermelon, some fresh figs, a sliced banana, and occasionally, one of the more exotic fresh fruits found in fine markets—the mangoes, papayas, persimmons, and so on.

A salad of almost any kind—fruit, vegetable, cheese, or tossed greens—makes a perfect lunch when accompanied by a slice of high-protein bread or a wheatgerm muffin or cornbread square hot from the oven and spread with dairy-fresh sweet butter.

For snacks or appetizers, you can't top something as simple and healthful as a bowl of firm red radishes, crisp stalks of celery or fennel, cucumber or carrot strips, cherry tomatoes, or almost any young vegetable served just with a bowl of coarse salt, or with a favorite dip if you prefer, or after having been marinated for a couple of hours in a light salad dressing.

When you buy vegetables to eat raw, seek out the young, tender ones. The smaller vegetables have more flavor than the larger overgrown ones, which are also apt to be tough. Try paper-thin slices of peeled young kohlrabi, small button mushrooms, finger-size strips of small firm zucchini, or tiny eggplants.

Soups

When fresh garden vegetables are at the height of their season, remember the intriguing Spanish Gazpachos, raw vegetable soups or "liquid salads," and enjoy them as luncheon dishes or as first courses before dinner. Use the reddest, vine-ripened tomatoes you can buy.

GAZPACHO

Serves 6

BUY

2 slim firm cucumbers
1 large sweet Bermuda onion
2 green peppers
8 ripe tomatoes

HAVE ON HAND

Garlic
Tarragon red wine vinegar
Olive oil
Salt
Coarsely cracked pepper
Bread

COOKWARE

Small skillet

IN ADVANCE:

1. Peel, seed, and finely dice *1 cucumber*. Peel and finely chop *half the onion*. Seed and sliver *1 green pepper*. Peel, quarter, squeeze out seeds, and chop *6 tomatoes*. Mince *2 cloves garlic*.

2. Combine all these vegetables in a bowl or pitcher, and stir in *6 tablespoons wine vinegar, ¼ cup olive oil, 1 teaspoon salt, ½ teaspoon coarsely cracked pepper,* and *1½ cups cold water.*

3. Chill in refrigerator for several hours before serving.

4. Meanwhile prepare the garnish. Peel, seed, and dice the *remaining cucumber;* chop the *remaining half onion;* seed and chop the *remaining green pepper;* and peel, seed, and chop the *remaining 2 tomatoes.* Put each vegetable in a separate bowl and refrigerate until ready to serve.

PREPARE CROUTONS:

5. Cut *3 slices bread* into cubes. Brown the cubes lightly in *2 tablespoons olive oil,* and empty onto absorbent paper to drain.

WHEN READY TO SERVE:

6. Stir soup well, and pour into soup plates. Put *1 ice cube* in the center of each serving, and pass the croutons and chopped vegetables separately.

CRAIG CLAIBORNE'S GAZPACHO

Serves 4

BUY

2 slim cucumbers
3 large ripe tomatoes
2 green peppers

HAVE ON HAND	*COOKWARE*
Onions	Electric blender
Garlic	Small skillet
4 eggs	
Vinegar	
Olive oil	
Salt	
Cayenne pepper	
Tomato juice	
Bread	

1. Peel and slice *1 medium onion* and *1 clove garlic*. Peel and slice *1 cucumber* and the *3 tomatoes,* and seed and slice *1 green pepper*. Put these vegetables along with *4 eggs* into the container of an electric blender and blend to a purée.

2. Pour the blended vegetables into a bowl, and add *¼ cup vinegar, ¼ cup olive oil, ⅛ teaspoon salt, ⅛ teaspoon cayenne pepper,* and *¾ cup tomato juice*. Chill.

3. Meanwhile cut *2 slices bread* into cubes. They should measure 1 cup. Peel and mince *1 clove garlic*. Heat *2 tablespoons olive oil* with the minced garlic in a small skillet. Brown the bread lightly in this, then empty onto absorbent paper to drain.

4. Peel and dice *1 cucumber* and *1 medium onion*. Seed, peel, and chop the *remaining green pepper*.

5. When ready to serve, add the diced vegetables to the chilled soup. Pass the croutons separately, or top each serving of soup with a spoonful of croutons.

ICED CUCUMBER SOUP

Serves 4

BUY	*HAVE ON HAND*
2 cucumbers	Milk
1 pint yogurt	Garlic
Parsley *or* chives	Salt

1. Peel and seed the *cucumbers*. Chop *1½ of the cucumbers,* then combine with the *yogurt* and *½ cup milk*.

2. Peel and mince *1 clove garlic* and add to soup. Add *½ teaspoon salt*. Chop and add *1 tablespoon parsley or chives,* and correct seasoning with *salt*. Chill.

3. When ready to serve, shred the *remaining ½ cucumber*. Serve the soup with *1 ice cube* in each bowl, and garnish with the shredded cucumber.

ICED TOMATO SOUP

Serves 4. Try this in early September, when tomatoes are lush and juicy. Of course, you can substitute bottled tomato juice, but taste it just once made with the fresh. It's heaven.

BUY	*HAVE ON HAND*
3 pounds ripe tomatoes	Onion
8-ounce container heavy cream	Tabasco
Bunch green onions	Salt
Sour cream	
Parsley *or* fresh sweet basil	

1. Peel the *tomatoes;* then chop them in a large mixing bowl or pot and mash well with a potato masher. Strain through a sieve, stirring and pressing through as much of the soft pulp as possible. Discard the seeds.

2. Into 3 cups of the fresh tomato juice, stir the *heavy cream, 2 tablespoons minced green onion, 2 good dashes of tabasco,* and *salt to taste.*

3. Chill thoroughly; then pour into chilled cups, and top with *sour cream* and *a sprinkling of finely chopped parsley or sweet basil.*

Unusual & International Salads

One of the most luscious, nutritious, and satisfying fruits is the avocado. And the smallish, black, hard-shelled ones from California, known as calavos, are by far the best, being the richest in flavor and natural oils (and in calories, too!). The ways to serve avocados are many. The simplest is to cut an avocado in half lengthwise, remove the seed, and serve half to a person, with the hollow filled with lemon-juice Vinaigrette Sauce (page 127).

Guacamole is perhaps the most popular recipe for the avocado, served as a spread or dip. It also makes an excellent stuffing for small peeled tomatoes.

GUACAMOLE

Serves 4 as a dip or spread.

BUY	*HAVE ON HAND*
1 firm ripe California avocado	Garlic
	Lemon
	Tabasco
	Olive oil
	Salt and pepper
	Lettuce leaves
	Fritos *or* tortillas
	(*or* raw vegetables)

1. Peel the *avocado* and remove the seed. Chop the flesh coarsely into a mixing bowl.

2. Add *1 large peeled and minced clove garlic,* the *juice of ½ lemon,* about *20 drops Tabasco,* and *2 tablespoons olive oil.* Mix and mash the ingredients coarsely. It should not be a smooth spread. Mash in a *little salt and pepper* to taste.

3. Pile in a bowl lined with *lettuce leaves,* and serve with *Fritos, toasted tortillas, or raw vegetables.*

YIAOURTO SKODALIA

Makes about 1 cup. This Greek dip made with yogurt is a favorite to serve with crisp raw vegetables. Use tender hearts of romaine, strips of Belgian endive, raw cauliflowerets, carrot or cucumber sticks, scallions, small raw mushrooms, and radishes.

BUY	*HAVE ON HAND*
1 small slim cucumber	Garlic
8-ounce container unflavored	Walnut meats
yogurt	Olive oil
	Vinegar *or* lemon juice
	Salt and pepper

1. In a small mixing bowl combine *1 minced clove garlic, 3 minced walnut halves,* and *1 tablespoon olive oil.* Beat well with a fork.

2. Peel, seed, and shred the *cucumber* and add to bowl.

3. Gradually stir in the *yogurt,* and *about 1 teaspoon vinegar or lemon juice,* and *salt and pepper* to taste. Chill several hours or overnight before serving.

NOTE: See page 342 for Homemade Yogurt.

SWEDISH CUCUMBERS

Select *6 small slim, very firm cucumbers.* Peel and slice as thinly as possible into a salad bowl. Sprinkle with *1 teaspoon sugar, 1 teaspoon coarse salt,* and *some freshly ground black pepper.* Add *2 tablespoons white vinegar* and *6 ice cubes.* Refrigerate for several hours. Before serving, sprinkle lavishly with *chopped fresh dill or parsley.*

CUCUMBERS IN SOUR CREAM

Again, use *small slim, firm cucumbers.* Peel and slice thinly into a bowl. Combine to taste *sour cream, wine vinegar,* and *salt and pepper.* Pour over the cucumbers and chill for at least an hour before serving, tossing the cucumbers in the cream mixture occasionally. *Chopped fresh dill* is frequently added.

ONION SALAD

Peel and slice *several large sweet red onions* and soak in *ice water* for 2 to 3 hours. Drain well and sprinkle with *lots of chopped fresh parsley* and *freshly ground black pepper*. Add vinegar and salad oil in the proportion of *1 part vinegar to 3 parts salad oil,* and keep cold until ready to serve. Just before serving, sprinkle with *coarse salt*.

ONION ORANGE SALAD

Serves 3

Peel and thinly slice *1 orange* and *1 medium onion*. Sprinkle with *salt,* and add *1 tablespoon wine vinegar* and *3 tablespoons salad oil*. Chill for at least 30 minutes. Serve on *crisp lettuce leaves* with *a sprinkling of cayenne pepper* on top.

RAW MUSHROOM SALAD

Serves 4 to 6

BUY	HAVE ON HAND
½ pound very fresh button mushrooms	Wine vinegar
	Olive oil
	Dry mustard
	Dried tarragon
	Salt
	Coarsely ground pepper

1. Wash *mushrooms* and dry on paper towels. Cut stems off close to the caps and reserve for another use. Slice the *caps*.

2. In a mixing bowl combine *3 tablespoons wine vinegar, ½ cup olive oil, ¼ teaspoon dry mustard, ½ teaspoon dried tarragon, ¼ teaspoon salt* and *ground pepper to taste*. Add the sliced mushroom caps and toss lightly. Let marinate at room temperature for several hours before serving, tossing the mushrooms occasionally in the dressing.

MUSHROOMS IN CREAM DRESSING

Serves 4 to 6

Prepare *½ pound mushrooms* as in preceding recipe and add *1 small onion*, grated, *¼ cup heavy cream, 1 tablespoon each olive oil and lemon juice, ¼ teaspoon sugar,* and *salt and pepper to taste*. Marinate several hours or overnight before serving.

SPANISH SALAD

Serves 4

BUY	HAVE ON HAND
Head of romaine *or* lettuce	1 small onion
1 large orange	Olive oil
2 medium tomatoes	Salt and pepper
1 ripe avocado	Wine vinegar
Bunch firm radishes	
Small jar pimiento-stuffed green olives	

1. Wash and separate leaves from *head of romaine or lettuce*. Chill.

2. Peel *orange* deeply, removing all white pithy substance under the rind, right down to the fruit. Slice thinly. Peel and thinly slice *1 small onion*. Peel and quarter the *tomatoes*.

3. Put orange slices, onion, and tomatoes in a mixing bowl. Add *½ cup olive oil, ¼ teaspoon each salt and pepper,* and *3 tablespoons vinegar*. Marinate for 30 minutes, tossing ingredients once or twice.

4. Just before serving, peel the *avocado;* cut it in half and discard the seed. Slice the avocado into the bowl. Slice and add *8 radishes* and *8 olives.*

5. Toss salad and arrange it on a bed of the salad greens.

SPANISH CAULIFLOWER SALAD

Serves 6

BUY	HAVE ON HAND
Small jar ripe olives	Wine vinegar
1 small head cauliflower	Olive oil
1 green pepper	Salt
Jar pimientos	Freshly ground pepper
Green onions	
Romaine *or* crisp lettuce	

1. Slice *enough ripe olives to measure ½ cup* and empty into salad bowl.

2. Wash and trim the *cauliflower;* set half aside for another use and shred the other half thinly. Add shredded cauliflower to olives.

3. Add *⅓ cup finely chopped green pepper, ¼ cup chopped pimiento,* and *3 tablespoons chopped green onions.*

4. Add *1 tablespoon wine vinegar* and *3 tablespoons salad oil,* and chill for several hours.

5. When ready to serve, line individual salad plates with *crisp romaine or lettuce leaves.* Sprinkle the salad with *salt* and *freshly ground pepper,* toss again, and spoon a nest of the salad on each bed of greens.

SWISS CHEESE AND VEGETABLE SALAD

Serves 4

Dice *½ pound Swiss cheese,* and toss with *2 cucumbers,* peeled and diced,

12 radishes, thinly sliced, *1 sweet red onion,* peeled and thinly sliced, *1 cup sour cream,* and *2 tablespoons chopped fresh dill.* Mix gently, then season to taste with *salt, pepper,* and *lemon juice.* Keep cold until ready to serve. Serve on *shredded lettuce.*

CELERY ROOT RÉMOULADE

Serves 6

BUY	HAVE ON HAND
1 pound medium-size celery roots (about 3)	Mayonnaise
	Prepared mustard (preferably Dijon)
	Lemon juice
	Salt

1. Peel the *celery roots* with a sharp paring knife and cut them into sticks about the size of toothpicks.

2. Combine *1 cup mayonnaise, 1 tablespoon mustard,* and *lemon juice* and *salt to taste.* Add the celery root, mix well, and chill for several hours before serving.

TABOOLEY
(Parsley and Bulgur Salad)

Serves 4 to 6

BUY	HAVE ON HAND
1-pound box bulgur (cracked wheat)	Onions
Large bunch fresh parsley	Olive oil
Fresh mint leaves	Lemons
1 large ripe tomato	Salt and pepper
Bunch of romaine	

1. Soak *1 cup bulgur* in *water to cover* for 1 hour. Drain well and press out excess water.

2. Combine soaked wheat with *1 cup chopped onions, 1½ cups finely chopped parsley, ½ cup finely chopped fresh mint leaves, ¾ cup olive oil, ½ cup lemon juice,* and *salt and pepper to taste.* Chill.

3. Wash and separate the leaves of the *romaine* and chill.

4. Peel, seed, and chop the *tomato.* Serve the salad on a bed of romaine leaves, garnished with the chopped tomato.

CHINESE CABBAGE SALAD

Serves 6

BUY	*HAVE ON HAND*
1 head Chinese cabbage	Salt and pepper
Bunch scallions	1 lemon
Bunch radishes	Salad oil
Bunch parsley	

1. Wash the *head of cabbage,* discarding any discolored leaves. Shred the cabbage very thinly and put into a large salad bowl.

2. Wash and mince the *scallions,* using as much as possible of the tender green stalks. Wash, trim, and thinly slice the *radishes.* Chop ¼ *cup parsley.*

3. Add scallions, radishes, and parsley to the cabbage, and sprinkle with *salt and pepper to taste.* Add *juice of ½ lemon* and *⅓ cup salad oil,* and toss lightly. Chill for about 1 hour before serving.

COTTAGE CHEESE is one of the most versatile of cheeses. It's a high-protein food and provides important calcium. Team it with fruits and vegetables for a main-dish salad. Fresh garden vegetables such as tomatoes and radishes, green peppers and cucumbers, also carrots, celery, and lettuce —and chives—all make good foils for cottage cheese.

RED CABBAGE AND COTTAGE CHEESE SALAD

Serves 4

BUY	*HAVE ON HAND*
1-pound can diced beets	Mayonnaise
Small bunch celery	1 lemon
Small head red cabbage	Salt and pepper
8-ounce carton creamed cottage cheese	Nutmeg

1. Drain liquid from can of *beets* and empty beets into a large mixing bowl.

2. Wash, trim, and dice the *celery* and add to beets.

3. Discard any outer wilted or discolored leaves from *cabbage* and slice enough thinly to measure 3 cups. Add cabbage to celery and beets and mix lightly.

4. In another bowl combine the *cottage cheese* with *1 cup mayonnaise, 2 tablespoons lemon juice, 2 teaspoons salt, or to taste, ½ teaspoon pepper,* and *a dash of nutmeg.* Spoon mayonnaise mixture over vegetables and toss lightly to mix. Chill for at least 1 hour before serving.

PAPAYA AND AVOCADO SALAD

Serves 6. Here's a fabulous fruit salad combination to try when papayas are in season.

BUY	*HAVE ON HAND*
1 head romaine	Olive oil
Limes	Salt
1 ripe papaya	Black pepper
2 ripe calavo avocados	

1. Wash and separate leaves from the *head of romaine.* Chill well.

2. Combine ¼ *cup freshly squeezed lime juice* with ½ *cup olive oil,* *1 teaspoon salt,* and ¼ *teaspoon freshly ground black pepper.*

3. Arrange romaine leaves on six individual salad plates. Peel and slice the *papaya* and *avocados,* and arrange alternate slices of the fruits on each plate.

4. Whip the lime juice dressing briefly with a fork, then spoon a little over each salad. Serve immediately.

STRAWBERRY SALAD

Line a salad platter with *romaine or other crisp greens,* and spoon *a mound of cottage cheese* in the center. Surround the cheese with *large hulled strawberries.* Serve with a salad dressing made by combining ½ *cup each heavy cream and sour cream, 1 tablespoon lemon juice, 2 tea-spoons sugar,* and *a dash of salt.*

DR. RISER'S PERSIMMON AND AVOCADO SALAD WITH BUTTERMILK DRESSING

Serves 4. An even more exotic fruit salad combines the sensuous persimmon with avocado.

BUY	HAVE ON HAND
1 head romaine	Mayonnaise
4 very ripe persimmons	Buttermilk
2 ripe avocados	Lemon

1. Separate leaves from the *head of romaine,* wash well, then dry and chill.

2. Combine ½ *cup mayonnaise* and ¼ *cup buttermilk* and chill.

3. Line individual salad plates with romaine leaves. Do not peel the *persimmons;* wash them, then cut them into 8 sections—slicing from the pointed end down to, but not completely through, the calyx of the fruit. Open up each persimmon like a flower and place on the romaine.

4. Peel the *avocados,* remove seeds, and slice each half avocado lengthwise into 8 thin slices. Place a slice of avocado between each two "petals" of the persimmons and sprinkle the avocado with a *little lemon juice.*

5. Serve immediately with the *buttermilk salad dressing.*

Green Salads

THE TRADITIONAL TOSSED SALAD

The first requirement is the finest of raw ingredients: crisp greens of several varieties, fully matured ripe tomatoes, crunchy cucumbers, flavorful herbs, good salad oil (part olive), and a mild vinegar, preferably wine. Then it must be seasoned just right, tossed with a light hand, and served very cold.

THE GREENS:

These are varied and abundant during a great part of the year. There are water cress, firm heads of Belgian endive, tender sprouts of field salad, oak lettuce, Bibb lettuce, romaine, escarole, curly endive or chicory, and, that wonderfully pungent green known as arugala or Italian water cress, found in most Italian vegetable markets. Buy several different varieties.

Wash your greens thoroughly, leaf by leaf, and drain just as thoroughly. If you don't have a salad basket to drain them in, spread them out on absorbent toweling and pat dry with more towels. Tear larger leaves into medium pieces, leave the small tender leaves whole. Wrap all in a dry terry-cloth towel, and place in your salad crisper. Here they will stay fresh, crisp, and cold until salad-making time.

OPTIONAL INGREDIENTS:

To these salad greens you may add an extra touch—chopped chives, chopped fresh basil or tarragon, a ripe tomato, peeled, carefully seeded and chopped, a crisp cucumber, peeled, seeded and thinly sliced, some chopped spring onions, thin slices of firm radishes, a little crumbled Roquefort-type cheese, and so on.

THE SALAD DRESSING:

Now to the dressing, which is so simple, it's unbelievable that so many poor salads are served in homes and particularly in restaurants. Alexandre Dumas gave the clue, when he wrote, "No matter what the method adopted in the preparation of salads, it is always necessary to be very restrained in the use of vinegar." Some years later, Escoffier specified the correct amount of vinegar as 1 part vinegar to 3 parts oil, but Escoffier did not take into consideration that American vinegars are higher in acidity than the French ones are, so a better proportion, unless you are using an imported wine vinegar, is 1 part vinegar to 4 parts oil. Lemon juice is a good alternative to vinegar, but some lemons are much more tart than others, so the proportion of lemon juice to oil depends on the acidity of the lemon.

Then there is the question of garlic. To many persons, a little fresh garlic is essential to a perfect salad, but never use too much as it will overpower the subtle flavor of tender greens.

The salad dressing can be made directly in the salad bowl. A large wooden bowl is best. And I do not go along with the theory that it should never be washed. Nonsense! Who wants a salad bowl with its pores filled with rancid oil? Scrub it with salt, rinse thoroughly in warm water, then dry with paper towels.

SAUCE VINAIGRETTE
(French Dressing)

Peel and cut *1 clove of garlic*. Rub the inside of the salad bowl with the cut clove. Discard the garlic. Sprinkle the bottom of the bowl with *½ teaspoon salt* and *¼ teaspoon freshly ground black pepper*. Add *½ teaspoon dry mustard or 1 teaspoon prepared Dijon-type mustard*. Now use your salad spoon to measure the vinegar and oil. Add *1 spoonful of vinegar or lemon juice, or a combination of them both,* and blend this thoroughly with the mustard and seasonings, swirling and mixing with the back of the spoon. Then stir in *3 to 4 spoonfuls of salad oil or a mixture of oils,* always including at least 1 part olive oil. Set bowl aside until ready to serve.

To SERVE: Fill the bowl with the prepared greens, add herbs or chopped raw vegetables, and toss lightly.

CAESAR SALAD

Serves 4. This popular variation of the simple tossed salad is the creation of an imaginative chef in Tijuana, Mexico. Caesar salad depends primarily on the flavor and texture of romaine for its character. Traditionally it includes anchovy fillets but it can be enjoyed without these if one wants to be strictly "meatless."

BUY

2 heads romaine lettuce
Small can anchovy fillets (optional)

HAVE ON HAND	*COOKWARE*
Garlic	Small skillet
Olive oil	Small saucepan
Bread	
Parmesan cheese	
Salt	
Dry mustard	
Cayenne pepper *or* Tabasco	
1 large lemon	
1 egg	
Coarsely cracked pepper	

1. The day before you want to serve the salad, peel and crush *1 clove garlic* and let it soak overnight in *½ cup olive oil.*

2. Prepare *romaine leaves:* Wash and drain each leaf thoroughly; then tear them into medium-size pieces, wrap in a towel, and put into refrigerator to chill.

3. Trim crusts off *4 slices bread,* and cut the slices into cubes.

4. Heat *3 tablespoons of the garlic-olive oil* in a small skillet, and in it sauté the bread cubes over moderate heat until golden brown on all sides, tossing them frequently with a wooden spoon. Drain on paper towels and set aside.

5. If using *anchovies,* slice them into small pieces. Grate *1 tablespoon Parmesan cheese* and set aside.

6. Sprinkle the bottom of a wooden salad bowl with ½ *teaspoon salt.* Add *1 teaspoon dry mustard, dash cayenne pepper or Tabasco,* and the *juice of 1 large lemon.* Stir with wooden salad spoon until the salt dissolves. Add *remaining garlic-olive oil* and stir rapidly until blended. Set aside.

7. Gently lower *1 egg* into a small saucepan of *rapidly boiling water* and boil for 1 minute. Remove to cool a little.

8. Pile the romaine leaves into the salad bowl, sprinkle with the Parmesan cheese, add the anchovies, and break the coddled egg over the greens. Sprinkle with ½ *teaspoon coarsely cracked pepper* and toss everything together gently but thoroughly until each leaf is coated with the oil.

9. Sprinkle with the garlic croutons and toss again gently.

GOOD VARIATION OF A CAESAR SALAD

Serves 4

BUY

1 large firm cucumber
2 heads romaine lettuce
8-ounce container sour cream

HAVE ON HAND	*COOKWARE*
Bread	Small skillet
Garlic	Small saucepan
Olive oil	
Parmesan cheese	
1 egg	
Salt	
Freshly ground black pepper	
1 large lemon	

1. Trim crusts from *2 slices bread.* Rub the slices with *a cut clove of garlic,* then cut them into cubes. Sauté the cubes in a *little hot olive oil* until golden brown on all sides. Drain on absorbent paper.

2. Grate *enough Parmesan cheese to measure ½ cup.* Peel and dice

1 large cucumber. Boil *1 egg* for 1 minute; remove from water and set aside.

3. Wash and dry the romaine; then tear the leaves into bite-size pieces and put them into a large salad bowl rubbed with *garlic.* Add the *sour cream, 2 tablespoons olive oil, 1 teaspoon salt,* and *lots of freshly ground black pepper.*

4. Scoop the egg from the shell into the salad, and squeeze the *juice of 1 large lemon* on top of the egg. Mix gently but well. Sprinkle with the Parmesan cheese and toss again.

5. Toss in the croutons and serve.

SPINACH SALAD WITH CROUTONS

Serves 4

BUY

1 pound fresh young spinach

HAVE ON HAND	COOKWARE
Bread	Small skillet
Olive oil	
Garlic	
Salt	
Dry mustard	
Peppercorns	
Wine vinegar	

1. Wash *spinach,* cut off the stems, and refrigerate the leaves.

2. Dice *enough bread to measure 1½ cups.* Sauté the cubes in a *little olive oil* until lightly browned on all sides. Drain on absorbent paper.

3. Peel and mince *2 cloves garlic,* then sprinkle them into the bottom of a salad bowl. Add *½ teaspoon salt, ¼ teaspoon each dry mustard and freshly ground pepper,* and *2 tablespoons wine vinegar.* Stir ingredients with back of spoon. Gradually stir in *½ cup olive oil.* Set bowl aside.

4. When ready to serve, pile the spinach leaves into the bowl, add the croutons, and toss briefly but well.

EGGS & CHEESE

Eggs

Eggs are nature's most perfect food. Every baby chick is evidence of the nutritional perfection packed into the egg from which it came. Out of the protective shell emerges a bird that can see, hear, walk, cheep, and eat adult food at birth. And, moreover, in its tiny furry body at the time it is hatched are stored enough nutrients for it to sustain itself for the first three days of its life.

How any food as perfect as the egg could be condemned by physicians and nutritionists is hard to understand, but until the past few years eggs were restricted in the diets of anyone suffering from high cholesterol. Today they are decidedly back in favor and are recommended in the diets of heart patients.

Adelle Davis, one of the country's leading nutritionists, states in her book *Let's Stay Well:* "Because eggs are particularly rich in methionine and lecithin, they should never be restricted in the diets of persons with atherosclerosis," and she supports this statement with convincing clinical evidence. Eggs are also high on the list of foods to help cure anemia, and the time-honored practice of serving eggnogs to the ill and elderly should be encouraged.

Eggs and cheese are perfect flavor mates, and they are combined in a number of the recipes which follow (see also Quiches & Tarts, page 48). But I begin this chapter with eggs in general and poached eggs in particular. When perfectly cooked, a poached egg is, perhaps, the epitome of egg cookery, and the egg which poaches best is the freshest that money can buy. That's not much, for, penny for penny, eggs are the best protein value in our markets today.

Poached Eggs

Poaching means to cook an egg, out of its shell, in hot liquid. The liquid may be water, milk, cream, broth, tomato juice, or wine. The important rule to remember in poaching an egg is that the liquid should NEVER BOIL. The white of an egg coagulates at 140° F.; the yolk, at 149° F. Therefore, it is obvious that boiling liquid is not necessary to poach an egg. Too high temperatures can, in fact, toughen the egg white and make the yolk less digestible.

HOW TO POACH EGGS

1. Use a shallow saucepan or skillet at least 2 inches deep. Oil the bottom lightly, unless it has a non-stick coating, and fill with water to a depth of 1½ inches. Add a little salt, bring the water to a boil, then reduce to barely a simmer.

2. Use 2 eggs per person. Break eggs one at a time into a saucer or shallow dish and slip them carefully into the water, with the edge of the dish placed as close to the water level as possible. The addition of the cold eggs will immediately lower the temperature, so increase heat until bubbles begin to rise again from bottom of the pan, or to about 185° F., the perfect simmering temperature to set a perfectly poached egg. If the temperature is allowed to remain *too* low, the egg white will not set quickly enough and will spread out into the liquid.

3. Cook the eggs for 3 to 5 minutes, or until the white is delicately firm and the yolk is set to the desired firmness.

4. Carefully remove eggs with a slotted spoon and, if the edges are jagged, trim neatly with a round cooky cutter.

5. Serve immediately on hot buttered toast or English muffin halves. If you wish to gild the lily, spoon a tablespoon of luscious Hollandaise Sauce over each egg.

TO HOLD POACHED EGGS:

If poached eggs are to be part of a more elaborate dish, or if you wish to serve poached eggs to several people at the same time, gently place each one after poaching into a pan of warm salted water; they will stay moist there but not continue to cook.

To reheat: Lift the eggs, one at a time, out of the water with a perforated or slotted spoon, lower them into a second saucepan containing hot water (140° F.), and let them warm for about 1 minute.

HOLLANDAISE SAUCE is a gorgeous egg sauce and not nearly so tricky as most people believe. If you use an electric blender, it can literally be made in seconds. I give you both the traditional and the blender recipes and methods for making it, for no good cook should have qualms about whipping up this sauce. Serve it not just on special occasions but also as a nutritious egg dish for the family. When fresh asparagus is in the markets, perch a poached egg atop a few cooked stalks and cover with Hollandaise. Heaven!

SAUCE HOLLANDAISE

Serves 6

HAVE ON HAND	*COOKWARE*
4 egg yolks	Small Pyrex bowl
Cream	8-inch skillet
Lemon	
Salt	
Cayenne pepper	
½ pound butter	

1. Into the small bowl put *4 egg yolks, 2 tablespoons cream, 1 tablespoon lemon juice, ¼ teaspoon salt,* and *a pinch of cayenne pepper.* Set bowl into a skillet containing hot water, and beat the mixture over low heat until it begins to thicken. The water should not boil, only barely

simmer. Use a wire whisk if possible, otherwise beat with two forks held in one hand.

2. Beat in *½ pound butter,* bit by bit. When all the butter has been added, turn off the heat, and pour a little cold water into the water in the skillet to reduce the temperature and prevent further cooking of the sauce. It will stay warm while the eggs are poaching.

BLENDER HOLLANDAISE

Serves 6

HAVE ON HAND	*COOKWARE*
½ pound butter	Small saucepan
4 egg yolks	Electric blender
Lemon	
Salt	
Tabasco	

1. In saucepan heat *butter* until melted and very hot, but do not let it brown. The entire success of making blender Hollandaise is the temperature of the butter, which must be hot enough to cook the egg as it blends, but not hot enough to curdle it. Bubbling butter is no indication of temperature. It means merely that the liquid contained in the butter is evaporating. The point at which the bubbles subside and the butter is very golden is just right.

2. Into the blender container put *4 egg yolks, 1 tablespoon lemon juice, ¼ teaspoon salt,* and *¼ teaspoon Tabasco.* Cover container. Turn motor on low speed. If the blender is a multiple-speed unit, use lowest speed. As soon as the blades reach full motion, remove cover and pour in the hot butter in a steady stream. When all butter is added, turn blender off.

3. To keep the sauce hot until serving time, set the container with the sauce into a saucepan containing about 2 inches of hot but not boiling water. If the sauce becomes too thick to pour when ready to use, return container to blender. Add *1 tablespoon hot water* and blend briefly.

EGGS SARDOU

Serves 4 or 8

BUY

2 packages frozen chopped spinach (10 ounces each)
8-ounce container heavy cream
14-ounce can imported artichoke bottoms

HAVE ON HAND	COOKWARE
Nutmeg	Cookware for Hollandaise
Ingredients for Hollandaise	2 small saucepans
8 eggs	1 skillet for poaching

1. Cook *spinach* according to package directions. Drain well in a sieve and press out excess moisture with back of a wooden spoon. Return to saucepan, and stir in *a pinch of nutmeg* and *¼ cup heavy cream*. Place over very low heat.

2. Make *Hollandaise* and keep warm.

3. Heat *artichoke bottoms* in *liquid from can.*

4. Poach *8 eggs* (page 133).

5. Place 1 or 2 artichoke bottoms per serving on warm plate, hollow side up. Fill hollows with creamed spinach, and top each with a poached egg. Cover each egg with a blanket of Hollandaise.

EGGS FLORENTINE

Serves 6

BUY

2 packages frozen chopped spinach
   (10-ounces each)
Heavy cream

HAVE ON HAND

Butter
Flour
Salt
Cayenne pepper
Milk
6 eggs
Parmesan cheese, freshly grated

COOKWARE

2 small saucepans
6 individual baking dishes *or* 1½-quart shallow baking dish

1. In saucepan melt *⅓ cup butter.* Stir in *⅓ cup flour, ¾ teaspoon salt,* and *⅛ teaspoon cayenne.* Gradually stir in *2 cups milk* and cook, stirring constantly, until sauce is smooth and thickened. Stir in *½ cup cream* and cook over low heat until ready to use, stirring occasionally.

2. Cook *spinach* according to package directions. Drain well and stir in *½ cup of the sauce.* Spread spinach onto bottom of the baking dish, or dishes.

3. Poach *6 eggs.*

4. Stir *½ cup grated Parmesan cheese* into *remaining cream sauce.*

5. Make six depressions in the spinach and put a poached egg in each. Pour sauce over eggs and spinach, and place under broiler heat until sauce is lightly browned and bubbly.

HUEVOS RANCHEROS

Serves 6. Eggs poached in a sauce. Good with a hot corn muffin.

BUY

1 large green pepper
Mozzarella cheese
1-pound can whole tomatoes

HAVE ON HAND

Large onion
Garlic
Olive oil
Chili powder

Cumin, ground
Oregano   *COOKWARE*
Red pepper *or* cayenne   10-inch skillet
6 eggs

1. Peel and chop *1 large onion*. Seed and slice thinly the *green pepper*. Peel and mince *2 cloves garlic*. Cut 6 thin slices *mozzarella cheese*. Set aside.

2. In skillet heat *3 tablespoons olive oil* and in it sauté the onion, green pepper, and garlic until vegetables are tender and onion is golden.

3. Add *2 tablespoons chili powder,* ½ *teaspoon cumin,* and ½ *teaspoon oregano*. Drain and add the *tomatoes* and ¼ *teaspoon red pepper or cayenne*. Bring to a simmer and cook over medium heat for 20 minutes, stirring and mashing the tomatoes occasionally.

4. Make 6 depressions in the vegetable mixture and break *1 egg* into each depression. Cover each egg with a slice of mozzarella. Cover the skillet and poach the eggs over low heat until they reach the desired degree of firmness.

Scrambled Eggs

Among the most delicious dishes in all the world are properly scrambled eggs. On the other hand, there is no dish which suffers more often from overcooking. They must be heated slowly and stirred constantly, until they are cooked through yet are still moist and creamy. All it takes is strictly fresh eggs—and enough love and care to want them to be perfect. If you don't feel you can devote the few minutes of constant stirring to assure perfection, you can resort to the use of a double saucepan. Eggs scrambled in this fashion are called Rumbled Eggs. They cook practically unattended and may be kept waiting for a short time before being served. Count on 2 to 3 eggs per serving, depending on appetites.

HOW TO SCRAMBLE EGGS FOR TWO

1. Break *6 fresh eggs* into a bowl and sprinkle with a *little salt* and *a dash of white pepper.* Beat quickly but lightly with a fork or rotary beater. Mix thoroughly if you like a uniform yellow, or slightly if you like streaks of white and yellow.

2. Melt *2 tablespoons butter* in the bottom of an 8-inch skillet over moderate heat. Swirl the pan so that the butter coats sides as well as bottom. Give one last beat to the eggs and, before the butter begins to sizzle, pour them into the pan.

3. Stir with a wooden spoon gently, constantly, scraping the bottom and sides of the skillet in order to prevent any one portion from becoming overcooked. Cook for 3 to 5 minutes, or until the eggs are thickened throughout, but are still soft, creamy, and glossy.

4. Remove pan immediately from heat and stir in *1 tablespoon butter or cream, or,* to be extra magnanimous, *1 tablespoon of each.*

5. Serve on warm plates IMMEDIATELY, since the heat of the eggs will cause them to continue to cook. If desired, sprinkle with a *little minced parsley or chives.*

RUMBLED EGGS FOR TWO

1. Put a baking dish or casserole on top of a saucepan of *boiling water.* For *4 eggs,* put *1 tablespoon butter* in the casserole to melt. Meanwhile beat eggs with *a pinch each of salt and pepper.* Pour eggs into the hot butter and stir for a moment. You can leave them over gently bubbling water while you attend to other duties, giving them an occasional stir as you pass the stove.

2. As soon as the eggs have reached a thick, creamy consistency, remove saucepan from the heat and the eggs will keep hot for a few minutes. But don't decide at this point to make muffins to go with them!

EGGS AND SPINACH HELSCHER

Serves 2

BUY

10-ounce package frozen chopped spinach
Parmesan cheese

HAVE ON HAND   *COOKWARE*

Garlic   Medium saucepan
Olive oil   10-inch skillet
Salt and pepper
2 eggs

1. Cook *spinach* according to package directions. Empty into a sieve to drain and, with the back of a wooden spoon, press out as much of the liquid from the spinach as possible. Set aside.

2. Grate *¼ cup Parmesan cheese.* Peel and mince *1 clove garlic.*

3. In skillet heat *3 tablespoons olive oil.* Add the garlic, and sauté until pale gold. Be careful it does not over-brown.

4. Add the spinach and spread it over the bottom of the skillet. Sprinkle spinach with *¼ teaspoon salt, some pepper,* and *2 tablespoons of the grated Parmesan.* Cook for 2 to 3 minutes, turning the spinach over with a spatula until it is very hot.

5. Break in *2 eggs,* then keep tossing and turning the spinach until the eggs are lightly scrambled into it.

6. Drain off any excess oil or liquid from skillet, turn spinach and eggs onto a warm serving plate, and sprinkle with the *remaining grated cheese.*

EGGS SOUTH OF THE BORDER

Serves 4 to 6

BUY

4 green peppers
2 large sweet onions
4 ripe tomatoes
Chives *or* green onions
8-ounce container cream

HAVE ON HAND   COOKWARE

Garlic   2 medium skillets
Olive oil
Salt
Coarsely cracked pepper
Butter
Bread
1 dozen eggs

1. Remove stems and seeds from *green peppers* and slice thinly. Peel *onions* and slice thinly. Peel and quarter the *tomatoes* and squeeze out excess seeds. Peel and mince *1 large clove garlic.*

2. In skillet heat *4 tablespoons olive oil,* and in it sauté the peppers and onions until onions are transparent. Add tomatoes, garlic, *½ teaspoon*

salt, and *a good sprinkling of pepper.* Cook, stirring, until all the vegetables are tender, but not overcooked.

3. Meanwhile *toast and butter 6 slices bread,* and cut into triangles. Chop *some chives or green onion tops* and set aside.

4. Beat *1 dozen eggs* with *½ cup of the cream.* In the second skillet melt *4 tablespoons butter.* Just as the butter begins to bubble, turn heat to low and pour in the eggs. Cook, stirring constantly, until eggs are set but not dry. Sprinkle with a *little more salt and pepper.*

5. Turn the eggs out into the center of a warm serving platter, and surround with the vegetables and pan juice. Sprinkle with the chopped chives or green onion tops and serve with the toast triangles.

EGGS SCRAMBLED WITH GREEN PEPPER AND MUSHROOMS

Serves 4

BUY

1 green pepper
¼ pound fresh mushrooms
Parsley

HAVE ON HAND	COOKWARE
Onion	Medium skillet
Olive oil	
4 eggs	
Salt and pepper	

1. Seed and finely chop the *green pepper.* Trim, wash, and slice the *mushrooms.* Peel and chop *1 medium onion.* Chop *2 tablespoons parsley.*

2. In skillet heat *3 tablespoons olive oil,* and in it sauté onion, green pepper, and mushrooms for about 5 minutes, or until onion and green pepper are soft and mushrooms are tender.

3. Beat *4 eggs* with *1 tablespoon water, ½ teaspoon salt,* and *a sprinkling of pepper.* Pour egg mixture over the vegetables and cook over low heat, stirring constantly until the eggs are just set, but still soft. Sprinkle with the chopped parsley and serve with toast, muffins, or hot biscuits.

PISTO CON HUEVOS REVUELTOS
(Sautéed Vegetables with Scrambled Eggs)

Serves 4. Serve with fresh crusty bread.

BUY
1 green pepper
3 small zucchini
1 medium eggplant
4 large tomatoes

HAVE ON HAND

Medium onion
Large potato
Olive oil
Salt
6 eggs

COOKWARE

10-inch skillet

1. Halve, seed, and dice the *green pepper*. Trim the *zucchini* and cut into ½-inch thick slices. Peel and dice the *eggplant*. Peel and chop *1 medium onion* and the *tomatoes*. Peel *1 large potato* and cut into ½-inch thick rounds.

2. In heavy skillet, heat *⅓ cup olive oil*. Add the green pepper, zucchini, eggplant, onion, potato, and *1 tablespoon salt*. Sauté for 10 to 15 minutes, stirring occasionally, or until vegetables are lightly browned. Add tomatoes and cook over low heat for 15 to 20 minutes, or until all vegetables are soft.

3. Beat *6 eggs*. Pour eggs into the vegetable mixture and stir constantly until they begin to thicken. The mixture should not be allowed to set in the bottom of the skillet. Serve immediately.

Baked or Shirred Eggs

These are a delicate and beautiful dish IF they are taken from the oven before they are overcooked. And this takes care on your part. The eggs should be cooked both underneath and on top; the whites should be still creamy and soft, and the yolks barely set with just a film of transparent white over them. Baked eggs will continue to cook from the heat of the dish, so err on the undercooked side rather than on the overcooked if you must err. And if your partner likes his eggs well done, skip over to the hard-cooked egg section that follows.

Baked eggs may be cooked in a shallow baking dish large enough to accommodate the number of eggs you wish to cook, or in shallow individual baking dishes of a size to hold 2 eggs. You can use various sizes of skillets, too, if you prefer, providing the handle either is ovenproof or has been protected by a tight wrapping of aluminum foil. The oven temperature used for baking eggs is a moderate one, so a wood handle will not char. Don't forget, however, that it will be hot when you take the skillet from the oven. Use your pot holder!

HOW TO BAKE OR SHIRR EGGS
FOR ONE INDIVIDUAL DISH

1. Preheat oven to 325° F.

2. In an individual baking dish melt *1 tablespoon butter* over low heat. Don't let the butter brown. When it is melted, slip *2 eggs* into the dish and sprinkle them with a *little salt*.

3. Using a pot holder, tip the dish and spoon a little of the melted butter over the yolks.

4. Bake in the preheated oven for 15 to 20 minutes, or until the whites are milky but still creamy and the yolks are lightly set.

5. Serve from the baking dish.

EGGS SHIRRED IN CREAM

Melt *1 teaspoon butter* in bottom of a small, shallow baking dish and when butter is melted slip in *2 eggs*. Spoon a *little hot heavy cream* over the eggs, then place dish in a preheated 325° F. oven. Bake for 15 to 20 minutes, or until perfectly cooked.

SWISS EGGS

Serves 3

HAVE ON HAND	*COOKWARE*
Butter	Shallow baking dish
6 eggs	
Swiss cheese, thinly sliced	
Heavy cream	
Salt and pepper	

1. Melt *3 tablespoons butter* in a shallow heatproof baking dish large enough to accommodate *6 eggs*. Slip eggs into the melted butter, and cook over low heat for about 2 minutes.

2. Cover each egg with *a slice of cheese;* pour *½ cup cream* over the cheese slices; and sprinkle with *salt and pepper*. Bake in a preheated 325° F. oven for about 15 minutes, or until eggs are just set and cheese is melted.

HUEVOS CAMPESINOS

Serves 4

BUY

A good cheese, such as Parmesan,
    mozzarella, Swiss, *or* Cheddar
4 slightly green tomatoes

HAVE ON HAND	*COOKWARE*
Garlic	8- or 10-inch skillet
Parsley	
Olive oil	
Salt	
4 eggs	

1. Preheat oven to 350° F.

2. Grate or shred *½ cup cheese.*

3. Cut and discard a thin slice from both top and bottom of each *tomato,* then remove the hard stem core and slice the tomatoes thickly. Peel and chop *2 large cloves garlic.* Chop *2 tablespoons parsley.*

4. In skillet with handle that is ovenproof (or has been wrapped in foil) heat *6 tablespoons olive oil,* and in it sauté the tomato slices for 2 to 3 minutes on each side or until fork tender.

5. Sprinkle tomato slices with the garlic and parsley and *½ teaspoon salt.*

6. Break *4 eggs* into the skillet on top of the tomatoes, keeping each egg separate from the other. Sprinkle eggs with the cheese.

7. Bake in preheated oven for about 20 minutes, or until eggs are set.

Hard-Cooked Eggs

The following recipe is in my last book, *Ann Seranne's Good Food & How to Cook It*. I have tried to avoid repeating recipes, but the simple technique of hard-cooking and peeling an egg is so often ignored or abused that it is worth repeating.

THE RIGHT WAY TO HARD COOK AN EGG AND PEEL IT

Put fresh eggs into a saucepan with sufficient water to cover the eggs by at least 1 inch. Bring to a rapid boil, reduce heat, and simmer the eggs for exactly 10 minutes.

Drain immediately and cover with cold water to stop further cooking and prevent the unattractive thin layer of gray which often coats the brilliant gold of the yolks.

Peel as soon as the eggs are cool enough to handle as follows: Crack the egg all over in a myriad of little cracks—easy does it—then hold the cracked egg under cold running water and the shell and thin inner membrane will come cleanly away. If you don't believe me, try it!

Hard-cooked eggs are a joy either as an appetizer or as an accompaniment to a salad luncheon. There are dozens of savory mayonnaise sauces to serve with them, and the eggs may be sliced, halved, or quartered before saucing. One of my favorite dishes featuring hard-cooked eggs is:

EGGS CRESSONNIÈRE

Hard cook *6 eggs,* then peel and cut in half lengthwise. Arrange the halves, cut side down, in a serving dish and cover generously with *Watercress Mayonnaise.* Cover dish with transparent film and refrigerate until serving time.

WATERCRESS MAYONNAISE: Combine *1 cup mayonnaise* with *¼ cup finely chopped watercress, 1 tablespoon lemon juice,* and *salt to taste.*

EGGS ANDALOUSE

Another simple favorite: Hard cook *12 eggs,* then peel, and cut in half lengthwise. Arrange the halves, cut side down, in a serving dish, and cover generously with *Sauce Andalouse.* Garnish with *strips of pimiento* and *capers.* Cover dish with transparent film and refrigerate until serving time.

SAUCE ANDALOUSE: Combine *2 cups mayonnaise* with *2 tablespoons tomato ketchup* and *2 tablespoons finely chopped pimiento.*

SPEAKING OF MAYONNAISE, why not make your own in a blender? It takes about 1 minute, and it's much cheaper and much better than any mayonnaise you can buy. For a special treat, use all fresh olive oil, or use half olive oil and half safflower oil.

BLENDER MAYONNAISE

Makes about 1½ cups. Please don't try to double this recipe—it won't work!

HAVE ON HAND
Salad oils (part olive oil, please)
1 egg

Vinegar *or* lemon juice
Dry mustard
Salt

1. Measure *1 cup of mixed salad oils* and set aside.

2. Into blender container break *1 egg.* Add *2 tablespoons vinegar or lemon juice, ½ teaspoon dry mustard, ½ teaspoon salt, and ¼ cup of the measured oil.*

3. Cover blender container and begin blending on medium or low-medium speed. IMMEDIATELY remove cover and pour in the *remaining oil* in a steady stream. All oil must be added within 18 seconds from the start.

4. Turn off blender and stir mayonnaise with a rubber spatula.

VARIATIONS:

Green Mayonnaise: Add to *egg* in container *½ small clove garlic, 1 tablespoon fresh dill, 1 tablespoon chopped chives or green onion tops.*

Aïoli Sauce (if you like garlic); try this sometime on a baked potato! Add to *egg* in container *4 cloves garlic,* peeled and sliced.

Tarragon Mayonnaise: Add to egg in container *1 tablespoon fresh tarragon leaves or 1 teaspoon dried tarragon.*

CREAMED EGGS

Serves 2 or 4. Serve on hot buttered toast or on split and buttered corn bread.

HAVE ON HAND	*COOKWARE*
Milk	Small saucepan
Butter	2-quart saucepan
Flour	
Cream	
Parsley	
Worcestershire sauce	
Tabasco	
Salt	
4 hard-cooked eggs	

1. In small saucepan measure *1 cup milk* and heat to steaming.

2. In larger saucepan melt *3 tablespoons butter*. Stir in *3 tablespoons flour,* and cook, stirring, until mixture is smooth and bubbling. Remove from heat and add hot milk, all at once. Stir vigorously until mixture is smooth. Return to medium heat and cook, stirring, for 3 minutes, or until sauce is smooth and thick. Stir in *½ cup cream.*

3. Stir in *2 tablespoons chopped parsley, ½ teaspoon Worcestershire sauce, a good dash Tabasco,* and *½ teaspoon salt, or to taste.*

4. Slice and stir in the *eggs,* and heat to serving temperature. Do not let the sauce boil after eggs are added.

CURRIED EGGS

Add *1 tablespoon good curry powder* along with the flour to the hot butter.

CURRIED EGG CAKES

Serves 6. Serve plain or with a favorite sauce such as cream, tomato or mushroom.

HAVE ON HAND	COOKWARE
1 dozen plus 3 eggs	Shallow baking pan
Chutney	Small saucepan
Butter	8- or 10-inch skillet
Flour	
Curry powder	
Cayenne pepper	
Salt	
Milk	
Fine bread, *or* cracker, crumbs	
Salad oil for frying	

IN ADVANCE:

1. Hard cook and peel *1 dozen eggs,* then chop coarsely. Chop *2 tablespoons chutney.*

2. In saucepan melt *4 tablespoons butter;* stir in *6 tablespoons flour, 1 tablespoon curry powder, ⅛ teaspoon cayenne,* and *1 teaspoon salt.*

Cook, stirring, for about 1 minute. Then gradually stir in *1¼ cups milk,* and cook over moderate heat, stirring constantly, until sauce is smooth and very thick.

3. Remove sauce from heat, and beat in *2 egg yolks.* Stir in chopped hard-cooked eggs and chutney. Spread mixture in a shallow baking pan and chill.

WHEN READY TO COOK:

4. Form the chilled mixture into 6 flat cakes.

5. Beat *1 egg with 1 tablespoon water.* Coat the egg cakes with *flour,* then with beaten egg, and finally roll in *bread crumbs,* coating the cakes well on all sides.

6. In skillet heat *enough salad oil to cover bottom of skillet by ¼ inch.* When oil is hot but not smoking, add the egg cakes and fry until golden and crisp on both sides, turning once.

7. Drain on absorbent paper and serve hot.

Omelets

An omelet can be described as scrambled eggs enclosed in their own soft blanket of coagulated egg. The actual cooking is a question of 30 seconds, and the omelet should be served golden, light, and plump while the consistency of the interior is for the most part semiliquid or, as the French would say, *baveuse.* When overcooked an omelet becomes dry and tough.

Actually there is little reason for anyone to make a poor or overcooked omelet, but anyone who tells you that it is altogether easy is an optimist. It *is* tricky, and practice is the only way to master the technique. But why not try? The worst you can end up with is scrambled eggs, and they're nothing to turn one's nose up at—unless, again, they are overcooked.

Once you have learned to make a plain omelet, you can make variations *ad infinitum* by adding chopped herbs, or vegetables (or chopped meats, fish, or seafood) to the egg mixture before cooking, by filling the omelet with a savory purée or diced mixture of your choice, or by garnishing it with sour cream or a sauce.

In addition to very fresh eggs, three things are necessary for a good omelet. These are: A correct omelet pan, brisk heat, and some courage. The relatively new non-stick omelet pans of porcelain-covered cast iron have solved the first requirement. Every cook has brisk heat, and most have courage. So let's make an omelet.

For a 3-egg omelet, use a pan with a bottom diameter of 7 to 8 inches. A smaller pan, with a bottom diameter of 5 to 6 inches, is perfect for a 2-egg omelet.

HOW TO MAKE A PLAIN OR FRENCH OMELET

1. Break *3 fresh eggs* into a bowl, add *a pinch of salt* and *1 tablespoon cold water,* and beat lightly with a fork until whites and yolks are thoroughly blended but not foamy.

2. Heat an omelet pan over brisk heat until a drop of water flicked on it sizzles and evaporates immediately. Add *a good tablespoon of sweet butter,* and when it begins to foam and give off a nutty aroma but before it browns, pour in the eggs.

3. With the left hand, shake the pan continually back and forth over the heat; at the same time, with a fork held in the right hand, stir the eggs so that you heat all the liquid evenly. (It's a little like rubbing your tummy and patting your head at the same time.)

4. When eggs are thickened but still soft and moist, continue to shake the pan, but stop stirring with the fork—instead, use the fork to smooth the egg evenly in the pan.

5. If the omelet is to be filled, now is the time to sprinkle the filling over the surface of the eggs, fold the omelet, and turn it out onto a warm serving plate. To do this neatly, grasp the handle of the omelet pan in the left hand, thumb and fingers uppermost. Then tip the pan over the plate as, with the fork in the right hand, you roll the omelet onto the plate.

If you're lucky, you have an omelet; if not, you have scrambled eggs. Don't get discouraged, try again!

CHEESE OMELET

Add *3 tablespoons grated mixed Gruyère and Parmesan cheese* to *3 beaten eggs*. Use *very little salt*.

MUSHROOM OMELET

Add *3 tablespoons minced sautéed mushrooms* to *3 beaten eggs*. Garnish omelet with *sautéed mushroom caps*.

OMELETTE FINES HERBS

Add *½ teaspoon each minced parsley, chives, tarragon, and chervil* to *3 beaten eggs*.

TOMATO OMELET

Fill omelet with *peeled, diced, and seeded ripe tomatoes* stewed in a *little butter* until reduced to a thick purée. Season to taste with *salt and pepper*.

SPANISH OMELET

Simmer *1 chopped onion, 2 peeled and chopped tomatoes* or *½ cup canned tomatoes, 1 chopped sweet green pepper*, and *1 minced clove garlic*, in *2 tablespoons salad oil* for about 10 minutes, or until vegetables are tender. Fill omelet with *half the vegetable mixture,* turn out onto warm plate, and pour *remaining mixture* over and around it.

SPINACH OMELET

Sauté *1 minced small onion,* in *1 tablespoon butter* until golden. Combine onion mixture with *½ cup cooked, well-drained spinach, 2 tablespoons heavy cream,* and *a pinch of marjoram.* Season to taste with *salt and pepper.* Fill omelet with the spinach mixture, turn onto warm plate, and serve with *sour cream.*

SORREL OMELET

Sauté *a dozen or so shredded sorrel leaves* and *2 tablespoons chopped chives* in *1 tablespoon butter* until sorrel is wilted and mushy. Fill omelet with the tart sorrel mixture, turn onto warm plate, and serve with *sour cream* and lots of *chopped chives* sprinkled on top.

PRINCESS OMELET

Serves 2. The method described in step 3 is the American one for making an omelet. You may find it easier, but it is not "correct." Garnish with cooked buttered asparagus or peas.

HAVE ON HAND	*COOKWARE*
3-ounce package fresh cream cheese	8-inch skillet *or* omelet pan
Onion	
4 eggs	
Commercial dairy sour cream	
Crushed red pepper	
Salt	
Butter	

1. Cut the *cheese* into ½-inch cubes. Peel *1 small onion* and mince *enough to measure 2 teaspoons.*

2. Combine *4 eggs, ¼ cup sour cream,* the onion, *¼ teaspoon crushed red pepper,* and *½ teaspoon salt.* Beat well and fold in the cream cheese.

3. In skillet or omelet pan, heat *1 tablespoon butter* until it just begins to brown. Pour egg mixture into the hot butter. As the mixture thickens at the edges, draw these portions with a fork toward the center of the pan so that the uncooked portions flow to the bottom. Shake pan back and forth over the heat to keep the omelet from sticking.

4. When eggs are set but still moist, fold and turn onto a warm serving dish. Serve at once.

CHINESE VEGETABLE OMELET SCRAMBLE

Serves 3

BUY

Small can bean sprouts
4 medium mushrooms
1 red *or* green sweet pepper
Small can bamboo shoots
Celery

HAVE ON HAND

Garlic
Peanut oil
Sugar
Soy sauce
6 eggs
Salt
Ground ginger
Dry sherry

COOKWARE

Two 8-inch skillets *or* Chinese woks
One lid

1. Drain the *bean sprouts.* Trim, wash, and slice the *mushrooms.* Seed the *sweet pepper* and cut into ¾-inch squares. Drain and dice *½ cup bamboo shoots.* Slice *½ cup celery.* Peel and mince *1 clove garlic.*

2. In a skillet or wok, heat *2 tablespoons peanut oil* until very hot. Add bean sprouts, mushrooms, the sweet pepper, bamboo shoots, and celery, and cook over high heat for 3 to 4 minutes, stirring constantly. Remove from heat and stir in *½ teaspoon sugar* and *1 tablespoon soy sauce.*

3. In mixing bowl beat *6 eggs* lightly with *½ teaspoon salt* and *½ teaspoon ginger.*

4. In a second skillet or wok, heat *another 2 tablespoons peanut oil*—this time to medium hot. Add garlic and sauté for 1 minute. Pour in eggs, cover pan, and cook for 1 minute. Add the vegetables and give the whole mixture a gentle stir. Then flip over egg-and-vegetables with a broad spatula. When mixture is almost set, pour over it *¼ cup dry sherry;* then give the omelet another flip over, and scramble lightly. Serve immediately on warm plates.

Savory Soufflés

The basis of all savory soufflés is a thick sauce made of butter and flour and, usually, milk. The secret of a soufflé is nothing more or less than the proper beating of the eggs and the incorporation of these beaten eggs into the basic mixture.

The yolks should be beaten until light and lemon-colored and should be stirred into the sauce while the sauce is still hot; the heat of the sauce partly cooks the yolks. However, you should let the mixture cool a little before you go on to add the whites.

The egg whites should be beaten until stiff but not dry, and there should be more egg whites than egg yolks, the usual proportion being 4 whites to each 3 yolks. Even larger quantities of egg whites will not hurt, but the way the whites are beaten and the manner in which they are mixed into the egg yolk base are the most important. Also, care should be taken that the bowl and beater are absolutely clean and that the egg whites do not contain any particle of yolk, for if they do, or if either the bowl or beater is greasy, the eggs will not mound stiffly.

A round-bottomed copper bowl is the perfect bowl in which to beat egg whites, but lacking that, use porcelain, glass, stainless steel, or plastic—anything except aluminum, for that is likely to discolor the whites. Also egg whites will mound faster and to greater volume if they are hand-beaten with a large balloon whip. This large whisk can keep all the egg whites in constant motion so that they reach the right degree of stiffness in about 3 minutes, as against 8 minutes with an electric or rotary beater.

BASIC SOUFFLÉ PROCEDURES

TO BEAT EGG WHITES BY HAND:

Use a large, clean, round-bottomed bowl and a large wire whisk. Start beating with a circular motion, about 2 strokes per second until the egg whites become frothy. Then increase the strokes to 4 per second, keeping the motion in as large circles as the bowl will permit, and turning the bowl frequently. Continue to beat until a large, graceful peak will hold its shape on the end of the whip when the whisk is withdrawn. The egg whites should be glossy, not overbeaten and dry-looking.

TO BEAT WITH ELECTRIC BEATER:

Begin beating on low speed until egg whites are frothy. Gradually increase speed to moderate. If using a hand electric beater, tilt the bowl and move the beater up from the center and around the sides of the bowl until whites are stiff enough to hold a large peak. If using a stationary beater, push whites from sides of bowl into the beater with a rubber spatula while they are being beaten.

FOLDING EGG WHITES INTO EGG YOLK MIXTURE:

The way the beaten egg whites are added to the yolk mixture is an important step in a successful soufflé. They must be mixed in gently and delicately in order to retain as much of the air beaten into them as possible. First, STIR in a couple of large spoonfuls of the beaten whites (about ¼ of the total amount) to thin down the yolk mixture. Then FOLD in remaining egg whites as follows: using the palm of one hand (the best method), or a large rubber scraper, cut down from top of mixture to the bottom of the bowl, then up against the side of the bowl. Rotate the bowl frequently and continue until all the whites have been incorporated into the yolk mixture. A few unblended patches of egg whites do not matter, but there should be no visible streaks of egg yolk mixture.

PREPARING THE SOUFFLÉ DISH:

Butter bottom and sides generously; then, if desired, coat them lightly with grated Parmesan cheese or dry bread crumbs. Pour soufflé mixture into the prepared mold. The mixture should fill the mold at least ¾ full, but it should not exceed ⅞ full.

TO HOLD A PREPARED SOUFFLÉ:

Bake immediately. Or, if necessary, you can hold the soufflé for as long as 1 hour before baking if you cover it with a large soup kettle to keep drafts from dissipating the air in the mixture.

TO BAKE A SOUFFLÉ:

Preheat oven to 400° F. Place the soufflé on rack in the center of the oven, close door, and immediately turn oven temperature down to 375° F. Bake until soufflé is done to the point desired—either completely set or still creamy in the center. *To test for doneness:* Open oven door and, with a pot holder, grasp the rim of the soufflé dish and shake it gently. If the soufflé shimmies just a little in the center, it is what the French call *baveuse,* creamy in the middle. If you don't like it this way, bake for 3 or 4 minutes longer.

CHEESE SOUFFLÉ

Serves 4

BUY

2-ounces aged Parmesan cheese
4-ounces aged Cheddar *or* imported Swiss
   or Gruyère chesee

HAVE ON HAND

Milk
Butter
Flour
Cornstarch

Dry mustard *or* prepared Dijon
Salt
Cayenne pepper
6 eggs

COOKWARE

1½-quart soufflé dish
Small saucepan
1-quart saucepan

1. Grate the *Parmesan.* Shred the *Cheddar, Swiss, or Gruyère.*

2. Preheat oven to 400° F. *Butter* the soufflé dish, then sprinkle it with *1 tablespoon of the grated Parmesan.*

3. In small saucepan heat *1 cup milk* to steaming hot.

4. In larger saucepan melt *3 tablespoons butter.* Stir in *2 tablespoons flour* and cook, stirring, until mixture is bubbly. Remove saucepan from heat; add hot milk and beat vigorously until mixture is well blended and smooth. Return to moderate heat and cook, stirring, for about 1 minute, or until sauce is thickened.

5. Combine *2 teaspoons cornstarch* and *2 tablespoons water* and stir into the hot sauce. Add the shredded cheese and cook, stirring, until cheese is melted.

6. Remove from heat, and beat in *½ teaspoon dry mustard or 1 teaspoon Dijon,* and *a dash each of salt and cayenne.*

7. Separate *4 eggs,* beating the *yolks, one at a time,* into the hot sauce, and dropping the *whites* into a mixing bowl. Separate *2 more eggs;* reserve the yolks for another purpose and add the whites to the other whites in the bowl. Return sauce to low heat and cook, stirring, for 3 minutes, without letting it boil. Set aside.

8. Beat the egg whites with a rotary beater until stiff, but still glossy and BY NO MEANS DRY. Add about *¼ of the beaten whites* to the yolk mixture and stir in thoroughly. Add *remaining whites* and fold in gently.

9. Turn soufflé mixture into the prepared dish, and put into the preheated oven. IMMEDIATELY REDUCE HEAT to 375° F., and bake the soufflé for 30 to 35 minutes, or until set to taste.

VEGETABLE SOUFFLÉ

Follow preceding recipe, but in place of the cheese use *1 cup cooked, finely chopped or mashed vegetable,* such as spinach, broccoli, cauliflower, carrots, peas, eggplant, mushrooms, artichoke bottoms.

BLACK WALNUT SOUFFLÉ

Serves 4. You may substitute hazelnuts or pecans for the black walnuts if you prefer, but there is something about the flavor of black walnuts that makes this soufflé unique.

BUY

6 ounces shelled black walnuts
3 fresh medium-size mushrooms
6 very fresh eggs

HAVE ON HAND

Onion
Garlic
Butter
Milk
Flour
Salt and cayenne pepper
Dry mustard
Brandy

COOKWARE

Mortar *or* electric blender
Small skillet
Small saucepan
1-quart saucepan
1½-quart soufflé dish

1. Crush *walnuts* to a paste in a mortar, or grind very finely in a blender. Set aside. Peel and mince *1 large onion* and *1 small clove garlic.* Wash, trim, and mince the *mushrooms.*

2. In small skillet melt *3 tablespoons butter,* and in it sauté onion, garlic, and mushrooms until onion is golden. Set aside.

3. Preheat oven to 400° F. *Butter* the soufflé dish.

4. In small saucepan heat *1 cup milk* to steaming hot. Separate the *6 eggs.*

5. In larger saucepan melt *4 tablespoons butter.* Stir in *4 tablespoons flour, a dash each of salt and cayenne,* and *½ teaspoon dry mustard.* Cook, stirring, until mixture bubbles, then remove from heat. Add hot milk all at once, and stir rapidly until mixture is blended. Return to heat and cook for about 2 minutes, stirring rapidly, until sauce is smooth and thickened.

6. Remove saucepan from heat, and beat in the *egg yolks,* onion mixture, and the crushed nuts.

7. In mixing bowl beat *egg whites* until stiff but still glossy. Add *about ¼ of the beaten whites* to the nut mixture and stir in thoroughly. Fold in *remaining whites*.

8. Turn soufflé mixture into prepared dish and put into the pre-heated oven. IMMEDIATELY REDUCE OVEN TEMPERATURE to 375° F., and bake the soufflé for 35 to 40 minutes, or until set to taste.

9. Remove from oven. Pour *1 ounce of brandy* over the soufflé, ignite the brandy, and serve the soufflé flaming.

CHEESE STRATA

Serves 6. Called a soufflé in some parts of the country because it has a similar consistency, this mixture of bread, cheese, and custard is a good, homey, inexpensive dish that can stand on its own merit without borrowing its reputation from a real soufflé.

BUY

Loaf of bread
½ pound Cheddar cheese
1 pint milk
8-ounce container light *or* heavy cream
1 large ripe tomato (optional)

HAVE ON HAND	*COOKWARE*
Butter	9 x 13 inch baking dish
Paprika	
6 eggs	
Salt	
Cayenne	
Parsley	

1. *Butter* the baking dish. Spread *12 slices bread* thinly with *butter*. Shred or thinly slice the *cheese*.

2. Line baking dish with *half the bread slices* and top with a layer of *half the cheese*. Repeat bread and cheese layers and sprinkle generously with *paprika*.

3. In mixing bowl beat *6 eggs* lightly, and stir in *2 cups milk,* the *cream, ½ teaspoon salt,* and *⅛ teaspoon cayenne pepper.*

4. Pour egg mixture over the bread and cheese, being careful that every slice of bread is thoroughly moistened. Refrigerate for at least 3 hours, or overnight.

5. When ready to bake, preheat oven to 325° F. and bake the strata for 35 minutes. Sprinkle with a *little chopped parsley,* and, if desired, arrange slices of the *tomato* on top. Return to oven and bake for 15 minutes longer. Serve hot and puffed.

SPINACH MOUSSE RING

Serves 4. Serve filled with Creamed or Curried Eggs.

BUY

2 packages frozen chopped spinach (10 ounces each)

HAVE ON HAND	COOKWARE
Eggs	Saucepan
Cream *or* milk	1-quart ring mold
Butter	Shallow baking pan
Salt and pepper	
Soft bread crumbs	

1. Cook *spinach* according to package directions. Drain in a sieve, pressing out as much excess liquid as possible with back of a spoon.

2. Empty spinach into a mixing bowl and add *3 eggs, ¼ cup cream or milk, ¼ cup melted butter, ¼ teaspoon pepper, 1 teaspoon salt,* and *1½ cups soft bread crumbs.*

3. *Butter* the ring mold. Preheat oven to 350° F.

4. Set mold into a shallow pan containing about *1 inch of hot water.* Fill the mold with the spinach mixture, and bake in the preheated oven for 40 minutes, or until set.

5. Remove mold from oven. Run a knife around the edges and unmold the ring onto a serving platter. Fill the center with Creamed or Curried Eggs (page 149).

There's Nothing Quite Like Good Cheese

If I had to select one food, and one only, to live on for the rest of my life, it would be cheese. If I were allowed a second food, I would choose whole-grain breads. You can undoubtedly guess the third choice—wine, of course. Wine, bread, and cheese have been staple foods of the world since Biblical times.

Cheese is to milk what wine is to grapes: both are the end results of the preservation of the raw food. And cheese, like wine, has infinite varieties of textures, flavors, and formulae, no two cheeses or wines being identical unless made from the harvest of the same pastureland or vineyard.

To many Americans, unfortunately, cheese means those neat, convenient, relatively inexpensive, pre-packaged processed cheeses, with their unique plastic quality, so readily available in supermarkets. They come in endless flavorless flavors, colors, and shapes, and even in aerosol spray cans!

The cheese used in such products is of very little value in the first place. It is young cheese, and the very soul of cheese lies in its maturity. It is ground, along with any reject cheeses lying around, heated to stringy sterility, and homogenized with artificial flavors, colors, and other additives, until any small virtue it had in the beginning is lost forever. Finally packaged, it remains in its impotent, flavorless, waxy state for a long time in the refrigerator section of the supermarket or at home—but it will never mature.

To some Americans, however, including a rapidly growing group of rebellious truth-seekers, cheese means any one of a vast number of honest unprocessed cheeses, either properly aged or dairy fresh. They may be imported from France, Italy, Denmark, England, Switzerland, Holland, or Greece, or they may be made right here in America, for America need take no second place with the Cheddars and other carefully produced cheeses it has to offer. A fine Port-Salut is made in Wisconsin; California is famous for its Monterey Jack; our domestic Tilsit, Munster, and Brick are excellent, and our native Liederkranz can hold its own against such famous soft-ripening cheeses as Brie and Camembert.

BUYING CHEESE

Because of the growing interest in good cheeses, supermarkets are being forced to stock, among the pre-sliced packages, some respectable wedges of Cheddar (aged more than six months), Munster, and Danish Blue, boxes of Liederkranz or domestic Camembert, and real Switzerland Swiss cheese, and by popular demand new unpackaged types and flavors are added to delicatessen counters every week.

The best sources, however, of quality and variety are the speciality cheese stores and the delicacy departments of large department stores. Here the turnover is quick enough so that the cheeses are in good condition. You can be sure of the cheese you buy if you can see it being cut from bulk, and especially if you can taste a sliver before you buy. Many good cheese stores offer a sample not only to the buyer, but also to the next person waiting in line to be served. Even local grocery stores that sell cheese from bulk will seldom begrudge a sample. If the cheese you buy is good, it looks good in its own special way—moist, of typical color, and pleasantly plump, fitting its wrappings or box snugly. It is not dry (except in the case of certain aged Cheddars), or shriveled, or sunken in the middle.

WHEN TO SERVE CHEESE

Wedges of good cheese make perfect snacks or appetizers to serve with cocktails and should be part of every buffet table. In addition to these usual ways of serving cheese, many Americans are adopting the European custom of serving it as a last course, along with a bowl of ripe fruit or berries, or as the next-to-last course in a meal, with or without a tossed salad.

HOW TO SERVE CHEESE

ALL CHEESE should be served at ROOM TEMPERATURE. In warm weather, firm or semisoft cheese does not need to be out of the refrigerator for more than an hour or so, and soft cheeses like Brie and Camembert require only 30 minutes. In cooler weather, allow at least 2 hours for firm or semisoft varieties and 1 hour for the soft ones.

Bread and wine, the traditional accompaniments, should be chosen to complement the cheese. Strong cheeses, such as Cheddar, Limburger, or Liederkranz need a good rough bread such as pumpernickel and beer or a robust red wine as a beverage. A young firm cheese, such as Gruyère or the semisoft Bel Paese or Port-du-Salut, and the soft-ripening Brie and Camembert call for unsalted crackers or French or Italian bread and sweet butter. A light wine, either red or white, is appropriate. Cream-type and dairy-fresh cheeses are best with a well-chilled white wine or champagne and are often served, for dessert, with a sprinkling of sugar and fresh berries in season. Poached peaches or apricots, or preserved guavas, or even a good fruit jelly also make good accompaniments to the cream-type cheeses. The blue-veined cheeses and the soft-ripening and semisoft cheeses have a great affinity for fresh fruit, particularly apples pears, or figs, but they are also excellent with a lightly tossed salad.

HOW TO STORE CHEESES

Keep all cheese under refrigeration and return any unused portion as soon as possible to the refrigerator. Wrap it tightly in plastic film to keep it moist and to keep its flavor from penetrating other foods. Most firm and semisoft cheeses will keep well for several weeks. Fresh cheeses and soft-ripening cheese should be enjoyed as soon as possible.

Varieties of Cheese
& What Goes with Them

FRESH OR CREAM-TYPE "GREEN" CHEESES:

Usually considered dessert cheeses, these are best when served with fresh berries, stewed fruits, or fruit jellies. They deserve a well-chilled, not too dry white wine.

Boursault (France)
Boursin (France)
Brillat Savarin (France)
Cottage (U.S.)
Cream (U.S.)
Crèma Danica (Denmark)
Crème Chantilly (France)
Double Crème Gervais (France)

Fontainebleau (France)
Fromage de Monsieur (France)
Le Roi (France)
Mozzarella (Italy)
Neufchâtel (France)
Petit Suisse (France)
Ricotta (Italy, U.S.)
Une Gourmandise!!! (France)

MILD SOFT-RIPENING CHEESES:

Traditionally served after the main course and before dessert, with French or Italian bread and a dry red wine. A tossed salad may accompany them, but very little lemon juice or vinegar should be used in the dressing.

Brie (France)
Camembert (France, U.S.)
Crèma Danica (Denmark)

Crèma Royale (Denmark)
Caprice des Dieux (France)
Liederkranz (U.S.)

BLUE-VEINED CHEESES:

Beautiful served as accompaniment to a tossed salad or crumbled into the dressing; excellent as dessert with French or Italian bread and a fresh pear, apple, or peach. A dry red wine is most suitable.

Bleu d'Auvergne (France)
Bleu de Bresse (France)
Blue Cheshire (England)

Danish Blue (Denmark)
Fourme d'Ambert (France)
Gorgonzola (Italy)

Minnesota Blue (U.S.)

Norwegian Blue (Norway)

Pipo Crem' (France)

Roquefort (France)

Saingorlon (France)

Stilton (England)

STRONG CHEESES:

May be served before dessert or as a snack, with buttered dark bread. Beer is the best beverage.

Bierkase (Germany, U.S.)

Liederkranz, fully ripened (U.S.)

Limburger (Belgium, Germany, U.S.)

Livarot (France)

Maroilles (France)

Old Brick (U.S.)

Romadur (Germany)

SEMISOFT CHEESES:

Serve before dessert with French or Italian bread or as a dessert with fresh fruit. Dry red wine is the best beverage.

Beaumont (France)

Bel Paese (Italy)

Creamy Cheddars (U.S.)

Curé Nantais (France

Fontina (Italy)

Fondue de Raisin, or La Grappe (France)

Monterey Jack (U.S.)

Kernhem (Holland)

Munster (Germany, U.S.)

Pont l'Évêque (France)

Port-du-Salut (France, U.S.)

Port-Salut (Denmark)

Queijo da Serra (Portugal)

Reblochon (France)

St.-Paulin (France)

St.-Nectaire (France)

St.-Rémy (France)

Tête de Moine, or Bellelay (France)

Tilsiter (Germany, Denmark, U.S.)

White Wensleydale (England)

FIRM CHEESES:

Serve before dessert; accompany with French or Italian bread or a good dark bread, and with salad if desired. A dry red wine is the best beverage. Note, however, that in England beer is traditional with Cheddars.

Cacciocavallo (Italy)

Cheddar (England, U.S.)

Cheshire (England)

Christian IX (Denmark)

Coon Cheddar (U.S.)

Double Cream Gloucester (England)

Emmentaler (Switzerland, Austria)

Edam (Holland)

Gouda (Holland)

Grand Murols (France)

Gruyère (Switzerland, France)

Kefalotyrie (Greece)

Lancashire (England)

Leicester (England)

Provolone (Italy)

Raclette (Switzerland)   Vacherin (Switzerland)
Swiss (Switzerland, Finland, U.S.)

HARD GRATING CHEESES:

Used primarily to serve freshly grated with pasta, or sparingly in sauces, or sprinkled over the top of dishes to be gratinéed. But they can also be enjoyed as appetizers if sliced paper thin and served on buttered bread with a little freshly ground pepper.

Asiago (Italy)   Romano (Italy, U.S.)
Parmesan (Italy)   Sap Sago (Switzerland)
Pecorino Romano (Italy)   Sardo (Italy)
Pepato (Sicily)

PICKLED OR SALTED CHEESES:

Used in cooking, but excellent as appetizers served with ripe olives, hot peppers, and crisp radishes.

Feta (Greece)   Kasseri (Greece)
Bryndza de Braila (Romania)   Kash Kaval (Bulgaria)

SPICED AND FLAVORED:

Best served for dessert with fresh fruit, but they may also be presented on a buffet table or served as hors d'oeuvres on toast or crackers.

American Munster Caraway (flavored with caraway seeds)
American Pineapple (flavored with pineapple)
Dutch Leyden (spiced with clove)
French Gourmandise (flavored with cherry or kirsch)
German Kuminkase (flavored with cumin seeds)
German Kummelkase (flavored with caraway seeds)
Norwegian Gjetost (flavored with caramel or brown sugar)
Norwegian Nokkelost (flavored with cumin or caraway and clove)
Vermont Sage (flavored with sage)

MELTING CHEESES:

Cheddars   Gruyère
Emmentaler   Mozzarella
Fondue de Raisin or La Grappe   Raclette
Fontina   Switzerland Swiss
Gourmandise

Cooking with Cheese

Cheese should always be melted over low heat or simmering water. If cooked at too high temperature or for too long a time, it becomes unmanageable and stringy.

Melting cheeses should be shredded or grated before they are added to a sauce or combined with other ingredients as in a rarebit or fondue. Cheese, of course, is a prime ingredient of *quiches* and savory tarts (page 48).

Four ounces of cheese will make a generous cupful when shredded or grated.

THE FONDUE

Contrary to what most people think, fondue means "melted," not "cheese." Swiss Fondue, the original and best-known fondue, is a blend of melted cheese, white wine, and Kirschwasser. It is enjoyed as a communal dish. A large bowl containing the fondue is placed in the middle of a table and kept warm by a low-burning spirit lamp. Chunks of French bread are speared onto fondue forks and dipped into the hot cheese mixture. The fondue is stirred often to keep it smooth, and should it become too thick, a little more wine or kirsch is stirred in.

Serve the fondue with white wine, rosé wine, or beer.

In Switzerland, traditionally, anyone who loses his chunk of bread in the fondue must either drink his glass empty or kiss the person on his left. For the sake of sobriety, it's probably safest to give the kiss.

SWISS FONDUE

Serves 4 or 6

BUY

1 pound Switzerland Swiss or Gruyère cheese; DO NOT USE PROCESSED CHEESE
Long flute of French bread
1 bottle, or more, white wine such as Neufchâtel

HAVE ON HAND	*COOKWARE*
Cornstarch	Fondue casserole
Garlic	
Kirschwasser	
Freshly ground black pepper	

1. Shred the *cheese* and toss it lightly with *2 teaspoons cornstarch*. Slice the *bread* into bite-size chunks. Set aside.

2. Peel and split a *clove of garlic* and rub the casserole with the cut pieces. Add *1 cup wine* and heat until bubbles begin to rise. Do not let the wine boil.

3. Add cheese to the hot wine, a handful at a time, and cook over low heat until cheese is melted and smooth, stirring constantly with a wooden spoon. Stir in *4 tablespoons kirsch,* and sprinkle with *pepper*.

4. Keep the fondue warm over low heat, preferably by means of an alcohol burner in a chafing dish or buffet warmer.

5. Serve with the chunks of French bread, and supply each diner with a long-handled fork.

WELSH RABBIT

Serves 4 or 6. This is a variety of fondue in which sharp natural Cheddar cheese is melted with beer or cream. It is usually quite highly seasoned with mustard, cayenne, and Worcestershire. Ladle the melted mixture over hot buttered toast.

BUY

1 pound sharp natural Cheddar cheese

HAVE ON HAND	*COOKWARE*
Beer *or* ale	Heavy skillet
Worcestershire sauce	
Dry mustard	
Cayenne	
Hot buttered toast	

1. Shred the *cheese* and set aside.

2. In skillet combine *½ cup ale or beer, 2 teaspoons Worcestershire sauce, ½ teaspoon dry mustard,* and *a good dash of cayenne pepper.* Place over low heat until beer is hot but not boiling.

3. Gradually add the shredded cheese, and stir constantly until it is smooth and melted. Serve immediately on the *toast.*

In many European countries, cheese is served hot and melting without being mixed with any liquid at all. In France, slices of Swiss cheese are coated lightly with flour and pan-fried. In Italy, strips of mozzarella are dipped into a fritter batter and deep-fried. In Switzerland, a wheel of Swiss cheese known as Raclette is cut in half and then placed before an open wood fire; as the cheese melts, it is scraped off and eaten immediately. Here is an unusual Greek recipe for a melting cheese appetizer.

FLAMING KASSERI

Serves 4

BUY

½ pound wedge of Kasseri *or* mozzarella cheese
Italian *or* French bread

HAVE ON HAND	*COOKWARE*
Lemon	Ovenproof skillet *or*
Brandy (the Greeks use Metaxa)	shallow au gratin dish

1. Slice *cheese* ¼ inch thick. Slice and toast the *bread*. Cut *1 lemon* in half.

2. Arrange the cheese in an ovenproof skillet, or a shallow au gratin dish, and place 4 inches beneath broiler heat. Broil for about 6 minutes, or until cheese is soft and the surface is bubbly. Remove from oven.

3. Immediately pour *4 tablespoons brandy* over the cheese and ignite. When the flame has spread over the entire surface, extinguish it by squeezing the juice of the lemon over all.

4. Serve immediately on warm plates with the *pan juices*. Serve the hot toast on the side.

BEANS & PEAS,
GRAINS & CEREALS

Beans & Peas

Most beans and grains are incomplete protein foods, lacking some of the essential amino acids, but they gain substantially in food value when combined with complete protein foods such as eggs, milk, or cheese, or with one another. For instance, neither beans nor rice alone provides all the necessary amino acids, but what is lacking in one is present in the other, so that in combination they add up to be good nutritionally.

The poor peoples of many countries instinctively combine beans with grains or cereals, thereby providing good, low-cost protein dishes for their tables. American Indians cooked lima beans with corn in a dish known as *sauquaquatash,* which later became New England succotash. Black beans and rice is a popular dish in South American countries. Soybean curd, known as *tofu,* is frequently teamed with rice in Japan. And beans and pasta are a happy combination in *minestrone* and *pasta e fagioli* all through Italy. Knowledge of nutrition aside, beans and cereals have nourished the human race since long before Esau sold his birthright for a mess of lentil soup.

Many varieties of dried and canned beans are readily available to us today and, usually, they are interchangeable in recipes. Dried kidney beans may be substituted for dried black beans, dried pea beans or navy beans for dried pinto beans, and canned garbanzos make an excellent (often more interesting) substitute for canned kidney beans. It helps to know, however, that in making substitutions 1 pound of dried beans makes about 5 cups of cooked beans—and that 5 cups of canned cooked beans are the equivalent of the 1 pound of dried beans that is generally specified in a recipe to serve 6.

BAKED SOYBEANS

Serves 6. Here's a "quick" method of cooking dried beans which has recently been publicized. Wash *1 pound of beans* and put them into a saucepan with *1 quart water.* Bring water to a boil, and boil hard for 1 minute. Remove from heat, cover, and let stand for 1 hour. Then simmer for about 1 hour, or until tender, adding *more water* if needed. You don't save much actual cooking time, but the method is a convenience when you forget to soak your beans overnight in advance.

BUY

1 pound soybeans
Bunch green onions
1 green pepper
¼ pound fresh mushrooms

HAVE ON HAND	*COOKWARE*
Cooking oil	3-quart saucepan
Butter	Small skillet
Tomato juice	2-quart baking dish
Oregano *or* marjoram	
Brown sugar	
Salt	

1. Wash *2 cups soybeans* and soak overnight in *plenty of water* to cover.

2. Next day, bring beans to a boil, then simmer for 1 to 1½ hours or until tender, adding *additional water* if needed. Drain and set aside.

3. Meanwhile chop *½ cup green onions, ½ cup green pepper,* and *¾ cup mushrooms.* Sauté these vegetables in *2 tablespoons cooking oil* until onion is transparent. Add vegetables and pan oil to the drained beans and mix well.

4. Add *2 tablespoons butter, ¾ cup tomato juice, ½ teaspoon oregano or marjoram, ¼ cup brown sugar,* and *salt to taste.*

5. Preheat oven to 325° F. *Butter* a baking dish.

6. Empty bean mixture into the baking dish, and bake in the preheated oven for 40 to 50 minutes.

TEXAS BEANS

Serves 5 to 6. Serve over cooked rice.

BUY

1 pound dried pinto beans
4-ounce can roasted green chili peppers
8-ounce can taco sauce
1-pound can tomatoes

HAVE ON HAND	COOKWARE
Salt	4-quart saucepan with lid
Large onion	
Garlic	
Black pepper	
Cumin seeds	

1. A day in advance, soak the *pinto beans* in *water* to cover generously.

2. Next day, drain beans, and add *fresh water* to cover by 2 inches. Add *1 teaspoon salt,* bring to a boil, cover, and simmer for about 1 hour, adding *more water* if necessary.

3. Peel and chop *1 large onion* and *2 large cloves garlic.* Chop *half the chili peppers* and set aside. Refrigerate remaining chili peppers for another use.

4. To beans add *½ teaspoon black pepper, 1 teaspoon cumin seeds,* the chopped onion, garlic, and chili peppers, the *taco sauce,* and the *tomatoes.* Cook over low heat for 1 to 1½ hours longer, or until beans are tender and sauce is reduced.

FRIED BEANS WITH SOUR CREAM

Serves 6. You may use any kind of dried beans, but the small pinkish ones, known as pinto beans, are most frequently used in Mexico for this popular and simple recipe.

BUY

1 pound dry pinto beans
Container of sour cream

HAVE ON HAND	*COOKWARE*
Cooking oil	3- to 4-quart saucepan with lid
Salt	Large heavy skillet

1. Pick over *beans,* discarding any shriveled ones or any foreign particles which may be found among them. Wash, then cover generously with *water* in a large saucepan, and let soak overnight.

2. Drain beans, cover with *2 quarts fresh cold water,* and bring to a boil. Cover and simmer for about 1½ hours, or until beans are tender. Set aside (but do not drain) until ready to fry.

3. To fry beans, heat *½ cup cooking oil* in a heavy skillet. Use a slotted spoon to spoon some of the beans into the hot oil. Mash the beans with the back of a heavy spoon and add a *little of the bean liquor.* Continue to add beans and liquid and continue mashing until all beans are used. Add *salt to taste,* and cook until the mashed beans reach the desired consistency, dry or moist or soupy—according to your preference.

4. Serve hot with a topping of *sour cream.*

BEANS WITH RED WINE

Serves 6

BUY

1 pound dried kidney beans
8-ounce can tomato sauce

HAVE ON HAND   COOKWARE

Large onion   2-quart saucepan
Garlic   2-quart casserole with cover
Red wine
Salt and pepper
Bay leaves
Thyme
Fresh parsley
Butter

1. A day in advance, wash *beans* and soak overnight in *water* to cover generously.

2. Next day, drain beans. Preheat oven to 325° F.

3. Chop *1 large onion* and *2 cloves garlic,* and add to beans along with *1 cup red wine,* the *tomato sauce, 1 teaspoon salt, 1 teaspoon pepper, 1 bay leaf,* crumbled, *a dash of thyme,* and *2 tablespoons chopped parsley.*

4. Put bean mixture into a 2-quart casserole and add *enough water* to cover the beans by 2 inches. Cover and bake in preheated oven for 4 hours. Add *4 tablespoons butter* and, if necessary, *additional water* to keep beans moist. Continue to bake for 2 hours longer.

SPLIT PEA AND TOMATO CASSEROLE

Serves 4

BUY

Box green split peas
1-pound can stewed tomatoes

HAVE ON HAND

Onion
Salt
Butter
Flour
Pepper
Bread
1 cup cooked *or* leftover rice

COOKWARE

2-quart saucepan
2 small skillets
2-quart baking dish

1. Soak *1 cup green split peas* overnight in *water*. Drain the peas, and cook in *fresh water* with *2 tablespoons chopped onion* and *1 teaspoon salt* until tender. Drain, reserving *1 cup of the liquid*.

2. Melt *2 tablespoons butter* in skillet. Stir in *3 tablespoons flour*. Gradually stir in the *reserved liquid*, and cook, stirring, until sauce is smooth and thick. Stir in *salt and pepper to taste*.

3. Crumble *enough bread to make 1 cup crumbs*. In second skillet, sauté crumbs in *2 tablespoons butter* until golden.

4. *Butter* baking dish. Preheat oven to 350° F.

5. In baking dish, place alternate layers of the peas, sauce, the *stewed tomatoes*, and *1 cup cooked rice*. Sprinkle with the buttered bread crumbs and bake in the preheated oven for 30 minutes.

BLACK BEAN PURÉE

Serves 8. Black beans are difficult to buy in my section of northern New Jersey, so I have frequently substituted kidney beans in this recipe with excellent results.

BUY

1 pound dried Cuban black beans *or* kidney beans
1 green pepper
Bunch of green onions
1-pint container sour cream

HAVE ON HAND	COOKWARE
Large onion	4-quart saucepan
Garlic	
Olive *or* peanut oil	
Bay leaves	
Salt	
Coarsely cracked pepper	

1. A day in advance, wash *beans* and soak overnight in *6 cups cool water.*

2. Next day, DO NOT DRAIN BEANS. Peel and chop *1 large onion* and *2 cloves garlic.* Seed and chop the *green pepper.* Sauté these vegetables in *½ cup oil* until onion is transparent.

3. Add vegetables and pan oil to the beans and soaking water, and bring to a boil. Add *1 bay leaf, 1 teaspoon salt,* and *½ teaspoon cracked pepper.* Simmer for 1 to 1½ hours, or until beans are tender. Drain off any excess water, leaving the beans fairly dry.

4. Press the beans through a food mill, or, easier still, blend 2 cups of them at a time in an electric blender. Empty into a serving dish and keep warm.

5. Wash and trim the *scallions* and chop the *white part and as much of the green stalks as is tender.* Sprinkle the chopped scallions over the bean purée, and serve with *sour cream.*

LIMA BEANS IN SOUR CREAM

Serves 6. This is good whether served as a cold salad or as a hot casserole.

BUY

1 pound dried lima beans
1 pint sour cream
Bunch of fresh chives
Fresh dill, if possible
Parsley

HAVE ON HAND	*COOKWARE*
Lemons	Large saucepan
Salt and pepper	1½-quart casserole dish
Butter	

1. Wash and pick over the *beans,* and soak overnight in *water* to cover generously.

2. Next day, bring beans and soaking water to a boil and simmer for about 1 hour, or until tender, adding *more water* if necessary. Drain well.

3. Combine the cooked beans with the *sour cream, ¼ cup lemon juice, ½ cup minced chives, 1 tablespoon chopped fresh dill, ¼ cup chopped parsley, 1 teaspoon salt,* and *a good dash pepper.*

4. To serve cold, refrigerate for several hours before serving on a bed of salad greens. To serve hot, pile the bean mixture into a 1½-quart casserole, dot with *3 tablespoons butter,* and bake in a preheated 375° F. oven for 30 minutes.

KIDNEY BEAN CREOLE

Serves 2 or 4. Serve with either cooked rice or garlic bread, plus a green salad.

BUY

1 large green pepper
1-pound can kidney beans
1-pound can stewed tomatoes

HAVE ON HAND	*COOKWARE*
1 large onion	2-quart saucepan
Garlic	
Cooking oil	
Salt	
Cayenne pepper	

1. Peel and thinly slice the *onion,* peel and mince *1 large clove garlic.* Trim, seed, and slice the *green pepper.* In saucepan, sauté the vegetables in *2 tablespoons cooking oil* until onion is lightly browned.

2. Drain *kidney beans* and add to saucepan. Add *stewed tomatoes with liquid, 1 teaspoon salt,* and ⅛ *teaspoon cayenne pepper.* Bring to a boil and simmer for 10 minutes, stirring occasionally, or until pepper slices are almost tender (they should still be slightly crisp). Correct seasoning and serve.

BLACK-EYED PEAS WITH TOMATOES

Serves 8

BUY

2 cans black-eyed peas, 1 pound each
2 cans tomatoes, 1 pound each

HAVE ON HAND

HAVE ON HAND   *COOKWARE*

Onion   2-quart saucepan with lid
Butter
Flour
Milk
Salt and pepper
Worcestershire sauce

1. Peel and finely chop *1 medium onion.*

2. In saucepan heat *2 tablespoons butter,* and in it sauté the onion until tender.

3. Stir in *3 tablespoons flour.* Gradually stir in *1 cup milk* and cook, stirring, until sauce is smooth and thickened.

4. Drain and add the *peas* and *tomatoes,* and add *½ teaspoon salt or to taste, ½ teaspoon pepper,* and *1 teaspoon Worcestershire.* Cover and simmer over low heat for 15 minutes.

SOPA SECA

Serves 6

BUY

1 green pepper
8-ounce can Italian plum tomatoes
8-ounce can garbanzos *or* chick peas

HAVE ON HAND   *COOKWARE*

Onion   2-quart saucepan with lid
Garlic
Cooking oil
Rice
Salt and pepper

1. Peel and chop *1 onion* and *1 large clove garlic.* Seed and chop *half the green pepper.*

2. Heat *3 tablespoons oil* in the saucepan, and in it sauté the chopped vegetables over low heat until onion is transparent.

3. Add *1 cup rice* and continue to cook for a couple of minutes, stirring constantly, until rice is golden.

4. Add the *tomatoes with their liquid, 1 cup water,* and *½ teaspoon salt,* and bring to a rapid boil. Cover saucepan tightly, reduce heat to very low, and cook for 20 minutes.

5. Drain the *garbanzos* and add to rice mixture. Toss mixture with a fork, partially cover, and let cook over low heat for 5 minutes longer, or until rice is fluffy and all of the liquid has been absorbed.

Corn Meal & Hominy

GNOCCHI DI SEMOLINA

Serves 6. The tender dumplings known by the Italian name of *gnocchi* are a great favorite in European countries. In Germany (and sometimes in France) they are made with potatoes. In many countries, semolina, corn meal, or farina is used to make the paste. *Gnocchi* are really glorified Italian *polenta* (which bears a remarkable resemblance to our own old-fashioned corn-meal mush).

HAVE ON HAND	*COOKWARE*
Parmesan cheese	2-quart saucepan
Milk	Jelly-roll pan
Salt	˙6 individual ovenproof ramekins
Fine yellow corn meal	
Sweet butter	
1 egg	

1. Grate *enough cheese to measure 1⅓ cups.*

2. In saucepan combine *2 cups milk* and *½ cup water.* Bring to a boil. Remove from heat and stir in *1 teaspoon salt,* then slowly stir in *1*

cup corn meal, mixing well. Return to low heat and cook, stirring constantly, until thick and smooth. Cook over low heat for 20 minutes, stirring occasionally. If too thick, stir in a *little boiling water.*

3. Remove from heat and stir in *2 tablespoons butter, 1 egg,* and *⅓ cup of the grated cheese.* Mix well.

4. Moisten a jelly-roll pan with cold water and, using a rubber spatula, spread the corn-meal mixture on it in a smooth layer ½ inch thick. Cool, then cover with waxed paper and refrigerate for at least 30 minutes. Cut the chilled mixture into 1½-inch rounds with a cooky cutter.

5. *Butter* individual ramekins, and in each one place 6 or 8 rounds—they should slightly overlap. Dot each ramekin with *½ tablespoon butter* (you will use 3 tablespoons in all). Sprinkle with *remaining cheese,* and place under broiler until golden, watching carefully so they do not burn.

FARINA GNOCCHI

Serves 8

HAVE ON HAND	*COOKWARE*
Parmesan cheese	2-quart saucepan
Milk	1-quart loaf pan
Butter	Shallow baking dish
Salt	
Farina *or* Cream of Wheat	
2 eggs	

1. Grate and set aside *2 cups Parmesan cheese.*

2. In saucepan combine *3 cups milk, ½ cup butter,* and *1 teaspoon salt.* Bring to a simmer.

3. Gradually stir in *1 cup plus 2 tablespoons farina;* cook, continuing to stir, until mixture is thick.

4. Beat in *2 eggs,* one at a time, and beat in *1 cup of the grated cheese.*

5. Pour into *buttered* loaf pan. Cool, turn out, then slice into strips.

6. *Butter* baking dish. Preheat oven to 425° F.

7. Arrange strips in baking dish, dot with *3 tablespoons butter,* and sprinkle with *remaining grated Parmesan.*

8. Bake in the hot oven for 10 to 15 minutes, or until hot and lightly browned.

POLENTA CASSEROLE

Serves 6

HAVE ON HAND

Yellow *or* white corn meal
Salt
4 egg yolks
Swiss *or* Gruyère cheese
Cream

COOKWARE

2-quart saucepan with lid
2-quart casserole dish

1. In saucepan blend *1 cup corn meal* and *1 cup cold water.* Gradually stir in *3 cups hot water* and *1 teaspoon salt.* Bring to a boil, stirring constantly, then cover and cook over low heat for 30 minutes, stirring occasionally.

2. Meanwhile, separate *4 eggs,* reserving the whites for another use. Shred *1 cup cheese. Butter* the casserole, and preheat oven to 350° F.

3. Remove corn-meal mixture from heat, then beat in the *4 egg yolks, ½ cup cream,* and the *shredded cheese.*

4. Spoon into the casserole, and bake in the moderate oven for 25 minutes.

FRITELLE DI POLENTA

Serves 8. Serve with maple syrup for breakfast; or with melted butter and grated Parmesan cheese as a starch accompaniment for lunch or dinner.

HAVE ON HAND	*COOKWARE*
Yellow *or* white corn meal	2-quart saucepan with lid
Salt	1-quart loaf pan
2 eggs	Medium skillet
Flour	
Fine bread crumbs	
Cooking oil *or* butter	
Butter (optional)	

1. In a small bowl, mix *1 cup corn meal* with *1 teaspoon salt* and *1 cup cold water* to a smooth paste.

2. In saucepan bring *3 cups water* to a boil. Gradually stir the *corn-meal paste* into the boiling water; cook, stirring constantly, until thick. Then cover the saucepan and cook over low heat for 10 minutes, stirring occasionally.

3. Spoon mixture into the loaf pan and pack down firmly. Cool, then chill thoroughly.

4. Remove the corn-meal loaf from the pan and cut it in slices ½ inch thick.

5. Beat *2 eggs with 2 tablespoons water.* Coat the polenta slices evenly on both sides with *flour,* dip into the egg mixture, then roll in *bread crumbs.*

6. Sauté the slices in *cooking oil or butter* for about 2 minutes on each side, or until golden.

MUSHROOM POLENTA

Follow preceding recipe for Polenta Casserole, but make this addition: Wash, trim, and slice *½ pound fresh mushrooms.* Sauté them in *2 tablespoons butter* for 5 minutes, or until just tender, stirring frequently. Fold into the *corn mixture* at the same time as the *shredded cheese.*

BUTTERMILK SPOON BREAD

Serves 8

BUY

Buttermilk

HAVE ON HAND	*COOKWARE*
Milk	2-quart saucepan
Yellow corn meal	2-quart casserole
Baking soda	
Salt	
Butter at room temperature	
2 eggs	

1. In saucepan combine *2 cups each milk* and *buttermilk* and heat to steaming. Gradually stir in *1 cup corn meal,* and cook over moderate heat, stirring frequently, for 15 minutes. Cool slightly.

2. Preheat oven to 350° F. *Butter* the casserole.

3. Stir *1 teaspoon baking soda, 1 teaspoon salt,* and *3 tablespoons butter* into corn-meal mixture. Stir in *2 egg yolks,* one by one.

4. Beat the *2 egg whites* until stiff but not dry; fold into corn-meal mixture.

5. Turn batter into casserole, and bake in moderate oven for 30 minutes. Serve hot from the casserole with a large spoon.

VIRGINIA SPOON BREAD

Serves 4

HAVE ON HAND

Butter
Milk
Corn meal

3 eggs
Salt
Sugar
Baking powder
Cayenne pepper

COOKWARE

2-quart saucepan
1½-quart baking dish

1. Preheat oven to 375° F. Generously *butter* the baking dish.

2. Heat *2½ cups milk* to steaming hot. Gradually stir *1 cup corn meal* into the hot milk. Add *2 tablespoons butter* and cook, stirring, until mixture is very thick and smooth. Remove from heat and cool slightly.

3. Add *3 egg yolks,* one by one, beating well after each addition; reserve the whites.

4. Stir in *1 teaspoon salt, 1 teaspoon sugar, ½ teaspoon baking powder,* and *a dash of cayenne pepper.*

5. Beat the *3 egg whites* until stiff but not dry, and fold into yolk mixture.

6. Turn batter into prepared baking dish. Bake in preheated oven for 30 to 40 minutes. Serve hot from the dish, dipping out large spoonfuls. Serve with a *little hot melted butter* if desired.

BAKED GRITS

Serves 6

BUY

Grits (hominy grits, to Northerners)

HAVE ON HAND

Salt
1 egg
Milk
Sugar

COOKWARE

2-quart saucepan
1½-quart casserole

1. Combine *1 quart boiling water* and *¼ teaspoon salt* in saucepan. Gradually stir in *1 cup grits* and cook over moderate heat, stirring occasionally, for 1 hour. Cool.

2. Preheat oven to 400° F. *Butter* casserole.

3. Into hominy mixture, stir *1 egg, 1 cup milk,* and *½ teaspoon sugar.* Turn into the buttered casserole; bake in the hot oven for 30 minutes.

HOMINY CHEESE CASSEROLE

Serves 4 to 6

BUY

1-pound 12-ounce can whole hominy

HAVE ON HAND	*COOKWARE*
Bread	2-quart casserole
Cheddar cheese	
Parsley	
Butter	
2 eggs	
Milk	
Salt	

1. Crumb *enough bread to measure 1 cup crumbs.* Shred *1 cup cheese.* Chop *2 tablespoons parsley.* Drain the *hominy.*

2. Preheat oven to 325° F. *Butter* casserole.

3. In mixing bowl beat *2 eggs.* Stir in *1 cup milk,* the bread crumbs and cheese, *1 teaspoon salt,* the drained hominy, and the parsley.

4. Turn into casserole; bake in preheated oven for 55 to 60 minutes, or until firm.

Rice

There are several types of white rice—the long-grained; the round-grained, or Japanese; and the short-grained, or Italian. Then there is brown rice, which is more nutritious than the white ones, since it retains the coat of bran that is normally removed in the hulling and milling of white rice. "Converted" rice lies in between brown and white, as it retains some but not all of the bran.

All these rices may be cooked in the same way, with some variation in cooking time. I find I can make the best rice, tender and with each grain separate from the other, if I use the converted. It is never mushy when cooked by the classic method.

Many of the great international methods of cooking rice involve a rich broth, rather than water, for the necessary liquid. Chicken broth is the most usual, but a well-seasoned Vegetable Broth, rich in leeks and other vegetables (page 97), is something even the non-vegetarian cook will appreciate.

But first:

HOW TO COOK PLAIN RICE

Serves 4. Use a heavy 2-quart saucepan with a tightly fitting lid. In it put *1 cup rice, 1 teaspoon salt,* and *2 cups water.* Bring the water to a boil over high heat. Stir only once with a fork, and cover tightly. Turn heat to very low; without removing the lid, let the rice steep in the hot liquid for 15 to 20 minutes. Then remove the lid, add *a good chunk of butter,* and toss rice lightly with a fork. Partially cover with the lid, and let stand over the low heat to steam-dry for another 10 to 30 minutes, or until you are ready to serve it.

CHINESE RICE

Serves 6. The Chinese method of cooking rice is equally good, but no salt or butter is used.

Rinse *1½ cups rice* in a sieve under *cold running water* for 10 seconds, then empty into a heavy 3-quart saucepan with a tightly fitting lid. Add *1½ cups cold water.* Bring water to a boil, and boil hard for 1 minute. Lower heat to a minimum and let the rice simmer, uncovered, for 7 to 8 minutes, or until all water has been absorbed and the rice is quite dry. Pour in *1 cup boiling water,* cover tightly, and cook for about 6 minutes longer. Turn off heat and let the rice cook in its own heat for another 5 minutes—do not remove lid during this time. The rice is now ready to serve. Fluff it with a fork, and serve; accompany with tiny bowls of soy sauce—one for each person.

RICE SALAD

Serves 6. Combine *3 cups cold Chinese rice* with *1 sweet green pepper,* seeded and thinly sliced; *1 sweet red onion,* peeled and thinly sliced; *1 clove garlic,* minced; and *½ cup French dressing* (page 127). Refrigerate for several hours. Before serving, fold in *4 ripe tomatoes,* peeled and cut into slim wedges, and *1 cup finely chopped fresh parsley.*

PIERRE'S OVEN RICE

Serves 6 to 8. This is the method of my good friend Pierre Franey.

HAVE ON HAND

Onion
Butter
Long-grain *or* converted rice
Tabasco

Bay leaf
Broth, vegetable (page 97)
  or chicken.
Parsley
Salt

COOKWARE

Heavy 2-quart casserole with lid

1. Preheat oven to 425° F. Chop *3 tablespoons onion.*

2. In casserole melt *4 tablespoons butter.* Add the chopped onion and cook, stirring, until onion is wilted but not brown.

3. Add *2 cups rice,* and cook, stirring, for about 30 seconds.

4. Add *4 drops Tabasco, 3 cups broth (or part broth and part water), 1 bay leaf, 4 sprigs parsley,* and *a little salt* if necessary. Bring liquid to a boil over direct heat.

5. Cover casserole tightly and transfer to the hot oven. Bake for 20 minutes—no longer. The rice should now be done. When it is cooked, all the water will be absorbed and the grains tender. If not, continue baking for 1 to 10 minutes longer.

6. Remove rice from oven. It will stay hot for at least half an hour if need be, providing you leave it covered. When ready to serve, add *3 tablespoons butter,* and toss lightly with a two-pronged fork.

SAFFRON-RICE VARIATION: Cook *1 clove garlic,* peeled and minced, along with the chopped onion. Add *½ teaspoon saffron threads* along with the liquid.

RICE PILAF

Serves 3, but recipe may be doubled.

HAVE ON HAND

Butter
Onion
Garlic
Converted rice
Broth (page 97) *or* water
Salt

COOKWARE

2-quart heavy saucepan with
  tight-fitting lid

AN HOUR OR SO BEFORE DINNER:

1. Melt *1 stick butter (½ cup)* in saucepan, and in it sauté *1 medium onion,* minced, and *1 clove garlic,* minced, for 3 minutes or until onion is transparent.

2. Add *1 cup raw rice,* and cook, stirring, until rice grains are thoroughly coated with the butter mixture.

3. Add *1¾ cups broth or water* and *salt to taste,* and bring to a rapid boil. Cover tightly. Reduce heat to its very lowest point, and cook without raising the lid for 20 to 30 minutes.

4. Remove lid, toss rice with a fork, and partially cover. Let rice steam on very low heat until ready to serve. If it forms a golden crust on the bottom, you are lucky. No pilaf in the Near East would be worth its garlic if it didn't have that golden crust.

AT SERVING TIME:

5. Fluff the rice again with a fork, then empty into a hot serving dish. With a spoon scrape the golden crust from the bottom of the pan and pile it on top of the pilaf.

NOTE: Cooking rice this way—the perfect way—often makes the saucepan a problem to wash. If you don't want to have to soak it overnight, invest in a heavy 2-quart porcelain-coated iron saucepan. It cleans quickly and you'll use it for dozens of other dishes.

RISOTTO

Serves 6

HAVE ON HAND	*COOKWARE*
Onion	Heavy saucepan with tight-fitting
Parmesan cheese	lid
Butter	
Converted rice	
Water *or* Broth (page 97)	
Saffron	
Salt	

1. Peel and chop *1 medium onion*. Grate *½ cup Parmesan cheese*.

2. In saucepan melt *4 tablespoons butter*. Add onion and sauté for 5 minutes, or until onion is transparent.

3. Add *2 cups rice,* then cook, stirring, for 2 minutes, or until rice is well coated with butter.

4. Add *3 cups water or broth, ½ teaspoon saffron,* and *1 teaspoon salt*. Bring to a rapid boil. Cover tightly. Reduce heat to very low and cook without removing cover for 20 minutes.

5. Remove cover and fluff rice with a fork. Keep warm, partially covered, until ready to serve.

6. When ready to serve, add *2 tablespoons butter* and toss rice again. Empty into serving dish and sprinkle generously with grated Parmesan.

CURRIED RICE

Serves 6

BUY

Major Grey chutney
Small can slivered toasted almonds

HAVE ON HAND

Onion
Peanut *or* cooking oil
Good curry powder
Converted rice
Water *or* Broth (page 97)
Bay leaves
Salt

COOKWARE

Heavy 3-quart saucepan with tight-fitting lid

1. Chop *1 medium onion* finely. Measure and chop *½ cup chutney*. Set aside.

2. Heat *3 tablespoons oil,* and in it sauté the chopped onion for 3 minutes. Stir in *1 tablespoon good curry powder,* and sauté for 3 minutes longer.

3. Add *1½ cups raw rice;* cook and stir for 2 to 3 minutes, or until rice is coated with the oil.

4. Add *3 cups water or broth, 1 small bay leaf,* the chutney, and *1½ teaspoons salt.* Reduce heat to very, very low, cover saucepan tightly, and cook for 20 to 25 minutes. Toss rice, partially cover, and keep warm until ready to serve.

5. Fluff with a fork, discard bay leaf, turn into a serving dish, and sprinkle with *almonds.*

ALMOND RICE

Serves 6. In a heavy saucepan combine *1½ cups converted rice, 4 table-spoons butter, 2 tablespoons ground blanched almonds, 1 teaspoon salt,* and *3 cups water.* Bring to a boil over high heat, cover tightly, and cook, without stirring, for 20 minutes. Remove lid, toss mixture with a fork, partially cover, and keep over low heat for 10, but no more than 30, minutes.

NASI GORENG

Serves 6

HAVE ON HAND	COOKWARE
Garlic	Kettle
Salad oil	8-inch skillet
Rice	2-quart casserole with tight-
Ground coriander	fitting cover
Ground turmeric	
Ground cumin	
Salt	
3 eggs	
Pepper	
Butter	

1. Peel and mince *1 large clove garlic*. Preheat oven to 350° F. Put kettle of water on to boil.

2. In skillet heat *3 tablespoons salad oil*. Add *1½ cups rice,* and cook, stirring, until rice is golden. Empty rice and oil into casserole.

3. Add garlic, *1½ teaspoons each coriander, turmeric, and cumin,* and *1 teaspoon salt*. Pour *3 cups boiling water* over rice, stir well, cover, and bake in the preheated oven for 50 minutes.

4. Meanwhile beat *3 eggs lightly* with *½ teaspoon salt* and *¼ teaspoon pepper*. Heat *1 tablespoon butter* in the skillet, add the eggs, and cook over low heat until eggs are set like a large flat omelet. Turn omelet out onto a chopping board and cut into long strips.

5. When rice is cooked, remove from oven, uncover, and add egg strips. Toss well with two forks and serve hot.

PARSLEY RICE RING

Serves 4. Fill with creamed eggs or mushrooms or any colorful sauced vegetable. Serve with a tossed salad.

HAVE ON HAND

Butter, at room temperature
Rice
Salt
Parsley *or* water cress

COOKWARE

8-inch ring mold
2-quart heavy saucepan with tight-fitting lid

1. *Butter* ring mold.

2. In saucepan combine *1 cup rice, 1 teaspoon salt,* and *2 cups water*. Bring water to a rapid boil, cover tightly, reduce heat to low, and cook for 20 minutes, or until water is absorbed. Remove lid, add *¼ cup butter (½ stick),* and toss until butter is melted.

3. Stir in *1 cup chopped parsley or water cress*.

4. Spoon into ring mold and press down well with back of a wooden spoon. Let stand in a warm place for 5 minutes, then invert onto a serving dish.

Our American Indian rice, or wild rice, is regarded by many persons as the most delicious of all grains. Certainly it is the most expensive, for even in a good year the crop is limited by the whims of nature. So, when you do buy a box of wild rice, please make the most of it by cooking it in Indian fashion. This method transforms 1 cup wild rice into 6 cups of large tender kernels.

WILD RICE, INDIAN FASHION

Serves 6. The day before serving: wash *1 cup wild rice* thoroughly, add *8 cups boiling water,* and let soak overnight.

Next day: drain rice, pour *4 cups boiling water* over it, cover, and let stand for 20 minutes; drain. Repeat this procedure 3 times.

A few minutes before serving, again cover the rice with *boiling water,* add *1 teaspoon salt,* cover the pan, and simmer for 5 minutes. Then drain the rice and place in a hot oven for a few minutes to dry out.

Toss with *a big nugget of butter* and season to taste with *salt and pepper.*

WILD RICE WITH MUSHROOMS AND
SOUR CREAM

Serves 6. Cook *1 cup wild rice* in Indian fashion described above.

Trim, wash, and dry *1 pound whole button mushrooms,* then sauté them in *½ stick hot butter* until lightly browned on all sides. Add *1½ cups sour cream,* and heat to serving temperature. Toss into the wild rice just before serving.

Wheat & Other Cereals

BULGUR, or cracked wheat, has been around for centuries. Although underappreciated by Americans, it is well known to other peoples, particularly of the Near East and North Africa, who prize it as the staff of life. It is either soft or hard wheat that has been processed by being soaked in water, then cooked and dried.

BULGUR PILAF

Serves 6

BUY

Box or bag of cracked wheat (bulgur)

HAVE ON HAND	*COOKWARE*
Butter	Heavy 2-quart casserole with cover
Onion	
Salt	
Pepper	
Water *or* Broth (page 97)	

1. Preheat oven to 350° F.

2. In casserole melt *½ cup butter (1 stick)* and in it sauté *1 medium onion*, chopped, until golden. Add *2 teaspoons salt* and *a little pepper*, and stir in *2 cups cracked wheat.* Cover the casserole and cook over low heat for 10 minutes.

3. Add *1 quart water or vegetable broth;* cover, and bake in the preheated oven for 30 minutes. Fluff gently with a fork and bake for 15 minutes longer, or until liquid is absorbed and bulgur is moist and fluffy.

MUSHROOM BULGUR PILAF

Serves 4

BUY

½ pound mushrooms
Bunch green onions
Box or bag of cracked wheat (bulgur)

HAVE ON HAND	*COOKWARE*
Garlic	Large heavy skillet with tight-
Butter	fitting lid
Salt	
White wine *or* dry vermouth	

1. Wash, trim, and slice the *mushrooms.* Chop the *green onions* and *1 clove garlic.*

2. In saucepan or skillet melt *¼ cup butter (½ stick),* and in it sauté the mushrooms, onions, and garlic until soft but not brown.

3. Add *1 teaspoon salt* and *1 cup cracked wheat.* Stir in *½ cup white wine or dry vermouth* and *1 cup water.* Cover tightly and cook over very low heat for about 30 minutes, or until wheat is dry and cooked.

4. Fluff with a fork, partially cover, and keep over low heat for a few minutes before serving.

BAKED BARLEY

Serves 4

BUY

½ pound fresh mushrooms
1 large sweet onion
1 box medium pearl barley
Chives *or* parsley

HAVE ON HAND   *COOKWARE*

Butter   8-inch skillet
2 cups Vegetable Broth (page 97) 2-quart casserole with cover
Salt and pepper

1. Wash, trim, and slice the *mushrooms*. Peel and finely chop the *onion*.

2. In skillet melt *2 tablespoons butter,* and in it sauté mushrooms over moderately high heat for about 5 minutes, or until mushrooms are lightly browned; stir occasionally. Empty mushrooms into the casserole.

3. In same skillet melt *another 2 tablespoons butter;* in it sauté the onion for about 5 minutes, or until golden; stir occasionally. Empty onion into casserole.

4. In skillet melt *1 more tablespoon butter.* Add *1 cup barley;* cook for 8 to 10 minutes, or until barley becomes nut brown; stir frequently. Add barley to casserole.

5. Preheat oven to 350° F.

6. Add *2 cups broth* to skillet and bring to a boil. Empty into casserole, add *½ cup chopped chives or parsley,* and stir well to combine all ingredients.

7. Cover casserole and bake for 30 minutes. Add *2 cups water* and *salt and pepper to taste;* then cover and cook for 1 hour longer. Serve, or reduce oven heat to very low and keep warm until ready to serve.

BAKED KASHA

Serves 6

BUY   *COOKWARE*

Buckwheat groats (kasha)   Kettle
                                  Large heavy skillet
                                  Casserole with cover

1. Preheat oven to 400° F. Boil *water* in kettle.

2. In heavy skillet melt *2 tablespoons butter.* Add *2 cups kasha,* and cook over moderate heat, stirring constantly, for 10 minutes.

3. Empty into casserole, and add *enough boiling water* to cover kasha by 1 inch. Cover, and bake in preheated oven for 30 minutes.

4. Remove cover, and add a *little more water* if kasha seems dry. Replace cover, turn temperature down to 300° F., and bake for 30 minutes longer.

Couscous is the name of *the* native dish of North Africa, a savory stew of lamb or chicken containing many vegetables and often fruit and nuts. But *couscous* is also the Arab word for the finely ground hard wheat, or semolina, which is steamed and served with the stew. It is an excellent cereal which should be more widely known. There is no reason to serve it only with North African stews! The recipe for the complete dish is given in ANN SERANNE'S GOOD FOOD & HOW TO COOK IT. Here I am repeating only the method for cooking the cereal.

COUSCOUS

Serves 4. Serve with additional butter or any savory sauce.

BUY
1-pound box imported *couscous*

HAVE ON HAND
Butter
Salt and pepper

COOKWARE
Saucepan
Large kettle with lid
Colander with handles that can sit
    on top of kettle without falling in

Empty *couscous* into a saucepan and moisten with *enough boiling water (about ½ cup) to make the grains swell.* Stir with a fork and let stand for 20 minutes. Break up any lumps which form with fingertips, and repeat the moistening and stirring three times at 20-minute intervals. By this time the semolina will have more than doubled in bulk. Empty it into a colander lined with cheesecloth. Sprinkle with *¼ cup melted butter* and *salt (about 1 teaspoon) and pepper to taste.* Set colander over kettle of *simmering water,* cover, and steam for 1 hour.

PASTA

A Whole World of Pasta

It's a cinch to be a vegetarian and yet eat a balanced, interesting diet if you are a pasta lover! There are so many types of pasta and so many variations of the recipes for them that one could eat pasta every day for years without repeating the same dish.

The word pasta is a generic term for a multitude of products made of semolina (a nutritious fine, hard, and pure flour milled from the heart of durum wheat) plus either water alone or water and egg.

Not so very long ago, the average supermarket carried elbow macaroni in several thicknesses, one or two types of spaghetti, and fine, medium, and wide egg noodles. Today it stocks pasta in a bewildering variety of shapes and sizes. Since the names for these products can vary not only from manufacturer to manufacturer but from location to location, the result may often be utter confusion for the cook.

But don't panic. If you understand that there are basically four different types of pasta and four basic methods of cooking them, you can vary the pasta within a recipe to please your palate and your mood.

THE TYPES OF PASTA

1. SPAGHETTI

Spaghetti, meaning "string," is a solid round rod and comes in various thicknesses from very thin *vermicelli,* to the larger *spaghettini* and *spaghetti,* to the largest form, *spaghettoni.*

2. LINGUINE

Linguine, meaning "small tongues," is a form of spaghetti, but the rods are slightly flattened or oval rather than round. They also are named according to their size, from the fine *bavettine* to the largest form, *lingue di passeri.*

3. MACARONI

Macaroni (Italian: *maccheroni*) is a general term for hollow pasta products. These, too, range from thicknesses no larger than that of spaghetti, to larger tubes like *cannelle* and the grooved tubes called *rigatoni,* to *cannelloni* or *tufoli* which are still larger tubes that are generally stuffed and baked.

4. NOODLES

These are ribbons of egg pasta ranging in size from the smallest, ⅛ inch wide, called *tagliarini;* to ¼ inch wide, *fettuccine;* ¾ inch wide, *tagliatelli;* broad noodles, or *lasagnette,* about ½ inch wide; to the extra-broad, 2-inch-wide *lasagne* or ripple-edged *mafalda.*

When noodle paste is cut into squares or rectangles it is known as *ravioli, manicotti,* or *cannelloni.*

In addition to these basic types, there is a wide range of shapes and sizes of small pasta. Some are used primarily in broths and soups; rings, threads, shells, stars, alphabets, and so on. A myriad of other shapes, like bows, snails, and shells, are boiled and sauced or they are baked in a sauce.

METHODS OF COOKING PASTA

1. Boil and serve in soups or broths: small pasta of plain or fancy shape.

2. Boil, then toss with a sauce and grated cheese: such pasta as *linguine,* spaghetti, and noodles.

3. Boil, then bake with a sauce: such pasta as macaroni, *lasagne,* and *ziti.*

4. Stuff, then boil and sauce: such pasta as *ravioli* and *agnolotti.*

5. Boil, stuff, sauce, and bake: such pasta as *manicotti, cannelloni,* and *rigatoni.*

HOW TO COOK PASTA

Generally it is best to follow the manufacturer's directions on the package, but here are some basic rules that will assure the best possible flavor.

1. Use a large, deep, heavy, pot (10- to 12-quart capacity), and *at least 6 to 7 quarts of water* for *1 pound of pasta.* The pasta needs room to swim in the water so the strands will not stick together.

2. Bring the water to a rolling boil, then add *2 tablespoons salt.* The salt should be added just before the pasta goes in. Let the water return to an active boil.

3. Add the pasta gradually so that the water continues to boil at all times, gently pushing each handful down into the boiling water until it is all submerged.

4. With a wooden fork, stir the pasta frequently as it boils, taking care to separate the strands or pieces. Stir gently.

5. Cook the minimum amount of time given in package directions, then test for doneness. Tasting the pasta is the only way to tell if it has boiled sufficiently that it has no remaining flavor of uncooked flour and yet is still *al dente,* or just firm "to the tooth." It should be a little chewy and by no means soft or mushy.

6. Drain the pasta into a large colander that has just been rinsed in hot water. Then empty immediately into a large mixing bowl to be tossed with butter or sauce and cheese. Or, fork it directly from the boiling water into individual serving dishes. In either case the mixing bowl or serving dishes should be piping hot. (By forking the pasta directly out of the boiling water, you can be certain that the pasta is as hot as it can possibly be. Also each strand is moist, so there is no chance of strands drying and sticking together. The fork-from-pot method applies only to strands of pasta. For macaroni, shells, or other broken or cut lengths, use a slotted spoon.)

When the pasta is ready, all your other ingredients—*and* your guests—must also be ready.

TO HOLD COOKED PASTA:

Drain off all but enough of the boiling water to cover the pasta, then add just enough cold water to prevent further cooking yet still keep the pasta hot until ready to serve.

HOW MUCH PASTA TO COOK?

This is a difficult question. I know a young man who can happily consume an entire pound of spaghetti bathed in a quart of sauce! But he is the exception to the general rule that: *1 pound of dry pasta will, when cooked, serve 3 to 4 persons as a main dish; 4 to 6 as an appetizer.*

NOODLES

There are many varieties of excellent commercially made noodles available, and my favorites, at the moment, are the crinkly ones, a recent addition to the vast array of pasta products in my local market. They are exceptionally tender and really sop up the sauce. But none of them can compare in texture and flavor to homemade noodles, and unless I am very pressed for time, I make them frequently and usually have a couple of bags of them in the freezer.

I have a little noodle maker which goes everywhere with me. When I sold my summer house in Saltaire, I left a fully equipped kitchen. The only pieces of equipment I took with me were my noodle maker and a very inexpensive little slicer which I use to slice potatoes for pommes Anna and cucumbers for salad.

The noodle maker is fairly expensive, around $35.00, but well worth it. If you are a noodle lover you might like to invest in one, but I'll give you methods of rolling and cutting the noodle dough both with and without mechanical aid. In either case the ingredients are the same.

HOMEMADE EGG PASTA

Makes about 1 pound. For noodles, manicotti, fettuccine, lasagne, cannelloni, tagliatelle, and tagliarini.

HAVE ON HAND

Semolina flour, *or* unbleached all-purpose flour
4 large eggs
Salt

1. In mixing bowl combine *3 cups flour* and *1 teaspoon salt.* Make a well in the center, and into the well break *4 large eggs.*

2. Using just one hand, begin to work the flour into the eggs until all of it is moistened and the the dough can be gathered together into a rough ball. If dough is too moist, add a *little flour;* if too dry, add *2 teaspoons warm water.*

TO HAND-KNEAD, ROLL, AND CUT:

3. Remove ball and place on *floured* surface. Begin kneading with both hands; knead vigorously, pulling and pressing the hard dough with the heels of the hands until it is smooth, or for about 10 minutes.

4. Return dough to the bowl, cover with a towel, and let it rest for half an hour. During this time the moisture in the dough will equalize throughout and the dough will lose its elasticity.

5. Cut dough in half, and work with one half at a time. Roll out on *floured* surface until the dough is as thin as possible, no more than ⅛ inch thick and preferably thinner, turning dough over frequently and keeping both sides lightly floured.

6. For Noodles: cut the dough into strips of the desired width. Toss the strips lightly with flour and drop lightly and loosely onto a *floured* towel to dry.
    For *tagliarini:* cut ⅛ inch wide.
    For *fettuccine:* cut ¼ inch wide.
    For *tagliatelle:* cut ¾ inch wide.
    For *lasagne:* cut 2 inches wide, then cut 4 to 6 inches in length.
    For *manicotti* or *cannelloni:* cut sheet of dough into 3-inch squares for manicotti and 4-inch squares for cannelloni. Arrange squares on *floured* towel, cover lightly with another towel, and let dry for 1 hour.

TO MACHINE-KNEAD, ROLL, AND CUT:

1. The dough must be very hard. I've never found it necessary to add even a drop of warm water. Gather it together and then pull it apart into a dozen small pieces. Keep the pieces in the bowl covered with a towel and work with one piece at a time.

2. Set up the noodle maker, attaching it firmly to the edge of a table or chopping block. Set the rollers as wide apart as possible, and the handle so it turns the rollers.

3. Run *one piece of dough* through the rollers two or three times to knead it until it is a smooth rather thickish band, folding it in half crosswise between each roll. This process, too, equalizes the moisture from the eggs; however, if the dough sticks to the rollers or comes out crinkled, sprinkle each side with a little flour until the band is smooth and not sticky. Place the band on a lightly floured surface just behind the noodle maker and sprinkle with a little flour. Repeat this kneading process with the *other chunks of dough,* stacking each band, one on top of the other, with flour in between.

4. When all the pieces of dough have been kneaded in this way, they must be rolled thinly—in three successive runs:

Bring the rollers together a couple of notches, then run each of the bands through the rollers. Again stack the bands (which will have become a little longer) on top of each other with a little flour sprinkled between.

Reduce size of space between rollers another couple of notches, and repeat the rolling, and stacking.

Once again through the rollers, set as closely as possible, will give you very thin, very long bands of smooth dough.

5. Cutting the noodles is fun. Change the handle from the rollers to the cutting blades. There are two sets of cutting blades: the very fine blades which make tagliarini, and the ¼-inch blades which make fettuccine. As you turn the handle, slip one end of a band of dough into the cutters and continue to turn until the dough drops out in narrow strips on the other side. Pick noodles up and drop lightly onto a floured towel. Repeat until all bands of dough are cut.

FOR FRESH NOODLES: Let dry for 1 hour, then cook or freeze.

To FREEZE: Place noodles and towel in freezer until noodles are frozen stiff, then pack in freezer bags.

To COOK: Fresh noodles cook very quickly. Use *a large quantity of rapidly boiling water.* Add *1 tablespoon salt,* then the *noodles.* Cook for no more than 5 minutes, testing frequently to make sure they do not become overcooked.

FOR DRY NOODLES: Let noodles dry on the floured towel for 12 hours, or overnight. Dry noodles will take from 8 to 10 minutes to cook.

GREEN PASTA
(*Pasta Verde*)

Makes about 1 pound green noodles or lasagne

BUY

¾ pound fresh (*or* 10-ounce package frozen chopped) spinach

HAVE ON HAND

Semolina *or* unbleached all-purpose flour
2 eggs
Salt

1. Wash *spinach* well and place in saucepan without any more water than is clinging to the leaves; cook for 5 minutes, or until tender. Or cook frozen chopped spinach according to package directions.

2. Drain spinach well, pressing out moisture with back of a spoon. Then chop FINELY.

3. Measure *3 cups flour* into mixing bowl and make a well in the center. Into the well put *2 eggs, 1 teaspoon salt,* and the finely chopped spinach. Mix center ingredients, then gradually work in the flour to make a rough dough. Turn dough out on lightly floured board and knead for 10 minutes; add a *little water* if dough is too dry, and *some flour* if dough is too soft.

4. Separate dough into 4 pieces and let rest for 30 minutes.

5. Flatten each piece, one at a time, and roll out on floured surface into very thin sheets, ⅛ inch thick or thinner. For noodles cut into strips ¼ inch wide; for lasagne into strips 2 inches wide.

6. Let pasta dry on floured towels for 1 hour.

7. Cook the pasta in large quantity of *rapidly boiling salted water* for 8 minutes or until just al dente. Drain and serve as desired.

PASTA FOR RAVIOLI AND TORTELLINI

Makes about 1½ pounds. This is a slightly softer, smoother dough, and easier to roll out.

HAVE ON HAND
Semolina *or* unbleached all-purpose flour
Salt
4 eggs
Olive oil
Ingredients for filling (see recipes on pp. 248-250)

1. Into mixing bowl measure *3 cups flour* and *1 teaspoon salt*. Make a well in the center, and into the well put *4 eggs, 1 tablespoon olive oil,* and *4 teaspoons warm water*. Mix center ingredients, then gradually work in flour to make a rough dough.

2. Turn dough out on floured board and knead for about 10 minutes, adding a few more drops of warm water if dough is too dry; a little more flour if dough is too moist.

3. Cut dough into 4 parts, cover, and let rest for 30 minutes.

4. Roll out one part at a time on floured surface, turning dough frequently and keeping both sides lightly floured, to a rectangle less than ⅛ inch thick; the thinner the better.

5. FOR RAVIOLI: Cut the rectangle lengthwise into 3-inch wide strips. Place *teaspoonfuls of the desired filling* 2½ inches apart along one strip. Cover with another strip and press the strips firmly together around each spoonful of filling. With a fluted pastry wheel or ravioli cutter, cut into 2- or 3-inch squares, depending on how large you want the ravioli. Cover with a cloth, and let dry for 1½ hours.

FOR TORTELLINI: With a floured cooky cutter or tortellini cutter, cut sheet of dough into 2-inch circles. Place *1 teaspoon of filling* on top of each circle, then fold in half to form a half circle. Press edges of dough together firmly; then bend the half circle, seam side out, to form a ring. To maintain this shape, overlap the points of the dough and press them firmly together. Cover with a towel and let the tortellini dry for half an hour.

6. For cooking directions, see individual recipes, pp 248-250.

CHEESES FOR PASTA

Several kinds of hard cheeses are popular with pasta. Top of the list, and the best to many, is Parmesan. Asiago has a nuttier flavor, while Pecorino Romano is saltier. Some pasta connoisseurs like to mix half Parmesan and half Romano; others prefer Parmesan, Romano, and Asiago in equal proportions.

Whatever you select, make sure it is well aged, for good well-aged cheese makes all the difference between a really great pasta dish and a mediocre one.

GRATE YOUR OWN CHEESE, PLEASE!

Don't ruin a good dish with commercial grated cheese! The cheese isn't very good in the first place, and secondly, grated cheese loses its flavor quickly unless frozen.

Buy your pasta cheese in big chunks and grate it in one of those efficient and inexpensive little Mouli cheese graters imported from France. You may freeze any left-over part of a chunk if you wish after wrapping it carefully in foil, but once cheese has been frozen it is never quite as fluffy when you grate it. If you have time, it's better to grate the entire chunk and then package the grated cheese in several small freezer bags. It will stay free-flowing and flavorful in the freezer for many months.

Pastas with Simple Sauces

We begin the recipes in this chapter with some of the simplest and very best dishes—perfectly cooked pastas, always *al dente,* tossed with several of the following: olive oil, garlic, butter, cheese, cream, spices, herbs, and nuts. Although each recipe specifies either a noodle or spaghetti, use your imagination and vary the pasta according to your mood. Keep on hand a wide variety of linguine, vermicelli, spaghetti, tagliolini, tagliatelle, fettuccine, and so on.

FETTUCCINE AL BURRO
(with Butter Sauce)

Serves 4 to 6 as a first course

HAVE ON HAND	*COOKWARE*
Parmesan cheese	Pasta pot
Fettuccine *or* spaghetti	Large skillet
Butter	
Black peppercorns	

1. Grate *½ cup Parmesan cheese* and set aside.

2. Cook *1 pound pasta* according to directions (page 206).

3. Meanwhile, put *1 stick (½ cup) butter* in a large skillet over very low heat to melt.

4. As soon as the pasta is cooked al dente, drain and empty into the skillet with the melted butter. Begin tossing, and then gradually add the grated cheese and *lots of freshly grated black pepper.*

BUTTERED FINE NOODLES

Serves 4 or 6

BUY

8-ounce package fine noodles

HAVE ON HAND	*COOKWARE*
Salt	Large saucepan
Butter, at room temperature	
Freshly ground pepper	

1. Bring *4 quarts water* to a rapid boil in large saucepan. Add *1 tablespoon salt* and drop in the *noodles*. When water returns to a boil, boil for 8 minutes.

2. Drain noodles in a hot colander and empty into a hot serving dish. Add *4 tablespoons butter* and toss well. Add *salt and pepper to taste*. Toss again and serve immediately.

NOODLES POLONAISE

Serves 4 as an accompaniment to other foods.

BUY

8 ounces broad egg noodles *or* curly noodles

HAVE ON HAND	*COOKWARE*
Bread	Large saucepan
Garlic	Small skillet
Butter	

1. *Crumb enough bread to measure ½ cup.* Peel and mince *1 large clove garlic.*

2. Cook the *noodles* according to package directions.

3. While noodles are cooking, melt *1 stick (½ cup) butter* in a small skillet. When butter is foaming, add garlic and bread crumbs; cook, stirring constantly, until crumbs and garlic are golden brown. Set aside.

4. Drain noodles and empty into hot serving dish. Pour the crumb mixture over the noodles and toss lightly.

NOODLES FINES HERBS

Serves 4 as an accompaniment to other foods. Cook *8-ounce package egg noodles.* While noodles are cooking, melt *1 stick (½ cup) butter* with *1 tablespoon chopped chives* and *2 tablespoons chopped parsley.* Drain noodles and empty into hot serving bowl. Add butter-herb mixture and toss. Sprinkle with *salt and pepper* to taste.

FETTUCCINE ALFREDO

Serves 6 for appetizer, 4 for main course

BUY OR MAKE
½ pound aged Parmesan cheese
1 pound fettuccine *or* curly noodles
8-ounce container heavy cream

HAVE ON HAND
Butter
Salt
Black peppercorns

COOKWARE
Pasta pot
Small saucepan

1. Grate the *cheese* and set aside.

2. Cook *pasta* in *rapidly boiling salted water* until just barely tender.

3. While pasta is cooking, in small saucepan melt *1 stick (½ cup) butter* together with the *cream* over very low heat. You just want the cream hot enough to melt the butter.

4. Drain the pasta and empty into a warm bowl. Pour the butter and

cream over the noodles and start tossing. Gradually toss in *1 cup of the grated cheese.*

5. Sprinkle with a *little salt, if necessary,* and season generously with *lots of freshly ground black pepper.*

6. Serve on warm plate with *additional grated cheese* on the side.

FETTUCCINE CON TARTUFI

When you feel in an expansive mood or have a special reason to celebrate, buy *a 1-ounce can of white Italian truffles.* Make Fettuccine Alfredo (preceding recipe), but add the juice from the can of truffles to the butter-and-cream mixture. Slice the truffle (you will have 1 medium-size truffle or 2 small ones in the can) as paper-thin as possible, and toss into the noodles along with the cheese. Heaven!

NOODLES WITH BLACK PEPPER

Serves 4 or 6. This one is for pepper lovers. Cook *1 pound noodles or tagliolini* until just al dente. While noodles are cooking, melt *¼ pound sweet butter* over very low heat. Do not let it get hot. It's ready when most of the butter is melted or mushy. Empty the butter into a warm serving dish. Drain noodles, and empty them into the butter. Add *1 tablespoon coarsely cracked black pepper* and toss gently. Serve on hot plates with *grated Parmesan* on the side.

PASTA WITH OLIVE OIL AND GARLIC SAUCE

Serves 3 or 4. This is a robust sauce, good for garlic lovers. It's easy to make, yet tricky. The tricks are to use very fresh olive oil of the best quality, to slice the garlic paper thin, and to cook it very slowly until just lightly toasted in the hot oil. If the garlic is allowed to overbrown even slightly, there goes a lovely dish right down the disposal.

BUY

Chunk of Parmesan cheese
1 pound thin spaghetti, linguine, *or* vermicelli

HAVE ON HAND	*COOKWARE*
Large head fresh garlic	Small skillet
Olive oil	Pasta pot
Freshly ground black pepper	

1. Grate *a bowlful of cheese* and set aside.

2. Peel *10 to 12 large cloves garlic* and slice them paper thin.

3. Measure *¾ cup fresh olive oil* into a small skillet. Add the garlic and place over moderate heat. Stand by! Do not leave the stove! As soon as the oil begins to bubble around the edge of the garlic slices, turn heat to low, then cook and watch, stirring occasionally, until garlic slices become crisp and pale gold, like toasted nut flakes. Remove from heat.

4. Meanwhile cook the *pasta* in *boiling salted water* until al dente. Just before pasta is done, return garlic and oil to very low heat.

5. Drain pasta into a colander and, while it is still dripping wet, empty it immediately into a hot mixing bowl. Pour the garlic and oil over the pasta and toss with wooden spoons. Add *lots of freshly ground black pepper* and serve with grated Parmesan.

SPAGHETTI VERDE

Serves 4 to 6

BUY

Bunch fresh parsley
1 pound thin spaghetti *or* vermicelli

HAVE ON HAND

Garlic
Parmesan cheese

Butter
Olive oil
Black peppercorns

COOKWARE

Pasta pot
Small skillet

1. Peel and lightly crush *3 cloves garlic.* Mince *1 cup parsley,* and grate *1 cup cheese.* Set aside.

2. Cook the *pasta* al dente according to package directions.

3. Meanwhile in small skillet heat *12 tablespoons butter (1½ sticks)* and *2 tablespoons olive oil.* Add the cloves of garlic and sauté until lightly brown. Discard garlic, stir in parsley, and remove from heat.

4. Drain pasta and empty into hot mixing bowl. Add the butter-parsley sauce, the cheese, and *freshly ground pepper to taste.* Toss well and serve on hot plates.

PESTO ALLA GENOVESE

Serves 4. A glorious pasta sauce, if you like garlic and fresh sweet basil, is this speciality of Genoa. Dried basil cannot be substituted, so plan to make it only in the warm months when fresh sweet basil is available. If you like it as well as I do, you may want to freeze some in small plastic containers. I defrost it a few hours before needed by setting the plastic container into a small saucepan of warm water.

BUY

Large bunch fresh sweet basil
1 pound spaghetti, linguini, *or* fettuccine
Parmesan cheese
Bunch of Italian parsley
Jar pine nuts

HAVE ON HAND

COOKWARE

Garlic
Salt
Olive oil
Butter

Electric blender
Pasta pot

1. Wash the *basil* and dry on absorbent toweling; put *20 of the largest leaves* into container of an electric blender.

2. Add *3 large cloves garlic*, peeled, *¾ cup grated Parmesan*, *½ cup parsley leaves*, *⅓ cup pine nuts*, *½ teaspoon salt*, and *½ cup olive oil.* Cover and blend on high speed until ingredients are reduced to a thick paste. Scrape paste into a large mixing bowl.

3. Cook the *pasta* according to directions. As soon as it is al dente, fork it out of the hot water directly into the mixing bowl with the cheese paste; toss well. Add *a chunk (2 tablespoons) butter* and *4 tablespoons of the hot water from the pasta pot,* and toss again. Serve hot with *additional grated Parmesan.*

FETTUCCINE WITH CREAM AND EGGS

Serves 4 to 6

BUY

Chunk of Asiago cheese
1 pound fettuccine
8-ounce container heavy cream

HAVE ON HAND	*COOKWARE*
Butter	Pasta pot
Black pepper	Large skillet
2 egg yolks	Small saucepan

1. Grate *½ cup cheese.* Set aside.

2. Cook *fettuccine* al dente according to package directions.

3. While pasta is cooking melt *1 stick (½ cup) butter* in a skillet, and warm *½ cup cream* in a small saucepan.

4. Drain fettuccine and empty into the hot butter in the skillet. Toss briefly, then gradually toss in the grated cheese, and *some freshly ground pepper.*

5. Break the *yolks of 2 eggs* into the pasta; toss again, while gradually adding the warm cream. Serve on warm plates.

PASTA WITH RICOTTA SAUCE

Serves 3 or 4

>   *BUY*

Chunk of Parmesan cheese
Fresh parsley
8 ounces noodles (curly ones are great with this), vermicelli, *or* linguine
8-ounce container ricotta cheese
8-ounce container heavy cream

HAVE ON HAND	*COOKWARE*
Butter	Pasta pot
Peppercorns	Small saucepan

1. Grate *½ cup Parmesan cheese. Chop ½ cup parsley.* Set aside.

2. Cook the *pasta* al dente according to package directions.

3. Meanwhile combine the *ricotta cheese* with *1 tablespoon butter* and the *cream,* place over low heat, and stir occasionally.

4. Drain the pasta and toss with *2 tablespoons butter.* Add the warm cheese-and-cream mixture, the Parmesan cheese, the parsley, and *freshly ground pepper to taste.* Toss well and serve on warm plates.

Hearty Tomato-Sauced Pasta Dishes

There are many good brands of tomato sauces available, but somehow they never taste as flavorful as ones made from vine-ripened tomatoes, or from canned tomatoes, when fresh ones are out of season. To me, commercial sauces are too dense and pasty. I prefer a lighter, chunkier sauce such as this first one. It's a very easy sauce to make and uses prepared marinara sauce as a base. Vegetables and spices give it character, and you may vary it according to what vegetables are the freshest in the market— mushrooms, celery, zucchini, and diced eggplant are all good.

CHUNKY TOMATO SAUCE FOR PASTA

Makes about 6 cups

BUY

2 jars marinara sauce (15½ ounces each) *or* 4 cans tomato sauce (8 ounces each)
1-pound can stewed tomatoes
Parsley *or* sweet basil

HAVE ON HAND

Large onion
Garlic
Cooking oil
Hot red pepper flakes
Fennel seeds
Coarsely cracked pepper
Oregano

COOKWARE

Large skillet

1. Peel and chop *1 large onion* and *2 large cloves garlic.* In large skillet, heat *2 tablespoons oil,* and in it sauté onion and garlic for 5 to 10 minutes, or until transparent but not brown.

2. Add *½ teaspoon hot pepper flakes, 1 teaspoon fennel, ½ teaspoon coarsely cracked pepper, ½ teaspoon oregano, the marinara or tomato sauce,* and the *stewed tomatoes.* Stir well and bring to a simmer; continue to simmer for 20 to 30 minutes, stirring occasionally.

3. Just before serving, stir in *2 tablespoons chopped parsley or sweet basil.* Serve immediately over the hot spaghetti.

LIGHT TOMATO SAUCE

Makes about 4 cups

BUY

2-pound, 3-ounce can Italian plum tomatoes

HAVE ON HAND	*COOKWARE*
Garlic	Large heavy skillet
Olive oil	
Salt	
Black peppercorns	
Dried sweet basil	

1. Press the *tomatoes and juice* through a food mill, or blend in an electric blender and then strain to remove seeds. Set aside.

2. Mince *2 cloves garlic (or more, if desired),* and add them to a skillet containing *2 tablespoons olive oil.* Simmer over low heat until garlic is golden (DO NOT BROWN).

3. Add the *tomatoes.* Add *1 teaspoon salt, lots of freshly ground black pepper,* and *1 teaspoon dried sweet basil.* Cook over low heat, stirring frequently with a wooden spoon, until sauce is bubbling. Raise heat to medium and simmer sauce for about 30 minutes, or until excess water has evaporated and the sauce is thickened.

EGGPLANT SAUCE

For 1 pound pasta. This is a rich and hearty sauce for spaghetti or linguine.

BUY

2 pounds very ripe tomatoes *or* a 2-pound, 3-ounce can Italian plum tomatoes
1 large eggplant
Parsley
6-ounce can tomato paste

<table>
<tr><td>*HAVE ON HAND*</td><td>*COOKWARE*</td></tr>
<tr><td>Garlic</td><td>Large heavy skillet *or* saucepan</td></tr>
<tr><td>Onion</td><td>Small skillet</td></tr>
<tr><td>Olive oil</td><td></td></tr>
<tr><td>Salt</td><td></td></tr>
<tr><td>Crushed red pepper</td><td></td></tr>
<tr><td>Dried basil</td><td></td></tr>
<tr><td>Oregano</td><td></td></tr>
</table>

1. If using *fresh tomatoes,* peel and chop them coarsely. Peel and chop *2 large cloves garlic* and *1 medium onion.* Peel and dice the *eggplant.* Chop *¼ cup parsley.*

2. In large heavy skillet or saucepan sauté onion and garlic in *1 tablespoon olive oil* for about 3 minutes, or until golden brown. Add the fresh or canned tomatoes, *tomato paste, ½ cup water, 2 teaspoons salt, ¼ teaspoon crushed red pepper, 1 teaspoon basil,* and *½ teaspoon oregano.* Simmer for 20 minutes, stirring occasionally.

3. In another skillet sauté eggplant in *4 tablespoons olive oil* until lightly browned. Add to tomato sauce and cook over low heat for 30 minutes longer. Stir in *parsley,* and keep the sauce hot until ready to serve.

BASIL AND TOMATO SPAGHETTI SAUCE

Makes about 3 cups

BUY

2-pound, 3-ounce can Italian plum tomatoes
2 cans tomato purée (8 ounces each)

HAVE ON HAND

2 large onions
Garlic
Olive oil
Celery
Carrots
Fresh *or* dried basil

Oregano
Bay leaves
Salt
Coarsely ground black pepper

COOKWARE

2-quart heavy saucepan

1. Thinly slice *2 large onions.* Peel and mince *4 cloves garlic.*

2. In heavy saucepan heat *6 tablespoons olive oil,* and in it sauté onions and garlic until transparent but not brown. Add *6 stalks celery,* coarsely chopped, *2 carrots,* scraped and sliced, *1 tablespoon chopped fresh basil or 1 teaspoon dried basil, ½ teaspoon oregano, 2 bay leaves,* the *canned Italian tomatoes,* the *2 cans of tomato purée,* and *1 cup water.* Stir in *1 teaspoon salt* and *1 teaspoon coarsely ground pepper.*

3. Bring mixture to a boil; then partially cover, and simmer over low heat for 3 hours, stirring occasionally. Press sauce though a sieve, or blend it about 1 cup at a time in an electric blender.

VELVETY MARINARA SAUCE

Makes 7 cups

BUY

Two 2-pound, 3-ounce cans Italian plum tomatoes

HAVE ON HAND

Small onions
Garlic
Carrots
Olive oil
Black peppercorns
Salt
Butter
Cayenne pepper

COOKWARE

Medium skillet
Large saucepan

1. Peel and finely chop *2 small onions;* peel and mince *1 clove garlic;* scrape and chop *2 small carrots.*

2. In skillet heat *2 tablespoons olive oil,* and in it sauté onions, garlic, and carrots until onions are soft but not brown.

3. Add the *tomatoes* and *1 teaspoon freshly ground black pepper.* Stir in *salt to taste,* and cook over moderate heat for 20 minutes.

4. Rub sauce through a food mill, or blend 1 cup at a time in an electric blender. The sauce will emerge velvety.

5. Melt *3 tablespoons butter* in saucepan and add the puréed sauce. Cook, stirring frequently, for 15 minutes. Stir in *cayenne pepper to taste.*

RED-HOT TOMATO SAUCE

For 1 pound pasta

BUY

Fresh parsley
2-pound, 3-ounce can Italian plum tomatoes

HAVE ON HAND	*COOKWARE*
Garlic	Large heavy skillet
Olive oil	
Salt	
Crushed dried red peppers *or* 2 large fresh chili peppers	
Butter	
Grated Parmesan *or* Pecorino Romano cheese	

1. Chop *½ cup parsley.* Peel and mince *2 large cloves garlic.*

2. Sauté the garlic in *2 tablespoons olive oil* until just golden. Add the *tomatoes, 1 teaspoon salt,* the parsley, and *1 teaspoon of the crushed red peppers, or 2 large fresh chili peppers, seeded and chopped;* stir well. Simmer uncovered for 35 minutes, stirring frequently.

3. Keep hot until ready to serve. Just before serving add *2 table-spoons butter* to the sauce and swirl until butter is melted. Ladle over hot pasta, and accompany with *grated Parmesan or Pecorino Romano.*

MIXED VEGETABLE SAUCE

For 1 pound pasta

BUY

2 large green peppers
6 large ripe tomatoes
2 medium zucchini
1 small eggplant

HAVE ON HAND

Celery
Onions
Olive oil
Salt
Coarsely cracked pepper

COOKWARE

3-quart heavy saucepan *or* skillet

1. Wash, stem, and seed the *green peppers* and cut into thin strips. Peel *tomatoes* and cut each into 8 sections. Wash, trim, and slice rather thickly the *zucchini*. Peel *eggplant* and cut into 1-inch dice. Slice *3 stalks celery* thickly. Peel and dice *3 medium onions*.

2. Combine all the vegetables in the saucepan or skillet, and add *2 tablespoons olive oil, 1½ teaspoons salt,* and *1 teaspoon cracked pepper.* Cover and simmer over low heat for 1 hour, stirring frequently. Correct seasoning before serving over hot pasta.

RAW TOMATO SAUCE

For 1 pound pasta

BUY

2 pounds ripe tomatoes
Fresh parsley
Fresh sweet basil

HAVE ON HAND

Lemon
Olive oil
Garlic
Salt
Coarsely cracked pepper

1. Peel *tomatoes* and slice thinly. Put them in a bowl and add *¼ cup chopped parsley, ¼ cup chopped fresh basil, the juice of 1 large lemon, 3 tablespoons olive oil, 1 large clove garlic,* minced, and *½ teaspoon each of salt and pepper.* Toss well.

2. Serve over hot elbow macaroni or linguine.

Pasta with
Sauces & Vegetables

It's very hard to think of any vegetable that would not combine with pasta. Some are better at this than others, certainly, but do not let the specification of one vegetable in a recipe prevent you from changing to another. Buy the freshest vegetables possible and use those which are in season.

LINGUINE WITH ZUCCHINI

Serves 2 or 4

BUY

2 medium zucchini
1 pound linguine

HAVE ON HAND	*COOKWARE*
Butter	Large heavy skillet
Olive oil	Pasta pot
Salt	
Black peppercorns	
Parmesan cheese, freshly grated	

1. Wash and slice the *zucchini;* then sauté in a large skillet in *4 table-spoons each butter and olive oil* for about 10 minutes, or until zucchini is barely tender.

2. Meanwhile cook *pasta* al dente according to package directions.

3. Drain pasta and empty into skillet with the zucchini. Sprinkle with *½ teaspoon salt, lots of freshly ground black pepper,* and *¼ cup grated cheese;* toss well. Serve on warm plates.

VARIATION: Substitute *two dozen small button mushrooms,* washed and trimmed, for the zucchini.

CAULIFLOWER WITH NOODLES OR SPAGHETTI

Serves 2 to 4

BUY

1 small cauliflower
Parsley or chives

HAVE ON HAND	*COOKWARE*
Butter	Saucepan with cover *or* vegetable steamer
Salt	
Freshly ground pepper	12-inch heavy skillet
6 ounces medium noodles, spaghetti *or* other pasta	Pasta pot
Parmesan cheese, freshly grated	

1. Trim the *cauliflower,* breaking away all leaves and cutting out and discarding the hard center core. Separate the cauliflower into bite-size flowers or pieces. Simmer in *water to cover* (or cook over steaming water) for 8 to 10 minutes, or until barely tender.

2. Meanwhile melt *1 stick (½ cup) butter* in skillet over low heat. When cauliflower is barely tender, drain, and empty into butter in the skillet. Sprinkle with *a good ½ teaspoon salt* and *lots of pepper*. Cover and set aside.

3. Chop *2 tablespoons parsley or chives* and set aside.

4. Cook the *noodles or other pasta* according to package directions until just tender. While noodles are cooking, set the skillet containing the cauliflower over low heat for 5 minutes and shake it frequently.

5. Drain noodles and empty into the skillet. Add the chopped parsley or chives and *½ cup grated cheese* and toss well.

VARIATIONS: Substitute *sliced Chinese cabbage* for the cauliflower. Substitute *2 cups fresh lima beans or peas* for the cauliflower.

BROCCOLI IN NOODLE RING

Serves 6

BUY

1 large bunch broccoli
8 ounces medium egg noodles
Pint milk

HAVE ON HAND	*COOKWARE*
Swiss *or* Cheddar cheese	1-quart saucepan
Butter	Saucepan with cover *or* vegetable
Flour	steamer
Salt and pepper	Pasta pot
Paprika	
Dry mustard	
1 egg yolk	

1. Wash and trim the *broccoli* and cut into manageable pieces. Shred *1 cup cheese*. Set aside.

2. In saucepan melt *3 tablespoons butter*. Stir in *3 tablespoons flour, ½ teaspoon salt, ⅛ teaspoon pepper, ¼ teaspoon paprika,* and *½ teaspoon dry mustard*. Gradually stir in *2 cups milk* and cook, stirring, until sauce is smooth and thickened.

3. Combine *1 egg yolk* with a *little of the hot sauce,* then stir into *remaining sauce.* Add the shredded cheese and cook over low heat, stirring constantly, for 3 minutes, or until cheese is melted. Keep warm over hot water.

4. Meanwhile steam broccoli for 10 minutes or until just fork tender.

5. Cook noodles according to package directions.

6. Drain noodles, toss with *2 tablespoons butter,* and arrange in a ring on a hot serving platter. Empty steamed broccoli into center and pour cheese sauce over all.

PASTA WITH MUSHROOMS

Serves 4. This is a delicate dish when made with fresh homemade noodles or fettuccine.

BUY

½ pound fresh mushrooms
Chunk of Parmesan cheese
1 pound noodles, fettuccine, *or* linguine

HAVE ON HAND	*COOKWARE*
Butter	Medium skillet
Coarsely cracked pepper	Pasta pot

1. Wash, trim, and slice the *mushrooms.* Grate *½ cup cheese.*

2. Sauté the mushrooms in *½ stick (¼ cup) butter* for 5 minutes, or until just tender. Set aside.

3. Cook *pasta* al dente according to package directions. If using home-made fresh noodles, do not cook them more than 5 minutes.

4. When the pasta is put into the boiling water, set mushrooms over low heat.

5. Drain cooked pasta and empty into warm serving bowl; toss with *2 tablespoons butter* and the cheese. Add the mushrooms and *cracked pepper to taste,* and toss again. Serve on warm plates.

VERMICELLI WITH GREEN PEPPERS

Serves 4 to 6

BUY

4 medium green peppers
1 pound vermicelli

HAVE ON HAND	*COOKWARE*
1 medium onion	Small skillet
Garlic	Pasta pot
Olive oil	
Butter	
Salt and pepper	
Parmesan cheese, freshly grated	

1. Remove stems from the *green peppers,* discard seeds and either dice the flesh or cut it into narrow strips. Peel and chop *1 medium onion* and *1 clove garlic.*

2. Sauté onion and garlic in *2 tablespoons olive oil* and *4 tablespoons butter* until onion is soft. Add peppers, then cover and cook for 10 minutes. Add *1 teaspoon salt* and *lots of pepper,* and keep warm over low heat.

3. Cook *vermicelli* al dente. Drain, and empty into mixing bowl.

4. Pour pepper mixture over the pasta and toss lightly. Serve hot on warm plates, sprinkling each serving generously with *grated Parmesan.*

NOODLES WITH GARDEN PEAS
AND MUSHROOMS

Serves 2 to 4

BUY

¼ pound fresh mushrooms
1 pound fresh peas in the pod
8-ounce container heavy cream
8 ounces fettuccine *or* crinkly egg noodles

HAVE ON HAND	*COOKWARE*
Butter	1-quart saucepan
Parmesan cheese, freshly grated	Small saucepan
Black peppercorns	Large skillet
	Pasta pot

1. Wash, trim, dry, and slice the *mushrooms*. Set aside.

2. Shell *peas* and cook in *a very small amount of lightly salted water* for 8 to 10 minutes, or until barely tender. Drain and set aside.

3. Warm *½ cup cream* in small saucepan over low heat.

4. In large skillet melt *1 stick (½ cup) butter* and in it sauté the mushrooms for 3 minutes, or until just tender. Keep warm.

5. Cook the *pasta* al dente.

6. Drain the pasta; empty into skillet with the mushrooms and butter; and toss. Then gradually toss in *½ cup grated Parmesan cheese* and *freshly ground pepper to taste*. Add the peas and the warm cream and toss again. Serve immediately on warm plates.

LINGUINE WITH MIXED VEGETABLES

Serves 4 to 6

BUY

2 small young carrots
2-pound, 3-ounce can Italian plum tomatoes with basil
1 small eggplant
Jar pine nuts
1 pound linguine

HAVE ON HAND

2 small white onions
Olive oil
Butter

Salt
Pepper   *COOKWARE*
Parmesan cheese, freshly grated   Large skillet
                                             1 medium skillet
                                             Pasta pot

1. Peel and chop *2 small white onions;* scrape and chop the *2 carrots.*

2. In large skillet heat *2 tablespoons olive oil* and *2 tablespoons butter,* and in it sauté onions and carrots until onions are soft. Add *tomatoes,* breaking them with a wooden spoon. Add *1 teaspoon salt* and *lots of pepper.* Cook, uncovered, over moderate heat for 25 minutes, stirring frequently, until sauce is velvety and thickened.

3. Peel *eggplant* and cut into pieces. Sauté in *3 tablespoons butter,* in medium skillet, until lightly browned. Stir eggplant mixture and *2 tablespoons pine nuts* into tomato sauce, and simmer for 5 minutes longer.

4. Cook *pasta* al dente.

5. Fork pasta onto warm serving plates and spoon on the sauce. Serve *grated Parmesan* separately.

MACARONI WITH GREEN TOMATOES

Serves 4 to 6

BUY

6 green tomatos, just beginning to ripen
1 pound elbow macaroni *or* mezzani (medium-size macaroni)

HAVE ON HAND   *COOKWARE*
Flour   Large skillet
Salt   Pasta pot
Coarsely cracked black pepper
Olive oil
Butter

1. Discard a thin slice from both the stem end and the bottom of the *tomatoes,* then slice them about ½ inch thick. *Flour* each slice on both sides, and sprinkle with *salt and pepper.*

2. In large skillet heat *6 tablespoons olive oil,* and in it sauté the tomato slices until lightly browned on each side and just fork tender. Keep warm.

3. Cook *macaroni* al dente according to package directions.

4. Drain macaroni and toss with *3 tablespoons butter* and *more pepper if desired.* Serve on warm plates, topping each portion with several tomato slices.

Pasta Salads

MACARONI SALAD SLAW

Serves 6 to 8

BUY

8 ounces elbow macaroni
1 bunch celery
1 small cabbage
Small jar pimientos
1 green pepper
Water cress

HAVE ON HAND

Onion
Salt and pepper
1 lemon
Mayonnaise

COOKWARE

Pasta pot

1. Cook *macaroni* according to package directions; drain; and rinse with *cold water*.

2. Peel *1½ cups celery*, and shred *1½ cups cabbage*. Peel and mince *1 small onion* and mince *2 pimientos*. Wash, seed, and chop the *green pepper*.

3. Combine macaroni with prepared vegetables. Stir in *2 teaspoons salt, ¼ teaspoon pepper, 2 tablespoons lemon juice,* and *1 cup mayonnaise*. Chill thoroughly.

4. Garnish atractively with *water cress* and serve.

PATIO SALAD WITH SOUR CREAM DRESSING

Serves 6 to 8

BUY

8 ounces elbow macaroni
Celery
1 green pepper
2 large tomatoes
8-ounce container sour cream
Water cress and salad greens

HAVE ON HAND

4 eggs
Onion
Salt and pepper
Lemon
Mayonnaise

COOKWARE

Pasta pot
Small saucepan

1. Cook *macaroni* according to package directions; drain; and rinse with *cold water*. Set aside.

2. Hard cook *4 eggs,* then cool and peel (page 147).

3. Dice *½ cup each of celery and green pepper*. Peel and chop *tomatoes*. Peel and mince *enough onion to measure 2 tablespoons*.

4. Combine cooked macaroni with the prepared vegetables, and stir in *2 teaspoons salt, ¼ teaspoon pepper, 2 tablespoons lemon juice, ½ cup sour cream,* and *½ cup mayonnaise.*

5. Pile the salad into a bowl lined with *crisp greens,* and garnish with the hard-cooked eggs and *water cress.*

MACARONI VINAIGRETTE

Serves 6

BUY

8 ounces elbow macaroni
1 head romaine
1 cucumber
2 large tomatoes

HAVE ON HAND	*COOKWARE*
Onion	Pasta pot
Parsley	
Salt	
Pepper	
Dry mustard	
Wine vinegar	
Salad oil	

1. Cook *macaroni* according to package directions; drain and rinse with *cold water.*

2. Peel and mince *1 small onion.* Chop *¼ cup parsley.* Peel and dice the *cucumber.* Combine cooked macaroni with the onion, parsley, and cucumber. Add *2 teaspoons salt, ¼ teaspoon pepper, ½ teaspoon dry mustard, 2 tablespoons wine vinegar,* and *6 tablespoons salad oil.* Marinate in refrigerator for 30 minutes or longer.

3. Peel and cut *tomatoes* into wedges. Separate *romaine leaves* and wash. Dry well. Line a salad bowl with the crisp romaine leaves and turn the macaroni salad into the center. Garnish with tomato wedges.

Baked Pasta Dishes

Noodles, macaroni, and other pasta products lend themselves well to being cooked in advance, sauced in a casserole, and baked when needed. There are many such dishes combining pasta, sauce, cheese, and vegetables but, in my view, it's hard to beat a really well-prepared dish of macaroni and fine, aged Cheddar cheese. Here's the best recipe for it that I know.

GOOD MACARONI AND CHEESE

Serves 1 to 6

BUY

½ pound aged sharp Cheddar cheese
8 ounces elbow macaroni

HAVE ON HAND	*COOKWARE*
Milk	2 small saucepans
Butter	Pasta pot
Flour	2-quart baking dish
Salt and pepper	

1. Shred *cheese* and set aside.

2. In saucepan, heat *2 cups milk* to simmering.

3. In second saucepan, melt *2 tablespoons butter*. Stir in *2 tablespoons flour* and cook until mixture bubbles. Remove saucepan from heat and add hot milk. Return to heat and cook, stirring rapidly, for about 3 minutes or until sauce is smooth and thickened. Add cheese and cook, stirring, until cheese is melted. Season with salt and pepper.

4. Cook *macaroni* al dente according to package directions. Drain and empty into the baking dish. Pour cheese sauce over macaroni and mix well.

5. When ready to bake, place in oven preheated 375° F.

6. Bake macaroni and cheese in the moderate oven for 25 to 30 minutes, or until sauce is bubbling and lightly browned.

WITH CRUMB TOPPING:

Brown *½ cup fresh bread crumbs* in *2 tablespoons butter.* Sprinkle on top of macaroni before baking.

BAKED NOODLE DISH

Serves 4

BUY

6-ounce package medium noodles
1 pint dairy sour cream
1 container heavy cream

HAVE ON HAND	*COOKWARE*
Fresh bread	Pasta pot
Butter	Medium skillet
Salt and pepper	1½-quart casserole
Parmesan cheese, freshly grated	

1. Crumb *enough bread to measure ¾ cup.* Lightly brown the crumbs in *2 tablespoons butter.* Set aside.

2. Boil *noodles* in *large quantity of salted water* for 8 minutes, or until barely tender. Drain and rinse with *hot water.* Empty into casserole.

3. Combine the *sour cream* with *½ cup heavy sweet cream, ½ cup grated Parmesan cheese, a sprinkling of salt to taste,* and *lots of freshly ground black pepper.* Add to noodles and mix well. Sprinkle bread crumbs on top.

4. When ready to bake, place in oven preheated to 350° F.

5. Bake noodles in the moderate oven for 30 minutes.

COTTAGE CHEESE AND NOODLE CASSEROLE

Serves 4 to 6

BUY

Green onions *or* chives
8-ounce package egg noodles
16 ounces cottage cheese
1 pint dairy sour cream

HAVE ON HAND	*COOKWARE*
Parmesan cheese	Small skillet
Salt and pepper	Pasta pot
Bread	2-quart baking dish
Butter	

1. Chop *¼ cup green onions or chives.* Grate *enough Parmesan cheese to measure ½ cup.* Set aside.

2. Prepare *1 cup fresh bread crumbs;* heat *2 tablespoons butter* in small skillet; add crumbs and sauté until golden. Set aside.

3. Cook *noodles* according to package directions. Drain and empty into mixing bowl. Stir in *1½ cups cottage cheese,* the *sour cream,* the green onions or chives, *1 teaspoon salt,* and *¼ teaspoon pepper.*

4. Empty noodle mixture into baking dish, and sprinkle the crumbs and grated cheese on top.

5. When ready to bake, place in oven preheated to 350° F.

6. Bake noodles in the moderate oven for 30 minutes.

NOODLES BARBAN

Serves 3 or 4

BUY

8 ounces egg noodles
8-ounce container ricotta *or* small-curd cottage cheese
8-ounce container heavy cream

HAVE ON HAND

Parmesan cheese
Butter
Black pepper
Salt
Flour
Milk

COOKWARE

Pasta pot
Small saucepan
2-quart baking dish

1. Grate *½ cup Parmesan cheese* and set aside.

2. Parboil *noodles* in *boiling salted water* for just 8 minutes. They should be chewy and not quite cooked. Drain into a warm bowl and toss with *4 tablespoons butter* and *½ teaspoon coarsely grated pepper.*

3. In smaller bowl mash the *ricotta or cottage cheese* with *¼ cup of the cream* and *½ teaspoon salt* to make a creamy mixture.

4. *Butter* baking dish. Cover bottom of dish with *half the cheese mixture,* then add layer of *half the noodles.* Sprinkle with *half the Parmesan.* Add *another layer of the cheese mixture* and cover it with the *remaining noodles;* do NOT add remaining Parmesan yet.

5. In a small saucepan melt *3 tablespoons butter* and stir in *3 tablespoons* flour. Slowly stir in *1½ cups milk;* cook, stirring, until sauce is smooth and thickened. Stir in *remaining cream, 1 tablespoon Parmesan cheese,* and *½ teaspoon salt.*

6. Pour the sauce over the noodles, and sprinkle with *remaining Parmesan.* Dot with *2 tablespoons butter.*

7. When ready to bake, place in oven preheated to 400° F.

8. Bake the noodles in the hot oven for 20 to 25 minutes.

SCALLOPED SPINACH AND MACARONI

Serves 6

BUY

8-ounce package elbow macaroni
2 packages frozen chopped spinach (10 ounces each)
8-ounce container heavy cream

HAVE ON HAND	*COOKWARE*
Swiss *or* Cheddar cheese	Pasta pot
Butter	Two 1-quart saucepans
Flour	2-quart baking dish
Salt and pepper	
Nutmeg	
Milk	
Paprika	

1. Cook *macaroni* according to package directions; drain; and rinse with *hot water*. Set aside.

2. Cook *spinach* according to package directions and drain well. Set aside. Shred *1 cup cheese*.

3. In saucepan melt *4 tablespoons butter*. Stir in *4 tablespoons flour, 1 teaspoon salt, ¼ teaspoon pepper,* and *¼ teaspoon nutmeg.* Gradually stir in *2 cups milk;* continue to stir until sauce is smooth and thickened. Stir in *½ cup cream* and *half the cheese;* cook, stirring, until cheese is melted.

4. *Butter* baking dish, and in it arrange alternate layers of macaroni, sauce, and spinach, ending with sauce. Sprinkle with *remaining cheese* and a *little paprika.*

5. When ready to bake, place in oven preheated to 350° F.

6. Bake macaroni in the moderate oven for 30 minutes, or until cheese is melted and sauce is bubbling.

MACARONI BAKED WITH TOMATO SAUCE

Serves 4

BUY

Parmesan cheese
8-ounce package cut ziti, mezzani, *or* elbow macaroni
1 pint milk
1-pound can stewed tomatoes

HAVE ON HAND	COOKWARE
Onions	Pasta pot
Butter	1-quart saucepan
Flour	2-quart casserole
Salt	
Black peppercorns	
Thyme *or* oregano	

1. Grate and set aside *1 cup Parmesan cheese.* Chop *2 tablespoons onion.*

2. Cook the *pasta* the least amount of time given on package. Drain; then rinse with *cold water.* Set aside.

3. In saucepan melt *2 tablespoons butter,* and in it sauté the onion for 3 minutes, or until onion is transparent. Stir in *2 tablespoons flour.* Slowly stir in *1½ cups milk;* cook, stirring, until sauce is smooth and slightly thickened. Stir in *½ teaspoon salt, ½ teaspoon freshly ground black pepper, ¼ teaspoon thyme or oregano,* and *¾ cup of the cheese.*

4. Pour the cheese sauce over the macaroni and mix well.

5. In baking dish spread a layer of *half the stewed tomatoes.* Spoon the macaroni on top, then pour *remaining stewed tomatoes* over the macaroni. Sprinkle with the *remaining ¼ cup Parmesan.*

6. When ready to bake, preheat oven to 375° F.

7. Bake macaroni for 20 minutes, or until sauce is bubbling.

Stuffed Pasta Dishes

There is little reason to give you the more-or-less ordinary ways of preparing manicotti and lasagne since good recipes for them usually appear on the packages. Also there are some quite acceptable frozen manicotti and ravioli products available, especially the unsauced ones (to which you can add your own homemade sauces). So I'll give you just a few different and favorite stuffed pasta dishes, limiting my selection, of course, to ones calling for cheese and vegetables.

MANICOTTI WITH MUSHROOM CHEESE SAUCE

Serves 4. Recipe may be doubled. If you wish to take a short cut, buy 8 frozen manicotti already stuffed with cheese and keep them frozen until you are ready to sauce them. This will eliminate steps 1 and 2 except for grating some Parmesan cheese. You'll need only ½ cup.

BUY

½ pound aged Parmesan cheese
Parsley
Chives
8 ounces mozzarella
1 pound ricotta cheese
8 manicotti tubes
Ingredients for the Mushroom Cheese Sauce

HAVE ON HAND	*COOKWARE*
2 eggs	Pasta pot
Salt	14 x 8½ x 2 lasagne dish
Freshly ground black pepper	
Olive oil	
Butter	

1. Grate *1½ cups Parmesan cheese.* Chop *2 tablespoons each parsley and chives.* Shred the *mozzarella.*

2. Into mixing bowl pour *1 cup of the Parmesan cheese* (reserve remaining ½ cup to sprinkle on top of the sauce). Then add the mozzarella, the *ricotta,* the chopped parsley and chives, *2 eggs, 1½ teaspoons salt, ½ teaspoon pepper.* Mix well.

3. Make Mushroom Cheese Sauce (see recipe below).

4. Put manicotti into *rapidly boiling salted water* to which *1 tablespoon olive oil* has been added; cook for the least amount of time specified in box directions. Drain, then cover with *cool water.*

5. *Butter* the lasagne dish. Fill the manicotti, one at a time, with the

cheese mixture. The best way to do this is to slit each cooked tube, lay it out flat, spread surface thickly with the cheese filling, and then roll the tube.

6. Arrange the filled manicotti side by side in the prepared dish. Spoon the Mushroom Cheese Sauce over all, and sprinkle with the *reserved ½ cup Parmesan cheese.*

7. When ready to bake, place in oven preheated to 350° F. Bake for 25 to 30 minutes, or until sauce is bubbling and hot throughout. Serve each person 2 manicotti with plenty of sauce.

MUSHROOM CHEESE SAUCE

Makes about 4 cups

BUY

¾ pound fresh mushrooms
¼ pound Gruyère *or* Swiss cheese
¼ pound aged Parmesan cheese
1 pint milk
1 pint heavy cream

HAVE ON HAND	*COOKWARE*
Shallots if possible; otherwise onion	2-quart saucepan
Butter	
Flour	
Salt	
Freshly ground black pepper	

1. Peel and mince *enough shallots or onion to measure ¼ cup.* Wash, trim, and slice the *mushrooms.* Shred *enough Gruyère or Swiss cheese to make 1 cup.* Grate *1 cup Parmesan.*

2. In saucepan melt *1 stick (½ cup) butter,* and in it sauté the shallots or onion for 3 to 4 minutes, or until transparent. Add mushrooms and sauté for 5 to 6 minutes longer, stirring frequently.

3. Stir in *6 tablespoons flour.* Gradually stir in *1 pint of milk;* cook, stirring constantly, until sauce is smooth and thick. Gradually stir in the *cream.* Add the cheeses, *1½ teaspoons salt,* and *pepper to taste;* cook, stirring, until cheeses are melted.

MANICOTTI WITH TOMATO SAUCE

Serves 4

BUY

Package manicotti tubes
15½-ounce jar marinara sauce
8-ounce can tomato sauce
½ pound mozzarella cheese
1-pound container ricotta cheese

HAVE ON HAND

Salt
Parsley
Oregano
Coarsely cracked pepper
Parmesan cheese
2 eggs

COOKWARE

Pasta pot
Small saucepan
11¾ x 7½ x 1¾-inch baking dish

1. *Cook 8 manicotti* in *boiling salted water* until just tender. Drain, then keep moist in a *little warm water.*

2. In saucepan combine *marinara sauce, tomato sauce, 2 tablespoons chopped parsley, ¼ teaspoon oregano, ¼ teaspoon pepper,* and *½ cup water.* Bring to a boil and simmer for 10 to 15 minutes.

3. Meanwhile grate *enough Parmesan cheese to measure ½ cup.* Shred the *mozzarella cheese.* Combine *1 cup of the shredded mozzarella* with *all of the ricotta, 2 eggs,* and *½ teaspoon salt.*

4. Drain manicotti tubes, then stuff them with cheese mixture, using about ¼ cupful for each.

5. Spread *about 1 cup of the spaghetti sauce* in bottom of baking dish. Arrange the stuffed manicotti side by side on top of the sauce. Pour *remaining sauce* over the manicotti, and sprinkle with *remaining mozzarella* and the Parmesan cheese.

6. To cook: Preheat oven to 350° F. Bake the manicotti, uncovered, for 30 minutes, or until cheese is melted and sauce is bubbling.

MEATLESS LASAGNE WITH HOMEMADE MARINARA SAUCE

Serves 8

BUY FOR THE SAUCE

4 large yellow onions
Two 2-pound, 3-ounce cans Italian plum tomatoes
1 pound mushrooms

BUY FOR THE LASAGNE

½ pound Parmesan cheese
1 pound mozzarella cheese
1 pound ricotta cheese
1-pound package of lasagne

HAVE ON HAND

Garlic
Carrow
Olive oil
Salt
Freshly ground pepper
Oregano
Basil
Butter
Parsley
3 eggs

COOKWARE

Large skillet
Pasta pot
Small saucepan
Large lasagne baking dish

MAKE MUSHROOM MARINARA SAUCE:

1. Peel and chop *enough onions to measure 4 cups.* Peel and mince *4 large cloves garlic.* Chop *2 small carrots.*

2. In large skillet heat *½ cup olive oil,* and in it sauté onion, garlic, and carrot for about 10 minutes, or until vegetables are lightly browned; stir frequently. Add *tomatoes* and *salt and pepper to taste.* Bring to a boil and simmer for 30 minutes.

3. Meanwhile wash, trim, and chop the *mushrooms.*

4. At end of half hour rub sauce through a sieve or food mill. Add

2 teaspoons oregano and *2 teaspoons basil* to strained sauce, then set it aside. Wash skillet.

5. In skillet melt *2 tablespoons butter,* and in it sauté the mushrooms for 5 minutes, or until just tender; stir frequently. Add tomato sauce, bring to a simmer, and continue to simmer for 45 minutes.

FOR THE LASAGNE:

1. Grate *enough Parmesan to measure 1½ cups.* Chop *2 tablespoons parsley.* Dice or shred the *mozzarella.*

2. Combine the *ricotta* with *3 eggs, 1 cup of the grated Parmesan,* the parsley, and *salt and pepper to taste.*

3. Cook the *lasagne* according to package directions until barely tender. Drain immediately and rinse in *cold water.*

4. Melt *6 tablespoons butter* in a small saucepan.

5. Assemble the lasagne: Spoon a layer of sauce over bottom of lasagne dish. Add a layer of lasagne. Spoon another layer of sauce over this, and add a layer of mozzarella cheese, and a sprinkling of Parmesan. Spoon *1 tablespoon melted butter* over this. Next, another layer of lasagne another of sauce, then a layer of ricotta, and a sprinkling of *1 tablespoon butter.* Repeat these two sets of layers until the lasagne dish is almost full, and end with mozzarella, Parmesan, and melted butter.

6. When ready to bake, place in oven preheated to 375° F. Bake lasagne in the moderate oven for 45 minutes, or until sauce is bubbling and mixture is piping hot throughout.

RAVIOLI WITH SPINACH AND RICOTTA

Serves 4 to 6

BUY

½ pound Parmesan cheese
½ pound fresh spinach
½ pound ricotta cheese

HAVE ON HAND

COOKWARE

Ingredients for Fresh Pasta for
  ravioli (page 212)
1 egg
Salt
Pepper
Nutmeg
Butter

1-quart saucepan with cover
Small saucepan
Large heavy pot

1. Make *fresh pasta dough*. Grate and set aside *1½ cups Parmesan cheese*.

2. Wash *spinach* thoroughly and cook in covered pan without water until tender. Drain and press out as much liquid as possible.

3. Put spinach and *ricotta* through food chopper, then mix in *1 egg*, and *1 cup of the Parmesan cheese*. Season with *salt, pepper,* and *nutmeg*.

4. Roll out dough into thin sheets. Place a teaspoon of filling on bottom sheet every 2 inches. Cover with second sheet of dough, press firmly around filling, and cut into squares with a pastry cutter.

5. Dry for 45 minutes.

6. Melt *1 stick (½ cup) butter* in small saucepan over low heat.

7. Cook ravioli a half dozen at a time in *simmering salted water*. Remove with a slotted spoon as they rise to surface of water and are cooked al dente. Drain on paper towels. Serve immediately with the hot melted butter. Pass *additional grated Parmesan*.

RAVIOLI WITH FIVE CHEESES

Serves 4 to 6

  BUY

4 ounces Parmesan cheese
4 ounces Romano cheese
4 ounces mozzarella cheese
4 ounces Gruyère *or* Swiss cheese
½ pound ricotta cheese
8-ounce container heavy cream

HAVE ON HAND	*COOKWARE*
Ingredients for Fresh Pasta for ravioli (page 212)	Small saucepan
1 egg	Large heavy saucepot
Nutmeg	
Pepper	
Butter	

1. Make *fresh pasta dough.*

2. Grate the *Parmesan* and *Romano.* Shred the *mozzarella* and the *Swiss* or *Gruyère.*

3. In mixing bowl combine the *ricotta* with *1 cup of the Parmesan* (reserve the rest) and the other three cheeses. Stir in *1 egg,* the *cream, a dash of nutmeg,* and *freshly ground pepper to taste.* Mix well.

4. Roll out dough into thin sheets. Place a spoonful of the cheese filling on the bottom sheet of dough every 2 inches. Cover with second sheet of dough, press firmly around filling, and cut into squares with pastry cutter.

5. Let filled ravioli dry for 45 minutes.

6. Melt *1 stick (½ cup) butter* in small pan over low heat.

7. Cook a half dozen ravioli at a time in *simmering salted water* until they rise to the surface and are cooked al dente, or to taste. Remove with a slotted spoon to drain on paper towels.

8. Serve on hot plates, drenched with the melted butter and topped with *a generous sprinkling of the reserved grated Parmesan.*

BREADS

Nutritious Homemade Breads— The Basics

Julia Child may well go down in history for her classic remark, "How can a society be great when its bread tastes like Kleenex?"

How, indeed? The spongy refined white breads found today in our markets are made of poison-sprayed, degerminated, over-bleached wheat, hydrogenated shortening, refined white sugar, and water. The initial dough is nutritionally worthless. Then chemicals are added to condition it, and more chemicals are added to prevent spoilage. You can push both ends of the baked bread together like an accordion, and when the pressure is released, the loaf bounces back to its original shape! I kept such a loaf on my kitchen counter for weeks to see how long it would remain soft until I got tired of looking at it. It didn't mold; it didn't dry out. It remained in the same spongy condition it had the day I bought it!

So, if you are not already among the many rebels who have learned to make and bake their own fresh, nutritious, whole-grain breads, it's time you started.

Making a loaf of yeast bread is easier than apple pan dowdy. It takes only a few minutes to stir up the dough and to form it into a loaf or pan rolls. It does take time for the infinitesimal living organisms known as yeast to grow and give off the carbon dioxide which raises the bread and makes it light—but the yeast does this by itself.

Once the miracle of yeast is understood, it's almost impossible to turn out a poor loaf, and there are all the satisfactions of working and kneading the living dough and feeling it respond to the touch, the unforgettable aroma of fresh yeast bread baking in the oven, the crunch of the crisp crust crumbling between the teeth, and the substantial, honest flavor of yeast mingled with the nutritious whole-grain texture beneath.

Nowadays, you don't have to go far to seek out stone-ground whole-grain flours. Country stores and health-food markets which stock a large variety of whole-grain products are multiplying. It won't be long before all the supermarkets will be forced to supply either the flours themselves or some honest bread, or both, and even then, it will be much more economical to bake your own than to buy theirs.

So promise yourself that you will bake bread at least once a week from whole grains with all their God-given goodness.

Once you learn to make a basic loaf of whole-wheat bread, you can go on to use all kinds of flour, you can alterate brown sugars, maple syrup, honey, or molasses to suit your mood, and you can add seeds, nuts, raisins, or herbs to create new and interesting flavors and textures.

WHAT MAKES A GOOD LOAF OF BREAD?

YEAST is the essential ingredient, and the fresh yeast cakes or the packets of dry active yeast are equally satisfactory. Like all living substances, yeast needs food, moisture, and warmth (75° to 85° F.) to develop, and when these three conditions are met, the yeast spores multiply rapidly.

FLOUR is the chief ingredient in all breads, and your bread is only as nutritious as the kind of flour you use. You will need to keep on hand some all-purpose flour, but buy only the unbleached kind, which is already in the supermarkets. Then seek out a variety of stone-ground or water-ground whole-grain flours: whole wheat, rye, barley, millet, soy, gluten, graham, buckwheat. Buy them in small quantities and be sure to store them in your refrigerator or freezer, for the germ of the cereal has been left in these flours and the oil contained in the germ becomes rancid quickly. Also, since no chemicals have been added, tiny insects develop and grow fat in such a happy environment, especially in warm weather. They know a good thing when they smell it!

In addition to these flours, you may want to keep on hand some oats, either quick-cooking or long-cooking, some corn meal, cracked wheat, bran flakes or 100% bran, soy grits, farina, wheat flakes, and wheat germ.

SUGAR provides quick food for the yeast, adds flavor to the bread, and is partly responsible for the golden color of the crust. Sweetening can also contribute to the nutrition of the loaf if you use brown sugars, molasses, honey, corn syrup, or maple syrup in place of refined white sugar. These may be interchanged at will.

MILK, WATER, OR POTATO WATER supplies the moisture.

SHORTENING lubricates the delicate meshwork of the dough so it can expand smoothly and easily. Our grandmothers had no such thing as hydrogenated shortening. They used butter or oil and you may do the same.

These ingredients plus a little salt and a little time are all it takes to make a loaf of bread that is vital, healthful, and utterly delicious.

Kneading the dough is guaranteed to reduce any hostility or neuroses you may be harboring.

Make two loaves, always, rather than one—a loaf to refrigerate or freeze and another one to eat hot from the oven. Slice it in good-size chunks, spread it lavishly with sweet butter, and top it occasionally with some homemade peanut butter (page 341). Heaven!

BASIC FORMULA FOR ONE LOAF

Although we are going to begin, on page 255, by making *two* loaves of bread, you might like to memorize the following very easy quantities that any single loaf of bread requires:

1 cup liquid (usually half milk plus half water *or* potato water)
1 cake yeast *or* 1 package active dry yeast
1 tablespoon sugar (preferably brown)
1 tablespoon molasses *or* dark corn syrup
1 tablespoon shortening *or* oil
1 teaspoon salt
3 cups flour

While breadmaking is one of the most creative forms of culinary art —not only in its flour variations and its texture and flavor changes, but also in its shaping—if you remember these standard quantities you cannot fail. Double, triple, or quadruple them for 2, 3, or 4 loaves, but remember the formula for the single loaf.

Generally, the dough for 12 buns or rolls is equivalent to the quantity used to make one loaf.

FOUR RULES OF BREADMAKING TO REMEMBER:

1. Yeast is living! Don't kill it with too hot a liquid. For yeast cakes the liquid should be just lukewarm (80° to 85° F.). For active dry yeast the water can be slightly hot to the hand or as high as 120° F.

2. Don't knead in any more flour than necessary. The dough should be soft but not sticky.

3. Don't let the bread over-rise in the pans. If you do, it may collapse a little during baking. When the dough is just nicely rounded over sides of the pans, it is ready for the oven.

4. Don't overbake the loaves. They are done when they sound hollow when rapped with the knuckle and the crust is golden.

BASIC 100% WHOLE-WHEAT BREAD

Makes 2 loaves

BUY

2 yeast cakes *or* 2 packages active dry yeast
2-pound bag stone-ground whole-wheat flour

HAVE ON HAND	*COOKWARE*
Milk	Small saucepan
Brown sugar	Two 8½ x 4½-inch loaf pans
Molasses	(1½-quart capacity)
Salt	
Butter	
Salad oil	

1. Heat *1 cup milk* to scalding.

2. Add the *yeast* to *¼ cup lukewarm water* and let soak for 5 minutes, then stir mixture until well blended.

3. Into large mixing bowl measure *2 tablespoons each brown sugar and molasses, 2 teaspoons salt,* and *2 tablespoons butter.* Pour the hot milk over these ingredients and stir, mashing the butter against sides of bowl until melted or broken into small lumps. Stir in *¾ cup cool water.*

4. Stir in *1 cup of the flour* and beat with a wooden spoon for 1 minute. Add the yeast and *2 more cups flour* and continue to beat until batter is smooth and elastic. Stir in *another 2 cups flour.* Then, with floured fingers, work in *enough additional flour to make a dough that does not stick to the fingers yet is still soft.*

5. Turn dough out onto a floured surface and knead about 100 kneading strokes, or until dough becomes elastic.

HOW TO KNEAD:

Kneading is a three-step rhythm that quickly becomes automatic. On the floured surface, fold dough over onto itself toward you, then push dough away with heels of your hands. Give dough a quarter turn; repeat.

6. When you've finished kneading the dough, shape it into a ball and rub the surface with a *little salad oil*.

7. Cover lightly with a towel and let dough rise for about 1½ hours, or until double in bulk. *Oil* bread pans and set aside.

8. Plunge a floured fist into the center of the dough to deflate it and knead again briefly. Cut ball of dough in half and shape each half into a loaf.

TO SHAPE LOAF:

Flatten the ball of dough with palms of hands, fold in half lengthwise, and flatten again. Take one end of the dough in each hand, then stretch the dough gently to elongate it. Overlap ends at center and press firmly together. Now roll dough lengthwise, turn it seam side down, and seal the ends. Place each loaf, seam side down, in prepared bread pan. Cover loaves with the towel and let dough rise for about 1 hour, or until puffed and nicely rounded above sides of pans.

9. Preheat oven to 375° F. Bake the loaves for 45 to 50 minutes, or until tops are golden brown and loaves test done.

TO TEST BREAD FOR DONENESS:

Rap the top of the bread with your knuckles. If it sounds hollow the loaf is done.

10. Turn loaves from pans immediately to keep the crust crisp, and cool on cake rack.

FOR A SOFT CRUST:

Brush loaves with a little melted butter as soon as they come from the oven.

FOR ONE LOAF AND ONE DOZEN ROLLS:

Shape half the dough into a loaf and follow recipe directions for raising and baking.

Divide remaining dough into 12 portions. Shape each portion into a round ball. Place balls 2 inches apart on an oiled cake pan or baking sheet; cover and let rise for about 45 minutes, or until puffed and double in bulk. Bake along with the bread in preheated 375° F. oven for 20 to 25 minutes, or until golden.

IF DESIRED, SPRINKLE TOPS OF ROLLS WITH SEEDS

Sesame, caraway, and poppy seeds, any one of these toppings is good. Before baking the rolls, brush the tops lightly with melted butter and sprinkle generously with seeds.

BREAD FREEZES BEAUTIFULLY:

If you freeze a loaf in one of the new plastic ovenproof bags, you can remove it from the freezer and then put it, bag and all, in a 325° F. oven. The bread will be hot and ready to serve in 20 to 30 minutes. Frozen bread that has been partially thawed slices more easily than bread at room temperature, so remove a loaf from the freezer about 1 hour before slicing.

VARIATIONS ON BASIC 100% WHOLE-WHEAT BREAD (page 255)

WHITE BREAD: Use unbleached all-purpose flour in place of the whole wheat; white sugar in place of the brown; and honey in place of the molasses.

OATMEAL BREAD: Substitute 2 cups oats (quick- or long-cooking) for 2 cups of the flour.

SWEDISH RYE BREAD: Use half stone-ground rye flour and half unbleached all-purpose flour in basic recipe. Add 1 tablespoon caraway seeds to the hot milk.

BRAN BREAD: Substitute 2 cups bran flakes or 100% all bran for 2 cups of the flour.

CRACKED WHEAT BREAD: Add 2 tablespoons honey and 2 cups cracked wheat to hot-milk mixture before adding necessary flour to make a dough that does not stick to the hands.

WHEAT GERM BREAD: Add 1 cup wheat germ to hot-milk mixture before adding necessary flour to make a dough that does not stick to the hands.

SOY BREAD: Use half stone-ground soy flour and half unbleached all-purpose flour in basic recipe.

BUCKWHEAT BREAD: Substitute 1 cup buckwheat flour for 1 cup whole-wheat or all-purpose flour.

CORN BREAD: Add 1 cup stone-ground corn meal to hot-milk mixture before adding necessary flour to make a dough that does not stick to the hands. To give a nice crunch to the bread, sprinkle bottom of the bread pans with corn meal before the dough is placed in them.

GLUTEN BREAD: Like whole-wheat flour, all gluten flour (a low-starch, high-protein corn product) may be used in breadmaking and combines well with soy, rye and other specialty flours used in breadmaking.

GRAHAM BREAD: Substitute 2 cups graham flour for 2 cups whole wheat or all-purpose flour in making bread.

RYE CORNMEAL BREAD: Substitute 1 cup each rye flour and corn meal for 2 cups of the all-purpose flour.

RYE SOY BREAD: Substitute 1 cup each rye flour and soy flour for 2 cups of the all-purpose flour.

MILLET BREAD: Substitute 2 cups millet flour for 2 cups of the all-purpose flour.

WHOLE-WHEAT RYE BREAD: Substitute 2 cups rye flour for 2 cups whole-wheat flour.

Bread & Roll Recipes

HALF AND HALF BREAD

Makes 2 loaves

BUY

2 envelopes active dry yeast *or* 2 yeast cakes
1-pound bag whole-wheat flour

HAVE ON HAND	*COOKWARE*
Milk	Small saucepan
Butter	Two 8½ x 4½-inch loaf pans
Sugar	
Salt	
Unbleached all-purpose flour	
Molasses	
Salad oil	

1. In small saucepan measure *2 cups milk.* Add *¼ cup butter (½ stick)* and heat until milk is scalding hot and butter is melted. Remove from heat and pour in *½ cup cold water.*

2. Pour *½ cup lukewarm water* into a large mixing bowl and sprinkle, or crumble, in the *yeast.* Let stand for about 5 minutes, or until yeast is softened and mixture is bubbling.

3. Stir in *⅓ cup sugar, 1 tablespoon salt,* and the milk mixture. Beat in *2 cups all-purpose flour,* then divide the dough in half.

4. Into one half stir *enough additional all-purpose flour to make a light dough.* Turn out on floured board and knead until dough is smooth and elastic.

5. Into the other half stir *4 tablespoons molasses* and *2½ to 3 cups*

whole-wheat flour. Turn out onto floured board and knead until smooth and elastic.

6. *Oil* surface of each mound of dough, cover lightly with a towel, and let rise for 1¼ to 1½ hours. Punch down and knead again briefly. Cover and let rest for 10 minutes.

7. Oil loaf pans.

8. Cut each mound of dough in half. Roll out half the white dough and half the whole-wheat dough, making two rectangles about 12 x 8 inches. Place the whole-wheat rectangle on top of the white rectangle, then roll up, starting with the short side of the dough. Repeat with remaining dough.

9. Place in 2 oiled loaf pans. Cover and let rise for 45 to 60 minutes, or until double in bulk.

10. Bake in preheated 375° F. oven for 45 to 50 minutes, or until loaves are brown and crusty and test done.

NOTE: You can adapt this recipe to make many interesting light-and-dark breads. For instance, change the plain white dough to *a rich egg dough* (page 269), and use rye, soy, or wheat-germ dough in place of the whole-wheat. To vary the flavor, add caraway, poppy, or toasted sesame seeds (page 273).

WHOLE-WHEAT BREAD WITH WHEAT GERM

Makes 2 loaves

BUY

2 packages active dry yeast *or* 2 yeast cakes
2-pound package stone-ground whole-wheat flour

HAVE ON HAND	*COOKWARE*
Brown sugar	Two 8½ x 4½-inch loaf pans
Salt	
Wheat germ	
Non-fat instant dry milk solids	
Butter	
Unbleached all-purpose flour	
Salad oil	

1. In small bowl soften the *yeast* in *½ cup lukewarm water*.

2. In large mixing bowl combine *¼ cup brown sugar, 2 teaspoons salt, ½ cup wheat germ, 1 cup non-fat instant dry milk powder*. Slice in *2 tablespoons butter*, and stir in *2 cups hot water*. Gradually stir in *3 cups unbleached all-purpose flour*, then stir in the yeast mixture. Gradually work in *about 4 cups whole-wheat flour*, or enough to make a dough that is stiff enough to handle.

3. Turn dough out on floured board and knead until smooth and elastic. *Oil* the top of the dough, cover lightly with a towel, and let rise for 1¼ to 1½ hours, or until doubled in bulk.

4. Oil loaf pans.

5. Punch dough and knead again briefly. Shape dough into two loaves and put each into a prepared pan. Let rise again about 45 minutes, or until well rounded above sides of pans.

6. Bake in preheated 400° F. oven for 40 minutes, or until golden brown, and hollow-sounding when tapped with the knuckles. Remove from pans to cool on racks.

OATMEAL MOLASSES BREAD

Makes 2 loaves

BUY

2 yeast cakes *or* 2 packages active dry yeast

HAVE ON HAND	*COOKWARE*
Milk	Small saucepan
Butter	Two 8½ x 4½-inch loaf pans
Molasses	
Salt	
Oats, instant *or* long-cooking	
Unbleached all-purpose flour	
Salad oil	

1. In saucepan measure *1 cup milk*. Add *¼ cup butter (½ stick)* and heat until milk is scalding hot and butter is melted.

2. Soften the *yeast* in *½ cup lukewarm water*.

3. In large mixing bowl put *½ cup molasses, 2 teaspoons salt,* and *2 cups oats (instant or long-cooking).* Pour the hot milk mixture over the oats and mix thoroughly. Stir in *½ cup cold water,* and gradually stir in *3 cups unbleached all-purpose flour.* Stir in yeast mixture, and gradually work in *about 2 more cups unbleached flour,* or enough to make a soft dough.

4. Turn dough out on floured board and knead until smooth and elastic. *Oil* top, cover with a towel and let rise for about 1½ hours, or until double in bulk.

5. Oil loaf pans and set aside.

6. Punch dough and knead again briefly. Divide dough in half. Shape each half into a loaf and put it into a prepared pan. Cover and let rise for 45 minutes, or until well rounded over sides of pan.

7. Bake in preheated 375° F. oven for 45 to 50 minutes, or until bread tests done. Remove loaves from pans to cool on wire racks.

RYE PUMPERNICKEL

Makes two 2-pound loaves. This is the favorite bread in our household.

BUY

3 large Idaho baking potatoes
2 yeast cakes *or* 2 packages active dry yeast
2-pound package stone-ground rye flour

HAVE ON HAND	*COOKWARE*
Salt	Two 9 x 5-inch loaf pans *or*
Molasses	9-inch round cake pans
Caraway seeds	
Unbleached all-purpose flour	
Salad oil	

1. Peel and dice *3 large Idaho potatoes;* boil in *salted water to cover* for about 20 minutes, or until potato is very tender. Drain, leaving *a couple of tablespoons of water* on the potatoes; mash thoroughly with a potato masher. Let cool.

2. In large mixing bowl, soften the *yeast* in ½ *cup warm water.*

3. Stir yeast and water until well mixed, then stir in *2 cups warm water.* Stir in *3 cups rye flour, 1 teaspoon salt, 2 tablespoons molasses,* the mashed potatoes, and *2 tablespoons caraway seeds.*

4. Stir in *3 cups all-purpose flour* to make a soft dough. Turn dough out onto floured surface and knead well, kneading in *about 1 more cup of all-purpose flour,* or enough to make a dough that is smooth and elastic. The amount of flour required at this point depends on the amount of moisture in the mashed potatoes.

5. *Oil* surface of dough, cover with a towel, and let rise for about 1 hour, or until double in bulk.

6. Oil baking pans.

7. Punch dough down and divide in half. Knead each half for a few minutes, then shape it into loaf. Place dough in two prepared loaf pans, or in two round cake pans if you wish round loaves. Cover and let rise again for about 40 minutes, or until double in bulk.

8. Bake in a preheated 425° F. oven for 10 minutes; then reduce oven temperature to 375° F. and continue to bake for 40 minutes longer, or until bread tests done.

OVERNIGHT WHITE OR WHOLE-WHEAT BUNS

Makes 2 to 3 dozen. Recipe may be doubled.

BUY

1 yeast cake *or* 1 package active dry yeast

HAVE ON HAND	*COOKWARE*
Sugar	Saucepan
Butter	9 x 13-inch cake pans
Unbleached all-purpose *or*	
stone-ground whole-wheat flour	
2 eggs	
Salad oil	

1. First day: In early afternoon combine *2 cups water* and *½ cup sugar* in saucepan. Bring to a boil and boil for 5 minutes. Remove from heat and add *1 stick (½ cup) butter*. Pour into mixing bowl and let cool to lukewarm.

2. Meanwhile soften *yeast in ¼ cup lukewarm water*.

3. When mixture in bowl is lukewarm, stir in *2 cups flour (all-purpose or whole-wheat)*, then beat in yeast and *2 eggs*. Gradually stir in *enough additional flour (3 to 3½ cups) to make a soft dough*. Turn out on floured board and knead for about 10 minutes, or until dough is smooth and satiny. Cover dough and let rise for 3 hours.

4. Punch dough, and let rise again for about 2 hours.

5. *Oil* cake pans.

6. Punch the twice-risen dough down again and shape into rolls. Place rolls in prepared pans. Cover with a towel and refrigerate until morning.

7. Next morning: Preheat oven to 400° F. Bake the rolls for 12 to 15 minutes.

HIGH PROTEIN WHOLE-WHEAT RYE BREAD

Makes 4 loaves. A gutsy, heavy-crusted bread—marvelous!

BUY

4 yeast cakes *or* 4 packages active dry yeast
2-pound bag stone-ground whole-wheat flour
2-pound bag stone-ground rye flour

HAVE ON HAND	*COOKWARE*
Milk	Small saucepan
Butter	Four 8½ x 4½-inch baking pans *or*
Salt	8-inch round cake pans
Non-fat instant dry milk solids	
Molasses	
Caraway seeds	
Unbleached all-purpose flour	
Salad oil	

1. In small saucepan heat *2 cups milk* and *1 stick (½ cup) butter* together until milk is scalding hot and butter is melted.

2. In large mixing bowl measure *2 teaspoons salt, 1 cup non-fat instant dry milk solids, 4 tablespoons molasses,* and *4 tablespoons caraway seeds.* Pour hot milk mixture over and stir until ingredients are well mixed. Add *1 cup cool water,* then cool to lukewarm.

3. Meanwhile soften *4 yeast cakes or packages of dry yeast* in *1 cup lukewarm water.*

4. When mixture in large bowl is lukewarm, stir in *4 cups whole-wheat flour,* then the softened yeast, and then *4 cups rye flour* to make a soft batter.

5. Stir and work in with the hands *enough all-purpose flour (from 4 to 5 cups) to make a soft dough that does not stick to the hands.*

6. Turn dough out on floured surface; knead until dough is smooth and elastic. *Grease* surface, cover with towel, and let rise for 2 hours.

7. *Oil* baking pans.

8. Punch dough down, knead again briefly, and cut into quarters. Shape each quarter into loaf and place it in prepared pan. Cover again and let rise for 45 minutes to 1 hour, or until dough is well puffed over sides of pans.

9. Preheat oven to 375° F. Bake loaves for 50 minutes, or until they are golden and test done. Remove from pans to cool on racks.

REFRIGERATOR WHOLE-WHEAT ROLLS

Makes 2 to 3 dozen. Here is a great dough if you like fresh rolls every day. It will keep in the refrigerator for at least 4 days.

BUY

2 yeast cakes *or* 2 packages active dry yeast
Package stone-ground whole-wheat flour

HAVE ON HAND	*COOKWARE*
Milk	Small saucepan
Butter	Cake pans
Brown sugar	
Salt	
Unbleached all-purpose flour	
2 eggs	
Salad oil	

1. In ADVANCE: Soften the *yeast* in *½ cup warm water.*

2. In small saucepan measure *1 cup milk;* add *½ stick (¼ cup) butter;* heat over low heat until butter is melted and milk is scalding hot.

3. Pour hot milk mixture into large mixing bowl, preferably of an electric mixer; and add *½ cup brown sugar,* and *1 tablespoon salt.* Stir until sugar is melted. Then stir in *¾ cup cold water, 1 cup all-purpose flour,* and *1 cup whole-wheat flour.* Set mixer at medium speed and beat mixture for 2 minutes (or beat 5 minutes with a hand rotary beater), scraping the sides and bottom of bowl occasionally. Beat in yeast and *2 eggs.*

4. Now stir in *4 cups whole-wheat flour* and *enough all-purpose flour (1 to 1½ cups) to make a soft dough.* Turn the dough into an *oiled* bowl and oil surface of dough. Cover with plastic film and store in refrigerator.

5. ABOUT 2 HOURS BEFORE BAKING: Butter cake pans. Remove required quantity of dough from refrigerator; place on floured board and knead until dough is smooth and elastic. Shape into rolls, and place in prepared pans. Brush surface with *melted butter;* cover dough, and let rise for about 1½ hours.

6. Bake in preheated 400° F. oven for 20 minutes, or until brown.

RICH POTATO SWEET ROLLS

Makes 3 dozen rolls

BUY

1 yeast cake *or* 1 package dry active yeast

HAVE ON HAND	*COOKWARE*
1 cup unseasoned mashed potatoes	Baking sheets
Sugar	
Butter (1 stick)	
4 eggs	
Salt	
Unbleached all-purpose flour	

1. FIRST DAY: In large mixing bowl soften the *yeast* in *1 cup luke-warm water.* Stir in *1 cup potatoes mashed with a little cooking water* and *1 cup sugar;* stir until sugar is dissolved. Cover with a towel and let stand in a warm place overnight. Remove *1 stick (½ cup) butter* from refrigerator and set aside.

2. NEXT DAY: beat into the potato mixture *4 eggs,* the stick of soft butter, and *1 teaspoon salt.*

3. Stir in *about 3 cups flour* to make a stiff dough that is difficult to stir. Then, with your hands, mix in another *2 to 3 cups flour* to make a soft light dough. Be careful not to add any more flour than necessary.

4. Butter baking sheets.

5. Turn dough out on floured surface and, with floured rolling pin, roll the dough out about ½ inch thick. Cut out small rounds with a floured cooky cutter. Place the rounds 1 inch apart on the buttered baking sheets.

TO BAKE WITHOUT REFRIGERATING:

Cover rolls with a towel, then let them rise at room temperature until double in bulk—about 2 hours.

Preheat oven to 400° F. Bake the rolls for just 10 minutes. Do not overbake. The rolls should be just lightly tinged with brown. Serve warm with sweet butter and honey.

TO REFRIGERATE:

The shaped rolls will keep in the refrigerator for several days before baking. Allow 3 hours rising time after removing rolls from refrigerator. Bake as above.

VARIATIONS: Substitute whole-wheat flour in place of all-purpose; or use half rye flour and half whole-wheat or all-purpose.

BRIOCHE EGG BREAD
(*Rich Egg Bread*)

Makes 2 loaves. This recipe is made with exactly the same ingredients as the French *brioche* but the method has been simplified and the dough is baked in conventional bread pans. It's a divine bread to slice thinly and make into watercress or onion-and-cucumber sandwiches, with lots of mayonnaise. Since it dries out quickly, store the extra loaf in the freezer. If it becomes stale, don't throw it away. Slice it paper thin (it slices easily and evenly) and make it into the best Melba toast you ever put in your mouth.

BUY

½ pound butter (2 sticks)
2 packages active dry yeast *or* 2 yeast cakes
6 large eggs

HAVE ON HAND

Sugar
Salt
Unbleached all-purpose flour
Salad oil

COOKWARE

Two 8½ x 4½-inch loaf pans

1. Soften *butter* to room temperature.

2. Soften *yeast* in *½ cup lukewarm water* with *1 teaspoon sugar.*

3. In mixing bowl measure *½ teaspoon salt,* and *¼ cup sugar.* Add *6 whole eggs* and beat with a rotary beater until eggs are fluffy and sugar and salt are dissolved.

4. Beat in *2 cups flour,* then stir in yeast.

5. Divide butter into chunks and add to yeast mixture. Add *another cup flour* and beat well. Work in *1 more cup flour,* or enough to make a soft dough that doesn't stick to the hands—be careful when adding this fourth and last cup of flour not to add more than is necessary.

6. Turn dough out onto floured board and knead until dough is smooth. Cover with towel and let rise for 1½ hours.

7. *Oil* loaf pans.

8. Punch dough down and cut into two parts. Knead each part briefly and shape into a thick loaf. Put loaves into oiled loaf pans, cover again with towel, and let rise for about 45 minutes, or until well rounded in pans. Bake in preheated 375° F. oven for 45 to 50 minutes.

SALLY LUNN EGG BREAD

Makes 2 loaves. This fine-textured bread is delicious sliced and toasted for breakfast.

BUY

1 yeast cake *or* 1 envelope active dry yeast

HAVE ON HAND	*COOKWARE*
Milk	Two 8½ x 4½-inch loaf pans
Butter	
Sugar	
Salt	
Unbleached all-purpose flour	
2 eggs	
Salad oil	

1. Scald *1 cup milk.* Add *½ cup butter, 2 tablespoons sugar,* and *2 teaspoons salt.* Stir over low heat until butter is melted. Remove from heat and cool to lukewarm.

2. Soften the *yeast* in *½ cup lukewarm water.* Add to milk mixture. Beat in *2 cups all-purpose flour.* Stir in *2 eggs,* lightly beaten. Add *3 cups flour* and beat until batter is smooth and elastic. Then work in an additional *1 cup flour* to make a dough that is soft but not sticky. Cover and let rise for 1½ hours, or until double in bulk.

3. *Oil* loaf pans.

4. Punch dough down and turn out on a lightly floured board. Knead dough until it is smooth and elastic. Cut in half. Shape each half into a loaf and put into oiled loaf pan. Cover and let rise for 1 hour, or until dough is well rounded over sides of pans.

5. Preheat oven to 425° F. Bake loaves in the hot oven for 30 minutes, or until lightly browned. Remove from pans to cool on racks. Serve warm with sweet butter and jam or jelly.

PAIN PARISIEN
(*Real French Bread*)

Makes 2 large or 3 small loaves. All unbleached flour may be used in this recipe, but the gluten flour is concentrated high protein and makes a more authentic French loaf.

BUY

2 yeast cakes *or* 2 packages active dry yeast
1-pound package gluten flour

HAVE ON HAND	*COOKWARE*
Salt	Baking sheet
Sugar	Large shallow pan
Corn *or* safflower oil	
Unbleached all-purpose flour	
Corn meal	
1 egg white	

1. Pour *2 cups lukewarm water* into a large mixing bowl. Add the *yeast* and let soak for 5 minutes. Stir to mix yeast thoroughly with water. Add *1 tablespoon salt, 2 tablespoons sugar,* and *2 tablespoons oil.*

2. Stir in *3 cups all-purpose flour* and beat well with a wooden spoon. Stir in *1 cup of the gluten flour* and beat again.

3. Turn dough out onto floured surface and knead in *1 to 1½ cups all-purpose flour* to make a soft dough that does not stick to hands. Shape into a ball; cover with a towel; and let rise for 1 hour, or until double in bulk.

4. Punch dough down, then knead for a few minutes, or until smooth and elastic. Cover and let rest for 10 minutes.

5. *Oil* baking sheet, then sprinkle it lightly with *corn meal.*

6. Cut dough either in half or in thirds. To shape each part into a long loaf, first roll the dough out into a rectangle about 16 inches long. Then roll the dough lengthwise, seal the edges, and press into shape. Place loaves, seam side down, one alongside another, on prepared baking sheet. Let rise for 20 minutes.

7. With a sharp knife score the surface of each loaf diagonally down its length, making shallow cuts at intervals of about 1 inch. Brush loaves with *lightly beaten egg white*.

8. Do NOT PREHEAT OVEN. Place a large shallow pan of boiling water on lower shelf of oven. Place bread on center shelf of oven. Set oven temperature at 400° F., and bake the loaves for 40 to 50 minutes, or until golden brown and crusty.

GARLIC BREAD

Cream *1 stick butter* until light and fluffy. Beat in *1 large clove minced garlic*. Cut long loaf of French bread diagonally into 1-inch slices, cutting well down toward the bottom but leaving bottom crust intact. Spread garlic butter generously between slices and on top. Shape heavy-duty aluminum foil around the loaf, boat-fashion, twisting ends and leaving top open. Bake in a preheated 400° F. oven for 10 to 12 minutes.

ITALIAN BREAD

Make as above but cream the *stick of butter* and *garlic* with *½ teaspoon crumbled oregano* and *1 teaspoon dry parsley flakes.* Just before baking, sprinkle top of loaf with *¼ cup grated Parmesan cheese.*

CHEESE LOAF

Split a long loaf of French bread lengthwise. Combine *2 cups shredded sharp Cheddar cheese (8 ounces)* with *⅓ cup butter, ½ cup chopped chives or green onions, ½ cup minced parsley,* and *a few drops Tabasco.* Toast the cut sides of the bread under broiler heat. Remove from boiler and spread thickly with the cheese mixture. Return to broiler and broil just long enough to melt the cheese. Slice into serving portions while bubbling hot.

PARSLEY BREAD

Trim the top and side crusts from a loaf of homemade bread and slice it very thinly down to, but not through, the bottom crust.

Chop *enough fresh parsley to measure 1 full cup.* Empty it into a towel and squeeze out excess juice, leaving the parsley dry and fluffy. Cream *1 stick butter* until soft, then beat in the parsley. If desired, also beat in *1 tablespoon chopped chives, fresh dill, or tarragon,* or *1 clove minced garlic.* Spread the parsley butter on each slice and over top and sides. Place the loaf in a baking pan and bake in a preheated 300° F. oven for 1¼ hours, or until loaf spreads open and edges are crisp and brown.

SESAME SEED BREAD

Sprinkle *½ cup sesame seeds* thinly on bottom of a baking pan and bake in a preheated 350° F. oven for 10 minutes, or until golden. Beat *1 stick butter* until light and fluffy, then beat in *2 minced cloves garlic* and the toasted sesame seeds. Split a long loaf of French bread lengthwise and toast cut sides lightly under the broiler. Remove from broiler, and while bread is hot spread it lavishly with the seed butter. Cut into serving portions and serve immediately, or keep warm in a warm oven.

MIRACLE CROISSANTS

Makes 36. Here is a miracle recipe for those wonderfully flaky *croissants* that you enjoy in France and at some of our better restaurants. Perhaps you have been sufficiently interested to look up a recipe, but have given up right there, for the technique is lengthy and difficult, or perhaps you've tried to make *croissants* and had little success. Try again. This recipe is an easy one and it's foolproof if you measure the ingredients exactly.

What's more, you can chill the dough and roll it out a day or two later; or you can roll it out, cut and form the *croissants,* and bake them, or keep them cold in the refrigerator on a baking sheet for several days until ready to bake; or you can freeze the baked rolls and reheat them when needed—a most obliging and versatile recipe for a hot bread that will make you famous.

BUY

8-ounce container light cream
1 cake yeast *or* 1 package active dry yeast

HAVE ON HAND	COOKWARE
1 egg	Baking sheets
Sugar	
Salt	
Unbleached all-purpose flour	
½ pound butter (2 sticks)	

TO MAKE THE DOUGH:

1. Measure *¾ cup cream* into a 1-cup measure. Crumble or sprinkle the *yeast* into the cream and let soak for 10 minutes.

2. Meanwhile put *1 egg, 2 tablespoons sugar,* and *1 teaspoon salt* into a mixing bowl and beat with a rotary beater until blended.

3. Stir yeast-cream mixture to blend, then stir it into egg mixture. Stir in *2* LEVEL *cups flour, 1 cup at a time,* to make a moist dough.

4. Turn dough out onto a well-floured board, sprinkle with flour, and knead gently about 12 kneading strokes.

5. With floured rolling pin, roll out dough into a square about ¼ inch thick, keeping both sides lightly floured. Unwrap *1 stick cold butter* and slice thickly. Arrange slices in center of the square. Fold all four sides of the dough over the butter, completely enclosing it. Seal edges.

6. Now begin rolling out the dough. (You'll want to do this 5 times, always keeping both sides of the dough floured.) Roll out into a band about 12 inches long and ¼ inch thick. Turn one third of the dough over center third. Fold other third on top, making three layers of dough. Turn dough ¼ turn to left. Repeat the rolling and turning four times. Don't roll too thinly.

7. Wrap dough in transparent film and store in refrigerator if croissants are not to be made until later.

TO FORM CROISSANTS:

8. Before rolling and forming dough into crescents, melt *1 stick butter.*

9. Place dough on floured board. With floured rolling pin, roll the dough into a rectangle 8 inches wide and 16 inches long and about ⅛ inch thick. Cut it lengthwise in half, then crosswise in half, making four small rectangles.

10. Work with one piece at a time. Roll it out as thinly as possible into a rectangle 6 inches wide and 12 inches long. Cut into 8 triangles with wide sides about 3 inches wide. Brush surface of each triangle with melted butter and roll, beginning at wide side and rolling to the point. Brush baking sheets with butter. Curve each roll into crescent shape and place on baking sheet. Repeat process with the three remaining pieces of dough.

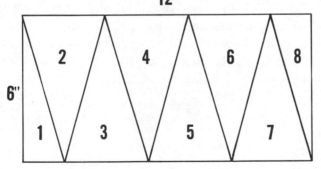

11. Brush crescents with melted butter. Cover with plastic film and refrigerate.

TO BAKE:

12. When ready to bake, preheat oven to 375° F. Bake rolls in center of the hot oven for 20 minutes and serve hot.

Quick Breads & Pancakes

No other bread offers more eating pleasure, for the amount of effort expended, than a quick bread served hot from the oven and slathered with sweet butter and honey. There are many recipes for quick breads in basic cookbooks, so I am including only a few of my special favorites in this chapter.

Recipes for quick breads in most books specify all-purpose flour. There is little reason to abide by this. Whole-wheat flour may be used in place of the all-purpose flour, and other whole-grain cereals, bran, corn meal, wheat germ and so on may be substituted for half the quantity of all-purpose flour specified in a general recipe, making these quick breads into real nutritional assets and augmenting the protein in the milk and eggs which most quick-bread recipes contain.

Also there is no need to use refined white sugar just because a recipe lists this in the ingredients. Use brown sugar, honey, maple syrup, or molasses in place of it. All of these contain B vitamins which the body needs to "burn" sugar, thereby converting it into energy.

With imagination, you can serve a variety of nutritious quick breads. They are an excellent way to begin the day, and they complement almost any soup or salad supper.

CRISP CORN DOLLARS

Makes about 36

HAVE ON HAND

Butter
White corn meal

Salt
Sugar   *COOKWARE*
Boiling water   Baking pan

1. Preheat oven to 450° F. *Butter* a baking pan generously.

2. In mixing bowl combine *1 cup corn meal, 1 teaspoon salt,* and *¼ teaspoon sugar.* Gradually stir into the corn-meal mixture *1¾ to 2 cups boiling water* to make a batter having the consistency of a heavy pancake batter.

3. Put baking pan in the hot oven until butter sizzles, then remove. Drop or pour batter onto the hot pan in little cakes about the size of a silver dollar. Return pan to hot oven and bake for 15 minutes, or until corn dollars are lightly browned. Serve hot.

BASIC HIGH-PROTEIN MUFFINS

Makes one dozen 2½-inch muffins

HAVE ON HAND   *COOKWARE*

Vegetable oil   Small saucepan
Butter   12-cup muffin pan
Unbleached all-purpose flour
Stone-ground whole-wheat *or* other
    whole-grain flour; *or* wheat germ
Baking powder
Salt
Brown sugar
Milk
1 egg

1. Preheat oven to 400° F. *Oil* muffin cups.

2. In small saucepan, put *½ stick (¼ cup) butter* over low heat to melt.

3. In mixing bowl combine (no need to sift) *1 cup all-purpose flour, 1 cup whole-grain flour or wheat germ, 3 teaspoons baking powder, 1 teaspoon salt,* and *2 tablespoons brown sugar.*

4. In small bowl combine *1 cup milk* and *1 egg;* add flour mixture

and stir gently just until dry ingredients are moistened. Stir in melted butter.

5. Fill muffin cups ⅔ full of batter. Bake in the preheated oven for 20 to 25 minutes. Serve hot with sweet butter and jam or jelly or peanut butter.

FOR SWEETER MUFFINS: Increase sugar to ¼ or ½ cup.

FOR BUTTERMILK MUFFINS: Use only 2 teaspoons baking powder, add ½ teaspoon baking soda, and substitute buttermilk for the sweet milk.

BERRY MUFFINS: Increase sugar to ¼ or ½ cup. Fold in 1 cup washed and drained blueberries or raspberries before spooning batter into pans.

CRANBERRY MUFFINS: Cut 1 cup fresh or frozen cranberries in half and sprinkle with 2 tablespoons sugar. Make muffin batter, but increase sugar to ¼ or ½ cup. Fold cranberries into batter before spooning it into the pans.

RAISIN OR DATE BRAN MUFFINS: Increase sugar to ¼ or ½ cup. Substitute 1 cup bran flakes or 100% bran for the whole-grain flour. Fold 1 cup seedless raisins (or pitted and cut dates) and ½ cup chopped nuts into the batter.

CORNMEAL MUFFINS: Substitute 1 cup stone-ground yellow corn meal for the whole-grain flour.

APPLE PECAN MUFFINS: Increase sugar to ¼ or ½ cup. Add ½ teaspoon cinnamon or nutmeg. Fold in 1 cup peeled, chopped apples and ½ cup chopped pecans.

BASIC WHOLE-WHEAT BISCUITS

Makes sixteen 2-inch biscuits

HAVE ON HAND	COOKWARE
Unbleached all-purpose flour	Baking sheet
Stone-ground whole-wheat flour	
Baking powder	
Salt	
Shortening	
Milk	

1. Preheat oven to 425° F.

2. Measure (no need to sift) *1 cup all-purpose flour* and *1 cup whole-wheat flour;* combine these in mixing bowl with *3 teaspoons baking powder* and *1 teaspoon salt.*

3. With a pastry blender or two knives, cut in *½ cup shortening* until shortening is broken into small particles.

4. Add *⅔ cup milk* and stir gently with a fork until dough holds together. Gather dough into a ball, place on a lightly floured surface, and knead gently, about 12 kneading strokes.

5. Roll dough out ½ inch thick on the floured surface, then cut into biscuits with a floured biscuit cutter.

6. Place biscuits about 1 inch apart on baking sheet. Bake in the hot oven for 12 to 15 minutes.

BUTTERMILK BISCUITS: Reduce baking powder to 2 teaspoons and add ½ teaspoon baking soda to dry ingredients. Use buttermilk in place of the milk.

WHEAT-GERM OR SOY BISCUITS: Substitute ½ cup wheat germ or soy granules for ½ cup of the all-purpose flour. Increase milk to ¾ cup.

CORN-MEAL BISCUITS: Substitute ⅔ cup corn meal for ⅔ cup of the whole-wheat flour.

PEANUT BUTTER BISCUITS: Omit salt, and substitute peanut butter for the shortening.

DUBLIN SCONES

Makes 8

BUY

Small box seedless raisins *or* currants

HAVE ON HAND

Flour
Baking soda
Cream of tartar

Salt
Vegetable shortening
Milk

COOKWARE

Baking sheet

1. Preheat oven to 400° F.

2. In a mixing bowl combine *2 cups flour, 1 teaspoon baking soda, 1 teaspoon cream of tartar,* and *½ teaspoon salt.*

3. Add *½ cup shortening;* using a pastry blender or two knives, cut in shortening until mixture looks like coarse meal. Stir in *½ cup raisins or currants.*

4. Add, all at once, *¾ cup milk* and stir gently with a fork until dough holds together.

5. With hands, gather dough into a ball, turn it out into a lightly floured board, and knead gently with floured fingers about 12 kneading strokes. Roll dough out on floured surface into a circle ½ inch thick, then cut into 8 pie-shaped wedges with a floured knife.

6. Place wedges on baking sheet about 1 inch apart. Bake in the hot oven for 15 minutes.

SCOTCH OAT SCONES

Makes 6 servings

HAVE ON HAND

All-purpose flour
Oats
Salt
Baking soda
Sugar
Butter
Buttermilk

COOKWARE

Baking sheet

1. Preheat oven to 400° F.

2. In mixing bowl combine *1 cup flour, 1 cup oats, ½ teaspoon salt, 1 teaspoon baking soda,* and *1 tablespoon sugar.* Add *1 tablespoon butter* and rub in with tips of fingers. Add *¾ cup buttermilk* and mix lightly with a fork to make a fairly soft dough that can be gathered together.

3. Turn dough out on lightly floured board and pat into a large circle about ½ inch thick. Place circle on *greased* baking sheet. Prick at frequent intervals with a fork and score into six triangles.

4. Bake in preheated oven for 15 minutes, or until lightly browned. Serve warm with butter and honey or jelly.

THE POPPINGEST POPOVERS

Makes 4. There's a lot of meaningless hokus-pokus around trying to make a mystery of how to make a popover pop. You don't need any special recipe; you don't have to preheat your oven or use special cast-iron popover pans. One basic recipe works for everyone. The trick is to use ordinary 6-ounce pyrex custard cups set wide apart on a baking sheet, and to make 4 popovers instead of 6 or 8 from the recipe. This means filling the cups three-quarters full of batter.

HAVE ON HAND	COOKWARE
Butter	Four 6-ounce custard cups
2 eggs	
Salt	
Milk	
All-purpose flour	

1. *Butter* custard cups lavishly.

2. If you have an electric blender, put *2 eggs, ½ teaspoon salt, 1 cup milk,* and *1 level cup all-purpose flour* (no need to sift) into container in order given; otherwise measure them into a mixing bowl. Blend or beat until batter is smooth.

3. Pour batter into prepared custard cups set wide apart on a baking sheet, filling cups ¾ full.

4. Set baking sheet in a cold oven until ready to bake—and this means until next morning, if you wish, for the batter can remain safely in the oven overnight. Turn oven to 450° F., and bake popovers for 30 minutes. Toward end of baking time, but not before, check popovers and if they are becoming too brown, turn temperature down to 400° F. and bake until popovers are crisp.

POPOVER PANCAKE

Serves 2 or 4

HAVE ON HAND	*COOKWARE*
Unbleached all-purpose flour	12 x 8-inch oval top-of-the stove
Milk	au gratin dish *or* 12-inch round
2 eggs	skillet with heatproof handle
Butter	
Confectioners' sugar	
Lemon	
Honey, jam, *or* marmalade	

1. Preheat oven to 425° F.

2. In mixing bowl combine *½ cup flour, ½ cup milk,* and *2 eggs.* Beat lightly, leaving the batter slightly lumpy.

3. In au gratin dish or skillet heat *¼ cup butter (½ stick)* until very hot. Pour in the batter. Place the dish in the hot oven and bake for 20 minutes, or until pancake is puffed all around sides of dish and golden brown. Remove from oven and sprinkle with *2 tablespoons sugar* and *juice of ½ lemon.* Return to oven for 2 to 3 minutes, or until pancake is glazed.

4. Serve immediately with honey, jam, or marmalade.

LAPLAND CAKES

Makes 12 medium cakes

BUY

8-ounce container heavy cream

HAVE ON HAND	*COOKWARE*
Butter	12-cup muffin pan
Flour	
Salt	
3 eggs	

1. Preheat oven to 375° F. Generously *butter* muffin cups.

2. Combine (no need to sift) *1 cup flour* and *¼ teaspoon salt.*

3. *Separate 3 eggs,* dropping whites into one bowl and yolks into another. Beat *egg whites* with rotary beater until stiff, but not dry. With the same beater, beat *egg yolks* thoroughly. In a third bowl, with same beater, beat *heavy cream* until stiff.

4. Fold flour mixture into egg yolks alternately with the whipped cream, then fold in egg whites.

5. Spoon batter into prepared muffin cups (about 2 rounded table-spoons per cup), and bake in preheated oven for 20 to 25 minutes, or until lightly brown. Serve hot.

BASIC WHOLE-WHEAT BREAKFAST BREAD

Makes 1 square. Homemade fruit and nut quick breads are a treat for breakfast, or for an afternoon snack. Thinly slice and toast any leftover loaf on another day.

HAVE ON HAND	*COOKWARE*
Stone-ground whole-wheat flour	Small saucepan
Baking powder	Loaf pan
Salt	
Brown sugar	
Butter	
Milk	
1 egg	

1. In small saucepan put *1 stick (½ cup) butter* over low heat to melt. *Oil* baking pan.

2. Preheat oven to 375° F.

3. In mixing bowl combine *2 cups whole-wheat flour, 3 teaspoons baking powder, 1 teaspoon salt,* and *½ cup sugar.*

4. Combine *1 cup milk* and *1 egg* and stir gently into flour mixture to make a slightly lumpy batter. Stir in melted butter.

5. Spoon batter into prepared pan. Spread top evenly and bake in the hot oven for 25 to 30 minutes. Serve hot or remove from pan to cool on rack.

CINNAMON NUT BREAD: Before baking breakfast bread, combine ½ cup brown sugar, 1 teaspoon cinnamon, and ½ cup chopped pecans or walnuts, and sprinkle on top of batter.

STREUSEL BREAD: Before baking breakfast bread, combine and sprinkle on top ½ cup brown sugar, 1 teaspoon cinnamon, 2 tablespoons all-purpose flour, ½ cup chopped almonds, and 2 tablespoons butter.

APRICOT NUT BREAD: Fold into batter 1 cup coarsely chopped nuts and ½ cup cut, dried apricots.

POPPY SEED BREAD: Before making breakfast bread, add 1 tablespoon each grated lemon rind and poppy seeds to the milk.

ORANGE SUNFLOWER BREAD: Use ½ cup orange juice and ½ cup milk in place of all milk. Just before spooning batter into pan, fold in 1 table-spoon grated orange rind and ½ cup chopped toasted sunflower seeds.

BANANA BRAN BREAD

Makes 8½ x 4½-inch loaf

BUY

2 bananas
1 box bran flakes

HAVE ON HAND	*COOKWARE*
Vegetable oil	Loaf pan
Butter	
Brown sugar	
2 eggs	
All-purpose flour	
Baking powder	
Salt	
Milk	
Vanilla	

1. Preheat oven to 350° F. *Oil* loaf pan. Peel and slice *bananas*. Chop ½ *cup nuts*.

2. Cream together ⅓ *cup butter*, ⅔ *cup brown sugar*, and the sliced bananas.

3. Add *2 eggs* and beat until well blended.

4. Combine *1 cup all-purpose flour, 1 cup bran flakes, 2 teaspoons baking powder*, and *1 teaspoon salt*. Stir the dry ingredients into the banana mixture alternately with ½ *cup milk*. Stir in *1 teaspoon vanilla* and the nuts. Spoon mixture into prepared pan.

5. Bake in moderate oven for 1 hour, or until done. Serve hot, or remove from baking pan to cool on rack.

DATE NUT BREAD

Makes 8½ x 4½-inch loaf

BUY

1 pound pitted dates
8-ounce can walnuts

HAVE ON HAND

Vegetable oil
Butter
Baking soda
Brown sugar
Vanilla
1 egg
Unbleached all-purpose flour
Baking powder
Salt

COOKWARE

Loaf pan

1. Chop or cut *dates*. Chop *walnuts*.

2. Preheat oven to 350° F. *Oil* loaf pan.

3. Put dates, nuts, and *1 cup boiling water* into large mixing bowl. Add *⅓ cup butter* and beat until butter is broken into small pieces.

4. Add *5 tablespoons cold water* and stir in *1 teaspoon soda, ¾ cup brown sugar, 1 teaspoon vanilla, 1 egg* and *2 cups flour.* Add *1 teaspoon baking power* and *½ teaspoon salt,* beat until all ingredients are well blended.

5. Spoon batter into prepared pan and bake in the moderate oven for about 1 hour, or until loaf tests done. Remove loaf from pan to cool on rack.

BOSTON BROWN BREAD

Makes 3 small loaves or 2 large loaves

BUY

Yellow corn meal
Graham flour
Rye flour
Buttermilk
Seedless raisins

HAVE ON HAND

Baking soda
Salt
Molasses
Sugar

COOKWARE

Three 1-pound coffee cans *or*
    two 1-quart pudding molds
Large kettle with rack and lid

1. In mixing bowl combine *1 cup yellow corn meal, 1 cup graham flour, 1 cup rye flour, 1 teaspoon baking soda,* and *1 teaspoon salt.* Stir in *¾ cup molasses, 1 tablespoon sugar, 2 cups buttermilk,* and *¾ cup raisins.*

2. Place rounds of greased paper in bottom of the coffee cans or pudding molds. Grease cans or molds and fill ⅔ full of batter. Place lids on the molds, or tie aluminum foil tightly over tops of cans.

3. Place containers on a rack in a large kettle and add enough warm water to reach half way up their sides. Cover kettle, bring water to a boil, and continue to boil gently for 2 hours, or until bread tests done, adding more boiling water from time to time if needed. Remove molds or cans, cool slightly, then remove bread from containers.

CORN-MEAL BUTTERMILK PANCAKES

Makes about 20

HAVE ON HAND	*COOKWARE*
White *or* yellow stone-ground corn meal	Griddle
All-purpose flour	
Salt	
Baking soda	
2 eggs	
Buttermilk	
Butter	
Vegetable oil	

1. In mixing bowl combine *1⅓ cups corn meal, ¼ cup flour, 1 teaspoon salt,* and *½ teaspoon baking soda.*

2. In another bowl beat *2 eggs* lightly with *2 cups buttermilk.* Stir into corn-meal mixture. Stir in *¼ cup melted butter.*

3. Heat a griddle until a drop of water on it sputters and evaporates almost immediately (350° F.).

4. Grease griddle lightly with *oil,* and spoon batter onto it to make small pancakes no larger than 2 inches in diameter. When surface of the cakes becomes bubbly and underside is lightly browned, turn cakes and brown lightly on the other side.

PINEAPPLE NUT BREAD

Makes 2 loaves

BUY

8 ounces shelled nuts (pecans, walnuts, *or* macadamia)
1 pound light brown sugar
1-pound can crushed pineapple

HAVE ON HAND

Vegetable oil
All-purpose flour
Baking powder
Baking soda
Salt
Butter, at room temperature
2 eggs

COOKWARE

Two 1-pound loaf pans

1. Preheat oven to 350° F. *Oil* loaf pans.

2. Chop *nuts* and set aside.

3. In mixing bowl combine *3½ cups flour, 4 teaspoons baking powder, ½ teaspoon baking soda,* and *½ teaspoon salt.* Stir in the chopped nuts.

4. In another mixing bowl cream *6 tablespoons butter* and *1½ cups brown sugar* until well blended. Beat in *2 eggs,* one at a time, and continue to beat until mixture is smooth. Stir in *half the flour mixture.* Stir in *pineapple and juice.* Stir in *remaining flour mixture.*

5. Divide batter into prepared loaf pans. Bake in the preheated oven for 50 to 60 minutes, or until bread tests done. Let loaves cool for 5 minutes, then turn out on racks to cool completely.

WHOLE-WHEAT PANCAKES

Makes about 18

HAVE ON HAND

All-purpose flour
Stone-ground whole-wheat flour
Salt
Sugar
Baking powder
Molasses
2 eggs
Milk
Butter *or* vegetable oil

COOKWARE

Griddle

1. In mixing bowl combine ¾ *cup all-purpose flour, 1 cup whole-wheat flour, 1 teaspoon salt, 2 tablespoons sugar,* and *1 teaspoon baking powder.*

2. In another mixing bowl combine *3 tablespoons molasses, 2 eggs, 1 cup milk,* and ¼ *cup melted butter or oil.*

3. Gradually stir liquid ingredients into dry ingredients, and continue to stir until batter is smooth.

4. Heat a griddle until a drop of water sputters and evaporates almost immediately (350° F.).

5. *Grease* griddle lightly. Spoon batter onto it to make cakes about 3 inches in diameter. When surface of cakes becomes bubbly and underside is nicely browned, turn cakes and cook until brown on other side.

RAISED BUCKWHEAT CAKES

Makes about 18

BUY

1 pound stone-ground buckwheat flour
1 yeast cake *or* 1 envelope active dry yeast

HAVE ON HAND

HAVE ON HAND	COOKWARE
Milk	Small saucepan
Salt	Griddle
Baking soda	
Molasses	
1 egg	
Butter *or* vegetable oil	

NIGHT BEFORE:

1. Scald *2 cups milk,* then cool to lukewarm.

2. In mixing bowl crumble or sprinkle the *yeast;* add the lukewarm milk; stir until yeast is softened and mixed with the milk. Stir in *2 cups buckwheat flour* and ½ *teaspoon salt.*

3. Cover bowl with a towel and let stand at room temperature overnight.

NEXT DAY:

4. Combine ½ *teaspoon baking soda* and ¼ *cup lukewarm water.* Stir the mixture into the batter. Stir in *2 tablespoons molasses, 1 egg,* and ¼ *cup melted butter or vegetable oil.*

5. Heat griddle until a drop of water on it sputters and evaporates almost immediately (350° F.).

6. *Grease* griddle lightly, then pour or spoon the pancake mixture onto the griddle to make cakes about 3 inches in diameter. Cook until surface becomes bubbly and underside is lightly browned. Turn and brown the other side.

DESSERTS

Fruit Desserts

According to the French, there are some desserts that are interesting, some that are presumptuous, some that are memorable, and a few that are truly great. I'm going to try to give you a few of each of these in this chapter, beginning with a fresh melon—about which François de Malherbe, court poet to Henri IV, once wrote: "There are only two beautiful things in the world, roses and women; and two good morsels, women and melons."

MELON ORIENTALE

Serves 6

BUY

1 pound mixed fresh fruits in season, such as sweet cherries, peaches, apricots, strawberries, pineapple, raspberries, or blueberries
1 large cantaloupe, honeydew, *or* cassaba melon

HAVE ON HAND

Confectioners' sugar
Kirsch, Madeira, port, sherry, *or* Sauternes

1. Prepare the fresh fruits: Peel and dice the *pineapple, peaches, or apricots.* Wash and pit the *cherries,* hull the *strawberries,* or pick over the *raspberries* or *blueberries.*

2. Cut a circular piece from the stem end of the *melon,* reserving the piece, and scoop out seeds and filaments. With a French ball scoop,

carve melon balls out of the pulp, being careful not to cut through the rind.

3. Cut the thinnest possible slice from opposite end of the melon, just enough to allow it to stand upright on a serving plate. Dust the inside of the melon shell with *confectioners' sugar,* then fill the cavity with alternate layers of the mixed fruit and the melon balls.

4. Add *½ cup kirsch or wine,* and replace the top plug. Chill for 2 hours before serving. To serve, remove the plug, spoon out the fruit mélange onto serving plates, and ladle over it a little of the liquid.

Any seasonal fruit makes a perfect dessert providing it is fully ripe and at its peak. What could be better than a big bowl of fresh raspberries or strawberries in spring, a slice of red ripe watermelon in June, a juicy peach or apricot in August, a basket of fresh Concord grapes in mid-September, a shiny red apple in October, or a soft, ultrasweet persimmon during the holiday season? Fortunately, when no special fruits are available, there are always bananas.

RHUBARB STEWED IN ITS JUICE

Serves 4

BUY OR PICK

2 pounds fresh rhubarb

HAVE ON HAND	*COOKWARE*
Sugar	Double saucepan *or* baking dish; tight-fitting cover

1. Break off and discard rhubarb leaves. Wipe *rhubarb stalks* and slice into ½-inch lengths. Do not peel. Put the rhubarb and *1½ cups sugar* into the upper part of a double saucepan or into a baking dish. Stir thoroughly, then cover tightly.

2. If using a double saucepan, bring water just to simmering and cook for 30 minutes, stirring occasionally. Otherwise bake the dish in a

325° F. oven for 50 minutes, removing the cover and stirring after 20 minutes of baking.

Cherry Cobbler, Apple Pan Dowdy, Peach Brown Betty, Blueberry Grunt —all such wonderfully homespun early American names—are among my favorite desserts. A few of them are in Good Food & How to Cook It. Another is:

FRUIT SLUMP

Serves 4

BUY

2 pounds fresh rhubarb, blueberries, apples, *or* peaches
Heavy cream

HAVE ON HAND

Butter
Sugar
Ginger
All-purpose flour
Salt
Baking powder
Milk

COOKWARE

Small saucepan
Shallow baking dish,
    8 inches in diameter

1. Preheat oven to 375° F. Melt *½ stick (4 tablespoons) butter* in small saucepan over low heat.

2. Prepare the *fruit,* washing and peeling if necessary; dice *enough to measure 4 cups.* Put the fruit in the baking dish and mix it with *1 cup sugar* and *½ teaspoon ground ginger.*

3. In mixing bowl combine *1 cup flour, ½ teaspoon salt, 1½ teaspoons baking powder,* and *¼ cup sugar.* Stir in *¾ cup milk* and the melted butter.

4. Pour the batter over the fruit and bake in the moderate oven for 45 minutes.

5. Serve hot or warm with *heavy cream.*

STRAWBERRY FLUMMERY

Serves 6. And how about that for a marvelous name?

BUY

2 pints fresh strawberries
8-ounce container heavy cream

HAVE ON HAND	*COOKWARE*
Light brown sugar	2-quart saucepan
Cornstarch	
Salt	
Lemon juice	

1. Wash *strawberries* in a colander placed under cool running water. Remove hulls.

2. In saucepan combine the strawberries, *1 cup light brown sugar, 2 tablespoons cornstarch, a dash of salt, ½ cup water,* and *¼ cup lemon juice.* Bring slowly to a boil, stirring constantly, then boil for 1 minute.

3. Pour into an attractive serving dish and chill thoroughly. Before serving whip the *cream* and spoon large dollops of it on top of the flummery.

BLUEBERRY COBBLER

Serves 6. And don't forget a topping of homemade ice cream.

BUY

2 pints fresh blueberries

HAVE ON HAND	*COOKWARE*
Butter	1½-quart baking dish
Flour	
Sugar	
Baking powder	
Milk	

1. Wash and pick over the *berries,* discarding any wilted or green ones.

2. Preheat oven to 425° F. Place *1 stick (½ cup) butter* in baking dish over low heat to melt.

3. In mixing bowl combine *1 cup flour* with *1 cup sugar* and *1 teaspoon baking powder*. Stir in *¾ cup milk* to make a smooth batter. Pour batter over the hot butter in the baking dish, and sprinkle the blueberries on top.

4. Bake in the preheated oven for 25 to 30 minutes, or until puffed and golden.

APPLE TART

Makes one 8-inch tart. Let's forget the American double-crust apple pie in favor of this luscious apple tart from Italy, where it is called *Crostate di Mele*. We like to serve it with a smooth sour-cream sauce that closely resembles the glorious Crème Fraîche of France.

BUY

6 fresh cooking apples (2 pounds)
4 ounces blanched slivered almonds *or* broken walnuts *or* pecans
12-ounce jar apricot preserves

HAVE ON HAND	COOKWARE
Ingredients for Rich Dessert Pastry	8-inch pie plate
Granulated sugar	
Butter	
Confectioners' sugar	

1. Make *pastry* and chill as directed (page 298).

2. Meanwhile, peel, halve, and core the *apples*.

3. Preheat oven to 425° F.

4. Roll out ⅔ of the pastry thinly on a lightly floured pastry cloth, using a rolling pin with floured stocking. Transfer the pastry to the pie plate and trim off overhanging edge.

5. Slice the apples and, as you do so, arrange them in circles over the

pastry, each slice slightly overlapping the next. Sprinkle the apples with *2 tablespoons granulated sugar* and *½ cup of the almonds.* Then spread the *apricot preserves* over the apples and nuts. Dot with *2 tablespoons butter.*

6. Roll out remaining pastry thinly and cut into strips ½ inch wide. Arrange 10 strips, lattice-fashion, over filling, and trim overhanging edges. Place a strip of pastry all around edge of pie so that it covers the ends of lattice strips; flute this edge along with the bottom pastry.

6. Bake in the hot oven for 15 minutes; then reduce oven temperature to 375° F. and continue to bake for 40 to 45 minutes longer.

7. Remove from oven and, while hot, sift a little confectioners' sugar over the top. Serve with Sour-Cream Sauce.

SOUR-CREAM SAUCE
(Simulated Crème Fraîche)

Makes about 1¼ cups

Combine *1 cup dairy sour cream* with *2 tablespoons confectioners' sugar* and *¼ cup light cream, or enough to make a sauce consistency.* Flavor with *½ teaspoon vanilla,* or *1 tablespoon brandy,* or *2 tablespoons Grand Marnier.*

RICH DESSERT PASTRY

Makes enough pastry for a 1-crust and lattice-topped pie or tart

HAVE ON HAND
Flour
Sugar
2 egg yolks
Salt
Lemon
Butter

1. Empty *1¼ cups flour* onto a pastry board or into a mixing bowl and make a well in center. In the well put *4 tablespoons sugar, 2 egg yolks* (reserve whites for another use), *a dash of salt,* and the *grated rind of 1 lemon.* Slice *1 stick butter* on top of these ingredients.

2. Work the center ingredients to a paste with one hand, then knead in enough additional flour to make a stiff dough. Form dough into a ball, wrap in waxed paper, and refrigerate for 30 minutes.

3. See page 49 for the techniques of rolling out pastry.

HONEY RHUBARB PIE

Serves 6

BUY OR PICK

1½ pounds fresh rhubarb

HAVE ON HAND	*COOKWARE*
Rich Dessert Pastry (page 297)	9-inch pie plate
Sugar	
Honey	
Salt	
Ginger, nutmeg, or cinnamon	
Butter	
Cornstarch	

1. Line the pie plate with *pastry.*

2. Preheat oven to 425° F.

3. Wash and slice *enough rhubarb to measure 4 cups.* Combine it with *1 cup sugar, 2 tablespoons honey, ½ teaspoon salt, ½ teaspoon ginger, nutmeg, or cinnamon,* and *3 tablespoons cornstarch.* Pile fruit mixture into the prepared pie plate and dot with *1 tablespoon butter.*

4. Cover with a lattice topping, and sprinkle the topping with *2 tablespoons sugar.*

5. Bake in the preheated oven for 20 minutes; then reduce oven temperature to 350° F. and continue to bake for 20 to 25 minutes longer. Serve the pie warm.

Rich Desserts

REAL GOOEY CHOCOLATE CAKE

Serves 8. For those of you to whom dessert means chocolate cake, here is the best recipe that I know.

BUY

Box of unsweetened chocolate
1 quart buttermilk

HAVE ON HAND

Walnuts or pecans (optional)
Cooking oil
Butter, at room temperature
Sugar
3 eggs
All-purpose flour
Baking soda
Salt
Vanilla extract
Lemon
Ingredients for Chocolate Butter Cream
Ingredients for Meringue Frosting

COOKWARE

Small saucepan
Medium saucepan
3 8-inch layer cake pans *or*
a 13 x 9 x 2-inch oblong cake pan

1. Put *3 squares unsweetened chocolate* into a small saucepan and set in another saucepan of simmering water until chocolate is melted; stir occasionally. Coarsely chop *½ cup nuts, if desired.*

2. Preheat oven to 350° F. *Oil* pan or pans and line with waxed paper.

3. In mixing bowl, cream *1½ sticks butter (¾ cup)* with *2 cups sugar*

until light and fluffy. Add *3 eggs,* one at a time, beating well after each addition. Set aside.

4. Combine *3 cups flour, 1½ teaspoons baking soda,* and *1 teaspoon salt.* Add these dry ingredients alternately with *1½ cups buttermilk* to the egg mixture, stirring well after each addition until batter is smooth.

5. Stir in *1 teaspoon vanilla, 1½ teaspoons lemon juice,* and the melted chocolate. Stir in nuts, if using them.

6. Pour batter into the oblong pan, or divide it evenly among the 3 layer-cake pans.

7. Bake the layer-cake pans in the preheated oven for 30 to 35 minutes; the oblong pan for 45 minutes, or until cake is done when tested with a wooden pick or cake tester.

8. Remove cake from oven, let cool a couple of minutes, then run a knife around edge and turn cake out onto wire rack.

9. When cake is completely cool, put the layers together with Chocolate Butter Cream; frost top and sides lavishly with Meringue Frosting. Or, spread the oblong cake thickly with the butter cream.

CHOCOLATE BUTTER CREAM

In small saucepan over very low heat melt *6 ounces semi-sweet chocolate pieces* and *¼ cup hot water or coffee,* stirring occasionally until smooth. Remove from heat and beat in *3 egg yolks* (reserve the whites to make the Meringue Frosting for the 3-layer cake). Beat in *1 tablespoon vanilla or Jamaica rum,* and gradually beat in *1 stick soft butter,* bit by bit. If butter cream is too soft, chill in refrigerator for an hour.

MERINGUE FROSTING

In saucepan combine *1½ cups sugar, ½ cup water,* and *1 teaspoon lemon juice.* Bring to a boil over low heat, then boil rapidly until bubbles get thick and the syrup spins a thread when a little is dripped off the tines of a fork (236° F. on candy thermometer). Remove from heat. Beat *3 egg whites* until thick and glossy. Gradually beat in the hot syrup and continue to beat until the frosting is thick enough to hold its shape. Use an electric beater for this if you have one.

CHOCOLATE ROLL CONTAINS NO FLOUR

A favorite dessert of mine is chocolate roll, or *roulade au chocolat,* which seems as light as a breath of sweet air, literally melts in the mouth, and has never failed to bring applause whenever I have served it.

The reason for its lightness is that it is really a chocolate soufflé mixture, spread thinly on a large baking sheet, rather than a cake batter. After baking, it is allowed to deflate as a soufflé typically will do, and then is filled with whipped cream and rolled.

It's actually an easy dessert but to make it is very difficult to describe in a recipe. It would be easy to show you how, but since that is not possible, I have tried to write the technique in great detail. The drawings show what words perhaps cannot make altogether clear.

The roll may be made a day in advance and refrigerated until serving time, or it may be made several weeks in advance, wrapped loosely and carefully in aluminum foil, and frozen. Remove it from its wrappings and onto a serving board about 3 hours before you need it.

In addition to a long, narrow jelly-roll board or tray to serve it on, you will need to have on hand: waxed paper, a rimmed baking sheet or jelly-roll pan, a small covered saucepan for melting chocolate, a second and somewhat larger saucepan, 2 mixing bowls, an electric or rotary beater, and a small sieve for sifting cocoa.

ROULADE AU CHOCOLAT

Serves 8 to 10

BUY

6-ounce package semi-sweet chocolate pieces
6 eggs
1 pint heavy cream
Small can cocoa, without sugar or powdered milk

HAVE ON HAND	*COOKWARE*
Cooking oil	Small saucepan with cover
Instant coffee	Rimmed baking sheet or jelly-roll
Hot water	pan approximately
Sugar	15½ x 10½ x 1 inch
Vanilla	
Confectioners' sugar	

1. *Oil* the baking sheet, line with waxed paper, and *oil* the paper. Use your fingertips to oil sheet and paper, for this is the only way you can be sure that all surfaces are evenly coated.

2. Put *chocolate pieces, 1 teaspoon instant coffee,* and *3 tablespoons hot water* into a small saucepan, cover tightly, and set saucepan into a larger pan or a skillet containing a couple of inches of simmering (not boiling) water. Stir occasionally until chocolate is melted and mixture is smooth, then set aside to cool. Rinse two mixing bowls with hot water and dry.

3. Preheat oven to 350° F.

4. Separate the eggs, putting yolks into one bowl and whites into another. Be careful not to let the slightest speck of yolk fall into the whites, otherwise they will not beat. If you are a novice at breaking eggs, separate one at a time, letting the white fall into a cup before transferring it to the bowl. Should you break the yolk of one egg, you haven't ruined all your egg whites.

5. Add ⅔ *cup sugar* to the *egg yolks* and begin beating. Use an electric beater for this if possible, for the egg yolks and sugar must be beaten at top speed for at least 5 minutes, or until mixture is very pale in color and as thick as cake batter. The mixture should take some time to level out when the beater is withdrawn. This is known as a "ribbon stage."

6. To this thick yolk mixture add the melted and cooled chocolate, and stir until well blended.

7. Beat the *egg whites* with a clean beater until glossy and thick enough to hold a stiff peak. Do NOT beat until they are dry. Pour the chocolate mixture on top of the egg whites, scraping out all of the chocolate mixture with a rubber spatula; then use the spatula to fold chocolate mixture into the egg whites. To FOLD: Cut down through the mixture with the side of the spatula, bring spatula along bottom of the bowl, then up and over the top. Repeat this down-across-up-and-over motion until egg whites completely disappear into the chocolate mixture.

8. Pour batter onto the prepared baking sheet, again scraping bowl well; spread evenly in a thin layer over the sheet and well into the corners of the pan. Bake in center of preheated oven for 15 minutes. Do *not* over-bake.

9. Remove baking sheet from oven, then cover top of the cake with a sheet of waxed paper. Cover the waxed paper with a damp towel and let the cake cool for 1 hour.

10. Remove towel and waxed paper. The cake will look pretty sad, but don't worry—it won't taste that way! Run a knife around edge of pan to loosen cake. Overlap two strips of waxed paper lengthwise on work table. The strips should be longer than the length of the cake and, over-lapping, they should be wider than the width of the cake. Sift enough *cocoa* over surface of the cake to coat it generously, then, with one motion, flip baking sheet and cake upside down onto the center of the waxed paper strips. The long side of the baking sheet should be horizontal to you.

11. Now remove the baking sheet. Grasp edge of waxed paper that lines the sheet on your right, and gently raise the baking sheet from right to left until it is off. Again, carefully, remove waxed paper from the bottom of the cake. If you oiled the paper well, you'll have no trouble, but if you didn't or if you left any little lumps of egg whites in the batter you may find the cake will stick a little in spots. Free these spots of cake with a knife.

12. Beat *1½ cups of the cream until stiff*, then beat in *2 tablespoons confectioners' sugar* and *1 tablespoon vanilla*. With spatula spread the cream in an even layer over surface of the cake.

13. You're ready to roll. Using both hands, grasp the wide side of the waxed paper closest to you on the table, raise the edge of the cake, and turn about 1 inch of it over on top of the filling. Continue to lift the waxed paper and at the same time roll cake and filling, making a long roll about 4 inches in diameter and 15 inches long. Don't be upset if the cake cracks a little, especially on your first attempt. It usually does, but this doesn't hurt the flavor. The last roll of the cake should deposit the "log" well into the center of the back sheet of waxed paper. Place the serving board on the far side of the roll and parallel to it, and lift the

waxed paper and the roll onto the serving board. I usually leave the waxed paper under the roll until I am ready to serve the dessert. The roll will firm a little when it chills in the refrigerator.

14. Now sift a *little more cocoa* over the roll to coat it generously. This helps disguise any cracks in the cake. Place in refrigerator. When ready to serve, cut away all visible waxed paper with a sharp knife, leaving a small strip under the roll. This may be discarded as the cake is served. To serve, cut into thick slices.

JELLY ROLL

Serves 8. Another cake, a favorite at the turn of the century, is a delicate jelly roll. Serve in thin slices, alone or accompanied by ice cream or fruit compote, or use it as the basis of the glorious Savoy Trifle (page 306).

HAVE ON HAND	COOKWARE
Cooking oil	Jelly roll pan *or* baking sheet
5 eggs	18 x 12 inches
Sugar	
All-purpose flour	
Vanilla	
Red currant jelly or raspberry jam	

1. *Oil* the baking sheet, line with waxed paper, and *oil* the paper evenly. Preheat oven to 350° F.

2. Separate *5 large eggs.* To the *egg yolks* add *4 tablespoons sugar;* beat until mixture is thick and pale in color. Carefully fold in *3 tablespoons flour.* Stir in *1 teaspoon vanilla.*

3. Beat the *egg whites* until thick and glossy, but be careful not to overbeat. The whites should be just stiff enough to hold a peak when the beater is withdrawn. Fold the egg-yolk batter into the egg whites gently but thoroughly.

4. Spread the batter evenly on the prepared baking sheet, and bake in the center of the preheated oven for 12 minutes, or until surface is a pale golden brown. Do not overbake. Remove from oven and sprinkle the surface lightly with *sugar.* Loosen waxed paper from the baking pan and turn the cake out onto a long sheet of waxed paper. Carefully peel waxed paper off bottom of cake. Spread with about *3 tablespoons of the jelly or jam,* and roll lengthwise into a long roll. Cut into thin slices to serve, or to use in the following recipe.

JUST A "LITTLE" SAVOY TRIFLE
(also known as Tipsy Pudding)

Serves 6

BUY

1 pink milk
3 containers heavy cream, 8 ounces each
1 dozen eggs

<table>
<tr><td>*HAVE ON HAND*</td><td>*COOKWARE*</td></tr>
</table>

HAVE ON HAND	COOKWARE
Sugar	2 heavy saucepans
Flour	
Vanilla	
Jelly Roll (page 305)	
Madeira *or* port wine	
Dark rum *or* cognac	
Confectioners' sugar	

1. MAKE PASTRY CREAM: In saucepan heat *2 cups milk* and *2 of the containers of cream* to steaming hot.

2. In another saucepan beat *9 egg yolks* (reserve the whites for another use) and *¾ cup sugar*. Beat in *½ cup flour*. Gradually beat in (use a wire whisk if possible) the hot milk-cream mixture; then cook over moderate heat, stirring rapidly, for about 2 minutes, or until cream is smooth and thick. Reduce heat to low and cook for 3 minutes longer. Be careful not to let the cream boil. If it starts to simmer around the edges, remove from heat but continue to stir. Cool, stirring occasionally; then stir in *1 tablespoon vanilla*.

3. Slice the *Jelly Roll* thinly, and line a 6 cup bowl with about half of the slices. Combine *¼ cup Madeira* or *port with ¼ cup rum or cognac*, and moisten the slices of jelly roll with half of this mixture. Pour in half the pastry cream and place a layer of jelly roll slices on top. Moisten with the remaining wine mixture and cover with remaining pastry cream. Cover top with remaining slices of jelly roll.

4. Chill the trifle. Before serving, beat the *third container of heavy cream* until stiff, and fold in *2 tablespoons confectioners' sugar* and *1 teaspoon vanilla*. Garnish the top of the trifle with the whipped cream. Serve with a large spoon, dipping deeply to bottom of bowl to include some of the jelly roll slices from bottom in each serving.

CHARLOTTE RUSSE

Serves 4 to 6. Still another famous combination of cake and cream is Charlotte Russe. It may be kept for a day in the refrigerator before serving, or it may be frozen. Remove it from the freezer about 3 hours before serving.

BUY

3-ounce package ladyfingers
1 pint heavy cream
Additional heavy cream for garnish (optional)

HAVE ON HAND	*COOKWARE*
Butter	1-quart mold
Unflavored gelatin	2-quart saucepan plus
Milk	pan of larger diameter
Confectioners' sugar	
Vanilla	

1. *Butter* a 1-quart charlotte or timbale mold and line bottom with waxed paper. Split the *ladyfingers*. Place a small round of ladyfinger in center of bottom of mold; then, working outward from the center, cover bottom with close-fitting triangles of ladyfingers. Arrange remaining ladyfingers upright and close together all around inside wall of mold. Set aside.

2. *Soften 2 tablespoons gelatin in ¼ cup cold water.*

3. In saucepan heat *1 cup milk.* Add the softened gelatin and stir until gelatin is thoroughly dissolved. Remove saucepan from heat and stir into milk mixture *⅔ cup confectioners' sugar* and *1 tablespoon vanilla.* Set the saucepan into a pan of ice water and stir constantly until cream begins to set and thicken.

4. Whip the *cream* until stiff. Beat the vanilla cream until light and fluffy, then fold in the whipped cream. Turn mixture into the prepared mold and chill until set.

5. When ready to serve, unmold onto serving plate and, if desired, garnish with *rosettes of whipped cream.*

STRAWBERRY BAVARIAN CREAM

Serves 8. Rich and delicate, this is another scrumptious French favorite. For variety, it may be molded in a 2-quart charlotte or timbale mold lined with ladyfingers, as in the preceding recipe, to make a Strawberry Charlotte Russe.

BUY

1 quart fresh strawberries
1 pint heavy cream
Additional berries and cream for garnish (optional)

HAVE ON HAND	*COOKWARE*
Lemon	Small saucepan plus pan of larger
Sugar	diameter
Unflavored gelatin	2-quart mold

1. Wash and hull *berries,* then force them through a sieve, or purée them in an electric blender. To this purée, add *1 tablespoon lemon juice* and *½ cup sugar;* stir until sugar is completely dissolved.

2. Soften *2 envelopes gelatin* in *¼ cup cold water,* then stir over hot water until gelatin is clear and thoroughly dissolved. Stir dissolved gelatin into the strawberry purée. Set mixture into a pan of cracked ice, or chill in refrigerator until it begins to thicken, stirring occasionally. Do not let it set.

3. Whip the *heavy cream* and fold into the strawberry mixture. Pour the dessert into a serving dish. Chill until set. If desired, chill the cream in a decorative mold.
To mold: Rinse a 2-quart mold with cold water. Pour in the mixture and chill for at least 2 hours.
To unmold: Run a knife around the edge of the cream to loosen it from the sides of the mold. Dip the mold slowly in and out of a pan of hot-to-the-hand water three times, being careful that the water does not flow over the side of the mold into the cream. Invert on chilled serving platter.

4. Garnish with whole strawberries and whipped cream, if desired.

COEUR À LA CRÈME

Serves 6. This favorite French dessert molds cream cheese into a heart shape and sets it in a sea of fresh strawberries. When served in traditional French manner, it is accompanied by crusty French bread and a slightly sweet wine or a *vin rosé.* You should have a heart-shaped basket in which to mold the cheese mixture and to allow the excess moisture, or *petit lait,* to drain from it while it chills.

BUY

1 pint small-curd cottage cheese
1 pound cream cheese
1 pint heavy cream
1 quart fresh strawberries
Small loaf French bread

HAVE ON HAND	*COOKWARE*
Salt	Heart-shaped basket mold
Cheesecloth	

1. Beat *cottage cheese* well with a rotary beater. Use an electric one if possible. Gradually add *the cream cheese,* beating constantly at high speed until all of it has been added and the mixture is smooth. Add *a dash of salt.* Reduce speed to medium and gradually beat in the *heavy cream.*

2. Line a heart-shaped basket mold with moist cheesecloth. Pour the blended cheese mixture into the lined mold. Place mold on a plate and store in the refrigerator overnight to drain.

3. To serve, unmold carefully on a chilled serving platter, and surround with *fresh strawberries.* Serve with *French bread.*

FLOATING ISLAND
(Oeufs à la Neige)

Serves 4 or 8. Here is my favorite custard dessert which should serve 8 but is so good that it serves only 4! It has a fancy French name but it is a real old-fashioned dish.

BUY

6 eggs
1 quart milk
8-ounce container heavy cream

HAVE ON HAND	*COOKWARE*
Lemon	Large skillet
Sugar	2-quart saucepan
Cornstarch	
Vanilla extract	

1. Separate *5 eggs,* and set the yolks aside. Beat the *egg whites* with *½ teaspoon lemon juice* until light and fluffy. Gradually beat in *⅔ cup sugar,* one tablespoon at a time, and continue to beat until you have a meringue that is glossy and holds a stiff peak when the beater is withdrawn.

2. In the skillet heat *2 cups milk,* the *heavy cream,* and *1 teaspoon vanilla* to simmering. Drop into the hot milk *heaping rounded spoonfuls of the meringue.* Let the meringues poach for 5 minutes. Turn with a slotted spoon and poach for 5 minutes longer. The milk must not boil, just barely simmer. Remove the cooked meringues with a slotted spoon to paper toweling to drain.

3. Strain the milk mixture into a quart measuring cup, then add *enough milk to make a total of 2½ cups liquid.*

4. Beat *the 5 egg yolks* with *4 tablespoons sugar, 2 teaspoons cornstarch,* and *1 teaspoon vanilla* until sugar is dissolved; then gradually beat in the hot milk mixture.

5. Pour the custard into the saucepan and cook over quite high heat, stirring vigorously, until it begins to steam. Remove from heat, but continue to stir. Repeat this cooking and stirring until custard is thick enough to coat the spoon. It will be thin, but will set a little as it cools. It should NOT be a thick custard, rather a custard sauce.

6. Pour the hot custard sauce into a serving bowl and pile the meringues on top. Cool, then chill until ready to serve.

SOUR CREAM CHEESECAKE

Serves 6

BUY

1 pound cream cheese
Box of graham crackers
1 pint dairy sour cream

HAVE ON HAND

Butter
Sugar

Cinnamon
Lemon
2 eggs

COOKWARE

Small saucepan
9-inch pie plate

1. Set *cream cheese* out at room temperature to soften. Melt *6 tablespoons butter* in small saucepan over low heat. Preheat oven to 325° F.

2. Crumb *16 graham crackers,* then mix them with *½ cup sugar, ½ teaspoon cinnamon,* and *4 tablespoons of the melted butter.* Line the pie plate with the crumbs.

3. In large mixing bowl mash the cream cheese with *½ cup sugar, 1 tablespoon lemon juice,* and *2 eggs.* Gradually beat in *1½ cups of the sour cream* and continue to beat until mixture is smooth. Beat in the *remaining 2 tablespoons melted butter.*

4. Pour mixture into the crumb-lined pan and bake in the preheated oven for 30 to 40 minutes, or until set in center. The filling will still be very soft but will firm as it cools. Chill thoroughly before serving.

CRÊPES, those delicate, paper-thin pancakes which are such fun to make, are just about perfection as a dessert. They may be served hot from the crêpe pan with a simple sprinkling of fine granulated sugar and a squeeze of lemon juice. Or they may be made well in advance (they freeze well and defrost quickly) and rolled around any number of sweet fillings. The latter process results in especially luxurious desserts.

The technique for making crêpes is included in the chapter on appetizers (see page 68). The batter is almost the same and a little sugar is added.

DESSERT CRÊPES

Makes 18 to 20 crêpes

HAVE ON HAND

All-purpose flour
Sugar
Salt
3 eggs

COOKWARE

5- *or* 6-inch crêpe pan

Milk
Butter
Cognac

1. Combine *1 cup flour, 4 tablespoons sugar,* and *a dash of salt.* In separate bowl beat *3 eggs,* then stir in *1½ cups milk.* Gradually stir egg-milk mixture into the dry ingredients, and continue to stir until batter is smooth. It should have the consistency of heavy cream and just coat the spoon.

2. Add *1 tablespoon each of melted butter and cognac.*

3. Strain the batter through a fine sieve to remove any lumps which might remain.

4. Let batter stand for 1 to 2 hours before using it. This improves the texture of the crêpes.

5. To COOK THE CRÊPES: Heat crêpe pan until very hot. Crêpes must cook quickly, otherwise they may become tough. Put *½ teaspoon butter* in pan, and swirl pan to coat bottom and sides with butter. Pour in about *2 tablespoons crêpe batter,* and again tilt pan with a circular motion to spread batter evenly and thinly to the edges. This must be done quickly before the batter has a chance to set. Cook crêpes for about 1 minute, or until set and brown on one side. Turn and brown the other side. Tip the crêpe out onto waxed paper to cool.

CRÊPES TRIUMPHANTE

Serves 4. Here is my interpretation of the ultra-rich crêpes dessert served at the Forum of the Twelve Caesars in New York City.

HAVE ON HAND	*COOKWARE*
1 orange	10-inch skillet
Butter	
Sugar	
Cognac	
2 squares (2 ounces) bitter chocolate	
Vanilla ice cream	
8 crêpes (page 312)	
Toasted slivered almonds	

1. Cut rind from ½ *orange* in one continuous piece, just as in peeling an apple.

2. In the skillet melt *4 tablespoons butter*. Add *6 tablespoons sugar* and *the spiral of orange rind,* and cook over medium heat, stirring constantly, until the mixture caramelizes to a dark brown color.

3. Immediately squeeze in about *2 tablespoons orange juice* from the half orange, and add *½ cup cognac*. Set the cognac aflame and as soon as the flame dies out, discard orange rind and add the *2 squares of bitter chocolate*. Cook, stirring, until chocolate is melted and the sauce is smooth.

4. Put a large spoonful of *vanilla ice cream* on the lower third of each crêpe, and roll the crêpes into cylinders.

5. Place two rolls side by side on each serving plate, cover with the hot chocolate sauce, and sprinkle with *almonds*.

Fruit and berries make delicious fillings for crêpes. Fresh strawberries and stewed lingonberries are especially good. Imported jars of lingonberries are sold in many food specialty shops. If you can't find them, you may substitute stewed and sweetened cranberries or cranberry preserves.

CRÊPES WITH STRAWBERRIES AND CURAÇAO

Serves 6

BUY

1 pint fresh strawberries
8-ounce container heavy cream
1 pint vanilla ice cream
4-ounce can toasted slivered almonds

HAVE ON HAND	COOKWARE
Butter	10-inch heavy skillet
Sugar	
Curaçao	
Maraschino, framboise, *or* kirsch	
6 crêpes (page 312)	

1. Wash, hull, and halve the *berries*. Whip the *heavy cream* and refrigerate until needed.

2. In skillet melt *½ cup butter.* Add *2 tablespoons sugar* and *3 table-spoons Curaçao.* Heat to simmering. Add the strawberries; cook, stirring, until berries and their juice are warm.

3. Add *½ cup maraschino, framboise, or kirsch* and set aflame.

4. When the flame burns out, dip a *crêpe* into the sauce, turning it to coat both sides. Roll it around a scoop of *vanilla ice cream,* place on serving dish, and top with the strawberries and their sauce. Garnish each serving with a dollop of the whipped cream and sprinkle with almonds.

CRÊPES WITH LINGONBERRIES

Sprinkle a *crêpe* thickly with *confectioners' sugar* and lightly with a little *powdered cinnamon* and *lemon juice.* Spread with *hot lingonberries* and roll into a cylinder. Place 2 crêpes on each serving plate, pour over *1 ounce warm Jamaica rum,* and serve flaming.

Homemade Ice Cream & Sherbet

In keeping with the trend toward honest, wholesome, unadulterated food is the revival of making ice cream at home. The old-fashioned hand-cranked ice-cream freezer invented sometime around 1840 by a woman named Nancy Johnson is still the most common device used for making homemade ice cream—with all members of the family or commune taking turns at the crank. Now there are also the new electric ice-cream freezers, which do an admirable job and require much less effort than the hand-crank ones.

I became an ice-cream enthusiast in the past year when a friend presented me with a recipe for Buttermilk Ice Cream. It sounded so intriguing that I invested in an electric ice-cream freezer, and since then I have made many daring combinations into frozen creams and sherbets—all delicious and all a heck of a lot better and less expensive than even the best of the commercial ones. Naturally, now I heartily recommend *everyone* getting on the homemade-ice-cream band wagon.

With a couple of basic formulas, it's almost impossible to go wrong, and the varieties of flavors and textures are innumerable, limited only by one's imagination. I'll begin the recipes with the one that captured my interest. But first, a few basic how-to's:

HOW TO MAKE ICE CREAM IN AN ELECTRIC OR HAND-CRANK FREEZER

Don't make a big production out of it unless you want to—it can all be so simple. You don't need to crack or crush ice. Just use ice cubes—but you'll need a lot of them on hand in order to keep the bucket filled at all times. You don't need rock salt, either. It's cheaper, of course, but table salt works just as well.

1. Read the instructions, in the booklet that comes with the freezer, as to assembling, cleaning, and caring for the freezer.

2. Wash ice-cream can, cover, and dasher in hot soapy water, and rinse thoroughly in hot, then cold, water.

3. Have all liquid ingredients or fruit purées cold before combining them in the freezer can.

4. Insert dasher in can.

5. Put ingredients in the can, filling it only ¾ full so that there will be room for the mixture to expand. Position the can in the freezer, and then add the cover.

6. Position the motor or hand-crank unit over the can, and lock it in place.

7. Fill the bucket with layers of ice cubes and salt, alternating each

2 inches of ice with 3 tablespoons salt until ice and salt are level with top of can. As the brine settles, add more ice and salt.

8. Allow the ice cream to churn for 30 to 60 minutes, or until either the motor slows or stops or the hand crank becomes difficult to turn. Freezing time varies according to the type of ice-cream mixture being churned, the temperature of the mix before it was put into the can, and the amount of salt used. If too much salt is used, the cream will freeze too quickly and end up with a coarse texture.

9. When ice cream is the consistency of whipped cream or mush, it's ready either to be ripened or hardened or to be spooned out onto plates and enjoyed as "soft" ice cream.

10. Clear away ice and salt from around can cover. Remove motor or crank, then wipe cover free of any salt and remove. Lift out dasher and scrape clean with a rubber spatula.

TO RIPEN OR HARDEN ICE CREAM:

The easiest way to do this is in your food freezer, if you have one. Re-cover the ice-cream can, put a cork in the hole in the cover, and put the can in the freezer. Or, you can spoon the mush into plastic containers, allowing ⅛ inch of space at the top for expansion, then cover with tight-fitting lids and freeze.

If you don't have a freezer, push the ice cream down into the can, cover with aluminum foil, replace cover, and put a cork in the hole. Drain the brine from the bucket, and add salt and ice to completely cover can and lid. For insulation, put a few newspapers on top of the bucket. Let the ice cream ripen for 2 to 3 hours.

HOW MUCH SALT AND ICE?

For a gallon container, you will need approximately *20 pounds of ice cubes* and a total of *3 cups table salt* (1½ cups while churning the ice cream and 1½ cups while ripening it). If you use *rock salt,* you will need a total of *5 cups*.

AD LIB ICE CREAM (General Formula)

Almost any combination is possible: The liquid can include a combination of cream plus milk, sour cream, yogurt, or buttermilk, eggs, and fruit juice and/or fruit purée. Then add sugar and flavoring. Some heavy cream should be used for a smooth texture, and the more heavy cream you use, of course, the richer and more delicious the ice cream.

For 1 gallon of ice cream you will need:

10 cups total liquid
2 cups sugar, white *or* brown
2 tablespoons vanilla extract *or* other flavoring

Try the following basic recipes, then let your imagination take over.

BUTTERMILK ICE CREAM

Makes almost 4 quarts, and costs less then 50¢ per quart!

In freezer can, churn together:

1½ quarts buttermilk
1 pint half-and-half
1 cup heavy cream
2 cups sugar
1 to 2 tablespoons vanilla extract

BASIC CUSTARD ICE CREAM

Makes 4 quarts

In freezer can, churn together:

4 eggs
2 cups sugar, white *or* light brown
5 cups milk
4 cups heavy cream
2 tablespoons vanilla extract

LIGHT-AND-EASY ICE CREAM

Makes 4 quarts

In freezer can, churn together:

10 cups light cream *or* half-and-half
2 cups sugar
2 tablespoons vanilla extract

BASIC COOKED-CUSTARD VANILLA ICE CREAM

Makes 1 gallon

In saucepan combine *2 cups sugar, 6 tablespoons flour,* and *a dash of salt.* Slowly stir in *5 cups hot milk* and cook over low heat for about 10 minutes, stirring constantly, until mixture is thickened.

Beat *6 eggs* with *a little of the hot milk mixture;* add to *remaining milk mixture* and cook for 1 minute longer, stirring rapidly. Cool; then chill in refrigerator.

In freezer can, churn together the *chilled custard* and *4 cups heavy cream.*

FRESH FRUIT ICE CREAM

In basic recipes, substitute 3 to 4 cups puréed fresh fruit, such as peaches, strawberries, or raspberries, for an equal quantity of the milk or light cream specified in the recipe.

FROZEN FRUIT ICE CREAM

Defrost three 12-ounce packages frozen peaches, strawberries, or raspberries and mash thoroughly. Substitute the mashed fruit for 4 cups of the milk or light cream, and reduce amount of sugar to 1½ cups.

CHOCOLATE SWIRL ICE CREAM

Swirl 2 cups chocolate sauce through ice cream after dasher is removed. Repack and allow to ripen.

PRUNE WALNUT ICE CREAM

Makes 3 quarts

Put *12 ounces pitted prunes* in *water to cover* and cook until soft. Purée prunes and liquid in electric blender or press them through a food mill. Chill the purée. You will have about 2 cups. In freezer can, churn together:

The chilled prune purée
4 cups half-and-half
1 cup heavy cream
2 eggs
1½ cups brown sugar
1 tablespoon vanilla
½ cup broken walnuts

APRICOT YOGURT ICE CREAM

Makes 1 gallon

Simmer *11 ounces dried apricots* in *1 quart water* for 30 minutes. Mash the apricots or purée them in a blender or a food mill. You will have about 3 cups purée. Chill. In freezer can, churn together:

The chilled apricot purée
1 pint plain yogurt
1 quart buttermilk
1 cup heavy cream

BANANA ICE CREAM

Makes 2 quarts

In freezer can, churn together:

5 bananas, sliced and slightly mashed
3 cups heavy cream
1 pint half-and-half *or* light cream
1 cup sugar
2 tablespoons vanilla

BITTER-CHOCOLATE ICE CREAM

Makes 1 gallon

In advance, heat *5 squares (ounces) unsweetened chocolate* and *5 cups milk* until scalding. In another, larger saucepan beat *4 eggs,* then stir in *2 cups sugar, 5 tablespoons flour,* and *dash of salt.* Pour the hot chocolate milk over the egg mixture, stirring constantly, and cook over low heat just until mixture thickens enough to coat the spoon. Be careful not to let it boil. Cool the chocolate custard, then chill. In freezer can, churn together:

The chilled chocolate custard
5 cups light *or* heavy cream
1 tablespoon vanilla

THREE-IN-ONE SHERBET

Makes 3 quarts

In advance, boil *1½ cups sugar* and *3 cups water or cranberry juice cocktail* for 5 minutes. Cool, then chill. In freezer can, churn together:

The chilled syrup
3 large bananas, sliced
1-pound can crushed pineapple
½ cup lemon juice
1 cup orange juice
3 egg whites beaten until stiff but still glossy

LEMON ICE

Makes 2 quarts

In advance, combine *1½ cups sugar* and *1 cup water* in saucepan. Bring to a boil and simmer for 5 minutes. Cool then chill. In freezer can, churn together:

The chilled syrup
¾ cup lemon juice
2 teaspoons grated lemon rind
4 cups water

FOR LEMON SHERBET

Add to above ingredients *2 egg whites* beaten until stiff but still glossy.

MINT SHERBET

Makes 2 quarts

In advance, combine *1½ cups sugar* and *2 cups water* in saucepan. Bring slowly to a boil and simmer for 5 minutes. Shred *2 cups fresh mint leaves*. Add to the boiling hot syrup, cover and cool, then chill. In freezer can, churn together:

The chilled mint syrup
1 cup lemon juice
2 cups water
A couple of drops of green food coloring
4 egg whites beaten until stiff but still glossy

PARFAIT AU CAFÉ

Makes 2 quarts

In freezer can, churn together:

1 cup sugar
1 cup strong black coffee
8 egg yolks, beaten
3 cups heavy cream, whipped

With homemade ice cream in your freezer and a few good dessert sauces in the refrigerator, you can make any number of fancy coupes, parfaits, and other yummy ice-cream desserts for gala occasions—or simply to please the family. By the way, those big brandy snifters that you use so rarely make elegant containers for these fun and fancy desserts.

RASPBERRY SAUCE

Makes 1 cup

Defrost a *10-ounce package frozen raspberries.* Purée in an electric blender, and strain to remove the seeds; or press the defrosted berries through a food mill. Stir *¼ cup sugar or sugar to taste* into the purée.

RICH CHOCOLATE SAUCE FOR ICE CREAM

Makes 2 cups

This sauce will keep in the refrigerator for several weeks. Into a small saucepan empty *6 ounces semi-sweet chocolate pieces.* Add *1 cup cream, 1 cup light brown sugar,* and *4 tablespoons grated orange rind,* and stir over low heat until chocolate is melted and sauce is smooth. Remove from heat and, if desired, stir in *4 tablespoons Jamaica rum.*

❀

CHERRIES JUBILEE

Serves 4 to 6

BUY

1 pound dark sweet cherries

HAVE ON HAND

Sugar
Cornstarch
Kirsch *or* cognac
Vanilla ice cream

1. Wash stem, and pit the *cherries.*

2. In saucepan combine *1 cup sugar* and *½ cup water.* Bring to a boil and boil rapidly for 5 minutes. Add cherries and simmer for 5 minutes.

3. Combine *2 teaspoons cornstarch* and *1 tablespoon water;* add to cherries. Cook, stirring constantly, for 1 minute longer, or until syrup is clear and slightly thickened.

4. Just before serving, add *2 ounces kirsch or cognac,* ignite the liquor, and serve the flaming cherries over vanilla ice cream.

CARAMEL PECAN DESSERT

Cook *an unopened can of sweetened condensed milk* in *boiling water to cover* for 2 hours. Cool before opening. The milk will have turned to a rich caramel sauce which will keep for several weeks in the refrigerator. Break *ladyfingers* into a serving dish, add *a scoop of vanilla ice cream,* cover with the *caramel sauce,* sprinkle with *pecan halves,* and top with *whipped cream!*

APPENDIX

Everyone Should Know
a Little About Nutrition

Good health is the greatest asset anyone can have. Without it we cannot go about our daily work or play with enthusiasm and pleasure, and no single factor is more important to the achievement and maintenance of good health than nutrition. Therefore it is important that everyone know a little about the subject, for the kinds of food we eat can make the difference between feeling just all right and radiant good health, true *joie de vivre*.

Generally speaking, as I have said before, good food is nutritious food, and the more flavorful it is, the more nutritious it is. Yet, a knowledge of the essentials of nutrition, and an understanding of how they work, can bring about a revolutionary improvement in health and vitality and can do much to alleviate the stresses and strains of modern-day living.

So whether you bought this book for economy reasons, because you are a vegetarian, or just because you enjoy good food, you should have a nutritional blueprint from which you can build your daily menus, and I'm going to try to give it to you. This does not mean that you cannot eat the dishes you enjoy most; it simply means that you should combine these favorite dishes in balanced meals that contain all the essential nutrients that your body requires.

The subject of nutrition today is especially important, for our vegetables are grown on exhausted soil, chemically fertilized, sprayed with pesticides, then travel long exhausting miles from processor to warehouse, from warehouse to market. Our grains are processed to remove the germ and along with it a dozen or more essential nutrients contained in the germ, then bleached to further rob them of more valuable properties. Stabilizers, dyes, emulsifiers, and other chemicals are added to our foods, some containing as much as twenty or more different chemical additives. Our bean and seed oils and our nut butters are hydrogenated, and our frozen products are mishandled in transportation and at their destination, so that serious thawing can and does take place.

Therefore we must work intelligently at supplying our bodies each day with the nutrients they require. Forty such nutrients are known.

Supplementing our meals with vitamin pills can assure us of an adequate supply of these, BUT it is more than possible that forty or more additional essential nutrients are still undiscovered, and these can be supplied only by natural, unrefined foods. Nature has a way of putting all living substances together in pretty perfect packages, with all the nutrients in the correct proportion one to the other to nurture and sustain life. A lack of any one of the essential nutrients can result in the underproduction of an estimated ten thousand compounds that work together in perfect harmony to give us good health, vitality, and longevity.

OUR DAILY MEALS SHOULD INCLUDE THE BIG FIVE

These are complete proteins, carbohydrates (starches and sugars), fats (essential fatty acids), vitamins, and minerals. Let's deal with each of these individually.

PROTEINS PROVIDE THE MATERIAL NEEDED FOR OUR BODIES TO BUILD AND REPAIR LIVING TISSUE

All living tissue—nails, hair, skin, muscles—are made of proteins, and without them our bodies cannot replace the cells which are constantly dying.

There are two types of proteins: complete proteins, such as eggs, milk and milk products, and liver and other organ foods, such as muscle meats, fish, seafood, fowl, wheat germ, soy beans or soy flour, and natural cheeses. These contain all the essential amino acids, of which there are twenty-two known. Digestion breaks protein foods down into these acids, so the body can use what it needs.

Other grains, beans, and most nuts are incomplete protein, lacking some of the amino acids, and are of food value only when combined with a complete protein food.

Half as many grams of complete protein as our ideal weight are needed daily. If your normal weight is one hundred twenty pounds, you need sixty grams of protein; if your normal weight is one hundred eighty pounds, then you need ninety grams of protein. So it is just is important that you learn to count grams of proteins as it is calories.

If you are not a big meat eater, or do not eat meat at all, a good way to ensure adequate protein is to eat wheat germ or soy granules in preference to other breakfast cereals, and to add these highly nutritious natural grains to muffins, breads, pancakes, waffles, omelets, scrambled eggs, and vegetable croquettes and loaves. One-half cup of wheat germ contains twenty-four grams of complete proteins, and a half cup of soy granules contains thirty grams. Another easy way is to add natural desiccated liver tablets to your diet, along with natural grains, legumes, and nuts, combined with eggs and milk products.

CARBOHYDRATES SUPPLY BODY ENERGY

These are the sugars and starches, which are converted into sugar in in our intestines and supply very necessary body energy. They are normally associated with problems of overweight, and rightly so if we are thinking of the refined flours that go into commercial baked goods, cookies, pastries, and packaged mixes, or the refined white sugars used in candy, soft drinks, and in tea and coffee. These are "empty" carbohydrates that have been robbed of their natural vitamins and minerals. When such carbohydrates are eaten, the blood-sugar level rises quickly, but the body cannot assimilate them, so they are stored as fat and the blood-sugar level drops quickly, leaving fatigue in its path.

On the other hand there are GOOD carbohydrates, the natural ones containing B vitamins, which the body needs to "burn" or metabolize them into body energy. These are found in whole grains and whole-grain cereals, potatoes, fresh fruits and juices, dried fruits, honey, molasses, and brown sugars. Some of these natural carbohydrates should be included at each meal for balanced diet, even if only in small amounts. When proteins and some fat are included in a meal with some natural carbohydrates, the blood-sugar level rises slowly and the level of energy is properly maintained.

Is it so very difficult to substitute good starches and sugars in place of empty ones? It really isn't, and if weight is a serious problem, learn moderation not only in your intake of carbohydrates, but of all foods.

GOOD CARBOHYDRATES	EMPTY CARBOHYDRATES
Whole grains and cereals	"Enriched" cereals
Breads made from whole grains	Commercial white bread
Root vegetables, such as yams	Canned fruits
Potatoes	Soft drinks
Fresh fruits and juices	Instant puddings and desserts
Dried fruits	Commercial candy
Pure maple syrup and maple sugar	Refined white sugar
Honey	Packaged mixes
Dark molasses	Ready-whipped toppings
Brown sugars	
Unrefined crystallized sugars	
Malted-milk tablets	

FATS COMBINE WITH PHOSPHORUS TO FORM EVERY CELL

Just as there are good and bad carbohydrates, there are good and bad fats, and the right kinds are essential to stimulate the flow of bile and promote good health.

The bad fats are the saturated ones such as the hard or solid fats on meats and margarines, lards, and hydrogenated cooking fats, which cannot dissolve in the blood at body temperature. These are the fats that turn into a fatty substance known as cholesterol which is deposited on the walls of the arteries, narrowing the channels through which the blood passes and decreasing circulation. When such a condition exists in the body it is known as atherosclerosis and, if not corrected, can result in premature senility, strokes, or death by heart attack.

The good fats are the unsaturated liquid fats from vegetables. In these clear liquid oils are essential fatty acids which are necessary to utilize cholesterol and the saturated fats. According to the noted nutritionist, Adelle Davis, the most essential of fatty acid is linoleic acid—contained in safflower seeds and oil—which if sufficient, and with the help of many vitamins and minerals, can synthesize the two other essential fatty acids and increase a substance in the blood known as lecithin, an agent which emulsifies cholesterol and breaks it down into minute particles. These particles are small enough to be held in suspension in the blood and can then pass through the walls of the arteries and be utilized in the tissues.

Lecithin is naturally available in such food products as egg yolks, liver, some nuts, soy oil, and wheat germ oil and is available in capsule form. However, it can also be manufactured in our bodies from the essential fatty acids, the B vitamins known as choline and inositol vitamin B 6 (pyridoxine), plus magnesium and other nutrients found in a balanced diet.

GOOD FATS

Safflower oil
Poppy-seed and sesame-seed oils
Sunflower seed oil
Soybean and corn oil
Peanut oil
Wheat germ oil
Peanut butter (natural)
Mayonnaise (made of the above oils)
Fresh butter and cream

BAD FATS

Hard animal fats on roasts and chops
Hydrogenated fats
Hard oil margarines or peanut butters
Processed cheeses

A most enjoyable way to include essential fatty acids in the daily diet is by tossing salads with your own dressing made of wine vinegar or lemon juice and a mixture of fresh vegetable oils. They must be fresh, for even a slight rancidity in oils can destroy many of the nutrients. Buy the oils in small quantities and combine in one jar equal parts of safflower, soy, peanut, and olive oil (for flavor). Use the mixture for both salads and cooking.

To dress vegetables and for a spread on breads and biscuits, fresh butter should be used in preference to margarine. With an adequate supply of linoleic acid, there is no need whatsoever to hold back on butter and rich cream sauces. Again, if you are a weight watcher, just use in moderation.

VITAMINS AND MINERALS REGULATE BODY PROCESSES AND ARE ESSENTIAL FOR HEALTH AND GROWTH

VITAMIN A

This important vitamin is needed to prevent certain infections, to promote appetite, digestion, and longevity and to maintain vigor. It aids in the development of body cells, prevents night blindness, and keeps the skin healthy. The best natural sources of vitamin A are: liver, fish-liver oils, eggs, butter, cream, whole milk, dark-green leafy vegetables, carrots, apricots, cantaloupe, papaya, prunes, sweet potatoes, winter squash, and Swiss or Roquefort-type cheeses.

Nobody really knows how many units of vitamin A a person should consume each day, but it's possible that as many as fifty thousand units are not too many. In order to supply this amount in natural foods, a person would have to consume four and one-half pounds of butter or three and one-half quarts of heavy cream, four dozen eggs, three cups of cooked diced carrots or dried apricots, or one quart of steamed spinach! It's obviously easier to depend on a single vitamin A capsule each day.

VITAMIN C

This is another very important vitamin that is difficult to consume in adequate amounts via the table. One hundred mgs. daily are adequate, but more—even a great deal more—cannot do any harm, for it is a water-soluble vitamin and is expelled in the urine. It is generally believed that the body is unable to store it and therefore it is better taken several times daily in small doses.

Vitamin C is necessary for the health of the tissues which surround and cushion bones and joints and for healthy bones, gums, teeth, and capillary walls. It speeds up the production of natural cortisones in the body, and guards against infections of the head and chest and some allergies, especially those produced by insect bites. It is especially important in the detoxification of dangerous substances formed in the body during times of stress.

The best natural sources of vitamin C are citrus juices, strawberries, raw green peppers, dark-green leafy vegetables, avocados, tomatoes, pineapple, cantaloupe, bean sprouts, and rose hips, and it is available as ascorbic acid in tablets ranging from fifty to five hundred mgs. each.

Vitamin D

The "sunshine" vitamin regulates the metabolism of calcium and phosphorus, the elements that form strong bones and teeth. The body manufactures its own vitamin D in the skin from the direct rays of the sun. Twenty-five hundred units of vitamin D daily are not too much. This is more than the amount recommended by the Food and Nutrition Board, but the daily allowances suggested by various government agencies are based on simply staying alive and not necessarily on promoting vigorous health. If your body cannot absorb or use twenty-five hundred units, any excess is detoxified by vitamin C.

The best sources of vitamin D are: fish-liver oils, irradiated vegetable oils, yeast, canned salmon, moderate sun tanning in summer, and careful use of a sun lamp in winter months.

Vitamin E

After forty years of intensive research, this vitamin is the last to be officially recognized as nutritionally necessary, and may turn out to be one of the most important of all vitamins to children and adults for reproduction and longevity. It is known to supply vascular muscle tone, and recent experiments indicate that it may be a possible cure for gout and for muscular distrophy. Although no minimum daily requirement has yet been set for vitamin E, most doctors recommend at least one hundred units of water-soluble vitamin E per day for adults. It is found naturally in eggs and wheat germ.

Vitamin K

This is the vitamin responsible for the clotting of blood and is normally manufactured in the body by intestinal bacteria. In synthetic form it should only be taken on the advice of a doctor. The best food sources of vitamin K are all green leafy vegetables and vegetables belonging to the cabbage family.

THE VITAMIN B COMPLEX

And complex it is indeed, so I have left it until the last of the vitamins to explain. More than fifteen different nutrients make up the B complex, which is necessary to convert sugar to energy, and a lack of it can produce great fatigue and accompanying irritability.

No complete B complex is available in tablet form, so supplements of any of the B vitamins should be taken only if accompanied by natural foods which are a source of the complete complex. These are liver, wheat germ, yeast, whole grains, and soy beans.

However, by the simple expedient of developing sound eating habits, the B complex can be quite easily supplied via our daily meals. And these sound eating habits include fortifying breads, pancakes, waffles, and muffins with wheat germ and powdered milk, AND it means including the occasional cup of yogurt for a snack or as a dessert.

WHY YOGURT?

All the B vitamins can be synthesized in the intestines by means of the bacteria found in yogurt. These are lactic acid organisms which destroy the harmful·bacteria that produce gas and odor. Once you supply your system with these organisms, in much the same way as you seed your garden, they will grow and thrive for a long time providing they are well fed. They are nurtured by the cellulose found in whole-grain cereals and raw vegetables and on the milk sugars readily available in powdered or malted milk, in buttermilk, or in yogurt itself. They provide your body with the ability to manufacture the B complex, including the essential vitamin, pantothenic acid, or calcium pantothenate.

So stock your system with the valuable organisms found in yogurt and maintain these organisms and keep them vigorous with the cellulose in raw vegetables and natural grains and with milk sugars.

THE MOST IMPORTANT VITAMINS IN THE B COMPLEX
AND THEIR FUNCTIONS AND SOURCES

Vitamin	*Function*	*Best Natural Sources*
VITAMIN B 1 (thiamin)	For the relief of fatigue and depression	Salad greens, eggs, meats, nuts, seeds, soybeans, and brewer's yeast
VITAMIN B 2 (riboflavin)	For healthy nerves and skin, good blood, and normal functions	Nuts, eggs, milk, molasses, green vegetables, liver, poultry, and fish

VITAMIN B 6 (pyridoxine)	For metabolism of fats	Nuts, milk, and eggs
VITAMIN B 12	For prevention of anemia	Eggs, milk, yogurt, and liver
NIACIN	For healthy nerves, skin, and digestion	Powdered milk, peanuts, seeds, whole grains, fish, and lean meats
PARA-AMINOBENZOIC ACID	For preventing allergies and graying hair	Fish, fruits, nuts, and whole grains
CALCIUM PANTOTHENATE (Pantothenic Acid)	Essential to every cell in the body, keeps the glands alive and active, and contributes to healthy digestive system	Eggs, molasses, peanuts, lean beef, salmon, potatoes, and vegetables belonging to the cabbage family
INOSITOL AND CHOLINE	Metabolize fats and are essential in preventing the accumulation of cholesterol in the arteries	Whole grains, fruits, seeds, peanuts, liver, yeast, wheat germ, and lecithin (eggs)

WHAT ABOUT MINERALS?

The organic substances in our foods, the proteins, fats and carbohydrates, are constantly forming acids, such as lactic acid and carbonic acid, but in addition to these acid-producing foods, there are seven acid-producing minerals, such as sulphur which forms sulphuric acid, phosphorus which forms phosphoric acid, and others.

Dr. Louis Berman explains in his *Food and Character* that there are seven alkaline minerals which assume a most important role in nutrition by counteracting overacidity. These are sodium, potassium, calcium, magnesium, iron, manganese, and copper, but the most important of these are the first four—sodium, potassium, calcium, and magnesium. The latter three are important to the manufacture of red blood cells in the marrow of the bone. If our bodies are deficient in any one of this important trio, anemia can result.

In addition to balancing the chemical composition of the cells, each of the minerals has other duties to perform. Calcium, for instance, combined with phosphorus and vitamin D makes strong bones and teeth.

Phosphorus soothes nerves and quickens muscular responses through the brain. The intake of phosphorus should not be more than one-third higher than the intake of calcium.

Magnesium is associated with cellular functions and needed to synthesize lecithin. The intake of this mineral should not be more than half that of calcium. The magnesium content in raw foods, however, can be destroyed by the use of chemical fertilizers containing potassium, which prevents plants from absorbing magnesium. It may be further reduced by refining processes, so it is often difficult for this important mineral to be obtained in sufficient quantities from our daily foods.

Iodine is needed to regulate the function of the thyroid gland, while iron increases energy, encourages the body's economy of several of the vitamins, and is necessary for the formation of the red blood-cell pigment.

In general fruits, vegetables, and salad greens furnish most of the alkali-producing minerals, while cereals and animal foods contain mostly acid ones. Milk and milk products are the best sources of calcium and phosphorus (one quart of milk furnishes one thousand mgs. of calcium and nine hundred mgs. of phosphorus). Iodized salt, kelp, fish, and seafood supply adequate iodine, and iron is present in good quantities in liver, eggs, wheat germ, yeast, soybeans, lentils, and molasses.

Eggs are by far the richest source of sulphur, containing the important amino acid methionine, and seafoods and yeast are dependable sources of the trace minerals—copper, manganese, zinc, cobalt, and others that are poorly absorbed by vegetables growing in commercially fertilized soil.

WHAT YOU SHOULD KNOW ABOUT DRUGS

Any drug, even one as mild as aspirin, is toxic to some extent, preventing the absorption of nutrients in the body and increasing their excretion. In large amounts, drugs can cause serious dietary deficiencies and damage to the kidneys and liver.

An adequate diet can do much to offset drug toxicity, and it's not a bad idea at all to accompany any drug with a 250 mg. tablet of ascorbic acid (vitamin C).

During infections or any illness calling for the use of antibiotics, adequate vitamin E is also recommended, and the time-honored practice of serving eggnogs to the ill and feverish should never be forgotten. Nor should we forget to replenish our systems with the yogurt bacteria during illness and the recovery period, for while the twentieth-century miracle drugs destroy many otherwise killing bacteria, they also destroy the beneficial bacteria in the intestines which can be resupplied by yogurt and which, if not replenished, can result in a serious deficiency of the vitamin B complex.

WHAT ABOUT ALCOHOL AND COFFEE?

Alcohol and coffee are both drugs but, just as I believe you can eat whatever you want to eat providing you include essentials to balance the diet, I feel that a quiet, relaxing cocktail before dinner can do much to stimulate the appetite, relax frazzled nerves, and alleviate the stresses and strains of an average busy day, and that alcohol in moderation is probably more beneficial than harmful.

You should know, however, in case you are a heavy drinker that alcohol contains a lot of "empty" calories, which are quickly deposited in the body as fat, and not only slows down the flow of blood but can cause the amount of cholesterol in the blood to double. Alcohol also increases the excretion of all the water-soluble vitamins and minerals, especially magnesium. So, if you are a heavy drinker, at least take the precaution to eat the right foods and supplement your diet with vitamin and mineral pills.

It may be that the caffeine in coffee, especially in the instant varieties, may prove to be more harmful to one's system than alcohol. But, again, I cannot advocate complete abstinence from something as truly wonderful as a good cup of coffee. I can suggest however that you serve and drink only coffee brewed from freshly ground beans, freshly made, and served for breakfast as it is done in France—half hot, strong coffee and half hot milk. And if you add sugar, take a tip from the Latin-American countries and use unrefined crystallized sugar, or brown sugar, or even honey. Honey is a delicious sweetener for freshly brewed tea.

DRINK A LITTLE WINE FOR THY STOMACH'S SAKE

Louis Pasteur said that wine "is the most healthful and hygenic of beverages." Unhappily, in the United States wine is classified as a liquor, whose main purpose is to intoxicate rather than to be used as a food, which is where it should be placed. Throughout the ages man has looked on wine as food. Even Noah cultivated grapes for wine, and Isaiah made the promise, "Until I come and take you away to a land like your own land, a land of corn and wine, a land of bread and vineyards."

The process of fermentation is a natural phenomenon which transforms grape juice into wine, and grape juice is a healthful, fragrant solution of water, grape sugars, acids, vitamins B and C, and many minerals, particularly potassium.

Harold Grossman, in his invaluable *Guide,* writes that wine has been looked upon as a natural remedy for man's ills since earliest days. In ancient times it was invaluable to physicians whose medical knowledge was limited, and European doctors still prescribe various wines in cases of arteriosclerosis, constipation, diarrhea, malaria, pneumonia, and illnesses of the liver, kidneys, and gall bladder.

Fortified wines, such as sherry, Madeira, port, and Tokay, all rich in minerals, are easily assimilated and are most helpful to people who are run down and fatigued. Grandmother knew well the value of red wine as a cure for anemia.

In France, wine is called the "milk of the aged," and claret forms a part of the daily diet of the many octogenarians in the Médoc district of Bordeaux, who attribute their longevity to "half a bottle" of red wine a day.

THE NUTRITIONAL VALUE OF HERBS AND SEEDS

Our remote ancestors were well versed in the magic of herbs and seeds. Whether they learned about the medicinal value of many of our common field plants by experimenting on themselves or by observing the effect of them on birds and animals is not known, but today we know that scientists have proved the medicinal and nutritional value of many of our herbs through chemical analysis and have found that the seeds of many plants contain as perfect a balance of nutrients as can be found in any natural foods.

Seeds are concentrated packets of protein, vitamins, and minerals, containing rich amounts of phosphorus, iron, magnesium, the B complex, vitamins E, and essential fatty acids. And what is the vital element in seeds, such as the seed of the melon, which can sprout into roots, stems, leaves, and fruit, after thirty years of lying dormant? Seeds alone do not form a completely nutritious diet for man, but when combined with eggs, fruit, and milk, the diet is nutritionally complete, perhaps containing the very essence of life itself.

There are excellent dried herbs and seeds available in quality food markets, but as good as they are they cannot come close to the flavor and freshness of home-grown ones. If you have a small plot of ground in a sunny, but partially shaded area, there are many herbs and seed plants that can be grown. Parsley, both curly and Italian, and chervil are easily grown from packets of seeds available in hardware and seed stores. So too are dill, basil, thyme, sweet marjoram, summer savory, sage, the highly-prized French sorrel, which is nothing more than the field weed known as sour grass, cumin, fennel, and coriander. But it takes some of the seedlings of these plants so long to reach usable size that you are farther ahead if you can buy small plants from a nursery. Occasionally, you may be lucky enough to find small pots of dill, sweet basil, and parsley in rural vegetable markets along with pots of chives.

Otherwise seek out a nursery which cultivates root herbs. Here, if you are lucky, you will find tarragon, a hardy perennial once you get it started which grows to a bushy plant about two feet high. You might also want to buy a couple of roots each of rosemary, thyme, mint, winter savory, and sage. Most of these are perennials, but, in very cold climates, will be frosted out, along with your precious tarragon, unless well mulched before the first heavy frost. Parsley and chervil are biennials and can survive one winter if mulched. Sorrel and mint seem to withstand the most severe low temperatures.

Fresh tarragon and sweet basil leaves will give a marvelous flavor to wine or cider vinegar to last you during the winter, but basil leaves lose their flavor easily and are better preserved if packed tightly into a jar and covered with olive oil. In a couple of weeks, strain the wonderfully flavored basil oil off the leaves, and use it for your salads and for flavoring soups, stews, and pasta sauces.

Home-frozen parsley is better than anything you can buy in dried or frozen form. Pick the clusters after a nice rain, when they are clean and have just had enough time to dry off. Spread them on a baking sheet and put them in the freezer for 1 hour. Remove from the freezer and crumble into plastic pouches, and return to the freezer for winter use.

THE BEST WAY TO PRESERVE OTHER FRESH HERBS

Remove the leaves from the stems and pack leaves tightly into small jars with tight-fitting tops. (Empty baby-food jars are perfect.) Cover tightly, drop the jars into boiling water, and simmer for forty-five minutes. Remove jars, cool, and store in the freezer.

TWENTY-SIX EASY WAYS TO GOOD NUTRITION

Eat the foods you like, but eat wisely. Learn moderation in all things and, if you have a weight problem, eat a balanced diet of good foods, but eat a little less and always leave the table just a little hungry. Learn to count protein grams as well as calories.

REMEMBER THE BASICS: Your body needs all the building blocks of *complete proteins,* with their built-in supply of B vitamins, to convert sugar to energy, *natural sugars, natural unsaturated fats* that provide essential fatty acids to put cholesterol into suspension in the blood stream, and the *vitamins* and *minerals* that the body cannot manufacture to regulate and stimulate the body processes.

If you will follow the twenty-six rules for good daily nutrition, such common complaints as high blood pressure, nervous disorders, disorders of the digestive system, and even heart disease may be prevented.

1. EAT LOTS OF RAW FRUIT AND VEGETABLES. Begin each meal with some raw fruit or fruit juice, raw vegetable, or vegetable juice.

2. ENJOY A GREEN SALAD at least once a day.

3. USE NATURAL SUGARS whenever possible. Substitute brown sugar, crystallized sugars, honey, or molasses or maple syrup in place of refined white sugar, which interferes with the absorption of proteins, calcium, and other minerals and retards the growth of valuable intestinal bacteria. Good natural sugars are supplied by bananas, dried fruit, fruit juices, whole grain cereals, and root vegetables.

4. START THE DAY RIGHT by eating a bowl of bran flakes or toasted wheat germ instead of so-called "enriched" cereals. Top it off with one-half sliced banana or fresh berries in season, or with a spoonful of dried prunes or apricots, cooked and sweetened with brown sugar, honey, or maple syrup.

5. AVOID SATURATED FATS. This means the hard fats on meat, hydrogenated fats, such as lard or margarine, or margarine or peanut butter made with "hard" oils. It also means to avoid packaged mixes, deep-fried frozen foods, and whipped toppings.

6. EAT 1 TO 2 TABLESPOONS OF VEGETABLE OILS DAILY. Buy small bottles of fresh soy oil, safflower oil, peanut oil, and olive oil (for flavor), and combine them in one large bottle in equal proportions, or one-quarter of each. Each supplies a different fatty acid needed to put saturated fats into suspension in the blood. Use the combined oils for cooking and for salads.

7. USE DARK GREENS IN SALADS WHENEVER POSSIBLE—spinach leaves, water cress, field salad, and others, and MAKE YOUR OWN SALAD DRESSING. It's so simple! Just salt, freshly ground pepper, lemon juice or vinegar, and your combined oils.

8. USE FRESH CHOPPED GARLIC AND HERBS LAVISHLY. Grow your own fresh herbs if you have a patch of good earth.

9. MAKE YOUR OWN BREADS from whole-grain cereals. The nutrients necessary for energy are supplied in whole grains, while commercial breads and baked goods are "empty" foods, lacking these essential nutrients and causing obesity.

10. ADD WHEAT GERM OR SOY GRANULES to omelets, scrambled eggs, pancakes, muffins, biscuits, croquettes, or loaves.

11. AVOID PROCESSED CHEESES. Eat instead whole or skim-milk fresh cheeses and natural aged cheeses such as Parmesan, Cheddar, Gruyère, Swiss, and Roquefort-type.

12. USE IODIZED SALT (if not on a salt-restricted diet).

13. FORGET BOTTLED SOFT DRINKS and substitute fresh fruit juices, vegetable juices, milk, or a glass of good wine.

14. DON'T ELIMINATE BUTTER, CREAM, AND WHOLE MILK. These are the best way to get vitamin A. Butterfat can be a problem only when other nutrients necessary to utilize it are not supplied.

15. EAT ONE OR TWO EGGS DAILY. Eggs are rich in methionine and lecithin and, according to many food authorities, should not be restricted even in heart diets. Use them in cooking, or poach or scramble them in a little fresh butter, or lightly shirr them in your mixed vegetable oils.

16. EAT ONE SERVING OF LEAN MEAT, FISH, FOWL, CHEESE, OR MEAT SUBSTITUTE DAILY.

17. EAT LIVER OFTEN (if you eat meat), or supplement your diet daily with desiccated liver pills and vitamin D, or with one teaspoon of food yeast stirred into a glass of orange or vegetable juice.

18. EAT YOGURT. Try it plain, or flavored, or frozen on a stick. You just might like it. Or try the recipe for yogurt ice cream (page 320). Delicious! There is no substitute for the cultured bacteria in yogurt so essential for the complete assimilation of nutrients in the digestive system. To make your own yogurt see recipe, page 342.

19. DRINK AT LEAST ONE GLASS OF MILK OR BUTTERMILK DAILY, and supplement homemade baked goods with powdered milk.

20. EAT ONE OR TWO SERVINGS OF FRESH COOKED VEGETABLES DAILY.

21. EAT ONE SERVING OF NATURAL GRAINS DAILY, such as buckwheat grits (kasha), bulgur, natural brown rice or wild rice, or cous-cous.

22. POTATOES ARE A VITAMIN-RICH FOOD, but don't forget other mop-up-the-sauce carbohydrates such as high-protein spaghetti, macaroni, noodles, hominy, or hominy grits, or cornmeal (mush or polenta).

23. KEEP ALL MEALS LIGHT AND EAT A SNACK BETWEEN EACH MEAL. Make the snack a good one. Forget the doughnuts, cookies, candies, and potato chips. Snack on fresh fruit or dried apricots, prunes or dates,

peanuts, almonds with their skins, walnuts, pecans, natural cheeses, yogurt, or sunflower seeds. Peanut butter on crackers supplies high-quality protein, but should not contain hard oils. Buy it at a health store or make your own (page 341).

24. USE SEEDS OFTEN IN COOKING. Poppy seeds, sesame seeds, cumin seeds on buttered vegetables, on top of breads and biscuits and in pie crusts and muffins. Seeds are small packets of concentrated protein and minerals and are especially high in phosphorus and calcium.

25. LEARN TO DRINK COFFEE IN THE FRENCH MANNER, half hot strong, freshly brewed coffee and half hot milk.

26. A HOT MILK DRINK BEFORE BED IS NATURE'S PILL and the best way to assure a good night's sleep.

P.S. Take short and frequent sunbaths during summer and invest in a sun lamp for use during winter months. Supplement your diet with vitamins and minerals whenever a satisfactory diet is not or cannot be consumed daily. This is your best life insurance.

SAMPLE OF BALANCED MEALS FOR A DAY

It's so easy if you just think good health. The following meals supply more than adequate complete proteins (at least 80 grams) with all the essential nutrients.

BREAKFAST

Half a grapefruit or a glass of orange or cranberry juice, or a serving of berries in season, or stewed apricots or prunes.

One-fourth cup of wheat germ cereal or soy granules with brown sugar and milk or half-and-half.

Café au lait.

LUNCH

Cup of homemade soup or vegetable juice.

Two eggs, scrambled in a little butter or an omelet, and a slice of whole-wheat bread or a bran muffin.

or

Egg, salmon, or chicken salad (with mayonnaise) sandwich on whole-wheat bread.

Green or vegetable salad with vegetable-oil dressing, or cole slaw with mayonnaise dressing.

Yogurt topped with fresh or stewed fruit, or homemade ice cream.

Café au lait or, preferably, milk.

DINNER

Raw vegetable or fruit appetizer, or seafood cocktail, or half an avocado with vegetable-oil dressing, or a cooked artichoke vinaigrette, or tossed green salad with vegetable-oil dressing.

Serving of liver, or lamb chops, or steak, or fish, or seafood, or meat substitute.

Serving of a cooked whole grain or pasta, or a potato, plus a slice of whole-grain bread.

Serving of a green vegetable tossed with a little butter.

Glass of good red or white wine.

Maple syrup custard, or crème brûlée, or fresh fruit with an aged cheese, or homemade ice cream.

Coffee, tea, or milk.

HOMEMADE PEANUT BUTTER IN AN ELECTRIC BLENDER

Makes 6 ounces peanut butter. Be sure your blender container is completely dry.

1. Empty *1 cup shelled fresh or vacuum-packed peanuts* into the container. Cover and blend on highest speed for 5 seconds. Turn off motor.

2. Add *1 tablespoon vegetable oil* to the ground nuts, cover container, and blend on medium speed for about 60 seconds, or until nuts are ground and churned into peanut butter.

3. If necessary, stop the motor occasionally and stir down the ground mixture with a thin rubber spatula.

4. Remove peanut butter from container with the spatula and pack into a jar with a tight-fitting cover. Store in refrigerator.

HOMEMADE YOGURT

1. Pour *1 quart milk* into a heavy saucepan and bring to a boil. Watch carefully not to let it boil over the pan. Reduce heat and simmer the milk for 5 minutes, stirring constantly.

2. Remove from heat, and stir in *1 cup instant dried milk* and let cool to lukewarm (110° F.).

3. Stir in *½ cup commercial yogurt*. Cover saucepan with a tight-fitting lid and wrap in a heavy towel. Set it in an oven (heat off) for 6 to 8 hours or overnight. (Or, easier still, pour the lukewarm mixture into a wide-mouthed thermos and seal tightly until the next day.)

4. Spoon the yogurt into pint jars. Store in refrigerator where it will keep fresh for several days.

Index

The following example illustrates how these questions can guide an evaluation of a research study.

EXAMPLE 2.4   The newspaper article entitled "Spray Away Flu" (*Omaha World-Herald,* June 8, 1998) reported on a study of the effectiveness of a new flu vaccine that is administered by nasal spray rather than by injection. The article states the following:

> Researchers gave the spray to 1070 healthy children 15 months to 6 years old before the flu season two winters ago. One percent developed confirmed influenza, compared with 18 percent of the 532 children who received a placebo. And only one vaccinated child developed an ear infection after coming down with influenza. . . . Typically 30 percent to 40 percent of children with influenza later develop an ear infection.

The researchers concluded that the nasal flu vaccine was effective in reducing the incidence of flu and also in reducing the number of children with flu who subsequently get ear infections.

In this study, the researchers were trying to find out whether the nasal flu vaccine was effective in reducing the number of flu cases and in reducing the number of ear infections in children who do get the flu. The researchers recorded whether a child received the nasal vaccine or a placebo. A **placebo** is a treatment that has no active ingredients. Whether the child developed the flu and subsequent ear infection was also recorded. These are appropriate measurements to make to answer the research question of interest. We typically cannot tell much about the data collection process from a newspaper article. As we will see in Section 2.5, to fully evaluate this study, we would also want to know how the participating children were selected, how it was determined whether a particular child received the vaccine or the placebo, and how the subsequent diagnoses of flu and infection were made.

We will also have to delay discussion of the data analysis and the appropriateness of the conclusions to a later chapter, since we don't yet have the necessary tools to evaluate these aspects of the study.

Other interesting examples of statistical studies can be found in the books *Statistics: A Guide to the Unknown* and *Forty Studies That Changed Psychology: Exploration into the History of Psychological Research* (listed in the chapter references).

2.3   Collecting Data Sensibly: Observation and Experimentation

During the week of August 10, 1998, articles with the following headlines appeared in *USA Today*:

> Prayer Can Lower Blood Pressure (August 11, 1998)
> Wired Homes Watch 15% Less Television (August 13, 1998)

In each of these articles, a conclusion is drawn from data. In the study on prayer and blood pressure, 2391 people 65 years or older were followed for 6 years. The article states that people who attended a religious service once a week and prayed or studied the Bible at least once a day were less likely to have high blood pressure. The researcher then concluded that "attending religious services lowers blood pressure." The second article reported on a study of 5000 families, some of whom had on-line Internet services. The researcher concluded that TV use was lower in homes that were wired for the Internet, compared to nonwired homes. The researcher who conducted the study cautioned that the study does not answer the question of whether higher family income could be another factor in lower TV usage. Are these conclusions reasonable? As we will see, the answer in each case depends in a critical way on how the data was collected.

Observation and Experimentation

Data collection is an important step in the data analysis process. When we set out to collect information, it is important to keep in mind the questions we hope to answer on the basis of the resulting data. Sometimes we are interested in answering questions about characteristics of an existing population or in comparing two or more well-defined populations. To accomplish this, a sample is selected from each population under consideration, and the sample information is used to gain insight into characteristics of the population(s).

For example, an ecologist might be interested in estimating the average shell thickness of bald eagle eggs. A social scientist studying a rural community may want to determine whether there is a relationship between gender and attitude toward abortion. A city council member in a college town may want to ascertain whether student residents of the city differ from nonstudent residents with respect to their support for various community projects. These are examples of studies that are **observational** in nature. We want to observe characteristics of members of an existing population or several populations and then use the resulting information to draw conclusions.

In an observational study, it is important to obtain a sample that is representative of the corresponding population. To be reasonably certain of this, the way in which the sample is selected must be carefully considered.

Sometimes the questions we are trying to answer deal with the effect of certain explanatory variables on some response and cannot be answered using data from an observational study. Such questions are often of the form, What happens when . . . ? or, What is the effect of . . . ? For example, an educator may wonder what would happen to test scores if the required lab time for a chemistry course were increased from 3 hours to 6 hours per week. To answer questions like this, the researcher conducts an experiment to collect relevant data. The value of some response variable (test score in the chemistry example) is recorded under different experimental conditions (3-hour lab and 6-hour lab in the chemistry example). In an experiment, the researcher manipulates one or more variables, called **factors,** to create the experimental conditions.

A study is an **observational study** if the investigator observes characteristics of a subset of the members of one or more existing populations. The usual goal of an observational study is to draw conclusions about the corresponding population or about differences between two or more populations.

A study is an **experiment** if the investigator observes how a response variable behaves when the researcher manipulates one or more factors. The usual goal of an experiment is to determine the effect of the manipulated factors on some response variable.

The type of conclusion that may be drawn from a research study depends on the study design. Both observational studies and experiments can be used to compare groups, but in an experiment the researcher controls who is in which group, whereas this is not the case in an observational study. This seemingly small difference is critical when it comes to the interpretation of results from the study.

A well-designed experiment can result in data that provides evidence for a cause-and-effect relationship — this is an important difference between an observational study and an experiment. In an observational study, it is impossible to draw cause-and-effect conclusions because we cannot rule out the possibility that the observed effect is due to some other variable rather than to the factor being studied. Such variables are called *confounding variables*.

A **confounding variable** is one that is related both to group membership and to the response variable of interest in the research study.

Both of the studies from the *USA Today* articles discussed previously in this section were observational studies. In the TV-viewing example, the researcher merely observes the TV-viewing behavior of individuals in two groups (wired and non-wired) but does not control which individuals are in which group. A possible confounding variable here is family income. In the prayer example, two groups are compared (those who attend church at least once a week and those who do not), but the researcher does not manipulate this factor to observe the effect on blood pressure by assigning people to church or no-church groups. As a result, cause-and-effect conclusions such as "Prayer Can Lower Blood Pressure," are not reasonable based on the observed data. It is possible that some other variable, such as lifestyle, is related both to church attendance and to blood pressure. In this case, lifestyle is an example of a potential confounding variable.

Both observational studies and experiments must be carefully designed if the resulting data is to be useful. In the next two sections, we will describe the data collection process and discuss what constitutes good practice in this area.

Exercises 2.5 – 2.9

2.5 The Associated Press (Dec. 10, 1999) reported that researchers have found that women who suffer severe morning sickness early in pregnancy are more likely to have a girl. This conclusion was reached by researchers in Sweden based on a "scientific study." How do you think the researchers might have collected data that would have enabled them to reach such a conclusion? Do you think that the scientific study referred to in the article was an experiment or an observational study? Explain.

2.6 "Attending Church Found Factor in Longer Life" is the title of an article that appeared in *USA Today* (Aug. 9, 1999). Based on a "nationally representative survey of 3617 Americans," the article concludes that "Attending services extends the life span about as much as moderate exercise or not smoking." Comment on the validity of this conclusion.

2.7 An article that appeared in the *San Luis Obispo Tribune* (Nov. 11, 1999) was titled "Study Points Out Dangerous Side to SUV Popularity: Half of All 1996 Ejection Deaths Occur in SUVs." This article states that sports utility vehicles (SUVs) have a much higher rate of passengers being thrown from a window during an accident than do automobiles. The article also states that more than half of all deaths caused by ejection involved sports utility vehicles — the basis for the conclusion that SUVs are more dangerous than cars. Later in the article, there is a comment that about 98% of those injured or killed in ejection accidents were not wearing seat belts. Com-

ment on the conclusion that SUVs are more dangerous than cars.

2.8 Does living in the South cause high blood pressure? Data from a group of 6278 whites and blacks questioned in the Third National Health and Nutritional Examination Survey between 1988 and 1994 (see CNN.com Website article of January 6, 2000, entitled "High Blood Pressure Greater Risk in U.S. South, Study Says") indicates that a greater percentage of Southerners have high blood pressure than do people in any other region of the United States. This difference in rate of high blood pressure was found in every race, gender, and age category studied. List at least two possible reasons we cannot conclude that living in the South causes high blood pressure.

2.9 Does eating broccoli reduce the risk of prostate cancer? According to an observational study from the Fred Hutchinson Cancer Research Center (see CNN.com Website article entitled "Broccoli, Not Pizza Sauce, Cuts Cancer Risk, Study Finds," January 5, 2000), men who ate more cruciferous vegetables (broccoli, cauliflower, brussels sprouts, and cabbage) had a lower risk of prostate cancer. This study made separate comparisons for men who ate different levels of vegetables. According to one of the authors, "at any given level of total vegetable consumption, as the percent of cruciferous vegetables increased, the prostate cancer risk decreased." Based on this study, is it reasonable to conclude that eating cruciferous vegetables causes a reduction in prostate cancer risk? Explain.

2.4 Sampling

There are many reasons for selecting a sample rather than obtaining information from an entire population (a **census**). The most common is limited resources: Restrictions on available time or money usually prohibit observation of an entire population. Sometimes the process of measuring the characteristics of interest is destructive, as with the measurement of the breaking strength of soda bottles, the lifetime of flashlight batteries, or the sugar content of oranges, and it would be foolish to study the entire population.

An observational study usually involves an attempt to generalize from a sample to the corresponding population. As a result, it is important that the sample be representative of the population. To be reasonably certain of this, the way in which the sample is selected must be carefully considered. It is sometimes tempting to take the easy way out and gather data in a haphazard way; but if a sample is chosen on the basis of convenience alone, it becomes impossible to interpret the resulting data with confidence. For example, it might be easy to use the students in your statistics class as a sample of students at your university. However, in doing so, you may introduce problems. Not all majors include a statistics course in their curriculum, and most students take statistics in their sophomore or junior year. It is not clear whether or how these factors (and others of which we might not be aware) affect inferences based on information from such a sample. There is no way to tell just by looking at a sample whether it is representative of the population from which it was drawn. Our only assurance comes from the method used to select the sample.

Bias in Sampling

Bias is the tendency for a sample to differ from the corresponding population in some systematic way. The most common types of bias encountered in sampling situations are selection bias, measurement or response bias, and nonresponse bias. **Selection bias** is introduced when some part of the population is systematically excluded from the sample. This problem is sometimes also called *undercoverage*. For example, a researcher may wish to generalize from the results of a study to the population consisting of all residents of a particular city, but the method of selecting individuals may exclude the homeless or those without telephones. If those who are excluded from the sampling process differ in some systematic way from those who are included, the sample will not be representative of the population. If this difference between the included and the excluded occurs on a variable that is important to the study, conclusions based on the sample data may not be valid. Selection bias also occurs if only volunteers or self-selected individuals are used in a study, since self-selected individuals (for example, those who choose to participate in a call-in telephone poll) usually differ from those who choose not to participate.

Measurement or **response bias** occurs when our method of observation tends to produce values that systematically differ from the true population value in some way. This might happen if an improperly calibrated scale is used to weigh items or if questions on a survey are worded in a way that tends to influence the response. For example, a May 1994 Gallup survey sponsored by the American Paper Institute (*Wall Street Journal,* May 17, 1994) included the following question:

> It is estimated that disposable diapers account for less than 2 percent of the trash in today's landfills. In contrast, beverage containers, third-class mail and yard waste are estimated to account for about 21 percent of trash in landfills. Given this, in your opinion, would it be fair to tax or ban disposable diapers?

It is likely that the wording of this question prompted people to respond in a particular way.

Other things that might contribute to response bias are the appearance or behavior of the person asking the question, the group or organization conducting the study, and the tendency for people to lie when asked about illegal behavior or unpopular beliefs.

Although the terms *measurement bias* and *response bias* are often used interchangeably, the term *measurement bias* is usually used to describe systematic deviation from the true value as a result of a faulty measurement instrument (as with the improperly calibrated scale).

Nonresponse bias occurs when responses are not actually obtained from all individuals selected for inclusion in the sample. Like selection bias, nonresponse can distort results if those who respond differ in important ways from those who do not respond. Although some level of nonresponse is unavoidable in most surveys, the biasing effect on the resulting sample is lowest when the response rate is high. It is very important that a serious effort be made to follow up with individuals who do not respond to an initial request for information.

The nonresponse rate for surveys or opinion polls varies dramatically depending on how the data is collected. Surveys are commonly conducted by mail, by phone, or by personal interview. Mail surveys are inexpensive, but often have high nonresponse rates. Telephone surveys can also be inexpensive and can be implemented quickly, but they work well only for short surveys and they can also have high nonresponse rates. Personal interviews are generally expensive but tend to have better response rates.

Types of Bias

Selection Bias
Tendency for samples to differ from the corresponding population as a result of systematic exclusion of some part of the population

Measurement or Response Bias
Tendency for samples to differ from the corresponding population because the method of observation tends to produce values that differ from the true value

Nonresponse Bias
Tendency for samples to differ from the corresponding population because data is not obtained from all individuals selected for inclusion in the sample

---

It is important to note that bias is introduced by the way in which a sample is selected or by the way in which the data is collected from the sample. Increasing the size of the sample, although possibly desirable for other reasons, does nothing to reduce bias. A good discussion of types of bias appears in the book by Lohr listed in the chapter references.

Random Sampling

Most of the inferential methods introduced in this text are based on the idea of random selection. The simplest of these methods is called *simple random sampling*. A simple random sample is one chosen using a method that ensures that each different possible sample of the desired size has an equal chance of being the one chosen. Suppose we want a simple random sample of ten employees chosen from all those who work at a particular department store. For the sample to be a simple random sample, each of the many different sets of ten employees must be equally likely to be the one selected. A sample taken from only full-time employees would not be a simple random sample of *all* employees, since someone who works part-time is still considered an employee but has no chance of being selected. Although a simple random sample may, by chance, include only full-time employees, it must be selected in such a way that *every* employee has the same chance of inclusion in the sample. It is the selection process, not the final sample, that determines whether the sample is a simple random sample.

The letter n is used to denote the sample size; it is the number of individuals or objects in the sample.

Definition

A **simple random sample of size** n is a sample that is selected from a population in a way that ensures that every different possible sample of the desired size has the same chance of being selected.

The definition implies that every individual member of the population has an equal chance of being selected. **However, the fact that every individual has an equal chance of selection, by itself, is not enough to guarantee that the sample is a simple random sample.** For example, suppose that a class is made up of 100 students, 60 of whom are female. A researcher decides to select 6 of the female students by writing all 60 names on slips of paper, mixing the slips, and then picking 6. She then selects 4 male students from the class using a similar procedure. Even though every student in the class has an equal chance of being included in the sample (6 of 60 females are selected and 4 of 40 males are chosen), the resulting sample is *not* a simple random sample because not all different possible samples of 10 students from the class have the same chance of selection. There are many possible samples of 10 students that consist of 7 females and 3 males or that consist of all females that have no chance of being selected. The sample selection method described here is not necessarily a bad choice (in fact, it is an example of a stratified sample, to be discussed in more detail shortly), but it is not a simple random sample; this must be considered when a method is chosen for analyzing data from such a sample.

There are a number of different methods for selecting a simple random sample. One way is to use a slip of paper to identify each member of the population. Names or numbers are commonly used to label the different population members. The process of thoroughly mixing the slips and then selecting n slips one by one (without replacement) yields a random sample of size n. This method is easy to understand, but it has obvious drawbacks. The mixing must be adequate, and producing the necessary slips of paper can be extremely tedious, even for populations of moderate size.

A commonly used method for selecting a random sample is to first create a list, called a **sampling frame,** of the objects or individuals in the population. Each item on the list can then be identified by a number, and a table of random digits or a random number generator can be used to select the sample. A random number generator is an algorithm that produces a sequence of numbers that satisfy all reasonable properties associated with the notion of randomness. Most statistics software packages include a random number generator, as do many calculators. A small table of random digits can be found in Appendix Table I.

When selecting a random sample, sampling can be done with or without replacement. **Sampling with replacement** means that after each successive item is selected for the sample, the item is "replaced" back into the population and may therefore be selected again at a later stage. Thus, sampling with replacement allows for the possibility of having the same item or individual appear more than once in the sample. In practice, sampling with replacement is rarely used. Instead, the more common method is to not allow the same individual to be included in the sample more than once. After being included in the sample, an individual or object would not be considered for further selection. Sampling in this manner is called **sampling without replacement.** Although these two forms of sampling are different, when the sample size is small relative to the population size, as is typically the case in most applications, there is little practical difference between them.

EXAMPLE 2.5

Breaking strength is an important characteristic of glass soda bottles. If the strength is too low, a bottle may burst — not a desirable outcome. Suppose that we want to measure the breaking strength of a random sample of three bottles selected from four crates containing a total of 100 bottles (the population). Each crate contains five rows of five bottles each. We can identify each bottle with a number from 1 to 100 by numbering across the rows, starting with the top row of crate 1, as pictured.

Crate 1

1	2	3	4	5
6	...			

Crate 2

26	27	28	...	

⋮

Crate 4

Using a random number generator from a calculator or statistical software package, we could generate three random numbers between 1 and 100 to determine which bottles would be included in our sample. This might result in bottles 15 (row 3 column 5 of crate 1), 89 (row 3 column 4 of crate 4), and 60 (row 2 column 5 of crate 3) being selected. (Alternately, we could write the numbers from 1 to 100 on slips of paper, place them in a container, mix them well, and then select three.)

The goal of random sampling is to produce a sample that is representative of the population. Although random sampling does not *guarantee* that the sample will be representative, probability-based methods can be used to assess the risk of an unrepresentative sample. It is the ability to quantify this risk that allows us to generalize with confidence from a random sample to the corresponding population.

Other Sampling Methods

Simple random sampling provides researchers with a sampling method that is objective and free of selection bias. In some settings, however, alternative sampling methods may be less costly, may be easier to implement, or may result in more accurate results. When the entire population can be divided into a set of nonoverlapping groups, a method known as stratified sampling often proves to be easier to implement and more cost-effective than random sampling. Stratified random sampling is a method that independently selects a separate simple random sample from each subgroup. For example, for the purpose of estimating average cost of malpractice insurance, it might be convenient to view the population of all doctors practicing in a particular community as being made up of the four subpopulations: (1) surgeons, (2) internists and family practitioners, (3) obstetricians, and (4) a group that includes all other areas of specialization. Rather than taking a simple random sample from the population of all doctors, we could take four separate random samples — one from the group of surgeons, another from the internists and family practitioners, and so on. These four samples would provide information about the four subgroups as well as information about the overall population of doctors.

When the population is divided in this way, the subpopulations are called **strata.** **Stratified sampling** entails selecting a separate simple random sample from each of the strata. Stratified sampling can be used instead of random sampling if it is important to obtain information about characteristics of the individual strata as well as of the entire population.

Stratified sampling usually allows more accurate inferences about a population than does simple random sampling. In general, it is much easier to estimate characteristics of a homogeneous group than of a heterogeneous group. For example, even with a small sample, it is possible to obtain a very accurate estimate of the average grade point average (GPA) of students graduating with high honors from a university. This is a very homogeneous group with respect to GPA. The individual GPAs of group members are all quite similar, and even a sample of three or four individuals from this subpopulation should be representative. On the other hand, estimating the average GPA of *all* seniors at the university, a much more diverse group of GPAs, is a more difficult task.

If a varied population can be divided into strata each of which is more homogeneous than the population with respect to the characteristic of interest, stratified sampling tends to produce more accurate estimates of population characteristics than does simple random sampling. This is because when the strata are relatively homogeneous, a small sample from each stratum can provide reasonably accurate information about strata characteristics. The strata information can then be used to obtain better information about the population as a whole than might have been possible using a simple random sample of the same total size.

Exercises 2.10 – 2.22

2.10 The psychology department at a university produced 140 graduates in 1999. As part of a curriculum review, the department would like to select a simple random sample of 20 1999 graduates to obtain information on how graduates perceived the value of the curriculum. Describe two different methods that might be used to select the sample.

2.11 During the previous calendar year, a county's small-claims court processed 870 cases. A legal researcher would like to select a simple random sample of 50 cases to obtain information regarding the average award in such cases. Describe how a simple random sample of size 50 might be selected from the case files.

2.12 A petition with 500 signatures is submitted to a university's student council. The council president would like to determine the proportion of those who signed the petition who are actually registered students at the university. There is not enough time to check all 500 names with the registrar, so it is decided to select a simple random sample of 30 signatures. Describe how this might be done.

2.13 The financial aid office of a university wishes to estimate the average amount of money that students spend on textbooks each term. They are considering taking a stratified sample. For each of the proposed stratification schemes, discuss whether you think it would be worthwhile to stratify the university students in this manner.
a. Strata corresponding to class standing (freshman, sophomore, junior, senior, graduate student)
b. Strata corresponding to field of study, using the following categories: engineering, architecture, business, other
c. Strata corresponding to first letter of last name: A–E, F–K, etc.

2.14 Devise a procedure for selecting a random sample of words from a dictionary. Explain why your procedure guarantees that, for any *n*, each collection of *n* words has an equal chance of being selected.

2.15 Citrus trees are usually grown in orderly arrangements of rows to facilitate automated farming and harvesting practices. Suppose a group of 1000 trees is laid out in 40 rows of 25 trees each. To determine the sugar content of fruit from a sample of 30 trees, researcher A suggests randomly selecting five rows and then randomly selecting six trees from each sampled row. Researcher B suggests numbering each tree on a map of the trees from

1 to 1000 and using random numbers to select 30 of the trees. Is there a reason for preferring one of these sample selection methods over the other? Explain.

2.16 If liquor stores accept credit cards, does alcohol consumption change? The article "Changes in Alcohol Consumption Patterns Following the Introduction of Credit Cards in Ontario Liquor Stores" (*Journal of Studies on Alcohol* (1999): 378–382) attempted to answer this question with data based on a telephone survey. The sample was obtained by generating random phone numbers.

   a. What are some potential drawbacks of using random phone numbers for sampling? Do any of these drawbacks seem critical for answering this question about alcohol and credit cards?
   b. What time of day would be best for such calls?

2.17 The article "Drinking-Driving and Riding with Drunk Drivers among Young Adults: An Analysis of Reciprocal Effects" (*Journal of Studies on Alcohol* (1999): 615–621) concludes that although 16–24-year olds who drive drunk are more likely to ride with drunk drivers, those who ride with drunk drivers are not more likely to drive drunk themselves. These results are based on a sample of 993 young adults from the state of New York, excluding New York City residents. The article explains the exclusion of New York City by saying that the proportion of young adults is higher but that the driving rate of young adults is far lower.

   a. Describe the population of interest for this study.
   b. Explain how this sample would (or would not) be representative of New York City young adults.
   c. Explain how this sample would (or would not) be representative of adults from the entire United States.

2.18 The study described in Exercise 2.17 actually used a stratified sample with strata determined by age. Why do you think the stratification was desirable?

2.19 According to the article "Effect of Preparation Methods on Total Fat Content, Moisture Content, and Sensory Characteristics of Breaded Chicken Nuggets and Beef Steak Fingers" (*Family and Consumer Sciences Research Journal* (1999): 18–27), sensory tests were conducted using 40 college student volunteers at Texas Women's University. Give three reasons apart from the relatively small sample size why this sample may not be ideal as the basis for generalizing to the population of all college students.

2.20 According to an article on the CNN.com Website dated September 17, 1998, entitled "Majority of U.S. Teens Are Not Sexually Active Study Shows," 52% of surveyed teens had never had sexual intercourse. A very large random sample of 16,262 high school students were the source of these data. If the population of interest is teens in the United States, are there individuals in the population who had no chance of being included in the sample? What is the name for this type of bias?

2.21 A new and somewhat controversial polling procedure that replaces the phone with the Internet is being employed in the conduct of public opinion polls. The article "Pollsters Fear Internet Numbers Offer Warped View" (*Knight Ridder Newspapers,* Oct. 18, 1999) states

> Many pollsters say Internet users as a whole are still too upper-income, highly educated, white and urban to produce results that accurately reflect all Americans. What's more, while 94% of U.S. households had a telephone in 1998, only 26% had Internet access, according to a U.S. Department of Commerce study.

What type of bias is being described in this statement? Do you think that this bias is a serious problem? Explain.

2.22 The article "Study Provides New Data on the Extent of Gambling by College Athletes" (*The Chronicle of Higher Education,* Jan. 22, 1999) reported that "72 percent of college football and basketball players had bet money at least once since entering college." This conclusion was based on a study in which "Copies of the survey were mailed to 3000 athletes at 182 Division I institutions, 25 percent of whom responded." What types of bias might have influenced the results of this study? Explain.

2.5   Simple Comparative Experiments

Sometimes the questions we are trying to answer deal with the effect of certain explanatory variables on some response. Such questions are often of the form, What happens when . . . ? or, What is the effect of . . . ? For example, an educator may wonder what happens to test scores if an activity-based method of instruction is used rather than a traditional lecture method. An industrial engineer may be considering two different workstation designs and might want to know whether the choice of design affects work performance. A medical researcher may want to determine how a proposed treatment for a disease compares to a standard treatment. A nutritionist working for a commercial bakery may want to determine the effect of baking time and baking temperature on the nutritional content of bread.

To address these questions, the researcher conducts an experiment to collect the relevant information. The value of some response variable (test score, assembly time, bread density, etc.) is recorded under different experimental conditions. Such experiments must be carefully planned to obtain information that will give unambiguous answers to questions of interest.

Definition

An **experiment** is a planned intervention undertaken to observe the effects of one or more explanatory variables, often called **factors**, on a response variable. The fundamental purpose of the intervention is to increase understanding of the nature of the relationships between the explanatory and response variables. Any particular combination of values for the explanatory variables is called an **experimental condition** or **treatment.**

The **design** of an experiment is the overall plan for conducting an experiment. A good design minimizes ambiguity in the interpretation of the results.

Suppose that we are interested in determining how student performance on a first-semester calculus exam is affected by room temperature. There are four sections of calculus being offered next term. We might design an experiment in this way: Set the room temperature (in degrees Fahrenheit) to 65° in two of the rooms and to 75° in the other two rooms on test day, and then compare the exam scores for the 65° group and the 75° group. Suppose that the average exam score for the students in the 65° group was noticeably higher than the average for the 75° group. Could we conclude that the increased temperature resulted in a lower average score? The answer is no because many other factors might be related to exam score. Were the sections at different times of the day? Did they have the same instructor? Different textbooks? Was one section required to do more homework than the other sections? Did the sections differ with respect to the abilities of the students? Any of these other factors could be a plausible explanation (having nothing to do with room temperature) of why the average test score was different for the two groups. It is not possible to separate the effect of temperature from the effects of these other factors. As a consequence, simply setting the room temperatures as described makes for a poorly designed experiment. A well-designed experiment requires more than just manipulating the explanatory variables; the design must also eliminate rival explanations or the experimental results will be ambiguous.

The goal of experimentation is to design an experiment that will allow us to determine the effects of the relevant factors on the chosen response variable. To do this, we must take into consideration other factors that, although not of interest in the current study, might also affect the response variable. These are called *extraneous factors*.

Definition

An **extraneous factor** is one that is not of interest in the current study but is thought to affect the response variable.

A researcher can directly **control** some extraneous factors. In the calculus test example, the textbook used is an extraneous factor since part of the differences in test result might be attributed to this factor. We might choose to control this factor directly, by requiring that all sections participating in the study use the same text. If this were the case, any observed differences between temperature groups could not be explained by the use of different texts, since all sections would have used the same text. The extraneous factor *time of day* might also be directly controlled in this way by having all sections meet at the same time.

The effect of some extraneous factors can be filtered out by a process known as **blocking.** Extraneous factors that are addressed through blocking are called *blocking factors.* Blocking creates groups (called *blocks*) that are similar with respect to blocking factors; then all treatments are tried in each block. In our example, we might use *instructor* as a blocking factor. If two instructors are each teaching two sections of calculus, we would make sure that for each instructor, one section was part of the 65° group and the other was part of the 75° group. With this design, if we see a difference in exam scores for the two temperature groups, the factor *instructor* can be ruled out as a possible explanation, because both instructors' students were present in each temperature group. If one instructor taught both 65° sections and the other taught both 75° sections, we would be unable to distinguish the effect of temperature from the effect of instructor. These two factors (temperature and instructor) are said to be *confounded*.

Two factors are **confounded** if their effects on the response variable cannot be distinguished from one another.

We can directly control some extraneous factors by holding them constant, and we can use blocking to create groups that are similar to essentially block out the effect of others. What about factors, such as student ability in our calculus test example, that cannot be controlled by the experimenter and would be difficult to use as blocking factors? These extraneous factors are handled by the use of random assignment to experimental groups—a process called **randomization.** Randomization ensures that our experiment does not favor one experimental condition over any other and attempts to create "equivalent" experimental groups (groups that are as much alike as possible). For example, if the students requesting calculus could be assigned to one of the four available sections using some sort of random mechanism, we would expect the resulting groups to be similar with respect to student ability, as well as similar with respect to other extraneous factors that we are not directly controlling or using as a basis for blocking.

Not all experiments require the use of human subjects to evaluate different experimental conditions. For example, a researcher might be interested in comparing three different gasoline additives with respect to automobile performance as measured by gasoline mileage. The experiment might consist of using a single car with an empty tank. One gallon of gas with one of the additives will be put in the tank and the car driven along a standard route at a constant speed until it runs out of gas. The total distance traveled on the gallon of gas could then be recorded. This could be repeated a number of times, ten for example, with each additive.

The experiment just described can be viewed as consisting of a sequence of trials. Because there are a number of extraneous factors that might have an effect on gas mileage (such as variations in environmental conditions like wind speed or humidity and small variations in the condition of the car), it would not be a good idea to use additive 1 for the first ten trials, additive 2 for the next ten, and so on. An approach that would not unintentionally favor any one of the additives would be to randomly assign additive 1 to 10 of the 30 planned trials, then randomly assign additive 2 to 10 of the remaining 20 trials. The resulting plan for carrying out the experiment might look as follows:

Trial	1	2	3	4	5	6	7	...	30
Additive	2	2	3	3	2	1	2	...	1

When an experiment can be viewed as a sequence of trials, randomization involves the random assignment of treatments to trials. **Just remember that random assignment — either of subjects to treatments or of treatments to trials — is a critical component of a good experiment.**

Randomization can be effective in evening out the effects of extraneous variables only if the number of subjects or observations in each treatment or experimental condition is large enough for each experimental group to reliably reflect variability in the population. For example, if there were only eight students requesting calculus, it is unlikely that we would get equivalent groups for comparison, even with random assignment to the sections. **Replication** is the design strategy of making multiple observations for each experimental condition. Together, replication and randomization allow the researcher to be reasonably confident of comparable experimental groups.

Key Concepts in Experimental Design

Randomization

Random assignment (of subjects to treatments or of treatments to trials) to ensure that the experiment does not systematically favor one experimental condition over another

Blocking

Using extraneous factors to create groups (blocks) that are similar. All experimental conditions are then tried in each block.

Direct Control

Holding extraneous factors constant so that their effects are not confounded with those of the experimental conditions

Replication

Ensuring that there is an adequate number of observations in each experimental condition

These four concepts — randomization, blocking, control, and replication — are the fundamental principles of experimental design. When collecting data through experimentation, you should give careful thought to the role that each of these principles plays in your design.

It is an unremarkable event when we read in our newspapers or see on the news or perhaps read in one of our textbooks that a scientist performed an experiment. The subject matter may be a new therapy for arthritis, a promising drug for asthma control, or a substance that holds promise of longer lasting tires for automobiles, but the stories are very similar. A scientist, doctor, or engineer has performed an experiment and some new or unexpected result has brought new knowledge or refined our understanding of some scientific puzzle or, in some cases, caused rethinking about a heretofore "settled" issue in some area of human endeavor.

Although we may be aware of the results of experiments, the details of carrying out experiments are not usually reported, and, in all likelihood, we have little or no understanding of how experiments are performed or just how they provide the scientific information they do. To illustrate the design of a simple experiment, consider the dilemma of Anna, a waitress in a local restaurant. Anna is saving money for college, and she depends on tips from her customers in the restaurant. She would like to increase the amount of her tips, and her strategy is very simple: In addition to prompt and courteous service, she will project a positive image of herself to her customers by writing "Thank you" on the back of the check before she gives it to the patron. She reasons that friendly waitresses are likely to result in satisfied customers and that this satisfaction would result in higher tips. She will write "Thank you" on some of the checks, and on others she will write nothing. She plans to calculate the percentage of the tip as her measure of success. (For instance, a 15% tip is common.) She will compare the average percentage of the tip calculated from checks with and without thank you.

Writing thank you consumes a bit more time in her already hectic serving activities, and so she has a stake in the outcome of her experiment. If the extra time does not produce higher tips, she may try a different strategy; in any case it is of value to her to have at least a tentative answer to the question: Will writing thank you produce the desired outcome of higher tips? Anna is untrained in the art of planning experiments, but already she has taken some common sense steps in the right direction to answer her question.

1. **Identification of a specific problem**
   Anna has defined a manageable problem, and collecting the appropriate data is feasible. It should be very easy to gather data as a normal part of her work.

2. **Definition of the variables of interest**
   Anna reasons that writing thank you on the customers' bills will have an effect on the amount of tipping. Moreover, it seems logical to her that such a communication could produce this desired effect. In the language of experimentation we would refer to the writing of thank you and the not writing of thank you as **treatments** (the two experimental conditions to be compared in the experiment). The two treatments together are the possible values of the **explanatory** variable. The tipping percentage is the **response** variable. The idea behind this terminology is that the outcome of the experiment (the tipping percentage) is a *response* to the treatments *writing thank you* or *not writing thank you.* Anna's experiment may be thought of as an attempt to explain the variability in the response variable in terms of its presumed cause, the variability in the explanatory variable. That is, as she manipulates the explanatory variable, she expects the response by her customers to vary in a manner consistent with her theory.

3. **Formulation of the measurement**
   Writing or not writing is a categorical variable, which is easily measured. It is possible that Anna may write more or less legibly depending on how hectic her day is, but with practice she should be able to dash off a thank you in a standard manner. The tipping percentage is easily calculated from the tip and the original bill: % tip = (tip/bill total) $\times$ 100.

4. **Interpretation of the results**
   In general, if the tip sizes are higher for the *thank you* treatment, Anna will regard this as evidence in favor of her hypothesis that such activity ought to increase tipping. If the tip sizes are very similar, she will regard the writing as a waste of time with respect to increasing tip percentages.

Anna has a good start, but now she must consider the four fundamental design principles.

Replication   Anna cannot run a successful experiment by gathering tipping information on only one person for each treatment. There is no reason to believe that any single tipping incident is representative of what would happen in other incidents (since customers vary in their tipping practices), and therefore it would be impossible to evaluate the two treatments with only two subjects. To interpret the effects of a particular treatment, she must **replicate** each treatment in the experiment.

Control and Randomization   There are a number of extraneous variables in this example — variables that might have an effect on the size of tip. Some restaurant patrons will be seated near the window with a nice view, some will have to wait for a table while others may be seated immediately, some may be on a fixed income and cannot afford a large tip, and so on. Some of these variables can be controlled. For example, Anna may choose to only use window tables in her experiment, thus eliminating table location as a potential confounding variable. Other variables, such as length of wait and customer income, cannot be easily controlled. As a result, it is important that Anna use randomization to decide which of the window tables will be in the thank you group and which will be in the no thanks group. She might do this by flipping a coin as she prepares the check for each window table. If the coin lands with the head side up, she could write thank you on the bill, omitting the thank you when a tail is observed.

Blocking   Suppose that Anna works on both Thursdays and Fridays. Because day of the week might affect tipping behavior, Anna should block on day of the week and make sure that observations for both treatments are made on each of the two days.

Evaluating an Experimental Design

The key concepts of experimental design provide a framework for evaluating an experimental design, as illustrated in the following two examples.

EXAMPLE 2.6   The article "The Most Powerful Manipulative Messages Are Hiding in Plain Sight" (*Chronicle of Higher Education,* Jan. 29, 1999) reported the results of an experiment on "priming" — the effect of subliminal messages on how we behave. In the experiment, a researcher asked subjects to complete a language test in which the subject was asked to construct a sentence using each word in a list of words. One group of subjects received a list of words related to politeness, and a second group was given a list of words related to rudeness. Subjects were asked to complete the language test and then come into the hall and find the researcher so that he could explain the next part of the test. When each subject came into the hall, he or she found the researcher engaged in conversation. The researcher wanted to see whether the subject would interrupt the conversation. The researcher found that 63% of those primed with words related to rudeness interrupted the conversation, whereas only 17% of those primed with words related to politeness interrupted.

If we assume that the researcher randomly assigned the subjects to the two groups, then this study is an experiment that compares two treatments (primed with words related to rudeness and primed with words related to politeness). The response variable, *politeness,* has the values *interrupted conversation* and *did not interrupt conversation.* The experiment uses replication (many subjects in each treatment group) and randomization to control for extraneous variables that might affect the response.

Many experiments compare a group that receives a particular treatment to a group that receives no treatment. An experimental group that receives no treatment or that receives a placebo treatment (something that looks like the treatment, but which has no active ingredients) is called a **control group.** An experiment that illustrates the use of a control group is described in Example 2.7.

EXAMPLE 2.7   Researchers at the University of North Carolina studied 422 third- and fourth-grade children to determine whether a program of health education and exercise was effective in reducing cholesterol level (*San Luis Obispo Telegram-Tribune,* Aug. 4, 1998). Children with high cholesterol levels were divided into three groups. One group attended classes in healthy nutrition twice a week and exercised three times a week. A second group received individualized instruction from a nurse and exercised three times a week. The third group, a control group, received no specialized instruction and participated in the school's regular physical education classes. After 2 months, cholesterol levels were measured. The researchers concluded that the classroom-based program (group 1) was most effective in lowering cholesterol.

If the researchers randomly assigned the 422 children to the three experimental conditions (treatments), the study was an experiment that employed both replication and randomization.

When planning an experiment or evaluating a design by someone else, be sure to keep the basics in mind:

1. Replication: Design strategy of making multiple observations for each experimental treatment
2. Direct control: Holding the value of an extraneous variable constant so that its effect is not potentially confounded with factors in the experiment
3. Blocking: Using extraneous variables to create groups (blocks) that are similar, and then making sure that all treatments are tried in each block
4. Randomization (**a must!**): The strategy for dealing with all extraneous variables not taken into account through direct control or blocking. We count on randomization to create "equivalent" experimental groups.

Before proceeding with an experiment, you should be able to give a satisfactory answer to each of the following ten questions.

1. What is the research question that data from the experiment will be used to answer?
2. What is the response variable?

3. How are the values of the response variable to be determined?

4. What are the factors (explanatory variables) for the experiment?

5. For each factor, how many different values are there, and what are these values?

6. What are the treatments for the experiment?

7. What extraneous variables might influence the response?

8. How does the design incorporate random assignment of subjects to treatments (or treatments to subjects) or random assignment of treatments to trials?

9. For each extraneous variable listed in question 7, how does the design protect against its potential influence on the response through blocking, direct control, or randomization?

10. Will you be able to answer the research question using the data collected in this experiment?

Exercises 2.23 – 2.32

2.23 The head of the quality control department at a publishing company is interested in factors that affect the strength of the binding on books that it publishes. In particular, she would like to carry out an experiment to determine which of three different glues results in the greatest binding strength. Although they are not of interest in the current investigation, other factors thought to affect binding strength are the number of pages in the book and whether the book is being bound as a paperback or a hardback.
  a. What is the response variable in this experiment?
  b. What factor will determine the experimental conditions?
  c. What two extraneous factors are mentioned in the problem description? Can you think of other extraneous factors that might be considered?

2.24 Based on observing more than 400 drivers in the Atlanta area, two investigators at Georgia State University concluded that people exiting parking spaces did so more slowly when a driver in another car was waiting for the space than when no one was waiting ("Territorial Defense in Parking Lots: Retaliation Against Waiting Drivers," *J. Applied Social Psych.* (1997): 821–834). Describe how you might design a study to collect information that would allow you to determine whether this phenomenon is true for your city. What is the response variable for your study? What extraneous factors might have an effect on the response variable, and how does your design control for them?

2.25 An article in the *San Luis Obispo Tribune* (Sept. 7, 1999) described an experiment designed to investigate the effect of creatine supplements on the development of muscle fibers. The article states that the researchers

  . . . looked at 19 men, all about 25 years of age and similar in weight, lean body mass and capacity to lift weights. Ten were given creatine — 25 grams a day for the first week, followed by 5 grams a day for the rest of the study. The rest were given a fake preparation. No one was told what they were getting. All the men worked out under the guidance of the same trainer.

The response variable measured was gain in fat-free mass (in percent).
  a. What extraneous variables are identified in the statement above, and what strategy did the researchers use to deal with them?
  b. Do you think it was important that the men participating in the experiment were not told whether they were receiving creatine or the placebo? Explain. This type of study, where subjects do not know what treatment they are receiving, is called a **blinded study.**
  c. In a **double-blind study,** not only do the subjects not know which treatment they are receiving, but nei-

ther does the person who measures the response variable. This particular experiment was not conducted in a double-blind manner. Do you think it would have been a good idea to have made this a double-blind experiment? Explain.

2.26 In 1993, researchers proclaimed that listening to Mozart can make you smarter. Dubbed the "Mozart Effect," this conclusion was based on a study that showed college students temporarily gained up to nine IQ points after listening to a Mozart piano sonata. This research has since been criticized by a number of researchers who have been unable to confirm this result in other similar studies. Suppose you wanted to see whether there is a Mozart effect for students at your school.
  a. Describe how you might design an experiment for this purpose.
  b. Does your experimental design include direct control of any extraneous variables? Explain.
  c. Does your experimental design use blocking? Explain why you did or did not include blocking in your design.
  d. What role does randomization play in your design?

2.27 Do race and gender influence the type of care that a heart patient receives? The following passage is from the article "Heart Care Reflects Race and Sex, Not Symptoms" (© 1999, *USA Today,* Feb. 25, 1999. Reprinted with permission.):

> Previous research suggested blacks and women were less likely than whites and men to get cardiac catheterization or coronary bypass surgery for chest pain or a heart attack. Scientists blamed differences in illness severity, insurance coverage, patient preference and health care access. The researchers eliminated those differences by videotaping actors — two black men, two black women, two white men and two white women — describing chest pain from identical scripts. They wore identical gowns, used identical gestures and were taped from the same position. Researchers asked 720 primary care doctors at meetings of the American College of Physicians or the American Academy of Family Physicians to watch a tape and recommend care. The doctors thought the study was on clinical decision making.

Evaluate this experimental design. Do you think this is a good design or a poor design, and why? If you were designing such a study, what, if anything, would you propose to do differently?

2.28 Four new word-processing software programs are to be compared by measuring the speed with which various standard tasks can be completed. Before conducting the tests, researchers note that the level of a person's computer experience is likely to have a large influence on the test results. Discuss how you would design an experiment that fairly compares the word-processing programs while simultaneously accounting for possible differences in users' computer proficiency.

2.29 Is status related to a student's understanding of science? The article "From Here to Equity: The Influence of Status on Student Access to and Understanding of Science" (*Culture and Comparative Studies* (1999): 577–602) described a study on the effect of group discussions on learning biology concepts. An analysis of the relationship between status and "rate of talk" (the number of on-task talk speech acts per minute) during group work included gender as a blocking variable. Do you think that gender is a useful blocking variable? Explain.

2.30 In an experiment to determine whether suggesting a number of items to purchase (for example, "limit 12 per person") increases the number of items purchased [see "An Anchoring and Adjustment Model of Purchase Quantity Decision" (*Journal of Marketing Research* (1999): 71–81)], data was collected at three separate stores. At one store the display of sale soup had a sign that said "no limit per person," at another store the sign read "limit four per person," and at the third the sign read "limit 12 per person." On the second and third days of the experiment the signs were switched so that each store had each treatment one day only.
  a. Why did the researchers rotate the three treatments across the three different stores for the three days?
  b. The results of this study showed that there were no day-to-day or store-to-store differences in the quantity of soup purchased. Also, in the stores with the "limit 12 per person" soup display, the average number of cans purchased per person was twice that of the "no limit" or "limit 4 per person" (7 instead of 3.5). This difference was large enough for the researchers to conclude that the results were not due to chance alone. If a grocery store manager asked you how she should market soup, what would you say?
  c. If a grocer asked you about how she should market lettuce, would you say (based on the results of this study) that "limit 12 per person" would increase sales over "no limit per person"? Explain.

2.31 Does alcohol cause increased cravings for cigarettes? Research at Purdue University suggests so (see

CNN.com Website article dated June 13, 1997 entitled "Researchers Find Link Between Cigarette Cravings and Alcohol"). In an experiment, 60 heavy smokers and moderate drinkers were divided into two groups. One group drank vodka tonics and the other group drank virgin tonics (tonic water alone), but all subjects were told they were drinking vodka tonics. The researchers then measured the level of nicotine cravings (by monitoring heart rate, skin conductance, etc.). Those who had consumed the vodka tonics had 35% higher cravings than those who did not. Assuming that the assignment of subjects to treatment (vodka) or control was made at random, do you think that there might be any confounding factors that would make conclusions based on this experiment questionable?

2.32   The level of lead in children's blood should be kept low, and one way to reduce a child's exposure to lead is to control dust in the home. Researchers at the University of Rochester studied the effects of families' dust control on children with low to mild elevations in blood lead levels

("A Randomized Trial of the Effect of Dust Control on Children's Blood Lead Levels," *Pediatrics* (1996): 35). They designed an experiment in which they randomly assigned families whose children had elevated lead levels to two groups: intervention and control. The intervention group was given cleaning supplies and a demonstration of proper cleaning techniques. The control group was given a pamphlet on how to avoid lead exposure. The researchers measured lead levels in the child's blood and in the household dust at the beginning of the study and 7 months later.

a. Identify the population in this experiment.
b. Discuss the role and importance of randomization in this study.
c. Discuss the purpose of a control group.
d. Identify the treatments and response variable(s).
e. Discuss possible extraneous factors and how they could be controlled.
f. Discuss whether and how blocking should be used in this experiment.

Summary of Key Concepts and Formulas

Term or Formula	Comment
Categorical data	Individual observations are categorical responses (nonnumerical).
Numerical data	Individual observations are numerical in nature.
Discrete numerical data	Possible values are isolated points along the number line.
Continuous numerical data	Possible values form an entire interval along the number line.
Bivariate and multivariate data	Each observation consists of two (bivariate) or more (multivariate) responses or values.
Observational study	A study that observes characteristics of an existing population.
Simple random sample of size n	A sample selected in a way that gives every different sample of size n an equal chance of being selected.
Stratified sampling	Dividing a population into subgroups (strata) and then taking a separate random sample from each stratum.
Confounding variable	A variable that is related both to group membership and to the response variable.
Measurement or response bias	The tendency for a sample to differ from the population because the method of observation tends to produce values that differ from the true value.
Selection bias	The tendency for a sample to differ from the population due to systematic exclusion of some part of the population.

Term or Formula	Comment
Nonresponse bias	The tendency for a sample to differ from the population because measurements are not obtained from all individuals selected for inclusion in the sample.
Experiment	A procedure for investigating the effect of an *experimental condition* (which is manipulated by the experimeter) on a *response variable.*
Extraneous factor	A variable that is not of interest in the current study but is thought to affect the response variable.
Direct control	Holding extraneous factors constant so that their effects are not confounded with those of the experimental conditions.
Blocking	Using extraneous factors to create experimental groups that are similar with respect to those factors, thereby filtering out their effect.
Randomization	Random assignment to experimental conditions.
Replication	Ensuring that there is an adequate number of observations on each experimental treatment.
Placebo treatment	A treatment that resembles the other treatments in an experiment, but which has no active ingredients.
Control group	A group that receives no treatment or a placebo treatment.

Supplementary Exercises 2.33 – 2.40

2.33 The article "Heavy Drinking and Problems among Wine Drinkers" (*Journal of Studies on Alcohol* (1999): 467–471) attempts to answer the question of whether wine drinkers tend to drink less excessively than those who drink beer and spirits. A sample of Canadians, stratified by province of residence and other socioeconomic factors, was selected.

  a. Why might stratification by province be a good thing?

  b. List two socioeconomic factors that would be appropriate to use for stratification. Explain how each would relate to the consumption of alcohol in general and wine in particular.

2.34 According to Social Security Administration information on the names given to all babies born in the United States, the most popular name for girls born in 1982 is Jennifer, with 30.6 per 1000 girls being given that name. By 1998 Jennifer had fallen in popularity to 20th with 8569 Jennifers of the 1,579,399 females born nationwide. The 1982 results are based on a "one-percent sample of Social Security Number card applications" (required for every baby born in the United States within a year of birth). The 1998 results are based on a 100% sample of Social Security records.

  a. Calculate the rate per 1000 of Jennifers in 1998.

  b. What is another name for a 100% sample, such as the one of 1998 birth names?

  c. The one-percent sample from 1992 is "based on the last four digits of the Social Security Number, which are random and not correlated with a particular geographical region." Would you say that this sample is a simple random sample of names of girls? Explain.

2.35 The general manager of a four-star hotel decides to check the quality of housekeeping by inspecting 15 rooms himself. Discuss how the manager should determine which rooms to check. Consider that the hotel offers economy- and business-class rooms, and suites; would a simple random sample or a stratified sample be more appropriate? Also discuss possible extraneous factors.

2.36 The size of a tip that a restaurant server receives is determined, in part, by the behavior of the server. Researchers at the University of Houston ("Effect of Server Posture on Restaurant Tipping," *Journal of Applied Social Psychology* (1993): 678–685) decided to test the hypothesis that servers who squat down to the level of their customers would receive a larger tip. In the experiment, the waiter would flip a coin to determine whether he would stand or squat down next to the table. The waiter would record the amount of the bill and tip, and whether he stood or squatted down.

a. Describe the treatments and response variable.

b. Discuss possible extraneous factors and how they could be controlled.

c. Discuss whether blocking would be necessary.

d. Identify possible confounding variables.

e. Discuss the role of randomization in this experiment.

2.37   You have been asked to determine on what types of grasslands two species of birds, northern harriers and short-eared owls, build nests. The types of grasslands to be used include undisturbed, native grasses; managed, native grasses; undisturbed, nonnative grasses; and managed, nonnative grasses. You are allowed a plot of land 500 meters square to study. Explain how you would determine where to plant the four types of grasses. What role would randomization play in this determination? Identify any confounding variables. Would this study be considered observational or an experiment? (Based on the article "Response of Northern Harriers and Short-Eared Owls to Grassland Management in Illinois," *Journal of Wildlife Management* (1999): 517–523.)

2.38   Clay tiles are fired in a kiln. Unfortunately, some of the tiles crack during the firing process. A manufacturer of clay roofing tiles would like to investigate the effect of clay type on the proportion of cracked tiles. Two different types of clay are to be considered. One hundred tiles can be placed in the kiln at any one time. There will be slight variations in firing temperature at different locations in the kiln, and firing temperature may also affect cracking. Discuss the design of an experiment to collect information that could be used to decide between the two clay types. How does your proposed design deal with the extraneous factor *temperature*?

2.39   A mortgage lender routinely places advertisements in a local newspaper. The advertisements are of three different types: one focusing on low interest rates, one featuring low fees for first-time buyers, and one appealing to people who may want to refinance their homes. The lender would like to determine which advertisement format is most successful in attracting customers to call for more information. Describe an experiment that would provide the information needed to make this determination. Be sure to consider extraneous factors such as the day of the week that the advertisement appears in the paper, the section of the paper in which the advertisement appears, daily fluctuations in the interest rate, and so forth. What role does randomization play in your design?

2.40   The headline "Men Cause More Car Accidents" appeared in the Australian newspaper *The Mercury* (Sept. 12, 1995). The article stated that men were twice as likely as women to be involved in a car accident. This conclusion was based on a sample of 4000 insurance claims. Do you think the headline is justified based on this study? Explain.

References

Cobb, George. *Introduction to the Design and Analysis of Experiments,* Springer-Verlag, 1997. (An interesting and thorough introduction to the design of experiments.)

Freedman, David, Robert Pisani, and Roger Purves. *Statistics,* 3rd ed. New York: W. W. Norton, 1997. (The first two chapters contain some interesting examples of both well-designed and poorly designed experimental studies.)

Hock, Roger R. *Forty Studies That Changed Psychology: Exploration into the History of Psychological Research.* New York: Prentice-Hall, 1995.

Lohr, Sharon. *Sampling Design and Analysis.* Belmont, CA: Duxbury Press, 1996. (A very nice discussion of sampling and sources of bias at an accessible level.)

Moore, David. *Statistics: Concepts and Controversies,* 4th ed. New York: W. H. Freeman, 1997. (Contains an excellent chapter on the advantages and pitfalls of experimentation and another one in a similar vein on sample surveys and polls.)

Scheaffer, Richard L., William Mendenhall, and Lyman Ott. *Elementary Survey Sampling,* 5th ed. Belmont, CA: Duxbury Press, 1996. (An accessible yet thorough treatment of the subject.)

Tanur, Judith, ed. *Statistics: A Guide to the Unknown.* Belmont, CA: Duxbury Press, 1989. (Short articles by a number of well-known statisticians and users of statistics, all very nontechnical, on the application of statistics in various disciplines and subject areas.)

3

Graphical Methods for Describing Data

INTRODUCTION

One interesting characteristic of a book is its length. Some books have very few pages, others are exceedingly long, and most fall between these two extremes. Even within books of a given type, such as science fiction, romance, biography, or cooking, there is variation in length. One of the authors, being addicted to reading mysteries, decided to investigate the lengths of such books. A sample of 40 paperback mysteries was randomly selected from the shelves of a local bookstore — this was only a small fraction of the population of mysteries at the store — and the number of pages in each one was recorded. The resulting data is displayed in the order in which observations were obtained:

229	247	347	246	307	181	198	214	234	340	314
260	202	320	360	320	200	414	262	248	376	211
214	218	276	628	255	352	197	308	203	371	203
406	261	378	223	181	284	196				

Here are some interesting questions about the data. What is a typical or representative book length? Are the observations highly concentrated near the typical value or quite spread out? Do short or long books predominate, or are there roughly equal numbers of these two types? Are there any books whose lengths are somehow unusual when compared to the rest of the data? What proportion or fraction of observed lengths are at most 200 pages? At least 500 pages?

Questions such as these are most easily answered if the data can be organized in a sensible manner. In this chapter, we introduce some useful tabular and graphical techniques for organizing and describing data.

3.1 Displaying Categorical Data: Frequency Distributions, Bar Charts, and Pie Charts

Frequency Distributions for Categorical Data

An appropriate graphical or tabular display of data can be an effective way to summarize and communicate information. When the data set is categorical, a common way to present the data is in the form of a table, called a *frequency distribution.*

Definition

A **frequency distribution for categorical data** is a table that displays the possible categories along with the associated frequencies or relative frequencies.

The **frequency** for a particular category is the number of times the category appears in the data set.

The **relative frequency** for a particular category is the fraction or proportion of the time that the category appears in the data set. It is calculated as

$$\text{relative frequency} = \frac{\text{frequency}}{\text{number of observations in the data set}}$$

When the table includes relative frequencies, it is sometimes referred to as a **relative frequency distribution.**

EXAMPLE 3.1

Many public health efforts are directed toward increasing levels of physical activity. The article "Physical Activity in Urban White, African-American, and Mexican-American Women" (*Medicine and Science in Sports and Exercise* (1997): 1608–1614) reported on physical activity patterns in urban women. The accompanying data set gives the preferred leisure-time physical activity for each of 30 Mexican-American women. The following coding is used: W = walking, T = weight training, C = cycling, G = gardening, A = aerobics.

```
W   T   A   W   G   T   W   W   C   W   T
W   A   T   T   W   G   W   W   C   A   W
A   W   W   W   T   W   W   T
```

The corresponding frequency distribution appears as Table 3.1.

From the frequency distribution, we can see that 15 women indicated a preference for walking and that this was by far the most popular response. Equivalently, using the relative frequencies, we can say that .5 (half or 50%) of the women preferred walking.

A frequency distribution gives a tabular display of a data set. It is also common to display categorical data graphically. Bar charts and pie charts are the two most widely used types of graphic displays to use with categorical data.

Table 3.1 *Frequency Distribution for Type of Injury*

Category	Frequency	Relative Frequency
Walking	15	.500 ← 15/30
Weight training	7	.233 ← 7/30
Cycling	2	.067
Gardening	2	.067
Aerobics	4	.133
	30	1.000
	Total number of observations	*Should total 1, but in some cases may be slightly off due to rounding*

Bar Charts

A bar chart is a graph of the frequency distribution of categorical data. Each category in the frequency distribution is represented by a bar or rectangle, and the picture is constructed in such a way that the *area* of the bar is proportional to the corresponding frequency or relative frequency.

Bar Charts

When to Use: Categorical data

How to Construct:

1. Draw a horizontal line, and write the category names or labels below the line at regularly spaced intervals.

2. Draw a vertical line, and label the scale using either frequency or relative frequency.

3. Place a rectangular bar above each category label. The height is determined by the category's frequency or relative frequency, and all bars should have the same width. With the same width, both the height and the area of the bar are proportional to the relative frequency.

What to Look For: Frequently and infrequently occurring categories

---

EXAMPLE 3.2

Example 3.1 gave data on preferred leisure time physical activity for a sample of 30 Mexican-American women. Figure 3.1 (page 44) shows the bar chart corresponding to the frequency distribution constructed for this data (Table 3.1).

The bar chart provides a visual representation of the information in the frequency distribution. From the bar chart, it is easy to see that walking occurred most often in the data set, followed by weight training. The bar for walking is about twice as tall (and therefore has twice the area) as the bar for weight training, because approximately twice as many women preferred walking to weight training.

FIGURE 3.1 Bar chart of
preferred leisure activity
from MINITAB

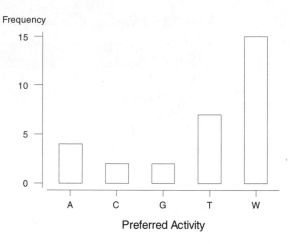

Bar charts can also be used to give a visual comparison of two or more groups. This is done by constructing two or more bar charts that use the same set of horizontal and vertical axes. The article referenced in Example 3.1 also gave data on preferred leisure physical activity for samples of white and African-American women, and included a graph like the one in Figure 3.2. Since the sample sizes for the three groups were not equal, it is important to use relative frequency to construct the scale on the vertical axis so that we can make meaningful comparisons between the groups. It is easy to discern differences among the three groups with respect to preferred leisure activity from the graph.

FIGURE 3.2 Bar chart of preferred leisure physical activity by ethnic group

EXAMPLE 3.3

The article "So Close, Yet So Far: Predictors of Attrition in College Seniors" (*J. College Student Development* (1998): 343–348) examined the reasons that college seniors leave their college programs before graduating. Forty-two college seniors at a large public university who dropped out prior to graduation were interviewed and asked the main reason for discontinuing enrollment at the university. Data consistent with that given in the article is summarized in the accompanying frequency distribution.

Reason for Leaving the University	Frequency
Academic problems	7
Poor advising or teaching	3
Needed a break	2
Economic reasons	11
Family responsibilities	4
To attend another school	9
Personal problems	3
Other	3

The corresponding bar chart is shown in Figure 3.3. From the bar chart, it is easy to see that more students reported leaving the university for economic reasons or to attend another school than for academic reasons.

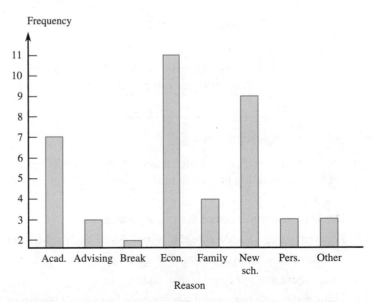

FIGURE 3.3 Bar chart for data of Example 3.3, reason for leaving university

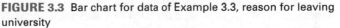

Pie Charts

A categorical data set can also be summarized using a pie chart. In a pie chart, a circle is used to represent the whole data set, with "slices" of the pie representing the possible categories. The size of the slice for a particular category is proportional to the corresponding frequency or relative frequency.

EXAMPLE 3.4

The Chronicle of Higher Education (Jan. 29, 1999) published data collected in a survey of a very large number of students who were college freshmen in the fall of 1998. One question asked whether the student was attending his or her first, second, or third choice of university. Fourth or higher choice were combined in a category called "other." The resulting data is summarized in the pie chart of Figure 3.4.

FIGURE 3.4 Pie chart of data on college choice

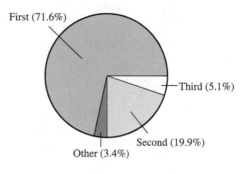

Pie charts are most effective for summarizing data sets when there are not too many different categories.

Pie Chart for Categorical Data

When to Use: Categorical data with a relatively small number of possible categories. Pie charts are most useful for illustrating proportions of the whole data set for various categories.

How to Construct:

1. Draw a circle to represent the entire data set.
2. For each category, calculate the "slice" size. This is done by computing

   slice size = category relative frequency · 360

   (since there are 360 degrees in a circle).
3. Draw a slice of appropriate size for each category. This can be tricky, so most pie charts are generated using a graphing calculator or a statistical software package.

What to Look For: Categories that form large and small proportions of the data set

EXAMPLE 3.5   Night herons and cattle egrets are species of birds that feed on aquatic prey in shallow water. These birds stalk submerged prey while wading in shallow water, and then strike rapidly and downward through the water in an attempt to catch the prey. The article "Cattle Egrets Are Less Able to Cope with Light Refraction Than Are Other Herons" (*Animal Behaviour* (1999): 687–694) gave data on outcome when 240 cattle egrets attempted to capture submerged prey. The data is summarized in the accompanying frequency distribution.

Outcome	Frequency	Relative Frequency
prey caught on first attempt	103	.43
prey caught on second attempt	41	.17
prey caught on third attempt	2	.01
prey not caught	94	.39

To draw a pie chart by hand, we must first compute the slice size for each category. This is done as follows:

Category	Slice Size
first attempt	$(.43)(360) = 154.8$
second attempt	$(.17)(360) = 61.2$
third attempt	$(.01)(360) = 3.6$
not caught	$(.39)(360) = 140.4$

We would then draw a circle and use a protractor to mark off a slice corresponding to about 155 degrees, as illustrated here:

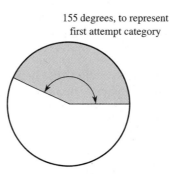

155 degrees, to represent
first attempt category

Continuing to add slices in this way leads to a completed pie chart.

It is much easier to use a statistical software package to construct pie charts. A MINITAB pie chart for the cattle egret data is shown in Figure 3.5(a) on page 48. Figure 3.5(b) shows a pie chart constructed using similar data on outcome for 180 night herons. Although some differences between night herons and cattle egrets can be seen by comparing the pie charts in Figures 3.5(a) and (b), it is difficult to actually compare category proportions using pie charts. A bar chart (Figure 3.6) makes this type of comparison easier.

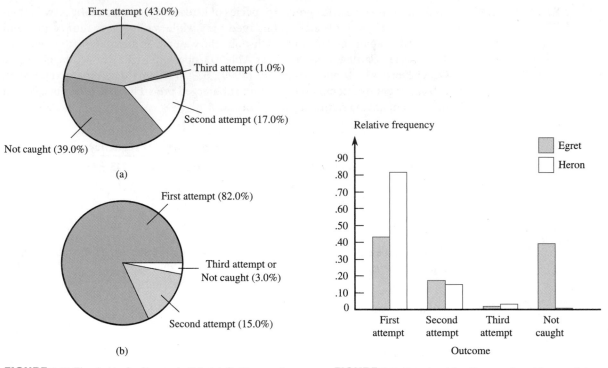

FIGURE 3.5 Pie charts for Example 3.5: (a) Cattle egret data; (b) Night heron data

FIGURE 3.6 Bar chart for the egret and heron data

Other Uses of Bar Charts and Pie Charts

As we have seen in previous examples, bar charts and pie charts can be used to summarize categorical data sets. However, they are occasionally also used for other purposes, as illustrated in the following example.

EXAMPLE 3.6   The 1998 Grape Crush Report for San Luis Obispo and Santa Barbara Counties gave the accompanying information on grape production for each of seven different types of grapes used to make wine (*San Luis Obispo Telegram-Tribune*, Feb. 12, 1999).

Type of Grape	Tons Produced
Chardonnay	39,582
Chenin Blanc	1,601
Sauvignon Blanc	5,868
Cabernet Sauvignon	21,656
Merlot	11,210
Pinot Noir	2,856
Zinfandel	7,330
Total	90,103

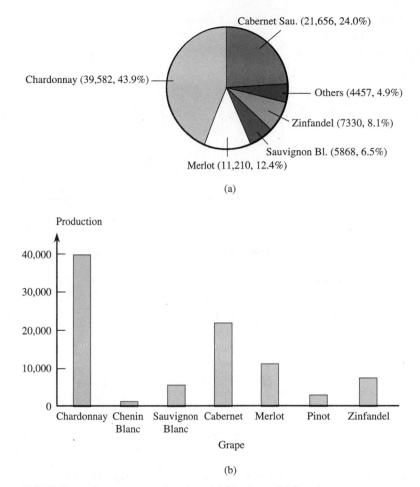

FIGURE 3.7 Grape production data: (a) Pie chart; (b) Bar chart

Although this table is not a frequency distribution for a categorical data set, it is common to represent information of this type graphically using either a pie chart or a bar chart. A pie chart is shown in Figure 3.7(a). The pie represents the total grape production, and the slices show the proportion of the total production for each of the seven types of grapes. Figure 3.7(b) shows a bar chart representation of the grape production data.

The article also gave grape production information for 1997 and commented on the effect of harsh weather on the counties' grape crop. Figure 3.8 (page 50) is a bar chart of grape production in 1997 and 1998. The bar chart clearly shows decreased production in 1998 for all but two of the seven types of grape.

FIGURE 3.8 Bar chart comparing 1997 and 1998 grape production

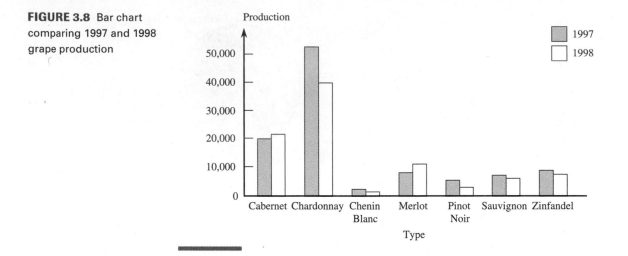

Exercises 3.1 – 3.11

3.1 Many adolescent boys aspire to be a professional athlete. The paper "Why Adolescent Boys Dream of Becoming Professional Athletes" (*Psychological Reports* (1999): 1075–1085) examined some of the reasons. A sample of teenage boys was asked the following question: "Previous studies have shown that more teenage boys say that they are considering becoming professional athletes than any other occupation. In your opinion, why do these boys want to become professional athletes?" The resulting data is shown in the accompanying table.

Response	Frequency
Fame and celebrity	94
Money	56
Attract women	29
Like sports	27
Easy life	24
Don't need an education	19
Other	19

a. Construct a bar chart to display this data.
b. Would a pie chart be a better way to display this data? Why or why not?

3.2 The paper "Profile of Sport/Leisure Injuries Treated at Emergency Rooms of Urban Hospitals" (*Canadian J. of Sports Science* (1991): 99–102) classified non-contact sports injuries by sport, resulting in the accompanying table. Calculate relative frequencies and draw the corresponding bar chart.

Sport	No. of Injuries	Sport	No. of Injuries
Touch football	38	Jogging/running	11
Soccer	24	Bicycling	11
Basketball	19	Volleyball	7
Baseball/softball	11	Others	47

3.3 The paper "Exploring the Factors that Influence Men and Women to Form Medical Career Aspirations" (*J. College Student Development* (1998): 417–421) gave estimates of the percent of college freshmen nationwide who hoped to have a medical career. These percentages were based on "a nationally representative sample of all entering college students" that is conducted each year.

	Percent with Medical Career Aspirations			
	1975	**1980**	**1985**	**1990**
Men	3.9	4.4	4.1	3.9
Women	2.5	2.9	3.4	3.7

Construct a comparative bar graph that shows the proportion with medical career aspirations for men and women over time. (*Hint*: Mark the years on the horizontal axis, and then construct a bar for each gender for each year). Comment on any interesting features of the graph.

3.4 The paper referenced in the previous exercise also gave information on parent's occupation for those who aspire to a medical career. Construct two pie charts, one for men and one for women, to display this information, and comment on the similarities and differences between the two.

Parent Occupation	Male	Female
Only mother is a physician	596	712
Only father is a physician	504	350
Both parents are physicians	734	824
Neither parent is a physician	166	114

3.5 The percentage of the U.S. gross domestic product spent on health care over the period from 1960 to 1995 was given in the paper "Building the Next Generation of Healthy People" (*Public Health Reports* (1999): 213–216). Construct a bar graph for this data and comment on the interesting features of this graph. Be sure to comment on the trend over time.

Year	Percent Spent on Health Care
1960	5.1
1965	5.7
1970	7.1
1975	8.0
1980	8.9
1985	10.3
1990	12.2
1995	13.7

3.6 Nonresponse is a common problem facing researchers who rely on mail questionnaires. In the paper "Reasons for Nonresponse on the Physicians' Practice Survey" (*Proc. Social Statistics Amer. Stat. Assoc.* (1980): 202), 811 doctors who did not respond to the AMA Survey of Physicians were contacted about the reason for their non-participation. The results are summarized in the accompanying relative frequency distribution. Draw the corresponding histogram.

Reason	Relative Frequency
1. No time to participate	.264
2. Not interested	.300
3. Don't like surveys in general	.145
4. Don't like this particular survey	.025
5. Hostility toward the government	.054
6. Desire to protect privacy	.056
7. Other reason for refusal	.053
8. No reason given	.103

3.7 The article "Physicians Accessing the Internet: The PAI project" (*J. Amer. Med. Assn.* (1999): 633–634) gave the following information on Internet usage by doctors.

The data is from a survey of 324 randomly selected doctors, who were asked to indicate the category that best described how often they used the Internet.

Internet Usage Pattern	Frequency
Never	31
Rarely (about 3 times per year)	15
Occasionally (about once a month)	52
Often (about once a week)	109
Daily	117

Construct a pie chart for this data and write a brief summary that describes Internet usage for physicians who participated in this survey.

3.8 The paper "Sexual Content of Top-Grossing Motion Pictures" (*J. of Health Education* (1998): 354–357) gave the accompanying information on the ratings of the ten movies that made the most money in the years 1987 and 1992.

	Rating		
	G	**PG/PG-13**	**R**
1987	0	3	7
1992	1	5	4

a. Construct a pie chart to show the distribution of ratings for 1987.

b. Construct a pie chart to show the distribution of ratings for 1992, and comment on the differences between this chart and the one based on the 1987 data.

3.9 Each murder committed in Utah during the period 1978–1990 was categorized by day of the week, resulting in the following frequencies: Sunday, 109; Monday, 73; Tuesday, 97; Wednesday, 95; Thursday, 83; Friday, 107; Saturday, 100.

a. Obtain the corresponding frequency distribution.

b. What proportion of these murders were committed on a "weekend day"—i.e., Friday, Saturday, or Sunday?

c. Does this data suggest that a murder is more likely to be committed on some days than on other days? Explain your reasoning.

3.10 The paper "Fire Doors: A Potential Weak Link in the Protection Chain" (*Fire Technology* (1992): 177–179) reported on a survey of companies that use fire doors to subdivide major plant facilities in case of uncontrolled fires. Four types of doors were in use: rolling steel (R), single metal-clad sliding (M), swinging with door closer (C), and single swinging (S). Suppose the data was as shown in the accompanying table. Determine frequencies and relative frequencies for the four categories (percentages agree with those given in the paper).

R   M   M   S   R   R   C   R   M   R   M
M   M   C   S   R   R   C   C   M   R   R
C   S   R   C   C   M   S   M   M   M   R
S   R   R   C   C   S   R   M   C   R   M
C   M   R   C   M   S

3.11 The use of anabolic steroids (synthetic derivatives of the male sex hormone testosterone) among athletes is believed to have increased dramatically in recent years. A survey of college athletes was carried out to gather relevant data, which was then summarized in the paper "Associations between Academic Performance of Division 1 College Athletes and Their Perceptions of the Effects of Anabolic Steroids" (*Perceptual and Motor Skills* (1995): 284–286). Each athlete was asked for an opinion concerning the severity of the steroid use problem in his or her sport. Responses were also categorized by student grade point average (GPA). (See the accompanying table.)

Response Category	Grade Point Average		
	3.0–4.0	2.0–<3.0	1.0–<2.0
Very great problem	40	73	3
A problem	84	184	11
A small problem	149	170	4
Not a problem	276	317	9
Don't know	146	156	11

a. Construct a separate bar chart of the responses for each GPA category. Compare and contrast the three graphs.

b. Data from any particular GPA category can be summarized in a single rectangular bar, as in the accompanying diagram. The length of each segment is the relative frequency of the corresponding response category. Construct three of these bars above one another for the three different GPA groups. Is it easier to compare and contrast with this picture than with the three separate bar charts?

Figure for Exercise 3.11b

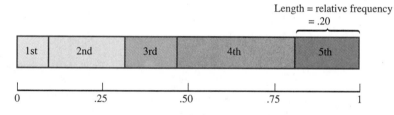

3.2   Displaying Numerical Data: Dotplots and Stem-and-Leaf Displays

Dotplots

A dotplot is a simple way to display numerical data when the data set is reasonably small. Each observation is represented by a dot above the location corresponding to its value on a horizontal measurement scale. When a value occurs more than once, there is a dot for each occurrence and these dots are stacked vertically.

Dotplots

When to Use: Small numerical data sets

How to Construct:
1. Draw a horizontal line and mark it with an appropriate measurement scale.
2. Locate each value in the data set along the measurement scale, and represent it by a dot. If there are two or more observations with the same value, stack the dots vertically.

(continued)

What to Look For: Dotplots convey information about a representative or typical value in the data set, the extent to which the data values spread out, the nature of the distribution of values along the number line, and the presence of unusual values in the data set.

EXAMPLE 3.7   The accompanying data on gender and birth weight (in kilograms) of foals born to 15 thoroughbred mares appeared in the article "Suckling Behavior Does Not Measure Milk Intake in Horses" (*Animal Behaviour* (1999): 673–678). Figure 3.9 shows a MINITAB dotplot of the weight values.

Foal	1	2	3	4	5	6	7	8	9	10
Gender	F	M	M	F	F	M	F	F	M	F
Weight	129	119	132	123	112	113	95	104	104	93

Foal	11	12	13	14	15
Gender	M	F	M	F	F
Weight	108	95	117	128	127

A typical birth weight is around 113. The 15 observations are quite spread out around this value. A gap separates the three smallest values from the rest of the data. Figure 3.10 shows the dotplots of male and female foal weights. Although the weights for male and female foals seem similar in the main part of the data, it is interesting to note that all three of the foals with low birth weight were female.

FIGURE 3.9 Dotplot of foal birth weights

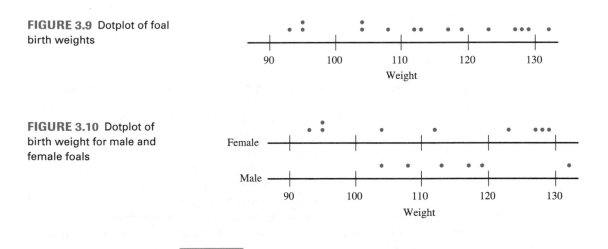

FIGURE 3.10 Dotplot of birth weight for male and female foals

Stem-and-Leaf Displays

A stem-and-leaf display is an effective and compact way to summarize numerical data. Each number in the data set is broken into two pieces called a stem and a leaf.

The **stem** is the first part of the number and consists of the beginning digit(s). The **leaf** is the last part of the number and consists of the final digit(s). For example, the number 213 might be split into a stem of 2 and a leaf of 13 or a stem of 21 and a leaf of 3. The resulting stems and leaves are then used to construct the display.

EXAMPLE 3.8

The use of alcohol by college students is of great concern, not only to those in the academic community, but also, because of potential health and safety consequences, to society at large. The article "Health and Behavioral Consequences of Binge Drinking in College" (*J. of the Amer. Med. Assoc.* (1994): 1672–1677) reported on a comprehensive study of heavy drinking on campuses across the country. A binge episode was defined as five or more drinks in a row for males and four or more for females. Figure 3.11 shows a stem-and-leaf display of 140 values of the percentage of undergraduate students who are binge drinkers at various colleges. (These values were not given in the cited article, but our display agrees with a picture of the data that did appear.)

FIGURE 3.11 Stem-and-leaf display for percentage of binge drinkers at each of 140 colleges

```
0 | 4
1 | 1345678889
2 | 1223456666777889999
3 | 0112233344555666677777888899999        Stem:   Tens digit
4 | 111222223344445566666677788888999       Leaf:   Ones digit
5 | 0011122223345566666777788889 99
6 | 01111244455666778
```

The numbers in the vertical column on the left of the display are the **stems.** Each number to the right of the vertical line is a **leaf** corresponding to one of the observations in the data set. The legend

Stem: Tens digit

Leaf: Ones digit

tells us that the observation that had a stem of 2 and a leaf of 1 corresponds to a college where 21% (as opposed to 2.1% or .21%) of the students were binge drinkers.

The display in Figure 3.11 suggests that a typical or representative value is in the stem 4 row, perhaps someplace in the low 40% range. The observations are not highly concentrated about this typical value, as would be the case if all values were between 20% and 49%. The display rises to a single peak as we move downward and then declines, and there are no gaps in the display. The shape of the display is not perfectly symmetric but rather appears to stretch out a bit more in the direction of low stems than in the direction of high stems. The most surprising feature of this data is that at most colleges in the sample, at least one-quarter of the students are binge drinkers.

The leaves on each line of the display in Figure 3.11 have been arranged in order from smallest to largest. Most statistical software packages order the leaves this way, but it is not necessary to do so to get an informative display that still shows many of the important characteristics of the data set, such as shape and spread.

Stem-and-leaf displays can be useful in getting a sense of a typical value for the data set, as well as how spread out the values in the data set are. It is also easy to spot data values that are far away from the rest of the values in the data set. Such values are called **outliers.**

Definition

An **outlier** is an unusually small or large data value. A more formal definition of outliers is given in Chapter 4.

The stem-and-leaf display of the data on binge drinking does not show any outliers.

Stem-and-Leaf Displays

When to Use: Numerical data sets with a small to moderate number of observations (does not work well for very large data sets)

How to Construct:
1. Select one or more leading digits for the stem values. The trailing digits (or sometimes just the first one of the trailing digits) become the leaves.
2. List possible stem values in a vertical column.
3. Record the leaf for every observation beside the corresponding stem value.
4. Indicate the units for stems and leaves someplace in the display.

What to Look For: The display conveys information about a representative or typical value in the data set, the extent of spread about such a value, the presence of any gaps in the data, the extent of symmetry in the distribution of values, the number and location of peaks, and the presence of any outliers.

EXAMPLE 3.9   The chapter introduction gave data on page length for a sample of 40 paperback mysteries. The data is reproduced here. The page lengths ranged from a low value of 181 to a high value of 628.

229	247	347	246	307	181	198	214	234	340	314
260	202	320	360	320	200	414	262	248	376	211
214	218	276	628	255	352	197	308	203	371	203
406	261	378	223	181	284	196				

A natural choice for the stem is the leading (hundreds) digit. This would result in a display with 6 stems (1, 2, 3, 4, 5, 6). Using the first two digits of a number as the stem would result in 45 stems (18, 19, . . ., 62). A stem-and-leaf display with 45 stems would not be a very effective summary of the data. In general, stem-and-leaf displays that use between 5 and 20 stems tend to work well.

If we choose the hundreds digit as the stem, the remaining two digits (the tens and ones) digits would form the leaf. For example, for the first few data values

$$229 \rightarrow \text{stem} = 2, \text{leaf} = 29$$
$$247 \rightarrow \text{stem} = 2, \text{leaf} = 47$$
$$347 \rightarrow \text{stem} = 3, \text{leaf} = 47$$

The leaves have been entered in the display of Figure 3.12 in the order they are encountered in the data set.

Commas are used to separate the leaves only when each leaf has two or more digits. This display shows that most mysteries had page lengths in the two and three hundreds, and that a typical page length is around 300. There is one outlier, 638 pages, that stands out as being unusually large compared to the page lengths of the other books in the sample.

An alternative display (Figure 3.13) results from dropping all but the first digit of the leaf. This is what most statistical computer packages do when generating a display; little information about a typical value, spread, or shape is lost in this truncation.

FIGURE 3.12 Stem-and-leaf display of page length

1	81,98,97,81,96
2	29,47,46,14,34,60,02,00,62,48,11,14,18,76,55,03,03,61,23,84
3	47,07,40,14,20,60,20,76,52,08,71,78
4	14,06
5	
6	28

Stem: Hundreds
Leaf: Tens and ones

FIGURE 3.13 Stem-and-leaf display of the page length data using truncated leaves

1	89989
2	24413600641117500628
3	404126275077
4	10
5	
6	2

Stem: Hundreds
Leaf: Tens

Repeated Stems to Stretch a Display

Sometimes a natural choice of stems gives a display in which too many observations are concentrated on just a few stems. A more informative picture may be obtained by dividing the leaves at any given stem into two groups: those that begin with 0, 1, 2, 3, or 4 (the "low" leaves) and those that begin with 5, 6, 7, 8, or 9 (the "high" leaves). Then each stem is listed twice when constructing the display, once for the low leaves and once again for the high leaves.

EXAMPLE 3.10

The accompanying data on daily protein intake (in grams of protein per kilogram of body weight) for 20 competitive athletes was obtained from a plot in the article "A Comparison of Plasma Glutamine Concentration in Athletes from Different Sports" (*Medicine and Science in Sports and Exercise* (1998): 1693–1697):

| 1.4 | 2.2 | 2.7 | 1.5 | 2.3 | 1.7 | 2.3 | 1.5 | 1.8 | 2.8 |
| 1.8 | 1.9 | 2.0 | 2.3 | 1.5 | 1.9 | 1.7 | 1.8 | 1.6 | 3.0 |

Since each value in the data set has only two digits, we must use the first digit for the stem and the last digit for the leaf. The corresponding stem-and-leaf display is shown in Figure 3.14; the display has only three stems (1, 2, and 3), and all but one of the leaves are located at the 1 and 2 stems.

A more informative display using repeated stems is shown in Figure 3.15.

FIGURE 3.14 Stem-and-leaf display for the protein intake data

```
1 | 457588959786
2 | 2733803        Stem:  Ones
3 | 0               Leaf:  Tenths
```

FIGURE 3.15 Stem-and-leaf display for protein intake data using repeated stems

```
1L | 4
1H | 57588959786
2L | 23303
2H | 78              Stem:  Ones
3L | 0               Leaf:  Tenths
```

It is also possible to repeat a stem more than twice. For example, each stem might be repeated five times, once for each of the leaf groupings {0, 1}, {2, 3}, {4, 5}, {6, 7}, and {8, 9}.

Comparative Stem-and-Leaf Displays

Frequently an analyst wishes to see whether two groups of data differ in some fundamental way. A comparative stem-and-leaf display, in which the leaves for one group extend to the right of the stem values and those from the second group to the left, can provide preliminary visual impressions and insights.

EXAMPLE 3.11

The article "Tobacco and Alcohol Use in G-Rated Children's Animated Films (*J. American Medical Assn.* (1999): 1131–1136) investigated exposure to tobacco and alcohol use in all G-rated animated films released between 1937 and 1997 by five major film studios. The researchers found that tobacco use was shown in 56% of the films reviewed. Data on the total tobacco exposure time (in seconds) for films with tobacco use produced by Walt Disney, Inc., were

| 223 | 176 | 548 | 37 | 158 | 51 | 299 | 37 | 11 | 165 |
| 74 | 9 | 2 | 6 | 23 | 206 | 9 | | | |

Data for 11 G-rated animated films showing tobacco use that were produced by MGM/United Artists, Warner Brothers, Universal, and Twentieth Century Fox was also given. The tobacco exposure times (in seconds) for these films was

| 205 | 162 | 6 | 1 | 117 | 5 | 91 | 155 | 24 | 55 | 17 |

To construct a stem-and-leaf display, think of each observation as a three-digit number. For example, 2 would be 002 and 37 would be 037. We then use the first digit of each number as the stem and the remaining two digits as the leaf. For simplicity, let's truncate the leaves to one digit:

$$223 \rightarrow \text{stem} = 2, \text{leaf} = 2 \quad (\text{truncated from } 23)$$
$$37 \rightarrow 037 \rightarrow \text{stem} = 0, \text{leaf} = 3 \quad (\text{truncated from } 37)$$
$$9 \rightarrow 009 \rightarrow \text{stem} = 0, \text{leaf} = 0 \quad (\text{truncated from } 09)$$

The resulting comparative stem-and-leaf display, using repeated stems, is shown in Figure 3.16.

FIGURE 3.16 Comparative stem-and-leaf display for tobacco exposure times

Other Studios		Disney
12000	0L	33100020
59	0H	57
1	1L	
56	1H	756
All Dogs Go to Heaven 0	2L	20 *Pinocchio, James and the Giant Peach*
	2H	9 *101 Dalmatians*
	3L	
	3H	Stem: Hundreds
	4L	Leaf: Tens
	4H	
	5L	4 *The Three Caballeros*

One first impression is that there are many films where the tobacco exposure time is small, both for Disney films and for those made by the other studios. Disney has more films with longer exposure to tobacco, and there is an obvious outlier in the Disney data (the 548-second exposure in the 1945 film *The Three Caballeros*).

Exercises 3.12 – 3.20

3.12 The article "Can We Really Walk Straight?" (*Amer. J. of Physical Anthropology* (1992): 19–27) reported on an experiment in which each of 20 healthy men was asked to walk as straight as possible to a target 60 meters away at normal speed. Consider the following observations on cadence (number of strides per second):

Figure for Exercise 3.13

Acc. Rate

.95 .85 .92 .95 .93 .86 1.00 .92 .85 .81
.78 .93 .93 1.05 .93 1.06 1.06 .96 .81 .96

Construct a dotplot for the cadence data. Do any data values stand out as being unusual?

3.13 Each year *U.S. News and World Report* publishes a ranking of U.S. business schools. The accompanying data gives the acceptance rates (percent of applicants admitted) for the best 25 programs in the most recent survey. Construct a dotplot and compare it to the accompanying MINITAB dotplot (see top of this page).

16.3 12.0 25.1 20.3 31.9 20.7 30.1 19.5 36.2 46.9 25.8
36.7 33.8 24.2 21.5 35.1 37.6 23.9 17.0 38.4 31.2 43.8
28.9 31.4 48.9

3.14 Here is data on both yield and average maturity (in days) for the ten largest tax-free money-market funds, as reported in the Jan. 4, 1996 *Los Angeles Times*:

Yield   4.8 4.3 4.2 4.2 4.2 4.1 4.0 4.0 4.0 3.6
Maturity 26   64   63   48   71   37   55   64   50   48

a. Construct a dotplot of the yield data.
b. Construct a dotplot of the maturity data.
c. The first yield and maturity are for the highest-yielding fund, the second yield and maturity are for the second-highest-yielding fund, and so on. Does it appear that decreasing yield is associated either with longer average maturity or with shorter average maturity? That is, does the value of one variable tend to increase or to decrease as the other one decreases? Explain your reasoning. (You might find it helpful to replace the dots in the dotplot of part **b** with the characters 1, 2, . . . , 9, and 0 corresponding to 26, . . . , 48. This type of question will be addressed more formally in Chapter 5.)

3.15 The accompanying stem-and-leaf display shows observations on average shower flow rate (l/min) for a sample of 129 houses in Perth, Australia ("An Application of Bayes Methodology to the Analysis of Diary Records from a Water Use Study," *J. Amer. Stat. Assoc.* (1987): 705–711).

2	23
3	2344567789
4	01356889
5	00001114455666789
6	0000122223344456667789999
7	00012233455555668
8	02233448
9	012233335666788
10	2344455688
11	2335999
12	37
13	8
14	36
15	0035
16	
17	
18	9

Stem: Ones
Leaf: Tenths

a. What is the smallest flow rate in the sample?
b. If one additional house yielded a flow rate of 8.9, where would this observation be placed on the display?
c. What is a typical, or representative, flow rate?
d. Does the display appear to be highly concentrated, or quite spread out?
e. Does the distribution of values in the display appear to be reasonably symmetric? If not, how would you describe the departure from symmetry?
f. Does the data set appear to contain any outliers (observations far removed from the bulk of the data)?

3.16 The accompanying observations are maximum flow rates (at 80 pounds per square inch, or psi) for 34 different shower heads evaluated in a *Consumer Reports* article (July 1990).

2.9 2.8 2.0 3.6 2.7 2.5 2.6 2.9 2.7 2.8 2.5
2.8 2.2 2.5 2.5 2.8 1.8 2.7 2.7 4.7 2.8 2.7
3.1 2.9 3.4 2.6 2.6 2.7 2.4 2.5 5.4 4.9 2.8
2.5

Construct a stem-and-leaf display using stems 1, 2, 3, 4, and 5. What is the most prominent feature of the display?

3.17 Return to the previous exercise, and construct a stem-and-leaf display using repeated stems (1H, 2L, 2H, 3L, . . .).

3.18 Each observation in the accompanying data set is the number of housing units (homes or condominiums) sold during November 1992 in a region corresponding to a particular Orange County, California, ZIP code. Construct a stem-and-leaf display, and comment on any interesting features.

25	18	16	6	26	11	29	7	5	15	12
37	35	11	16	35	20	27	17	30	10	16
28	13	26	11	12	8	9	29	0	20	30
12	45	26	21	30	18	31	0	46	47	14
13	29	11	18	10	27	5	18	67	21	35
48	42	70	43	0	30	17	35	40	61	18
17	17									

3.19 The accompanying observations are yardages for a sample of golf courses recently listed by *Golf Magazine* as being among the most challenging in the United States. Construct a stem-and-leaf display, and explain why your choice of stems seems preferable to any of the other possible choices.

6526	6770	6936	6770	6583	6464	7005	6927	6790	7209	7040
6850	6700	6614	7022	6506	6527	6470	6900	6605	6873	6798
6745	7280	7131	6435	6694	6433	6870	7169	7011	7168	6713
7051	6904	7105	7165	7050	7113	6890				

3.20 An article on peanut butter in *Consumer Reports* (Sept. 1990) reported the following scores for various brands:

Creamy

56	44	62	36	39	53	50	65	45
40	56	68	41	30	40	50	56	30
22								

Crunchy

62	53	75	42	47	40	34	62	52
50	34	42	36	75	80	47	56	62

Construct a comparative stem-and-leaf display, and discuss similarities and differences for the two types.

3.3 Displaying Numerical Data: Frequency Distributions and Histograms

A stem-and-leaf display is not always an effective summary technique because it is unwieldy when the data set contains a great many observations. Frequency distributions and histograms are displays that are useful for summarizing even a very large data set in a compact fashion.

Frequency Distributions and Histograms for Discrete Numerical Data

Discrete numerical data almost always results from counting. In such cases, each observation is a whole number. As in the case of categorical data, a frequency distribution for discrete numerical data lists each possible value (either individually or grouped into intervals), the associated frequency, and sometimes the corresponding relative frequency. Recall that relative frequency is calculated by dividing the frequency by the total number of observations in the data set.

EXAMPLE 3.12

The authors of the article "Behavioral Aspects of the Raccoon Mating System: Determinants of Consortship Success" (*Animal Behaviour* (1999): 593–601) monitored raccoons in southern Texas during the 1990–1992 mating seasons in an effort to describe mating behavior. Twenty-nine female raccoons were observed, and the number of male partners during the time the female was accepting partners (generally 1 to 4 days each year) was recorded for each female. The resulting data follows:

1	3	2	1	1	4	2	4	1	1	1	3	1	1	1
1	2	2	1	1	4	1	1	2	1	1	1	1	3	

The corresponding frequency distribution is given in Table 3.2.

Table 3.2 *Frequency Distribution for Number of Partners*

Number of Partners	Frequency	Relative Frequency
1	18	.621
2	5	.172
3	3	.103
4	3	.103
	29	.999
		Differs from 1 due to rounding

From the frequency distribution, we can see that 18 of the female raccoons had a single partner. The corresponding relative frequency, .621, tells us that the proportion of female raccoons in the sample with a single partner was .621, or equivalently 62.1% of the females had a single partner. Adding the relative frequencies for the values of 1 and 2 gives

.621 + .172 = .793

indicating that 79.3% of the raccoons had two or fewer partners.

A histogram for discrete numerical data is a graph of the frequency distribution that is very similar to the bar chart for categorical data. Each frequency or relative frequency is represented by a rectangle centered over the corresponding value (or range of values) and with area proportional to the corresponding frequency or relative frequency.

Histogram for Discrete Numerical Data

When to Use: Discrete numerical data. Works well even for large data sets.

How to Construct:

1. Draw a horizontal scale, and mark the possible values.

2. Draw a vertical scale, and mark it with either frequencies or relative frequencies.

3. Above each possible value, draw a rectangle centered at that value (so that the rectangle for 1 is centered at 1, the rectangle for 5 is centered at 5, and so on). The height of each rectangle is determined by the corresponding frequency or relative frequency. Often possible values are consecutive whole numbers, in which case the base width for each rectangle is 1.

What to Look For: Central or typical value, extent of spread or variation, general shape, location and number of peaks, and presence of gaps and outliers

---

EXAMPLE 3.13   The raccoon data of Example 3.12 was summarized in a frequency distribution. The corresponding histogram is shown in Figure 3.17 on page 62.

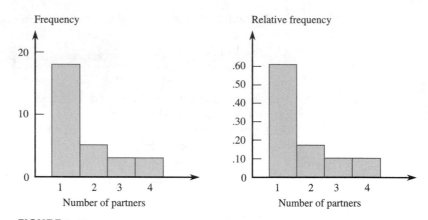

FIGURE 3.17 Histogram and relative frequency histogram of raccoon data

Note that each rectangle in the histogram is centered over the corresponding value. When relative frequency instead of frequency is used for the vertical scale, the scale on the vertical axis is different but all essential characteristics of the graph (shape, location, spread) are unchanged.

Sometimes a discrete numerical data set contains a large number of possible values and may also have a few large or small values that are far away from most of the data. In this case, rather than forming a frequency distribution with a very long list of possible values, it is common to group the observed values into intervals or ranges. This is illustrated in the following example.

EXAMPLE 3.14   Each student in a sample of 176 students at a large public university was asked about alcohol use, and the resulting data appeared in the article "Alcohol, Tobacco, and Marijuana Use: Relationships to Undergraduate Students' Creative Achievement" (*J. College Student Development* (1998): 472–479). The frequency distribution in Table 3.3 summarizes data on number of drinks consumed per week.

Table 3.3 *Frequency Distribution for Number of Drinks per Week*

Drinks per Week	Frequency
0 to 1	52
2 to 5	38
6 to 9	17
10 to 15	35
16 or more	34

The authors of this article chose to group the observed values (rather than list them all: 0, 1, 2, . . .), and they also created an open-ended group of "16 or more." This results in a much more compact table that still communicates one of the important features of the data: the large numbers of individuals at both the low and the high ends. Also note that we could not draw a histogram based on this frequency distribution because of the open-ended group (16 or more). Also, since the number of possible values included differs from group to group (2 in the "0 or 1" group, 4 in the "2 to 5" group, 6 in the "10 to 15" group, etc.), even without the open-ended group drawing a correct histogram is a bit more complicated. You cannot just use frequency or relative frequency for the vertical scale. One method of drawing a histogram that would work, as long as there are no open-ended groups, is described later in this section.

Frequency Distributions and Histograms for Continuous Numerical Data

The difficulty in constructing tabular or graphical displays with continuous data, such as observations on reaction time (seconds) or fuel efficiency (miles per gallon), is that there are no natural categories. The way out of this dilemma is to define our own categories. For fuel efficiency data, suppose that we mark some intervals on a horizontal miles-per-gallon measurement axis, as pictured in Figure 3.18. Each data value should fall in exactly one of these intervals. If the smallest observation were 25.3 and the largest were 29.8, we might use intervals of width .5, with the first one starting at 25.0 and the last one ending at 30.0. The resulting intervals are called **class intervals,** or just **classes.** The class intervals play the same role that the categories or individual values played in frequency distributions for categorical or discrete numerical data.

| 25.0 | 25.5 | 26.0 | 26.5 | 27.0 | 27.5 | 28.0 | 28.5 | 29.0 | 29.5 | 30.0 |

FIGURE 3.18 Suitable class intervals for miles-per-gallon data

There is one further difficulty. Where should we place an observation such as 27.0, which falls on a boundary between classes? Our convention will be to define intervals so that such an observation is placed in the upper rather than the lower class interval. Thus, in our frequency distribution, a typical class will be 26.5 to <27.0, where the symbol < is a substitute for the phrase *less than.* This class will contain all observations that are greater than or equal to 26.5 and less than 27.0. The observation 27.0 would then fall in the class 27.0 to <27.5.

EXAMPLE 3.15 The trace element zinc is an important dietary constituent, partly because it aids in the maintenance of the immune system. The accompanying data on zinc intake (mg) for a sample of 40 patients with rheumatoid arthritis was read from a graph in the article "Plasma Zinc and Copper Concentrations in Rheumatoid Arthritis: Influence of Dietary Factors and Disease Activity" (*American J. Clinical Nutrition* (1991): 1082–1086):

8.0	12.9	13.0	8.9	10.1	7.3	11.1	10.9	6.2	8.1	8.8
10.4	15.7	13.6	19.3	9.9	8.5	11.1	10.7	8.8	10.7	6.8
7.4	4.8	11.8	13.0	9.5	8.1	6.9	11.5	11.2	13.6	4.9
18.8	15.7	10.8	10.7	11.5	16.1	9.9				

The smallest observation is 4.8, and the largest is 19.3. It seems reasonable to start the first class interval at 3.0 and let each interval have a width of 3.0. This gives the class intervals

3 to <6   6 to <9   9 to <12   12 to <15   15 to <18   18 to <21

Table 3.4 displays the resulting frequency distribution.

Various relative frequencies can be added together to yield other interesting information. For example,

proportion of individuals with intake <12 = (proportion in 3 to <6)
$$+ \text{(proportion in 6 to } <9) + \text{(proportion in 9 to } <12)$$
$$= .050 + .300 + .400$$
$$= .750 \quad (75\%)$$

and

proportion of individuals with intake between 6 and 15 = (proportion in 6 to <9)
$$+ \text{(proportion in 9 to } <12)$$
$$+ \text{(proportion in 12 to } <15)$$
$$= .300 + .400 + .125$$
$$= .825 \quad (82.5\%)$$

Table 3.4 *Frequency distribution for zinc intake (mg)*

Class Interval	Frequency	Relative Frequency
3 to <6	2	.050
6 to <9	12	.300
9 to <12	16	.400
12 to <15	5	.125
15 to <18	3	.075
18 to <21	2	.050
	40	1.000

There are no set rules for selecting either the number of class intervals or the length of the intervals. Using a few relatively wide intervals will bunch the data, whereas using a great many relatively narrow intervals may spread the data over too many intervals, so that no interval contains more than a few observations. Neither type of distribution will give an informative picture of how values are distributed over the range of measurement, and interesting features of the data set may be missed. Generally speaking, with a small amount of data, relatively few intervals, perhaps between five and ten, should be used, whereas with a large amount of data, a distribution based on 15 to 20 (or even more) intervals is often recommended. The quantity

$$\sqrt{\text{number of observations}}$$

often gives a rough estimate for an appropriate number of intervals: 5 intervals for 25 observations, 10 intervals when the number of observations is 100, and so on. Two people making reasonable and similar choices for the number of intervals, their width, and the starting point of the first interval should obtain very similar summaries of the data.

Cumulative Relative Frequencies

Rather than wanting to know what proportion of the data falls in a particular class, we often wish to determine the proportion falling below a specified value. This is easily done when the value is a class boundary. Consider the following classes and relative frequencies:

Class	0 to <25	25 to <50	50 to <75	75 to <100	100 to <125	. . .
Relative frequency	.05	.10	.18	.25	.20	. . .

Then

proportion of observations less than 75 = proportion in one of the first three classes

$$= .05 + .10 + .18$$
$$= .33$$

Similarly,

proportion of observations less than 100 = .05 + .10 + .18 + .25 = .33 + .25 = .58

Each such sum of relative frequencies is called a **cumulative relative frequency.** Notice that the cumulative relative frequency .58 is the sum of the previous cumulative relative frequency .33 and the "current'" relative frequency .25. These calculations can also be done for discrete data (e.g., the proportion of observations that are at most 5, at most 6, and so on).

EXAMPLE 3.16   The strength of welds used in aircraft construction has been of great concern to aeronautical engineers in recent years. Table 3.5 (page 66) gives a frequency distribution for shear strengths (force in pounds required to break the weld) of ultrasonic

Table 3.5 *Frequency distribution with cumulative relative frequencies*

Class Interval	Frequency	Relative Frequency	Cumulative Relative Frequency
4000 to <4200	1	.01	.01
4200 to <4400	2	.02	.03
4400 to <4600	9	.09	.12
4600 to <4800	14	.14	.26
4800 to <5000	17	.17	.43
5000 to <5200	22	.22	.65
5200 to <5400	20	.20	.85
5400 to <5600	7	.07	.92
5600 to <5800	7	.07	.99
5800 to <6000	1	.01	1.00
	100	1.00	

spot welds ("Comparison of Properties of Joints Prepared by Ultrasonic Welding and Other Means," *J. Aircraft* (1983): 552–556).

Thus, the proportion of welds with strength values less than 5400 is .85 (that is, 85% of the observations are below 5400). What about the proportion of observations less than 4700? Because 4700 is not a class boundary, we must make an educated guess. Since it is halfway between the boundaries of the 4600–4800 class, let's estimate that half of the relative frequency of .14 for this class, or .07, belongs in the 4600–4700 range. Thus,

estimate of proportion less than 4700 = .01 + .02 + .09 + .07 = .12 + .07 = .19

Similarly, since 5250 is one-fourth of the way from 5200 to 5400,

estimate of proportion less than 5250 = .65 + .25(.20) = .70

In Examples 3.15 and 3.16, the class intervals in the frequency distribution were all of equal width. When this is the case, it is easy to construct a histogram using the information in a frequency distribution.

Histogram for Continuous Numerical Data When the Class Interval Widths Are Equal

When to Use: Continuous numerical data. Works well, even for large data sets.

How to Construct:
  1. Mark the boundaries of the class intervals on a horizontal axis.
  2. Use either frequency or relative frequency on the vertical axis.

(continued)

3. Draw a rectangle for each class directly above the corresponding interval (so that the edges are at the class boundaries). Use frequency or relative frequency to determine the height of the rectangle.

What to Look For: Central or typical value, extent of spread or variation, general shape, location and number of peaks, and presence of gaps and outliers

EXAMPLE 3.17

Mercury contamination is a serious environmental concern. Mercury levels are particularly high in certain types of fish. Citizens of the Republic of Seychelles, a group of islands in the Indian Ocean, are among those who consume the most fish in the world. The article "Mercury Content of Commercially Important Fish of the Seychelles, and Hair Mercury Levels of a Selected Part of the Population" (*Environ. Research* (1983): 305–312) reported the following observations on mercury content (ppm) in the hair of 40 fishermen:

13.26	32.43	18.10	58.23	64.00	68.20	35.35	33.92	23.94	18.28	22.05	39.14
31.43	18.51	21.03	5.50	6.96	5.19	28.66	26.29	13.89	25.87	9.84	26.88
16.81	37.65	19.63	21.82	31.58	30.13	42.42	16.51	21.16	32.97	9.84	10.64
29.56	40.69	12.86	13.80								

A reasonable choice for class intervals is to start the first interval at zero and set the interval width as 10. The resulting frequency distribution is displayed in Table 3.6, and the corresponding histogram appears in Figure 3.19 (page 68). If it were not for the slight dip in the interval 50 to <60, the histogram would have a single peak; this dip might well disappear with a larger sample size. The upper or right end of the histogram is much more stretched out than the lower or left end. Typical mercury content is somewhere between 20 and 30, but the data exhibits a substantial amount of variability about the center.

Table 3.6 *Frequency distribution for hair mercury content of Seychelles fishermen (ppm)*

Class Interval	Frequency	Relative Frequency
0 to <10	5	.125
10 to <20	11	.275
20 to <30	10	.250
30 to <40	9	.225
40 to <50	2	.050
50 to <60	1	.025
60 to <70	2	.050
	40	1.000

FIGURE 3.19 Histogram for hair mercury content of Seychelles fishermen

Figure 3.20 is a histogram generated by the MINITAB statistical package. Notice that the classes are different from the ones we chose and that the centers of the intervals, rather than the class boundaries, are marked. There is now a gap toward the upper end of the data; this discrepancy in the two graphical displays may well be attributable to the small sample size. With larger samples, the choice of intervals has less impact on the appearance of the histogram.

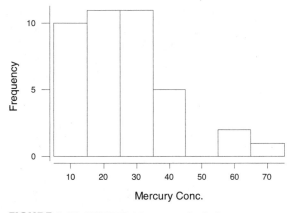

FIGURE 3.20 MINITAB histogram for hair mercury content of Seychelles fishermen

Class Intervals of Unequal Width

Figure 3.21 shows a data set in which a great many observations are concentrated at the center of the set, with only a few outlying, or stray, values both below and above

FIGURE 3.21 Three choices of class intervals for a data set with outliers: (a) Many short intervals of equal width; (b) A few wide intervals of equal width; (c) Intervals of unequal width

the main body of data. If a frequency distribution is based on short intervals of equal width, a great many intervals will be required to capture all observations, and many of them will contain no observations (zero frequency). On the other hand, only a few wide intervals will capture all values, but then most of the observations will be grouped into a very few intervals. Neither choice will yield an informative distribution. In such a situation, it is best to use a few, relatively wide class intervals at the ends of the distribution and some shorter intervals in the middle.

Constructing a Histogram for Continuous Data When Class Widths Are Unequal

In this case, frequencies or relative frequencies *should not* be used on the vertical axis. Instead, the height of each rectangle, called the **density** for the class, is given by

$$\text{density} = \text{rectangle height} = \frac{\text{relative frequency of class}}{\text{class width}}$$

The vertical axis is called the **density scale**; it should be marked so that each rectangle can be drawn to the calculated height.

The use of the density scale to construct the histogram ensures that the area of each rectangle in the histogram will be proportional to the corresponding relative frequency. The formula for rectangle height can also be used when class widths are identical; the denominator is then the same for each density calculation. The resulting histogram will look exactly like the one based on relative frequencies, except for the vertical scaling. In the case of equal-width intervals, the extra arithmetic required to obtain the densities is unnecessary.

EXAMPLE 3.18   When people are asked for the values of characteristics such as age or weight, they sometimes shade the truth in their responses. The article "Self-Reports of Academic Performance" (*Soc. Methods and Research* (Nov. 1981): 165–185) focused on such characteristics as SAT scores and grade point average (GPA). For each student in a sample, the difference in GPA (reported − actual) was determined. Positive differences resulted from individuals reporting grade point averages larger than the correct values. Most differences were close to zero, but there were some rather

Table 3.7 *Frequency distribution for errors in reported GPA*

Class Interval	Relative Frequency	Width	Density
−2.0 to <−.4	.023	1.6	.014
−.4 to <−.2	.055	.2	.275
−.2 to <−.1	.097	.1	.970
−.1 to <0	.210	.1	2.100
0 to <.1	.189	.1	1.890
.1 to <.2	.139	.1	1.390
.2 to <.4	.116	.2	.580
.4 to <2.0	.171	1.6	.107

gross errors. Because of this, a frequency distribution based on unequal class widths gives an informative yet concise summary. Table 3.7 displays such a distribution based on classes with boundaries at −2.0, −.4, −.2, −.1, 0, .1, .2, .4, and 2.0.

Figure 3.22 displays two histograms based on this frequency distribution. The histogram of part (a) is correctly drawn, with height = relative frequency/interval width.

The histogram of part (b) has height = relative frequency and is therefore not correct. In particular, this second histogram considerably exaggerates the incidence of grossly overreported and underreported values — the areas of the two most extreme rectangles are much too large. The eye is naturally drawn to large areas, so it is important that the areas correctly represent the relative frequencies.

———

The formula for rectangle height given in the last box implies that

relative frequency = (rectangle height)(class width) = area of rectangle

That is, a histogram can always be drawn so that the area of each rectangle is the relative frequency of the corresponding class (thus the total area of all rectangles is 1).

Histogram Shapes

The general shape of a histogram is an important characteristic. In describing various shapes, it is convenient to approximate the histogram itself with a smooth curve (called a *smoothed histogram*). This is illustrated in Figure 3.23.

One characterization of general shape relates to the number of peaks, or **modes.** A histogram is said to be **unimodal** if it has a single peak, **bimodal** if it has two peaks, and **multimodal** if it has more than two peaks. These shapes are illustrated in Figure 3.24. Bimodality often occurs when data consists of observations made on two different kinds of individuals or objects. For example, a histogram of heights of college students would show one peak at a typical male height of roughly 70 in. and another at a typical female height of about 67 in. The majority of histograms encountered in practice are unimodal, and multimodality is rather rare.

FIGURE 3.22 Histograms for errors in reporting GPA: (a) A correct picture (height = density); (b) An incorrect picture (height = relative frequency)

(a)

(b)

FIGURE 3.23 Approximating a histogram with a smooth curve

FIGURE 3.24 Smoothed histograms with various numbers of modes: (a) Unimodal; (b) Bimodal; (c) Multimodal

(a)   (b)   (c)

Unimodal histograms come in a variety of shapes. A unimodal histogram is **symmetric** if there is a vertical line of symmetry such that the part of the histogram to the left of the line is a mirror image of the part to the right. (Bimodal and multimodal histograms can also be symmetric in this way.) Several different symmetric smoothed histograms are shown in Figure 3.25. Proceeding to the right from the peak of a unimodal histogram, we move into what is called the **upper tail** of the histogram. Going in the opposite direction moves us into the **lower tail.**

FIGURE 3.25 Several symmetric unimodal smoothed histograms

A unimodal histogram that is not symmetric is said to be **skewed.** If the upper tail of the histogram stretches out much farther than the lower tail, then the distribution of values is **positively skewed.** If, on the other hand, the lower tail is much longer than the upper tail, the histogram is **negatively skewed.** These two types of skewness are illustrated in Figure 3.26. Positive skewness is much more frequently encountered than is negative skewness. An example of positive skewness occurs in the distribution of single-family home prices in Los Angeles County; most homes are moderately priced (at least for California), whereas the relatively few homes in Beverly Hills and Malibu have much higher price tags.

FIGURE 3.26 Two examples of skewed smoothed histograms: (a) Positive skew; (b) Negative skew

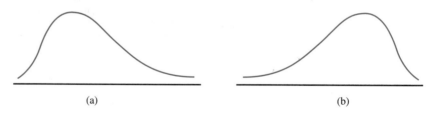

(a)   (b)

One rather specific shape, a **normal curve,** arises more frequently than any other in statistical applications. Many histograms can be well approximated by a normal curve (for example, characteristics such as blood pressure, brain weight, adult male height, adult female height, and IQ score). We briefly mention several of the most important qualitative properties of such a curve, postponing a more detailed discussion until Chapter 7. A normal curve is not only symmetric but also bell shaped; it looks like the curve in Figure 3.27(a). However, not all bell-shaped curves are normal. From the top of the bell, the height of the curve decreases at a well-defined rate when moving into either tail. (This rate of decrease is specified by a certain mathematical function.)

A curve with tails that do not decline as rapidly as the tails of a normal curve is said to specify a **heavy-tailed** distribution (compared to the normal curve). Similarly, a curve with tails that decrease more rapidly than the normal tails is called

FIGURE 3.27 Three examples of bell-shaped histograms: (a) Normal; (b) Heavy-tailed; (c) Light-tailed

(a)   (b)   (c)

light-tailed. Parts (b) and (c) of Figure 3.27 illustrate these possibilities. Many inferential procedures that work well (that is, result in accurate conclusions) when the population distribution is approximately normal do poorly when the population distribution is heavy tailed. This has spurred development of methods that are not so sensitive to the nature of the tails.

Do Sample Histograms Resemble the Population Histogram?

Sample data is usually collected to make inferences about a population. The resulting conclusions may be in error if the sample is somehow unrepresentative of the population. So how similar might a histogram of sample data be to the histogram of all population values? Will the two histograms be centered at roughly the same place and spread out to about the same extent? Will they have the same number of peaks, and will these occur at approximately the same places?

A related issue concerns the extent to which histograms based on different samples from the same population resemble one another. If two different sample histograms can be expected to differ from one another in obvious ways, then at least one of them will differ substantially from the population histogram. If the sample differs substantially from the population, conclusions about the population based on the sample are likely to be incorrect. **Sampling variability** — the extent to which samples differ from one another and from the population — is a central idea in statistics. We present an example to illustrate such variability in histogram shapes.

EXAMPLE 3.19

A sample of 708 bus drivers employed by public corporations was selected, and the number of traffic accidents in which each bus driver was involved during a 4-year period was determined ("Application of Discrete Distribution Theory to the Study of Noncommunicable Events in Medical Epidemiology," *Random Counts in Biomedical and Social Sciences,* G. P. Patil, ed., University Park, Pa.: Penn. State Univ. Press, 1970). A listing of the 708 sample observations might look like this:

3 0 6 0 0 2 1 4 1 . . . 6 0 2

The frequency distribution (Table 3.8) shows that 117 of the 708 drivers had no accidents, a relative frequency of 117/708 = .165 (or 16.5%). Similarly, the proportion of sampled drivers who had one accident is .222 (or 22.2%). The largest sample observation was 11.

Although the 708 observations actually constituted a sample from the population of all bus drivers, we will regard the 708 observations as constituting the entire population. The first histogram in Figure 3.28 then represents the population histogram. The other four histograms in Figure 3.28 are based on four different samples of 50 observations each from this population. The five histograms certainly

Table 3.8 *Frequency distribution for number of accidents by bus drivers*

Number of accidents	Frequency	Relative frequency
0	117	.165
1	157	.222
2	158	.223
3	115	.162
4	78	.110
5	44	.062
6	21	.030
7	7	.010
8	6	.008
9	1	.001
10	3	.004
11	1	.001
	708	.998

resemble one another in a general way, but there are also some obvious dissimilarities. The population histogram rises to a peak and then declines smoothly, whereas the sample histograms tend to have more peaks, valleys, and gaps. Although the population data set contained an observation of 11, none of the four samples did. In fact, in the first two samples, the largest observations were 7 and 8, respectively. In subsequent chapters, we will see how sampling variability can be described and incorporated into conclusions based on inferential methods.

FIGURE 3.28 A comparison of population and sample histograms for number of accidents

(continued)

FIGURE 3.28 (Continued)

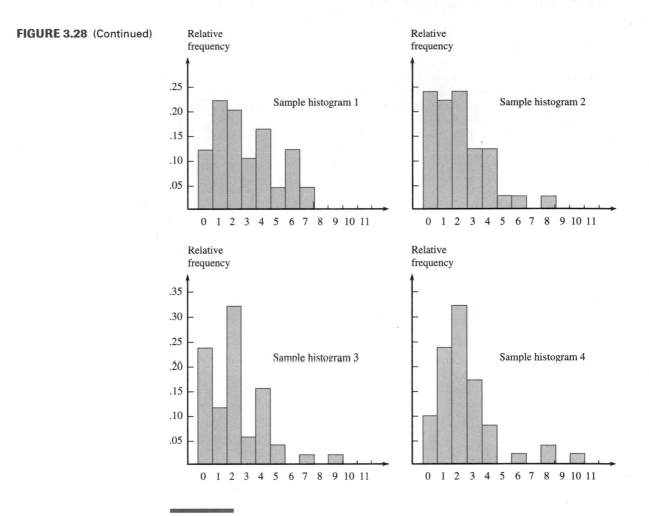

Exercises 3.21 – 3.38

3.21 People suffering from Alzheimer's disease often have difficulty performing basic activities of daily living (ADLs). In one study ("Functional Status and Clinical Findings in Patients with Alzheimer's Disease," *J. of Gerontology* (1992): 177–182), investigators focused on six such activities: dressing, bathing, transferring, toileting, walking, and eating. Here is data on the number of ADL impairments for each of 240 patients.

Number of impairments	0	1	2	3	4	5	6
Frequency	100	43	36	17	24	9	11

a. Determine the corresponding relative frequencies.
b. What proportion of these patients had at most two impairments?
c. Use the result of part **b** to determine what proportion of patients had more than two impairments.
d. What proportion of these patients had at least four impairments?
e. Do you notice anything especially interesting about the frequencies and relative frequencies?

Note: The investigators proposed statistical models from which the number of impairments could be predicted from various patient characteristics and symptoms.

3.22 Is it really the case, as it might seem to an unsuccessful and frustrated angler, that 10% of those fishing reel in 90% of the fish caught? More generally, how is the number of fish caught distributed among those who are trying to catch them? The accompanying table presents data from a survey of 911 anglers done during a particular period on the lower Current River in Canada ("Fisherman's Luck," *Biometrics* (1976): 265–271).

Number of Fish Caught	Number of Anglers (frequency)
0	515
1	65
2	60
3	66
4	53
5	55
6	27
7	25
8	25
9	20
	911

a. Calculate the relative frequencies. (Express each one using four digits of decimal accuracy.)
b. What proportion of those in the sample caught no fish? One fish? At most one fish?
c. What proportion of the 911 anglers caught at least five fish? More than five fish?
d. Calculate the cumulative relative frequencies for the sample of 911 fishermen. Then use them to answer the questions posed in part **c**.
e. Suppose the sample had included an additional four anglers, with numbers of fish caught being 12, 14, 19, and 25. Construct a frequency distribution that has exactly one more row than the one just displayed.

3.23 How unusual is a game with no hits in major-league baseball, and how frequently does a game have more than 10, 15 or even 20 hits? The accompanying table is a frequency distribution for the number of hits per game for all nine-inning games that were played between 1989 and 1993.

Hits/ Game	Frequency
0	20
1	72
2	209
3	527
4	1048
5	1457
6	1988
7	2256
8	2403
9	2256
10	1967
11	1509

(*continued*)

Hits/ Game	Frequency
12	1230
13	834
14	569
15	393
16	253
17	171
18	97
19	53
20	31
21	19
22	13
23	5
24	1
25	0
26	1
27	1

a. Calculate the relative frequencies and then construct a relative frequency histogram.
b. Describe the key features of the histogram.
c. What proportion of games had at most two hits?
d. What proportion of games had between 5 and 10 hits?
e. What proportion of games had more than 15 hits?

3.24 The concentration of suspended solids in river water is an important environmental characteristic. The paper "Water Quality in Agricultural Watershed: Impact of Riparian Vegetation during Base Flow" (*Water Resources Bull.* (1981): 233–239) reported on concentration (in parts per million, or ppm) for several different rivers. Suppose that the accompanying 50 observations had been obtained for a particular river.

55.8	60.9	37.0	91.3	65.8	42.3	33.8	60.6	76.0	69.0	45.9
39.1	35.5	56.0	44.6	71.7	61.2	61.5	47.2	74.5	83.2	40.0
31.7	36.7	62.3	47.3	94.6	56.3	30.0	68.2	75.3	71.4	65.2
52.6	58.2	48.0	61.8	78.8	39.8	65.0	60.7	77.1	59.1	49.5
69.3	69.8	64.9	27.1	87.1	66.3					

a. Why can't you base a frequency distribution on the class intervals 0–10, 10–20, 20–30, . . . , 90–100?
b. Construct a frequency distribution using class intervals 20–<30, 30–<40, . . . , 90–<100. (The resulting distribution agrees with that for one of the rivers discussed in the paper.)
c. What proportion of the concentration observations were less than 50? At least 60?
d. Just from the frequency distribution, can you determine the proportion of sample observations less than 65? Explain. Can you *estimate* this proportion from the distribution? How does your estimate compare with the actual value of the proportion?

3.25 Refer to the concentration data given in Exercise 3.24.
a. Obtain the cumulative relative frequencies for the class intervals specified in part **b** of that problem.
b. Use the cumulative relative frequencies to calculate the proportions described in part **c** of Exercise 3.24.

c. Use cumulative relative frequencies to calculate the proportion of observations in the interval 40–<70.
d. Just from the frequency distribution, can you determine the proportion of observations that are at most 40? Explain.

3.26 The results of the 1990 census included a state-by-state listing of population density. The accompanying table gives the number of people per square mile for each of the 50 states.

AL	79.6	LA	96.9	OH	264.9
AK	1.0	ME	39.8	OK	45.8
AZ	32.3	MD	489.2	OR	29.6
AR	45.1	MA	767.6	PA	265.1
CA	190.8	MI	163.6	RI	960.3
CO	31.8	MN	55.0	SC	115.8
CT	678.4	MS	54.9	SD	9.2
DE	340.8	MO	74.3	TN	118.3
FL	239.6	MT	5.5	TX	64.9
GA	111.9	NB	20.5	UT	21.0
HI	172.5	NV	10.9	VT	60.8
ID	12.2	NH	123.7	VA	156.3
IL	205.6	NJ	1042.0	WA	73.1
IN	154.6	NM	12.5	WV	74.5
IA	49.7	NY	381.0	WI	90.1
KS	30.3	NC	136.1	WY	4.7
KY	92.8	ND	9.3		

a. Construct a relative frequency distribution for state population density.
b. In your relative frequency distribution, did you use class intervals of equal widths? Why or why not?
c. Use the relative frequency distribution to give an approximate value for the proportion of states that have a population density of more than 100 people per square mile. Is this value close to the actual value?

3.27 The paper "Lessons from Pacemaker Implantations" (*J. Amer. Med. Assoc.* (1965): 231–232) gave the results of a study that followed 89 heart patients who had received electronic pacemakers. The time (in months) to the first electrical malfunction of the pacemaker was recorded.

24	20	16	32	14	22	2	12	24	6
10	20	8	16	12	24	14	20	18	14
16	18	20	22	24	26	28	18	14	10
12	24	6	12	18	16	34	18	20	22
24	26	18	2	18	12	12	8	24	10
14	16	22	24	22	20	24	28	20	22
26	20	6	14	16	18	24	18	16	6
16	10	14	18	24	22	28	24	30	34
26	24	22	28	30	22	24	22	32	

a. Summarize this data in the form of a frequency distribution, using class intervals of 0–<6, 6–<12, and so on.
b. Compute the relative frequencies and cumulative relative frequencies for each class interval of the frequency distribution of part **a.**
c. Show how the relative frequency for the class interval 12–<18 could be obtained from the cumulative relative frequencies.

Use the cumulative relative frequencies to give approximate answers to the following questions.
d. What proportion of those who participated in the study had pacemakers that did not malfunction within the first year?
e. If the pacemaker must be replaced as soon as the first electrical malfunction occurs, approximately what proportion required replacement between 1 and 2 years after implantation?
f. Estimate the time at which about 50% of the pacemakers had failed.
g. Estimate the time at which only about 10% of the pacemakers initially implanted were still functioning.

3.28 A student obtained data on fuel efficiency (mpg) and constructed a frequency distribution using the eight class intervals 27.0–<27.5, 27.5–<28.0, . . . , 30.5–<31.0. He then calculated and reported the following cumulative relative frequencies: .09, .23, .38, .35, .72, .80, .93, 1.00. Comment.

3.29 The clearness index was determined for the skies over Baghdad for each of the 365 days during a particular year ("Contribution to the Study of the Solar Radiation Climate of the Baghdad Environment," *Solar Energy* (1990): 7–12). The accompanying table summarizes the resulting data.

Clearness Index	Number of Days (frequency)
.15–<.25	8
.25–<.35	14
.35–<.45	28
.45–<.50	24
.50–<.55	39
.55–<.60	51
.60–<.65	106
.65–<.70	84
.70–<.75	11

a. Determine the relative frequencies and draw the corresponding histogram. (Be careful here — the intervals do not all have the same width.)
b. Cloudy days are those with a clearness index smaller than .35. What proportion of the days were cloudy?

c. Clear days are those for which the index is at least .65. What proportion of the days were clear?

3.30   The article "Associations between Violent and Nonviolent Criminality" (*Multivariate Behavioral Research* (1981): 237–242) reported the number of previous convictions for 283 adult males arrested for felony offenses. The accompanying frequency distribution is a summary of the data given in the paper. Draw the histogram corresponding to this frequency distribution, and comment on its shape.

Number of Previous Convictions	Frequency
0	0
1	16
2	27
3	37
4	46
5	36
6	40
7	31
8	27
9	13
10	8
11	2

3.31   How does the speed of a runner vary over the course of a marathon (a distance of 42.195 km)? Consider determining both the time to run the first five kilometers and the time to run between the 35 km and 40 km points, and then subtracting the former time from the latter time. A positive value of this difference corresponds to a runner slowing down toward the end of the race. The accompanying histogram is based on times of runners who participated in several different Japanese marathons ("Factors Affecting Runners' Marathon Performance,"

Chance (Fall, 1993): 24–30). What are some interesting features of this histogram? What is a typical difference value? Roughly what proportion of the runners ran the late distance more quickly than the early distance?

3.32   The article "Determination of Most Representative Subdivision" (*J. of Energy Engr.* (1993): 43–55) gave data on various characteristics of subdivisions that could be used in deciding whether to provide electrical power using overhead lines or underground lines. Below is data on the variable x = total length of streets within a subdivision.

1280	5320	4390	2100	1240	3060	4770
1050	360	3330	3380	340	1000	960
1320	530	3350	540	3870	1250	2400
960	1120	2120	450	2250	2320	2400
3150	5700	5220	500	1850	2460	5850
2700	2730	1670	100	5770	3150	1890
510	240	396	1419	2109		

a. Construct a stem-and-leaf display for this data using the thousands digit as the stem. Comment on the various features of the display.
b. Construct a histogram using class boundaries of 0–<1000, 1000–<2000, etc. How would you describe the shape of the histogram?
c. What proportion of subdivisions have total length less than 2000? Between 2000 and 4000?

3.33   The article cited in the previous exercise also gave the following values of the variable y = number of culs-de-sac and z = number of intersections.

y	1	0	1	0	0	2	0	1	1
z	1	8	6	1	1	5	3	0	0

y	1	2	1	0	0	1	1	0	1	1
z	4	4	0	0	1	2	1	4	0	4

(*continued*)

Figure for Exercise 3.31

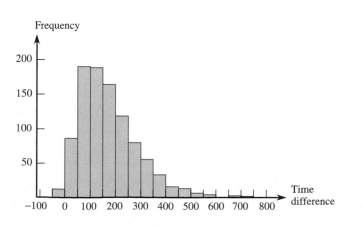

y	1	1	0	0	0	1	1	2	0	
z	0	3	0	1	1	0	1	3	2	

y	1	2	2	1	1	0	2	1	1	0
z	4	6	6	0	1	1	8	3	3	5

y	1	5	0	3	0	1	1	0	0
z	0	5	2	3	1	0	0	0	3

a. Construct a histogram for the number of culs-de-sac. What proportion of these subdivisions had no cul-de-sac? At least one?

b. Construct a histogram for the number of intersections. What proportion of these subdivisions had at most five intersections? Fewer than five?

3.34 Disparities among welfare payments by different states have been the source of much political controversy. The accompanying table reports average payment per person (in dollars) in the Aid to Families with Dependent Children Program for the 1990 fiscal year. Construct a relative frequency distribution for this data using equal interval widths. Draw the histogram corresponding to your frequency distribution.

Alaska	244.90	Tennessee	65.93
California	218.31	Wisconsin	155.04
Arizona	93.57	Ohio	115.26
Montana	114.95	Vermont	183.36
Texas	56.79	Connecticut	205.86
Nebraska	115.15	Pennsylvania	127.70
Minnesota	171.75	Maryland	132.86
Arkansas	65.96	South Carolina	71.91
Alabama	39.62	Hawaii	187.71
Illinois	112.28	Oregon	135.99
Indiana	92.43	Nevada	100.25
New Hampshire	164.20	Wyoming	113.84
Rhode Island	179.37	New Mexico	81.87
New Jersey	121.99	Kansas	113.88
Delaware	113.66	North Dakota	130.49
North Carolina	91.95	Missouri	91.93
Florida	95.43	Mississippi	40.22
Washington	160.41	Kentucky	85.21
Idaho	97.93	Michigan	154.75
Utah	118.36	Maine	150.12
Colorado	111.20	Massachusetts	200.99
Oklahoma	96.98	New York	193.48
South Dakota	95.52	West Virginia	82.94
Iowa	129.58	Virginia	97.98
Louisiana	55.81	Georgia	91.31

3.35 The behavior of children watching television has been a much-studied phenomenon. Now the same attention is being given to children engaged in playing with toys. The paper "A Temporal Analysis of Free Toy Play

and Distractibility in Young Children" (*J. of Exp. Child Psychology* (1991): 41–69) reported the accompanying data on play-episode lengths (in seconds) for a particular 5-year-old boy.

Class	Frequency
0–<5	54
5–<10	44
10–<15	28
15–<20	21
20–<40	31
40–<60	15
60–<90	16
90–<120	5
120–<180	8

a. Display this information in a histogram.

b. What proportion of episodes lasted at least 20 sec?

c. Roughly what proportion of episodes lasted between 40 and 75 sec?

3.36 An exam is given to students in an introductory statistics course. What is likely to be true of the shape of the histogram of scores if

a. the exam is quite easy?

b. the exam is quite difficult?

c. half the students in the class have had calculus, the other half have had no prior college math courses, and the exam emphasizes mathematical manipulation?

Explain your reasoning in each case.

3.37 Construct a histogram corresponding to each of the five frequency distributions given in the following table, and state whether each histogram is symmetric, bimodal, positively skewed, or negatively skewed.

	Frequency				
Class Interval	I	II	III	IV	V
0–<10	5	40	30	5	6
10–<20	10	25	10	25	5
20–<30	20	10	8	8	6
30–<40	30	8	7	7	9
40–<50	20	7	7	20	9
50–<60	10	5	8	25	23
60–<70	5	5	30	10	42

3.38 Using the five class intervals 100–<120, 120–<140, ..., 180–<200, devise a frequency distribution based on 70 observations whose histogram could be described as follows.

a. Symmetric

b. Bimodal

c. Positively skewed

d. Negatively skewed

3.4   Interpreting the Results of Statistical Analyses

The use of graphical data displays is quite common in newspapers, magazines, and journals, so it is important to be able to extract information from such displays. For example, data on test scores for a standardized math test given to eighth-graders in 37 states, two territories (Guam and the Virgin Islands), and the District of Columbia was presented in the August 13, 1992, edition of *USA Today*. Figure 3.29 gives both a stem-and-leaf display and a histogram summarizing this data. Careful examination of these displays reveals the following:

1. Most of the participating states had average eighth-grade math scores between 240 and 280. We would describe the shape of this display as negatively skewed, because of the longer tail on the low end of the distribution.

2. Three of the average scores differed substantially from the others. These turn out to be for the Virgin Islands (218), the District of Columbia (229), and Guam (230). These three could be described as outliers. It is interesting to note that the three unusual values are from the areas that are not states.

3. There do not appear to be any outliers on the high side.

4. A "typical" average math score for the 37 states would be somewhere around 260.

5. There is quite a bit of variability in average score from state to state.

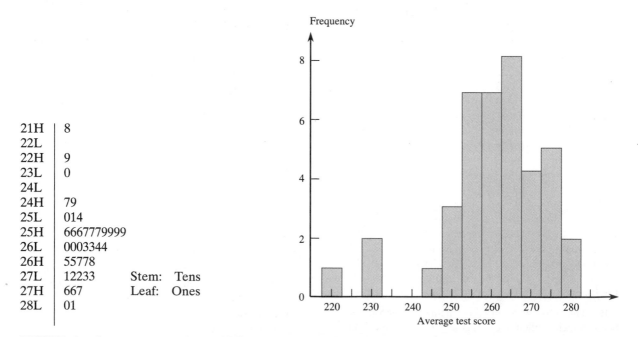

FIGURE 3.29 Stem-and-Leaf display and histogram for math test data

How would the displays have been different if the two territories and the District of Columbia had not participated in the testing? The resulting histogram is shown in Figure 3.30. Note that the display is now more symmetric, with no noticeable outliers. The display still reveals quite a bit of state-to-state variability in average score, and 260 still looks reasonable as a "typical" average score.

Now suppose that the two highest values among the 37 states (Montana and North Dakota) had been even higher. The stem-and-leaf display might then look like the one given in Figure 3.31. In this stem-and-leaf display, two values stand out from the main part of the display. This would catch our attention and might cause us to look carefully at these two states to determine what factors may be related to high math scores. Researchers at Educational Testing Service found math scores to be associated with such factors as amount of time spent reading and amount of time spent watching TV.

FIGURE 3.30 A histogram for the modified math score data

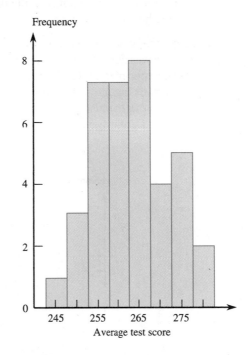

FIGURE 3.31 Stem-and-leaf display for modified math score data

```
24H | 79
25L | 014
25H | 6667779999
26L | 0003344
26H | 55778
27L | 12233        Stem:  Tens
27H | 667          Leaf:  Ones
28L |
28H |
29L |
29H | 68
```

What to Look for in Published Data

Here are some questions you might ask yourself when attempting to extract information from a graphical data display.

■ Is the chosen display appropriate for the type of data collected?

■ How would you describe the shape of the distribution, and what does this say about the variable being summarized?

■ Are there any outliers (noticeably unusual values) in the data set? Is there any plausible explanation for why these differ from the rest of the data? (This often leads to further avenues of investigation.)

■ Where do most of the data values fall? What is a typical value for the data set? What does this say about the variable being summarized?

■ Is there much variability in the data values? What does this say about the variable being summarized?

Of course, you should always think carefully about how the data was collected. If the data was not gathered in a reasonable manner (based on sound sampling methods or experimental design principles), you should be cautious in formulating any conclusions based on the data.

Consider the histogram in Figure 3.32, which is based on data published by the National Center for Health Statistics. The data set summarized by this histogram

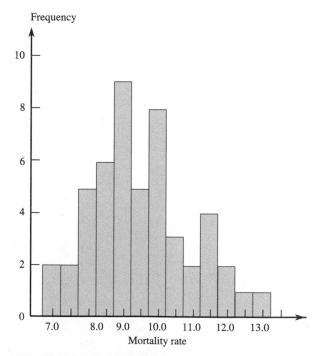

FIGURE 3.32 Histogram of infant mortality rates

consisted of 1990 infant mortality rates (deaths per 1000 live births) for the 50 states in the United States. A histogram is an appropriate way of summarizing this data (although with only 50 observations, a stem-and-leaf display would also have been reasonable). The histogram itself is slightly positively skewed, with most mortality rates between 7.5 and 12. There is quite a bit of variability in infant mortality rate from state to state — perhaps more than we might have expected. This variability might be explained by differences in economic conditions or in access to health care. We may want to look further into these issues. Although there are no obvious outliers, the upper tail is a little longer than the lower tail. The three largest values in the data set are 12.1 (Alabama), 12.3 (Georgia), and 12.8 (South Carolina) — all southern states. Again, this may suggest some interesting questions that deserve further investigation. A typical infant mortality rate would be about 9.5 deaths per 1000 live births. This represents an improvement, since researchers at the National Center for Health Statistics stated that the overall rate for 1988 was 10 deaths per 1000 live births. However, they also point out that the United States still ranked 22nd out of 24 industrialized nations surveyed, with only New Zealand and Israel having higher infant mortality rates.

Summary of Key Concepts and Formulas

Term or Formula	Comment
Frequency distribution	A table that displays frequencies, and sometimes relative and cumulative relative frequencies, for categories (categorical data), possible values (discrete data), or class intervals (continuous data).
Bar chart	A graph of a frequency distribution for a categorical data set. Each category is represented by a bar and the area of the bar is proportional to the corresponding frequency or relative frequency.
Pie chart	A graph of a frequency distribution for a categorical data set. Each category is represented by a slice of the pie and the area of the slice is proportional to the corresponding frequency or relative frequency.
Dotplot	A picture of numerical data in which each observation is represented by a dot on or above a horizontal measurement axis.
Stem-and-leaf display	A method of organizing numerical data in which the stem values (leading digit(s) of the observations) are listed in a column, and the leaf (trailing digit(s)) for each observation is then listed beside the corresponding stem. Sometimes stems are repeated to stretch the display.
Histogram	A picture of the information in a frequency distribution for a numerical data set. A rectangle is drawn above each possible value (discrete data) or class interval. The rectangle's area is proportional to the corresponding frequency or relative frequency.
Histogram shapes	A (smoothed) histogram may be unimodal (a single peak), bimodal (two peaks), or multimodal. A unimodal histogram may be symmetric, positively skewed (a long right or upper tail), or negatively skewed. A frequently occurring shape is the normal curve.

Supplementary Exercises 3.39 – 3.52

3.39 One advantage that margarine has over butter is that it is typically much lower in saturated fat content. (Unfortunately, you can usually taste the difference!) The accompanying MINITAB stem-and-leaf display contains saturated fat contents (in percent) for 37 different margarines (*Consumer Reports,* June 1989). Explain how MINITAB constructed the display. (*Note:* The butters investigated all had fat contents of 64%, 65%, or 66%.)

```
Stem-and-leaf of satfat N = 37
Leaf Unit = 1.0
    2    0   99
    3    1   0
    3    1
    8    1   44444
   10    1   77
    b.   1   88888888888888888899
    7    2   0000
    3    2   2
    2    2   5
    1    2   7
```

3.40 A sample of 50 individuals who recently joined a certain travel club yielded the responses on occupation shown in the accompanying table (C = clerical, M = manager/executive, P = professional, R = retired, S = sales, T = skilled tradesperson, O = other). Summarize this data.

P	R	R	M	S	R	P	R	C	P	M
R	T	O	R	S	R	S	P	M	R	P
C	R	R	S	T	P	P	C	M	S	R
R	P	R	S	R	R	P	M	P	R	R
S	C	P	R	S	M

3.41 The accompanying frequency distribution of the number of years of continuous service at the time of resignation from a job with an oil company appeared in the paper "The Role of Performance in the Turnover Process" (*Academy of Management J.* (1982): 137–147). Construct the histogram corresponding to this frequency distribution. Which terms introduced in this chapter (*symmetric, skewed,* and so on) would you use to describe the histogram?

Duration of service	Frequency
0–<1	4
1–<2	41
2–<3	67

(*continued*)

Duration of Service	Frequency
3–<4	82
4–<5	28
5–<6	43
6–<7	14
7–<8	17
8–<9	11
9–<10	7
10–<11	14
11–<12	6
12–<13	14
13–<14	5
14–<15	2

3.42 Many nutritional experts have expressed concern about the high levels of sodium in prepared foods. The accompanying data on sodium content (mg) per frozen meal appeared in the article "Comparison of 'Light' Frozen Meals" (*Boston Globe,* April 24, 1991).

```
720  530  800  690  880  1050  340  810  760  300  400
680  780  390  950  520   500  630  480  940  450  990
910  420  850  390  600
```

MINITAB gave the two accompanying histograms; we selected the classes for the second histogram and let MINITAB do so for the first one.

a. Do the two histograms give different impressions about the distribution of values?

b. Use each histogram to determine approximately the proportion of observations that are less than 800, and compare to the actual proportion.

(*continued*)

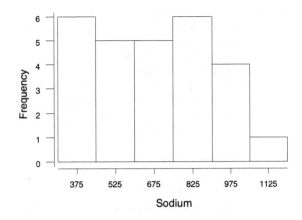

3.43 The paper "Paraquat and Marijuana Risk Assessment" (*Amer. J. of Public Health* (1983): 784–788) reported the results of a 1978 telephone survey on marijuana usage. The accompanying frequency distribution gives the amount of marijuana (in grams) smoked per week for those respondents who indicated that they did use the drug.

Amount Smoked	Frequency
0–<3	94
3–<11	269
11–<18	70
18–<25	48
25–<32	31
32–<39	10
39–<46	5
46–<53	0
53–<60	1
60–<67	0
67–<74	1

a. Display the information given in the frequency distribution in the form of a histogram.
b. What proportion of respondents smoked 25 or more grams per week?
c. Use the histogram to estimate the proportion of respondents who smoked more than 15 g per week.
d. Calculate the cumulative relative frequencies, and use them to determine the proportion of respondents who smoked at least 25 g per week.

3.44 A *Pareto diagram* is a variation of a histogram for categorical data resulting from a quality-control study. Each category represents a different type of product nonconformity or production problem. The categories are or-

dered so that the one with the largest frequency appears on the far left, then the one with the second largest frequency, and so on. Suppose the following information on nonconformities in circuit packs is obtained: failed component, 126; incorrect component, 210; insufficient solder, 67; excess solder, 54; missing component, 131. Construct a Pareto diagram.

3.45 Data on engine emissions for 46 vehicles is given in the accompanying table (*Technometrics* (Nov. 1980): 487).

Vehicle	HC	CO	Vehicle	HC	CO
1	.50	5.01	24	1.10	22.92
2	.65	14.67	25	.65	11.20
3	.46	8.60	26	.43	3.81
4	.41	4.42	27	.48	3.45
5	.41	4.95	28	.41	1.85
6	.39	7.24	29	.51	4.10
7	.44	7.51	30	.41	2.26
8	.55	12.30	31	.47	4.74
9	.72	14.59	32	.52	4.29
10	.64	7.98	33	.56	5.36
11	.83	11.53	34	.70	14.83
12	.38	4.10	35	.51	5.69
13	.38	5.21	36	.52	6.35
14	.50	12.10	37	.57	6.02
15	.60	9.62	38	.51	5.79
16	.73	14.97	39	.36	2.03
17	.83	15.13	40	.49	4.62
18	.57	5.04	41	.52	6.78
19	.34	3.95	42	.61	8.43
20	.41	3.38	43	.58	6.02
21	.37	4.12	44	.46	3.99
22	1.02	23.53	45	.47	5.22
23	.87	19.00	46	.55	7.47

a. Construct a frequency distribution and histogram for the hydrocarbon (HC) emissions data. Do any of the observations appear to be outliers?
b. Construct a frequency distribution and histogram for the carbon monoxide (CO) data.
c. Are the HC and CO histograms symmetric or skewed? If they are both skewed, is the direction of the skew the same?

3.46 The table at the top of page 86 gives data on the cost per ounce (in cents) for 31 shampoos intended for "normal" hair and 29 shampoos intended for "fine" hair (*Consumer Reports,* 1992). Use methods developed in this chapter to describe and compare the two cost distributions.

Normal

79	63	19	9	37	49	20	16	55	69	23
14	9	87	44	13	16	23	20	64	28	18
32	81	85	47	50	8	13	21	9		

Fine

69	9	23	22	8	12	32	12	18	74	19
63	49	37	55	85	44	87	17	11	23	50
65	51	35	14	20	28	8				

3.47 Reconsider the data on lengths of mystery novels given in the chapter introduction.

a. Use various methods developed in this chapter to organize and describe the data.

b. Visit a bookstore with a good selection of science fiction books, select a sample, record page lengths, and compare the data to the mystery novels data.

3.48 The two given frequency distributions of storm duration (in minutes) are based on data appearing in the article "Lightning Phenomenology in the Tampa Bay Area" (*J. of Geophysical Research* (1984): 789–805). Construct a histogram for each of the frequency distributions, and discuss the similarities and differences between the two with respect to shape.

Storm Duration	Single-peak Storms Frequency	Multiple-peak Storms Frequency
0–<25	1	0
25–<50	17	1
50–<75	14	1
75–<100	11	3
100–<125	8	2
125–<150	8	2
150–<175	5	1
175–<200	4	3
200–<225	3	1
225–<250	2	6
250–<275	0	4
275–<300	1	2

3.49 The paper "The Acid Rain Controversy: The Limits of Confidence" (*Amer. Statistician* (1983): 385–394) gave the accompanying data on average SO_2 (sulfur dioxide) emission rates from utility and industrial boilers (lb/million Btu) for 47 states. (Data from Idaho, Alaska, and Hawaii was not given.)

2.3	2.7	1.5	1.5	.3	.6	4.2	1.3	1.2	.4	.5
2.2	4.5	3.8	1.2	.2	1.0	.7	.2	1.4	.7	3.6
1.0	.7	1.7	.5	.1	.6	2.5	2.7	1.5	1.4	2.9
1.0	3.4	2.1	.9	1.9	1.0	1.7	1.8	.6	1.7	2.9
1.8	1.4	3.7								

a. Summarize this set of data by constructing a relative frequency distribution.

b. Draw the histogram corresponding to the frequency distribution in part **a.** Would you describe the histogram as symmetric or skewed?

c. Use the relative frequency distribution of part **a** to compute the cumulative relative frequencies.

d. Use the cumulative relative frequencies to give the approximate proportion of states with SO_2 emission rates that

    i. were below 1.0 lb/million Btu.

    ii. were between 1.0 and 2.0 lb/million Btu.

    iii. were at least 2.0 lb/million Btu.

3.50 Americium 241 (^{241}Am) is a radioactive material used in the manufacture of smoke detectors. The article "Retention and Dosimetry of Injected ^{241}Am in Beagles" (*Radiation Research* (1984): 564–575) described a study in which 55 beagles were injected with a dose of ^{241}Am (proportional to the animals' weights). Skeletal retention of ^{241}Am (μCi/kg) was recorded for each beagle, resulting in the accompanying data.

.196	.451	.498	.411	.324	.190	.489	.300	.346	.448	.188
.399	.305	.304	.287	.243	.334	.299	.292	.419	.236	.315
.447	.585	.291	.186	.393	.419	.335	.332	.292	.375	.349
.324	.301	.333	.408	.399	.303	.318	.468	.441	.306	.367
.345	.428	.345	.412	.337	.353	.357	.320	.354	.361	.329

a. Construct a frequency distribution for this data, and draw the corresponding histogram.

b. Write a short description of the important features of the shape of the histogram.

3.51 In the paper "Reproduction in Laboratory Colonies of Bank Vole" (*Oikos* (1983): 184), the authors presented the results of a study on litter size. (A vole is a small rodent with a stout body, blunt nose, and short ears.) As each new litter was born, the number of babies was recorded, and the accompanying results were obtained.

Size of Litter

3	6	5	6	5	7	5	7	6	6	6
4	6	5	6	4	3	5	6	4	5	9
6	5	6	1	9	7	8	3	7	4	5
5	6	7	3	6	6	9	4	5	7	5
6	8	6	4	7	5	7	4	5	8	6
7	2	7	7	3	3	5	4	6	4	6
3	7	8	5	7	7	7	7	9	8	7
6	7	6	4	7	10	5	2	3	6	6
4	7	6	7	5	5	5	7	5	8	8
4	9	7	5	4	6	5	8	4	5	6
6	3	6	8	6	8	6	5	8	6	11

(*continued*)

4	7	6	8	9	7	3	8	3	4	6
4	5	7	5	6	5	7	6	9	3	5
9	7	5	6	7	5	8	6	8	8	6
5	7	4	8	7	7	7	5	3	8	6
10	4	5	5	5						

a. Construct a relative frequency distribution for this data.

b. What proportion of the litters had more than 6 babies? Between 3 and 8 (inclusive)?

c. Is it easier to answer questions like those posed in part **b** using the relative frequency distribution or the raw data given in the table? Explain.

3.52 Compute the cumulative relative frequencies for the data of Exercise 3.51 and use them to answer the following questions.

a. What proportion of observations are at most 8? At least 8?

b. What proportion of litters contain between 5 and 10 (inclusive) offspring?

References

Chambers, John, William Cleveland, Beat Kleiner, and Paul Tukey. *Graphical Methods for Data Analysis.* Belmont, CA: Wadsworth, 1983. (This is an excellent survey of methods, illustrated with numerous interesting examples.)

Cleveland, William. *The Elements of Graphing Data,* 2d ed. Summit, NJ: Hobart Press, 1994. (An informal and informative introduction to various aspects of graphical analysis.)

Freedman, David, Robert Pisani, and Roger Purves. *Statistics,* 3d ed. New York: W. W. Norton, 1997. (An excellent, very informal introduction to concepts, with some insightful cautionary examples concerning misuses of statistical methods.)

Moore, David. *Statistics: Concepts and Controversies,* 4th ed. New York: W. H. Freeman, 1997. (A nonmathematical yet highly entertaining introduction to our discipline — two thumbs up!)

Velleman, Paul, and David Hoaglin. *Applications, Basics, and Computing of Exploratory Data Analysis.* Boston: Duxbury, 1981. (Subtitled *ABCs of EDA,* this book contains a good treatment of exploratory methods.)

4

Numerical Methods for Describing Data

INTRODUCTION

Exposure to various chemical substances can pose substantial health risks. Evidence from recent years suggests that high indoor radon concentration may be linked to the development of childhood cancers. The article "Indoor Radon and Childhood Cancer" (*The Lancet* (1991): 1537–1538) presented the accompanying data on radon concentration (Bq/m^3) in two different samples of houses. The first sample consisted of houses in which a child diagnosed with cancer had been residing. Houses in the second sample had no recorded cases of childhood cancer.

Cancer

10	21	5	23	15	11	9	13	27	13	39	22
7	20	45	12	15	3	8	11	18	16	23	16
34	10	15	11	18	210	22	11	6	17	33	10
9	57	16	21	18	38						

No Cancer

9	38	11	12	29	5	7	6	8	29	24	12
17	11	3	9	33	17	55	11	29	13	24	7
11	21	6	39	29	7	8	55	9	21	9	3
85	11	14									

What is a representative or typical radon concentration value for each sample, and how do these values compare for the two samples? Do the two samples show similar amounts of variability, or are the observations in one sample substantially more spread out than those in the other sample? As we have seen, a stem-and-leaf display, a frequency distribution, or a histogram gives general impressions about where each data set is centered and how much it spreads out about its center. This chapter shows how to calculate numerical summary measures that describe more precisely both the center and the extent of spread. Section 4.1 introduces the mean and median, the two most popular measures of the center of a distribution. The variance and the standard deviation are presented in Section 4.2 as measures of variability. Later sections discuss several techniques for using such summary measures to describe other features of the data.

4.1   Describing the Center of a Data Set

An informative way to describe the location of a numerical data set is to report a value that is representative of the observations in the set. This number describes roughly where the data set is located or "centered" along the number line, and it is called a measure of center. The two most popular measures of center are the *mean* and the *median*.

The Mean

The **mean** of a set of numerical observations is just the familiar arithmetic average, the sum of the observations divided by the number of observations. Values in such a data set are observations on a numerical variable. The variable might be number of traffic accidents, number of pages in a book, reaction time, yield from a chemical reaction, etc. When working with sample data, it is helpful to have concise notation for the variable, sample size, and individual observations. Let

x = the variable for which we have sample data

n = the number of sample observations (sample size)

x_1 = the first sample observation

x_2 = the second sample observation

$\vdots$

x_n = the nth (last) sample observation

For example, we might have a sample consisting of $n = 4$ observations on $x =$ battery lifetime (hr):

$x_1 = 5.9$ $x_2 = 7.3$ $x_3 = 6.6$ $x_4 = 5.7$

Notice that the value of the subscript on x has no relationship to the magnitude of the observation. In this example, x_1 is just the first observation in the data set and not necessarily the smallest observation.

The sum of $x_1, x_2, \ldots, x_n$ can be denoted by $x_1 + x_2 + \cdots + x_n$, but this is cumbersome. The Greek letter Σ is traditionally used in mathematics to denote summation. In particular, $\Sigma\, x$ will denote the sum of all of the x values in the data set under consideration.*

Definition

The **sample mean** of a numerical sample $x_1, x_2, \ldots, x_n$, denoted by $\bar{x}$, is

$$\bar{x} = \frac{\text{sum of all observations in the sample}}{\text{number of observations in the sample}} = \frac{x_1 + x_2 + \cdots + x_n}{n} = \frac{\Sigma\, x}{n}$$

EXAMPLE 4.1

Traumatic knee dislocation often requires surgery to repair ruptured ligaments. One measure of recovery is range of motion (measured by the angle formed when, starting with the leg straight, the knee is bent as far as possible). The article "Reconstruction of the Anterior and Posterior Cruciate Ligaments after Knee Dislocation" (*American Journal of Sports Medicine* (1999): 189–197) reported the following postsurgical range of motion for a sample of 13 patients.

Range of Motion (degrees)

$x_1 = 154 \quad x_2 = 142 \quad x_3 = 137 \quad x_4 = 133 \quad x_5 = 122 \quad x_6 = 126 \quad x_7 = 135$

$x_8 = 135 \quad x_9 = 108 \quad x_{10} = 120 \quad x_{11} = 127 \quad x_{12} = 134 \quad x_{13} = 122$

The sum of these sample values is $154 + 142 + 137 + \cdots + 122 = 1695$, and the sample mean range of motion is

$$\bar{x} = \frac{\Sigma\, x}{n} = \frac{1695}{13} = 130.38$$

We would report 130.38 degrees as a representative value of range of motion for this sample (even though there is no patient in the sample that actually had a range of motion of 130.38 degrees).

The data values in Example 4.1 were all integers, yet the mean was given as 130.38. It is common to use more digits of decimal accuracy for the mean. This allows the value of the mean to fall between possible observable values (for example, the average number of children per family could be 1.8, whereas no single family will have 1.8 children). It could also be argued that the mean carries with it more precision than does any single observation.

The sample mean $\bar{x}$ is computed from sample observations, so it is a characteristic of the particular sample in hand. It is customary to use Roman letters to denote *sample* characteristics, as we have done with $\bar{x}$. Characteristics of the entire

---

*It is also common to see $\Sigma\, x$ written as $\sum_{i=1}^{n} x_i$, but for simplicity we will usually omit the summation indices.

population are usually denoted by Greek letters. One of the most important such characteristics is the population mean.

Definition

The **population mean,** denoted by μ, is the average of all x values in the entire population.

For example, the true average fuel efficiency for all 600,000 cars of a certain type under specified conditions might be $\mu = 27.5$ mpg. A sample of $n = 5$ cars might yield efficiencies of

$$27.3 \quad 26.2 \quad 28.4 \quad 27.9 \quad 26.5$$

from which we obtain $\bar{x} = 27.26$ for this particular sample (somewhat smaller than μ). However, a second sample might give $\bar{x} = 28.52$, a third $\bar{x} = 26.85$, and so on. The value of $\bar{x}$ varies from sample to sample, whereas there is just one value for μ. We shall see subsequently how the value of $\bar{x}$ from a particular sample can be used to draw various conclusions about the value of μ.

EXAMPLE 4.2   The 50 states plus the District of Columbia contain a total of 3137 counties. Let x denote the number of residents of a county. Then there are 3137 values of the variable x in the population. The sum of these 3137 values is 248,709,873 (1990 census), so the population average value of x is

$$\mu = \frac{248,709,873}{3137} = 79,282.7 \text{ residents per county}$$

We used *The World Almanac and Book of Facts* to select three different samples at random from this population of counties, with each sample consisting of five counties. The results appear in Table 4.1, along with the sample mean for each sample.

Table 4.1 *Three samples from the population of all U.S. counties (x = number of residents)*

Sample 1		Sample 2		Sample 3	
County	**x value**	**County**	**x value**	**County**	**x value**
Fayette, TX	20,095	Stoddard, MO	28,895	Chattahoochee, GA	16,934
Monroe, IN	108,978	Johnston, OK	10,032	Petroleum, MT	519
Greene, NC	15,384	Sumter, AL	16,174	Armstrong, PA	73,478
Shoshone, ID	13,931	Milwaukee, WI	959,275	Smith, MI	14,798
Jasper, IN	24,960	Albany, WY	30,797	Benton, MO	13,859
$\Sigma x = 183,348$		$\Sigma x = 1,045,173$		$\Sigma x = 119,588$	
$\bar{x} = 36,669.6$		$\bar{x} = 209,034.6$		$\bar{x} = 23,917.6$	

Not only are the three $\bar{x}$ values different from one another — because they are based on three different samples and the value of $\bar{x}$ depends on the x values in the sample — but none of the three comes close to the value of the population mean, μ. If we did not know the value of μ but had only sample 1 available, we might use $\bar{x} = 36,669.6$ as an *estimate* of μ, but our estimate would be far off the mark. Alternatively, we could combine the three samples into a single sample with $n = 15$ observations:

$$x_1 = 20,095, \ldots, x_5 = 24,960, \ldots, x_{15} = 13,859$$
$$\Sigma x = 1,348,109$$
$$\bar{x} = \frac{1,348,109}{15} = 89,873.9$$

This is closer to the value of μ but still not very satisfactory as an estimate. The problem here is that there is so much variability in the population of x values (the largest is $x = 8,863,164$ for Los Angeles County, California, and the smallest is $x = 107$ for Loving County, Texas, which evidently few people love). Therefore, it is difficult for a sample of 15 observations, let alone just 5, to be reasonably representative of the population. But don't lose hope! Once we learn how to measure it, we will also see how to take variability into account in making accurate inferences.

One potential drawback to the mean as a measure of center for a data set is that its value can be greatly affected by the presence of even a single *outlier* (an unusually large or small observation) in the data set.

EXAMPLE 4.3

The following data on x = savings rate for a sample of Southern California financial institutions appeared in the August 15, 1994, *Los Angeles Times*. The values are listed here in increasing order:

2.15	2.20	2.20	2.22	2.22	2.23	2.25	2.25	2.27	2.28
2.28	2.28	2.29	2.30	2.30	2.32	2.32	2.33	2.33	2.33
2.33	2.33	2.33	2.38	2.43	2.55	2.79	3.05	3.68	4.35

The sample mean was reported as $\bar{x} = 2.45$. Figure 4.1 is a MINITAB dotplot of the data. Many would argue that since it is larger than 25 of the 30 observations, 2.45 is not a very representative value for this sample. The two largest rates, 3.68 and 4.35, are unusually large (i.e., outliers) and have a substantial impact on $\bar{x}$.

FIGURE 4.1 A MINITAB dotplot of the data in Example 4.3

We now turn our attention to a measure of center that is not so sensitive to outliers.

The Median

The median strip of a highway divides the highway in half, and the median of a numerical data set does the same thing. Once the data values have been listed in order from smallest to largest, the **median** is the middle value in the list and divides the list into two equal parts. It turns out that the median is found differently, depending on whether the sample size n is even or odd. When n is an odd number (say, 5), the sample median is the single middle value. But when n is even (say, 6), there are two middle values in the ordered list, and we average these two middle values to obtain the sample median.

Definition

The **sample median** is obtained by first ordering the n observations from smallest to largest (with any repeated values included, so that every sample observation appears in the ordered list). Then

$$\text{sample median} = \begin{cases} \text{the single middle value if } n \text{ is odd} \\ \text{the average of the middle two values if } n \text{ is even} \end{cases}$$

EXAMPLE 4.4

(Example 4.3 continued)   The sample size for the savings rate data was $n = 30$, an even number. The median is the average of the 15th and 16th values (the middle two) in the ordered list of the data. Note that the savings rate data is already arranged in numerical order. If this were not the case, we would have had to put the data values in order first before determining the median, as follows:

$$\text{sample median} = \frac{2.30 + 2.32}{2} = 2.31$$

Looking at the dotplot, we see that this value appears to be somewhat more typical of the data than does $\bar{x} = 2.45$.

The **population median** plays the same role for the population as the sample median plays for the sample. It is the middle value in the ordered list consisting of all population observations. We previously noted that the mean — population or sample — is very sensitive to even a single value that lies far above or below the rest of the data. The value of the mean is pulled out toward such an outlying value or values. The median, on the other hand, is quite *in*sensitive to outliers. For example, the largest sample observation (4.35) in Example 4.3 can be increased by an arbitrarily large amount without changing the value of the median. Similarly, an increase in the second or third largest observations does not affect the median, nor would a decrease in several of the smallest observations.

This stability of the median is what sometimes justifies its use as a measure of center in some situations. For example, the July 5, 1999, issue of *The Los Angeles Times* reported that the average earnings for stock brokers in 1997 was $158,201, whereas the median earnings was only $119,010. Income distributions are commonly summarized by reporting the median rather than the mean, since otherwise a few very high salaries could result in a mean that is not representative of a typical salary.

Comparing the Mean and the Median

Figure 4.2 presents several smoothed histograms that might represent either a distribution of sample values or a population distribution. Pictorially, the median is the value on the measurement axis that separates the histogram into two parts, with .5 (50%) of the area under each part of the curve. The mean is a bit harder to visualize. If the histogram were balanced on a triangle with a sharp point (a fulcrum), it would tilt unless the triangle were positioned exactly at the mean. The mean is the balance point for the distribution.

When the histogram is symmetric, the point of symmetry is both the dividing point for equal areas and the balance point, and the mean and median are equal. However, when the histogram is unimodal (single-peaked) with a longer upper tail, the relatively few outlying values in the upper tail pull the mean up, so it generally lies above the median. For example, an unusually high exam score raises the mean but does not affect the median. Similarly, when a unimodal histogram is negatively skewed, the mean is generally smaller than the median (see Figure 4.3).

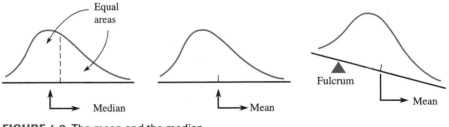

FIGURE 4.2 The mean and the median

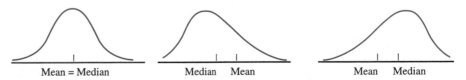

FIGURE 4.3 Relationship between the mean and the median

Categorical Data

The natural numerical summary quantities for a categorical data set are the relative frequencies for the various categories. Each relative frequency is the proportion (fraction) of responses that are in the corresponding category. Often there are only two possible responses (a *dichotomy*)—male or female, does or does not have a driver's license, did or did not vote in the last election, and so on. It is convenient in such situations to label one of the two possible responses S (for success) and the other F (for failure). As long as further analysis is consistent with the labeling, it is immaterial which category is assigned the S label. When the data set is a sample, the fraction of S's in the sample is called the *sample proportion of successes.*

Definition

The **sample proportion of successes,** denoted by p, is

$$p = \text{sample proportion of successes} = \frac{\text{number of } S\text{'s in the sample}}{n}$$

where S is the label used for the response designated as success.

EXAMPLE 4.5

The use of antipollution equipment on automobiles has substantially improved air quality in certain areas. Unfortunately, many car owners have tampered with smog control devices to improve performance. Suppose a sample of $n = 15$ cars was selected, and each was classified as S or F, according to whether or not tampering had taken place. The resulting data was

$$S \quad F \quad S \quad S \quad S \quad F \quad F \quad S \quad S \quad F \quad S \quad S \quad S \quad F \quad F$$

This sample contains nine S's, so

$$p = \frac{9}{15} = .60$$

That is, 60% of the sample responses are S's. In 60% of the cars sampled, there has been tampering with the air pollution control devices.

The Greek letter π is used to denote the **population proportion of S's.*** We will see later how the value of p from a particular sample can be used to make inferences about π.

Trimmed Means

The extreme sensitivity of the mean to even a single outlier and the extreme insensitivity of the median to a substantial proportion of outliers can make both of them suspect as a measure of center. Statisticians have proposed a *trimmed mean* as a compromise between these two extremes.

---

* Note that we are using the symbol π to represent a population proportion and *not* as the mathematical constant $\pi = 3.14 \ldots$. Many other sources use the symbol p for the population proportion and $\hat{p}$ for the sample proportion.

> ### Definition
>
> A **trimmed mean** is computed by first ordering the data values from smallest to largest, deleting a selected number of values from each end of the ordered list, and finally averaging the remaining values. The **trimming percentage** is the percentage of values deleted from each end of the ordered list.

EXAMPLE 4.6

The film industry has been criticized for its depiction of alcohol and tobacco use in children's movies. The article "Tobacco and Alcohol Use in G-Rated Animated Films" (*J. American Medical Assn.* (1999): 1131–1136) gave the following data on the number of seconds showing alcohol use in each of 30 animated films released between 1980 and 1997.

Alcohol Exposure (seconds)

34	414	0	0	76	123	3	0	7	0	46	38	13	73
0	72	0	5	0	0	0	0	74	0	28	0	0	0
0	39												

A MINITAB dotplot of this data is shown in Figure 4.4. Since the dotplot shows that the data distribution is not symmetric and that there is an outlier, a trimmed mean is a reasonable choice for describing this data set.

FIGURE 4.4 A MINITAB dotplot of the data in Example 4.6

Since 10% of 30 is 3, a 10% trimmed mean results from deleting the three largest and three smallest data values and then averaging the remaining 24 data values. The ordered data values are

0	0	0	0	0	0	0	0	0	0	0	0	0	0	0
3	5	7	13	28	34	38	39	46	72	73	74	76	123	414

Deleting three of the 0's (the smallest 10%) and 76, 123, and 414 (the largest 10%) and averaging the remaining values gives

$$10\% \text{ trimmed mean} = \frac{0 + 0 + \cdots + 74}{24} = \frac{432}{24} = 18.00$$

The mean, $\bar{x} = 34.53$, is much larger than the trimmed mean because of the unusually large value (414) in the data set. The 10% trimmed mean, which is 1.5 for this data set, falls between the mean and the median.

Sometimes the number of observations to be deleted from each end of the data set is specified and then the corresponding trimming percentage is calculated as

$$\text{trimming percentage} = \left(\frac{\text{number deleted from each end}}{n} \right) \cdot 100$$

In other cases, the trimming percentage is specified and then used to determine how many observations to delete from each end, with

$$\text{number deleted from each end} = (\text{trimming percentage}) \cdot n$$

If the number of observations to be deleted from each end resulting from this calculation is not an integer, it can be rounded to the nearest integer.

A trimmed mean with a small to moderate trimming percentage — between 5% and 25% — is less affected by outliers than the mean, but it is not as insensitive as the median. Trimmed means are therefore being used more and more often.

Exercises 4.1 – 4.18

4.1 The risk of developing iron deficiency is especially high during pregnancy. Detecting such deficiency is complicated by the fact that some methods for determining iron status can be affected by the state of pregnancy itself. Consider the following data on transferrin receptor concentration for a sample of women with laboratory evidence of overt iron-deficiency anemia ("Serum Transferrin Receptor for the Detection of Iron Deficiency in Pregnancy," *Amer. J. of Clinical Nutrition* (1991): 1077–1081): $x_1 = 15.2$, $x_2 = 9.3$, $x_3 = 7.6$, $x_4 = 11.9$, $x_5 = 10.4$, $x_6 = 9.7$, $x_7 = 20.4$, $x_8 = 9.4$, $x_9 = 11.5$, $x_{10} = 16.2$, $x_{11} = 9.4$, $x_{12} = 8.3$. Compute the values of the sample mean and median. Why are these values different here? Which one do you regard as more representative of the sample, and why?

4.2 The paper "The Pedaling Technique of Elite Endurance Cyclists" (*Int. J. of Sport Biomechanics* (1991): 29–53) reported the accompanying data on single-leg power at a high workload.

244 191 160 187 180 176 174 205 211 183 211 180 194 200

a. Calculate and interpret the sample mean and median.
b. Suppose the first observation had been 204, not 244. How would the mean and median change?
c. Calculate a trimmed mean by eliminating the smallest and largest sample observations. What is the corresponding trimming percentage?

d. Suppose that the largest observation had been 204 rather than 244. How would the trimmed mean in part **c** change? What if the largest value had been 284?

4.3 The paper cited in Exercise 4.2 also reported values of single-leg power for a low workload. The sample mean for $n = 13$ observations was $\bar{x} = 119.8$ (actually 119.7692), and the 14th observation, somewhat of an outlier, was 159. What is the value of $\bar{x}$ for the entire sample?

4.4 According to an article about buying Viagra via the Internet (see "Direct Sale of Sildenafil (Viagra) to Consumers over the Internet," *New England Journal of Medicine* (1999): 1389–1392), of 77 Web sites offering to sell Viagra, 55 were in the United States, and 11 were from the United Kingdom. Furthermore, 42 of the 77 provided information about contraindications (reasons a patient should not use Viagra, for example, concomitant use of nitrates).
a. What proportion of the sampled Web sites were in the United Kingdom?
b. What proportion of the sampled Web sites were outside the United States?
c. What proportion of the sampled Web sites did not warn consumers about possible contraindications?

4.5 A sample of 26 offshore oil workers took part in a simulated escape exercise, resulting in the accompanying data on time (sec) to complete the escape ("Oxygen Consumption and Ventilation During Escape from an Offshore Platform," *Ergonomics* (1997): 281–292):

389	356	359	363	375	424	325	394	402
373	373	370	364	366	364	325	339	393
392	369	374	359	356	403	334	397	

a. Construct a stem-and-leaf display of the data. How does it suggest that the sample mean and median will compare?

b. Calculate the values of the sample mean and median.

c. By how much could the largest time be increased without affecting the value of the sample median? By how much could this value be decreased without affecting the sample median?

4.6 Did Civil War veterans have different levels of wealth than those who did not fight after the war was over? The article "The Civil War Generation: Military Service and Mobility in Dubuque, Iowa, 1860–1870" (*Journal of Social History* (1999): 791–820) discusses this issue. One bit of information presented in this article is the average property value (in dollars) of each of 123 non-soldier sons of business-class parents and 14 soldier sons of these same parents in Dubuque, Iowa. The average property value of the 123 non-soldier sons was 14,905.69, whereas the average property value of the 14 soldier sons was 17,678.57.

a. What is the mean income of all 137 sons?

b. If one of the soldier sons had no property at all, what is the mean property value of the remaining 13 sons?

4.7 According to the September 1999 *Survey of Current Business,* the top five metropolitan regions by per capita personal income in 1997 were:

Area Name	Total Personal Income (in millions of dollars)	Per Capita Personal Income	Rank
San Francisco	68,671	41,128	1
New Haven/ Bridgeport/ Stamford/ Danbury/ Waterbury	66,562	40,928	2
West Palm Beach/ Boca Raton	39,269	38,772	3
San Jose	61,345	37,856	4
Bergen/ Passaic	49,111	36,769	5

a. Why would areas be ranked by per capita personal income rather than total personal income?

b. How can an area like West Palm Beach–Boca Raton

with such a relatively low personal income still have a very high per capita personal income? Explain.

c. Approximately how many people live in the San Jose area?

4.8 Calculate both the 10% trimmed mean and the 20% trimmed mean for the savings rate data of Example 4.3. Compare these values to $\bar{x}$ and the sample median.

4.9 Consider the following statement: More than 65% of the residents of Los Angeles earn less than the average wage for that city. Could this statement be correct? If so, how? If not, why not?

4.10 Five experimental animals were put on a certain diet for several weeks, and another five animals were put on a second diet. The resulting weight gains (in pounds) at the end of the period were as follows:

Diet 1	12	13	7	5	15
Diet 2	11	14	3	13	4

Without doing any calculation, decide which group of animals achieved the larger average weight gain. (*Hint*: Base your reasoning on the ordered values from each sample.)

4.11 Reconsider the situation described in Exercise 4.10, but suppose now that the weight gains for the second diet are 5, 13, 11, 10, and 3 lb. Without doing any calculation, say how the average gain for the first diet compares to that for the second diet. (*Hint*: Again order the observations from smallest to largest within each sample.)

4.12 A sample consisting of four pieces of luggage was selected from among those checked at an airline counter, yielding the following data on x = weight (lb):

$$x_1 = 33.5 \qquad x_2 = 27.3 \qquad x_3 = 36.7 \qquad x_4 = 30.5$$

Suppose one more piece is selected; denote its weight by x_5. Find a value of x_5 such that $\bar{x}$ = sample median.

4.13 The October 1, 1994, issue of the *San Luis Obispo Telegram-Tribune* reported the following monthly salaries for supervisors from six different counties: $5354 (Kern), $5166 (Monterey), $4443 (Santa Cruz), $4129 (Santa Barbara), $2500 (Placer), and $2220 (Merced). San Luis Obispo County supervisors are supposed to be paid the average of the two counties among these six in the middle of the salary range. Which measure of center determines this salary, and what is its value? Why is the other measure of center featured in this section not as favorable to these supervisors (though it might appeal to taxpayers)?

4.14 Suppose that ten patients with meningitis received treatment with large doses of penicillin. Three days later, temperatures were recorded, and the treatment was considered successful if there had been a reduction in a patient's temperature. Denoting success by *S* and failure by *F,* the ten observations are

S   S   F   S   S   S   F   F   S   S

a. What is the value of the sample proportion of successes?
b. Replace each *S* with 1 and each *F* with a 0. Then calculate $\bar{x}$ for this numerically coded sample. How does $\bar{x}$ compare to *p*?
c. Suppose it is decided to include 15 more patients in the study. How many of these would have to be *S*'s to give *p* = .80 for the entire sample of 25 patients?

4.15 An experiment to study the lifetime (in hours) for a certain type of component involved putting ten components into operation and observing them for 100 hr. Eight of the components failed during that period, and those lifetimes were recorded. Denote the lifetimes of the two components still functioning after 100 hr by 100+. The resulting sample observations were

48   79   100+   35   92   86   57   100+   17   29

Which of the measures of center discussed in this section can be calculated, and what are the values of those measures? (*Note*: The data from this experiment is said to be "censored on the right.")

4.16 An instructor has graded 19 exam papers submitted by students in a certain class of 20 students, and the average so far is 70. (The maximum possible score is 100.) How high would the score on the last paper have to be to raise the class average by one point? By two points?

4.17 "The Motley Fool," an investment column that appears in newspapers (*San Luis Obispo Tribune*, Oct. 16, 1999), made the following statement about mutual funds:

Funds with a great three or five or even 10-year average are likely to have that great average because of one amazing year. After all, a five-year average is just an average of five numbers. If one of them is unusually high, the average will be high. Let's consider an example. If in each of five years, a fund earns 8 percent, 11 percent, 4 percent, 12 percent, and 33 percent, its average annual return will be about 13 percent. That might look respectable, but note that in reality it exceeded 13 percent in only one of five years. That 33 percent return (an "outlier" in statistical terms) has skewed the average.

Calculate the median return for the five years mentioned in the above quote. Do you think that the median would be a better indication of a typical return in this case? Explain.

4.18 A certain college has two sections of introductory statistics during a particular semester. One section has 20 students, and the other has 100 students.
a. What is the mean number of students per section (the average over sections)?
b. Let x_1 denote the number of students in the first student's class, x_2 the number of students in the second student's class, and so on (up through x_{120}). What is the average of these *x* values? (This is the mean class size when averaged over students rather than classes.)
c. From a student perspective, which of the two averages, the one calculated in part **a** or the one in part **b,** is more pertinent?

4.2   Describing Variability in a Data Set

Reporting a measure of center gives only partial information about a data set. It is also important to describe the spread of values about the center. The three different samples displayed in Figure 4.5 all have mean = median = 45. There is much variability in the first sample compared to the third sample. The second sample shows less variability than the first and more than the third; most of the variability in the second sample is due to the two extreme values being so far from the center.

The simplest numerical measure of variability is the **range,** which is defined as the difference between the largest and smallest values. Generally speaking, more variability will be reflected in a larger range. However, variability depends on more than just the distance between the two most extreme values. Variability is a characteristic of the entire data set, and each observation contributes to the variability.

Sample

1. 20, 40, 50, 30, 60, 70

2. 47, 43, 44, 46, 20, 70

3. 44, 43, 40, 50, 47, 46

Mean = Median

FIGURE 4.5 Three samples with the same center and different amounts of variability

The first two samples plotted in Figure 4.5 both have a range of 50, but there is substantially less dispersion in the second sample.

Deviations from the Mean

The most common measures of variability describe the extent to which the sample observations deviate from the sample mean $\bar{x}$. Subtracting $\bar{x}$ from each observation gives a set of deviations from the mean.

Definition

The n **deviations from the sample mean** are the differences

$$x_1 - \bar{x}, x_2 - \bar{x}, \ldots, x_n - \bar{x}$$

A particular deviation is positive if the x value exceeds $\bar{x}$ and negative if the x value is less than $\bar{x}$.

EXAMPLE 4.7

The $n = 30$ savings rate observations from Example 4.3 are displayed in Table 4.2 (page 102), along with the corresponding deviations calculated from $\bar{x} = 2.452$.

Only 5 of the deviations are positive, because only 5 of the 30 observations exceed $\bar{x}$. Most of the negative deviations are quite small in magnitude, corresponding to observations slightly smaller than the mean.

Generally speaking, the greater the amount of variability in the sample, the larger the magnitudes (ignoring the sign) of the deviations. Thus, the magnitudes of the deviations for the first sample in Figure 4.5 substantially exceed those for the third sample, implying more variability in sample 1.

Table 4.2 *Deviations of savings rates from the mean*

Observation (x)	Deviation $(x - \bar{x})$	Observation	Deviation $(x - \bar{x})$
2.15	−.302	2.32	−.132
2.20	−.252	2.32	−.132
2.20	−.252	2.33	−.122
2.22	−.232	2.33	−.122
2.22	−.232	2.33	−.122
2.23	−.222	2.33	−.122
2.25	−.202	2.33	−.122
2.25	−.202	2.33	−.122
2.27	−.182	2.38	−.072
2.28	−.172	2.43	−.022
2.28	−.172	2.55	.098
2.28	−.172	2.79	.338
2.29	−.162	3.05	.598
2.30	−.152	3.68	1.228
2.30	−.152	4.35	1.898

We now consider how to combine the deviations into a single numerical measure. Our first thought might be to calculate the average deviation, by adding the deviations together — this sum can be denoted compactly by $\Sigma (x - \bar{x})$ — and dividing by n. This does not work, though, because negative and positive deviations counteract one another in the summation.

Except for the effects of rounding in computing the deviations, it is always true that $\Sigma (x - \bar{x}) = 0$. Since this sum is zero, the average deviation is always zero and so cannot be used as a measure of variability.

As a result of rounding the value of $\bar{x}$, the sum of the 30 deviations in Example 4.7 is $\Sigma (x - \bar{x}) = .01$. If we used even more decimal accuracy in computing $\bar{x}$, the sum would be closer to zero.

The Variance and Standard Deviation

The standard way to prevent negative and positive deviations from counteracting one another is to square them before combining. Then deviations with opposite signs but with the same magnitude, such as +20 and −20, will make identical contributions to variability. The squared deviations are $(x_1 - \bar{x})^2$, $(x_2 - \bar{x})^2$, . . . , $(x_n - \bar{x})^2$, and their sum is

$$(x_1 - \bar{x})^2 + (x_2 - \bar{x})^2 + \cdots + (x_n - \bar{x})^2 = \Sigma (x - \bar{x})^2$$

A common shorthand notation for $\Sigma (x - \bar{x})^2$ is S_{xx}. Dividing this sum by the sample size n gives the average squared deviation. Although this seems to be a reasonable measure of variability, a divisor slightly smaller than n will be used. (The reason for this will be explained subsequently.)

Definition

The **sample variance,** denoted by s^2, is the sum of squared deviations from the mean divided by $n - 1$. That is,

$$s^2 = \frac{\Sigma (x - \bar{x})^2}{n - 1} = \frac{S_{xx}}{n - 1}$$

The **sample standard deviation** is the positive square root of the sample variance and is denoted by **s.**

A large amount of variability in the sample is indicated by a relatively large value of s^2 or s, whereas a small value of s^2 or s indicates a small amount of variability. For most statistical purposes, s is the desired quantity, but s^2 must be computed first. Notice that whatever unit is used for x (such as lb or sec), the squared deviations and therefore s^2 are in squared units. Taking the square root gives a measure expressed in the same units as x. Thus, for a sample of heights, the standard deviation might be $s = 3.2$ in., and for a sample of textbook prices, it might be $s = \$12.43$.

EXAMPLE 4.8   (Example 4.1 continued)   To illustrate the calculation of the sample variance and standard deviation, let's look again at the range of motion data from Example 4.1. Table 4.3 shows squared deviations (obtained by subtracting $\bar{x} = 130.38$ from each observation), which are then combined to compute the values of s^2 and s.

Table 4.3 *Deviations and squared deviations for the range of motion data*

Observation	Deviation $(x - \bar{x})$	Squared Deviation $(x - \bar{x})^2$
154	23.62	557.9044
142	11.62	135.0244
137	6.62	43.8244
133	2.62	6.8644
122	−8.38	70.2244
126	−4.38	19.1844
135	4.62	21.3444
135	4.62	21.3444
108	−22.38	500.8644
120	−10.38	107.7444
127	−3.38	11.4244
134	3.62	13.1044
122	−8.38	70.2244
		Sum = 1579.0772

So,

$$\Sigma (x - \bar{x})^2 = S_{xx} = 1579.0772$$

and

$$s^2 = \frac{\Sigma (x - \bar{x})^2}{n - 1} = \frac{1579.0722}{12} = 131.5898$$

$$s = \sqrt{131.5898} = 11.4713$$

The computation of s^2 can be a bit tedious. Fortunately, many calculators and computer software packages compute the variance and standard deviation. One commonly used statistical computer package is MINITAB. Output resulting from using the MINITAB Describe command with the range of motion data follows. MINITAB gives a variety of numerical descriptive measures, including the mean, median, and standard deviation.

Descriptive Statistics

Variable	N	Mean	Median	TrMean	StDev	SE Mean
Motion	13	130.38	133.00	130.27	11.47	3.18

Variable	Minimum	Maximum	Q1	Q3
Motion	108.00	154.00	122.00	136.00

Interpretation and Properties

A standard deviation may be informally interpreted as the size of a "typical" deviation from the mean. Thus, in Example 4.8, a typical deviation from $\bar{x} = 130.38$ is about 11.47; some observations are closer than 11.47 to $\bar{x}$, and others are farther away. We computed $s = 11.47$ in Example 4.8 without saying whether this value indicated a large or small amount of variability. At this point, it is better to use s for comparative purposes than for an absolute assessment of variability. If we obtained a sample of range of motion values for a second group of patients and computed $s = 9.1$ for those patients, then we would conclude that there is more variability in our original sample than in this second sample. A particular value of s can be judged large or small only in comparison to something else.

There are measures of variability for the entire population that are analogous to s^2 and s for a sample. These measures are called the **population variance** and **population standard deviation,** and are denoted by σ^2 and σ, respectively. (We again use a lowercase Greek letter for a population characteristic.) The population standard deviation σ is expressed in the same units of measurement as are the values in the population. As with s, the value of σ can be used for comparative purposes.

In many statistical procedures, we would like to use the value of σ, but unfortunately it is not usually available. Therefore, in its place we must use a value computed from the sample that we hope is close to σ (that is, a good *estimate* of σ). We use the divisor $n - 1$ in s^2 rather than n because, on average, it tends to be a bit closer to σ^2. We will say more about this in Chapter 9.

An alternative rationale for using $n - 1$ is based on the property $\Sigma(x - \bar{x}) = 0$. Suppose that $n = 5$ and four of the deviations are

$$x_1 - \bar{x} = -4 \qquad \dot{x}_2 - \bar{x} = 6 \qquad x_3 - \bar{x} = 1 \qquad x_5 - \bar{x} = -8$$

Then, since the sum of these four deviations is -5, the remaining deviation must be $x_4 - \bar{x} = 5$ (so that the sum of all five is 0). Although there are five deviations, only four of them contain independent information about variability. More generally, once any $n - 1$ of the deviations are available, the value of the remaining deviation is determined. The n deviations actually contain only $n - 1$ independent pieces of information about variability. Statisticians express this by saying that s^2 and s are based on $n - 1$ *degrees of freedom* (df). Many inferential procedures encountered in later chapters are based on some appropriate number of df.

The Interquartile Range

As with $\bar{x}$, the value of s can be greatly affected by the presence of even a single unusually small or large observation. The *interquartile range* is a measure of variability that is resistant to the effects of outliers. It is based on quantities called *quartiles*. The *lower quartile* separates the bottom 25% of the data set from the upper 75%, and the *upper quartile* separates the top 25% from the bottom 75%. The *middle quartile* is the median, and it separates the bottom 50% from the top 50%. Figure 4.6 illustrates the locations of these quartiles for a smoothed histogram.

The quartiles for sample data are obtained by dividing the n ordered observations into a lower half and an upper half; if n is odd, the median is excluded from both halves. The two extreme quartiles are then the medians of the two halves.

FIGURE 4.6 The quartiles for a smoothed histogram

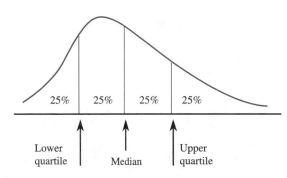

Lower quartile   Median   Upper quartile

25%   25%   25%   25%

Definition*

    lower quartile = median of the lower half of the sample
    upper quartile = median of the upper half of the sample

(If n is odd, the median of the entire sample is excluded from both halves.)

The **interquartile range (iqr)**, a resistant measure of variability, is given by

    iqr = upper quartile − lower quartile

---

* There are several other sensible ways to define quartiles. Some calculators and software packages use an alternate definition.

EXAMPLE 4.9   Cardiac output and maximal oxygen capacity typically decrease with age in sedentary individuals, but these decreases are at least partially arrested in middle-aged individuals who engage in a substantial amount of physical exercise. To understand better the effects of exercise and aging on various circulatory functions, the article "Cardiac Output in Male Middle-Aged Runners" (*J. of Sports Medicine* (1982): 17–22) presented data from a study of 21 middle-aged male runners. Figure 4.7 is a stem-and-leaf display of oxygen capacity values (mL/kg · min) while pedaling at a specified rate on a bicycle ergometer.

FIGURE 4.7 MINITAB stem-and-leaf display of oxygen capacity (mL/kg · min)

```
12 | 81
13 |
14 | 95
15 | 97,83
16 |
17 | 90
18 | 34,27
19 | 94,82
20 | 99,93,98,62,88
21 | 15
22 | 16,24          Stem:   Ones
23 | 16,56          Leaf:   Hundreths
```
HI: 35.78, 36.73 *These are outliers.*

The sample size $n = 21$ is an odd number, so the median, 20.88, is excluded from both halves of the sample:

Lower half   12.81 14.95 15.83 15.97 17.90 18.27 18.34 19.82 19.94 20.62
Upper half   20.93 20.98 20.99 21.15 22.16 22.24 23.16 23.56 35.78 36.73

Each half of the sample contains 10 observations, so each quartile is the average of the fifth and sixth values of the corresponding half. This gives us

$$\text{lower quartile} = \frac{17.90 + 18.27}{2} = 18.085 \qquad \text{upper quartile} = \frac{21.16 + 22.24}{2} = 22.200$$

and $\text{iqr} = 22.200 - 18.085 = 4.115$

The sample mean and standard deviation are 21.10 and 5.75, respectively. If we were to change the two largest values from 35.78 and 36.73 to 25.78 and 26.73 (so that they are still the two largest values), the median and the interquartile range would not be affected, whereas the mean and the standard deviation would change to 20.14 and 3.44, respectively.

The resistant nature of the iqr follows from the fact that up to 25% of the smallest sample observations and up to 25% of the largest can be made more extreme without affecting its value.

The **population interquartile range** is the difference between the upper and lower population quartiles. If a histogram of the data set under consideration (whether a population or a sample) can be reasonably well approximated by a normal curve, then the relationship between the standard deviation (sd) and interquartile range is roughly sd = iqr/1.35. A value of the standard deviation much larger than iqr/1.35 suggests a histogram with heavier (or longer) tails than a normal curve. For the oxygen uptake data of Example 4.9, we had $s = 5.75$, whereas iqr/1.35 = 4.115/1.35 = 3.05. This suggests that the distribution of sample values is indeed heavy tailed compared to a normal curve.

A Note Concerning Computation (Optional)

Hand calculation of s^2 using the defining formula can be a bit tedious. An alternative expression for the numerator of s^2 simplifies the arithmetic by eliminating the need to calculate the deviations. In this alternative, it is necessary to distinguish between two quantities that are similar in appearance but very different in value:

1. Sum the x values, then square the sum to obtain $(\Sigma x)^2$.

2. Square each x value, then sum the squares to obtain Σx^2.

If, for example, $x_1 = 3$ and $x_2 = 5$, then

$$(\Sigma x)^2 = (3 + 5)^2 = 8^2 = 64$$
$$\Sigma x^2 = x_1^2 + x_2^2 = 3^2 + 5^2 = 9 + 25 = 34$$

So the order in which the two operations, squaring and summation, are carried out makes a difference!

A computational formula for the sum of squared deviations is

$$S_{xx} = \Sigma (x - \overline{x})^2 = \Sigma x^2 - \frac{(\Sigma x)^2}{n}$$

Thus, a **computational formula for the sample variance** is

$$s^2 = \frac{S_{xx}}{n - 1} = \frac{\Sigma x^2 - \dfrac{(\Sigma x)^2}{n}}{n - 1}$$

According to this formula, after squaring each x value and adding these to obtain Σx^2, the single quantity $(\Sigma x)^2/n$ is subtracted from the result. Instead of the n subtractions required to obtain the deviations, just one subtraction now suffices.

The computed value of s^2, whether obtained from the defining formula or the computational formula, can sometimes be greatly affected by rounding in $\overline{x}$ or $(\Sigma x)^2/n$. Protection against adverse rounding effects can almost always be achieved by using four or five digits of decimal accuracy beyond the decimal accuracy of the data values themselves.

We now illustrate the use of the computational formula with the range of motion data of Example 4.8. For efficient computation, it is convenient to place the x

values in a single column and the x^2 values in a second column. Adding the numbers in these two columns then gives $\Sigma\, x$ and $\Sigma\, x^2$, respectively.

x	x^2
154	23,716
142	20,164
137	18,769
133	17,689
122	14,884
126	15,876
135	18,225
135	18,225
108	11,664
120	14,400
127	16,129
134	17,956
122	14,844
Sum = 1695	Sum = 222,581

Thus,

$$\frac{(\Sigma\, x)^2}{n} = \frac{(1695)^2}{13} = 221{,}001.9231$$

$$s^2 = \frac{222{,}581 - 221{,}001.9231}{13 - 1} = \frac{1579.0769}{12} = 131.5897$$

$$s = \sqrt{131.5897} = 11.4713$$

Note that the values of s^2 and s obtained using the computational formulas agree with those found previously in Example 4.8.

Exercises 4.19 – 4.28

4.19 A sample of $n = 5$ college students yielded the following observations on number of traffic citations for a moving violation during the previous year:

$$x_1 = 1 \quad x_2 = 0 \quad x_3 = 0 \quad x_4 = 3 \quad x_5 = 2$$

Calculate s^2 and s.

4.20 A study of the relationship between age and various visual functions (such as acuity and depth perception) reported the following observations on area of scleral lamina (mm^2) from human optic nerve heads ("Morphometry of Nerve Fiber Bundle Pores in the Optic Nerve

Head of the Human," *Experimental Eye Research* (1988): 559–568).

2.75	2.62	2.74	3.85	2.34	2.74
3.93	4.21	3.88	4.33	3.46	4.52
2.43	3.65	2.78	3.56	3.01	

It is easily verified that $S_{xx} = 8.025176$. Use this to compute the sample variance s^2 and then the sample standard deviation s. How can the value of s be interpreted?

4.21 **a.** Give two sets of five numbers that have the same mean but different standard deviations.

b. Give two sets of five numbers that have the same standard deviation but different means.

4.22 Although bats are not known for their eyesight, they are able to locate prey (mainly insects) by emitting high-pitched sounds and listening for echoes. A paper appearing in *Animal Behaviour* ("The Echolocation of Flying Insects by Bats" (1960): 141–154) gave the following distances (in cm) at which a bat first detected a nearby insect:

62 23 27 56 52 34 42 40 68 45 83

a. Compute the sample mean distance at which the bat first detects an insect.

b. Compute the sample variance and standard deviation for this data set. Interpret these values.

4.23 For the data in Exercise 4.22, add -10 to each sample observation. (This is the same as subtracting 10.) For the new set of values, compute the mean and the deviations from the mean. How do these deviations compare to the deviations from the mean for the original sample? How does s^2 for the new values compare to s^2 for the old values? In general, what effect does adding the same number to each observation have on s^2 and s? Explain.

4.24 For the data of Exercise 4.22, multiply each data value by 10. How does s for the new values compare to s for the original values?

4.25 The paper "The Pedaling Technique of Elite Endurance Cyclists" (*Int. J. of Sport Biomechanics* (1991): 29–53) reported the accompanying data on single-leg power at a high workload. Calculate and interpret the sample variance and standard deviation.

244 191 160 187 180 176 174
205 211 183 211 180 194 200

4.26 Refer to the data in Exercise 4.20 on scleral lamina areas.

a. Determine the lower and upper quartiles.

b. Calculate the value of the interquartile range.

c. If the two largest sample values, 4.33 and 4.52, had instead been 5.33 and 5.52, how would this affect the iqr? Explain.

d. By how much could the observation 2.34 be increased without affecting the iqr? Explain.

e. If an eighteenth observation, $x_{18} = 4.60$, is added to the sample, what is the iqr?

4.27 The sample standard deviation of the savings rate data given in Example 4.3 is $s = .469$. Calculate the value of iqr/1.35 and compare this to s. What does this comparison suggest about the shape of the histogram of this data?

4.28 The standard deviation alone does not measure relative variation. For example, a standard deviation of $1 would be considered large if it is describing the variability from store to store in the price of an ice cube tray. On the other hand, a standard deviation of $1 would be considered small if it is describing store-to-store variability in the price of a particular brand of freezer. A quantity designed to give a relative measure of variability is the *coefficient of variation*. Denoted by CV, the coefficient of variation expresses the standard deviation as a percent of the mean. It is defined by the formula

$$CV = 100 \cdot \frac{s}{x}$$

Consider the two samples below. Sample 1 gives the actual weight (in ounces) of the contents of cans of pet food labeled as having a net weight of 8 oz. Sample 2 gives the actual weight (in pounds) of the contents of bags of dry pet food labeled as having a net weight of 50 lb.

Sample 1:
8.3	7.1	7.6	8.1	7.6
8.3	8.2	7.7	7.7	7.5

Sample 2:
52.3	50.6	52.1	48.4	48.8
47.0	50.4	50.3	48.7	48.2

a. For each of the given samples, calculate the mean and the standard deviation.

b. Compute the coefficient of variation for each sample. Do the results surprise you? Why or why not?

4.3 Summarizing a Data Set: Boxplots

In the previous two sections, we looked at ways of describing the center and variability of a data set using numerical measures. It would be nice to have a method of summarizing data that gives more detail than just a measure of center and spread and yet less detail than a stem-and-leaf display or histogram. A *boxplot* is one such technique. It is compact, yet it provides information about the center, spread, and symmetry or skewness of the data. A boxplot is based on the median and interquartile range rather than on the mean and standard deviation. We will consider two types of boxplots: the skeletal and the modified boxplot.

Construction of a Skeletal Boxplot

1. Draw a horizontal (or vertical) measurement scale.

2. Construct a rectangular box whose left (or lower) edge is at the lower quartile and whose right (or upper) edge is at the upper quartile (so box width = iqr).

3. Draw a vertical (or horizontal) line segment inside the box at the location of the median.

4. Extend horizontal (or vertical) line segments from each end of the box to the smallest and largest observations in the data set. (These line segments are called *whiskers*.)

EXAMPLE 4.10

Let's reconsider the savings rate data first given in Example 4.3. Recall that savings rate was reported for a sample of 30 financial institutions in Southern California. The ordered observations are

2.15	2.20	2.20	2.22	2.22	2.23	2.25	2.25	2.27	2.28
2.28	2.28	2.29	2.30	2.30	2.32	2.32	2.33	2.33	2.33
2.33	2.33	2.33	2.38	2.43	2.55	2.79	3.05	3.68	4.35

To construct a boxplot of this data, we need the following information: the smallest observation, the lower quartile, the median, the upper quartile, and the largest observation. This collection of summary measures is often referred to as a five-number summary. For this data set,

smallest observation = 2.15

lower quartile = median of the lower half = 2.25

median = average of the 15th and 16th observations in the ordered list

$$= \frac{2.30 + 2.32}{2} = 2.31$$

upper quartile = median of the upper half = 2.33

largest observation = 4.35

Figure 4.8 shows the corresponding boxplot. The median line is somewhat closer to the upper edge of the box than to the lower edge, suggesting a concentration of values in the upper part of the middle half. The upper whisker is much longer than the lower whisker, giving the impression of positive skewness in the extremes of the data. These conclusions are consistent with the dotplot of Figure 4.1.

FIGURE 4.8 Skeletal boxplot for the savings rate data

The sequence of steps used to construct a skeletal boxplot is easily modified to give information about outliers.

Definition

An observation is an **outlier** if it is more than 1.5 iqr away from the closest end of the box (the closest quartile). An outlier is **extreme** if it is more than 3 iqr from the closest end of the box, and it is **mild** otherwise. A **modified boxplot** represents mild outliers by shaded circles and extreme outliers by open circles. Whiskers extend on each end to the most extreme observations that are *not* outliers.

EXAMPLE 4.11

The accompanying data came from an anthropological study of rectangular shapes (*Lowie's Selected Papers in Anthropology,* Cora Dubios, ed., Berkeley, Calif.: Univ. of Calif. Press, 1960: 137–142). Observations were made on the variable x = width/length for a sample of $n = 20$ beaded rectangles used in Shoshoni Indian leather handicrafts.

.553 .570 .576 .601 .606 .606 .609 .611 .615 .628 .654 .662
.668 .670 .672 .690 .693 .749 .844 .933

The quantities needed for constructing the modified boxplot follow:

median = .641   iqr = .681 − .606 = .075
lower quartile = .606   1.5 iqr = .1125
upper quartile = .681   3 iqr = .225

Thus,

upper edge of box (upper quartile) + 1.5 iqr = .681 + .1125 = .7935
lower edge of box (lower quartile) − 1.5 iqr = .606 − .1125 = .4935

so .844 and .933 are both outliers on the upper end, and there are no outliers on the lower end. Since

upper edge of box + 3 iqr = .681 + .225 = .906

.933 is an extreme outlier, and .844 is only a mild outlier. The upper whisker extends to the largest observation that is not an outlier, .749, and the lower whisker extends to .553. The boxplot is presented in Figure 4.9. The median line is not at the center of the box, so there is a slight asymmetry in the middle half of the data. However, the most striking feature is the presence of the two outliers. These two x values considerably exceed the "golden ratio" .618, used since antiquity as an aesthetic standard for rectangles.

FIGURE 4.9 Modified boxplot for rectangle data

With two or more data sets consisting of observations on the same variable (for example, fuel efficiencies for two types of car, weight gains for a control group and a treatment group, and so on), side-by-side boxplots convey initial impressions concerning similarities and differences between the data sets.

EXAMPLE 4.12

An article in the October 1994 issue of *Consumer Reports* compared various brands of brewed coffee. The study included 31 regular-roast caffeinated brands, 9 decaffeinated brands, and 13 dark-roast brands. Figure 4.10 is a comparative boxplot of cost per cup for the three types. The median marker for the first type (above 6.0) is barely discernible at the lower end of the box, and the same is true at the higher end (above 8.0) for the second type. The box for the third type is much wider than for the other two types (much larger iqr), indicating much more variability in the middle half of the data. However, there are no outliers for the third type, whereas the second type has one extreme outlier and the first type has three extreme and four mild outliers (two of these outlier brands have the same value: 4¢ per cup).

FIGURE 4.10 Comparative boxplot for cost per cup

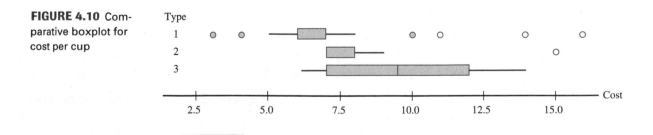

Exercises 4.29 – 4.34

4.29   The percentage of juice lost after thawing for 19 different strawberry varieties appeared in the article "Evaluation of Strawberry Cultivars with Different Degrees of Resistance to Red Scale" (*Fruit Varieties J.* (1991): 12–17):

46	51	44	50	33	46	60	41	55	46
53	53	42	44	50	54	46	41	48	

a. Are there any observations that are mild outliers? Extreme outliers?

b. Construct a boxplot and comment on the important features of the plot.

4.30   A *Consumer Reports* article on peanut butter (Sept. 1990) reported the following scores for various brands:

Creamy   56 44 62 36 39 53 50 65 45 22
         40 56 68 41 30 40 50 56 30

Crunchy 62 53 75 42 47 40 34 62 52
         50 34 42 36 75 80 47 56 62

The statistical package S-Plus was used to obtain the accompanying comparative boxplot. Comment on the similarities and differences in the two data sets.

4.31   The paper "Sodium–Calcium Exhange Equilibria in Soils as Affected by Calcium Carbonate and Organic Matter" (*Soil Science* (1984): 109) gave ten observations on soild pH. The data resulted from analysis of ten samples of soil from the Central Soil Salinity Research experimental farm.

8.53	8.52	8.01	7.99	7.93
7.89	7.85	7.82	7.80	7.72

a. Compute the upper quartile, lower quartile, and interquartile range.

b. Construct a skeletal boxplot and comment.

4.32   The amount of aluminum contamination (ppm) in plastic of a certain type was determined for a sample of 26 plastic specimens, resulting in the following data ("The LogNormal Distribution for Modeling Quality Data When the Mean Is Near Zero," *J. of Quality Technology* (1990): 105–110):

30	30	60	63	70	79	87	90	101
102	115	118	119	119	120	125	140	145
172	182	183	191	222	244	291	511	

Construct a boxplot that shows outliers, and comments on the interesting features of this plot.

4.33   The article "Compression of Single-Wall Corrugated Shipping Containers Using Fixed and Floating Test Platens" (*J. of Testing and Evaluation* (1992): 318–320) described an experiment in which several different types of boxes were compared with respect to compressive strength. Consider the following observations on four different types of boxes (this data is consistent with summary quantities given in the paper):

Type of Box	Compression Strength (lb)					
1	655.5	788.3	734.3	721.4	679.1	699.4
2	789.2	772.5	786.9	686.1	732.1	774.8
3	737.1	639.0	696.3	671.7	717.2	727.1
4	535.1	628.7	542.4	559.0	586.9	520.0

Construct a boxplot for each type of box. Use the same scale for all four boxplots. Discuss the similarities and differences in the boxplots.

4.34   Blood cocaine concentration (mg/L) was determined both for a sample of individuals who had died from cocaine-induced excited delirium and for a sample of those who had died from a cocaine overdose without excited delirium. The accompanying data is consistent with summary values given in the paper "Fatal Excited Delirium Following Cocaine Use" (*J. of Forensic Sciences* (1997): 25–31).

Excited Delirium:

0	0	0	0	.1	.1	.1	.1	.2
.2	.3	.3	.3	.4	.5	.7	.7	1.0
1.5	2.7	2.8	3.5	4.0	8.9	9.2	11.7	21.0

No Excited Delirium:

0	0	0	0	0	.1	.1	.1	.1	.2
.2	.2	.3	.3	.3	.4	.5	.5	.6	.8
.9	1.0	1.2	1.4	1.5	1.7	2.0	3.2	3.5	4.1
4.3	4.8	5.0	5.6	5.9	6.0	6.4	7.9	8.3	8.7
9.1	9.6	9.9	11.0	11.5	12.2	12.7	14.0	16.6	17.8

a. Determine the median, quartiles, and iqr for each of the two samples.

b. Are there any outliers in either sample? Any extreme outliers?

c. Construct a boxplot for each of the samples, and use them as a basis for comparing and contrasting the two samples.

4.4 Interpreting Center and Variability: Chebyshev's Rule, the Empirical Rule, and z Scores

The mean and standard deviation can be combined to obtain informative statements about how the values in a data set are distributed and about the relative position of a particular value in a data set. To do this, it is useful to be able to describe how far away a particular observation is from the mean in terms of the standard deviation. For example, we might say that an observation is 2 standard deviations above the mean or that an observation is 1.3 standard deviations below the mean. In this way, the standard deviation functions as a unit of measurement for describing distance from the mean. This is illustrated in the following example.

EXAMPLE 4.13

Consider a data set of scores on a standardized test with mean and standard deviation 100 and 15, respectively. We can make the following statements:

1. Because $100 - 15 = 85$, we say that a score of 85 is "1 standard deviation *below* the mean." Similarly, $100 + 15 = 115$ is "1 standard deviation *above* the mean." (See Figure 4.11.)

2. Since 2 standard deviations is $2(15) = 30$ and $100 + 30 = 130$, $100 - 30 = 70$, scores between 70 and 130 are those *within* 2 standard deviations of the mean. (See Figure 4.12.)

3. Because $100 + (3)(15) = 145$, scores above 145 exceed the mean by more than 3 standard deviations.

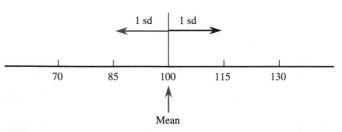

FIGURE 4.11 Values within 1 standard deviation of the mean

FIGURE 4.12 Values within 2 standard deviations of the mean

Sometimes in published articles, the mean and standard deviation are reported, but a graphical display of the data is not given. The following result enables us to get a sense of the distribution of data values based on knowledge of the mean and standard deviation only.

Chebyshev's Rule

Consider any number *k*, where k ≥ 1. Then *the percentage of observations that are within k standard deviations of the mean is at least* $100(1 - 1/k^2)\%$.

Substituting selected values of *k* gives the following results.

Number of Standard Deviations, *k*	$1 - \dfrac{1}{k^2}$	Percentage Within *k* sd's of the Mean
2	1 − 1/4 = .75	at least 75%
3	1 − 1/9 = .89	at least 89%
4	1 − 1/16 = .94	at least 94%
4.472	1 − 1/20 = .95	at least 95%
5	1 − 1/25 = .96	at least 96%
10	1 − 1/100 = .99	at least 99%

EXAMPLE 4.14   The article "Piecing Together Child Care with Multiple Arrangements: Crazy Quilt or Preferred Pattern for Employed Parents of Preschool Children?" (*J. of Marriage and the Family* (1994): 669–680) examined various modes of care for preschool children. For a sample of families with one such child, it was reported that the mean and standard deviation of child care time per week (hours) were approximately 36 and 12, respectively. Figure 4.13 displays values that are 1, 2, and 3 standard deviations from the mean.

FIGURE 4.13 Measurement scale for child care time

0	12	24	36	48	60	72
$\bar{x} - 3s$	$\bar{x} - 2s$	$\bar{x} - s$	$\bar{x}$	$\bar{x} + s$	$\bar{x} + 2s$	$\bar{x} + 3s$

Chebyshev's Rule allows us to assert the following:

1. At least 75% of the sample observations must be between 12 and 60 hours (within 2 sd's of the mean).

2. Because at least 89% of the observations must be between 0 and 72, at most 11% are outside this interval. Time cannot be negative, so we conclude that at most 11% of the observations exceed 72.

3. The values 18 and 52 are 1.5 sd's to either side of $\bar{x}$ ($1.5s = 18$), so using $k = 1.5$ in Chebyshev's Rule implies that at least 55.6% of the observations must be between these two values. Thus, at most 44.4% of the observations are less than 18 — *not* at most 22.2%, since the distribution of values may not be symmetric.

Because Chebyshev's Rule is applicable to any data set (distribution), whether symmetric or skewed, we must be careful when making statements about the proportion above a particular value, below a particular value, or inside or outside an interval that is not centered at the mean. The rule must be used in a conservative fashion. There is another aspect of this conservatism. Whereas the rule states that at least 75% of the observations are within 2 standard deviations of the mean, in many data sets substantially more than 75% of the values satisfy this condition. The same sort of understatement is frequently encountered for other values of k (numbers of standard deviations).

EXAMPLE 4.15   Figure 4.14 gives a stem-and-leaf display of IQ scores of 112 children in one of the early studies that used the Stanford revision of the Binet–Simon intelligence scale (*The Intelligence of School Children,* L. M. Terman, 1919).

Summary quantities include

$$\bar{x} = 104.5 \qquad s = 16.3 \qquad 2s = 32.6 \qquad 3s = 48.9$$

FIGURE 4.14 Stem-and-leaf display of IQ scores

```
 6 | 1
 7 | 25679
 8 | 0000124555668
 9 | 00001123333446666778889
10 | 000112222233335666677778899999
11 | 00001122333344444477899
12 | 01111123445669
13 | 006
14 | 26                        Stem:  Tens
15 | 2                         Leaf:  Ones
```

Table 4.4 shows how Chebyshev's Rule considerably understates actual percentages.

Table 4.4 *Summarizing the distribution of IQ scores*

k = no. of sd's	$\bar{x} \pm ks$	Chebyshev	Actual
2	71.9 to 137.1	at least 75%	96% (108)
2.5	63.7 to 145.3	at least 84%	97% (109)
3	55.6 to 153.4	at least 89%	100% (112)

The Empirical Rule

The fact that statements based on Chebyshev's Rule are frequently very conservative suggests that we should look for rules that are less conservative and more precise. The most useful such rule is the **Empirical Rule,** which can be applied whenever the distribution of data values can be reasonably well described by a normal curve. The word *empirical* means deriving from practical experience, and practical experience has shown that a normal curve gives a reasonable fit to many data sets.

Empirical Rule

If the histogram of values in a data set can be reasonably well approximated by a normal curve, then

Approximately 68% of the observations are within 1 standard deviation of the mean.

Approximately 95% of the observations are within 2 standard deviations of the mean.

Approximately 99.7% of the observations are within 3 standard deviations of the mean.

The Empirical Rule makes "approximately" instead of "at least" statements, and the percentages for $k = 1, 2$, and 3 standard deviations are much higher than those allowed by Chebyshev's Rule. Figure 4.15 illustrates the percentages given in

FIGURE 4.15 Approximate percentages implied by the Empirical Rule

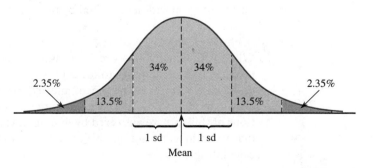

the Empirical Rule. In contrast to Chebyshev's Rule, dividing the percentages in half is permissible, because a normal curve is symmetric.

EXAMPLE 4.16   One of the earliest articles to argue for the wide applicability of the normal distribution was "On the Laws of Inheritance in Man. I. Inheritance of Physical Characters" (*Biometrika* (1903): 375–462). Among the data sets discussed in the article was one consisting of 1052 measurements of the heights of mothers. The mean and standard deviation were

$$\bar{x} = 62.484 \text{ in.} \qquad s = 2.390 \text{ in.}$$

A normal curve did provide a good fit to the data. Table 4.5 contrasts actual percentages with those from Chebyshev's Rule and the Empirical Rule. Clearly, the Empirical Rule is much more successful and informative in this case than Chebyshev's Rule.

Table 4.5 *Summarizing the distribution of mothers' heights*

No. of sd's	Interval	Actual	Empirical Rule	Chebyshev Rule
1	60.094 to 64.874	72.1%	68%	at least 0%
2	57.704 to 67.264	96.2%	95%	at least 75%
3	55.314 to 69.654	99.2%	99.7%	at least 89%

Our detailed study of the normal distribution and areas under normal curves in Chapter 7 will enable us to make statements analogous to those of the Empirical Rule for values other than $k = 1, 2,$ or 3 standard deviations. For now, note that it is rather rare to see an observation from a normally distributed population that is farther than 2 standard deviations from the mean (only 5%), and it is very surprising to see one that is more than 3 standard deviations away. If you encountered a mother whose height was 72 in., you might reasonably conclude that she was not part of the population described by the data set in Example 4.16.

Measures of Relative Standing

When you obtain your score after taking an achievement test, you probably want to know how it compares to the scores of others who have taken the test. Is your score above or below the mean, and by how much? Does your score place you among the top 5% of those who took the test, or only among the top 25%? Questions of this sort are answered by finding ways to measure the position of a particular value in a data set relative to all values in the set. One such measure involves calculating a *z score*.

> **Definition**
>
> The *z* **score** corresponding to a particular observation in a data set is
>
> $$z \text{ score} = \frac{\text{observation} - \text{mean}}{\text{standard deviation}}$$
>
> The *z* score tells us how many standard deviations the observation is from the mean. It is positive or negative according to whether the observation lies above or below the mean.

The process of subtracting the mean and then dividing by the standard deviation is sometimes referred to as *standardization,* and a *z* score is one example of what is called a *standardized score.*

EXAMPLE 4.17   Suppose that two graduating seniors, one marketing major and one accounting major, are comparing job offers. The accounting major has an offer for $35,000 per year, and the marketing student has one for $33,000 per year. Summary information about the distribution of offers follows:

Accounting: mean = 36,000   standard deviation = 1500

Marketing: mean = 32,500   standard deviation = 1000

Then,

$$\text{accounting } z \text{ score} = \frac{35,000 - 36,000}{1500} = -.67$$

(so $35,000 is .67 standard deviation below the mean), whereas

$$\text{marketing } z \text{ score} = \frac{33,000 - 32,500}{1000} = .5$$

Relative to the appropriate data sets, the marketing offer is actually more attractive than the accounting offer (though this may not offer much solace to the marketing major).

The *z* score is particularly useful when the distribution of observations is approximately normal. In this case, by the Empirical Rule, a *z* score outside the interval from -2 to $+2$ will occur in about 5% of all cases, whereas a *z* score outside the interval from -3 to $+3$ will occur only about .3% of the time.

A particular observation can be located even more precisely by giving the percentage of the data that fall at or below that observation. If, for example, 95% of all test scores are at or below 650, whereas only 5% are above 650, then 650 is called the *95th percentile* of the data set (or of the distribution of scores). Similarly, if 10% of all scores are at or below 400 and 90% are above 400, then the value 400 is the 10th percentile.

Definition

For any particular number *r* between 0 and 100, the *r*th percentile is a value such that *r* percent of the observations in the data set fall at or below that value.

Figure 4.16 illustrates the 90th percentile. We have already met several percentiles in disguise. The median is the 50th percentile, and the lower and upper quartiles are the 25th and 75th percentiles, respectively.

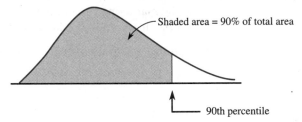

FIGURE 4.16 90th percentile from a smoothed histogram

EXAMPLE 4.18 Variable cost as a percentage of operating revenue is an important indicator of a company's financial health. The article "A Credit Limit Decision Model for Inventory Floor Planning and Other Extended Trade Credit Arrangements" (*Decision Sciences* (1992): 200–220) reported the following summary data for a sample of 350 corporations:

> sample mean = 90.1%   sample median = 91.2%
> 5th percentile = 78.3%   95th percentile = 98.6%

Thus, half of the sampled firms had variable costs that were less than 91.2% of operating revenues because 91.2 is the 50th percentile. If the distribution of values were perfectly symmetric, the mean and median would be identical. Further evidence against symmetry is provided by the two other given percentiles. The 5th percentile is 12.9 below the median, whereas the 95th percentile is only 7.4 above the median. The histogram given in the article had roughly the shape of the negatively skewed smoothed histogram in Figure 4.17. (The total area under the curve is 1.)

FIGURE 4.17 The distribution of variable costs from Example 4.18

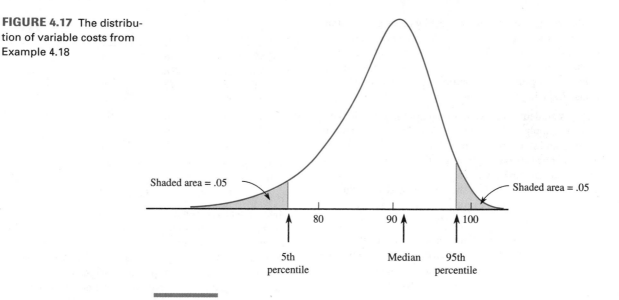

Exercises 4.35 – 4.48

4.35 The average playing time of compact discs in a large collection is 35 min, and the standard deviation is 5 min.
  a. What value is 1 standard deviation above the mean? 1 standard deviation below the mean? What values are 2 standard deviations away from the mean?
  b. Without assuming anything about the distribution of times, at least what percentage of the times are between 25 and 45 min?
  c. Without assuming anything about the distribution of times, what can be said about the percentage of times that are either less than 20 min or greater than 50 min?
  d. Assuming that the distribution of times is normal, approximately what percentage of times are between 25 and 45 min? Less than 20 min or greater than 50 min? Less than 20 min?

4.36 In a study investigating the effect of car speed on accident severity, 5000 reports of fatal automobile accidents were examined, and the vehicle speed at impact was recorded for each one. It was determined that the average speed was 42 mph and that the standard deviation was 15 mph. In addition, a histogram revealed that vehicle speed at impact could be described by a normal curve.
  a. Roughly what proportion of vehicle speeds were between 27 mph and 57 mph?

  b. Roughly what proportion of vehicle speeds exceeded 57 mph?

4.37 Mobile homes are very tightly constructed for energy conservation. This may lead to a buildup of pollutants generated indoors. The paper "A Survey of Nitrogen Dioxide Levels Inside Mobile Homes" (*J. Air Pollut. Control Assoc.* (1988): 647–651) discussed various aspects of NO_2 concentration in these structures.
  a. In one sample of homes in the Los Angeles area, the mean NO_2 concentration in kitchens during the summer was 36.92 ppb, and the standard deviation was 11.34. Making no assumptions about the shape of the histogram, what can be said about the percentage of observations between 14.24 and 59.60?
  b. Inside what interval is it guaranteed that at least 89% of the concentration observations will lie?
  c. In a sample of non–Los Angeles homes, the average kitchen concentration during the winter was 24.76 ppb, and the standard deviation was 17.20. Do these values suggest that the histogram of sample observations did not closely resemble a normal curve? (*Hint*: What is $\bar{x} - 2s$?)

4.38 The article "Taxable Wealth and Alcoholic Beverage Consumption in the United States" (*Psychological Reports* (1994): 813–814) reported that the mean annual adult consumption of wine was 3.15 gallons and the standard deviation was 6.09 gallons. Would you use the Empirical Rule to approximate the proportion of adults who consume more than 9.24 gallons (i.e., whose consumption value exceeds the mean by more than 1 standard deviation)? Explain your reasoning.

4.39 A student took two national aptitude tests in the course of applying for admission to colleges. The national average and standard deviation for the first test were 475 and 100, respectively, whereas for the second test the average and standard deviation were 30 and 8, respectively. The student scored 625 on the first test and 45 on the second. Use z scores to determine on which exam the student performed better.

4.40 Suppose that your younger sister is applying for entrance to college and has taken the SAT exams. She scored at the 83rd percentile on the verbal section of the test and at the 94th percentile on the math section of the test. Since you have been studying statistics, she asks you for an interpretation of these values. What would you tell her?

4.41 A sample of concrete specimens of a certain type is selected, and the compressive strength of each one is determined. The mean and standard deviation are calculated as $\bar{x} = 3000$ and $s = 500$, and the sample histogram is found to be very well approximated by a normal curve.

a. Approximately what percentage of the sample observations are between 2500 and 3500, and what result justifies your assertion?

b. Approximately what percentage of sample observations are outside the interval from 2000 to 4000?

c. What can be said about the approximate percentage of observations between 2000 and 2500?

d. Why would you not use Chebyshev's Rule to answer the questions posed in parts **a–c**?

4.42 The paper "Modeling and Measurements of Bus Service Reliability" (*Trans. Research* (1978): 253–256) studied various aspects of bus service and presented data on travel times from several different routes. We give here a frequency distribution for bus travel times from origin to destination on one particular route in Chicago during peak morning traffic periods.

Class	Frequency	Relative Frequency
15–<16	4	.02
16–<17	0	.00
17–<18	26	.13
18–<19	99	.49

(*continued*)

Class	Frequency	Relative Frequency
19–<20	36	.18
20–<21	8	.04
21–<22	12	.06
22–<23	0	.00
23–<24	0	.00
24–<25	0	.00
25–<26	16	.08

a. Construct the corresponding histogram.

b. Compute the following (approximate) percentiles.
i. 86th **ii.** 15th **iii.** 90th **iv.** 95th **v.** 10th

4.43 An advertisement for the "30-in. wonder" that appeared in the September 1983 issue of the journal *Packaging* claimed that the 30-in. wonder weighs cases and bags up to 110 lb and provides accuracy to $\frac{1}{4}$ oz. Suppose that a 50-oz weight was repeatedly weighed on this scale and the weight readings recorded. The mean value was 49.5 oz, and the standard deviation was .1. What can be said about the proportion of the time that the scale actually showed a weight that was within $\frac{1}{4}$ oz of the true value of 50 oz? (*Hint*: Try to make use of Chebyshev's Rule.)

4.44 Suppose that your statistics professor returned your first midterm exam with only a z score written on it. She also told you that a histogram of the scores was closely described by a normal curve. How would you interpret each of the following z scores?
a. 2.2 **b.** −.4 **c.** −1.8 **d.** 1.0 **e.** 0

4.45 The paper "Answer Changing on Multiple-Choice Tests" (*J. of Experimental Education* (1980): 18–21) reported that for a group of 162 college students, the average number of responses changed from the correct answer to an incorrect answer on a test containing 80 multiple-choice items was 1.4. The corresponding standard deviation was reported to be 1.5. Based on this mean and standard deviation, what can you tell about the shape of the distribution of the variable *number of answers changed from right to wrong*? What can you say about the number of students who changed at least six answers from correct to incorrect?

4.46 The average reading speed of students completing a speed-reading course is 450 words per minute (wpm). If the standard deviation is 70 wpm, find the z score associated with each of the following reading speeds.
a. 320 wpm **b.** 475 wpm **c.** 420 wpm **d.** 610 wpm

4.47 The accompanying data values are 1989 per capita expenditures on public libraries for each of the 50 states. (New York is the highest and Arkansas the lowest.)

29.48	24.45	23.64	23.34	22.10	21.16	19.83
18.01	17.95	17.23	16.53	16.29	15.89	15.85
13.64	13.37	13.16	13.09	12.66	12.37	11.93
10.99	10.55	10.24	10.06	9.84	9.65	8.94
7.70	7.56	7.46	7.04	6.58	5.98	19.81
19.25	19.18	18.62	14.74	14.53	14.46	13.83
11.85	11.71	11.53	11.34	8.72	8.22	8.13
8.01						

a. Summarize this data set with a frequency distribution. Construct the corresponding histogram.

b. Use the histogram in part **a** to find approximate values of the following percentiles:

  i. 50th   **ii.** 70th   **iii.** 10th   **iv.** 90th   **v.** 40th

4.48 The accompanying table gives the mean and standard deviation of reaction times (sec) for each of two different stimuli.

	Stimulus 1	Stimulus 2
Mean	6.0	3.6
Standard deviation	1.2	.8

If your reaction time for the first stimulus is 4.2 sec and for the second stimulus 1.8 sec, to which stimulus are you reacting (when compared to all other individuals) relatively more quickly?

4.5   Interpreting the Results of Statistical Analyses

It is relatively rare to find raw data in published sources. Most of the time, only a few numerical summary quantities are reported. We must be able to interpret these values and understand what they tell us about the underlying data set.

For example, a university recently conducted an investigation of the amount of time required to enter the information contained in an application for admission into the university computer system. One of the individuals who performs this task was asked to note starting time and completion time for 50 randomly selected application forms. The resulting entry times (minutes) were summarized using the mean, median, and standard deviation:

$$\bar{x} = 7.854 \qquad \text{median} = 7.423 \qquad s = 2.129$$

What do these summary values tell us about entry times? The average time required to enter admissions data was 7.854 minutes, but the relatively large standard deviation suggests that there was quite a bit of variability among the 50 observed times. The median tells us that half of the applications required less than 7.423 minutes for entry. The fact that the mean exceeds the median suggests that some unusually large values in the data set affected the value of the mean. This last conjecture is confirmed by the stem-and-leaf display of the data given in Figure 4.18.

FIGURE 4.18 Stem-and-leaf display of data entry times

```
 4 | 8
 5 | 0234579
 6 | 00001234566779
 7 | 223556688
 8 | 23334
 9 | 002
10 | 011168
11 | 134
12 | 2            Stem:  Ones
13 |              Leaf:  Tenths
14 | 3
```

Those conducting the study looked at the outlier 14.3 and at the other relatively large values in the data set; they found that the five largest values came from applications that were entered before lunch. After talking with the individual entering the data, administrators speculated that morning entry times might differ from afternoon entry times because there tended to be more distractions and interruptions (phone calls, etc.) during the morning hours, when the admissions office generally was busier. When morning and afternoon entry times were separated, the following summary statistics resulted:

Morning (*based on n* = 20 applications): $\bar{x}$ = 9.093   median = 8.743   s = 2.329

Afternoon (*based on n* = 30 applications): $\bar{x}$ = 7.027   median = 6.737   s = 1.529

From these summary values, we see that the average entry time is higher for applications entered in the morning and also that the individual entry times differ more from one another in the mornings than in the afternoons (since the standard deviation for morning entry times is about 1.5 times as large as that for afternoon entry times).

What to Look for in Published Data

Here are a few questions to ask yourself when interpreting numerical summary measures.

- Is the chosen summary measure appropriate for the type of data collected? In particular, watch for inappropriate use of the mean and the standard deviation with categorical data that has simply been coded numerically.

- If both the mean and the median are reported, how do the two values compare? What does this suggest about the distribution of values in the data set? If only the mean or the median was used, was the appropriate measure selected?

- Is the standard deviation large or small? Is the value consistent with your expectations regarding variability? What does the value of the standard deviation tell you about the variable being summarized?

- Can anything of interest be said about the values in the data set by applying Chebyshev's Rule or the Empirical Rule?

The journal article "Smoking During Pregnancy and Lactation and Its Effects on Breast Milk Volume" (*Amer. J. of Clinical Nutrition* (1991): 1011–1016) reported the following summary values for data collected on daily breast milk volume for two groups of nursing mothers. For a group of mothers who smoked, the mean milk volume was 693 g and the standard deviation was 110. Based on data given in the article, the median milk volume was 589.5 g. For a group of nonsmoking mothers, the mean was 961 g, the standard deviation 120, and the median 946 g.

	Mean	Standard Deviation
Smokers	693	110
Nonsmokers	589	120

Since milk volume is a numerical variable, these descriptive measures reasonably summarize the data set. For smoking mothers, the mean and median are similar, indicating that the milk volume distribution is approximately symmetric. The average milk volume for this group is 693, whereas for nonsmoking mothers the mean milk volume is 961 — quite a bit higher than for the smoking mothers. The standard deviations for the two groups are similar, suggesting that, although the average milk volume may be lower for smokers, the variability in mothers' milk volume is about the same. Since the median for the nonsmoking group is smaller than the corresponding mean, we suspect that the distribution of milk volume for nonsmoking mothers is positively skewed.

Summary of Key Concepts and Formulas

Term or Formula	Comment
$x_1, x_2, \ldots, x_n$	Notation for sample data consisting of observations on a variable x, where n is the sample size.
Sample mean, $\bar{x} = \dfrac{\Sigma x}{n}$	The most frequently used measure of center of a sample. It can be very sensitive to the presence of even a single outlier (unusually large or small observation).
Population mean, μ	The average x value in the entire population.
Sample median	The middle value in the ordered list of sample observations. (For n even, the median is the average of the two middle values.) It is very insensitive to outliers.
Trimmed mean	A measure of center in which the observations are first ordered from smallest to largest, one or more observations are deleted from each end, and the remaining ones are averaged. In terms of sensitivity to outliers, it is a compromise between the mean and the median.
Deviations from the mean: $x_1 - \bar{x}, x_2 - \bar{x}, \ldots, x_n - \bar{x}$	Quantities used to assess variability in a sample. Except for rounding effects, $\Sigma (x - \bar{x}) = 0$.
The sample variance $s^2 = \dfrac{\Sigma(x - \bar{x})^2}{n - 1}$ and standard deviation $s = \sqrt{s^2}$	The most frequently used measures of variability for sample data.
$S_{xx} = \Sigma x^2 - \dfrac{(\Sigma x)^2}{n}$	The computing formula for S_{xx}, the numerator of s^2.
The population variance σ^2 and standard deviation σ	Measures of variability for the entire population.
Quartiles and the interquartile range	The lower quartile separates the smallest 25% of the data from the remaining 75%, and the upper quartile separates the largest 25% from the smallest 75%. The interquartile range (iqr), a measure of variability less sensitive to outliers than s, is the difference between the upper and lower quartiles.
Chebyshev's Rule	This rule states that for any number $k \geq 1$, *at least* $100(1 - 1/k^2)\%$ of the observations in *any* data set are within k standard deviations of the mean. It is typically conservative in that the actual percentages often considerably exceed $100(1 - 1/k^2)$.

Empirical Rule	This rule gives the approximate percentage of observations within 1 standard deviation (68%), 2 standard deviations (95%), and 3 standard deviations (99.7%) of the mean when the histogram is well approximated by a normal curve.
z score	This quantity gives the distance between an observation and the mean expressed as a certain number of standard deviations. It is positive (negative) if the observation lies above (below) the mean.
rth percentile	The value such that r percent of the observations in the data set fall at or below that value.
Boxplot	A picture that conveys information about the most important features of a data set: center, spread, extent of skewness, and presence of outliers.

Supplementary Exercises 4.49–4.64

4.49 Reconsider the radon concentration data given in the chapter introduction.

a. Construct a comparative stem-and-leaf display with 210 shown separately as a high value, and comment on similarities and differences.

b. $\Sigma x = 958$ for the cancer sample and 747 for the no-cancer sample. Calculate the two sample means and medians, and comment.

c. $S_{xx} = 41,084.476$ for the cancer sample and 10,969.077 for the no-cancer sample. What do the values of the two sample standard deviations suggest about variability in the two samples?

d. Determine the value of iqr for each sample. What do these values tell you about variability in the two samples? Is the conclusion here different from the conclusion in part **c**? Explain. (*Hint:* Without 210 and 85, cancer $s = 11.4$ and no-cancer $s = 13.3$.)

e. Construct comparative boxplots.

4.50 The article "Can We Really Walk Straight?" (*Amer. J. of Physical Anthropology* (1992): 19–27) reported on an experiment in which each of 20 healthy men was asked to walk as straight as possible to a target 60 meters away at normal speed. Consider the accompanying data on cadence (number of strides per second).

.95   .85   .92   .95   .93   .86   1.00   .92   .85   .81   .78
.93   .93   1.05   .93   1.06   1.06   .96   .81   .96

Use the methods developed in this chapter to summarize the data; include an interpretation or discussion wherever appropriate. (*Note:* The author of the paper used a rather sophisticated statistical analysis to conclude that people cannot walk in a straight line, and suggested several explanations for this.)

4.51 The *San Luis Obispo Telegram-Tribune* (Dec. 18, 1992) reported that for the 1992 season, the average major-league baseball salary was just over $1 million, whereas only 267 of the 772 players made at least this much money. What does this imply about the median salary and the shape of a histogram of salaries?

4.52 The article "Comparing the Costs of Major Hotel Franchises" (*Real Estate Review* (1992): 46–51) gave the accompanying data on franchise cost as a percentage of total room revenue for chains of three different types.

Budget	2.7	2.8	3.8	3.8	4.0	4.1	5.5	5.9	6.7
	7.0	7.2	7.2	7.5	7.5	7.7	7.9	7.9	8.1
	8.2	8.5							
Midrange	1.5	4.0	6.6	6.7	7.0	7.2	7.2	7.4	7.8
	8.0	8.1	8.3	8.6	9.0				
First-class	1.8	5.8	6.0	6.6	6.6	6.6	7.1	7.2	7.5
	7.6	7.6	7.8	7.8	8.2	9.6			

Construct a boxplot for each type of hotel, and comment on interesting features, similarities, and differences.

4.53 In recent years, many teachers have been subject to increased levels of stress, contributing to disenchantment with teaching as a profession. The paper "Professional Burnout Among Public School Teachers" (*Public Personnel Mgmt.* (1988): 167–189) looked at various aspects of this problem. Consider the accompanying information on total psychological effects scores for a sample of 937 teachers.

Burnout Level	Range of Scores	Frequency
Low	0–21	554
Moderate	22–43	342
High	44–65	41

$\bar{x} = 19.93$ $s = 12.89$

a. Draw a histogram.

b. Mark the value of $\bar{x}$ on the measurement scale, and use the histogram to locate the approximate value of the median. Why are the two measures of center not identical?

c. In what interval of values are we guaranteed to find at least 75% of the scores, irrespective of the histogram shape? From the histogram, roughly what percentage of the scores actually fall in this interval?

4.54 The amount of radiation received at a greenhouse plays an important role in determining the rate of photosynthesis. The accompanying observations on incoming solar radiation were read from a graph in the paper "Radiation Components over Bare and Planted Soils in a Greenhouse" (*Solar Energy* (1990): 1–6).

6.3	6.4	7.1	7.7	8.4	8.5	8.8	8.9	9.0
9.1	10.0	10.1	10.2	10.6	10.6	10.7	10.7	10.8
10.9	11.1	11.2	11.2	11.4	11.9	11.9	12.2	13.1

Use some of the methods discussed in this chapter and the previous one to describe this data.

4.55 The accompanying data on milk volume (g/day) was taken from the paper "Smoking during Pregnancy and Lactation and Its Effects on Breast Milk Volume" (*American J. of Clinical Nutrition* (1991): 1011–1016).

Smoking mothers	621	793	593	545	753	655
	895	767	714	598	693	
Nonsmoking mothers	947	945	1086	1202	973	981
	930	745	903	899	961	

Compare and contrast the two samples.

4.56 **a.** Suppose that n, the number of sample observations, is an odd number. Under what conditions will $\bar{x}$ and the sample median be identical?

b. If $n = 10$, when will $\bar{x}$ and the 10% trimmed mean be identical?

4.57 **a.** A statistics instructor informed her class that the median exam score was 78 and the mean was 70. Sketch a picture of what the smoothed histogram of scores might look like.

b. Suppose that the majority of students in the class studied for the exam, but a few students did not. How might this be reflected in a smoothed histogram of exam scores?

4.58 Suppose that an auto dealership employs clerical workers, salespeople, and mechanics. The average monthly salaries of the clerical employees, salespeople, and mechanics are $1700, $2200, and $2900, respectively. If the dealership has three clerical employees, ten sales-

people, and eight mechanics, find the average monthly wage for all employees of the dealership.

4.59 The *Los Angeles Times* (July 17, 1995) reported that in a sample of 364 lawsuits in which punitive damages were awarded, the sample median damage award was $50,000, and the sample mean was $775,000. What does this suggest about the distribution of values in the sample?

4.60 The paper "Sodium–Calcium Exchange Equilibria in Soils as Affected by Calcium Carbonate and Organic Matter" (*Soil Science* (1984): 109) gave ten observations on soil pH. The data resulted from analysis of ten samples of soil from the Central Soil Salinity Research Institute experimental farm.

Soil pH 8.53 8.52 8.01 7.99 7.93 7.89 7.85 7.82 7.80 7.72

a. Calculate and interpret the values of the sample mean, variance, and standard deviation.

b. Compute the 10% trimmed mean and the sample median. Do either of these values differ much from the value of the sample mean?

c. Find the upper quartile, the lower quartile, and the interquartile range.

d. Illustrate the location and spread of this sample using a boxplot.

4.61 Age at diagnosis for each of 20 patients under treatment for meningitis was given in the paper "Penicillin in the Treatment of Meningitis" (*J. Amer. Med. Assoc.* (1984): 1870–1874). The ages (in years) were as follows:

18	18	25	19	23	20	69	18	21	18
20	18	18	20	18	19	28	17	18	18

a. Calculate the values of the sample mean and the standard deviation.

b. Calculate the 10% trimmed mean. How does the value of the trimmed mean compare to that of the sample mean? Which would you recommend as a measure of location? Explain.

c. Compute the upper quartile, the lower quartile, and the interquartile range.

d. Are there any mild or extreme outliers present in this data set?

e. Construct the boxplot for this data set.

4.62 Although blood pressure is a continuous variable, its value is often reported to the nearest 5 mm Hg (for example, 100, 105, 110, and so on). Suppose that the actual blood pressure values for nine randomly selected individuals are as follows.

118.6 127.4 138.4 130.0 113.7 122.0 108.3 131.5 133.2

a. If values are reported as suggested (rounded to the nearest 5 mm Hg), what is the sample of the *reported* values, and what is the median of this sample?

b. Suppose that the second individual's blood pressure is 127.6 rather than 127.4 (a small change in a single value). How does this change the median of reported values? What does this say about the median's sensitivity to rounding or grouping of the data?

4.63 The accompanying observations are carbon monoxide levels (ppm) in air samples obtained from a certain region.

9.3 10.7   8.5 9.6 12.2 16.6 9.2 10.5 7.9 13.2 11.0
8.8 13.7 12.1 9.8

a. If a trimmed mean is calculated by first deleting the smallest and largest observations, what is the corresponding trimming percentage? What is it if the two smallest and two largest observations are deleted?

b. Calculate the two trimmed means referred to in part **a.**

c. Using the results of part **b,** how might you calculate a measure of center for this sample that could be regarded as a 10% trimmed mean?

4.64 Suppose that the distribution of scores on an exam is closely described by a normal curve with mean 100. The 16th percentile of this distribution is 80.

a. What is the 84th percentile?

b. What is the approximate value of the standard deviation of exam scores?

c. What z score is associated with an exam score of 90?

d. What percentile corresponds to an exam score of 140?

e. Do you think there were many scores below 40? Explain.

References

See the References at the end of Chapter 3.

5

Summarizing Bivariate Data

INTRODUCTION

How can the cost-effectiveness of schools be assessed? People inside and outside the education community have been arguing over this issue for years, and the debate has become more heated as spending for education has come under increasing scrutiny. The article "Cost-Effectiveness in Public Education" (*Chance* (1995): 38–41) considered data from various school districts in New Jersey. Part of this data consisted of observations on the two variables x = dollars spent per pupil and y = average SAT scores for 44 districts having only grade levels 7–12 or 9–12. Some representative observations (as read from a graph) are as follows:

x	7750	9900	10,870	12,080	. . .
y	878	893	966	950	. . .

What can be said about the general nature of the relationship between expenditure per pupil and SAT score? In particular, are high scores associated with high expenditure levels? Can average SAT score for a district be predicted once expenditure per pupil for the district is known? How accurate are predictions of average SAT score based just on expenditure per pupil?

Chapters 3 and 4 discussed methods for describing and summarizing univariate data. Often, however, an investigator is interested in two or more attributes of individuals or objects in a population, and how they are related to one another. For example, an environmental researcher might wish to know how the lead content of soil varies with distance from a major highway. Researchers in early childhood education might investigate how vocabulary size and age are related. College admissions officers, who must try to predict whether an applicant will succeed in college, might use a model relating college grade point average to high school grades, ACT or SAT scores, and various personal and family characteristics.

In this chapter, we introduce methods for describing relationships between two numerical variables and for assessing the strength of a relationship. Chapter 13 develops methods of statistical inference for drawing conclusions from data consisting of observations on two variables. The techniques introduced in this chapter are also important stepping stones for analyzing data consisting of observations on three or more variables, the topic of Chapter 14.

5.1   Scatter Plots

A **multivariate** data set consists of measurements or observations on each of two or more variables. An important special case, **bivariate** data, involves just two variables x and y. For example, x might be distance from a highway and y lead content of soil at that distance. When both x and y are numerical variables, each observation consists of a pair of numbers, such as (14, 5.2) or (27.63, 18.9). The first number in a pair is the value of x, and the second number is the value of y.

An unorganized list of such pairs yields little information about the distribution of either the x values or the y values separately, and even less information about how the two variables are related to one another. In Chapter 3, we saw how pictures could help make sense of univariate data. Pictures will help us with bivariate data also. The most important picture based on bivariate numerical data is a **scatter plot.** Each observation (pair of numbers) is represented by a point on a rectangular coordinate system, as shown in Figure 5.1(a). The horizontal axis is identified with values of x and is scaled so that any x value can be easily located. Similarly, the vertical or y axis is marked for easy location of y values. The point corresponding to any particular (x, y) pair is placed where a vertical line from the value on the x axis meets a horizontal line from the value on the y axis. Figure 5.1(b) shows the point representing the observation (4.5, 15); it is above 4.5 on the horizontal axis and to the right of 15 on the vertical axis.

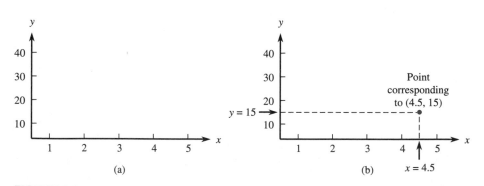

FIGURE 5.1 Constructing a scatter plot: (a) Rectangular coordinate system; (b) Point corresponding to (4.5, 15)

EXAMPLE 5.1

One method used by researchers to estimate the percentage of body fat is based on a measurement of total body electrical conductivity (TOBEC). The authors of the article "Comparing TOBEC-Derived Total Body Fat with Fat Pad Weights" (*Physiology & Behavior* (1995): 319–323) compared TOBEC body fat estimates with the actual weight of two fat deposits (called fat pads) for each rat in a sample of rats. The weight of these fat pads is known to be closely tied to overall body fat. The accompanying data on y = weight of fat pads and x = TOBEC estimate of body fat percentage is a subset of that given in the article. Figure 5.2 gives a scatter plot.

Observation	1	2	3	4	5	6	7	8	9
x	.1	1.9	4.0	4.6	4.2	4.2	7.1	5.4	6.2
y	216	233	251	272	282	295	298	303	311

Observation	10	11	12	13
x	4.6	3.6	7.1	5.4
y	318	318	327	335

FIGURE 5.2 Scatter plot for the data of Example 5.1

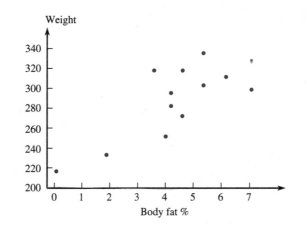

Examination of the data and plot reveals the following:

1. Several observations have identical x values yet different y values (for example, $x_5 = x_6 = 4.2$, but $y_5 = 282$ and $y_6 = 295$). Thus, the value of y is *not* determined *solely* by the value of x but by various other factors as well. That is, y is not a deterministic function of x.

2. There is a tendency for y to increase as x increases. That is, larger values of fat pad weight tend to be associated with larger values of TOBEC estimate of body fat percentage (a positive relationship between the variables).

3. It appears that the value of y could be predicted reasonably well from x by finding a line that is close to the points in the plot.

The horizontal and vertical axes in the scatter plot of Figure 5.2 do not intersect at the point $(0, 0)$. In many data sets, the values of x or of y or of both variables differ considerably from zero relative to the ranges of the values in the data set. For example, a study of how air conditioner efficiency is related to maximum daily outdoor temperature might involve observations at temperatures of $80°, 82°, \ldots, 98°$, and $100°$. In such cases, the plot will be more informative if the axes intersect at some point other than $(0, 0)$ and are marked accordingly. This is illustrated in the following example.

EXAMPLE 5.2

The growth and decline of forests is a matter of great public and scientific interest. The article "Relationships Among Crown Condition, Growth, and Stand Nutrition in Seven Northern Vermont Sugarbushes" (*Canad. J. of Forest Res.* (1995): 386–397) included a scatter plot of $y =$ mean crown dieback (%), which is one indicator of growth retardation, and $x =$ soil pH (higher pH corresponds to less acidic soil). The following observations were read from the scatter plot:

x	3.3	3.4	3.4	3.5	3.6	3.6	3.7	3.7	3.8	3.8
y	7.3	10.8	13.1	10.4	5.8	9.3	12.4	14.9	11.2	8.0

x	3.9	4.0	4.1	4.2	4.3	4.4	4.5	5.0	5.1
y	6.6	10.0	9.2	12.4	2.3	4.3	3.0	1.6	1.0

Figure 5.3 shows two scatter plots of this data, produced by the statistical computer package MINITAB. In Figure 5.3(a), we let MINITAB select the scale for both axes. We obtained Figure 5.3(b) by specifying minimum and maximum values for x and y such that the axes would intersect at (roughly) the point $(0, 0)$. The second plot is more crowded than the first one, and such crowding can make it more difficult to ascertain the general nature of any relationship. For example, it can be more difficult to spot curvature in a crowded plot.

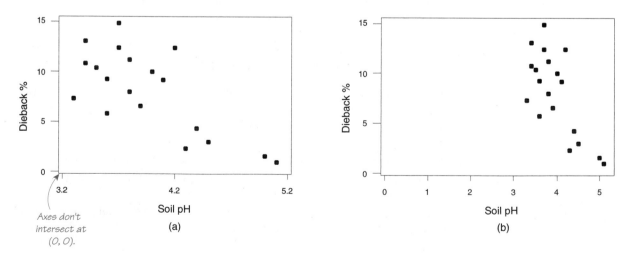

FIGURE 5.3 MINITAB scatter plots of data in Example 5.2

Large values of crown dieback tend to be associated with low soil pH, indicating a negative or inverse relationship. Furthermore, the two variables appear to be approximately linearly related, although the points would spread out quite a bit about any straight line drawn through the plot.

EXAMPLE 5.3

The focus of many agricultural experiments is to study how the yield of a crop varies with the time at which it is harvested. The accompanying data appeared in the article "Determination of Biological Maturity and Effect of Harvesting and Drying Conditions on Milling Quality of Paddy" (*J. of Agric. Engr. Research* (1975): 353–361). The variables are

x = time between flowering and harvesting (days)

y = yield of paddy, a type of grain farmed in India (kg/hectare)

x	16	18	20	22	24	26	28	30
y	2508	2518	3304	3423	3057	3190	3500	3883

x	32	34	36	38	40	42	44	46
y	3823	3646	3708	3333	3517	3214	3103	2776

Figure 5.4 is a MINITAB scatter plot. Notice that the axes do not intersect at $(0, 0)$. This is because zero lies well outside both the range of x values (16 to 46) and the range of y values (roughly 2500 to 3900). Had the scaling been chosen so that the axes did intersect at this point, all points in the plot would have been squeezed into the upper right-hand corner, obscuring somewhat the general pattern.

Although the pattern of the points in the plot is not linear, the scatter plot shows a fairly strong relationship between x and y: As x increases, y initially tends to increase, but after a certain point, y tends to decrease as x continues to increase. The shape of the plot is much like that of a parabola.

FIGURE 5.4 A scatter plot of the yield data from Example 5.3

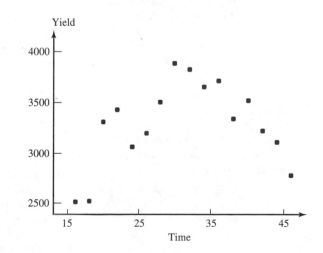

In the next three sections, we will develop methods for summarizing bivariate data when the scatter plot reveals a linear pattern (as in Examples 5.1 and 5.2). A curved pattern, such as the one in Example 5.3, is a bit more complicated to analyze, and methods for summarizing such nonlinear relationships will be discussed in Section 5.5.

Exercises 5.1 – 5.8

5.1 A number of studies concerning muscular efficiency in humans have utilized competitive cyclists as subjects. It had previously been observed that variation in efficiency could not be explained by differences in cycling technique. The paper "Cycling Efficiency Is Related to the Percentage of Type I Muscle Fibers" (*Med. and Sci. in Sports and Exercise* (1992): 782–788) reported the accompanying data on x = percentage of type I (slow twitch) muscle fibers and y = cycling gross efficiency (the ratio of work accomplished per minute to caloric expenditure).

Observation	1	2	3	4	5	6	7
x	32	37	38	40	45	50	50
y	18.3	18.9	19.0	20.9	21.4	20.5	20.1

Observation	8	9	10	11	12	13	14
x	54	54	55	61	63	63	64
y	20.1	20.8	20.5	19.9	20.5	20.6	22.1

Observation	15	16	17	18	19
x	64	70	70	75	76
y	21.9	21.2	20.5	22.7	22.8

a. Construct a scatter plot of the data in which the axes intersect at the point $(0, 16)$. How would you describe the pattern in the plot?
b. Does it appear that the value of cycling gross efficiency is determined solely by the percentage of type I muscle fibers? Explain.

5.2 The article "Exhaust Emissions from Four-Stroke Lawn Mower Engines (*J. of the Air and Water Mgmt. Assoc.* (1997): 945–952) reported data from a study in which both a baseline gasoline and a reformulated gasoline were used, Consider the following observations on age (yr) and NO_x emissions (g/kW-h):

Engine	1	2	3	4	5
Age	0	0	2	11	7
Baseline	1.72	4.38	4.06	1.26	5.31
Reformulated	1.88	5.93	5.54	2.67	6.53

(*continued*)

Engine	6	7	8	9	10
Age	16	9	0	12	4
Baseline	.57	3.37	3.44	.74	1.24
Reformulated	.74	4.94	4.89	.69	1.42

a. Construct a scatter plot of emissions versus age for the baseline gasoline.
b. Construct a scatter plot of emissions versus age for the reformulated gasoline.
c. Do age and emissions appear to be related? If so, in what way?
d. Comment on the similarities and differences in the two scatter plots of parts **a** and **b**.

5.3 A study to assess the capability of subsurface flow wetland systems to remove biochemical oxygen demand (BOD) and various other chemical constituents resulted in the accompanying data on x = BOD mass (kg/ha/d) and y = BOD removal (kg/ha/d) ("Subsurface Flow Wetlands — A Performance Evaluation," *Water Envir. Res.* (1995): 244–247).

x	3	8	10	11	13	16	27	30	35
y	4	7	8	8	10	11	16	26	21

x	37	38	44	103	142
y	9	31	30	75	90

a. Construct boxplots of both mass and mass removal, and comment on any interesting features.
b. Construct a scatter plot of the data and comment on any interesting features.

5.4 The paper "Objective Measurement of the Stretchability of Mozzarella Cheese" (*J. of Texture Studies* (1992): 185–194) reported on an experiment to investigate how the behavior of mozzarella cheese varied with temperature. Consider the data (at the top of page 135) on x = temperature and y = elongation (%) at failure of the cheese. (*Note*: The researchers were Italian and used *real* mozzarella, not the poor cousin widely available in the United States.)

x	59	63	68	72	74	78	83
y	118	182	247	208	197	135	132

a. Construct a scatter plot in which the axes intersect at the point (0, 0). (Mark 0, 20, 40, 60, 80, and 100 on the horizontal scale and 0, 50, 100, 150, 200, and 250 on the vertical scale.)

b. Construct a scatter plot in which the axes intersect at (55, 100) (as was done in the paper). Does this plot seem preferable to the one in part **a**? Explain.

c. What do the plots of parts **a** and **b** suggest about the nature of the relationship between x and y?

5.5 One factor in the development of tennis elbow, a malady that strikes fear into the hearts of all serious players of that sport (including one of the authors), is the impact-induced vibration of the racket-and-arm system at ball contact. It is well known that the likelihood of getting tennis elbow depends on various properties of the racket used. Consider the scatter plot of x = racket resonance frequency (Hz) and y = sum of peak-to-peak accelerations (a characteristic of arm vibration, in m/sec/sec) for n = 23 different rackets ("Transfer of Tennis Racket Vibrations into the Human Forearm," *Med. and Sci. in Sports and Exercise* (1992): 1134–1140). Discuss interesting features of the data and the scatter plot.

5.6 Stress can affect the physiology and behavior of animals, just as it can with humans (as many of us know all too well). The accompanying data on x = plasma cortisol concentration (ng cortisol/mL plasma) and y = oxygen consumption rate (mg/kg/hr) for juvenile steelhead after three 2-min disturbances was read from a graph in the paper "Metabolic Cost of Acute Physical Stress in Juvenile Steelhead" (*Trans. of Amer. Fish. Soc.* (1987): 257–263). The paper also included data for unstressed fish.

x	25	36	48	59	62
y	155	184	180	220	280

x	72	80	100	100	137
y	163	230	222	241	350

a. Is the value of y determined solely by the value of x? Explain your reasoning.

b. Construct a scatter plot of the data.

c. Does an increase in plasma cortisol concentration appear to be accompanied by a change in oxygen consumption rate? Comment.

5.7 Does the size of a transplanted organ matter? A study that attempted to answer this question ("Minimum Graft Size for Successful Living Donor Liver Transplantation," *Transplantation* (1999): 1112–1116) presented a scatter plot much like the following:

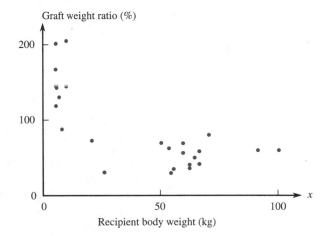

"Graft weight ratio" is the weight of the transplanted liver relative to the ideal size liver for the recipient.

a. Discuss interesting features of this scatter plot.

b. Why do you think the overall relationship is negative?

5.8 An article that appeared in *USA Today* (Dec. 20, 1999) gave the following data on the 25 largest counties in the United States.

County	Population	Number of Death Row Inmates
Los Angeles, CA	8,974,105	156
Cook, IL	5,109,887	81
Harris, TX	2,958,978	140
San Diego, CA	2,576,872	27

(continued)

County	Population	Number of Death Row Inmates
Orange, CA	2,503,996	41
Maricopa, AZ	2,328,217	53
Kings, NY	2,283,622	0
Dade, FL	1,979,145	50
Queens, NY	1,958,299	0
Dallas, TX	1,917,501	37
King, WA	1,553,110	2
Philadelphia, PA	1,541,039	125
Santa Clara, CA	1,535,916	27
New York, NY	1,501,014	1
San Bernardino, CA	1,497,816	28
Cuyahoga, OH	1,410,021	37
Suffolk, NY	1,337,486	0

(continued)

County	Population	Number of Death Row Inmates
Broward, FL	1,337,001	26
Alameda, CA	1,323,155	33
Allegheny, PA	1,321,002	8
Nassau, NY	1,297,132	0
Riverside, CA	1,275,338	36
Bexar, TX	1,245,209	29
Tarrant, TX	1,227,122	25
Bronx, NY	1,198,220	0

Construct a scatter plot of this data and comment on any unusual features. How would you describe the relationship between county population and number of death row inmates? How are the unusual features of the plot incorporated into your description of the relationship?

5.2   Correlation

A scatter plot of bivariate numerical data gives a visual impression of how strongly *x* values and *y* values are related. However, to make precise statements and draw conclusions from data, we must go beyond pictures. A **correlation coefficient** (from *co-relation*) is a quantitative assessment of the strength of relationship between the *x* and *y* values in a set of (*x, y*) pairs. In this section, we introduce the most commonly used correlation coefficient.

Figure 5.5 displays several scatter plots that indicate different types of relationships between the *x* and *y* values. The plot in Figure 5.5(a) suggests a strong *positive relationship* between *x* and *y*; for every pair of points in the plot, the one with the larger *x* value also has the larger *y* value. That is, an increase in *x* is inevitably paired with an increase in *y*. The plot in Figure 5.5(b) shows a strong *tendency* for *y* to increase as *x* does, but there are a few exceptions. For example, the *x* and *y* values of the two points in the extreme upper right-hand corner of the plot go in opposite directions (*x* increases, but *y* decreases). Nevertheless, a plot such as this would again indicate a rather strong positive relationship. Figure 5.5(c) suggests that *x* and *y* are *negatively related* — as *x* increases, there is a tendency for *y* to decrease. Obviously, the negative relationship in this plot is not as strong as the positive relationship in Figure 5.5(b), although both plots show a well-defined linear pattern. The plot of Figure 5.5(d) is indicative of no strong relationship between *x* and *y*; there is no tendency for *y* either to increase or to decrease as *x* increases. Finally, as illustrated in Figure 5.5(e), a scatter plot can show evidence of a strong positive (or negative) relationship through a pattern that is curved rather than linear in character.

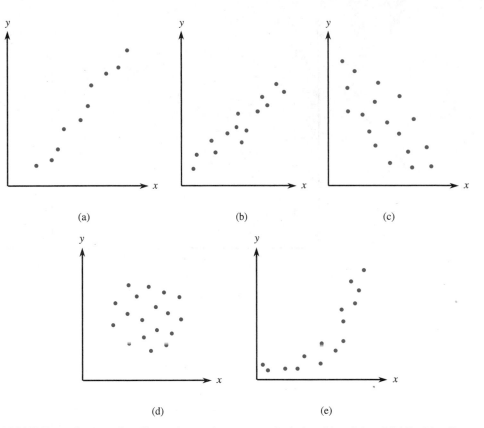

FIGURE 5.5 Scatter plots illustrating various types of relationships: (a) and (b) Positive linear relation; (c) Negative linear relation; (d) No relation; (e) Curved relation

Pearson's Sample Correlation Coefficient

Let $(x_1, y_1), (x_2, y_2), \ldots, (x_n, y_n)$ denote a sample of (x, y) pairs. Consider replacing each x value by the corresponding z score, z_x, (by subtracting $\bar{x}$ and then dividing by s_x) and similarly replacing each y value by its z score. Note that x values that are larger than the mean x value will have a positive z score and those smaller than $\bar{x}$ will have negative z scores. The same will be true for the y values: Those larger than $\bar{y}$ will have positive z scores and those smaller will have negative z scores. A common measure of the strength of linear relationship, called Pearson's sample correlation coefficient, is based on $\Sigma \, z_x z_y$, the sum of the product of z_x and z_y for each observation in the bivariate data set.

The scatter plot in Figure 5.6(a) on page 138 indicates a substantial positive relationship. A vertical line through $\bar{x}$ and a horizontal line through $\bar{y}$ divide the plot into four regions. In region I, both x and y exceed their mean values, so the z score for x and the z score for y are both positive numbers. It follows that $z_x z_y$ is positive. The product of the z scores is also positive for any point in region III, because both z scores are negative there, and multiplying two negative numbers gives a positive

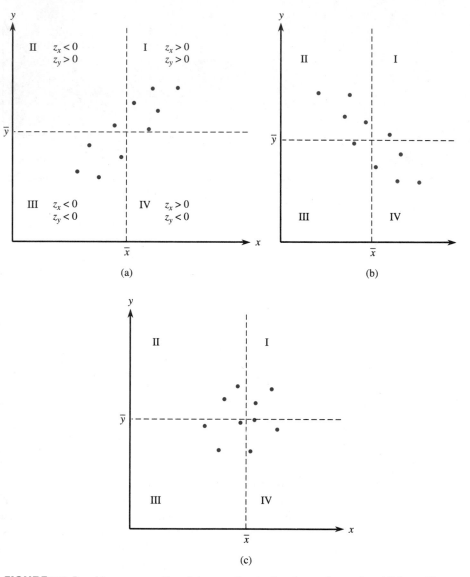

FIGURE 5.6 Breaking up a scatter plot according to the signs of z_x and z_y: (a) A positive relation; (b) A negative relation; (c) No strong relation

number. In each of the other two regions, one z score is positive and the other negative, so $z_x z_y$ is negative. But because almost all points lie in regions I and III, almost all products of z scores are positive. Thus, the *sum* of products, $\Sigma\, z_x z_y$, will be a large positive number.

Similar reasoning for the data displayed in Figure 5.6(b), which exhibits a strong negative relationship, implies that $\Sigma\, z_x z_y$ will be a large negative number. When there is no strong relationship, as in Figure 5.6(c), positive and negative products tend to counteract one another, producing a value of $\Sigma\, z_x z_y$ that is close to zero. In summary, $\Sigma\, z_x z_y$ seems to be a reasonable measure of the degree of association between x and y; it will be a large positive number, a large negative number, or a number close to zero, depending on whether there is a strong positive, a strong negative, or no strong linear relationship.

Pearson's sample correlation coefficient, denoted by r, is obtained by dividing $\Sigma\, z_x z_y$ by $n-1$.

Definition

Pearson's sample correlation coefficient r is given by

$$r = \frac{\Sigma\, z_x z_y}{n-1}$$

Although there are several different types of correlation coefficients, Pearson's correlation coefficient is by far the most commonly used, and so the name Pearson's is often omitted and it is referred to as simply "the correlation coefficient."

Hand calculation of the correlation coefficient is illustrated in the following example; such calculation can be quite tedious. Fortunately, all statistical software packages and most scientific calculators will compute r from sample data.

EXAMPLE 5.4

The article "Parents' and Adolescents' Perceptions of a Strong Family" (*Psych. Reports* (1999): 1219–1224) examined the relationship between family strength and other characteristics such as commitment, time spent together, and crisis management skills. Adolescents in what the researchers called "intact families" (those with both of the parents present in the home) rated their families with respect to the degree that the family exhibited effective crisis management and also with respect to family strength. Data consistent with findings that appeared in the article is given here:

Observation	1	2	3	4	5	6	7	8	9	10
Crisis management score	20	13	27	18	19	21	0	21	21	11
Family strength score	50	60	67	57	49	72	52	68	60	58

Figure 5.7 (page 140) is a scatter plot of this data.

Let x denote the crisis management score and y denote the family strength score. It is easy to verify that

$$\bar{x} = 17.10 \qquad s_x = 7.48 \qquad \bar{y} = 59.30 \qquad s_y = 7.82$$

To illustrate the calculation of the correlation coefficient, we begin by computing z scores for each (x, y) pair in the data set. For example, the first observation is $(20, 50)$. The corresponding z scores are

$$z_x = \frac{20 - 17.10}{7.48} = .39 \qquad z_y = \frac{50 - 59.30}{7.82} = -1.19$$

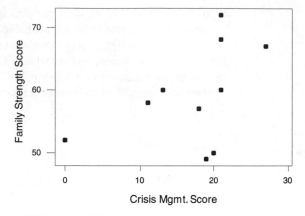

FIGURE 5.7 MINITAB scatter plot for data of Example 5.4

The accompanying table shows the z scores as well as the product $z_x z_y$ for each observation.

x	y	z_x	z_y	$z_x z_y$
20	50	.39	−1.19	−.46
13	60	−.55	.09	−.05
27	67	1.32	.98	1.29
18	57	.12	−.29	−.03
19	49	.25	−1.32	−.33
21	72	.52	1.62	.84
0	52	−2.29	−.93	2.13
21	68	.52	1.11	.58
21	60	.52	.09	.05
11	58	−.82	−.17	.14

$$4.16 = \Sigma\, z_x z_y$$

Then, with $n = 10$

$$r = \frac{\Sigma\, z_x z_y}{n - 1} = \frac{4.16}{9} = .46$$

Based on the scatter plot and the properties of the correlation coefficient presented in the discussion that follows this example, there is only a weak positive linear relationship between crisis management score and family strength score.

Properties of *r*

1. *The value of r does not depend on the unit of measurement for either variable.* For example, if *x* is height, the corresponding *z* score will be the same whether height is expressed in inches, meters, or miles, and thus the value of the correlation coefficient is not affected. The correlation coefficient measures the inherent strength of the relationship between two numerical variables.

2. *The value of r does not depend on which of the two variables is labeled x.* Thus, if we had let *x* = family strength score and *y* = crisis management score in Example 5.4, the same value, *r* = .46, would have resulted.

3. *The value of r is between −1 and +1.* A value near the upper limit, +1, is indicative of a substantial positive relationship, whereas an *r* close to the lower limit, −1, suggests a prominent negative relationship. Figure 5.8 shows a useful way to describe the strength of relationship based on *r*.

FIGURE 5.8 Describing the strength of relationship

It may seem surprising that a value of *r* as extreme as −.5 or .5 should be in the "weak" category; an explanation for this is given later in the chapter. Even a weak correlation may indicate a meaningful relationship.

4. *The correlation coefficient r = 1 only when all the points in a scatter plot of the data lie exactly on a straight line that slopes upward. Similarly, r = −1 only when all the points lie exactly on a downward-sloping line.* Only when there is a perfect linear relationship between *x* and *y* in the sample will *r* take on one of its two possible extreme values.

5. *The value of r is a measure of the extent to which x and y are linearly related* — that is, the extent to which the points in the scatter plot fall close to a straight line. A value of *r* close to zero does not rule out any strong relationship between *x* and *y*; there could still be a strong relationship but one that is not linear.

EXAMPLE 5.5

College administrators and instructors have long puzzled over what factors affect student performance. The article "The Impact of Athletics, Part-Time Employment, and Other Activities on Academic Achievement" (*J. of College Student Devel.* (1992): 447–453) summarized the results of one large-scale study.

With *x* = grade point average and *y* = time spent working at a job (hr/week), it was reported that *r* = −.08 (based on *n* = 528). It appears that the linear relationship between time spent working at a job and grade point average is extremely weak: There is a very slight tendency for those who work more to have lower grades. If time spent working were reexpressed in min/week, *r* would still be −.08.

EXAMPLE 5.6   Economists sometimes use what is called the Misery Index to reflect the gloominess of the U.S. population. The Misery Index is defined as the sum of the inflation rate and the unemployment rate. The article "The Misery Index and Suicide" (*Psych. Reports* (1999): 1086) examined the relationship between suicide rate and both the Misery Index and a proposed revised misery index (the sum of the inflation rate and 2 times the unemployment rate). The revised index was proposed based on the belief that "unemployment inflicts twice the pain of inflation on the general public."

Using inflation, unemployment, and suicide rates for 1958–1992, the authors reported that

Pearson correlations between the Misery Indices and suicide rate were .97 for the original Misery Index and .61 for the revised index.

Based on the correlation coefficient, which measures the strength of any linear relationship, it appears that although there is a positive relationship between suicide rate and both indices, the relationship is much stronger for the original index than for the revised index.

EXAMPLE 5.7   Foal weight at birth is an indicator of health, therefore it is of interest to breeders of thoroughbred horses. Is foal weight related to the weight of the mare (mother)? The accompanying data are from the article "Suckling Behaviour Does Not Measure Milk Intake in Horses" (*Animal Behaviour* (1999): 673–678).

Observation	1	2	3	4	5	6	7	8	9
Mare weight (x, in kg)	556	638	588	550	580	642	568	642	556
Foal weight (y, in kg)	129	119	132	123.5	112	113.5	95	104	104

Observation	10	11	12	13	14	15
Mare weight (x, in kg)	616	549	504	515	551	594
Foal weight (y, in kg)	93.5	108.5	95	117.5	128	127.5

MINITAB was used to compute the value of the correlation coefficient for this data, with the following result.

Correlations (Pearson)
Correlation of Mare Weight and Foal Weight = 0.001, P-Value = 0.996

A correlation coefficient this close to zero indicates no linear relationship between mare weight and foal weight. The conclusion that mare weight and foal weight are unrelated is supported by a scatter plot of this data, which appears as Figure 5.9. From the correlation coefficient alone, we can conclude only that there is no *linear* relationship. We cannot rule out a more complicated curved relationship without examining the scatter plot.

FIGURE 5.9 A MINITAB scatter plot of the mare and foal weight data

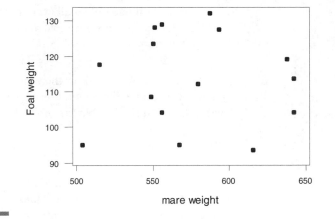

EXAMPLE 5.8

(Example 5.3 continued) Let's reconsider the data on

x = time between planting and harvesting

and

y = yield

for the grain data of Example 5.3. The scatter plot for this data set appeared in Figure 5.4 and showed a strong curved pattern. Using MINITAB to compute the correlation coefficient between time and yield results in the following:

Correlations (Pearson)
Correlation of Time and Yield = 0.274, P-Value = 0.304

This shows the importance of interpreting r as a measure of the strength of any linear association. Here, r is not large, but there is a strong nonlinear relationship between time and yield. We should not conclude that there is no relationship whatsoever just because r is near 0.

The Population Correlation Coefficient

The sample correlation coefficient r measures how strongly the x and y values in a *sample* of pairs are related to one another. There is an analogous measure of how strongly x and y are related in the entire population of pairs from which the sample $(x_1, y_1), \ldots, (x_n, y_n)$ was obtained. It is called the **population correlation coefficient** and is denoted by $\boldsymbol{\rho}$. (Notice again the use of a Greek letter for a population characteristic and Roman letter for a sample characteristic.) We will never have to calculate ρ from the entire population of pairs, but it is important to know that ρ satisfies properties paralleling those of r:

1. ρ is a number between -1 and $+1$ that does not depend on the unit of measurement for either x or y or on which variable is labeled x and which is labeled y.

2. $\rho = +1$ or -1 if and only if all (x, y) pairs in the population lie exactly on a straight line, so ρ measures the extent to which there is a linear relationship in the population.

In Chapter 13, we show how the sample characteristic r can be used to make an inference concerning the population characteristic ρ. In particular, r can be used to decide whether it is plausible that $\rho = 0$ (no linear relationship in the population).

Correlation and Causation

A value of r close to 1 indicates that relatively large values of one variable tend to be associated with relatively large values of the other variable. This is far from saying that a large value of one variable *causes* the value of the other variable to be large. Correlation (Pearson's or any other) measures the extent of association, but **association does not imply causation.** It frequently happens that two variables are highly correlated not because one is causally related to the other but because they are both strongly related to a third variable. Among all elementary school children, there is a strong positive relationship between the number of cavities in a child's teeth and the size of his or her vocabulary. Yet no one advocates eating foods that result in more cavities to increase vocabulary size (or working to decrease vocabulary size to protect against cavities). Number of cavities and vocabulary size are both strongly related to age, so older children tend to have higher values of both variables than do younger ones.

Scientific experiments can frequently make a strong case for causality by carefully controlling the values of all variables that might be related to the ones under study. Then, if y is observed to change in a "smooth" way as the experimenter changes the value of x, the most plausible explanation would be a causal relationship between x and y. In the absence of such control and ability to manipulate values of one variable, we must admit the possibility that an unidentified underlying third variable is influencing both the variables under investigation. A high correlation in many uncontrolled studies carried out in different settings can marshal support for causality — as in the case of cigarette smoking and cancer — but proving causality is often a very elusive task.

Spearman's Rank Correlation Coefficient (Optional)

Pearson's correlation coefficient r identifies a strong linear relationship between x and y but may miss a strong relationship that is not linear. In addition, the value of r can be greatly affected by the presence of even one or two outlying (x, y) pairs that are far from the main part of the scatter plot. Spearman's correlation coefficient r_S is a measure that is not as sensitive as r to outlying points and identifies both linear and nonlinear relationships. It does so by using the *ranks* of the x and y observations rather than the observations themselves.

To compute r_S, first replace the smallest x value by its rank, 1, the second smallest x value by its rank, 2, and so on. Similarly, the smallest y value is replaced by its rank, 1, the second smallest by its rank, 2, and so on. Suppose, for example, that $n = 4$ and the data pairs are

(110, 24.7)   (125, 24.2)   (116, 22.6)   (95, 23.5)

Then we have

x value	110	125	116	95		y value	24.7	24.2	22.6	23.5
Rank	2	4	3	1		Rank	4	3	1	2

The resulting rank pairs are

(2, 4)   (4, 3)   (3, 1)   (1, 2)

If there is a strong positive relationship between x and y, the x observations with small ranks tend to be paired with y observations having small ranks. An extreme case of this, the rank pairs $(1, 1), (2, 2), (3, 3), (4, 4)$, occurs whenever a larger x value is always associated with a larger y value. Alternatively, large x ranks paired with small y ranks indicate a negative relationship, the most extreme case being $(1, 4), (2, 3), (3, 2)$, and $(4, 1)$ for $n = 4$ observations. Once the rank pairs have been determined, Spearman's r_S is just Pearson's coefficient r applied to these rank pairs. It can be computed by converting the ranks to z scores and then using the formula introduced earlier in this section, or by using the equivalent formula in the accompanying box.

Definition

Spearman's rank correlation coefficient r_S is Pearson's correlation coefficient applied to the rank pairs obtained by replacing each x value by its rank and each y value by its rank. An equivalent computing formula is

$$r_S = \frac{\Sigma\,(x \text{ rank})(y \text{ rank}) - \dfrac{n(n + 1)^2}{4}}{\dfrac{n(n - 1)(n + 1)}{12}}$$

As with r, the value of r_S is between -1 and 1. A value close to 1 or -1 indicates a strong relationship, whereas a value close to 0 indicates a weak relationship.

To illustrate the computation of Spearman's rank correlation coefficient, we will consider data from the paper "The Relation Between Freely Chosen Meals and Body Habits" (*Amer. J. Clinical Nutrition* (1983): 32–40). This article reported results of an investigation into the relationship between body build and energy intake of an individual's diet. A measure of body build is the Quetelet index (x), with a high value of x indicating a thickset individual. The variable reflecting energy intake is y = dietary energy density. There were nine subjects in the investigation, and the resulting (x, y) pairs and corresponding $(x$ rank, y rank) pairs were as shown at the top of page 146.

Subject	x	y	x Rank	y Rank	(x Rank)·(y Rank)
1	221	.67	3	3	9
2	228	.86	6	5	30
3	223	.78	4	4	16
4	211	.54	1	2	2
5	231	.91	7	7	49
6	215	.44	2	1	2
7	224	.90	5	6	30
8	233	.94	8	9	72
9	268	.93	9	8	72
					Sum = 282

Then

$$r_{\text{S}} = \frac{282 - \dfrac{9(10)^2}{4}}{\dfrac{(9)(8)(10)}{12}} = \frac{57}{60} = .95$$

This indicates a very strong positive relationship between the x and y values in the sample. The accompanying figure displays a scatter plot of the data. The point (268, .93) is a clear outlier and considerably distorts the linear pattern in the plot. The value of Pearson's r is only .658. Consider the effect on r and r_{S} of changing x_9. If 268 is replaced by 234, then (234, .93) is no longer an outlier. The value of r_{S} remains at .95, since 234 has the same x rank as 268, but the value of r for the altered data set rises dramatically to .92.

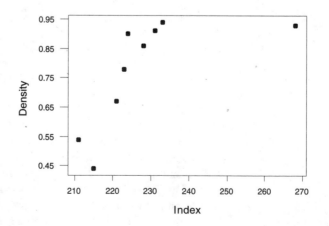

The objective of some experiments is to make comparisons by having individuals rank the objects or entities in a specified group. Thus, some television viewers might be asked to rank a group of programs in order of decreasing preference, or some wine connoisseurs might convene for the purpose of ranking a group of wines in order of descending quality. In such cases, the data values consist of sets of rankings rather than observations on numerical variables. Spearman's r_S can be applied directly to two sets of such rankings to measure the extent to which those doing the rating agree in their judgments. Several examples of this type are given in the exercises.

The procedure for calculating r_S must be modified somewhat if there are ties in either the x values or the y values (for example, three pairs with $x = 27.5$). One of the chapter references can be consulted to find out how this is done.

Exercises 5.9 – 5.25

5.9 For each of the following pairs of variables, indicate whether you would expect a positive correlation, a negative correlation, or no correlation. Explain your choice.
  a. Maximum daily temperature and cooling costs
  b. Interest rate and number of loan applications
  c. Incomes of husbands and wives when both have full-time jobs
  d. Height and IQ
  e. Height and shoe size
  f. Score on the math section of the SAT exam and score on the verbal section of the same test
  g. Time spent on homework and time spent watching television during the same day by elementary school children
  h. Amount of fertilizer used per acre and crop yield (*Hint:* As the amount of fertilizer is increased, yield tends to increase for a while but then tends to start decreasing.)

5.10 Is the following statement correct? Explain why or why not. A correlation coefficient of zero implies that no relationship exists between the two variables under study.

5.11 Draw two scatter plots, one for which $r = 1$ and a second for which $r = -1$.

5.12 Peak heart rate (beats per minute) was determined both during a shuttle run and during a 300-yard run for a sample of $n = 10$ individuals afflicted with Down Syndrome ("Heart Rate Responses to Two Field Exercise Tests by Adolescents and Young Adults with Down Syndrome," *Adapted Phys. Act. Quarterly* (1995): 43–51), resulting in the following data.

Shuttle	168	168	188	172	184
300-yd	184	192	200	192	188
Shuttle	176	192	172	188	180
300-yd	180	182	188	196	196

a. A scatter plot of the data is shown. What does it suggest about the nature of the relationship between the two variables?

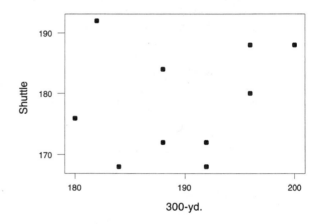

b. With x = shuttle run peak rate and y = 300-yd run peak rate, calculate r. Is the value of r consistent with your answer in part **a**?
c. With x = 300-yd peak rate and y = shuttle run peak rate, how does the value of r compare to what you calculated in part **b**?

5.13 The detection of anemia requires an accurate method for the determination of hemoglobin level. The accompanying scatter plot is for observations on hemoglobin level, determined both by the standard spectrophometric method (x) and by a new, simpler method based on a color scale (y) ("A Simple and Reliable Method for Estimating Hemoglobin," *Bull. World Health Org.* (1995): 369–373).

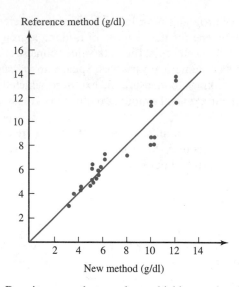

Reference method (g/dl)

New method (g/dl)

a. Does it appear that x and y are highly correlated?

b. The paper reported that $r = .9366$. How would you describe the relationship between the two variables?

c. The line pictured in the scatter plot has a slope of 1 and passes through $(0, 0)$. If x and y were always identical, all points would lie exactly on this line. The authors of the paper claimed that perfect correlation ($r = 1$) would result in this line. Do you agree? Explain your reasoning.

5.14 Is there a correlation between test anxiety and exam score performance? Data on $x =$ score on a measure of test anxiety and $y =$ exam score consistent with summary quantities given in the paper "Effects of Humor on Test Anxiety and Performance" (*Psych. Reports* (1999): 1203–1212) appears below.

| x | 23 | 14 | 14 | 0 | 7 | 20 | 20 | 15 | 21 |
| y | 43 | 59 | 48 | 77 | 50 | 52 | 46 | 51 | 51 |

Higher values for x indicate higher levels of anxiety.

a. Construct a scatter plot and comment on the features of the plot.

b. Does there appear to be a linear relationship between the two variables? Based on the scatter plot, would you characterize the relationship as positive or negative? Strong or weak?

c. Compute the value of the correlation coefficient. Is the value of r consistent with your answer to part **b**?

d. Based on the value of the correlation, is it reasonable to conclude that text anxiety caused poor exam performance? Explain.

5.15 According to the article "First-Year Academic Success: A Prediction Combining Cognitive and Psychosocial

Variables for Caucasian and African-American Students" (*Journal of College Student Development* (1999): 599–605), there is a mild correlation between high school GPA (x) and first-year college GPA (y). The data, which were collected from a "Southeastern public research university," can be summarized as follows:

$$n = 2600 \qquad \Sigma x = 9620 \qquad \Sigma y = 7436$$
$$\Sigma xy = 27{,}918 \qquad \Sigma x^2 = 36{,}168 \qquad \Sigma y^2 = 23{,}145$$

An alternative formula for computing the correlation coefficient that is algebraically equivalent to the one given in the text is

$$r = \frac{\Sigma xy - \dfrac{(\Sigma x)(\Sigma y)}{n}}{\sqrt{\Sigma x^2 - \dfrac{(\Sigma x)^2}{n}}\sqrt{\Sigma y^2 - \dfrac{(\Sigma y)^2}{n}}}$$

Use this formula to compute the value of the correlation coefficient and interpret this value.

5.16 An employee of an auction house has a list of 25 recently sold paintings. Eight artists were represented in these sales. The sale price of each painting appears on the list. Would the correlation coefficient be an appropriate way to summarize the relationship between artist (x) and sale price (y)? Why or why not?

5.17 Each individual in a sample was asked to indicate on a quantitative scale how willing he or she was to spend money on the environment and also how strongly he or she believed in God ("Religion and Attitudes Toward the Environment," *J. for the Scient. Study of Religion* (1993): 19–28). (This article was authored by Andrew Greeley, who also writes entertaining mysteries with religious themes.) The resulting value of the sample correlation coefficient was $r = -.085$. Would you agree with the stated conclusion that stronger support for environmental spending is associated with a weaker degree of belief in God? Explain your reasoning.

5.18 A sample of automobiles traversing a certain stretch of highway is selected. Each one travels at roughly a constant rate of speed, though speed does vary from auto to auto. Let $x =$ speed and $y =$ time needed to traverse this segment of highway. Would the sample correlation coefficient be closest to .9, .3, $-.3$, or $-.9$? Explain.

5.19 A sample of $n = 5$ (x, y) pairs gives $(1, 1)$, $(2, 2)$, $(3, 3)$, $(4, 4)$, and $(5, y_5)$. It must be the case that $y_5 \geq 0$. Could r be negative?

5.20 Nine students currently taking introductory statistics are randomly selected, and both the first midterm exam score (x) and the second midterm exam score (y) are determined. Three of the students have the class at 8 A.M., another three have it at noon, and the remaining three have a night class. The resulting (x, y) pairs are as follows:

8 A.M.	(70, 60)	(72, 83)	(94, 85)
Noon	(80, 72)	(60, 74)	(55, 58)
Night	(45, 63)	(50, 40)	(35, 54)

a. Calculate the sample correlation coefficient for the nine (x, y) pairs.

b. Let $\bar{x}_1$ = the average score on the first midterm for the 8 A.M. students and $\bar{y}_1$ = the average score on the second midterm for these students. Let $\bar{x}_2$ and $\bar{y}_2$ be these averages for the noon students and $\bar{x}_3$ and $\bar{y}_3$ these averages for the evening students. Calculate r for these three ($\bar{x}$, $\bar{y}$) pairs.

c. Construct a scatter plot of the nine (x, y) pairs and construct another one of the three ($\bar{x}$, $\bar{y}$) pairs. Can you see why r in part **a** is smaller than r in part **b**? Does this suggest that a correlation coefficient based on averages (an "ecological" correlation) might be misleading? Explain.

5.21 An article titled "When it Comes to Sex, We Score" in the newspaper *The Australian* (May 20, 1996) used the results of a large multination survey to rank 15 countries on the variables x = frequency of sex and y = partner's reported satisfaction.

Country	Rank for y	Rank for x
France	5	3
Britain	3	5
United States	11	1
Australia	6	7
Russia	7	2
Italy	4	11
Brazil	10	9
Mexico	2	12
South Africa	9	8
Canada	1	10
Germany	12	4
Thailand	13	15
Spain	8	14
Poland	14	6
Hong Kong	15	13

Is there a correlation between partner satisfaction and frequency? Since only the ranks are given, use Spearman's rank correlation coefficient to describe the strength of the relationship between these two variables.

5.22 In a study of variables thought to be related to urban gang activity, seven Chicago-area communities were

ranked according to prevalence of ganging, percent of residents who are African-American, median family income, and percent of families below poverty level ("Youth Gangs," *Pacific Sociol. Rev.* (1981): 366). See the accompanying table. The authors of this paper analyzed this data using Spearman's rank correlation coefficient.

Community	Prevalence of Ganging	Percent African-American	Median Income	% Below Poverty Level
A	2	3	7	1
B	4	6	6	4
C	7	7	1	7
D	5	5	2	5
E	6	4	3	6
F	3	2	5	3
G	1	1	4	2

a. Calculate r_S for the following pairs of variables.
  i. Ganging prevalence and percent African-American
  ii. Ganging prevalence and median income
  iii. Ganging prevalence and percent below poverty level

b. Based on the coefficients in part **a,** which of the variables seems to exhibit the strongest relationship with ganging prevalence?

5.23 The article "Perceived Importance of Self-Determination Factors by Consumers in Substance-Abuse Treatment" (*Perceptual and Motor Skills* (1994): 284–286) reported the accompanying data on ranking of importance of variables related to self-determination. Verify that $r_S = .95$ as stated in the paper, and interpret this value.

Variable	1993 Rank	1994 Rank
Self-confidence	1	1
Positive attitude	2	2
Listening skills	3	3
Responsibility	4	4
Speaking ability	5	7
Know legal rights	6	5
Health and hygiene	7	12
Think about self	8	8
Getting help	9	11
Solve problems	10	6
Planning	11	9
Reading skills	12	14
Persistence	13	16
Getting information	14	10
Strong family	15	15

(continued)

Variable	1993 Rank	1994 Rank
Know needs	16	13
Change plans	17	20
Accepting support	18	17
Negotiate with others	19	19
Writing ability	20	21
Being creative	21	18
Using humor	22	22
Transportation	23	24
Role model	24	23

5.24 Ranking wines is a common practice at wine tastings. Suppose that after tasting nine wines, two judges rank the wines as in the accompanying table. Compute r_S as a measure of agreement between the two judges.

Wine	A	B	C	D	E	F	G	H	I
Judge 1	7	1	3	2	8	5	9	6	4
Judge 2	9	4	1	3	7	5	6	8	2

5.25 Let d_1 denote the difference (x rank $-$ y rank) for the first (x, y) pair, d_2 denote this difference for the second (x, y) pair, and so on. It can be shown that

$$r_S = 1 - \frac{6 \Sigma d^2}{n(n^2 - 1)}$$

a. Use this formula to compute r_S for the Quetelet index data given on page 146.
b. What does this formula imply about the value of r_S when there is a perfect positive relationship? Explain.

5.3 Fitting a Line to Bivariate Data

Given two variables x and y, the general objective of *regression analysis* is to use information about x to draw some type of conclusion concerning y. Often an investigator will want a prediction of the y value that would result from making a single observation at a specified x value — for example, predict product sales y during a given period when shelf space for displaying the product is $x = 6$ ft^2. The different roles played by the two variables are reflected in standard terminology: y is called the **dependent** or **response variable,** and x is referred to as the **independent,** or **predictor,** or **explanatory variable.**

A scatter plot of y versus x (that is, of the (x, y) pairs in a sample) will frequently exhibit a linear pattern. It is natural in such cases to summarize the relationship between the variables by finding a line that is as close as possible to the points in the plot. Before doing so, let's review some elementary facts about lines and linear relationships.

Suppose that a car dealership advertises that a particular model of car can be rented for a flat fee of $25 plus an additional $.30 per mile. If this type of car is rented and driven for 100 miles, the dealer's revenue y is

$$y = 25 + (.30)(100) = 25 + 30 = 55$$

More generally, if x denotes distance driven (miles), then

$$y = 25 + .30x$$

That is, x and y are linearly related.

The general form of a linear relation between x and y is $y = a + bx$. A particular relation is specified by choosing values of a and b. Thus, one such relationship is $y = 10 + 2x$, whereas another is $y = 100 - 5x$. If we choose some x values and compute $y = a + bx$ for each value, the points in the plot of the resulting (x, y) pairs will fall exactly on a straight line.

Definition

The relationship

Intercept
↓
$$y = a + bx$$
↑
Slope

is the equation of a straight line. The value of b, called the **slope** of the line, is the amount by which y increases when x increases by 1 unit. The value of a, called the **intercept** (or sometimes the **vertical intercept**) of the line, is the height of the line above the value $x = 0$.

The equation $y = 10 + 2x$ has slope $b = 2$, so each 1-unit increase in x is paired with an increase of 2 in y. When $x = 0$, $y = 10$, and the height at which the line crosses the vertical axis (where $x = 0$) is 10. This is illustrated in Figure 5.10(a). The slope of the line determined by $y = 100 - 5x$ is -5, so y increases by -5 (that is, decreases by 5) when x increases by 1. The height of the line above $x = 0$ is $a = 100$. The resulting line is pictured in Figure 5.10(b).

It is easy to draw the line corresponding to any particular linear equation. First choose any two x values and substitute them into the equation to obtain the corresponding y values. Then plot the resulting two (x, y) pairs as two points. The desired line is the one passing through these points. For the equation $y = 10 + 2x$, substituting $x = 5$ yields $y = 20$, whereas using $x = 10$ gives $y = 30$. The two points are then $(5, 20)$ and $(10, 30)$. The line in Figure 5.10(a) does indeed pass through these points.

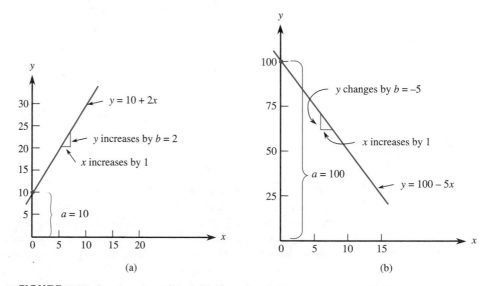

FIGURE 5.10 Graphs of two lines: (a) Slope $b = 2$, intercept $a = 10$; (b) Slope $b = -5$, intercept $a = 100$

Fitting a Straight Line: The Principle of Least Squares

Figure 5.11 shows a scatter plot with two lines superimposed on the plot. The line that gives the most effective summary of the approximate linear relationship is the one that in some sense is the best-fitting line, the one closest to the sample data. Line II clearly gives a better fit to the data than does Line I. To measure the extent to which a particular line provides a good fit, we focus on the vertical deviations from the line. For example, Line II in Figure 5.11 has equation $y = 10 + 2x$, and the third and fourth points from the left in the scatter plot are $(15, 44)$ and $(20, 45)$. For these two points, the vertical deviations from this line are

$$\text{3rd deviation} = y_3 - \text{height of the line above } x_3$$
$$= 44 - [10 + 2(15)]$$
$$= 4$$

and

$$\text{4th deviation} = 45 - [10 + 2(20)] = -5$$

FIGURE 5.11 Lines I and II
give poor and good fits,
respectively, to the data.

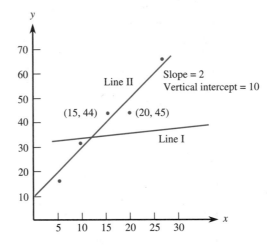

A positive vertical deviation results from a point that lies above the chosen line, and a negative deviation from a point that lies below this line. A particular line is said to be a good fit to the data if the deviations from the line are small in magnitude. Line I in Figure 5.11 fits poorly, because all deviations from that line are larger in magnitude (some are much larger) than the corresponding deviations from Line II.

We now need a way to combine the n deviations into a single measure of fit. The standard approach is to square the deviations (to obtain nonnegative numbers) and sum these squared deviations.

Definition

The most widely used criterion for measuring the goodness of fit of a line $y = a + bx$ to bivariate data $(x_1, y_1), \ldots, (x_n, y_n)$ is the sum of the squared deviations about the line:

$$\Sigma\, [y - (a + bx)]^2 = [y_1 - (a + bx_1)]^2 + [y_2 - (a + bx_2)]^2 + \cdots + [y_n - (a + bx_n)]^2$$

The line that gives the best fit to the data is the one that minimizes this sum; it is called the **least squares line** or **sample regression line.**

Fortunately, the equation of the least squares line can be obtained without having to calculate deviations from any particular line. This is because mathematical techniques can be applied to obtain relatively simple formulas for the slope and vertical intercept of the least squares line. The formula for b involves $\Sigma\, (x - \bar{x})(y - \bar{y})$, which is the sum of products of the x and y deviations from their respective means.

The slope of the least squares line is

$$b = \frac{\Sigma\, (x - \bar{x})(y - \bar{y})}{\Sigma\, (x - \bar{x})^2}$$

and the y intercept is

$$a = \bar{y} - b\bar{x}$$

We write the equation of the least squares line as

$$\hat{y} = a + bx$$

where the $\hat{}$ above y emphasizes that $\hat{y}$ (read as y-hat) is a prediction of y resulting from the substitution of a particular x value into the equation.

Statistical software packages and many calculators will compute the slope and intercept of the least squares line. If the slope and intercept are to be computed by hand, the following computational formula can be used to reduce the amount of time required to perform the calculations.

Calculating Formula for the Slope of the Least Squares Line

$$b = \frac{\Sigma\, xy - \dfrac{(\Sigma\, x)(\Sigma\, y)}{n}}{\Sigma\, x^2 - \dfrac{(\Sigma\, x)^2}{n}}$$

EXAMPLE 5.9   Corrosion of the steel frame is the most important factor affecting the durability of reinforced concrete buildings. It is believed that carbonation of the concrete (caused by a chemical reaction that lowers the pH of the concrete) leads to corrosion of the steel frame and thus reduces the strength of the concrete.

Representative data on

$$x = \text{carbonation depth (mm)}$$
$$\text{and} \quad y = \text{strength of concrete (Mpa)}$$

for a sample of core specimens taken from a particular building were read from a plot in the article "The Carbonation of Concrete Structures in the Tropical Environment of Singapore" (*Magazine of Concrete Research* (1996): 293–300):

Depth, x	8.0	20.0	20.0	30.0	35.0	40.0	50.0	55.0	65.0
Strength, y	22.8	17.1	21.5	16.1	13.4	12.4	11.4	9.7	6.8

A scatter plot of this data (Figure 5.12) shows that the relationship between corrosion depth and strength could be summarized by a line.

FIGURE 5.12 MINITAB scatter plot for data of Example 5.9

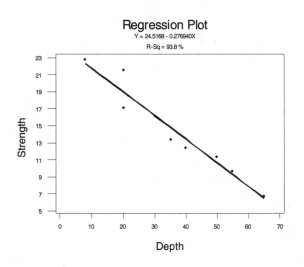

The summary quantities necessary to compute the equation of the least squares line are

$$\Sigma x = 323 \qquad \Sigma x^2 = 14{,}339 \qquad \Sigma y = 131.2 \qquad \Sigma y^2 = 2137.3 \qquad \Sigma xy = 3947.9$$

From these quantities, we compute

$$\bar{x} = 35.89 \qquad \bar{y} = 14.58$$

$$b = \frac{\Sigma xy - \dfrac{(\Sigma x)(\Sigma y)}{n}}{\Sigma x^2 - \dfrac{(\Sigma x)^2}{n}} = \frac{3947.9 - \dfrac{(323)(131.2)}{9}}{14{,}339 - \dfrac{(323)^2}{9}} = -.277$$

and

$$a = \bar{y} - b\bar{x} = 14.58 - (-.277)(35.89) = 24.5$$

The least squares line is then

$$\hat{y} = 24.5 - .277x$$

This line is also shown on the scatter plot of Figure 5.12.

If we wanted to predict the strength of concrete that had a depth of corrosion of 25, we could use the point on the least squares line above $x = 25$:

$$\hat{y} = 24.5 - (.277)(25) = 17.575$$

Predicted strengths for other corrosion depths could be obtained in a similar way. **However, the least squares line should not be used to predict strength for corrosion depths much outside the range 8 to 59 (the range of x values in the data set) since we do not know whether the linear pattern observed in the scatter plot continues outside this range.** This is sometimes referred to as the **danger of extrapolation.**

Calculations involving the least squares line can obviously be quite tedious, and fitting a function to multivariate data is even worse. This is where the computer comes to our rescue. All the standard statistical packages fit a straight line to bivariate data when asked to do so. To accomplish this, a regression command or option is used. (This terminology is explained shortly.)

EXAMPLE 5.10

Millions of Muslims all over the world participate in controlled or partial fasting during the month of Ramadan. The article "Body Weight Loss and Changes in Blood Lipid Levels in Normal Men on Hypo-caloric Diets During Ramadan Fasting" (*Amer. J. of Clinical Nutrition* (1988): 1197–1210) reported on a study carried out to assess the physiological effects of such fasting. The accompanying table gives selected data (read from a graph in the article) on x = percentage change in body weight during phase two of the fasting period (in this phase, experimental subjects received a high-fat, low-carbohydrate diet) and y = high-density lipoprotein cholesterol level (mg/dl):

x	−5	−3.2	−2.2	−1.7	−1.6	−1.5	−.9	0	0	1.2	1.6	1.7	2.8
y	43	50	61	63	47	57	51	60	67	76	70	51	74

Figure 5.13 (page 156) is a scatter plot. The predominant pattern is linear, though the points in the plot spread out about *any* line (even the least squares line).

MINITAB was used to fit the least squares line, and Figure 5.14 shows part of the resulting output. Instead of x and y, the variable labels **perchgwt** (*percent change in weight*) and **chollevl** (*cholesterol level*) are used. The equation at the top is that of the least squares line. In the rectangular table just below the equation, the first row gives information about the intercept, *a*, and the second row gives information concerning the slope, *b*. In particular, the coefficient column labeled **Coef** contains the values of *a* and *b* using more significant figures than appear in the rounded equation.

FIGURE 5.13 Scatter plot and least squares line for the data of Example 5.10

The regression equation is
chollevl = 61.5 + 3.41 perchgwt ← Equation $\hat{y} = a + bx$

Predictor	Coef	Stdev	t-ratio	p
Constant	61.537	2.268	27.13	0.000
perchgwt	3.407	1.028	3.31	0.007

Value of a   Value of b

FIGURE 5.14 Partial MINITAB output for Example 5.10

The least squares line should not be used here to predict cholesterol level for values of percentage change in body weight such as $x = -10$ or $x = 8$. These x values are well outside the range of the data, and there is no evidence to support extrapolation of the linear relationship.

Regression

The least squares line is often called the **sample regression line.** This terminology comes from the relationship between the least squares line and Pearson's correlation coefficient. To understand this relationship, we first need alternative expressions for the slope b and the equation of the line itself. With s_x and s_y denoting the sample standard deviations of the x's and y's, respectively, a bit of algebraic manipulation gives

$$b = r \cdot \frac{s_y}{s_x}$$

$$\hat{y} = \bar{y} + r \cdot \frac{s_y}{s_x}(x - \bar{x})$$

You do not need to use these formulas in any computations, but several of their implications are important for appreciating what the least squares line does.

1. When $x = \bar{x}$ is substituted in the equation of the line, $\hat{y} = \bar{y}$ results. That is, the least squares line passes through the *point of averages* $(\bar{x}, \bar{y})$.

2. Suppose for the moment that $r = 1$, so that all points lie exactly on the line whose equation is

$$\hat{y} = \bar{y} + \frac{s_y}{s_x}(x - \bar{x})$$

Now substitute $x = \bar{x} + s_x$, which is 1 standard deviation above $\bar{x}$:

$$\hat{y} = \bar{y} + \frac{s_y}{s_x}(\bar{x} + s_x - \bar{x}) = \bar{y} + s_y$$

That is, with $r = 1$, when x is 1 standard deviation above its mean, we predict that the associated y value will be 1 standard deviation above its mean. Similarly, if $x = \bar{x} - 2s_x$ (2 standard deviations below its mean), then

$$\hat{y} = \bar{y} + \frac{s_y}{s_x}(\bar{x} - 2s_x - \bar{x}) = \bar{y} - 2s_y$$

also 2 standard deviations below the mean. If $r = -1$, then $x = \bar{x} + s_x$ results in $\hat{y} = \bar{y} - s_y$, so the predicted y is also 1 standard deviation from its mean but on the opposite side of $\bar{y}$ from where x is relative to $\bar{x}$. In general, if x and y are perfectly correlated, the predicted y value associated with a given x value will be the same number of standard deviations (of y) from its mean, $\bar{y}$, as x is from its mean, $\bar{x}$.

3. Suppose that x and y are not perfectly correlated. To be specific, take $r = .5$, so the least squares line has the equation

$$\hat{y} = \bar{y} + .5\left(\frac{s_y}{s_x}\right)(x - \bar{x})$$

Then substituting $x = \bar{x} + s_x$ gives

$$\hat{y} = \bar{y} + .5\left(\frac{s_y}{s_x}\right)(\bar{x} + s_x - \bar{x}) = \bar{y} + .5s_y$$

That is, for $r = .5$, when x lies 1 standard deviation above its mean, we predict that y will be only .5 standard deviation above its mean.

Similarly, we can predict y when r is negative. If $r = -.5$, then the predicted y value will be only half the number of standard deviations from $\bar{y}$ that x is from $\bar{x}$, but x and the predicted y will now be on opposite sides of their respective means.

Consider using the least squares line to predict the value of y associated with an x value some speci-fied number of standard deviations away from $\bar{x}$. Then the predicted y value will be only r times this number of standard deviations from $\bar{y}$. In terms of standard deviations, except when $r = 1$ or -1, the predicted y will always be closer to $\bar{y}$ than x is to $\bar{x}$.

Using the least squares line for prediction results in a predicted y that is pulled back in, or regressed, toward its mean compared to where x is relative to its mean. This regression effect was first noticed by Sir Francis Galton (1822–1911), a famous biologist, while studying the relationship between the heights of fathers and their sons. He found that the predicted height of a son whose father was above average in height would also be above average (because r is positive here) but not by as much as the father's; he found a similar relationship for a father whose height was below average. This regression effect has led to the term **regression analysis** for the collection of methods involving the fitting of lines, curves, and more complicated functions to bivariate and multivariate data.

The alternate form of the regression (least squares) line emphasizes that predicting y from knowledge of x is not the same problem as predicting x from knowledge of y. The slope of the least squares line for predicting x is $r \cdot (s_x/s_y)$ rather than $r \cdot (s_y/s_x)$, and the intercepts of the lines are also usually different. It makes a difference whether y is regressed on x, as we have done, or whether x is regressed on y. The regression line of y on x should not be used to predict x, since it is not the line that minimizes the sum of squared x deviations.

Exercises 5.26 – 5.36

5.26 In the article "Reproductive Biology of the Aquatic Salamander *Amphiuma tridactylum* in Louisiana (*Journal of Herpetology* (1999): 100–105), 14 female salamanders were studied. Using regression, the author predicted y = clutch size (number of salamander eggs) from x = snout-vent length (measured in cm) as follows:

$$\hat{y} = -147 + 6.175x$$

It is interesting to note that for the salamanders studied, the range of snout-vent lengths was from approximately 30 to 70. Because the scatter plot looked linear, the authors thought a simple linear regression was a reasonable way of describing the relationship between x and y.

a. What is the value of the y intercept of the least squares line? What is the value of the slope of the least squares line? Give an interpretation of the slope in the context of this problem.

b. Would you be reluctant to predict the clutch size when snout-vent length is 22 cm? Explain.

5.27 A number of studies have shown lichens (certain plants composed of an alga and a fungus) to be excellent bioindicators of air pollution. The article "The Epiphytic Lichen Hypogymnia Physodes as a Bioindicator of Atmospheric Nitrogen and Sulphur Deposition in Norway" (*Envir. Monitoring and Assessment* (1993): 27–47) gives the following data (read from a graph in the paper) on x = NO_3 wet deposition (g/m^3) and y = lichen (% dry weight):

x	.05	.10	.11	.12	.31	.37	.42
y	.48	.55	.48	.50	.58	.52	1.02

x	.58	.68	.68	.73	.85	.92
y	.86	.86	1.00	.88	1.04	1.70

a. What is the equation of the least squares regression line?

b. Predict lichen for an NO_3 deposition of .5.

5.28 According to the article "First-Year Academic Success: A Prediction Combining Cognitive and Psychosocial Variables for Caucasian and African-American Students" (*Journal of College Student Development* (1999): 599–

605) there is a mild correlation between high school GPA (x) and first-year college GPA (y). The data, which was collected from a "Southeastern public research university," can be summarized:

$$n = 2600 \qquad \Sigma x = 9620 \qquad \Sigma y = 7436$$

$$\Sigma xy = 27{,}918 \qquad \Sigma x^2 = 36{,}168 \qquad \Sigma y^2 = 23{,}145$$

a. Find the equation of the least squares regression line.
b. Interpret the value of b, the slope of the least squares line, in the context of this problem.
c. What first-year GPA would you predict for a student with a 4.0 high school GPA?

5.29 Shells of molluscs function as both part of the skeletal system and as protective armor. It has been argued that many features of these shells were the result of natural selection in the constant battle against predators. The paper "Postmortem Changes in Strength of Gastropod Shells" (*Paleobiology* (1992): 367–377) included scatter plots of data on x = shell height (cm) and y = breaking strength (newtons). The least squares line for a sample of n = 38 hermit crab shells was $\hat{y} = -275.1 + 244.9x$.

a. What are the slope and intercept of this line?
b. When shell height increases by 1 cm, by how much does breaking strength tend to change?
c. What breaking strength would you predict when shell height is 2 cm?
d. Does this approximate linear relationship appear to hold for shell heights as small as 1 cm? Explain your reasoning.

5.30 It has been observed that Andean high-altitude natives have larger chest dimensions and lung volumes than do sea-level residents. Is this also true of lifelong Himalayan residents? The paper "Increased Vital and Total Lung Capacities in Tibetan Compared to Han Residents of Lhasa" (*Amer. J. Phys. Anthro.* (1991): 341–351) reported on the results of an investigation into this question. Included in the paper was a plot of vital capacity (y) versus chest circumference (x) for a sample of 16 Tibetan natives, from which the accompanying data was read.

x	79.4	81.8	81.8	82.3	83.7	84.3	84.3	85.2
y	4.3	4.6	4.8	4.7	5.0	4.9	4.4	5.0

x	87.0	87.3	87.7	88.1	88.1	88.6	89.0	89.5
y	6.1	4.7	5.7	5.7	5.2	5.5	5.0	5.3

a. Construct a scatter plot. What does it suggest about the nature of the relationship between x and y?
b. The summary quantities are

$$\Sigma x = 1368.1 \qquad \Sigma y = 80.9 \qquad \Sigma x^2 = 117{,}123.85$$

$$\Sigma y^2 = 412.81 \qquad \Sigma xy = 6933.48$$

Verify that the equation of the least squares line is $\hat{y} = -4.54 + .1123x$; draw this line on your scatter plot.
c. Roughly what change in vital capacity is associated with a 1-cm increase in chest circumference? with a 10-cm increase?
d. What vital capacity would you predict for a Tibetan native whose chest circumference is 85 cm?
e. Is vital capacity completely determined by chest circumference? Explain.

5.31 Example 5.2 gave data on x = soil pH and y = crown dieback (an indicator of forest growth retardation). Consider the accompanying MINITAB output.

The regression equation is
dieback = 31.0 - 5.79 soil ph

Predictor	Coef	Stdev	t-ratio	p
Constant	31.040	5.445	5.70	0.000
soil ph	−5.792	1.363	-4.25	0.001
s = 2.981	R-sq = 51.5%			

a. What is the equation of the least squares line?
b. Roughly what change in crown dieback would be associated with an increase of 1 in soil pH (for pH within the range of the data)?
c. What value of crown dieback would you predict when soil pH = 4.0?
d. Would it be sensible to use the least squares line to predict crown dieback when soil pH = 5.6? Explain.

5.32 Athletes competing in a triathlon participated in a study described in the paper "Myoglobinemia and Endurance Exercise" (*Amer. J. of Sports Med.* (1984): 113–118). The accompanying data on finishing time x (hr) and myoglobin level y (ng/mL) was read from a scatter plot in the paper.

x	4.90	4.70	5.35	5.22	5.20
y	1590	1550	1360	895	865

x	5.40	5.70	6.00	6.20	6.10
y	905	895	910	700	675

x	5.60	5.35	5.75	5.35	6.00
y	540	540	440	380	300

$$\Sigma (x - \bar{x})(y - \bar{y}) = -1561.227 \qquad \Sigma (x - \bar{x})^2 = 2.702$$

a. Obtain the equation of the least squares line.
b. Interpret the value of b.
c. What happens if the line in part a is used to predict the myoglobin level for a finishing time of 8 hr? Is this reasonable? Explain.

5.33 Explain why it can be dangerous to use the least squares line to obtain predictions for x values that are substantially larger or smaller than those contained in the sample.

5.34 The sales manager of a large company selected a random sample of $n = 10$ salespeople and determined for each one the values of x = years of sales experience and y = annual sales (in thousands of dollars). A scatter plot of the resulting (x, y) pairs showed a marked linear pattern.

a. Suppose that the sample correlation coefficient is $r = .75$ and average annual sales is $\bar{y} = 100$. If a particular salesperson is 2 standard deviations above the mean in terms of experience, what would you predict for that person's annual sales?

b. If a particular person whose sales experience is 1.5 standard deviations below average experience is predicted to have an annual sales value that is 1 standard deviation below average annual sales, what is the value of r?

5.35 Explain why the slope b of the least squares line always has the same sign (positive or negative) as does the sample correlation coefficient r.

5.36 The accompanying data resulted from an experiment in which weld diameter, x, and shear strength, y (lb), were determined for five different spot welds on steel. A scatter plot shows a pronounced linear pattern. With $\Sigma (x - \bar{x})^2 = 1000$ and $\Sigma (x - \bar{x})(y - \bar{y}) = 8577$, the least squares line is $\hat{y} = -936.22 + 8.577x$.

x	200	210	220	230	240
y	813.7	785.3	960.4	1118.0	1076.2

a. Since 1 lb = .4536 kg, strength observations can be reexpressed in kilograms through multiplication by this conversion factor: new y = .4536·(old y). What is the equation of the least squares line when y is expressed in kilograms?

b. More generally, suppose that each y value in a data set consisting of n (x, y) pairs is multiplied by a conversion factor c (which changes the units of measurement for y). What effect does this have on the slope b (that is, how does the new value of b compare to the value before conversion), on the intercept $a,$ and on the equation of the least squares line? Verify your conjectures by using the given formulas for b and a. (*Hint:* Replace y with cy and see what happens — and remember, this conversion will affect $\bar{y}$.)

5.4 Assessing the Fit of a Line

Once the least squares regression line has been obtained, it is natural to examine how effectively the line summarized the relationship between x and y. Important questions to consider are

1. Is a line an appropriate way to summarize the relationship between the two variables?

2. Are there any unusual aspects of the data set that we need to consider before proceeding to use the regression line to make predictions?

3. If we decide that it is reasonable to use the regression line as a basis for prediction, how accurate can we expect predictions based on the regression line to be?

In this section, we look at graphical and numerical methods that will allow us to answer these questions. Most of these methods are based on the vertical deviations of the data points from the regression line. These vertical deviations are called *residuals,* and each represents the difference between an actual y value and the corresponding predicted value, $\hat{y},$ that would have resulted from using the regression line to make a prediction.

Predicted Values and Residuals

If the x value for the first observation is substituted in the equation for the least squares line, the result is $a + bx_1$, the height of the line above x_1. The point (x_1, y_1) in the scatter plot also lies above x_1, so the difference

$$y_1 - (a + bx_1)$$

is the vertical deviation from this point to the line (see Figure·5.15). A point lying above the line gives a positive deviation, and a point below the line results in a negative deviation. The remaining vertical deviations come from repeating this process for $x = x_2$, then $x = x_3$, and so on.

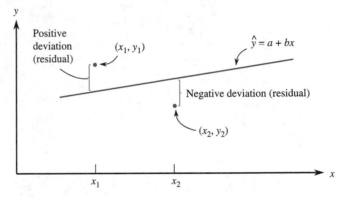

FIGURE 5.15 Positive and negative deviations (residuals) from the least squares line

Definition

The **predicted** or **fitted values** result from substituting each sample x value in turn into the equation for the least squares line. This gives

$\hat{y}_1 = $ 1st predicted value $= a + bx_1$

$\hat{y}_2 = $ 2nd predicted value $= a + bx_2$

$\vdots$

$\hat{y}_n = n$th predicted value $= a + bx_n$

The residuals from the least squares line are the n quantities

$$y_1 - \hat{y}_1, y_2 - \hat{y}_2, \ldots, y_n - \hat{y}_n$$

Each residual is the difference between an observed y value and the corresponding predicted y value.

EXAMPLE 5.11   One measure of the success of knee surgery is postsurgical range of motion for the knee joint. Postsurgical range of motion was recorded for 12 patients who had surgery following a knee dislocation. The age of each patient was also recorded ("Reconstruction of the Anterior and Posterior Cruciate Ligaments after Knee

Dislocation," *Amer. J. of Sports Medicine* (1999): 189–194). The data is given in Table 5.1.

Table 5.1 *Predicted values and residuals for the data of Example 5.11*

Patient	Age x	Range of Motion y	Predicted Range of Motion $\hat{y}$	Residual $y - \hat{y}$
1	32	154	138.07	15.93
2	24	142	128.49	13.51
3	40	137	142.42	−5.42
4	31	133	134.58	−1.58
5	28	122	131.97	−9.97
6	25	126	129.36	−3.36
7	26	135	130.23	4.77
8	16	135	121.52	13.48
9	14	108	119.78	−11.78
10	20	120	125.00	−5.00
11	21	127	125.87	1.13
12	30	122	133.71	−11.71

MINITAB was used to fit the least squares regression line; partial computer output is shown. The resulting least squares regression line is $\hat{y} = 107.58 + .871$age.

Regression Analysis
The regression equation is
Range of Motion = 108 + 0.871 Age

Predictor	Coef	StDev	T	P
Constant	107.58	11.12	9.67	0.000
Age	0.8710	0.4146	2.10	0.062

S = 10.42   R-Sq = 30.6%   R-Sq(adj) = 23.7%

A scatter plot that also includes the regression line is shown in Figure 5.16. The residuals for this data set are the vertical distances from the points to the regression line.

For the youngest patient (patient 9 with $x_9 = 14$ and $y_9 = 108$), the corresponding predicted value and residual are

predicted value $= \hat{y}_9 = 107.58 + .871$age $= 119.78$

residual $= y_9 - \hat{y}_9 = 108 - 119.78 = -11.78$

The other predicted values and residuals are computed in a similar manner and are included in Table 5.1.

Computing the predicted values and residuals by hand can be tedious, but MINITAB and other statistical software packages, as well as many graphing calculators, include them as part of the output, as shown in Figure 5.17. The predicted

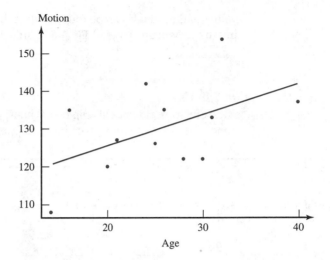

FIGURE 5.16 Scatter plot of the data from Example 5.11

The regression equation is

Range of Motion = 108 + 0.871 Age

Predictor	Coef	StDev	T	P
Constant	107.58	11.12	9.67	0.000
Age	0.8710	0.4146	2.10	0.062

S = 10.42   R-Sq = 30.6%   R-Sq(adj) = 23.7%

Analysis of Variance

Source	DF	SS	MS	F	P
Regression	1	479.2	479.2	4.41	0.062
Residual Error	10	1085.7	108.6		
Total	11	1564.9			

Obs	Age	Range of	Fit	StDev Fit	Residual	St Resid
1	35.0	154.00	138.07	4.85	15.93	1.73
2	24.0	142.00	128.49	3.10	13.51	1.36
3	40.0	137.00	142.42	6.60	-5.42	-0.67
4	31.0	133.00	134.58	3.69	-1.58	-0.16
5	28.0	122.00	131.97	3.14	-9.97	-1.00
6	25.0	126.00	129.36	3.03	-3.36	-0.34
7	26.0	135.00	130.23	3.01	4.77	0.48
8	16.0	135.00	121.52	5.07	13.48	1.48
9	14.0	108.00	119.78	5.75	-11.78	-1.36
10	20.0	120.00	125.00	3.86	-5.00	-0.52
11	21.0	127.00	125.87	3.61	1.13	0.12
12	30.0	122.00	133.71	3.47	-11.71	-1.19

FIGURE 5.17 MINITAB output for the data of Example 5.11

values and residuals can be found in the table at the bottom of the MINITAB output in the columns labeled **Fit** and **Residual,** respectively.

━━━━━━

Plotting the Residuals

A careful look at residuals can reveal many potential problems. A *residual plot* is a good place to start when assessing the appropriateness of the regression line.

Definition

A **residual plot** is a scatter plot of the (*x*, residual) pairs.

Isolated points or a pattern of points in the residual plot indicate potential problems. A desirable plot is one that exhibits no particular pattern, such as curvature. Curvature in the residual plot is an indication that the relationship between *x* and *y* is not linear and that a curve would be a better choice than a line for describing the relationship between *x* and *y*. This is sometimes easier to see in a residual plot than in a scatter plot of *y* versus *x,* as illustrated in the next example.

EXAMPLE 5.12

Consider the accompanying data on *x* = height (in) and *y* = average weight (lb) for American females aged 30–39 (from *The World Almanac and Book of Facts*). The scatter plot displayed in Figure 5.18(a) appears rather straight. However, when the

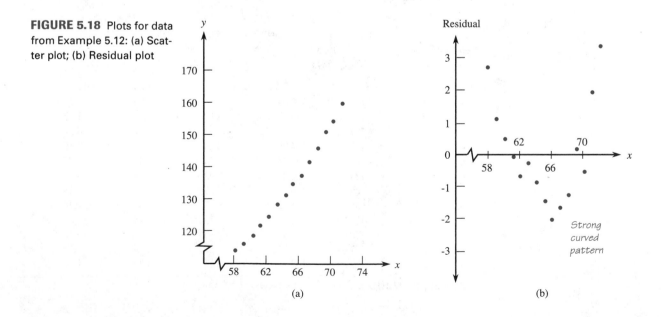

FIGURE 5.18 Plots for data from Example 5.12: (a) Scatter plot; (b) Residual plot

residuals from the least squares line ($\hat{y} = 98.23 + 3.596x$) are plotted, substantial curvature is apparent (even though $r \approx .99$). It is not accurate to say that weight increases in direct proportion to height (linearly with height). Instead, average weight increases somewhat more rapidly for relatively large heights than it does for relatively small heights.

x	58	59	60	61	62	63	64	65
y	113	115	118	121	124	128	131	134

x	66	67	68	69	70	71	72
y	137	141	145	150	153	159	164

There is another common type of residual plot — one that plots the residuals versus the corresponding $\hat{y}$ values rather than versus the x values. Since $\hat{y} = a + bx$ is simply a linear function of x, the only real difference between the two types of residual plots is the scale on the horizontal axis. The pattern of points in the residual plots will be the same, and it is this pattern of points that is important, not the scale. Thus the two plots give equivalent information, as can be seen in Figure 5.19, which gives both plots for the data of Example 5.11.

FIGURE 5.19 (a) Plot of residuals versus x; (b) Plot of residuals versus $\hat{y}$

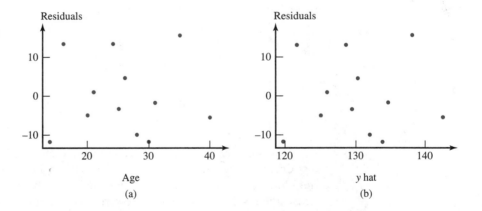

It is also important to look for unusual values in the scatter plot or the residual plot. A point falling far above or below the horizontal line at height zero corresponds to a large residual, which may indicate some type of unusual behavior, such as a recording error, nonstandard experimental condition, or atypical experimental subject. A point whose x value differs greatly from others in the data set may have exerted excessive influence in determining the fitted line. One method for assessing the impact of such an isolated point on the fit is to delete it from the data set and then recompute the best-fit line.

EXAMPLE 5.13

One factor in the development of tennis elbow is the impact-induced vibration of the racket and arm at ball contact. The likelihood of developing tennis elbow is known to depend on various properties of the tennis racket used. The accompanying data is a subset of that analyzed in the article "Transfer of Tennis Racket Vibrations into the Human Forearm" (*Med. and Sci. in Sports and Exercise* (1992): 1134–1140). Measurements on

x = racket resonance frequency (Hz)

and

y = sum of peak-to-peak accelerations (a characteristic of arm vibration in m/sec/sec) are given for $n = 14$ different rackets.

Racket	Resonance (x)	Acceleration (y)
1	105	36.0
2	106	35.0
3	110	34.5
4	111	36.8
5	112	37.0
6	113	34.0
7	113	34.2
8	114	33.8
9	114	35.0
10	119	35.0
11	120	33.6
12	121	34.2
13	126	36.2
14	189	30.0

A scatter plot and residual plot are shown in Figures 5.20(a) and (b), respectively.

One observation in the data set is far to the right of the other points in the scatter plot. Because the least squares line minimizes the sum of squared residuals, the least squares line is pulled down toward this discrepant point. This single observation plays a big role in determining the slope of the least squares line, and it is therefore called an *influential* observation. Notice that an influential observation is not necessarily the one with the largest residual, since the least squares line actually passes very near this point.

Figure 5.20(c) and (d) show what happens when the influential observation is removed from the sample. Both the slope and intercept of the least squares line are quite different from the slope and intercept of the line when this observation is included.

Deletion of the observation corresponding to the largest residual (1.955 for observation 13) also changes the value of the slope and intercept of the least squares line, but these changes are not profound. For example, the least squares line for the

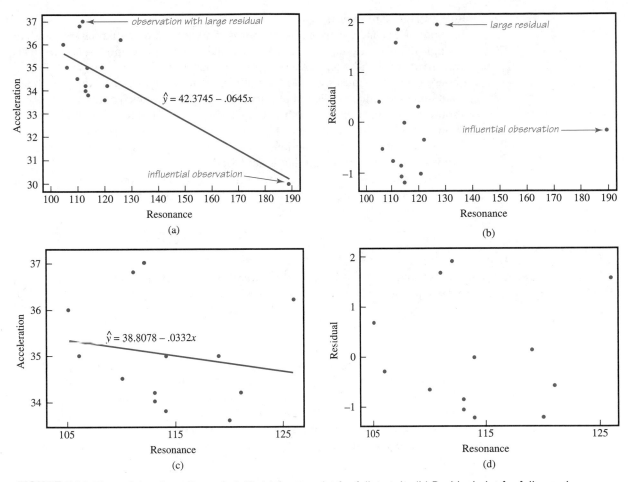

FIGURE 5.20 Plots of data from Example 5.13: (a) Scatter plot for full sample; (b) Residual plot for full sample; (c) Scatter plot when influential observation is deleted; (d) Residual plot when influential observation is deleted

data set consisting of the 13 points that remain when observation 13 is deleted is $\hat{y} = 42.5 - .0670x$. This observation does not appear to be all that influential.

Careful examination of a scatter plot and a residual plot can help us determine the appropriateness of a line for summarizing a relationship. If we decide that a line is appropriate, the next step is to think about assessing the accuracy of predictions to be based on the least squares line and whether these predictions (based on the value of x) are better in general than those made without knowledge of the value of x. Two numerical measures that are helpful in this assessment are the coefficient of determination and the standard deviation about the regression line.

The Coefficient of Determination

Suppose we would like to predict the price of homes in a particular city. A random sample of 20 homes that are for sale is selected and y = price and x = size (sq ft) is recorded for each house in the sample. Undoubtedly, there will be variability in house price (the houses will differ with respect to price), and it is this variability that makes accurate prediction of price a challenge. How much of the variability in house price can be explained by the fact that price is related to house size and houses differ in size? If differences in size account for a large proportion of the variability in price, a price prediction that takes house size into account is a big improvement over a prediction that is not based on size.

The **coefficient of determination** is a measure of the proportion of variability in the y variable that can be "explained by" a linear relationship between x and y.

Definition

The **coefficient of determination,** denoted by r^2, gives the proportion of variation in y that can be attributed to an approximate linear relationship between x and y.

Variation in y can effectively be explained by an approximate straight-line relationship when the points in the scatter plot fall close to the least squares line — that is, when the residuals are small in magnitude. A natural measure of variation about the least squares line is the sum of the squared residuals. (Squaring before combining prevents negative and positive residuals from counteracting one another.) A second sum of squares assesses the total amount of variation in observed y values.

Definition

The **total sum of squares,** denoted by **SSTo,** is defined as

$$\text{SSTo} = (y_1 - \bar{y})^2 + (y_2 - \bar{y})^2 + \cdots + (y_n - \bar{y})^2 = \Sigma (y - \bar{y})^2$$

The **residual sum of squares** (sometimes referred to as the error sum of squares), denoted by **SSResid,** is defined as

$$\text{SSResid} = (y_1 - \hat{y}_1)^2 + (y_2 - \hat{y}_2)^2 + \cdots + (y_n - \hat{y}_n)^2 = \Sigma (y - \hat{y})^2$$

These sums of squares can be found as part of the regression output from most standard statistical packages or can be obtained using the following computational formulas:

$$\text{SSTo} = \Sigma y^2 - \frac{(\Sigma y)^2}{n}$$

$$\text{SSResid} = \Sigma y^2 - a \Sigma y - b \Sigma xy$$

EXAMPLE 5.14

(Example 5.11 continued)   Figure 5.21 displays part of the MINITAB output that results from fitting the least squares line to the data on range of motion and age of Example 5.11. From the output,

SSTo = 1564.9   and   SSResid = 1085.7

Notice that SSResid is relatively large compared to SSTo.

FIGURE 5.21 MINITAB output for the data of Example 5.14

Regression Analysis

The regression equation is
Range of Motion = 108 + 0.871 Age

Predictor	Coef	StDev	T	P
Constant	107.58	11.12	9.67	0.000
Age	0.8710	0.4146	2.10	0.062

S = 10.42   R-Sq = 30.6%   R-Sq(adj) = 23.7%

Analysis of Variance

Source	DF	SS	MS	F	P
Regression	1	479.2	479.2	4.41	0.062
Residual Error	10	1085.7	108.6		
Total	11	1564.9			

SSResid

SSTo

The residual sum of squares is the sum of squared vertical deviations from the least squares line. As Figure 5.22 illustrates, SSTo is also a sum of squared vertical

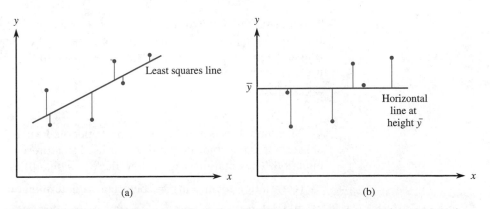

FIGURE 5.22 Interpreting sums of squares: (a) SSResid = sum of squared vertical deviations from the least squares line; (b) SSTo = sum of squared vertical deviations from the horizontal line at height $\bar{y}$

deviations from a line — the horizontal line at height $\bar{y}$. The least squares line is by definition the one having the smallest sum of squared deviations. It follows that SSResid $\leq$ SSTo. The two sums of squares will be equal only when the least squares line *is* the horizontal line.

SSResid is often referred to as a measure of "unexplained" variation — the amount of variation in y that cannot be attributed to the linear relationship between x and y. The more points in the scatter plot deviate from the least squares line, the larger will be the value of SSResid, and the greater the amount of y variation that cannot be explained by the approximate linear relationship. Similarly, SSTo is interpreted as a measure of total variation. The larger the value of SSTo, the greater the amount of variability in $y_1, y_2, \ldots, y_n$. The ratio SSResid/SSTo is the fraction or proportion of total variation that is unexplained by a straight-line relation. Subtracting this ratio from 1 gives the proportion of total variation that *is* explained.

The coefficient of determination, r^2, can be computed as

$$r^2 = 1 - \frac{\text{SSResid}}{\text{SSTo}}$$

Multiplying r^2 by 100 gives the percentage of y variation attributable to the approximate linear relationship. The closer this percentage is to 100%, the more successful is the relationship in explaining variation in y.

EXAMPLE 5.15   (Example 5.14 continued)   For the data on range of motion and age of Example 5.14, we found SSTo = 1564.9 and SSResid = 1085.7, so

$$r^2 = 1 - \frac{\text{SSResid}}{\text{SSTo}} = 1 - \frac{1085.7}{1564.9} = .306$$

This means that only 30.6% of the observed variability in postsurgical range of motion can be explained by an approximate linear relationship between range of motion and age. Note that the r^2 value can be found in the MINITAB output of Figure 5.21 labeled as **R-Sq.**

The symbol r was used in Section 5.2 to denote Pearson's sample correlation coefficient. It is not coincidental that r^2 is used to represent the coefficient of determination. The notation suggests how these two quantities are related:

(correlation coefficient)^2 = coefficient of determination

Thus, if $r = .8$ or $r = -.8$, then $r^2 = .64$, so 64% of the observed variation in the dependent variable can be attributed to the linear relationship. Because the value of r does not depend on which variable is labeled x, the same is true of r^2. The coefficient of determination is one of the few quantities calculated in the course of a regression analysis whose value remains the same when the role of dependent and independent variables are interchanged. When $r = .5$, we get $r^2 = .25$, so only 25% of the observed variation is explained by a linear relation. This is why a value of r between $-.5$ and $.5$ is not considered as evidence of a strong linear relationship.

Standard Deviation About the Least Squares Line

The coefficient of determination measures the extent of variation about the best-fit line *relative* to overall variation in y. A high value of r^2 does not by itself promise that the deviations from the line are small in an absolute sense. A typical observation could deviate from the line by quite a bit, yet these deviations might still be small relative to overall y variation. Recall that in Chapter 4 the sample standard deviation

$$s = \sqrt{\frac{\sum (x - \bar{x})^2}{n - 1}}$$

was used as a measure of variability in a single sample; roughly speaking, s is the typical amount by which a sample observation deviates from the mean. There is an analogous measure of variability when a line is fit by least squares.

Definition

The **standard deviation about the least squares line** is given by

$$s_e = \sqrt{\frac{\text{SSResid}}{n - 2}}$$

Roughly speaking, s_e is the typical amount by which an observation deviates from the least squares line. Justification for division by $n - 2$ and the use of the subscript e are given in Chapter 13.

EXAMPLE 5.16

The values of x = commuting distance and y = commuting time were determined for workers in samples from three different regions. The data is given in Table 5.2; the three scatter plots are displayed in Figure 5.23 on page 172.

Table 5.2 *Data for Example 5.16*

Region 1		Region 2		Region 3	
x	y	x	y	x	y
15	42	5	16	5	8
16	35	10	32	10	16
17	45	15	44	15	22
18	42	20	45	20	23
19	49	25	63	25	31
20	46	50	115	50	60

FIGURE 5.23 Scatter plots for Example 5.16: (a) Region 1; (b) Region 2; (c) Region 3

For sample 1, a rather small proportion of variation in y can be attributed to an approximate linear relationship, and a typical deviation from the least squares line is roughly 4. The amount of variability about the line for sample 2 is the same as for sample 1, but the value of r^2 is much higher, because y variation is much greater overall in sample 2 than in sample 1. Sample 3 yields roughly the same high value of r^2 as does sample 2, but the typical deviation from the line for sample 3 is only half that for sample 2. For a complete picture of variation, both r^2 and s_e must be computed.

Exercises 5.37 – 5.51

5.37 Exercise 5.26 gave the least squares regression line for predicting y = clutch size from x = snout-vent length ("Reproductive Biology of the Aquatic Salamander *Amphiuma tridactylum* in Louisiana," *Journal of Herpetology* (1999): 100–105). The paper also reported r^2 = .7664 and SSTo = 43,951.

   a. Interpret the value of r^2.
   b. Find and interpret the value of s_e. (The sample size was n = 14.)

5.38 The article "Characterization of Highway Runoff in Austin, Texas, Area" (*J. of Envir. Engr.* (1998)) gave a scatter plot, along with the least squares line for x = rainfall volume (m³) and y = runoff volume (m³) for a particular location. The accompanying data was read from the plot in the paper.

x	5	12	14	17	23	30	40	47
y	4	10	13	15	15	25	27	46

x	55	67	72	81	96	112	127
y	38	46	53	70	82	99	100

a. Does a scatter plot of the data suggest a linear relationship between x and y?
b. Estimate the slope and intercept of the least squares line.
c. Compute an estimate of the average runoff volume when rainfall volume is 80.
d. Compute the estimated standard deviation about the regression line.
e. What proportion of the observed variation in runoff volume can be explained by the linear relationship to rainfall volume?

5.39 The article cited in the chapter introduction reported that for a regression of y = average SAT score on x = expenditure per pupil, based on data from n = 44 New Jersey school districts, a = 766, b = .015, r^2 = .160, and s_e = 53.7.

   a. One observation in the sample was (9900, 893). What average SAT score would you predict for this district, and what is the corresponding residual?
   b. Interpret the value of s_e.

c. How effectively do you think the least squares line summarizes the relationship between x and y? Explain your reasoning.

5.40 The paper "Root Dentine Transparency: Age Determination of Human Teeth Using Computerized Densitometric Analysis" (*Amer. J. Phys. Anthro.* (1991): 25–30) reported on an investigation of methods for age determination based on tooth characteristics. With $y =$ age (years) and $x =$ percentage of root with transparent dentine, a regression analysis for premolars using an image-analyser method to determine x gave $n = 36$, SSResid = 5987.16, and SSTo = 17,409.60. Calculate and interpret the values of r^2 and s_e.

5.41 The paper cited in Exercise 5.40 gave a scatter plot in which x values were for anterior teeth. Consider the accompanying representative subset of the data.

x	15	19	31	39	41
y	23	52	65	55	32

x	44	47	48	55	65
y	60	78	59	61	60

$\Sigma x = 404 \qquad \Sigma x^2 = 18{,}448 \qquad \Sigma y = 545$

$\Sigma y^2 - 31{,}993 \qquad \Sigma xy - 23{,}198$

$a = 32.080888 \qquad b = .554929$

a. Calculate the predicted values and residuals.
b. Use the results of part a to obtain SSResid and r^2.
c. Does the least squares line appear to give very accurate predictions? Explain your reasoning.

5.42 The decline of salmon fisheries along the Columbia River in Oregon has caused great concern among commercial and recreational fishermen. The paper "Feeding of Predaceous Fishes on Out-Migrating Juvenile Salmonids in John Day Reservoir, Columbia River" (*Trans. Amer. Fisheries Soc.* (1991): 405–420) gave the accompanying data on $y =$ maximum size of salmonids consumed by a northern squawfish (the most abundant salmonid predator) and $x =$ squawfish length, both in mm.

x	218	246	270	287	318	344
y	82	85	94	127	141	157

x	375	386	414	450	468
y	165	216	219	238	249

Use the accompanying output from MINITAB to answer the following questions.

The regression equation is
size = -89.1 + 0.729 length

Predictor	Coef	Stdev	t ratio	p
Constant	-89.09	16.83	-5.29	0.000
length	0.72907	0.04778	15.26	0.000

s = 12.56   R-sq = 96.3%   R-sq(adj) = 95.9%

Analysis of Variance

SOURCE	DF	SS	MS	F	p
Regression	1	36736	36736	232.87	0.000
Error	9	1420	158		
Total	10	38156			

a. What maximum size would you predict for a squawfish whose length is 375 mm, and what is the residual corresponding to the observation (375, 165)?
b. What proportion of observed variation in y can be attributed to the approximate linear relationship between the two variables?

5.43 There have been numerous studies on the effects of radiation. The accompanying data on the relationship between degree of exposure to ^{242}Cm alpha particles (x) and the percentage of exposed cells without aberrations (y) appeared in the paper "Chromosome Aberrations Induced in Human Lymphocytes by D-T Neutrons" (*Radiation Research* (1984): 561–573).

x	.106	.193	.511	.527	1.08	1.62
y	98	95	87	85	75	72

x	1.73	2.36	2.72	3.12	3.88	4.18
y	64	55	44	41	37	40

Summary quantities are

$n = 12 \qquad \Sigma x = 22.027 \qquad \Sigma y = 793$

$\Sigma x^2 = 62.600235 \qquad \Sigma xy = 1114.5 \qquad \Sigma y^2 = 57{,}939$

a. Obtain the equation of the least squares line.
b. Calculate SSResid and SSTo.
c. What percentage of observed variation in y can be explained by the approximate linear relationship between the two variables?
d. Calculate and interpret the value of s_e.
e. Using just the results of parts a and c, what is the value of Pearson's sample correlation coefficient?

5.44 The paper "Crop Improvement for Tropical and Subtropical Australia: Designing Plants for Difficult Climates" (*Field Crops Research* (1991): 113–139) gave the accompanying data on $x =$ crop duration (days) for soybeans and $y =$ crop yield (tons/ha).

x	92	92	96	100	102
y	1.7	2.3	1.9	2.0	1.5

x	102	106	106	121	143
y	1.7	1.6	1.8	1.0	.3

$\Sigma x = 1060 \qquad \Sigma y = 15.8 \qquad \Sigma xy = 1601.1$

$\Sigma x^2 = 114{,}514 \qquad \Sigma y^2 = 27.82$

$a = 5.20683380 \qquad b = -0.3421541$

a. Construct a scatter plot of the data. Do you think the least squares line will give accurate predictions?

b. The largest x value in the sample greatly exceeds the remaining ones. Delete the corresponding observation from the sample and recalculate the equation of the least squares line. Does this observation greatly affect the equation of the line?

c. What effect does the deletion suggested in part **b** have on the value of r^2? Can you explain why this is so?

5.45 A study was carried out to investigate the relationship between the hardness of molded plastic (y, in Brinell units) and the amount of time elapsed since termination of the molding process (x, in hours). Summary quantities include

$$n = 15 \qquad \text{SSResid} = 1235.470 \qquad \text{SSTo} = 25{,}321.368$$

Calculate and interpret the coefficient of determination.

5.46 There has been an ongoing debate in recent years as to whether various species of wolves are endangered and what steps should be taken to prevent their demise. Disease can certainly pose a serious threat to such wildlife populations. The paper "Effects of Canine Parvovirus (CPV) on Gray Wolves in Minnesota" (*J. of Wildlife Manage.* (1995): 565–570) summarized a regression of y = percentage of pups in a capture on x = percentage of CPV prevalence among adults and pups. The equation of the least squares line, based on $n = 10$ observations, was $\hat{y} = 62.9476 - .54975x$, with $r^2 = .57$.

a. One observation was (25, 70). What is the corresponding residual?

b. What is the value of the sample correlation coefficient?

c. Suppose that SSTo = 2520.0 (this value was not given in the paper). What is the value of s_e?

5.47 Construct a residual plot for the data of Exercise 5.43, and comment on any interesting features.

5.48 Anthropologists often study soil composition for clues as to how the land was used during different periods. The accompanying data on x = soil depth (cm) and y = percent montmorillonite in the soil was taken from a scatter plot in the paper "Ancient Maya Drained Field Agriculture: Its Possible Application Today in the New River Floodplain, Belize, C.A." (*Ag. Ecosystems and Environ.* (1984): 67–84).

x	40	50	60	70	80	90	100
y	58	34	32	30	28	27	22

a. Draw a scatter plot of y versus x.

b. The equation of the least squares line is $\hat{y} =$ 64.50 − .45x. Draw this line on your scatter plot. Do there appear to be any large residuals?

c. Compute the residuals and construct a residual plot. Are there any unusual features in the plot?

5.49 **a.** Is it possible that both r^2 and s_e could be large for a bivariate data set? Explain. (A picture might be helpful.)

b. Is it possible that a bivariate data set could yield values of r^2 and s_e that are both small? Explain. (Again, a picture might be helpful.)

c. Explain why it is desirable to have r^2 large and s_e small if the relationship between two variables x and y is to be described using a straight line.

5.50 **a.** Show that the sum of the residuals $\Sigma \, [y - (a + bx)]$ is zero. [*Hint:* Substitute $a = \bar{y} - b\bar{x}$ and then use facts about $\Sigma \, (x - \bar{x})$ and $\Sigma \, (y - \bar{y})$.]

b. Let the residuals be denoted by $e_1, e_2, \ldots, e_n$ and consider fitting a line to the (x, e) pairs — that is, to the points in the residual plot — using the method of least squares. Then the slope of the least squares line is

$$\frac{\Sigma \, (x - \bar{x})(e - \bar{e})}{\Sigma \, (x - \bar{x})^2}$$

From part **a**, $\bar{e} = 0$, so $e - \bar{e} = e = y - (a + bx) = y - \bar{y} - b(x - \bar{x})$. Use this to show that the slope in the given expression is zero, so the residual plot has no tilt (though it may still have a nonlinear pattern if a straight-line fit is not appropriate).

5.51 Some straightforward but slightly tedious algebra shows that

$$\text{SSResid} = (1 - r^2) \, \Sigma \, (y - \bar{y})^2$$

from which it follows that

$$s_e = \sqrt{\frac{n - 1}{n - 2}} \sqrt{1 - r^2} \, s_y$$

Unless n is quite small, $(n - 1)/(n - 2) \approx 1$, so $s_e \approx \sqrt{1 - r^2} \, s_y$.

a. For what value of r is s_e as large as s_y? What is the least squares line in this case?

b. For what values of r will s_e be much smaller than s_y?

c. A study by the Berkeley Institute of Human Development (see the book *Statistics* by Freedman et al., listed in the Chapter 2 references) reported the following summary data for a sample of $n = 66$ California boys:

$$r \approx .80$$

At age 6, average height ≈ 46 in., standard deviation ≈ 1.7 in.

At age 18, average height ≈ 70 in., standard deviation ≈ 2.5 in.

What would s_e be for the least squares line used to predict 18-year-old height from 6-year-old height?

d. Referring to part **c,** suppose you wanted to predict the past value of 6-year-old height from knowledge of 18-year-old height. Find the equation for the appropriate least squares line. What is the corresponding value of s_e?

5.5 Nonlinear Relationships and Transformations

As we have seen in the previous sections, when the points in a scatter plot exhibit a linear pattern and the residual plot does not reveal any problems with the linear fit, the least squares line is a sensible way to summarize the relationship between x and y. A linear relationship is easy to interpret, departures from the line are easily detected, and using the line to predict y from our knowledge of x is straightforward. Often, though, a scatter plot or residual plot exhibits a curved pattern, indicating a more complicated relationship between x and y. In this case, finding a curve that fits the observed data well is a more complex task. In this section, we will consider two common approaches to fitting nonlinear relationships: polynomial regression and transformations.

Polynomial Regression

Let's reconsider the data on

   $x = $ time between flowering and harvesting

and

   $y = $ yield of paddy (a type of grain)

from Example 5.3. The scatter plot of this data is reproduced here as Figure 5.24. Since this plot shows a marked curved pattern, it is clear that no straight line would do a reasonable job of describing the relationship between x and y. However, the

FIGURE 5.24 Scatter plot for the paddy data

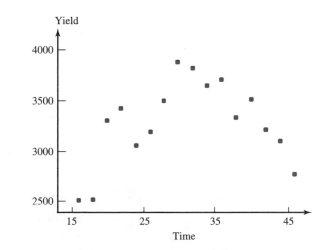

relationship could be described by a curve, and in this case the curved pattern in the scatter plot looks like a parabola (the graph of a quadratic function). This suggests trying to find a quadratic function of the form

$$\hat{y} = a + b_1 x + b_2 x^2$$

that would reasonably describe the relationship. That is, the values of the coefficients a, b_1, and b_2, in this equation must be selected to obtain a good fit to the data.

What are the best choices for the values of a, b_1, and b_2? In fitting a line to data, we used the principle of least squares to guide our choice of slope and intercept. Least squares can be used to fit a quadratic function as well. The deviations, $y - \hat{y}$, are still represented by vertical distances in the scatter plot, but now they are vertical distances from the points to a parabolic curve (the graph of a quadratic equation) rather than to a line, as shown in Figure 5.25. We then choose values for the coefficients in the quadratic equation so that the sum of squared deviations is as small as possible.

For a quadratic regression, the least squares estimates of a, b_1, and b_2 are those values that minimize the sum of squared deviations $\Sigma (y - \hat{y})^2$.

For quadratic regression, a measure that is useful for assessing fit is $R^2 = 1 - \text{SSResid}/\text{SSTo}$, where $\text{SSResid} = \Sigma (y - \hat{y})^2$. The measure R^2 is defined in a way similar to r^2 for simple linear regression and is interpreted in a similar fashion. The notation r^2 is used only with linear regression to emphasize the relationship between r^2 and the correlation coefficient, r, in the linear case.

The general expressions for computing the least squares estimates are somewhat complicated, so we will rely on a statistical software package or graphing calculator to do the computations for us.

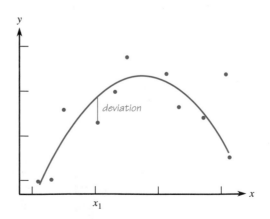

FIGURE 5.25 Deviations for a quadratic function

EXAMPLE 5.17

(Example 5.3 continued)   For the paddy yield data, the scatter plot (see Figure 5.24) showed a marked curved pattern. If the least squares line is fit to this data, it is no surprise that the line does not do a good job of describing the relationship ($r^2 = .075$ or 7.5% and $s_e = 416.7$), and the residual plot shows a distinct curved pattern as well (Figure 5.26).

FIGURE 5.26 Paddy data of Example 5.17: (a) Fitted line plot; (b) Residual plot

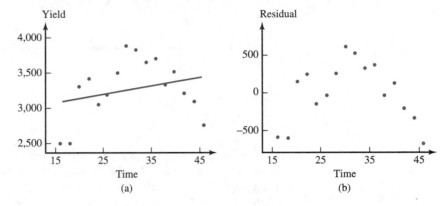

Partial MINITAB output from fitting a quadratic function to this data follows.

Polynomial Regression

$Y = -1074.63 + 293.924X - 4.54644X**2$

R-Sq = 79.4 %

Analysis of Variance

SOURCE	DF	SS	MS	F	P
Regression	2	2086388	1043194	25.0334	3.48E-05
Error	13	541738	41672		
Total	15	2628126			

The least squares coefficients are

$$a = -1074.63 \qquad b_1 = 293.924 \qquad b_2 = -4.54644$$

and the least squares quadratic is $\hat{y} = -1074.63 + 293.924x - 4.54644x^2$.

A plot showing the curve and the corresponding residual plot for the quadratic regression are given in Figure 5.27 (page 178). Notice that there is no strong pattern in the residual plot for the quadratic case as there was in the linear case. For the quadratic regression, $R^2 = .794$ (as opposed to .075 for the least squares line), which means that 79.4% of the variability in yield can be explained by an approximate quadratic relationship between yield and time between flowering and harvesting.

Linear and quadratic regression are special cases of polynomial regression. A polynomial regression curve is described by a function of the form

$$\hat{y} = a + b_1x + b_2x^2 + b_3x^3 + \cdots + b_kx^k$$

FIGURE 5.27 Quadratic regression of Example 5.17: (a) Scatter plot; (b) Residual plot

which is called a kth degree polynomial. The case of $k = 1$ results in linear regression ($\hat{y} = a + b_1 x$), and $k = 2$ yields a quadratic regression ($\hat{y} = a + b_1 x + b_2 x^2$). A quadratic curve has only one bend (see Figure 5.28(a) and (b)). A less frequently encountered special case is for $k = 3$, $\hat{y} = a + b_1 x + b_2 x^2 + b_3 x^3$, which is called a cubic regression curve. Cubic curves have two bends, as shown in Figure 5.28(c).

FIGURE 5.28 Polynomial regression curves: (a) Quadratic curve with $b_2 < 0$; (b) Quadratic curve with $b_2 > 0$; (c) Cubic curve

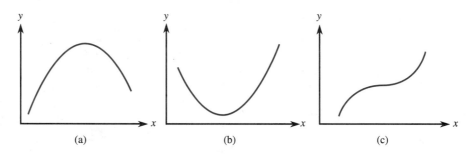

EXAMPLE 5.18

Researchers have examined a number of climatic variables in an attempt to understand the mechanisms that govern rainfall runoff. The article "The Applicability of Morton's and Penman's Evapotranspiration Estimates in Rainfall-Runoff Modeling" (*Water Resources Bull.* (1991): 611–620) reported on a study that examined the relationship between

x = cloud cover index   and y = sunshine index

Suppose that cloud cover index can have values between 0 and 1. Consider the accompanying data that is consistent with some of the summary quantities in the article:

Cloud Cover Index (x)	Sunshine Index (y)
.2	10.98
.5	10.94
.3	10.91
.1	10.94
.2	10.97
.4	10.89
0	10.88
.4	10.92
.3	10.86

The authors of the article used a cubic regression to describe the relationship between cloud cover and sunshine. Using the given data, MINITAB was instructed to fit a cubic regression to this data, resulting in the following output.

Polynomial Regression

Y = 10.8801 + 1.43140X - 7.20079X**2 + 9.19225X**3

R-Sq = 57.9 %

Analysis of Variance

SOURCE	DF	SS	MS	F	P
Regression	3	8.02E-03	2.67E-03	2.28796	0.195998
Error	5	5.84E-03	1.17E-03		
Total	8	1.39E-02			

The least squares cubic regression is then $\hat{y} = 10.8801 + 1.4314x - 7.20079x^2 + 9.19225x^3$. To predict the sunshine index for a day when the cloud cover index is .45, we use the regression equation to obtain

$$\hat{y} = 10.8801 + 1.4314x - 7.20079x^2 + 9.19225x^3$$
$$= 10.8801 + 1.4314(.45) - 7.20079(.45)^2 + 9.19225(.45)^3 = 10.91$$

The least squares cubic regression and the corresponding residual plot are shown in Figure 5.29 (page 180). The residual plot does not reveal any troublesome patterns that would suggest modification of the choice of cubic regression.

Transformations

An alternative to finding a curve to fit the data is to find a way to "transform" the x values and/or y values so that a scatter plot of the transformed data has a linear appearance. A **transformation** (sometimes called a reexpression) involves using a simple function of a variable in place of the variable itself. For example, instead of trying to describe the relationship between x and y, it might be easier to describe the relationship between $\sqrt{x}$ and y or between x and $\log(y)$. And, if we can describe the relationship between, say, $\sqrt{x}$ and y, it will still be possible for us to give a prediction

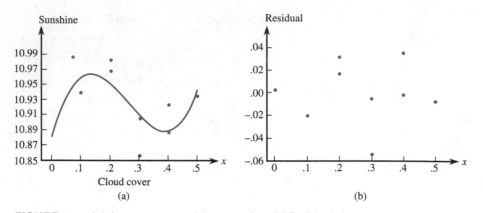

FIGURE 5.29 (a) Least squares cubic regression; (b) Residual plot

of the value of y for a given x value. Common transformations involve taking square roots, logs, or reciprocals.

EXAMPLE 5.19

As fans of white-water rafting know, a river flows more slowly close to its banks (due to friction between the river bank and the water). To study the nature of the relationship between water velocity and the distance from the shore, data is gathered on velocity (cm/sec) of a river at different distances (meters) from the bank. Suppose that the resulting data was as follows:

Distance	.5	1.5	2.5	3.5	4.5	5.5	6.5	7.5	8.5	9.5
Velocity	22.00	23.18	25.48	25.25	27.15	27.83	28.49	28.18	28.50	28.63

A graph of the data exhibits a curved pattern, as seen in both the scatter plot of Figure 5.30(a) and the residual plot from a linear fit shown in Figure 5.30(b).

Let's try transforming the x values by replacing each x value by its square root. We define

$$x' = \sqrt{x}$$

The resulting transformed data is given in Table 5.3.

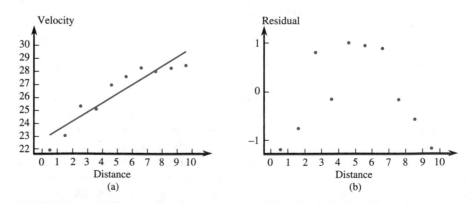

FIGURE 5.30 (a) Scatter plot of the river data; (b) Residual plot from linear fit

Table 5.3 *Original and transformed data of Example 5.19*

Original Data		Transformed Data	
x	*y*	*x'*	*y*
.5	22.00	0.7071	22.00
1.5	23.18	1.2247	23.18
2.5	25.48	1.5811	25.48
3.5	25.25	1.8708	25.25
4.5	27.15	2.1213	27.15
5.5	27.83	2.3452	27.83
6.5	28.49	2.5495	28.49
7.5	28.18	2.7386	28.18
8.5	28.50	2.9155	28.50
9.5	28.63	3.0822	28.63

Figure 5.31(a) shows a scatter plot of y versus x' (or equivalently y versus $\sqrt{x}$). The pattern of points in this plot looks linear, and so we can fit a least squares line using the transformed data. The MINITAB output from this regression follows.

Regression Analysis

The regression equation is
velocity = 20.1 + 3.01 sqrt distance

Predictor	Coef	StDev	T	P
Constant	20.1102	0.6097	32.99	0.000
sqrt dis	3.0085	0.2726	11.03	0.000

S = 0.6292   R-Sq = 93.8%   R-Sq(adj) = 93.1%

Analysis of Variance

Source	DF	SS	MS	F	P
Regression	1	48.209	48.209	121.76	0.000
Residual Error	8	3.168	0.396		
Total	9	51.376			

FIGURE 5.31 (a) Scatter plot of *y* versus *x'* for data of Example 5.19; (b) Residual plot resulting from a linear fit to transformed data

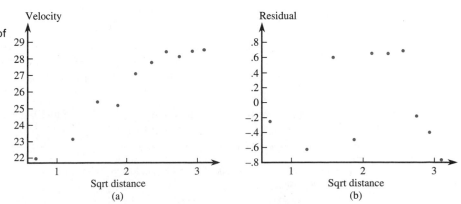

The residual plot in Figure 5.31(b) shows no indication of a pattern. The resulting regression equation is

$$\hat{y} = 20.1 + 3.01x'$$

or, equivalently,

$$\hat{y} = 20.1 + 3.01\sqrt{x}$$

The values of r^2 and s_e (see the MINITAB output) indicate that a line is a reasonable way to describe the relationship between y and x'. To predict velocity of the river at a distance of 9 meters from shore, we first compute $x' = \sqrt{x} = \sqrt{9} = 3$ and then use the sample regression line to obtain a prediction of y:

$$\hat{y} = 20.1 + 3.01x' = 20.1 + (3.01)(3) = 29.14$$

In Example, 5.19, transforming the x values using the square root function worked well. In general, how can we choose a transformation that will result in a linear pattern? Table 5.4 gives some guidance and summarizes some of the properties of the most commonly used transformations.

Table 5.4 *Commonly used transformations*

Transformation	Mathematical Description	Try This Transformation When
No transformation	$\hat{y} = a + bx$	The change in y is constant as x changes. A 1-unit increase in x is associated with, on average, an increase of b in the value of y.
Square root of x	$\hat{y} = a + b\sqrt{x}$	The change in y is not constant. A 1-unit increase in x is associated with smaller increases or decreases in y for larger x values.
Log of x*	$\hat{y} = a + b\log_{10}(x)$ or $\hat{y} = a + b\ln(x)$	The change in y is not constant. A 1-unit increase in x is associated with smaller increases or decreases in the value of y for larger x values.
Reciprocal of x	$\hat{y} = a + b(\frac{1}{x})$	The change in y is not constant. A 1-unit increase in x is associated with smaller increases or decreases in the value of y for larger x values. In addition, y has a limiting value of a as x increases.
Log of y* (Exponential growth or decay)	$\log(\hat{y}) = a + bx$ or $\ln(\hat{y}) = a + bx$	The change in y associated with a 1-unit change in x is proportional to x.

*The values of a and b in the regression equation will depend on whether $\log_{10}$ or ln is used, but the $\hat{y}$'s and r^2 values will be identical.

EXAMPLE 5.20

No tortilla chip lover likes soggy chips, so it is important to find characteristics of the production process that produce chips with an appealing texture. The following data on

x = frying time (sec)

and

y = moisture content (%)

appeared in the article "Thermal and Physical Properties of Tortilla Chips as a Function of Frying Time" (*J. of Food Processing and Preservation* (1995): 175–189).

Frying time, x	5	10	15	20	25	30	45	60
Moisture content, y	16.3	9.7	8.1	4.2	3.4	2.9	1.9	1.3

Figure 5.32(a) on page 184 shows a scatter plot of the data. The pattern in this plot is typical of exponential decay, with the change in y as x increases much smaller for large x values than for small x values. You can see that a 5-second change in frying time is associated with a much larger change in moisture content in the part of the plot where the x values are small than in the part of the plot where the x values are large. Table 5.4 suggests transforming the y values (moisture content in this example) by taking logarithms.

Two standard logarithmic functions are commonly used for such transformations — the common log (log base 10, denoted by log) and the natural log (log base e, denoted by ln). Either the common or natural log can be used; the only difference in the resulting scatter plots is the scale of the transformed y variable. This can be seen in Figures 5.32(b) and (c). These two scatter plots show the same pattern, and it looks like a line would be appropriate to describe this relationship.

Table 5.5 displays the original data along with the transformed y values using $y' = \log(y)$.

The MINITAB output at the top of page 184 shows the result of fitting the least squares line to the transformed data.

Table 5.5 *Transformed data from Example 5.20*

Frying Time x	Moisture y	Log(moisture) y'
5	16.3	1.21219
10	9.7	.98677
15	8.1	.90849
20	4.2	.62325
25	3.4	.53148
30	2.9	.46240
45	1.9	.27875
60	1.3	.11394

Regression Analysis

The regression equation is
log(moisture) = 1.14 - 0.0192 frying time

Predictor	Coef	StDev	T	P
Constant	1.14287	0.08016	14.26	0.000
frying t	-0.019170	0.002551	-7.52	0.000

S = 0.1246   R-Sq = 90.4%   R-Sq(adj) = 88.8%

Analysis of Variance

Source	DF	SS	MS	F	P
Regression	1	0.87736	0.87736	56.48	0.000
Residual Error	6	0.09320	0.01553		
Total	7	0.97057			

The resulting regression equation is

$$y' = 1.14 - .0192x$$

or, equivalently,

$$\log(y) = 1.14 - .0192x$$

FIGURE 5.32 (a) Scatter plot of the tortilla chip data; (b) Scatter plot of transformed data with $y = \log(y)$

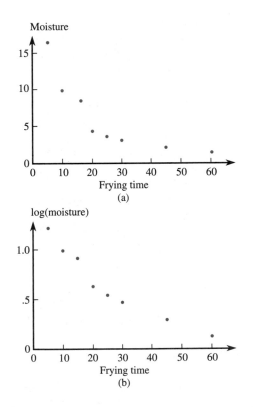

(a)

(b)

(*continued*)

FIGURE 5.32 (continued)
(c) Scatter plot of transformed data with $y' = \ln(y)$

(c)

Fitting a Curve Using Transformations

The objective of a regression analysis is usually to describe the approximate relationship between x and y with an equation of the form

$$y = \text{some function of } x$$

If we have transformed only x, fitting a least squares line to the transformed data
will result in an equation of the desired form, for example, something like

$$\hat{y} = 5 + 3x' = 5 + 3\sqrt{x} \qquad \text{where } x' = \sqrt{x}$$

or

$$\hat{y} = 4 + .2x' = 4 + .2\left(\frac{1}{x}\right) \qquad \text{where } x' = \frac{1}{x}$$

These functions specify lines when graphed using y and x', and they specify curves
when graphed using y and x, as illustrated in Figure 5.33 for the case of the square-
root transformation.

FIGURE 5.33 (a) A plot of $\hat{y} = 5 + 3x'$, where $x' = \sqrt{x}$ (b) A plot of $\hat{y} = 5 + 3\sqrt{x}$

If the y values have been transformed, after obtaining the least squares line, the transformation can be "undone" to yield an expression of the form $y =$ some function of x (as opposed to $y' =$ some function of x). For example, to reverse a log transformation ($y' = \log(y)$), we can take the antilog of each side of the equation. To reverse a square-root transformation ($y' = \sqrt{y}$), we can square both sides of the equation, and to reverse a reciprocal transformation ($y' = 1/y$), we can take the reciprocal of each side of the equation. This is illustrated in the following example.

EXAMPLE 5.21 (Example 5.20 continued)   For the tortilla chip data of Example 5.20, $y' = \log(y)$ and the least squares line relating y' and x was

$$y' = 1.14 - .0192x$$

or, equivalently,

$$\log(y) = 1.14 - .0192x$$

To reverse this transformation, we take the antilog of both sides of the equation:

$$10^{\log(y)} = 10^{1.14 - .0192x}$$

Using the properties of logs and exponents

$$10^{\log(y)} = y$$
$$10^{1.14 - .0192x} = (10^{1.14})(10^{-.0192x})$$

We get

$$\hat{y} = (10^{1.14})(10^{-.0192x}) = (13.8038)(10^{-.0192x})$$

This equation can now be used to predict the y value (moisture content) for a given x (frying time). For example, the predicted moisture content when frying time is 35 seconds is

$$\hat{y} = (13.8038)(10^{-.0192x}) = (13.8038)(.2128) = 2.9376$$

It should be noted that the process of transforming data, fitting a line to the transformed data, and then "undoing" the transformation to get an equation for a curved relationship between x and y usually results in a curve that provides a reasonable fit to the sample data, but it is not the "least squares" curve for the data. For example, in Example 5.21, a transformation was used to fit the curve $\hat{y} = (13.8038)(10^{-.0192x})$. However, there may be another equation of the form $\hat{y} = a(10^{bx})$ that has a smaller sum of squared residuals for the *original* data than the one we obtained using transformations. Finding the least squares estimates for a and b in an equation of this form is complicated. Fortunately, the curves found using transformations usually provide reasonable predictions of y.

Power Transformations

Frequently, an appropriate transformation will be suggested by the data. One type of transformation that statisticians have found useful for straightening a plot is a

Table 5.6 *Power transformation ladder*

Power	Transformed Value*	Name
3	(Original value)^3	Cube
2	(Original value)^2	Square
1	Original value	No transformation
$\frac{1}{2}$	$\sqrt{\text{Original value}}$	Square root
$\frac{1}{3}$	$\sqrt[3]{\text{Original value}}$	Cube root
0	Log(original value)	Logarithm
-1	1/(original value)	Reciprocal

*Transformed value = (original value)^{power}

power transformation. A power (exponent) is first selected, and each original value is raised to that power to obtain the corresponding transformed value. Table 5.6 displays a "ladder" of the most frequently used power transformations. The power 1 corresponds to no transformation at all. Using the power 0 would transform every value to 1, which is certainly not informative, so statisticians use the logarithmic transformation in its place in the ladder of transformations. Other powers intermediate to or more extreme than those listed can be used, of course, but they are less frequently needed than those on the ladder. Notice that all of the transformations previously presented are included in this ladder.

Figure 5.34 is designed to suggest where on the ladder we should go to find an appropriate transformation. The four curved segments labeled 1, 2, 3, and 4 represent shapes of curved scatter plots that are commonly encountered. Suppose that a scatter plot looks like the curve labeled 1. Then to straighten the plot, we should use a power on x that is up the ladder from the no-transformation row (x^2 or x^3) and/or

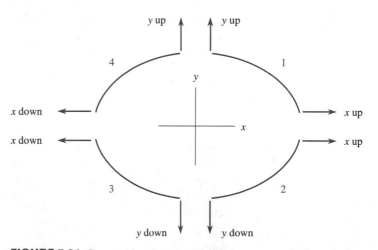

FIGURE 5.34 Scatter plot shapes and where to go on the transformation ladder to straighten the plot

a power on y that is also up the ladder from the power 1. Thus, we might be led to squaring each x value, cubing each y, and plotting the transformed pairs. If the curvature looks like curved segment 2, a power up the ladder from no transformation for x and/or a power down the ladder for y (for example, $\sqrt{y}$ or $\log(y)$) should be used.

Note that the scatter plot for the tortilla chip data (Figure 5.32(a)) has the pattern of segment 3 in Figure 5.34. This suggests going down the ladder of transformations for x and/or for y. We found that transforming the y values in this data set by taking logs worked well, and this is consistent with the suggestion of going down the ladder of transformations for y.

EXAMPLE 5.22

In many parts of the world, a typical diet consists mainly of cereals and grains, and many individuals suffer from a substantial iron deficiency. The article "The Effects of Organic Acids, Phytates, and Polyphenols on the Absorption of Iron from Vegetables" (*British J. Nutrition* (1983): 331–342) reported the data in Table 5.7 on

x = proportion of iron absorbed

and

y = polyphenol content (mg/g)

when a particular vegetable is consumed. The scatter plot of the data in Figure 5.35(a) shows a clear curved pattern, which resembles the curved segment 3 in

Table 5.7 *Original and transformed data for Example 5.22*

Vegetable	x	y	$\sqrt{x}$	$\sqrt{y}$
Wheat germ	.007	6.4	.083666	2.52982
Aubergine	.007	3.0	.083666	1.73205
Butter beans	.012	2.9	.109545	1.70294
Spinach	.014	5.8	.118322	2.40832
Brown lentils	.024	5.0	.154919	2.23607
Beetroot greens	.024	4.3	.154919	2.07364
Green lentils	.032	3.4	.178885	1.84391
Carrot	.096	.7	.309839	.83666
Potato	.115	.2	.339116	.44721
Beetroot	.185	1.5	.430116	1.22474
Pumpkin	.206	.1	.453872	.31623
Tomato	.224	.3	.473286	.54772
Broccoli	.260	.4	.509902	.63246
Cauliflower	.263	.7	.512835	.83666
Cabbage	.320	.1	.565685	.31623
Turnip	.327	.3	.571839	.54772
Sauerkraut	.327	.2	.571839	.44721

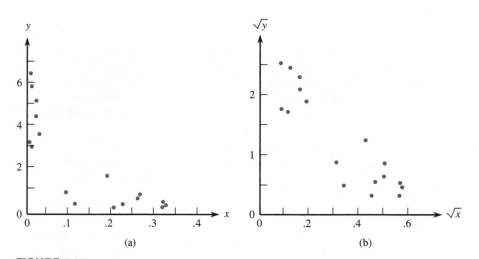

FIGURE 5.35 Scatter plot of data from Example 5.22: (a) Original data; (b) Data transformed by taking square roots

Figure 5.34. This suggest that x and/or y should be transformed by a power transformation down the ladder from 1. The authors of the article applied a square-root transformation to both x and y. The resulting scatter plot in Figure 5.35(b) is reasonably straight.

Using MINITAB to fit a least squares line to the transformed data $(y' = \sqrt{y}$ and $x' = \sqrt{x})$ results in the following output:

Regression Analysis

The regression equation is
sqrt y = 2.45 - 3.72 sqrt x

Predictor	Coef	StDev	T	P
Constant	2.4483	0.1833	13.35	0.000
sqrt x	-3.7247	0.4836	-7.70	0.000

S = 0.3695   R-Sq = 79.8%   R-Sq(adj) = 78.5%

The corresponding least squares line is

$$\hat{y}' = 2.45 - 3.72x'$$

This transformation can be reversed by squaring both sides (to obtain an equation of the form $y = $ some function of x) to obtain

$$\hat{y}'^2 = (2.45 - 3.72x')^2$$

Since $y'^2 = y$ and $x' = \sqrt{x}$, we get

$$\hat{y} = (2.45 - 3.72\sqrt{x})^2$$

Exercises 5.52 – 5.59

5.52 The following data on x = frying time (sec) and y = moisture content (%) appeared in the paper "Thermal and Physical Properties of Tortilla Chips as a Function of Frying Time" (*J. of Food Processing and Preservation* (1995): 175–189).

x	5	10	15	20	25	30	45	60
y	16.3	9.7	8.1	4.2	3.4	2.9	1.9	1.3

a. Construct a scatter plot of the data. Would a straight line provide an effective summary of the relationship?
b. Here are the values of $x' = \log(x)$ and $y' = \log(y)$. Construct a scatter plot of this transformed data and comment on the pattern.

x'	.70	1.00	1.18	1.30	1.40	1.48	1.65	1.78
y'	1.21	.99	.91	.62	.53	.46	.28	.11

c. Based on the accompanying MINITAB output, does the least squares line effectively summarize the relationship between y' and x'?

The regression equation is
logmoist = 2.01 - 1.05 logtime

Predictor	Coef	Stdev	t-ratio	p
Constant	2.01444	0.09166	21.98	0.000
logtime	-1.04920	0.06786	-15.46	0.000

s = 0.06293   R-sq = 97.6%   R-sq(adj) = 97.1%

Analysis of Variance

SOURCE	DF	SS	MS	F	p
Regression	1	0.94680	0.94680	239.06	0.000
Error	6	0.02376	0.00396		
Total	7	0.97057			

d. Use the MINITAB output in part **c** to predict moisture content when frying time is 35 seconds.
e. Do you think that predictions of moisture content using the model in part **c** will be better than those using the model fit in Example 5.20, which used transformed y values but did not transform x? Explain.

5.53 The article "Reduction in Soluble Protein and Chlorophyll Contents in a Few Plants as Indicators of Automobile Exhaust Pollution" (*Int. J. of Environ. Studies* (1983): 239–244) reported the accompanying data on x = distance from a highway (m) and y = lead content of soil at that distance (ppm).

x	.3	1	5	10	15	20
y	62.75	37.51	29.70	20.71	17.65	15.41

x	25	30	40	50	75	100
y	14.15	13.50	12.11	11.40	10.85	10.85

a. Use a statistical computer package to construct scatter plots of y versus x, y versus $\log(x)$, $\log(y)$ versus $\log(x)$, and $1/y$ versus $1/x$.
b. Which transformation considered in part **a** does the best job of producing an approximately linear relationship? Use the selected transformation to predict lead content when distance is 25 m.

5.54 The paper "Aspects of Food Finding by Wintering Bald Eagles" (*The Auk* (1983): 477–484) examined the relationship between the time that eagles spend aerially searching for food (indicated by the percentage of eagles soaring) and relative food availability. The accompanying data is taken from a scatter plot that appeared in this paper. Let x denote salmon availability and y denote the percent of eagles in the air.

x	0	0	.2	.5	.5	1.0
y	28.2	69.0	27.0	38.5	48.4	31.1

x	1.2	1.9	2.6	3.3	4.7	6.5
y	26.9	8.2	4.6	7.4	7.0	6.8

a. Draw a scatter plot for this data set. Would you describe the plot as linear or curvilinear?
b. One possible transformation that might lead to a straighter plot involves taking the square root of both the x and y values. Use Figure 5.34 to explain why this might be a reasonable transformation.
c. Construct a scatter plot using the variables $\sqrt{x}$ and $\sqrt{y}$. Is this scatter plot straighter than that in part **a**?
d. Using Table 5.6, suggest another transformation that might be used to straighten the original plot.

5.55 Data on salmon availability (x) and the percent of eagles in the air (y) is given in the previous exercise.
a. Calculate the correlation coefficient for this data.
b. Since the scatter plot of the original data appeared curved, transforming both the x and y values by taking square roots was suggested. Calculate the correlation coefficient for the variables $\sqrt{x}$ and $\sqrt{y}$. How does this value compare with that of part **a**? Does this indicate that the transformation was successful in straightening the plot?

5.56 Penicillin was administered orally to five horses, and the concentration of penicillin in the blood was determined after five different lengths of time (a different horse was used each time). The accompanying data appeared in the paper "Absorption and Distribution Patterns of Oral Phenoxymethyl Penicillin in the Horse" (*Cornell Veterinarian* (1983): 314–323).

x (Time elapsed, hr)		1	2	3	6	8
y (Penicillin concentration, mg/mL)		1.8	1.0	.5	.1	.1

Construct scatter plots using the following variables. Which transformation, if any, would you recommend?

a. x and y
b. $\sqrt{x}$ and y
c. x and $\sqrt{y}$
d. $\sqrt{x}$ and $\sqrt{y}$
e. x and $\log(y)$ (Values of $\log(y)$ are .26, 0, $-.30$, -1, -1.)

5.57 The paper "Population Pressure and Agricultural Intensity" (*Annals of the Assoc. of Amer. Geog.* (1977): 384–396) reported a positive association between population density and agricultural intensity. The accompanying data consists of measures of population density (x) and agricultural intensity (y) for 18 different subtropical locations.

x	1.0	26.0	1.1	101.0	14.9	134.7
y	9	7	6	50	5	100

x	3.0	5.7	7.6	25.0	143.0	27.5
y	7	14	14	10	50	14

x	103.0	180.0	49.6	140.6	140.0	233.0
y	50	150	10	67	100	100

a. Construct a scatter plot of y versus x. Is the scatter plot compatible with the statement of positive association made in the paper?
b. The scatter plot in part **a** is curved upward like segment 2 in Figure 5.34, suggesting a transformation that is up the ladder for x or down the ladder for y. Try a scatter plot that uses y and x^2. Does this transformation straighten the plot?
c. Draw a scatter plot that uses $\log(y)$ and x. The $\log(y)$ values, given in order corresponding to the y values, are .95, .85, .78, 1.70, .70, 2.00, .85, 1.15, 1.15, 1.00, 1.70, 1.15, 1.70, 2.18, 1.00, 1.83, 2.00, and 2.00. How does this scatter plot compare with that of part **b**?
d. Next consider a scatter plot that uses transformations on both x and y: $\log(y)$ and x^2. Is this effective in straightening the plot? Explain.

5.58 Determining the age of an animal can sometimes be a difficult task. One method of estimating the age of harp seals is based on the width of the pulp canal in the seal's canine teeth. To investigate the relationship between age and the width of the pulp canal, age and canal width were measured for seals of known age. The accompanying data is a portion of a larger data set that appeared in the paper "Validation of Age Estimation in the Harp Seal Using Dentinal Annuli" (*Canadian J. of Fisheries and Aquatic Sci.* (1983): 1430–1441). Let x denote age (years) and y denote canal length (mm).

x	.25	.25	.50	.50	.50	.75	.75	1.00
y	700	675	525	500	400	350	300	300

x	1.00	1.00	1.00	1.00	1.25	1.25	1.50	1.50
y	250	230	150	100	200	100	100	125

x	2.00	2.00	2.50	2.75	3.00	4.00	4.00	5.00
y	60	140	60	50	10	10	10	10

x	5.00	5.00	5.00	6.00	6.00
y	15	10	10	15	10

Construct a scatter plot for this data set. Would you describe the relationship between age and canal length as linear? If not, suggest a transformation that might straighten the plot.

5.59 A frequently encountered problem in crop planting situations involves deciding when to harvest in order to maximize yield. The accompanying data on x = date of harvesting (number of days after flowering) and y = yield (kg/ha) of paddy, a grain farmed in India, appeared in the paper "Determination of Biological Maturity and Effect of Harvesting and Drying Conditions on Milling Quality of Paddy" (*J. of Ag. Eng.* (1975): 353–361). Construct a scatter plot of this data. Can the methodology discussed in this section be used to select a straightening transformation? Why or why not? What kind of a curve might provide a reasonable fit to the plot?

x	16	18	20	22	24	26	28	30
y	2508	2518	3304	3423	3057	3190	3500	3883

x	32	34	36	38	40	42	44	46
y	3823	3646	3708	3333	3517	3241	3103	2776

5.6   Interpreting the Results of Statistical Analyses

Using either a least squares line to summarize a relationship or a correlation coefficient to describe the strength of a linear relationship is common in investigations that focus on more than a single variable. In fact, the methods described in this chapter are among the most widely used of all statistical tools. When numerical bivariate data is analyzed in journal articles and other published sources, it is common to find a scatter plot of the data and a least squares line or a correlation coefficient.

What to Look for in Published Data

Here are a few things to consider when you read an article that includes an analysis of bivariate data:

■ What two variables are being studied? Are they both numerical? Is a distinction made between a dependent variable and an independent variable?

■ Does the article include a scatter plot of the data? If so, does the relationship between the two variables appear to be linear or curved?

■ Does the relationship between the two variables appear to be weak or strong? Is the value of a correlation coefficient reported?

■ If the least squares line is used to summarize the relationship between the dependent and independent variables, is any measure of goodness of fit reported, such as r^2 or s_e? How are such values interpreted, and what do they imply about the usefulness of the least squares line?

■ If a correlation coefficient is reported, is it interpreted properly? Be cautious of interpretations that claim a causal relationship.

The article "Rubbish Regression and the Census Undercount" (*Chance* (1992): 33) describes work done by the Garbage Project at the University of Arizona. Project researchers had analyzed different categories of garbage for a number of households. They were asked by the Census Bureau to see whether any of the garbage data variables were related to household size. They reported the following:

> The weight data for different categories of garbage were plotted on graphs against data on household size, dwelling by dwelling, and the resulting scatter plots were analyzed to see in which categories the weight showed a steady, monotonic rise relative to household size.

They determined that the strongest linear relationship appeared to be that between the amount of plastic discarded and household size. The line used to summarize this relationship was stated to be $y = .2815x$, where y = household size and x = weight (in lb) of plastic during a 5-week collection. Note that the line reported has an intercept of zero. Scientists at the Census Bureau believed that this relationship would extend to entire neighborhoods, and so the amount of plastic discarded by a neighborhood could be measured (rather than having to measure house to house) and then used to approximate the neighborhood size.

An example of the use of r^2 and the correlation coefficient is found in the article "Affective Variables Related to Mathematics Achievement Among High-Risk College Freshmen" (*Psychological Reports* (1991): 399–403). The authors write the following:

> An examination of the Pearson correlations indicated that the two scales, Confidence in Learning Mathematics and Mathematics Anxiety, were highly related, with values ranging from .87 to .91 for the men, women, and for the total group. Such a high relationship indicates that the two scales are measuring essentially the same concept, so for further analysis, one of the two scales could be eliminated.

The correlation coefficients reported (from .87 to .91) indicate a strong positive linear relationship between scores on the two scales. Students who scored high on the Confidence in Learning Mathematics scale tended also to score high on the Mathematics Anxiety scale. (The authors explain that a high score on the Mathematics Anxiety scale corresponds to low anxiety toward mathematics.) We should be cautious of the statement that the two scales are measuring essentially the same concept. Although that interpretation may make sense in this context given what the researchers know about these two scales, it does not follow solely from the fact that the two are highly correlated. (For example, there might be a correlation between number of years of education and income, but it would be hard to argue that these two variables are measuring the same thing!)

The same article also states that Mathematics Anxiety score accounted for 27% of the variability in first-quarter math grades. The value of 27% reported is the value of r^2 converted to a percentage. Although a value of 27% ($r^2 = .27$) may not seem particularly large, it is in fact surprising that the variable *Math Anxiety score* would be able to explain more than one-fourth of the student-to-student variability in first-quarter math grades.

Summary of Key Concepts and Formulas

Term or Formula	Comment
Scatter plot	A picture of bivariate numerical data in which each observation (x, y) is represented as a point located with respect to a horizontal x axis and a vertical y axis.
Pearson's sample correlation coefficient $$r = \frac{\Sigma z_x z_y}{n - 1}$$	A measure of the extent to which sample x and y values are linearly related; $-1 \leq r \leq 1$, so values close to 1 or -1 indicate a strong linear relationship.
Spearman's correlation coefficient r_S	Pearson's r applied to the *ranks* of the x and y values. It will detect both linear and nonlinear relationships and is not as sensitive to outliers as is r.
Principle of least squares	The method used to select a line that summarizes an approximate linear relationship between x and y. The least squares line is the line that minimizes the sum of the squared vertical deviations from the points in the scatter plot.

Term or Formula	Comment
$$b = \frac{\Sigma(x - \bar{x})(y - \bar{y})}{\Sigma(x - \bar{x})^2} = \frac{\Sigma xy - \dfrac{(\Sigma x)(\Sigma y)}{n}}{\Sigma x^2 - \dfrac{(\Sigma x)^2}{n}}$$ $$a = \bar{y} - b\bar{x}$$	The slope and intercept of the least squares line.
Predicted (fitted) values $\hat{y}_1, \ldots, \hat{y}_n$	Obtained by substituting the x value for each observation into the least squares line; $\hat{y}_1 = a + bx_1, \ldots, \hat{y}_n = a + bx_n$
Residuals	Obtained by subtracting each predicted value from the corresponding observed y value: $y_1 - \hat{y}_1, \ldots, y_n - \hat{y}_n$. These are the vertical deviations from the least squares line.
Residual plot	Scatter plot of the (x, residual) pairs. Isolated points or a pattern of points in a residual plot are indicative of potential problems.
Residual (error) sum of squares $\text{SSResid} = \Sigma(y - \hat{y})^2$	The sum of the squared residuals is a measure of y variation that cannot be attributed to an approximate linear relationship (unexplained variation).
Total sum of squares $\text{SSTo} = \Sigma(y - \bar{y})^2$	The sum of squared deviations from the sample mean $\bar{y}$ is a measure of total variation in the observed y values.
Coefficient of determination $r^2 = 1 - \dfrac{\text{SSResid}}{\text{SSTo}}$	The proportion of variation in observed y's that can be attributed to an approximate linear relationship.
Standard deviation about the least squares line, $s_e = \sqrt{\dfrac{\text{SSResid}}{n - 2}}$	The size of a "typical" deviation from the least squares line.
Transformation	A simple function of the x and/or y variable which is then used in a regression.
Power transformation	An exponent, or power, p, is first specified, and then new (transformed) data values are calculated as *transformed value* = (original value)^p. A logarithmic transformation is identified with $p = 0$. When the scatter plot of original data exhibits curvature, a power transformation of x and/or y will often result in a scatter plot that has a linear appearance.

Supplementary Exercises 5.60 – 5.71

5.60 The sample correlation coefficient between annual raises and teaching evaluations for a sample of $n = 353$ college faculty was found to be $r = .11$ ("Determination of Faculty Pay: An Agency Theory Perspective," *Academy of Mgmt. J.* (1992): 921–955).
  a. Interpret this value.
  b. If a straight line were fit to the data using least squares, what proportion of variation in raises could be attributed to the approximate linear relationship between raises and evaluations?

5.61 An accurate assessment of oxygen consumption provides important information for determining energy-expenditure requirements for physically demanding tasks. The paper "Oxygen Consumption During Fire Suppression: Error of Heart Rate Estimation" (*Ergonomics* (1991): 1469–1474) reported on a study in which oxygen consumption (mL/kg/min) during a treadmill test was determined for a sample of ten firefighters. Then oxygen consumption at a comparable heart rate was measured for each of the ten individuals while performing a fire-suppression simulation. This resulted in the following data and scatter plot.

Firefighter	1	2	3	4	5
x = treadmill consumption	51.3	34.1	41.1	36.3	36.5
y = fire-simulation consumption	49.3	29.5	30.6	28.2	28.0

Firefighter	6	7	8	9	10
x = treadmill consumption	35.4	35.4	38.6	40.6	39.5
y = fire-simulation consumption	26.3	33.9	29.4	23.5	31.6

a. Does the scatter plot suggest an approximate linear relationship?

b. The investigators fit a least squares line. The resulting MINITAB output is shown. Predict fire-simulation consumption when treadmill consumption is 40.

The regression equation is
firecon = -11.4 + 1.09 treadcon

Predictor	Coef	Stdev	t-ratio	p
Constant	-11.37	12.46	-0.91	0.388
treadcon	1.0906	0.3181	3.43	0.009

s = 4.70   R-sq = 59.5%   R-sq(adj) = 54.4%

c. How effectively does a straight line summarize the relationship?

d. Delete the observation (51.3, 49.3) and calculate the new equation of the least squares line and the value of r^2. What do you conclude? (*Hint*: For the original data, $\Sigma x = 388.8$, $\Sigma y = 310.3$, $\Sigma x^2 = 15,338.54$, $\Sigma xy = 12,306.58$, and $\Sigma y^2 = 10,072.41$.)

5.62 Silane coupling agents have been used in the rubber industry to improve the performance of fillers in rubber compounds. The accompanying data on y = tensile modulus (in MPa, a measure of silane coupling effectiveness) and x = bound rubber content (%) appeared in the paper "The Effect of the Structure of Sulfur-Containing

Silane Coupling Agents on Their Activity in Silica-Filled SBR" (*Rubber Chem. and Tech.* (1984): 675–685).

x	16.1	31.5	21.5	22.4	20.5	28.4
y	4.41	6.81	5.26	5.99	5.92	6.14

x	30.3	25.6	32.7	29.2	34.7
y	6.84	5.87	7.03	6.89	7.87

$n = 11$ $\Sigma y = 69.03$ $\Sigma x = 292.9$
$\Sigma y^2 = 442.1903$ $\Sigma x^2 = 8141.75$ $\Sigma xy = 1890.200$

a. Construct a scatter plot. Does it look linear?
b. Find the equation of the least squares line.
c. Compute and interpret the value of r^2.

5.63 The relationship between the depth of flooding and the amount of flood damage was examined in the paper "Significance of Location in Computing Flood Damage" (*J. of Water Resources Planning and Mgmt.* (1985): 65–81). The accompanying data on x = depth of flooding (feet above first-floor level) and y = flood damage (as a percent of structure value) was obtained using a sample of flood insurance claims.

x	1	2	3	4	5	6
y	10	14	26	28	29	41

x	7	8	9	10	11	12	13
y	43	44	45	46	47	48	49

a. Obtain the equation of the least squares line.
b. Construct a scatter plot and draw the least squares line on the plot. Does it look as though a straight line provides an adequate description of the relationship between y and x? Explain.
c. Predict flood damage for a structure subjected to 6.5 ft of flooding.
d. Would you use the least squares line to predict flood damage when depth of flooding is 18 ft? Explain.

5.64 An investigation was carried out to study the relationship between speed (ft/sec) and stride rate (number of steps taken/sec) among female marathon runners. Resulting summary quantities included

$n = 11$ $\Sigma (\text{speed}) = 205.4$ $\Sigma (\text{speed})^2 = 3880.08$
$\Sigma (\text{rate}) = 35.16$ $\Sigma (\text{rate})^2 = 112.681$
$\Sigma (\text{speed})(\text{rate}) = 660.130$

a. Calculate the equation of the least squares line that you would use to predict stride rate from speed.
b. Calculate the equation of the least squares line that you would use to predict speed from stride rate.
c. Calculate the coefficient of determination for the "stride rate on speed" regression of part **a** and for the "speed on stride rate" regression of part **b**. How are these related?

5.65 Consider the four (x, y) pairs $(0, 0)$, $(1, 1)$, $(1, -1)$, and $(2, 0)$.

a. What is the value of the sample correlation coefficient r?

b. If a fifth observation is made at the value $x = 6$, find a value of y for which $r > .5$.

c. If a fifth observation is made at the value $x = 6$, find a value of y for which $r < -.5$.

5.66 It is certainly plausible that workers are less likely to quit their jobs when wages are high than when they are low. The paper "Investigating the Causal Relationship Between Quits and Wages: An Exercise in Comparative Dynamics" (*Economic Inquiry* (1986): 61–83) presented the accompanying data on x = average hourly wage and y = quit rate (number of employees per 100 who left jobs during 1986). Each observation is for a different industry.

x	8.20	10.35	6.18	5.37	9.94	9.11	10.59	13.29
y	1.4	.7	2.6	3.4	1.7	1.7	1.0	.5

x	7.99	5.54	7.50	6.43	8.83	10.93	8.80
y	2.0	3.8	2.3	1.9	1.4	1.8	2.0

a. Does the data demonstrate unequivocally that quit rate is determined at least in part by factors other than wages? What does your intuition suggest?

b. Construct a scatter plot of the data. What does the plot suggest about the nature of the relationship?

c. Use the summary quantities $\Sigma x = 129.05$, $\Sigma x^2 = 1178.9601$, $\Sigma y = 28.2$, $\Sigma y^2 = 64.34$, and $\Sigma xy = 218.806$ to obtain the equation of the least squares line.

d. Predict the quit rate for an industry with an average hourly wage of $7.50, and calculate the corresponding residual.

e. What proportion of observed variation in quit rate can be attributed to the linear relationship?

5.67 The paper "Biomechanical Characteristics of the Final Approach Step, Hurdle, and Take-Off of Elite American Springboard Divers" (*J. Human Movement Studies* (1984): 189–212) gave the accompanying data on y = judge's score and x = length of final step (m) for a sample of seven divers performing a forward pike with a single somersault.

y	7.40	9.10	7.20	7.00	7.30	7.30	7.90
x	1.17	1.17	.93	.89	.68	.74	.95

a. Construct a scatter plot.

b. Calculate the slope and intercept of the least squares line. Draw this line on your scatter plot.

c. Calculate and interpret the value of Pearson's sample correlation coefficient.

d. Compute the value of Spearman's rank correlation coefficient, r_S. [For tied scores, assign the av-

erage of the ranks that would have been assigned had they differed slightly; for example, if the values of 7.3 in the score row were slightly different, they would be ranked 4 and 5, so each is assigned rank $(4 + 5)/2 = 4.5$.] How does the value of r_S compare to that of r from part **c**?

5.68 The accompanying data on y = concentration of penicillin-G in pig's blood plasma (units/mL) and x = time (min) from administration of a dose of penicillin (22 mg/kg body weight) appeared in the paper "Calculation of Dosage Regimens of Antimicrobial Drugs for Surgical Prophylaxis" (*J. Amer. Vet. Med. Assoc.* (1984): 1083–1087).

x	5	15	45	90	180	240	360	480	1440
y	32.6	43.3	23.1	16.7	5.7	6.4	9.2	.4	.2

a. Construct a scatter plot for this data.

b. Using the ladder of transformations of Section 5.5, suggest a transformation that might straighten the plot. Give reasons for your choice of transformation.

5.69 The accompanying data resulted from an experiment in which x was the amount of catalyst added to accelerate a chemical reaction and y was the resulting reaction time.

x	1	2	3	4	5
y	49	46	41	34	25

a. Calculate r. Does the value of r suggest a strong linear relationship?

b. Construct a scatter plot. From the plot, does the word *linear* really provide the most effective description of the relationship between x and y? Explain.

5.70 The least squares intercept a and slope b come from solving a system of two linear equations called the **normal equations**:

$$na + (\Sigma x)b = \Sigma y$$
$$(\Sigma x)a + (\Sigma x^2)b = \Sigma xy$$

a. Verify by direct substitution that

$$a = \bar{y} - b\bar{x} = \frac{\Sigma y}{n} - b\frac{\Sigma x}{n}$$

$$b = \frac{\Sigma xy - \dfrac{(\Sigma x)(\Sigma y)}{n}}{\Sigma x^2 - \dfrac{(\Sigma x)^2}{n}}$$

is the solution to this system of equations.

b. Show that the first normal equation implies that the sum of the residuals from the least squares line is zero — that is, that $\Sigma (y - \hat{y}) = 0$. (*Hint:* Recall that $\hat{y} = a + bx$.)

5.71 **a.** Show that

SSResid = SSTo − b(numerator of b)

(*Hint*: Use the computational formula for SSResid and the fact that $a = \bar{y} - b\bar{x}$.)

b. Argue that the expression for SSResid in part **a** implies that SSResid ≤ SSTo. (*Hint*: Both b and the numerator of b have the same sign.)

References

Chatterjee, Samprit and Bertram Price. *Regression Analysis by Example,* 2nd edition. New York, Wiley Inter-Science, 1991.

Hamilton, Lawrence C. *Regression with Graphics: A Second Course in Applied Statistics.* Belmont, CA, Duxbury Press, 1992.

Neter, John, William Wasserman, and Michael Kutner. *Applied Linear Statistical Models,* 4th edition. New York: McGraw Hill, 1996. (The first half of this book gives a comprehensive treatment of regression analysis without overindulging in mathematical development; a highly recommended reference.)

6

Probability

INTRODUCTION

We make decisions based on uncertainty every day. Should you buy an extended warranty for your new CD player? It depends on the likelihood that it will malfunction during the warranty period. Should you put off taking a required course until the last term before graduation? It depends on the likelihood that all sections will be full before it is your turn to register or that the course won't be offered during that term. Should you allow 45 minutes to get to your 8 A.M. class, or is 35 minutes enough? From experience, you may know that most mornings you can drive to campus and find a parking place in 25 minutes or less. Most of the time, you can walk from your parking space to class in 10 minutes or less. But how often will one of these two activities take longer than you expect? How often will both take longer? When it takes longer to drive to campus, is it more likely that it will take you longer to walk to class? Some situations have more serious consequences: If an artificial heart has four key systems, how likely is each one to fail? How likely is it that at least one will fail? If a satellite has a backup solar power system, how likely is it that both the main and the backup parts will fail?

We can answer questions like these using the ideas and methods of probability, the systematic study of uncertainty. From its roots in the analysis of games of chance, probability has evolved into a science that enables us to make important decisions with confidence. This chapter introduces the basic rules of probability that are most widely used in statistics, and it explains two ways of estimating probabilities when it is difficult to derive them analytically.

6.1   Interpreting Probabilities and Basic Probability Rules

In many situations, it is uncertain what outcome will occur. For example, when a ticketed passenger shows up at the airport, she may be denied a seat on the flight as a result of overbooking by the airline. There are two possible outcomes of interest for the passenger: (1) she is able to take the flight or (2) she is denied a seat on the plane and must take a later flight. Before she arrives at the airport, there is uncertainty about which outcome will occur. Based on past experience with this particular flight, the passenger may know that one outcome is more likely than the other. She may believe that the chance of being denied a seat is quite small; she may not be overly concerned about this possibility. Although this outcome is possible, she views it as unlikely. Assigning a probability to such an outcome is an attempt to quantify what is meant by "likely" or "unlikely." We do this by using a number between 0 and 1 to indicate the likelihood of occurrence of some outcome.

There is more than one way to interpret such numbers. One is a subjective interpretation. A probability is interpreted as a personal measure of the strength of belief that the outcome will occur. A probability of 1 represents a belief that the outcome will certainly occur. A probability of 0 then represents a belief that the outcome will certainly not occur — that it is impossible. Other probabilities are intermediate to these two extremes. This interpretation is common in ordinary speech. We say, for example, "There's about a 50–50 chance," or "My chances are nil." In the airline flight example, suppose that the passenger reported her subjective assessment of the probability of being denied a seat to be .01. Since this probability is close to 0, she believes it is very unlikely that she would be denied a seat. The subjective interpretation, however, presents some difficulties. For one thing, different people may assign different probabilities to the same outcome, since each person could have a different subjective belief.

Wherever possible, we will use instead the objective *relative frequency* interpretation of probability. A probability is the *long-run proportion* of the time that an outcome will occur, given many repetitions under identical circumstances. A probability of 1 corresponds to an outcome that occurs 100% of the time — that is, a certain outcome. A probability of 0 corresponds to an outcome that occurs 0% of the time — an impossible outcome.

Relative Frequency Interpretation of Probability

A **probability** is a number between 0 and 1 that reflects the likelihood of occurrence of some outcome.

The **probability of an outcome,** denoted by P**(outcome),** is interpreted as the long-run proportion of the time that the outcome will occur when the experiment is performed repeatedly under identical conditions.

To illustrate the relative frequency interpretation of probability, consider the following situation. A package delivery service promises two-day delivery between two cities in California but is often able to deliver packages in just one day. Suppose the company reports that there is a 50–50 chance that a package will arrive in one day. Alternatively, they might report that the probability of next-day delivery is .5, implying that in the long run, 50% of all packages arrive in one day.

Suppose we track the delivery of packages shipped with this company. With each new package shipped, we could compute the relative frequency of packages shipped so far that arrived in one day:

$$\frac{\text{number of packages that arrived in one day}}{\text{total number of packages shipped}}$$

The results for the first ten packages might be as follows:

Package number	1	2	3	4	5	6	7	8	9	10
Arrived next day	N	Y	Y	Y	N	N	Y	Y	N	N
Relative frequency delivered next day	0	.5	.667	.75	.6	.5	.571	.625	.556	.5

Figure 6.1 illustrates how the relative frequency of packages arriving in one day fluctuates during a sample sequence of 50 shipments. As the number of packages in the sequence increases, the relative frequency does not continue to fluctuate wildly, but instead stabilizes and approaches some fixed number, called the *limiting*

FIGURE 6.1 The fluctuation of relative frequency

value. This limiting value is the true probability. Figure 6.2 illustrates this process of stabilization for a sample sequence of 1000 shipments.

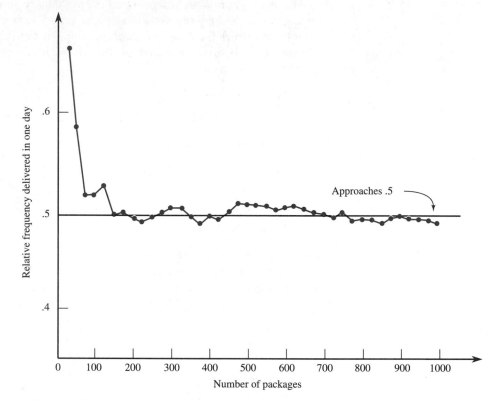

FIGURE 6.2 The stabilization of relative frequency

The stabilization of the relative frequency of occurrence illustrated in Figure 6.2 is not unique to this particular example. The general phenomenon of stabilization makes the relative frequency interpretation of probabilities possible.

Some Basic Properties

The relative frequency interpretation of probability makes it easy to understand the following basic properties of probability.

1. *The probability of any outcome is a number between 0 and 1.* A relative frequency, which is the number of times the outcome occurs divided by the total number of repetitions, cannot be less than 0 (you cannot have a negative number of occurrences) or greater than 1 (the outcome cannot occur more often than the total number of repetitions).

2. *If outcomes cannot occur simultaneously, the probability that any one of them will occur is the sum of their outcome probabilities.* For example, a hotel near Disney World offers three different rental options to its guests. Package A includes hotel room only; package B includes hotel room and meals; and package C includes hotel room, meals, and admission to Disney World. From past

experience, the hotel knows that about 30% of those who stay at the hotel choose package A (room only) and about 25% choose package B (room and meals). Interpreting these percentages, which are really long-run relative frequencies, as probabilities, we can say that

P(next person calling to make reservations will choose package A) = .30

and

P(next person calling to make reservations will choose package B) = .25

Since no one can choose more than one package for a single visit, the probability that the next person calling for a reservation will choose either package A or package B is

P(package A *or* package B) = .30 + .25 = .55

3. *The probability that an outcome will not occur is equal to* 1 *minus the probability that the outcome will occur.* By this property, the probability that the next person calling the hotel for a reservation will not choose either package A or package B is

P(*not* (package A *or* package B)) = 1 − P(package A *or* package B)
$$= 1 - .55 = .45$$

Since there are only three packages available, if the next reservation is not for package A or B, it must be for package C. Thus, we have used this property to calculate the probability that the next person calling for a reservation chooses package C.

Remember that, in probability, 1 represents an outcome that is certain — one that will occur 100% of the time. At this hotel, it is certain that a reservation will be for one of the three packages, since these are the only options available. So

P(package A *or* B *or* C) = .30 + .25 + .45 = 1

Similarly, it is certain that any event either will or will not occur. Thus,

P(package A *or* B) + P(*not* (package A *or* B)) = .55 + .45 = 1

Independence

Suppose that the incidence rate for a particular disease in a certain population is known to be 1 in 1000. Then the probability that a randomly selected individual from this population has the disease is .001. A diagnostic test for the disease is given to the selected individual, and the test result is positive. However, suppose that the diagnostic test is not infallible; it returns a false positive about 10% of the time. That is, about 90% of those without the disease get a correct (negative) response, but the other 10% of people without the disease incorrectly test positive. When we learn that the outcome *positive test result* has occurred, we obviously want to revise the probability that the selected individual has the disease upward from .001. Knowing that one outcome has occurred (the selected person has a positive test result) changes the probability of another outcome (the selected person has the disease).

As another example, consider a university's course registration system, which consists of 12 priority groups. Overall, only 5% of all students receive all requested classes, but 75% of those in the first priority group receive all requested classes. Interpreting these figures as probabilities, we say that the probability that a randomly selected student at this university receives all requested classes is .05. However, if we know that the selected student is in the first priority group, we revise the probability that the selected student received all requested classes to .75. Knowing that the outcome *selected person is in the first priority group* has occurred changes the probability of the outcome *selected person received all requested classes.* These two outcomes are said to be **dependent.**

It is often the case, however, that the likelihood of one outcome is not affected by the occurrence of another outcome. For example, suppose you purchase a computer system with a separate monitor and keyboard. Two possible outcomes of interest are

Outcome 1:   The monitor needs service while under warranty.

Outcome 2:   The keyboard needs service while under warranty.

Because the two components operate independently of one another, learning that the monitor has needed warranty service should not affect our assessment of the likelihood of the keyboard needing repair. If we know that 1% of all keyboards need repair while under warranty, we say that the probability that a keyboard needs warranty service is .01. Knowing that the monitor has needed warranty service would not affect this probability. We say that *monitor failure* (outcome 1) and *keyboard failure* (outcome 2) are **independent** outcomes.

Definition

Independent outcomes: Two outcomes are said to be **independent** if the chance that one outcome occurs is not affected by knowledge of whether the other has occurred. If there are more than two outcomes under consideration, they are independent if knowledge that some of the outcomes have occurred does not change the probabilities that any of the other outcomes occur.

Dependent outcomes: If the occurrence of one outcome changes the probability that the other outcome occurs, the outcomes are **dependent.**

In the previous examples, the outcomes *has disease* and *tests positive* are dependent; the outcomes *receives all requested classes* and *is in first priority group* are dependent; but the outcomes *monitor needs warranty service* and *keyboard needs warranty service* are independent.

A Multiplication Rule for Independent Outcomes

An individual who purchases a computer system might wonder how likely it is that *both* the monitor and the keyboard will need service while under warranty. A student who must take a chemistry or a physics course to fulfill a science requirement might be concerned about the chance that both are full. In each of these cases, interest is centered on the probability that two different outcomes occur together. In the case of independent events, a simple rule relates the individual outcome probabilities to the probability that the outcomes occur together.

The Multiplication Rule for Independent Outcomes

If two outcomes are independent, the probability that *both* outcomes occur is the product of the individual outcome probabilities. Denoting the outcomes as *A* and *B*,

$$P(A \ and \ B) = P(A) \cdot P(B)$$

More generally, if there are *k* independent outcomes, the probability that all of the outcomes occur is simply the product of all of the individual outcome probabilities.

EXAMPLE 6.1

The Diablo Canyon nuclear power plant in Avila Beach, California, has a warning system that includes a network of sirens in the vicinity of the plant. Sirens are located approximately $\frac{1}{2}$ mile from each other. When the system is tested, individual sirens sometimes fail. The sirens operate independently of one another. That is, knowing that a particular siren has failed does not change the probability that any other siren fails.

Imagine that you live near Diablo Canyon (as do the authors of this book) and that there are two sirens that can be heard from your home. We will call these siren 1 and siren 2. You might be concerned about the probability that *both* siren 1 *and* siren 2 fail. Suppose that when the siren system is activated, about 5% of the individual sirens fail. Then

$$P(\text{siren 1 fails}) = .05 \qquad P(\text{siren 2 fails}) = .05$$

and the two outcomes *siren 1 fails* and *siren 2 fails* are independent. Using the multiplication rule for independent outcomes,

$$P(\text{siren 1 fails } and \text{ siren 2 fails}) = P(\text{siren 1 fails}) \cdot P(\text{siren 2 fails}) = (.05) \cdot (.05) = .0025$$

Even though the probability that any individual siren will fail is .05, the probability that two sirens will both fail is much smaller. This would happen in the long run only about 25 times in 10,000 times that the system is activated.

In Example 6.1, the two outcomes *siren 1 fails* and *siren 2 fails* are independent outcomes, so using the multiplication rule for independent outcomes is justified. It is not so easy to calculate the probability that both outcomes occur when two outcomes are dependent, and we won't go into the details here. Be careful to use this rule only when outcomes are independent!

EXAMPLE 6.2

DNA testing has become very prominent in the arsenal of criminal detection techniques. It illustrates a somewhat controversial application of the multiplication rule for independent outcomes. Let's focus on three different characteristics (such as blue eye color or blood type B), each of which might or might not occur in a given DNA specimen. Define the following three outcomes:

Outcome 1: The first characteristic occurs in the specimen.

Outcome 2: The second characteristic occurs in the specimen.

Outcome 3: The third characteristic occurs in the specimen.

Suppose that the long-run frequency of occurrence is 1 in 10 people for the first characteristic, 1 in 20 for the second, and 1 in 5 for the third. *Assuming independence of the three characteristics,* we calculate the probability that all three characteristics appear in the specimen (all three outcomes occur together) to be

$$P(1\text{st } and \text{ 2nd } and \text{ 3rd all occur}) = (.10)(.05)(.20) = .001$$

That is, in the long run, only 1 in every 1000 individuals will yield DNA specimens with all three characteristics. For more than three characteristics, the probability that all are present would be very small. So if an accused individual has all characteristics present in a DNA specimen found at the scene of a crime, it is extremely unlikely that another person would have such a genetic profile.

The assumption of independence in this situation makes computing probabilities in this manner controversial. Suppose, for example, that the three characteristics considered above had been as follows:

Outcome 1: The gene for blue eyes occurs in the DNA specimen.

Outcome 2: The gene for blond hair occurs in the DNA specimen.

Outcome 3: The gene for fair skin occurs in the DNA specimen.

Is it reasonable to believe that knowing that outcome 2 (gene for blond hair) has occurred would not affect your assessment of the probability of outcome 1 (gene for blue eyes)? If these outcomes are in fact dependent, we are not justified in using the multiplication rule for independent outcomes to compute the probability that all three outcomes occur together.

Using Probability Rules

The probability rules introduced so far are summarized in the accompanying box.

Probability Rules

Addition Rule for Outcomes That Cannot Occur at the Same Time
$$P(\text{outcome 1 } or \text{ outcome 2}) = P(\text{outcome 1}) + P(\text{outcome 2})$$

Complement Rule
$$P(not \text{ outcome}) = 1 - P(\text{outcome})$$

Multiplication Rule for Independent Outcomes
$$P(\text{outcome 1 } and \text{ outcome 2}) = P(\text{outcome 1}) \cdot P(\text{outcome 2})$$

The chapter introduction posed several questions that can be addressed by using these probability rules. These questions are considered in the examples that follow.

EXAMPLE 6.3

A satellite has both a main and a backup solar power system, and these systems function independently of one another. (It is common to design such redundancy into products to increase their reliability.) Suppose that the probability of failure during the 10-year lifetime of the satellite is .05 for the main power system and .08 for the backup system. What is the probability that both systems will fail? Since whether one of these systems functions properly has no effect on whether the other one does, it is reasonable to assume that

Outcome 1:   Main system fails

and

Outcome 2:   Backup system fails

are independent outcomes. It is then appropriate to use the multiplication rule for independent outcomes to compute

$$P(\text{main system fails } and \text{ backup system fails}) = P(\text{main system fails}) \cdot P(\text{backup system fails})$$

Multiply because outcomes are independent.
$$= (.05) \cdot (.08) = .004$$

The probability that the satellite has at least one workable power system is, using the complement rule,

$$P(not \text{ (main system fails } and \text{ backup system fails)}) = 1 - P(\text{main system fails } and \text{ backup fails})$$
$$= 1 - .004 = .996$$

EXAMPLE 6.4

A certain type of artificial heart has four independent, critical components. Failure of any of these four components is a serious problem. Suppose that 5-year failure rates (expressed as the proportion that fail within 5 years) for these components are known to be:

Component 1:   .01   Component 2:   .06

Component 3:   .04   Component 4:   .02

What is the probability that an artificial heart functions for 5 years? For the heart to function for 5 years, all four components must not fail during that time. Let's define the following outcomes:

Outcome 1:   Component 1 does not fail in the first 5 years.

Outcome 2:   Component 2 does not fail in the first 5 years.

Outcome 3:   Component 3 does not fail in the first 5 years.

Outcome 4:   Component 4 does not fail in the first 5 years.

These outcomes are independent (since the components function independently of one another), so

$$P(\text{no components fail}) = P(1 \text{ does not fail } and\ 2 \text{ does not fail } and\ 3 \text{ does not fail } and\ 4 \text{ does not fail})$$
$$= P(1 \text{ does not fail}) \cdot P(2 \text{ does not fail}) \cdot P(3 \text{ does not fail}) \cdot P(4 \text{ does not fail})$$

To compute $P(\text{component 1 does not fail})$, we use the complement rule:

$$P(\text{component 1 does not fail}) = 1 - P(\text{component 1 does fail}) = 1 - .01 = .99$$

The corresponding probabilities for the other three components are computed in a similar fashion. Then the desired probability is

$$P(\text{no components fail}) = (.99)(.94)(.96)(.98) = .8755$$

This probability, interpreted as a long-run relative frequency, tells us that in the long run, 87.55% of these artificial hearts will function for 5 years with no failures of critical components.

Exercises 6.1 – 6.13

6.1   An article in the *New York Times* (March 2, 1994) reported that people who suffer cardiac arrest in New York City have only a 1 in 100 chance of survival. Using probability notation, an equivalent statement would be

$$P(\text{survival}) = .01$$

for people who suffer a cardiac arrest in New York City. (The article attributed this poor survival rate to factors common in large cities: traffic congestion and the difficulty of finding victims in large buildings. Similar studies in smaller cities showed higher survival rates.)
a. Give a relative frequency interpretation of the given probability.
b. The research that was the basis for the *New York Times* article was a study of 2329 consecutive cardiac arrests in New York City. To justify the "1 in 100 chance of survival" statement, how many of the 2329 cardiac arrest sufferers do you think survived? Explain.

6.2   Many fire stations handle emergency calls for medical assistance as well as those requesting firefighting equipment. A particular station says that the probability that an incoming call is for medical assistance is .85. This can be expressed as

$$P(\text{call is for medical assistance}) = .85$$

a. Give a relative frequency interpretation of the given probability.
b. What is the probability that a call is not for medical assistance?
c. Assuming that successive calls are independent of one another (that is, knowing that one call is for medi-

cal assistance doesn't influence our assessment of the probability that the next call will be for medical assistance), calculate the probability that two successive calls will both be for medical assistance.
d. Still assuming independence, calculate the probability that for two successive calls, the first is for medical assistance and the second is not for medical assistance.
e. Still assuming independence, calculate the probability that exactly one of the next two calls will be for medical assistance. (*Hint*: There are two different possibilities that you should consider. The one call for medical assistance might be the first call, or it might be the second call.)
f. Do you think it is reasonable to assume that the requests made in successive calls are independent?

6.3   The Associated Press (*San Luis Obispo Telegram-Tribune,* Aug. 23, 1995) reported on the results of mass screening of school children for tuberculosis (TB). It was reported that for Santa Clara County, California, the proportion of all kindergartners tested who were found to have TB was .0006. The corresponding proportion for recent immigrants (thought to be a high-risk group) was .0075. Suppose that a Santa Clara County kindergartner is to be selected at random. Are the outcomes *selected student is a recent immigrant* and *selected student has TB* independent or dependent outcomes? Justify your answer using the given information.

6.4   The article "Men, Women at Odds on Gun Control" (*Cedar Rapids Gazette,* Sept. 8, 1999) includes the following statement:

The survey found that 56 percent of American adults favored stricter gun control laws. Sixty-six percent of women favored the tougher laws, compared with 45 percent of men.

These figures are based on a large telephone survey conducted by Associated Press Polls. If an adult is selected at random, are the outcomes *selected adult is female* and *selected adult favors stricter gun control* independent or dependent outcomes? Explain.

6.5 The Australian newspaper *The Mercury* (May 30, 1995) reported that, based on a survey of 600 reformed and current smokers, 11.3% of those who had attempted to quit smoking in the previous two years had used a nicotine aid (such as a nicotine patch). It also reported that 62% of those who quit smoking without a nicotine aid began smoking again within two weeks and 60% of those who used a nicotine aid began smoking again within two weeks. If a smoker who is trying to quit smoking is selected at random, are the outcomes *selected smoker who is trying to quit uses a nicotine aid* and *selected smoker who has attempted to quit begins smoking again within two weeks* independent or dependent outcomes? Justify your answer using the given information.

6.6 In a small city, approximately 15% of those eligible are called for jury duty in any one calendar year. People are selected for jury duty at random from those eligible, and the same individual can't be called more than once in the same year. What is the probability that an eligible person in this city is selected two years in a row? Three years in a row?

6.7 Jeanie is a bit forgetful, and if she doesn't make a "to do" list, the probability that she forgets something she is supposed to do is .1. Tomorrow she intends to run three errands, and she fails to write them on her list.
  a. What is the probability that Jeanie forgets all three errands? What assumptions did you make in order to calculate this probability?
  b. What is the probability that Jeanie remembers at least one of the three errands?
  c. What is the probability that Jeanie remembers the first errand but not the second or third?

6.8 Approximately 30% of the calls to an airline reservation phone line result in a reservation being made.
  a. Suppose that an operator handles 10 calls. What is the probability that none of the 10 results in a reservation?
  b. What assumption did you make in order to calculate the probability in part **a**?
  c. What is the probability that at least one call results in a reservation being made?

6.9 Of the 10,000 students at a certain university, 7000 have Visa cards, 6000 have MasterCards, and 5000 have both. Suppose that a student is randomly selected.
  a. What is the probability that the selected student has a Visa card?
  b. What is the probability that the selected student has both cards?
  c. Suppose you learn that the selected individual has a Visa card (was one of the 7000 with such a card). Now what is the probability that this student has both cards?
  d. Are the outcomes *has a Visa card* and *has a Master-Card* independent? Explain.
  e. Answer the question posed in part **d** if only 4200 of the students have both cards.

6.10 The article "Baseball: Pitching No-Hitters" (*Chance,* Summer 1994: 24–30) gives information on the number of hits per team per game for all nine-inning major league games played between 1989 and 1993. Each game resulted in two observations, one for each team. No distinction was made between the home and the visiting team. The data is summarized in the accompanying table.

Hits per team per game	0	1	2	3	4
Number of observations	20	72	209	527	1048
Hits per team per game	5	6	7	8	9
Number of observations	1457	1988	2256	2403	2256
Hits per team per game	10	11	12	13	14
Number of observations	1967	1509	1230	843	569
Hits per team per game	15	>15			
Number of observations	393	633			

  a. If one of these games is selected at random, what is the probability that the visiting team got fewer than 3 hits?
  b. What is the probability that the home team got more than 13 hits?
  c. Assume that the following outcomes are independent:

  Outcome 1: Home team got 10 or more hits.
  Outcome 2: Visiting team got 10 or more hits.

What is the probability that both teams got 10 or more hits?
  d. Calculation of the probability in part **c** required that we assume independence of outcomes 1 and 2. If the

outcomes are independent, knowing that one team had 10 or more hits would not change the probability that the other team had 10 or more hits. Do you think that the independence assumption is reasonable? Explain.

6.11 This case study is reported in the article "Parking Tickets and Missing Women," which appears in the book *Statistics: A Guide to the Unknown,* Judith Tanur, ed. (see Chapter 1 references). In a Swedish trial on a charge of overtime parking, a police officer testified that he had noted the position of the two air valves on the tires of a parked car: To the closest hour, one was at the one o'clock position and the other was at the six o'clock position. After the allowable time for parking in that zone had passed, the policeman returned, noted that the valves were in the same position, and ticketed the car. The owner of the car claimed that he had left the parking place in time and had returned later. The valves just happened by chance to be in the same positions. An "expert" witness computed the probability of this occurring as $(1/12)(1/12) = 1/144$.

   a. What reasoning did the expert use to arrive at the probability of $1/144$?

   b. Can you spot the error in the reasoning that leads to the stated probability of $1/144$? What effect does this error have on the probability of occurrence? Do you think that $1/144$ is larger or smaller than the correct probability of occurrence?

6.12 Three friends (A, B, and C) will participate in a round-robin tournament in which each one plays both of the others. Suppose that $P(\text{A beats B}) = .7$, $P(\text{A beats C}) = .8$, $P(\text{B beats C}) = .6$, and that the outcomes of the three matches are independent of one another.

   a. What is the probability that A wins both her matches and B beats C?

   b. What is the probability that A wins both her matches?

   c. What is the probability that A loses both her matches?

   d. What is the probability that each person wins one match? (*Hint*: There are two different ways for this to happen. Calculate the probability of each separately, and then add.)

6.13 Consider a system consisting of four components, as pictured in the accompanying diagram. Components 1 and 2 form a series subsystem, as do components 3 and 4. The two subsystems are connected in parallel. Suppose $P(1 \text{ works}) = .9$, $P(2 \text{ works}) = .9$, $P(3 \text{ works}) = .9$, and $P(4 \text{ works}) = .9$, and that these four outcomes are independent (the four components work independently of one another).

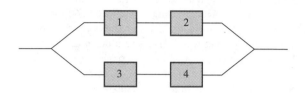

   a. The 1–2 subsystem works only if both components work. What is the probability of this happening?

   b. What is the probability that the 1–2 subsystem doesn't work? That the 3–4 subsystem doesn't work?

   c. The system won't work if the 1–2 subsystem doesn't work and the 3–4 subsystem also doesn't work. What is the probability that the system won't work? That it will work?

   d. How would the probability of the system working change if a 5–6 subsystem were added in parallel with the other two subsystems?

   e. How would the probability that the system works change if there were three components in series in each of the two subsystems?

6.2   Probability as a Basis for Making Decisions

The concepts of probability play a critical role in developing statistical methods that allow us to draw conclusions based on available information, as we see in the following two examples.

EXAMPLE 6.5   Table 6.1 shows the proportions of the student body who fall in various age–gender combinations at a university. These numbers can be interpreted as probabilities if

Table 6.1 *Age and gender distribution*

	Age					
	Under 17	**17–20**	**21–24**	**25–30**	**31–39**	**40 and over**
Male	.006	.15	.16	.08	.04	.01
Female	.004	.18	.14	.10	.04	.09

we think of selecting a student at random from the student body. For example, the probability (long-run proportion of the time) that a male age 21–24 will be selected is .16.

Suppose that you are told that a 43-year-old student from this university is waiting to meet you. You are asked to decide whether the student is male or female. How would you respond? What if the student had been 27 years old? What about 33 years old? Are you equally confident in all three of your choices?

A reasonable response to these questions could be based on the probability information in Table 6.1. We would decide that the 43-year-old student was female. We cannot be certain that this is correct, but we can see that a male is much less likely in the 40-and-over age group than a female. We would also decide that the 27-year-old was female. However, we would be less confident in our conclusion than we were for the 43-year-old student. For the age group 30–39, males and females constitute the same proportion of the student body, so we would think it equally likely that a 33-year-old student would be male or female. We could decide in favor of male (or female), but with little confidence in our conclusion; in other words, there is a good chance of being incorrect.

EXAMPLE 6.6   A professor planning to give a quiz that consists of 20 true–false questions is interested in knowing how someone who answers by guessing will do on such a test. To investigate, he asks the 500 students in his introductory psychology course to write the numbers from 1 to 20 on a piece of paper and then to arbitrarily write T or F next to each number. The students are forced to guess at the answer to each question, since they are not even told what the questions are. These answer sheets are then collected and graded using the key for the quiz. The results are summarized in Table 6.2 on page 212.

Since probabilities are long-run proportions, an entry in the right-hand column of Table 6.2 can be considered as an estimate of the probability of correctly guessing a specific number of responses. For example, a proportion of .122 (or 12.2%) of the 500 students got 12 of the 20 correct when guessing. We then estimate the long-run proportion of guessers who would get 12 correct to be .122; we say that the probability that a student who is guessing will get 12 correct is (approximately) .122.

Table 6.2 *Quiz "guessing" distribution*

Number of Correct Responses	Number of Students	Proportion of Students
0	0	.000
1	0	.000
2	1	.002
3	1	.002
4	2	.004
5	8	.016
6	18	.036
7	37	.074
8	58	.116
9	81	.162
10	88	.176
11	79	.158
12	61	.122
13	39	.078
14	18	.036
15	7	.014
16	1	.002
17	1	.002
18	0	.000
19	0	.000
20	0	.000

Let's use the information in Table 6.2 to answer the following questions.

1. Would you be surprised if someone who is guessing on a 20-question true–false quiz were to get only 3 correct? The approximate probability of a guesser getting 3 correct is .002. This means that, in the long run, only about 2 in 1000 guessers would score exactly 3 correct. This would be an unlikely outcome, and we would consider its occurrence to be surprising.

2. If a score of 15 or more correct is required to receive a passing grade on the quiz, is it likely that someone who is guessing will be able to pass? The long-run proportion of guessers who would pass is the sum of the proportions for all of the passing scores (15, 16, 17, 18, 19, and 20). Thus,

    probability of passing ≈ .014 + .002 + .002 + .000 + .000 + .000 = .018

It would be unlikely that a student who is guessing would be able to pass.

3. The professor actually gives the quiz, and a student scores 16 correct. Do you think that the student was just guessing? Let's begin by assuming that the stu-

dent was guessing and determine whether a score as high as 16 would be a likely or an unlikely occurrence. Table 6.2 tells us that the approximate probability of getting a score at least as high as this student's score is

probability of scoring 16 or higher $\approx$ .002 + .002 + .000 + .000 + .000 = .004

That is, in the long run, only about 4 times in 1000 would a guesser score 16 or higher. This would be a very rare outcome. There are two possible explanations for the observed score: (1) the student was guessing and was really lucky, and (2) the student was not just guessing. Given that the first explanation is very unlikely, a more plausible choice would be the second explanation. We would conclude that the student was not just guessing at the answers. Although we cannot be certain that we are correct in this conclusion, the evidence is very compelling.

4. What score on the quiz would it take to convince you that a student was not just guessing? We would be convinced that a student was not just guessing if his or her score was high enough that it was unlikely that a guesser would have been able to do as well. Consider the following approximate probabilities (computed from the entries in Table 6.2):

Score	Approximate Probability
20	.000
19 or better	.000 + .000 = .000
18 or better	.000 + .000 + .000 = .000
17 or better	.002 + .000 + .000 + .000 = .002
16 or better	.002 + .002 + .000 + .000 + .000 = .004
15 or better	.014 + .002 + .002 + .000 + .000 + .000 = .018
14 or better	.036 + .014 + .002 + .002 + .000 + .000 + .000 = .054
13 or better	.078 + .036 + .014 + .002 + .002 + .000 + .000 + .000 = .132

We might say that a score of 14 or higher would be reasonable evidence that someone is not guessing, since the approximate probability that a guesser would score this high is only .054. Of course, if we conclude that a student is not guessing based on a quiz score of 14 or higher, there is a risk that we are incorrect (about 1 in 20 guessers would score this high by chance). About 13.2% of the time, a guesser will score 13 or more correct. This would happen by chance often enough that most people would not rule out the student's being a guesser.

Examples 6.5 and 6.6 show how probability information can be used to make a decision. This is a primary goal of statistical inference. Later chapters look more formally at the problem of drawing a conclusion based on available, but often incomplete, information and then assessing the reliability of such a conclusion.

Exercises 6.14 – 6.15

6.14 Researchers at UCLA were interested in whether working mothers were more likely to suffer workplace injuries than women without children. They studied 1400 working women, and a summary of their findings was reported in the *San Luis Obispo Telegram-Tribune* (Feb. 28, 1995). The information in the accompanying table is consistent with summary values reported in the article.

	No Children	Children Under 6	Children, but None Under 6	Total
Injured on the Job in 1989	32	68	56	156
Not Injured on the Job in 1989	368	232	644	1244
Total	400	300	700	1400

The researchers drew the following conclusion: Women with children younger than age 6 are much more likely to be injured on the job than childless women or mothers with older children. Provide a justification for the researchers' conclusion. Use the information in the table to calculate estimates of any probabilities that are relevant to your justification.

6.15 Students at a particular university use a telephone registration system to select their courses for the next term. There are four different priority groups, with students in group 1 registering first, followed by those in group 2, and so on. Suppose that the university provided the accompanying information on registration for the fall semester. The entries in the table represent the proportion of students falling into each of the 20 priority–unit combinations.

Number of Units Secured During First Call to Registration System

Priority Group	0–3	4–6	7–9	10–12	More Than 12
1	.01	.01	.06	.10	.07
2	.02	.03	.06	.09	.05
3	.04	.06	.06	.06	.03
4	.04	.08	.07	.05	.01

a. What proportion of students at this university got 10 or more units during the first call?
b. Suppose that a student reports receiving 11 units during the first call. Is it more likely that he or she is in the first or the fourth priority group?
c. If you are in the third priority group next term, is it likely that you will get more than 9 units during the first call? Explain.

6.3   Estimating Probabilities

In the examples presented so far, reaching conclusions required knowledge of the probabilities of various outcomes. This is reasonable when we know the true long-run proportion of the time that each outcome will occur. In other situations, these probabilities are not known and must be determined. Sometimes probabilities can be determined analytically, by employing mathematical rules and probability properties, including the basic ones introduced in this chapter. When an analytical approach is impossible or impractical, we can *estimate* probabilities empirically through observation or by using simulation.

Estimating Probabilities Empirically

It is fairly common practice to use observed long-run proportions to estimate probabilities. In Example 6.6, information from a group of 500 students was used to approximate the probabilities of obtaining particular scores on a 20-question true–false quiz when guessing at the answers. Intuitively, we feel that estimates are likely to be more accurate when more information is available. If the proportions in Table 6.2 were based on a group of 50 students rather than 500, we would be more hesitant to use these proportions as estimates of the corresponding long-run proportions. The use of observed proportions to estimate probabilities is illustrated in the following two examples.

EXAMPLE 6.7

The Biology Department at a university plans to recruit a new faculty member and intends to advertise for someone with a Ph.D. in biology and at least 10 years of college-level teaching experience. One member of the department expresses the belief that requiring at least 10 years of teaching experience will exclude most potential applicants and will exclude far more of the female applicants than of the male applicants. The Biology Department would like to determine the probability that a Ph.D. in biology who is looking for an academic position would be eliminated from consideration because of the experience requirement.

A similar university just completed a search in which there was no requirement for prior teaching experience, but the information about prior teaching experience was recorded. The 410 applications yielded the following:

Number of Applicants

	Less Than 10 Years Experience	10 or More Years Experience	Total
Male	178	112	290
Female	99	21	120
Total	277	133	410

Assuming that the populations of applicants for the two positions can be regarded as the same, we will use the available information to approximate the probability that an applicant will fall in each of the four gender–experience combinations. The estimated probabilities (obtained by dividing the number of applicants for each gender–experience combination by 410) are given in Table 6.3. From Table 6.3,

estimate of P(candidate excluded) = .4341 + .2415 = .6756

Table 6.3 *Estimated probabilities for Example 6.7*

	Less Than 10 Years Experience	10 or More Years Experience
Male	.4341	.2732
Female	.2415	.0512

We can also assess the impact of the experience requirement separately for male and for female applicants. From the data, we calculate that the proportion of male applicants who have less than 10 years of experience is 178/290 = .6138, whereas the corresponding proportion for females is 99/120 = .8250. Therefore, approximately

61% of the male applicants would be eliminated by the experience requirement, and about 82% of the female applicants would be eliminated.

These subgroup proportions — .6138 for males and .8250 for females — are examples of *conditional probabilities*. As discussed in Section 6.1, outcomes are dependent if the occurrence of one outcome changes our assessment of the probability that the other outcome will occur. A conditional probability shows how the original probability changes in light of new information. In this example, the probability that a potential candidate has less than 10 years experience is .6756, but this probability changes to .8250 if we know that a candidate is female. These probabilities can be expressed as an unconditional probability

$$P(\text{less than 10 years experience}) = .6756$$

and a conditional probability

$$P(\text{less than 10 years experience, given female}) = .8250$$

For a more formal discussion of conditional probability and probability in general, consult one of the chapter references.

EXAMPLE 6.8

Consider a state lottery in which six numbers are drawn from the numbers $1, 2, \ldots,$ 54. Suppose that we want to determine the probability that our two favorite numbers (18 and 36) are both drawn. That is, we wish to determine the proportion of the time, in the long run, that 18 and 36 will both be among the six numbers selected. We will use simulation to estimate this probability. Suppose that we have access to lottery records for the last 5 years and that drawings occur twice each week (for a total of 520 drawings). For each drawing, we determine whether the numbers 18 and 36 were both among the six selected. For example, consider the first few drawings:

Drawing	Numbers Selected	18	36	Both
1	6 17 23 36 38 51	no	yes	no
2	4 12 22 29 48 53	no	no	no
3	14 21 27 32 33 41	no	no	no

Summarizing the data year by year resulted in the following information:

Year	Number of Drawings	Number with 18 and 36	Cumulative Proportion with 18 and 36
1	104	0	0/104 = 0
2	104	3	3/208 = .0144
3	104	0	3/312 = .0096
4	104	2	5/416 = .0120
5	104	1	6/520 = .0115

Based on the available data (the 520 observed drawings), we would estimate the probability that both 18 and 36 are drawn to be .0115. This is reasonably close to the actual value of .0105.*

If we had used only the first 104 observations, our estimate would have been 0. As we saw in the package delivery example of Section 6.1 (see Figures 6.1 and 6.2), increasing the number of observations tends to increase the reliability of an estimated probability.

—————

Estimating Probabilities Using Simulation

Simulation provides a means of estimating probabilities when we are unable (or do not have the time or resources) to determine probabilities analytically and it is impractical to estimate them empirically by observation. Simulation is a method that generates "observations" by performing an experiment that is as similar as possible in structure to the real situation of interest.

To illustrate the idea of simulation, recall Example 6.6, in which a professor estimated the probabilities of different possible scores on a 20-question true–false quiz when students were merely guessing at the answers. Observations were collected by having 500 students actually guess at the answers to 20 questions and then scoring the resulting papers. Obtaining the probability estimates in this way requires considerable time and effort; simulation provides an alternative approach.

Since each question on the quiz is a true–false question, a person who is guessing is equally likely to answer correctly or incorrectly on any given question. Rather than asking a student to select T or F and then comparing the choice to the correct answer, an equivalent process would be to pick a ball at random from a box that contains half red balls and half blue balls, with a blue ball representing a correct answer. Making 20 selections from the box (replacing each ball selected before picking the next one) and then counting the number of correct choices (the number of times a blue ball is selected) is a physical substitute for an observation from a student who has guessed at the answers to 20 true–false questions. The number of blue balls in 20 selections, with replacement, from a box that contains half red and half blue balls should have the same probability as the number of correct responses to the quiz when a student is guessing. For example, 20 selections of balls might yield the following results:

Selection	1	2	3	4	5	6	7	8	9	10
	R	R	B	R	B	B	R	R	R	B
Selection	11	12	13	14	15	16	17	18	19	20
	R	R	B	R	R	B	B	R	R	B

—————

*If the lottery selection equipment is fair, this probability can be determined analytically to be .0105.

This would correspond to a quiz with eight correct responses, and it would provide us with one observation for estimating the probabilities of interest. This process could then be repeated a large number of times to generate additional observations. For example, we might find the following:

Repetition	Number of "Correct" Responses
1	8
2	11
3	10
4	12
⋮	⋮
1000	11

The 1000 simulated quiz scores would then be used to construct a table of estimated probabilities similar to Table 6.2.

Taking this many balls out of a box and writing down the results would be cumbersome and tedious. The process can be simplified by using random digits to substitute for drawing balls from the box. For example, a single digit could be selected at random from the ten digits 0, 1, 2, 3, 4, 5, 6, 7, 8, 9. When using random digits, each of the ten possibilities is equally likely to occur, so we can use the even digits (including 0) to indicate a correct response and the odd digits to indicate an incorrect response. This would maintain the important property that a correct response and an incorrect response are equally likely, since correct and incorrect are each represented by five of the ten digits.

To aid in carrying out such a simulation, tables of random digits (such as Appendix Table I) or computer-generated random digits can be used. The numbers in Table I were generated using a computer's random number generator. You can think of the table as being produced by repeatedly drawing a chip from a box containing ten chips numbered 0, 1, . . . , 9. After each selection, the result is recorded, the chip returned to the box, and the chips mixed. Thus, any of the digits is equally likely to occur on any of the selections.

To see how a table of random numbers can be used to carry out a simulation, let's reconsider the quiz example. We will use a random digit to represent the guess on a single question, with an even digit representing a correct response. A series of 20 digits will represent the answers to the 20 quiz questions. We pick an arbitrary starting point in Table I. Suppose that we start at row 10 and take the 20 digits in a row to represent one quiz. The first five "quizzes" and the corresponding number correct are

Correct response

Quiz	Random Digits	Number Correct
1	* * * * * * * * * * * * * 9 4 6 0 6 9 7 8 8 2 5 2 9 6 0 1 4 6 0 5	13
2	6 6 9 5 7 4 4 6 3 2 0 6 0 8 9 1 3 6 1 8	12
3	0 7 1 7 7 7 2 9 7 8 7 5 8 8 6 9 8 4 1 0	9
4	6 1 3 0 9 7 3 3 6 6 0 4 1 8 3 2 6 7 6 8	11
5	2 2 3 6 2 1 3 0 2 2 6 6 9 7 0 2 1 2 5 8	13

This process would be repeated to generate a large number of observations, which would then be used to construct a table of estimated probabilities.

The method for generating observations must preserve the important characteristics of the actual process being considered if simulation is to be successful. For example, it would be easy to adapt the simulation procedure for the true–false quiz to one for a multiple-choice quiz. Suppose that each of the 20 questions on the quiz has five possible responses, only one of which is correct. For any particular question, we would expect a student to be able to guess the correct answer only $\frac{1}{5}$ of the time in the long run. To simulate this situation, we could select at random from a box that contained four red balls and only one blue ball (or, more generally, four times as many reds as blues). If we are using random digits for the simulation, we could use 0 and 1 to represent a correct response and 2, 3, . . . , 9 to represent an incorrect response.

Using Simulation to Approximate a Probability

1. Design a method that uses a random mechanism (such as a random number generator or table, the selection of a ball from a box, the toss of a coin, etc.) to represent an observation. Be sure that the important characteristics of the actual process are preserved.

2. Generate an observation using the method from step 1, and determine whether the outcome of interest has occurred.

3. Repeat step 2 a large number of times.

4. Calculate the estimated probability by dividing the number of observations for which the outcome of interest occurred by the total number of observations generated.

The simulation process is illustrated in the three examples that follow.

EXAMPLE 6.9   Many California cities limit the number of building permits that are issued each year. Because of limited water resources, one such city plans to issue permits for only ten dwelling units in the upcoming year. The city will decide who is to receive permits by holding a lottery. Suppose that you are one of a total of 39 individuals who apply for permits. Thirty of these individuals are requesting permits for a single-family home, eight are requesting permits for a duplex (which counts as two dwelling units), and one person is requesting a permit for a small apartment building with eight units (which counts as eight dwelling units). Each request will be entered into the lottery. Requests will be selected at random one at a time, and if there are enough permits remaining, the request will be granted. This process will continue until all ten permits have been issued. If your request is for a single-family home, what are you chances of receiving a permit? Let's use simulation to estimate this probability. (It is not easy to determine analytically.)

To carry out the simulation, we can view the requests as being numbered from 1 to 39 as follows:

01–30	Requests for single-family homes
31–38	Requests for duplexes
39	Request for 8-unit apartment

For ease of discussion, let's assume that your request is numbered 1.

One method for simulating the permit lottery follows:

1. Choose a random number between 1 and 39 to indicate which permit request is selected first, and grant this request.

2. Select another random number between 1 and 39 to indicate which permit request will be considered next. Determine the number of dwelling units for the selected request. Grant the request only if there are enough permits remaining to satisfy the request.

3. Repeat step 2 until permits for 10 dwelling units have been granted.

We used MINITAB to generate random numbers between 1 and 39 to imitate the lottery drawing. (The random number table in Appendix Table I could also be used, by selecting two digits and ignoring 00 and any value over 39). For example, the first sequence generated by MINITAB is shown here.

Random Number	Type of Request	Total Number of Units So Far
25	Single-family home	1
7	Single-family home	2
38	Duplex	4
31	Duplex	6
26	Single-family home	7
12	Single-family home	8
33	Duplex	10

We would stop at this point, since permits for 10 units would have been issued. In this simulated lottery, request number 1 was not selected, so you would not have received a permit.

The next simulated lottery (using MINITAB to generate the selections) is as follows.

Random Number	Type of Request	Total Number of Units So Far
38	Duplex	2
16	Single-family home	3
30	Single-family home	4
39	Apartment — not granted, since there are not 8 permits remaining	4

(continued)

Random Number	Type of Request	Total Number of Units So Far
14	Single-family home	5
26	Single-family home	6
36	Duplex	8
13	Single-family home	9
15	Single-family home	10

Again, request number 1 was not selected, so you would not have received a permit in this simulated lottery.

Now that a strategy for simulating a lottery has been devised, the tedious part of the simulation begins. We would now have to simulate a large number of lottery drawings, determining for each whether request number 1 was granted. We simulated 500 such drawings and found that request number 1 was selected in 85 of the lotteries. Thus,

$$\text{estimated probability of receiving a permit} = \frac{85}{500} = .17$$

EXAMPLE 6.10

Suppose that couples who wanted children were to continue having children until a boy is born. If we assume that each newborn child is equally likely to be a boy or a girl, would this behavior change the proportion of boys in the population? This question was posed in an article in *The American Statistician* (1994: 290–293), and many people answer the question incorrectly. We will use simulation to estimate the long-run proportion of boys in the population if families were to continue to have children until they have a boy. This proportion is an estimate of the probability that a randomly selected child from this population is a boy. Note that every sibling group would have exactly one boy.

We will use a single-digit random number to represent a child. The odd digits (1, 3, 5, 7, 9) will represent a male birth, and the even digits will represent a female birth. An observation will be constructed by selecting a sequence of random digits. If the first random number obtained is odd (a boy), the observation is complete. If the first selected number is even (a girl), another digit will be chosen. We continue in this way until an odd digit is obtained. For example, reading across row 15 of the random number table (Appendix Table I), the first 10 digits are

0 7 1 7 4 2 0 0 0 1

Using these numbers to simulate sibling groups, we would get

Sibling group 1	0 7	girl, boy
Sibling group 2	1	boy
Sibling group 3	7	boy
Sibling group 4	4 2 0 0 0 1	girl, girl, girl, girl, girl, boy

Continuing along row 15 of the random number table, we get

Sibling group 5	3				boy
Sibling group 6	1				boy
Sibling group 7	2	0	4	7	girl, girl, girl, boy
Sibling group 8	8	4	1		girl, girl, boy

After simulating eight sibling groups, we have 8 boys among 19 children. The proportion of boys is 8/19, which is close to .5. Continuing the simulation to obtain a large number of observations suggests that the long-run proportion of boys in the population would still be .5, which is indeed the case.

EXAMPLE 6.11

Can a close friend read your mind? Try the following experiment. Write the word *blue* on one piece of paper and the word *red* on another, and place the two slips of paper in a box. Select one slip of paper from the box, look at the word written on it, and then try to convey the word by sending a mental message to a friend who is seated in the same room. Ask your friend to select either red or blue, and record whether the response is correct. Repeat this ten times, and total the number of correct responses. How did your friend do? Is your friend receiving your mental messages or just guessing?

Let's investigate this issue by using simulation to get the approximate probabilities of the various possible numbers of correct responses for someone who is guessing. Someone who is guessing should have an equal chance of responding correctly or incorrectly. We can use a random digit to represent a response, with an even digit representing a correct response (C) and an odd digit representing an incorrect response (X). A sequence of ten digits can be used to simulate one execution of the experiment.

For example, using the last ten digits in row 25 of the random number table gives

5	2	8	3	4	3	0	7	3	5
X	C	C	X	C	X	C	X	X	X

a simulated experiment resulting in four correct responses. We used MINITAB to generate 150 sequences of 10 random digits and obtained the following results:

Sequence Number	Digits	Number Correct
1	3996285890	5
2	1690555784	3
3	9133190550	2
⋮	⋮	⋮
149	3083994450	5
150	9202078546	7

Table 6.4 summarizes the results of our simulation.

Table 6.4 *Estimated probabilities for Example 6.11*

Number Correct	Number of Sequences	Estimated Probability
0	0	.0000
1	1	.0067
2	8	.0533
3	16	.1067
4	30	.2000
5	36	.2400
6	35	.2333
7	17	.1133
8	7	.0467
9	0	.0000
10	0	.0000
Total	150	1.0000

The estimated probabilities in Table 6.4 are based on the assumption that a correct and an incorrect response are equally likely (guessing). Evaluate your friend's performance in light of the information in Table 6.4. Is it likely that someone who is guessing would have been able to get as many correct as your friend did? Do you think your friend was receiving your mental messages? How are the estimated probabilities in Table 6.4 used to support your answer?

Exercises 6.16 – 6.24

6.16 The *Los Angeles Times* (June 14, 1995) reported that the U.S. Postal Service is getting speedier, with higher overnight on-time delivery rates than in the past. Postal Service standards call for overnight delivery within a zone of about 60 miles for any first-class letter deposited by the last collection time posted on a mailbox. Two-day delivery is promised within a 600-mile zone, and three-day delivery is promised for distances over 600 miles. The Price Waterhouse accounting firm conducted an independent audit by "seeding" the mail with letters and recording on-time delivery rates for these letters. Suppose the results of the Price Waterhouse study were as follows. (These numbers are fictitious, but are compatible with summary values given in the article.)

	Number of Letters Mailed	Number Arriving on Time
Los Angeles	500	425
New York	500	415
Washington, D.C.	500	405
Nationwide	6000	5220

Use the given information to estimate the following probabilities.
a. The probability of an on-time delivery in Los Angeles
b. The probability of late delivery in Washington, D.C.
c. The probability that two letters mailed in New York are both delivered on time
d. The probability of on-time delivery nationwide

6.17 Five hundred first-year students at a state university were classified according to both high school GPA and whether they were on academic probation at the end of their first semester.

High School GPA

Probation	2.5–<3.0	3.0–<3.5	3.5 and Above	Total
Yes	50	55	30	135
No	45	135	185	365
Total	95	190	215	500

a. Construct a table of the estimated probabilities for each GPA–probation combination by dividing the number of students in each of the six cells of the given table by 500.

b. Use the table constructed in part **a** to approximate the probability that a randomly selected first-year student at this university will be on academic probation at the end of the first semester.

c. What is the estimated probability that a randomly selected first-year student at this university had a high school GPA of 3.5 or above?

d. Are the two outcomes *selected student has a GPA of 3.5 or above* and *selected student is on academic probation at the end of the first semester* independent outcomes? How can you tell?

e. Estimate the proportion of first-year students with high school GPAs between 2.5 and 3.0 who are on academic probation at the end of the first semester.

f. Estimate the proportion of those first-year students with high school GPAs of 3.5 and above who are on academic probation at the end of the first semester.

6.18 The table below describes (approximately) the distribution of students by gender and college at a midsized public university in the West. If we were to randomly select one student from this university:

a. What is the probability the selected student is a male?

b. What is the probability the selected student is in the College of Agriculture?

c. What is the probability the selected student is a male in the College of Agriculture?

d. What is the probability that the selected student is a male who is not from Agriculture?

6.19 On April 1, 2000, the Bureau of the Census in the United States attempted to count every U.S. citizen and every resident. When counting such a large number of people, however, there are likely to be mistakes of various sorts. In the year 2000 the Bureau of the Census employed many people to verify some of the information obtained by other census workers. Suppose that the table at the bottom of the page gives counts obtained in one region.

a. If a census fact-checker selects one person at random from this region, what is the probability that the selected person is from Ventura County?

b. If one person is selected at random from Ventura County, what is the probability that the selected person is Hispanic?

c. If one Hispanic person is selected at random from this region, what is the probability that the selected individual is from Ventura?

d. If one person is selected at random from this region, what is the probability that the selected person is an Asian from San Luis Obispo County?

e. If one person is selected at random from this region, what is the probability that the person is either Asian or from San Luis Obispo County?

f. If one person is selected at random from this region,

Table for Exercise 6.18

College

Gender	Education	Engineering	Liberal Arts	Science and Math	Agriculture	Business	Architecture
Female	300	3200	1500	1500	2100	1500	200
Male	200	800	1500	1500	900	1500	300

Table for Exercise 6.19

Race/Ethnicity

County	Caucasian	Hispanic	Black	Asian	American Indian
Monterey	163,000	139,000	24,000	39,000	4000
San Luis Obispo	180,000	37,000	7000	9000	3000
Santa Barbara	230,000	121,000	12,000	24,000	5000
Ventura	430,000	231,000	18,000	50,000	7000

what is the probability that the person is Asian or from San Luis Obispo County but not both?

g. If two people are selected at random from this region, what is the probability that both are Caucasians?

h. If two people are selected at random from this region, what is the probability that neither is Caucasian?

i. If two people are selected at random from this region, what is the probability that exactly one is a Caucasian?

j. If two people are selected at random from this region, what is the probability that both are residents of the same county?

k. If two people are selected at random from this region, what is the probability that both are from different racial/ethnic groups?

6.20 A medical research team wishes to evaluate two different treatments for a disease. Subjects are selected two at a time, and then one of the pair is assigned to each of the two treatments. The treatments are applied, and each is either a success (S) or a failure (F). The researchers keep track of the total number of successes for each treatment. They plan to continue the experiment until the number of successes for one treatment exceeds the number of successes for the other treatment by 3. For example, they might observe the results in the accompanying table. The experiment would stop after the sixth pair, because treatment 1 has 3 more successes than treatment 2. The researchers would conclude that treatment 1 is preferable to treatment 2. Suppose that treatment 1 has a success rate of .7 (that is, P(success) = .7 for treatment 1) and that treatment 2 has a success rate of .4. Use simulation to estimate the following probabilities (see the hint that follows).

a. The probability that more than 5 pairs must be treated before a conclusion can be reached

b. The probability that the researchers will incorrectly conclude that treatment 2 is the best treatment

[*Hint*: Use a pair of random digits to simulate one pair of subjects. Let the first digit represent treatment 1 and use 1–7 as an indication of a success and 8, 9, and 0 to indi-

cate a failure. Let the second digit represent treatment 2, with 1–4 representing a success. For example, if the two digits selected to represent a pair were 8 and 3, you would record failure for treatment 1 and success for treatment 2. Continue to select pairs, keeping track of the total number of successes for each treatment. Stop the trial as soon as the number of successes for one treatment exceeds that for the other by 3. This would complete one trial. Now repeat this whole process until you have results for at least 20 trials (more is better). Finally, use the simulation results to estimate the desired probabilities.]

6.21 Many cities regulate the number of taxi licenses, and there is a great deal of competition for both new and existing licenses. Suppose that a city has decided to sell 10 new licenses for $25,000 each. A lottery will be held to determine who gets the licenses, and no one may request more than 3 licenses. Twenty individuals and taxi companies have entered the lottery. Six of the 20 entries are requests for 3 licenses, 9 are requests for 2 licenses, and the rest are requests for a single license. The city will select requests at random, filling as much of the request as possible. For example, the city might fill requests for 2, 3, 1, and 3 licenses and then select a request for 3. Since there is only one license left, the last request selected would receive a license, but only one.

a. An individual who wishes to be an independent driver has put in a request for a single license. Use simulation to approximate the probability that the request will be granted. Perform *at least* 20 simulated lotteries (more is better!).

b. Do you think that this is a fair way of distributing licenses? Can you propose an alternative procedure for distribution?

6.22 Four students must work together on a group project. They decide that each will take responsibility for a particular part of the project, as follows:

Person	Maria	Alex	Juan	Jacob
Task	Survey design	Data collection	Analysis	Report writing

Table for Exercise 6.20

Pair	Treatment 1	Treatment 2	Total Number of Successes for Treatment 1	Total Number of Successes for Treatment 2
1	S	F	1	0
2	S	S	2	1
3	F	F	2	1
4	S	F	3	1
5	F	F	3	1
6	S	F	4	1

Because of the way the tasks have been divided, one student must finish before the next student can begin work. To ensure that the project is completed on time, a timeline is established, with a deadline for each team member. If any one of the team members is late, the timely completion of the project is jeopardized. Assume the following probabilities:

1. The probability that Maria completes her part on time is .8.
2. If Maria completes her part on time, the probability that Alex completes on time is .9, but if Maria is late, the probability that Alex completes on time is only .6.
3. If Alex completes his part on time, the probability that Juan completes on time is .8, but if Alex is late, the probability that Juan completes on time is only .5.
4. If Juan completes his part on time, the probability that Jacob completes on time is .9, but if Juan is late, the probability that Jacob completes on time is only .7.

Use simulation (with at least 20 trials) to estimate the probability that the project is completed on time. Think carefully about this one. For example, you might use a random digit to represent each part of the project (four in all). For the first digit (Maria's part), 1–8 could represent

on time and 9 and 0 could represent *late*. Depending on what happened with Maria (late or on time), you would then look at the digit representing Alex's part. If Maria was on time, 1–9 would represent *on time* for Alex, but if Maria was late, only 1–6 would represent *on time* for Alex. The parts for Juan and Jacob could be handled similarly.

6.23   In Exercise 6.22, the probability that Maria completes her part on time was .8. Suppose that this probability is really only .6. Use simulation (with at least 20 trials) to estimate the probability that the project is completed on time.

6.24   Refer back to Exercises 6.22 and 6.23. Suppose that the probabilities of timely completion are as in Exercise 6.22 for Maria, Alex, and Juan, but that Jacob has a probability of completing on time of .7 if Juan is on time and .5 if Juan is late.

a. Use simulation (with at least 20 trials) to estimate the probability that the project is completed on time.

b. Compare the probability from part **a** to the one computed in Exercise 6.23. Which decrease in the probability of on-time completion (Maria's or Jacob's) made the bigger change in the probability that the project is completed on time?

Summary of Key Concepts and Formulas

Term or Formula	Comment
Probability	A number between 0 and 1 that reflects the likelihood of occurrence of some outcome.
Independent outcomes	Two outcomes are independent if the chance that one outcome occurs is not affected by knowledge of whether or not the other occurred.
$P(not\ outcome) = 1 - P(outcome)$	Complement rule.
$P(outcome\ 1\ or\ outcome\ 2)$ $= P(outcome\ 1) + P(outcome\ 2)$	Addition rule for outcomes that can't occur at the same time.
$P(outcome\ 1\ and\ outcome\ 2)$ $= P(outcome\ 1) \cdot P(outcome\ 2)$	Multiplication rule for independent outcomes.
Simulation	A technique for estimating probabilities that generates observations by performing an experiment that is similar in structure to the real situation of interest.

Supplementary Exercises 6.25 – 6.30

6.25 Consider the five outcomes (at the bottom of the page) for an experiment in which the type of ice cream purchased by the next customer at a certain store is noted.

a. What is the probability that Dreyer's ice cream is purchased?

b. What is the probability that Von's brand is not purchased?

c. What is the probability that the size purchased is larger than a pint?

6.26 A radio station that plays classical music has a "by request" program each Saturday evening. The percentages of requests for composers on a particular night are as follows:

Bach	5%	Mozart	21%
Beethoven	26%	Schubert	12%
Brahms	9%	Schumann	7%
Dvorak	2%	Tchaikovsky	14%
Mendelssohn	3%	Wagner	1%

Suppose that one of these requests is randomly selected.

a. What is the probability that the request is for one of the three B's?

b. What is the probability that the request is not for one of the two S's?

c. Neither Bach nor Wagner wrote any symphonies. What is the probability that the request is for a composer who wrote at least one symphony?

6.27 Suppose that the accompanying information on births in the United States over a given period of time is available to you.

Type of Birth	Number of Births
Single birth	41,500,000
Twins	500,000
Triplets	5,000
Quadruplets	100

Use this information to approximate the probability that a randomly selected pregnant woman who reaches full term

a. Delivers twins

b. Delivers quadruplets

c. Gives birth to more than a single child

6.28 Two individuals, A and B, are finalists for a chess championship. They will play a sequence of games, each of which can result in a win for A, a win for B, or a draw. Suppose that the outcomes of successive games are independent, with $P(A \text{ wins game}) = .3$, $P(B \text{ wins game}) = .2$, and $P(\text{draw}) = .5$. Each time a player wins a game, he earns one point and his opponent earns no points. The first player to win 5 points wins the championship. For the sake of simplicity, assume that the championship will end in a draw if both players obtain 5 points at the same time.

a. What is the probability that A wins the championship in just five games?

b. What is the probability that it takes just five games to obtain a champion?

c. If a draw earns $\frac{1}{2}$ point for each player, describe how you would perform a simulation experiment to estimate $P(A \text{ wins the championship})$.

d. If neither player earns any points from a draw, would the simulation requested in part **c** take longer to perform? Explain your reasoning.

6.29 Consider a clinical trials experiment for comparing two treatments, A and B, and suppose that patients arrive for treatment one by one. If the result of treating each patient, success or failure, is determined before the next patient arrives, a "play the winner" rule is often used to assign treatments. The first patient is equally likely to be assigned A or B. Suppose that A is assigned. Then, if the treatment is a success, A is assigned to the next patient, but if the treatment is a failure, the treatment is switched to B for the next patient. Continuing in this manner, treatment is switched from A to B or from B to A if the previous patient was a failure and remains the same otherwise. If $P(A \text{ is a success}) = .7$, $P(B \text{ is a success}) = .4$, and the experiment is continued until one treatment has achieved 5 successes, perform a simulation experiment to estimate $P(A \text{ is the "winner"})$.

6.30 A single-elimination tournament with four players is to be held. A total of three games will be played. In game 1, the players seeded (rated) first and fourth play. In game 2, the players seeded second and third play. In game 3, the winners of games 1 and 2 play, with the winner

Data for Exercise 6.25

Brand	Steve's	Ben and Jerry's	Dreyer's	Dreyer's	Von's
Size of container	Pint	Pint	Quart	Half-gallon	Half-gallon
Probability	.10	.15	.20	.25	.30

of game 3 declared the tournament winner. Suppose that the following probabilities are given:

P(seed 1 defeats seed 4) = .8

P(seed 1 defeats seed 2) = .6

P(seed 1 defeats seed 3) = .7

P(seed 2 defeats seed 3) = .6

P(seed 2 defeats seed 4) = .7

P(seed 3 defeats seed 4) = .6

a. Describe how you would use a selection of random digits to simulate game 1 of this tournament.

b. Describe how you would use a selection of random digits to simulate game 2 of this tournament.

c. How would you use a selection of random digits to simulate the third game in the tournament? (This will depend on the outcomes of games 1 and 2.)

d. Simulate one complete tournament, giving an explanation for each step in the process.

e. Simulate 10 tournaments and use the resulting information to estimate the probability that the first seed wins the tournament.

f. Ask four classmates for their simulation results. Along with your own results, this should give you information on 50 simulated tournaments. Use this information to estimate the probability that the first seed wins the tournament.

g. Why do the estimated probabilities from parts **e** and **f** differ? Which do you think is a better estimate of the true probability? Explain.

Reference

Peck, Roxy, Chris Olsen, and Jay Devore. *Introduction to Statistics and Data Analysis.* Belmont, CA: Duxbury Press, 2001. (Contains a more comprehensive treatment of probability than what appears here, but still at a modest mathematical level.)

7

Population Distributions

This chapter is the first of two that together link the basic ideas of probability explored in the previous chapter with the techniques of statistical inference. Chapter 6 used probability to describe the long-run frequency of occurrence of various types of outcomes. Here we introduce probability models that can be used to describe the distribution of characteristics of individuals in a population. Such models are essential to help us reach conclusions based on a sample from the population.

The chapter begins by distinguishing between categorical and numerical variables and between discrete and continuous numerical variables. We show how a continuous numerical variable can be described by a probability distribution curve, which can also be used to make probability statements about values of the variable. Finally, one particular probability model, the normal distribution, is presented in detail.

7.1   Describing the Distribution of Values in a Population

In Chapter 1, statistical inference was described as the branch of statistics that involves generalizing from a sample to the population from which it was selected. A population is the entire collection of individuals or objects about which information is desired. Interest usually centers on the value of one or more variables. For example, if one wants to obtain information about the performance of a new telephone registration system for selecting college courses, the population would consist of all students at the university who use the phone registration system. The variable of interest (a characteristic of each individual member of the population) might be *time to complete registration.*

A variable can be either categorical or numerical, depending on the possible values of the variable that occur in the population. The variable *time to complete registration* is numerical, since it associates a number with each individual in the population. If interest instead had centered on whether a student was able to complete registration for classes with a single phone call, rather than on the time required to complete registration, the variable of interest, which we might name *first call,* would be categorical. This variable associates a categorical response (successful completion or unsuccessful) with each individual in the population. The variable *class standing* is also categorical, with the four categories freshman, sophomore, junior, and senior.

Definition

A **variable** associates a value with each individual or object in a population. A variable may be either **categorical** or **numerical,** depending on its possible values.

The distribution of categories or values in a population provides important information about the population. For example, if we knew something about the distribution of registration completion times for the population of all students, we might be able to give students an idea of how much time to allow (e.g., most students require between 8 and 13 minutes to complete the registration process) or determine a reasonable amount of time after which a student should be automatically disconnected from the system. The distribution of all the values of a numerical variable or categories of a categorical variable is called a **population distribution.**

Categorical Variables

Categorical variables are often dichotomous (having only two possible categories). For example, each individual in the population of students at a state university may be classified as a resident of the state or as a nonresident, or each owner of a Mazda automobile might be classified according to whether they would consider purchasing a Mazda as their next car. Each of these variables (*residence status* for the college population or *future purchase* for the population of Mazda owners) is a categorical variable with two possible categories.

EXAMPLE 7.1 Consider the variable *residence status* for the population of students at a state university. This variable associates a category (resident or nonresident) with each individual in the population. The population distribution for this variable can be summarized in a histogram, with a rectangle for each possible category. The height of

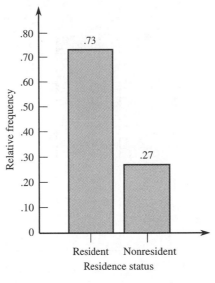

FIGURE 7.1 Population distribution of *residence status*

each rectangle will correspond to the relative frequency (proportion) for the corresponding value in the population. Figure 7.1 shows a possible population distribution for the variable *residence status*. If an individual is randomly selected from this population, the two relative frequencies can be interpreted as the probabilities of observing each of the two possible categories of *residence status*. Thus, in the long run, a resident will be selected about 73% of the time, and a nonresident will be selected about 27% of the time.

EXAMPLE 7.2

In a study of factors related to air quality, monitors were posted at every entrance to a university campus on October 10, 1999. From 6 A.M. to 10 P.M., monitors recorded the mode of transportation for each person entering the campus. Based on the information collected, the population distribution of the variable

x = mode of transportation

was constructed; it is shown in Figure 7.2 (page 232). In this example, the population consists of all individuals entering campus on October 10, 1999. The variable x is categorical, with the following possible categories: car or motorcycle (driver), car or motorcycle (passenger), bike, bus, foot, and skateboard or rollerblades. (This was in California!)

If an individual is selected at random from those who were on campus on October 10, 1999, the probability that the selected individual arrived as the driver of a car or motorcycle is .529. The probability that the selected individual arrived by car

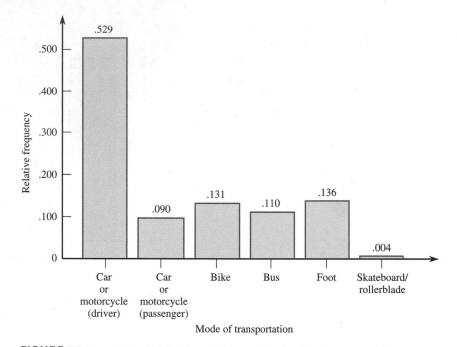

FIGURE 7.2 Population distribution of the variable *mode of transportation*

or motorcycle (either as the driver or as a passenger) is .529 + .090 = .619. The probability that the selected individual arrived on foot is .136.

It is common practice to use special notation when writing probability statements, such as those at the end of Example 7.2. The probability of an outcome is denoted by P(outcome). The outcome can be described with words or by using a variable name. Thus, continuing Example 7.2 where the outcome of interest is mode of transportation, we write:

P(selected individual arrives by bus) = .110   or $P(x = \text{bus}) = .110$

P(selected individual arrives by bike) = .131   or $P(x = \text{bike}) = .131$

and so on.

Numerical Variables

Before considering examples of numerical variables, we must distinguish between two types of such variables.

> **Definition**
>
> Numerical variables can be either discrete or continuous.
>
> A **discrete numerical variable** is one whose possible values are isolated points along the number line.
>
> A **continuous numerical variable** is one whose possible values form an interval along the number line.

The population distribution for a discrete numerical variable can be summarized by a relative frequency histogram, whereas a density histogram is used to summarize the distribution of a continuous numerical variable. The examples that follow demonstrate how this is done.*

EXAMPLE 7.3   The Department of Animal Regulation released information on pet ownership for the population of all households in a particular county. The variable considered was

x = number of licensed dogs or cats for a household

This variable associates a numerical value with each household in the population; possible x values are 0, 1, 2, 3, 4, and 5 (county regulations prohibit more than five dogs or cats per household). Since possible values of x are isolated points along the number line, it is a discrete numerical variable.

One way to summarize the population distribution for a discrete numerical variable is to use a relative frequency histogram. The population distribution for the variable

x = number of licensed dogs or cats

is shown in Figure 7.3 on page 234.

The most common value of x in the population is $x = 0$, and $P(x = 0) = .52$. Only 1% of all households have five licensed dogs or cats, so if a household were selected at random from this population, it would be unusual to observe five licensed dogs or cats. The probability of observing a household with three or more licensed dogs or cats is

$P(3 \text{ or more licensed dogs or cats}) = P(x \geq 3) = .09 + .03 + .01 = .13$

---

*One frequently encountered discrete distribution, the **binomial distribution,** is discussed in the Appendix at the end of this text.

FIGURE 7.3 Population distribution of the variable *number of licensed dogs or cats*

EXAMPLE 7.4

Birth weight was recorded for all full-term babies born during 1995 in a semirural county. The variable

x = birth weight for a full-term baby

for the population of all full-term babies in this county is an example of a continuous numerical variable. One way to describe the population distribution of x values for this population is to construct a density histogram. Recall from Chapter 3 that, in a density histogram, the measurement scale (here, the range that includes all possible birth weights) is divided into class intervals. Each value in the data set (here, each birth weight) is classified in one of the intervals. For each interval, the resulting relative frequency is used to compute

$$\text{density} = \frac{\text{relative frequency}}{\text{interval width}}$$

The density histogram has a rectangle for each interval; the height of the rectangle is determined by the corresponding density. (Review Section 3.3 of Chapter 3 for a more detailed description of density histograms.)

Figure 7.4 is a density histogram of the birth-weight values. This density histogram shows the distribution of birth weights for all full-term babies in this county, so it can be viewed as the population distribution of the variable x = birth weight.

From Figure 7.4, we can see that most birth weights are between 5 and 9 pounds, and that it would be unusual for a full-term baby born in this county to have a birth weight over 10 pounds. In the next section, we will see how this distribution can be used to calculate various probabilities regarding the birth weight of a randomly selected child.

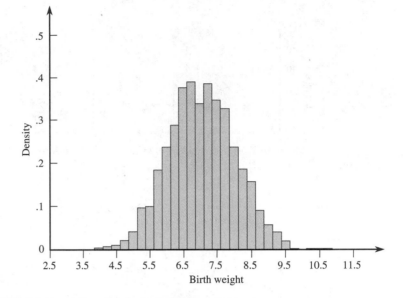

FIGURE 7.4 Population distribution of birth-weight values

The population distribution for a numerical variable is useful for describing the distribution of its values in the population. Such a population distribution can also be summarized by a mean and a standard deviation. The mean describes where the distribution of values is centered, and the standard deviation describes how much the distribution spreads out about this central value.

Definition

The **mean value of a numerical variable x,** denoted by **μ,** describes where the population distribution of x is centered.

The **standard deviation of a numerical variable x,** denoted by **σ,** describes variability in the population distribution. When σ is close to 0, the values of x in the population tend to be close to the mean value (little variability). When the value of σ is large, there is more variability in the population of x values.

Figure 7.5(a) on page 236 shows two discrete distributions with the same standard deviation (spread) but different means (center). One distribution has a mean of $\mu = 6$; the other has $\mu = 10$. Which is which? Figure 7.5(b) shows two continuous distributions that have the same mean but different standard deviations. Smooth curves have been used to approximate the shape of the underlying density

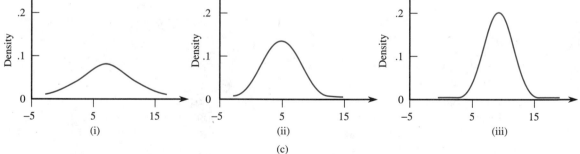

FIGURE 7.5 (a) Different values of μ with the same value of σ; (b) Different values of σ with the same value of μ; (c) Different values of μ and σ

histograms. Which distribution, (i) or (ii), has the larger standard deviation? Finally, Figure 7.5(c) shows three continuous distributions with different means and standard deviations. Which of the three distributions has the largest mean? Which has a mean of about 5? Which distribution has the smallest standard deviation? (Check your answers to the previous questions: 7.5(a)(ii) has a mean of 6, and 7.5(a)(i) has a mean of 10; 7.5(b)(ii) has the larger standard deviation; 7.5(c)(iii) has the largest mean, 7.5(c)(ii) has a mean of about 5, and 7.5(c)(iii) has the smallest standard deviation.)

We will not concern ourselves with how to compute the values of μ and σ (it is handled differently for discrete and for continuous variables), but we will look at how these values are interpreted. For the population distribution of Example 7.3, the mean value of x turns out to be $\mu = .92$. This value is interpreted as the average number of licensed dogs or cats for the population of households in the county considered. Notice that μ is not a possible value of x. If another county (another population) had a mean of $\mu = .5$, we would know that the average number of licensed pets per household was smaller for the second county than for the first, so the distribution for the second county would be centered to the left of the first county's distribution.

For the population distribution in Example 7.4, $\mu = 7$ and $\sigma = 1$. The value of μ tells us that the average (mean) birth weight of full-term babies in the population is 7 pounds. The value of the standard deviation provides information on the extent to which individual birth weights vary in the population. Since the population distribution is roughly bell shaped and symmetric, the Empirical Rule tells us that about 68% of the birth weights fall between 6 and 8 pounds, and that it would be extremely rare for a full-term baby to have a birth weight under 4 pounds (or over 10 pounds). If the birth-weight distribution for a different population (for example, an urban county) had $\mu = 7.4$ and $\sigma = 1.3$, we would know that the average birth weight for the urban population was higher and that individual birth weights varied more than for the semirural area considered in Example 7.4 (that is, the urban distribution is more spread out than the semirural distribution).

If the population distribution for a variable is known, it is possible to determine the values of μ and σ. Most often, however, the population distribution is not fully known, and the mean and standard deviation are estimated using sample data. In later chapters, we will us $\bar{x}$ and s for this purpose.

Exercises 7.1 – 7.10

7.1 State whether each of the following numerical variables is discrete or continuous.
  a. The number of defective tires on a car
  b. The body temperature of a hospital patient
  c. The number of pages in a book
  d. The number of checkout lines operating at a large grocery store
  e. The lifetime of a lightbulb

7.2 Classify each of the following numerical variables as either discrete or continuous.
  a. The fuel efficiency (mpg) of an automobile
  b. The amount of rainfall at a particular location during the next year
  c. The distance that a person throws a baseball
  d. The number of questions asked during a one-hour lecture

  e. The tension (lb/in^2) at which a tennis racket is strung
  f. The amount of water used by a household during a given month
  g. The number of traffic citations issued by the highway patrol in a particular county on a given day

7.3 Consider the variable x = earthquake insurance status for the population of homeowners in an earthquake-prone California county. This variable associates a category (insured or not insured) with each individual in the population.
  a. Construct a relative frequency histogram that represents the population distribution for x for the case where 60% of the county homeowners have earthquake insurance.
  b. If an individual is randomly selected from this

population, what is the probability that the selected homeowner does not have earthquake insurance?

7.4 Based on past history, a fire station reports that 25% of the calls to the station are false alarms, 60% are for small fires that can be handled by station personnel without outside assistance, and 15% are for major fires that require outside help.

a. Construct a relative frequency histogram that represents the distribution of the variable x = type of call, where *type of call* has three categories: false alarm, small fire, and major fire. What is the underlying population for this variable?

b. Based on the information given, we can write $P(x$ = false alarm$)$ = .25. Use the other two relative frequencies shown in the histogram from part **a** to write two other probability statements.

7.5 Suppose that fundraisers at a university call recent graduates to request donations for the campus outreach programs. They report the following information for last year's graduates.

Size of donation	0	$10	$25	$50
Proportion of calls	.45	.30	.20	.05

Three attempts were made to contact each graduate; a donation of 0 was recorded both for those who were contacted but who declined to make a donation and for those who were not reached in three attempts. Consider the variable x = amount of donation for the population of last year's graduates of this university.

a. Construct a relative frequency histogram to represent the population distribution of this variable.

b. What is the most common value of x in this population?

c. What is $P(x \geq 25)$?

d. What is $P(x > 0)$?

7.6 A pizza shop sells pizzas in four different sizes. The 1000 most recent orders for a single pizza gave the following proportions for the various sizes.

Size	12″	14″	16″	18″
Proportion	.20	.25	.50	.05

With x denoting the size of a pizza in a single-pizza order, the above table is an approximation to the population distribution of x.

a. Construct a relative frequency histogram to represent the approximate distribution of this variable.

b. Approximate $P(x < 16)$.

c. Approximate $P(x \leq 16)$.

d. It can be shown that the mean value of x is approxi-

mately 14.8″. What is the approximate probability that x is within 2″ of this mean value?

7.7 Airlines sometimes overbook flights. Suppose that for a plane with 100 seats, an airline takes 110 reservations. Define the variable x as the number of people who actually show up for a sold-out flight. From past experience, the population distribution of x is given in the following table.

x	95	96	97	98
Proportion	.05	.10	.12	.14

x	99	100	101	102
Proportion	.24	.17	.06	.04

x	103	104	105	106
Proportion	.03	.02	.01	.005

x	107	108	109	110
Proportion	.005	.005	.0037	.0013

a. What is the probability that the airline can accommodate everyone who shows up for the flight?

b. What is the probability that not all passengers can be accommodated?

c. If you are trying to get a seat on such a flight and you are number 1 on the standby list, what is the probability that you will be able to take the flight? What if you are number 3?

7.8 Homicide rate (homicides per 100,000 population) for each of the 50 states appeared in the *San Luis Obispo Telegram-Tribune* (Feb. 2, 1995). A frequency distribution constructed from the 50 observations is shown.

Homicide Rate	Frequency
0–<3	5
3–<6	16
6–<9	9
9–<12	9
12–<15	9
15–<18	1
18–<21	1

a. Calculate the relative frequency and density for each of the seven intervals in the frequency distribution. Use the computed densities to construct a density histogram for the variable x = homicide rate for the population consisting of the 50 states.

b. Is the population distribution symmetric or skewed?

c. Use the population distribution to determine the following probabilities.

i. $P(x \geq 15)$ **ii.** $P(x < 9)$ **iii.** $P(12 \leq x < 18)$

7.9 A company receives lightbulbs from two different suppliers. Define the variables x and y by

x = lifetime of a bulb from supplier 1

y = lifetime of a bulb from supplier 2

Five hundred bulbs from each supplier are tested, and the lifetime of each bulb is recorded. The accompanying density histograms are constructed from these two sets of observations. Although these histograms are constructed using data from only 500 bulbs, they can be considered as approximations to the corresponding population distributions.

a. Which population distribution has the larger mean?

b. Which population distribution has the larger standard deviation?

c. Assuming the cost of the bulbs is the same for both suppliers, which supplier would you recommend? Explain.

d. One of the two distributions pictured has a mean of approximately 1000, and the other has a mean of about 900. What is the mean of the distribution for the variable x (lifetime for a bulb made by supplier 1)?

e. One of the two distributions pictured has a standard deviation of approximately 100, and the other has a standard deviation of about 175. What is the standard deviation of the distribution for the variable x (lifetime for a bulb made by supplier 1)?

7.10 A certain basketball player makes 70% of his free throws. Assume that results of successive free throws are independent of one another. At the end of a particular practice, the coach tells the player to begin shooting free throws and to stop only when he has made two consecutive shots. Let x denote the number of shots until the player can stop. Describe how you would carry out a simulation experiment to estimate the probability distribution of x.

Figure for Exercise 7.9

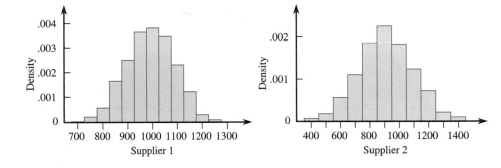

7.2   Population Models for Continuous Numerical Variables

In Example 7.4 of Section 7.1, we saw how a density histogram could be used to summarize a population distribution when the variable of interest is numerical and continuous. When this is done, the exact shape of the histogram and any approximate probability statements that we may make based on the population distribution depend somewhat on the number and location of intervals used in constructing the density histogram.

For example, let's look again at the distribution of birth weights for the population of all full-term babies born in 1995 in a particular county (see Example 7.4). Suppose that 2000 full-term babies were born. Then the population consists of 2000 individuals, and each has an associated value of the variable x = birth weight. Figure 7.6(a) on page 240 shows a density histogram for the population distribution of x based on seven intervals: 3.5–<4.5, 4.5–<5.5, etc.

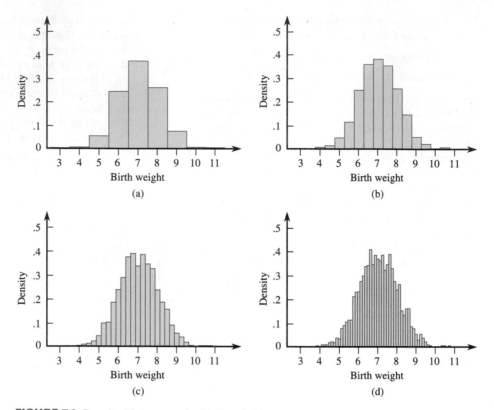

FIGURE 7.6 Density histograms for birth weight

The area of any rectangle in such a histogram can be interpreted as the probability of observing a variable value in the corresponding interval, if an individual is selected at random from the population. This follows from the fact that, for any interval,

$$\text{density} = \frac{\text{relative frequency}}{\text{interval width}}$$

By construction, the corresponding rectangle has height equal to density, so the area of the rectangle is

$$
\begin{aligned}
\text{area} &= (\text{height}) \cdot (\text{interval width}) \\
&= (\text{density}) \cdot (\text{interval width}) \\
&= \left(\frac{\text{relative frequency}}{\text{interval width}} \right)(\text{interval width}) \\
&= \text{relative frequency}
\end{aligned}
$$

Thus, the area of the rectangle above each interval is equal to the relative frequency of values that fall in the interval. Since the area of a rectangle in the density histogram specifies the proportion of the population values that fall in the corresponding interval, it can be interpreted as the long-run proportion of time that a value in the interval would occur if individual after individual were randomly selected from the population.

Thus, for the interval 4.5 to <5.5 in Figure 7.6(a), the probability that the weight of a randomly selected individual falls in the interval is

$$P(4.5 < x < 5.5) = \text{area of rectangle above the interval from 4.5 to 5.5}$$
$$= (\text{density})(1)$$

Height of rectangle ↗   ↖ *Width of rectangle*

$$= (.05)(1)$$
$$= .05$$

Similarly,

$$P(7.5 < x < 8.5) = .255$$

The probability of observing a value in an interval other than those used to construct the density histogram can be approximated. For example, to approximate the probability of observing a birth weight between 7 and 8 pounds, we could add half the area of the rectangle for the 6.5–7.5 interval and half the area for the 7.5–8.5 interval. This gives only an approximate probability, since the area of each rectangle in the density histogram is equal to the proportion of the population falling in the corresponding interval. So

$$P(7 < x < 8) \approx \tfrac{1}{2}(\text{area of rectangle for 6.5–7.5}) + \tfrac{1}{2}(\text{area of rectangle for 7.5–8.5})$$
$$= \tfrac{1}{2}(.370)(1) + \tfrac{1}{2}(.255)(1)$$
$$= .3125$$

The approximation of probabilities can be improved by increasing the number of intervals on which the density histogram is based. As Figure 7.6(a) shows, a density histogram based on a small number of intervals can be quite jagged. Figures 6.6(b)–(d) show density histograms based on 14, 28, and 56 intervals, respectively. As the number of intervals increases, the rectangles in the density histogram become much narrower, and the histogram appears smoother.

Two very important ideas were presented in the foregoing discussion. First, when summarizing a population distribution with a density histogram, the area of any rectangle in the histogram can be interpreted as the probability of observing a variable value in the corresponding interval when an individual is selected at random from the population. The second important idea is that when a density histogram based on a small number of intervals is used to summarize a population distribution for a continuous numerical variable, the histogram can be quite jagged. However, when the number of intervals is increased, the resulting histograms become much smoother in appearance. (You can see this in the histograms of Figure 7.6.)

It is often useful to represent a population distribution for a continuous variable by using a simple smooth curve that approximates the actual population distribution. For example, Figure 7.7 (page 242) shows a smooth curve superimposed over the density histogram of Figure 7.6(d). Such a curve is called a **continuous probability distribution.** Since the total area of the rectangles in a density histogram

FIGURE 7.7 A smooth curve specifies a continuous distribution for birth weight.

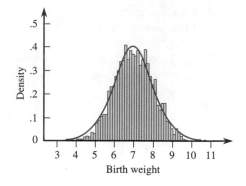

is equal to 1, we will consider only smooth curves for which the total area under the curve is equal to 1.

A continuous probability distribution is an abstract but simplified description of the population distribution that preserves important population characteristics (general shape, center, spread, etc.). Thus, it can serve as a model for the distribution of values in the population. Because the area under the curve approximates the areas of rectangles in the density histogram, the area under the curve and above any particular interval can be interpreted as the approximate probability of observing a value in that interval when an individual is selected at random from the population.

A **continuous probability distribution** is a smooth curve, called a **density curve,** that serves as a model for the population distribution of a continuous variable.

Properties of continuous probability distributions are:

1. The total area under the curve is equal to 1.
2. The area under the curve and above any particular interval is interpreted as the (approximate) probability of observing a value in the corresponding interval when an individual or object is selected at random from the population.

The following examples show how a continuous probability distribution can be used to make probability statements about a variable.

EXAMPLE 7.5   A morning commuter train never leaves before its scheduled departure time. The length of time that elapses between the scheduled departure time and the actual departure is recorded on 200 occasions. The resulting observations are summarized in the density histogram shown in Figure 7.8(a). This histogram can serve as an approximation to the population distribution of the variable $x =$ elapsed time (min).

Since the histogram is fairly flat, a reasonable model (smooth curve) for the population distribution is the probability distribution "curve" shown in Figure 7.8(b). This model is sometimes referred to as a *uniform distribution*. The height of the

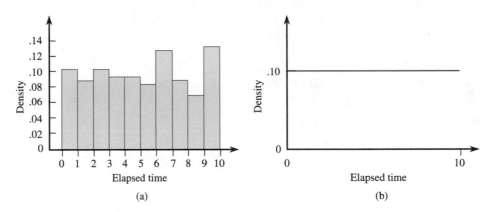

FIGURE 7.8 (a) Histogram of elapsed time values; (b) Continuous probability distribution for elapsed time

curve (density = .1) is chosen so that the total area under the density curve is equal to 1.

The model can be used to approximate probabilities involving the variable x. For example, the probability that between 5 and 7 minutes elapse between scheduled and actual departure is the area under the density curve and above the interval from 5 to 7, as shown in the accompanying illustration.

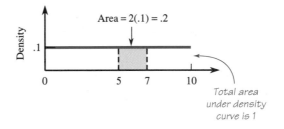

So

$$P(\text{elapsed time is between 5 and 7}) = P(5 < x < 7) = (2)(.1) = .2$$

Other probabilities are determined in a similar fashion. For example,

$$P(\text{elapsed time is less than 2.5}) = P(x < 2.5)$$
$$= \text{area under curve and above interval from 0 to 2.5}$$
$$= (2.5)(.1)$$
$$= .25$$

For continuous numerical variables, probabilities are represented by an area under a probability distribution curve and above an interval. The area above an interval is not changed by including the interval endpoints, since there is no area above a single point. In Example 7.5, we found $P(x < 2.5) = .25$. It is also true that $P(x \leq 2.5) = .25$.

For continuous numerical variables and any particular numbers a and b,

$$P(x \leq a) = P(x < a)$$
$$P(x \geq b) = P(x > b)$$
$$P(a < x < b) = P(a \leq x \leq b)$$

EXAMPLE 7.6

Two hundred packages shipped using the Priority Mail rate for packages under 2 pounds were weighed, resulting in a sample of 200 observations of the variable

x = package weight (lb)

from the population of all Priority Mail packages under 2 pounds. A density histogram constructed from the 200 weights is shown in Figure 7.9(a). Since the histogram is based on a sample of 200 packages, it provides only an approximation to the population histogram. However, the shape of the sample density histogram does suggest that a reasonable model for the population might be the triangular distribution shown in Figure 7.9(b).

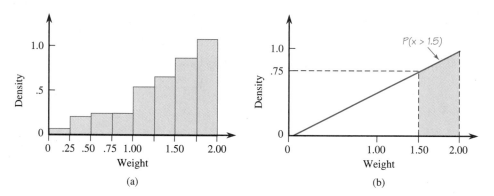

FIGURE 7.9 (a) Histogram of package weight values; (b) Continuous probability distribution for package weight

Note that the total area under the probability distribution curve (the density curve) is equal to

total area of triangle = $\frac{1}{2}$(base)(height) = $\frac{1}{2}(2)(1) = 1$

The probability model can be used to compute the proportion of packages over 1.5 lb, $P(x > 1.5)$. This corresponds to the area of the shaded trapezoid in Figure 7.9(b). In this case, it is easier to compute the area of the unshaded region (which corresponds to $P(x \leq 1.5)$), since this is just the area of a triangle:

$$P(x \leq 1.5) = \frac{1}{2}(1.5)(.75) = .5625$$

Since the total area under a probability density curve is 1,

$$P(x > 1.5) = 1 - .5625 = .4375$$

It is also the case that

$$P(x \geq 1.5) = .4375$$

and that

$$P(x = 1.5) = 0$$

The latter probability is a consequence of the fact that there is zero area under the density curve above a single x value.

EXAMPLE 7.7   An airline's toll-free reservation number recorded the length of time required to provide service to each of 500 callers. This resulted in 500 observations of the continuous numerical variable

x = service time

A density histogram is shown in Figure 7.10(a).

The population of interest is all callers to the reservation line. After studying the density histogram, we might think that a model for the population distribution would be flat over the interval from 0 to 3 and higher but also flat over the interval from 3 to 10. This type of model was thought to be reasonable, since service requests were usually one of two types: (1) requests to make a flight reservation and (2) requests to cancel a reservation. Canceling a reservation, which accounted for about $\frac{1}{8}$ of the calls to the reservation line, could usually be accomplished fairly quickly, whereas making a reservation ($\frac{7}{8}$ of the calls) required more time.

Figure 7.10(b) shows the probability distribution curve proposed as a model for the variable x = service time. The height of the curve for each of the two segments was chosen so that the total area under the curve would be 1 and that $P(x \leq 3) = \frac{1}{8}$ (these were thought to be cancellation calls) and $P(x > 3) = \frac{7}{8}$.

FIGURE 7.10 (a) Histogram of service times; (b) Continuous distribution of service times

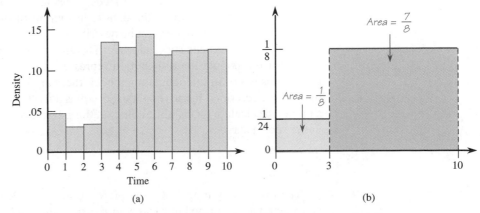

(a)   (b)

Once the model has been developed, it can be used to compute probabilities. For example,

$P(x > 8)$ = area under curve and above interval from 8 to 10

$$= 2\left(\frac{1}{8}\right) = \frac{2}{8} = \frac{1}{4}$$

In the long run, one-fourth of all service requests will require more than 8 minutes. Similarly,

$P(2 < x < 4)$ = area under curve and above interval from 2 to 4

= (area under curve and above interval from 2 to 3)

  + (area under curve and above interval from 3 to 4)

$$= 1\left(\frac{1}{24}\right) + 1\left(\frac{1}{8}\right)$$

$$= \frac{1}{24} + \frac{3}{24}$$

$$= \frac{4}{24}$$

$$= \frac{1}{6}$$

In each of the previous examples, the continuous probability distribution used as a model for the population distribution was simple enough that we were able to calculate probabilities (evaluate areas under the curve) using simple geometry. The next example shows that this is not always the case.

EXAMPLE 7.8   Students at a university use a telephone registration system to register for courses. The variable

x = length of time required for a student to register

was recorded for a large number of students using the system, and the resulting values were used to construct the density histogram of Figure 7.11. The general form of the density histogram can be described as bell shaped and symmetric, and a smooth curve has been superimposed. This smooth curve serves as a reasonable model for the population distribution represented by the density histogram. Although this is a common population model (there are many variables whose distributions are described by curves of this sort), it is not obvious how we could use such a model to calculate probabilities, since at this point it is not clear how to find areas under such a curve.

The probability model of Example 7.8 is an example of a type of symmetric bell-shaped distribution known as a *normal probability distribution*. Normal distri-

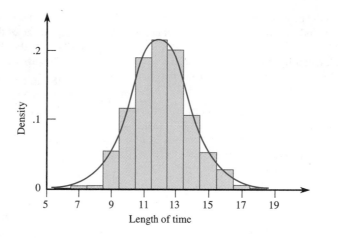

FIGURE 7.11 Histogram and continuous probability distribution for time to register

butions have many and varied applications, and they are investigated in more detail in the next section.

Exercises 7.11 – 7.15

7.11 Consider the population of batteries made by a particular manufacturer. The accompanying density curve represents the probability distribution for the variable x = lifetime (hours).

Shade the region under the curve corresponding to each of the following probabilities (draw a new curve for each part).

a. $P(10 < x < 25)$ **b.** $P(10 \le x \le 25)$ **c.** $P(x < 30)$
d. The probability that the lifetime is at least 25 hours
e. The probability that the lifetime exceeds 30 hours

7.12 A particular professor never dismisses class early. Let x denote the amount of time past the hour (in minutes) that elapses before the professor dismisses class.

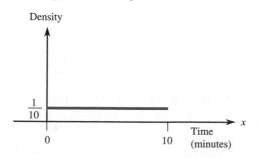

Suppose that the density curve shown in the accompanying figure is an appropriate model for the probability distribution of x.

a. What is the probability that at most 5 minutes elapse before dismissal?
b. What is the probability that between 3 and 5 minutes elapse before dismissal?
c. What do you think is the value of the mean of this distribution?

7.13 Consider the population that consists of all soft contact lenses made by a particular manufacturer and define the variable x = thickness (in mm). Suppose that a reasonable model for the population distribution is the one shown in the accompanying figure.

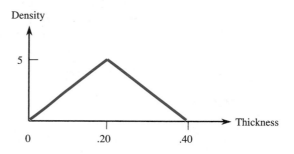

a. Verify that the total area under the density curve is equal to 1. [*Hint*: The area of a triangle is equal to .5(base) · (height).]
b. What is the probability that x is less than .20? Less than .10? More than .30?

c. What is the probability that x is between .10 and .20? (*Hint*: First find the probability that x is *not* between .10 and .20.)

d. Since the density curve is symmetric, the mean of the distribution is .20. What is the probability that thickness is within .05 mm of the mean thickness?

7.14 A delivery service charges a special rate for any package that weighs less than 1 lb. Let x denote the weight of a randomly selected parcel that qualifies for this special rate. The probability distribution of x is specified by the accompanying density curve.

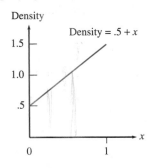

Use the fact that

area of a trapezoid = (base) · (average of two side lengths)

to answer each of the following questions.

a. What is the probability that a randomly selected package of this type weighs at most .5 lb?

b. What is the probability that a randomly selected package of this type weighs between .25 lb and .5 lb?

c. What is the probability that a randomly selected package of this type weighs at least .75 lb?

7.15 Let x denote the time (sec) necessary for an individual to react to a certain stimulus. The probability distribution of x is specified by the accompanying density curve.

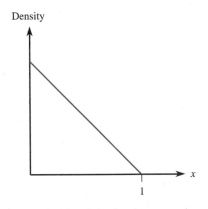

a. What is the height of the density curve above $x = 0$? (*Hint*: Total area = 1.)

b. What is the probability that reaction time exceeds .5 sec?

c. What is the probability that reaction time is at most .25 sec?

7.3 Normal Distributions

Normal distributions formalize the notion of mound-shaped distributions introduced in Chapter 4. Normal distributions are widely used as population models because they provide a reasonable approximation to the distribution of many different variables. They also play a central role in many of the inferential procedures that will be discussed in later chapters. Normal distributions are continuous, bell shaped, and symmetric, as shown in Figure 7.12. Normal distributions are sometimes referred to as a *normal curves*.

FIGURE 7.12 A normal distribution

There are many different normal distributions, and they are distinguished from one another by their mean μ and standard deviation σ. The mean μ of a normal distribution describes where the corresponding curve is centered, and the standard deviation σ describes how much the curve spreads out around the center. As with all continuous probability distributions, the total area under any normal curve is equal to 1. Several normal distributions are shown in Figure 7.13. Notice that the smaller the standard deviation, the taller and narrower is the corresponding curve. Areas under a continuous probability distribution curve represent probabilities, so when the standard deviation is small, a larger area is concentrated near the center of the curve, which means that there is a much greater chance of observing a value near the mean (since μ is at the center).

FIGURE 7.13 Three normal distributions

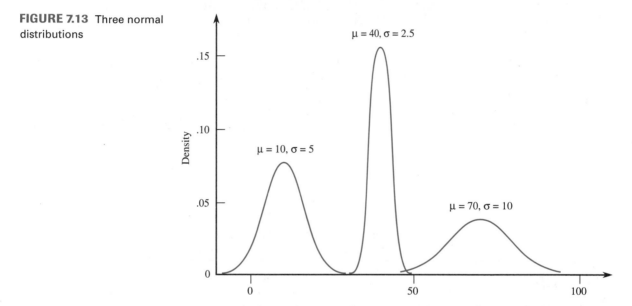

The value of μ is the number on the measurement axis lying directly below the top of the bell. The value of σ can also be ascertained from a picture of the curve. Consider the normal curve shown in Figure 7.14. Starting at the top of the bell (above 100) and moving to the right, the curve turns downward until it is above the value 110. After that point, it continues to decrease in height but is turning up rather than down. Similarly, to the left of 100 it turns down until it reaches 90 and then begins to turn up. The curve changes from turning down to turning up at a distance of 10 on either side of μ, so $\sigma = 10$. In general, σ is the distance to either side of μ at which a normal curve changes from turning downward to turning upward.

FIGURE 7.14 Illustrating μ and σ for a normal curve

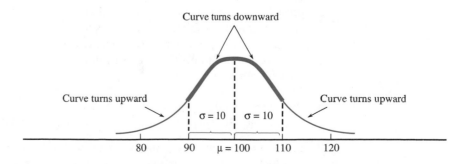

If a normal distribution is to be used as a population model, a mean and standard deviation must be specified. For example, a normal distribution with mean 7 and standard deviation 1 might be used as a model for the population distribution of birth weights from Example 7.4. If this model is a reasonable description of the population distribution, we could use areas under the normal curve with $\mu = 7$ and $\sigma = 1$ to approximate various probabilities related to birth weight. Letting x represent the variable *birth weight,* the probability that a birth weight is over 8 lb (expressed symbolically as $P(x > 8)$) corresponds to the shaded area in Figure 7.15(a). The shaded area in Figure 7.15(b) is the (approximate) probability $P(6.5 < x < 8)$ of a birth weight falling between 6.5 and 8 lb.

FIGURE 7.15 Normal distribution model for birth weight:
(a) Shaded area = $P(x > 8)$;
(b) Shaded area = $P(6.5 < x < 8)$

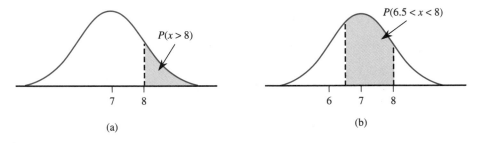

Unfortunately, direct computation of such probabilities (areas under a normal curve) is not simple. To overcome this difficulty, we rely on a table of areas for a reference normal distribution called the *standard normal distribution.*

Definition

The **standard normal distribution** is the normal distribution with

$$\mu = 0 \quad \text{and} \quad \sigma = 1$$

It is customary to use the letter z to represent a variable whose distribution is described by the standard normal curve. The term z *curve* is often used in place of *standard normal curve.*

Few naturally occurring variables have distributions that are well described by the standard normal distribution, but it is important because it is used in probability calculations for other normal distributions as well. When interested in finding a probability based on some other normal curve, we first translate our problem into an "equivalent" problem that involves finding an area under the standard normal curve. A table for the standard normal distribution is then used to find the desired area. To be able to do this, we must first learn to work with the standard normal distribution.

The Standard Normal Distribution

In working with normal distributions, two general skills are required:

1. We must be able to use the normal distribution to compute probabilities, which are areas under a normal curve and above given intervals.

2. We must be able to describe extreme values in the distribution, such as the largest 5%, the smallest 1%, the most extreme 5% (which would include the largest 2.5% and the smallest 2.5%), etc.

Let's begin by looking at how to accomplish these tasks when the distribution of interest is the standard normal distribution.

The standard normal or z curve is shown in Figure 7.16(a). It is centered at $\mu = 0$, and the standard deviation, $\sigma = 1$, is a measure of the extent to which it spreads out about its mean (in this case, 0). Note that this picture is consistent with the Empirical Rule of Chapter 4, with about 95% of the area (probability) associated with values that are within 2 standard deviations of the mean (between -2 and 2) and almost all of the area associated with values that are within 3 standard deviations of the mean (between -3 and 3).

FIGURE 7.16 (a) Standard normal (z) curve; (b) Cumulative z curve area

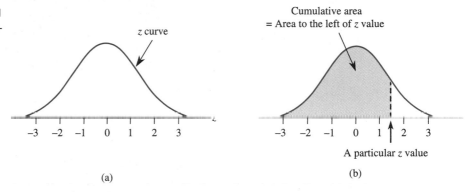

(a)

(b)

Appendix Table II tabulates cumulative z curve areas of the sort shown in Figure 7.16(b) for many different values of z. The smallest value for which the cumulative area is given is -3.89, a value quite far out in the lower tail of the z curve. The next smallest value for which the area appears is -3.88, then -3.87, then -3.86, and so on in increments of .01, terminating with the cumulative area to the left of 3.89.

Using the Table of Standard Normal Curve Areas

For any number z^* between -3.89 and 3.89 and rounded to two decimal places, Appendix Table II gives

(area under z curve to the left of z^*) $= P(z < z^*) = P(z \leq z^*)$

where the letter z is used to represent a variable whose distribution is the standard normal distribution.

To find this probability, locate:

1. The row labeled with the sign of z^* and the digit to either side of the decimal point (for example, -1.7 or 0.5)

2. The column identified with the second digit to the right of the decimal point in z^* (for example, .06 if $z^* = -1.76$)

The number at the intersection of this row and column is the desired probability, $P(z < z^*)$.

FIGURE 7.17

z^*	.00	.01	.02	.03	.04	.05
0.0	.5000	.5040	.5080	.5120	.5160	.5199
0.1	.5398	.5438	.5478	.5517	.5557	.5596
0.2	.5793	.5832	.5871	.5910	.5948	.5987
0.3	.6179	.6217	.6255	.6293	.6331	.6368
0.4	.6554	.6591	.6628	.6664	.6700	.6736
0.5	.6915	.6950	.6985	.7019	.7054	.7088
0.6	.7257	.7291	.7324	.7357	.7389	.7422
0.7	.7580	.7611	.7642	.7673	.7704	.7734
0.8	.7881	.7910	.7939	.7967	.7995	.8023
0.9	.8159	.8186	.8212	.8238	.8264	.8289
1.0	.8413	.8438	.8461	.8485	.8508	.8531
1.1	.8643	.8665	.8686	.8708	.8729	.8749
1.2	.8849	.8869	.8888	.8907	.8925	.8944
1.3	.9032	.9049	.9066	.9082	.9099	.9115
1.4	.9192	.9207	.9222	.9236	.9251	.9265
1.5	.9332	.9345	.9357	.9370	.9382	.9394
1.6	.9452	.9463	.9474	.9484	.9495	.9505
1.7	.9554	.9564	.9573	.9582	.9591	.9599
1.8	.9641	.9649	.9656	.9664	.9671	.9678

$P(z < 1.42)$

A portion of the table of standard normal curve areas is shown in Figure 7.17. To find the z curve area to the left of 1.42, look in the row labeled 1.4 and the column labeled .02 (the highlighted row and column in Figure 7.17). From the table, the corresponding cumulative area is .9222. So

$$P(z < 1.42) = z \text{ curve area to the left of } 1.42 = .9222$$

Since the total area under the z curve is 1, it follows that

$$z \text{ curve area to the right of } 1.42 = 1 - (z \text{ curve area to the left of } 1.42)$$
$$= 1 - .9222$$
$$= .0778$$

These probabilities can be interpreted as meaning that, in a long sequence of observations selected from the standard normal distribution, roughly 92.22% of the observed values will be smaller than 1.42, and 7.78% will be larger than 1.42.

EXAMPLE 7.9

The probability $P(z < -1.76)$ is found at the intersection of the -1.7 row and the .06 column of the z table. The result is

$$P(z < -1.76) = .0392$$

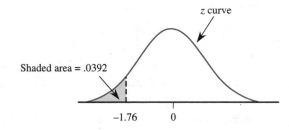

In other words, in a long sequence of observations selected from the standard normal distribution, roughly 3.9% of the observed values will be smaller than -1.76. Similarly,

$P(z \leq 0.58) =$ entry in 0.5 row and .08 column of Table II $= .7190$

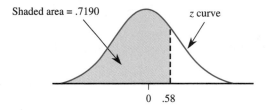

Consider $P(z < -4.12)$. This probability does not appear in Appendix Table II; there is no -4.1 row. However, $P(z < -4.12)$ must be less than $P(z < -3.89)$, the smallest z value in the table, because -4.12 is farther out in the lower tail of the z curve. Since $P(z < -3.89) = .0000$ (that is, zero to four decimal places), it follows that

$P(z < -4.12) \approx 0$

Similarly,

$P(z < 4.18) > P(z < 3.89) = 1.0000$

from which we conclude that

$P(z < 4.18) \approx 1$

We can also use the probabilities tabulated in Appendix Table II to calculate other probabilities involving z. The probability that z is larger than a value c is

$P(z > c) =$ area under the z curve to the right of $c = 1 - P(z \leq c)$

In words, the area to the right of a value (a right-tail area) is 1 minus the corresponding cumulative area. This is illustrated in Figure 7.18 on page 254.

Similarly, the probability that z falls in the interval between a lower limit a and an upper limit b is

$P(a < z < b) =$ area under the z curve and above the interval from a to b
$= P(z < b) - P(z < a)$

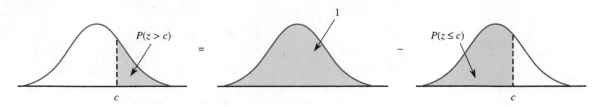

FIGURE 7.18 The relationship between an upper-tail area and a cumulative area

That is, $P(a < z < b)$ is the difference between two cumulative areas, as illustrated in Figure 7.19.

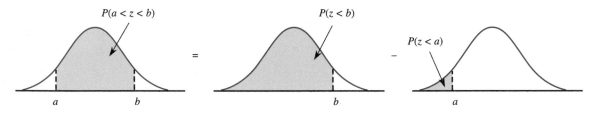

FIGURE 7.19 $P(a < z < b)$ as a difference of two cumulative areas

EXAMPLE 7.10

The probability that z is between -1.76 and 0.58 is

$$P(-1.76 < z < 0.58) = P(z < 0.58) - P(z < -1.76)$$
$$= .7190 - .0392$$
$$= .6798$$

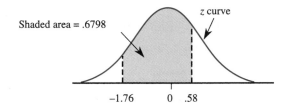

The probability that z is between -2 and $+2$ (within 2 standard deviations of its mean, since $\mu = 0$ and $\sigma = 1$) is

$$P(-2.00 < z < 2.00) = P(z < 2.00) - P(z < -2.00)$$
$$= .9772 - .0228$$
$$= .9544$$
$$\approx .95$$

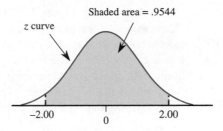

Shaded area = .9544

z curve

−2.00   0   2.00

This last probability is the basis for one part of the Empirical Rule, which states that when a histogram is well approximated by a normal curve, roughly 95% of the values are within 2 standard deviations of the mean.

The probability that the value of z exceeds 1.96 is

$$P(z > 1.96) = 1 - P(z \le 1.96)$$
$$= 1 - .9750$$
$$= .0250$$

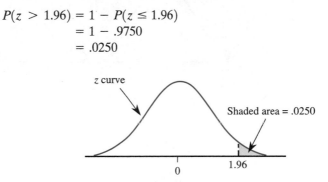

z curve

Shaded area = .0250

0   1.96

That is, 2.5% of the area under the z curve lies to the right of 1.96 in the upper tail. Similarly,

$$P(z > -1.28) = \text{area to the right of } -1.28$$
$$= 1 - P(z \le -1.28)$$
$$= 1 - .1003$$
$$= .8997$$
$$\approx .90$$

Identifying Extreme Values

Let's now see how we can identify extreme values in the distribution. For example, we might want to describe the values included in the smallest 2% of the distribution or the values making up the most extreme 5% (which includes the largest 2.5% and the smallest 2.5%).

EXAMPLE 7.11   Suppose we want to describe the values that make up the smallest 2% of the standard normal distribution. Symbolically, we are trying to find a value (call it z^*) such that

$$P(z < z^*) = .02$$

This is illustrated in Figure 7.20. The figure shows that the cumulative area for $z*$ is .02, so we look for a cumulative area of .0200 in the body of Appendix Table II. The closest cumulative area in the table is .0202, in the -2.0 row and .05 column; so we will use $z* = -2.05$, the best approximation from the table. Variable values less than -2.05 make up the smallest 2% of the standard normal distribution.

Suppose that we had been interested in the largest 5% of all z values. We would then be trying to find a value of $z*$ for which

$$P(z > z*) = .05$$

as illustrated in Figure 7.21.

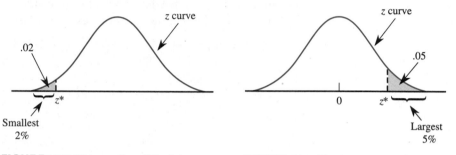

FIGURE 7.20 The smallest 2% of the standard normal distribution

FIGURE 7.21 The largest 5% of the standard normal distribution

Since Appendix Table II always works with cumulative area (area to the left), the first step is to determine

area to the left of $z* = 1 - .05 = .95$

Looking for the cumulative area closest to .95 in Table II, we find that .95 falls exactly halfway between .9495 (corresponding to a z value of 1.64) and .9505 (corresponding to a z value of 1.65). Since .9500 is exactly halfway between the two areas, we will use a z value that is halfway between 1.64 and 1.65. (If one had been closer to .9500 than the other, we would just use the z value corresponding to the closest area.) This gives

$$z* = \frac{1.64 + 1.65}{2} = 1.645$$

Values greater than 1.645 make up the largest 5% of the standard normal distribution. By symmetry, -1.645 separates the smallest 5% of all z values from the others.

EXAMPLE 7.12

Sometimes we are interested in identifying the most extreme (unusually large *or* small) values in a distribution. Consider describing the values that make up the most extreme 5% of the standard normal distribution. That is, we want to separate the middle 95% from the extreme 5%. This is illustrated in Figure 7.22.

FIGURE 7.22 The most extreme 5% of the standard normal distribution

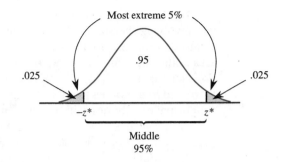

Since the standard normal distribution is symmetric, the most extreme 5% would be equally divided between the high side and the low side of the distribution, resulting in an area of .025 for each of the tails of the z curve. Symmetry about 0 implies that if z^* denotes the value that separates the largest 2.5%, the value that separates the smallest 2.5% will be simply $-z^*$.

To find z^*, first determine the cumulative area for z^*, which is

area to the left of $z^* = .95 + .025 = .975$

The cumulative area .9750 appears in the 1.9 row and .06 column of Table II, so $z^* = 1.96$. For the standard normal distribution, 95% of the variable values fall between -1.96 and 1.96; the most extreme 5% are those values that are either greater than 1.96 or less than -1.96.

═══════════

Other Normal Distributions

We will now show how z curve areas can be used to calculate probabilities and describe extreme values for any normal distribution. Remember that the letter z is reserved for those variables whose distribution is standard normal; the letter x is used more generally for any variable whose distribution is described by a normal curve with mean μ and standard deviation σ.

Suppose that we want to compute $P(a < x < b)$, the probability that the variable x lies in a particular range. This probability corresponds to an area under a normal curve and above the interval from a to b, as shown in Figure 7.23(a).

FIGURE 7.23 Equality of nonstandard and standard normal curve areas

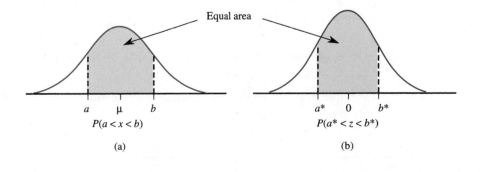

Our strategy for obtaining this probability will be to find an "equivalent" problem involving the standard normal distribution. Finding an equivalent problem means determining an interval (a^*, b^*) that has the same probability for z (same area under the z curve) as does the interval (a, b) in our original normal distribution (see Figure 7.23(b)). The * notation is used to distinguish a and b from a^* and b^*; a^* and b^* are values from the z curve, whereas a and b are values from the original normal distribution with mean μ and standard deviation σ. To find a^* and b^*, we simply calculate z scores for the endpoints of the interval for which a probability is desired. This process is called **standardizing** the endpoints. For example, suppose that the variable x has a normal distribution with mean $\mu = 100$ and standard deviation $\sigma = 5$. To calculate

$$P(98 < x < 107)$$

we first translate this problem into an equivalent problem for the standard normal distribution. Recall from Chapter 4 that a z score, or standardized score, tells how many standard deviations away from the mean a value lies; it is calculated by first subtracting the mean and then dividing by the standard deviation. Converting the lower endpoint $a = 98$ to a z score gives

$$a^* = \frac{98 - 100}{5} = \frac{-2}{5} = -.40$$

and converting the upper endpoint yields

$$b^* = \frac{107 - 100}{5} = \frac{7}{5} = 1.40$$

Then

$$P(98 < x < 107) = P(-.40 < z < 1.40)$$

The probability $P(-.40 < z < 1.40)$ can now be evaluated using Appendix Table II.

Finding Probabilities

To calculate probabilities for any normal distribution, standardize the relevant values and then use the table of z curve areas.

More specifically, if x is a variable whose behavior is described by a normal distribution with mean μ and standard deviation σ, then

$$P(x < b) = P(z < b^*)$$
$$P(a < x) = P(a^* < z) \quad \text{or, equivalently,} \quad P(x > a) = P(z > a^*)$$
$$P(a < x < b) = P(a^* < z < b^*)$$

where z is a variable whose distribution is standard normal and

$$a^* = \frac{a - \mu}{\sigma} \qquad b^* = \frac{b - \mu}{\sigma}$$

EXAMPLE 7.13   In poor countries, the growth of children can be an important indicator of general levels of nutrition and health. Data from the article "The Osteological Paradox: Problems in Inferring Prehistoric Health from Skeletal Samples" (*Current Anthropology* (1992): 343–370) suggests that a reasonable model for the population distribution of the continuous numerical variable x = height of a randomly selected 5-year-old child is a normal distribution with a mean of μ = 100 cm and standard deviation σ = 6 cm. What proportion of the population has height between 94 cm and 112 cm? To answer this question, we must find

$$P(94 < x < 112)$$

Translating to an equivalent problem for the standard normal distribution,

$$a^* = \frac{a - \mu}{\sigma} = \frac{94 - 100}{6} = -1.00 \qquad b^* = \frac{b - \mu}{\sigma} = \frac{112 - 100}{6} = 2.00$$

Then

$$
\begin{aligned}
P(94 < x < 112) &= P(-1.00 < z < 2.00) \\
&= (z \text{ curve area to the left of } 2.00) - (z \text{ curve area to the left of } -1.00) \\
&= .9772 - .1587 \\
&= .8185
\end{aligned}
$$

The probabilities for x and z are shown in Figure 7.24. If heights for many children from this population were determined, about 82% of them would fall between 94 and 112 cm.

FIGURE 7.24
$P(94 < x < 112)$ and corresponding z curve area

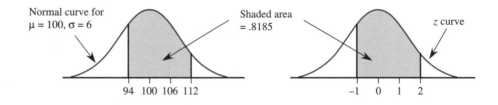

What is the probability that a randomly chosen child will be taller than 110 cm? To evaluate $P(x > 110)$, we first compute

$$a^* = \frac{a - \mu}{\sigma} = \frac{110 - 100}{6} = 1.67$$

Then, as shown in Figure 7.25,

FIGURE 7.25 $P(x > 110)$ and corresponding z curve area

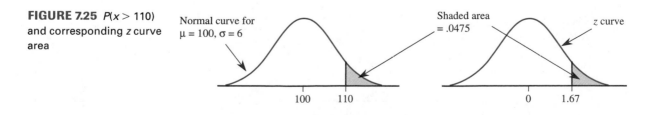

$$P(x > 110) = P(z > 1.67)$$
$$= z \text{ curve area to the right of } 1.67$$
$$= 1 - (z \text{ curve area to the left of } 1.67)$$
$$= 1 - .9525$$
$$= .0475$$

EXAMPLE 7.14   Although there is some controversy regarding the appropriateness of IQ scores as a measure of intelligence, they are commonly used for a variety of purposes. IQ scores are scaled so that the mean is 100 and the standard deviation is 15, and the scores are approximately normally distributed. (IQ score is actually a discrete variable, but its population distribution closely resembles a normal curve.) If we define

x = IQ score of a randomly selected individual

then x has a normal distribution with $\mu = 100$ and $\sigma = 15$.

To be eligible for membership in MENSA, an organization purportedly for those of high intelligence, an individual must have an IQ above 130. What proportion of the population would quality for MENSA membership? An answer to this question requires evaluating $P(x > 130)$. This probability is shown in Figure 7.26. With $a = 130$,

$$a^* = \frac{130 - 100}{15} = 2.00$$

So, as shown in Figure 7.27,

$$P(x > 130) = P(z > 2.00)$$
$$= z \text{ curve area to the right of } 2.00$$
$$= 1 - (z \text{ curve area to the left of } 2.00)$$
$$= 1 - .9772$$
$$= .0228$$

Only 2.28% of the population would qualify for MENSA membership.

FIGURE 7.26 Normal distribution and desired proportion for Example 7.14

FIGURE 7.27 $P(x > 130)$ and corresponding z curve area

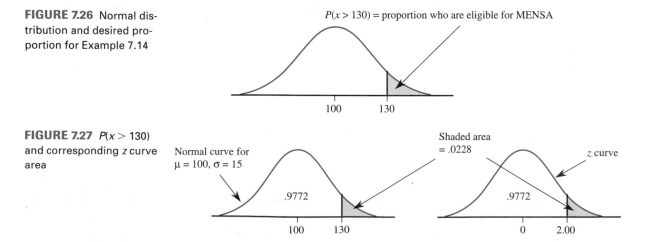

Suppose that we were interested in the proportion of the population with IQ scores below 80 — that is, $P(x < 80)$. With $b = 80$,

$$b^* = \frac{80 - 100}{15} = -1.33$$

So

$$P(x < 80) = P(z < -1.33)$$
$$= z \text{ curve area to the left of } -1.33$$
$$= .0918$$

as shown in Figure 7.28. This probability (.0918) tells us that just a little over 9% of the population have IQ scores below 80.

FIGURE 7.28 $P(x < 80)$ and corresponding z curve area

Shaded area = .0918

Now consider the proportion of the population with IQs between 75 and 125. Using $a = 75$ and $b = 125$,

$$a^* = \frac{75 - 100}{15} = -1.67 \qquad b^* = \frac{125 - 100}{15} = 1.67$$

so

$$P(75 < x < 125) = P(-1.67 < z < 1.67)$$
$$= z \text{ curve area between } -1.67 \text{ and } 1.67$$
$$= (z \text{ curve area to the left of } 1.67) - (z \text{ curve area to the left of } -1.67)$$
$$= .9525 - .0475$$
$$= .9050$$

as illustrated in Figure 7.29. This tells us that 90.5% of the population have IQ scores between 75 and 125. Of the 9.5% whose IQ score is not between 75 and 125, half (4.75%) would have scores over 125, and the other half would have scores below 75.

FIGURE 7.29
$P(75 < x < 125)$ and corresponding z curve area

Shaded area = .9050

When we translate from a problem involving a normal distribution with mean μ and standard deviation σ to one involving the standard normal, we convert interval endpoints to z scores:

$$z = \frac{x - \mu}{\sigma}$$

Since a z score can be interpreted as giving the distance of an x value from the mean in units of the standard deviation, a z score of 1.4 corresponds to an x value that is 1.4 standard deviations above its mean, and a z score of -2.1 corresponds to an x value that is 2.1 standard deviations below its mean.

Suppose that we are trying to evaluate $P(x < 60)$ for a variable whose distribution is normal with $\mu = 50$ and $\sigma = 5$. Converting the endpoint 60 to a z score gives

$$z = \frac{60 - 50}{5} = 2$$

which tells us that the value 60 is 2 standard deviations above its mean. We then have

$$P(x < 60) = P(z < 2)$$

where z is a standard normal variable. Notice that for the standard normal distribution, the value 2 is 2 standard deviations above the mean, since the mean is 0 and the standard deviation is 1. The value $z = 2$ is located the same distance (measured in standard deviations) from the mean of the standard normal as is the value $x = 60$ from the mean in the normal distribution with $\mu = 50$ and $\sigma = 5$. This is why the translation using z scores results in an "equivalent" problem involving the standard normal distribution.

Describing Extreme Values in a Normal Distribution

To describe the extreme values for a normal distribution with mean μ and standard deviation σ, we first solve the corresponding problem for the standard normal distribution and then translate our answer into one for the normal distribution of interest. This process is illustrated in the following example.

EXAMPLE 7.15

Data on the length of time required to complete registration for classes using a telephone registration system suggests that the distribution of the variable

$x = $ time to register

for students at a particular university can be well approximated by a normal distribution with mean $\mu = 12$ minutes and standard deviation $\sigma = 2$ minutes. (The normal distribution might not be an appropriate model for $x = $ time to register at another university. Many factors influence the shape, center, and spread of such a distribution.) Because some students do not sign off properly, the university would like to disconnect students automatically after some amount of time has elapsed. It is decided to choose this time such that only 1% of the students will be disconnected while they are still attempting to register. To determine the amount of time that should be allowed before disconnecting a student, we need to describe the largest 1% of the distribution of time to register. These are the individuals who will be mistakenly disconnected. This is illustrated in Figure 7.30(a). To determine the value of x^*, we first solve the analogous problem for the standard normal distribution, as shown in Figure 7.30(b).

FIGURE 7.30 Capturing the largest 1% in a normal distribution

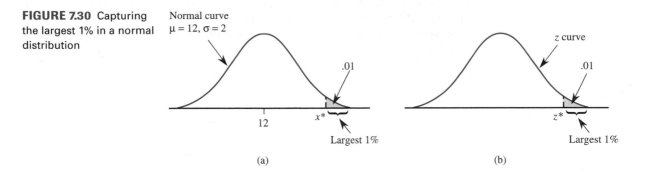

Looking in Table II for a cumulative area of .99, the closest entry (.9901) we find is in the 2.3 row and the .03 column, from which $z^* = 2.33$. For the standard normal distribution, the largest 1% of the distribution is made up of those values greater than 2.33. An equivalent statement is that the largest 1% are those with z scores greater than 2.33. This implies that in the *time to register* (x) distribution (or any other normal distribution), the largest 1% will be those values with z scores greater than 2.33 or, equivalently, those x values more than 2.33 standard deviations above the mean. Here, the standard deviation is 2, so 2.33 standard deviations is 2.33(2), and it follows that

$$x^* = 12 + 2.33(2) = 12 + 4.66 = 16.66$$

The largest 1% of the *time to register* distribution is made up of values that are greater than 16.66 minutes. If the university system were set to disconnect students after 16.66 minutes, only 1% of the students registering would be disconnected before completing their registration.

To convert a z score z^* back to an x value, use

$$x^* = \mu + z^*\sigma$$

EXAMPLE 7.16   The Environmental Protection Agency (EPA) has developed a testing program to monitor vehicle emissions levels of several pollutants. The article "Determining Statistical Characteristics of a Vehicle Emissions Audit Procedure" (*Technometrics* (1980): 483–493) describes the program, which measures pollutants from various types of vehicles, all following a fixed driving schedule. Data in the article suggests that the emissions of oxides of nitrogen, which are major constituents of smog, can be plausibly modeled using a normal distribution. Let x denote the amount of this pollutant emitted by a randomly selected vehicle. The distribution of x can be described by a normal distribution with $\mu = 1.6$ and $\sigma = .4$.

Suppose that the EPA wants to offer some sort of incentive to get the worst polluters off the road. What emissions levels constitute the worst 10% of the vehicles? The worst 10% would be the 10% with the highest emissions level, as shown in the illustration.

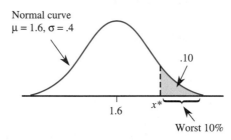

For the standard normal distribution, the largest 10% are those with z values greater than $z^* = 1.28$ (from Table II, based on a cumulative area of .90). Then

$$x^* = \mu + z^*\sigma$$
$$= 1.6 + 1.28(.4)$$
$$= 1.6 + .512$$
$$= 2.112$$

In the population of vehicles of the type considered, about 10% would have oxide emissions levels greater than 2.112.

Exercises 7.16 – 7.32

7.16 Determine the following standard normal (z) curve areas.
  a. The area under the z curve to the left of 1.75
  b. The area under the z curve to the left of $-.68$
  c. The area under the z curve to the right of 1.20
  d. The area under the z curve to the right of -2.82
  e. The area under the z curve between -2.22 and .53
  f. The area under the z curve between -1 and 1
  g. The area under the z curve between -4 and 4

7.17 Determine each of the areas under the standard normal (z) curve.
  a. To the left of -1.28
  c. Between -1 and 2
  e. To the right of -5
  g. To the left of .23
  b To the right of 1.28
  d. To the right of 0
  f. Between -1.6 and 2.5

7.18 Let z denote a random variable having a standard normal distribution. Determine each of the following probabilities.
  a. $P(z < 2.36)$
  b. $P(z \le 2.36)$
  c. $P(z < -1.23)$
  d. $P(1.14 < z < 3.35)$
  e. $P(-.77 \le z \le -.55)$
  f. $P(z > 2)$
  g. $P(z \ge -3.38)$
  h. $P(z < 4.98)$

7.19 Let z denote a random variable having a normal distribution with $\mu = 0$ and $\sigma = 1$. Determine each of the following probabilities.
  a. $P(z < .10)$
  b. $P(z < -.10)$
  c. $P(.40 < z < .85)$
  d. $P(-.85 < z < -.40)$
  e. $P(-.40 < z < .85)$
  f. $P(z > -1.25)$
  g. $P(z < -1.50 \; or \; z > 2.50)$

7.20 Let z denote a variable that has a standard normal distribution. Determine the value $z*$ to satisfy the following conditions.

    a. $P(z < z*) = .025$ **b.** $P(z < z*) = .01$
    c. $P(z < z*) = .05$ **d.** $P(z > z*) = .02$
    e. $P(z > z*) = .01$ **f.** $P(z > z* \text{ or } z < -z*) = .20$

7.21 Determine the value $z*$ that
    a. Separates the largest 3% of all z values from the others
    b. Separates the largest 1% of all z values from the others
    c. Separates the smallest 4% of all z values from the others
    d. Separates the smallest 10% of all z values from the others

7.22 Determine the value of $z*$ such that
    a. $z*$ and $-z*$ separate the middle 95% of all z values from the most extreme 5%
    b. $z*$ and $-z*$ separate the middle 90% of all z values from the most extreme 10%
    c. $z*$ and $-z*$ separate the middle 98% of all z values from the most extreme 2%
    d. $z*$ and $-z*$ separate the middle 92% of all z values from the most extreme 8%

7.23 Because $P(z < .44) = .67$, 67% of all z values are less than .44, and .44 is the 67th percentile of the standard normal distribution. Determine the value of each of the following percentiles for the standard normal distribution. (If the cumulative area that you must look for does not appear in the z table, use the closest entry.)
    a. The 91st percentile (*Hint*: Look for area .9100.)
    b. The 77th percentile
    c. The 50th percentile
    d. The 9th percentile
    e. What is the relationship between the 70th z percentile and the 30th z percentile?

7.24 Consider the population of all 1-gallon cans of dusty rose paint manufactured by a particular paint company. Suppose that a normal distribution with mean $\mu = 5$ ml and standard deviation $\sigma = .2$ ml is a reasonable model for the distribution of the variable x = amount of red dye in the paint mixture. Use the normal distribution model to calculate the following probabilities.
    a. $P(x < 5.0)$ **b.** $P(x < 5.4)$
    c. $P(x \leq 5.4)$ **d.** $P(4.6 < x < 5.2)$
    e. $P(x > 4.5)$ **f.** $P(x > 4.0)$

7.25 Consider babies born in the "normal" range of 37–43 weeks gestational age. Extensive data supports the assumption that for such babies born in the United States,

birth weight is normally distributed with mean 3432 g and standard deviation 482 g. [The article "Are Babies Normal" (*The American Statistician* (1999): 298–302) analyzed data from a particular year; for a sensible choice of class intervals, a histogram did not look at all normal but after further investigations it was determined that this was due to some hospitals measuring weight in grams and others measuring to the nearest ounce and then converting to grams. A modified choice of class intervals that allowed for this gave a histogram that was well described by a normal distribution.]
    a. What is the probability that the birth weight of a randomly selected baby of this type exceeds 4000 grams? Is between 3000 and 4000 grams?
    b. What is the probability that the birth weight of a randomly selected baby of this type is either less than 2000 grams or greater than 5000 grams?
    c. What is the probability that the birth weight of a randomly selected baby of this type exceeds 7 lb?
    d. How would you characterize the most extreme .1% of all birth weights?
    e. If x is a random variable with a normal distribution and a is a numerical constant ($a \neq 0$), then $y = ax$ also has a normal distribution. Use this to determine the distribution of birth weight expressed in pounds (shape, mean, and standard deviation), and then recalculate the probability from part **c**. How does this compare to your previous answer?

7.26 A machine that cuts corks for wine bottles operates in such a way that the distribution of the diameter of the corks produced is well approximated by a normal distribution with mean 3 cm and standard deviation .1 cm. The specifications call for corks with diameters between 2.9 and 3.1 cm. A cork not meeting the specifications is considered defective. (A cork that is too small leaks and causes the wine to deteriorate; a cork that is too large doesn't fit in the bottle.) What proportion of corks produced by this machine are defective?

7.27 Refer to Exercise 7.26. Suppose that there are two machines available for cutting corks. The one described in the preceding problem produces corks with diameters that are approximately normally distributed with mean 3 cm and standard deviation .1 cm. The second machine produces corks with diameters that are approximately normally distributed with mean 3.05 cm and standard deviation .01 cm. Which machine would you recommend? (*Hint*: Which machine would produce the fewest defective corks?)

7.28 A gasoline tank for a certain car is designed to hold 15 gallons of gas. Suppose that the variable x = actual capacity of a randomly selected tank has a distribution that is well approximated by a normal curve with mean 15.0 gal and standard deviation .1 gal.

  a. What is the probability that a randomly selected tank will hold at most 14.8 gal?

  b. What is the probability that a randomly selected tank will hold between 14.7 and 15.1 gal?

  c. If two such tanks are independently selected, what is the probability that both hold at most 15 gal?

7.29 The time that it takes a randomly selected job applicant to perform a certain task has a distribution that can be approximated by a normal distribution with a mean value of 120 sec and a standard deviation of 20 sec. The fastest 10% are to be given advanced training. What task times qualify individuals for such training?

7.30 A machine that produces ball bearings has initially been set so that the true average diameter of the bearings it produces is .500 in. A bearing is acceptable if its diameter is within .004 in. of this target value. Suppose, however, that the setting has changed during the course of production, so that the distribution of the diameters produced is well approximated by a normal distribution with mean .499 in and standard deviation .002 in. What percentage of the bearings produced will not be acceptable?

7.31 Suppose that the distribution of net typing rate in words per minute (wpm) for experienced typists can be approximated by a normal curve with mean 60 wpm and standard deviation 15 wpm. [The paper "Effects of Age and Skill in Typing" (*J. of Exper. Psych.* (1984): 345–371)

describes how net rate is obtained from gross rate by using a correction for errors.]

  a. What is the probability that a randomly selected typist's net rate is at most 60 wpm? Less than 60 wpm?

  b. What is the probability that a randomly selected typist's net rate is between 45 and 90 wpm?

  c. Would you be surprised to find a typist in this population whose net rate exceeded 105 wpm? (*Note:* The largest net rate in a sample described in the paper cited is 104 wpm.)

  d. Suppose that two typists are independently selected. What is the probability that both their typing rates exceed 75 wpm?

  e. Suppose that special training is to be made available to the slowest 20% of the typists. What typing speeds would qualify individuals for this training?

7.32 Consider the variable x = time required for a college student to complete a standardized exam. Suppose that for the population of students at a particular university, the distribution of x is well approximated by a normal curve with mean 45 min and standard deviation 5 min.

  a. If 50 minutes is allowed for the exam, what proportion of students at this university would be unable to finish in the allotted time?

  b. How much time should be allowed for the exam if we wanted 90% of the students taking the test to be able to finish in the allotted time?

  c. How much time is required for the fastest 25% of all students to complete the exam?

7.4   Checking for Normality and Normalizing Transformations

Some of the most frequently used statistical methods are valid only when a sample $x_1, x_2, \ldots, x_n$ has come from a population distribution that is at least approximately normal. One way to see whether an assumption of population normality is plausible is to construct a **normal probability plot.** One version of this plot utilizes certain quantities called **normal scores.** The values of the normal scores depend on the sample size n. For example, the normal scores when $n = 10$ are as follows:

−1.539	−1.001	−.656	−.376	−.123
.123	.376	.656	1.001	1.539

To interpret these numbers, think of selecting sample after sample from a standard normal distribution, each one consisting of $n = 10$ observations. Then -1.539 is the long-run average of the smallest observation from each sample, -1.001 is the long-run average of the second smallest observation from each sample, and so on. In other words, -1.539 is the mean value of the smallest observation in a sample of size 10 from the z distribution, -1.001 is the mean value of the second smallest observation, etc.

Extensive tabulations of normal scores for many different sample sizes are available. Alternatively, many software packages (such as MINITAB and SAS) and some graphing calculators can compute these scores on request and then construct a normal probability plot. Some graphing calculators and software packages use a slightly different algorithm to compute normal scores. This does not change the overall character of a normal probability plot, so either the tabled values or those given by the computer or calculator can be used.

After ordering the sample observations from smallest to largest, the smallest normal score is paired with the smallest observation, the second smallest normal score with the second smallest observation, and so on. The first number in a pair is the normal score, and the second is the observed data value. A normal probability plot is just a scatter plot of the (normal score, observed value) pairs.

If the sample has actually been selected from a *standard* normal distribution, the second number in each pair should be reasonably close to the first number (ordered observation $\approx$ corresponding mean value). Then the n plotted points will fall near a line with slope equal to 1 (a 45° line) passing through (0, 0). When the sample has been obtained from *some* normal population distribution, the plotted points should be close to *some* straight line.

Definition

A **normal probability plot** is a scatter plot of the (normal score, observation) pairs.

A substantial linear pattern in a normal probability plot suggests that population normality is plausible. On the other hand, a systematic departure from a straight-line pattern (such as curvature in the plot) casts doubt on the legitimacy of assuming a normal population distribution.

EXAMPLE 7.17

The following ten observations are widths of contact windows in integrated circuit chips:

| 3.21 | 2.49 | 2.94 | 4.38 | 4.02 | 3.62 | 3.30 | 2.85 | 3.34 | 3.81 |

The ten pairs for the normal probability plot are then

$(-1.539, 2.49)$	$(.123, 3.34)$
$(-1.001, 2.85)$	$(.376, 3.62)$
$(-.656, 2.94)$	$(.656, 3.81)$
$(-.376, 3.21)$	$(1.001, 4.02)$
$(-.123, 3.30)$	$(1.539, 4.38)$

The normal probability plot is shown in Figure 7.31 on page 268. The linearity of the plot supports the assumption that the distribution of window widths from which these observations were drawn is normal.

FIGURE 7.31 A normal probability plot for Example 7.17

The judgment as to whether a plot does or does not show a substantial linear pattern is somewhat subjective. Particularly when *n* is small, normality should not be ruled out unless the departure from linearity is very clear-cut. Figure 7.32 displays several plots that suggest a nonnormal population distribution.

FIGURE 7.32 Plots suggesting nonnormality: (a) Indication that the population distribution is skewed; (b) Indication that the population distribution has heavier tails than a normal curve; (c) Presence of an outlier

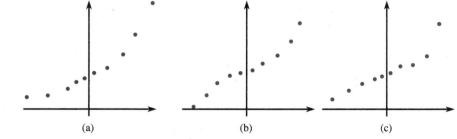

Using the Correlation Coefficient to Check Normality

The correlation coefficient *r* was introduced in Chapter 5 as a quantitative measure of the extent to which the points in a scatter plot fall close to a straight line. Let's denote the *n* (normal score, observation) pairs as follows:

(smallest normal score, smallest observation)

⋮

(largest normal score, largest observation)

Then the correlation coefficient can be computed using the defining equation for *r* given in Chapter 5. The normal probability plot always slopes upward (since it is based on values ordered from smallest to largest), so r will be a positive number. A value of r quite close to 1 indicates a very strong linear relationship in the normal probability plot. If r is too much smaller than 1, normality of the underlying distribution is questionable.

How far below 1 does r have to be before we begin to doubt seriously the plausibility of normality? The answer depends on the sample size n. If n is small, an r value somewhat below 1 would not be surprising even when the distribution is normal, but if n is large, only an r value very close to 1 would support the assumption of normality. For selected values of n, Table 7.1 gives critical values to which r can be compared in checking for normality.

If

$r <$ critical r for corresponding n

considerable doubt is cast on the assumption of population normality.

If the sample size is between two tabled values of n, use the critical value for the larger sample size (for example, if $n = 46$, use the value .966 for sample size 50). In addition to providing a normal probability plot, MINITAB will automatically compute r on request.

Table 7.1 *Values to which r can be compared to check for normality**

n	5	10	15	20	25	30	40	50	60	75
Critical r	.832	.880	.911	.929	.941	.949	.960	.966	.971	.976

*Source: MINITAB User's Manual.

How were the critical values in Table 7.1 obtained? Consider the critical value .941 for $n = 25$. Suppose that the underlying distribution is actually normal. Consider obtaining a large number of different samples, each one consisting of 25 observations, and computing the value of r for each one. Then it can be shown that only 1% of the samples result in an r value less than the critical value .941. That is, .941 was chosen to guarantee a 1% error rate: In only 1% of all cases will we judge normality implausible when the distribution is really normal. The other critical values are also chosen to yield a 1% error rate for the corresponding sample sizes. It might have occurred to you that another type of error is possible: obtaining a large value of r and concluding that normality is a reasonable assumption when the distribution is actually quite nonnormal. This type of error is more difficult to control than the type mentioned previously, but the procedure we have described does a good job in both respects.

EXAMPLE 7.18   (Example 7.17 continued)   The sample size for the data on contact window width of Example 7.17 is $n = 10$. The critical r, from Table 7.1, is then .880. The correlation coefficient calculated using the (normal score, observation) pairs is $r = .995$.

Since *r* is larger than the critical *r* for a sample of size 10, it is plausible that the population distribution of window widths from which this sample was drawn is approximately normal.

Transforming Data to Obtain a Distribution That Is Approximately Normal

Many of the most frequently used statistical methods are valid only when the sample is selected at random from a population whose distribution is at least approximately normal. When the sample histogram shows a distinctly nonnormal shape, it is common to use a transformation or reexpression of the data. By *transforming* data, we mean using some specified mathematical function (such as square root, logarithm, or reciprocal) on each data value to produce a set of transformed data. We can then study and summarize the distribution of these transformed values. We saw in Chapter 5 that, with bivariate data, one or both of the variables might be transformed in an attempt to find two variables that are linearly related. With univariate data, a transformation is usually chosen to yield a distribution of transformed values that is more symmetric and more closely approximated by a normal curve than was the original distribution.

EXAMPLE 7.19

A data set that has been used by several authors to introduce the concept of transformation (see "Exploratory Methods for Choosing Power Transformations," *J. Amer. Stat. Assoc.* (1982): 103–108, for example) consists of values of March precipitation for Minneapolis–St. Paul over a period of 30 years. These values are displayed in Table 7.2, along with the square root of each value, and histograms

Table 7.2 *Original and square-root transformed values of March precipitation in Minneapolis–St. Paul over a 30-year period*

Year	Precipitation	$\sqrt{\text{Precipitation}}$	Year	Precipitation	$\sqrt{\text{Precipitation}}$
1	.77	.88	16	1.62	1.27
2	1.74	1.32	17	1.31	1.14
3	.81	.90	18	.32	.57
4	1.20	1.10	19	.59	.77
5	1.95	1.40	20	.81	.90
6	1.20	1.10	21	2.81	1.68
7	.47	.69	22	1.87	1.37
8	1.43	1.20	23	1.18	1.09
9	3.37	1.84	24	1.35	1.16
10	2.20	1.48	25	4.75	2.18
11	3.00	1.73	26	2.48	1.57
12	3.09	1.76	27	.96	.98
13	1.51	1.23	28	1.89	1.37
14	2.10	1.45	29	.90	.95
15	.52	.72	30	2.05	1.43

of both the original and transformed data appear in Figure 7.33. The distribution of the original data is clearly skewed, with a long upper tail. The square-root transformation has resulted in a substantially more symmetric distribution, with a typical (that is, central) value near the 1.25 boundary between the third and fourth class intervals.

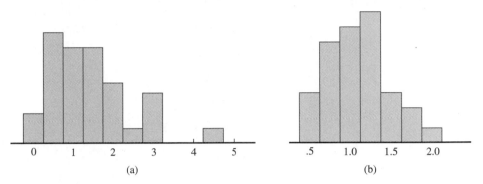

FIGURE 7.33 Histograms of precipitation data: (a) Untransformed data; (b) Square-root transformed data

Logarithmic transformations are also common and, as with bivariate data, either the natural log or $\log_{10}$ can be used. A log transformation is usually applied to data that is positively skewed (a long upper tail). This affects values in the upper tail substantially more than values in the lower tail, yielding a more symmetric — and often more normal — distribution.

EXAMPLE 7.20   Exposure to beryllium is known to produce adverse effects on lungs as well as on other tissues and organs in both laboratory animals and humans. The article "Time Lapse Cinematographic Analysis of Beryllium—Lung Fibroblast Interactions" (*Envir. Research* (1983): 34–43) reported the results of experiments designed to study the behavior of certain individual cells that had been exposed to beryllium. An important characteristic of such an individual cell is its interdivision time (IDT). IDTs were determined for a large number of cells under both exposed (treatment) and unexposed (control) conditions. The authors of the article state, "The IDT distributions are seen to be skewed, but the natural logs do have an approximate normal distribution." The same property holds for $\log_{10}$-transformed data. We give representative IDT data in Table 7.3 (page 272) and the resulting histograms in Figure 7.34, which are in agreement with the authors' statement.

The sample size for the IDT data is $n = 40$. The correlation coefficient for the (normal score, original (untransformed) data) pairs is .950, which is less than the critical r for $n = 40$ (critical $r = .960$). The correlation coefficient using the trans-

Table 7.3 *Original and log₁₀(IDT) values*

IDT	$\log_{10}(\text{IDT})$	IDT	$\log_{10}(\text{IDT})$	IDT	$\log_{10}(\text{IDT})$
28.1	1.45	31.2	1.49	13.7	1.14
46.0	1.66	25.8	1.41	16.8	1.23
34.8	1.54	62.3	1.79	28.0	1.45
17.9	1.25	19.5	1.29	21.1	1.32
31.9	1.50	28.9	1.46	60.1	1.78
23.7	1.37	18.6	1.27	21.4	1.33
26.6	1.42	26.2	1.42	32.0	1.51
43.5	1.64	17.4	1.24	38.8	1.59
30.6	1.49	55.6	1.75	25.5	1.41
52.1	1.72	21.0	1.32	22.3	1.35
15.5	1.19	36.3	1.56	19.1	1.28
38.4	1.58	72.8	1.86	48.9	1.69
21.4	1.33	20.7	1.32	57.3	1.76
40.9	1.61				

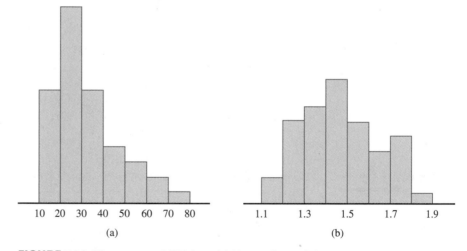

FIGURE 7.34 Histograms of IDT data: (a) Untransformed data; (b) Log₁₀-transformed data

formed data is .998, which is much larger than the critical *r*, supporting the assertion that $\log_{10}(\text{IDT})$ has approximately a normal distribution. Figure 7.35 displays MINITAB normal probability plots for the original data and for the transformed data. The plot for the transformed data is clearly much more linear than the plot for the original data.

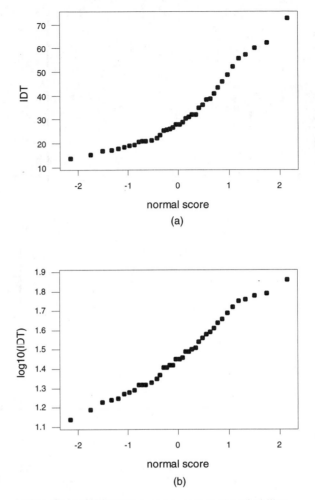

FIGURE 7.35 MINITAB-generated normal probability plots: (a) Original IDT data; (b) Log$_{10}$-transformed IDT data

Selecting a Transformation

A particular transformation may on occasion be dictated by some theoretical argument, but often this is not the case. Then you may wish to try several different transformations to find one that is satisfactory. Figure 7.36 (page 274), from the article "Distribution of Sperm Counts in Suspected Infertile Men" (*J. of Reproduction and Fertility* (1983): 91–96), shows what can result from such a search. Other workers in this field had previously used all three of the transformations illustrated, but these investigators strongly favored the square root transformation for their data.

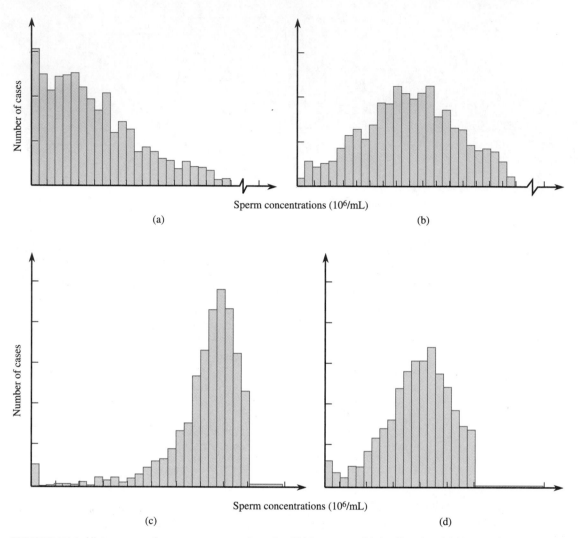

FIGURE 7.36 Histograms of sperm concentrations for 1711 suspected infertile men: (a) Untransformed (highly skewed); (b) Log transformed (reasonably symmetric); (c) Square-root transformed; (d) Cube-root transformed

Exercises 7.33 – 7.44

7.33 Ten measurements of the steam rate (lb/hr) of a distillation tower were used to construct the normal probability plot at the top of page 275 ("A Self-Descaling Distillation Tower" (*Chem. Eng. Process* (1968): 79–84)).

Based on the accompanying plot, do you think it is reasonable to assume that the normal distribution provides an adequate description of the steam rate distribution? Explain.

Observation

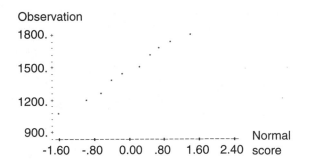

x	Normal Score	x	Normal Score
47.1	−1.867	240.0	.062
68.1	−1.408	240.0	.187
68.1	−1.131	278.0	.315
90.8	−.921	278.0	.448
103.6	−.745	289.0	.590
106.0	−.590	289.0	.745
115.0	−.448	367.0	.921
126.0	−.315	385.9	1.131
146.6	−.187	392.0	1.408
229.0	−.062	305.0	1.867

7.34 The accompanying normal probability plot was constructed using part of the data appearing in the paper "Trace Metals in Sea Scallops" (*Environ. Concentration and Toxicology* 19: 1326–1334). The variable under study was the amount of cadmium in North Atlantic scallops. Does the sample data suggest that the cadmium concentration distribution is not normal? Explain.

Observation

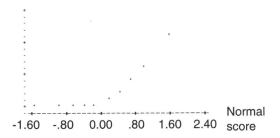

7.35 Consider the following ten observations on the lifetime (hr) for a certain type of component:

152.7	172.0	172.5	173.3	193.0
204.7	216.5	234.9	262.6	422.6

Construct a normal probability plot, and comment on the plausibility of a normal distribution as a model for component lifetime.

7.36 The article "The Load-Life Relationship for M50 Bearings with Silicon Nitride Ceramic Balls" (*Lubric. Eng.* (1984): 153–159) reported the accompanying data on bearing load life (million revs); the corresponding normal scores are also given. Construct a normal probability plot. Is normality plausible?

7.37 The accompanying observations are DDT concentrations in the blood of 20 people.

24	26	30	35	35	38	39	40	40	41
42	52	56	58	61	75	79	88	102	42

Use the normal scores from Exercise 7.36 to construct a normal probability plot, and comment on the appropriateness of a normal probability model.

7.38 Consider the following sample of 25 observations on the diameter x (cm) of a disk used in a certain system:

16.01	16.08	16.13	15.94	16.05	16.27	15.89
15.84	16.15	16.19	16.22	15.95	16.10	15.92
16.04	15.82	16.15	16.06	15.66	16.07	16.13
16.11	15.78	15.99	16.29			

The 13 largest normal scores for a sample of size 25 are 1.965, 1.524, 1.263, 1.067, .905, .764, .637, .519, .409, .303, .200, .100, and 0. The 12 smallest scores result from placing a negative sign in front of each of the given nonzero scores. Construct a normal probability plot. Does it appear plausible that disk diameter is normally distributed? Explain.

7.39 The first example in this section examined rainfall data for Minneapolis–St. Paul. The square-root transformation was used to obtain a distribution of values that was more symmetric than the distribution of the original data. Another power transformation that has been suggested by meteorologists is the cube root: Transformed value = (original value)$^{1/3}$. The original values and their cube roots (the transformed values) are given on page 276. Construct a histogram of the transformed data. Compare your histogram to those given in Figure 7.33. Which of the cube-root and the square-root transformations appears to result in the more symmetric histogram?

Data for Exercise 7.39	Original	.32	.47	.52	.59	.77	.81	.81	.90
	Transformed	.68	.78	.80	.84	.92	.93	.93	.97
	Original	.96	1.18	1.20	1.20	1.31	1.35	1.43	1.51
	Transformed	.99	1.06	1.06	1.06	1.09	1.11	1.13	1.15
	Original	1.62	1.74	1.87	1.89	1.95	2.05	2.10	2.20
	Transformed	1.17	1.20	1.23	1.24	1.25	1.27	1.28	1.30
	Original	2.48	2.81	3.00	3.09	3.37	4.75		
	Transformed	1.35	1.41	1.44	1.46	1.50	1.68		

7.40 The table gives a sample of survival times (days from diagnosis) for patients suffering from chronic leukemia of a certain type (*Statistical Methodology for Survival Time Studies,* National Cancer Institute, 1986).

7	47	58	74	177	232	273
285	317	429	440	445	455	468
495	497	532	571	579	581	650
702	715	779	881	900	930	968
1077	1109	1314	1334	1367	1534	1712
1784	1877	1886	2045	2056	2260	2429
2509						

a. Construct a relative frequency distribution for this data set, and draw the corresponding histogram.
b. Would you describe this histogram as having a positive or a negative skew?
c. Would you recommend transforming the data? Explain.

7.41 In a study of warp breakage during the weaving of fabric (*Technometrics* (1982): 63), 100 pieces of yarn were tested. The number of cycles of strain to breakage was recorded for each yarn sample, as follows:

86	146	251	653	98	249	400
292	131	169	175	176	76	264
15	364	195	262	88	264	157
220	42	321	180	198	38	20
61	121	282	224	149	180	325
250	196	90	229	166	38	337
65	151	341	40	40	135	597
246	211	180	93	315	353	571
124	279	81	186	497	182	423
185	229	400	338	290	398	71
246	185	188	568	55	55	61
244	20	284	93	396	203	829
239	236	286	194	277	143	198
264	105	203	124	137	135	350
193	188					

a. Construct a frequency distribution using the class intervals 0–<100, 100–<200, and so on.
b. Draw the histogram corresponding to the frequency distribution in part **a.** How would you describe the shape of this histogram?
c. Find a transformation for this data that results in a more symmetric histogram than what you obtained in part **b.**

7.42 The article "The Distribution of Buying Frequency Rates" (*J. of Marketing Research* (1980): 210–216) reported the results of a $3\frac{1}{2}$-year study of dentifrice purchases. The authors conducted their research using a national sample of 2071 households and recorded the number of toothpaste purchases for each household participating in the study. The results are given in the accompanying frequency distribution.

Number of Purchases	Number of Households (frequency)
10–<20	904
20–<30	500
30–<40	258
40–<50	167
50–<60	94
60–<70	56
70–<80	26
80–<90	20
90–<100	13
100–<110	9
110–<120	7
120–<130	6
130–<140	6
140–<150	3
150–<160	0
160–<170	2

a. Draw a histogram for this frequency distribution. Would you describe the histogram as positively or negatively skewed?

b. Does the square-root transformation result in a histogram that is more symmetric than that of the original data? (Be careful — this one is a bit tricky, since you don't have the raw data. Transforming the endpoints of the class intervals will result in class intervals that are not necessarily of equal widths, so the histogram of the transformed values will have to be drawn with this in mind.)

7.43 Ecologists have long been interested in factors that might explain how far north or south particular animal species are found. As part of one such study, the paper "Temperature and the Northern Distributions of Wintering Birds" (*Ecology* (1991): 2274–2285) gave the accompanying body masses (in grams) for 50 different bird species that had previously been thought to have northern boundaries corresponding to a particular isotherm.

7.7	10.1	21.6	8.6	12.0
11.4	16.6	9.4	9.8	10.2
15.9	11.5	9.0	8.2	20.2
48.5	21.6	26.1	6.2	93.9
31.0	12.5	19.1	21.0	28.1
10.6	31.6	6.7	5.0	68.8
10.9	21.5	14.5	23.9	19.8
20.1	6.0	99.6	19.8	16.5
9.0	19.6	11.9	32.5	448.0
21.3	17.4	36.9	34.0	41.0

a. Construct a stem-and-leaf display in which 448.0 is shown beside the display as a HI value, the stem of an observation is the tens digit, the leaf is the ones digit, and the tenths digit is suppressed (so, e.g., 21.5 has stem 2 and leaf 1). What do you perceive as the most prominent feature of the display?

b. Draw a histogram based on class intervals 5–<10, 10–<15, 15–<20, 20–<25, 25–<30, 30–<40, 40–<50, 50–<100, and 100–<500. Is a transformation of the data desirable? Explain.

c. Use a calculator or statistical computer package to calculate logarithms of these observations and construct a histogram. Is the log transformation satisfactory?

d. Consider

$$\text{transformed value} = 1/\sqrt{\text{original value}}$$

and construct a histogram of the transformed data. Does it appear to resemble a normal curve?

7.44 The figure at the bottom of the page appeared in the paper "EDTA-Extractable Copper, Zinc and Manganese in Soils of the Canterbury Plains" (*New Zealand J. of Ag. Res.* (1984): 207–217). A large number of topsoil samples were analyzed for manganese (Mn), zinc (Zn), and copper (Cu), and the resulting data was summarized using histograms. The authors transformed each data set using logarithms in an effort to obtain more symmetric distributions of values. Do you think the transformations were successful? Explain.

Figure for Exercise 7.44

 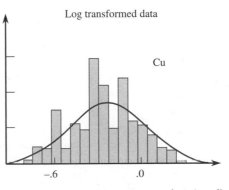

(*continued*)

Figure for Exercise 7.44—*continued*

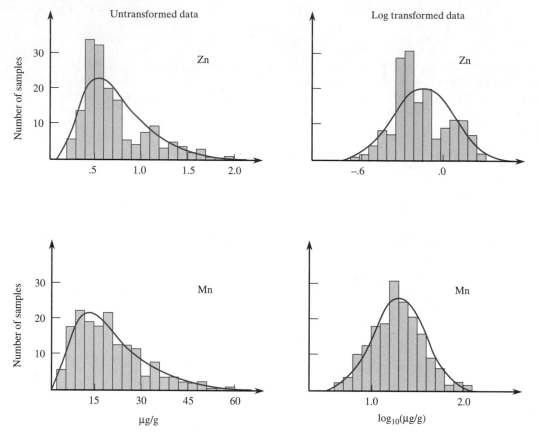

Summary of Key Concepts and Formulas

Term or Formula	Comment
Population distribution	The distribution of all the values of a numerical variable or categories of a categorical variable.
Discrete numerical variable	A numerical variable whose possible values are isolated points along the number line
Continuous numerical variable	A numerical variable whose possible values form an interval along the number line.
Continuous probability distribution density curve	A smooth curve that serves as a model for the population distribution of a continuous numerical variable. Areas under this curve are interpreted as probabilities.
μ, σ	The mean and standard deviation, respectively, of a probability distribution. The mean describes the center, and the standard deviation describes the spread of the probability distribution.

Term or Formula	Comment
Normal distribution	A continuous probability distribution that is specified by a particular type of bell-shaped density curve.
Standard normal distribution (z curve)	The normal distribution with $\mu = 0$ and $\sigma = 1$.
$z = \dfrac{x - \mu}{\sigma}$	The formula for a z score. When x has a normal distribution, z has a standard normal distribution.
Normal probability plot	A scatter plot of the (normal score, observation) pairs. A linear pattern in the plot suggests that it is plausible that the data is from a normal population distribution. Curvature in the plot suggests that the population distribution is not normal.

Supplementary Exercises 7.45 – 7.52

7.45 A machine producing vitamin E capsules operates in such a way that the distribution of x = actual amount of vitamin E in a capsule can be modeled by a normal curve with mean 5 mg and standard deviation .05 mg. What is the probability that a randomly selected capsule contains less than 4.9 mg of vitamin E? At least 5.2 mg?

7.46 Accurate labeling of packaged meat is difficult because of weight decrease due to moisture loss (defined as a percentage of the package's original net weight). Suppose that the normal distribution with mean value 4.0% and standard deviation 1.0% is a reasonable model for the variable x = moisture loss for a package of chicken breasts. (This model is suggested in the paper "Drained Weight Labeling for Meat and Poultry: An Economic Analysis of a Regulatory Proposal" (*J. of Consumer Affairs* (1980): 307–325).)
   a. What is the probability that x is between 3.0% and 5.0%?
   b. What is the probability that x is at most 4.0%?
   c. What is the probability that x is at least 7%?
   d. Describe the largest 10% of the moisture loss distribution.
   e. Describe the most extreme 10% of the moisture loss distribution. (*Hint*: The most extreme 10% consists of the largest 5% and the smallest 5%.)

7.47 The *Wall Street Journal* (Feb. 15, 1972) reported that General Electric was being sued in Texas for sex discrimination because of a minimum height requirement of 5 ft 7 in. The suit claimed that this restriction eliminated more than 94% of adult females from consideration. Let x represent the height of a randomly selected adult woman. Suppose that the probability distribution of x is approximately normal with mean 66 in and standard deviation 2 in.
   a. Is the claim that 94% of all women are shorter than 5 ft 7 in correct?
   b. What proportion of adult women would be excluded from employment due to the height restriction?

7.48 Your statistics professor tells you that the distribution of scores on a midterm exam was approximately normal with a mean of 78 and a standard deviation of 7. The top 15% of all scores have been designated as A's. Your score was 89. Did you receive an A? Explain.

7.49 Suppose the distribution of pH readings for soil samples taken in a certain geographical region can be approximated by a normal distribution with mean 6.00 and standard deviation .10. The pH of a randomly selected soil sample from this region is to be determined.
   a. What is the probability that the resulting pH is between 5.90 and 6.15?
   b. What is the probability that the resulting pH exceeds 6.10?
   c. What is the probability that the resulting pH is at most 5.95?
   d. Describe the largest 5% of the pH distribution.

7.50 The lightbulbs used to provide exterior lighting for a large office building have an average lifetime of 700 hr. If the distribution of the variable x = length of bulb life can be modeled as a normal distribution with a standard deviation of 50 hr, how often should all of the bulbs be replaced so that only 20% of the bulbs will have already burned out?

7.51 Let x denote the duration of a randomly selected pregnancy (the time elapsed between conception and birth). Accepted values for the mean value and standard deviation of x are 266 days and 16 days, respectively. Suppose that a normal distribution is an appropriate model for the probability distribution of x.

a. What is the probability that the duration of pregnancy is between 250 and 300 days?

b. What is the probability that the duration of pregnancy is at most 240 days?

c. What is the probability that the duration of pregnancy is within 16 days of the mean duration?

d. A *Dear Abby* column dated Jan. 20, 1973, contained a letter from a woman who stated that the duration of her pregnancy was exactly 310 days. (She wrote that the last visit with her husband, who was in the Navy, occurred 310 days prior to birth.) What is the probability that the duration of a pregnancy is at least 310 days? Does this probability make you a bit skeptical of the claim?

e. Some insurance companies will pay the medical expenses associated with childbirth only if the insurance has been in effect for more than 9 months (275 days). This restriction is designed to ensure that the insurance company has to pay benefits only for those pregnancies where conception occurred during coverage. Suppose that conception occurred two weeks after coverage began. What is the probability that the insurance company will refuse to pay benefits because of the 275-day insurance requirement?

7.52 Let x denote the systolic blood pressure (mm Hg) of an individual selected at random from a certain population. Suppose that the normal distribution with mean $\mu = 120$ mm and standard deviation $\sigma = 10$ mm is a reasonable model for describing the population distribution of x. [The article "Oral Contraceptives, Pregnancy, and Blood Pressure" (*J. of the Amer. Med. Assoc.* 222 (1972): 1507–1510) reported on the results of a large study in which a sample histogram of blood pressures among women of similar ages was found to be well approximated by a normal curve.]

a. Calculate $P(110 < x < 140)$. How does this compare to $P(110 \le x \le 140)$, and why?

b. Calculate $P(x < 75)$.

c. Calculate $P(x < 95 \ or \ x > 145)$, the probability that x is more than 2.5 standard deviations from its mean value.

Reference

McClave, James, and Terry Sincich. *Statistics,* 8th ed. Englewood Cliffs, NJ: Prentice-Hall, 2000. (Chapters 4 and 5 present a good exposition of discrete and continuous distributions at a modest mathematical level.)

8

Sampling Variability and Sampling Distributions

INTRODUCTION

The inferential methods presented in subsequent chapters will use information contained in a sample to reach conclusions about one or more characteristics of the population from which the sample was selected. For example, let μ denote the true mean fat content of quarter-pound hamburgers marketed by a national fast-food chain. To learn something about μ, a sample of $n = 50$ hamburgers might be obtained and the fat content determined for each burger in the sample. The sample data might produce a mean of $\bar{x} = 28.4$ grams. How close is this sample mean to the population mean, μ? If another sample of 50 were selected and $\bar{x}$ computed, would this second $\bar{x}$ value be near 28.4, or might it be quite different?

These questions can be addressed by studying what is called the *sampling distribution* of $\bar{x}$. Just as the distribution of a numerical variable describes its long-run behavior, the sampling distribution of $\bar{x}$ provides information about the long-run behavior of $\bar{x}$.

Later in the text, properties of the sampling distribution of $\bar{x}$ will be used to develop inferential procedures for drawing conclusions about μ. In a similar manner, we will study the sampling distribution of a sample proportion (the fraction of individuals or objects in a sample who have some characteristic of interest). This will enable us to describe procedures for making inferences about the corresponding population proportion, π.

281

8.1   Statistics and Sampling Variability

Many investigations and research projects try to draw conclusions about how the values of some variable x are distributed in a population. Often, attention is focused on a single characteristic of that distribution. Examples include the following:

1. x = fat content (grams) of an Oscar Mayer beef hot dog, with interest centered on the mean fat content μ of all such hot dogs

2. x = fuel efficiency (miles per gallon) for a 2000 Honda Accord, with interest focused on the variability in fuel efficiency as described by σ, the standard deviation for the fuel efficiency population distribution

3. x = time to first recurrence of skin cancer for a patient treated using a particular therapy, with attention focused on the proportion π of such individuals whose first recurrence is within 5 years of treatment

4. x = marital status (a categorical variable) of a student at a particular university, with interest centered on π, the proportion of all students at the university who are married

The usual way of obtaining information regarding the value of a population characteristic is by selecting a sample from the population. For example, to gain insight about the mean value of the fat content distribution for the population of all Oscar Mayer beef hot dogs, we might select a sample of 50 hot dogs for analysis. Each item in the sample could be tested to yield a value of x = fat content. As in Chapter 7, we could construct a histogram of the 50 sample x values, and we could view this histogram as a rough approximation of the population distribution of x. In a similar way, we could view the sample mean, $\bar{x}$ (the mean of the sample of n values) as an approximation of μ, the mean of the population distribution. It would be nice if the value of $\bar{x}$ were equal to the value of μ. It could happen that $\bar{x} = \mu$, but this would be an unusual occurrence; $\bar{x}$ is only an *estimate* of μ. An important question addressed later in this chapter is, How good is this estimate?

Not only does the value of $\bar{x}$ for a particular sample from a population usually differ from μ, but the $\bar{x}$ values from different samples also typically differ from one another. (For example, two different samples of 50 hot dogs will usually result in different $\bar{x}$ values.) This sample-to-sample variability makes it challenging to generalize from a sample to the population from which it was selected. To meet this challenge, we must understand sample-to-sample variability.

EXAMPLE 8.1   When we sample from a population, many different samples might result. Consider a small population consisting of the board of directors of a day care center. (Also listed are the values of x = number of children for each board member.)

Board member	Jay	Carol	Allison	Teresa	Lygia	Bob	Roxy	Kyle
Number of children	2	2	0	0	2	2	0	3

The average number of children for the entire group of eight (the population) is

$$\mu = \frac{2 + 2 + 0 + 0 + 2 + 2 + 0 + 3}{8} = \frac{11}{8} = 1.38$$

There are 28 different possible outcomes when a sample of size 2 is selected (without replacement) from the board; these are shown in Table 8.1. If sample 1 (Jay, Carol) is selected, the associated sample mean is $\bar{x}_1 = (2 + 2)/2 = 2$; if sample 14 (Allison, Teresa) is selected, the associated sample mean is $\bar{x}_{14} = (0 + 0)/2 = 0$. Each of the different possible samples has an $\bar{x}$ value associated with it. The $\bar{x}$ values not only differ from μ (neither $\bar{x}_1$ nor $\bar{x}_{14}$ is equal to 1.38), but they may also differ from sample to sample (for example, $\bar{x}_1 \neq \bar{x}_{14}$).

Table 8.1 *All possible samples of size 2 and their respective means*

Sample	$\bar{x}$	Sample	$\bar{x}$	Sample	$\bar{x}$	Sample	$\bar{x}$
1. Jay, Carol	2	8. Carol, Allison	1	15. Allison, Lygia	1	22. Teresa, Kyle	1.5
2. Jay, Allison	1	9. Carol, Teresa	1	16. Allison, Bob	1	23. Lygia, Bob	2
3. Jay, Teresa	1	10. Carol, Lygia	2	17. Allison, Roxy	0	24. Lygia, Roxy	1
4. Jay, Lygia	2	11. Carol, Bob	2	18. Allison, Kyle	1.5	25. Lygia, Kyle	2.5
5. Jay, Bob	2	12. Carol, Roxy	1	19. Teresa, Lygia	1	26. Bob, Roxy	1
6. Jay, Roxy	1	13. Carol, Kyle	2.5	20. Teresa, Bob	1	27. Bob, Kyle	2.5
7. Jay, Kyle	2.5	14. Allison, Teresa	0	21. Teresa, Roxy	0	28. Roxy, Kyle	1.5

Table 8.1 also gives the value of $\bar{x}$ for each of the 28 different possible samples, and a dotplot of $\bar{x}$ values in the table is shown in Figure 8.1.

Figure 8.1 provides some insight into the behavior of the mean of a sample of size 2 from this population. We see that the value $\bar{x} = 1$ is more common than any other value. However, $\bar{x}$ values can differ greatly not only from one sample to another, but also from the value of the population mean μ. If we were to select a random sample of size 2 (so that each different sample has the same chance of being selected), we could not count on the resulting value of $\bar{x}$ being very close to the population mean $\mu = 1.38$.

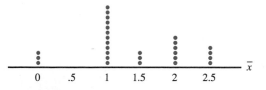

FIGURE 8.1 A dotplot of the $\bar{x}$ values in Example 8.1

To formalize these ideas, we must introduce some terminology.

> **Definition**
>
> Any quantity computed from values in a sample is called a **statistic.**
>
> The observed value of a statistic depends on the particular sample selected from the population; typically, it varies from sample to sample. This variability is called **sampling variability.**

The statistic considered in Example 8.1 was $\bar{x}$, the sample mean. Values of statistics such as $\bar{x}, s$, the sample median, the sample interquartile range, and so on, will be our primary source of information regarding various population characteristics.

Sampling Distributions

It is possible to view a statistic as a random variable and to use a distribution to describe its behavior. Before examining how this is done, let's review how a population distribution is used to describe the distribution of the values of some variable in a particular population. For example, suppose that we are studying the population of all mail carriers in Los Angeles County. Each carrier has an assigned route, and so associated with each carrier is a value of the variable

x = length of route (in miles)

One carrier might have a 3.8-mile route ($x = 3.8$), whereas for another carrier, we might find that $x = 2.4$. If we knew the x value for every individual in the population, we could construct a density histogram that would represent the population distribution for the variable x. The distribution might look like the histogram in Figure 8.2. The population distribution tells us about the distribution of individual x values in the population. If a single carrier were randomly selected from the population, the population distribution could be used to evaluate probabilities such as $P(x > 4)$ or $P(2 < x < 3)$.

FIGURE 8.2 Histogram of x = length of route

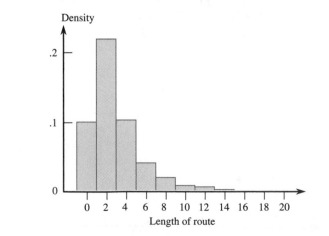

Now suppose that we are interested in μ, the mean value of x (the average route length) for this population. If the population distribution is known, the value of μ can be determined. For the distribution in Figure 8.2, $\mu \approx 3$.

What if the population distribution is not known? Then we must estimate μ using information in a sample. Suppose that we plan to take a random sample of size $n = 100$ from the population of all mail carriers in Los Angeles County. There are many, many different possible samples that might result (many more than the 28 from the day care example). We now define a hypothetical "population," which consists of all the different possible samples of a given size n. That is, we consider a *population of samples*. (This is a bit abstract, but it is a very important idea!) The population of samples is viewed as a population because it consists of *every* different sample; it is the complete collection of all possible samples.

Just as a variable associates a value with every individual or object in a population and can be described by its distribution, a statistic associates a value with each individual sample in the population of samples. Thus, a statistic can also be described by a distribution.

Definition

The distribution of a statistic is called its **sampling distribution.**

EXAMPLE 8.2

(Example 8.1 continued)   In Example 8.1, we considered a small population consisting of the board of directors of a day care center. The variable of interest was x = number of children, and the statistic of interest was the sample mean $\bar{x}$. Figure 8.1 showed a plot of the $\bar{x}$ values for the population of all 28 samples of size $n = 2$. The corresponding density histogram appears in Figure 8.3; this is the sampling

FIGURE 8.3 Sampling distribution of $\bar{x}$ for Example 8.2

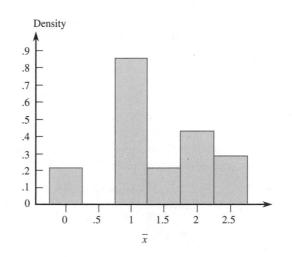

distribution of the statistic $\bar{x}$ when a random sample of size 2 is selected from the original population of eight people.

Looking at the sampling distribution of $\bar{x}$ depicted in Figure 8.3 helps us to understand what happens when a random sample of size 2 is selected from this population. For example, we can compute the probability of observing a sample mean that is within .5 of $\mu = 1.38$, the mean number of children in the population. This probability is

$$P(\bar{x} \text{ is within } .5 \text{ of } \mu) = P(\bar{x} = 1 \text{ or } \bar{x} = 1.5)$$
$$= \frac{12}{28} + \frac{3}{28}$$
$$= .4286 + .1071$$
$$= .5357$$

The probabilities $P(\bar{x} = 1) = 12/28$ and $P(\bar{x} = 1.5) = 3/28$ were computed using the information in Figure 8.1. Note that they are also the areas of the corresponding rectangles in the density histogram of Figure 8.3.

The sampling distribution of $\bar{x}$ can also be displayed in table form in this case (because there are only a few different possible $\bar{x}$ values), as shown below.

$\bar{x}$	0	1	1.5	2	2.5
$p(\bar{x})$	$\frac{3}{28}$	$\frac{12}{28}$	$\frac{3}{28}$	$\frac{6}{28}$	$\frac{4}{28}$

The sampling distribution of $\bar{x}$ provides important information about the behavior of the statistic $\bar{x}$ and how it relates to μ. However, you may have noticed that obtaining the sampling distribution of $\bar{x}$, even for a population of just eight individuals and a sample size of 2, was a lot of work. For realistic examples with larger population and sample sizes, the situation becomes worse, since there are so many possible samples. Fortunately, as we look at more examples, patterns emerge that enable us to describe some important aspects of the sampling distribution of the statistic $\bar{x}$ without actually having to look at all possible samples.

EXAMPLE 8.3   Consider a small population consisting of the 20 students enrolled in an upper-division class. The students are numbered from 1 to 20, and the amount of money (dollars) each student spent on textbooks for the current semester is shown in the accompanying table.

Student	Amount Spent on Books	Student	Amount Spent on Books
1	267	3	342
2	258	4	261
			(*continued*)

Student	Amount Spent on Books	Student	Amount Spent on Books
5	275	13	265
6	295	14	262
7	222	15	333
8	270	16	184
9	278	17	231
10	168	18	159
11	319	19	230
12	263	20	323

For this population,

$$\mu = \frac{267 + 258 + \cdots + 323}{20} = 260.25$$

Suppose that the value of the population mean is unknown to us and that we want to estimate μ by taking a random sample of five students and computing the sample mean amount spent on textbooks, $\bar{x}$. Is this a reasonable thing to do? Will the estimate that we produce be close to the true population mean? To answer these questions, we can perform a simple experiment that allows us to look at the behavior of the statistic $\bar{x}$ when random samples of size five are taken from the population. (Note that this is not a realistic example. If a population consisted of only 20 individuals, we would probably conduct a census rather than select a sample. However, this small population size makes it easier to work with as we develop the ideas of sampling distributions.)

Let's select a random sample of size 5 from this population. This can be done by writing the numbers from 1 to 20 on slips of paper, mixing them well, and then selecting five slips without replacement. The numbers on the slips selected identify which of the 20 students will be included in our sample. Alternatively, either a table of random digits or a random number generator can be used to determine which five should be selected. We used MINITAB to obtain five numbers between 1 and 20, resulting in

17   20   7   11   9

Selecting students numbered 17, 20, 7, 11, and 9 gives the following sample of amounts spent on books:

231   323   222   319   278

For this sample,

$$\bar{x} = \frac{1373}{5} = 274.60$$

The sample mean is larger than the population mean of 260.25 by about $15. Is this difference typical, or is this sample mean unusually far away from μ? Taking additional samples could provide some insight.

Four more random samples (samples 2–5) from this same population are shown here.

Sample 2		Sample 3		Sample 4		Sample 5	
Student	x	Student	x	Student	x	Student	x
4	261	15	333	20	323	18	159
15	333	12	263	16	184	8	270
12	263	3	342	19	230	9	278
1	267	7	222	1	267	7	222
18	159	18	159	8	270	14	262

The value of $\bar{x}$ can be computed for each sample:

Sample	2	3	4	5
$\bar{x}$	256.60	263.80	254.80	238.20

Since $\mu = 260.25$, we can see the following:

1. The value of $\bar{x}$ differs from one random sample to another (sampling variability).

2. Some samples produced $\bar{x}$ values larger than μ (samples 1 and 3), whereas others produced $\bar{x}$ values smaller than μ (samples 2, 4, and 5).

3. Samples 2, 3, and 4 produced $\bar{x}$ values that were fairly close to the population mean, but sample 5 resulted in an $\bar{x}$ value that was $22 below the population mean.

Continuing with the experiment, we selected 45 additional random samples (each of size 5). The resulting sample means are as follows:

Sample	$\bar{x}$	Sample	$\bar{x}$	Sample	$\bar{x}$
1	274.6	16	255.0	31	253.4
2	256.6	17	307.2	32	279.6
3	263.8	18	280.0	33	252.6
4	254.8	19	277.4	34	242.2
5	238.2	20	241.2	35	262.6
6	275.6	21	216.0	36	215.4
7	279.2	22	270.0	37	266.2
8	241.6	23	301.0	38	261.4
9	255.4	24	247.0	39	275.0
10	263.8	25	273.8	40	301.4
11	239.6	26	282.8	41	237.0
12	248.2	27	220.4	42	287.4
13	330.8	28	213.6	43	249.2
14	288.8	29	287.6	44	236.8
15	252.8	30	214.8	45	264.6

Figure 8.4, a MINITAB density histogram of the 45 sample means, provides us with a lot of information about the behavior of the statistic $\bar{x}$. Most samples resulted in sample means that were reasonably near $\mu = 260.25$, falling between 235 and 295. A few samples, however, produced $\bar{x}$ values that were very far from μ. If we were to take a sample of size 5 from this population and use $\bar{x}$ as an estimate of the population mean μ, we should not expect $\bar{x}$ to be really close to μ.

FIGURE 8.4 $\bar{x}$ values from 45 random samples

If we had continued sampling indefinitely, the resulting histogram of $\bar{x}$ values would represent the sampling distribution of $\bar{x}$ for samples of size 5 from this population. The information provided by this sampling distribution enables us to evaluate the behavior of the statistic $\bar{x}$ and is critical for developing inferential procedures based on $\bar{x}$. You may have noticed some general patterns emerging as we did this type of sampling experiment with different sample sizes and different populations, so we do not actually have to carry out such experiments on a regular basis! These general results are described in the next section.

Exercises 8.1 – 8.13

8.1 Explain the difference between a population characteristic and a statistic.

8.2 What is the difference between $\bar{x}$ and μ? between σ and s?

8.3 For each of the following statements, identify the number that appears in boldface type as the value of either a population characteristic or a statistic.

a. A department store reports that **84%** of all customers who use the store's credit plan pay their bills on time.
b. A sample of 100 students at a large university had a mean age of **24.1** years.
c. The Department of Motor Vehicles reports that **22%** of all vehicles registered in a particular state are imports.

d. A hospital reports that based on the ten most recent cases, the mean length of stay for surgical patients is **6.4** days.

e. A consumer group, after testing 100 batteries of a certain brand, reported an average life of **63** hours of use.

8.4 Consider the following "population": {1, 2, 3, 4}. Note that the population mean is

$$\mu = \frac{1 + 2 + 3 + 4}{4} = 2.5$$

a. Suppose that a random sample of size 2 is to be selected without replacement from this population. There are 12 possible samples (provided that the order in which observations are selected is taken into account):

1, 2	1, 3	1, 4	2, 1	2, 3	2, 4
3, 1	3, 2	3, 4	4, 1	4, 2	4, 3

Compute the sample mean for each of the 12 possible samples. Use this information to construct the sampling distribution of $\bar{x}$. (Display it in table form.)

b. Suppose that a random sample of size 2 is to be selected, but this time sampling will be done with replacement. Using a method similar to that of part **a,** construct the sampling distribution of $\bar{x}$. (*Hint:* There are 16 different possible samples in this case.)

c. In what ways are the two sampling distributions of parts **a** and **b** similar? In what ways are they different?

8.5 Simulate sampling from the population of Exercise 8.4 by using four slips of paper individually marked 1, 2, 3, and 4. Select a sample of size 2 without replacement, and compute $\bar{x}$. Repeat this process 50 times, and construct a relative frequency distribution of the 50 $\bar{x}$ values. How does the relative frequency distribution compare to the sampling distribution of $\bar{x}$ derived in Exercise 8.4, part **a**?

8.6 Use the method of Exercise 8.4 to find the sampling distribution of the sample range when a random sample of size 2 is to be selected with replacement from the population {1, 2, 3, 4}. (Recall that sample range = largest observation − smallest observation.)

8.7 On four different occasions, you have borrowed money from a friend in the amounts $1, $5, $10, and $20. The friend has four IOU slips with each of these amounts written on a different slip. He will randomly select two slips from among the four and ask that those IOUs be repaid immediately. Let t denote the amount that you must repay immediately.

a. List all possible outcomes and the value of t for each, and then determine the sampling distribution of t.

b. Calculate μ_t, the mean value of t. How is μ_t related to the "population" mean μ?

8.8 Refer to Exercise 8.7. Suppose that instead of asking that the total amount on the two selected slips be repaid immediately, the maximum m of the two selected amounts is to be repaid immediately (e.g., $m = 10$ if the $5 and $10 slips are drawn). Obtain the sampling distribution of m if the two slips are selected

a. without replacement

b. with replacement

8.9 Consider the following population: {2, 3, 3, 4, 4}. The value of μ is 3.2, but suppose that this is not known to an investigator, who therefore wants to estimate μ from sample data. Three possible statistics for estimating μ are

Statistic no. 1: the sample mean, $\bar{x}$
Statistic no. 2: the sample median
Statistic no. 3: the average of the largest and the smallest values in the sample

A random sample of size 3 will be selected without replacement. Provided that we disregard the order in which observations are selected, there are ten possible samples that might result (writing 3 and 3*, 4 and 4* to distinguish the two 3's and the two 4's in the population):

2, 3, 3*	2, 3, 4	2, 3, 4*	2, 3*, 4	2, 3*, 4*
2, 4, 4*	3, 3*, 4	3, 3*, 4*	3, 4, 4*	3*, 4, 4*

For each of these ten samples, compute statistics 1, 2, and 3. Construct the sampling distribution of each of these statistics. Which statistic would you recommend for estimating μ? Explain the reasons for your choice.

8.10 On your shelf, you have four books that you are planning to read in the near future. Two are fictional works, containing 212 and 379 pages, respectively, and the other two are nonfiction, with 350 and 575 pages, respectively.

a. Suppose that you randomly select two books from among these four to take on a one-week ski trip (in case you injure yourself). Let $\bar{x}$ denote the sample average number of pages for the two books selected. Obtain the sampling distribution of $\bar{x}$ for this sampling method, and determine the mean of the $\bar{x}$ distribution.

b. Suppose that you randomly select one of the two fiction books and also randomly select one of the two nonfiction books. Determine the sampling distribution of $\bar{x}$, and then calculate the mean of the $\bar{x}$ distribution.

8.11 Consider a population consisting of the following five values, which represent the number of video rentals during the academic year for each of five housemates.

8	14	16	10	11

a. Compute the mean of this population.

b. Select a random sample of size 2 by writing the numbers on slips of paper and selecting two. Compute the mean of your sample.

c. Repeatedly select samples of size 2, and compute the associated $\bar{x}$ values until you have looked at 25 samples.

d. Construct a histogram using the 25 $\bar{x}$ values. Are most of the sample $\bar{x}$ values near the population mean? Do the $\bar{x}$ values differ a lot from sample to sample, or do they tend to be similar?

8.12 Select 10 additional random samples of size 5 from the population of 20 students given in Example 8.3, and compute the mean amount spent on books for each of the 10 samples. Are the $\bar{x}$ values consistent with the results of the sampling experiment summarized in Figure 8.4?

8.13 Suppose the sampling experiment described in Example 8.3 had used samples of size 10 rather than size 5. If 45 samples of size 10 were selected, $\bar{x}$ computed, and a histogram constructed, how do you think this histogram would differ from that for samples of size 5 (Figure 8.4)? In what way would it be similar?

8.2   The Sampling Distribution of a Sample Mean

When the objective of a statistical investigation is to make an inference about the population mean, μ, it is natural to consider the sample mean, $\bar{x}$. To understand how inferential procedures based on $\bar{x}$ work, we must first study how sampling variability causes $\bar{x}$ to vary in value from one sample to another. The behavior of $\bar{x}$ is described by its sampling distribution. The sample size n and characteristics of the population — its shape, mean value μ, and standard deviation σ — are important in determining properties of the sampling distribution of $\bar{x}$.

It is helpful first to consider the results of some sampling experiments. In the two examples that follow, we start with a specified x population distribution, fix a sample size n, and select 500 different random samples of this size. We then compute $\bar{x}$ for each sample and construct a sample histogram of these 500 $\bar{x}$ values. Because 500 is reasonably large (a reasonably long sequence of samples), the sample histogram should rather closely resemble the true sampling distribution of $\bar{x}$ (which would be obtained from an unending sequence of $\bar{x}$ values). We repeat the experiment for several different values of n to see how the choice of sample size affects the sampling distribution. Careful examination of these sample histograms will aid in understanding the general properties to be stated shortly.

EXAMPLE 8.4   The article "Platelet Size in Myocardial Infarction" (*Brit. Med. J.* (1983): 449–451) presented evidence suggesting that the distribution of platelet volume was approximately normal in shape both for patients after acute myocardial infarction (a heart attack) and for control subjects who had no history of serious illness. The suggested values of μ and σ for the control-subject distribution were $\mu = 8.25$ and $\sigma = .75$. Figure 8.5 (page 292) shows the corresponding normal curve centered at 8.25, the mean value of platelet volume. The value of the population standard deviation, .75, determines the extent to which the x distribution spreads out about its mean value.

We first used MINITAB to select 500 random samples from this normal distribution, with each sample consisting of $n = 5$ observations. A histogram of the resulting 500 $\bar{x}$ values appears in Figure 8.6(a). This procedure was repeated for samples of size $n = 10$, again for $n = 20$, and finally for $n = 30$. The resulting sample histograms of $\bar{x}$ values are displayed in Figures 8.6(b)–(d).

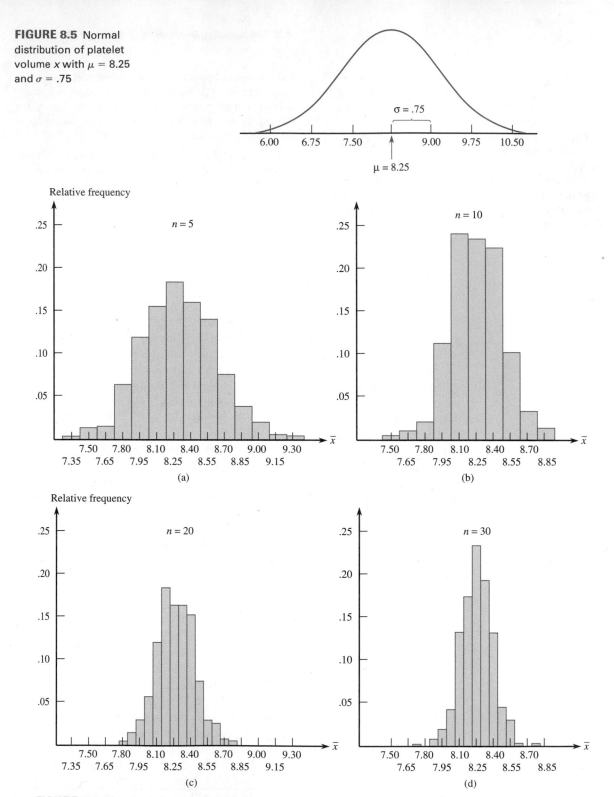

FIGURE 8.5 Normal distribution of platelet volume x with $\mu = 8.25$ and $\sigma = .75$

(a)

(b)

(c)

(d)

FIGURE 8.6 Sample histograms for $\bar{x}$ based on 500 samples, each consisting of n observations: (a) $n = 5$; (b) $n = 10$; (c) $n = 20$; (d) $n = 30$

The first thing to notice about the histograms is their shape. To a reasonable approximation, each of the four looks like a normal curve. The resemblance would be even more striking if each histogram had been based on many more than 500 $\bar{x}$ values. Second, each histogram is centered approximately at 8.25, the mean of the population being sampled. Had the histograms been based on an unending sequence of $\bar{x}$ values, their centers would have been exactly the population mean, 8.25.

The final aspect of the histograms to note is their spread relative to one another. The smaller the value of n, the greater the extent to which the sampling distribution spreads out about the population mean value. This is why the histograms for $n = 20$ and $n = 30$ are based on narrower class intervals than those for the two smaller sample sizes. For the larger sample sizes, most of the $\bar{x}$ values are quite close to 8.25. This is the effect of averaging. When n is small, a single, unusual x value can result in an $\bar{x}$ value far from the center. With a larger sample size, any unusual x values, when averaged with the other sample values, still tend to yield an $\bar{x}$ value close to μ. Combining these insights yields a result that should appeal to your intuition: $\bar{x}$ **based on a large n tends to be closer to μ than does $\bar{x}$ based on a small n.**

EXAMPLE 8.5

Now consider properties of the $\bar{x}$ distribution when the population is quite skewed (and thus very unlike a normal distribution). The Winter 1995 issue of *Chance* magazine gave data on the length of the overtime period for all 251 National Hockey League play-off games between 1970 and 1993 that went into overtime. In hockey, the overtime period ends as soon as either team scores a goal. Figure 8.7 displays a histogram of the data. The histogram has a very long upper tail, indicating that although most overtimes lasted less than 20 minutes, there were a few games with long overtime periods.

If we think of the 251 values as a population, the histogram in Figure 8.7 shows the distribution of values in that population. The skewed shape makes identification of the mean value from the picture more difficult than for a normal distribution.

FIGURE 8.7 The population distribution for Example 8.5 ($\mu = 9.841$)

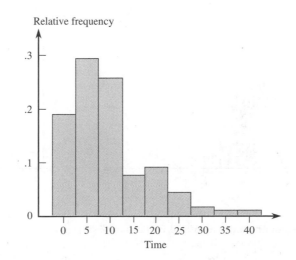

We found the average of these 251 values to be $\mu = 9.841$, so that is the balance point for the population histogram. The median value for the population, 8.000, is less than μ as a result of the distribution's positively skewed nature.

For each of the sample sizes $n = 5, 10, 20$, and 30, we selected 500 random samples of size n. This was done with replacement to approximate more nearly the usual situation in which the sample size n is only a small fraction of the population size. We then constructed a histogram of the 500 $\bar{x}$ values for each of the four sample sizes. These histograms are displayed in Figure 8.8.

As with samples from a normal population, the averages of the 500 $\bar{x}$ values for the four different sample sizes are all close to the population mean $\mu = 9.841$. If each histogram had been based on an unending sequence of sample means, rather than just 500 of them, each one would have been centered at exactly 9.841. Comparison of the four $\bar{x}$ histograms in Figure 8.8 also shows that as n increases, the

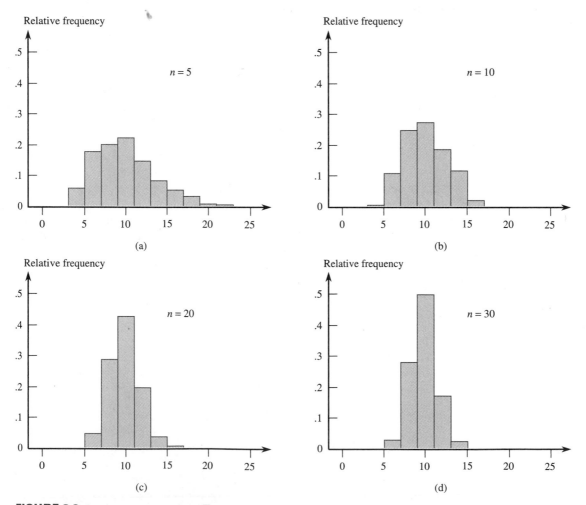

FIGURE 8.8 Four histograms of 500 $\bar{x}$ values for Example 8.5

histogram's spread about its center decreases. This was also true of increasing sample sizes from a normal population: $\bar{x}$ is less variable for a large sample size than it is for a small sample size.

Another aspect of these histograms distinguishes them from the distribution of $\bar{x}$ based on a sample from a normal population. They are skewed and differ in shape more, but they become progressively more symmetric as the sample size increases. The four histograms in Figure 8.8 were drawn using the same horizontal scale, to make it easy to see the decrease in spread as n increases. However, this makes it harder to see how the histograms' shapes change with sample size. Figure 8.9 is a histogram based on narrower class intervals for the $\bar{x}$ values from samples of size 30. This figure shows that for $n = 30$, the histogram has a shape much like a normal curve. Again this is the effect of averaging. Even when n is large, one of the few large x values in the population appears infrequently in the sample. When one does appear, its contribution to $\bar{x}$ is swamped by the contributions of more typical sample values. The normal-curve shape of the histogram for $n = 30$ is what is predicted by the Central Limit Theorem, which will be introduced shortly. According to this theorem, even if the population distribution bears no resemblance whatsoever to a normal curve, the $\bar{x}$ sampling distribution is approximately normal when the sample size n is reasonably large.

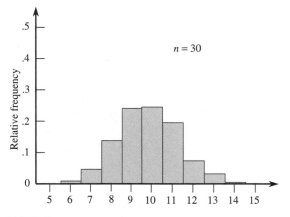

FIGURE 8.9 Histogram of 500 $\bar{x}$ values

General Properties of the Sampling Distribution of $\bar{x}$

Examples 8.4 and 8.5 suggest that for any n, the center of the $\bar{x}$ distribution (the mean value of $\bar{x}$) coincides with the mean of the population being sampled, and the spread of the $\bar{x}$ distribution decreases as n increases, indicating that the standard deviation of $\bar{x}$ is smaller for large n than for small n. The sample histograms also suggest that in some cases, the $\bar{x}$ distribution is approximately normal in shape. These observations are stated more formally in the following general rules.

General Properties of the Sampling Distribution of $\bar{x}$

Let $\bar{x}$ denote the mean of the observations in a random sample of size n from a population having mean μ and standard deviation σ. Denote the mean value of the $\bar{x}$ distribution by $\mu_{\bar{x}}$ and the standard deviation of the $\bar{x}$ distribution by $\sigma_{\bar{x}}$. Then the following rules hold.

Rule 1. $\mu_{\bar{x}} = \mu$

Rule 2. $\sigma_{\bar{x}} = \dfrac{\sigma}{\sqrt{n}}$ This rule is approximately correct as long as no more than 5% of the population is included in the sample.

Rule 3. When the population distribution is normal, the sampling distribution of $\bar{x}$ is also normal for any sample size n.

Rule 4. (**Central Limit Theorem**)   When n is sufficiently large, the sampling distribution of $\bar{x}$ is well approximated by a normal curve, even when the population distribution is not itself normal.

Rule 1, $\mu_{\bar{x}} = \mu$, states that the sampling distribution of $\bar{x}$ is always centered at the mean of the population sampled. Rule 2, $\sigma_{\bar{x}} = \sigma/\sqrt{n}$, not only states that the spread of the sampling distribution of $\bar{x}$ decreases as n increases, but also gives a precise relationship between the standard deviation of the $\bar{x}$ distribution and the population standard deviation. When $n = 4$, for example,

$$\sigma_{\bar{x}} = \frac{\sigma}{\sqrt{n}} = \frac{\sigma}{\sqrt{4}} = \frac{\sigma}{2}$$

so the $\bar{x}$ distribution has a standard deviation only half as large as the population standard deviation. Rules 3 and 4 specify circumstances under which the $\bar{x}$ distribution is normal or approximately normal: when the population is normal or when the sample size is large. Figure 8.10 illustrates these rules by showing several $\bar{x}$ distributions superimposed over a graph of the population distribution.

The Central Limit Theorem of rule 4 states that when n is sufficiently large, the $\bar{x}$ distribution is approximately normal, no matter what the population distribution

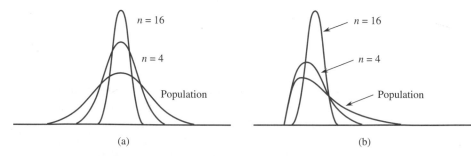

FIGURE 8.10 Population distribution and sampling distributions of $\bar{x}$: (a) A symmetric population; (b) A skewed population

looks like. This result has enabled statisticians to develop large-sample procedures for making inferences about a population mean μ even when the shape of the population distribution is unknown.

Recall that a variable is standardized by subtracting the mean value and then dividing by its standard deviation. Using rules 1 and 2 to standardize $\bar{x}$ gives an important consequence of the last two rules.

If n is large or the population distribution is normal, the standardized variable

$$z = \frac{\bar{x} - \mu_{\bar{x}}}{\sigma_{\bar{x}}} = \frac{\bar{x} - \mu}{\sigma/\sqrt{n}}$$

has (approximately) a standard normal (z) distribution.

Application of the Central Limit Theorem in specific situations requires a rule of thumb for deciding whether n is indeed sufficiently large. Such a rule is not as easy to come by as you might think. Look back at Figure 8.8, which shows the approximate sampling distribution of $\bar{x}$ for $n = 5, 10, 20,$ and 30 when the population distribution is quite skewed. Certainly the histogram for $n = 5$ is not well described by a normal curve, and this is still true of the histogram for $n = 10$, particularly in the tails of the histogram (far away from the mean value). Among the four histograms, only the one for $n = 30$ has a reasonably normal shape.

On the other hand, when the population distribution is normal, the sampling distribution of $\bar{x}$ is normal for any n. If the population distribution is somewhat skewed but not to the extent of Figure 8.7, we might expect the $\bar{x}$ sampling distribution to be a bit skewed for $n = 5$ but quite well fit by a normal curve for n as small as 10 or 15. How large an n is needed for the $\bar{x}$ distribution to approximate a normal curve will depend on how much the population distribution differs from a normal distribution. The closer the population distribution is to being normal, the smaller will be the value of n necessary for the Central Limit Theorem approximation to be accurate.

The following conservative rule is recommended by many statisticians.

The Central Limit Theorem can safely be applied if n exceeds 30.

If the population distribution is believed to be reasonably close to a normal distribution, an n of 15 or 20 is often large enough for $\bar{x}$ to have approximately a normal distribution. At the other extreme, we can imagine a distribution with a much longer tail than that of Figure 8.7, in which case even $n = 40$ or 50 would not suffice for approximate normality of $\bar{x}$. In practice, however, very few population distributions are likely to be this badly behaved.

EXAMPLE 8.6

Let x denote the duration of a randomly selected song (in minutes) for a certain type of songbird. Suppose that the mean value of song duration is $\mu = 1.5$ min and that the standard deviation of song duration is $\sigma = .9$ min. (These values are suggested by the results of a large random sample of house finch songs, as reported in "Song Dialects and Colonization in the House Finch" (*Condor* (1975): 407–422).) The sampling distribution of $\bar{x}$ based on a random sample of $n = 25$ song durations then also has mean value

$$\mu_{\bar{x}} = 1.5 \text{ min}$$

That is, the sampling distribution of $\bar{x}$ is centered at 1.5. The standard deviation of $\bar{x}$ is

$$\sigma_{\bar{x}} = \frac{\sigma}{\sqrt{n}} = \frac{.9}{\sqrt{25}} = .18$$

which is only one-fifth as large as the population standard deviation, σ.

EXAMPLE 8.7

A soft-drink bottler claims that, on average, cans contain 12 oz of soda. Let x denote the actual volume of soda in a randomly selected can. Suppose that x is normally distributed with $\sigma = .16$ oz. Sixteen cans are to be selected and the soda volume determined for each one; let $\bar{x}$ denote the resulting sample average soda volume. Because the x distribution is normal, the sampling distribution of $\bar{x}$ is also normal. *If the bottler's claim is correct,* the sampling distribution of $\bar{x}$ has mean value

$$\mu_{\bar{x}} = \mu = 12$$

and standard deviation

$$\sigma_{\bar{x}} = \frac{\sigma}{\sqrt{n}} = \frac{.16}{\sqrt{16}} = .04$$

To calculate a probability involving $\bar{x}$, we simply standardize by subtracting the mean value, 12, and dividing by the standard deviation (of $\bar{x}$), which is .04. For example, the probability that the sample average soda volume is between 11.96% and 12.08% is calculated by first standardizing the interval limits:

Lower limit: $a^* = \dfrac{11.06 - 12}{.04} = -1.0$

Upper limit: $b^* = \dfrac{12.08 - 12}{.04} = 2.0$

Then

$$P(11.96 \le \bar{x} \le 12.08) = \text{area under the } z \text{ curve between } -1.0 \text{ and } 2.0$$
$$= (\text{area to the left of } 2.0) - (\text{area to the left of } -1.0)$$
$$= .9772 - .1587$$
$$= .8185$$

The probability that the sample average soda volume is at least 12.1 oz is

$$P(\bar{x} \ge 12.1) = P\left(z \ge \frac{12.1 - 12}{.04} = 2.5 \right) = (\text{area under the } z \text{ curve to the right of } 2.5) = .0062$$

If the x distribution is as described and the claim is correct, a sample average soda volume based on 16 observations exceeds 12.1 oz for less than 1% of all such samples. Thus, observation of an $\bar{x}$ value that exceeds 12.1 oz casts doubt on the bottler's claim that the average soda volume is 12 oz.

EXAMPLE 8.8

A hot dog manufacturer asserts that one of its brands of hot dogs has an average fat content of $\mu = 18$ grams per hot dog. Consumers of this brand would probably not be disturbed if the mean was less than 18, but would be unhappy if it exceeded 18. Let x denote the fat content of a randomly selected hot dog, and suppose that σ, the standard deviation of the x distribution, is 1.

An independent testing organization is asked to analyze a random sample of 36 hot dogs. Let $\bar{x}$ be the average fat content for this sample. The sample size, $n = 36$, is large enough to invoke the Central Limit Theorem and regard the $\bar{x}$ distribution as being approximately normal. The standard deviation of the $\bar{x}$ distribution is

$$\sigma_{\bar{x}} = \frac{\sigma}{\sqrt{n}} = \frac{1}{\sqrt{36}} = .1667$$

If the manufacturer's claim is correct, we know that

$$\mu_{\bar{x}} = \mu = 18 \text{ grams}$$

Suppose the sample resulted in a mean of $\bar{x} = 18.4$. Does this result indicate that the manufacturer's claim is incorrect?

We can answer this question by looking at the sampling distribution of $\bar{x}$. Because of sampling variability, even if $\mu = 18$, we know that $\bar{x}$ will typically deviate somewhat from this value. Is it likely that we would see a sample mean at least as large as 18.4 when the population mean is really 18? If the company's claim is correct,

$$P(\bar{x} \ge 18.4) \approx P\left(z \ge \frac{18.4 - 18}{.1667} \right)$$
$$= P(z \ge 2.4)$$
$$= \text{area under the } z \text{ curve to the right of } 2.4$$
$$= .0082$$

The value $\bar{x} = 18.4$ exceeds 18 by enough to cast substantial doubt on the manufacturer's claim. Values of $\bar{x}$ at least as large as 18.4 will be observed only about .82% of the time when a random sample of size 36 is taken from a population with mean 18 and standard deviation 1.

Other Cases

We now know a great deal about the sampling distribution of $\bar{x}$ in two cases, that of a normal population distribution and that of a large sample size. What happens when the population distribution is not normal and n is small? Although it is still true that $\mu_{\bar{x}} = \mu$ and $\sigma_{\bar{x}} = \sigma/\sqrt{n}$, unfortunately there is no general result about the shape of the $\bar{x}$ distribution. When the objective is to make an inference about the center of such a population, one way to proceed is to replace the normality assumption with some other distributional model for the population. Statisticians have proposed and studied a number of such models. Theoretical methods or simulation can be used to describe the $\bar{x}$ distribution corresponding to the assumed model. One alternative strategy is to use one of the transformations presented in Chapter 7 to create a data set that more closely resembles a sample from a normal population and then base inferences on the transformed data. Yet another path is to use an inferential procedure based on statistics other than $\bar{x}$.

Exercises 8.14 – 8.26

8.14 A random sample is to be selected from a population with mean $\mu = 100$ and standard deviation $\sigma = 10$. Determine the mean and standard deviation of the $\bar{x}$ sampling distribution for each of the following sample sizes.

   a. $n = 9$ **b.** $n = 15$
   c. $n = 36$ **d.** $n = 50$
   e. $n = 100$ **f.** $n = 400$

8.15 For which of the sample sizes given in Exercise 8.14 would it be reasonable to think that the $\bar{x}$ sampling distribution will be approximately normal in shape?

8.16 Explain the difference between σ and $\sigma_{\bar{x}}$. Between μ and $\mu_{\bar{x}}$.

8.17 Suppose that a random sample of size 64 is to be selected from a population with mean 40 and standard deviation 5.

   a. What are the mean and standard deviation of the $\bar{x}$ sampling distribution? Describe the shape of the $\bar{x}$ sampling distribution.

   b. What is the approximate probability that $\bar{x}$ will be within .5 of the population mean μ?

   c. What is the approximate probability that $\bar{x}$ will differ from μ by more than .7?

8.18 The time that a randomly selected individual waits for an elevator in an office building has a uniform distribution over the interval from 0 to 1 min. It can be shown that for this distribution, $\mu = .5$ and $\sigma = .289$.

   a. Let $\bar{x}$ be the sample average waiting time for a random sample of 16 individuals. What are the mean value and standard deviation of the sampling distribution of $\bar{x}$?

   b. Answer part **a** for a random sample of 50 individuals. In this case, sketch a picture of a good approximation to the actual $\bar{x}$ distribution.

8.19 Let x denote the time (min) that it takes a fifth-grade student to read a certain passage. Suppose that the mean value and standard deviation of x are $\mu = 2$ min and $\sigma = .8$ min, respectively.

   a. If $\bar{x}$ is the sample average time for a random sample of $n = 9$ students, where is the $\bar{x}$ distribution centered, and how much does it spread out about the center (as described by its standard deviation)?

   b. Repeat part **a** for a sample of size of $n = 20$ and again for a sample of size $n = 100$. How do the centers and spreads of the three $\bar{x}$ distributions compare to one another? Which sample size would be most likely to result in an $\bar{x}$ value close to μ, and why?

8.20 In the library on a university campus, there is a sign in the elevator that indicates a limit of 16 persons. Furthermore, there is a weight limit of 2500 pounds. Assume the average weight of students, faculty, and staff on campus is 150 pounds, the standard deviation is 27 pounds, and that the distribution of weights of individuals on campus is approximately normal. If a random sample of 16 persons from the campus is taken:

a. What is the expected value of the sample mean of their weights?

b. What is the standard deviation of the sampling distribution?

c. What average weight for these 16 people will result in the total weight exceeding the weight limit of 2500 pounds?

d. What is the chance that a random sample of 16 persons on the elevator will exceed the weight limit?

8.21 Suppose that the mean value of interpupillary distance for all adult males is 65 mm, and the population standard deviation is 5 mm.

a. If the distribution of interpupillary distance is normal and a sample of $n = 25$ adult males is selected, what is the probability that the sample average distance $\bar{x}$ for these 25 will be between 64 and 67 mm? At least 68 mm?

b. Suppose that a sample of 100 adult males is obtained. Without assuming that interpupillary distance is normally distributed, what is the approximate probability that the sample average distance is between 64 and 67 mm? At least 68 mm?

8.22 Suppose that a sample of size 100 is to be drawn from a population with standard deviation 10.

a. What is the probability that the sample mean will be within 2 of the value of μ?

b. For this example ($n = 100, \sigma = 10$), complete each statement by computing the appropriate value.

i. Approximately 95% of the time, $\bar{x}$ is within _____ of μ.

ii. Approximately .3% of the time, $\bar{x}$ is farther than _____ from μ.

8.23 A manufacturing process is designed to produce bolts with a .5-in diameter. Once each day, a random sample of 36 bolts is selected and the diameters recorded. If the resulting sample mean is less than .49 in or greater than .51 in, the process is shut down for adjustment. The standard deviation for diameter is .02 in. What is the probability that the manufacturing line will be shut down unnecessarily? (*Hint*: Find the probability of observing an $\bar{x}$

in the shut-down range when the true process mean really is .5 in.)

8.24 College students with a checking account typically write relatively few checks in any given month, whereas full-time residents typically write many more checks during a month. Suppose that 50% of a bank's accounts are held by students and 50% by full-time residents. Let x denote the number of checks written in a given month by a randomly selected bank customer.

a. Give a sketch of what the probability distribution of x might look like.

b. Suppose the mean value of x is 22.0 and the standard deviation is 16.5. If a random sample of $n = 100$ customers is selected and $\bar{x}$ denotes the sample average number of checks written during a particular month, where is the sampling distribution of $\bar{x}$ centered, and what is the standard deviation of the $\bar{x}$ distribution? Sketch a rough picture of the sampling distribution.

c. Referring to part **b**, what is the approximate probability that $\bar{x}$ is at most 20? At least 25? What result are you using to justify your computations?

8.25 An airplane with room for 100 passengers has a total baggage limit of 6000 lb. Suppose that the total weight of the baggage checked by an individual passenger is a random variable x with mean value 50 lb and standard deviation 20 lb. If 100 passengers board a flight, what is the approximate probability that the total weight of their baggage will exceed the limit? (*Hint*: With $n = 100$, the total weight exceeds the limit when the average weight $\bar{x}$ exceeds 6000/100.)

8.26 The thickness (mm) of the coating applied to disk drives is a characteristic that determines the usefulness of the product. When no unusual circumstances are present, the thickness (x) has a normal distribution with mean 3 mm and standard deviation .05 mm. Suppose that the process will be monitored by selecting a random sample of 16 drives from each shift's production and determining $\bar{x}$, the mean coating thickness for the sample.

a. Describe the sampling distribution of $\bar{x}$ (for a sample size 16).

b. When no unusual circumstances are present, we expect $\bar{x}$ to be within $3\sigma_{\bar{x}}$ of 3 mm, the desired value. An $\bar{x}$ value farther from 3 than $3\sigma_{\bar{x}}$ is interpreted as an indication of a problem that needs attention. Compute $3 \pm 3\sigma_{\bar{x}}$. (A plot over time of $\bar{x}$ values with horizontal lines drawn at the limits $\mu \pm 3\sigma_{\bar{x}}$ is called a process control chart.)

c. Referring to part **b**, what is the probability that a

sample mean will be outside $3 \pm 3\sigma_{\bar{x}}$ just by chance (that is, when there are no unusual circumstances)?

d. Suppose that a machine used to apply the coating is out of adjustment, resulting in a mean coating thick-

ness of 3.05 mm. What is the probability that a problem will be detected when the next sample is taken? (*Hint:* This will occur if $\bar{x} > 3 + 3\sigma_{\bar{x}}$ or $\bar{x} < 3 - 3\sigma_{\bar{x}}$ when $\mu = 3.05$.)

8.3 The Sampling Distribution of a Sample Proportion

The objective of many statistical investigations is to draw a conclusion about the proportion of individuals or objects in a population that possess a specified property; for example, Maytag washers that don't require service during the warranty period, Europeans who favor the deployment of a certain type of missile, or coffee drinkers who regularly drink decaffeinated coffee. Traditionally, any individual or object that possesses the property of interest is labeled a success (*S*), and one that does not possess the property is termed a failure (*F*). The letter π denotes the proportion of *S*'s in the population. The value of π is a number between 0 and 1, and 100π is the percentage of *S*'s in the population. If $\pi = .75$, 75% of the population members are *S*'s, and if $\pi = .01$, this means that a population contains only 1% *S*'s and 99% *F*'s.

The value of π is usually unknown to an investigator. When a random sample of size *n* is selected from this type of population, some of the individuals in the sample are *S*'s, and the remaining individuals in the sample are *F*'s. The statistic that will provide a basis for making inferences about π is *p*, the **sample proportion of *S*'s**:

$$p = \frac{\text{number of } S\text{'s in the sample}}{n}$$

For example, if $n = 5$ and three *S*'s result, then $p = 3/5 = .6$.

Just as making inferences about μ requires knowing something about the sampling distribution of the statistic $\bar{x}$, making inferences about π requires first learning about properties of the sampling distribution of the statistic *p*. For example, when $n = 5$, the six possible values of *p* are 0, .2 (from 1/5), .4, .6, .8, and 1. The sampling distribution of *p* gives the probability of each of these six possible values, the long-run proportion of the time that each value would occur if samples with $n = 5$ were selected over and over again. Similarly, when $n = 100$, the 101 possible values of *p* are 0, .01, .02, . . . , .98, .99, and 1. The sampling distribution of *p* can then be used to calculate probabilities such as $P(.3 \le p \le .7)$ and $P(.75 \le p)$.

As we did for the distribution of the sample mean, we will look at some simulation experiments to develop an intuitive understanding of the distribution of the sample proportion before stating general rules. In each example, 500 random samples (each of size *n*) are selected from a population having a specified value of π. We compute *p* for each sample and then construct a sample histogram of the 500 values.

EXAMPLE 8.9   In the fall of 1999, there were 16,250 students enrolled at Cal Poly, San Luis Obispo. Of these students, 6825 (42%) were female. To illustrate properties of the sampling distribution of a sample proportion, we decided to simulate sampling from Cal

Poly's student population. With S denoting a female student and F a male stude n-t, the proportion of S's in the population is $\pi = .42$. A statistical software package was used to select 500 samples of size $n = 5$, then 500 samples of size $n = 10$, then 500 samples with $n = 25$, and finally 500 samples with $n = 50$. The sample histo-grams of the 500 values of p for the four sample sizes are displayed in Figure 8.11.

The most noticeable feature of the histogram shapes is the progression toward the shape of a normal curve as n increases. The histogram for $n = 10$ is more bell shaped than the histogram for samples of size 5, although it still has a slight posi-tive skew. The histograms for $n = 25$ and $n = 50$ look much like a normal curve.

Although the skewness of the first two histograms makes it a bit difficult to lo-cate their centers, all four histograms appear to be centered at roughly .42, the value of π for the population sampled. Had the histograms been based on an unending sequence of samples, each histogram would have been centered at exactly .42. Fi-nally, as was the case with the sampling distribution of $\bar{x}$, the histograms spread out

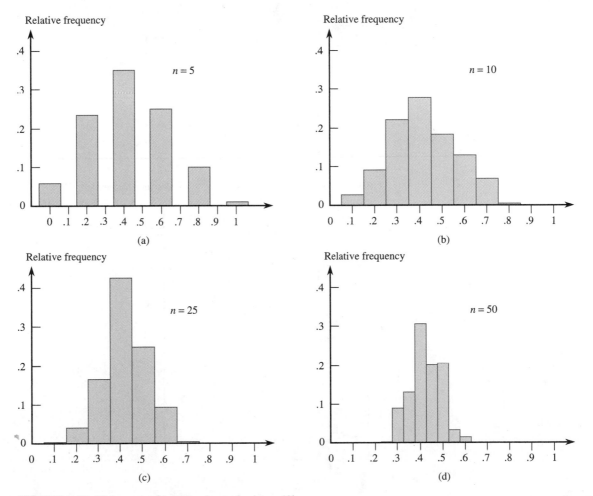

FIGURE 8.11 Histograms for 500 values of p ($\pi = .42$)

more for small n than for large n. The value of p based on a large sample size tends to be closer to π, the population proportion of S's, than does p from a small sample.

EXAMPLE 8.10

The development of viral hepatitis subsequent to a blood transfusion can cause serious complications for a patient. The article "Hepatitis in Patients with Acute Non-lymphatic Leukemia" (*Amer. J. of Med.* (1983): 413–421) reported that in spite of careful screening for those having a hepatitis antigen, viral hepatitis occurs in 7% of blood recipients. Here we simulate sampling from the population of blood re-

FIGURE 8.12 Histograms of 500 values of p ($\pi = .07$)

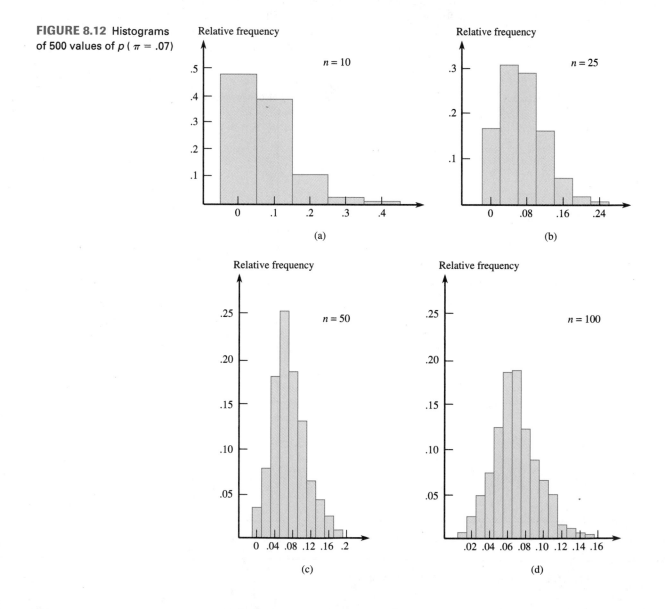

cipients, with S denoting a recipient who contracts hepatitis (not the sort of characteristic one usually thinks of as a success, but the S–F labeling is arbitrary), so $\pi = .07$. Figure 8.12 displays histograms of 500 values of p for the four sample sizes $n = 10, 25, 50$, and 100.

As was the case in Example 8.9, all four histograms are centered at approximately the value of π for the population being sampled. (The average values of p for these simulations are .0690, .0677, .0707, and .0694.) If the histograms had been based on an unending sequence of samples, they would all have been centered at exactly $\pi = .07$. Again, the spread of a histogram based on a large n is smaller than the spread of a histogram resulting from a small sample size. The larger the value of n, the closer the sample proportion, p, tends to be to the value of the population proportion, π.

Furthermore, there is a progression toward the shape of a normal curve as n increases. However, the progression is much slower here than in the previous example, because the value of π is so extreme. (The same thing would happen for $\pi = .93$, except that the histograms would be negatively rather than positively skewed.) The histograms for $n = 10$ and $n = 25$ exhibit substantial skew, and the skew of the histogram for $n = 50$ is still moderate (compare Figure 8.12(c) to Figure 8.11(d)). Only the histogram for $n = 100$ is reasonably well fit by a normal curve. It appears that whether a normal curve provides a good approximation to the sampling distribution of p depends on the values of both n and π. Knowing only that $n = 50$ is not enough to guarantee that the shape of the histogram is approximately normal.

General Properties of the Sampling Distribution of p

The previous two examples suggest that the sampling distribution of p depends both on n, the sample size, and on π, the proportion of S's in the population. These results are stated more formally in the following general rules.

General Properties of the Sampling Distribution of p

Let p be the proportion of successes in a random sample of size n from a population whose proportion of S's is π. Denote the mean value of p by μ_p and the standard deviation by σ_p. Then the following rules hold.

Rule 1. $\mu_p = \pi$

Rule 2. $\sigma_p = \sqrt{\dfrac{\pi(1 - \pi)}{n}}$

Rule 3. When n is large and π is not too near 0 or 1, the sampling distribution of p is approximately normal.

Thus, the sampling distribution of p is always centered at the value of the population success proportion π, and the extent to which the distribution spreads out about π decreases as the sample size n increases.

Examples 8.9 and 8.10 indicate that both π and n must be considered in judging whether the sampling distribution of p is approximately normal.

The farther the value of π is from .5, the larger n must be for a normal approximation to the sampling distribution of p to be accurate. A conservative rule of thumb is that if both $n\pi \geq 10$ and $n(1 - \pi) \geq 10$, then it is safe to use a normal approximation.

A sample size of $n = 100$ is not by itself sufficient to justify the use of a normal approximation. If $\pi = .01$, the distribution of p will be very positively skewed, so a bell-shaped curve will not give a good approximation. Similarly, if $n = 100$ and $\pi = .99$ (so $n(1 - \pi) = 1 < 10$), the distribution of p will have a substantial negative skew. The conditions $n\pi \geq 10$ and $n(1 - \pi) \geq 10$ ensure that the sampling distribution of p is not too skewed. If $\pi = .5$, the normal approximation can be used for n as small as 20, whereas for $\pi = .05$ or .95, n should be at least 200.

EXAMPLE 8.11

The proportion of all blood recipients stricken with viral hepatitis was given as .07 in the article referenced in Example 8.10. Suppose that a new treatment is believed to reduce the incidence rate of viral hepatitis. This treatment is given to $n = 200$ blood recipients. Only 6 of the 200 patients contract hepatitis. This appears to be a favorable result, since $p = 6/200 = .03$. The question of interest to medical researchers is: Does this result indicate that the true (long-run) proportion of patients who contract hepatitis after the experimental treatment is less than .07, or could this result be plausibly attributed to sampling variability (i.e., the fact that p will typically deviate from its mean value, π)? If the treatment is ineffective,

$$\mu_p = \pi = .07 \qquad \sigma_p = \sqrt{\frac{\pi(1 - \pi)}{200}} = \sqrt{\frac{(.07)(.93)}{200}} = .018$$

Furthermore, since

$$n\pi = 200(.07) = 14 \geq 10$$

and

$$n(1 - \pi) = 200(.93) = 186 \geq 10$$

the sampling distribution of p is approximately normal. Then

$$P(p < .03) \approx P\left(z < \frac{.03 - .07}{.018}\right)$$
$$= P(z < -2.22)$$
$$= .0132$$

Thus, it is unlikely that a sample proportion .03 or smaller would be observed if the treatment really were ineffective. The new treatment appears to yield a smaller incidence rate for the disease than occurs without any treatment.

Exercises 8.27 – 8.33

8.27   A random sample is to be selected from a population that has a proportion of successes $\pi = .65$. Determine the mean and standard deviation of the sampling distribution of p for each of the following sample sizes.
  a. $n = 10$ **b.** $n = 20$ **c.** $n = 30$
  d. $n = 50$ **e.** $n = 100$ **f.** $n = 200$

8.28   For which of the sample sizes given in Exercise 8.27 would the sampling distribution of p be approximately normal if $\pi = .65$? If $\pi = .2$?

8.29   A certain chromosome defect occurs in only one out of 200 Caucasian adult males. A random sample of $n = 100$ adult Caucasian males is obtained.
  a. What is the mean value of the sample proportion p, and what is the standard deviation of the sample proportion?
  b. Does p have approximately a normal distribution in this case? Explain.
  c. What is the smallest value of n for which the sampling distribution of p is approximately normal?

8.30   The article "Should Pregnant Women Move? Linking Risks for Birth Defects with Proximity to Toxic Waste Sites" (*Chance* (1992): 40–45) reported that in a large study carried out in the state of New York, approximately 30% of the study subjects lived within 1 mile of a hazardous waste site. Let π denote the proportion of all New York residents who live within 1 mile of such a site, and suppose that $\pi = .3$.
  a. Would p based on a random sample of only 10 residents have approximately a normal distribution? Explain why or why not.
  b. What are the mean value and standard deviation of p based on a random sample of size 400?
  c. When $n = 400$, what is $P(.25 \leq p \leq .35)$?
  d. Is the probability calculated in part **c** larger or

smaller than would be the case if $n = 500$? Answer without actually calculating this latter probability.

8.31   The article "Thrillers" (*Newsweek,* Apr. 22, 1985) states, "Surveys tell us that more than half of America's college graduates are avid readers of mystery novels." Let π denote the actual proportion of college graduates who are avid readers of mystery novels. Consider p to be based on a random sample of 225 college graduates.
  a. If $\pi = .5$, what are the mean value and standard deviation of p? Answer this question for $\pi = .6$. Does p have approximately a normal distribution in both cases? Explain.
  b. Calculate $P(p \geq .6)$ both for $\pi = .5$ and for $\pi = .6$.
  c. Without doing any calculations, how do you think the probabilities in part **b** would change if n were 400 rather than 225?

8.32   Suppose that a particular candidate for public office is in fact favored by 48% of all registered voters in the district. A polling organization takes a random sample of 500 voters and will use p, the sample proportion, to estimate π. What is the approximate probability that p will be greater than .5, causing the polling organization to incorrectly predict the result of the upcoming election?

8.33   A manufacturer of computer printers purchases plastic ink cartridges from a vendor. When a large shipment is received, a random sample of 200 cartridges is selected, and each is inspected. If the sample proportion of defectives is more than .02, the entire shipment will be returned to the vendor.
  a. What is the approximate probability that the shipment will be returned if the true proportion of defectives in the shipment is .05?
  b. What is the approximate probability that the shipment will not be returned when the true proportion of defectives in the shipment is .10?

Summary of Key Concepts and Formulas

Term or Formula	Comment
Statistic	Any quantity whose value is computed from sample data.
Sampling distribution	The probability distribution of a statistic: The sampling distribution describes the long-run behavior of the statistic.
Sampling distribution of $\bar{x}$	The probability distribution of the sample mean $\bar{x}$, based on a random sample of size n. Properties of the $\bar{x}$ sampling distribution: $\mu_{\bar{x}} = \mu$ and $\sigma_{\bar{x}} = \sigma/\sqrt{n}$

Term or Formula	Comment
	(where μ and σ are the population mean and standard deviation, respectively). In addition, when the population distribution is normal or the sample size is large, the sampling distribution of $\bar{x}$ is (approximately) normal.
Central Limit Theorem	This important theorem states that when n is sufficiently large, the $\bar{x}$ distribution will be approximately normal. The standard rule of thumb is that the theorem can safely be applied when n exceeds 30.
Sampling distribution of p	The probability distribution of the sample proportion p, based on a random sample of size n. When the sample size is sufficiently large, the sampling distribution of p is approximately normal, with $\mu_p = \pi$ and $\sigma_p = \sqrt{\pi(1-\pi)/n}$ (where π is the true population proportion).

Supplementary Exercises 8.34 – 8.40

8.34 The nicotine content in a single cigarette of a particular brand has a distribution with mean .8 mg and standard deviation .1 mg. If 100 of these cigarettes are analyzed, what is the probability that the resulting sample mean nicotine content will be less than .79? Less than .77?

8.35 Let $x_1, x_2, \ldots, x_{100}$ denote the actual net weights (in lb) of 100 randomly selected bags of fertilizer. Suppose that the weight of a randomly selected bag has a distribution with mean 50 lb and variance 1 lb². Let $\bar{x}$ be the sample mean weight ($n = 100$).
   a. Describe the sampling distribution of $\bar{x}$.
   b. What is the probability that the sample mean is between 49.75 lb and 50.25 lb?
   c. What is the probability that the sample mean is less than 50 lb?

8.36 Suppose that 20% of the subscribers of a cable television company watch the shopping channel at least once a week. The cable company is trying to decide whether to replace this channel with a new local station. A survey of 100 subscribers will be undertaken. The cable company has decided to keep the shopping channel if the sample proportion is greater than .25. What is the approximate probability that the cable company will keep the shopping channel, even though the true proportion who watch it is only .20?

8.37 Although a lecture period at a certain university lasts exactly 50 minutes, the actual lecture time of a statistics instructor on any particular day has a distribution with mean value 52 min and standard deviation 2 min. Suppose that times of different lectures are independent

of one another. Let $\bar{x}$ represent the mean of 36 randomly selected lecture times.
   a. What are the mean value and standard deviation of the sampling distribution of $\bar{x}$?
   b. What is the probability that the sample mean exceeds 50 min? 55 min?

8.38 Water permeability of concrete is an important characteristic in assessing suitability for various applications. Permeability can be measured by letting water flow across the surface and determining the amount lost (in/hr). Suppose that the permeability index x for a randomly selected concrete specimen of a particular type is normally distributed with mean value 1000 and standard deviation 150.
   a. How likely is it that a single specimen will have a permeability index between 850 and 1300?
   b. If the permeability index is determined for each specimen in a random sample of size 10, how likely is it that the sample average permeability index will be between 950 and 1100? Between 850 and 1300?

8.39 *Newsweek* (Nov. 23, 1992) reported that 40% of all U.S. employees participate in "self-insurance" health plans ($\pi = .40$).
   a. In a random sample of 100 employees, what is the approximate probability that at least half of those in the sample participate in such a plan?
   b. Suppose you were told that at least 60 of the 100 employees in a sample from your state participated in such a plan. Would you think $\pi = .40$ for your state?

8.40 The amount of money spent by a customer at a discount store has a mean of $100 and a standard deviation of $30. What is the probability that a randomly selected group of 50 shoppers will spend a total of more than $5300? (*Hint*: The total will be more than $5300 when the sample average exceeds what value?)

References

Freedman, David, Robert Pisani, Roger Purves. *Statistics,* 3rd ed. New York: W. W. Norton, 1997. (This book gives an excellent informal discussion of sampling distributions.)

9

Estimation Using
a Single Sample

INTRODUCTION

Despite protests from civil libertarians and gay rights activists, many people favor mandatory AIDS testing of certain at-risk groups, and some even believe that all citizens should be tested. What proportion of the adults in the United States favor mandatory testing for all citizens? For doctors, dentists, and other health care workers? For those convicted of a crime? To assess public opinion on this issue, researchers conducted a survey of 1014 adult U.S. citizens ("Large Majorities Continue to Back AIDS Testing," *Gallup Poll Monthly* (1991): 25–28). The researchers wanted to use the resulting information to estimate the true proportion in favor of testing various groups. The methods introduced in this chapter are used to produce the desired estimates. Since the estimates are based only on a sample rather than on a census of all U.S. adults, it is important that these estimates are constructed in a way that also conveys information about the anticipated accuracy.

The objective of inferential statistics is to use sample data to decrease our uncertainty about the corresponding population. Often, data is collected to obtain information that allows the investigator to estimate the value of some population characteristic, such as a population mean, μ, or a population proportion, π. One way to accomplish this uses the sample data to arrive at a single number that represents a plausible value for the characteristic of interest. Alternatively, an entire range of plausible values for the characteristic can be reported. These two estimation techniques, *point estimation* and *interval estimation,* are introduced in this chapter.

9.1   Point Estimation

The simplest approach to estimating a population characteristic involves using sample data to compute a single number that can be regarded as a plausible value of the characteristic. For example, sample data might suggest that 1000 hours is a plausible value for μ, the true mean lifetime for lightbulbs of a particular brand. In a different setting, a sample survey of students at a particular university might lead to the statement that .41 is a plausible value for π, the true proportion of students who favor a fee for recreational activities.

Definition

A **point estimate** of a population characteristic is a single number that is based on sample data and represents a plausible value of the characteristic.

In the examples just given, 1000 is a point estimate of μ, and .41 is a point estimate of π. The adjective *point* reflects the fact that the estimate corresponds to a single point on the number line.

A point estimate is obtained by first selecting an appropriate statistic. The estimate is then the value of the statistic for the given sample. For example, the computed value of the sample mean $\bar{x}$ provides a point estimate of a population mean μ.

EXAMPLE 9.1   One of the purposes of the survey on AIDS testing described in the chapter introduction was to estimate the proportion of the U.S. population who believe that every citizen should be tested for AIDS. The article reported that 466 of the 1014 people surveyed believed that all citizens should be tested. Let's use this information to estimate π, where

π = true proportion of all U.S. adults who favor AIDS testing of all citizens

With "success" identified as a person who favors testing, π is then just the population proportion of successes. The statistic

$$p = \frac{\text{number of successes in the sample}}{n}$$

which is the sample proportion of successes, is an obvious choice for obtaining a point estimate of π. Based on the reported information, the point estimate of π is

$$p = \frac{466}{1014} = .460$$

That is, based on the sample, we estimate that 46% of the adults in the United States favor AIDS testing of all citizens.

For purposes of estimating a population proportion π, it would be difficult to suggest a statistic other than p that could reasonably be used. In other situations, such as the one illustrated in Example 9.2, there may be several statistics that can be used to obtain an estimate.

EXAMPLE 9.2

The article "Effects of Roadside Conditions on Plants and Insects" (*J. Appl. Ecology* (1988): 709–715) reported the results of an experiment to evaluate the effect of nitrous oxide from automobile exhaust on roadside soil. The concentration of soluble nitrogen (in mg/g) was recorded at 20 roadside locations. Suppose that the observed readings are as follows (data is compatible with summary values given in the article):

1.7	1.9	2.0	1.7	1.6	1.7	1.8	1.7	1.8	1.8
1.6	1.7	2.1	1.7	1.8	1.7	1.8	1.4	1.9	1.7

A dotplot of the data is shown here:

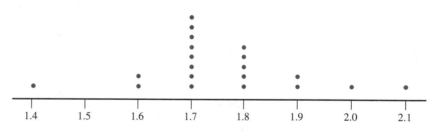

Suppose further that a point estimate of μ, the true mean soluble nitrogen concentration, is desired. An obvious choice of a statistic for estimating μ is the sample mean, $\bar{x}$. However, there are other possibilities. We might consider using a trimmed mean or even the sample median, since the data set exhibits some symmetry. (If the corresponding population distribution is symmetric, μ is also the population median.)

The three statistics and the resulting estimates of μ calculated from the data are

$$\text{sample mean} = \bar{x} = \frac{\Sigma x}{n} = \frac{35.1}{20} = 1.76$$

$$\text{sample median} = \frac{1.7 + 1.7}{2} = 1.70$$

$$10\% \text{ trimmed mean} = \left(\begin{array}{c}\text{average of middle} \\ \text{16 observations}\end{array}\right) = \frac{28.0}{16} = 1.75$$

The estimates differ somewhat from one another. The choice from among them should depend on which statistic tends, on average, to produce an estimate closest to the true value. The following subsection discusses criteria for choosing among competing statistics.

Choosing a Statistic for Computing an Estimate

The point of the previous example is that there may be more than one statistic that can reasonably be used to obtain a point estimate of a specified population characteristic. Loosely speaking, the statistic used should be one that tends to yield an accurate estimate — that is, an estimate close to the value of the population characteristic. Information about the accuracy of estimation for a particular statistic is provided by the statistic's sampling distribution. Figure 9.1 displays the sampling distributions of three different statistics. The value of the population characteristic, which we refer to as the *true value,* is marked on the measurement axis.

The distribution pictured in Figure 9.1(a) is that of a statistic unlikely to yield an estimate close to the true value. The distribution is centered to the right of the true value, making it very likely that an estimate (a value of the statistic for a particular sample) will be larger than the true value. If this statistic is used to compute an estimate based on a first sample, then another estimate based on a second sample, and another estimate based on a third sample, and so on, the long-run average value of these estimates will exceed the true value.

The sampling distribution of Figure 9.1(b) is centered at the true value. Thus, while one estimate may be smaller than the true value and another may be larger, when this statistic is used many times over with different samples, there will be no long-run tendency to over- or underestimate the true value. Note that even though the sampling distribution is correctly centered, it spreads out quite a bit about the true value. Because of this, some estimates resulting from the use of this statistic will be far above or below the true value — even though there is no systematic tendency to underestimate or overestimate the true value. In contrast, the mean value of the statistic with the distribution shown in Figure 9.1(c) is exactly the true value of the population characteristic (implying no systematic error in estimation), and the statistic's standard deviation is relatively small. Estimates using this third statistic will almost always be quite close to the true value — certainly more often than estimates resulting from the statistic with the sampling distribution shown in Figure 9.1(b).

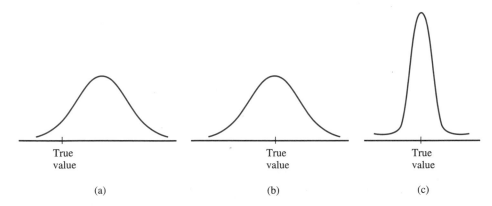

FIGURE 9.1 Sampling distributions of three different statistics for estimating a population characteristic

Definition

A statistic with mean value equal to the value of the population characteristic being estimated is said to be an **unbiased statistic.** A statistic that is not unbiased is said to be **biased.**

Let $x_1, x_2, \ldots, x_n$ represent the values in a random sample. One of the general results concerning the sampling distribution of $\bar{x}$, the sample mean, is that $\mu_{\bar{x}} = \mu$. This result says that the $\bar{x}$ values from many different random samples of size n center around μ, the population mean. For example, if $\mu = 100$, the $\bar{x}$ distribution is centered at 100, whereas if $\mu = 5200$, then the $\bar{x}$ distribution is centered at 5200. Therefore, $\bar{x}$ is an unbiased statistic for estimating μ. Similarly, since $\mu_p = \pi$, the sampling distribution of p is centered at π, and it follows that p is an unbiased statistic for estimating a population proportion.

Using an unbiased statistic that has a small standard deviation guarantees that there will be no systematic tendency to under- or overestimate the value of the population characteristic *and* that estimates will almost always be relatively close to the true value.

Given a choice between several unbiased statistics that could be used for estimating a population characteristic, the best statistic to use is the one with the smallest standard deviation.

Consider the problem of estimating a population mean, μ. The obvious choice of statistic for obtaining a point estimate of μ is the sample mean, $\bar{x}$, an unbiased statistic for this purpose. However, when the population distribution is symmetric, $\bar{x}$ is not the only choice. Other unbiased statistics for estimating μ in this case include the sample median and any trimmed mean (with the same number of observations trimmed from each end of the ordered sample). Which statistic should be used? The following facts may be helpful in making a choice.

1. If the population distribution is normal, then $\bar{x}$ has a smaller standard deviation than any other unbiased statistic for estimating μ. However, in this case, a trimmed mean with a small trimming percentage (such as 10%) performs almost as well as $\bar{x}$.

2. When the population distribution is symmetric with heavy tails compared to the normal curve, a trimmed mean is a better statistic than $\bar{x}$ for estimating μ.

When the population distribution is unquestionably normal, the choice is clear: Use $\bar{x}$ to estimate μ. But with a heavy-tailed distribution, a trimmed mean gives protection against one or two outliers in the sample that might otherwise have a large effect on the value of the estimate.

Now consider estimating another population characteristic, the population variance σ^2. The sample variance

$$s^2 = \frac{\Sigma(x - \bar{x})^2}{n - 1}$$

is a good choice for obtaining a point estimate of the population variance σ^2. It can be shown that s^2 is an unbiased statistic for estimating σ^2; that is, whatever the value of σ^2, the sampling distribution of s^2 is centered at that value. It is precisely for this reason — to obtain an unbiased statistic — that the divisor $n - 1$ is used. An alternative statistic is the average squared deviation

$$\frac{\Sigma(x - \bar{x})^2}{n}$$

which one might think has a more natural divisor than s^2. However, the average squared deviation is biased, with its values tending to be smaller, on average, than σ^2.

EXAMPLE 9.3

The article "Sensory and Mechanical Assessment of the Quality of Frankfurters" (*J. of Texture Studies* (1990): 395–409) reported the following salt content (percentage by weight) for ten frankfurters:

2.26   2.11   1.64   1.17   1.64   2.36   1.70   2.10   2.19   2.40

Then

$$\Sigma x = 19.57 \qquad \Sigma x^2 = 39.7335 \qquad n = 10$$

and

$$\Sigma(x - \bar{x})^2 = \Sigma x^2 - \frac{(\Sigma x)^2}{n}$$

$$= 39.7335 - \frac{(19.57)^2}{10}$$

$$= 1.435$$

Let σ^2 denote the true variance in salt content for frankfurters. Using the sample variance s^2 to provide a point estimate of σ^2 yields

$$s^2 = \frac{\Sigma(x - \bar{x})^2}{n - 1} = \frac{1.435}{9} = .1594$$

Using the average squared deviation (with divisor $n = 10$), the resulting point estimate is

$$\frac{\Sigma(x - \bar{x})^2}{n} = \frac{1.435}{10} = .1435$$

Because s^2 is an unbiased statistic for estimating σ^2, most statisticians would recommend using the point estimate .1594.

An obvious choice of a statistic for estimating the population standard deviation σ is the sample standard deviation s. For the data given in Example 9.3,

$$s = \sqrt{.1594} = .3992$$

Unfortunately, the fact that s^2 is an unbiased statistic for estimating σ^2 does not imply that s is an unbiased statistic for estimating σ. The sample standard deviation tends to underestimate slightly the true value of σ. However, unbiasedness is not the only criterion by which a statistic can be judged, and there are other good reasons for using s to estimate σ. In what follows, whenever we need to estimate σ based on a single random sample, we use the statistic s to obtain a point estimate.

Exercises 9.1 – 9.9

9.1 Three different statistics are being considered for estimating a population characteristic. The sampling distributions of the three statistics are shown in the illustration at the bottom of the page. Which statistic would you recommend? Explain your choice.

9.2 Why is an unbiased statistic generally preferred over a biased statistic for estimating a population characteristic? Does unbiasedness alone guarantee that the estimate will be close to the true value? Explain. Under what circumstances might you choose a biased statistic over an unbiased statistic if two statistics are available for estimating a population characteristic?

9.3 Radon, an odorless gas that can cause lung cancer, is released in the decay of radium, which is naturally present in soil and rocks. The Environmental Protection Agency (EPA) considers radon to be the second leading cause of lung cancer (behind cigarette smoking). One radon hot spot has been identified on the Spokane Indian reservation in Washington. The Associated Press (June 10, 1991) reported that of 270 randomly selected homes on the reservation, 68 showed radon readings above 4 pCi (the level that the EPA considers hazardous). Estimate π, the proportion of all homes on the reservation with a radon level above 4 pCi.

9.4 The article "Diallel Analysis of Pod Length and Shelling Percent of Winged Beans" (Field Crops Research (1987): 209–216) reported the following lengths for nine winged bean pods:

12.1   18.5   17.2   27.7   17.9   12.9   17.0   15.0   14.5

a. Use the given data to produce a point estimate of μ, the true mean length for winged bean pods. (*Hint:* $\Sigma x = 152.8$)

b. Use the given data to produce a point estimate of σ^2, the variance of pod length for all winged bean pods. (*Hint:* $\Sigma x^2 = 2762.86$)

Figure for Exercise 9.1

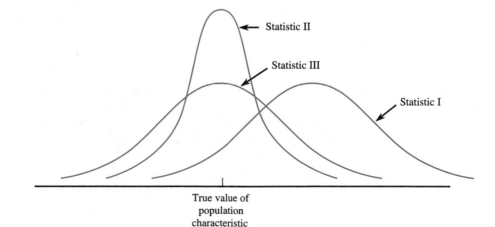

Statistic II

Statistic III

Statistic I

True value of
population
characteristic

c. Use the given data to produce an estimate of σ, the standard deviation of pod length. Is the statistic you used to produce your estimate unbiased?

9.5 A study reported in *Newsweek* (Dec. 23, 1991) involved a sample of 935 smokers. Each individual received a nicotine patch, which delivers nicotine to the bloodstream but at a much slower rate than cigarettes. Dosage was decreased to zero over a 12-week period. Suppose that 245 of the subjects were still not smoking 6 months after treatment (this figure is consistent with information given in the article). Estimate the percentage of all smokers who, when given this treatment, would refrain from smoking for at least 6 months.

9.6 The following data on gross efficiency (ratio of work accomplished per minute to calorie expenditure per minute) for trained endurance cyclists was given in the article "Cycling Efficiency Is Related to the Percentage of Type I Muscle Fibers" (*Medicine and Science in Sports and Exercise* (1992): 782–788).

18.3 18.9 19.0 20.9 21.4 20.5 20.1
20.1 20.8 20.5 19.9 20.5 20.6 22.1
21.9 21.2 20.5 22.6 22.6

a. Assuming that the distribution of gross energy in the population of all endurance cyclists is normal, give a point estimate of μ, the population mean gross efficiency. (*Hint*: $\Sigma x = 392.4$)
b. Making no assumptions about the shape of the population distribution, estimate the proportion of all such cyclists whose gross efficiency is at most 20.

9.7 A random sample of $n = 12$ 4-year-old red pine trees was selected, and the diameter (in) of each tree's main stem was measured. The resulting observations are as follows:

11.3   10.7   12.4   15.2   10.1   12.1
16.2   10.5   11.4   11.0   10.7   12.0

a. Compute a point estimate of σ, the population standard deviation of main stem diameter. What statistic did you use to obtain your estimate?
b. Making no assumptions whatsoever about the shape of the population distribution of diameter, give a point estimate for the population median diameter (that is, for the middle diameter value in the entire population

of 4-year-old red pine trees). What statistic did you use to obtain the estimate?
c. Suppose that the population distribution of diameter is symmetric but with heavier tails than the normal distribution. Give a point estimate of the population mean diameter based on a statistic that gives some protection against the presence of outliers in the sample. What statistic did you use?
d. Suppose that the diameter distribution is normal. Then the 90th percentile of the diameter distribution is $\mu + 1.28\sigma$ (so 90% of all trees have diameters less than this value). Compute a point estimate for this percentile. (*Hint*: First compute an estimate of μ in this case; then use it along with your estimate of σ from part **a**.)

9.8 Each person in a random sample of 20 students at a particular university was asked whether he or she was registered to vote. The responses (R = registered, N = not registered) are given here:

| R | R | N | R | N | N | R | R | R | N |
| R | R | R | R | R | N | R | R | R | N |

Use this data to estimate π, the true proportion of all students at the university who were registered to vote.

9.9 a. A random sample of ten houses in a particular area, each of which is heated with natural gas, is selected, and the amount of gas (therms) used during the month of January is determined for each house. The resulting observations are as follows:

103   156   118   89   125   147   122   109   138   99

Let μ_J denote the average gas usage during January by all houses in this area. Compute a point estimate of μ_J.
b. Suppose that there are 10,000 houses in this area that use natural gas for heating. Let τ denote the total amount of gas used by all of these houses during January. Estimate τ using the data of part **a**. What statistic (sample-based quantity) did you use in computing your estimate?
c. Use the data in part **a** to estimate π, the proportion of all houses that used at least 100 therms.
d. Give a point estimate of the population median usage (the middle value in the population of all houses) based on the sample of part **a**. Which statistic did you use?

9.2 A Large-Sample Confidence Interval for a Population Proportion

In Section 9.1, we saw how to use a statistic to produce a point estimate of a population characteristic. The value of a point estimate depends on which sample, out of all the possible samples, happens to be selected. Different samples will usually yield different estimates due to chance differences from one sample to another. Because of sampling variability, rarely is the point estimate from a sample exactly equal to the true value of the population characteristic. We must hope that the chosen statistic produces an estimate that is close, on average, to the true value. Although a point estimate may represent our best single-number guess for the value of the population characteristic, it is not the only plausible value. These considerations suggest the need to indicate in some way how precisely the population characteristic has been estimated. A point estimate by itself does not provide this information.

As an alternative to a point estimate, suppose that we report not just a single credible value for the population characteristic, but an entire interval of reasonable values based on the sample data. For example, we might be confident that for all calls made from AT&T pay phones, the proportion, π, of calls that are billed to a credit card is in the interval from .53 to .57. The narrowness of this interval implies that we have rather precise information about the value of π. If, with the same high degree of confidence, we could state only that π was between .32 and .74, it would be clear that we had relatively imprecise knowledge of the value of π.

> **Definition**
>
> A **confidence interval** for a population characteristic is an interval of plausible values for the characteristic. It is constructed so that, with a chosen degree of confidence, the value of the characteristic will be captured inside the interval.

Associated with each confidence interval is a *confidence level*. The confidence level provides information on how much "confidence" we can have in the *method* used to construct the interval estimate, *not* our confidence in any one particular interval. Usual choices for confidence levels are 90%, 95%, and 99%, although other levels are also possible. If we were to construct a 95% confidence interval using the technique to be described shortly, we would be using a method that is "successful" 95% of the time. That is, if this method were used to generate an interval estimate over and over again with different samples, in the long run, 95% of the resulting intervals would capture the true value of the characteristic being estimated. Similarly, a 99% confidence interval is one that is constructed using a method that is, in the long run, successful in capturing the true value of the population characteristic 99% of the time.

> **Definition**
>
> The **confidence level** associated with a confidence interval estimate is the success rate of the *method* used to construct the interval.

Many factors influence the choice of confidence level. These factors will be discussed after we develop the method for constructing confidence intervals. We will first consider a large-sample confidence interval for a population proportion, π.

Often an investigator wishes to make an inference about the proportion of individuals or objects in a population that possesses a particular property of interest. For example, a university administrator might be interested in the proportion of students who prefer a new web-based computer registration system to the previous registration method. In a different setting, a quality control engineer might be concerned about the proportion of defective parts manufactured using a particular process.

Let

$$\pi = \text{proportion of the population that possesses the property of interest}$$

In this section, we consider the problem of estimating π using information in a random sample of size n from the population. Previously, we used the sample proportion

$$p = \frac{\text{number in sample that possesses property of interest}}{n}$$

to calculate a point estimate of π. We can also use p to form a confidence interval for π.

Although a small-sample confidence interval for π can be obtained, our focus will be on the large-sample case. The justification for the large-sample interval rests on properties of the sampling distribution of the statistic p:

1. The sampling distribution of p is centered at π; that is, $\mu_p = \pi$. Therefore, p is an unbiased statistic for estimating π.
2. The standard deviation of p is $\sigma_p = \sqrt{\pi(1 - \pi)/n}$.
3. As long as n is large ($n\pi \geq 10$ and $n(1 - \pi) \geq 10$), the sampling distribution of p is well approximated by a normal curve.

The accompanying box summarizes these properties.

> When n is large, the statistic p has a sampling distribution that is approximately normal with mean π and standard deviation $\sqrt{\pi(1 - \pi)/n}$.

The development of a confidence interval for π is easier to understand if we select a particular confidence level (say, 95%). Appendix Table II, the table of standard normal (z) curve areas, can be used to determine a value z^* such that a central area of .95 falls between $-z^*$ and z^*. In this case, the remaining area of .05 is divided equally between the two tails, as shown in Figure 9.2. The total area to the left of the desired z^* is .975 (.95 central area + .025 area below $-z^*$). Locating .9750 in the body of Appendix Table II, we find that the corresponding z critical value is 1.96.

FIGURE 9.2 Capturing a central area of .95 under the z curve

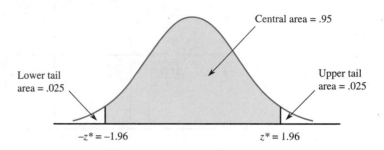

Central area = .95

Lower tail
area = .025

Upper tail
area = .025

$-z^* = -1.96$ $z^* = 1.96$

Generalizing this result to normal distributions other than the standard normal tells us that for *any* normal distribution, about 95% of the values are within 1.96 standard deviations of the mean. Since (for large samples) the sampling distribution of p is approximately normal with mean $\mu_p = \pi$ and standard deviation $\sigma_p = \sqrt{\pi(1 - \pi)/n}$, we get the following result.

Approximately 95% of all large samples will result in a value of p that is within $1.96\sigma_p = 1.96\sqrt{\pi(1 - \pi)/n}$ of the true population proportion π.

If p is within $1.96\sqrt{\pi(1 - \pi)/n}$ of π, the interval

$$p - 1.96\sqrt{\frac{\pi(1 - \pi)}{n}} \quad \text{to} \quad p + 1.96\sqrt{\frac{\pi(1 - \pi)}{n}}$$

will capture π (and this will happen for 95% of all possible samples). However, if p is farther away from π than $1.96\sqrt{\pi(1 - \pi)/n}$ (which will happen for about 5% of all possible samples), the interval will not include the true value of π. This is shown in Figure 9.3 on page 322.

Since p is within $1.96\sigma_p$ of π 95% of the time, this implies that in repeated sampling, 95% of the time the interval

$$p - 1.96\sqrt{\frac{\pi(1 - \pi)}{n}} \quad \text{to} \quad p + 1.96\sqrt{\frac{\pi(1 - \pi)}{n}}$$

FIGURE 9.3 The population proportion π is captured in the interval from $p - 1.96\sqrt{\pi(1 - \pi)/n}$ to $p + 1.96\sqrt{\pi(1 - \pi)/n}$ when p is within $1.96\sqrt{\pi(1 - \pi)/n}$ of π.

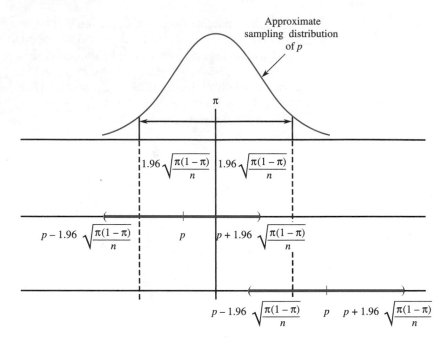

will contain π. Since π is unknown, $\sqrt{\pi(1 - \pi)/n}$ must be estimated. As long as the sample size is large, the value of $\sqrt{p(1 - p)/n}$ should be close to $\sqrt{\pi(1 - \pi)/n}$ and can be used in its place.

When n is large, a 95% confidence interval for π is

$$\left(p - 1.96\sqrt{\frac{p(1 - p)}{n}}, \quad p + 1.96\sqrt{\frac{p(1 - p)}{n}} \right)$$

An abbreviated formula for the interval is

$$p \pm 1.96\sqrt{\frac{p(1 - p)}{n}}$$

where + gives the upper endpoint of the interval and − gives the lower endpoint of the interval. The interval can be used as long as $np \geq 10$ and $n(1 - p) \geq 10$.

EXAMPLE 9.4   Let's return to the information gathered by the Gallup Organization in the survey on attitudes towards AIDS testing (see the chapter introduction and Example 9.1):

Total number of people surveyed:	1014
Number favoring testing of every citizen:	466
Number favoring testing of doctors and dentists:	882

A point estimate of π = true proportion who favor AIDS testing of all citizens is

$$p = \frac{466}{1014} = .460$$

Since

$$np = (1014)(.46) = 466 \geq 10 \quad \text{and} \quad n(1 - p) = (1014)(.54) = 548 \geq 10$$

the large-sample interval can be used. For a 95% confidence level, the appropriate z critical value is 1.96, and a 95% confidence interval for π is

$$p \pm 1.96\sqrt{\frac{p(1 - p)}{n}} = .460 \pm 1.96\sqrt{\frac{(.460)(.540)}{1014}}$$
$$= .460 \pm (1.96)(.016)$$
$$= .460 \pm .031$$
$$= (.429, .491)$$

Based on what was seen in this sample, we can be 95% confident that π, the true proportion favoring AIDS testing of all citizens, is between .429 and .491. That is, we used a *method* to construct this estimate that is successful in capturing the true value of π 95% of the time.

The calculations for a 95% confidence interval for the proportion who favor testing of doctors and dentists are

$$p = \frac{882}{1014} = .870$$

Since $np = 1014(.870) = 882 \geq 10$ and $n(1 - p) = 1014(.130) = 132 \geq 10$, the large-sample interval can be used. Then

$$p \pm 1.96\sqrt{\frac{p(1 - p)}{n}} = .870 \pm 1.96\sqrt{\frac{(.870)(.130)}{1014}}$$
$$= .870 \pm .021$$
$$= (.849, .891)$$

Based on this interval, we conclude that between 84.9% and 89.1% of the population favors AIDS testing of doctors and dentists. A comparison of these intervals indicates that the sentiment for testing doctors and dentists is much stronger than that for testing the general public.

The second 95% confidence interval for π calculated in Example 9.4 is (.849, .891). It is tempting to say that there is a probability of .95 that π is between .849 and .891. **Do not yield to this temptation!** The 95% refers to the percentage of *all* possible samples resulting in an interval that includes π. In other words, if we take sample after sample from the population and use each one separately to compute a 95% confidence interval, in the long run roughly 95% of these intervals will capture π. Figure 9.4 on page 324 illustrates this for intervals generated from

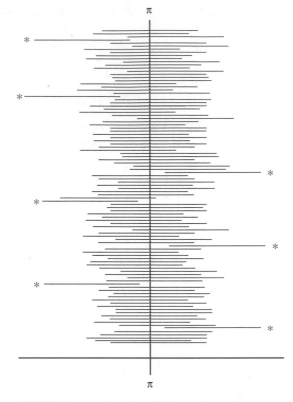

FIGURE 9.4 One hundred 95% confidence intervals for π computed from 100 different random samples (Asterisks identify intervals that do not include π.)

100 different random samples; 93 of the intervals include π, whereas 7 do not. Any specific interval, and our interval (.849, .891) in particular, either includes π or it does not (remember, the value of π is fixed but not known to us). We cannot make a chance (probability) statement concerning this particular interval. *The confidence level 95% refers to the **method** used to construct the interval rather than to any particular interval, such as the one we obtained.*

The formula given for a 95% confidence interval can easily be adapted for other confidence levels. The choice of a 95% confidence level led to the use of the z value 1.96 (chosen to achieve a central area of .95 under the standard normal curve) in the formula. Any other confidence level can be obtained by using an appropriate z critical value in place of 1.96. For example, suppose we wanted to achieve a confidence level of 99%. To obtain a central area of .99, the approximate z critical value would have a cumulative area (area to the left) of .995, as illustrated in Figure 9.5. From Appendix Table II, we find that the corresponding z critical value is 2.58. A 99% confidence interval for π is then obtained by using 2.58 in place of 1.96 in the formula for the 95% confidence interval.

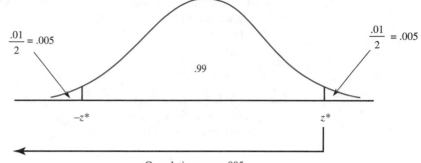

Cumulative area = .995

FIGURE 9.5 Finding the *z* critical value for a 99% confidence level

---

The Large-Sample Confidence Interval for π

The general formula for a confidence interval for a population proportion π when

1. p is the sample proportion from a **random sample,** and
2. the sample size **n is large** ($np \geq 10$ and $n(1 - p) \geq 10$)

is

$$p \pm (z \text{ critical value})\sqrt{\frac{p(1 - p)}{n}}$$

The desired confidence level determines which z critical value is used. The three most commonly used confidence levels, 90%, 95%, and 99%, use z critical values 1.645, 1.96, and 2.58, respectively.

Note: This interval is not appropriate for small samples. It is possible to construct a confidence interval in the small-sample case (based on the binomial distribution), but this is beyond the scope of this text.

Why settle for 95% confidence when 99% confidence is possible? Because the higher confidence level comes with a price tag. The resulting interval is wider than the 95% interval. The width of the 95% interval is $2(1.96\sqrt{p(1 - p)/n})$, whereas the 99% interval has width $2(2.58\sqrt{p(1 - p)/n})$. The higher *reliability* of the 99% interval (where "reliability" is specified by the confidence level) entails a loss in precision (as indicated by the wider interval). In the opinion of many investigators, a 95% interval gives a reasonable compromise between reliability and precision.

EXAMPLE 9.5   An Associated Press article on potential violent behavior reported the results of a survey of 750 workers who were employed full time (*San Luis Obispo Tribune,* Sept. 7, 1999). Of those surveyed, 125 indicated that they were so angered by a coworker during the past year that he or she felt like hitting the person (but didn't). Assuming that it is reasonable to regard this sample of 750 as a random sample from the population of full-time workers, we can use this information to construct an estimate π, the true proportion of full-time workers so angered in the last year that they wanted to hit a colleague.

For this sample

$$p = \frac{125}{750} = .167$$

Since $np = 125$ and $n(1 - p) = 625$ are both greater than or equal to 10, the sample size is large enough to use the formula for a large-sample confidence interval. A 90% confidence interval for π is then

$$p \pm (z \text{ critical value})\sqrt{\frac{p(1 - p)}{n}} = .167 \pm 1.645\sqrt{\frac{(.167)(.833)}{750}}$$
$$= .167 \pm (1.645)(.014)$$
$$= .167 \pm .022$$
$$= (.145, .189)$$

Based on this sample data, we can be 90% confident that the true proportion of full-time workers who have been angry enough in the last year to consider hitting a coworker is between .145 and .189. We have used a *method* to construct this interval estimate that has a 10% error rate.

The General Form of a Confidence Interval

Many confidence intervals have the same general form as the large-sample intervals for π just considered. We started with a statistic p, from which a point estimate for π was obtained. The standard deviation of this statistic is $\sqrt{\pi(1 - \pi)/n}$. This resulted in a confidence interval of the form

$$\left(\begin{array}{c} \text{point estimate using} \\ \text{a specified statistic} \end{array}\right) \pm \left(\begin{array}{c} \text{critical} \\ \text{value} \end{array}\right) \cdot \left(\begin{array}{c} \text{standard deviation} \\ \text{of the statistic} \end{array}\right)$$

Since π was unknown, we estimated the standard deviation of the statistic by $\sqrt{p(1 - p)/n}$, which yielded the interval

$$\left(\begin{array}{c} \text{point estimate using} \\ \text{a specified statistic} \end{array}\right) \pm \left(\begin{array}{c} \text{critical} \\ \text{value} \end{array}\right) \cdot \left(\begin{array}{c} \text{estimated standard} \\ \text{deviation of the} \\ \text{statistic} \end{array}\right)$$

For a population characteristic other than π, a statistic for estimating the characteristic will be selected. Then (drawing on statistical theory) a formula for the standard deviation of the statistic will be given. In practice, it will almost always be necessary to estimate this standard deviation (using something analogous to $\sqrt{p(1 - p)/n}$ rather than $\sqrt{\pi(1 - \pi)/n}$), so the second interval will be the prototype confidence interval. The estimated standard deviation of the statistic is usually referred to as the *standard error* in the statistical literature.

> **Definition**
>
> The **standard error** of a statistic is the estimated standard deviation of the statistic.

Choosing the Sample Size

The 95% confidence interval for π is based on the fact that, for approximately 95% of all random samples, p will be within $1.96\sqrt{\pi(1-\pi)/n}$ of π. The quantity $1.96\sqrt{\pi(1-\pi)/n}$ is sometimes called the *bound on the error of estimation* associated with a 95% confidence level — we have 95% confidence that the point estimate p will be no farther than this from π.

> **Definition**
>
> The **bound on error of estimation, B,** associated with a 95% confidence interval is $(1.96) \cdot$ (standard error of the statistic).

Before collecting any data, an investigator may wish to determine a sample size for which a particular value of the bound is achieved. For example, with π representing the true proportion of students at a university who purchase textbooks over the Internet, the objective of an investigation may be to estimate π to within .05 with 95% confidence. The value of n necessary to achieve this is obtained by equating .05 to $1.96\sqrt{\pi(1-\pi)/n}$ and solving for n.

In general, suppose that we wish to estimate π to within an amount B (the specified bound on error of estimation) with 95% confidence. Finding the necessary sample size requires solving the equation

$$B = 1.96\sqrt{\frac{\pi(1-\pi)}{n}}$$

Solving this equation for n results in

$$n = \pi(1-\pi)\left(\frac{1.96}{B}\right)^2$$

Unfortunately, the use of this formula requires the value of π, which is unknown. One possible way to proceed is to carry out a preliminary study and use the resulting data to get a rough estimate of π. In other cases, prior knowledge may suggest a reasonable estimate of π. If there is no reasonable basis for estimating π and a preliminary study is not feasible, a conservative solution follows from the observation that $\pi(1 - \pi)$ is never larger than .25 (its value when $\pi = .5$). Replacing $\pi(1 - \pi)$ with .25, the maximum value, yields

$$n = .25\left(\frac{1.96}{B}\right)^2$$

Using this formula to obtain n gives us a sample size for which we can be 95% confident that p will be within B of π, no matter what the value of π.

The sample size required to estimate a population proportion π to within an amount B with 95% confidence is

$$n = \pi(1 - \pi)\left(\frac{1.96}{B}\right)^2$$

The value of π may be estimated using prior information. In the absence of any such information, using $\pi = .5$ in this formula gives a conservatively large value for the required sample size (this value of π gives a larger n than would any other value).

EXAMPLE 9.6

The 1991 publication of the book *Final Exit,* which includes chapters on doctor-assisted suicide, caused a great deal of controversy in the medical community. The Society for the Right to Die and the American Medical Association quoted very different figures regarding the proportion of primary-care physicians who have participated in some form of doctor-assisted suicide for terminally ill patients (*USA Today,* July 1991). Suppose that a survey of physicians is to be designed to estimate this proportion to within .05 with 95% confidence. How many primary-care physicians should be included in a random sample?

Using a conservative value of $\pi = .5$ in the formula for required sample size gives

$$n = \pi(1 - \pi)\left(\frac{1.96}{B}\right)^2 = .25\left(\frac{1.96}{.05}\right)^2 = 384.16$$

Thus, a sample of at least 385 doctors should be used.

Exercises 9.10 – 9.28

9.10 For each of the following, indicate which would result in a wider large-sample confidence interval for π.
  a. 90% confidence level or 95% confidence level
  b. $n = 100$ or $n = 400$

9.11 The formula used to compute a confidence interval for π is

$$p \pm (z \text{ critical value}) \cdot \sqrt{\frac{p(1 - p)}{n}}$$

What is the appropriate z critical value for each of the following confidence levels?
  a. 95%   **b.** 90%   **c.** 99%   **d.** 80%   **e.** 85%

9.12 The use of the interval

$$p \pm (z \text{ critical value}) \cdot \sqrt{\frac{p(1 - p)}{n}}$$

requires a large sample. For each of the following combinations of n and p, indicate whether the given interval would be appropriate.

a. $n = 50$ and $p = .30$ b. $n = 50$ and $p = .05$
c. $n = 15$ and $p = .45$ d. $n = 100$ and $p = .01$
e. $n = 100$ and $p = .70$ f. $n = 40$ and $p = .25$
g. $n = 60$ and $p = .25$ h. $n = 80$ and $p = .10$

9.13 Discuss how each of the following factors affects the width of the confidence interval for π.
   a. The confidence level
   b. The sample size
   c. The value of p

9.14 Retailers report that the use of cents-off coupons is increasing. The Scripps Howard News Service (July 9, 1991) reported the proportion of all households that use coupons as .77. Suppose that this estimate was based on a random sample of 800 households (that is, $n = 800$ and $p = .77$). Construct a 95% confidence interval for π, the true proportion of all households that use coupons.

9.15 The article "Ban on Smoking Shown to Improve Lung Health" (*Los Angeles Times,* Dec. 9, 1998) reported the results of a study of San Francisco bartenders. Of 39 bartenders who reported respiratory problems before a ban on smoking in bars, 21 were symptom-free 2 months after the ban began. Suppose that it is reasonable to regard this group of 39 bartenders as a random sample of bartenders with reported respiratory problems. Use this information to construct a 95% confidence interval for the proportion of bartenders with respiratory problems who were symptom-free 2 months after the smoking ban.

9.16 The *Princeton Metro Times* (Sept. 25, 1999) reported that 48% of a random sample of 369 students at The College of New Jersey indicated that they were "binge drinkers." Binge drinking was defined to be consuming five to six drinks in one sitting for men and four to five drinks for women. Construct and interpret a 90% confidence interval for π, the proportion of students at The College of New Jersey who are binge drinkers.

9.17 An article in the *Chicago Tribune* (Aug. 29, 1999) reported that in a poll of residents of the Chicago suburbs, 43% felt that their financial situation had improved during the last year. The following statement is from the article:

> The findings of this Tribune poll are based on interviews with 930 randomly selected suburban residents. The sample included suburban Cook County plus DuPage, Kane, Lake, McHenry and Will Counties. In a sample of this size, one can say with 95% certainty that results will differ by no more than 3 percent from results obtained if all residents had been included in the poll.

Comment on this statement. Give a statistical argument to justify the claim that the estimate of 43% is within 3% of the true proportion of residents who feel that their financial situation has improved.

9.18 According to a 1998 survey of 4000 randomly selected teachers, many full-time public school teachers feel inadequately prepared for various classroom situations. Of those surveyed, 21% indicated that they felt unprepared to address the needs of students with disabilities, and 20% stated that they felt unprepared to integrate technology into the grade or subject they taught.
   a. Construct a 99% confidence interval for the true proportion of teachers who feel unprepared to integrate technology into the classroom. Is your interval relatively narrow or wide? What aspect of this problem explains the interval width?
   b. Construct and interpret a 95% confidence interval for the proportion of teachers who feel unprepared to address the needs of students with disabilities.
   c. Since a higher percentage of the sample reported that they felt unprepared to address the needs of students with disabilities (21%) than reported that they felt unprepared to integrate technology (20%), is it reasonable to conclude that this proportion is also higher for the entire population of teachers? Use the results of parts **a** and **b** to justify your answer.

9.19 In an article titled "Fluoridation Brushed off by Utah" (Associated Press, Aug. 24, 1998), it was reported that a small but vocal minority in Utah has been successful in keeping fluoride out of Utah water supplies in spite of evidence that fluoridation reduces tooth decay and the fact that a clear majority of Utah residents favor fluoridation. To support this statement, the article included the result of a survey of Utah residents that found 65% to be in favor of fluoridation. Suppose that this result was based on a random sample of 150 Utah residents. Construct and interpret a 90% confidence interval for π, the true proportion of Utah residents who favor fluoridation. Is this interval consistent with the statement that fluoridation is favored by a clear majority of residents?

9.20 In a study of 1710 school children in Australia (*The Herald Sun,* Oct. 27, 1994), 1060 indicated that they normally watch TV before school in the morning. (Interestingly, only 35% of the parents said their children watched TV before school!). Construct a 95% confidence interval for the true proportion of Australian children who say they watch TV before school. What assumption about the sample must be true for the method used to construct the interval to be valid?

9.21 The *Chronicle of Higher Education* (Jan. 13, 1993) reported that 72.1% of those responding to a national survey of college freshmen were attending the college of their first choice. Suppose that $n = 500$ students responded to the survey (the actual sample size was much larger).

a. Using the sample size $n = 500$, calculate a 99% confidence interval for the proportion of college students who are attending their first choice of college.

b. Compute and interpret a 95% confidence interval for the proportion of students who are *not* attending their first choice of college.

c. The actual sample size for this survey was much larger than 500. Would a confidence interval based on the actual sample size have been narrower or wider than the one computed in part **a**?

9.22 The Gallup Organization conducted a telephone survey on attitudes towards AIDS (*Gallup Monthly,* 1991). A total of 1014 individuals were contacted. Each was asked whether they agreed with the following statement: "Landlords should have the right to evict a tenant from an apartment because that person has AIDS." One hundred one individuals in the sample agreed with this statement. Use this data to construct a 90% confidence interval for the proportion who are in agreement with this statement. Give an interpretation of your interval.

9.23 Many Americans think it does not matter which political party controls Congress. In an Associated Press article (*San Luis Obispo Telegram-Tribune,* Sept. 6, 1995), it was reported that 442 individuals in a random sample of 1005 U.S. adults said it wouldn't make a difference which party is in power.

a. Construct a 90% confidence interval for the proportion of U.S. adults who believe that it wouldn't make a difference which party is in power.

b. Based on your interval in part **a**, is it plausible that a majority of U.S. adults feel that it makes no difference which party is in control? Explain your reasoning.

9.24 Recent high-profile legal cases have many people reevaluating the jury system. Many believe that juries in criminal trials should be able to convict on less than a unanimous vote. To assess support for this idea, each individual in a random sample of Californians was asked whether they favored allowing conviction by a 10–2 verdict in criminal cases not involving the death penalty. The Associated Press (*San Luis Obispo Telegram-Tribune,* Sept. 13, 1995) reported that 71% supported the 10–2 verdict. Suppose that the sample size for this survey was $n = 900$. Compute and interpret a 99% confidence interval for the proportion of Californians who favor the 10–2 verdict.

9.25 The article "What Kinds of People Do Not Use Seat Belts?" (*Amer. J. of Public Health* (1977): 1043–1049) reported on a survey with the objective of studying characteristics of drivers and seat belt usage. Let π denote the proportion of all drivers of cars with seat belts who use them. Suppose that at the outset of the study, the investigators wished to estimate π to within an amount .02 with 95% confidence. What is the required sample size? Why is the recommended sample size so large?

9.26 The article "Television and Human Values: A Case for Cooperation" (*J. of Home Econ.* (Summer 1982): 18–23) reported that 48% of U.S. homes had more than one television set.

a. Suppose that the statistic reported in this article was based on a random sample of 200 homes. Construct a 95% confidence interval for π, the proportion of all U.S. homes that have more than one television set.

b. The same article reported that the average viewing time per household was about 6 hours per day. If you wanted to construct an interval estimate for the average television viewing time for all U.S. households, would you use the following interval? Explain your answer.

$$p \pm (z \text{ critical value}) \cdot \sqrt{\frac{p(1 - p)}{n}}$$

9.27 A consumer group is interested in estimating the proportion of packages of ground beef sold at a particular store that have an actual fat content exceeding the fat content stated on the label. How many packages of ground beef should be tested to estimate this proportion to within .05 with 95% confidence?

9.28 A manufacturer of small appliances purchases plastic handles for coffeepots from an outside vendor. If a handle is cracked, it is considered defective and must be discarded. A very large shipment of plastic handles is received. The proportion of defective handles, π, is of interest. How many handles from the shipment should be inspected to estimate π to within .1 with 95% confidence?

9.3   A Confidence Interval for a Population Mean

The purpose of an investigation is often to estimate the population mean, μ. In this section, we consider how to use information from a random sample to construct a confidence interval estimate of a population mean.

We begin by considering the case where (1) **σ, the population standard deviation, is known** (not realistic, but we will see shortly how to handle the more common situation where σ is unknown) and (2) **the sample size, n, is large** enough for the Central Limit Theorem to apply. In this case, the following three properties about the sampling distribution of $\bar{x}$ hold:

1. The sampling distribution of $\bar{x}$ is centered at μ, so $\bar{x}$ is an unbiased statistic for estimating μ.
2. The standard deviation of $\bar{x}$ is $\sigma_{\bar{x}} = \sigma / \sqrt{n}$.
3. As long as n is large (generally $n \geq 30$), the sampling distribution of $\bar{x}$ is approximately normal, even when the population distribution itself is not normal.

The same reasoning that was used to develop the large-sample confidence interval for a population proportion π can be used to obtain a confidence interval estimate for μ.

The One-Sample z Confidence Interval for μ

The general formula for a confidence interval for a population mean μ when

1. $\bar{x}$ is the sample mean from a **random sample,**
2. the **sample size n is large** (generally $n \geq 30$), and
3. **σ, the population standard deviation, is known**

is

$$\bar{x} \pm (z \text{ critical value})\left(\frac{\sigma}{\sqrt{n}}\right)$$

EXAMPLE 9.7   Public Citizens, a consumer group, ranks the 111 U.S. nuclear reactors according to employee exposure to radiation. Based on a sample of workers at Diablo Canyon Nuclear Power Plant, Public Citizens rated Diablo's Unit 2 reactor as the 28th worst in the country. They reported (*San Luis Obispo Telegram-Tribune,* April 11, 1990) a mean annual radiation exposure of .481 rems for a sample of Unit 2 workers. Suppose that this mean was based on a random sample of 100 workers.

Let μ denote the true mean radiation exposure for Unit 2 workers at Diablo Canyon. Although σ, the true population standard deviation, is not usually known, suppose for illustrative purposes that $\sigma = .35$. Then a 95% confidence interval for μ is

$$\bar{x} \pm (z \text{ critical value})\left(\frac{\sigma}{\sqrt{n}}\right) = .481 \pm (1.96)\left(\frac{.35}{\sqrt{100}}\right)$$
$$= .481 \pm .069$$
$$= (.412, .550)$$

Based on this sample, *plausible* values of μ, the true mean annual radiation exposure for Diablo's Unit 2 workers, are between .412 and .550 rems. A 95% confidence level is associated with the method used to produce this interval estimate.

───

The confidence interval just introduced is appropriate when σ is known and n is large, and it can be used irrespective of the shape of the population distribution. This is because it is based on the Central Limit Theorem, which says that when n is sufficiently large, the sampling distribution of $\bar{x}$ is approximately normal for any population distribution. When n is small, the Central Limit Theorem cannot be used to justify the normality of the sampling distribution of $\bar{x}$, therefore the interval we developed previously should not be used. One way to proceed in the small-sample case is to make a specific assumption about the shape of the population distribution and then to use a method of estimation that is valid only under this assumption.

The one instance where this is easy to do is when it is reasonable to think that the population distribution is normal in shape. Recall that in the case of a normal population distribution, the sampling distribution of $\bar{x}$ is normal even for small sample sizes. So, if n is small but the population distribution is normal, the same confidence interval formula just introduced can still be used.

If n is small (generally $n < 30$) but it is reasonable to believe that the distribution of values in the population is normal, a confidence interval for μ (when σ is known) is

$$\bar{x} \pm (z \text{ critical value})\left(\frac{\sigma}{\sqrt{n}}\right)$$

Sample data can be used in several ways to assess the plausibility of normality. The two most common ways are to look at a normal probability plot of the sample data (looking for a plot that is reasonably straight) and to construct a boxplot of the data (looking for approximate symmetry and no outliers).

A Confidence Interval for μ When σ Is Unknown

The confidence intervals just developed have one major drawback: To compute the interval endpoints, σ must be known. Unfortunately, this is rarely the case. We now turn our attention to the situation when σ is unknown. The development of the confidence interval in this instance depends on the assumption that the population distribution is normal. Although this assumption is not critical if the sample size is large, it is important when the sample size is small.

To understand the derivation of this confidence interval, it is instructive to begin by taking another look at the 95% confidence interval. When σ is known, we know that $\mu_{\bar{x}} = \mu$ and $\sigma_{\bar{x}} = \sigma/\sqrt{n}$; also, when the population distribution is normal, the $\bar{x}$ distribution is normal. These facts imply that the standardized variable

$$z = \frac{\bar{x} - \mu}{\dfrac{\sigma}{\sqrt{n}}}$$

has approximately a standard normal distribution. Since the interval from -1.96 to 1.96 captures an area of .95 under the z curve, approximately 95% of all samples result in an $\bar{x}$ value that satisfies

$$-1.96 < \frac{\bar{x} - \mu}{\dfrac{\sigma}{\sqrt{n}}} < 1.96$$

Manipulating these inequalities to isolate μ in the middle results in the equivalent inequalities

$$\bar{x} - 1.96\left(\frac{\sigma}{\sqrt{n}}\right) < \mu < \bar{x} + 1.96\left(\frac{\sigma}{\sqrt{n}}\right)$$

The term $\bar{x} - 1.96(\sigma/\sqrt{n})$ is the lower endpoint of the 95% large-sample confidence interval for μ, and $\bar{x} + 1.96(\sigma/\sqrt{n})$ is the upper endpoint.

However, if σ is unknown, we must use the sample data to estimate σ. If we use the sample standard deviation as our estimate, the result is a different standardized variable denoted by t:

$$t = \frac{\bar{x} - \mu}{\dfrac{s}{\sqrt{n}}}$$

The value of s may not be all that close to σ, especially when n is small. As a consequence, the use of s in place of σ introduces extra variability, so the distribution of t is more spread out than the standard normal (z) curve. (The value of z will vary from sample to sample, because different samples generally result in different $\bar{x}$ values. There is even more variability in t, because different samples may result in different values of both $\bar{x}$ and s.)

To develop an appropriate confidence interval, we must know about the probability distribution of the standardized variable t for a sample from a normal population. This requires that we first learn about probability distributions called *t distributions*.

t Distributions

Just as there are many different normal distributions, there are also many different *t* distributions. Although normal distributions are distinguished from one another by their mean μ and standard deviation σ, the t distributions are distinguished by a positive whole number called the number of *degrees of freedom* (df). There is a t distribution with 1 df, another with 2 df, and so on.

Important Properties of t Distributions

1. The t curve corresponding to any fixed number of degrees of freedom is bell shaped and centered at zero (just like the standard normal (z) curve).

2. Each t curve is more spread out than the z curve.

3. As the number of degrees of freedom increases, the spread of the corresponding t curve decreases.

4. As the number of degrees of freedom increases, the corresponding sequence of t curves approaches the z curve.

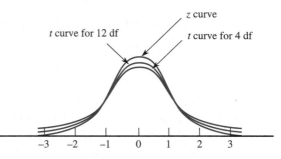

FIGURE 9.6 Comparison of the z curve and t curves for 12 df and 4 df

These properties are illustrated in Figure 9.6, which shows two t curves along with the z curve.

Appendix Table III gives selected critical values for various t distributions. The central areas for which values are tabulated are .80, .90, .95, .98, .99, .998, and .999. To find a particular critical value, go down the left margin of the table to the row labeled with the desired number of degrees of freedom. Then move over in that row to the column headed by the desired central area. For example, the value in the 12-df row under the column corresponding to central area .95 is 2.18, so 95% of the area under the t curve with 12 df lies between -2.18 and 2.18. Moving over two columns, we find the critical value for central area .99 (still with 12 df) to be 3.06 (see Figure 9.7). Moving down the .99 column to the 20-df row, we see the critical value is 2.85, so the area between -2.85 and 2.85 under the t curve with 20 df is .99. Notice that the critical values increase as you move to the right in each row. This is necessary to capture a larger central area and a smaller tail area. In each column, the critical values decrease as you move downward, reflecting decreasing spread for t distributions with larger degrees of freedom.

The larger the number of degrees of freedom, the more closely the t curve re-

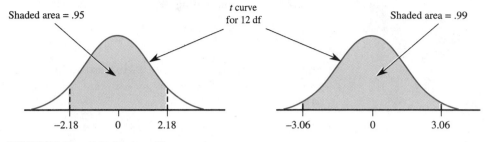

FIGURE 9.7 *t* critical values illustrated

sembles the *z* curve. To emphasize this, we have included the *z* critical values as the last row of the *t* table. Furthermore, once the number of degrees of freedom exceeds 30, the critical values change very little as the number of degrees of freedom increases. For this reason, Table III jumps from 30 df to 40 df, then to 60 df, then to 120 df, and finally to the row of *z* critical values. If we need a critical value for a number of degrees of freedom between those tabulated, we just use the critical value for the closest df. For df > 120, we use the *z* critical values. Many graphing calculators calculate *t* critical values for any df; so, if you are using such a calculator, it will not be necessary to approximate the *t* critical values as described.

The One-Sample *t* Confidence Interval

The fact that the sampling distribution of $(\bar{x} - \mu)/(\sigma/\sqrt{n})$ is approximately the *z* (standard normal) distribution when *n* is large is what led to the *z* interval when σ is known. In the same way, the following proposition provides the key to obtaining a confidence interval when the population distribution is normal and σ is unknown.

Let $x_1, x_2, \ldots, x_n$ constitute a random sample from a normal population distribution. Then the probability distribution of the standardized variable

$$t = \frac{\bar{x} - \mu}{\dfrac{s}{\sqrt{n}}}$$

is the *t* distribution with $n - 1$ df.

To see how this result leads to the desired confidence interval, consider the case $n = 25$, so we use the *t* distribution with df = 24. From Table III, the interval between -2.06 and 2.06 captures a central area of .95 under the *t* curve with 24 df. Then 95% of all samples (with $n = 25$) from a normal population result in values of $\bar{x}$ and s for which

$$-2.06 < \frac{\bar{x} - \mu}{\dfrac{s}{\sqrt{n}}} < 2.06$$

Algebraically manipulating these inequalities to isolate μ yields

$$\bar{x} - 2.06\left(\frac{s}{\sqrt{25}}\right) < \mu < \bar{x} + 2.06\left(\frac{s}{\sqrt{25}}\right)$$

The 95% confidence interval for μ in this situation extends from the lower endpoint $\bar{x} - 2.06(s/\sqrt{25})$ to the upper endpoint $\bar{x} + 2.06(s/\sqrt{25})$. This interval can be written

$$\bar{x} \pm 2.06\left(\frac{s}{\sqrt{25}}\right)$$

The major difference between this interval and the interval when σ is known is the use of the t critical value 2.06 rather than the z critical value 1.96. The extra uncertainty that results from estimating σ causes the t interval to be wider than the z interval.

If the sample size is something other than 25 or if the desired confidence level is something other than 95%, a different t critical value (obtained from Table III) is used in place of 2.06.

The One-Sample t Confidence Interval for μ

The general formula for a confidence interval for a population mean μ based on a sample of size n when

1. $\bar{x}$ is the sample mean from a **random sample,**
2. the **population distribution is normal,** OR the **sample size n is large** (generally $n \geq 30$), and
3. σ, **the population standard deviation, is unknown**

is

$$\bar{x} \pm (t \text{ critical value})\left(\frac{s}{\sqrt{n}}\right)$$

where the t critical value is based on $n - 1$ df. Appendix Table III gives critical values appropriate for each of the confidence levels 90%, 95%, and 99%, as well as several other less frequently used confidence levels.

If n is large (generally $n \geq 30$), the normality of the population distribution is not critical. *However, this confidence interval is appropriate for small n only when the population distribution is (at least approximately) normal.* If this is not the case, as might be suggested by a normal probability plot or boxplot, another method should be used.

EXAMPLE 9.8   "Executives whose wives stay at home earn more" was the headline for an article that appeared in the *San Luis Obispo Telegram-Tribune* (Oct. 14, 1994). To support this claim, the article presented data from a random sample of 231 married men who received MBA degrees in the late 1970s. For this sample, the mean salary in 1993 for married men in two-income families was $95,140, whereas the mean for the married men who were the sole source of family income was $124,510. The article did not give the sample standard deviations, but suppose for purposes of this example that they were as given in the accompanying table.

	n	Mean Salary	Standard Deviation
Two-income family	140	95,140	15,000
Sole source of income	91	124,510	18,000

If we had access to the raw data (the 140 + 91 = 231 salary observations), we might begin by looking at boxplots. Data consistent with the given summary quantities was used to generate the boxplots of Figure 9.8. The boxplots show that salaries for the one-income group tend to be higher than those for the two-income group. There is some overlap, and the smallest salary in each group is similar. The outliers in the boxplots indicate that the income distributions may not be normal, but because the sample sizes are large, we can still use the t confidence interval.

FIGURE 9.8 Boxplots for Example 9.8

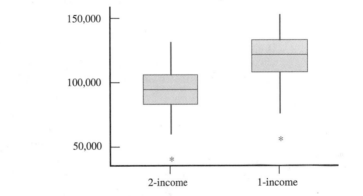

As a next step, we can use the confidence interval of this section to estimate the true mean salary of each group. Let's first focus on the sample of men from two-income families. For this group,

sample size = n = 140

sample mean salary = $\bar{x}$ = 95,140

sample standard deviation = s = 15,000

The newspaper article generalized from this sample to the population of "executives whose wives work." Is this appropriate? Remember that everyone in the sample received an MBA degree in the late 1970s. A more cautious approach would be to consider this group as a sample from the population of married men who received MBAs in the late 1970s and whose wives also work. Then, with μ denoting the mean salary for this population, we can estimate μ using a 90% confidence interval.

From Appendix Table III, we will use t critical value = 1.645 (from the z critical value row since df = 139 > 120, the largest tabled df). The 90% confidence interval for μ is

$$\bar{x} \pm (t \text{ critical value})\left(\frac{s}{\sqrt{n}}\right) = 95{,}140 \pm (1.645)\left(\frac{15{,}000}{\sqrt{140}}\right)$$
$$= 95{,}140 \pm 2085.42$$
$$= (\$93{,}054.58, \$97{,}225.42)$$

Based on this sample, we are confident that μ is between \$93,054.58 and \$97,225.42. This interval is fairly narrow given the context of this problem; the interval spans a range of only \$4200. This indicates that our information about the value of μ is relatively precise.

A 90% confidence interval estimate for the mean of the population of married men who received MBAs in the late 1970s and who are the sole source of family income is (\$121,406.03, \$127,613.97). This interval is wider than the first interval for two reasons: The sample size is smaller (91 rather than 140), and the sample standard deviation is larger (18,000 rather than 15,000).

Based on these two interval estimates, it does appear that the mean salary for the two-income family group is lower than the mean for the one-income group. However, this analysis does not prove the existence of a cause-and-effect relationship between wife's work status and increased salary. The cited article falls into this trap by speculating that "the upper ranks of corporate America favor men whose wives stay at home" and that stay-at-home wives "actually further their husbands careers." Can you see the flaw in this argument?

EXAMPLE 9.9

Misconceptions about everyday scientific phenomena, such as the seasons, gravity, and light, are common in the general population. To assess the degree to which university students about to receive a middle school teaching credential shared these misconceptions, a science quiz consisting of 10 multiple-choice questions was given to a random sample of 52 such students ("Assessing Selected Physical Science and Earth Science Misconceptions of Middle School Through University Preservice Teachers," *J. College Science Teaching* (1994): 38–42). Let x denote the number of correct responses (out of 10), and let μ denote the mean value of x in the population of students about to receive a middle school teaching credential. For this sample of $n = 52$ students,

sample mean number of correct responses = $\bar{x} = 5.14$

sample standard deviation = $s = 1.30$

(For the purpose of this example, we approximated the standard deviation, but it is consistent with information given in the article.) A histogram for sample data consistent with the given summary quantities is shown in Figure 9.9. Even though the histogram suggests that the corresponding population distribution may be positively skewed, we can use the t confidence interval formula, because the sample size is large.

FIGURE 9.9 Histogram for Example 9.9

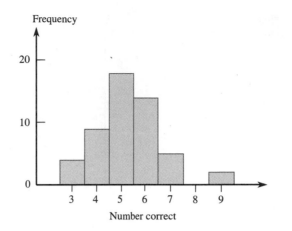

Since df = 51, we will use the t critical value for df = 60 (the closest df value in Appendix Table III). A 95% confidence interval for μ is then

$$\bar{x} \pm (t\text{ critical value})\left(\frac{s}{\sqrt{n}}\right) = 5.14 \pm (2.00)\left(\frac{1.30}{\sqrt{52}}\right)$$
$$= 5.14 \pm .36$$
$$= (4.78, 5.50)$$

Based on this sample, we believe that the mean number of correct responses for preservice middle school teachers is somewhere between 4.78 and 5.50.

EXAMPLE 9.10

A study of the ability of individuals to walk in a straight line ("Can We Really Walk Straight?" *Amer. J. of Physical Anthropology* (1992): 19–27) reported the accompanying data on *cadence* (strides per second) for a sample of n = 20 randomly selected healthy men.

| .95 | .85 | .92 | .95 | .93 | .86 | 1.00 | .92 | .85 | .81 |
| .78 | .93 | .93 | 1.05 | .93 | 1.06 | 1.06 | .96 | .81 | .96 |

Figure 9.10 (page 340) is a normal probability plot of this data. The plot is reasonably straight, so it seems plausible that the population distribution is approximately normal. Calculation of a confidence interval for the population mean cadence requires $\bar{x}$ and s:

$$\bar{x} = .926 \qquad s^2 = .006552 \qquad s = \sqrt{.006552} = .0809$$

The t critical value for a 99% confidence interval based on 19 df is 2.86. The interval is

$$\bar{x} \pm (t\text{ critical value})\left(\frac{s}{\sqrt{n}}\right) = .926 \pm (2.86)\left(\frac{.0809}{\sqrt{20}}\right)$$
$$= .926 \pm .052$$
$$= (.874, .978)$$

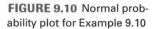

FIGURE 9.10 Normal probability plot for Example 9.10

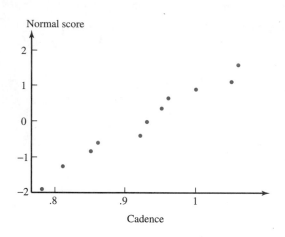

With 99% confidence, we estimate the population mean cadence to be between .874 and .978 strides per second. Remember that the 99% confidence level implies that if the same formula is used to calculate intervals for sample after sample randomly selected from the population, in the long run 99% of these intervals will capture μ between the lower and upper confidence limits.

Any of the commercially available statistical computing packages will produce a one-sample t confidence interval upon request. The following is an example of output from MINITAB. The slight discrepancy between the previous interval and MINITAB's interval occurs because MINITAB uses more decimal accuracy in $\bar{x}$, s, and t critical values.

	N	MEAN	STDEV	SE MEAN	99.0 PERCENT C.I.
CADENCE	20	0.9255	0.0809	0.0181	(0.8737, 0.9773)

EXAMPLE 9.11

How much time do school-age children spend helping with housework? The article "The Three Corners of Domestic Labor: Mothers', Fathers', and Children's Weekday and Weekend Housework" (*J. Marriage and the Family* (1994): 657–668) gave information on the number of minutes per weekday spent on housework. The mean and standard deviation in the accompanying table are for a random sample of girls in two-parent families where both parents work full-time.

Sample Size	Mean Time Spent per Weekday (minutes)	Standard Deviation
26	14.0	8.6

The authors of the article analyzed this data using methods designed for population distributions that are approximately normal. This assumption appears a bit questionable based on the reported mean and standard deviation (it is impossible to spend less than 0 minutes per day on housework, so the smallest possible value, 0, is only 1.63 standard deviations below the mean). However, since the authors reported that there were no outliers in the data and since n is relatively close to 30, we will use the t confidence interval formula of this section to compute a 95% confidence interval.

Since $n = 26$, df $= 25$, and the appropriate t critical value is 2.06. The confidence interval is then

$$\bar{x} \pm (t \text{ critical value})\left(\frac{s}{\sqrt{n}}\right) = 14.0 \pm (2.06)\left(\frac{8.6}{\sqrt{26}}\right)$$
$$= 14.0 \pm 3.5$$
$$= (10.5, 17.5)$$

Based on the sample data, we believe that the true mean time per weekday spent on housework is between 10.5 minutes and 17.5 minutes for girls in two-parent families where both parents work. We used a method that has a 5% error rate to construct this interval. We should be somewhat cautious in interpreting this confidence interval because of the concern expressed about the normality of the population distribution.

Choosing the Sample Size

When estimating μ using a large sample or a small sample from a normal population, the bound on error of estimation, B, associated with a 95% confidence interval is

$$B = 1.96\left(\frac{\sigma}{\sqrt{n}}\right)$$

Before collecting any data, an investigator may wish to determine a sample size for which a particular value of the bound is achieved. For example, with μ representing the average fuel efficiency (mpg) for all cars of a certain type, the objective of an investigation may be to estimate μ to within 1 mpg with 95% confidence. The value of n necessary to achieve this is obtained by equating 1 to $1.96(\sigma/\sqrt{n})$ and solving for n.

In general, suppose that we wish to estimate μ to within an amount B (the specified bound on error of estimation) with 95% confidence. Finding the necessary sample size requires solving the equation $B = 1.96(\sigma/\sqrt{n})$ for n. The result is

$$n = \left[\frac{1.96\sigma}{B}\right]^2$$

Notice that a large value of σ forces n to be large, as does a small value of B. Use of the sample-size formula requires that σ be known, but this is rarely the case. One possibility is to carry out a preliminary study and use the resulting sample standard deviation (or a somewhat larger value, to be conservative) to determine n for the main part of the study. Another possibility is simply to make an educated guess about the value of σ and use it in calculating n. For a population distribution that is not too skewed, dividing the range (the difference between the largest and smallest values) by 4 often gives a rough idea of the value of the standard deviation.

The sample size required to estimate a population mean μ to within an amount B with 95% confidence is

$$n = \left[\frac{1.96\sigma}{B}\right]^2$$

If σ is unknown, it may be estimated based on previous information or, for a population that is not too skewed, by using (range)/4.

If the desired confidence level is something other than 95%, 1.96 is replaced by the appropriate z critical value (e.g., 2.58 for 99% confidence).

EXAMPLE 9.12   The financial aid office wishes to estimate the mean cost of textbooks per quarter for students at a particular university. For the estimate to be useful, it should be within $20 of the true population mean. How large a sample should be used to be 95% confident of achieving this level of accuracy?

To determine the required sample size, we must have a value for σ. The financial aid office is pretty sure that the amount spent on books varies widely, with most values between $50 and $450. A reasonable estimate of σ is then

$$\frac{\text{range}}{4} = \frac{450 - 50}{4} = \frac{400}{4} = 100$$

The required sample size is

$$n = \left[\frac{196\sigma}{B}\right]^2 = \left[\frac{(1.96)(100)}{20}\right]^2 = [9.8]^2 = 96.04$$

Rounding up, a sample size of 97 or larger is recommended.

Exercises 9.29 – 9.49

9.29   Given a variable that has a t distribution with the specified degrees of freedom, what percentage of the time will its value fall in the indicated region?
   a. 10 df, between −1.81 and 1.81
   b. 10 df, between −2.23 and 2.23
   c. 24 df, between −2.06 and 2.06
   d. 24 df, between −2.80 and 2.80
   e. 24 df, outside the interval from −2.80 to 2.80
   f. 24 df, to the right of 2.80
   g. 10 df, to the left of −1.81

9.30   The formula used to compute a confidence interval for the mean of a normal population when n is small is

$$\bar{x} \pm (t \text{ critical value}) \cdot \frac{s}{\sqrt{n}}$$

What is the appropriate t critical value for each of the following confidence levels and sample sizes?
   a. 95% confidence, $n = 17$
   b. 90% confidence, $n = 12$
   c. 99% confidence, $n = 24$
   d. 90% confidence, $n = 25$
   e. 90% confidence, $n = 13$
   f. 95% confidence, $n = 10$

9.31   Each of the following is a confidence interval for μ = true average resonance frequency (in Hz) for all tennis rackets of a certain type: (114.4, 115.6) and (114.1, 115.9).
   a. What is the value of the sample mean resonance frequency?

b. The confidence level for one of these intervals is 90% and for the other it is 99%. Which is which, and why?

9.32 Samples of two different types of automobiles were selected, and the actual speed for each car was determined when the speedometer registered 50 mph. The resulting 95% confidence intervals for true average actual speed were (51.3, 52.7) and (49.4, 50.6). Assuming that the two sample standard deviations were identical, which confidence interval is based on the larger sample size? Explain your reasoning.

9.33 Suppose that a random sample of 50 bottles of a particular brand of cough medicine is selected and the alcohol content of each bottle is determined. Let μ denote the average alcohol content for the population of all bottles of the brand under study. Suppose that the sample of 50 results in a 95% confidence interval for μ of (7.8, 9.4).

a. Would a 90% confidence interval have been narrower or wider than the given interval? Explain your answer.

b. Consider the following statement: There is a 95% chance that μ is between 7.8 and 9.4. Is this statement correct? Why or why not?

c. Consider the following statement: If the process of selecting a sample of size 50 and then computing the corresponding 95% confidence interval is repeated 100 times, 95 of the resulting intervals will include μ. Is this statement correct? Why or why not?

9.34 The McClatchy News Service (*San Luis Obispo Telegram-Tribune*, June 13, 1991) reported on a sample of prime-time television hours. The following table summarizes the information reported for four networks.

Network	Mean Number of Violent Acts per Hour
ABC	15.6
CBS	11.9
FOX	11.7
NBC	11.0

Suppose that each of these sample means was computed on the basis of viewing $n = 50$ randomly selected prime-time hours and that the population standard deviation for each of the four networks is known to be $\sigma = 5$.

a. Compute a 95% confidence interval for μ_{ABC}, the true mean number of violent acts per prime-time hour for ABC.

b. Compute 95% confidence intervals for the mean number of violent acts per prime-time hour for each of the other three networks.

c. The National Coalition on Television Violence claims that shows on ABC are more violent than on the other networks. Based on the confidence intervals from parts **a** and **b,** do you agree with this conclusion? Explain.

9.35 Seventy-seven students at the University of Virginia were asked to keep a diary of a conversation with their mothers, recording any lies they told during these conversations (*San Luis Obispo Telegram-Tribune*, August 16, 1995). It was reported that the mean number of lies per conversation was .5. Suppose that the standard deviation (which was not reported) was .4.

a. Suppose that this group of 77 is a random sample from the population of students at this university. Construct a 95% confidence interval for the mean number of lies per conversation for this population.

b. The interval in part **a** does not include 0. Does this imply that all students lie to their mothers? Explain.

9.36 The article "Selected Characteristics of High-Risk Students and their Enrollment Persistence" (*J. of College Student Development* (1994): 54–60) examined factors that affect whether students stay in college. The accompanying summary statistics are based on data from a sample of 44 students who did not return to college after the first quarter (the nonpersisters) and a sample of 257 students who did return (the persisters).

	Number of Hours Worked per Week During the First Quarter	
	Mean	**Standard Deviation**
Nonpersisters	25.62	14.41
Persisters	18.10	15.31

a. Consider the 44 nonpersisters as a random sample from the population of all nonpersisters at the university where the data was collected. Compute a 98% confidence interval for the mean number of hours worked per week for nonpersisters.

b. Consider the 257 persisters as a random sample from the population of all persisters at the university where the data was collected. Compute a 98% confidence interval for the mean number of hours worked per week for persisters.

c. The 98% confidence interval for persisters is narrower than the corresponding interval for nonpersisters even though the standard deviation for persisters is larger than that for nonpersisters. Explain why this happened.

d. Based on the interval in part **a,** do you think that the mean number of hours worked per week for nonpersisters is greater than 20? Explain.

9.37 The article "Financial Characteristics of Leveraged Buyouts" (*J. of Business Research* (1992): 241–252) reported summary data covering the period 1986–1988 for random samples of two different types of companies. Consider the accompanying data on net income per share of common stock. (*Note*: Standard error = $s/\sqrt{n}$)

Type of Firm	Sample Size	Sample Mean	Standard Error of Mean
Involved in leveraged buyout	45	.6214	.4000
Not involved	297	.9504	.2076

a. Calculate confidence intervals at the 95% confidence level for true average earnings per share both for leveraged buyout (LBO) firms and for non-LBO firms.
b. Why is the non-LBO interval narrower than the LBO interval?

9.38 Increases in worker injuries and disability claims have prompted renewed interest in workplace design and regulation. As one particular aspect of this, employees required to do regular lifting should not have to handle unsafe loads. The article "Anthropometric, Muscle Strength, and Spinal Mobility Characteristics as Predictors of the Rating of Acceptable Loads in Parcel Sorting" (*Ergonomics* (1992): 1033–1044) reported on a study involving a random sample of $n = 18$ male postal workers. The sample mean rating of acceptable load attained with a work-simulating test was found to be $\bar{x} = 9.7$ kg, and the sample standard deviation was $s = 4.3$ kg. Suppose that in the population of all male postal workers, the distribution of rating of acceptable load can be modeled approximately using a normal distribution with mean value μ. Construct and interpret a 95% confidence interval for μ.

9.39 A number of cities have implemented needle exchange programs in an attempt to slow the spread of AIDS among intravenous drug users. These programs are designed to remove infected needles from circulation. One such program in New Haven kept information on the length of time a needle remained in circulation. It was reported that the mean circulation time (in days) was 2.2 ("What Happened to HIV Transmission Among Drug Injectors in New Haven?" *Chance* (Spring 1993)). The sample size and standard deviation for circulation time were not given in the article, but suppose that they were $n = 25$ needles and $s = 1.2$ days. Compute a 90% confidence interval for μ, the mean circulation time for needles recovered by this exchange program.

9.40 The eating habits of 12 bats were examined in the article "Foraging Behavior of the Indian False Vampire Bat" (*Biotropica* (1991): 63–67). These bats consume insects and frogs. For these 12 bats, the mean time to consume a frog was $\bar{x} = 21.9$ min. Suppose the standard deviation was $s = 7.7$ min. Construct and interpret a 90% confidence interval for the mean suppertime of a vampire bat whose meal consists of a frog. What assumptions must be reasonable for the one-sample t interval to be appropriate?

9.41 Fat content (in percentage) for ten randomly selected hot dogs was given in the article "Sensory and Mechanical Assessment of the Quality of Frankfurters" (*J. of Texture Studies* (1990): 395–409). Use the given data to construct a 90% confidence interval for the true mean fat percentage of hot dogs.

25.2 21.3 22.8 17.0 29.8 21.0 25.5 16.0 20.9 19.5

9.42 A triathlon consisting of swimming, cycling, and running is one of the more strenuous amateur sporting events. The article "Cardiovascular and Thermal Response of Triathlon Performance" (*Medicine and Science in Sports and Exercise* (1988): 385–389) reported on a research study involving nine randomly selected male triathletes. Maximum heart rate (beats/min) was recorded while performing each of the three events.

	$\bar{x}$	s
Swimming	188	7.2
Biking	186	8.5
Running	194	7.8

a. Assuming that the heart-rate distribution for each event is approximately normal, construct 95% confidence intervals for the true mean heart rate of triathletes for each event.
b. Do the intervals in part **a** overlap? Based on the computed intervals, do you think there is evidence that the mean maximum heart rate is higher for running than for the other two events? Explain.

9.43 Five students visiting the student health center for a free dental examination during National Dental Hygiene Month were asked how many months had passed since their last visit to a dentist. Their responses were as follows:

6   17   11   22   29

Assuming that these five students can be considered to be a random sample of all students participating in the free checkup program, construct a 95% confidence interval for the mean number of months elapsed since the last visit to a dentist for the population of students participating in the program.

9.44 The article "First Year Academic Success: A Prediction Combining Cognitive and Psychosocial Variables for Caucasian and African American Students" (*J. College Student Devel.* (1999): 599) reported that the sample mean and standard deviation for high school grade point average for students enrolled at a large research university were 3.73 and .45, respectively. Suppose that the mean and standard deviaition were based on a random sample of 900 students at the university.

a. Construct a 95% confidence interval for the mean high school GPA for students at this university.

b. Suppose you wanted to make a statement about the range of GPAs for students at this university. Is it reasonable to say that 95% of the students at the university have GPAs in the interval you computed in part **a**? Explain.

9.45 The following data are the calories per $\frac{1}{2}$-cup serving for 17 popular chocolate ice cream brands reviewed by *Consumer Reports* (July 1999).

270   150   170   140   160   160   160   290
190   190   160   170   150   110   180   170

Is it reasonable to use the *t* confidence interval of this section to compute a confidence interval for μ, the true mean calories per $\frac{1}{2}$-cup serving of chocolate ice cream? Explain why or why not.

9.46 The Bureau of Alcohol, Tobacco, and Firearms (BATF) has been concerned about lead levels in California wines. In a previous testing of wine specimens, lead levels ranging from 50 to 700 parts per billion were recorded (*San Luis Obispo Telegram-Tribune,* June 11, 1991). How many wine specimens should be tested if

BATF wishes to estimate the true mean lead level for California wines to within 10 parts per billion with 95% confidence?

9.47 A manufacturer of college textbooks is interested in estimating the strength of the bindings produced by a particular binding machine. Strength can be measured by recording the force required to pull the pages from the binding. If this force is measured in pounds, how many books should be tested to estimate with 95% confidence to within .1 lb the average force required to break the binding? Assume that σ is known to be .8 lb.

9.48 The article "*National Geographic,* the Doomsday Machine," which appeared in the *Journal of Irreproducible Results* (yes, there really is a journal by that name — it's a spoof of technical journals!) predicted dire consequences resulting from a nationwide buildup of *National Geographic.* The author's predictions are based on the observation that the number of subscriptions for *National Geographic* is on the rise and that no one ever throws away a copy of *National Geographic.* A key to the analysis presented in the article is the weight of an issue of the magazine. Suppose that you were assigned the task of estimating the average weight of an issue of *National Geographic.* How many issues should you sample to estimate the average weight to within .1 oz with 95% confidence? Assume that σ is known to be 1 oz.

9.49 The formula described in this section for determining sample size corresponds to a confidence level of 95%. What would be the appropriate formula for determining sample size when the desired confidence level is 90%? 98%?

9.4   Interpreting the Results of Statistical Analyses

The purpose of most surveys and many research studies is to produce estimates of population characteristics. Unfortunately, there is no customary way of reporting the resulting estimates. Possibilities include

confidence interval

estimate $\pm$ bound on error

estimate $\pm$ standard error

and, if the population characteristic is a population mean,

mean $\pm$ sample standard deviation

If the interval reported is described as a confidence interval, it should be accompanied by a confidence level. These intervals can be interpreted just as we have interpreted the confidence intervals in this chapter, and the confidence level specifies the long-run error rate associated with the method used to construct the interval (for example, a 95% confidence level specifies a 5% long-run error rate).

A form particularly common in news articles is estimate ± bound on error, where bound on error is also sometimes called **margin of error.** The bound on error reported is usually two times the standard deviation of the estimate. This method of reporting is a little more informal than a confidence interval and, if the sample size is reasonably large, is roughly equivalent to reporting a 95% confidence interval. You can interpret these intervals like a confidence interval with approximate confidence level of 95%.

You must use care in interpreting intervals reported in the form

estimate ± standard error

Recall from Section 9.2 that the general form of a confidence interval is

estimate ± (critical value)(standard deviation of the estimate)

In journal articles, the estimated standard deviation of the estimate is usually referred to as the *standard error.* The critical value in the confidence interval formula was determined by the form of the sampling distribution of the estimate and by the confidence level. Note that the reported form, estimate ± standard error, is equivalent to a confidence interval with the critical value set equal to 1. For an estimate whose sampling distribution is (approximately) normal (such as the mean of a large sample or a large-sample proportion), a critical value of 1 corresponds to an approximate confidence level of 68%. Since a confidence level of 68% is rather low, you may want to use the given information and the confidence interval formula to convert to an interval with a higher confidence level.

When researchers are trying to estimate a population mean, they sometimes report

sample mean ± sample standard deviation

Be particularly careful here. To convert this information into a useful interval estimate of the population mean, you must first convert the sample standard deviation to the standard error of the sample mean (by dividing by $\sqrt{n}$) and then use the standard error and an appropriate critical value to construct a confidence interval.

For example, suppose that a random sample of size 100 is to be used to estimate the population mean. If the sample resulted in a sample mean of 500 and a sample standard deviation of 20, you might find the published results summarized in any of the following ways:

95% confidence interval for the population mean: (496.08, 503.92)

mean ± bound on error: 500 ± 4

mean ± standard error: 500 ± 2

mean ± standard deviation: 500 ± 20

What to Look for in Published Data

Here are some questions to ask when you encounter interval estimates in research reports.

■ Is the reported interval a confidence interval, mean ± bound on error, mean ± standard error, or mean ± standard deviation? If the reported interval is not a confidence interval, you may want to construct a confidence interval from the given information.

■ What confidence level is associated with the given interval? Is the choice of confidence level reasonable? What does the confidence level say about the long-run error rate of the method used to construct the interval?

■ Is the reported interval relatively narrow or relatively wide? Has the population characteristic been estimated precisely?

For example, the article "Increased Vital and Total Lung Capacity in Tibetan Compared to Han Residents of Lhasa" (*Amer. J. of Physical Anthro.* (1991): 341–351) compared various physical characteristics of people who live at high altitudes to those of people who live a sea level. The article includes the following statements:

> We studied 38 Tibetan and 43 Han residents. . . . The Tibetan compared with the Han subjects had a larger total lung capacity [6.80 ± 0.19 (mean ± SEM) vs. 6.24 ± 0.18 liters].

The reported intervals are of the form estimate ± standard error. We can use this information to construct a confidence interval for the mean total lung capacity for residents of each of the two locations. Since the sample sizes are both large, we can use the *t* confidence interval formula

mean ± (*t* critical value)(standard deviation of the mean)

The Tibetan sample has df = 38 − 1 = 37 and the Han sample has df = 43 − 1 = 42. For both of these df's, the closest df value in Appendix Table III is for df = 40, and the corresponding *t* critical value for a 95% confidence level is 2.02. The corresponding intervals are

Tibetan residents: 6.80 ± 2.02(0.19) = 6.80 ± .38 = (6.42, 7.18)

Han residents: 6.24 ± 2.02(0.18) = 6.24 ± .36 = (5.88, 6.60)

The chosen confidence level of 95% implies that the method used to construct each of the intervals has a 5% long-run error rate. Assuming it is reasonable to view these samples as random samples, we can interpret these intervals as follows:

■ Based on the information provided in the sample of Tibetan residents, we can be 95% confident that the mean total lung capacity of Tibetan residents is between 6.42 and 7.18 liters.

■ Based on the information provided in the sample of Han residents, we can be 95% confident that the mean total lung capacity of Han residents is between 5.88 and 6.60 liters.

These intervals are relatively wide, indicating that the value of the population mean has not been estimated precisely in either case. This is not surprising given the reported sample sizes. Note that the two intervals overlap. This may cause us to be skeptical of the statement that Tibetans have a higher total lung capacity than Han residents. Formal methods for directly comparing two groups, covered in Chapter 11, could be used to further investigate this issue.

Summary of Key Concepts and Formulas

Term or Formula	Comment
Point estimate	A single number, based on sample data, that represents a plausible value of a population characteristic.
Unbiased statistic	A statistic that has a sampling distribution with a mean equal to the value of the population characteristic to be estimated.
Confidence interval	An interval that is computed from sample data and provides a range of plausible values for a population characteristic.
Confidence level	A number that provides information on how much "confidence" we can have in the method used to construct a confidence interval estimate. The confidence level specifies the percentage of all possible samples that will produce an interval containing the true value of the population characteristic.
$p \pm (z \text{ critical value})\sqrt{\dfrac{p(1-p)}{n}}$	A formula used to construct a confidence interval for π when the sample size is large.
$n = \pi(1-\pi)\left[\dfrac{1.96}{B}\right]^2$	A formula used to compute the sample size necessary for estimating π to within an amount B with 95% confidence. (For other confidence levels, replace 1.96 with an appropriate z critical value.)
$\bar{x} \pm (z \text{ critical value})\dfrac{\sigma}{\sqrt{n}}$	A formula used to construct a confidence interval for μ when σ is known and either the sample size is large or the population distribution is normal.
$\bar{x} \pm (t \text{ critical value})\dfrac{s}{\sqrt{n}}$	A formula used to construct a confidence interval for μ when σ is unknown and either the sample size is large or the population distribution is normal.
$n = \left[\dfrac{1.96\sigma}{B}\right]^2$	A formula used to compute the sample size necessary for estimating μ to within an amount B with 95% confidence. (For other confidence levels, replace 1.96 with an appropriate z critical value.)

Supplementary Exercises 9.50 – 9.58

9.50 Scripps News Service (Sept. 14, 1991) reported that 4% of the members of the American Bar Association (ABA) are African American. Suppose that this figure is based on a random sample of 400 ABA members.

a. Is the sample size large enough to justify the use of the large-sample confidence interval for a population proportion?
b. Construct and interpret a 90% confidence interval

for π, the true proportion of all ABA members who are African American.

9.51 The Center for Urban Transportation Research released a report stating that the average commuting distance in the United States is 10.9 mi (*USA Today,* Aug. 13, 1991). Suppose that this average is actually the mean of a random sample of 300 commuters and that the sample standard deviation was 6.2 mi. Estimate the true mean commuting distance using a 99% confidence interval.

9.52 In 1991, California imposed a "snack tax" (a sales tax on snack food) in an attempt to help balance the state budget. A proposed alternative tax was a 12¢-per-pack increase in the cigarette tax. In a poll of 602 randomly selected California registered voters, 445 responded that they would have preferred the cigarette tax increase to the snack tax (*Reno Gazette-Journal,* Aug. 26, 1991). Estimate the true proportion of California registered voters who preferred the cigarette tax increase; use a 95% confidence interval.

9.53 Systolic blood pressure (mm Hg) was determined for each individual in a random sample of nine athletes who had used anabolic steroids ("The Blood Pressure Response to Exercise in Anabolic Steroid Users," *Medicine and Science in Sports and Exercise* (1992): 633–637), resulting in a sample mean and sample standard deviation of 207.8 and 10.9, respectively.

   a. Calculate and interpret a confidence interval for mean blood pressure in the population of all athletes who used anabolic steroids; use a confidence level of 95%.

   b. Does the validity of the interval calculated in part **a** require any assumptions about the population distribution? Explain.

9.54 The confidence intervals presented in this chapter give both lower and upper bounds on plausible values for the population characteristic being estimated. In some instances, only an upper bound or only a lower bound is appropriate. Using the same reasoning that gave the large-sample interval in Section 9.3, we can say that when n is large, 99% of all samples have

$$\mu < \bar{x} + 2.33\frac{s}{\sqrt{n}}$$

(because the area under the z curve to the left of 2.33 is .99). Thus, $\bar{x} + 2.33(s/\sqrt{n})$ is a 99% upper confidence bound for μ. Use the data of Example 9.8 to calculate the 99% upper confidence bound for the true average salary for married men in two-income families.

9.55 The Associated Press (Dec. 16, 1991) reported that in a random sample of 507 people, only 142 correctly described the Bill of Rights as the first ten amendments to the U.S. Constitution. Calculate a 95% confidence interval for the proportion of the entire population that could give a correct description.

9.56 When n is large, the statistic s is approximately unbiased for estimating σ and has approximately a normal distribution. The standard deviation of this statistic when the population distribution is normal is $\sigma_s \approx \sigma/\sqrt{2n}$, which can be estimated by $s/\sqrt{2n}$. A large-sample confidence interval for the population standard deviation σ is then

$$s \pm (z \text{ critical value})\frac{s}{\sqrt{2n}}$$

Use the data of Exercise 9.51 to obtain a 95% confidence interval for the true standard deviation of commuting distance.

9.57 The interval from -2.33 to 1.75 captures an area of .95 under the z curve. This implies that another large-sample 95% confidence interval for μ has lower limit $\bar{x} - 2.33(\sigma/\sqrt{n})$ and upper limit $\bar{x} + 1.75(\sigma/\sqrt{n})$. Would you recommend using this 95% interval over the 95% interval $\bar{x} \pm 1.96(\sigma/\sqrt{n})$ discussed in the text? Explain. (*Hint:* Look at the width of each interval.)

9.58 Suppose that an individual's waiting time for a morning bus is known to have a uniform distribution on the interval from 0 min to an unknown upper limit θ min. A 95% confidence interval for θ based on a random sample of n waiting times can be shown to have lower limit $\max(x)$ and upper limit $\max(x)/(.05)^{1/n}$. Assuming that $n = 5$ and that the resulting waiting times are 4.2, 3.5, 1.7, 1.2, and 2.4, obtain the confidence interval. (*Hint:* $(.05)^{1/5} = .5493$) Notice that the confidence interval here is not of the form (estimate) $\pm$ (critical value)(standard deviation).

References

Devore, Jay L. *Probability and Statistics for Engineering and the Sciences,* 5th ed. Pacific Grove, CA: Brooks/Cole, 2000. (This book gives a somewhat general introduction to confidence intervals.)

Freedman, David, Robert Pisani, and Roger Purves, *Statistics,* 3rd ed. New York: W. W. Norton, 1997. (This book contains a very informal discussion of confidence intervals.)

10

Hypothesis Testing Using a Single Sample

INTRODUCTION

In the previous chapter, we considered situations in which the primary goal was to estimate the unknown value of some population characteristic. Sample data may also be used to decide whether some claim or *hypothesis* about a population characteristic is plausible. For example, the lead story in the August 27, 1995, *San Francisco Examiner* focused on health care problems resulting from an increase in the number of Americans without health insurance. Serious difficulties for state and local agencies arise if the coverage rate for the entire population is less than 90%. The same day, the *Los Angeles Times* reported that in its survey of 3297 California adults, 2750, or 83.4%, had health insurance coverage. Let π denote the proportion of all California adults who have health insurance. The hypothesis-testing methods presented in this chapter could be used to decide whether the sample data provides strong support for the hypothesis $\pi < .90$.

As another example, a report released by the National Association of Colleges and Employers stated that the average starting salary for students graduating in 1999 with a degree in marketing was $31,542 (*San Luis Obispo Tribune,* Sept. 8, 1999). Suppose that you are interested in determining whether the mean starting salary for students graduating with a marketing degree from your university is greater than the national average of $31,542. You select a random sample of $n = 10$ marketing graduates from the 1999 graduating class of your university and determine the starting salary of each one. If this sample produced a mean starting salary of $31,758 and a standard deviation of $1214, is it reasonable to conclude that μ, the true mean starting salary for marketing graduates at your university, is greater than $31,542 (that is, $\mu > 31,542$)? We will see in this chapter how this sample data might be analyzed to decide whether $\mu > 31,542$ is an appropriate conclusion.

10.1   Hypotheses and Test Procedures

A hypothesis is a claim or statement either about the value of a single population characteristic or about the values of several population characteristics. The following are examples of legitimate hypotheses:

$\mu = 1000$ where μ is the mean number of characters in an e-mail message

$\pi < .01$ where π is the proportion of e-mail messages that are undeliverable

In contrast, the statements $\bar{x} > 1000$ and $p = .01$ are *not* hypotheses, because $\bar{x}$ and p are *sample* characteristics.

A **test of hypotheses** or **test procedure** is a method for using sample data to decide between two competing claims (hypotheses) about a population characteristic. One hypothesis might be $\mu = 1000$ and the other $\mu \neq 1000$, or one might be $\pi = .01$ and the other $\pi < .01$. If it were possible to carry out a census of the entire population, we would know which of the two hypotheses is correct, but usually we must decide between them using information from a sample.

A criminal trial is a familiar situation in which a choice between two contradictory claims must be made. The person accused of the crime must be judged either guilty or not guilty. Under the U.S. system of justice, the individual on trial is initially presumed not guilty. Only strong evidence to the contrary will cause the not guilty claim to be rejected in favor of a guilty verdict. The burden is thus put on the prosecution to prove the guilty claim. The French perspective in criminal proceedings is the opposite of ours. There, once enough evidence has been presented to justify bringing an individual to trial, the initial assumption is that the accused is guilty. The burden of proof then falls on the accused to establish otherwise.

As in a judicial proceeding, we shall initially assume that a particular hypothesis, called the *null hypothesis,* is the correct one. We then consider the evidence (the sample data) and reject the null hypothesis in favor of the competing hypothesis, called the *alternative hypothesis,* only if there is *convincing* evidence against the null hypothesis.

Definition

The **null hypothesis,** denoted by H_0, is a claim about a population characteristic that is initially assumed to be true.

The **alternative hypothesis,** denoted by H_a, is the competing claim.

In carrying out a test of H_0 versus H_a, the hypothesis H_0 will be rejected in favor of H_a only if sample evidence strongly suggests that H_0 is false. If the sample does not contain such evidence, H_0 will not be rejected. The two possible conclusions are then *reject H_0* or *fail to reject H_0*.

EXAMPLE 10.1   Because of variation in the manufacturing process, tennis balls produced by a particular machine do not have identical diameters. Let μ denote the true average diameter for tennis balls currently being produced. Suppose that the machine was initially calibrated to achieve the design specification $\mu = 3$ in However, the manufacturer is now concerned that the diameters no longer conform to this specification. That is, $\mu \neq 3$ in must now be considered a possibility. If sample evidence suggests that $\mu \neq 3$ in, the production process will have to be halted while recalibration takes place. Because this is costly, the manufacturer wants to be quite sure that $\mu \neq 3$ in before undertaking recalibration. Under these circumstances, a sensible choice of hypotheses is

H_0: $\mu = 3$ (the specification is being met, so recalibration is unnecessary)

H_a: $\mu \neq 3$

Only compelling sample evidence would then result in H_0 being rejected in favor of H_a.

EXAMPLE 10.2

K mart-brand 60-watt lightbulbs state on the package "Avg. Life 1000 Hr." Let μ denote the true mean life of K mart 60-watt lightbulbs. Then the advertised claim is $\mu = 1000$ hr. People who purchase this brand would be unhappy if μ is actually less than the advertised value. Suppose that a sample of K mart lightbulbs is selected and the lifetime for each bulb in the sample is recorded. The sample results can then be used to test the hypothesis $\mu = 1000$ hr against the hypothesis $\mu < 1000$ hr. The accusation that the company is overstating the mean lifetime is a serious one, and it is reasonable to require compelling evidence from the sample before concluding that $\mu < 1000$. This suggests that the claim $\mu = 1000$ should be selected as the null hypothesis and $\mu < 1000$ selected as the alternative hypothesis. Then

H_0: $\mu = 1000$

would be rejected in favor of

H_a: $\mu < 1000$

only when sample evidence strongly suggests that the initial assumption $\mu = 1000$ hr is no longer tenable.

Since the alternative hypothesis in Example 10.2 asserted that $\mu < 1000$ (true average lifetime is less than the advertised value), it might have seemed sensible to state H_0 as the inequality $\mu \geq 1000$. This assertion is in fact the *implicit* null hypothesis, but we will state H_0 explicitly as a claim of equality. There are several reasons for this. First of all, the development of a decision rule is most easily understood if there is only a single value of μ (or π, or whatever other population characteristic is under consideration) when H_0 is true. Secondly, suppose that the sample data provided compelling evidence that H_0: $\mu = 1000$ should be rejected in favor of H_a: $\mu < 1000$. This means that we were convinced by the sample data that the true mean was smaller than 1000. It follows that we would have also been convinced that the true mean could not have been 1001 or 1010 or any other value that was larger than 1000. As a consequence, the conclusion when testing H_0: $\mu = 1000$ versus H_a: $\mu < 1000$ will always be the same as the conclusion for a test where the null hypothesis is H_0: $\mu \geq 1000$. For the sake of simplicity, we will state the null hypothesis, H_0, as a claim of equality.

The form of a null hypothesis is

H_0:   population characteristic = hypothesized value

where the hypothesized value is a specific number determined by the problem context.

The alternative hypothesis will have one of the following three forms:

H_a: population characteristic > hypothesized value

H_a: population characteristic < hypothesized value

H_a: population characteristic ≠ hypothesized value

Thus, we might test H_0: $\pi = .1$ versus H_a: $\pi < .1$; but we won't test H_0: $\mu = 50$ versus H_a: $\mu > 100$. The number appearing in the alternative hypothesis must be identical to the hypothesized value in H_0.

The following example illustrates how the selection of H_0 (the claim initially believed true) and H_a depend on the objectives of a study.

EXAMPLE 10.3   A medical research team has been given the task of evaluating a new laser treatment for certain types of tumors. Consider the following two scenarios:

Scenario 1:   The current standard treatment is considered reasonable and safe by the medical community, has no major side effects, and has a known success rate of .85 (85%).

Scenario 2:   The current standard treatment sometimes has serious side effects, is very costly, and has a known success rate of .30 (30%).

In the first scenario, research efforts would probably be directed toward determining whether the new treatment has a higher success rate than the standard treatment. Unless convincing evidence of this is presented, it is unlikely that current medical practice would be changed. With π representing the true proportion of successes for the laser treatment, the following hypotheses would be tested:

$$H_0: \quad \pi = .85 \qquad \text{versus} \qquad H_a: \quad \pi > .85$$

In this case, rejection of the null hypothesis would be indicative of compelling evidence that the success rate is higher for the new treatment.

In the second scenario, the current standard treatment does not have much to recommend it. The new laser treatment may be considered preferable because of cost or because it has fewer or less serious side effects, as long as the success rate for the new procedure is no worse than that of the standard treatment. Here, researchers might decide to test the hypothesis

$$H_0: \quad \pi = .30 \quad \text{versus} \quad H_a: \quad \pi < .30$$

If the null hypothesis is rejected, the new treatment will not be put forward as an alternative to the standard treatment, because there is strong evidence that the laser method has a lower success rate.

If the null hypothesis is not rejected, we are able to conclude only that there is not convincing evidence that the success rate for the laser treatment is lower than that for the standard. This is *not* the same as saying we have evidence that the laser treatment is as good as the standard. If medical practice were to embrace the new procedure, it would not be because it has a higher success rate but rather because it costs less or has fewer side effects, and there is not strong evidence that it has a lower success rate than the standard.

You should be careful in setting up the hypotheses for a test. Remember that a statistical hypothesis test is only capable of demonstrating strong support for the alternative hypothesis (by rejection of the null hypothesis). When the null hypothesis is not rejected, it does not mean strong support for H_0— only lack of strong evidence against it. In the lightbulb scenario of Example 10.2, if $H_0: \mu = 1000$ is rejected in favor of $H_a: \mu < 1000$, we have strong evidence for believing that true average lifetime is less than the advertised value. However, nonrejection of H_0 does not necessarily provide strong support for the advertised claim. If the objective is to demonstrate that the average lifetime is greater than 1000 hours, the hypothesis tested should be $H_0: \mu = 1000$ versus $H_a: \mu > 1000$. Now rejection of H_0 indicates strong evidence that $\mu > 1000$. *Keep the research objectives in mind when selecting the hypotheses to be tested.*

Exercises 10.1 – 10.9

10.1 Explain why the statement $\bar{x} = 50$ is not a legitimate hypothesis.

10.2 For the following pairs, indicate which do not comply with our rules for setting up hypotheses, and explain why.
   a. $H_0: \mu = 15, H_a: \mu = 15$
   b. $H_0: \pi = .4, H_a: \pi > .6$
   c. $H_0: \mu = 123, H_a: \mu < 123$
   d. $H_0: \mu = 123, H_a: \mu = 125$
   e. $H_0: p = .1, H_a: p \neq .1$

10.3 To determine whether the pipe welds in a nuclear power plant meet specifications, a random sample of welds is selected, and tests are conducted on each weld in the sample. Weld strength is measured as the force required to break the weld. Suppose that the specifications state that the mean strength of welds should exceed 100 lb/in². The inspection team decides to test $H_0: \mu = 100$ versus $H_a: \mu > 100$. Explain why this alternative was chosen rather than $\mu < 100$.

10.4 The mean length of long-distance telephone calls placed with a particular phone company was known to be 7.3 minutes under an old rate structure. In an attempt to be more competitive with other long-distance carriers, the phone company lowered long-distance rates, thinking that its customers would be encouraged to make longer calls, so there would not be a big loss in revenue. Let μ

denote the true mean length of long-distance calls after the rate reduction. What hypotheses should the phone company test to determine whether the mean length of long-distance calls increased with the lower rates?

10.5 A certain university has decided to introduce the use of + and − with letter grades, as long as there is evidence that more than 60% of the faculty favor the change. A random sample of faculty will be selected and the resulting data used to test the relevant hypotheses. If π represents the true proportion of all faculty that favor a change to +/− grading, which of the following pair of hypotheses should the administration test? Explain your choice.

$$H_0: \quad \pi = .6 \quad \text{versus} \quad H_a: \quad \pi < .6$$

or

$$H_0: \quad \pi = .6 \quad \text{versus} \quad H_a: \quad \pi > .6$$

10.6 A certain television station has been providing live coverage of a particularly sensational criminal trial. The station's program director wishes to know whether more than half the potential viewers prefer a return to regular daytime programming. A survey of randomly selected viewers is to be conducted. Let π represent the true proportion of viewers who prefer regular daytime programming. What hypotheses should the program director test to answer the question of interest?

10.7 Researchers have postulated that because of differences in diet, Japanese children have a lower mean

blood cholesterol level than U.S. children. Suppose that the mean level for U.S. children is known to be 170. Let μ represent the true mean blood cholesterol level for Japanese children. What hypotheses should the researchers test?

10.8 A county commissioner must vote on a resolution that would commit substantial resources to the construction of a sewer in an outlying residential area. Her fiscal decisions have been criticized in the past, so she decides to take a survey of constituents to find out whether they favor spending money for a sewer system. She will vote to appropriate funds only if she can be fairly certain that a majority of the people in her district favor the measure. What hypotheses should she test?

10.9 Many older homes have electrical systems that use fuses rather than circuit breakers. A manufacturer of 40-amp fuses wants to make sure that the mean amperage at which its fuses burn out is in fact 40. If the mean amperage is lower than 40, customers will complain because the fuses require replacement too often. If the mean amperage is higher than 40, the manufacturer might be liable for damage to an electrical system as a result of fuse malfunction. To verify the mean amperage of the fuses, a sample of fuses is to be selected and inspected. If a hypothesis test is to be performed using the resulting data, what null and alternative hypotheses would be of interest to the manufacturer?

10.2 Errors in Hypothesis Testing

Once hypotheses have been formulated, we need a method for using sample data to determine whether H_0 should be rejected. The method that we use for this purpose is called a **test procedure.** Just as a jury may reach the wrong verdict in a trial, there is some chance that the use of a test procedure with sample data may lead us to the wrong conclusion about a population characteristic. This section discusses the kinds of errors that may occur and considers how the choice of a test procedure influences the chances of these errors.

One erroneous conclusion in a criminal trial is for a jury to convict an innocent person, and another is for a guilty person to be set free. Similarly, there are two different types of errors that might be made when making a decision in a hypothesis-testing problem. One type of error involves rejecting H_0 even though H_0 is true. The second type of error results from failing to reject H_0 when it is false.

Definition

type I error	the error of rejecting H_0 when H_0 is true
type II error	the error of failing to reject H_0 when H_0 is false

---

The only way to guarantee that neither type of error will occur is to make such decisions on the basis of a census of the entire population. The risk of error is introduced when we try to make an inference about a population using incomplete information. This is the price paid for basing an inference on a sample. With any reasonable procedure, there is some chance that a type I error will be made and some chance that a type II error will result.

EXAMPLE 10.4

The U.S. Department of Transportation reported that during a recent period, 77% of all domestic passenger flights arrived "on time" (meaning within 15 minutes of the scheduled arrival). Suppose that an airline with a poor on-time record decides to offer its employees a bonus if, in an upcoming month, the airline's proportion of on-time flights exceeds the overall industry rate of .77. Let π be the true proportion of the airline's flights that are on time during the month of interest. A random sample of flights might be selected and used as a basis for choosing between

$$H_0: \quad \pi = .77 \quad \text{and} \quad H_a: \quad \pi > .77$$

In this context, a type I error (rejecting a true H_0) would result in the airline's rewarding its employees when in fact their true proportion of on-time flights did not exceed .77. A type II error (not rejecting a false H_0) would result in the airline employees *not* receiving a reward that in fact they deserved.

EXAMPLE 10.5

Researchers at the National Cancer Institute announced plans to begin studies of a cancer treatment thought to slow the growth of tumors (Associated Press, March 30, 1993). Having tested the treatment on only 13 patients, the researchers had very little information, but they stated that the treatment appears to be less toxic than standard chemotherapy treatments. An experiment to study the treatment more extensively was reported as being in the planning stages.

Let μ denote the true mean growth rate of tumors for patients receiving the new treatment. Data resulting from the planned experiments could be used to test

$H_0: \quad \mu =$ mean growth rate of tumors without treatment

$H_a: \quad \mu <$ mean growth rate of tumors without treatment

The null hypothesis states that the new treatment is not effective — that the mean growth rate of tumors for patients receiving the new treatment is the same as for patients who are not treated. The alternative hypothesis states that the new treatment is effective in reducing the mean growth rate of tumors. In this context, a type I error consists of incorrectly concluding that the new treatment is effective in slowing the growth rate of tumors. A type II error consists of concluding that the new treatment is ineffective when, in fact, the mean growth rate of tumors is reduced.

Examples 10.4 and 10.5 illustrate the two different types of error that might occur when testing hypotheses. Type I and type II errors, and the associated consequences of making such errors, are quite different. In choosing a test procedure (a method for deciding whether to reject H_0), we would like a small probability of drawing an incorrect conclusion. The accompanying box introduces the terminology and notation used to describe error probabilities.

Definition

The probability of a type I error is denoted by α and is called the **level of significance** of the test. Thus, a test with $\alpha = .01$ is said to have a level of significance of .01 or to be a level .01 test.

The probability of a type II error is denoted by β.

EXAMPLE 10.6   A type of lie detector that measures brain waves was developed by a professor of neurobiology at Northwestern University (Associated Press, July 7, 1988). He said, "It would probably not falsely accuse any innocent people and it would probably pick up 70% to 90% of guilty people." Suppose that the result of this lie detector test is allowed as evidence in a criminal trial as the sole basis of a decision between two rival hypotheses:

H_0:   accused is innocent

H_a: accused is guilty

[*Note*: Although these are not "statistical hypotheses" (statements about a population characteristic), the possible decision errors are analogous to type I and type II errors.]

In this situation, a type I error would be finding an innocent person guilty — rejecting the null hypothesis of innocence when it was, in fact, true. A type II error would be finding a guilty person innocent — not rejecting the null hypothesis of innocence when it was, in fact, false. If the developer of the lie detector is correct in his statements, the probability of a type I error, α, is approximately 0, and β, the probability of type II error, is somewhere between .1 and .3.

The ideal test procedure has both $\alpha = 0$ and $\beta = 0$. However, if we must base our decision on incomplete information — a sample rather than a census — it is impossible to achieve this ideal. The standard test procedures do allow the user to control α, but they provide no direct control over β. Since α represents the probability of rejecting a true null hypothesis, selecting a significance level $\alpha = .05$ results in a test procedure that, used over and over with different samples, rejects a *true* H_0 about five times in a hundred. Selecting $\alpha = .01$ results in a test procedure with a type I error rate of 1% in long-term repeated use. Choosing a small value for α implies that the user wants to employ a procedure for which the risk of a type I error is quite small.

One question arises naturally at this point: If the user can select α, the probability of making a type I error, why would anyone ever select $\alpha = .05$ rather than $\alpha = .01$? Why not always select a very small value for α? To achieve a small probability of making a type I error, the corresponding test procedure will require the evidence against H_0 to be very strong before the null hypothesis can be rejected. Although this makes a type I error unlikely, it increases the risk of a type II error (*not* rejecting H_0 when it should have been rejected). Frequently the investigator must balance the consequences of type I and type II errors. If a type II error has serious consequences, it may be a good idea to select a somewhat larger value for α.

In general, there is a compromise between small α and small β, leading to the following widely accepted principle for specifying a test procedure.

After assessing the consequences of type I and type II errors, identify the largest α that is tolerable for the problem. Then employ a test procedure that uses this maximum acceptable value — rather than anything smaller — as the level of significance (because using a smaller α increases β). In other words, don't make α smaller than it needs to be.

Thus, if you decide that $\alpha = .05$ is tolerable, you should not use a test with $\alpha = .01$, because the smaller α inevitably results in a larger β. The values of α most commonly used in practical problems are .05 and .01 (a 1-in-20 or 1-in-100 chance of rejecting H_0 when it is actually true), but the choice in any given problem depends on the seriousness of a type I error relative to a type II error in that context.

EXAMPLE 10.7

The Associated Press (May 13, 1993) reported that the Environmental Protection Agency (EPA) had warned 819 communities that their tap water contained too much lead. Drinking water is considered unsafe if the mean concentration of lead is 15 parts per billion or greater. The EPA requires the cited communities to take corrective actions and to monitor lead levels. With μ denoting the mean concentration of lead, a cited community could test

$$H_0: \quad \mu = 15 \qquad \text{versus} \qquad H_a: \quad \mu < 15$$

The null hypothesis (which is equivalent to the assertion $\mu \geq 15$) states that the mean lead concentration is excessive by EPA standards. The alternative hypothesis states that the mean lead concentration is at an acceptable level and that the water system meets EPA standards for lead.

In this context, a type I error would lead to the conclusion that a water source meets EPA standards for lead when, in fact, it does not. Possible consequences of this type of error include health risks associated with excessive lead consumption (for example, increased blood pressure, hearing loss, and, in severe cases, anemia and kidney damage). A type II error would be to conclude that the water does not meet EPA standards for lead when, in fact, it actually does. Possible consequences of a type II error include elimination of a community water source. Since a type I error might result in potentially serious public health risks, a small value of α (type I error probability), such as $\alpha = .01$, could be selected. Of course, selecting a small value for α increases the risk of a type II error. If the community has only one water source, a type II error could also have very serious consequences for the community, and we might want to rethink our choice of α.

Exercises 10.10 – 10.19

10.10 Researchers at the University of Washington and Harvard University analyzed records of breast cancer screening and diagnostic evaluations ("Mammogram Cancer Scares More Frequent Than Thought," *USA Today*, April 16, 1998). Discussing the benefits and downsides of the screening process, the article states that, although the rate of false positives is higher than previously thought, if radiologists were less aggressive in following up on suspicious tests, the rate of false positives would fall but the rate of missed cancers would rise. Suppose that such a screening test is to be used to decide between a null hypothesis of H_0: no cancer is present and an alternative hypothesis of H_a: cancer is present.

a. Would a false positive (thinking that cancer is present when in fact it is not) be a type I error or a type II error?

b. Describe a type I error in the context of this problem, and discuss the consequences of making a type I error.

c. Describe a type II error in the context of this problem, and discuss the consequences of making a type II error.

d. What aspect of the relationship between the probability of type I and II errors is being described by the statement in the article that if radiologists were less aggressive in following up on suspicious tests, the rate of false positives would fall but the rate of missed cancers would rise?

10.11 The National Cancer Institute conducted a 2-year study to determine whether cancer death rates for areas near nuclear power plants were higher than for areas without nuclear facilities (*San Luis Obispo Telegram-Tribune*, Sept. 17, 1990). A spokesperson for the Cancer Institute said, "From the data at hand, there was no convincing evidence of any increased risk of death from any of the cancers surveyed due to living near nuclear facilities. However, no study can prove the absence of an effect."

a. Let π denote the true proportion of the population in areas near nuclear power plants who die of cancer during a given year. The researchers at the Cancer Institute might have considered the two rival hypotheses of the form

H_0: π = value for areas without nuclear facilities

H_a: π > value for areas without nuclear facilities

Did the Cancer Institute reject H_0 or fail to reject H_0?

b. If the Cancer Institute was incorrect in its conclusion that there is no increased cancer risk associated with living near a nuclear power plant, would they be making a type I or a type II error? Explain.

c. Comment on the spokesperson's last statement that no study can *prove* the absence of an effect. Do you agree with this statement?

10.12 Ann Landers, in her advice column of Oct. 24, 1994 (*San Luis Obispo Telegram-Tribune*), described the reliability of DNA paternity testing as follows: "To get a completely accurate result, you would have to be tested, and so would (the man) and your mother. The test is 100 percent accurate if the man is NOT the father and 99.9 percent accurate if he is."

a. Consider using the results of DNA paternity testing to decide between the following two hypotheses:

H_0: a particular man is the father

H_a: a particular man is not the father

In the context of this problem, describe type I and II errors. (Although these are not hypotheses about a population characteristic, this exercise illustrates the definitions of type I and type II errors.)

b. Based on the information given, what are the values of α, the probability of type I error, and β, the probability of type II error?

c. Ann Landers also states, "If the mother is not tested, there is a 0.8 percent chance of a false positive." For the hypotheses given in part **a,** what are the values of α and β if the decision will be based on DNA testing where the mother is not tested?

10.13 Pizza Hut, after test-marketing a new product called the Bigfoot Pizza, concluded that introduction of the Bigfoot nationwide would increase its sales by more than 14% (*USA Today,* April 2, 1993). This conclusion was based on recording sales information for a random sample of Pizza Hut restaurants selected for the marketing trial. With μ denoting the mean percentage increase in sales for all Pizza Hut restaurants, consider using the sample data to decide between

$$H_0: \quad \mu = 14 \quad \text{and} \quad H_a: \quad \mu > 14$$

a. Is Pizza Hut's conclusion consistent with a decision to reject H_0 or to fail to reject H_0?

b. If Pizza Hut is incorrect in its conclusion, is the company making a type I or a type II error?

10.14 A television manufacturer claims that (at least) 90% of its sets will need no service during the first 3 years of operation. A consumer agency wishes to check this claim, so it obtains a random sample of $n = 100$ purchasers and asks each whether the set purchased needed repair during the first 3 years. Let p be the sample proportion of responses indicating no repair (so that no repair is identified with a success). Let π denote the true proportion of successes. The agency does not want to claim false advertising unless sample evidence strongly suggests that $\pi < .9$. The appropriate hypotheses are then

$$H_0: \quad \pi = .9 \quad \text{versus} \quad H_a: \quad \pi < .9$$

a. In the context of this problem, describe type I and type II errors, and discuss the possible consequences of each.

b. Would you recommend a test procedure that uses $\alpha = .10$ or one that uses $\alpha = .01$? Explain.

10.15 A manufacturer of handheld calculators receives very large shipments of printed circuits from a supplier. It is too costly and time-consuming to inspect all incoming circuits, so when each shipment arrives, a sample is selected for inspection. Information from the sample is then

used to test $H_0: \pi = .05$ versus $H_a: \pi > .05$, where π is the true proportion of defectives in the shipment. If the null hypothesis is not rejected, the shipment is accepted, and the circuits are used in the production of calculators. If the null hypothesis is rejected, the entire shipment is returned to the supplier because of inferior quality. (A shipment is defined to be of inferior qualify if it contains more than 5% defectives.)

a. In this context, define type I and type II errors.

b. From the calculator manufacturer's point of view, which type of error would be considered more serious?

c. From the printed circuit supplier's point of view, which type of error would be considered more serious?

10.16 Water samples are taken from water used for cooling as it is being discharged from a power plant into a river. It has been determined that as long as the mean temperature of the discharged water is at most 150°F, there will be no negative effects on the river's ecosystem. To investigate whether the plant is in compliance with regulations that prohibit a mean discharge water temperature above 150°, 50 water samples will be taken at randomly selected times and the temperature of each sample recorded. The resulting data will be used to test the hypotheses

$$H_0: \quad \mu = 150° \quad \text{versus} \quad H_a: \quad \mu > 150°$$

In the context of this example, describe type I and type II errors. Which type of error would you consider to be more serious? Explain.

10.17 Occasionally, warning flares of the type contained in most automobile emergency kits fail to ignite. A consumer advocacy group is to investigate a claim against a manufacturer of flares brought by a person who claims that the proportion of defectives is much higher than the value of .1 claimed by the manufacturer. A large number of flares will be tested and the results used to decide between $H_0: \pi = .1$ and $H_a: \pi > .1$, where π represents the true proportion of defectives for flares made by this manufacturer. If H_0 is rejected, charges of false advertising will be filed against the manufacturer.

a. Explain why the alternative hypothesis was chosen to be $H_a: \pi > .1$.

b. In this context, describe type I and type II errors, and discuss the consequences of each.

10.18 Suppose that you are an inspector for the Fish and Game Department, and you are given the task of determining whether to prohibit fishing along part of the Oregon coast. You will close an area to fishing if it is determined that fish in that region have an unacceptably high mercury content.

a. Assuming that a mercury concentration of 5 ppm is considered to be the maximum safe concentration, which of the following pairs of hypotheses would you test? Give the reasons for your choice.

$$H_0: \quad \mu = 5 \quad \text{versus} \quad H_a: \quad \mu > 5$$

or

$$H_0: \quad \mu = 5 \quad \text{versus} \quad H_a: \quad \mu < 5$$

b. Would you prefer a significance level of .1 or .01 for your test? Explain.

10.19 An automobile manufacturer is considering using robots for part of its assembly process. Converting to robots is an expensive process, so it will be undertaken only if there is strong evidence that the proportion of defective installations is lower for the robots than for human assemblers. Let π denote the true proportion of defective installations for the robots. It is known that human assemblers have a defect proportion of .02.

a. Which of the following pairs of hypotheses should the manufacturer test? Explain your answer.

$$H_0: \quad \pi = .02 \quad \text{versus} \quad H_a: \quad \pi < .02$$

or

$$H_0: \quad \pi = .02 \quad \text{versus} \quad H_a: \quad \pi > .02$$

b. In the context of this example, describe type I and type II errors.

c. Would you prefer a test with $\alpha = .01$ or $\alpha = .1$? Explain your reasoning.

10.3 Large-Sample Hypothesis Tests for a Population Proportion

Now that some general concepts of hypothesis testing have been introduced, we are ready to turn our attention to the development of procedures for using sample information to decide between the null and alternative hypotheses. There are two possibilities: We will either reject H_0 or else fail to reject H_0. The fundamental idea behind hypothesis-testing procedures is this: *We reject the null hypothesis if the observed sample is very unlikely to have occurred when H_0 is true.* In this section, we consider testing hypotheses about a population proportion when the sample size n is large.

Let π denote the proportion of individuals or objects in a specified population that possess a certain property. A random sample of n individuals or objects is to be selected from the population. The sample proportion

$$p = \frac{\text{number in the sample that possess property}}{n}$$

is the natural statistic for making inferences about π.

The large-sample test procedure is based on the same properties of the sampling distribution of p that were used previously to obtain a confidence interval for π, namely,

1. $\mu_p = \pi$

2. $\sigma_p = \sqrt{\dfrac{\pi(1 - \pi)}{n}}$

3. When n is large, the sampling distribution of p is approximately normal.

These three results imply that the standardized variable

$$z = \frac{p - \pi}{\sqrt{\dfrac{\pi(1 - \pi)}{n}}}$$

has approximately a standard normal distribution when n is large. With this background, let's look at an example.

EXAMPLE 10.8

The authors of the article "Perceived Risks of Heart Disease and Cancer Among Cigarette Smokers" (*J. Amer. Medical Assn.* (1999): 1019–1021) expressed the concern that a majority of smokers do not view themselves as being at increased risk of heart disease or cancer. Because of this, the authors call for a public health campaign to educate smokers about the associated risks. In support of this recommendation, the authors offered the results of a study of 737 current smokers selected at random from U.S. households with telephones. Of the 737 smokers surveyed, 295 indicated that they believed they have a higher than average risk of cancer. Does this data suggest that π, the true proportion of smokers who view themselves as being at increased risk of cancer is, in fact, less than .5 as claimed by the authors of the paper?

This question can be answered by testing hypotheses, where

π = true proportion of smokers who believe that they are at increased risk of cancer

H_0: $\pi = .5$

H_a: $\pi < .5$ (The proportion of smokers who believe that they are at increased risk of cancer is less than .5. That is, less than half of all smokers believe that they are at increased risk of cancer.)

Recall that in a hypothesis test, the null hypothesis will be rejected only if there is convincing evidence against it — in this case, convincing evidence that $\pi < .5$. If H_0 is rejected, the authors would have strong support for the claim made in the article and for their recommended action.

For this sample,

$$p = \frac{295}{737} = .400$$

The observed sample proportion is certainly less than .5, but this could just be due to sampling variability. That is, when $\pi = .5$ (meaning H_0 is true), the sample proportion p will usually differ somewhat from .5 simply because of chance variation from one sample to another. Is it plausible that a sample proportion of $p = .40$ occurred as a result of this chance variation, or is it unusual to observe a sample proportion this small when $\pi = .5$?

To answer this question, we form a *test statistic,* the quantity used as a basis for making a decision between H_0 and H_a, by replacing π by the hypothesized value in the foregoing z variable:

$$z = \frac{p - .5}{\sqrt{\dfrac{(.5)(.5)}{n}}}$$

If the null hypothesis is true, this statistic should have approximately a standard normal distribution, because when the sample size is large and H_0 is true,

1. $\mu_p = .5$

2. $\sigma_p = \sqrt{\dfrac{(.5)(.5)}{n}}$

3. p has approximately a normal distribution.

The calculated value of z expresses the distance between p and the hypothesized value as a number of standard deviations. If, for example, $z = -3$, then the value of p that came from the sample is 3 standard deviations (of p) less than what we would have expected if the null hypothesis were true. How likely is it that a z value at least this contradictory to H_0 would be observed if in fact H_0 is true? Because the test statistic z is constructed using the hypothesized value from the null hypothesis, when H_0 is true it has (approximately) a standard normal distribution, so

$$P(z \leq -3 \text{ when } H_0 \text{ is true}) = \text{area under the } z \text{ curve to the left of } -3.00$$
$$= .0013$$

That is, if H_0 were true, very few samples (much less than 1% of all samples) would produce a value of z at least as contradictory to H_0 as $z = -3$. Since this z value is in the most extreme 1%, it would be sensible to reject H_0.

For our data,

$$z = \frac{p - .5}{\sqrt{\dfrac{(.5)(.5)}{n}}} = \frac{.40 - .5}{\sqrt{\dfrac{(.5)(.5)}{737}}} = \frac{-.10}{.018} = -5.56$$

That is, $p = .40$ is more than 5.5 standard deviations less than what we would expect it to be if H_0: $\pi = .5$ were true. The sample data appears to be much more consistent with H_a: $\pi < .5$. In particular,

$$P(\text{value of } z \text{ is at least as contradictory to } H_0 \text{ as } -5.56 \text{ when } H_0 \text{ is true})$$
$$= P(z \leq -5.56 \text{ when } H_0 \text{ is true})$$
$$= \text{area under the } z \text{ curve to the left of } -5.56$$
$$\approx 0$$

There is virtually no chance of seeing a sample proportion and hence a z value this extreme as a result of chance variation alone when H_0 is true. If p is more than 5.5 standard deviations away from .5, how can we possibly believe that $\pi = .5$? The evidence for rejecting H_0 in favor of H_a is very compelling.

The preceding example illustrates the rationale behind large-sample procedures for testing hypotheses about π (and other test procedures as well). We begin by assuming that the null hypothesis is correct. The sample is then examined in light of this assumption. If the observed sample proportion would not be unusual when H_0

is true, then chance variability from one sample to another is a plausible explanation for what has been observed, and H_0 should not be rejected. On the other hand, if the observed sample proportion would have been quite unlikely were H_0 true, we take the sample as convincing evidence against the null hypothesis and we should reject H_0. We base a decision to reject or to fail to reject the null hypothesis on an assessment of how extreme or unlikely the observed sample is when H_0 is true.

The assessment of how contradictory the observed data is to H_0 is based on first computing the value of the test statistic

$$z = \frac{p - \text{hypothesized value}}{\sqrt{\dfrac{(\text{hypothesized value})(1 - \text{hypothesized value})}{n}}}$$

We then calculate the *P-value*, the probability, assuming that H_0 is true, of obtaining a z value at least as contradictory to H_0 as what was actually observed.

Definition

A **test statistic** is the function of sample data on which a conclusion to reject or fail to reject H_0 is based.

The *P-value* (also sometimes called the **observed significance level**) is a measure of inconsistency between the hypothesized value for a population characteristic and the observed sample. It is the probability, assuming that H_0 is true, of obtaining a test statistic value at least as inconsistent with H_0 as what actually resulted.

EXAMPLE 10.9

A number of initiatives on the topic of legalized gambling have appeared on state ballots in recent years. Suppose that a political candidate has decided to support legalization of casino gambling if he is convinced that more than 2/3 of U.S. adults approve of casino gambling. *USA Today* (June 17, 1999) reported the results of a Gallup poll in which 1523 adults (selected at random from households with telephones) were asked if they approved of casino gambling. The number in the sample who approved was 1035. Does the sample provide convincing evidence that more than 2/3 approve?

With

π = true proportion of U.S. adults who approve of casino gambling

the relevant hypotheses are

H_0: $\pi = 2/3 = .667$
H_a: $\pi > 2/3 = .667$

The sample proportion is

$$p = \frac{1035}{1523} = .680$$

Does the value of p exceed 2/3 by enough to cast substantial doubt on H_0?

Since the sample size is large, the statistic

$$z = \frac{p - .667}{\sqrt{\dfrac{(.667)(1 - .667)}{n}}}$$

has approximately a standard normal distribution when H_0 is true. The calculated value of the test statistic is

$$z = \frac{.680 - .667}{\sqrt{\dfrac{(.667)(1 - .667)}{1523}}} = \frac{.013}{.012} = 1.08$$

The probability that a z value at least this inconsistent with H_0 would be observed if in fact H_0 is true is

P-value $= P(z \geq 1.08$ when H_0 is true)

     = area under the z curve to the right of 1.08

     $= 1 - .8599$

     $= .1401$

This probability indicates that when $\pi = .667$, it would not be all that unusual to observe a sample proportion as large as .680. When H_0 is true, roughly 14% of all samples would have a sample proportion larger than .680, so a sample proportion of .680 is reasonably consistent with the null hypothesis. Although .680 is larger than the hypothesized value of $\pi = .667$, chance variation from sample to sample is a plausible explanation for what was observed. There is not strong evidence that the proportion who favor casino gambling is greater than 2/3.

―――――――――

As illustrated by Examples 10.8 and 10.9, small P-values indicate that sample results are inconsistent with H_0, whereas larger P-values are interpreted as meaning that the data is consistent with H_0 and that sampling variability alone is a plausible explanation for what was observed in the sample. As you probably noticed, the two cases examined (P-value ≈ 0 and P-value $= .1401$) were such that a decision between rejecting or not rejecting H_0 was clear-cut. A decision in other cases might not be so obvious. For example, what if the sample had resulted in P-value $= .04$? Is this unusual enough to warrant rejection of H_0? How small must the P-value be before H_0 should be rejected?

The answer depends on the significance level α (the probability of a type I error) selected for the test. For example, suppose that $\alpha = .05$. This means that the probability of rejecting a true null hypothesis is to be .05. To obtain a test procedure with this probability of type I error, the null hypothesis should be rejected if the sample result is among the most unusual 5% of all samples when H_0 is true. That is, H_0 will be rejected if the computed P-value $\leq .05$. If $\alpha = .01$ had been selected, H_0 would be rejected only if we observed a sample result so extreme that it would be among the most unusual 1% if H_0 is true (that is, if P-value $\leq .01$).

A decision as to whether H_0 should be rejected results from comparing the P-value to the chosen α:

H_0 should be rejected if P-value $\leq \alpha$.

H_0 should not be rejected if P-value $> \alpha$.

Suppose, for example, that P-value $= .0352$ and that a significance level of .05 is chosen. Then, since

$$P\text{-value} = .0352 \leq .05 = \alpha$$

H_0 would be rejected. This would not be the case, though, for $\alpha = .01$, since then P-value $> \alpha$.

Computing a P-value for a Large-Sample Test Concerning π

The computation of the P-value depends on the form of the inequality in H_a. Suppose, for example, that we wish to test:

$$H_0: \quad \pi = .6 \qquad \text{versus} \qquad H_a: \quad \pi > .6$$

based on a large sample. The appropriate test statistic is

$$z = \frac{p - .6}{\sqrt{\dfrac{(.6)(1 - .6)}{n}}}$$

Values of p contradictory to H_0 and much more consistent with H_a are those much *larger* than .6 (since $\pi = .6$ when H_0 is true and $\pi > .6$ when H_0 is false and H_a is true). Such values of p correspond to z values considerably greater than zero. If

$$n = 400 \qquad p = .679$$

then

$$z = \frac{.679 - .6}{\sqrt{\dfrac{(.6)(.4)}{400}}} = \frac{.079}{.025} = 3.16$$

The value $p = .687$ is a bit more than 3 standard deviations larger than what we would have expected were H_0 true. Thus,

$$
\begin{aligned}
P\text{-value} &= P(z \text{ at least as contradictory to } H_0 \text{ as } 3.16 \text{ when } H_0 \text{ is true}) \\
&= P(z \geq 3.16 \text{ when } H_0 \text{ is true}) \\
&= \text{area under the } z \text{ curve to the right of } 3.16 \\
&= 1 - .9992 \\
&= .0008
\end{aligned}
$$

This P-value is illustrated in Figure 10.1 (page 368). If H_0 were true, in the long run only 8 out of 10,000 samples would result in a z value more extreme than what

P-value = .0008

0

Calculated $z = 3.16$

FIGURE 10.1 Calculating a P-value

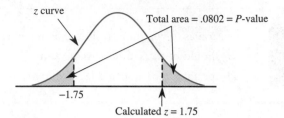

Total area = .0802 = P-value

-1.75

Calculated $z = 1.75$

FIGURE 10.2 P-value as the sum of two tail areas

actually resulted; most of us would consider such a z quite unusual. Using a significance level of .01, we would reject H_0 because P-value $= .0008 \le .01 = \alpha$.

Now consider testing H_0: $\pi = .3$ versus H_a: $\pi \ne .3$. A value of p either much greater than .3 *or* much less than .3 is inconsistent with H_0 and provides support for H_a. Such a p corresponds to a z value far out in *either* tail of the z curve. If

$$z = \frac{p - .3}{\sqrt{\dfrac{(.3)(1 - .3)}{n}}} = 1.75$$

then (as shown in Figure 10.2)

P-value $= P(z$ value at least as inconsistent with H_0 as 1.75 when H_0 is true)
$= P(z \ge 1.75$ or $z \le -1.75$ when H_0 is true)
$= (z$ curve area to the right of 1.75) + (z curve area to the left of -1.75)
$= (1 - .9599) + .0401$
$= .0802$

The P-value in this situation would also be .0802 if $z = -1.75$, since 1.75 and -1.75 are equally inconsistent with H_0 and consistent with H_a: $\pi \ne .3$.

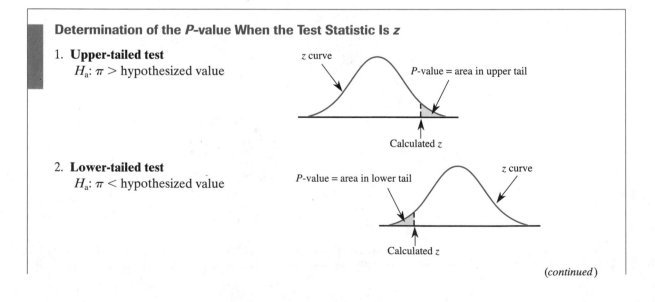

Determination of the P-value When the Test Statistic Is z

1. **Upper-tailed test**
   H_a: $\pi >$ hypothesized value

   z curve

   P-value = area in upper tail

   Calculated z

2. **Lower-tailed test**
   H_a: $\pi <$ hypothesized value

   P-value = area in lower tail

   z curve

   Calculated z

(*continued*)

3. **Two-tailed test**
   H_a: $\pi \neq$ hypothesized value

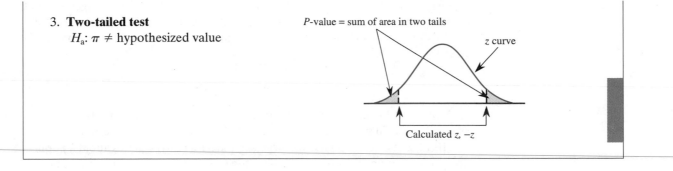

P-value = sum of area in two tails

z curve

Calculated *z*, −*z*

The symmetry of the *z* curve implies that when the test is two-tailed (the $\neq$ alternative), it is not necessary to add two curve areas. Instead,

If *z* is positive, *P*-value = 2 · (area to the right of *z*).

If *z* is negative, *P*-value = 2 · (area to the left of *z*).

EXAMPLE 10.10

In December 1999, a countywide water conservation campaign was conducted in a particular county. In January 2000, a random sample of 500 homes was selected, and water usage was recorded for each home in the sample. The county supervisors would like to know whether the data supports the claim that fewer than half of the households in the county reduced water consumption. The relevant hypotheses are

$$H_0: \quad \pi = .5 \qquad \text{versus} \qquad H_a: \quad \pi < .5$$

where π = true proportion of households in the county with reduced water usage.
   Suppose that the sample results were

$$n = 500 \qquad p = .440$$

Since the sample size is large and this is a lower-tailed test, we can compute the *P*-value by first calculating the value of the *z* test statistic

$$z = \frac{p - .5}{\sqrt{\dfrac{(.5)(1 - .5)}{n}}}$$

and then finding the area under the *z* curve to the left of this *z*.
   Based on the observed sample data,

$$z = \frac{.440 - .5}{\sqrt{\dfrac{(.5)(1 - .5)}{500}}} = \frac{-.060}{.0224} = -2.68$$

The *P*-value is then equal to the area under the *z* curve and to the left of −2.68. From the entry in the −2.6 row and .08 column of Appendix Table II, we find

$$P\text{-value} = .0037$$

Using a .01 significance level, we would reject H_0 (since $.0037 < .01$), suggesting that the proportion with reduced water usage was less than .5. Notice that rejection of H_0 would not be justified if a *very* small significance level, such as .001, had been selected.

Example 10.10 illustrates the calculation of a *P*-value for a lower-tailed test. The use of *P*-values in upper-tailed and two-tailed tests is illustrated in Examples 10.11 and 10.12. But first we summarize large-sample tests of hypotheses about a population proportion and introduce a step-by-step procedure for carrying out a hypothesis test.

Summary of Large-Sample *z* Test for π

Null hypothesis: $H_0: \pi =$ hypothesized value

Test statistic: $z = \dfrac{p - \text{hypothesized value}}{\sqrt{\dfrac{(\text{hypothesized value})(1 - \text{hypothesized value})}{n}}}$

Alternative hypothesis: *P-value*:

$H_a: \pi >$ hypothesized value   Area under *z* curve to right of calculated *z*

$H_a: \pi <$ hypothesized value   Area under *z* curve to left of calculated *z*

$H_a: \pi \neq$ hypothesized value   (i) $2 \cdot$ (area to right of *z*) if *z* is positive
                                                                    (ii) $2 \cdot$ (area to left of *z*) if *z* is negative

Assumptions: 1. *p* is the sample proportion from a *random sample*.
                           2. The *sample size is large*. This test can be used if *n* satisfies both
                               $n(\text{hypothesized value}) \geq 10$ and $n(1 - \text{hypothesized value}) \geq 10$.

We recommend that the following sequence of steps be used when carrying out a hypothesis test.

Steps in a Hypothesis-Testing Analysis

1. Describe the population characteristic about which hypotheses are to be tested.
2. State the null hypothesis, H_0.
3. State the alternative hypothesis, H_a.
4. Select the significance level α for the test.
5. Display the test statistic to be used, with substitution of the hypothesized value identified in step 2 but without any computation at this point.
6. Check to make sure that any assumptions required for the test are reasonable.

(continued)

7. Compute all quantities appearing in the test statistic and then the value of the test statistic itself.

8. Determine the *P*-value associated with the observed value of the test statistic.

9. State the conclusion (which will be to reject H_0 if *P*-value $\leq \alpha$ and not to reject H_0 otherwise). The conclusion should then be stated in the context of the problem, and the level of significance should be included.

Steps 1–4 constitute a statement of the problem, steps 5–8 give the analysis that will lead to a decision, and step 9 provides the conclusion.

EXAMPLE 10.11 The article "Credit Cards and College Students: Who Pays, Who Benefits?" (*J. College Student Development* (1998): 50–56) described a study of credit card payment practices of college students. According to the authors of the article, the credit card industry asserts that at most 50% of college students carry a credit card balance from month to month. However, the authors of the article report that, in a random sample of 310 college students, 217 carried a balance each month. Does this sample provide sufficient evidence to reject the industry claim? We will answer this question by carrying out a hypothesis test using a .05 significance level.

1. *Population characteristic of interest*:

   π = true proportion of college students who carry a balance from month to month

2. *Null hypothesis*: $H_0: \pi = .5$

3. *Alternative hypothesis*: $H_a: \pi > .5$ (the proportion of students who carry a balance from month to month is greater than .5)

4. *Significance level*: $\alpha = .05$

5. *Test statistic*:

$$z = \frac{p - \text{hypothesized value}}{\sqrt{\dfrac{(\text{hypothesized value})(1 - \text{hypothesized value})}{n}}} = \frac{p - .5}{\sqrt{\dfrac{(.5)(.5)}{n}}}$$

6. *Assumptions*:   This test requires a random sample and a large sample size. The given sample was a random sample with a sample size of $n = 310$. Since $310(.5) \geq 10$ and $310(1 - .5) \geq 10$, the large-sample test is appropriate.

7. *Computations*: $n = 310$ and $p = 217/310 = .700$, so

$$z = \frac{.700 - .5}{\sqrt{\dfrac{(.5)(.5)}{310}}} = \frac{.200}{.028} = 7.14$$

8. *P-value*:   This is an upper-tailed test (the inequality in H_a is $>$), so the *P*-value is the area to the right of the computed z value. Since $z = 7.14$ is so far out in

the upper tail of the standard normal distribution, the area to its right is negligible. Thus,

$$P\text{-value} \approx 0$$

9. *Conclusion*:   Since P-value $\leq \alpha$ $(0 \leq .05)$, H_0 is rejected at the .05 level of significance. We conclude that the proportion of students who carry a credit card balance from month to month is greater than .5. That is, the sample provides convincing evidence that the industry claim is not correct.

EXAMPLE 10.12   The Associated Press (Feb. 27, 1995) reported that 71% of Americans age 25 and older are overweight, a substantial increase over the 58% figure from 1983. Although this information came from a Harris Poll (a survey) rather than a census of the population, let's assume for purposes of this example that the nationwide population proportion is exactly .71. Suppose that an investigator wishes to know whether the proportion of such individuals in her state that are overweight differs from the national proportion. A random sample of size $n = 600$ results in 450 who are classified as overweight. What can the investigator conclude? We will answer this question by carrying out a hypothesis test with $\alpha = .01$.

1. π = proportion of all residents of a particular state age 25 and over who are overweight
2. H_0: $\pi = .71$
3. H_a: $\pi \neq .71$ (differs from the national proportion)
4. *Significance level*: $\alpha = .01$
5. *Test statistic*:

$$z = \frac{p - \text{hypothesized value}}{\sqrt{\dfrac{(\text{hypothesized value})(1 - \text{hypothesized value})}{n}}} = \frac{p - .71}{\sqrt{\dfrac{(.71)(.29)}{n}}}$$

6. *Assumptions*:   This test requires a random sample and a large sample size. The given sample was a random sample and had sample size $n = 600$. Since $600(.71) \geq 10$ and $600(.29) \geq 10$, the large-sample test is appropriate.
7. *Computations*: $p = 450/600 = .750$, from which

$$z = \frac{.750 - .71}{\sqrt{\dfrac{(.71)(.29)}{600}}} = \frac{.040}{.01852} = 2.16$$

8. *P-value*:   The area under the z curve to the right of 2.16 is $1 - .9846 = .0154$, so P-value $= 2(.0154) = .0308$.

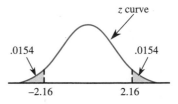

9. *Conclusion*: At significance level .01, H_0 cannot be rejected, because *P*-value $= .0308 > .01 = \alpha$. The data does not convince us that the proportion in this state differs from the nationwide proportion. (Notice that the opposite conclusion would be reached had we used $\alpha = .05$.)

Most statistical computer packages and graphing calculators will calculate and report *P*-values for a variety of hypothesis-testing situations, including the large-sample test for a proportion. MINITAB was used to carry out the test of Example 10.10, and the resulting computer output follows. (MINITAB uses p instead of π to denote the population proportion.)

Test and Confidence Interval for One Proportion

Test of p = 0.5 vs p < 0.5

Sample	X	N	Sample p	95.0 % CI	Z-Value	P-Value
1	220	500	0.440000	(0.396491, 0.483509)	-2.68	0.004

From the MINITAB output, $z = -2.68$ and the associated *P*-value is .004. The small difference in the value of the test statistic is the result of rounding in the hand computations of Example 10.10.

It is also possible to compute the value of the z test statistic and then use a statistical computer package or graphing calculator to determine the corresponding *P*-value as an area under the standard normal curve. For example, the user can specify a value, and MINITAB will determine the area to the left of this value for any particular normal distribution. Because of this, the computer can be used in place of Appendix Table II. In Example 10.12 (a two-tailed test), the computed z was 2.16. Using MINITAB gives

z	area to left
-2.16	0.015386
2.16	0.984614

from which

$$\text{area to the left of } -2.16 = .015386$$
$$\text{area to the right of } 2.16 = 1 - .984614 = .015386$$

and

$$P\text{-value} = .015386 + .015386 = .030772$$

which agrees with the value obtained by using the tables.

Exercises 10.20 – 10.37

10.20 **a.** Use the definition of the *P*-value to explain why H_0 would certainly be rejected if *P*-value $= .0003$.
b. Use the definition of the *P*-value to explain why H_0 would definitely not be rejected if *P*-value $= .350$.

10.21 For which of the given *P*-values will the null hypothesis be rejected when performing a level .05 test?

    a. .001   **b.** .021   **c.** .078   **d.** .047   **e.** .148

10.22 Pairs of *P*-values and significance levels, α, are given. For each pair, state whether the observed *P*-value will lead to rejection of H_0 at the given significance level.
  a. *P*-value $= .084$, $\alpha = .05$
  b. *P*-value $= .003$, $\alpha = .001$
  c. *P*-value $= .498$, $\alpha = .05$
  d. *P*-value $= .084$, $\alpha = .10$
  e. *P*-value $= .039$, $\alpha = .01$
  f. *P*-value $= .218$, $\alpha = .10$

10.23 Let π denote the proportion of grocery store customers that use the store's "club card." For a large-sample *z* test of H_0: $\pi = .5$ versus H_a: $\pi > .5$, find the *P*-value associated with each of the given values of the test statistic.
  a. 1.40 **b.** .93 **c.** 1.96 **d.** 2.45 **e.** $-.17$

10.24 For which of the following null hypotheses H_0 and sample sizes *n* is the large-sample *z* test appropriate?
  a. H_0: $\pi = .2$, $n = 25$
  b. H_0: $\pi = .6$, $n = 10$
  c. H_0: $\pi = .9$, $n = 100$
  d. H_0: $\pi = .05$, $n = 75$

10.25 Although arsenic is known to be a poison, it also has some beneficial medicinal uses. In one study of the use of arsenic to treat a rare type of blood cell cancer denoted by APL (for acute promyelocytic leukemia), APL patients were given an arsenic compound as part of their treatment. Of those receiving arsenic, 42% were in remission and showed no signs of leukemia in a subsequent examination (*The Washington Post,* Nov. 5, 1998). It is known that 15% of APL patients are in remission after the conventional treatment. Suppose that the study had included 40 randomly selected patients (the actual number in the study was much smaller). Is there sufficient evidence to conclude that the proportion in remission for the arsenic treatment is greater than .15, the remission proportion for the conventional treatment? Test the relevant hypotheses using a .01 significance level.

10.26 According to the article "Which Adults Do Underage Youth Ask for Cigarettes?" (*American Journal of Public Health* (1999): 1561–1564), 43.6% of the 149 18- to 19-year-olds in a random sample have been asked to buy cigarettes for an underage smoker.
  a. Is there convincing evidence that fewer than half of 18- to 19-year-olds have been approached to buy cigarettes by an underage smoker? Be sure to calculate the *P*-value for your hypothesis test.
  b. The article went on to state that of the 110 non-smoking 18- to 19-year-olds, only 38.2% had been approached to buy cigarettes for an underage smoker. Is there evidence that less than half of nonsmoking 18- to 19-year-olds have been approached to buy cigarettes?

10.27 Many people have misconceptions about how profitable small, consistent investments can be. In a survey of 1010 randomly selected U.S. adults (Associated Press, Oct. 29, 1999), only 374 responded that they thought that an investment of $25 per week over 40 years with a 7% annual return would result in a sum of over $100,000 (the correct amount is $286,640). Is there sufficient evidence to conclude that fewer than half of U.S. adults are aware that such an investment would result in a sum of over $100,000? Test the relevant hypotheses using $\alpha = .05$.

10.28 The same survey described in Exercise 10.27 also asked the individuals in the sample what they thought was their best chance to obtain more than $500,000 in their lifetime. Twenty eight percent responded "win a lottery or sweepstakes." Does this provide convincing evidence that more than a fourth of U.S. adults see a lottery or sweepstakes win as their best chance at accumulating $500,000? Test using a significance level of .01.

10.29 "Clerk Tosses Out Two Recall Petitions — Random Check Fails to Confirm Enough Valid Signatures" was the headline of an article that appeared in the *San Luis Obispo Tribune* (Sept. 9, 1999). The article states that a random check of the petitions showed that there were not enough valid signatures to force a recall election. For one of the petitions, 11,800 signatures were submitted and 10,384 valid signatures were required to force a recall election. There would be enough valid signatures to force a recall if 88% or more of the signatures could be verified. The county clerk selected a random sample of 592 signatures and verified the signature, address, and registration status against voter registration records. It was determined that 411 of the 592 were valid.
  a. Is there sufficient evidence to conclude that the proportion of valid signatures on the petition is less than .88? Test the relevant hypotheses using $\alpha = .01$.
  b. For the hypotheses in part **a,** describe a type I error and discuss the consequence of making such an error.
  c. Describe a type II error, and discuss the consequence of making such an error.
  d. If the conclusion to the test in part **a** is in error, which type of error (I or II) would you be making?
  e. Is the result of your hypothesis test consistent with the county clerk's decision to "toss out" the recall petition? Explain.

10.30 Duck hunting in populated areas faces opposition on the basis of safety and environmental issues. The *San Luis Obispo Telegram-Tribune* (June 18, 1991) reported the results of a survey to assess public opinion regarding duck hunting on Morro Bay (located along the central coast of California). A random sample of 750 local residents included 560 who strongly opposed hunting on the bay. Does this sample provide sufficient evidence to conclude that the majority of local residents oppose hunting on Morro Bay? Test the relevant hypotheses using $\alpha = .01$.

10.31 Drug testing of job applicants is becoming increasingly common. The Associated Press (May 24, 1990) reported that 12.1% of those tested in California tested positive. Suppose that this figure had been based on a random sample of size 600, with 73 testing positive. Does this sample support a claim that more than 10% of job applicants in California test positive for drug use?

10.32 In an experiment, ("Effect of Preparation Methods on Total Fat Content, Moisture Content, and Sensory Characteristics of Breaded Chicken Nuggets and Beef Steak Fingers," *Family and Consumer Sciences Research Journal* (1999): 18–27), 25 of 37 panelists preferred the flavor of deep-fat fried chicken nuggets to baked chicken nuggets.
a. Is there evidence to show that a clear majority of consumers prefer either baked or deep-fat fried chicken nuggets? Assume that the 37 panelists can be viewed as a random sample of consumers.
b. Describe a type I error.
c. Which sort of error, type I or type II, could not have been committed in this test.
d. In another part of this experiment, it was noted that 23 of 37 panelists preferred the flavor of baked beef steak fingers to hot-air fried beef steak fingers. Is there evidence to show that the majority of consumers prefer the flavor of baked beef steak fingers to hot-air fried beef steak fingers?

10.33 The state of Georgia's HOPE scholarship program guarantees fully paid tuition to Georgia public universities for Georgia high school seniors who have a B average in academic requirements as long as they maintain a B average in college. Of 137 randomly selected students enrolling in the Ivan Allen College at Georgia Tech (social science and humanities majors) in 1996 who had a B average going into college ("Who Loses HOPE? Attrition from Georgia's College Scholarship Program,"

Southern Economic Journal (1999): 379-390) 53.2% had a GPA below 3.0 at the end of their first year. Does this data provide convincing evidence that a majority of students at Ivan Allen College who enroll with a HOPE scholarship will lose their scholarship?

10.34 Seat belts help prevent injuries in automobile accidents, but they certainly don't offer complete protection in extreme situations. A random sample of 319 front-seat occupants involved in head-on collisions in a certain region resulted in 95 who sustained no injuries ("Influencing Factors on the Injury Severity of Restrained Front Seat Occupants in Car-to-Car Head-on Collisions," *Accid. Anal. and Prev.* (1995): 143–150). Does this suggest that the true (population) proportion of uninjured occupants exceeds .25? State and test the relevant hypotheses using a significance level of .05.

10.35 Academic dishonesty continues to be a problem on college and university campuses. One study ("Cheating at Small Colleges: An Examination of Student and Faculty Behaviors," *J. of College Student Devel.* (1994): 255–260) reported that in a random sample of 480 students, 124 said that they had looked at notes during an exam. Assuming that the survey was designed and carried out in a manner resulting in truthful responses, does it appear that more than 20% of all students in the population sampled engaged in this particular form of cheating?

10.36 White remains the most popular car color in the United States, but its popularity appears to be slipping relative to other colors. According to an annual survey by DuPont (*Los Angeles Times,* Feb. 22, 1994), white was the color of 20% of the vehicles purchased during 1993, a decline of 4% from the previous year. (According to a DuPont spokesperson, white represents "innocence, purity, honesty, and cleanliness.") A random sample of 400 cars purchased during this period in a certain metropolitan area resulted in 100 that were white. Does the proportion of all cars purchased in this area that were white appear to differ from the national percentage? Test the relevant hypotheses using $\alpha = .05$. Does your conclusion change if $\alpha = .01$ is used?

10.37 A random sample of 2700 California lawyers revealed only 1107 who felt that the ethical standards of most lawyers are high (Associated Press, Nov. 12, 1994). Does this provide strong evidence for concluding that fewer than 50% of all California lawyers feel this way? Carry out a test of appropriate hypotheses.

10.4 Hypothesis Tests for a Population Mean

We will now turn our attention to developing a method for testing hypotheses about a population mean. The test procedures in this case are based on the same two results that led to the z and t confidence intervals in Chapter 9. These results follow:

1. When either n is large or the population distribution is approximately normal, then

$$z = \frac{\bar{x} - \mu}{\dfrac{\sigma}{\sqrt{n}}}$$

has approximately a standard normal distribution.

2. When either n is large or the population distribution is approximately normal, then

$$t = \frac{\bar{x} - \mu}{\dfrac{s}{\sqrt{n}}}$$

has approximately a t distribution with df $= n - 1$.

A consequence of these two results is that if we are interested in testing a null hypothesis of the form

$H_0: \quad \mu =$ hypothesized value

then, depending on whether σ is known or unknown, we can use (as long as n is large or the population distribution is approximately normal) either the accompanying z or t test statistic:

Case 1 σ known

Test statistic: $z = \dfrac{\bar{x} - \text{hypothesized value}}{\dfrac{\sigma}{\sqrt{n}}}$

P-value: Computed as an area under the z curve

Case 2 σ unknown

Test statistic: $t = \dfrac{\bar{x} - \text{hypothesized value}}{\dfrac{s}{\sqrt{n}}}$

P-value: Computed as an area under the t curve with df $= n - 1$

Since it is rarely the case that σ, the population standard deviation, is known, we will focus our attention on the test procedure for the σ unknown case.

When testing a hypothesis about a population mean, the null hypothesis will specify a particular hypothesized value for μ:

H_0: μ = hypothesized value

The alternative hypothesis will have one of the following three forms

H_a: μ > hypothesized value

H_a: μ < hypothesized value

H_a: μ ≠ hypothesized value

depending on the research question being addressed. If n is large or the population distribution is approximately normal, the test statistic

$$t = \frac{\bar{x} - \text{hypothesized value}}{\dfrac{s}{\sqrt{n}}}$$

can be used. For example, if the null hypothesis to be tested is H_0: μ = 100, the test statistic becomes

$$t = \frac{\bar{x} - 100}{\dfrac{s}{\sqrt{n}}}$$

Consider the alternative hypothesis H_a: μ > 100, and suppose that a sample of size n = 24 gives $\bar{x}$ = 104.20 and s = 8.23. The resulting test statistic value is

$$t = \frac{104.20 - 100}{\dfrac{8.23}{\sqrt{24}}} = \frac{4.20}{1.6799} = 2.50$$

Since this is an upper-tailed test, if the test statistic had been z rather than t, the P-value would be the area under the z curve to the right of 2.50. With a t statistic, the P-value is the area under an appropriate t curve (here with df = 24 − 1 = 23) to the right of 2.50. The 23-df row of the t table (Appendix Table III) used previously for calculating confidence intervals shows that 2.50 is the critical value for a central t curve area of .98. Thus, the area to the right of 2.50 under this t curve is .01 (see Figure 10.3), and this area is the P-value. That is, if H_0 were true, only 1% of all

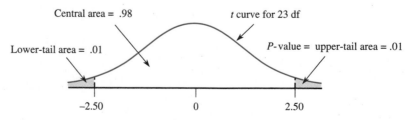

FIGURE 10.3 *P*-value for an upper-tailed *t* test

samples of size 24 would result in a value of t at least as extreme as the one we obtained. Using a significance level of .05, H_0 would be rejected, because

P-value $= .01 < .05 = \alpha$

Suppose that we had calculated $t = 2.7$ for an upper-tailed test based on 23 df. The 23-df row of Table III contains 2.50 (upper-tail area .01) and 2.81 (upper-tail area .005), but not 2.7. We can therefore not determine exactly the P-value (captured tail area); at best, we can say that it is between .005 and .01. More generally, because any particular row of Table III contains only seven critical values, for most calculated values of t the captured tail area cannot be determined exactly. To remedy this deficiency, we have included as Appendix Table IV a tabulation of t curve tail areas. Each column of the table is for a different number of degrees of freedom: 1, 2, 3, . . . , 30, 35, 40, 60, 120, and a last column for df $= \infty$, which is the same as for the z curve. The table gives the area under each t curve to the right of values ranging from 0.0 to 4.0 in increments of .1. Part of this table appears in Figure 10.4. For example,

area under the 23-df t curve to the right of 2.7 $= .006$

$= P$-value for an upper-tailed t test

Suppose that $t = -2.7$ for a lower-tailed test based on 23 df. Then, because any t curve is symmetric about 0,

P-value $=$ area to the left of $-2.7 =$ area to the right of 2.7 $= .006$

For a two-tailed z test, we had to double the captured tail area to obtain the P-value. This is also the case for a two-tailed t test. Thus, if $t = 2.7$ or if $t = -2.7$ for a 23-df two-tailed test,

P-value $= 2 \cdot (.006) = .012$

df ＼ t	1	2	. . .	22	23	24	. . .	60	120
0.0									
0.1									
⋮				⋮	⋮	⋮			
2.6			. . .	.008	.008	.008	. . .		
2.7			. . .	.007	.006	.006	. . .		
2.8			. . .	.005	.005	.005	. . .		
⋮				⋮	⋮	⋮			
4.0									

Area under 23-df t curve to right of 2.7

FIGURE 10.4 Part of Appendix Table IV: t curve tail areas

Once past 30 df, the tail areas change very little, so the last (z) column provides a very good approximation.

The following two boxes give a general description of the test procedure and show how the P-value is obtained as a t curve area or sum of areas.

Finding *P*-values for a *t* Test

1. **Upper-tailed test**
   H_a: $\mu >$ hypothesized value

2. **Lower-tailed test**
   H_a: $\mu <$ hypothesized value

3. **Two-tailed test**
   H_a: $\mu \neq$ hypothesized value

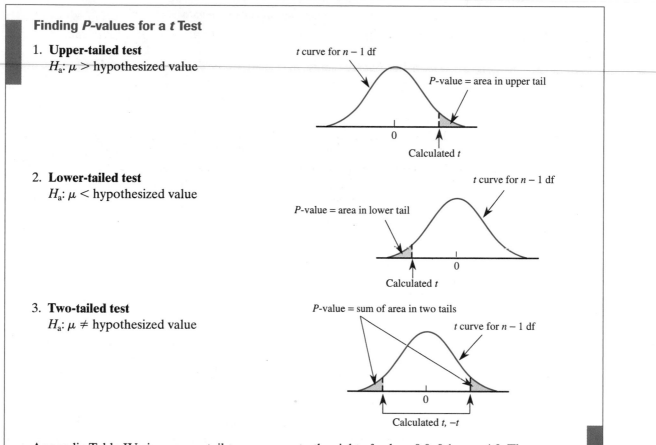

Appendix Table IV gives upper-tail t curve areas to the right of values 0.0, 0.1, . . . , 4.0. These areas are P-values for upper-tailed tests and, by symmetry, also for lower-tailed tests. Doubling an area gives the P-value for a two-tailed test.

The One-Sample *t* Test for a Population Mean

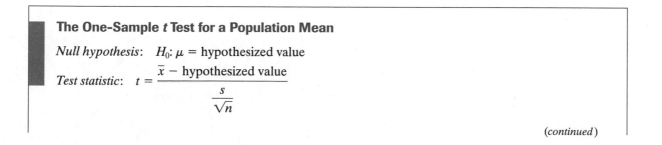

Null hypothesis: H_0: $\mu =$ hypothesized value

Test statistic: $t = \dfrac{\bar{x} - \text{hypothesized value}}{\dfrac{s}{\sqrt{n}}}$

(*continued*)

Alternative hypothesis:

H_a: μ > hypothesized value

H_a: μ < hypothesized value

H_a: μ ≠ hypothesized value

P-value:

Area under t curve with df = $n - 1$ to right of calculated t

Area under t curve with df = $n - 1$ to left of calculated t

(i) 2 · (area to right of t) if t is positive

(ii) 2 · (area to left of t) if t is negative

Assumptions: 1. $\bar{x}$ and s are the sample mean and sample standard deviation from a *random sample*.

2. The *sample size is large* (generally $n \geq 30$) or *the population distribution is at least approximately normal*.

EXAMPLE 10.13

The recommended daily dietary allowance (RDA) for zinc among males older than 50 years is 15 mg/day (*World Almanac*, 1992). The article "Nutrient Intakes and Dietary Patterns of Older Americans: A National Study" (*J. of Gerontology* (1992): M145–M150) reported the following data on zinc intake for a random sample of males age 65–74 years:

$$n = 115 \qquad \bar{x} = 11.3 \qquad s = 6.43$$

The researcher is concerned that males in this age group may not be getting the RDA for zinc in their diets. Is there evidence to support this concern? That is, does this data suggest that μ, the average daily zinc intake for the population of all males age 65–74, is less than the RDA? We will test

$$H_0: \quad \mu = 15 \qquad \text{versus} \qquad H_a: \quad \mu < 15$$

The null hypothesis will be rejected only if there is convincing evidence that $\mu < 15$ (that is, strong evidence against H_0).

Figure 10.5 shows a boxplot of data consistent with the given summary quantities. Roughly 75% of the sample observations are smaller than 15 (the top edge of the box is at the upper quartile). Furthermore, the observed $\bar{x}$ value, 11.3, is certainly smaller than 15, but this could be simply the result of sampling variability. That is, even when $\mu = 15$, meaning H_0 is true, the resulting $\bar{x}$ value will usually differ somewhat from 15 simply because of chance variation from one sample to another. Is it plausible that a sample mean of 11.3 occurred as a result of this chance variation, or is it unusual to observe a sample mean as small as 11.3 when $\mu = 15$?

FIGURE 10.5 Boxplot for zinc intake data

To answer this question, we will carry out a hypothesis test with a significance level of .05 using the same step-by-step procedure described in the previous section.

1. *Population characteristic of interest*:

   μ = true mean zinc intake for males age 65–74

2. *Null hypothesis*: H_0: $\mu = 15$

3. *Alternative hypothesis*: H_a: $\mu < 15$ (the mean is less than the RDA of 15)

4. *Significance level*: $\alpha = .05$

5. *Test statistic*: $t = \dfrac{\bar{x} - \text{hypothesized value}}{\dfrac{s}{\sqrt{n}}} = \dfrac{\bar{x} - 15}{\dfrac{s}{\sqrt{n}}}$

6. *Assumptions*:   This test requires a random sample and either a large sample size or approximately a normal population distribution. Since the given sample was a random sample and the sample size was $n = 115$, the t test is appropriate.

7. *Computations*: $n = 115$, $\bar{x} = 11.3$, and $s = 6.43$, so

   $$t = \frac{11.3 - 15}{\dfrac{6.43}{\sqrt{15}}} = \frac{-3.7}{.600} = -6.17$$

8. *P-value*:   This is a lower-tailed test (the inequality in H_a is <), so the P-value is the area to the left of the computed t value. Since df = $115 - 1 = 114$, we can use the df = 120 column (closest to df = 114) of Appendix Table IV to find the P-value. With $t = -6.17$,

   P-value = area to the left of $-6.17 \approx 0$

   (since 6.17 is greater than 4.0, the largest tabled value).

9. *Conclusion*:   Since P-value $\leq \alpha$, we reject H_0 at the .05 level of significance. There is virtually no chance of seeing a sample mean, and hence a t value, this extreme as a result of just chance variation when H_0 is true. There is convincing evidence that the mean zinc intake for males age 65–74 is less than the recommended daily allowance.

EXAMPLE 10.14

Speed, size, and strength are thought to be important factors in football performance. The article "Physical and Performance Characteristics of NCAA Division I Football Players" (*Research Quarterly for Exercise and Sport* (1990): 395–401) reported on physical characteristics of Division I starting football players in the 1988 football season. Information for teams ranked in the top 20 was easily obtained, and it was reported that the mean weight of starters on top-20 teams was 105 kg. A random sample of 33 starting players (various positions were represented) from Division I teams that were not ranked in the top 20 resulted in a sample mean weight of 103.3 kg and a sample standard deviation of 16.3 kg. Is there sufficient evidence to conclude that the mean weight for non–top-20 starters is less than 105, the known value for top-20 teams? Since the sample size is large, the $\bar{x}$ distribution will be approximately normal even though the distribution of weights of college football players is probably not normal in shape. We will carry out a test with significance level .01.

1. μ = true mean weight of starters on teams that are not ranked in the top 20

2. $H_0: \mu = 105$

3. $H_a: \mu < 105$

4. *Significance level*: $\alpha = .01$

5. *Test statistic*: $t = \dfrac{\bar{x} - \text{hypothesized value}}{\dfrac{s}{\sqrt{n}}} = \dfrac{\bar{x} - 105}{\dfrac{s}{\sqrt{n}}}$

6. *Assumptions*:   This test requires a random sample and either a large sample size or a normal population distribution. The given sample was a random sample and even though the population distribution may not be normal, the sample size was $n = 33$ so use of the t test is reasonable.

7. *Computations*: $n = 33, \bar{x} = 103.3$, and $s = 16.3$, so

$$t = \dfrac{103.3 - 105}{\dfrac{16.3}{\sqrt{33}}} = \dfrac{-1.7}{2.838} = -.60$$

8. *P-value*:   This is a lower-tailed test, so the P-value is the area under the t curve with $33 - 1 = 32$ df and to the left of the computed t value:

   P-value = area to the left of $-.60 = .277$

   (using the df = 30 column of Appendix Table IV).

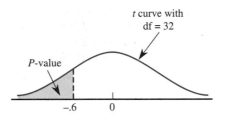

9. *Conclusion*:   Since P-value $> .01$, we fail to reject H_0 at the .01 level of significance. There is not sufficient evidence to conclude that the mean weight of non–top-20 starters is below that of top-20 teams.

EXAMPLE 10.15   A well-designed and safe workplace can contribute greatly to increasing productivity. It is especially important that workers not be asked to perform tasks, such as lifting, that exceed their capabilities. The accompanying data on maximum weight of lift (MWAL, in kg) for a frequency of four lifts per minute was reported in the article "The Effects of Speed, Frequency, and Load on Measured Hand Forces for a Floor-to-Knuckle Lifting Task" (*Ergonomics* (1992): 833–843):

    25.8   36.6   26.3   21.8   27.2

Subjects were randomly selected from the population of healthy males age 18–30. Does the data suggest that the population mean MWAL exceeds 25? Let's carry out a test of the relevant hypotheses using a .05 significance level.

1. μ = population mean MWAL

2. $H_0: \mu = 25$

3. $H_a: \mu > 25$

4. $\alpha = .05$

5. $t = \dfrac{\bar{x} - \text{hypothesized value}}{\dfrac{s}{\sqrt{n}}} = \dfrac{\bar{x} - 25}{\dfrac{s}{\sqrt{n}}}$

6. This test requires a random sample and either a large sample size or a normal population distribution. The given sample was a random sample. Since the sample size is only 5, for the t test to be appropriate, we must be able to assume that the population distribution of MWAL values is approximately normal. Is this reasonable? The accompanying graph gives a boxplot of the data.

MWAL

Although the boxplot is not perfectly symmetrical, there are no outliers. It is very difficult to assess the reasonableness of normality with only five observations. Based on their understanding of MWAL values, the authors of the article thought it was reasonable to assume that the population distribution was approximately normal. So, based on this judgment, we will proceed with the t test.

7. $\Sigma x = 137.7$ and $\Sigma x^2 = 3911.97$, from which $\bar{x} = 27.54$, $s = 5.47$, and

$$t = \frac{27.54 - 25}{\dfrac{5.47}{\sqrt{5}}} = 1.0$$

8. The test is based on $n - 1 = 4$ df. Appendix Table IV shows that the area under the 4-df curve to the right of 1.0 is .187. Because the test is upper-tailed, P-value = .187.

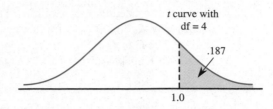

9. Since P-value $= .187 > .05 = \alpha$, H_0 cannot be rejected at this significance level. The data does not provide strong evidence for concluding that the population mean MWAL exceeds 25.

Output from MINITAB follows. The P-value differs slightly from ours because MINITAB uses more decimal accuracy in computing t. Thus, if H_0 were true, about 18% of all samples would yield a value of t more extreme than what we obtained. Since 1.04 is not in the most extreme 5% of all values, H_0 is not rejected.

TEST OF MU = 25.000 VS MU G.T. 25.000

N	MEAN	STDEV	SE MEAN	T	P VALUE
5	27.540	5.471	2.447	1.04	0.18

EXAMPLE 10.16

One concern employers have about the use of technology is the amount of time that employees spend each day making personal use of company technology, such as personal phone, e-mail, Internet, and computer games. The Associated Press (Sept. 7, 1999) reported that a management consultant believes that, on average, workers spend 75 minutes a day making personal use of company technology. Suppose that the CEO of a large corporation wanted to determine whether the average amount of time spent in personal use of company technology for her employees was greater than the reported value of 75 minutes. Each person in a random sample of 10 employees was contacted and asked about daily personal use of company technology. (Participants would probably have to be guaranteed anonymity to obtain truthful responses.) The resulting data is given along with some summary statistics.

Employee	1	2	3	4	5	6	7	8	9	10
Time	66	70	75	88	69	89	71	71	63	86

$n = 10$ $\bar{x} = 74.80$ $s = 9.45$

Does this data provide evidence that the mean for this company is greater than 75 minutes? To answer this question, let's carry out a hypothesis test with $\alpha = .05$.

1. μ = mean daily time spent in personal use of company technology for this company
2. $H_0: \mu = 75$
3. $H_a: \mu > 75$

4. $\alpha = .05$

5. $t = \dfrac{\overline{x} - \text{hypothesized value}}{\dfrac{s}{\sqrt{n}}} = \dfrac{\overline{x} - 75}{\dfrac{s}{\sqrt{n}}}$

6. This test requires a random sample and either a large sample or a normal population distribution. The given sample was a random sample of employees. Since the sample size is small, we must be willing to assume that the population distribution of times is approximately normal. The accompanying normal probability plot appears to be reasonably straight, and although a boxplot reveals some skewness in the sample, it does not reveal any outliers. Also, the correlation between the expected normal scores and the observed data for this sample is .943, which is well above the critical r value for $n = 10$ of .880. All of these observations support the assumption of a normal population distribution, so we will proceed with the t test.

Correlations (Pearson)
Correlation of Time and Normal Score = 0.943

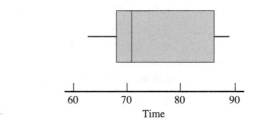

7. $t = \dfrac{74.80 - 75}{\dfrac{9.45}{\sqrt{10}}} = -.07$

8. From the df $= 9$ column of Appendix Table IV and rounding the test statistic value to $-.1$, we get

$$P\text{-value} = \text{area to the right of } -.1 = 1 - \text{area to the left of } -.1$$
$$= 1 - .461 = .539$$

9. Because the P-value $> \alpha$, we fail to reject H_0. There is not sufficient evidence to conclude that the mean time spent in personal use of company technology is greater than 75 minutes per day for this company.

MINITAB could also have been used to carry out the test, as shown in the accompanying output.

T-Test of the Mean
Test of mu = 75.00 vs mu > 75.00

Variable	n	Mean	StDev	SE Mean	t	P
Time	10	74.80	9.45	2.99	-0.07	0.53

Although we had to round the computed t value to $-.1$ to use Appendix Table IV, MINITAB was able to compute the P-value corresponding to the actual value of the test statistic.

Statistical Versus Practical Significance

Carrying out a test amounts to deciding whether the value obtained for the test statistic could plausibly have resulted when H_0 is true. If the value does not deviate too much from what is expected when H_0 is true, there is no compelling reason for rejecting H_0 in favor of H_a. But suppose that the observed value is quite far out in the appropriate tail of the test statistic's sampling distribution when H_0 is true (for example, a large positive value of t when H_a contains the inequality $>$). One could continue to believe that H_0 is true and that such a value arose just through chance variation (a very unusual and "unrepresentative" sample). However, in this case, a more plausible explanation for what was observed is that H_0 is false and H_a is true.

When the value of the test statistic leads to rejection of H_0, it is customary to say that the result is **statistically significant** at the chosen level α. The finding of statistical significance means that, in the investigator's opinion, the observed deviation from what was expected under H_0 cannot plausibly be attributed only to chance variation. However, statistical significance cannot be equated with the conclusion that the true situation differs from what H_0 states in any practical sense. That is, even after H_0 has been rejected, the data may suggest that there is no *practical* difference between the true value of the population characteristic and what the null hypothesis states that value to be.

EXAMPLE 10.17

Let μ denote the true average score on a standardized test for children in a certain region of the United States. The average score for all children in the United States is 100. Regional education authorities are interested in testing

$$H_0: \quad \mu = 100 \quad \text{versus} \quad H_a: \quad \mu > 100$$

using a significance level of .001. A sample of 2500 children resulted in the values

$$n = 2500 \quad \bar{x} = 101.0 \quad s = 15.0$$

Then

$$t = \frac{101.0 - 100}{\dfrac{15}{\sqrt{2500}}} = 3.3$$

This is an upper-tailed test, so (using the z column of Appendix Table IV since df = 2499)

P-value = area to the right of 3.33 = .000

Because P-value < .001, we reject H_0. The true mean score for this region does appear to exceed 100.

However, with $n = 2500$, the point estimate $\bar{x} = 101.0$ is almost surely very close to the true value of μ. So it looks as though H_0 was rejected because $\mu \approx 101$ rather than 100. And, from a practical point of view, a 1-point difference will most likely have no significance. A statistically significant result does not necessarily mean that there are any practical consequences.

Exercises 10.38 – 10.55

10.38 Newly purchased automobile tires of a certain type are supposed to be filled to a pressure of 30 lb/in^2. Let μ denote the true average pressure. Find the P-value associated with each given z statistic value for testing H_0: $\mu = 30$ versus H_a: $\mu \neq 30$ when σ is known.

  a. 2.10 **b.** −1.75 **c.** −.58 **d.** 1.44 **e.** −5.00

10.39 A soda manufacturer is interested in determining whether its bottling machine tends to overfill. Each bottle is supposed to contain 12 oz of fluid. A random sample of size 36 is taken from bottles coming off the production line, and the contents of each bottle are carefully measured. It is found that the mean amount of soda for the sample of bottles is 12.1 oz. Suppose it is known that $\sigma = .2$ oz. The manufacturer will use this information to test H_0: $\mu = 12$ versus H_a: $\mu > 12$. Use the accompanying MINITAB output to answer the following questions.

TEST OF MU = 12.0000 VS MU G.T. 12.0000

	N	MEAN	STDEV	SE MEAN	Z	P VALUE
soda	36	12.1001	0.1999	0.0333	3.00	0.0014

  a. What value does the z test statistic take for this data?
  b. What is the P-value associated with the computed value of z?
  c. If the manufacturer decides on a level .05 test, should H_0 be rejected in favor of the conclusion that the machine is overfilling?

10.40 The desired percentage of silicon dioxide in a certain type of cement is 5.0. A random sample of $n = 36$ specimens gave a sample average percentage of $\bar{x} = 5.21$. Let μ = the true average percentage of silicon dioxide in this type of cement, and suppose σ is known to be .38. Test H_0: $\mu = 5$ versus H_a: $\mu \neq 5$ using a significance level of .01.

10.41 Give as much information as you can about the P-value of a t test in each of the following situations:
  a. Upper-tailed test, df = 8, $t = 2.0$
  b. Upper-tailed test, $n = 14$, $t = 3.2$
  c. Lower-tailed test, df = 10, $t = -2.4$
  d. Lower-tailed test, $n = 22$, $t = -4.2$
  e. Two-tailed test, df = 15, $t = -1.6$
  f. Two-tailed test, $n = 16$, $t = 1.6$
  g. Two-tailed test, $n = 16$, $t = 6.3$

10.42 Give as much information as you can about the P-value of a t test in each of the following situations:
  a. Two-tailed test, df = 9, $t = .73$
  b. Upper-tailed test, df = 10, $t = -.5$
  c. Lower-tailed test, $n = 20$, $t = -2.1$
  d. Lower-tailed test, $n = 20$, $t = -5.1$
  e. Two-tailed test, $n = 40$, $t = 1.7$

10.43 Paint used to paint lines on roads must reflect enough light to be clearly visible at night. Let μ denote the true average reflectometer reading for a new type of paint under consideration. A test of $H_0: \mu = 20$ versus $H_a: \mu > 20$ based on a sample of 15 observations gave $t = 3.2$. What conclusion is appropriate at each of the following significance levels?

    a. $\alpha = .05$ **b.** $\alpha = .01$ **c.** $\alpha = .001$

10.44 A certain pen has been designed so that true average writing lifetime under controlled conditions (involving the use of a writing machine) is at least 10 hours. A random sample of 18 pens is selected, the writing lifetime of each is determined, and a normal probability plot of the resulting data supports the use of a one-sample t test. The relevant hypotheses are $H_0: \mu = 10$ versus $H_a: \mu < 10$.

    a. If $t = -2.3$ and $\alpha = .05$ is selected, what conclusion is appropriate?

    b. If $t = -1.83$ and $\alpha = .01$ is selected, what conclusion is appropriate?

    c. If $t = .47$, what conclusion is appropriate?

10.45 The true average diameter of ball bearings of a certain type is supposed to be .5 in. What conclusion is appropriate when testing $H_0: \mu = .5$ versus $H_a: \mu \neq .5$ in each of the following situations?

    a. $n = 13, t = 1.6, \alpha = .05$

    b. $n = 13, t = -1.6, \alpha = .05$

    c. $n = 25, t = -2.6, \alpha = .01$

    d. $n = 25, t = -3.6$

10.46 There is now broad evidence that stressful work conditions and critical personal characteristics contribute to the development of coronary dysfunction and disease. The article "Job Stressors and Coping Characteristics in Work-Related Disease" (*Work and Stress* (1994): 130–140) reported that, for a random sample of 42 blue-collar workers suffering from ischemic heart disease (IHD), the sample mean systolic blood pressure and sample standard deviation were 145.3 and 17.6, respectively. Suppose that for the population of all blue-collar non-IHD workers, the mean is 138 (a value consistent with information given in the article). Does it appear that true average blue-collar IHD pressure exceeds the non-IHD value? State and test the relevant hypotheses at significance level .01 using the suggested sequence of steps.

10.47 Typically, only very brave students are willing to speak out in a college classroom. Student participation may be especially difficult if the individual is from a different culture or country. The article "An Assessment of Class Participation by International Graduate Students" (*J. of College Student Development* (1995): 132–140) considered a numerical "speaking-up" scale, with possible values from 3 to 15 (a low value means that a student rarely speaks). For a random sample of 64 males from Asian countries where English is not the official language, the sample mean and sample standard deviation were 8.75 and 2.57, respectively. Suppose that the mean for the population of all males having English as their native language is 10.0 (suggested by data in the article). Does it appear that the population mean for males from non–English-speaking Asian countries is smaller than 10.0? Employ the sequence of nine steps to analyze the data and reach a conclusion.

10.48 Are young women delaying marriage and marrying at a later age? This question was addressed in a report issued by the Census Bureau (Associated Press, June 8, 1991). The report stated that in 1970 (based on census results) the mean age of brides marrying for the first time was 20.8 years. In 1990 (based on a sample, since census results were not yet available), the mean was 23.9. Suppose that the 1990 sample mean had been based on a random sample of size 100 and that the sample standard deviation was 6.4. Is there sufficient evidence to support the claim that women are now marrying later in life? Test the relevant hypotheses using $\alpha = .01$. (*Note*: It is probably not reasonable to think that the distribution of age at first marriage is normal in shape.)

10.49 In the article "Religious Outlook, Culture War Politics, and Antipathy Toward Christian Fundamentalists" (*Public Opinion Quarterly* (1999): 29–61), it is stated that nonfundamentalists have negative feelings overall toward Christian fundamentalists. The data offered to support this claim is that the mean "temperature" rating given to Christian fundamentalists for a random sample of 960 nonfundamentalists is 47 degrees (higher temperatures mean more approval). The sample standard deviation is 21. Test the hypothesis that the mean rating given by all nonfundamentalists to Christian fundamentalists is below 57 (the average rating given across all religious, racial, and political groups).

10.50 In recent years, female athletes have been identified as a population particularly at risk for developing eating disorders. The article "Disordered Eating in Female Collegiate Gymnasts" (*J. of Sport and Exercise Psychology* (1993): 424–436) reported that for a sample of 17 gymnasts who were classified as binge eaters, the sample mean difference between current weight and ideal weight was 6.65 lb. The accompanying boxplot is based on data consistent with this information; the sample standard deviation is 2.97 lb. Suppose that the true average weight difference for female gymnasts with normal eating habits is 4.5 lb (a value suggested in the article).

a. Does the boxplot indicate that μ, the true average weight difference for bingers, exceeds the value for normal eaters?

b. Carry out a test of the hypotheses suggested in part **a.**

10.51 An article titled "Teen Boys Forget Whatever it Was" appeared in the Australian newspaper *The Mercury* (April 21, 1997). It describes a study of academic performance and attention span, and reports that the mean time to distraction for teenage boys working on an independent task was 4 minutes. Although the sample size was not given in the article, suppose that this mean was based on a random sample of 50 teenage Australian boys and that the sample standard deviation was 1.4 min. Does this data provide convincing evidence that the average attention span for teenage boys is less than 5 minutes? Test the relevant hypotheses using $\alpha = .01$.

10.52 According to the article "Workaholism in Organizations: Gender Differences" (*Sex Roles* (1999): 333–346), the following data was reported on 1996 income for random samples of male and female MBA graduates from a certain Canadian business school:

	n	$\bar{x}$	s
Males	258	$133,442	$131,090
Females	233	$105,156	$98,525

(*Note:* These salary figures are in Canadian dollars.)

a. Test the hypothesis that the mean salary of a male MBA grad from this school was in excess of $100,000 in 1996.

b. Is there convincing evidence that the mean salary for all female MBA grads is above $100,000? Test using $\alpha = .10$.

c. If a significance level of .05 or .01 were used instead of .05 in the test of part **b,** would you still reach the same conclusion? Explain.

10.53 Many consumers pay careful attention to stated nutritional contents on packaged foods when making purchases. It is therefore important that the information on packages be accurate. A random sample of $n = 12$ frozen dinners of a certain type was selected from production during a particular period, and the calorie content of each one was determined. (This determination entails destroying the product, so a census would certainly not be desirable!) Here are the resulting observations, along with a boxplot and normal probability plot.

255	244	239	242	265	245
259	248	225	226	251	233

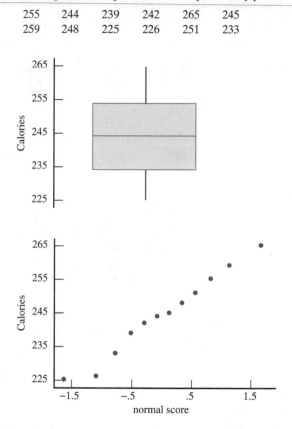

a. Is it reasonable to test hypotheses about true average calorie content μ by using a t test?

b. The stated calorie content is 240. Does the boxplot suggest that true average content differs from the stated value? Explain your reasoning.

c. Carry out a formal test of the hypotheses suggested in part **b.**

10.54 Much concern has been expressed in recent years regarding the practice of using nitrates as meat preservatives. In one study involving possible effects of these chemicals, bacteria cultures were grown in a medium containing nitrates. The rate of uptake of radio-labeled amino acid was then determined for each one, yielding the accompanying observations:

| 7251 | 6871 | 9632 | 6866 | 9094 | 5849 | 8957 | 7978 |
| 7064 | 7494 | 7883 | 8178 | 7523 | 8724 | 7468 |

Suppose that it is known that true average uptake for cultures without nitrates is 8000. Does the data suggest that the addition of nitrates results in a decrease in true average uptake? Test the appropriate hypotheses using a significance level of .10. Be sure to state any assumptions that are necessary to validate the use of your test.

10.55 The times of first sprinkler activation (sec) for a series of tests of fire-prevention sprinkler systems that use an aqueous film-forming foam were as follows:

| 27 | 41 | 22 | 27 | 23 | 35 | 30 |
| 33 | 24 | 27 | 28 | 22 | 24 | |

("Use of AFFF in Sprinkler Systems," *Fire Tech.* (1976): 5). The system has been designed so that the true average activation time is supposed to be at most 25 sec. Does the data strongly indicate that the design specifications have not been met?

a. Test the relevant hypotheses using a significance level of .05. What assumptions, if any, are you making about the distribution of activation times?

b. MINITAB was used to test H_0: $\mu = 25$ versus H_a: $\mu > 25$. Is the output consistent with your calculations in part **a**?

TEST OF MU = 25.000 VS MU G.T. 25.000

	N	MEAN	STDEV	SE MEAN	T	P VALUE
time	13	27.923	5.619	1.559	1.88	0.043

10.5 Power and Probability of Type II Error

In this chapter, we have introduced test procedures for testing hypotheses about a population characteristic. What characterizes a "good" test procedure? It makes sense to think that a good test procedure is one that has both a small probability of rejecting H_0 when it is true (a type I error) and a high probability of rejecting H_0 when it is false. The test procedures presented in this chapter allow us to directly control the probability of rejecting a true H_0 by our choice of the significance level, α. But what about the probability of rejecting H_0 when it is false? As we will see, several factors influence this probability. Let's begin by considering an example.

Suppose that the student body president at a university is interested in studying the amount of money that students spend on textbooks each semester. The director of the Financial Aid Office believes that the average amount spent on books is $300 per semester and uses this figure in determining the amount of financial aid for which a student is eligible. The student body president plans to ask each individual in a random sample of students how much he or she spent on books this semester and has decided to use the resulting data to test

$$H_0: \quad \mu = 300 \quad \text{versus} \quad H_a: \quad \mu > 300$$

using a significance level of .05. If the true mean is 300 (or less than 300), the correct decision would be to fail to reject the null hypothesis (incorrectly rejecting the null hypothesis would be a type I error). On the other hand, if the true mean is 325 or 310 or even 301, the correct decision would be to reject the null hypothesis (not rejecting would be a type II error). How likely is it that the null hypothesis will, in fact, be rejected? If the true mean is 301, the probability that we will reject H_0: $\mu = 300$ is not very great. This is because when we carry out the test, we are essentially looking at the sample mean and asking, Does this look like what we would have

FIGURE 10.6 Sampling distribution of $\bar{x}$ when $\mu =$ 300, 305, and 325

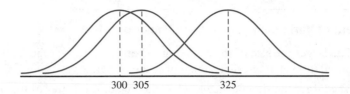

300 305   325

expected to see if the population mean were 300? As illustrated in Figure 10.6, if the true mean is greater than, but very close to, 300, chances are that the sample mean will look pretty much like what we would have expected to see if the population mean had been 300, and we will be unconvinced that the null hypothesis should be rejected. If the true mean is 325, it is less likely that the sample will be mistaken for a sample from a population with mean 300; sample means will tend to cluster around 325, and so it is more likely that we will correctly reject H_0. If the true mean is 350, rejection of H_0 is even more likely.

When we consider the probability of rejecting the null hypothesis, we are looking at what statisticians refer to as the **power** of the test.

The **power of a test** is the probability of rejecting the null hypothesis.

From the previous discussion, it should be apparent that the power of the test when a hypothesis about a population mean is being tested depends on the true value of the population mean, μ. Because the true value of μ is unknown (if we knew the value of μ, we wouldn't be doing the hypothesis test!), we cannot know what the power is for the actual true value of μ. It is possible, however, to gain some insight into the power of a test by looking at a number of "what if" scenarios. For example, we might ask, What is the power if the true mean is 325?, What is the power if the true mean is 310?, and so on. That is, we can calculate the power at $\mu = 325$, the power at $\mu = 310$, and at any other value of interest.

Although it is technically possible to consider power when the null hypothesis is true, an investigator is usually concerned about the power only at values for which the null hypothesis is false. In general, when testing a hypothesis about a population characteristic, there are three factors that influence the power of the test:

1. The size of the difference between the true value of the population characteristic and the hypothesized value (the value that appears in the null hypothesis)

2. The choice of significance level, α, for the test

3. The sample size

The effect of each of these factors on the power of a test is described in the accompanying box.

Effect of Various Factors on the Power of a Test

1. The larger the size of the discrepancy between the hypothesized value and the true value of the population characteristic, the higher the power.
2. The larger the significance level, α, the higher the power of the test.
3. The larger the sample size, the higher the power of the test.

Let's consider each of these three statements. The first has already been discussed in the context of the textbook example. Since power is the probability of rejecting the null hypothesis, it makes sense that power will be higher when the true value of a population characteristic is very different from the hypothesized value than when it is close to it.

The effect of significance level on power is not quite as obvious. To understand the relationship between power and significance level, it helps to see the relationship between power and β, the probability of a type II error.

When H_0 is false, power $= 1 - \beta$.

This relationship follows from the definitions of power and type II error. A type II error results from *not* rejecting a false H_0. Since power is the probability of rejecting H_0, it follows that *when H_0 is false*

power $=$ probability of rejecting a false H_0
$\qquad = 1 -$ probability of not rejecting a false H_0
$\qquad = 1 - \beta$

Recall from Section 10.2 that the choice of α, the type I error probability, affects the value of β, the type II error probability. Choosing a larger value for α results in a smaller value for β (and thus a larger value for $1 - \beta$). In terms of power, this means that choosing a larger value for α results in a larger value for the power of the test. That is, the larger the type I error probability we are willing to tolerate, the more likely it is that the test will be able to detect any particular departure from H_0.

The third factor that affects the power of a test is the sample size. When H_0 is false, the power of a test is the probability that we will "detect" that it is false and, based on the observed sample, reject H_0. Intuition suggests that we will be more likely to detect a departure from H_0 with a large sample than with a small sample. This is in fact the case — the larger the sample size, the higher the power.

Consider testing the hypotheses presented previously:

H_0: $\mu = 300$ versus H_a: $\mu > 300$

These observations about power imply the following, for example:

1. The power of a test based on a sample of size 100 will be higher than the power of a test based on a sample of size 75 (assuming the same significance level).

2. The power of a test using a significance level of .05 will be higher than the power of a test using a significance level of .01 (assuming the same sample size).

3. The power of the test will be greater if the true mean is 350 than if the true mean is 325 (assuming the same sample size and significance level).

As was mentioned previously in this section, it is impossible to calculate the *actual* power of a test because in practice we do not know the true value of population characteristics. However, we can evaluate the power at a selected alternative value if we want to know whether the power would be high or low if this were in fact the true value.

The following optional subsection shows how type II error probabilities and power can be evaluated for selected tests.

Calculating Power and Type II Error Probabilities for Selected Tests (Optional)

The test procedures presented in this chapter are designed to control the probability of a type I error (rejecting H_0 when H_0 is true) at the desired level α. However, little has been said so far about calculating the value of β, the probability of a type II error (not rejecting H_0 when H_0 is false). Here we consider the determination of β and power for the hypothesis tests previously introduced.

When we carry out a hypothesis test, we specify the desired value of α, the probability of a type I error. The probability of a type II error, β, is the probability of not rejecting H_0 even though it is false. Suppose we are testing

$$H_0: \quad \mu = 1.5 \qquad \text{versus} \qquad H_a: \quad \mu > 1.5$$

Since we do not know the true value of μ, we cannot calculate the actual value of β. However, the vulnerability of the test to type II error can be investigated by calculating β for several different values of μ, such as $\mu = 1.55$, $\mu = 1.6$, and $\mu = 1.7$. Once the value of β has been determined, the power of the test at the corresponding alternative value is just $1 - \beta$.

EXAMPLE 10.18

A cigarette manufacturer claims that the mean nicotine content of its cigarettes is 1.5 mg. We might investigate this claim by testing

$$H_0: \quad \mu = 1.5 \qquad \text{versus} \qquad H_a: \quad \mu > 1.5$$

where μ = true mean nicotine content. A random sample of $n = 36$ cigarettes is to be selected and the resulting data used to reach a conclusion. Suppose that the standard deviation of nicotine content (σ) is known to be .20 mg and that a significance level of .01 is to be used. Our test statistic is (since $\sigma = .20$)

$$z = \frac{\bar{x} - 1.5}{\dfrac{.20}{\sqrt{n}}} = \frac{\bar{x} - 1.5}{\dfrac{.20}{\sqrt{36}}} = \frac{\bar{x} - 1.5}{.0333}$$

The inequality in H_a implies that

P-value = area under z curve to the right of calculated z

From Appendix Table II, it is easily verified that the z critical value 2.33 captures an upper-tail z curve area of .01. Thus, rejecting H_0 if P-value $\leq$ .01 is equivalent to the decision rule

reject H_0 if calculated $z \geq 2.33$

This becomes

reject H_0 if $\dfrac{\bar{x} - 1.5}{.0333} \geq 2.33$

Solving this inequality for $\bar{x}$, we get

$\bar{x} \geq 1.5 + 2.33(.0333)$

or

$\bar{x} \geq 1.578$

So if $\bar{x} \geq 1.578$, we will reject H_0, and if $\bar{x} < 1.578$, we will fail to reject H_0. This decision rule corresponds to $\alpha = .01$.

Suppose now that $\mu = 1.6$ (H_0 is false). A type II error will then occur if $\bar{x} < 1.578$. What is the probability that this occurs? If $\mu = 1.6$, the sampling distribution of $\bar{x}$ is approximately normal, centered at 1.6, and has a standard deviation of .0333. The probability of observing an $\bar{x}$ value less than 1.578 can then be determined by finding an area under a normal curve with mean 1.6 and standard deviation .0333, as illustrated in Figure 10.7.

Since this is not the standard normal (z) curve, we must first convert to a z score before using Appendix Table II to find the area. Here,

z score for $1.578 = \dfrac{1.578 - \mu_{\bar{x}}}{\sigma_{\bar{x}}} = \dfrac{1.578 - 1.6}{.0333} = -.66$

and

area under z curve to left of $-.66 = .2546$

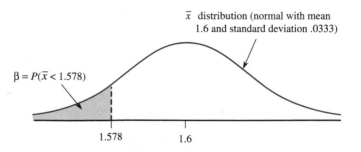

FIGURE 10.7 β when $\mu = 1.6$ in Example 10.18

So, if $\mu = 1.6$, $\beta = .2546$. This means that if μ is 1.6, about 25% of all samples would result in $\bar{x}$ values less than 1.578 and failure to reject H_0.

The power of the test at $\mu = 1.6$ is then

$$(\text{power at } \mu = 1.6) = 1 - (\beta \text{ when } \mu \text{ is } 1.6)$$
$$= 1 - .2546$$
$$= .7454$$

Thus, if the true mean is 1.6, the probability of rejecting H_0: $\mu = 1.5$ in favor of H_a: $\mu > 1.5$ is .7454. That is, if μ is 1.6 and the test is used repeatedly with random samples selected from the population, in the long run about 75% of the samples will result in the correct conclusion to reject H_0.

Now consider β and power when $\mu = 1.65$. The normal curve in Figure 10.7 would then be centered at 1.65. Since β is the area to the left of 1.578 and the curve has shifted to the right, β decreases. Converting 1.578 to a z score and using Appendix Table II gives $\beta = .0154$. Also

$$(\text{power at } \mu = 1.65) = 1 - .0154 = .9846$$

As expected, the power at $\mu = 1.65$ is higher than the power at $\mu = 1.6$ because 1.65 is farther from the hypothesized value of 1.5.

MINITAB will calculate power for specified values of σ, α, n, and the difference between the true and hypothesized value of μ. The accompanying output shows power calculations corresponding to those in Example 10.18.

1-Sample Z Test

Testing mean = null (versus > null)
Alpha = 0.01   Sigma = 0.2   Sample Size = 36

Difference	Power
0.10	0.7497
0.15	0.9851

The probability of a type II error and power for z tests concerning a population proportion is calculated in an analogous manner.

EXAMPLE 10.19

A package delivery service advertises that at least 90% of all packages brought to its office by 9 A.M. for delivery in the same city are delivered by noon that day. Let π denote the proportion of all such packages actually delivered by noon. The hypotheses of interest are

$$H_0: \quad \pi = .9 \quad \text{versus} \quad H_a: \quad \pi < .9$$

where the alternative hypothesis states that the company's claim is untrue. The value $\pi = .8$ represents a substantial departure from the company's claim. If the hypotheses are tested at level .01 using a sample of $n = 225$ packages, what is the probability that the departure from H_0 represented by this alternative value will go undetected?

At significance level .01, H_0 is rejected if P-value $\le .01$. For the case of a lower-tailed test, this is the same as rejecting H_0 if

$$z = \frac{p - \mu_p}{\sigma_p} = \frac{p - .9}{\sqrt{\frac{(.9)(.1)}{225}}} = \frac{p - .9}{.02} \le -2.33$$

(Since -2.33 captures a lower-tail z curve area of .01, the smallest 1% of all z values satisfy $z \le -2.33$.) This inequality is equivalent to $p \le .853$, so H_0 will *not* be rejected if $p > .853$. When $\pi = .8$, p has approximately a normal distribution with

$$\mu_p = .8 \qquad \sigma_p = \sqrt{\frac{(.8)(.2)}{225}} = .0267$$

Then β is the probability of obtaining a sample proportion greater than .853, as illustrated in Figure 10.8.

FIGURE 10.8 β when $\pi = .8$ in Example 10.19

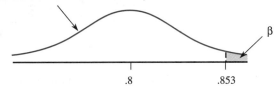

Sampling distribution of p (normal with mean .8 and standard deviation .0267)

β

.8   .853

Converting to a z score results in

$$z = \frac{.853 - .8}{.0267} = 1.99$$

and Appendix Table II gives

$$\beta = 1 - .9767 = .0233$$

When $\pi = .8$ and a level .01 test is used, less than 3% of all samples of size $n = 225$ will result in a type II error. The power of the test at $\pi = .8$ is $1 - .0233 = .9767$. This means that the probability of rejecting H_0: $\pi = .9$ in favor of H_a: $\pi < .9$ when π is really .8 is .9767, which is quite high.

β and Power for the t Test (Optional)

Power and β values for t tests can be determined by using a set of graphs specially constructed for this purpose. As with the z test, the value of β depends not only on the true value of μ, but also on the selected significance level α; β increases as α is made smaller. In addition, β depends on the number of degrees of freedom, $n - 1$. For any fixed level α, it should be easier for the test to detect a specific departure from H_0 when n is large than when n is small. This is indeed the case; for a fixed alternative value, β decreases as $n - 1$ increases.

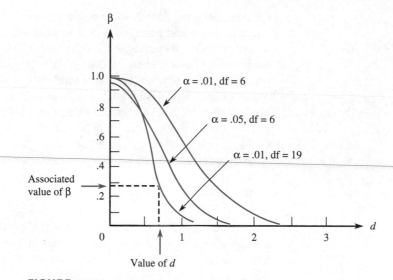

FIGURE 10.9 β curves for the one-tailed t test

Unfortunately, there is one other quantity on which β depends: the population standard deviation σ. As σ increases, so does $\sigma_{\bar{x}}$. This in turn makes it more likely that an $\bar{x}$ value far from μ will be observed, resulting in an erroneous conclusion. Once α is specified and n is fixed, the determination of β at a particular alternative value of μ requires that a value of σ be chosen, since each different value of σ yields a different value of β. (This did not present a problem with the z test because when using a z test the value of σ is known.) If the investigator can specify a range of plausible values for σ, then using the largest such value will give a pessimistic β (one on the high side) and a pessimistic value of power (one on the low side).

Figure 10.9 shows three different β curves for a one-tailed t test (appropriate for $H_a\colon \mu >$ hypothesized value or for $H_a\colon \mu <$ hypothesized value). A more complete set of curves for both one- and two-tailed tests when $\alpha = .05$ and when $\alpha = .01$ appears in Appendix Table V. To determine β, first compute the quantity

$$d = \frac{|\text{alternative value} - \text{hypothesized value}|}{\sigma}$$

Then locate d on the horizontal axis, move directly up to the curve for $n - 1$ df, and move over to the vertical axis to read β.

EXAMPLE 10.20   Consider testing

$$H_0\colon \quad \mu = 100 \qquad \text{versus} \qquad H_a\colon \quad \mu > 100$$

and focus on the alternative value $\mu = 110$. Suppose that $\sigma = 10$, the sample size is $n = 7$, and a significance level of .01 has been selected. For $\sigma = 10$,

$$d = \frac{|110 - 100|}{10} = \frac{10}{10} = 1$$

Figure 10.9 (using df $= 7 - 1 = 6$) gives $\beta \approx .6$. The interpretation is that if $\sigma = 10$ and a level .01 test based on $n = 7$ is used when $\mu = 110$ (and thus H_0 is false), roughly 60% of all samples will result in erroneously not rejecting H_0! Equivalently, the power of the test at $\mu = 110$ is only $1 - .6 = .4$. The probability of rejecting H_0 when $\mu = 110$ is not very large. If a level .05 test is used instead, then $\beta \approx .3$, which is still rather large. Using a level .01 test with $n = 20$ (df $= 19$) yields, from Figure 10.9, $\beta \approx .05$. At the alternative value $\mu = 110$, for $\sigma = 10$ the level .01 test based on $n = 20$ has smaller β than the level .05 test with $n = 7$. Substantially increasing n counterbalances using the smaller α.

Now consider the alternative $\mu = 105$, again with $\sigma = 10$, so that

$$d = \frac{|105 - 100|}{10} = \frac{5}{10} = .5$$

Then from Figure 10.9, $\beta \approx .95$ when $\alpha = .01, n = 7$; $\beta \approx .7$ when $\alpha = .05, n = 7$; and $\beta \approx .65$ when $\alpha = .01, n = 20$. These values of β are all quite large; with $\sigma = 10$, $\mu = 105$ is too close to the hypothesized value of 100 for any of these three tests to have a good chance of detecting such a departure from H_0. A substantial decrease in β necessitates using a much larger sample size. For example, from Table V, $\beta \approx .08$ when $\alpha = .05$ and $n = 40$.

The curves in Figure 10.9 also give β when testing $H_0: \mu = 100$ versus $H_a: \mu < 100$. If the alternative value $\mu = 90$ is of interest and $\sigma = 10$,

$$d = \frac{|90 - 100|}{10} = \frac{10}{10} = 1$$

and values of β are the same as those given in the first paragraph of this example.

Since curves for only selected degrees of freedom appear in Table V, other degrees of freedom require a visual approximation. For example, the 27-df curve (for $n = 28$) would lie between the 19- and 29-df curves, which do appear, and it would be closer to the latter. This type of approximation is adequate because it is the general magnitude of β—large, small, or moderate—that is of primary concern.

It is also possible to use MINITAB to evaluate power for the t test. For example, the accompanying output shows MINITAB calculations for power at $\mu = 110$ for samples sized 7 and 20 when $\alpha = .01$. The corresponding approximate values from Table V found in Example 10.20 are fairly close to the MINITAB values.

1-Sample t Test

Testing mean = null (versus > null)
Calculating power for mean = null + 10
Alpha = 0.01   Sigma = 10

Sample Size	Power
7	0.3968
20	0.9653

The β curves in Table V are those for t tests. When the alternative corresponds to a value of d relatively close to zero, β for a t test may be rather large. One might ask whether there is another type of test that has the same level of significance α as does the t test and smaller values of β. The following result provides the answer to this question.

When the population distribution is normal, the t test for testing hypotheses about μ has smaller β than does any other test procedure that has the same level of significance α.

Stated another way, among all tests with level of significance α, the t test makes β as small as it can possibly be. In this sense, the t test is a best test. Statisticians have also shown that when the population distribution is not too far from a normal distribution, no test procedure can improve on the t test (have the same α and substantially smaller β) by very much. But when the population distribution is believed to be very nonnormal (heavy-tailed, highly skewed, or multimodal), the t test should not be used. Then it's time to consult your friendly neighborhood statistician, who could provide you with alternative methods of analysis.

Exercises 10.56 – 10.62

10.56 The power of a test is influenced by the sample size and the choice of significance level.
  a. Explain how increasing the sample size affects the power (when significance level is held fixed).
  b. Explain how increasing the significance level affects the power (when sample size is held fixed).

10.57 Water samples are taken from water used for cooling as it is being discharged from a power plant into a river. It has been determined that as long as the mean temperature of the discharged water is at most 150°F, there will be no negative effects on the river ecosystem. To investigate whether the plant is in compliance with regulations that prohibit a mean discharge water temperature above 150°, 50 water samples will be taken at randomly selected times, and the water temperature of each sample will be recorded. A z statistic

$$z = \frac{\bar{x} - 150}{\dfrac{\sigma}{\sqrt{n}}}$$

will then be used to decide between the hypotheses

$$H_0: \quad \mu = 150 \quad \text{and} \quad H_a: \quad \mu > 150$$

where μ is the true mean temperature of discharged water. Assume that σ is known to be 10.
  a. Explain why use of the z statistic would be appropriate in this setting.
  b. Describe type I and type II errors in this context.
  c. The rejection of H_0 when $z \geq 1.8$ corresponds to what value of α? (That is, what is the area under the z curve to the right of 1.8?)
  d. Suppose that the true value for μ is 153 and that H_0 is to be rejected if $z \geq 1.8$. Draw a sketch (similar to that of Figure 10.7) of the sampling distribution of $\bar{x}$, and shade the region that would represent β, the probability of making a type II error.
  e. For the hypotheses and test procedure described, compute the value of β when $\mu = 153$.
  f. For the hypotheses and test procedure described, what value would β take if $\mu = 160$?
  g. If H_0 is rejected when $z \geq 1.8$ and $\bar{x} = 152.4$, what is the appropriate conclusion? What type of error might have been made in reaching this conclusion?

10.58 Let μ denote the true average lifetime for a certain type of pen under controlled laboratory conditions.

A test of $H_0: \mu = 10$ versus $H_a: \mu < 10$ will be based on a sample of size 36. Suppose that σ is known to be .6, from which $\sigma_{\bar{x}} = .1$. The appropriate test statistic is then

$$z = \frac{\bar{x} - 10}{.1}$$

a. What is α for the test procedure that rejects H_0 if $z \le -1.28$?

b. If the test procedure of part **a** is used, calculate β when $\mu = 9.8$, and interpret this error probability.

c. Without doing any calculation, explain how β when $\mu = 9.5$ compares to β when $\mu = 9.8$. Then verify your assertion by computing β when $\mu = 9.5$.

d. What is the power of the test when $\mu = 9.8$? When $\mu = 9.5$?

10.59 The city council in a large city has become concerned about the trend toward exclusion of renters with children in apartments within the city. The housing coordinator has decided to select a random sample of 125 apartments and determine for each whether children would be permitted. Let π be the true proportion of apartments that prohibit children. If π exceeds .75, the city council will consider appropriate legislation.

a. If 102 of the 125 sampled exclude renters with children, would a level .05 test lead you to the conclusion that more than 75% of all apartments exclude children?

b. What is the power of the test when $\pi = .8$ and $\alpha = .05$?

10.60 The amount of shaft wear after a fixed mileage was determined for each of seven randomly selected internal combustion engines, resulting in a mean of .0372 in and a standard deviation of .0125 in.

a. Assuming that the distribution of shaft wear is normal, test at level .05 the hypotheses $H_0: \mu = .035$ versus

$H_a: \mu > .035$.

b. Using $\sigma = .0125$, $\alpha = .05$, and Table V, what is the value of β, the probability of a type II error, when $\mu = .04$?

c. What is the power of the test when $\mu = .04$ and $\alpha = .05$?

10.61 Optical fibers are used in telecommunications to transmit light. Current technology allows production of fibers that will transmit light about 50 km (*Research at Rensselaer,* 1984). Researchers are trying to develop a new type of glass fiber that will increase this distance. In evaluating a new fiber, it would be of interest to test $H_0: \mu = 50$ versus $H_a: \mu > 50$, with μ denoting the true average transmission distance for the new optical fiber.

a. Assuming $\sigma = 10$ and $n = 10$, use Table V to find β, the probability of a type II error, for each of the given alternative values of μ when a level .05 test is employed.

   i. 52   **ii.** 55   **iii.** 60   **iv.** 70

b. What happens to β in each of the cases in part **a** if σ is actually larger than 10? Explain your reasoning.

10.62 Let μ denote the true average diameter for bearings of a certain type. A test of $H_0: \mu = .5$ versus $H_a: \mu \ne .5$ will be based on a sample of n bearings. The diameter distribution is believed to be normal. Determine the value of β in each of the following cases:

a. $n = 15$, $\alpha = .05$, $\sigma = .02$, $\mu = .52$
b. $n = 15$, $\alpha = .05$, $\sigma = .02$, $\mu = .48$
c. $n = 15$, $\alpha = .01$, $\sigma = .02$, $\mu = .52$
d. $n = 15$, $\alpha = .05$, $\sigma = .02$, $\mu = .54$
e. $n = 15$, $\alpha = .05$, $\sigma = .04$, $\mu = .54$
f. $n = 20$, $\alpha = .05$, $\sigma = .04$, $\mu = .54$
g. Is the way in which β changes as $n, \alpha, \sigma,$ and μ vary consistent with your intuition? Explain.

10.6   Interpreting the Results of Statistical Analyses

The step-by-step procedure that we have proposed for testing hypotheses provides a systematic approach for carrying out a complete test. However, when the results of such a test are reported in a journal article, it is common to find only the value of the test statistic and the associated P-value accompanying the discussion of conclusions drawn from the data analyzed. When a statistical computer package is used to perform a hypothesis test, the output generally includes the value of the test statistic and the P-value, leaving the rest of the analysis and interpretation to the user.

For example, the article "Forgeries Found on Jackson Petition" (*Austin American Statesman,* Jan. 23, 1988) indicates that forgeries were discovered on nominating petitions submitted to qualify Jesse Jackson for the 1988 Texas presidential primary. Five thousand valid signatures were required to qualify for the ballot, and 8500 signatures were submitted. However, because of the reported forgeries, it was unclear whether enough valid signatures were submitted. Jackson would qualify for the ballot as long as the proportion of valid signatures was greater than $5000/8500 = .588$. A sample of size 162 was randomly selected from the names that appeared on the petition, and 46 of the 162 individuals selected denied signing the petition. The article states that Jackson's spokesperson was sure that "the petition contained at least 5000 valid signatures." Is this a reasonable conclusion based on the sample data?

The z test for a population proportion would be appropriate for testing

$$H_0: \quad \pi = .588 \qquad \text{versus} \qquad H_a: \quad \pi > .588$$

where π represents the true proportion of valid signatures on the petition. Typical computer output for this test follows.

Test for One Proportion
Test of p = 0.588 vs p > 0.588

Sample	X	N	Sample p	Z-Value	P-Value
1	116	162	0.716049	3.31	0.0005

The stated P-value would lead to the rejection of H_0 for any $\alpha > .0005$, and so the data supports the statement by Jackson's spokesperson.

What to Look for in Published Data

Here are some questions to consider when you are reading a report that contains the results of a hypothesis test.

- What hypotheses are being tested? Are the hypotheses about a population mean, a population proportion, or some other population characteristic?
- Was the appropriate test used? Does the validity of the test depend on any assumptions about the population sampled? If so, are the assumptions reasonable?
- What is the P-value associated with the test? What is the significance level selected for the test? Is the chosen significance level reasonable?
- Are the conclusions drawn consistent with the results of the hypothesis test?

For example, consider the following statement (based on information in the article "Serum Transferrin Receptor for the Detection of Iron Deficiency in Pregnancy," *Amer. J. Clinical Nutrition* (1991): 1077–1081):

In a total sample of 176 pregnant women, mean serum receptor concentration did not differ significantly from 5.63, the mean for women who are not pregnant ($P > 0.10$).

The statement does not indicate what test was performed or what the value of the test statistics was. It appears that the hypotheses of interest are

$$H_0: \quad \mu = 5.63 \qquad \text{versus} \qquad H_a: \quad \mu \neq 5.63$$

where μ represents the true mean serum receptor concentration for pregnant women. Since the sample size is large, if the sample can be considered a random sample the one-sample t test would be appropriate. With the large sample size, no assumptions about the shape of the population distribution of serum receptor concentration values is necessary. Because the reported P-value is so large (P-value > .10), there is no reason to reject H_0. We cannot conclude that the mean for pregnant women differs from the known mean of 5.63 for women who are not pregnant.

Summary of Key Concepts and Formulas

Term or Formula	Comment
Hypothesis	A claim about the value of a population characteristic.
Null hypothesis, H_0	The hypothesis initially assumed to be true. It has the form H_0: population characteristic = hypothesized value.
Alternative hypothesis, H_a	A hypothesis that specifies a claim that is contradictory to H_0 and is judged the more plausible claim when H_0 is rejected.
Type I error	Rejection of H_0 when H_0 is true; the probability of a type I error is denoted by α and is referred to as the significance level for the test.
Type II error	Nonrejection of H_0 when H_0 is false; the probability of a type II error is denoted by β.
Test statistic	The quantity computed from sample data and used to make a decision between H_0 and H_a.
P-value	The probability, computed assuming H_0 to be true, of obtaining a value of the test statistic at least as contradictory to H_0 as what actually resulted. H_0 is rejected if P-value $\leq \alpha$ and not rejected if P-value $> \alpha$, where α is the chosen significance level.
$z = \dfrac{p - \text{hypothesized value}}{\sqrt{\dfrac{(\text{hyp. val})(1 - \text{hyp. val})}{n}}}$	A test statistic for testing H_0: π = hypothesized value when the sample size is large. The P-value is determined from the z curve.
$z = \dfrac{\bar{x} - \text{hypothesized value}}{\dfrac{\sigma}{\sqrt{n}}}$	A test statistic for testing H_0: μ = hypothesized value when σ is known and either the population distribution is normal or the sample size is large. The P-value is determined from the z curve.
$t = \dfrac{\bar{x} - \text{hypothesized value}}{\dfrac{s}{\sqrt{n}}}$	A test statistic for testing H_0: μ = hypothesized value when σ is unknown and either the population distribution is normal or the sample size is large. The P-value is determined from the t curve with df $= (n - 1)$.
Power	The power of a test is the probability of rejecting the null hypothesis. Power is affected by the size of the difference between the hypothesized value and the true value, the sample size, and the significance level.

Supplementary Exercises 10.63 – 10.75

10.63   When a published article reports the results of many hypothesis tests, the *P*-values are not usually given. Instead, the following type of coding scheme is frequently used ("Hostility in Depression," *Psychological Reports* (1994): 1391–1401): $*p < .05, ^\dagger p < .01, ^\ddagger p < .001,$ $^a p < .0001$. Which of the symbols would be used to code for each of the following *P*-values?

    a. .037   **b.** .0026   **c.** .072   **d.** .0003

10.64   A random sample of $n = 44$ individuals with a B.S. degree in accounting who had started with a "Big Eight" accounting firm and subsequently changed jobs resulted in a sample mean time to change of 35.02 months and a sample standard deviation of 18.94 months ("The Debate Over Post-Baccalaureate Education: One University's Experience," *Issues in Accounting Educ.* (1992): 18–36). Can it be concluded that the true average time to change exceeds 2 years? Test the appropriate hypotheses using a significance level of .01.

10.65   What motivates companies to offer stock ownership plans to their employees? In a random sample of 87 companies having such plans, 54 said that the primary rationale was tax-related ("The Advantages and Disadvantages of ESOPs: A Long-Range Analysis," *J. of Small Business Management* (1991): 15–21). Does this information provide strong support for concluding that more than half of all such firms feel this way?

10.66   Sixty-five randomly selected clerical workers at a large financial service organization participated in a health risk analysis, and the resulting data was summarized in the article "Workplace Stress and Indicators of Coronary-Disease Risk" (*Academy of Mgmt. J.* (1988): 686–698). For systolic blood pressure, the sample mean and standard deviation were 111.63 and 11.94, respectively. Is there sufficient evidence to conclude that the mean systolic blood pressure for all clerical workers at this business exceeds 110? Test the relevant hypotheses using a .01 significance level.

10.67   The article "Caffeine Knowledge, Attitudes, and Consumption in Adult Women" (*J. of Nutrition Educ.* (1992): 179–184) reported the following summary data on daily caffeine consumption for a random sample of adult women:

$$n = 47 \qquad \bar{x} = 215 \text{ mg} \qquad s = 235 \text{ mg} \qquad \text{range: 5 to 1176}$$

   a. Does it appear plausible that the population distribution of daily caffeine consumption is normal? Is it necessary to assume a normal population distribution to test hypotheses about the value of the population mean consumption? Explain your reasoning.

   b. Suppose that it had previously been believed that mean consumption was at most 200 mg. Does the given data contradict this prior belief? Test the appropriate hypotheses at significance level .10.

10.68   A standard method for recovering minerals and metals from biological materials results in a mean copper recovery of 63 ppm when used to treat oyster tissue. A new treatment method was described in the article "Simple Sample Digestion of Sewage and Sludge for Multi-Element Analysis" (*J. Environ. Sci. and Health* (1984): 959–972). Suppose that this new treatment is used to treat $n = 40$ bits of oyster tissue, resulting in a sample mean copper recovery and a sample standard deviation of 62.6 ppm and 3.7 ppm, respectively. Is there evidence to suggest that the mean copper recovery is lower for the new method than for the standard one? Use a .01 significance level.

10.69   Past experience has indicated that the true response rate is 40% when individuals are approached with a request to fill out and return a particular questionnaire in a stamped and addressed envelope. An investigator believes that if the person distributing the questionnaire is stigmatized in some obvious way, potential respondents would feel sorry for the distributor and thus tend to respond at a rate higher than 40%. To investigate this theory, a distributor is fitted with an eyepatch. Of the 200 questionnaires distributed by this individual, 109 were returned. Does this strongly suggest that the response rate in this situation does exceed the rate in the past? State and test the appropriate hypotheses at significance level .05.

10.70   An automobile manufacturer who wishes to advertise that one of its models achieves 30 miles per gallon (mpg) decides to carry out a fuel efficiency test. Six nonprofessional drivers are selected, and each one drives a car from Phoenix to Los Angeles. The resulting figures are, in mpg,

    27.2   29.3   31.2   28.4   30.3   29.6

Assuming that fuel efficiency (mpg) is normally distributed under these circumstances, does the data contradict the claim that true average fuel efficiency is (at least) 30? Use of MINITAB gave the output at the top of the next page.

TEST OF MU = 30.0 VS MU L.T. 30.0

N	MEAN	STDEV	SE MEAN	T	P VALUE
6	29.33	1.41	0.57	-1.16	0.15

What would you conclude, and why?

10.71 The effect of discharging wastewater from a dairy processing plant into groundwater used to irrigate kidney beans was examined in the article "Effect of Industrial Dairy Processing Effluent on Soil and Crop Plants" (*Environ. Pollution* (1984): 97–106). The wastewater was rich in bicarbonates and calcium, so it was thought that irrigating with a 50% solution of wastewater might promote growth. Suppose that 40 kidney bean plants were irrigated with this mixture, resulting in a sample mean root length of 5.46 cm and a sample standard deviation of .55 cm. The mean root length for kidney bean plants irrigated with uncontaminated water is known to be 5.20 cm. Does this data support the hypothesis that irrigation with the 50% wastewater solution results in a mean root length that is greater than 5.20? Use a .05 significance level.

10.72 The article referenced in Exercise 10.71 also gave information on root length for pearl millet. When irrigated with uncontaminated water, the mean root length is 6.40 cm. A sample of 40 plants irrigated with a 50% wastewater solution resulted in a sample mean root length of 4.76 cm and a sample standard deviation of .48 cm. Does the data strongly suggest that irrigation with the wastewater mixture results in a mean root length that differs from 6.40? Use a .05 level test.

10.73 A student organization uses the proceeds from a particular soft-drink dispensing machine to finance its activities. The price per can had been $.50 for a long time, and the average daily revenue during that period had been $50.00. The price was recently increased to $.60 per can. A random sample of $n = 20$ days subsequent to the price increase yielded a sample average revenue and sample standard deviation of $47.30 and $4.20, respectively. Does this data suggest that the true average daily revenue has decreased from its value prior to the price increase? Test the appropriate hypotheses using $\alpha = .05$.

10.74 A hot-tub manufacturer advertises that with its heating equipment, a temperature of 100°F can be achieved in at most 15 min. A random sample of 25 tubs is selected, and the time necessary to achieve a 100°F temperature is determined for each tub. The sample average time and sample standard deviation are 17.5 min and 2.2 min, respectively. Does this data cast doubt on the company's claim? Carry out a test of hypotheses using significance level .05.

10.75 Let π denote the proportion of voters in a certain state who favor a particular proposed constitutional amendment. Consider testing $H_0: \pi = .5$ versus $H_a: \pi > .5$ at significance level .05 based on a sample of size $n = 50$.
   a. Suppose that H_0 is in fact true. Use Appendix Table I (our table of random numbers) to simulate selecting a sample, and use the resulting data to carry out the test.
   b. If you repeated part **a** a total of 100 times (a simulation consisting of 100 replications), how many times would you expect H_0 to be rejected?
   c. Now suppose that H_0 is false because $\pi = .6$. Again use Appendix Table I to simulate selecting a sample, and carry out the test. If you repeated this a total of 100 times, would you expect H_0 to be rejected more frequently than when H_0 is true?

References

The books by Freedman et al. and by Moore listed in previous chapter references are excellent sources. Their orientation is primarily conceptual, with a minimum of mathematical development, and both sources offer many valuable insights.

11

Comparing Two Populations or Treatments

INTRODUCTION

Many investigations are carried out for the purpose of comparing two populations or treatments. For example, the article "Learn More, Earn More?" (ETS Policy Notes (1999)) described how the job market treats high school graduates who do not go to college. By comparing data from a random sample of students who had high grades in high school with data from a random sample of students who had low grades, the authors of the article were able to investigate whether the proportion employed for those with high grades was higher than the proportion employed for those with low grades. The authors were also interested in whether the mean monthly salary was higher for those with good grades than for those who did not earn good grades. To answer these questions, hypothesis tests that compare the proportions or means for two different populations were used. This chapter introduces hypothesis tests and confidence intervals that can be used when comparing two populations or treatments.

11.1   Inferences Concerning the Difference Between Two Population or Treatment Means Using Independent Samples

In this section, we consider using sample data to compare two population means or two treatment means. An investigator may wish to estimate the difference between two population means or to test hypotheses about this difference. For example, a university financial aid director may want to determine whether the mean cost of textbooks is different for students enrolled in the Engineering College than for students enrolled in the Liberal Arts College. Here, two populations (one consisting of all students enrolled in the Engineering College and the other consisting of all students enrolled in the Liberal Arts College) are to be compared on the basis of their respective means. Information from a random sample from each population could be the basis for making such a comparison.

In other cases, an experiment might be carried out to compare two different treatments or to compare the effect of a treatment with the effect of no treatment (treatment versus control). For example, an agricultural experimenter might wish to compare weight gains for animals placed on two different diets (each diet is a treatment), or an educational researcher might wish to compare on-line instruction to traditional classroom instruction by studying the difference in mean scores on a common final exam (each type of instruction is a treatment).

In previous chapters, the symbol μ was used to denote the mean of a single population under study. When comparing two populations or treatments, we must use notation that distinguishes between the characteristics of the first and those of the second. This is accomplished by using subscripts on quantities such as μ and σ^2. Similarly, subscripts on sample statistics, such as $\bar{x}$, indicate to which sample these quantities refer.

Notation

	Mean Value	Variance	Standard Deviation
Population or treatment 1	μ_1	σ_1^2	σ_1
Population or treatment 2	μ_2	σ_2^2	σ_2

	Sample Size	Mean	Variance	Standard Deviation
Sample from population or treatment 1	n_1	$\bar{x}_1$	s_1^2	s_1
Sample from population or treatment 2	n_2	$\bar{x}_2$	s_2^2	s_2

Comparison of means focuses on the difference, $\mu_1 - \mu_2$. When $\mu_1 - \mu_2 = 0$, the two population or treatment means are identical. That is,

$\mu_1 - \mu_2 = 0$ is equivalent to $\mu_1 = \mu_2$

Similarly,

$\mu_1 - \mu_2 > 0$ is equivalent to $\mu_1 > \mu_2$

and

$\mu_1 - \mu_2 < 0$ is equivalent to $\mu_1 < \mu_2$

We will first consider the problem of comparing two population means.

Before developing inferential procedures concerning $\mu_1 - \mu_2$, we must consider how the two samples, one from each population, are selected. Two samples are said to be **independent** if the selection of the individuals or objects that make up one sample does not influence the selection of those in the other sample. However, when observations from the first sample are paired in some meaningful way with observations in the second sample, the data is said to be **paired.** For example, to study the effectiveness of a speed-reading course, the reading speed of subjects could be measured before they take the class and again after they complete the course. This gives rise to two related samples — one from the population of individuals who have not taken this particular course (the "before" measurements) and one from the population of individuals who have had such a course (the "after" measurements). These samples are paired. The two samples are not independently chosen, since the selection of individuals from the first (before) population completely determines which individuals make up the sample from the second (after) population. In this section, we consider procedures based on independent samples. Methods for analyzing data resulting from paired samples are presented in Section 11.2.

Because $\bar{x}_1$ provides an estimate of μ_1 and $\bar{x}_2$ gives an estimate of μ_2, it is natural to use $\bar{x}_1 - \bar{x}_2$ as a point estimate of $\mu_1 - \mu_2$. The value of $\bar{x}_1$ varies from sample to sample (it is a *statistic*), as does the value of $\bar{x}_2$. Since the difference $\bar{x}_1 - \bar{x}_2$ is calculated from sample values, it is also a statistic and therefore has a sampling distribution. Our inferential methods will be based on information about the sampling distribution of $\bar{x}_1 - \bar{x}_2$.

Properties of the Sampling Distribution of $\bar{x}_1 - \bar{x}_2$

If the random samples on which $\bar{x}_1$ and $\bar{x}_2$ are based are selected independently of one another, then

1. $\mu_{\bar{x}_1 - \bar{x}_2} = \begin{pmatrix} \text{the mean value} \\ \text{of } \bar{x}_1 - \bar{x}_2 \end{pmatrix} = \mu_{\bar{x}_1} - \mu_{\bar{x}_2} = \mu_1 - \mu_2$

   Thus, the sampling distribution of $\bar{x}_1 - \bar{x}_2$ is always centered at the value of $\mu_1 - \mu_2$, so $\bar{x}_1 - \bar{x}_2$ is an unbiased statistic for estimating $\mu_1 - \mu_2$.

2. $\sigma^2_{\bar{x}_1 - \bar{x}_2} = \begin{pmatrix} \text{the variance of} \\ \bar{x}_1 - \bar{x}_2 \end{pmatrix} = \sigma^2_{\bar{x}_1} + \sigma^2_{\bar{x}_2} = \dfrac{\sigma^2_1}{n_1} + \dfrac{\sigma^2_2}{n_2}$

   and

   $\sigma_{\bar{x}_1 - \bar{x}_2} = \begin{pmatrix} \text{standard deviation of} \\ \bar{x}_1 - \bar{x}_2 \end{pmatrix} = \sqrt{\dfrac{\sigma^2_1}{n_1} + \dfrac{\sigma^2_2}{n_2}}$

3. If n_1 and n_2 are both large or the population distributions are (at least approximately) normal, $\bar{x}_1$ and $\bar{x}_2$ each have (at least approximately) a normal distribution. This implies that the sampling distribution of $\bar{x}_1 - \bar{x}_2$ is also normal or approximately normal.

Properties 1 and 2 follow from the following general results:

1. The mean value of a difference is the difference of the two individual mean values.

2. The variance of a difference of *independent* quantities is the *sum* of the two individual variances.

When the sample sizes are large or the population distributions are (at least approximately) normal, the properties of the sampling distribution of $\bar{x}_1 - \bar{x}_2$ imply that $\bar{x}_1 - \bar{x}_2$ can be standardized to obtain a variable with a sampling distribution that is (at least approximately) the standard normal (z) curve. This gives the following result.

When n_1 and n_2 are both large or the population distributions are (at least approximately) normal, the distribution of

$$z = \frac{\bar{x}_1 - \bar{x}_2 - (\mu_1 - \mu_2)}{\sqrt{\dfrac{\sigma_1^2}{n_1} + \dfrac{\sigma_2^2}{n_2}}}$$

is described (at least approximately) by the standard normal (z) distribution.

Although it is possible to base a test procedure and confidence interval on this result, the values of σ_1^2 and σ_2^2 are rarely known. As a result, the applicability of z is limited. When σ_1^2 and σ_2^2 are unknown, we must estimate them using the corresponding sample variances, s_1^2 and s_2^2. The result on which a test procedure and confidence interval are based is given in the accompanying box.

If n_1 and n_2 are both large or if the population distributions are normal and when the two random samples are independently selected, the standardized variable

$$t = \frac{\bar{x}_1 - \bar{x}_2 - (\mu_1 - \mu_2)}{\sqrt{\dfrac{s_1^2}{n_1} + \dfrac{s_2^2}{n_2}}}$$

has approximately a t distribution with

$$\text{df} = \frac{(V_1 + V_2)^2}{\dfrac{V_1^2}{n_1 - 1} + \dfrac{V_2^2}{n_2 - 1}} \quad \text{where } V_1 = \frac{s_1^2}{n_1} \text{ and } V_2 = \frac{s_2^2}{n_2}$$

df should be truncated (rounded down) to an integer.

If one or both sample sizes are small, normal probability plots or boxplots can be used to evaluate whether it is reasonable to assume that the population distributions are normal.

Test Procedures

In a test designed to compare two population means, the null hypothesis will be of the form

$$H_0: \quad \mu_1 - \mu_2 = \text{hypothesized value}$$

Often the hypothesized value will be zero, indicating that there is no difference between the population means. The alternative hypothesis will involve the same hypothesized value but will use one of the three inequalities $>$, $<$, or $\neq$. As an example, let μ_1 and μ_2 denote the average fuel efficiencies (mpg) for two models of a certain type of car, equipped with 4-cylinder and 6-cylinder engines, respectively. The hypotheses under consideration might be

$$H_0: \quad \mu_1 - \mu_2 = 5 \quad\quad \text{versus} \quad\quad H_a: \quad \mu_1 - \mu_2 > 5$$

With this null hypothesis, the researcher claims that average efficiency for the 4-cylinder engine exceeds the average efficiency for the 6-cylinder engine by exactly 5 mpg. The alternative hypothesis states that the difference between the true average efficiencies is more than 5 mpg.

A test statistic is obtained by replacing $\mu_1 - \mu_2$ in the standardized t variable (given in the previous box) by the hypothesized value which appears in H_0. Thus, the t statistic for testing $H_0: \mu_1 - \mu_2 = 5$ is

$$t = \frac{\bar{x}_1 - \bar{x}_2 - 5}{\sqrt{\dfrac{s_1^2}{n_1} + \dfrac{s_2^2}{n_2}}}$$

When H_0 is true and the sample sizes are large or the population distributions are normal, the sampling distribution of the test statistic is approximately a t distribution. The P-value for the test is obtained by first computing the appropriate df and then using Appendix Table IV. The next box gives a general description of the test procedure.

Summary of the Two-Sample t Test for Comparing Two Population Means

Null hypothesis: $H_0: \mu_1 - \mu_2 = \text{hypothesized value}$

Test statistic: $t = \dfrac{\bar{x}_1 - \bar{x}_2 - (\mu_1 - \mu_2)}{\sqrt{\dfrac{s_1^2}{n_1} + \dfrac{s_2^2}{n_2}}}$

The appropriate df for the two-sample t test is

$$df = \frac{(V_1 + V_2)^2}{\dfrac{V_1^2}{n_1 - 1} + \dfrac{V_2^2}{n_2 - 1}} \quad\quad \text{where } V_1 = \frac{s_1^2}{n_1} \text{ and } V_2 = \frac{s_2^2}{n_2}$$

df should be truncated (rounded down) to an integer.

(continued)

Alternative hypothesis:

$H_a: \mu_1 - \mu_2 >$ hypothesized value

$H_a: \mu_1 - \mu_2 <$ hypothesized value

$H_a: \mu_1 - \mu_2 \neq$ hypothesized value

P-value:

Area under appropriate t curve to the right of the computed t

Area under appropriate t curve to the left of the computed t

(i) $2 \cdot$ (area to the right of the computed t) if t is positive

or

(ii) $2 \cdot$ (area to the left of the computed t) if t is negative

Assumptions: 1. The two samples are *independently selected random samples.*
2. The *sample sizes are large* (generally 30 or larger)
OR
the population distributions are (at least approximately) normal.

EXAMPLE 11.1

The article "Affective Variables Related to Mathematics Achievement Among High-Risk College Freshmen" (*Psych. Reports* (1991): 399–403) examines the relationship between attitudes toward mathematics and success at college-level mathematics. Twenty men and thirty-eight women selected at random from those identified as being at high risk of failure (because they did not meet the usual admission requirements for the university) participated in the study. Each student was asked to respond to a series of questions, and the answers were combined to obtain a math anxiety score. For this particular scale, the higher the score, the lower the level of anxiety toward mathematics. Summary values appear in the accompanying table.

	n	$\bar{x}$	s
Males	20	35.9	11.9
Females	38	36.6	12.3

Does this data provide evidence that, as many researchers have hypothesized, the mean anxiety score for women is different than that for men? Using the nine-step procedure introduced in Chapter 10, we will test the relevant hypotheses using a .05 level of significance.

1. $\mu_1 =$ true mean math anxiety score for male at-risk students
$\mu_2 =$ true mean math anxiety score for female at-risk students
$\mu_1 - \mu_2 =$ difference in mean math anxiety scores

2. $H_0: \mu_1 - \mu_2 = 0$

3. $H_a: \mu_1 - \mu_2 \neq 0$

4. *Significance level*: $\alpha = .05$

5. *Test statistic*: $t = \dfrac{(\bar{x}_1 - \bar{x}_2) - \text{hypothesized value}}{\sqrt{\dfrac{s_1^2}{n_1} + \dfrac{s_2^2}{n_2}}} = \dfrac{(\bar{x}_1 - \bar{x}_2) - 0}{\sqrt{\dfrac{s_1^2}{n_1} + \dfrac{s_2^2}{n_2}}}$

6. *Assumptions*:   The samples were selected independently (the selection of men did not influence the selection of women), and we are told that the selec-

tion was random. Since the sample sizes are not both large, we must be willing to assume that the population distributions are approximately normal to justify using the t statistic. To decide whether this is reasonable, we would have to examine the actual data in each sample. The article gave only summary statistics (no raw data), but if the data from the two samples were available, we could construct boxplots or normal probability plots. For purposes of this example, let's suppose that the boxplots looked like those in the accompanying picture. Since the boxplots are reasonably symmetric and there are no outliers, the assumption of normality would be plausible.

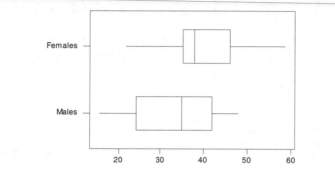

7. *Calculation:* $\quad t = \dfrac{(35.9 - 36.6) - 0}{\sqrt{\dfrac{(11.9)^2}{20} + \dfrac{(12.3)^2}{38}}} = \dfrac{-.70}{\sqrt{7.081 + 3.981}} = \dfrac{-.70}{3.326} = -.21$

8. *P-value:* We first compute the df for the two-sample t test:

$$V_1 = \frac{s_1^2}{n_1} = 7.081 \qquad V_2 = \frac{s_2^2}{n_2} = 3.981$$

$$\text{df} = \frac{(V_1 + V_2)^2}{\dfrac{V_1^2}{n_1 - 1} + \dfrac{V_2^2}{n_2 - 1}} = \frac{(7.081 + 3.981)^2}{\dfrac{(7.081)^2}{19} + \dfrac{(3.981)^2}{37}} = \frac{122.3678}{3.0673} = 39.89$$

We truncate df to 39. Appendix Table IV shows that the area under the t curve with 40 df (as close to 39 as possible in the table) to the right of .2 is .421. By symmetry, the area to the left of $-.2$ is also .421. Because this is a two-tailed test,

$\qquad$ P-value $\approx 2(.421) = .842$

9. *Conclusion:* Since .842 > .05, H_0 is not rejected. The data does not provide strong evidence that the mean math anxiety score of at-risk males differs from that of at-risk females.

EXAMPLE 11.2

Tennis elbow is thought to be aggravated by the impact experienced when hitting the ball. The article "Forces on the Hand in the Tennis One-Handed Backhand" (*Int. J. of Sport Biomechanics* (1991): 282–292) reported the force (*N*) on the hand just after impact on a one-handed backhand drive for six advanced players and for eight intermediate players. Summary statistics from the article, as well as data consistent with these summary quantities, appear in the accompanying table.

	Data							n	$\bar{x}$	s
Advanced	44.7	26.31	55.75	28.54	46.99	39.46		6	40.3	11.3
Intermediate	15.58	19.16	24.13	10.56	32.88	21.47	14.32	33.09	8	21.4	8.3

The authors of the article assumed in their analysis of the data that both force distributions (advanced and intermediate) were normal. We will use the given information to determine whether the mean force after impact is greater for advanced tennis players than it is for intermediate players.

1. μ_1 = mean force after impact for advanced players
    μ_2 = mean force after impact for intermediate players
    $\mu_1 - \mu_2$ = difference in mean force

2. H_0: $\mu_1 - \mu_2 = 0$

3. H_a: $\mu_1 - \mu_2 > 0$

4. *Significance level*: $\alpha = .01$

5. *Test statistic*: $t = \dfrac{(\bar{x}_1 - \bar{x}_2) - \text{hypothesized value}}{\sqrt{\dfrac{s_1^2}{n_1} + \dfrac{s_2^2}{n_2}}} = \dfrac{(\bar{x}_1 - \bar{x}_2) - 0}{\sqrt{\dfrac{s_1^2}{n_1} + \dfrac{s_2^2}{n_2}}}$

6. *Assumptions*:   For the two-sample t test to be appropriate, we must be willing to assume that the two samples can be viewed as independently selected random samples from the populations of advanced and intermediate tennis players. Since the sample sizes are both small, it is necessary to assume that the force distribution is approximately normal for each of these two populations. Boxplots constructed using the sample data are shown here, and they are consistent with the authors assumption of normal population distributions.

7. *Calculation*: $t = \dfrac{(40.3 - 21.4) - 0}{\sqrt{\dfrac{(11.3)^2}{6} + \dfrac{(8.3)^2}{8}}} = \dfrac{18.9}{5.467} = 3.46$

8. *P-value*: We first compute df for the two-sample *t* test:

$$V_1 = \frac{s_1^2}{n_1} = 21.282 \qquad V_2 = \frac{s_2^2}{n_2} = 8.611$$

$$\text{df} = \frac{(V_1 + V_2)^2}{\dfrac{V_1^2}{n_1 - 1} + \dfrac{V_2^2}{n_2 - 1}} = \frac{(21.282 + 8.611)^2}{\dfrac{(21.282)^2}{5} + \dfrac{(8.611)^2}{7}} = \frac{893.5914}{101.1775} = 8.8321$$

Truncating to an integer gives df = 8. Appendix Table IV shows that the area under the *t* curve with 8 df to the right of 3.5 is .004. Because this is an upper-tailed test,

$$P\text{-value} \approx .004$$

9. *Conclusion*: Since *P*-value $\leq \alpha$ (.004 $\leq$ .01), we reject H_0. There is sufficient evidence to conclude that the mean force after impact is greater for advanced players than it is for intermediate players.

Many statistical computer packages will perform the calculations for the two-sample *t* test. The accompanying MINITAB output shows the df, test statistic value, and *P*-value for the hypothesis test of Example 11.2.

Two sample T for Adv. vs Int.

	N	Mean	StDev	SE Mean
Adv.	6	40.3	11.3	4.6
Int.	8	21.40	8.30	2.9

T-Test mu Adv. = mu Int. (vs >): T = 3.46 P = 0.0043 DF = 8

Comparing Treatments

When an experiment is carried out to compare two treatments (or a single treatment with a control), the investigator is interested in the effect of the treatments on some response variable. The treatments are "applied" to individuals (as in an experiment to compare two different medications for decreasing blood pressure) or objects (as in an experiment to compare two different baking temperatures on the density of bread), and the value of some response variable (e.g., blood pressure, density) is recorded. Based on the resulting data, the investigator might wish to determine whether there is a difference in the mean response for the two treatments.

In many actual experimental situations, the individuals or objects to which the treatments will be applied are not selected at random from some larger population. A consequence of this is that it is not possible to generalize the results of the experiment to some larger population. However, *if the experimental design provides for random assignment of treatments to the individuals or objects used in the experiment (or random assignment of the individuals or objects to treatments), it is possible to test hypotheses about treatment differences.*

It is common practice to use the two-sample *t* test statistic previously described if the experiment employs random assignment and if either the samples sizes are large or it is reasonable to think that the treatment response distributions (the distributions of response values that would result if the treatments were applied to a *very* large number of individuals or objects) are approximately normal.

Two-Sample *t* Test for Comparing Two Treatments

When

1. *treatments are randomly assigned* to individuals or objects (or vice versa; that is, individuals or objects are randomly assigned to treatments), and

2. the *sample sizes are large* (generally 30 or larger) OR the *treatment response distributions are approximately normal,*

the two-sample *t* test can be used to test H_0: $\mu_1 - \mu_2 =$ *hypothesized value,* where μ_1 and μ_2 represent the mean response for treatments 1 and 2, respectively.

In this case, these two conditions replace the assumptions previously stated for comparing two population means. The validity of the assumption of normality of the treatment response distributions can be assessed by constructing a normal probability plot or a boxplot of the values in each sample.

Although the two-sample *t* test to compare two treatments when the individuals or objects used in the experiment are not randomly selected from some population is only an approximate test (the reported *P*-values are only approximate), this is still the most common way to analyze such data.

EXAMPLE 11.3

The article "Effects of Learning-Style Intervention on College Student's Achievement, Anxiety, Anger, and Curiosity" (*J. of College Student Development* (1994): 461–466) reported on an experiment designed to compare a treatment group with a control group. First-year nursing students enrolled in a science course were randomly assigned to one of two groups. Students in the control group were provided with conventional study-skill guidelines. Each student in the treatment group was evaluated to determine his or her preferred learning style. Students in the treatment group were then provided with homework prescriptions based on their identified learning style, as well as the conventional study-skill guidelines. Does the treatment (the homework prescriptions based on learning style) improve science grades? We will test the relevant hypotheses using a significance level of .01.

Group	Sample Size	Sample Mean	Sample SD
Control	100	2.75	.85
Treatment	103	3.28	.70

1. Let μ_1 denote the mean science score for the treatment *conventional study-skill guidelines* and define μ_2 analogously for the treatment *homework prescriptions based on learning style in addition to conventional study-skill guide-*

lines. Then $\mu_1 - \mu_2$ is the difference between the mean science scores for the two treatments.

2. $H_0: \mu_1 - \mu_2 = 0$

3. $H_a: \mu_1 - \mu_2 < 0$

4. *Significance level*: $\alpha = .01$

5. *Test statistic*: $t = \dfrac{(\bar{x}_1 - \bar{x}_2) - \text{hypothesized value}}{\sqrt{\dfrac{s_1^2}{n_1} + \dfrac{s_2^2}{n_2}}} = \dfrac{(\bar{x}_1 - \bar{x}_2) - 0}{\sqrt{\dfrac{s_1^2}{n_1} + \dfrac{s_2^2}{n_2}}}$

6. *Assumptions*: Subjects were randomly assigned to the treatment groups, and both sample sizes are large, so the two-sample t test is appropriate.

7. *Computation*: $t = \dfrac{(2.75 - 3.28) - 0}{\sqrt{\dfrac{(.85)^2}{100} + \dfrac{(.70)^2}{103}}} = \dfrac{-.53}{.1095} = -4.84$

8. *P-value*: We first compute the df for the two-sample t test:

$$V_1 = \frac{s_1^2}{n_1} = .0072 \qquad V_2 = \frac{s_2^2}{n_2} = .0048$$

$$\text{df} = \frac{(V_1 + V_2)^2}{\dfrac{V_1^2}{n_1 - 1} + \dfrac{V_2^2}{n_2 - 1}} = \frac{(.0072 + .0048)^2}{\dfrac{(.0072)^2}{99} + \dfrac{(.0048)^2}{102}} = \frac{.000144}{.00000075} = 192.69$$

This is a lower-tailed test, so the P-value is the area under the t curve with df = 192 and to the left of -4.84. Since -4.84 is so far out in the lower tail of this t curve, P-value ≈ 0.

9. *Conclusion*: Since P-value $\le \alpha$, H_0 is rejected. There is evidence that the mean science score for the treatment group is higher. The data supports the conclusion that homework prescriptions based on learning style are effective in raising the mean science score.

You have probably noticed that evaluating the formula for degrees of freedom for the two-sample t test involves quite a bit of arithmetic. An alternative approach is to compute a conservative estimate of the P-value — one that is close to but larger than the actual P-value. If H_0 were rejected using this conservative estimate, then it would also be rejected if the actual P-value had been used. **A conservative estimate of the P-value for the two-sample t test can be found by using the t curve with df equal to the smaller of $n_1 - 1$ and $n_2 - 1$.**

The Pooled t Test

The two-sample t test procedure just described is appropriate when it is reasonable to assume that the population distributions are approximately normal. If it is also known that the variances of the two populations are equal ($\sigma_1^2 = \sigma_2^2$), an alternative procedure known as the *pooled t test* can be used. This test procedure combines information from both samples to obtain a "pooled" estimate of the common variance and then uses this pooled estimate of the variance in place of s_1^2 and s_2^2 in the *t* test statistic. This test procedure was widely used in the past, but it has fallen into some disfavor because it is quite sensitive to departures from the assumption of equal population variances. If the population variances are equal, the pooled *t* procedure has a slightly better chance of detecting departures from H_0 than does the two-sample *t* test of this section. However, *P*-values based on the pooled *t* procedure can be seriously in error if the population variances are not equal, so in general the two-sample *t* procedure is a better choice.

Comparisons and Causation

If the assignment of treatments to the individuals or objects used in a comparison of treatments is not made by the investigators, the study is said to be **observational.**

As an example, the article "Lead and Cadmium Absorption among Children near a Nonferrous Metal Plant" (*Environ. Research* (1978): 290–308) reported data on blood-lead concentrations for two different samples of children. The first sample was drawn from a population residing within 1 km of a lead smelter, whereas those in the second sample were selected from a rural area much farther from the smelter. It was the parents of children, rather than the investigators, who determined whether the children would be in the close-to-smelter group or the far-from-smelter group. As a second example, a letter in the *Journal of the American Medical Association* (May 19, 1978) reported on a comparison of doctors' longevity after medical school graduation for those with an academic affiliation and those in private practice. (The letter writer's stated objective was to see whether "publish or perish" really meant "publish *and* perish.") Here again, an investigator did not start out with a group of doctors and assign some to academic and others to nonacademic careers. The doctors themselves selected their groups.

The difficulty with drawing conclusions based on an observational study is that a statistically significant difference may be due to some underlying factors that have not been controlled rather than to conditions that define the groups. Does the type of medical practice itself have an effect on longevity, or is the observed difference in lifetimes caused by other factors, which themselves led graduates to choose academic or nonacademic careers? Similarly, is the observed difference in blood-lead concentration levels due to proximity to the smelter? Perhaps there are other physical and socioeconomic factors related both to choice of living area and to concentration.

In general, rejection of $H_0: \mu_1 - \mu_2 = 0$ in favor of $H_a: \mu_1 - \mu_2 > 0$ suggests that, on the average, higher values of the variable are *associated* with individuals in the first population or receiving the first treatment than with those in the second population or receiving the second treatment. But *association does not imply causation.* Strong statistical evidence for a causal relationship can be built up over time through many different comparative studies that point to the same conclusions (as in the many investigations linking smoking to lung cancer). A **randomized controlled experiment,** in which investigators assign subjects in some prescribed random fashion to the treatments or conditions being compared, is particularly effective in suggesting causality. With such random assignment, the investigator and other interested parties will have more confidence in the conclusion that an observed difference was caused by the difference in treatments or conditions. (Recall the discussion in Chapter 2 of the role of randomization in designing an experiment.)

A Confidence Interval

A confidence interval for $\mu_1 - \mu_2$ is easily obtained from the basic t variable of this section. Both the derivation of and formula for the interval are very similar to that of the one-sample t interval discussed in Chapter 9.

The Two-Sample t Confidence Interval for the Difference Between Two Population or Treatment Means

The general formula for a confidence interval for $\mu_1 - \mu_2$ when

1. the two samples are *independently chosen random samples,* and
2. the *sample sizes are both large* (generally $n_1 \geq 30$ and $n_2 \geq 30$) OR the *population distributions are approximately normal*

is

$$\bar{x}_1 - \bar{x}_2 \pm (t \text{ critical value})\sqrt{\frac{s_1^2}{n_1} + \frac{s_2^2}{n_2}}$$

The t critical value is based on

$$df = \frac{(V_1 + V_2)^2}{\dfrac{V_1^2}{n_1 - 1} + \dfrac{V_2^2}{n_2 - 1}} \qquad \text{where } V_1 = \frac{s_1^2}{n_1} \text{ and } V_2 = \frac{s_2^2}{n_2}$$

df should be truncated (rounded down) to an integer. The t critical values for the usual confidence levels are given in Appendix Table III.

For a comparison of two treatments, when

1. *treatments are randomly assigned* to individuals or objects (or vice versa), and
2. the *sample sizes are large* (generally 30 or larger) OR the *treatment response distributions are approximately normal,*

the two-sample t confidence interval formula can be used to estimate $\mu_1 - \mu_2$.

EXAMPLE 11.4   Much research effort has been expended in studying possible causes of the pharmacological and behavioral effects resulting from smoking marijuana. The article "Intravenous Injection in Man of Δ^9THC and 11-OH-Δ^9THC" (*Science* (1982): 633) reported on a study of two chemical substances thought to be instrumental in marijuana's effects. Subjects were randomly assigned to one of two treatment groups. Individuals in each group were given one of the two substances in increasing amounts and asked to say when the effect was first perceived. The accompanying data values are necessary dose to perception per kilogram of body weight.

Δ^9THC   19.54   14.47   16.00   24.83   26.39   11.49   ($\bar{x}_1 = 18.79$, $s_1 = 5.91$)

11-OH-Δ^9THC   15.95   25.89   20.53   15.52   14.18   16.00   ($\bar{x}_2 = 18.01$, $s_2 = 4.42$)

Subjects were randomly assigned to treatments. Since both the sample sizes are small, we must first investigate whether it is reasonable to assume that the distribution of dose to perception is approximately normal for the two chemical substances. There are no outliers in either data set, and normal probability plots are reasonably straight, suggesting that the assumption of approximate normality is reasonable.

To estimate $\mu_1 - \mu_2$, the difference in mean dose to perception for the two substances, we will calculate a 95% confidence interval.

$$V_1 = \frac{s_1^2}{n_1} = \frac{(5.91)^2}{6} = 5.821 \qquad V_2 = \frac{s_2^2}{n_2} = \frac{(4.42)^2}{6} = 3.256$$

$$df = \frac{(V_1 + V_2)^2}{\dfrac{V_1^2}{n_1 - 1} + \dfrac{V_2^2}{n_2 - 1}} = \frac{(5.821 + 3.256)^2}{\dfrac{(5.821)^2}{5} + \dfrac{(3.256)^2}{5}} = \frac{82.392}{8.897} = 9.26$$

Truncating to an integer gives df = 9. In the 9-df row of Appendix Table III, the t critical value for a 95% confidence level is 2.26. The interval is then

$$\bar{x}_1 - \bar{x}_2 \pm (t \text{ critical value})\sqrt{\frac{s_1^2}{n_1} + \frac{s_2^2}{n_2}} = (18.79 - 18.01) \pm (2.26)\sqrt{\frac{(5.91)^2}{6} + \frac{(4.42)^2}{6}}$$

$$= .78 \pm (2.26)(3.01)$$
$$= .78 \pm 6.80$$
$$= (-6.02, 7.58)$$

This interval is rather wide, because the two sample variances are large and the sample sizes are small. Notice that the interval includes 0, so 0 is one of the plausible values for $\mu_1 - \mu_2$. That is, it is plausible that there is no difference in the mean dose to perception for the two substances.

Most statistical computer packages will compute the two-sample t confidence interval. MINITAB was used to construct a 95% confidence interval using the data of this example; the resulting output is shown here.

Two Sample T-Test and Confidence Interval

Two sample T for THC vs 11-OH-THC

	N	Mean	StDev	SE Mean
THC	6	18.79	5.91	2.4
11-OH-TH	6	18.01	4.42	1.8

95% CI for mu THC - mu 11-OH-TH: (-6.0, 7.6)

Exercises 11.1 – 11.31

11.1 Consider two populations for which $\mu_1 = 30$, $\sigma_1 = 2$, $\mu_2 = 25$, and $\sigma_2 = 3$. Suppose that two independent random samples of sizes $n_1 = 40$ and $n_2 = 50$ are selected. Describe the approximate sampling distribution of $\bar{x}_1 - \bar{x}_2$ (center, spread, and shape).

11.2 An article in the November 1983 *Consumer Reports* compared various types of batteries. The average lifetimes of Duracell Alkaline AA batteries and Eveready Energizer Alkaline AA batteries were given as 4.1 hr and 4.5 hr, respectively. Suppose that these are the population average lifetimes.

a. Let $\bar{x}_1$ be the sample average lifetime of 100 Duracell batteries and $\bar{x}_2$ be the sample average lifetime of 100 Eveready batteries. What is the mean value of $\bar{x}_1 - \bar{x}_2$; that is, where is the sampling distribution of $\bar{x}_1 - \bar{x}_2$ centered? How does your answer depend on the specified sample sizes?

b. Suppose that population standard deviations of lifetime are 1.8 hr for Duracell batteries and 2.0 hr for Eveready batteries. With the sample sizes as given in part **a**, what is the variance of the statistic $\bar{x}_1 - \bar{x}_2$, and what is its standard deviation?

c. For the sample sizes as given in part **a**, draw a picture of the approximate sampling distribution curve of $\bar{x}_1 - \bar{x}_2$ (include a measurement scale on the horizontal axis). Would the shape of the curve necessarily be the same for sample sizes of 10 batteries of each type? Explain.

11.3 An acquaintance of ours can take either a scenic route to work or a nonscenic route. She decides that use of the nonscenic route can be justified only if it reduces true average travel time by more than 10 min.

a. If μ_1 refers to the scenic route and μ_2 to the nonscenic route, which hypotheses should be tested?

b. If μ_1 refers to the nonscenic route and μ_2 to the scenic route, which hypotheses should be tested?

11.4 When a surgeon repairs injuries he uses sutures (stitched knots) to hold together and stabilize the injured area. If these knots elongate and loosen through use, the injury may not heal properly because the tissues would not be optimally positioned. Researchers at the University of California, San Francisco, tied a series of different types of knots with two types of suture material, Maxon and Ticron. Suppose that 112 tissue specimens were available and that for each specimen the type of knot and suture material were randomly assigned. The investigators tested the knots to see how much the loops elongated; the elongations were measured and the resulting data is summarized here.

Maxon	n	$\bar{x}$ (mm)	sd (mm)
Square (control)	10	10.0	.1
Duncan loop	15	11.0	.3
Overhand	15	11.0	.9
Roeder	10	13.5	.1
Snyder	10	13.5	2.0

Ticron	n	$\bar{x}$ (mm)	sd (mm)
Square (control)	10	2.5	.06
Duncan loop	11	10.9	.4
Overhand	11	8.1	1.0
Roeder	10	5.0	.04
Snyder	10	8.1	.06

a. Is there a significant difference in elongation between the square knot and the Duncan loop for Maxon thread?

b. Is there a significant difference between the square knot and the Duncan loop for Ticron thread?

c. For the Duncan loop data, is there a significant difference between the elongation of Maxon versus Ticron threads?

11.5 Snake experts believe that venomous snakes inject different amounts of venom when killing their prey. Researchers at the University of Wyoming tested this hypothesis to determine whether young prairie rattlesnakes use more venom to kill larger mice and less venom for smaller mice ("Venom Metering by Juvenile Prairie Rattlesnakes, Crotalus v. Viridis: Effects of Prey Size and Experience," *Animal Behavior* (1995): 33–40). In the first trial, the researchers used three groups of seven randomly selected snakes that were inexperienced hunters. In the second trial, three different groups of seven randomly selected "experienced" snakes were used. The amount (mg) of venom each snake injected was recorded and categorized according to the size of the mouse.

	Small Mouse		Medium Mouse		Large Mouse	
	$\bar{x}$	s	$\bar{x}$	s	$\bar{x}$	s
Inexperienced	3.1	1.0	3.4	.4	1.8	.3
Experienced	2.6	.3	2.9	.6	4.7	.3

For the small prey, is there a significant difference between the inexperienced and experienced snakes? For the medium prey? For the large prey?

11.6 The coloration of male guppies may affect the mating preference of the female guppy. To test this hypothesis, scientists first identified two types of guppies, Yarra and Paria, that display different colorations ("Evolutionary Mismatch of Mating Preferences and Male Colour Patterns in Guppies," *Animal Behaviour* (1997): 343–51). The relative area of orange was calculated for fish of each type. A random sample of 30 Yarra guppies resulted in a mean relative area of .106 and a standard deviation of .055. A random sample of 30 Paria guppies resulted in a mean relative area of .178 and a standard deviation .058. Is there evidence of a difference in coloration? Test the relevant hypotheses to determine whether the mean area of orange is different for the two types of guppies.

11.7 The article "Trial Lawyers and Testosterone: Blue-Collar Talent in a White-Collar World" (*J. Applied Social Psychology* (1998): 84–94) compared trial lawyers and nontrial lawyers on the basis of mean testosterone level. Random samples of 35 male trial lawyers, 31 male nontrial lawyers, 13 female trial lawyers, and 18 female nontrial lawyers were selected for study. The article includes the following statement:

> Trial lawyers had higher testosterone levels than did nontrial lawyers. This was true for men, $t(64) = 3.75$, $p < .001$, and for women, $t(29) = 2.26$, $p < .05$.

a. Based on the information given, is there a significant difference in the mean testosterone level for male trial and nontrial lawyers?
b. Based on the information given, is there a significant difference in the mean testosterone level for female trial and nontrial lawyers?
c. Do you have enough information to carry out a test to determine whether there is a significant difference in the mean testosterone levels of male and female trial lawyers? If so, carry out such a test. If not, what additional information would you need to be able to conduct the test?

11.8 The article "The Relevance of Sexual Orientation to Substance Abuse and Psychological Distress Among College Students" (*J. College Student Development* ((1998): 157–165) examined substance abuse patterns for individuals in a random sample of gay, lesbian, and bisexual students and in a random sample of heterosexual students at a particular university. One of the variables considered was frequency of marijuana use in the past year. It was reported that the mean and standard devia-

tion for this variable were 15.68 and 43.69, respectively for the sample of 37 gay, lesbian, and bisexual students, and 12.28 and 44.20 for the sample of 156 heterosexual students.

a. Based on the information given, is it reasonable to assume that the population distributions of the variable *frequency of marijuana use* are approximately normal. Explain why or why not.
b. Taking your answer to part **a** into account, do you think it is still reasonable to use the two-sample *t* test to determine whether there is sufficient evidence to conclude that the mean frequency of marijuana use differs for the two groups? Explain why or why not.
c. If you concluded in part **b** that the independent samples *t* test is appropriate, use it to carry out a test of the relevant hypotheses using $\alpha = .01$.

11.9 Do faculty and students have similar perceptions of what types of behavior are inappropriate in the classroom? This question was examined by the author of the article "Faculty and Student Perceptions of Classroom Etiquette" (*J. College Student Development* (1998): 515–516). Each individual in a random sample of 173 students in general education classes at a large public university was asked to judge various behaviors on a scale from 1 (totally inappropriate) to 5 (totally appropriate). Individuals in a random sample of 98 faculty members also rated the same behaviors. The mean rating for two of the behaviors studied are shown here (the means are consistent with data provided by the author of the article). The sample standard deviations were not given, but for purposes of this exercise, assume that they are all equal to 1.0.

Student Behavior	Student Mean Rating	Faculty Mean Rating
Wearing hats in the classroom	2.80	3.63
Addressing instructor by first name	2.90	2.11
Talking on a cell phone	1.11	1.10

a. Is there sufficient evidence to conclude that the mean "appropriateness" score assigned to wearing a hat in class differs for students and faculty?
b. Is there sufficient evidence to conclude that the mean "appropriateness" score assigned to addressing an instructor by his or her first name is higher for students than for faculty?
c. Is there sufficient evidence to conclude that the mean "appropriateness" score assigned to talking on a cell phone differs for students and faculty? Does the result of your test imply that students and faculty consider it acceptable to talk on a cell phone during class?

11.10 The article "So Close, Yet So Far: Predictors of Attrition in College Seniors" (*J. College Student Development* (1999): 343–354) attempts to describe differences between college seniors who disenroll before graduating and those who do graduate. Researchers randomly selected 42 nonreturning and 48 returning seniors, none of whom were transfer students. These 90 students rated themselves on personal contact and campus involvement. The resulting data is summarized here:

	Returning (n = 48)		Nonreturning (n = 42)	
	Mean	Standard Deviation	Mean	Standard Deviation
Personal contact	3.22	.93	2.41	1.03
Campus involvement	3.21	1.01	3.31	1.03

a. Construct and interpret a 95% confidence interval for the difference in mean campus involvement rating for returning and nonreturning students. Does your interval support the statement that students who do not return are less involved, on average, than those who do? Explain.

b. Do students who don't return have a lower mean personal contact rating than those who do return? Test the relevant hypotheses using a significance level of .01.

11.11 Does clear-cutting of trees in an area cause local extinction of the tailed frog? We don't really know, but an article that begins to address that issue attempts to quantify aspects of the habitat and microhabitat of streams with and without tailed frogs. The following data is from "Distribution and Habitat of *Ascaphus Truei* in Streams on Managed, Young Growth Forests in North Coastal California" (*Journal of Herpetology* (1999): 71–79).

Assume that the habitats and microhabitats examined were selected independently and at random from those that have tailed frogs and those that do not have tailed frogs. Use a significance level of .01 for any hypothesis tests required to answer the following questions.

Sites With Tailed Frogs		
	n	x̄	s
Habitat Characteristics			
Stream gradient (%)	18	9.1	6.00
Water temp. (°C)	18	12.2	1.71
Microhabitat Characteristics			
Depth (cm)	82	5.32	2.27

Sites Without Tailed Frogs		
	n	x̄	s
Habitat Characteristics			
Stream gradient (%)	31	5.9	6.29
Water temp. (°C)	31	12.8	1.33
Microhabitat Characteristics			
Depth (cm)	267	8.46	5.95

a. Is there evidence of a difference in mean stream gradient between streams with and streams without tailed frogs? (*Note*: Assume that it is reasonable to think that the distribution of stream gradients is approximately normal for both types of streams. It is possible for gradient % to be either positive or negative, so the fact that the mean $-$ 2 standard deviations is negative is not, by itself, an indication of nonnormality in this case.)

b. Is there evidence of a difference in the mean water temperature between streams with and streams without tailed frogs?

c. The article reported that the two depth distributions are both quite skewed. Does this imply that it would be unreasonable to use the independent samples t test to compare the mean depth for the two types of streams? If not, carry out a test to determine whether the sample data supports the claim that the mean depth of streams without tailed frogs is greater than the mean depth of streams with tailed frogs.

11.12 Are girls less inclined to enroll in science courses than boys? One recent study ("Intentions of Young Students to Enroll in Science Courses in the Future: An Examination of Gender Differences" (*Science Education* (1999): 55–76) asked randomly selected fourth, fifth, and sixth graders how many science courses they intend to take. The following data was obtained:

	n	Mean	Standard Deviation
Males	203	3.42	1.49
Females	224	2.42	1.35

Calculate a 99% confidence interval for the difference between males and females in mean number of science courses planned. Interpret your interval. Based on your interval, how would you answer the question posed at the beginning of the exercise?

11.13 The article "Workaholism in Organizations: Gender Differences" (*Sex Roles* (1999): 333–346) gave the following data on 1996 income for random samples of male and female MBA graduates from a particular Canadian business school:

	n	$\bar{x}$	s
Males	258	$133,442	$131,090
Females	233	$105,156	$98,525

(*Note*: These salary figures are in Canadian dollars.)

a. For what significance levels would you conclude that the mean salary of female MBA graduates of this business school is above $100,000?

b. Is there convincing evidence that the mean salary for female MBA graduates of this business school is lower than the mean salary for the male graduates?

11.14 The article "Movement and Habitat Use by Lake Whitefish During Spawning in a Boreal Lake: Integrating Acoustic Telemetry and Geographic Information Systems" (*Transactions of the American Fisheries Society*, (1999): 939–952) included the accompanying data on weights of 18 fish caught in 1995 and 1996:

1995	776	580	539	648	538	891	673	783	571	627
1996	571	627	727	727	867	1042	804	832	764	727

Is it reasonable to use the independent samples t test to compare the mean weight of fish for the 2 years? Explain why or why not.

11.15 The article "The Relationship of Task and Ego Orientation to Sportsmanship Attitudes and the Perceived Legitimacy of Injurious Acts" (*Research Quarterly for Exercise and Sport* (1991): 79–87) examined the extent of approval of unsporting play and cheating. High school basketball players completed a questionnaire that was used to arrive at an approval score, with higher scores indicating greater approval. A random sample of 56 male players resulted in a mean approval rating for unsportsmanlike play of 2.76, whereas the mean for a random sample of 67 female players was 2.02. Suppose that the two sample standard deviations were .44 for males and .41 for females. Is it reasonable to conclude that the mean approval rating is higher for male players than for female players by more than .5? Use $\alpha = .05$.

11.16 The article "Conflict Resolution Styles in Gay, Lesbian, Heterosexual Nonparent and Heterosexual Parent Couples" (*J. Marriage and Family* (1994): 705–722) reported the results of administering the Ineffective Arguing Inventory (IAI) to both partners of 75 gay, 51 lesbian, 108 married nonparent, and 99 married parent couples. The IAI is a measure of dysfunctionality in couple conflict resolution. The mean and standard deviation of the IAI scores for each group are given in the accompanying table.

	Type of Couple			
	Gay	**Lesbian**	**Heterosexual Nonparent**	**Heterosexual Parent**
Sample size	75	51	108	99
Mean	17.16	15.92	16.79	18.09
Standard deviation	6.19	5.93	5.81	6.55

a. Is there evidence to suggest that the mean IAI score is higher for heterosexual parent couples than for heterosexual nonparent couples? Test the relevant hypotheses using $\alpha = .01$.

b. Is there evidence to suggest that the mean IAI score is higher for gay couples than for lesbian couples? Test the relevant hypotheses using $\alpha = .05$.

c. Construct a 95% confidence interval for the difference in mean IAI score for gay couples and heterosexual nonparent couples. Interpret this interval.

d. Construct a 95% confidence interval for the difference in mean IAI score for heterosexual parent couples and heterosexual nonparent couples. Interpret this interval.

11.17 Techniques for processing poultry were examined in the article "Texture Profiles of Canned Boned Chicken as Affected by Chilling-Aging Times" (*Poultry Science* (1994): 1475–1478). Whole chickens were chilled 0, 2, 8, or 24 hours before being cooked and canned. To determine whether the chilling time affected the texture of the canned chicken, samples were evaluated by trained tasters. One characteristic of interest was hardness. The accompanying summary quantities were obtained. Each mean is based on 36 ratings.

	Chilling Time			
	0 hr	**2 hr**	**8 hr**	**24 hr**
Mean hardness	7.52	6.55	5.70	5.65
Standard deviation	.96	1.74	1.32	1.50

a. Does the data suggest that there is a difference in mean hardness for chicken chilled 0 hours before cooking and chicken chilled 2 hours before cooking? Use $\alpha = .05$.

b. Does the data suggest that there is a difference in mean hardness for chicken chilled 8 hours before cooking and chicken chilled 24 hours before cooking? Use $\alpha = .05$.

c. Use a 90% confidence interval to estimate the difference in mean hardness for chicken chilled 2 hours before cooking and chicken chilled 8 hours before cooking.

11.18 The Rape Myth Acceptance Scale (RMA) was administered to 333 male students at a public university. Of these students, 155 were randomly selected from students who did not belong to a fraternity, and 178 were randomly selected from students who belonged to a fraternity. The higher the score on the RMA, the greater the acceptance of rape myths, so lower scores are considered desirable. The accompanying data appeared in the article "Rape Supportive Attitudes Among Greek Students Before and After a Date Rape Prevention Program" (*J. of College Student Development* (1994): 450–455). Does the data support the researchers' claim that the mean RMA score is lower for fraternity members? Use $\alpha = .05$.

Sample	n	Mean RMA Score	sd
Fraternity members	178	25.63	6.16
Not fraternity members	155	27.40	5.51

11.19 The discharge of industrial wastewater into rivers affects water quality. To assess the effect of a particular power plant on water quality, 24 water specimens were taken 16 km upstream and 4 km downstream of the plant. Alkalinity (mg/L) was determined for each specimen, resulting in the summary quantities in the accompanying table. Does the data suggest that the true mean alkalinity is higher downstream than upstream by more than 50 mg/L? Use a .05 significance level.

Location	n	Mean	Standard Deviation
Upstream	24	75.9	1.83
Downstream	24	183.6	1.70

11.20 According to the Associated Press (*San Luis Obispo Telegram-Tribune,* June 23, 1995), a study by Italian researchers indicated that low cholesterol and depression were linked. The researchers found that among 331 randomly selected patients hospitalized because they had attempted suicide, the mean cholesterol level was 198. The mean cholesterol level of 331 randomly selected patients admitted to the hospital for other reasons was 217. The sample standard deviations were not reported, but suppose that they were 20 for the group who had attempted suicide and 24 for the other group. Does this data provide sufficient evidence to conclude that the mean cholesterol level is lower for those who have attempted suicide? Test the relevant hypotheses using $\alpha = .05$.

11.21 The article "The Sorority Rush Process: Self-Selection, Acceptance Criteria, and the Effect of Rejection" (*J. of College Student Development* (1994): 346–353) reported on a study of factors associated with the decision to rush a sorority. Fifty-four women who rushed a sorority and 51 women who did not were asked how often they drank alcoholic beverages. For the sorority rush group, the mean was 2.72 drinks per week and the standard deviation .86. For the group who did not rush, the mean was 2.11 and the standard deviation 1.02. Is there evidence to support the claim that those who rush a sorority drink more than those who do not rush? Test the relevant hypotheses using $\alpha = .01$. What assumptions are required in order for the two-sample t test to be appropriate?

11.22 The authors of the article "Dynamics of Canopy Structure and Light Interception in *Pinus elliottii,* North Florida" (*Ecological Monographs* (1991): 33–51) planned an experiment to determine the effect of fertilizer on a measure of leaf area. A number of plots were available for the study, and half were selected at random to be fertilized. To ensure that the plots to be treated with fertilizer and the control plots were similar, prior to beginning the experiment tree density (the number of trees per hectare) was recorded for eight plots to be fertilized and eight control plots, resulting in the given data.

Fertilizer plots	1024	1216	1312	1280	1216	1312	992	1120
Control plots	1104	1072	1088	1328	1376	1280	1120	1200

Based on the accompanying MINITAB output, would you conclude that there is a significant difference in the mean tree density for fertilizer and control plots? Use $\alpha = .05$.

Twosample T for fert. vs control

	N	Mean	StDev	SE Mean
Fert.	8	1184	126	44
Control	8	1196	118	42

95% C.I. for mu fert. - mu control: (-144, 120)
T-Test mu fert. = mu control (vs not =): T = -0.20 P = 0.85 DF = 13

11.23 British health officials have expressed concern about problems associated with vitamin D deficiency among certain immigrants. Doctors have conjectured that such a deficiency could be related to the amount of fiber in a person's diet. An experiment was designed to compare the vitamin D plasma half-life for two groups of healthy individuals. One group was placed on a normal diet, whereas the second group was placed on a high-fiber diet. The accompanying table gives the resulting data (from "Reduced Plasma Half-Lives of Radio-Labeled 25(OH)D3 in Subjects Receiving a High-Fibre Diet," *Brit. J. of Nutrit.* (1993): 213–216).

Normal diet	19.1	24.0	28.6	29.7	30.0	34.8	
High-fiber diet	12.0	13.0	13.6	20.5	22.7	23.7	24.8

Use the following MINITAB output to determine whether the data indicates that the mean half-life is higher for those on a normal diet than those on a high-fiber diet. Assume that treatments were assigned at random and the two plasma half-life distributions are normal. Test the appropriate hypotheses using $\alpha = .01$.

Twosample T for normal vs high

	N	Mean	StDev	SE Mean
Normal	6	27.70	5.44	2.2
High	7	18.61	5.55	2.1

95% C.I. for mu normal - mu high: (2.3, 15.9)
T-Test mu normal = mu high(vs >):T = 2.97 P = 0.0070 DF = 10

11.24 A researcher at the Medical College of Virginia conducted a study of 60 randomly selected male soccer players and concluded that frequently "heading" the ball in soccer lowers players' IQs (*USA Today,* Aug. 14, 1995). The soccer players were divided into two groups, based on whether they averaged 10 or more headers per game. Mean IQs were reported in the article, but the sample sizes and standard deviations were not given. Suppose that these values were as given in the accompanying table.

	n	Sample Mean	Sample sd
Fewer than 10 headers	35	112	10
10 or more headers	25	103	8

Does this data support the researcher's conclusion? Test the relevant hypotheses using $\alpha = .05$. Can you conclude that heading the ball *causes* lower IQ?

11.25 The effect of loneliness among college students was examined in the article "The Importance of Perceived Duration: Loneliness and Its Relationship to Self-Esteem and Academic Performance" (*J. College Student Development* (1994): 456–460). Based on reported frequency and duration of loneliness, subjects were divided into two groups. The first group ($n_1 = 72$) was the short-duration loneliness group, and the second ($n_2 = 17$) was the long-duration loneliness group. A self-esteem inventory was administered to students in both groups. For the short-duration group, the reported mean self-esteem score was 76.78 and the standard deviation was 17.80. For the long-duration group, the mean and standard deviation were 64.00 and 15.68, respectively. Does the data support the researcher's claim that mean self-esteem is lower for students classified as having long-duration loneliness? Test the relevant hypotheses using $\alpha = .01$. Be sure to state any assumptions that are necessary for your test to be valid.

11.26 The article referenced in Exercise 11.25 also gave information on college grade point average. Summary values appear in the accompanying table. Is there a significant difference in mean grade point average between students who experience short-duration loneliness and those who experience long-duration loneliness? Use $\alpha = .05$.

Group	n	Mean	sd
Short duration	72	2.58	.75
Long duration	17	2.80	.79

11.27 Wayne Gretzky was one of ice hockey's most prolific scorers when he played for the Edmonton Oilers. During his last season with the Oilers, Gretzky played in 41 games and missed 17 games due to injury. The article "The Great Gretzky" (*Chance* (1991): 16–21) looked at the number of goals scored by the Oilers in games with and without Gretzky, as shown in the accompanying table. If we view the 41 games with Gretzky as a random sample of all Oiler games in which Gretzky played and the 17 games without Gretzky as a random sample of all Oiler games in which Gretzky did not play, is there evidence that the mean number of goals scored by the Oilers is higher for games in which Gretzky played? Use $\alpha = .01$.

	n	Sample Mean	Sample sd
Games with Gretzky	41	4.73	1.29
Games without Gretzky	17	3.88	1.18

11.28 Here's one to sink your teeth into: The authors of the article "Analysis of Food Crushing Sounds During Mastication: Total Sound Level Studies" (*J. of Texture Studies* (1990): 165–178) studied the nature of sounds generated during eating. Peak loudness (in decibels at 20 cm away) was measured for both open-mouth and closed-mouth chewing of potato chips and of tortilla chips. Forty subjects participated, with ten assigned at random to each combination of conditions (such as closed-mouth, potato chip, and so on). We are not making this up! Summary values taken from plots given in the article appear in the accompanying table.

	n	$\bar{x}$	s
Potato chip			
Open mouth	10	63	13
Closed mouth	10	54	16
Tortilla chip			
Open mouth	10	60	15
Closed mouth	10	53	16

a. Construct a 95% confidence interval for the difference in mean peak loudness between open-mouth and closed-mouth chewing of potato chips. Interpret the resulting interval.

b. For closed-mouth chewing (the recommended

method!), is there sufficient evidence to indicate that there is a difference between potato chips and tortilla chips with respect to mean peak loudness? Test the relevant hypotheses using $\alpha = .01$.

c. The means and standard deviations given here were actually for stale chips. When ten measurements of peak loudness were recorded for closed-mouth chewing of fresh tortilla chips, the resulting mean and standard deviation were 56 and 14, respectively. Is there sufficient evidence to conclude that fresh tortilla chips are louder than stale chips? Use $\alpha = .05$.

11.29 Thirteen males and fourteen females participated in a study of grip and leg strength ("Sex Differences in Static Strength and Fatigability in Three Different Muscle Groups," *Research Quarterly for Exercise and Sport* (1990): 238–242). Right-leg strength (in newtons) was recorded for each participant, resulting in the summary statistics given in the accompanying table. Estimate the difference in mean right-leg strength between males and females, using a 95% confidence interval. Interpret the resulting interval.

	n	x	s
Males	13	2127	513
Females	14	1843	446

11.30 Are very young infants more likely to imitate actions that are modeled by a person or simulated by an object? This question was the basis of a research study summarized in the article "The Role of Person and Object in Eliciting Early Imitation" (*J. Experimental Child Psych.* (1991): 423–433). One action examined was mouth opening. This action was modeled repeatedly by either a person or a doll, and the number of times that the infant imitated the behavior was recorded. Twenty-seven infants participated, with 12 exposed to a human model and 15 exposed to the doll. Summary values are given here. Is there sufficient evidence to conclude that the mean number of imitations is higher for infants who watch a human model than for infants who watch a doll? Test the relevant hypotheses using a .01 significance level.

	Person Model	Doll Model
$\bar{x}$	5.14	3.46
s	1.6	1.3

11.31 Do certain behaviors result in a severe drain on energy resources because a great deal of energy is expended in comparison to energy intake? The article "The Energetic Cost of Courtship and Aggression in a Plethodontid Salamander" (*Ecology* (1983): 979–983) reported on one of the few studies concerned with behavior and energy expenditure. The accompanying table gives oxygen consumption (mL/g/hr) for male-female salamander pairs. (The determination of consumption values was rather complicated. It is partly for this reason that so few studies of this type have been carried out.)

Behavior	Sample Size	Sample Mean	Sample sd
Noncourting	11	.072	.0066
Courting	15	.099	.0071

a. The pooled t test is a test procedure for testing H_0: $\mu_1 - \mu_2 = hypothesized\ value$ when it is reasonable to assume that the two population distributions are normal with equal standard deviations ($\sigma_1 = \sigma_2$). The test statistic for the pooled t test is obtained by replacing both s_1 and s_2 in the two-sample t test statistic with s_p, where

$$s_p = \sqrt{\frac{(n_1 - 1)s_1^2 + (n_2 - 1)s_2^2}{n_1 + n_2 - 2}}$$

When the population distributions are normal with equal standard deviations and H_0 is true, the resulting pooled t statistic has a t distribution with df $= n_1 + n_2 - 2$. For the reported data, the two sample standard deviations are similar. Use the pooled t test with $\alpha = .05$ to determine whether the mean oxygen consumption for courting pairs is higher than the mean oxygen consumption for noncourting pairs.

b. Would the conclusion in part **a** have been different if the two-sample t test had been used rather than the pooled t test?

11.2 Inferences Concerning the Difference Between Two Population or Treatment Means Using Paired Samples

Two samples are said to be *independent* if the selection of the individuals or objects that make up one of the samples has no bearing on the selection of those in the other sample. In some situations, an experiment with independent samples is not the best way to obtain information concerning a possible difference between the populations. For example, suppose that an investigator wants to determine whether regular aerobic exercise affects blood pressure. A random sample of people who jog regularly and a second random sample of people who do not exercise regularly are selected independently of one another. The researcher then uses the two-sample *t* test to conclude that a significant difference exists between the average blood pressures for joggers and nonjoggers. Is it reasonable to think that the difference in mean blood pressure is attributable to jogging? It is known that blood pressure is related to both diet and body weight. Might it not be the case that joggers in the sample tend to be leaner and adhere to a healthier diet than the nonjoggers and that *this* might account for the observed difference? On the basis of this study, the researcher wouldn't be able to rule out the possibility that the observed difference in blood pressure is explained by weight differences between the people in the two samples and that aerobic exercise itself has no effect.

One way to avoid this difficulty would be to match subjects by weight. The researcher would find pairs of subjects so that the jogger and nonjogger in each pair were similar in weight (although weights for different pairs might vary widely). The factor *weight* could then be ruled out as a possible explanation for an observed difference in average blood pressure between the two groups. Matching the subjects by weight results in two samples for which each observation in the first sample is coupled in a meaningful way with a particular observation in the second sample. Such samples are said to be **paired.**

Experiments can be designed to yield paired data in a number of different ways. Some studies involve using the same group of individuals with measurements recorded both before and after some intervening treatment. Others use naturally occurring pairs, such as twins or husbands and wives, and some construct pairs by matching on factors with effects that might otherwise obscure differences (or the lack of them) between the two populations of interest (as might weight in the jogging example). Paired samples often provide more information than would independent samples, because extraneous effects are screened out.

EXAMPLE 11.5   It has been hypothesized that strenuous physical activity affects hormone levels. The article "Growth Hormone Increase During Sleep After Daytime Exercise" (*J. of Endocrinology* (1974): 473–478) reported the results of an experiment involving six healthy male subjects. For each participant, blood samples were taken during sleep on two different nights. The first blood sample (the control) was drawn after a day that included no strenuous activities, and the second was drawn after a day when the subject had engaged in strenuous exercise. The resulting data on growth hormone level (in mg/ml) follows. The samples are paired rather than independent, because both samples are composed of measurements on the same men.

	Subject					
	1	**2**	**3**	**4**	**5**	**6**
Postexercise	13.6	14.7	42.8	20.0	19.2	17.3
Control	8.5	12.6	21.6	19.4	14.7	13.6

Let μ_1 denote the mean nocturnal growth hormone level for the population of all healthy males who participated in strenuous activity on the previous day. Similarly, let μ_2 denote the mean nocturnal hormone level for the population consisting of all healthy males whose activities on the previous day did not include any strenuous physical exercise. The hypotheses of interest are then

$$H_0: \quad \mu_1 - \mu_2 = 0 \quad \text{versus} \quad H_a: \quad \mu_1 - \mu_2 \neq 0$$

Notice that in each of the six data pairs, the postexercise hormone level is higher than the corresponding control level. Intuitively, this suggests that there may be a difference between the population means.

Disregarding the paired nature of the samples results in a loss of information. Nocturnal growth hormone levels vary substantially from one individual to another. It is this variability that may obscure the difference in hormone level associated with strenuous exercise when the two-sample t test is used. If we were to (incorrectly) use the two-sample t test for independent samples on the given data, the resulting t test statistic value would be 1.28. This value would not allow for rejection of the hypothesis $\mu_1 - \mu_2 = 0$, even at level of significance .10. This result might surprise you at first, but remember that this test procedure ignores the fact that the samples are paired. Two plots of the data are given in Figure 11.1. The first one ignores the pairing, and the two samples look quite similar. The plot in which pairs are identified does suggest a difference, since for each pair the exercise observation exceeds the no-exercise observation.

FIGURE 11.1 Two plots of the paired data from Example 11.5: (a) Pairing ignored; (b) Pairs identified

Example 11.5 suggests that the methods of inference developed for independent samples are not adequate for dealing with paired samples. When sample observations from the first population are paired in some meaningful way with sample observations from the second population, inferences can be based on the differences between the two observations within each sample pair. The n sample differences can then be regarded as having been selected from a large population of differences. Thus, in Example 11.5, we can think of the six (postexercise − control) differences as having been selected from an entire population of differences. Let

μ_d = mean value of the difference population

and

σ_d = standard deviation of the difference population

The relationship between μ_d and the two individual population means is

$$\mu_d = \mu_1 - \mu_2$$

Therefore, when the samples are paired, inferences about $\mu_1 - \mu_2$ are equivalent to inferences about μ_d. Since inferences about μ_d can be based on the n observed sample differences, the original two-sample problem becomes a familiar one-sample problem.

The Paired t Test

To compare two population or treatment means when the samples are paired, we first translate the hypothesis of interest from one about the value of $\mu_1 - \mu_2$ to an equivalent one involving μ_d.

Hypothesis	Equivalent Hypothesis When Samples Are Paired
H_0: $\mu_1 - \mu_2$ = hypothesized value	H_0: μ_d = hypothesized value
H_a: $\mu_1 - \mu_2$ > hypothesized value	H_a: μ_d > hypothesized value
H_a: $\mu_1 - \mu_2$ < hypothesized value	H_a: μ_d < hypothesized value
H_a: $\mu_1 - \mu_2 \neq$ hypothesized value	H_a: $\mu_d \neq$ hypothesized value

Sample differences (sample 1 value − sample 2 value) are then computed and used as the basis for testing hypotheses about μ_d. When the sample size is large or it is reasonable to assume that the population of differences is approximately normal, the one-sample t test based on the differences is the recommended test procedure. Generally speaking, the difference population will be normal if each of the two individual populations is normal. A normal probability plot or boxplot of the differences can be used to validate this assumption.

Summary of the Paired t Test for Comparing Two Population or Treatment Means

Null hypothesis: H_0: μ_d = hypothesized value

Test statistic: $t = \dfrac{\bar{x}_d - \text{hypothesized value}}{\dfrac{s_d}{\sqrt{n}}}$

where n is the number of sample differences and $\bar{x}_d$ and s_d are the sample mean and standard deviation of the differences. This test is based on df $= n - 1$.

Alternative hypothesis:	*P-value*:
H_a: μ_d > hypothesized value	Area under the appropriate t curve to the right of the calculated t
H_a: μ_d < hypothesized value	Area under the appropriate t curve to the left of the calculated t
H_a: $\mu_d \neq$ hypothesized value	(i) 2 · (area to the right of t) if t is positive
	or
	(ii) 2 · (area to the left of t) if t is negative

(continued)

Assumptions: 1. The samples are *paired*.
2. The *n* sample differences can be viewed as a *random sample* from a population of differences.
3. The *number of sample differences is large* (generally at least 30) OR the *population distribution of differences is approximately normal*.

EXAMPLE 11.6   Children with Down syndrome generally show a pattern of retarded mental development, although some achieve higher intellectual levels than others. The intellectual achievements of Down syndrome children have been studied by numerous investigators, and several different types of chromosomal abnormalities associated with the syndrome have been identified. Two such abnormalities are called trisomy 21 and mosaicism. The levels of intellectual functioning of trisomy 21 and mosaic Down syndrome children were compared in the article "Mental Development in Down Syndrome Mosaicism" (*Amer. Journal on Mental Retardation* (1991): 345–351).

Thirty children with mosaic Down syndrome who were treated at USC Medical Center were selected to participate in the research project. The investigators then chose 30 children with trisomy 21 Down syndrome from among 350 who had been seen at the medical center. The 30 chosen were selected (with the help of a computer) to achieve the best possible matches for children in the mosaic group, using age, gender, and parental socioeconomic status as the criteria for matching. The result was 30 matched pairs of children. IQ levels for all of the children were determined.

The researchers proposed using this data to test the theory that children with mosaic Down syndrome generally achieve higher intellectual levels. These samples were not independently chosen, since the 30 trisomy 21 children were specifically selected to match the children in the mosaic sample. Since the data is paired, our analysis will focus on the mosaic–trisomy 21 IQ differences. The data and computed differences are shown in the accompanying table.

Pair	Mosaic	Trisomy 21	Difference	Pair	Mosaic	Trisomy 21	Difference
1	73	71	2	11	58	63	−5
2	43	53	−10	12	71	47	24
3	69	58	11	13	92	44	48
4	89	71	18	14	57	28	29
5	53	50	3	15	76	75	1
6	81	70	11	16	55	60	−5
7	59	55	4	17	61	48	13
8	71	18	53	18	63	55	8
9	65	31	34	19	87	59	28
10	53	57	−4	20	64	78	−14

(continued)

Pair	Mosaic	Trisomy 21	Difference		Pair	Mosaic	Trisomy 21	Difference
21	63	55	8		26	61	50	11
22	58	51	7		27	91	63	28
23	50	55	−5		28	43	46	−3
24	59	53	6		29	55	54	1
25	75	47	28		30	88	48	40

Let

μ_1 = mean IQ for children with mosaic Down syndrome

μ_2 = mean IQ for children with trisomy 21 Down syndrome

and

$\mu_d = \mu_1 - \mu_2$ = mean IQ difference between mosaic and trisomy 21 Down syndrome children

The question of interest can be answered by testing the hypothesis

H_0: $\mu_d = 0$ versus H_a: $\mu_d > 0$

Using the 30 differences, we compute

$$\Sigma \text{ diff} = 370 \qquad \Sigma (\text{diff})^2 = 13{,}134$$

$$\bar{x}_d = \frac{\Sigma \text{ diff}}{n} = \frac{370}{30} = 12.33$$

$$s_d^2 = \frac{\Sigma (\text{diff})^2 - \dfrac{(\Sigma \text{ diff})^2}{n}}{n-1} = \frac{13{,}134 - \dfrac{(370)^2}{30}}{29} = 295.54$$

$$s_d = \sqrt{s_d^2} = 17.19$$

We now use the paired t test with a significance level of .05 to carry out the hypothesis test.

1. $\mu_d = \mu_1 - \mu_2$ = mean IQ difference between mosaic and trisomy 21 Down syndrome children

2. H_0: $\mu_d = 0$

3. H_a: $\mu_d > 0$

4. *Significance level*: $\alpha = .05$

5. *Test statistic*: $t = \dfrac{\bar{x}_d - \text{hypothesized value}}{\dfrac{s_d}{\sqrt{n}}} = \dfrac{\bar{x}_d - 0}{\dfrac{s_d}{\sqrt{n}}}$

6. *Assumptions*:   The sample size is large ($n = 30$). The researchers believed that it was reasonable to view the 30 sample differences as a random sample of all such differences, and so we will proceed with the paired t test.

7. *Calculation*: $t = \dfrac{12.33 - 0}{\dfrac{17.19}{\sqrt{30}}} = 3.93$

8. *P-value*: This is an upper-tailed test, so the *P*-value is the area to the right of the computed *t* value. The appropriate df for this test is df = 30 − 1 = 29. From the 29-df column and the 3.9 row of Appendix Table IV, we find that

   P-value = .000

   The area to the right of 3.9 under the *t* curve with 29 df is so small that when it is rounded to 3 decimal places, the value is .000.

9. *Conclusion*: Since *P*-value ≤ α (.000 ≤ .05), we reject H_0. The data supports the theory that the mean IQ for mosaic Down syndrome children is higher than the mean IQ for trisomy 21 Down syndrome children.

To use the two-sample *t* test (for independent samples) for the data in Example 11.6 would have been incorrect, because the samples are not independent. Inappropriate use of the two-sample *t* test would have resulted in a computed test statistic value of 3.55. The conclusion would still be to reject the hypothesis of equal mean IQs in this particular example, but this is not always the case.

EXAMPLE 11.7

It has been estimated that between 1945 and 1971, as many as 2 million children were born to mothers treated with diethylstilbestrol (DES), a nonsteroidal estrogen. The FDA banned this drug in 1971 because research indicated a link with the incidence of cervical cancer. The article "Effects of Prenatal Exposure to Diethylstilbestrol (DES) on Hemispheric Laterality and Spatial Ability in Human Males" (*Hormones and Behavior* (1992): 62–75) discussed a study in which 10 males exposed to DES and their unexposed brothers underwent various tests. Here is the summary data on the results of a spatial ability test:

$$n = 10 \qquad \bar{x}_1 = \text{exposed mean} = 12.6 \qquad \bar{x}_2 = \text{unexposed mean} = 13.8$$

$$\bar{x}_d = -1.2 \qquad \text{standard error of difference} = \frac{s_d}{\sqrt{n}} = .5$$

The investigators used a one-tailed test to see whether DES exposure was associated with reduced spatial ability.

1. μ_d = difference between true average score for exposed males and true average score for unexposed males

2. $H_0: \mu_d = 0$

3. $H_a: \mu_d < 0$

4. *Significance level*: $\alpha = .05$

5. *Test statistic*: $t = \dfrac{\bar{x}_d - \text{hypothesized value}}{\dfrac{s_d}{\sqrt{n}}} = \dfrac{\bar{x}_d - 0}{\dfrac{s_d}{\sqrt{n}}}$

6. *Assumptions*: Without the raw data, it is difficult to assess the reasonableness of the assumptions. The author of the article judged the assumptions of the paired *t* test to be reasonable, so we will proceed.

7. *Calculation*: $t = \dfrac{-1.2 - 0}{.5} = -2.4$

8. *P-value*: This is a lower-tailed test. There are 10 sample differences, so df = 10 − 1 = 9. From the 9-df column and the 2.4 row of Appendix Table IV, we find that the area to the right of 2.4 is .020. Since the *t* curve is symmetric around 0, the area to the left of −2.4 is also .020, so

   P-value = .020

9. *Conclusion*: Since *P*-value ≤ α, H_0 is rejected. There is evidence that the mean spatial ability score is lower for those exposed to DES than for those who were unexposed.

The numerators $\bar{x}_d$ and $\bar{x}_1 - \bar{x}_2$ of the paired *t* and two-sample *t* test statistics are always equal. The difference lies in the denominator. The variability in differences is usually much smaller than the variability in each sample separately (because measurements in a pair tend to be similar). As a result, the value of the paired *t* statistic is usually larger in magnitude than the value of the two-sample *t* statistic. Pairing typically reduces variability that might otherwise obscure small but nevertheless significant differences.

A Confidence Interval

The one-sample *t* confidence interval for μ given in Chapter 9 is easily adapted to obtain an interval estimate for μ_d.

Paired *t* Confidence Interval for μ_d

When

1. the samples are *paired,*

2. the *n* sample differences can be viewed as a *random sample* from a population of differences, and

3. the *number of sample differences is large* (generally at least 30) OR the *population distribution of differences is approximately normal,*

the paired *t* confidence interval for μ_d is

$$\bar{x}_d \pm (t \text{ critical value}) \cdot \frac{s_d}{\sqrt{n}}$$

For a specified confidence level, the (*n* − 1) df row of Appendix Table III gives the appropriate *t* critical value.

EXAMPLE 11.8   The effect of exercise on the amount of lactic acid in the blood was examined in the article "A Descriptive Analysis of Elite-Level Racquetball" (*Research Quarterly for Exercise and Sport* (1991): 109–114). Eight males were selected at random from those attending a week-long training camp. Blood lactate levels were measured before and after playing three games of racquetball, as shown in the accompanying table. We will use this data to estimate the mean change in blood lactate level using a 95% confidence interval.

Player	Before	After	Difference
1	13	18	−5
2	20	37	−17
3	17	40	−23
4	13	35	−22
5	13	30	−17
6	16	20	−4
7	15	33	−18
8	16	19	−3

$$\bar{x}_d = -13.63 \qquad s_d = 8.28 \qquad n = 8$$

The eight men were selected at random from training camp participants. The accompanying boxplot of the eight sample differences is consistent with a difference population that is approximately normal, so the paired t confidence interval is appropriate.

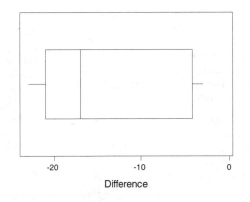

Difference

The t critical value for df = 7 and a 95% confidence level is 2.36, and so the confidence interval is

$$\bar{x}_d \pm (t \text{ critical value}) \cdot \frac{s_d}{\sqrt{n}} = -13.63 \pm (2.37) \cdot \frac{8.28}{\sqrt{8}}$$
$$= -13.63 \pm 6.938$$
$$= (-20.568, -6.692)$$

Based on the sample data, we can be 95% confident that the difference in mean blood lactate level is between −20.568 and −6.692. That is, we are 95% confident that the mean decrease in blood lactate level is somewhere between 6.692 and 20.568 after three games of racquetball.

When two populations must be compared to draw a conclusion on the basis of sample data, a researcher might choose to use independent samples or paired samples. In many situations, paired data provides a more effective comparison by screening out the effects of extraneous variables that might obscure differences between the two populations or that might suggest a difference when none exists.

Exercises 11.32 – 11.43

11.32 Suppose that you were interested in investigating the effect of a drug that is to be used in the treatment of patients who have glaucoma in both eyes. A comparison between the mean reduction in eye pressure for this drug and for a standard treatment is desired. Both treatments are applied directly to the eye.
  a. Describe how you would go about collecting data for your investigation.
  b. Does your method result in paired data?
  c. Can you think of a reasonable method of collecting data that would result in independent samples? Would such an experiment be as informative as a paired experiment? Comment.

11.33 Two different underground pipe coatings for preventing corrosion are to be compared. The effect of a coating (as measured by maximum depth of corrosion penetration on a piece of pipe) may vary with depth, orientation, soil type, pipe composition, etc. Describe how an experiment that filters out the effects of these extraneous factors could be carried out.

11.34 In a study of memory recall, eight students from a large psychology class were selected at random and given 10 min to memorize a list of 20 nonsense words. Each was asked to list as many of the words as he or she could remember both 1 hr and 24 hr later, as shown in the accompanying table. Is there evidence to suggest that the mean number of words recalled after 1 hr exceeds the mean recall after 24 hr by more than 3? Use a level .01 test.

Subject	1	2	3	4	5	6	7	8
1 hr later	14	12	18	7	11	9	16	15
24 hr later	10	4	14	6	9	6	12	12

11.35 Do girls think they don't need to take as many science classes as boys? The article "Intentions of Young Students to Enroll in Science Courses in the Future: An Examination of Gender Differences" (*Science Education* (1999): 55–76) gives information from a survey of children in grades 4, 5, and 6. The 224 girls participating in the survey each indicated the number of science courses they intended to take in the future, and they also indicated the number of science courses they thought boys

their age should take in the future. For each girl, the authors calculated the difference between the number of science classes she intends to take and the number she thinks boys should take.
  a. Explain why this data is paired.
  b. The mean of the differences was −.83 (indicating girls intended, on average, to take fewer classes than they thought boys should take), and the standard deviation was 1.51. Construct and interpret a 95% confidence interval for the mean difference.

11.36 As part of a study to determine the effects of allowing the use of credit cards for alcohol purchases in Canada (see "Changes in Alcohol Consumption Patterns Following the Introduction of Credit Cards in Ontario Liquor Stores," *Journal of Studies on Alcohol* (1999): 378–382), randomly selected individuals were given a questionnaire asking them (among other things) how many drinks they had consumed during the previous week. A year later (after liquor stores started accepting credit cards for purchases), these same individuals were again asked how many drinks they had consumed in the previous week. The data shown is consistent with summary statistics presented in the article.

	n	1994 Mean	1995 Mean	$\bar{d}$	s_d
Credit-Card Shoppers	96	6.72	6.34	.38	5.52
Non–Credit-Card Shoppers	850	4.09	3.97	.12	4.58

  a. The standard deviation of the difference was quite large. Explain how this could be the case.
  b. Calculate a 95% confidence interval for the mean difference in drink consumption for credit card shoppers between 1994 and 1995. Did the mean number of drinks decrease?
  c. Test the hypothesis that there was no change in the mean number of drinks between 1994 and 1995 for the non–credit-card shoppers. Be sure to calculate and interpret the *P*-value for this test.

11.37 The article "Agronomic Performance of Winter Versus Spring Wheat" (*Agronomy J.* (1991): 527–531) described the results of an experiment to compare the yield (kg/ha) of Sundance winter wheat and Manitou spring wheat. Data for nine test plots is given in the accompanying table. Is there sufficient evidence to conclude that the mean yield for the Sundance winter wheat is higher than that for the Manitou spring wheat? Use $\alpha = .01$.

	Location				
	1	**2**	**3**	**4**	**5**
Sundance	3201	3095	3297	3644	3604
Manitou	2386	2011	2616	3094	3069

	Location			
	6	**7**	**8**	**9**
Sundance	2860	3470	2042	3689
Manitou	2074	2308	1525	2779

11.38 The article referenced in Exercise 11.37 also gave information on the protein concentration of Sundance winter wheat and Manitou spring wheat grown at nine locations. Protein concentration was measured in grams of protein per kilogram of wheat.

a. Use the accompanying data to determine whether there is a significant difference in protein concentration for the two varieties of wheat.

b. Construct a 90% confidence interval for the true difference in mean protein concentration for the two varieties of wheat.

	Location				
	1	**2**	**3**	**4**	**5**
Sundance	77	84	116	145	100
Manitou	125	111	144	171	133

	Location			
	6	**7**	**8**	**9**
Sundance	154	144	149	137
Manitou	166	143	176	170

11.39 Several methods of estimating the number of seeds in soil samples have been developed by ecologists. An article in the *Journal of Ecology* ("A Comparison of Methods for Estimating Seed Numbers in the Soil" (1990): 1079–1093) considered three such methods. The accompanying data gives number of seeds detected by the direct method and by the stratified method for 27 soil specimens. Does the data provide sufficient evidence to conclude that the mean number of seeds detected differs for the two methods? Test the relevant hypotheses using $\alpha = .05$.

Sample	Direct	Stratified
1	24	8
2	32	36
3	0	8
4	60	56
5	20	52
6	64	64
7	40	28
8	8	8
9	12	8
10	92	100
11	4	0
12	68	56
13	76	68
14	24	52
15	32	28
16	0	0
17	36	36
18	16	12
19	92	92
20	4	12
21	40	48
22	24	24
23	0	0
24	8	12
25	12	40
26	16	12
27	40	76

11.40 The effect of exercise on the amount of lactic acid in the blood was examined in the article "A Descriptive Analysis of Elite-Level Racquetball" (*Research Quarterly for Exercise and Sport* (1991): 109–114). Eight men and seven women who were attending a week-long training camp participated in the experiment. Blood lactate levels were measured before and after playing three games of racquetball, as shown in the accompanying table.

Men				**Women**		
Player	**Before**	**After**		**Player**	**Before**	**After**
1	13	18		1	11	21
2	20	37		2	16	26
3	17	40		3	13	19
4	13	35		4	18	21
5	13	30		5	14	14
6	16	20		6	11	31
7	15	33		7	13	20
8	16	19				

a. Estimate the mean change in blood lactate level for male racquetball players using a 90% confidence interval. Why is this interval wider than the one in Example 11.8?

b. Estimate the mean change for female players using a 90% confidence interval.

c. Based on the intervals from parts **a** and **b,** do you think the mean change in blood lactate level is the same for men as it is for women? Explain.

11.41 Dentists make many people nervous (even more so than statisticians!). To see whether such nervousness elevates blood pressure, the blood pressure and pulse rates of 60 subjects were measured in a dental setting and in a medical setting ("The Effect of the Dental Setting on Blood Pressure Measurement," *Am. J. of Public Health* (1983): 1210–1214). For each subject, the difference (dental-setting blood pressure minus medical-setting blood pressure) was calculated. The analogous differences were also calculated for pulse rates. Summary data follows.

	Mean Difference	Standard Deviation of Differences
Systolic blood pressure	4.47	8.77
Pulse (beats/min)	−1.33	8.84

a. Does the data strongly suggest that true mean blood pressure is higher in a dental setting than in a medical setting? Use a level .01 test.

b. Is there sufficient evidence to indicate that true mean pulse rate in a dental setting differs from the true mean pulse rate in a medical setting? Use a significance level of .05.

11.42 Many people who quit smoking complain of weight gain. The results of an investigation of the relationship between smoking cessation and weight gain are given in the article "Does Smoking Cessation Lead to Weight Gain?" (*Amer. J. of Public Health* (1983): 1303–1305). Three hundred twenty-two subjects, selected at random from those who successfully participated in a program to quit smoking, were weighed at the beginning of the program and again 1 year later. The mean change in weight was 5.15 lb, and the standard deviation of the weight changes was 11.45 lb. Is there sufficient evidence to conclude that the true mean change in weight is positive? Use $\alpha = .05$.

11.43 The article "A Supplementary Behavioral Program to Improve Deficient Reading Performance" (*J. Abnormal Child Psych.* (1973): 390–399) reported the results of an experiment in which seven pairs of children reading below grade level were obtained by matching, so that within each pair the two children were equally deficient in reading ability. Then one child (selected at random) from each pair received experimental training, whereas the other received standard training. Based on the accompanying improvement scores, does the experimental training appear to be superior to the standard training? Use a .1 significance level.

	Pair						
	1	2	3	4	5	6	7
Experimental	.5	1.0	.6	.1	1.3	.1	1.0
Control	.8	1.1	−.1	.2	.2	1.5	.8

11.3 Large-Sample Inferences Concerning a Difference Between Two Population or Treatment Proportions

Large-sample methods for estimating and testing hypotheses about a single population proportion were presented in Chapters 9 and 10. The symbol π was used to represent the true proportion of individuals in the population who possess some characteristic (the "successes"). Inferences about the value of π were based on p, the corresponding sample proportion of successes.

Many investigations are carried out to compare the proportion of successes in one population (or resulting from one treatment) to the proportion of successes in a second population (or from a second treatment). As was the case for means, the subscripts 1 and 2 are used to distinguish between the two population proportions, sample sizes, and sample proportions.

Notation

Population or Treatment 1:   Proportion of "successes" = π_1

Population or Treatment 2:   Proportion of "successes" = π_2

	Sample Size	Proportion of Successes
Sample from population or treatment 1	n_1	p_1
Sample from population or treatment 2	n_2	p_2

When comparing two populations or treatments on the basis of "success" proportions, it is common to focus on the quantity $\pi_1 - \pi_2$, the difference between the two proportions. Since p_1 provides an estimate of π_1 and p_2 provides an estimate of π_2, the obvious choice for an estimate of $\pi_1 - \pi_2$ is $p_1 - p_2$.

Because p_1 and p_2 each vary in value from sample to sample, so will the difference $p_1 - p_2$. For example, a first sample from each of two populations might yield

$$p_1 = .69 \qquad p_2 = .70 \qquad p_1 - p_2 = -.01$$

A second sample from each might result in

$$p_1 = .79 \qquad p_2 = .67 \qquad p_1 - p_2 = .12$$

and so on. Since the statistic $p_1 - p_2$ will be the basis for drawing inferences about $\pi_1 - \pi_2$, we need to know something about its behavior.

Properties of the Sampling Distribution of $p_1 - p_2$

If two random samples are selected independently of one another, the following properties hold:

1. $\mu_{p_1-p_2} = \pi_1 - \pi_2$

   This says that the sampling distribution of $p_1 - p_2$ is centered at $\pi_1 - \pi_2$, so $p_1 - p_2$ is an unbiased statistic for estimating $\pi_1 - \pi_2$.

2. $\sigma^2_{p_1-p_2} = \sigma^2_{p_1} + \sigma^2_{p_2} = \dfrac{\pi_1(1 - \pi_1)}{n_1} + \dfrac{\pi_2(1 - \pi_2)}{n_2}$

   and

   $$\sigma_{p_1-p_2} = \sqrt{\dfrac{\pi_1(1 - \pi_1)}{n_1} + \dfrac{\pi_2(1 - \pi_2)}{n_2}}$$

3. If both n_1 and n_2 are large (that is, if $n_1\pi_1 \geq 10$, $n_1(1 - \pi_1) \geq 10$, $n_2\pi_2 \geq 10$, and $n_2(1 - \pi_2) \geq 10$), then p_1 and p_2 each have a sampling distribution that is approximately normal, and their difference, $p_1 - p_2$, also has a sampling distribution that is approximately normal.

The properties in the box imply that when the samples are independently selected and both sample sizes are large, the distribution of the standardized variable

$$z = \frac{p_1 - p_2 - (\pi_1 - \pi_2)}{\sqrt{\dfrac{\pi_1(1 - \pi_1)}{n_1} + \dfrac{\pi_2(1 - \pi_2)}{n_2}}}$$

is described approximately by the standard normal (z) curve.

A Large-Sample Test Procedure

Comparisons of π_1 and π_2 are often based on large, independently selected samples, and we restrict ourselves to this case. The most general null hypothesis of interest has the form

$$H_0: \quad \pi_1 - \pi_2 = \text{hypothesized value}$$

However, when the hypothesized value is something other than zero, the appropriate test statistic differs somewhat from the test statistic used for $H_0: \pi_1 - \pi_2 = 0$. Since this latter H_0 is almost always the relevant one in applied problems, we will focus exclusively on it.

Our basic testing principle has been to use a procedure that controls the probability of a type I error at the desired level α. This requires using a test statistic with a sampling distribution that is known when H_0 is true. That is, the test statistic should be developed under the assumption that $\pi_1 = \pi_2$ (as specified by the null hypothesis $\pi_1 - \pi_2 = 0$). In this case, π can be used to denote the common value of the two population proportions. The z variable obtained by standardizing $p_1 - p_2$ then simplifies to

$$z = \frac{p_1 - p_2}{\sqrt{\dfrac{\pi(1 - \pi)}{n_1} + \dfrac{\pi(1 - \pi)}{n_2}}}$$

Unfortunately, this cannot serve as a test statistic, because the denominator cannot be computed: H_0 says that there is a common value π but it does not specify the value. A test statistic can be obtained, though, by first *estimating* π from the sample data and then using this estimate in the denominator of z.

When $\pi_1 = \pi_2$, either p_1 or p_2 separately gives an estimate of the common proportion π. However, a better estimate than either of these is a weighted average of the two, in which more weight is given to the sample proportion based on the larger sample.

Definition

The **combined estimate of the common population proportion** is

$$p_c = \frac{n_1 p_1 + n_2 p_2}{n_1 + n_2} = \frac{\text{total number of } S\text{'s in two samples}}{\text{total sample size}}$$

The test statistic for testing $H_0: \pi_1 - \pi_2 = 0$ results from using p_c in place of π in the standardized variable z given previously. This z statistic has approximately a standard normal distribution when H_0 is true, so a test that has the desired significance level α can be obtained by calculating a P-value using the z table.

Summary of Large-Sample z Tests for $\pi_1 - \pi_2 = 0$

Null hypothesis: $H_0: \pi_1 - \pi_2 = 0$

Test statistic: $z = \dfrac{p_1 - p_2}{\sqrt{\dfrac{p_c(1 - p_c)}{n_1} + \dfrac{p_c(1 - p_c)}{n_2}}}$

Alternative hypothesis: *P-value*:

$H_a: \pi_1 - \pi_2 > 0$ Area under the z curve to the right of the computed z

$H_a: \pi_1 - \pi_2 < 0$ Area under the z curve to the left of the computed z

$H_a: \pi_1 - \pi_2 \neq 0$ (i) $2 \cdot$ (area to the right of z) if z is positive

                            or

                            (ii) $2 \cdot$ (area to the left of z) is z is negative

Assumptions: 1. The samples are *independently chosen random samples* OR *treatments were assigned at random to individuals or objects* (or vice versa).

              2. Both *sample sizes are large*:

$$n_1 p_1 \geq 10 \qquad n_1(1 - p_1) \geq 10 \qquad n_2 p_2 \geq 10 \qquad n_2(1 - p_2) \geq 10$$

EXAMPLE 11.9

Many investigators have studied the effect of the wording of questions on survey responses. Consider the following two versions of a question concerning gun control:

1. Would you favor or oppose a law that would require a person to obtain a police permit before purchasing a gun?

2. Would you favor or oppose a law that would require a person to obtain a police permit before purchasing a gun, or do you think that such a law would interfere too much with the right of citizens to own guns?

Let π_1 denote the proportion of all adults who would respond "favor" when asked question 1, and define π_2 similarly for question 2. The article "Attitude Measurement and the Gun Control Paradox" (*Public Opinion Quarterly* (1977–1978): 427–438) reported the accompanying sample data from two independently chosen random samples:

Sample size	$n_1 = 615$	$n_2 = 585$
Number who favor	463	403
Sample proportion	$p_1 = 463/615 = .753$	$p_2 = 403/585 = .689$

The extra phrase in question 2 that reminds individuals of the right to bear arms might elicit a smaller proportion of favorable responses than would the first question without the phrase. Does the data suggest that this is the case? We will test the relevant hypotheses using $\alpha = .01$. Suppose that $\pi_1 = \pi_2$; let π denote the common value. Then the combined estimate of π is

$$p_c = \frac{n_1 p_1 + n_2 p_2}{n_1 + n_2} = \frac{615(.753) + 585(.689)}{615 + 585} = .722$$

The nine-step procedure can now be used to perform the hypothesis test:

1. $\pi_1 - \pi_2$ is the difference between the true proportions of favorable responses to questions 1 and 2.

2. $H_0: \pi_1 - \pi_2 = 0 \quad (\pi_1 = \pi_2)$

3. $H_a: \pi_1 - \pi_2 > 0 \quad (\pi_1 > \pi_2,$ in which case the extra phrase *does* result in proportionately fewer favorable responses.)

4. *Significance level:* $\alpha = .01$

5. *Test statistic:* $z = \dfrac{p_1 - p_2}{\sqrt{\dfrac{p_c(1 - p_c)}{n_1} + \dfrac{p_c(1 - p_c)}{n_2}}}$

6. *Assumptions:* The two samples are independently chosen random samples. Checking to make sure that the sample sizes are large enough, we have

$$n_1 p_1 = 615(.753) = 463.10 \geq 10 \qquad n_1(1 - p_1) = 615(.247) = 151.91 \geq 10$$
$$n_2 p_2 = 585(.689) = 403.07 \geq 10 \qquad n_2(1 - p_2) = 585(.311) = 181.94 \geq 10$$

7. *Calculation:* $n_1 = 615, n_2 = 585, p_1 = .753, p_2 = .689,$ and $p_c = .722,$ so

$$z = \frac{.753 - .689}{\sqrt{\dfrac{(.722)(.278)}{615} + \dfrac{(.722)(.278)}{585}}} = \frac{.064}{.0259} = 2.47$$

8. *P-value:* This is an upper-tailed test, so the *P*-value is the area under the z curve and to the right of the computed $z = 2.47$. From Appendix Table II,

P-value $= 1 - .9932 = .0068$

9. *Conclusion:* Since *P*-value $\leq \alpha$, the hypothesis H_0 is rejected at level .01. Inclusion of the extra phrase about the right to bear arms *does* seem to result in fewer favorable responses than would be elicited without the phrase. This example points out the need to be particularly careful in wording survey questions.

EXAMPLE 11.10

The authors of the article "Accommodating Persons with AIDS: Acceptance and Rejection in Rental Situations" (*J. Applied Social Psychology* (1999): 261–270) state that even though landlords participating in a telephone survey indicated that they would generally be willing to rent to persons with AIDS, they wondered whether this was true in actual practice. To investigate, two random samples of 80 advertisements for rooms for rent were independently selected from newspaper advertisements in three large cities. An adult male caller responded to each ad in the first sample of 80 and inquired about the availability of the room and was told that the room was still available in 61 of these calls. The same caller also responded to each ad in the second sample. In these calls, the caller indicated that he was currently receiving some treatment for AIDS and was about to be released from the hospital and would require a place to live. The caller was told that a room was available in 32 of these calls. Based on this information, the authors concluded that "reference to AIDS substantially decreased the likelihood of a room being described as available." Does the data support this conclusion? Let's carry out a hypothesis test with $\alpha = .01$.

| No AIDS Reference | $n_1 = 80$ | $p_1 = 61/80 = .763$ |
| AIDS Reference | $n_2 = 80$ | $p_2 = 32/80 = .400$ |

1. π_1 = proportion of rooms available when there is no AIDS reference

   π_2 = proportion of rooms available with AIDS reference

2. $H_0: \pi_1 - \pi_2 = 0$

3. $H_a: \pi_1 - \pi_2 > 0$

4. *Significance level*: $\alpha = .01$

5. *Test statistic*: $z = \dfrac{p_1 - p_2}{\sqrt{\dfrac{p_c(1 - p_c)}{n_1} + \dfrac{p_c(1 - p_c)}{n_2}}}$

6. *Assumptions*: The two samples are independently chosen random samples. Checking to make sure that the sample sizes are large enough, we have

$$n_1 = 80 \qquad n_2 = 80 \qquad p_1 = .763 \qquad p_2 = .400$$

$$p_c = \frac{n_1 p_1 + n_2 p_2}{n_1 + n_2} = \frac{80(.763) + 80(.400)}{80 + 80} = .582$$

$$n_1 p_1 = 61.04 \geq 10 \qquad n_1(1 - p_1) = 18.96 \geq 10$$

$$n_2 p_2 = 32.00 \geq 10 \qquad n_2(1 - p_2) = 48.00 \geq 10$$

7. *Calculations*: $z = \dfrac{.763 - .400}{\sqrt{\dfrac{(.582)(.418)}{80} + \dfrac{(.582)(.418)}{80}}} = \dfrac{.363}{.078} = 4.65$

8. *P-value*: The *P*-value for this test is the area under the z curve and to the right of the computed $z = 4.65$. Since 4.65 is so far out in the upper tail of the z curve,

   P-value ≈ 0

9. *Conclusion*: Since *P*-value $\leq \alpha$, the hypothesis H_0 is rejected at level .01. There is strong evidence that the proportion of rooms reported as available is smaller with the AIDS reference than without it. This supports the claim made by the authors of the article.

   MINITAB can also be used to carry out a two-sample z test to compare two population proportions, as shown in the accompanying output.

Test and Confidence Interval for Two Proportions

Sample	X	N	Sample p
1	61	80	0.762500
2	32	80	0.400000

Estimate for p(1) - p(2): 0.3625
95% CI for p(1) - p(2): (0.220302, 0.504698)
Test for p(1) - p(2) = 0 (vs > 0): $z = 4.65$ P-Value = 0.000

A Confidence Interval

A large-sample confidence interval for $\pi_1 - \pi_2$ is a special case of the general z interval formula

$$\text{point estimate} \pm (z \text{ critical value})(\text{estimated standard deviation})$$

The statistic $p_1 - p_2$ gives a point estimate of $\pi_1 - \pi_2$, and the standard deviation of this statistic is

$$\sigma_{p_1 - p_2} = \sqrt{\frac{\pi_1(1 - \pi_1)}{n_1} + \frac{\pi_2(1 - \pi_2)}{n_2}}$$

An estimated standard deviation is obtained by using the sample proportions p_1 and p_2 in place of π_1 and π_2, respectively, under the square root symbol. Notice that this estimated standard deviation differs from the one used previously in the test statistic. Here, there isn't a null hypothesis that claims $\pi_1 = \pi_2$, so there is no common value of π to estimate.

A Large-Sample Confidence Interval for $\pi_1 - \pi_2$

When

1. the samples are *independently selected random samples* OR *treatments were assigned at random to individuals or objects* (or vice versa), and

2. both *sample sizes are large*:

$$n_1 p_1 \geq 10 \qquad n_1(1 - p_1) \geq 10 \qquad n_2 p_2 \geq 10 \qquad n_2(1 - p_2) \geq 10$$

a large-sample confidence interval for $\pi_1 - \pi_2$ is

$$(p_1 - p_2) \pm (z \text{ critical value})\sqrt{\frac{p_1(1 - p_1)}{n_1} + \frac{p_2(1 - p_2)}{n_2}}$$

EXAMPLE 11.11   Researchers at the National Cancer Institute released the results of a study that examined the effect of weed-killing herbicides on house pets (Associated Press, Sept. 4, 1991). The following data is compatible with summary values given in the report. Dogs, some of whom were from homes where the herbicide was used on a regular basis, were examined for the presence of malignant lymphoma. We will use the given

data to estimate the difference between the proportion of exposed dogs that develop lymphoma and the proportion of unexposed dogs that develop lymphoma.

Group	Sample Size	Number with Lymphoma	p
Exposed	827	473	.572
Unexposed	130	19	.146

Let π_1 denote the proportion of exposed dogs that develop lymphoma, and define
π_2 similarly for unexposed dogs. The sample sizes are large enough for the large-
sample interval to be valid ($n_1 p_1 = 827(.572) \geq 10, n_1(1 - p_1) = 827(.428) \geq 10$, and
so on). A 90% confidence interval for $\pi_1 - \pi_2$ is

$$(p_1 - p_2) \pm (z \text{ critical value})\sqrt{\frac{p_1(1 - p_1)}{n_1} + \frac{p_2(1 - p_2)}{n_2}}$$

$$= (.572 - .146) \pm (1.645)\sqrt{\frac{(.572)(.428)}{827} + \frac{(.146)(.854)}{130}}$$

$$= .426 \pm (1.645)(.0354)$$

$$= .426 \pm .058$$

$$= (.368, .484)$$

Based on the observed sample, we believe that the proportion of exposed dogs that
develop lymphoma exceeds that for unexposed dogs by somewhere between .36
and .48.

Exercises 11.44 – 11.58

11.44 Let π_1 and π_2 denote the proportions of all male
and all female shoppers, respectively, who buy only name-
brand grocery products (as opposed to generic or store
brands).
  a. Test H_0: $\pi_1 - \pi_2 = 0$ versus H_a: $\pi_1 - \pi_2 \neq 0$ at level
.05, using the following data: $n_1 = 200$, number of suc-
cesses (only name-brand purchases) = 87, $n_2 = 300$,
number of successes = 96.
  b. Use the data of part **a** to compute a 95% confidence
interval for $\pi_1 - \pi_2$.

11.45 A university is interested in evaluating registration
processes. Students can register for classes by using either
a telephone registration system or an on-line system that
is accessed through the university's Web site. Independent
random samples of 80 students who registered by phone
and 60 students who registered on-line were selected. Of
those who registered by phone, 57 reported that they
were satisfied with the registration process. Of those who
registered on-line, 50 reported that they were satisfied.

Based on this data, is it reasonable to conclude that the
proportion who are satisfied is higher for those who register on-line? Test the appropriate hypotheses using $\alpha = .05$.

11.46 Do teachers find their work rewarding and satisfying? The article "Work-Related Attitudes" (*Psychological Reports* (1991): 443–450) reported the results of a survey of random samples of 395 elementary school teachers
and 266 high school teachers. Of the elementary school
teachers, 224 said they were very satisfied with their jobs,
whereas 126 of the high school teachers were very satisfied with their work. Based on this data, is it reasonable
to conclude that the proportion very satisfied is different
for elementary school teachers than it is for high school
teachers? Test the appropriate hypotheses using a .05 significance level.

11.47 The article "Foraging Behavior of the Indian
False Vampire Bat" (*Biotropica* (1991): 63–67) reported
that 36 of 193 female bats in flight spent more than 5 min
in the air before locating food. For male bats, 64 of 168

spent more than 5 min in the air. Is there sufficient evidence to conclude that the proportion of flights longer than 5 min in length differs for males and females? Test the relevant hypotheses using $\alpha = .01$.

11.48 The article "Regrets on Early Sex" appeared in the Australian newspaper *The Herald* (Jan. 2, 1998). The article stated that "While 54% of women thought that they should have waited longer before having sex, only 16% of the men felt that way." Suppose that this statement had been based on interviews with independently chosen random samples of 50 women and 50 men from a particular city in New Zealand. (The article summarizes a survey conducted in New Zealand.) Construct and interpret a 90% confidence interval for the difference in the true proportions of men and women who think they should have waited longer before having sex.

11.49 Gender differences in student needs and fears were examined in the article "A Survey of Counseling Needs of Male and Female College Students" (*J. College Student Development* (1998): 205–208). Random samples of male and female students were selected from those attending a particular university. Of 234 males surveyed, 27.5% said that they were concerned about the possibility of getting AIDS. Of 568 female students surveyed, 42.7% reported being concerned about the possibility of getting AIDS. Is there sufficient evidence to conclude that the proportion of female students concerned about the possibility of getting AIDS is greater than the corresponding proportion for males?

11.50 In a study that was described by a writer for the *Washington Post* (*San Luis Obispo Tribune,* Feb. 2, 2000), 500 patients undergoing abdominal surgery were randomly assigned to breathe one of two oxygen mixtures during surgery and for 2 hours afterward. One group received a mixture containing 30% oxygen, a standard generally used in surgery. The other group was given 80% oxygen. Wound infections developed in 28 of the 250 patients who received 30% oxygen and in 13 of the 250 patients who received 80% oxygen. Is there sufficient evidence to conclude that the proportion of patients who develop wound infections is lower for the 80% oxygen treatment than for the 30% oxygen treatment? Test the relevant hypotheses using a significance level of .05.

11.51 The state of Georgia's HOPE scholarship program guarantees fully paid tuition to Georgia public universities for Georgia high school seniors who have a B average in academic requirements as long as they maintain a B average in college. (See "Who Loses HOPE? Attrition

from Georgia's College Scholarship Program" (*Southern Economic Journal* (1999): 379–390).) It was reported that 53.2% of a random sample of 137 students entering Ivan Allen College at Georgia Tech (social science and humanities) with a HOPE scholarship lost the scholarship at the end of the first year because they had a GPA of less than 3.0. It was also reported that 72 of a random sample of 111 students entering the College of Computing with a B average had lost their HOPE scholarship by the end of the first year. Is there evidence that the proportion who lose HOPE scholarships is different for the College of Computing than for the Ivan Allen College?

11.52 The article "Softball Sliding Injuries" (*Amer. J. of Diseases of Children* (1988): 715–716) provided a comparison of breakaway bases (designed to reduce injuries) and stationary bases. Consider the accompanying data (which agrees with summary values given in the paper).

	Number of Games Played	Number of Games Where a Player Suffered a Sliding Injury
Stationary bases	1250	90
Breakaway bases	1250	20

Does the use of breakaway bases reduce the proportion of games with a player suffering a sliding injury? Answer by performing a level .01 test. What assumptions are necessary in order for your test to be valid? Do you think they are reasonable in this case?

11.53 An Associated Press article (*San Luis Obispo Telegram-Tribune,* Sept. 23, 1995) examined the changing attitudes of Catholic priests. National surveys of priests aged 26 to 35 were conducted in 1985 and again in 1993. The priests surveyed were asked whether they agreed with the following statement: Celibacy should be a matter of personal choice for priests. In 1985, 69% of those surveyed agreed; in 1993, 38% agreed. Suppose that the samples were randomly selected and that the sample sizes were both 200. Is there evidence that the proportion of priests who agreed that celibacy should be a matter of personal choice declined from 1985 to 1993? Use $\alpha = .05$.

11.54 A *New York Times* article (Oct. 6, 1993) reported on an alternative sentencing program for those convicted of a crime. Those in the alternative program took a year-long course at the Dartmouth campus of the University of Massachusetts. Of 32 men who took the class, 6 were subsequently convicted of new crimes. Over the same time period, 18 of 40 other men with similar backgrounds were convicted of new crimes. Is there evidence that the proportion convicted of new crimes is lower for those taking the class? Test the appropriate hypotheses using $\alpha = .01$.

11.55 Are college students who take a freshman orientation course more or less likely to stay in college than those who do not take such a course? The article "A Longitudinal Study of the Retention and Academic Performance of Participants in Freshmen Orientation Courses" (*J. College Student Development* (1994): 444–449) reported that 50 of 94 randomly selected students who did not participate in an orientation course returned for a second year. Of 94 randomly selected students who did take the orientation course, 56 returned for a second year. Construct a 95% confidence interval for $\pi_1 - \pi_2$, the difference in the proportion returning for students who do not take an orientation course and those who do. Give an interpretation of this interval.

11.56 The article "Truth and DARE: Tracking Drug Education to Graduation" (*Social Problems* (1994): 448–456) compared the drug use of 238 randomly selected high school seniors exposed to a drug education program (DARE) and 335 randomly selected high school seniors who were not exposed to such a program. Data for marijuana use is given in the accompanying table. Is there evidence that the proportion using marijuana is lower for students exposed to the DARE program? Use $\alpha = .05$.

	n	Number Who Use Marijuana
Exposed to DARE	288	141
Not exposed to DARE	335	181

11.57 The positive effect of water fluoridation on dental health is well documented. One study that validates this is described in the article "Impact of Water Fluoridation on Children's Dental Health: A Controlled Study of Two Pennsylvania Communities" (*Amer. Stat. Assoc. Proc. of the Social Statistics Section* (1981): 262–265). Two communities were compared. One had adopted fluoridation in 1966, whereas the other had no such program. Of 143 randomly selected children from the town without fluoridated water, 106 had decayed teeth, and 67 of 119 randomly selected children from the town with fluoridated water had decayed teeth. Let π_1 denote the true proportion of children drinking fluoridated water who have decayed teeth, and let π_2 denote the analogous proportion for children drinking unfluoridated water. Estimate $\pi_1 - \pi_2$ using a 90% confidence interval. Does the interval contain 0? Interpret the interval.

11.58 A person released from prison before completing the original sentence is placed under the supervision of a parole board. If that person violates specified conditions of good behavior during the parole period, the board can order a return to prison. The article "Impulsive and Premeditated Homicide: An Analysis of the Subsequent Parole Risk of the Murderer" (*J. of Criminal Law and Criminology* (1978): 108–114) reported the accompanying data on parole behavior. One random sample of individuals had served time in prison for impulsive murder, and the other random sample had served time for premeditated murder. Construct a 98% confidence interval for the difference in the proportion who successfully completed parole for impulsive and premeditated murders.

	Crime	
	Impulsive	Premeditated
Sample size	$n_1 = 42$	$n_2 = 40$
Number with no violation	13	22
Sample proportion	$p_1 = 3.10$	$p_2 = .550$

11.4 Distribution-Free Procedures for Inferences Concerning a Difference Between Two Population or Treatment Means Using Independent Samples (Optional)

One approach to making inferences about $\mu_1 - \mu_2$ when n_1 and n_2 are small is to assume that the two population or treatment response distributions are normal and then use the two-sample t test or confidence interval presented in Section 11.1. In some situations, however, the normality assumption may not be reasonable. The validity of the procedures developed in this section does not depend on the normality of the population distributions. The procedures can be used to compare two populations or treatments when it is reasonable to assume that the population or treatment response distributions have the same shape and spread.

Basic Assumptions in This Section

The two population or treatment response distributions have the same shape and spread. The only possible difference between the distributions is that one may be shifted to one side or the other.

Distributions consistent with these assumptions are shown in Figure 11.2(a). The distributions shown in Figure 11.2(b) have different shapes and spreads, therefore the methods of this section would not be appropriate in this case. Inferences that involve comparing distributions with different shapes and spreads can be quite complicated. Good advice from a statistician is particularly important in this case.

(a)   (b)

FIGURE 11.2 Two possible population distribution pairs: (a) Same shape and spread, differing only in location; (b) Very different shape and spread

Procedures that do not require any overly specific assumptions about the population distributions are said to be **distribution-free** (some texts use the term *nonparametric* instead of distribution-free). The two-sample t test of Section 11.1 is not distribution-free, because its use is predicated on the specific assumption of (at least approximate) normality.

Inferences about $\mu_1 - \mu_2$ will be made from information in two independent random samples, one consisting of n_1 observations from the first population and the other consisting of n_2 observations from the second population. Suppose that the two population distributions are in fact identical (so that $\mu_1 = \mu_2$). In this case, each of the $n_1 + n_2$ observations is actually drawn from the same population distribution. The distribution-free procedure presented here is based on regarding the $n_1 + n_2$ observations as a single data set and assigning ranks to the ordered values. The assignment is easiest when there are no ties among the $n_1 + n_2$ values (each observation is different from every one of the others), so assume for the moment that this is the case. Then the smallest among the $n_1 + n_2$ values receives rank 1, the second smallest rank 2, and so on, until finally the largest value is assigned rank $n_1 + n_2$.

EXAMPLE 11.12   An experiment to compare fuel efficiencies for two types of subcompact automobile was carried out by first randomly selecting $n_1 = 5$ cars of type 1 and $n_2 = 5$ cars of type 2. Each car was then driven from Phoenix to Los Angeles by a nonprofessional driver, after which the fuel efficiency (in mpg) was determined. The resulting data, with observations in each sample ordered from smallest to largest, is given here:

Type 1	39.3	41.1	42.4	43.0	44.4
Type 2	37.8	39.0	39.8	40.7	42.1

The data and the associated ranks are shown in the accompanying dotplot.

The ranks of the five observations in the first sample are 3, 6, 8, 9, 10. If these five observations had all been larger than every value in the second sample, the corresponding ranks would have been 6, 7, 8, 9, and 10. On the other hand, if all five sample 1 observations had been less than each value in the second sample, the ranks would have been 1, 2, 3, 4, and 5. The ranks of the five observations in the first sample might be any set of five numbers from among $1, 2, 3, \ldots, 9, 10$ — there are actually 252 possibilities.

Testing Hypotheses

Let's first consider testing

$$H_0: \quad \mu_1 - \mu_2 = 0 \qquad (\mu_1 = \mu_2)$$

versus

$$H_a: \quad \mu_1 - \mu_2 > 0 \qquad (\mu_1 > \mu_2)$$

When H_0 is true, all $n_1 + n_2$ observations in the two samples are actually drawn from identical population distributions. We would then expect that the observations in the first sample would be intermingled with those of the second sample when plotted along the number line. In this case, the ranks of the observations should also be intermingled. For example, with $n_1 = 5$ and $n_2 = 5$, the set of sample 1 ranks 2, 3, 5, 8, 10 would be consistent with $\mu_1 = \mu_2$, as would the set 1, 4, 7, 8, 9. However, when $\mu_1 = \mu_2$, it would be quite unusual for all five values from sample 1 to be larger than every value in sample 2, resulting in the set 6, 7, 8, 9, 10 of sample 1 ranks.

A convenient measure of the extent to which the ranks are intermingled is the sum of the sample 1 ranks. These ranks in Example 11.12 were 3, 6, 8, 9, and 10, so

rank-sum = 3 + 6 + 8 + 9 + 10 = 36

The largest possible rank-sum when $n_1 = n_2 = 5$ is $6 + 7 + 8 + 9 + 10 = 40$. If μ_1 is much larger than μ_2, we would expect the rank-sum to be near its largest possible value. This suggests that we reject H_0 for unusually large values of the rank-sum.

Developing a test procedure requires information about the sampling distribution of the rank-sum statistic when H_0 is true. To illustrate this, consider again the case $n_1 = n_2 = 5$. There are 252 different sets of 5 from among the 10 ranks 1, 2, 3, . . . , 9, 10. The key point is that, when H_0 is true, any one of these 252 sets has the same chance of being the sample 1 ranks as does any other set, because all 10 observations come from the same population distribution. The chance under H_0 that any particular set occurs is 1/252 (because the possibilities are equally likely).

Table 11.1 displays the 12 sets of sample 1 ranks that yield the largest rank-sum values. Each of the other 240 possible rank sets has a rank-sum value less than 36.

Table 11.1 *The 12 rank sets that have the largest rank-sums when $n_1 = 5$ and $n_2 = 5$.*

Sample 1 Ranks	Rank-Sum
6 7 8 9 10	40
5 7 8 9 10	39
4 7 8 9 10	38
5 6 8 9 10	38
3 7 8 9 10	37
4 6 8 9 10	37
5 6 7 9 10	37
2 7 8 9 10	36
3 6 8 9 10	36
4 5 8 9 10	36
4 6 7 9 10	36
5 6 7 8 10	36

If we observe rank-sum = 36, we can compute

$P(\text{rank-sum} \geq 36 \text{ when } H_0 \text{ is true}) = 12/252 = .0476$

That is, when H_0 is true, a rank-sum at least as large as 36 would be observed only about 4.76% of the time. Thus, a test of H_0: $\mu_1 - \mu_2 = 0$ versus H_a: $\mu_1 - \mu_2 > 0$, based on $n_1 = 5$ and $n_2 = 5$ and a rank-sum of 36, would have an associated P-value of .0476. It is this type of reasoning that allows us to reach a conclusion about whether to reject H_0.

The process of looking at different rank-sum sets to carry out a test can be quite tedious. Fortunately, information about both one- and two-tailed P-values associated with values of the rank-sum statistic has been tabled. Appendix Table VI provides information on P-values for selected values of n_1 and n_2. For example, when

n_1 and n_2 are both 5, Appendix Table VI tells us that, for an upper-tailed test with a rank-sum statistic value of 36, P-value $< .05$. This is consistent with the value of .0476 computed previously. Had the rank-sum been 40, we would have concluded that the P-value was less than .01 (using the table). The use of this table is further illustrated in the examples that follow.

Summary of the Rank Sum Test*

Null hypothesis: $H_0: \mu_1 - \mu_2 = 0$

Test statistic: rank-sum = sum of ranks assigned to the observations in the first sample

Alternative hypothesis:	*Type of test*:
$H_a: \mu_1 - \mu_2 > 0$	Upper-tailed
$H_a: \mu_1 - \mu_2 < 0$	Lower-tailed
$H_a: \mu_1 - \mu_2 \neq 0$	Two-tailed

Information about the P-value associated with this test is given in Appendix Table VI.

Assumptions: 1. *The samples are independent random samples* OR *treatments are randomly assigned to individuals or objects* (or vice versa).
2. The two *population or treatment response distributions have the same shape and spread*.

EXAMPLE 11.13

The extent to which an infant's health is affected by parents' smoking is an important public health concern. The article "Measuring the Exposure of Infants to Tobacco Smoke" (*New Engl. J. of Med.* (1984): 1075–1078) reported on a study in which various measurements were taken both from a random sample of infants who had been exposed to household smoke and from a sample of unexposed infants. The accompanying data consists of observations on urinary concentration of cotanine, a major metabolite of nicotine. (The values constitute a subset of the original data and were read from a plot that appeared in the article.)

Unexposed ($n_1 = 7$)	8	11	12	14	20	43	111	
Rank	1	2	3	4	5	7	11	
Exposed ($n_2 = 8$)	35	56	83	92	128	150	176	208
Rank	6	8	9	10	12	13	14	15

Does the data suggest that the true average cotanine level is higher for exposed than for unexposed infants? The investigators used the rank-sum test to analyze the data.

1. $\mu_1 - \mu_2$ is the difference between true average cotanine concentration for unexposed and exposed infants.

2. $H_0: \mu_1 - \mu_2 = 0$

---

*This procedure is often called the *Wilcoxon rank-sum test* or the *Mann–Whitney test*, after the statisticians who developed it. Some sources use a slightly different (but equivalent) test statistic formula.

3. $H_a: \mu_1 - \mu_2 < 0$ (unexposed average is less than exposed average)

4. *Significance level*: $\alpha = .01$

5. *Test statistic*:   rank-sum = sum of sample 1 ranks

6. *Assumptions*:   The authors of the article indicated that they believe the assumptions of the rank-sum test were reasonable.

7. *Calculation*:   rank-sum = $1 + 2 + 3 + 4 + 5 + 7 + 11 = 33$

8. *P-value*:   This is a lower-tailed test. With $n_1 = 7$ and $n_2 = 8$, Appendix Table VI tells us that *P*-value $< .05$ if rank-sum ≤ 41 and *P*-value $< .01$ if rank-sum ≤ 36. Since rank-sum $= 33$, we conclude that

$$P\text{-value} < .01$$

9. *Conclusion*:   Since the *P*-value is less than α (.01), we reject H_0 and conclude that infants exposed to cigarette smoke do have a higher average cotanine level than do unexposed infants.

Many statistical computer packages will perform the rank-sum test and give exact *P*-values. Partial MINITAB output for the data of Example 11.13 follows. MINITAB uses the symbol **W** to denote the rank-sum statistic and uses the terms **ETA1** and **ETA2** in place of μ_1 and μ_2, but the test statistic value and the associated *P*-values are the same as for the test presented here. The output indicates that W = 33 and that the test "is significant at 0.0046." These two values, 33 and .0046, are the rank-sum statistic and the *P*-value, respectively. In Example 11.13, we used Appendix Table VI to determine that *P*-value $< .01$. This statement is consistent with the actual *P*-value given in the MINITAB output.

```
Unexpose    N = 7     Median =  14.00
Exposed     N = 8     Median = 110.00
Point estimate for ETA1-ETA2 is    -79.00
95.7 Percent CI for ETA1-ETA2 is (-156.00,-23.99)
W = 33.0
Test of ETA1 = ETA2 vs ETA1 < ETA2 is significant at 0.0046
```

The test procedure just described can be easily modified to handle a hypothesized value other than zero. Consider as an example testing $H_0: \mu_1 - \mu_2 = 5$. This hypothesis is equivalent to $H_0: (\mu_1 - 5) - \mu_2 = 0$. That is, if 5 is subtracted from each population 1 value, then according to H_0, the distribution of the resulting values coincides with the population 2 distribution. This suggests that, if the hypothesized value of 5 is first subtracted from each sample 1 observation, the test can then be carried out as before.

To test $H_0: \mu_1 - \mu_2 = $ *hypothesized value,* subtract the hypothesized value from each observation in the first sample and then determine the ranks of these when combined with the n_2 observations from the second sample.

EXAMPLE 11.14

(Example 11.13 continued)   Reconsider the cotanine concentration data introduced in Example 11.13. Suppose that a researcher wished to know whether average concentration for exposed children exceeds that for unexposed children by more than 25. Recall that μ_1 is the true average concentration for unexposed children. The exposed average exceeds the unexposed average by 25 when $\mu_1 - \mu_2 = -25$ and by more than 25 when $\mu_1 - \mu_2 < -25$. The hypotheses of interest are, therefore,

$$H_0: \quad \mu_1 - \mu_2 = -25 \qquad H_a: \mu_1 - \mu_2 < -25$$

These hypotheses can be tested by first subtracting -25 (or, equivalently, adding 25) to each sample 1 observation.

Sample 1

Unexposed	8	11	12	14	20	43	111
Unexposed $-$ (-25)	33	36	37	39	45	68	136
Rank	1	3	4	5	6	8	12

Sample 2

Exposed	35	56	83	92	128	150	176	208
Rank	2	7	9	10	11	13	14	15

1. $\mu_1 - \mu_2$ = difference in true mean cotanine concentration for unexposed and exposed infants

2. $H_0: \mu_1 - \mu_2 = -25$

3. $H_a: \mu_1 - \mu_2 < -25$

4. *Significance level*: $\alpha = .01$

5. *Test statistic*:   rank-sum = sum of sample 1 ranks

6. *Assumptions*:   Subtracting 25 does not change the shape or spread of a distribution, so if the assumptions were reasonable in Example 11.13, they are also reasonable here.

7. *Calculation*:   rank-sum = $1 + 3 + 4 + 5 + 6 + 8 + 12 = 39$

8. *P-value*:   This is a lower-tailed test. With $n_1 = 7$ and $n_2 = 8$, Appendix Table VI tells us that P-value $< .05$ if rank-sum ≤ 41 and P-value $< .01$ if rank-sum ≤ 36. Since rank-sum = 39, we conclude that

   $.01 < P\text{-value} < .05$

9. *Conclusion*:   Since P-value $> .01$, we fail to reject H_0. Sample evidence does not suggest that the mean concentration level for exposed infants is more than 25 higher than the mean for unexposed infants.

Frequently the $n_1 + n_2$ observations in the two samples are not all different from one another. When this occurs, the rank assigned to each observation in a tied group is the average of the ranks that would be assigned if the values in the group all differed slightly from one another. Consider, for example, the 10 ordered values

$$5.6 \quad 6.0 \quad 6.0 \quad 6.3 \quad 6.8 \quad 7.1 \quad 7.1 \quad 7.1 \quad 7.9 \quad 8.2$$

If the two 6.0 values differed slightly from each other, they would be assigned ranks 2 and 3. Therefore, each one is assigned rank $(2 + 3)/2 = 2.5$. If the three 7.1 observations were all slightly different, they would receive ranks 6, 7, and 8, so each of the three is assigned rank $(6 + 7 + 8)/3 = 7$. The ranks for the above 10 observations are then

$$1 \quad 2.5 \quad 2.5 \quad 4 \quad 5 \quad 7 \quad 7 \quad 7 \quad 9 \quad 10$$

If the proportion of tied values is quite large, it is recommended that the rank-sum statistic be multiplied by a *correction factor*. Several of the chapter references contain additional information.

Appendix Table VI contains information about P-values for the rank-sum test when $n_1 \leq 8$ and $n_2 \leq 8$. More extensive tables exist for other combinations of sample size. There is also a test procedure based on using a normal distribution to approximate the sampling distribution of the rank-sum statistic. This alternative procedure is often used when the two sample sizes are larger than 8. One of the chapter references can be consulted for details.

A Confidence Interval for $\mu_1 - \mu_2$

A confidence interval based on the rank-sum statistic is not nearly as familiar to users of statistical methods as is the hypothesis-testing procedure. This is unfortunate, because the confidence interval has the same virtues to recommend it as does the rank-sum test. It does not require the assumption that the population distributions are normal, as does the two-sample t interval.

The actual derivation of the rank-sum confidence interval is quite involved, and computing these intervals by hand can be very tedious, so we will rely on computer software.

The **rank sum confidence interval for $\mu_1 - \mu_2$** is the interval consisting of all hypothesized values for which

$$H_0: \mu_1 - \mu_2 = \text{hypothesized value}$$

cannot be rejected when using a two-tailed test.

A 95% confidence interval consists of those hypothesized values for which the previous null hypothesis is not rejected by a test with significance level $\alpha = .05$.

A 99% confidence interval is associated with a level $\alpha = .01$ test, and a 90% confidence interval is associated with a level $\alpha = .10$ test.

Thus, if $H_0: \mu_1 - \mu_2 = 100$ cannot be rejected at level .05, then 100 is included in the 95% confidence interval for $\mu_1 - \mu_2$.

EXAMPLE 11.15

The article "Some Mechanical Properties of Impregnated Bark Board" (*Forest Products J.* (1977): 31–38) reported the accompanying observations on crushing strength for epoxy-impregnated bark board (sample 1) and bark board impregnated with another polymer (sample 2). The sample values are displayed in the accompanying table:

Sample 1	10,860	11,120	11,340	12,130	13,070	14,380
Sample 2	4590	4850	5640	6390	6510	

A 95% confidence interval for $\mu_1 - \mu_2$ was requested using MINITAB. The resulting output follows:

```
Sample 1    N = 6    Median =  11735
Sample 2    N = 5    Median =   5640
Point estimate for ETA1-ETA2 is    6490
96.4 percent CI for ETA1-ETA2 is (4730, 8480)
```

Remember that MINITAB uses **ETA1 − ETA2** in place of $\mu_1 - \mu_2$. Also note that it was not possible to construct an interval for an exact 95% confidence level. MINITAB has calculated a 96.4% confidence interval. The reported interval is (4730, 8480). Based on the sample information, we estimate that the difference in mean crushing strength for epoxy-impregnated bark board and board impregnated with a different polymer is between 4730 and 8480 pounds per square inch.

There are many other distribution-free procedures, including some that allow inferences based on paired samples. The books mentioned in the chapter references can be consulted for further information.

Exercises 11.59 – 11.65

11.59 Urinary fluoride concentration (ppm) was measured both for a sample of livestock that had been grazing in an area previously exposed to fluoride pollution and for a similar sample that had grazed in an unpolluted region. Does the accompanying data indicate strongly that the true average fluoride concentration for livestock grazing in the polluted region is larger than for the unpolluted region? Assume that the distributions of urinary fluoride concentration for both grazing areas have the same shape and spread, and use a level .05 rank-sum test.

Polluted	21.3	18.7	23.0	17.1	16.8	20.9	19.7
Unpolluted	14.2	18.3	17.2	18.4	20.0		

11.60 A modification has been made to the process for producing a certain type of time-zero film (film that begins to develop as soon as a picture is taken). Because the modification involves extra cost, it will be incorporated only if sample data strongly indicates that the modification has decreased true average developing time by more than 1 sec. Assuming that the developing-time distributions differ only with respect to location, if at all, use the rank-sum test at level .05 on the accompanying data to test the appropriate hypotheses.

Original process	8.6	5.1	4.5	5.4	6.3	6.6	5.7	8.5
Modified process	5.5	4.0	3.8	6.0	5.8	4.9	7.0	5.7

11.61 The study reported in "Gait Patterns During Free Choice Ladder Ascents" (*Human Movement Sci.* (1983): 187–195) was motivated by publicity concerning the increased accident rate for individuals climbing ladders. A number of different gait patterns were used by subjects climbing a portable straight ladder according to specified instructions. The accompanying data consist of ascent times for seven subjects who used a lateral gait and six subjects who used a four-beat diagonal gait.

Lateral	.86	1.31	1.64	1.51	1.53	1.39	1.09
Diagonal	1.27	1.82	1.66	.85	1.45	1.24	

a. Use the rank-sum test to see whether the data suggests any difference in the true average ascent times for the two gaits.

b. Interpret the 95% confidence interval for the difference between the true average gait times, as indicated by the accompanying MINITAB output.

```
lateral    N = 7    Median = 1.3900
diagonal   N = 6    Median = 1.3600
Point estimate for ETA1 - ETA2 is   -0.0400
96.2 percent C.I. for ETA1 - ETA2 is (-0.4300, 0.3697)
```

11.62 A blood-lead level of 70 mg/mL has been commonly accepted as safe. However, researchers have noted that some neurophysiological symptoms of lead poisoning appear in people whose blood-lead levels are below 70 mg/mL. The article "Subclinical Neuropathy at Safe Levels of Lead Exposure" (*Arch. Environ. Health* (1975): 180) gives the following nerve-conduction velocities for a group of workers who were exposed to lead in the workplace but whose blood-lead levels were below 70 mg/mL and for a group of controls who had no exposure to lead:

Exposed to lead	46	46	43	41	38	36	31
Control	54	50.5	46	45	44	42	41

Use a level .05 rank-sum test to determine whether there is a significant difference in mean conduction velocity between workers exposed to lead and those not exposed to lead.

11.63 The effectiveness of antidepressants in treating the eating disorder bulimia was examined in the article "Bulimia Treated with Imipramine: A Placebo-Controlled Double-Blind Study" (*Amer. J. Psych.* (1983): 554–558). A group of patients diagnosed as bulimic were randomly assigned to one of two treatment groups, one receiving imipramine and the other a placebo. One of the variables recorded was binge frequency. The authors chose to analyze the data using a rank-sum test because it makes no assumption of normality. They state, "Because of the wide range of some measures, such as frequency of binges, the rank sum is more appropriate and somewhat more conservative." Data consistent with the findings of this article is given in the accompanying table.

Number of Binges During 1 Week								
Placebo	8	3	15	3	4	10	6	4
Imipramine	2	1	2	7	3	12	1	5

Does this data strongly suggest that imipramine is effective in reducing the mean number of binges per week? Use a level .05 rank-sum test.

11.64 In an experiment to compare the bond strength of two different adhesives, each adhesive was used in five bondings of two surfaces, and the force necessary to separate the surfaces was determined for each bonding. For adhesive 1, the resulting values were 229, 286, 245, 299, and 259, whereas the adhesive 2 observations were 213, 179, 163, 247, and 225. Let μ_1 and μ_2 denote the true average bond strengths of adhesives 1 and 2, respectively. Interpret the 90% distribution-free confidence interval estimate of $\mu_1 - \mu_2$ given in the MINITAB output shown here:

```
adhes. 1    N = 5    Median = 259.00
adhes. 2    N = 5    Median = 213.00
Point estimate for ETA1 - ETA2 is   61.00
90.5 Percent C.I. for ETA1 - ETA2 is (16.00, 95.98)
```

11.65 The article "A Study of Wood Stove Particulate Emissions" (*J. Air Poll. Control Assoc.* (1979): 724–728) reported the accompanying data on burn time (hr) for samples of oak and pine. An estimate of the difference between mean burn time for oak and mean burn time for pine is desired.

Oak	1.72	.67	1.55	1.56	1.42	1.23	1.77	.48
Pine	.98	1.40	1.33	1.52	.73	1.20		

Interpret the interval given in the MINITAB output.

```
Oak     N = 8    Median = 1.4850
Pine    N = 6    Median = 1.2650
Point estimate for ETA1 - ETA2 is   0.2100
95.5 Percent C.I. for ETA1 - ETA2 is (-0.4998, 0.5699)
```

11.5   Interpreting the Results of Statistical Analyses

Many different types of research involve comparing two populations or treatments. It is easy to find examples of the two-sample hypothesis tests introduced in this chapter in published sources in a wide variety of disciplines. As with the one-sample tests, it is common to find only the value of the test statistic and the associated *P*-value (or sometimes only the *P*-value) in reports.

What to Look for in Published Data

Here are some questions to consider when you are reading a report that contains the result of a two-sample hypothesis test:

- Are only two groups being compared? If more than two groups are being compared two at a time, a different type of analysis probably would be preferable (see Chapter 15).
- Were the samples selected independently, or are the samples paired? If the samples are paired, was the analysis performed appropriate for paired samples?
- What hypotheses are being tested? Is the test one- or two-sided?
- Does the validity of the test performed depend on any assumptions about the populations sampled (such as normality)? If so, do the assumptions appear to be reasonable?
- What is the *P*-value associated with the test? Does the *P*-value lead to rejection of the null hypothesis?
- Are the conclusions drawn consistent with the results of the hypothesis test? In particular, if H_0 was rejected, does this indicate practical significance or only statistical significance?

As an example, we consider a study reported in the article "The Relationship Between Distress and Delight in Males' and Females' Reactions to Frightening Films" (*Human Communication Research* (1991): 625–637). The investigators measured emotional responses of 50 males and 60 females after viewing a segment from a horror film. The article included the following statement:

> Females were much more likely to express distress than were males. While males did express higher levels of delight than females, the difference was not statistically significant.

The accompanying summary data was also contained in the article.

	Distress Index		**Delight Index**	
Gender	**Mean**	**SD**	**Mean**	**SD**
Males	31.2	10.0	12.02	3.65
Females	40.4	9.1	9.09	5.55
	P-value < .001		Not significant (*P*-value > .05)	

The *P*-values are the only evidence of the hypothesis tests that support the conclusions given. The *P*-value < .001 for the distress index means that the hypothesis

$$H_0: \quad \mu_F - \mu_M = 0$$

was rejected in favor of

$$H_a: \quad \mu_F - \mu_M > 0$$

where μ_F and μ_M are the true mean distress indexes for females and males, respectively.

The nonsignificant P-value (P-value $> .05$) reported for the delight index means that the hypothesis

$$H_0: \quad \mu_F - \mu_M = 0$$

(where μ_F and μ_M now refer to mean delight index for females and males, respectively) could not be rejected. Chance sample-to-sample variability is a plausible explanation for the observed difference in sample means ($12.02 - 9.09$). Thus we would not want to put much emphasis on the author's statement that males express higher levels of delight than females, which is based only on the fact that $12.02 > 9.09$ and could plausibly be due entirely to chance.

The article describes the samples as consisting of undergraduates selected from the student body of a large midwestern university. The authors extrapolate their results to American men and women in general. If it were considered unreasonable to make this type of generalization, we could be more conservative and view the sampled populations to be male and female university students, or male and female midwestern university students, or even male and female students at this particular university.

The comparison of males and females was based on two independently selected groups (not paired). Since the sample sizes were large, the two-sample t test for means could reasonably have been employed, and this would have required no specific assumptions about the two underlying populations.

Summary of Key Concepts and Formulas

Term or Formula	Comment
Independent samples	Two samples where the individuals or objects in the first sample are selected independently from those in the second sample.
Paired samples	Two samples for which each observation in the first sample is paired in a meaningful way with a particular observaton in the second sample.
$t = \dfrac{(\bar{x}_1 - \bar{x}_2) - \text{hyp. value}}{\sqrt{\dfrac{s_1^2}{n_1} + \dfrac{s_2^2}{n_2}}}$	The test statistic for testing $H_0: \mu_1 - \mu_2 =$ hypothesized value when the samples are independently selected and the sample sizes are large or it is reasonable to assume that both population distributions are normal.
$(\bar{x}_1 - \bar{x}_2) \pm (t \text{ crit. value})\sqrt{\dfrac{s_1^2}{n_1} + \dfrac{s_2^2}{n_2}}$	A formula for constructing a confidence interval for $\mu_1 - \mu_2$ when the samples are independently selected and the sample sizes are large or it is reasonable to assume that the population distributions are normal.

Term or Formula	Comment
$df = \dfrac{(V_1 + V_2)^2}{\dfrac{V_1^2}{n_1 - 1} + \dfrac{V_2^2}{n_2 - 1}}$ where $V_1 = \dfrac{s_1^2}{n_1}$ and $V_2 = \dfrac{s_2^2}{n_2}$	The formula for determining df for the two-sample t test and confidence interval.
$\bar{x}_d$	The sample mean difference.
s_d	The standard deviation of the sample differences.
μ_d	The mean value for the population of differences.
σ_d	The standard deviation for the population of differences.
$t = \dfrac{\bar{x}_d - \text{hypothesized value}}{\dfrac{s_d}{\sqrt{n}}}$	The paired t test statistic for testing $H_0: \mu_d = $ hypothesized value.
$\bar{x}_d \pm (t \text{ critical value})\dfrac{s_d}{\sqrt{n}}$	The paired t confidence interval formula.
$p_c = \dfrac{n_1 p_1 + n_2 p_2}{n_1 + n_2}$	p_c is the statistic for estimating the common population proportion when $\pi_1 = \pi_2$.
$z = \dfrac{p_1 - p_2}{\sqrt{\dfrac{p_c(1 - p_c)}{n_1} + \dfrac{p_c(1 - p_c)}{n_2}}}$	The test statistic for testing $H_0: \pi_1 - \pi_2 = 0$ when both sample sizes are large.
$(p_1 - p_2) \pm (z \text{ crit. value})\sqrt{\dfrac{p_1(1 - p_1)}{n_1} + \dfrac{p_2(1 - p_2)}{n_2}}$	A formula for constructing a confidence interval for $\pi_1 - \pi_2$ when both sample sizes are large.
Rank-sum = sum of sample 1 ranks	The distribution-free test statistic for testing $H_0: \mu_1 - \mu_2 = $ hypothesized value when it is reasonable to assume that the two populations have the same shape and spread.

Supplementary Exercises 11.66 – 11.89

11.66 An eating attitudes test (EAT) was administered both to a sample of female models and to a control group of females, resulting in the accompanying summary data ("Gender Differences in Eating Attitudes, Body Concept, and Self-Esteem Among Models," *Sex Roles* (1992): 413–437).

Group	Sample Size	Sample Mean	Sample sd
Models	30	8.63	7.1
Controls	30	10.97	8.9

Let μ_1 denote the true average EAT score for models and μ_2 the true average EAT score for controls.
a. Verify that the value of the test statistic for testing $H_0: \mu_1 - \mu_2 = 0$ versus $H_a: \mu_1 - \mu_2 < 0$ is $t = -1.13$.
b. Calculate the P-value, and then use it to reach a conclusion at significance level .05.
c. If μ_1 had been the true average score for controls and μ_2 the true average score for models, how would the hypotheses, value of t, and P-value have changed?

11.67 The authors of the article "Hostility, Aggression, and Anxiety Levels of Divorce and Nondivorce Children as Manifested in Their Responses to Projective Tests" (*J. of Personality Assessment* (1991): 438–452) speculated that children of divorced parents would show higher levels of hostility than children of married parents. To test this theory, Rorschach tests were used to compute a measure of hostility for 54 children of divorced parents and 54 children of married parents. All children who participated were between 10 and 12 years of age and lived in Sweden. Does the accompanying data support the researchers' theory?

Group	$\bar{x}$	s
Children of divorced parents	5.38	3.96
Children of married parents	1.94	3.10

11.68 Do teenage boys worry more than teenage girls? This is one of the questions addressed by the authors of the article "The Relationship of Self-Esteem and Attributional Style to Young People's Worries" (*J. of Psych.* (1987): 207–215). A scale called the Worries Scale was administered to a group of teenagers, and the results are summarized in the accompanying table.

Gender	n	Sample Mean Score	Sample sd
Girls	108	62.05	9.5
Boys	78	67.59	9.7

Is there sufficient evidence to conclude that teenage boys score higher on the Worries Scale than teenage girls? Use a significance level of $\alpha = .05$.

11.69 Some astrologers have speculated that people born under certain sun-signs are more extroverted than people born under other signs. The accompanying data was taken from the article "Self-Attribution Theory and the Sun-Sign" (*J. of Social Psych.* (1984): 121–126). The Eysenck Personality Inventory (EPI) was used to measure extroversion and neuroticism.

Sun-sign	Sample Size n	Extroversion $\bar{x}$	s	Neuroticism $\bar{x}$	s
Water signs	59	11.71	3.69	12.32	4.15
Other signs	186	12.53	4.14	12.23	4.11
Winter signs	73	11.49	4.28	11.96	4.22
Summer signs	49	13.57	3.71	13.27	4.04

a. Is there sufficient evidence to indicate that those born under water signs have a lower mean extroversion score than those born under other (nonwater) signs? Use a level .01 test.

b. Does the data strongly suggest that those born under winter signs have a lower mean extroversion score than those born under summer signs? Use a level .05 test.

c. Does the data indicate that those born under water signs differ significantly from those born under other signs with respect to mean neuroticism score? Use $\alpha = .05$.

d. Do those born under winter signs differ from those born under summer signs with respect to mean neuroticism score? Carry out a test of appropriate hypotheses using a significance level of .01.

11.70 Recorded speech can be compressed and played back at a faster rate. The article "Comprehension by College Students of Time-Compressed Lectures" (*J. of Exper. Educ.* (Fall 1975): 53–56) gave the results of a study designed to test comprehension of time-compressed speech. Fifty students listened to a 60-min lecture and took a comprehension test. Another 50 students heard the same lecture time-compressed to 40 min. The sample mean and standard deviation of comprehension scores for the normal-speed group were 9.18 and 4.59, respectively, and those for the time-compressed group were 6.34 and 4.93, respectively.

a. Use a level .01 test to determine whether the true mean comprehension score for students hearing a time-compressed lecture is significantly lower than the true mean score for students who hear a lecture at normal speed. What assumption must be reasonable in order for your test to be valid?

b. Estimate the difference in the true mean comprehension scores for normal and time-compressed lectures using a 95% confidence interval.

11.71 Should quizzes be given at the beginning or the end of a lecture period? The article "On Positioning the Quiz: An Empirical Analysis" (*Accounting Review* (1980): 664–670) provides some insight. Two sections of an introductory accounting class were given identical instructions to read and study assigned text materials. Three quizzes and a final exam were given during the term, with one section taking quizzes at the beginning of the lecture and the other section taking quizzes at the end. Final exam scores for the two groups are summarized. Does the accompanying data indicate that there is a significant difference in the true mean final exam scores for students who take quizzes at the beginning of class and those who take quizzes at the end? Do you think that the assumptions required for the two-sample t test are reasonable?

	Quiz at Beginning	Quiz at End
Sample size	40	40
Mean	143.7	131.7
Standard deviation	21.2	20.9

11.72 Data on self-esteem, leadership ability, and GPA was used to compare college students who were hired as resident assistants at Mississippi State University and those who were not hired ("Wellness as a Factor in University Housing," *J. of College Student Development* (1994): 248–254), as shown in the accompanying table.

	Self-esteem		Leadership		GPA	
	$\bar{x}$	s	$\bar{x}$	s	$\bar{x}$	s
Hired ($n = 69$)	83.28	12.21	62.51	3.05	2.94	.61
Not hired ($n = 47$)	81.96	12.78	62.43	3.36	2.60	.79

a. Does the data suggest that the true mean self-esteem score for students hired by the university as resident assistants differs from the mean for students who are not hired? Test the relevant hypotheses using $\alpha = .05$.
b. Does the data suggest that the true mean leadership score for students hired by the university as resident assistants differs from the mean for students who are not hired? Test the relevant hypotheses using $\alpha = .05$.
c. Does the data suggest that the true mean GPA for students hired by the university as resident assistants differs from the mean for students who are not hired? Test the relevant hypotheses using $\alpha = .05$.

11.73 The article "Religion and Well-Being Among Canadian University Students: The Role of Faith Groups on Campus" (*J. for the Scientific Study of Religion* (1994): 62–73) compared the self-esteem of students who belonged to Christian clubs and students who did not belong to such groups. Each student in a random sample of $n = 169$ members of Christian groups (the affiliated group) completed a questionnaire designed to measure self-esteem. The same questionnaire was also completed by each student in a random sample of $n = 124$ students who did not belong to a religious club (the unaffiliated group). The mean self-esteem score for the affiliated group was 25.08, and the mean for the unaffiliated group was 24.55.

The sample standard deviations weren't given in the article, but suppose that they were 10 for the affiliated group and 8 for the unaffiliated group. Is there evidence that the true mean self-esteem score differs for affiliated and unaffiliated students? Test using a significance level of .01.

11.74 The article "Social Science Research on Lay Definitions of Sexual Harassment" (*J. of Social Issues* (1995): 21–37) reported on a survey of randomly selected undergraduate and graduate students. Each student was asked whether he or she thought that unwanted pressure for a date from a faculty member was an example of sexual harassment. (See the accompanying table.)

	n	Number Who Perceived Pressure as Sexual Harassment
Undergraduates		
Males	1336	882
Females	1346	1104
Graduate students		
Males	565	469
Females	575	529

a. For undergraduate students, is there evidence that the proportion who perceive pressure for a date as sexual harassment is lower for males than for females? Test using $\alpha = .05$.
b. For graduate students, is there evidence that the proportion who perceive pressure for a date as sexual harassment is lower for males than for females? Test using $\alpha = .05$.
c. Estimate the difference between the proportion of male graduate students who perceive pressure for a date as sexual harassment and the corresponding proportion for male undergraduate students, using a 90% confidence interval. Interpret the resulting interval.

11.75 Meteorologists classify storms as either single-peak or multiple-peak. The total number of lightning flashes was recorded for seven single-peak and four multiple-peak storms, resulting in the accompanying data ("Lightning Phenomenology in the Tampa Bay Area," *J. of Geophys. Research* (1984): 11,789–11,805).

Single-peak	117	56	19	40	82	69	80
Multiple-peak	229	197	242	430			

a. Does the data suggest that the true mean number of lightning flashes differs for the two types of storms? Use a .05 significance level.

b. What assumptions about the distribution of number of flashes for each of the two types of storms are necessary if your test in part **a** is to be valid?

11.76 Nine observations of surface-soil pH were made at each of two different locations at the Central Soil Salinity Research Institute experimental farm, and the resulting data appeared in the article "Sodium-Calcium Exchange Equilibria in Soils as Affected by Calcium Carbonate and Organic Matter" (*Soil Sci.* (1984): 109). Does the accompanying data suggest that the true mean soil pH values differ for the two locations? Test the appropriate hypotheses using a .05 significance level.

Site		pH			
Location A	8.53	8.52	8.01	7.99	7.93
	7.89	7.85	7.82	7.80	
Location B	7.85	7.73	7.58	7.40	7.35
	7.30	7.27	7.27	7.23	

11.77 The accompanying summary data on the ratio of strength to cross-sectional area for knee extensors is taken from the article "Knee Extensor and Knee Flexor Strength: Cross-Sectional Area Ratios in Young and Elderly Men" (*J. of Gerontology* (1992): M204–M210).

Group	n	$\bar{x}$	Standard Error, $\dfrac{s}{\sqrt{n}}$
Young men	13	7.47	.22
Elderly men	12	6.71	.28

Does this data suggest that the true average ratio for young men exceeds that for elderly men? Carry out a test of appropriate hypotheses using $\alpha = .05$.

11.78 The authors of the article "The Color-a-Person Body Dissatisfaction Test" (*J. of Personality Assessment* (1991): 395–413) used a nonverbal measure of body dissatisfaction to compare students at two different universities. A random sample of 47 women at the University of Cincinnati and a random sample of 24 women at the University of New Mexico participated in the study. Mean and standard deviations for a measure of self-esteem are given in the accompanying table. Is it reasonable to conclude that women at the two universities differ with respect to mean self-esteem score? Use $\alpha = .05$.

	Self-esteem Score	
	$\bar{x}$	s
University of Cincinnati	32.55	4.41
University of New Mexico	31.25	4.92

11.79 An experiment to assess the effects of automobile pollution was described in the article "Effects of Roadside Conditions on Plants and Insects" (*J. of Appl. Ecology* (1988): 709–715). Twenty soil specimens taken .6 m from the roadside resulted in a mean nitrogen concentration of 1.70 mg/g. Twenty soil specimens taken 6 m from the roadside resulted in a mean nitrogen concentration of 1.35 mg/g. Suppose that the sample standard deviations were .4 (at .6 m) and .3 (at 6 m). Is there sufficient evidence to conclude that the mean nitrogen concentration in soil .6 m from the roadside is higher than that at 6 m? Test the relevant hypotheses using $\alpha = .01$.

11.80 The article "Effect of Carbohydrate and Vitamin B6 on Fuel Substrates during Exercise in Women" (*Medicine and Science in Sports and Exercise* (1988): 223–239) compared a group of women who participated in regular aerobic exercise with a group who did not. Data on percentage of body fat was obtained by skinfolds measured at seven sites, as summarized in the accompanying table.

	Sample Size	Mean Percent Body Fat	Sample sd
Aerobic exercise	5	20.1	4.2
No aerobic exercise	5	20.4	3.4

a. Estimate the true mean difference in percent body fat between the two groups, using a 90% confidence interval.
b. Does your interval in part **a** contain zero? How would you interpret the interval?
c. What assumptions are necessary for the interval of part **a** to be valid?

11.81 In an effort to assess the risk of brain damage in infants, the authors of the article "Neuropathologic Documentation of Prenatal Brain Damage" (*Amer. J. of Diseases of Children* (1988): 858–866) studied both infants born with brain damage and infants born without brain damage. They also looked at premature babies as well as those carried to term.

	Sample Size	Mean Birth Weight (g)	Sample sd
Term			
Brain damage	12	2998	707
No brain damage	13	2704	627
Premature			
Brain damage	10	1541	448
No brain damage	54	1204	656

a. Does the data indicate that the true mean birth weight for premature infants with brain damage differs from that of premature infants without brain damage? Test the relevant hypotheses using a significance level of .05.

b. Repeat part **a** for infants carried to term.

c. Use a 90% confidence interval to estimate the difference in mean weight between term and premature infants without brain damage.

d. Repeat part **c** for infants with brain damage.

11.82 The accompanying table gives data that appeared in the article "Development and Clinical Trial of a Minimal-Contact, Cognitive-Behavioral Treatment for Tension Headache" (*Cognitive Therapy and Research* (1988): 325–339). Two different treatments for headache (a relaxation therapy and a cognitive-behavioral therapy) were compared. Is there sufficient evidence to support the researchers' claim that the cognitive-behavioral therapy is more effective than relaxation in increasing the mean number of headache-free days (for a 1-week period)? Test the relevant hypotheses using a level .05 test.

Therapy	Sample Size	Mean Number of Headache-free Days	Sample sd
Relaxation	24	3.82	1.75
Cognitive-behavioral	24	5.71	1.43

11.83 Key terms in survey questions too often are not well understood, and such ambiguity can affect responses. As an example, the article "How Unclear Terms Affect Survey Data" (*Public Opinion Quarterly* (1992): 218–231) described a survey in which each individual in a sample was asked, "Do you exercise or play sports regularly?" But what constitutes exercise? The following revised question was then asked of each individual in the same sample: "Do you do any sports or hobbies involving physical activities, or any exercise, including walking, on a regular basis?" The resulting data is shown in the accompanying table.

	Yes	No
Initial question	48	52
Revised question	60	40

Is there any difference between the true proportions of yes responses to these questions? Can a procedure from this chapter be used to answer the question posed? If yes, use it; if not, explain why not.

11.84 An electronic implant that stimulates the auditory nerve has been used to restore partial hearing to a number of deaf people. In a study of implant acceptability (*Los Angeles Times,* Jan. 29, 1985), 250 adults born deaf and 250 adults who went deaf after learning to speak were followed for a period of time after receiving an implant. Of those deaf from birth, 75 had removed the implant, whereas only 25 of those who went deaf after learning to speak had done so. Does this suggest that the true proportion who remove the implants differs for those that were born deaf and those that went deaf after learning to speak? Test the relevant hypotheses using a .01 significance level.

11.85 Samples of both surface soil and subsoil were taken from eight randomly selected agricultural locations in a particular county. The soil samples were analyzed to determine both surface pH and subsoil pH, with the results shown in the accompanying table.

	Location			
	1	**2**	**3**	**4**
Surface pH	6.55	5.98	5.59	6.17
Subsoil pH	6.78	6.14	5.80	5.91

	Location			
	5	**6**	**7**	**8**
Surface pH	5.92	6.18	6.43	5.68
Subsoil pH	6.10	6.01	6.18	5.88

a. Compute a 90% confidence interval for the true average difference between surface and subsoil pH for agricultural land in this county.

b. What assumptions are necessary to validate the interval in part **a**?

11.86 The article "An Evaluation of Football Helmets Under Impact Conditions" (*Amer. J. of Sports Med.* (1984): 233–237) reported that when 44 padded football helmets and 37 suspension-type helmets were subjected to an impact test (a drop of 1.5 m onto a hard surface), 5 of the padded and 24 of the suspension-type helmets showed damage. Using a .01 significance level, test appropriate hypotheses to determine whether there is a difference between the two helmet types with respect to the true proportion of each type that would be damaged by a 1.5-m drop onto a hard surface.

11.87 The article "Post-Mortem Analysis of Neuropeptides in Brains from Sudden Infant Death Victims" (*Brain Research* (1984): 279–285) reported age (in days) at death for infants who died of sudden infant death syndrome (SIDS). Assuming that age at death for SIDS victims is normally distributed, use the accompanying data to construct a 95% confidence interval for the difference in the true mean age at death for female and male SIDS victims. Interpret the resulting interval. How does the interpretation depend on whether zero is included in the interval?

Age at Death (days)						
Females	55	120	135	154	54	
Males	56	60	60	60	105	140	147

11.88 The accompanying 1982 and 1983 net earnings (in millions of dollars) of ten food and beverage firms appeared in an article "Capital Expenditures Report" (*Food Engr.* (1984): 93–101). Is there sufficient evidence to indicate that mean net earnings increased from 1982 to 1983? Assume that the ten companies represent a random sample of all food and beverage firms. Perform the appropriate hypothesis test using a .01 significance level.

Firm	1983	1982
Coors	89.0	33.0
ConAgra	28.7	20.6
ADM	110.2	155.0
Heinz	237.5	214.3

(continued)

Firm	1983	1982
General Mills	130.7	134.1
Nestlé	113.4	93.7
Beatrice	292.1	320.8
Carnation	155.0	137.6
Hershey	100.2	94.2
Procter & Gamble	58.5	66.5

11.89 Many researchers have investigated the relationship between stress and reproductive efficiency. One such study is described in the article "Stress or Acute Adrenocorticotrophin Treatment Suppresses LHRH-Induced LH Release in the Ram" (*J. of Reprod. and Fertility* (1984): 385–393). Seven rams were used in the study, and LH (luteinizing hormone) release (ng/min) was recorded before and after treatment with ACTH (adrenocorticotrophin, a drug that results in stimulation of the adrenal gland). Use the accompanying data and $\alpha = .01$ to determine whether there is a significant reduction in mean LH release following treatment with ACTH.

Ram	1	2	3	4	5	6	7
Before	2400	1400	1375	1325	1200	1150	850
After	2250	1425	1100	800	850	925	700

References

Daniel, Wayne. *Applied Nonparametric Statistics,* 2nd ed. Boston: PWS-Kent, 1990. (An elementary presentation of distribution-free methods, including the rank-sum test discussed in the last section of this chapter.)

Devore, Jay. *Probability and Statistics for Engineering and the Sciences,* 5th ed. Belmont, Calif.: Duxbury Press, 2000. (Contains a somewhat more comprehensive treatment of the inferential material presented in this and the previous two chapters, although the notation is a bit more mathematical than that of the present text.)

Mosteller, Frederick, and Richard Rourke. *Sturdy Statistics.* Reading, Mass.: Addison-Wesley, 1973. (A very readable intuitive development of distribution-free methods, including those based on ranks.)

12

The Analysis of Categorical Data and Goodness-of-Fit Tests

INTRODUCTION

Most of the techniques presented in previous chapters are designed for numerical data. It is often the case, however, that information is collected on categorical variables, such as political affiliation, gender, or college major. As with numerical data, categorical data sets can be univariate (consisting of observations on a single categorical variable), bivariate (observations on two categorical variables), or even multivariate. In this chapter, we first consider inferential methods for analyzing univariate categorical data sets and then turn to techniques appropriate for use with bivariate data.

12.1   Chi-Squared Tests for Univariate Categorical Data

Univariate categorical data sets arise in a variety of settings. If each student in a sample of 100 is classified according to whether he or she is enrolled full-time or part-time, data on a categorical variable with two categories results. Each airline passenger in a sample of 50 might be classified into three categories based on the type of ticket — coach, business class, or first class. Each registered voter in a sample of 100 selected from those registered in a particular city might be asked which of the five city council members he or she favors for mayor. This would yield observations on a categorical variable with five categories.

Univariate categorical data is most conveniently summarized in a **one-way frequency table.** Suppose, for example, that each item returned to a department store is classified according to disposition — cash refund, credit to charge account, merchandise exchange, or return refused. Records of 100 randomly selected returns are examined and each disposition recorded. The first few observations might be

Cash refund   Return refused

Exchange   Cash refund

Exchange   Credit to account

Counting the number of observations of each type might then result in the following one-way table:

	Disposition			
	Cash	**Credit**	**Exchange**	**Refused**
Frequency	34	18	31	17

For a categorical variable with k possible values (k different levels or categories), sample data is summarized in a one-way frequency table consisting of k cells, displayed horizontally or vertically.

In this section, we consider testing hypotheses about the proportion of the population that fall into each of the possible categories. For example, the customer relations manager for a department store might be interested in determining whether the four possible dispositions for a return request occur with equal frequency. If this is indeed the case, the long-run proportion of returns falling into each of the four categories is 1/4, or .25. The test procedure to be presented shortly would allow the manager to decide whether this hypothesis is plausible.

Notation

k = number of categories of a categorical variable

π_1 = true proportion for category 1

π_2 = true proportion for category 2

$\vdots$

π_k = true proportion for category k

(*Note:* $\pi_1 + \pi_2 + \cdots + \pi_k = 1$)

The hypotheses to be tested have the form

H_0: π_1 = hypothesized proportion for category 1

π_2 = hypothesized proportion for category 2

$\vdots$

π_k = hypothesized proportion for category k

H_a: H_0 is not true, so at least one of the true category proportions differs from the corresponding hypothesized value.

For the example involving department store returns,

π_1 = proportion of all returns that result in a cash refund

π_2 = proportion of all returns that result in an account credit

π_3 = proportion of all returns that result in an exchange

π_4 = proportion of all returns that are refused

The null hypothesis of interest is then

$$H_0: \quad \pi_1 = .25, \pi_2 = .25, \pi_3 = .25, \pi_4 = .25$$

A null hypothesis of the type just described will be tested by first selecting a random sample of size n and then classifying each sample response into one of the k possible categories. To decide whether the sample data is compatible with the null hypothesis, we must compare the observed cell counts (frequencies) to the cell counts that would have been expected when the null hypothesis is true. In general, the expected cell counts are

expected cell count for category $1 = n\pi_1$

expected cell count for category $2 = n\pi_2$

and so on. The expected cell counts when H_0 is true result from substituting the corresponding hypothesized proportion for each π.

EXAMPLE 12.1

A number of psychological studies have considered the relationship between various deviant behaviors and other variables such as the lunar phase. The article "Psychiatric and Alcoholic Admissions Do Not Occur Disproportionately Close to Patients' Birthdays" (*Psychological Reports* (1992): 944–946) focused on the existence of any relationship between date of patient admission for specified treatment and patient's birthday. Admission date was partitioned into four categories according to how close it was to the patient's birthday:

1. Within 7 days of birthday

2. Between 8 and 30 days, inclusive, from the birthday

3. Between 31 and 90 days, inclusive, from the birthday

4. More than 90 days from the birthday

Let π_1, π_2, π_3, and π_4 denote the true proportions in categories 1, 2, 3, and 4, respectively. If there is no relationship between admission date and birthday, then since there are 15 days included in the first category (from 7 days prior to the patient's birthday to 7 days after, including, of course, the birthday itself),

$$\pi_1 = \frac{15}{365} = .041$$

(For simplicity, we are ignoring Feb. 29 of leap years.) Similarly, in the absence of any relationship,

$$\pi_2 = \frac{46}{365} = .126$$

$$\pi_3 = .329$$

$$\pi_4 = .504$$

The hypotheses of interest are then

H_0: $\pi_1 = .041, \pi_2 = .126, \pi_3 = .329, \pi_4 = .504$

H_a: H_0 is not true.

The cited article gave data for $n = 200$ patients admitted for alcoholism treatment. If H_0 is true, the expected counts are

$$\left(\begin{array}{c} \text{expected count} \\ \text{for category 1} \end{array} \right) = n \left(\begin{array}{c} \text{hypothesized proportion} \\ \text{for category 1} \end{array} \right) = 200(.041) = 8.2$$

$$\left(\begin{array}{c} \text{expected count} \\ \text{for category 2} \end{array} \right) = n \left(\begin{array}{c} \text{hypothesized proportion} \\ \text{for category 2} \end{array} \right) = 200(.126) = 25.2$$

$$\left(\begin{array}{c} \text{expected count} \\ \text{for category 3} \end{array} \right) = n \left(\begin{array}{c} \text{hypothesized proportion} \\ \text{for category 3} \end{array} \right) = 200(.329) = 65.8$$

$$\left(\begin{array}{c} \text{expected count} \\ \text{for category 4} \end{array} \right) = n \left(\begin{array}{c} \text{hypothesized proportion} \\ \text{for category 4} \end{array} \right) = 200(.504) = 100.8$$

Observed and expected cell counts are given in the following table.

	Category			
	1	**2**	**3**	**4**
Observed count	11	24	69	96
Expected count	8.2	25.2	65.8	100.8

Since the observed counts are based on a *sample* of admissions, it would be somewhat surprising to see *exactly* 4.1% of the sample falling in the first category, exactly 12.6% in the second, and so on, even when H_0 is true. If the differences between the observed and expected cell counts can reasonably be attributed to sampling variation, the data would be considered compatible with H_0. On the other hand, if the discrepancy between the observed and expected cell counts is too large to be attributed solely to chance differences from one sample to another, H_0 should be rejected in favor of H_a. Thus, we need an assessment of how different the observed and expected counts are.

The goodness-of-fit statistic, denoted by X^2, is a quantitative measure of the extent to which the observed counts differ from those expected when H_0 is true.*

---

*The Greek letter χ is often used in place of X. The symbol X^2 is referred to as the chi-squared (χ^2) statistic. In using X^2 rather than χ^2, we are adhering to the convention of denoting sample quantities by Roman letters.

The **goodness-of-fit statistic, X^2,** results from first computing the quantity

$$\frac{(\text{observed cell count} - \text{expected cell count})^2}{\text{expected cell count}}$$

for each cell, where, for a sample of size n,

$$\begin{pmatrix} \text{expected cell} \\ \text{count} \end{pmatrix} = n \begin{pmatrix} \text{hypothesized value of corresponding} \\ \text{population proportion} \end{pmatrix}$$

The X^2 is the sum of these quantities for all k cells:

$$X^2 = \sum_{\text{all cells}} \frac{(\text{observed cell count} - \text{ecpected cell count})^2}{\text{expected cell count}}$$

The value of the X^2 statistic reflects the magnitude of the discrepancies between observed and expected cell counts. When the differences are sizable, the value of X^2 tends to be large. Therefore, large values of X^2 suggest rejection of H_0. A small value of X^2 (it can never be negative) occurs when the observed cell counts are quite similar to those expected when H_0 is true and so would lend support to H_0.

As with previous test procedures, a conclusion will be reached by comparing a P-value to the significance level for the test. The P-value is computed as the probability of observing a value of X^2 at least as large as the observed value when H_0 is true. This requires information concerning the sampling distribution of X^2 when H_0 is true. A key result is that when the null hypothesis is correct and the sample size is sufficiently large, the behavior of X^2 is described approximately by a **chi-squared distribution.** A chi-squared curve has no area associated with negative values and is asymmetric, with a longer tail on the right. There are actually many chi-squared distributions, each one identified with a different number of degrees of freedom. Curves corresponding to several chi-squared distributions are shown in Figure 12.1.

FIGURE 12.1 Chi-squared curves

For a test procedure based on the X^2 statistic, the associated P-value is the area under the appropriate chi-squared curve and to the right of the computed X^2 value. Appendix Table IX gives upper-tail areas for chi-squared distributions with up to 20 df. Our chi-squared table has a different appearance from the t table used in previous chapters. In the t table, there is a single "value" column on the far left and then a column of P-values (tail areas) for each different df. A single column of t values works here because all t curves are centered at zero, and the t curves approach the z curve as the df increases. However, because the chi-squared curves move farther and farther to the right and spread out more as df increases, a single "value" column is impractical in this situation.

To find the area to the right for a particular X^2 value, locate the appropriate df column in Appendix Table IX. Determine which listed value is closest to the X^2 value of interest, and read the right-tail area corresponding to this value from the left-hand column of the table. For example, for a chi-squared distribution with df = 2, the area to the right of $X^2 = 4.93$ is .085, as shown in Figure 12.2. For this same chi-squared distribution (df = 2), the area to the right of 6.25 is approximately .045 (the area to the right of 6.20, the closest entry in the table for df = 2).

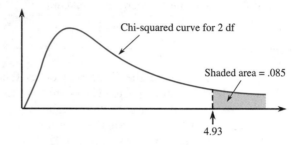

Chi-squared curve for 2 df

Shaded area = .085

4.93

FIGURE 12.2 A chi-squared upper-tail area

Goodness-of-Fit Tests

As long as none of the expected cell counts are too small, when H_0 is true, the X^2 goodness-of-fit statistic has approximately a chi-squared distribution with df = $(k - 1)$. *It is generally agreed that use of the chi-squared distribution is appropriate when the sample size is large enough for every expected cell count to be at least 5.* If any of the expected cell frequencies are less than 5, categories may be combined in a sensible way to create acceptable expected cell counts. Just remember to compute df based on the reduced number of categories.

Goodness-of-Fit Test Procedure

Hypotheses: H_0: π_1 = hypothesized proportion for category 1

$\vdots$

π_k = hypothesized proportion for category k

H_a: H_0 is not true.

Test statistic: $X^2 = \sum_{\text{all cells}} \dfrac{(\text{observed cell count} - \text{expected cell count})^2}{\text{expected cell count}}$

P-values: When H_0 is true and all expected counts are at least 5, X^2 has approximately a chi-squared distribution with df = $k - 1$. Therefore, the P-value associated with the computed test statistic value is the area to the right of X^2 under the df = $k - 1$ chi-squared curve. Upper-tail areas for chi-squared distribtuions are found in Appendix Table IX.

(continued)

Assumptions: 1. Observed cell counts are based on a *random sample*.
2. The *sample size is large*. The sample size is large enough for the chi-squared test to be appropriate as long as every expected count is at least 5.

EXAMPLE 12.2

(Example 12.1 continued)   We will use the admissions data of Example 12.1 to test the hypothesis that admission date is unrelated to birthday. Let's use a .05 level of significance and the nine-step hypothesis-testing procedure illustrated in previous chapters.

1. Let π_1, π_2, π_3, and π_4 denote the proportions of all admissions for treatment of alcoholism falling in the four categories.

2. H_0: $\pi_1 = .041$, $\pi_2 = .126$, $\pi_3 = .329$, $\pi_4 = .504$

3. H_a: H_0 is not true.

4. *Significance level*: $\alpha = .05$

5. *Test Statistic*: $X^2 = \sum_{\text{all cells}} \dfrac{(\text{observed cell count} - \text{expected cell count})^2}{\text{expected cell count}}$

6. *Assumptions*:   The expected cell counts (from Example 12.1) are 8.2, 25.2, 65.8, and 100.8, all of which are greater than 5. The article did not indicate how the patients were selected. We can proceed with the chi-squared test if it is reasonable to assume that the 200 patients in the sample can be regarded as a random sample of patients admitted for treatment of alcoholism.

7. *Calculation*:

$$X^2 = \frac{(11 - 8.2)^2}{8.2} + \frac{(24 - 25.2)^2}{25.5} + \frac{(69 - 65.8)^2}{65.8} + \frac{(96 - 100.8)^2}{100.8}$$
$$= .96 + .06 + .16 + .23$$
$$= 1.41$$

8. *P-value*:   The *P*-value is based on a chi-squared distribution with df = $4 - 1 = 3$. The computed value of X^2 is smaller than 6.25 (the smallest entry in the df = 3 column of Appendix Table IX), so *P*-value > .10.

9. *Conclusion*:   Since *P*-value > α, H_0 cannot be rejected. There is not sufficient evidence to conclude that a relationship exists between birthday and date admitted for treatment.

EXAMPLE 12.3

Does the color of a car influence the chance that it will be stolen? The Associated Press (*San Luis Obispo Telegram-Tribune*, Sept. 2, 1995) reported the following information for a random sample of 830 stolen vehicles: 140 were white, 100 were blue, 270 were red, 230 were black, and 90 were other colors. We will use the X^2 goodness-of-fit test and a significance level of $\alpha = .01$ to test the hypothesis that proportions stolen are identical to population color proportions. Suppose it is known that 15% of all cars are white, 15% are blue, 35% are red, 30% are black, and 5% are other colors. If these same population color proportions hold for stolen cars, the expected counts are

$$\text{expected count for white} = 830(.15) = 124.5$$
$$\text{expected count for blue} = 830(.15) = 124.5$$
$$\text{expected count for red} = 830(.35) = 290.5$$
$$\text{expected count for black} = 830(.30) = 249.0$$
$$\text{expected count for other colors} = 830(.05) = 41.5$$

These expected counts have been entered in Table 12.1.

Table 12.1

Category	Color	Observed Count	Expected Count
1	White	140	124.5
2	Blue	100	124.5
3	Red	270	290.5
4	Black	230	249.0
5	Other colors	90	41.5

1. Let $\pi_1, \pi_2, \ldots, \pi_5$ denote the true proportion of stolen cars that fall into the five color categories.

2. H_0: $\pi_1 = .15$, $\pi_2 = .15$, $\pi_3 = .35$, $\pi_4 = .30$, $\pi_5 = .05$

3. H_a: H_0 is not true.

4. *Significance level*: $\alpha = .01$

5. *Test statistic*: $X^2 = \sum_{\text{all cells}} \dfrac{(\text{observed cell count} - \text{expected cell count})^2}{\text{expected cell count}}$

6. *Assumptions*:   The sample was a random sample of stolen vehicles. All expected counts are greater than 5, so the sample size is large enough to use the chi-squared test.

7. *Calculation*:

$$X^2 = \frac{(140 - 124.5)^2}{124.5} + \frac{(100 - 124.5)^2}{124.5} + \frac{(270 - 290.5)^2}{290.5} + \frac{(230 - 249.0)^2}{249.0} + \frac{(90 - 41.5)^2}{41.5}$$
$$= 1.93 + 4.82 + 1.45 + 1.45 + 56.68$$
$$= 66.33$$

8. *P-value*:   All expected counts exceed 5, so the *P*-value can be based on a chi-squared distribution with df $= 5 - 1 = 4$. The computed X^2 value is larger than 18.46, the largest value in the df $= 4$ column of Appendix Table IX, so

   P-value $< .001$

9. *Conclusion*:   Since *P*-value $\leq \alpha$, H_0 is rejected. There is convincing evidence that at least one of the color proportions for stolen cars differs from the corresponding proportion for all cars.

Exercises 12.1 – 12.14

12.1   State what you know about the *P*-value for a chi-squared test in each of the following situations, and state the conclusion for a significance level of $\alpha = .01$.
  a. $X^2 = 7.5$, df $= 2$ **b.** $X^2 = 13.0$, df $= 6$
  c. $X^2 = 18.0$, df $= 9$ **d.** $X^2 = 21.3$, df $= 4$
  e. $X^2 = 5.0$, df $= 3$

12.2   A particular paperback book is published in a choice of four different covers. A certain bookstore keeps copies of each cover on its racks. To test the hypothesis that sales are equally divided among the four choices, a random sample of 100 purchases is identified.
  a. If the resulting X^2 value is 6.4, what conclusion would you reach when using a test with significance level .05?
  b. What conclusion would be appropriate at significance level .01 if $X^2 = 15.3$?
  c. If there were six different covers rather than just four, what would you conclude if $X^2 = 13.7$ and a test with $\alpha = .05$ was used?

12.3   Packages of mixed nuts made by a certain company contain four types of nuts. The percentages of nuts of types 1, 2, 3, and 4 are supposed to be 40%, 30%, 20%, and 10%, respectively. A random sample of nuts is selected, and each one is categorized by type.
  a. If the sample size is 200 and the resulting test statistic value is $X^2 = 19.0$, what conclusion would be appropriate for a significance level of .001?
  b. If the random sample had consisted of only 40 nuts, would you use the chi-squared test here? Explain your reasoning.

12.4   The article "Family Planning: Football Style. The Relative Age Effect in Football" (*Int. Rev. for Soc. of Sport* (1992): 77–88) investigated the relationship between month of birth and achievement in sports. Birth dates were collected for players on teams competing in the 1990 World Cup soccer games, and they are summarized in the accompanying table.

Birthday	Frequency
Quarter 1 (Aug.–Oct.)	150
Quarter 2 (Nov.–Jan.)	138
Quarter 3 (Feb.–Apr.)	140
Quarter 4 (May–July)	100

The authors of the article used a chi-squared goodness-of-fit test to determine whether the data was consistent with the hypothesis that the birthdays of world-class soccer players are evenly distributed across the four quarters.
  a. Perform a test of this hypothesis, using a .05 significance level.
  b. The article states that this analysis demonstrates that the distribution of player's birthdays is not random and that the number of players is related to the "quarters of the football year." Does your analysis support this conclusion? Explain.

12.5   The color vision of birds plays a role in their foraging behavior: Birds use color to select and avoid certain types of food. The authors of the article "Colour Avoidance in Northern Bobwhites: Effects of Age, Sex, and Previous Experience" (*Animal Behaviour* (1995): 519–526) studied the pecking behavior of 1-day-old bobwhites. In an area painted white, they inserted four pins with different colored heads. The color of the pin chosen on the birds first peck was noted for each of 33 bobwhites, resulting in the accompanying table. Does the data provide evidence of a color preference? Test using $\alpha = .01$.

Color	First Peck Frequency
Blue	16
Green	8
Yellow	6
Red	3

12.6 An article about the California lottery that appeared in the *San Luis Obispo Tribune* (Dec. 15, 1999) gave the following information on the age distribution of adults in California: 35% are between 18 and 34 years old, 51% are between 35 and 64 years old, and 14% are 65 years old or older. The article also gave information on the age distribution of those who purchase lottery tickets. The accompanying table is consistent with the values given in the article. Suppose that the data resulted from a random sample of 200 lottery ticket purchasers.

Age of Purchaser	Frequency
18–34	36
35–64	130
65 and over	34

Based on this sample data, is it reasonable to conclude that one or more of these three age groups buys a disproportionate share of lottery tickets? Use a chi-square goodness-of-fit test with $\alpha = .05$.

12.7 Drivers born under the astrological sign of Capricorn are the worst drivers in Australia, according to an article that appeared in the Australian newspaper *The Mercury* (Oct. 26, 1998). This statement was based on a study of insurance claims that resulted in the following data for male policyholders of a large insurance company.

Astrological Sign	Number of Policyholders
Aquarius	35,666
Aries	37,926
Cancer	38,126
Capricorn	54,906
Gemini	37,179
Leo	37,354
Libra	37,910
Pisces	36,677
Sagittarius	34,175
Scorpio	35,352
Taurus	37,179
Virgo	37,718

a. Assuming that it is reasonable to treat the policyholders of this particular insurance company as a random sample of insured drivers in Australia, is the observed data consistent with the hypothesis that the proportion of policyholders is the same for each of the 12 astrological signs?
b. Why do you think that the proportion of Capricorn policyholders is so much higher than would be expected if the proportions are the same for all astrological signs?
c. Suppose that a random sample of 1000 accident claims submitted to this insurance company is selected and each claim classified according to the astrological sign of the driver. (The accompanying table is consistent with accident rates given in the article.)

Astrological Sign	Observed Number in Sample
Aquarius	85
Aries	83
Cancer	82
Capricorn	88
Gemini	83
Leo	83
Libra	83
Pisces	82
Sagittarius	81
Scorpio	85
Taurus	84
Virgo	81

Test the null hypothesis that the proportion of accident claims submitted by drivers of each astrological sign is consistent with the proportion of policyholders of each sign. Use the information on the distribution of policyholders from part **a** to compute estimated expected frequencies and then carry out an appropriate test.

12.8 According to Census Bureau data, in 1998 the California population consisted of 50.7% whites, 6.6% blacks, 30.6% Hispanics, 10.8% Asians, and 1.3% other ethnic groups. Suppose that a random sample of 1000 students graduating from California colleges and universities in 1998 resulted in the accompanying data on ethnic group. This data is consistent with summary statistics contained in the article titled "Crumbling Public School System a Threat to California's Future (*Investor's Business Daily*, Nov. 12, 1999).

Ethnic Group	Number in Sample
White	679
Black	51
Hispanic	77
Asian	190
Other	3

Does this data provide evidence that the proportion of students graduating from colleges and universities in California for these ethnic group categories differs from the respective proportions in the population for California? Test the appropriate hypotheses using $\alpha = .01$.

12.9 Each person in a 1989 random sample of prison inmates was classified according to the type of offense committed, resulting in the following one-way frequency table. (These values are based on information in the article "Profile of Jail Inmates," *USA Today*, April 25, 1991). In 1983, it was reported that 30.7% of inmates had been convicted of violent crimes, 38.6% of crimes against property, 9.3% of drug-related crimes, 20.6% of public-order offenses, and .8% of other types of crimes. Does this data provide sufficient evidence to conclude that the true 1989 proportions falling in the various offense categories are not all the same as in 1983? Test the relevant hypotheses using $\alpha = .05$.

	Type of Offense				
	Violent Crime	Crimes Against Property	Drug-related Crimes	Public-order Offense	Other
Frequency	225	300	230	228	16

12.10 Criminologists have long debated whether there is a relationship between weather and violent crime. The author of the article "Is There a Season for Homicide?" (*Criminology* (1988): 287–296) classified 1361 homicides according to season, resulting in the accompanying data. Does this data support the theory that the homicide rate is not the same over the four seasons? Test the relevant hypotheses using a significance level of .05.

Season			
Winter	Spring	Summer	Fall
328	334	372	327

12.11 When public opinion surveys are conducted by mail, a cover letter explaining the purpose of the survey is usually included. To determine whether the wording of the cover letter influences the response rate, three different cover letters were used in a survey of students at a Midwestern university ("The Effectiveness of Cover-Letter Appeals," *J. of Soc. Psych.* (1984): 85–91). Suppose that each of the three cover letters accompanied questionnaires sent to an equal number of randomly selected students. Returned questionnaires were then classified according to the type of cover letter (I, II, or III). Use the accompanying data to test the hypothesis that $\pi_1 = 1/3$, $\pi_2 = 1/3$, and $\pi_3 = 1/3$, where π_1, π_2, and π_3 are the true proportions of all returned questionnaires accompanied by cover letters I, II, and III, respectively. Use a .05 significance level.

	Cover-letter Type		
	I	II	III
Frequency	48	44	39

12.12 A certain genetic characteristic of a particular plant can appear in one of three forms (phenotypes). A researcher has developed a theory, according to which the hypothesized proportions are $\pi_1 = .25$, $\pi_2 = .50$, and $\pi_3 = .25$. A random sample of 200 plants yields $X^2 = 4.63$.

a. Carry out a test of the null hypothesis that the theory is correct, using level of significance $\alpha = .05$.

b. Suppose that a random sample of 300 plants had resulted in the same value of X^2. How would your analysis and conclusion differ from those in part **a**?

12.13 The article "Linkage Studies of the Tomato" (*Trans. Royal Canad. Inst.* (1931): 1–19) reported the accompanying data on phenotypes resulting from crossing tall cut-leaf tomatoes with dwarf potato-leaf tomatoes. There are four possible phenotypes: (1) tall cut-leaf, (2) tall potato-leaf, (3) dwarf cut-leaf, and (4) dwarf potato-leaf. Mendel's laws of inheritance imply that $\pi_1 = 9/16$, $\pi_2 = 3/16$, $\pi_3 = 3/16$, and $\pi_4 = 1/16$. Is the data from this experiment consistent with Mendel's laws? Use a .01 significance level.

	Phenotype			
	1	2	3	4
Frequency	926	288	293	104

12.14 It is hypothesized that when homing pigeons are disoriented in a certain manner, they will exhibit no preference for any direction of flight after takeoff. To test this, 120 pigeons are disoriented and let loose, and the direction of flight of each is recorded. The resulting data is given in the accompanying table. Use the goodness-of-fit test with significance level .10 to determine whether the data supports the hypothesis.

Direction	Frequency
0°–45°	12
45°–90°	16
90°–135°	17
135°–180°	15
180°–225°	13
225°–270°	20
270°–315°	17
315°–360°	10

12.2 Tests for Homogeneity and Independence in a Two-Way Table

Data resulting from observations made on two different categorical variables can also be summarized using a tabular format. As an example, suppose that residents of a particular city can watch national news on affiliate stations of ABC, CBS, NBC, or PBS (the public television network). A researcher wishes to know whether there is any relationship between political philosophy (liberal, moderate, or conservative) and preferred news program among those residents who regularly watch the national news. Let x denote the variable *political philosophy* and y the variable *preferred network*. A random sample of 300 regular watchers is to be selected, and each one will be asked for his or her x and y values. The data set is bivariate and might initially be displayed as follows:

Observation	x value	y value
1	Liberal	CBS
2	Conservative	ABC
3	Conservative	PBS
⋮	⋮	⋮
299	Moderate	NBC
300	Liberal	PBS

Bivariate categorical data of this sort can most easily be summarized by constructing a **two-way frequency table,** or **contingency table.** This is a rectangular table that consists of a row for each possible value of x (each category specified by this variable) and a column for each possible value of y. There is then a cell in the table for each possible (x, y) combination. Once such a table has been constructed, the number of times each particular (x, y) combination occurs in the data set is determined, and these numbers (frequencies) are entered in the corresponding cells of the table. The resulting numbers are called **observed cell counts.** The table for the example relating political philosophy to preferred network discussed previously contains 3 rows and 4 columns (because x and y have 3 and 4 possible values, respectively). Table 12.2 is one possible table, with the rows and columns labeled with the possible x and y "values." These are often referred to as the *row* and *column categories.*

Table 12.2 *An example of a 3 × 4 frequency table*

	ABC	CBS	NBC	PBS	Row Marginal Total
Liberal	20	20	25	15	80
Moderate	45	35	50	20	150
Conservative	15	40	10	5	70
Column Marginal Total	80	95	85	40	300

Marginal totals are obtained by adding the observed cell counts in each row and also in each column of the table. The row and column marginal totals, along with the total of all observed cell counts in the table — the **grand total** — have been included in Table 12.2. The marginal totals provide information on the distribution of observed values for each variable separately. In this example, the row marginal totals reveal that the sample consisted of 80 liberals, 150 moderates, and 70 conservatives. Similarly, column marginal totals indicated how often each of the preferred program categories occurred: 80 preferred ABC news, 95 preferred CBS, and so on. The grand total, 300, is the number of observations in the bivariate data set — in this case, the sample size (although occasionally such a table results from a census of the entire population).

Two-way frequency tables are often characterized by the number of rows and columns in the table (specified in that order: rows first, then columns). Table 12.2 is called a 3 × 4 table. The smallest two-way frequency table is a 2 × 2 table, which has only two rows and two columns and thus four cells.

Two-way tables arise naturally in two different types of investigations. A researcher may be interested in comparing two or more groups on the basis of a single categorical variable and so may obtain a sample separately from each group. For example, data could be collected at a university to compare students, faculty, and staff on the basis of primary mode of transportation to campus (car, bicycle, motorcycle, bus, or on foot). One random sample of 200 students, another of 100 faculty, and a third of 150 staff might be chosen, and the selected individuals could be interviewed to obtain the necessary transportation information. Data from such a study could easily be summarized in a 3 × 5 two-way frequency table with row categories of student, faculty, and staff and column categories corresponding to the five possible modes of transportation. The observed cell counts could then be used to gain insight into differences and similarities among the three groups with respect to the means of transportation. This type of bivariate categorical data is characterized by having one set of marginal totals fixed (the sample sizes from the different groups), whereas each total in the other set is random. In the 3 × 5 situation just discussed, the row totals would be fixed at 200, 100, and 150, respectively.

A two-way table also arises when the values of two different categorical variables are observed for all individuals or items in a single sample. For example, a sample of 500 registered voters might be selected. Each voter could then be asked both if he or she favored a particular property tax initiative and if he or she was a registered Democrat, Republican, or independent. This would result in a bivariate data set with x representing the variable *political affiliation* (with categories Democrat, Republican, and independent) and y representing the variable *response* (favor initiative or oppose initiative). The corresponding 3 × 2 frequency table could then be used to investigate any association between position on the tax initiative and political affiliation. This type of bivariate categorical data is characterized by having both sets of marginal totals random and only the grand total fixed.

Comparing Two or More Populations: A Test of Homogeneity

When the value of a categorical variable is recorded for members of separate random samples obtained from each population under study, the central issue is whether the category proportions are the same for all of the populations. As in

Section 12.1, the test procedure uses a chi-squared statistic that compares the observed counts to those that would be expected if there were no differences between the populations.

EXAMPLE 12.4

In the past, a number of professions were prohibited from advertising. In 1977, the U.S. Supreme Court ruled that prohibiting doctors and lawyers from advertising violated their right to free speech. The article "Should Dentists Advertise?" (*J. of Ad. Research* (June 1982): 33–38) compared the attitudes of consumers and dentists toward the advertising of dental services. Separate random samples of 101 consumers and 124 dentists were asked to respond to the following statement: "I favor the use of advertising by dentists to attract new patients." Possible responses were strongly agree, agree, neutral, disagree, and strongly disagree. The data presented in the article appears in Table 12.3, a 2 × 5 frequency table. The authors were interested in determining whether the two groups — consumers and dentists — differed in their attitudes toward advertising.

Table 12.3 *Observed counts for Example 12.4*

	Response					Row Marg. Total
	Strongly Agree	Agree	Neutral	Disagree	Strongly Disagree	
Consumers	34	49	9	4	5	101
Dentists	9	18	23	28	46	124
Col. Marg. Total	43	67	32	32	51	225
Col. % of Total	19.11	29.78	14.22	14.22	22.67	

Estimates of expected cell counts can be thought of in the following manner: There were 225 responses, of which 43 were "strongly agree." The proportion of the total responding "strongly agree" is then

$$\frac{43}{225} = .19111$$

If there were no difference in response for consumers and dentists, we would then expect about 19.111% of the consumers and 19.111% of the dentists to have strongly agreed. Therefore, the expected cell counts* for the two cells in the "strongly agree" column are

expected count for consumer–strongly agree cell $= .19111(101) = 19.30$

expected count for dentist–strongly agree cell $= .19111(124) = 23.70$

---

*In this section, all expected cell counts will be estimated from sample data. All references to "expected counts" should be interpreted as *estimated* expected counts.

Note that the expected cell counts need not be whole numbers. The expected cell counts for the remaining cells can be computed in a similar manner. For example,

$$\frac{67}{225} = .29778$$

of all responses were in the "agree" category, so

expected count for consumer–agree cell $= .29778(101) = 30.08$

expected count for dentist–agree cell $= .29778(124) = 36.92$

It is common practice to display the observed cell counts and the corresponding estimated expected cell counts in the same table, with the estimated expected cell counts enclosed in parentheses. Expected cell counts for the remaining six cells have been computed and entered into Table 12.4. Except for small differences due to rounding, each marginal total for expected cell counts is identical to that of the corresponding observed counts.

A quick comparison of the observed and expected cell counts reveals large discrepancies. It appears that most consumers are more favorable toward advertising since the observed counts in the consumer–strongly agree and consumer–agree cells are substantially higher than would be expected if no difference exists, whereas the observed cell counts in the consumer–disagree and consumer–strongly disagree cells are lower than would be expected when no difference exists. The opposite relationship between observed and expected counts is exhibited by the dentists.

In Example 12.4, the expected count for a cell corresponding to a particular group–response combination was computed in two steps. First, the response *marginal proportion* was computed (for example, 43/225 for the "strongly agree" response). Then this proportion was multiplied by a marginal group total (for example, 101(43/225) for the consumer group). This is equivalent to first multiplying the row and column marginal totals and then dividing by the grand total:

$$\frac{(101)(43)}{225}$$

Table 12.4 *Observed and expected counts for Example 12.4*

Group	Observed and Expected Cell Counts					Row Marg. Total
	Strongly Agree	Agree	Neutral	Disagree	Strongly Disagree	
Consumers	34 (19.30)	49 (30.08)	9 (14.36)	4 (14.36)	5 (22.89)	101
Dentists	9 (23.70)	18 (36.92)	23 (17.64)	28 (17.64)	46 (28.11)	124
Col. Marg. Total	43	67	32	32	51	225

To compare two or more groups on the basis of a categorical variable, calculate an **expected cell count** for each cell by selecting the corresponding row and column marginal totals and then computing

$$\text{expected cell count} = \frac{(\text{row marginal total})(\text{column marginal total})}{\text{grand total}}$$

These quantities represent what would be expected when there is no difference between the groups under study.

The X^2 statistic, introduced in Section 12.1, can now be used to compare the observed cell counts to the expected cell counts. A large value of X^2 results when there are substantial discrepancies between the observed and expected counts, and suggests that the hypothesis of no differences between the populations should be rejected. A formal test procedure is described in the accompanying box.

Comparing Two or More Populations Using the X^2 Statistic

Null hypothesis: H_0: The true category proportions are the same for all the populations (homogeneity of populations).

Alternative hypothesis: H_a: The true category proportions are not all the same for all of the populations.

Test statistic: $X^2 = \sum_{\text{all cells}} \frac{(\text{observed cell count} - \text{expected cell count})^2}{\text{expected cell count}}$

The expected cell counts are estimated from the sample data (assuming that H_0 is true) using the formula

$$\text{expected cell count} = \frac{(\text{row marginal total})(\text{column marginal total})}{\text{grand total}}$$

P-values: When H_0 is true, X^2 has approximately a chi-squared distribution with

$\quad$ df = (number of rows $-$ 1)(number of columns $-$ 1)

The *P*-value associated with the computed test statistic value is the area to the right of X^2 under the chi-squared curve with the appropriate df. Upper-tail areas for chi-squared distributions are found in Appendix Table IX.

Assumptions: 1. The data consists of *independently chosen random samples*.
$\qquad\qquad$ 2. *The sample size is large*: all expected counts are at least 5. If some expected counts are less than 5, rows or columns of the table may be combined to achieve a table with satisfactory expected counts.

EXAMPLE 12.5

(Example 12.4 continued)   The following table of observed and expected cell counts appeared in Example 12.4.

Group	Strongly Agree	Agree	Neutral	Disagree	Strongly Disagree
Consumers	34 (19.30)	49 (30.08)	9 (14.36)	4 (14.36)	5 (22.89)
Dentists	9 (23.70)	18 (36.92)	23 (17.64)	28 (17.64)	46 (28.11)

Hypotheses:

H_0:   Proportions in each response category are the same for consumers and dentists.

H_a: H_0 is not true.

Significance level: A significance level of $\alpha = .05$ will be used.

Test statistic: $X^2 = \sum\limits_{\text{all cells}} \dfrac{(\text{observed cell count} - \text{expected cell count})^2}{\text{expected cell count}}$

Assumptions: All expected cell counts are at least 5, and the random samples were independently chosen, so use of the X^2 test is appropriate.

Calculation: $X^2 = \dfrac{(34 - 19.30)^2}{19.30} + \cdots + \dfrac{(46 - 28.11)^2}{28.11} = 84.47$

P-value: The two-way table for this example has 2 rows and 5 columns, so the appropriate df is $(2 - 1)(5 - 1) = 4$. Since 84.47 is greater than 18.46, the largest entry in the 4-df column of Appendix Table IX,

   P-value $< .001$

Conclusion: P-value $\leq \alpha$, so H_0 is rejected. There is strong evidence to support the claim that the proportions in the response categories are not the same for dentists and consumers.

EXAMPLE 12.6

The data on drinking behavior for independently chosen random samples of male and female students (Table 12.5, page 480) is similar to data that appeared in the article "Relationship of Health Behaviors to Alcohol and Cigarette Use by College Students" (*J. of College Student Development* (1992): 163–170). Does there appear to be a gender difference with respect to drinking behavior? (*Note*: Low = 1–7 drinks/week, moderate = 8–24 drinks/week, high = 25 or more drinks/week.)

Table 12.5 *Observed and expected counts for Example 12.6*

Drinking Level	Gender		Row Marginal Total
	Men	Women	
None	140 (158.6)	186 (167.4)	326
Low	478 (554.0)	661 (585.0)	1139
Moderate	300 (230.1)	173 (242.9)	473
High	63 (38.4)	16 (40.6)	79
Column Marginal Total	981	1036	2017

The relevant hypotheses are

H_0: True proportions for the four drinking levels are the same for males and females.

H_a: H_0 is not true.

Significance level: $\alpha = .01$

Test statistic: $X^2 = \sum_{\text{all cells}} \dfrac{(\text{observed cell count} - \text{expected cell count})^2}{\text{expected cell count}}$

Assumptions: Table 12.5 contains the computed expected counts, all of which are greater than 5. The data consists of independently chosen random samples.

Calculation: $X^2 = \dfrac{(140 - 158.6)^2}{158.6} + \cdots + \dfrac{(16 - 40.6)^2}{40.6} = 96.6$

P-value: The table has 4 rows and 2 columns, so df $= (4 - 1)(2 - 1) = 3$. The computed value of X^2 is greater than the largest entry of the 3-df column of Appendix Table IX, so

  P-value $< .001$

Conclusion: Since *P*-value $\leq \alpha$, H_0 is rejected. The data indicates that males and females differ with respect to drinking level.

Testing for Independence of Two Categorical Variables

The X^2 test statistic and test procedure can also be used to investigate association between two categorical variables in a single population. Suppose that each population member has a value of a first categorical variable and also of a second such variable. As an example, television viewers in a particular city might be categorized both with respect to preferred network (ABC, CBS, NBC, or PBS) and with respect to favorite type of programming (comedy, drama, or information-news). The question of interest is often whether knowledge of one variable's value provides any information about the value of the other variable — that is, are the two variables independent? Continuing the example, suppose that those who favor ABC prefer the three types of programming in proportions .4, .5, and .1 and that these proportions are also correct for individuals favoring any of the other three networks. Then learning an individual's preferred network provides no extra information concerning that individual's favorite type of programming. The categorical variables *preferred network* and *favorite program type* are independent.

To see how expected counts are obtained in this situation, recall from Chapter 6 that if two outcomes A and B are independent,

$$P(A \text{ and } B) = P(A) \cdot P(B)$$

so the proportion of time that they occur together in the long run is the product of the two individual long-run relative frequencies. Similarly, two categorical variables are independent in a population if, for each particular category of the first variable and each particular category of the second variable,

$$\begin{pmatrix} \text{proportion} \\ \text{of individuals} \\ \text{in a particular} \\ \text{category combination} \end{pmatrix} = \begin{pmatrix} \text{proportion in} \\ \text{specified category} \\ \text{of 1st variable} \end{pmatrix} \cdot \begin{pmatrix} \text{proportion in} \\ \text{specified category} \\ \text{of 2nd variable} \end{pmatrix}$$

Thus, if 30% of all viewers prefer ABC and the proportions of program type preferences are as previously given, assuming the two variables are independent, the proportion of individuals who both favor ABC and prefer comedy is $(.3)(.4) = .12$ (or 12%).

Multiplying the right-hand side of this expression by the sample size gives us the expected number of individuals in the sample who are in both specified categories of the two variables when the variables are independent. However, these expected counts cannot be calculated, because the individual population proportions are not known. The resolution of this dilemma is to estimate each population proportion using the corresponding sample proportion:

$$\begin{pmatrix} \text{estimated expected number} \\ \text{in specified categories} \\ \text{of the two variables} \end{pmatrix} = \begin{pmatrix} \text{sample} \\ \text{size} \end{pmatrix} \cdot \frac{\begin{pmatrix} \text{obs. number in} \\ \text{categ. of 1st var.} \end{pmatrix}}{\text{sample size}} \cdot \frac{\begin{pmatrix} \text{obs. number in} \\ \text{categ. of 2nd var.} \end{pmatrix}}{\text{sample size}}$$

$$= \frac{\begin{pmatrix} \text{obs. number in} \\ \text{categ. of 1st var.} \end{pmatrix} \cdot \begin{pmatrix} \text{obs. number in} \\ \text{categ. of 2nd var.} \end{pmatrix}}{\text{sample size}}$$

Suppose that the observed counts are displayed in a rectangular table in which rows correspond to the different categories of the first variable and columns to the categories of the second variable. Then the numerator in the preceding expression for estimated expected counts is just the product of the row and column marginal totals. This is exactly how estimated expected counts were computed in the test for homogeneity of several populations.

X^2 Test for Independence

Null hypothesis: H_0: The two variables are independent.

Alternative hypothesis: H_a: The two variables are not independent.

Test statistic: $X^2 = \sum_{\text{all cells}} \dfrac{(\text{observed cell count} - \text{expected cell count})^2}{\text{expected cell count}}$

The expected cell counts are estimated (assuming H_0 is true) by the formula

$$\text{expected cell count} = \frac{(\text{row marginal total})(\text{column marginal total})}{\text{grand total}}$$

P-values: When H_0 is true and the assumptions of the X^2 test are satisfied, X^2 has approximately a chi-squared distribution with

df = (number of rows − 1)(number of columns − 1)

The *P*-value associated with the computed test statistic value is the area to the right of X^2 under the chi-squared curve with the appropriate df. Upper-tail areas for chi-squared distributions are found in Appendix Table IX.

Assumptions: 1. The observed counts are from a *random sample*.
2. The *sample size is large*: All expected counts are at least 5. If some expected counts are less than 5, rows or columns of the table should be combined to achieve a table with satisfactory expected counts.

EXAMPLE 12.7

The article "Factors Associated with Sexual Risk-Taking Behaviors Among Adolescents" (*J. Marriage and Family* (1994): 622–632) examined the relationship between gender and contraceptive use by sexually active teens. Each person in a random sample of sexually active teens was classified according to gender and contraceptive use (with three categories: rarely or never use, use sometimes or most of the time, and always use), resulting in a 3 × 2 table. Data consistent with percentages given in the article is in Table 12.6.

Table 12.6 *Observed counts for Example 12.7*

Contraceptive Use	Gender		
	Female	Male	Row Marg. Total
Rarely/Never	210	350	560
Sometimes/Most Times	190	320	510
Always	400	530	930
Col. Marg. Total	800	1200	2000

The authors were interested in determining whether there is an association between gender and contraceptive use. Using a .05 significance level, we will test

H_0:   Gender and contraceptive use are independent.

H_a: Gender and contraceptive use are not independent.

Significance level: $\alpha = .05$

Test statistic: $X^2 = \sum_{\text{all cells}} \dfrac{(\text{observed cell count} - \text{expected cell count})^2}{\text{expected cell count}}$

Assumptions: Before we can check the assumptions we must first compute the expected cell counts.

Row	Cell Column	Expected Cell Count
1	1	$\dfrac{(560)(800)}{2000} = 224.0$
1	2	$\dfrac{(560)(1200)}{2000} = 336.0$
2	1	$\dfrac{(510)(800)}{2000} = 204.0$
2	2	$\dfrac{(510)(1200)}{2000} = 306.0$
3	1	$\dfrac{(930)(800)}{2000} = 372.0$
3	2	$\dfrac{(930)(1200)}{2000} = 558.0$

All expected cell counts are greater than 5 and the observed cell counts are based on a random sample, so the X^2 test can be used. The observed and expected counts are given together in Table 12.7.

Table 12.7 *Observed and expected counts for Example 12.7*

Contraceptive Use	Gender		Row Marg. Total
	Female	Male	
Rarely/Never	210 (224)	350 (336)	560
Sometimes/Most Times	190 (204)	320 (306)	510
Always	400 (372)	530 (558)	930
Col. Marg. Total	800	1200	2000

Calculation: $X^2 = \dfrac{(210 - 224)^2}{224} + \cdots + \dfrac{(530 - 558)^2}{558} = 6.572$

P-value: The table has 3 rows and 2 columns, so df = $(3 - 1)(2 - 1) = 2$. The entry closest to 6.572 in the 2-df column of Appendix Table IX is 6.70, so the approximate *P*-value for this test is

   P-value $\approx$ .035

Conclusion: Since *P*-value $\leq \alpha$, we reject H_0 and conclude that there is an association between gender and contraceptive use.

EXAMPLE 12.8

The accompanying two-way table (Table 12.8) was constructed using data in the article "Television Viewing and Physical Fitness in Adults" (*Research Quarterly for Exercise and Sport* (1990): 315–320). The author hoped to determine whether time spent watching television is associated with cardiovascular fitness. Subjects were asked about their television-viewing time (per day, rounded to the nearest hour) and were classified as physically fit if they scored in the excellent or very good category on a step test. Expected cell counts (computed under the assumption of no association between TV viewing and fitness) appear in parentheses in the table.

Table 12.8 *Observed and expected counts for Example 12.8*

TV Group	Fitness		
	Physically Fit	**Not Physically Fit**	
0	35 (25.5)	147 (156.5)	182
1–2	101 (102.2)	629 (627.8)	730
3–4	28 (35.0)	222 (215.0)	250
5 or More	4 (5.3)	34 (32.7)	38
	168	1032	1200

The X^2 test with a significance level of .01 will be used to test the relevant hypotheses:

   H_0:   Fitness and TV viewing are independent.

   H_a: Fitness and TV viewing are not independent.

Significance level: $\alpha = .01$

Test statistic: $X^2 = \displaystyle\sum_{\text{all cells}} \dfrac{(\text{observed cell count} - \text{expected cell count})^2}{\text{expected cell count}}$

Assumptions: All expected cell counts are at least 5. Assuming that the data can be viewed as a random sample of adults, the X^2 test can be used.

Calculation: $X^2 = \dfrac{(35 - 25.5)^2}{25.5} + \cdots + \dfrac{(34 - 32.7)^2}{32.7} = 6.13$

P-value: The table has 4 rows and 2 columns, so df $= (4 - 1)(2 - 1) = 3$. The computed value of $X^2 = 6.13$ is smaller than 6.25, the smallest entry in the 3-df column of Appendix Table IX. Therefore,

P-value $> .10$

Conclusion: Since P-value $> \alpha$, H_0 is not rejected. There is not sufficient evidence to conclude that an association exists between TV viewing and fitness.

Most statistical computer packages will calculate expected cell counts, the value of the X^2 statistic, and the associated P-value. MINITAB output for the data of Example 12.8 is given in Figure 12.3. The discrepancy between $X^2 = 6.13$ and $X^2 = 6.161$ is due to rounding in the hand calculations. Note also that MINITAB gives P-value $= .104$. This is consistent with the statement P-value $> .10$ from Example 12.8.

FIGURE 12.3 MINITAB output for Example 12.8

Chi-Square Test
Expected counts are printed below observed counts

	Fit	Not fit	Total
1	35	147	182
	25.48	156.52	
2	101	629	730
	102.20	627.80	
3	28	222	250
	35.00	215.00	
4	4	34	38
	5.32	32.68	
Total	168	1032	1200

Chi-Sq = 3.557 + 0.579 +
0.014 + 0.002 +
1.400 + 0.228 +
0.328 + 0.053 = 6.161
DF = 3, P-Value = 0.104

In some investigations, values of more than two categorical variables are recorded for each individual in the sample. For example, in addition to the variables *television-viewing time* and *fitness level,* the researchers in the study referenced in Example 12.8 might also have recorded age group (with categories under 21, 21–30, 31–40, and so on) for each subject. A number of interesting questions could then be explored: Are all three variables independent of one another? Is it possible that age and fitness level are dependent but that the relationship between them does not depend on TV-viewing time? For a particular age group, are TV-viewing time and fitness independent?

The X^2 test procedure described in this section for analysis of bivariate categorical data can be extended for use with *multivariate categorical data*. Appropriate hypothesis tests can then be used to provide insight into the relationships between variables. However, the computations required to calculate estimated expected cell counts and to compute the value of X^2 are quite tedious, so they are seldom done without the aid of a computer. Several statistical computer packages (including BMDP and SAS) can perform this type of analysis. Consult the chapter references for further information on the analysis of categorical data.

Exercises 12.15 – 12.33

12.15   A particular state university system has six campuses. On each campus, a random sample of students will be selected, and each student will be categorized with respect to political philosophy as liberal, moderate, or conservative. The null hypothesis of interest is that the proportion of students falling in these three categories is the same at all six campuses.

a. On how many degrees of freedom will the resulting X^2 test be based?

b. How does your answer in part **a** change if there are seven campuses rather than six?

c. How does your answer in part **a** change if there are four rather than three categories for political philosophy?

12.16   A random sample of 1000 registered voters in a certain county is selected, and each voter is categorized with respect to both educational level (four categories) and preferred candidate in an upcoming supervisorial election (five possibilities). The hypothesis of interest is that educational level and preferred candidate are independent factors.

a. If $X^2 = 7.2$, what would you conclude at significance level .10?

b. If there were only four candidates vying for election, what would you conclude if $X^2 = 14.5$ and $\alpha = .05$?

12.17   What factors influence people to respond to mail surveys? Researchers have found that the appearance of the survey and the nature of the first question have an influence on the overall response rate, but do they affect the speed of response? The article "The Impact of Cover Design and First Questions on Responses for a Mail Survey of Skydivers" (*Leisure Science* (1991): 67–76) presents the results of an experiment to investigate rate of response. Surveys with a plain cover were mailed to a random sample of 427 skydivers. Surveys with a cover graphic of a skydiver were mailed to a separate random sample of 414 skydivers. The postmark on the returned survey was used to classify each person who received a survey in one of the following response categories: returned in 1–7 days, returned in 8–14 days, returned in 15–31 days, returned in 32–60 days, and not returned. The resulting data is summarized in the two-way table below. Does the data support the theory that the proportions falling into the various response categories are not the same for the two cover designs? Use a significance level of .05 to test the relevant hypotheses.

12.18   The article "Heavy Drinking and Problems Among Wine Drinkers" (*Journal of Studies on Alcohol* (1999): 467–471) analyzed drinking problems among Canadians. The article gave the percentage of drinkers

Data for Exercise 12.17

Cover Design	Response Category					
	1–7	**8–14**	**15–31**	**32–60**	**Not Returned**	
Graphic	70	76	51	19	198	414
Plain	84	53	51	32	207	427
	154	129	102	51	405	841

who never drank to intoxication for seven different types of drinkers. From the information given in the article, we can obtain the following table:

	Never Intoxicated	Sometimes Intoxicated
Beer Only	515	741
Wine Only	875	232
Spirits Only	387	372
Beer and Wine	774	560
Beer and Spirits	312	727
Wine and Spirits	708	349
Beer, Wine, and Spirits	1032	1119

Assume that each of the seven samples studied can be viewed as a random sample from the respective group.

a. Is there sufficient evidence to conclude that the proportion who never become intoxicated is not the same for the seven groups?

b. Is the test that you performed in part **a** a test of independence or a test of homogeneity?

12.19 Do women have different patterns of work behavior than men? The article "Workaholism in Organizations: Gender Differences" (*Sex Roles: A Journal of Research* (1999): 333–346) attempts to answer this question. Each person in a random sample of 423 graduates of a business school in Canada were polled and classified by gender and workaholism type, resulting in the accompanying table:

	Gender	
Workaholism Types	**Female**	**Male**
Work Enthusiasts	20	41
Workaholics	32	37
Enthusiastic Workaholics	34	46
Unengaged Workers	43	52
Relaxed Workers	24	27
Disenchanted Workers	37	30

a. Test the hypothesis that gender and workaholism type are independent.

b. The author writes "women and men fell into each of the six workaholism types to a similar degree." Does the outcome of the test you performed in part **a** support this conclusion? Explain.

12.20 The following table is based on data reported in "Light-to-moderate Alcohol Consumption and Risk of Stroke Among U.S. Male Physicians" (*New England J. of Medicine* (1999): 1557–1564). The table is based on 21,870 male physicians age 40–84 who are participating in the Physicians Health Study.

	Alcohol Consumption (No. of Drinks)				
	<1/wk	**1/wk**	**2–4/wk**	**5–6/wk**	**1/day**
Never Smoked	3577	1711	2430	1211	1910
Smoked in the Past	1595	1068	1999	1264	2683
Currently Smokes	524	289	470	296	849

a. Calculate row percentages by dividing each observed count by the corresponding row total. Are the proportions falling in each of the alcohol consumption categories similar for the three smoking categories?

b. Test the hypothesis that smoking status and alcohol consumption are independent.

c. Is the result of your test in part **b** consistent with what you expected based on your answer to part **a**? If not, explain why your initial impression based on the percentages may not have been accurate? What aspect of the data set factors into your explanation?

12.21 The article "Motion Sickness in Public Road Transport: The Effect of Driver, Route and Vehicle" (*Ergonomics* (1999): 1646–1664) reported that seat position within a bus may have some effect on whether one experiences motion sickness. The accompanying table classifies each person in a random sample of bus riders by the location of his or her seat and whether nausea was reported.

	Nausea	No Nausea
Front	58	870
Middle	166	1163
Rear	193	806

Based on this data, can you conclude that there is an association between seat location and nausea? Test the relevant hypotheses using $\alpha = .05$.

12.22 The article "Mortality Among Recent Purchasers of Handguns" (*New England J. of Medicine* (1999): 1583–1589) examined the relationship between handgun purchases and cause of death. Suppose that a random sample of 4000 death records was examined and cause of death was noted for each individual in the sample. Gun registration records were also examined to determine which of these 4000 individuals had purchased a handgun within the previous year. Data consistent with summary values given in the article is shown in the accompanying table.

	Suicide	Not Suicide
Handgun Purchased	4	12
No Handgun Purchased	63	3921

Is it reasonable to use the chi-squared test to determine whether there is an association between handgun purchase within the year prior to death and whether the death was a suicide? Justify your answer.

12.23 When charities solicit donations, they must know what approach will encourage people to donate. Would a picture of a needy child tug at the heartstrings and convince someone to contribute to the charity? As reported in the article "The Effect of Photographs of the Handicapped on Donation" (*J. of Applied Social Psychology* (1979): 426–431), experimenters went door-to-door with four types of displays: a picture of a smiling child, a picture of an unsmiling child, a verbal message, and an identification of the charity only. At each door, they would randomly select which display to present. Suppose 18 of 30 subjects contributed when shown the picture of the smiling child, 14 of 30 contributed when shown the picture of an unsmiling child, 16 of 26 contributed when shown the verbal message, and 18 of 22 contributed when shown only the identification of the charity. What conclusions can be drawn from this data? Explain your procedure and reasoning.

12.24 The accompanying table is based on data given in the article "The Association Between Smoking and Unhealthy Behaviors Among a National Sample of Mexican-American Adolescents" (*J. of School Health* (1998): 376–379). Each boy in a sample of Mexican-American males age 10–18 was classified according to smoking status and response to a question asking whether he liked to do risky things. Assume that it is reasonable to regard the sample as a random sample of Mexican-American male adolescents.

	Smoking Status	
	Smoker	**Nonsmoker**
Likes Risky Things	45	46
Doesn't Like Risky Things	36	153

a. Is there sufficient evidence to conclude that there is an association between smoking status and desire to do risky things? Test the relevant hypotheses using $\alpha = .05$.
b. Based on your conclusion in part **a**, is it reasonable to conclude that smoking *causes* an increase in the desire to do risky things? Explain.

12.25 The article "Cooperative Hunting in Lions: The Role of the Individual" (*Behavioral Ecology and Sociobiology* (1992): 445–454) discusses the different roles taken by lionesses as they attack and capture prey. The authors were interested in the effect of the position in line as stalking occurs; an individual lioness may be in the center of the line or on the wing (end of the line) as they advance toward their prey. In addition to position, the role of the lioness was also considered. A lioness could initiate a chase (be the first one to charge the prey), or she could participate and join the chase after it has been initiated. Data from the article is summarized in the accompanying table.

	Role	
Position	**Initiate Chase**	**Participate in Chase**
Center	28	48
Wing	66	41

Is there evidence of an association between position and role? Test the relevant hypotheses using $\alpha = .01$. What assumptions about how the data was collected must be true for the chi-squared test to be an appropriate way to analyze this data?

12.26 The authors of the article "A Survey of Parent Attitudes and Practices Regarding Under Age Drinking" (*J. Youth and Adolescence* (1995): 315–334) conducted a telephone survey of parents with preteen and teenage children. One of the questions asked was "How effective do you think you are in talking to your children about drinking?" Responses are summarized in the accompanying 3×2 table. Using a significance level of .05, carry out a test to determine whether there is an association between age of children and parental response.

Response	Age of Children	
	Preteen	**Teen**
Very Effective	126	149
Somewhat Effective	44	41
Not at All Effective or Don't Know	51	26

12.27 The article "Regional Differences in Attitudes Toward Corporal Punishment" (*J. Marriage and Family* (1994): 314–324) presents data resulting from a random sample of 978 adults. Each individual in the sample was asked whether he or she agreed with the following statement: "Sometimes it is necessary to discipline a child with a good, hard spanking." Respondents were also classified according to the region of the United States in which they lived. The resulting data is summarized in the accompanying table. Is there an association between response (agree, disagree) and region of residence? Use $\alpha = .01$.

Response

Region	Agree	Disagree
Northeast	130	59
West	146	42
Midwest	211	52
South	291	47

12.28 A story describing a date rape was read by 352 high school students. To investigate the effect of the victim's clothing on subject's judgment of the situation described, the story was accompanied by either a photograph of the victim dressed provocatively, a photo of the victim dressed conservatively, or no picture. Each student was asked whether the situation described in the story was one of rape. Data from the article "The Influence of Victim's Attire on Adolescent Judgements of Date Rape" (*Adolescence* (1995): 319–323) is given in the accompanying table. Is there evidence that the proportion who believe that the story described a rape differs for the three different photo groups? Test the relevant hypotheses using $\alpha = .01$.

Picture

Response	Provocative	Conservative	No Picture
Rape	80	104	92
Not Rape	47	12	17

12.29 Can people tell the difference between a female nose and a male nose? This important (?) research question was examined in the article "You Can Tell by the Nose: Judging Sex from an Isolated Facial Feature" (*Perception* (1995): 969–973). Eight Caucasian males and eight Caucasian females posed for nose photos. The article states that none of the volunteers wore nose studs or had prominent nasal hair. Each person placed a black Lycra tube over his or her head in such a way that only the nose protruded through a hole in the material. Photos were then taken from three different angles: front view, three-quarter view, and profile. These photos were shown to a sample of undergraduate students. Each student in the sample was shown one of the nose photos and asked whether it was a photo of a male or a female; and the response was classified as either correct or incorrect. The accompanying table was constructed using summary val-

ues reported in the article. Is there evidence that the proportion of correct sex identifications differs for the three different nose views?

View

Sex ID	Front	Profile	Three-quarter
Correct	23	26	29
Incorrect	17	14	11

12.30 The accompanying table appeared in the article "Europe's Receptivity to New Religious Movements: Round Two" (*J. for the Scientific Study of Religion* (1993): 389–397). Suppose that the percentages in the table were based on random samples of size 200 from each of the six countries.

Country	Percent Who Believe in Fortune-Tellers
Great Britain	42
West Germany	32
East Germany	22
Slovenia	55
Ireland	27
Northern Ireland	33

a. Use the given percentages to construct a two-way table with rows corresponding to the six countries and columns corresponding to the categories "believe in fortune-tellers" and "don't believe in fortune-tellers." Enter the observed counts in the table. (*Hint:* The observed counts for Great Britain are $(.42)(200) = 84$ for the "believe" column and $(.58)(200) = 116$ for the "don't believe" column.)

b. Is there evidence that the proportion who believe in fortune-tellers is not the same for all six countries? Test the relevant hypotheses using $\alpha = .01$.

12.31 The two-way frequency table at the top of page 490 appeared in the article "Marijuana Use in College" (*Youth and Society* (1979): 323–334). Four hundred forty-five college students were classified according to both frequency of marijuana use and parental use of alcohol and psychoactive drugs. Use the accompanying SAS computer output to carry out a X^2 test with a significance level of .01 to determine whether there is an association between marijuana use and parental use of drugs and alcohol.

Data for Exercise 12.31

Parental Use of Alcohol and Drugs	Student Level of Marijuana Use			Row Marg. Total
	Never	Occasional	Regular	
Neither	141	54	40	235
One	68	44	51	163
Both	17	11	19	47
Col. Marg. Total	226	109	110	445

TABLE OF PRNT_USE BY STUD_USE

PRINT_USE   STUD_USE

Frequency
Percent
Row Pct

Col Pct	never	occasion	regular	Total
neither	141	54	40	235
	31.69	12.13	8.99	52.81
	60.00	22.98	17.02	
	62.39	49.54	36.36	
one	68	44	51	163
	15.28	9.89	11.46	36.63
	41.72	26.99	31.29	
	30.09	40.37	46.36	
both	17	11	19	47
	3.82	2.47	4.27	10.56
	36.17	23.40	40.43	
	7.52	10.09	17.27	
Total	226	109	110	446
	50.79	24.49	24.72	100.00

STATISTICS FOR TABLE OF PRINT_USE BY STUD_USE

Statistic	DF	Value	Prob
Chi-Square	4	22.373	0.000

12.32   Jail inmates can be classified into one of the following four categories according to the type of crime committed: violent crime, crime against property, drug offenses, and public-order offenses. Suppose that random samples of 500 male inmates and 500 female inmates are selected, and each inmate is classified according to type of offense. The data in the accompanying table is based on summary values given in the article "Profile of Jail Inmates" (*USA Today*, April 25, 1991). We would like to know whether male and female inmates differ with respect to type of offense.

Type of Crime	Gender	
	Male	Female
Violent	117	66
Property	150	160
Drug	109	168
Public-Order	124	106

a. Is this a test of homogeneity or a test of independence?
b. Test the relevant hypotheses using a significance level of .05.

12.33   Job satisfaction of professionals was examined in the article "Psychology of the Scientist: Work Related Attitudes of U.S. Scientists" (*Psychological Reports* (1991): 443–450). Each person in a random sample of 778 teachers was classified according to a job satisfaction variable and also by teaching level, resulting in the accompanying two-way table. Can we conclude that there is an association between job satisfaction and teaching level? Test the relevant hypotheses using $\alpha = .05$.

Teaching Level	Job Satisfaction	
	Satisfied	Unsatisfied
College	74	43
High School	224	171
Elementary	126	140

12.3   Interpreting the Results of Statistical Analyses

Many studies, particularly in the social sciences, result in categorical data. The questions of interest in such studies often lead to an analysis that involves using a chi-squared test. As with the other hypothesis tests considered, it is common to find the result of a chi-squared test summarized by giving the value of the chi-squared test statistic and an associated *P*-value. Because categorical data can be summarized compactly in frequency tables, the data often is given in the article (unlike data for numerical variables, which is rarely given).

What to Look for in Published Data

Here are some questions to consider when you are reading an article that contains the results of a chi-squared test:

- Are the variables of interest categorical rather than numerical?
- Is the data given in the article in the form of a frequency table?
- If a two-way frequency table is involved, is the question of interest one of homogeneity or one of independence?
- What null hypothesis is being tested? Are the results of the analysis reported in the correct context (homogeneity, etc.)?
- Is the sample size large enough to make use of a chi-squared test value? (Are all expected counts at least 5?)
- What is the value of the test statistic? Is the associated *P*-value given? Should the null hypothesis tested be rejected?
- Are the conclusions drawn by the authors consistent with the results of the test?
- How different are the observed and expected counts? Does the result have practical as well as statistical significance?

The authors of the article "Predicting Professional Sports Game Outcomes from Intermediate Game Scores" (*Chance* (1992): 18–22) used a chi-squared test to determine whether there was any merit to the idea that basketball games are not settled until the last quarter, whereas baseball games are over by the seventh inning. They also considered football and hockey. Data was collected for 189 basketball games, 92 baseball games, 80 hockey games, and 93 football games. The games analyzed were sampled randomly from all games played during the 1990 season for baseball and football and for the 1990–1991 season for basketball and hockey. For each game, the late-game leader was determined, and then it was noted whether the late-game leader actually ended up winning the game. The resulting data is summarized in the accompanying table.

Sport	Late-game Leader Wins	Late-game Leader Loses
Basketball	150	39
Baseball	86	6
Hockey	65	15
Football	72	21

The authors state

> *Late-game leader* is defined as the team that is ahead after three quarters in basketball and football, two periods in hockey, and seven innings in baseball. The chi-squared value (with three degrees of freedom) is 10.52 ($P < .015$).

They also conclude that

> the sports of basketball, hockey, and football have remarkably similar percentages of late-game reversals, ranging from 18.8% to 22.6%. The sport that is an anomaly is baseball. Only 6.5% of baseball games resulted in late reversals. . . . [The chi-squared test] is statistically significant due almost entirely to baseball.

In this particular analysis, the authors are comparing four populations (games from each of the four sports) on the basis of a categorical variable with two categories (late-game leader wins and late-game leader loses). The appropriate null hypothesis is then

H_0: The true proportion in each category (leader wins, leader loses) is the same for all four sports.

Based on the reported value of the chi-squared statistics and the associated *P*-value, this null hypothesis is rejected, leading to the conclusion that the category proportions are not the same for all four sports.

The validity of the chi-squared test requires that the sample sizes be large enough so that no expected counts are less than 5. Is this reasonable here? The accompanying MINITAB output shows the expected cell counts and the computation of the X^2 statistic.

Chi-Square Test

Expected counts are printed below observed counts

	leader w	leader l	Total
1	150	39	189
	155.28	33.72	
2	86	6	92
	75.59	16.41	
3	65	15	80
	65.73	14.27	
4	72	21	93
	76.41	16.59	
Total	373	81	454

Chi-Sq = 0.180 + 0.827 +
$\qquad$ 1.435 + 6.607 +
$\qquad$ 0.008 + 0.037 +
$\qquad$ 0.254 + 1.171 = 10.518
DF = 3, P-Value = 0.015

The smallest expected count is 14.27, so the sample sizes are large enough to justify the use of the X^2 test. Note also that the two cells in the table that correspond to baseball contribute a total of 1.435 + 6.607 = 8.042 to the value of the X^2 statistic of 10.518. This is due to the large discrepancies between the observed and expected counts for these two cells. There is reasonable agreement between the observed and the expected counts in the other cells. This is probably the basis for the authors' conclusion that baseball is the only anomaly and that the other sports were similar.

Summary of Key Concepts and Formulas

Term or Formula	Comment
One-way frequency table	A compact way of summarizing data on a categorical variable; it gives the number of times each of the possible categories in the data set occurs (the frequencies).
Goodness-of-fit statistic, $$X^2 = \sum_{\text{all cells}} \frac{\left(\begin{array}{cc}\text{observed} & \text{expected} \\ \text{cell count} & - \text{ cell count}\end{array}\right)^2}{\text{expected cell count}}$$	A statistic used to provide a comparison between observed counts and those expected when a given hypothesis is true. When none of the expected counts are too small, X^2 has approximately a chi-squared distribution.
X^2 test in a one-way frequency table: H_0: π_1 = hypothesized proportion for category 1 $\cdot$ π_k = hypothesized proportion for category k	A hypothesis test performed to determine whether the true category proportions are different from those specified by the given null hypothesis.
Two-way frequency table (contingency table)	A rectangular table used to summarize a bivariate categorical data set; two-way tables are used to compare several populations on the basis of a categorical variable or to identify whether an association exists between two categorical variables.
X^2 test for comparing two or more populations: H_0: The true category proportions are the same for all the populations.	The hypothesis test performed to determine whether the true category proportions are the same for all of the populations to be compared.
X^2 test for independence: H_0: The two variables defining the table are independent.	The hypothesis test performed to determine whether an association exists between two categorical variables.

Supplementary Exercises 12.34 – 12.42

12.34   In a study of 2989 cancer deaths, the location of death (home, acute-care hospital, or chronic-care facility) and age at death were recorded, resulting in the accompanying two-way frequency table ("Where Cancer Patients Die," *Public Health Reports* (1983): 173). Using a .01 significance level, test the null hypothesis that age at death and location of death are independent.

	Location		
Age	**Home**	**Acute-care**	**Chronic-care**
15–54	94	418	23
55–64	116	524	34
65–74	156	581	109
Over 74	138	558	238

12.35 Each driver in a sample of size 1024 was classified according to both seat-belt usage and gender to obtain the accompanying 2 × 2 frequency table ("What Kinds of People Do Not Use Seat Belts," *Amer. J. of Public Health* (1977): 1043–1049). Does the data strongly suggest an association between gender and seat-belt usage? Use a .05 significance level.

Seat-belt Usage

Gender	Don't Use	Use
Male	192	272
Female	284	276

12.36 The *Los Angeles Times* (July 29, 1983) conducted a survey to find out why some Californians don't register to vote. Random samples of 100 Latinos, 100 Anglos, and 100 African-Americans who were not registered to vote were selected. The resulting data is summarized in the accompanying table. Does the data suggest that the true proportion falling into each response category is not the same for Latinos, Anglos, and African-Americans? Use a .05 significance level.

Race

Reason For Not Registering	Latino	Anglo	African-American
Not a Citizen	45	8	0
Not Interested	19	33	19
Can't Meet Residency Requirements	9	35	23
Distrust of Politics	5	10	8
Too Difficult to Register	10	10	27
Other Reason	12	4	23

12.37 The relative importance attached to work and home life by high school students was examined in "Work Role Salience as a Determinant of Career Maturity in High School Students" (*J. Vocational Behavior* (1984): 30–44). Does the data summarized in the accompanying two-way frequency table suggest that gender and relative importance assigned to work and home are not independent? Test using a .05 level of significance.

Relative Importance

Gender	Work > Home	Work = Home	Work < Home
Female	68	26	94
Male	75	19	57

12.38 The accompanying 2 × 2 frequency table is the result of classifying random samples of 112 librarians and 108 faculty members of the California State University system with respect to gender ("Job Satisfaction Among

Faculty and Librarians: A Study of Gender, Autonomy, and Decision Making Opportunities," *J. of Library Admin.* (1984): 43–56). Does the data strongly suggest that librarians and faculty members differ with respect to the proportion of males and females? Test using a .05 level of significance.

	Faculty	Librarians
Male	56	59
Female	52	53

12.39 Is there any relationship between the age of an investor and the rate of return that the investor expects from an investment? A random sample of 972 common stock investors was selected, and each was placed in one of four age categories and in one of four categories according to rate believed attainable ("Patterns of Investment Strategy and Behavior Among Individual Investors," *J. of Business* (1977): 296–333). The resulting data is given in the accompanying table. Does there appear to be an association between age and rate believed attainable? Test the appropriate hypotheses using a .01 significance level.

Rate Believed Attainable

Investor Age	0–5%	6–10%	11–15%	Over 15%
Under 45	15	51	51	29
45–54	31	133	70	48
55–64	59	139	35	20
65 and Over	84	157	32	18

12.40 The article "Participation of Senior Citizens in the Swine Flu Inoculation Program" (*J. of Gerontology* (1979): 201–208) described a study of the factors thought to influence a person's decision to obtain a flu vaccination. Each member of a sample of 122 senior citizens was classified according to belief about the likelihood of getting the flu and vaccine status to obtain the two-way frequency table shown here. Using a .05 significance level, test to determine whether there is an association between belief and vaccine status.

Vaccine Status

Belief	Received Vaccine	Didn't Receive Vaccine
Very Unlikely	25	24
Unlikely	30	11
Likely	6	8
Don't Know	5	13

12.41 The article "An Instant Shot of 'Ah': Cocaine Use Among Methadone Clients" (*J. of Psychoactive Drugs*

(1984): 217–227) reported the accompanying data on frequency of cocaine use for individuals in three different treatment groups. Does the data suggest that the true proportion of individuals in each of the different cocaine-use categories differs for the three treatments? Carry out an appropriate test at level .05.

Treatment

Cocaine Use	A	B	C
None	149	75	8
1–2 Times	26	27	15
3–6 Times	6	20	11
At Least 7 Times	4	10	10

12.42 The article "Identification of Cola Beverages" (*J. of Appl. Psych.* (1962): 356–360) reported on an experiment in which each of 79 subjects was presented with glasses of cola in pairs and asked to identify which glass contained a specific brand of cola. The accompanying data appeared in the article. Does this data suggest that individuals' abilities to make correct identification differ for the different brands of cola?

Number of Correct Identifications

Cola	0	1	2	3 or 4
Coca-Cola	13	23	24	19
Pepsi Cola	12	20	26	21
Royal Crown	18	28	19	14

References

Agresti, Alan, and B. Finlay. *Statistical Methods for the Social Sciences,* 3rd ed. New Jersey: Prentice-Hall, 1997. (This book includes a good discussion of measures of association for two-way frequency tables.)

Everitt, B. S. *The Analysis of Contingency Tables.* New York: Halsted Press, 1977. (A compact but informative survey of methods for analyzing categorical data.)

Mosteller, Frederick, and Robert Rourke. *Sturdy Statistics.* Reading, Mass.: Addison-Wesley, 1973. (Contains several very readable chapters on the varied uses of the chi-squared statistic.)

13

Simple Linear Regression and Correlation: Inferential Methods

Regression and correlation were introduced in Chapter 5 as techniques for describing and summarizing bivariate data consisting of (x, y) pairs. For example, consider a regression of the dependent variable y = average SAT score on the independent variable x = spending per pupil (thousands of dollars) based on a sample of n = 44 New Jersey school districts ("Cost-Effectiveness in Public Education." *Chance* (1995): 38–41). A scatter plot of the data shows a linear pattern; the sample correlation coefficient is r = .4; and the equation of the least squares line is $\hat{y} = 766 + 15.0x$. When $x = 10$ is substituted into this equation, $\hat{y}$ is calculated to be 916. This number can be interpreted either as a *point estimate* of the average score for all districts that spend $10,000 per pupil or as a *point prediction* for the score in a single district that spends this amount of money per pupil. In this chapter, we develop inferential methods for this type of data, including a confidence interval (interval estimate) for a mean y value, a prediction interval for a single y value, and a test of hypotheses regarding the extent of correlation in the entire population of (x, y) pairs.

13.1 The Simple Linear Regression Model

A *deterministic relationship* is one in which the value of y is completely determined by the value of an independent variable x. Such a relationship can be described using traditional mathematical notation such as $y = f(x)$, where $f(x)$ is a specified function of x. For example, we might have

$$y = f(x) = 10 + 2x$$

or

$$y = f(x) = 4 - (10)^{2x}$$

However, in most situations, the variables of interest are not deterministically related. For example, the value of y = first-year-college grade point average is certainly not determined solely by x = high-school grade point average, and y = crop yield is determined partly by factors other than x = amount of fertilizer used.

A description of the relation between two variables x and y that are not deterministically related can be given by specifying a **probabilistic model.** The general form of an **additive probabilistic model** allows y to be larger or smaller than $f(x)$ by a random amount, e. The **model equation** is of the form

y = deterministic function of x + random deviation
  = $f(x) + e$

Let $x*$ denote some particular value of x, and suppose that an observation on y is made when $x = x*$. Then

$y > f(x*)$ if $e > 0$
$y < f(x*)$ if $e < 0$
$y = f(x*)$ if $e = 0$

Thinking geometrically, if $e > 0$, the observed point $(x*, y)$ will lie above the graph of $y = f(x)$; $e < 0$ implies that this point will fall below the graph. This is illustrated in Figure 13.1. If $f(x)$ is a function used in a probabilistic model relating y to x, and observations on y are made for various values of x, the resulting (x, y) points will be distributed about the graph of $f(x)$, some falling above it and others below it.

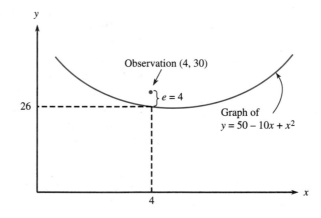

FIGURE 13.1 A deviation from the deterministic part of a probabilistic model

Simple Linear Regression

The simple linear regression model is a special case of the general probabilistic model in which the deterministic function $f(x)$ is linear (so its graph is a straight line).

Definition

The **simple linear regression model** assumes that there is a line with vertical or y intercept α and slope β, called the **true** or **population regression line.** When a value of the independent variable x is fixed and an observation on the dependent variable y is made,

$$y = \alpha + \beta x + e$$

Without the random deviation e, all observed (x, y) points would fall exactly on the population regression line. The inclusion of e in the model equation allows points to deviate from the line by random amounts.

Figure 13.2 shows several observations in relation to the population regression line.

FIGURE 13.2 Several observations resulting from the simple linear regression model

Before we make an observation on y for any particular value of x, we are uncertain about the value of e. It could be negative, positive, or even zero. Also, it might be quite large in magnitude (a point far from the population regression line) or quite small (a point very close to the line). In this chapter, we will make some assumptions about the distribution of e in repeated sampling at any particular x value.

Basic Assumptions of the Simple Linear Regression Model

1. The distribution of e at any particular x value has mean value 0 ($\mu_e = 0$).
2. The standard deviation of e (which describes the spread of its distribution) is the same for any particular value of x. This standard deviation is denoted by σ.

(continued)

3. The distribution of e at any particular x value is normal.

4. The random deviations $e_1, e_2, \ldots, e_n$ associated with different observations are independent of one another.

Randomness in e implies that y itself is subject to uncertainty. The foregoing assumptions about the distribution of e imply that the distribution of y values in repeated sampling satisfies certain properties. Consider y when x has some fixed value x^*, so that

$$y = \alpha + \beta x^* + e$$

Because α and β are fixed numbers, so is $\alpha + \beta x^*$. The sum of a fixed number and a normally distributed variable is again a normally distributed variable (the bell-shaped curve is simply relocated), so y itself has a normal distribution. Furthermore, $\mu_e = 0$ implies that the mean value of y is just $\alpha + \beta x^*$, the height of the population regression line above the value x^*. Lastly, because there is no variability in the fixed number $\alpha + \beta x^*$, the standard deviation of y is the same as that of e. These properties are summarized in the following box.

For any fixed x value, y itself has a normal distribution, with

$$\begin{pmatrix} \text{mean } y \text{ value} \\ \text{for fixed } x \end{pmatrix} = \begin{pmatrix} \text{height of the population} \\ \text{regression line above } x \end{pmatrix} = \alpha + \beta x$$

and

$$(\text{standard deviation of } y \text{ for fixed } x) = \sigma$$

The slope β of the population regression line is the *average* change in y associated with a 1-unit increase in x. The vertical intercept α is the height of the population line when $x = 0$. The value of σ determines the extent to which (x, y) observations deviate from the population line; when σ is small, most observations will be quite close to the line, but with large σ, there are likely to be some substantial deviations.

The key features of the model are illustrated in Figures 13.3 and 13.4. Notice that the three normal curves in Figure 13.3 have identical spreads. This is a consequence of $\sigma_e = \sigma$, which does not depend on x.

EXAMPLE 13.1   The authors of the article "On Weight Loss by Wrestlers Who Have Been Standing on Their Heads" (Sixth International Conference on Statistics, Combinatorics, and Related Areas, Forum for Interdisciplinary Mathematics, 1999) state

FIGURE 13.3 Illustration of the simple linear regression model

FIGURE 13.4 Data from the simple linear regression model: (a) σ small; (b) σ large

Amateur wrestlers who are overweight near the end of the weight certification period, but just barely so, have been known to stand on their heads for a minute or two, get on their feet, step back on the scale, and establish that they are in the desired weight class. Using a headstand as the method of last resort has become a fairly common practice in amateur wrestling.

Does this really work? Data was collected in an experiment where weight loss was recorded for each wrestler after exercising for 15 minutes and then doing a headstand for 1 minute and 45 seconds. Based on this data, the authors of the article concluded that there was in fact a demonstrable weight loss that was greater than that for a control group that exercised for 15 minutes but did not do the headstand.

(The authors give a plausible explanation for why this might be the case based on the way blood and other body fluids collect in the head during the headstand and the effect of weighing while these fluids are draining immediately after standing.) The authors also concluded that a simple linear regression model was a reasonable way to relate the variable

y = weight loss (in pounds)

and

x = body weight prior to exercise and headstand (in pounds)

Suppose that the actual model equation has

$\alpha = 0$ $\beta = .001$ $\sigma = .09$

(these values are consistent with the findings in the article). The population regression line is shown in Figure 13.5.

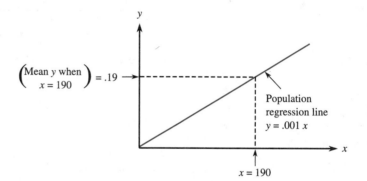

FIGURE 13.5 The population regression line for Example 13.1

If the distribution of the random errors at any fixed weight (x value) is normal, then the variable y = weight loss is normally distributed with

$\mu_y = 0 + .001x$ and $\sigma_y = .09$

For example, when $x = 190$ (corresponding to a 190-lb wrestler), weight loss has mean value

$\mu_y = 0 + .001(190) = .19$

Since the standard deviation of y is $\sigma = .09$, the interval $.19 \pm 2(.09) = (.01, .37)$ includes y values that are within 2 standard deviations of the mean value for y when $x = 190$. Roughly 95% of the weight loss observations made for 190-lb wrestlers will be in this range.

The slope $\beta = .001$ is the change in average weight associated with each additional pound of body weight.

More insight into model properties can be gained by thinking of the population of all (x, y) pairs as consisting of many smaller populations. Each one of these smaller populations contains pairs for which x has a fixed value. Suppose, for example, that the variables

x = grade point average in major courses

and

y = starting salary after graduation

are related according to the simple linear regression model. Then there is the population of all pairs with $x = 3.20$, the population of all pairs having $x = 2.75$, and so on. The model assumes that for each such population, y is normally distributed with the same standard deviation, and the *mean y value* (rather than y itself) is linearly related to x.

In practice, the judgment as to whether the simple linear regression model is appropriate must be based on how the data was collected and on a scatter plot of the data. The sample observations should be independent of one another. In addition, the scatter plot should show a linear rather than a curved pattern, and the vertical spread of points should be relatively homogeneous throughout the range of x values. Figure 13.6 shows plots with three different patterns; the first is consistent with the model assumptions.

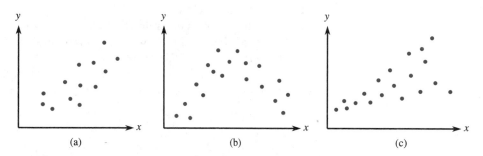

FIGURE 13.6 Some commonly encountered patterns in scatter plots: (a) Consistent with the simple linear regression model; (b) Suggests a nonlinear probabilistic model; (c) Suggests that variability in y changes with x

Estimating the Population Regression Line

The values of α and β (vertical intercept and slope of the population regression line) will almost never be known to an investigator. Instead, these values must first be estimated from the sample data $(x_1, y_1), \ldots, (x_n, y_n)$. We now assume that these n (x, y) pairs were obtained independently of one another, and that each observed y is related to the corresponding x via the model equation for simple linear regression.

Let a and b denote point estimates of α and β, respectively. These estimates come from applying the method of least squares introduced in Chapter 5; the least squares line has a smaller sum of squared vertical deviations from points in the scatter plot than does any other line.

The point estimates of β, the slope, and α, the y intercept of the population regression line, are the slope and y intercept, respectively, of the least squares line. That is,

$$b = \text{point estimate of } \beta = \frac{S_{xy}}{S_{xx}}$$

$$a = \text{point estimate of } \alpha = \bar{y} - b\bar{x}$$

where

$$S_{xy} = \Sigma xy - \frac{(\Sigma x)(\Sigma y)}{n} \quad \text{and} \quad S_{xx} = \Sigma x^2 - \frac{(\Sigma x)^2}{n}$$

The estimated regression line is then just the least squares line

$$\hat{y} = a + bx$$

Let x^* denote a specified value of the predictor variable x. Then $a + bx^*$ has two different interpretations:

1. It is a point estimate of the mean y value when $x = x^*$.

2. It is a point prediction of an individual y value to be observed when $x = x^*$.

EXAMPLE 13.2

Medical researchers have noted that adolescent females are much more likely to deliver low birth weight babies than are adult females. Because low birth weight babies have higher mortality rates, there have been a number of studies examining the relationship between birth weight and mother's age for babies born to young mothers. One such study is described in the article "The Risk of Teen Mothers Having Low Birth Weight Babies: Implications of Recent Medical Research for School Health Personnel" (*J. of School Health* (1998): 271–274). The accompanying data on

$x = $ maternal age (years)

and

$y = $ birth weight of baby (grams)

is consistent with summary values given in the referenced article and also with data published by the National Center for Health Statistics.

	Observation									
	1	**2**	**3**	**4**	**5**	**6**	**7**	**8**	**9**	**10**
x	15	17	18	15	16	19	17	16	18	19
y	2289	3393	3271	2648	2897	3327	2970	2535	3138	3573

A scatter plot (Figure 13.7) supports the appropriateness of the simple linear regression model.

The summary statistics are

$$n = 10 \qquad \Sigma x = 170 \qquad \Sigma y = 30{,}041$$
$$\Sigma x^2 = 2910 \qquad \Sigma xy = 515{,}600 \qquad \Sigma y^2 = 91{,}785{,}351$$

FIGURE 13.7 Scatter plot of the data from Example 13.2

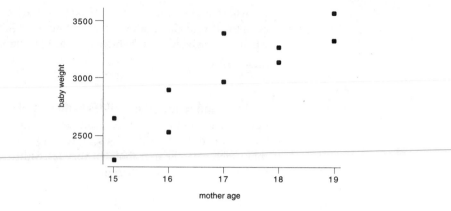

from which

$$S_{xy} = \Sigma\, xy - \frac{(\Sigma\, x)(\Sigma\, y)}{n} = 515{,}600 - \frac{(170)(30{,}041)}{10} = 4903.0$$

$$S_{xx} = \Sigma\, x^2 - \frac{(\Sigma\, x)^2}{n} = 2910 - \frac{(170)^2}{10} = 20.0$$

$$\bar{x} = \frac{170}{10} = 17.0 \qquad \bar{y} = \frac{30041}{10} = 3004.1$$

This gives

$$b = \frac{S_{xy}}{S_{xx}} = \frac{4903.0}{20.0} = 245.15$$

$$a = \bar{y} - b\bar{x} = 3004.1 - (245.15)(17.0) = -1163.45$$

The equation of the estimated regression line is then

$$\hat{y} = a + bx = -1163.45 + 245.15x$$

A point estimate of the average birth weight of babies born to 18-year-old mothers results from substituting $x = 18$ into the estimated equation:

$$\begin{aligned}(\text{estimated average } y \text{ value when } x = 18) &= a + bx \\ &= -1163.45 + 245.15(18) \\ &= 3249.25 \text{ grams}\end{aligned}$$

Similarly, we would predict the birth weight of a baby to be born to a particular 18-year-old mother to be

$$(\text{predicted } y \text{ value when } x = 18) = a + b(18) = 3249.25$$

The point estimate and the point prediction are identical, because the same x value was used in each calculation. However, the interpretation of each is different. One represents our prediction of the weight of a single baby whose mother is

18, whereas the other represents our estimate of the average weight of *all* babies born to 18-year-old mothers. This distinction will become important in Section 13.4 when we consider interval estimates and predictions.

In Example 13.2, the x values in the sample ranged from 15 to 19. An estimate or prediction should not be calculated for any x value much outside this range. Without sample data for such values, there is no hard evidence that the estimated linear relationship can be extrapolated very far. Statisticians refer to this potential pitfall as the **danger of extrapolation.**

Estimating σ^2 and σ

The value of σ determines the extent to which observed points (x, y) tend to fall close to or far away from the population regression line. A point estimate of σ is based on

$$\text{SSResid} = \Sigma (y - \hat{y})^2$$

where $\hat{y}_1 = a + bx_1, \ldots, \hat{y}_n = a + bx_n$ are the fitted or predicted y values and the residuals are $y_1 - \hat{y}_1, \ldots, y_n - \hat{y}_n$. SSResid is a measure of the extent to which the sample data spreads out about the estimated regression line.

Definition

The statistic for estimating the variance σ^2 is

$$s_e^2 = \frac{\text{SSResid}}{n - 2}$$

where

$$\text{SSResid} = \Sigma (y - \hat{y})^2 = \Sigma y^2 - a \Sigma y - b \Sigma xy$$

The subscript e in s_e^2 reminds us that we are estimating the variance of the "errors" or residuals.

The estimate of σ is the **estimated standard deviation**

$$s_e = \sqrt{s_e^2}$$

The number of degrees of freedom associated with estimating σ^2 or σ in simple linear regression is $n - 2$.

The estimates and number of degrees of freedom here have analogues in our previous work involving a single sample $x_1, x_2, \ldots, x_n$. The sample variance s^2 had numerator $\Sigma (x - \bar{x})^2$, a sum of squared deviations (residuals), and denominator $n - 1$, the number of degrees of freedom associated with s^2 and s. The use of $\bar{x}$ as an estimate of μ in the formula for s^2 reduces the number of degrees of freedom by 1, from n to $n - 1$. In simple linear regression, estimation of α and β results in a loss of 2 degrees of freedom, leaving $n - 2$ as df for SSResid, s_e^2, and s_e.

The coefficient of determination was defined previously (see Chapter 5) as

$$r^2 = 1 - \frac{\text{SSResid}}{\text{SSTo}}$$

where

$$\text{SSTo} = \Sigma (y - \bar{y})^2 = \Sigma y^2 - \frac{(\Sigma y)^2}{n} = S_{yy}$$

The value of r^2 can now be interpreted as the proportion of observed y variation that can be explained by (or attributed to) the model relationship. The estimate s_e also gives another assessment of model performance. Roughly speaking, the value of σ represents the magnitude of a typical deviation of a point (x, y) in the population from the population regression line. Similarly, in a rough sense, s_e is the magnitude of a typical sample deviation (residual) from the least squares line. The smaller the value of s_e, the closer the points in the sample fall to the line, and the better the line does in predicting y from x.

EXAMPLE 13.3   Forest managers are increasingly concerned about the damage done to animal populations when forests are clear-cut. Woodpeckers are a valuable forest asset, both because they provide nest and roost holes for other animals and birds and because they prey on many forest insect pests. The article "Artificial Trees as a Cavity Substrate for Woodpeckers" (*J. of Wildlife Mgmt.* (1983): 790–798) reported on a study of how woodpeckers behaved when provided with polystyrene cylinders as an alternative roost and nest cavity substrate. We give selected values of x = ambient temperature (°C) and y = cavity depth (cm); these values were read from a scatter plot that appeared in the article.

Obs.	Temp.	Depth	Pred. y value	Residual
1	−6	21.1	22.195	−1.095
2	−3	26.0	21.160	4.840
3	−2	18.0	20.815	−2.815
4	1	19.2	19.780	−.580
5	6	16.9	18.055	−1.155
6	10	18.1	16.675	1.425
7	11	16.8	16.330	.470
8	19	11.8	13.569	−1.769
9	21	11.0	12.879	−1.879
10	23	12.1	12.189	−.089
11	25	14.8	11.499	3.301
12	26	10.5	11.154	−.654

Our plot (Figure 13.8, page 508), as well as the original plot, gives evidence of a strong negative linear relationship between x and y.

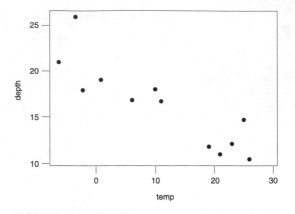

FIGURE 13.8 MINITAB scatter plot for Example 13.3

The summary statistics are

$$n = 12 \qquad \Sigma x = 131 \qquad \Sigma y = 196.3$$
$$\Sigma x^2 = 2939 \qquad \Sigma xy = 1622.3 \qquad \Sigma y^2 = 3445.25$$

from which we calculate

$$b = -.345043 \qquad a = 20.125053$$
$$\text{SSResid} = 54.4655 \qquad \text{SSTo} = 234.1093$$

Thus,

$$r^2 = 1 - \frac{\text{SSResid}}{\text{SSTo}} = 1 - \frac{54.4655}{234.1093} = 1 - .233 = .767$$
$$s_e^2 = \frac{\text{SSResid}}{n - 2} = \frac{54.4655}{10} = 5.447$$

and

$$s_e = \sqrt{5.447} = 2.33$$

Approximately 76.7% of the observed variation in cavity depth y can be attributed to the probabilistic linear relationship with ambient temperature. The magnitude of a typical sample deviation from the least squares line is about 2.3, which is reasonably small in comparison to the y values themselves. The model appears to be useful for estimation and prediction; in the next section, we show how a model utility test can be used to judge whether this is indeed the case.

A key assumption of the simple linear regression model is that the random deviation e in the model equation is normally distributed. In Section 13.3, we will indicate how the residuals can be used to determine whether this is plausible.

Exercises 13.1 – 13.11

13.1 Let x be the size of a house (sq ft) and y be the amount of natural gas used (therms) during a specified period. Suppose that for a particular community, x and y are related according to the simple linear regression model with

$$\beta = \text{slope of population regression line} = .017$$

$$\alpha = y \text{ intercept of population regression line} = -5.0$$

a. What is the equation of the population regression line?
b. Graph the population regression line by first finding the point on the line corresponding to $x = 1000$ and then the point corresponding to $x = 2000$, and drawing a line through these points.
c. What is the mean value of gas usage for houses with 2100 sq ft of space?
d. What is the average change in usage associated with a 1-sq-ft increase in size?
e. What is the average change in usage associated with a 100-sq-ft increase in size?
f. Would you use the model to predict mean usage for a 500-sq-ft house? Why or why not? (*Note*: There are no small houses in the community in which this model is valid.)

13.2 The flow rate y (m³/min) in a device used for air-quality measurement depends on the pressure drop x (in of water) across the device's filter. Suppose that for x values between 5 and 20, these two variables are related according to the simple linear regression model with true regression line $y = -.12 + .095x$.
a. What is the true average flow rate for a pressure drop of 10 in? A drop of 15 in?
b. What is the true average change in flow rate associated with a 1-in increase in pressure drop? Explain.
c. What is the average change in flow rate when pressure drop decreases by 5 in?

13.3 Data presented in the article "Manganese Intake and Serum Manganese Concentration of Human Milk-Fed and Formula-Fed Infants" (*Amer. J. of Clinical Nutrition* (1984): 872–878) suggests that a simple linear regression model is reasonable for describing the relationship between y = serum manganese (Mn) and x = Mn intake (μg/kg/day). Suppose that the true regression line is $y = -2 + 1.4x$ and that $\sigma = 1.2$. Then for a fixed x value, y has a normal distribution with mean $-2 + 1.4x$ and standard deviation 1.2.

a. What is the mean value of serum Mn when Mn intake is 4.0? When Mn intake is 4.5?
b. What is the probability that an infant whose Mn intake is 4.0 will have serum Mn greater than 5?
c. Approximately what proportion of infants whose Mn intake is 5 will have a serum Mn greater than 5? Less than 3.8?

13.4 A sample of small cars was selected, and the values of x = horsepower and y = fuel efficiency (mpg) were determined for each car. Fitting the simple linear regression model gave the estimated regression equation $\hat{y} = 44.0 - .150x$.
a. How would you interpret $b = -.150$?
b. Substituting $x = 100$ gives $\hat{y} = 29.0$. Give two different interpretations of this number.
c. What happens if you predict efficiency for a car with a 300 horsepower engine? Why do you think this has occurred?
d. Interpret $r^2 = .680$ in the context of this problem.
e. Interpret $s_e = 3.0$ in the context of this problem.

13.5 Suppose that a simple linear regression model is appropriate for describing the relationship between y = house price and x = house size (sq ft) for houses in a large city. The true regression line is $y = 23{,}000 + 47x$ and $\sigma = 5000$.
a. What is the average change in price associated with one extra sq ft of space? With an additional 100 sq ft of space?
b. What proportion of 1800-sq-ft homes would be priced over $110,000? Under $100,000?

13.6 **a.** Explain the difference between the line $y = \alpha + \beta x$ and the line $\hat{y} = a + bx$.
b. Explain the difference between β and b.
c. Let x^* denote a particular value of the independent variable. Explain the difference between $\alpha + \beta x^*$ and $a + bx^*$.
d. Explain the difference between σ and s_e.

13.7 Legumes, such as peas and beans, are important crops whose production is greatly affected by pests. The article "Influence of Wind Speed on Residence Time of *Uroleucon ambrosiae Alatae* on Bean Plants" (*Envir. Entom.* (1991): 1375–1380) reported on a study in which aphids were placed on a bean plant, and the elapsed time until half of the aphids had departed was observed. Data on x = wind speed (m/sec) and y = residence half-time was given and used to produce the following information.

$a = .0119$ $b = 3.4307$ $n = 13$

SSTo $= 73.937$ SSResid $= 27.890$

a. What percentage of observed variation in residence half-time can be attributed to the simple linear regression model?
b. Give a point estimate of σ and interpret the estimate.
c. Estimate the mean change in residence half-time associated with a 1-m/sec increase in wind speed.
d. Calculate a point estimate of true average residence half-time when wind speed is 1 m/sec.

13.8 The accompanying data on x = treadmill run time to exhaustion (min) and y = 20-km ski time (min) was taken from the article "Physiological Characteristics and Performance of Top U.S. Biathletes" (*Medicine and Science in Sports and Exercise* (1995): 1302–1310):

x	7.7	8.4	8.7	9.0	9.6	9.6
y	71.0	71.4	65.0	68.7	64.4	69.4

x	10.0	10.2	10.4	11.0	11.7
y	63.0	64.6	66.9	62.6	61.7

$\Sigma x = 106.3$ $\Sigma y = 1040.95$ $\Sigma x^2 = 728.70$

$\Sigma xy = 7009.91$ $\Sigma y^2 = 48,390.79$

a. Does a scatter plot suggest that the simple linear regression model is appropriate?
b. Determine the equation of the estimated regression line, and draw the line on your scatter plot.
c. What is your estimate of the average change in ski time associated with a 1-minute increase in treadmill time?
d. What would you predict ski time to be for an individual whose treadmill time is 10 min?
e. Should the model be used as a basis for predicting ski time when treadmill time is 15 min? Explain.
f. Calculate and interpret the value of r^2.
g. Calculate and interpret the value of s_e.

13.9 The accompanying summary quantities resulted from a study in which x was the number of photocopy machines serviced during a routine service call and y was the total service time (min):

$n = 16$ $\Sigma (y - \bar{y})^2 = 22,398.05$ $\Sigma (y - \hat{y})^2 = 2620.57$

a. What proportion of observed variation in total service time can be explained by a linear probabilistic relationship between total service time and the number of machines serviced?
b. Calculate the value of the estimated standard deviation s_e. What is the number of degrees of freedom associated with this estimate?

13.10 Exercise 5.45 described a regression situation in which y = hardness of molded plastic and x = amount of time elapsed since termination of the molding process. Summary quantities included $n = 15$, SSResid $= 1235.470$, and SSTo $= 25,321.368$.

a. Calculate a point estimate of σ. On how many degrees of freedom is the estimate based?
b. What percentage of observed variation in hardness can be explained by the simple linear regression model relationship between hardness and elapsed time?

13.11 The accompanying data on x = advertising share and y = market share for a particular brand of cigarettes during ten randomly selected years is from the article "Testing Alternative Econometric Models on the Existence of Advertising Threshold Effect" (*J. of Marketing Research* (1984): 298–308).

x	.103	.072	.071	.077	.086
y	.135	.125	.120	.086	.079

x	.047	.060	.050	.070	.052
y	.076	.065	.059	.051	.039

a. Construct a scatter plot for this data. Do you think the simple linear regression model would be appropriate for describing the relationship between x and y?
b. Calculate the equation of the estimated regression line and use it to obtain the predicted market share when the advertising share is .09.
c. Compute r^2. How would you interpret this value?
d. Calculate a point estimate of σ. On how many degrees of freedom is your estimate based?

13.2   Inferences Concerning the Slope of the Population Regression Line

The slope coefficient β in the simple linear regression model is the average or expected change in the dependent variable y associated with a 1-unit increase in the value of the independent variable x. For example, consider x = the size of a house (sq ft) and y = selling price of the house. If we assume that the simple linear regression model is appropriate for the population of houses in a particular city, β would be the average increase in selling price associated with a 1-sq-ft increase in size. As another example, if x = amount of time per week a computer system is used and y = the resulting annual maintenance expense, then β would be the expected change in expense associated with using the computer system one additional hour per week.

Since the value of β is almost always unknown, it will have to be estimated from sample data: n independently selected observations $(x_1, y_1), \ldots, (x_n, y_n)$. The slope of the least squares line gives a point estimate. As with any point estimate, though, it is desirable to have some indication of how accurately b estimates β. In some situations, the value of the statistic b may vary greatly from sample to sample, so b computed from a single sample may well be rather different from the true slope β. In other situations, almost all possible samples yield b values quite close to β, so the error of estimation is almost sure to be small. To proceed further, we need some facts about the sampling distribution of b: information concerning the shape of the sampling distribution curve, where the curve is centered relative to β, and how much the curve spreads out about its center.

Properties of the Sampling Distribution of b

When the four basic assumptions of the simple linear regression model are satisfied, the following conditions are met:

1. The mean value of b is β. That is, $\mu_b = \beta$, so the sampling distribution of b is always centered at the value of β. Thus, b is an unbiased statistic for estimating β.

2. The standard deviation of the statistic b is

$$\sigma_b = \frac{\sigma}{\sqrt{S_{xx}}}$$

3. The statistic b has a normal distribution (a consequence of the model assumption that the random deviation e is normally distributed).

The fact that b is unbiased means only that the sampling distribution is centered at the right place; it gives no information about dispersion. If σ_b is large, the normal sampling distribution curve will be quite spread out around β, and an estimate far from β may well result. For σ_b to be small, the numerator σ should be small (little variability about the population line) and/or the denominator $\sqrt{S_{xx}}$, or equivalently $S_{xx} = \Sigma (x - \bar{x})^2$ itself, should be large. Because $\Sigma (x - \bar{x})^2$ is a measure of how much the observed x values spread out, β will tend to be more precisely estimated when the x values in our sample are spread out than when they are close together.

The normality of b implies that the standardized variable

$$z = \frac{b - \beta}{\sigma_b}$$

has a standard normal distribution. However, inferential methods cannot be based on this variable, because the value of σ_b is not available (since the unknown σ appears in the numerator of σ_b). The obvious way out of this dilemma is to estimate σ with s_e, yielding an estimated standard deviation.

The **estimated standard deviation of the statistic b** is

$$s_b = \frac{s_e}{\sqrt{S_{xx}}}$$

When the four basic assumptions of the simple linear regression model are satisfied, the probability distribution of the standardized variable

$$t = \frac{b - \beta}{s_b}$$

is the t distribution with df $= (n - 2)$.

In the same way that $t = (\bar{x} - \mu)/(s/\sqrt{n})$ was used in Chapter 9 to develop a confidence interval for μ, the t variable in the preceding box can be employed to give a confidence interval (interval estimate) for β.

Confidence Interval for β

When the four basic assumptions of the simple linear regression model are satisfied, a **confidence interval for β,** the slope of the population regression line, has the form

$$b \pm (t \text{ critical value}) \cdot s_b$$

where the t critical value is based on df $= n - 2$. Appendix Table III gives critical values corresponding to the most frequently used confidence levels.

The interval estimate of β is centered at b and extends out from the center by an amount that depends on the sampling variability of b. When s_b is small, the interval will be narrow, implying that the investigator has relatively precise knowledge of β.

EXAMPLE 13.4

Is cardiovascular fitness (as measured by time to exhaustion running on a treadmill) related to an athlete's performance in a 20-km ski race? The accompanying data on

$$x = \text{treadmill run time to exhaustion (min)}$$

and

$$y = \text{20-km ski time (min)}$$

was taken from the article "Physiological Characteristics and Performance of Top U.S. Biathletes" (*Medicine and Science in Sports and Exercise* (1995): 1302–1310):

x	7.7	8.4	8.7	9.0	9.6	9.6	10.0	10.2	10.4	11.0	11.7
y	71.0	71.4	65.0	68.7	64.4	69.4	63.0	64.6	66.9	62.6	61.7

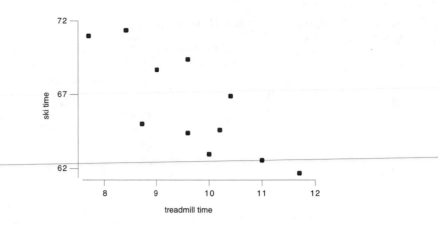

A scatter plot of the data appears in the preceding figure. The plot shows a linear pattern and the vertical spread of points does not appear to be changing over the range of x values in the sample. If we assume that the distribution of errors at any given x value is approximately normal, the simple linear regression model seems appropriate.

The slope β in this context is the average change in ski time associated with a 1-minute increase in treadmill time. The scatter plot shows a negative linear relationship, so the point estimate of β will be negative.

Straightforward calculation gives

$$n = 11 \qquad \Sigma x = 106.3 \qquad \Sigma y = 728.70$$
$$\Sigma x^2 = 1040.95 \qquad \Sigma xy = 7009.91 \qquad \Sigma y = 48{,}390.79$$

from which

$$b = -2.3335 \qquad a = 88.796$$
$$\text{SSResid} = 43.097 \qquad \text{SSSTo} = 117.727$$
$$r^2 = .634 \quad (63.4\% \text{ of the observed variation in ski time can be explained by the simple linear regression model})$$
$$s_e^2 = 4.789 \qquad s_e = 2.188$$
$$s_b = \frac{s_e}{\sqrt{S_{xx}}} = \frac{2.188}{3.702} = .591$$

Calculation of the 95% confidence interval for β requires a t critical value based on df $= n - 2 = 11 - 2 = 9$, which (from Appendix Table III) is 2.26. The resulting interval is then

$$b \pm (t \text{ critical value}) \cdot s_b = -2.3335 \pm (2.26)(.591)$$
$$= -2.335 \pm 1.336$$
$$= (-3.671, -.999)$$

We interpret this interval as follows: Based on the sample data, we are 95% confident that the true average decrease in ski time associated with a one-minute increase in treadmill time is between 1 and 3.7 minutes.

FIGURE 13.9 Partial MINITAB output for the data of Example 13.4

Regression Analysis

The regression equation is
ski time = 88.8 - 2.33 treadmill time

Equation $\hat{y} = a + bx$ of the estimated regression line

Estimated y intercept a

Estimated slope b

Predictor	Coef	StDev	T	P
Constant	88.796	5.750	15.44	0.000
treadmill	-2.3335	0.5911	-3.95	0.003

s_b = estimated standard deviation of b

S = 2.188   R-Sq = 63.4%   R-Sq (adj) = 59.3%

s_e

$100r^2$

Analysis of Variance

Source	DF	SS	MS	F	P
Regression	1	74.630	74.630	15.58	0.003
Residual Error	9	43.097	4.789		
Total	10	117.727			

$n - 2$ = residual df

SSResid

s_e^2

SSTo

Output from any of the standard statistical computer packages routinely includes the computed values of a, b, SSResid, s_e, SSTo, r^2, and s_b. Figure 13.9 displays partial MINITAB output for the data of Example 13.4. The format from other packages is very similar. Rounding will occasionally lead to small discrepancies between hand-calculated and computer-calculated values, but there are no such discrepancies for this example.

Hypothesis Tests Concerning β

Hypotheses about β can be tested using a t test very similar to the t tests discussed in previous chapters. The null hypothesis states that β has a specified hypothesized value. The t statistic results from standardizing b, the point estimate of β, under the assumption that H_0 is true. When H_0 is true, the sampling distribution of this statistic is the t distribution with df $= n - 2$.

Summary of Hypothesis Tests Concerning β

Null hypothesis: $H_0: \beta$ = hypothesized value

Test statistic: $t = \dfrac{b - \text{hypothesized value}}{s_b}$

The test is based on df $= n - 2$.

Alternative hypothesis:

P-value:

$H_a: \beta >$ hypothesized value   Area to the right of the computed t under the appropriate t curve

$H_a: \beta <$ hypothesized value   Area to the left of the computed t under the appropriate t curve

$H_a: \beta \neq$ hypothesized value   (i) $2 \cdot$ (area to the right of t) if t is positive

or

(ii) $2 \cdot$ (area to the left of the t) if t is negative

(continued)

Assumptions: For this test to be appropriate, the four basic assumptions of the simple linear regression model must be met:
1. The distribution of e at any particular x value has mean value 0 ($\mu_e = 0$).
2. The standard deviation of e is σ, which does not depend on x.
3. The distribution of e at any particular x value is normal.
4. The random deviations $e_1, e_2, \ldots, e_n$ associated with different observations are independent of one another.

Very frequently, the null hypothesis of interest is that $\beta = 0$. When this is the case, the population regression line is a horizontal line, and the value of y in the simple linear regression model does not depend on x. That is,

$$y = \alpha + 0 \cdot x + e$$

or equivalently,

$$y = \alpha + e$$

In this situation, knowledge of x is of no use in predicting y. On the other hand, if $\beta \neq 0$, there is a useful linear relationship between x and y, and knowledge of x is useful for predicting y. This is illustrated by the scatter plots of Figure 13.10.

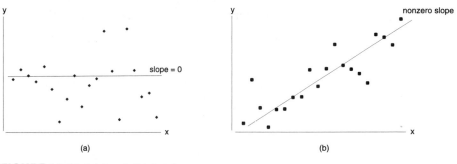

FIGURE 13.10 (a) $\beta = 0$; (b) $\beta \neq 0$

The test of $H_0: \beta = 0$ versus $H_a: \beta \neq 0$ is called the *model utility test for simple linear regression.*

The Model Utility Test for Simple Linear Regression

The **model utility test for simple linear regression** is the test of

$$H_0: \quad \beta = 0$$

versus

$$H_a: \quad \beta \neq 0$$

(continued)

The null hypothesis specifies that there is *no* useful linear relationship between x and y, whereas the alternative hypothesis specifies that there *is* a useful linear relationship between x and y. If H_0 is rejected, we conclude that the simple linear regression model is useful for predicting y. The test procedure in the previous box (with hypothesized value = 0) is used to carry out the model utility test; in particular, the test statistic is the *t* **ratio** $\dfrac{b}{s_b}$.

If a scatter plot and the value of r^2 do not provide convincing evidence for a useful linear relationship, we recommend that the model utility test be carried out before the estimated model is used to make other inferences.

EXAMPLE 13.5   Computers seem to have invaded almost every aspect of our lives. In recent years, this has led to an explosion in the number of investigations whose objective has been to study and document the varied effects of the computer revolution. Many of these have dealt with the work environment of people who spend a substantial amount of time staring at computer monitors. Image quality of monitors is an important characteristic, affecting, among other things, extent of eye strain and work efficiency. The article "Image Quality Determines Differences in Reading Performance and Perceived Image Quality with CRT and Hard Copy Displays" (*Human Factors* (1991): 459–469) reported on an experiment in which image quality (x) and average time for a group of subjects to read certain passages (y, in seconds) were determined. The accompanying data was read from a graph in the article:

x	4.30	4.55	5.55	5.65	5.95	6.30	6.45	6.45
y	8.0	8.3	7.8	7.25	7.7	7.5	7.6	7.2

The summary statistics necessary for a simple linear regression analysis are as follows:

$$n = 8 \qquad \Sigma x = 45.20 \qquad \Sigma x^2 = 260.215$$
$$\Sigma y = 61.35 \qquad \Sigma y^2 = 471.4325 \qquad \Sigma xy = 344.9425$$

from which

$$b = -.348501 \qquad a = 9.637778 \qquad \text{SSResid} = .367626$$
$$s_e = .247530 \qquad r^2 = .615 \qquad S_{xx} = 4.835$$

Since $r^2 = .615$, about 61.5% of observed variation in reading time can be explained by the simple linear regression model. It appears from this that there is a useful linear relation between the two variables, but a confirmation requires a formal model utility test. We will use a significance level of .05 to carry out this test.

1. β = the true average change in reading time associated with a 1-unit increase in image quality
2. $H_0: \beta = 0$
3. $H_a: \beta \neq 0$

4. $\alpha = .05$

5. *Test statistic*: $\quad t = \dfrac{b - \text{hypothesized value}}{s_b} = \dfrac{b - 0}{s_b} = \dfrac{b}{s_b}$

6. *Assumptions*: The accompanying scatter plot of the data shows a linear pattern and the variability of points does not appear to be changing with x. Assuming that the distribution of errors at any given x value is approximately normal, the assumptions of the simple linear regression model are appropriate.

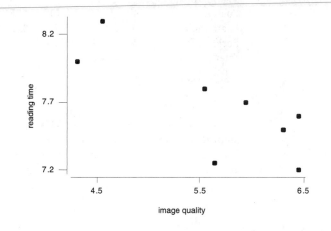

7. *Calculation*: The calculation of t requires

$$s_b = \frac{s_e}{\sqrt{S_{xx}}} = \frac{.247530}{2.1989} = .11257$$

yielding

$$t = \frac{-.348501 - 0}{.11257} = -3.10$$

8. *P-value*: Appendix Table IV shows that for a t test based on 6 df, $P(t > 3.10)$ $= P(t < -3.10) = .011$. The inequality in H_a requires a two-tailed test, so P-value $= 2(.011) = .022$.

9. *Conclusion*: Since .022 is smaller than the significance level .05, H_0 is rejected. We conclude, as did the investigators, that there is a useful linear relationship between image quality and reading time.

Figure 13.11 (page 518) shows partial MINITAB output from a simple linear regression analysis. The **Coef** column gives $b = -.3485$; $s_b = .1125$ is in the **Stdev** column; the **T** column (for t ratio) contains the value of the test statistic for testing H_0: $\beta = 0$, $t = (b - 0)/s_b = b/s_b$; and the P-value for the model utility test is given in the last column as .021 (slightly different from the one given in step 8 because of rounding). Other commonly used statistical packages also include this information in their output.

FIGURE 13.11 MINITAB
output for the data of
Example 13.5

Regression Analysis

The regression equation is
reading time = 9.64 - 0.349 image quality

Predictor	Coef	StDev	T	P
Constant	9.6378	0.6419	15.01	0.000
image qu	-0.3485	0.1125	-3.10	0.021

$S = 0.2475$ R-Sq = 61.5% R-Sq(adj) = 55.1%

Analysis of Variance

Source	DF	SS	MS	F	P
Regression	1	0.58722	0.58722	9.59	0.021
Residual Error	6	0.36746	0.06124		
Total	7	0.95469			

When H_0: $\beta = 0$ cannot be rejected by the model utility test at a reasonably small significance level, the search for a useful model must continue. One possibility is to relate y to x using a nonlinear model, an appropriate strategy if the scatter plot shows curvature. Alternatively, a multiple regression model using more than one predictor variable may be employed. The next chapter introduces such models.

Exercises 13.12 – 13.26

13.12 a. What is the difference between σ and σ_b?
b. What is the difference between σ_b and s_b?

13.13 a. Suppose that a single y observation is made at each of the x values 5, 10, 15, 20, and 25. If $\sigma = 4$, what is σ_b, the standard deviation of the statistic b?
b. Now suppose that a second observation is made at every x value listed in part **a** (for a total of 10 observations). Is the resulting value of σ_b half of what it was in part **a**?
c. How many observations at each x value in part **a** are required to yield a σ_b value that is half the value calculated in part **a**? Verify your conjecture.

13.14 Refer back to Example 13.3 in which the simple linear regression model was fit to data on x = ambient temperature and y = cavity depth. For the purpose of estimating β as accurately as possible, would it have been preferable to make observations at the x values $x_1 = -6$, $x_2 = -5$, $x_3 = -4$, $x_4 = -3$, $x_5 = -2$, $x_6 = -1$, $x_7 = 21$, $x_8 = 22$, $x_9 = 23$, $x_{10} = 24$, $x_{11} = 25$, and $x_{12} = 26$? Explain your reasoning.

13.15 Exercise 13.10 presented information from a study in which y was the hardness of molded plastic and x was the time elapsed since termination of the molding process. Summary quantities included

$$n = 15 \quad b = 2.50 \quad \text{SSResid} = 1235.470$$
$$\Sigma (x - \bar{x})^2 = 4024.20$$

a. Calculate s_b, the estimated standard deviation of the statistic b.
b. Obtain a 95% confidence interval for β, the slope of the true regression line.
c. Does the interval in part **b** suggest that β has been precisely estimated? Explain.

13.16 A study was carried out to relate sales revenue y (in thousands of dollars) to advertising expenditure x (also in thousands of dollars) for fast-food outlets during a 3-month period. A sample of 15 outlets yielded the accompanying summary quantities.

$$\Sigma x = 14.10 \quad \Sigma y = 1438.50 \quad \Sigma x^2 = 13.92$$
$$\Sigma y^2 = 140{,}354 \quad \Sigma xy = 1387.20$$
$$\Sigma (y - \bar{y})^2 = 2401.85 \quad \Sigma (y - \hat{y})^2 = 561.46$$

a. What proportion of observed variation in sales revenue can be attributed to the linear relationship between revenue and advertising expenditure?

b. Calculate s_e and s_b.

c. Obtain a 90% confidence interval for β, the average change in revenue associated with a $1000 (that is, 1-unit) increase in advertising expenditure.

13.17 An experiment to study the relationship between x = time spent exercising (min) and y = amount of oxygen consumed during the exercise period resulted in the following summary statistics.

$$n = 20 \quad \Sigma x = 50 \quad \Sigma y = 16{,}705 \quad \Sigma x^2 = 150$$

$$\Sigma y^2 = 14{,}194{,}231 \quad \Sigma xy = 44{,}194$$

a. Estimate the slope and y intercept of the population regression line.

b. One sample observation on oxygen usage was 757 for a 2-min exercise period. What amount of oxygen consumption would you predict for this exercise period, and what is the corresponding residual?

c. Compute a 99% confidence interval for the true average change in oxygen consumption associated with a 1-min increase in exercise time.

13.18 Exercise 5.66 presented data on x = average hourly wage and y = quit rate for a sample of industries. See the accompanying MINITAB output.

The regression equation is
quit rate = 4.86 - 0.347 wage

Predictor	Coef	Stdev	t-ratio	p
Constant	4.8615	0.5201	9.35	0.000
wage	-0.34655	0.05866	-5.91	0.000

s = 0.4862 R-sq = 72.9% R-sq(adj) = 70.8%

Analysis of Variance

SOURCE	DF	SS	MS	F	p
Regression	1	8.2507	8.2507	34.90	0.000
Error	13	3.0733	0.2364		
Total	14	11.3240			

a. Based on the given P-value, does there appear to be a useful linear relationship between average wage and quit rate? Explain your reasoning.

b. Calculate an estimate of the average change in quit rate associated with a $1 increase in average hourly wage, and do so in a way that conveys information about the precision and reliability of the estimate.

13.19 The article "Cost-Effectiveness in Public Education" cited in the chapter introduction reported that, for a sample of $n = 44$ school districts, a regression of y = average SAT score on x = expenditure per pupil (thousands of dollars) gave $b = 15.0$ and $s_b = 5.3$.

a. Does the simple linear regression model specify a useful relationship between x and y?

b. Calculate and interpret a confidence interval for β based on a 95% confidence level.

13.20 Exercise 5.40 described a study reported in the 1991 volume of the *Amer. J. of Phys. Anthropology* in which the objective was to predict age (y) from percentage of a tooth's root with transparent dentine. The accompanying data is for anterior teeth.

x	15	19	31	39	41	44	47	48	55	65
y	23	52	65	55	32	60	78	59	61	60

Use the accompanying MINITAB output to decide whether the simple linear regression model is useful.

The regression equation is
age = 32.1 + 0.555 percent

Predictor	Coef	Stdev	t-ratio	p
Constant	32.08	13.32	2.41	0.043
percent	0.5549	0.3101	1.79	0.111

s = 14.30 R-sq = 28.6% R-sq(adj) = 19.7%

Analysis of Variance

SOURCE	DF	SS	MS	F	p
Regression	1	654.8	654.8	3.20	0.111
Error	8	1635.7	204.5		
Total	9	2290.5			

13.21 The accompanying data was read from a plot (and is a subset of the complete data set) given in the article "Cognitive Slowing in Closed-Head Injury" (*Brain and Cognition* (1996): 429–440). The data represents the mean response times for a group of individuals with closed-head injury (CHI) and a matched control group without head injury on 10 different tasks. Each observation was based on a different study, and used different subjects, so it is reasonable to assume that the observations are independent.

	Mean Response Time	
Study	**Control**	**CHI**
1	250	303
2	360	491
3	475	659
4	525	683
5	610	922
6	740	1044
7	880	1421
8	920	1329
9	1010	1481
10	1200	1815

a. Fit a linear regression model that would allow you to predict the mean response time for those suffering a closed-head injury from the mean response time on the same task for individuals with no head injury.

b. Does the sample data support the hypothesis that there is a useful linear relationship between the mean response time for individuals with no head injury and the mean response time for individuals with CHI? Test the appropriate hypotheses using $\alpha = .05$.

c. It is also possible to test hypotheses about the y intercept in a linear regression model. For this data, the null hypothesis $H_0: \alpha = 0$ cannot be rejected at the .05 significance level, suggesting that a model with a y intercept of 0 might be an appropriate model. Fitting such a model results in an estimated regression equation of

CHI = 1.48 Control

Interpret the estimated slope of 1.48.

13.22 The article "Effects of Enhanced UV-B Radiation on Ribulose-1,5-Biphosphate, Carboxylase in Pea and Soybean" (*Environ. and Exper. Botany* (1984): 131–143) included the accompanying data on pea plants, with $y =$ sunburn index and $x =$ distance (cm) from an ultraviolet light source.

x	18	21	25	26	30	32	36	40
y	4.0	3.7	3.0	2.9	2.6	2.5	2.2	2.0

x	40	50	51	54	61	62	63
y	2.1	1.5	1.5	1.5	1.3	1.2	1.1

$\Sigma x = 609 \qquad \Sigma y = 33.1 \qquad \Sigma x^2 = 28,037$

$\Sigma xy = 1156.8 \qquad \Sigma y^2 = 84.45$

Estimate the mean change in the sunburn index associated with an increase of 1 cm in distance in a way that includes information about the precision of estimation.

13.23 Exercise 13.16 described a regression analysis in which $y =$ sales revenue and $x =$ advertising expenditure. Summary quantities given there yield

$n = 15 \qquad b = 52.57 \qquad s_b = 8.05$

a. Test the hypothesis $H_0: \beta = 0$ versus $H_a: \beta \neq 0$ using a significance level of .05. What does your conclusion say about the nature of the relationship between x and y?

b. Consider the hypothesis $H_0: \beta = 40$ versus $H_a: \beta > 40$. The null hypothesis states that the average change in sales revenue associated with a 1-unit increase in advertising expenditure is (at most) $40,000. Carry out a test using significance level .01.

13.24 The article "Technology, Productivity and Industry Structure" (*Tech. Forecasting and Social Change* (1983): 1–13) included the accompanying data on $x =$ research

and development expenditure and $y =$ growth rate for eight different industries.

x	2024	5038	905	3572	1157	327	378	191
y	1.90	3.96	2.44	.88	.37	−.90	.49	1.01

a. Would a simple linear regression model provide useful information for predicting growth rate from research and development expenditure? Use a .05 level of significance.

b. Use a 90% confidence interval to estimate the average change in growth rate associated with a 1-unit increase in expenditure. Interpret the resulting interval.

13.25 The article "Effect of Temperature on the pH of Skim Milk" (*J. of Dairy Research* (1988): 277–280) reported on a study involving $x =$ temperature (°C) under specified experimental conditions and $y =$ milk pH. The accompanying data (read from a graph) is a representative subset of that which appeared in the article:

x	4	4	24	24	25	38	38	40
y	6.85	6.79	6.63	6.65	6.72	6.62	6.57	6.52

x	45	50	55	56	60	67	70	78
y	6.50	6.48	6.42	6.41	6.38	6.34	6.32	6.34

$\Sigma x = 678 \qquad \Sigma y = 104.54 \qquad \Sigma x^2 = 36,056$

$\Sigma xy = 4376.36 \qquad \Sigma y^2 = 683.4470$

Does this data strongly suggest that there is a negative (inverse) linear relationship between temperature and pH? State and test the relevant hypotheses using a significance level of .01.

13.26 In anthropological studies, an important characteristic of fossils is cranial capacity. Frequently skulls are at least partially decomposed, so it is necessary to use other characteristics to obtain information about capacity. One such measure that has been used is the length of the lambda-opisthion chord. An article that appeared in the 1971 *Amer. Journal of Physical Anthropology* entitled "Vertesszollos and the Presapiens Theory" reported the accompanying data for $n = 7$ *Homo erectus* fossils.

x (chord length in mm)	78	75	78	81
y (capacity in cm³)	850	775	750	975

x (chord length in mm)	84	86	87
y (capacity in cm³)	915	1015	1030

Suppose that from previous evidence, anthropologists had believed that for each 1-mm increase in chord length, cranial capacity would be expected to increase by 20 cm³. Does this new experimental data strongly contradict prior belief?

13.3   Checking Model Adequacy

The simple linear regression model equation is

$$y = \alpha + \beta x + e$$

where e represents the random deviation of an observed y value from the population regression line $\alpha + \beta x$. The inferential methods presented in the previous section require some assumptions about e. Key assumptions follow:

1. At any particular x value, the distribution of e is a normal distribution.
2. At any particular x value, the standard deviation of e is σ, which is constant over all values of x.

Inferences based on the simple linear regression model continue to be reliable when model assumptions are slightly violated (for example, mild nonnormality of the random deviation distribution). However, using an estimated model in the face of grossly violated assumptions can result in very misleading conclusions. Therefore, it is desirable to have easily applied methods available for identifying such serious violations and for suggesting how a satisfactory model can be obtained.

Residual Analysis

If the deviations $e_1, e_2, \ldots, e_n$ from the population line were available, they could be examined for any inconsistencies with model assumptions. For example, a normal probability plot would suggest whether the normality assumption was tenable. But, since

$$e_1 = y_1 - (\alpha + \beta x_1)$$
$$\vdots$$
$$e_n = y_n - (\alpha + \beta x_n)$$

these deviations can be calculated only if the equation of the population line is known. In practice, this will never be the case. Instead, diagnostic checks must be based on the residuals

$$y_1 - \hat{y}_1 = y_1 - (a + b x_1)$$
$$\vdots$$
$$y_n - \hat{y}_n = y_n - (a + b x_n)$$

which are the deviations from the *estimated* line.

The values of the residuals will vary from sample to sample. When all model assumptions are met, the mean value of the residuals at any particular x value is zero. Any observation that gives a very large positive or negative residual should be examined carefully for any anomalous circumstances, such as a recording error or exceptional experimental conditions. Identifying residuals with unusually large magnitudes is made easier by inspecting **standardized residuals.**

Recall that a quantity is standardized by subtracting its mean value (zero in this case) and dividing by its true or estimated standard deviation. Thus,

$$\text{standardized residual} = \frac{\text{residual}}{\text{estimated standard deviation of residual}}$$

The value of a standardized residual tells how many standard deviations the corresponding residual lies from its expected value, zero.

Because residuals at different x values have different standard deviations (depending on the value of x for that observation),* computing the standardized residuals can be tedious. Fortunately, many computer regression programs provide standardized residuals as part of the output.

In Chapter 7, a normal probability plot was introduced as a technique for deciding whether the n observations in a random sample could plausibly have come from a normal population distribution. To assess whether the assumption that $e_1, e_2, \ldots ,$ e_n all come from the same normal distribution is reasonable, we recommend a normal probability plot of the standardized residuals.

EXAMPLE 13.6

Landslides are common events in tree-growing regions of the Pacific Northwest, so their effect on timber growth is of special concern to foresters. The article "Effects of Landslide Erosion on Subsequent Douglas Fir Growth and Stocking Levels in the Western Cascades, Oregon" (*Soil Science Soc. of Amer. J.* (1984): 667–671) reported on the results of a study in which growth in a landslide area was compared with growth in a previously clear-cut area. We present data on clear-cut growth, with x = tree age (years) and y = 5-year height growth (cm). The scatter plot in Figure 13.12 is consistent with the assumptions of the simple linear regression model.

FIGURE 13.12 MINITAB scatter plot for the data of Example 13.6

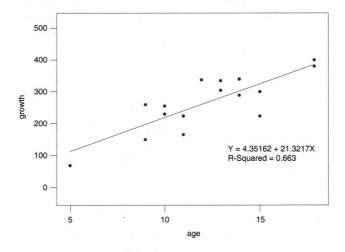

The residuals, their standard deviations, and the standardized residuals are given in Table 13.1. Except for $x = 5$ and $x = 18$, the two most extreme values, the residuals have roughly equal standard deviations. The residual with the largest magnitude, -99.2, initially seems quite extreme, but the corresponding standardized residual is only -2.04. That is, the residual is approximately 2 standard deviations below its expected value of zero, which is not terribly unusual in a sample of this size.

---

*The estimated standard deviation of the ith residual, $y_i - \hat{y}_i$, is $s_e\sqrt{1 - \dfrac{1}{n} - \dfrac{(x - \bar{x})^2}{S_{xx}}}$.

Table 13.1 *Data, residuals, and standardized residuals for Example 13.6*

Obs.	x	y	$\hat{y}$	Residual	Estimated Standard Deviation of Residual	Standardized Residual
1	5	70	111.0	−41.0	40.9	−1.00
2	9	150	196.2	−46.2	48.1	−.96
3	9	260	196.2	63.8	48.1	1.33
4	10	230	217.6	12.4	49.0	.25
5	10	255	217.6	37.4	49.0	.76
6	11	165	238.9	−73.9	49.5	−1.49
7	11	225	238.9	−13.9	49.5	−.28
8	12	340	260.2	79.8	49.8	1.60
9	13	305	281.5	23.5	49.7	.47
10	13	335	281.5	53.5	49.7	1.08
11	14	290	302.9	−12.9	49.4	−.26
12	14	340	302.9	37.1	49.4	.75
13	15	225	324.2	−99.2	48.7	−2.04
14	15	300	324.2	−24.2	48.7	−.50
15	18	380	388.1	−8.1	44.6	−.18
16	18	400	388.1	11.9	44.6	.27

On the standardized scale, no residual here is surprisingly large. Before standardization, there are some large residuals simply because there appears to be a substantial amount of variability about the true regression line ($s_e = 51.43$, $r^2 = .683$).

Figure 13.13 displays a normal probability plot of the standardized residuals and also one of the residuals. Notice that in this case the plots are nearly identical; it is usually the case that the two plots are similar. Although it is preferable to work with the standardized residuals, if you do not have access to a computer package or

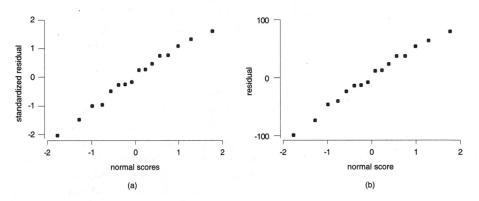

FIGURE 13.13 Normal probability plots for Example 13.6 (from MINITAB): (a) Standardized residuals; (b) Residuals

calculator that will produce standardized residuals, a plot of the unstandardized residuals should suffice. Few plots are straighter than these! The plots would not cause us to question the assumption of normality.

_____

Plotting the Residuals

A plot of the $(x,$ residual) pairs is called a **residual plot** and a plot of the $(x,$ standardized residual) pairs is a **standardized residual plot.** Residual and standardized residual plots typically exhibit the same general shapes. If you are using a computer package or graphing calculator that calculates standardized residuals, we recommend using the standardized residual plot. If not, it is acceptable to use the residual plot instead.

A standardized residual or residual plot is often helpful in identifying unusual or highly influential observations and in checking for violations of model assumptions. A desirable plot is one that exhibits no particular pattern (such as curvature or a much greater spread in one part of the plot than in another), and one that has no point that is far removed from all the others. A point falling far above or below the horizontal line at height zero corresponds to a large standardized residual, which may indicate some kind of unusual behavior, such as a recording error, a nonstandard experimental condition, or an atypical experimental subject. A point that has an x value that differs greatly from others in the data set could have exerted excessive influence in determining the fitted line.

A standardized residual plot such as the one pictured in Figure 13.14(a) is desirable, since no point lies much outside the horizontal band between -2 and 2 (so there is no unusually large residual corresponding to an outlying observation); there is no point far to the left or right of the others (thus no observation that might greatly influence the fit), and there is no pattern to indicate that the model should somehow be modified. When the plot has the appearance of Figure 13.14(b), the fitted model should be changed to incorporate curvature (a nonlinear model).

The increasing spread from left to right in Figure 13.14(c) suggests that the variance of y is not the same at each x value but rather increases with x. A straight-line model may still be appropriate, but the best-fit line should be selected by using _weighted least squares_ rather than ordinary least squares. This involves giving more weight to observations in the region exhibiting low variability and less weight to observations in the region exhibiting high variability. A specialized regression analysis text or a knowledgeable statistician should be consulted for details.

The standardized residual plots of Figure 13.14(d)–(e) show an extreme outlier and a potentially influential observation, respectively. Consider deleting the observation corresponding to such a point from the data set and refitting the same model. Substantial changes in estimates and various other quantities warn of instability in the data. The investigator should certainly carry out a more careful analysis and perhaps collect more data before drawing any firm conclusions. Improved computing power has allowed statisticians to develop and implement a variety of diagnostics for identifying unusual observations in a regression data set.

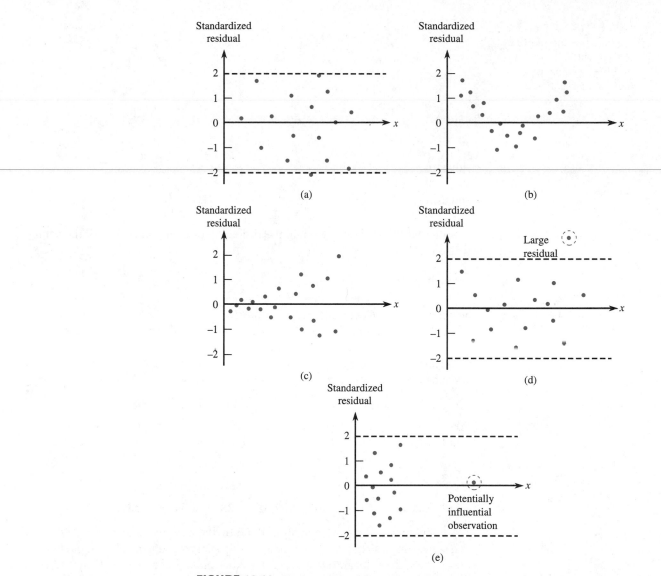

FIGURE 13.14 Examples of residual plots: (a) Satisfactory plot; (b) Plot suggesting that a curvilinear regression model is needed; (c) Plot indicating nonconstant variance; (d) Plot showing a large residual; (e) Plot showing a potentially influential observation

EXAMPLE 13.7   Figures 13.15(a) and (b) on page 526 display a standardized residual plot and a residual plot, respectively, for the data of Example 13.6 regarding tree age and 5-year growth. The first observation was at $x_1 = 5$ and the corresponding standardized residual was -1.00, so the first plotted point in the standardized residual plot is $(5, -1.00)$. Other points are similarly obtained and plotted. The plot shows no unusual behavior that might call for model modifications or further analysis.

FIGURE 13.15 Plots for the data of Example 13.6 (from MINITAB): (a) Standardized residual plot; (b) Residual plot

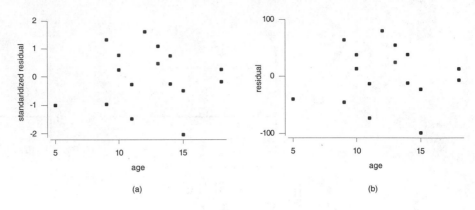

Note that the general pattern in the residual plot is similar to that of the standardized residual plot.

EXAMPLE 13.8

The article "Snow Cover and Temperature Relationships in North America and Eurasia" (*J. of Climate and Appl. Meteorology* (1983): 460–469) explored the relationship between October–November continental snow cover (x, in millions of km^2) and December–February temperature (y, in °C). The following data refers to Eurasia during the $n = 13$ time periods 1969–1970, 1970–1971, . . . , 1981–1982:

x	13.00	12.75	16.70	18.85	16.60	15.35	13.90
y	−13.5	−15.7	−15.5	−14.7	−16.1	−14.6	−13.4
Std. resid.	−.11	−2.19	−.36	1.23	−.91	−.12	.34

x	22.40	16.20	16.70	13.65	13.90	14.75
y	−18.9	−14.8	−13.6	−14.0	−12.0	−13.5
Std. resid.	−1.54	.04	1.25	−.28	1.54	.58

A simple linear regression analysis done by the authors yielded $r^2 = .52$, $r = −.72$, suggesting a significant linear relationship. This is confirmed by a model utility test. The scatter plot and standardized residual plot are displayed in Figure 13.16. There are no unusual patterns, although one standardized residual, −2.19, is a bit on the large side. The most interesting feature is the observation (22.40, −18.9), corresponding to a point far to the right of the others in these plots. This observation may have had a substantial influence on all aspects of the fit. The estimated slope when all 13 observations are included is $b = −.459$, and $s_b = .133$. When the potentially influential observation is deleted, the estimate of β based on the remaining 12 observations is $b = −.228$. Thus,

$$\text{change in slope} = \text{original } b − \text{new } b$$
$$= −.459 − (−.288)$$
$$= −.231$$

FIGURE 13.16 Plots for the data of Example 13.8 (from MINITAB): (a) Scatter plot; (b) Standardized residual plot

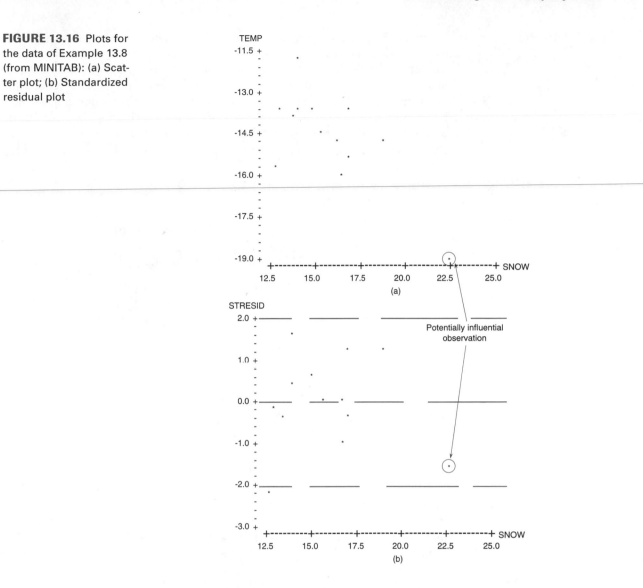

The change expressed in standard deviations is $-.231/.133 = -1.74$. Because b has changed by substantially more than 1 standard deviation, the observation under consideration appears to be highly influential.

Additionally, r^2 based just on the 12 observations is only .13, and the t ratio for testing $\beta = 0$ is not significant. Evidence for a linear relationship is much less conclusive in light of this analysis. The investigators should seek a climatological explanation for the influential observation and collect more data, which can be used to find an effective relationship.

EXAMPLE 13.9

Example 13.4 presented data on x = treadmill time and y = ski time. A simple linear regression model was fit to the data prior to constructing a confidence interval for β, the average change in ski time associated with a 1-minute increase in treadmill time. The validity of the t confidence interval depends on the assumptions that the distribution of the residuals from the population regression line at any fixed x is approximately normal and that the variance of this distribution does not depend on x. Constructing a normal probability plot of the standardized residuals and a standardized residual plot will provide insight as to whether these assumptions are in fact reasonable.

MINITAB was used to fit the simple linear regression model and compute the standardized residuals, resulting in the values shown in Table 13.2.

Table 13.2 *Data, residuals, and standardized residuals for Example 13.9*

Obs.	Treadmill	Ski Time	Residual	Std. Residual
1	7.7	71.000	.172	.10
2	8.4	71.400	2.206	1.13
3	8.7	65.000	−3.494	−1.74
4	9.0	68.700	.906	.44
5	9.6	64.400	−1.994	−.96
6	9.6	69.400	3.006	1.44
7	10.0	63.000	−2.461	−1.18
8	10.2	64.600	−.394	−.19
9	10.4	66.900	2.373	1.16
10	11.0	62.600	−.527	−.27
11	11.7	61.700	.206	.12

Figure 13.17 shows a normal probability plot of the standardized residuals and a standardized residual plot. The normal probability plot is quite straight and the standardized residual plot does not show evidence of any patterns or of increasing spread. These observations support the use of the t confidence interval in Example 13.4.

FIGURE 13.17 Normal probability plot and standardized residual plot for Example 13.9

(*continued*)

FIGURE 13.17 (Continued)

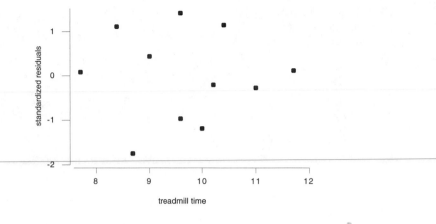

EXAMPLE 13.10

(Example 13.5 continued)   Use of the model utility test in Example 13.5 led to the conclusion that there was a useful linear relationship between

y = average reading time

and

x = image quality

The validity of this test requires that the random error distribution be normal and that the variability of the random error does not change with x. Let's construct a normal probability plot of the standardized residuals and a standardized residual plot to see whether these assumptions are reasonable. Table 13.3 gives the residuals and standardized residuals that are needed to construct the plots in Figure 13.18 (page 530).

Table 13.3 *Data, residuals, and standardized residuals for Example 13.10*

Obs	Image Quality	Reading Time	Residual	Std. Residual
1	4.30	8.0000	−.1392	−.80
2	4.55	8.3000	.2479	1.27
3	5.55	7.8000	.0964	.42
4	5.65	7.2500	−.4188	−1.81
5	5.95	7.7000	.1358	.59
6	6.30	7.5000	.0578	.26
7	6.45	7.6000	.2101	.98
8	6.45	7.2000	−.1899	−.89

FIGURE 13.18 Normal probability plot and standardized residual plot for Example 13.10

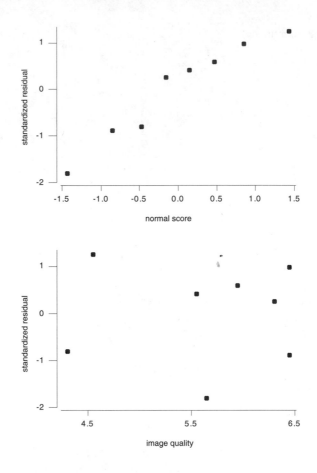

The normal probability plot is quite straight, and the standardized residual plot does·not show evidence of any pattern or increasing spread. This supports the use of the model utility test in Example 13.5.

Occasionally you will see a residual plot or a standardized residual plot with $\hat{y}$ plotted on the horizontal axis rather than x. Since $\hat{y}$ is just a linear function of x, using $\hat{y}$ rather than x will change the scale of the horizontal axis but will not change the pattern of the points in the plot. As a consequence, plots that use $\hat{y}$ on the horizontal axis can be interpreted in the same manner as plots that use x.

When the distribution of the random deviation e has heavier tails than does the normal distribution, observations with large standardized residuals are not that unusual. Such observations can have great effects on the estimated regression line when the least squares approach is used. In recent years, statisticians have proposed a number of alternative methods — called **robust,** or **resistant,** methods — for fitting a line. Such methods give less weight to outlying observations than does the method of least squares, without deleting them from the data set. The most widely used robust procedures require a substantial amount of computation, so a good computer program is necessary. Associated confidence-interval and hypothesis-testing procedures are still in the developmental stage.

Exercises 13.27 – 13.33

13.27 Exercise 13.8 gave data on x = treadmill run time to exhaustion and y = 20-km ski time. The x values and corresponding standardized residuals from a simple linear regression are as follows.

x	7.7	8.4	8.7	9.0	9.6	9.6
St. resid.	.10	1.13	−1.74	.44	−.96	1.44

x	10.0	10.2	10.4	11.0	11.7
St. resid.	−1.18	−.19	1.16	−.27	.12

Construct a standardized residual plot. Does the plot exhibit any unusual features?

13.28 The article "Vital Dimensions in Volume Perception: Can the Eye Fool the Stomach?" (*Journal of Marketing Research* (1999): 313–326) gave the accompanying data on the dimensions of 27 representative food products (Gerber baby food, Cheez Whiz, Skippy Peanut Butter, and Ahmed's tandoori paste, to name a few).

Row	Max. Width	Min. Width
1	2.50	1.80
2	2.90	2.70
3	2.15	2.00
4	2.90	2.60
5	3.20	3.15
6	2.00	1.80
7	1.60	1.50
8	4.80	3.80
9	5.90	5.00
10	5.80	4.75
11	2.90	2.80
12	2.45	2.10
13	2.60	2.20
14	2.60	2.60
15	2.70	2.60
16	3.10	2.90
17	5.10	5.10
18	10.20	10.20
19	3.50	3.50
20	2.70	1.20
21	3.00	1.70

(*continued*)

Row	Max. Width	Min. Width
22	2.70	1.75
23	2.50	1.70
24	2.40	1.20
25	4.40	1.20
26	7.50	7.50
27	4.25	4.25

a. Fit the simple linear regression model that would allow prediction of the maximum width (in cm) of a food container based on its minimum width (in cm).
b. Calculate the standardized residuals (or just the residuals if you don't have access to a computer program that gives standardized residuals), and plot them to determine whether there are any outliers. Would eliminating these outliers increase the accuracy of predictions using this regression? If so, eliminate the outlying data point (a 1-liter coke bottle) and refit the regression.
c. Interpret the estimated slope and, if appropriate, the intercept.
d. Do you think that the assumptions of the simple linear regression model are reasonable? Give statistical evidence for your answer.

13.29 The authors of the article "Age, Spacing and Growth Rate of *Tamarix* as an Indication of Lake Boundary Fluctuations at Sebkhet Kelbia, Tunisia" (*J. of Arid Environ.* (1982): 43–51) used a simple linear regression model to describe the relationship between y = vigor (average width in centimeters of the last two annual rings) and x = stem density (stems/m^2). The estimated model was based on the following data. Also given are the standardized residuals.

x	4	5	6	9	14
y	.75	1.20	.55	.60	.65
St. resid.	−.28	1.92	−.90	−.28	.54

x	15	15	19	21	22
y	.55	0	.35	.45	.40
St. resid.	.24	−2.05	−.12	.60	.52

a. What assumptions are required for the simple linear regression model to be appropriate?

b. Construct a normal probability plot of the standardized residuals. Does the assumption that the random deviation distribution is normal appear to be reasonable? Explain.

c. Construct a standardized residual plot. Are there any unusually large residuals?

d. Is there anything about the standardized residual plot that would cause you to question the use of the simple linear regression model to describe the relationship between x and y?

13.30 The article "Effects of Gamma Radiation on Juvenile and Mature Cuttings of Quaking Aspen" (*Forest Science* (1967): 240–245) reported the following data on x = exposure time to radiation (kR/16 hours) and y = dry weight of roots (mg):

x	0	2	4	6	8
y	110	123	119	86	62

a. Construct a scatter plot for this data. Does the plot suggest that the simple linear regression model might be appropriate?

b. The estimated regression line for this data is $\hat{y} = 127 - 6.65x$ and the standardized residuals are as given.

x	0	2	4	6	8
St. resid.	−1.55	.68	1.25	−.05	−1.06

Construct a standardized residual plot. What does the plot suggest about the adequacy of the simple linear regression model?

13.31 Carbon aerosols have been identified as a contributing factor in a number of air quality problems. In a chemical analysis of diesel engine exhaust, x = mass ($\mu g/cm^2$) and y = elemental carbon ($\mu g/cm^2$) were recorded ("Comparison of Solvent Extraction and Thermal Optical Carbon Analysis Methods: Application to Diesel Vehicle Exhaust Aerosol" *Environ. Science Tech.* (1984): 231–234). The estimated regression line for this data set is $\hat{y} = 31 + .737x$. The accompanying table gives the observed x and y values and the corresponding standardized residuals.

x	164.2	156.9	109.8	111.4	87.0
y	181	156	115	132	96
St. resid.	2.52	.82	.27	1.64	.08

(continued)

x	161.8	230.9	106.5	97.6	79.7
y	170	193	110	94	77
St. resid.	1.72	−.73	.05	−.77	−1.11

x	118.7	248.8	102.4	64.2	89.4
y	106	204	98	76	89
St. resid.	−1.07	−.95	−.73	−.20	−.68

x	108.1	89.4	76.4	131.7	100.8
y	102	91	97	128	88
St. resid.	−.75	−.51	.85	0.00	−1.49

x	78.9	387.8	135.0	82.9	117.9
y	86	310	141	90	130
St. resid.	−.27	−.89	.91	−.18	1.05

a. Construct a standardized residual plot. Are there any unusually large residuals? Do you think that there are any influential observations?

b. Is there any pattern in the standardized residual plot that would indicate that the simple linear regression model is not appropriate?

c. Based on your plot in part **a**, do you think that it is reasonable to assume that the variance of y is the same at each x value? Explain.

13.32 An investigation of the relationship between traffic flow x (thousands of cars per 24 hr) and lead content y of bark on trees near the highway ($\mu g/g$ dry weight) yielded the accompanying data. A simple linear regression model was fit, and the resulting estimated regression line was $\hat{y} = 28.7 + 33.3x$. Both residuals and standardized residuals are also given.

x	8.3	8.3	12.1	12.1	17.0
y	227	312	362	521	640
Residual	−78.1	6.9	−69.6	89.4	45.3
St. resid.	−.99	.09	−.81	1.04	.51

x	17.0	17.0	24.3	24.3	24.3
y	539	728	945	738	759
Residual	−55.7	133.3	107.2	−99.8	−78.8
St. resid.	−.63	1.51	1.35	−1.25	−.99

a. Plot the (x, residual) pairs. Does the resulting plot suggest that a simple linear regression model is an appropriate choice? Explain your reasoning.

b. Construct a standardized residual plot. Does the plot differ significantly in general appearance from the plot in part **a**?

13.33 The accompanying data on x = U.S. population (millions) and y = crime index (millions) appeared in the article "The Normal Distribution of Crime" (*J. of Police Science and Admin.* (1975): 312–318). The author comments that "The simple linear regression analysis remains one of the most useful tools for crime prediction." When observations are made sequentially in time, the residuals or standardized residuals should be plotted in time order (that is, first the one for time $t = 1$ (1963 here), then the one for time $t = 2$, and so on). Notice that here x increases with time, so an equivalent plot is of residuals or standardized residuals versus x. Using $\hat{y} = -47.26 + .260x$, calculate the residuals and plot the $(x,$ residual) pairs. Does the plot exhibit a pattern that casts doubt on the appropriateness of the simple linear regression model? Explain.

Year	1963	1964	1965	1966	1967	1968	1969	1970	1971	1972	1973
x	188.5	191.3	193.8	195.9	197.9	199.9	201.9	203.2	206.3	208.2	209.9
y	2.26	2.60	2.78	3.24	3.80	4.47	4.99	5.57	6.00	5.89	8.64

13.4 Inferences Based on the Estimated Regression Line (Optional)

The number obtained by substituting a particular x value x^* into the equation of the estimated regression line has two different interpretations. It is a point estimate of the average y value when $x = x^*$, and it is also a point prediction of a single y value to be observed when $x = x^*$. How precise is this estimate or prediction? That is, how close might $a + bx^*$ be to the actual mean value, $\alpha + \beta x^*$, or to a particular y observation? Because both a and b vary in value from sample to sample (each one is a statistic), the statistic $a + bx^*$ also has different values for different samples. The way in which this statistic varies in value with different samples is summarized by its sampling distribution. Properties of the sampling distribution are used to obtain both a confidence interval formula for $\alpha + \beta x^*$ and a prediction interval formula for a particular y observation. The width of the corresponding interval conveys information about the precision of the estimate or prediction.

Properties of the Sampling Distribution of $a + bx$ for a Fixed x Value

Let x^* denote a particular value of the independent variable x. When the four basic assumptions of the simple linear regression model are satisfied, the sampling distribution of the statistic $a + bx^*$ has the following properties:

1. The mean value of $a + bx^*$ is $\alpha + \beta x^*$, so $a + bx^*$ is an unbiased statistic for estimating the average y value when $x = x^*$.

2. The standard deviation of the statistic $a + bx^*$, denoted by σ_{a+bx^*}, is given by

$$\sigma_{a+bx^*} = \sigma\sqrt{\frac{1}{n} + \frac{(x^* - \bar{x})^2}{S_{xx}}}$$

3. The distribution of $a + bx^*$ is normal.

As you can see from the formula for σ_{a+bx^*}, the standard deviation of $a + bx^*$ is larger when $(x^* - \bar{x})^2$ is large than when it is small; that is, $a + bx^*$ tends to be a more precise estimate of $\alpha + \beta x^*$ when x^* is close to the center of the x values at which observations were made than when x^* is far from the center.

The standard deviation σ_{a+bx^*} cannot be calculated from the sample data, because the value of σ is unknown. However, it can be estimated by using s_e in place of σ. Using its mean and estimated standard deviation to standardize $a + bx^*$ gives a variable with a t distribution.

The **estimated standard deviation of the statistic $a + bx^*$**, denoted by s_{a+bx^*}, is given by

$$s_{a+bx^*} = s_e\sqrt{\frac{1}{n} + \frac{(x^* - \bar{x})^2}{S_{xx}}}$$

When the four basic assumptions of the simple linear regression model are satisfied, the probability distribution of the standardized variable

$$t = \frac{a + bx^* - (\alpha + \beta x^*)}{s_{a+bx^*}}$$

is the t distribution with df $= n - 2$.

Inferences About the Mean y Value $\alpha + \beta x^*$

In previous chapters, standardized variables were manipulated algebraically to give confidence intervals of the form

(point estimate) $\pm$ (critical value) $\cdot$ (estimated standard deviation)

A parallel argument leads to the following interval.

Confidence Interval for a Mean y Value

When the basic assumptions of the simple linear regression model are met, a **confidence interval for $\alpha + \beta x^*$,** the average y value when x has value x^*, is

$$a + bx^* \pm (t \text{ critical value}) \cdot s_{a+bx^*}$$

where the t critical value is based on df $= n - 2$. Appendix Table III gives critical values corresponding to the most frequently used confidence levels.

Because s_{a+bx^*} is larger the farther x^* is from $\bar{x}$, the confidence interval widens as x^* moves away from the center of the data.

EXAMPLE 13.11   Physical characteristics of sharks are of interest to surfers and scuba divers, as well as marine researchers. The accompanying data on $x =$ length (ft) and $y =$ jaw width (in) for 44 sharks was found in articles appearing in the magazines *Skin Diver* and *Scuba News*:

x	18.7	12.3	18.6	16.4	15.7	18.3	14.6	15.8	14.9	17.6	12.1
y	17.5	12.3	21.8	17.2	16.2	19.9	13.9	14.7	15.1	18.5	12.0
x	16.4	16.7	17.8	16.2	12.6	17.8	13.8	12.2	15.2	14.7	12.4
y	13.8	15.2	18.2	16.7	11.6	17.4	14.2	14.8	15.9	15.3	11.9
x	13.2	15.8	14.3	16.6	9.4	18.2	13.2	13.6	15.3	16.1	13.5
y	11.6	14.3	13.3	15.8	10.2	19.0	16.8	14.2	16.9	16.0	15.9
x	19.1	16.2	22.8	16.8	13.6	13.2	15.7	19.7	18.7	13.2	16.8
y	17.9	15.7	21.2	16.3	13.0	13.3	14.3	21.3	20.8	12.2	16.9

Because it is difficult to measure jaw width in living sharks, researchers would like to determine whether it is possible to estimate jaw width from body length, which is more easily measured. A scatter plot of the data (Figure 13.19) shows a linear pattern and is consistent with use of the simple linear regression model.

FIGURE 13.19 A scatter plot for the data of Example 13.11

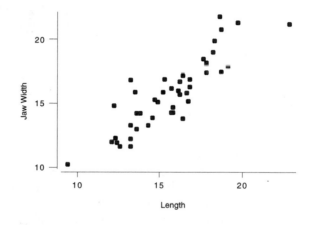

From the accompanying MINITAB output, it is easily verified that

$$a = .688 \qquad b = .96345 \qquad \text{SSResid} = 79.49$$
$$\text{SSTo} = 339.02 \qquad s_e = 1.376 \qquad r^2 = .766$$

Regression Analysis
The regression equation is
Jaw Width = 0.69 + 0.963 Length

Predictor	Coef	StDev	T	P
Constant	0.688	1.299	0.53	0.599
Length	0.96345	0.08228	11.71	0.000

S = 1.376   R-Sq = 76.6%   R-Sq(adj) = 76.0%

Analysis of Variance

Source	DF	SS	MS	F	P
Regression	1	259.53	259.53	137.12	0.000
Residual Error	42	79.49	1.89		
Total	43	339.02			

From the data, we can also compute $S_{xx} = 279.8718$. Since $r^2 = .766$, the simple linear regression model explains 76.6% of the variability in jaw width. The model utility test also confirms the usefulness of this model (P-value $= .000$).

Let's use the data to compute a 90% confidence interval for the mean jaw width for 15-ft-long sharks. The mean jaw width when length is 15 is $\alpha + \beta(15)$. The point estimate is

$$a + b(15) = .688 + .96345(15) = 15.140 \text{ in}$$

Since

$$\bar{x} = \frac{\Sigma x}{n} = \frac{685.80}{44} = 15.586$$

the estimated standard deviation of $a + b(15)$ is

$$s_{a+b(15)} = s_e \sqrt{\frac{1}{n} + \frac{(15 - \bar{x})^2}{S_{xx}}}$$

$$= (1.376)\sqrt{\frac{1}{44} + \frac{(15 - 15.586)^2}{279.8718}}$$

$$= .213$$

The t critical value for df $= 42$ is 1.68 (using the tabled value for df $= 40$). We now have all of the relevant quantities needed to compute a 90% confidence interval:

$$
\begin{aligned}
a + b(15) \pm (t \text{ critical value}) \cdot s_{a+b(15)} &= 15.140 \pm (1.68)(.213) \\
&= 15.140 \pm .358 \\
&= (14.782, 15.498)
\end{aligned}
$$

Based on this sample data, we can be 90% confident that the mean jaw width for sharks whose length is 15 ft is between 14.782 and 15.498 in. As with all confidence intervals, the 90% confidence level means that we have used a *method* to construct this interval estimate that has a 10% error rate.

––––––––––

We have just considered estimation of the mean y value at a fixed $x = x^*$. When the basic assumptions of the simple linear regression model are met, the true value of this mean is $\alpha + \beta x^*$. The reason that our point estimate, $a + bx^*$ is not exactly equal to $\alpha + \beta x^*$ is that the values of α and β are not known, so they have been estimated from sample data. As a result, the estimate $a + bx^*$ is subject to sampling variability and the extent to which the estimated line might differ from the true population line is reflected in the width of the confidence interval.

A Prediction Interval for a Single y

We now turn our attention to the problem of predicting a single y value at a particular $x = x^*$ (rather than estimating the mean y value when $x = x^*$). This is equivalent to trying to predict the y value of an individual point in a scatter plot of the population. If we use the estimated regression line to obtain a point prediction,

$a + bx*$, there are two reasons why this prediction will probably not be exactly equal to the true y value. First, as was the case when estimating a mean y value, the estimated line is not going to be exactly equal to the true population regression line. But, in the case of predicting a single y value, there is an additional source of error — even if we knew the true population line, individual points would not fall exactly on the population line. This implies that there is more uncertainty associated with predicting a single y value at a particular $x*$ than with estimating the mean y value at $x*$. This extra uncertainty is reflected in the width of the corresponding intervals.

An interval for a single y value, $y*$, is called a **prediction interval** (to distinguish it from the confidence interval for a mean y value). The interpretation of a prediction interval is very similar to the interpretation of a confidence interval. A 95% prediction interval for $y*$ is constructed using a method for which 95% of all possible samples would yield interval limits capturing $y*$; only 5% of all samples would give an interval that did not include $y*$.

Manipulation of a standardized variable similar to the one from which a confidence interval was obtained gives the following prediction interval.

Prediction Interval for a Single y Value

When the four basic assumptions of the simple linear regression model are met, a **prediction interval for $y*$**, a single y observation made when $x = x*$, has the form

$$a + bx* \pm (t \text{ critical value}) \cdot \sqrt{s_e^2 + s_{a+bx*}^2}$$

The prediction interval and confidence interval are centered at exactly the same place, $a + bx*$. The addition of s_e^2 under the square root symbol makes the prediction interval wider — often substantially so — than the confidence interval.

EXAMPLE 13.12   (Example 13.11 continued)   In Example 13.11, we computed a 90% confidence interval for the mean jaw width of sharks whose length is 15 ft. Suppose that we are interested in predicting the jaw width of a single shark of length 15 ft. The required calculations for a 90% prediction interval for $y*$ are

$$a + b(15) = .688 + .96245(15) = 15.140$$
$$s_e^2 = (1.376)^2 = 1.8934$$
$$s_{a+b(15)}^2 = (.213)^2 = .0454$$

The t critical value for df = 42 and a 90% prediction level is 1.68 (using the tabled value for df = 40). Substitution into the prediction interval formula then gives

$$
\begin{aligned}
a + b(15) \pm (t \text{ critical value})\sqrt{s_e^2 + s_{a+b(15)}^2} &= 15.140 \pm (1.68)\sqrt{1.9388} \\
&= 15.140 \pm 2.339 \\
&= (12.801, 17.479)
\end{aligned}
$$

We can be 90% confident that an individual shark with length 15 ft will have a jaw width between 12.801 and 17.479 in. Notice that, as expected, this 90% prediction

FIGURE 13.20 MINITAB output for the data of Example 13.12

Regression Analysis

The regression equation is

Jaw Width = 0.69 + 0.963 Length

Predictor	Coef	StDev	T	P
Constant	0.688	1.299	0.53	0.599
Length	0.96345	0.08228	11.71	0.000

S =1.376   R-Sq = 76.6%   R-Sq(adj) = 76.0%

Analysis of Variance

Source	DF	SS	MS	F	P
Regression	1	259.53	259.53	137.12	0.000
Residual Error	42	79.49	1.89		
Total	43	339.02			

Predicted Values

	Fit	StDev Fit	95.0% CI	95.0% PI
$x^* = 15 \rightarrow$	15.140	0.213	(14.710, 15.569)	(12.330, 17.949)
$x^* = 20 \rightarrow$	19.957	0.418	(19.113, 20.801)	(17.055, 22.859)

interval is much wider than the 90% confidence interval when $x^* = 15$ from Example 13.11.

Figure 13.20 gives MINITAB output that includes a 95% confidence interval and a 95% prediction interval both when $x^* = 15$ and $x^* = 20$. The intervals for $x^* = 20$ are both wider than the corresponding intervals for $x^* = 15$ because 20 is farther from $\bar{x}$ (the center of the sample x values) than is 15. Each prediction interval is wider than the corresponding confidence interval. Figure 13.21 is a MINITAB plot

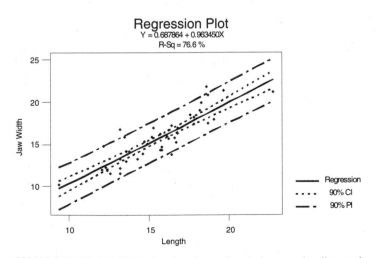

FIGURE 13.21 MINITAB plot showing estimated regression line and 90% confidence and prediction limits for the data of Example 13.12

that shows the estimated regression line as well as 90% confidence limits and prediction limits.

Exercises 13.34 – 13.48

13.34 Explain the difference between a confidence interval and a prediction interval. How can a prediction level of 95% be interpreted?

13.35 Suppose that a regression data set is given and you are asked to obtain a confidence interval. How would you tell from the phrasing of the request whether the interval is for β or for $\alpha + \beta x^*$?

13.36 In Exercise 13.17, we considered a regression of y = oxygen consumption on x = time spent exercising. Summary quantities given there yield

$$n = 20 \qquad \bar{x} = 2.50 \qquad S_{xx} = 25$$
$$b = 97.26 \qquad a = 592.10 \qquad s_e = 16.486$$

a. Calculate $s_{a+b(2.0)}$, the estimated standard deviation of the statistic $a + b(2.0)$.
b. Without any further calculation, what is $s_{a+b(3.0)}$, and what reasoning did you use to obtain it?
c. Calculate the estimated standard deviation of the statistic $a + b(2.8)$.
d. For what value x^* is the estimated standard deviation of $a + bx^*$ smallest, and why?

13.37 Example 13.3 gave data on x = ambient temperature (°C) and y = cavity depth (cm).
a. Calculate a confidence interval using a 95% confidence level for the true average change in depth associated with a 1° increase in temperature.
b. Calculate a confidence interval using a 95% confidence level for the true average depth when temperature is 1°C.

13.38 The data of Exercise 13.25, in which x = milk temperature and y = milk pH, yields

$$n = 16 \qquad \bar{x} = 43.375 \qquad S_{xx} = 7325.75$$
$$b = -.00730608 \qquad a = 6.843345 \qquad s_e = .0356$$

a. Obtain a 95% confidence interval for $\alpha + \beta(40)$, the true average milk pH when the milk temperature is 40°C.
b. Calculate a 99% confidence interval for the true average milk pH when the milk temperature is 35°C.
c. Would you recommend using the data to calculate a 95% confidence interval for the true average pH when the temperature is 90°C? Why or why not?

13.39 Return to the regression of y = milk pH on x = milk temperature described in Exercise 13.38.
a. Obtain a 95% prediction interval for a single pH observation to be made when milk temperature = 40°C.
b. Calculate a 99% prediction interval for a single pH observation when milk temperature = 35°C.
c. When the milk temperature is 60°C, would a 99% prediction interval be wider than the intervals of parts **a** and **b**? Answer without calculating the interval.

13.40 An experiment was carried out by geologists to see how the time necessary to drill a distance of 5 ft in rock (y, in min) depended on the depth at which the drilling began (x, in ft, between 0 and 400). We show part of the MINITAB output obtained from fitting the simple linear regression model ("Mining Information," *Am. Stat.* (1991): 4–9).

The regression equation is
time = 4.79 + 0.0144 depth

Predictor	Coef	Stdev	t-ratio	p
Constant	4.7896	0.6663	7.19	0.000
depth	0.014388	0.002847	5.05	0.000

s = 1.432   R-sq = 63.0%   R-sq(adj) = 60.5%

Analysis of Variance

SOURCE	DF	SS	MS	F	p
Regression	1	52.378	52.378	25.54	0.000
Error	15	30.768	2.051		
Total	16	83.146			

a. What proportion of observed variation in time can be explained by the simple linear regression model?
b. Does the simple linear regression model appear to be useful?
c. MINITAB reported that $s_{a+b(200)}$ = .347. Calculate a confidence interval at the 95% confidence level for the true average time when depth = 200 ft.
d. A single observation on time is to be made when drilling starts at a depth of 200 ft. Use a 95% prediction interval to predict the resulting value of time.

e. MINITAB gave (8.147, 10.065) as a 95% confidence interval for true average time when depth $= 300$. Calculate a 99% confidence interval for this average.

13.41 According to "Reproductive Biology of the Aquatic Salamander *Amphiuma tridactylum* in Louisiana" (*Journal of Herpetology*) 1999: 100–105, the size of a female salamander's snout is correlated with the number of eggs in her clutch. The following data is consistent with summary quantities reported in the article. MINITAB output is also included.

Snout-Vent Length	32	53	53	53	54
Clutch Size	45	215	160	170	190

Snout-Vent Length	57	57	58	58	59
Clutch Size	200	270	175	245	215

Snout-Vent Length	63	63	64	67
Clutch Size	170	240	245	280

The regression equation is
y = - 133 + 5.92 x

Predictor	Coef	StDev	T	P
Constant	-133.02	64.30	-2.07	0.061
x	5.919	1.127	5.25	0.000

S = 33.90   R-Sq = 69.7%   R-Sq(adj) = 67.2%

Additional summary statistics are

$n = 14$ $\bar{x} = 56.5$ $\bar{y} = 201.4$

$\Sigma x^2 = 45,958$ $\Sigma y^2 = 613,550$ $\Sigma xy = 164,969$

a. What is the equation of the regression line for predicting clutch size based on snout-vent length?
b. Calculate the standard deviation of b.
c. Test the hypothesis that the slope of the population line is positive.
d. Predict the clutch size for a salamander with a snout-vent length of 65 using a 95% interval.
e. Predict the clutch size for a salamander with snout-vent length of 105.

13.42 The article first introduced in Exercise 13.28 of Section 13.3 gave data on the dimensions of 27 representative food products.
a. Use the information given there to test the hypothesis that there is a positive linear relationship between the minimum width and the maximum width of an object.
b. Calculate and interpret s_e.
c. Calculate a 95% confidence interval for the mean maximum width of products with a minimum width of 6 cm.
d. Calculate a 95% prediction interval for the maximum width of a food package with a minimum width of 6 cm.

13.43 The shelf life of packaged food depends on many factors. Dry cereal is considered to be a moisture-sensitive product (no one likes soggy cereal!), with the shelf life determined primarily by moisture content. In a study of the shelf life of one particular brand of cereal, $x =$ time on shelf (stored at 73°F and 50% relative humidity) and $y =$ moisture content were recorded. The resulting data is from "Computer Simulation Speeds Shelf Life Assessments" (*Package Engr.* (1983): 72–73).

x	0	3	6	8	10	13	16
y	2.8	3.0	3.1	3.2	3.4	3.4	3.5

x	20	24	27	30	34	37	41
y	3.1	3.8	4.0	4.1	4.3	4.4	4.9

a. Summary quantities are

$\Sigma x = 269$ $\Sigma y = 51$ $\Sigma xy = 1081.5$

$\Sigma y^2 = 7745$ $\Sigma x^2 = 190.78$

Find the equation of the estimated regression line for predicting moisture content from time on the shelf.
b. Does the simple linear regression model provide useful information for predicting moisture content from knowledge of shelf time?
c. Find a 95% interval for the moisture content of an individual box of cereal that has been on the shelf 30 days.
d. According to the article, taste tests indicate that this brand of cereal is unacceptably soggy when the moisture content exceeds 4.1. Based on your interval in part **c**, do you think that a box of cereal that has been on the shelf 30 days will be acceptable? Explain.

13.44 For the cereal data of Exercise 13.43, the average x value is 19.21. Would a 95% confidence interval with $x^* = 20$ or $x^* = 17$ be wider? Explain. Answer the same question for a prediction interval.

13.45 High blood-lead levels are associated with a number of different health problems. The article "A Study of the Relationship between Blood Lead Levels and Occupational Lead Levels" (*Am. Stat.* (1983): 471) gave data on $x =$ air-lead level ($\mu g/m^3$) and $y =$ blood-lead level ($\mu g/dL$). Summary quantities (based on a subset of the data given in a plot in the article) are

$n = 15$ $\Sigma x = 1350$ $\Sigma y = 600$

$\Sigma x^2 = 155,400$ $\Sigma y^2 = 24,869.33$ $\Sigma xy = 57,760$

a. Find the equation of the estimated regression line.
b. Estimate the mean blood-lead level for people who work where the air-lead level is 100 $\mu g/m^3$ using a 90% interval.
c. Construct a 90% prediction interval for the blood-

lead level of a particular person who works where the air-lead level is 100 $\mu g/m^3$.

d. Explain the difference in interpretation of the intervals computed in parts **b** and **c**.

13.46 A regression of y = sunburn index for a pea plant on x = distance from an ultraviolet light source was considered in Exercise 13.22. The data and summary statistics presented there give

$$n = 15 \qquad \bar{x} = 40.60 \qquad \Sigma (x - \bar{x})^2 = 3311.60$$
$$b = -.0565 \qquad a = 4.500 \qquad \text{SSResid} = .8430$$

a. Calculate a 95% confidence interval for the true average sunburn index when the distance from the light source is 35 cm.

b. When two 95% confidence intervals are computed, it can be shown that the simultaneous confidence level is at least $[100 - 2(5)]\% = 90\%$. That is, if both intervals are computed for a first sample, for a second sample, yet again for a third, and so on, in the long run at least 90% of the samples will result in intervals both of which capture the values of the corresponding population characteristics. Calculate confidence intervals for the true mean sunburn index when the distance is 35 cm and when the distance is 45 cm in such a way that the simultaneous confidence level is at least 90%.

c. If two 99% intervals were computed, what do you think could be said about the simultaneous confidence level?

d. If a 95% confidence interval were computed for the true mean index when $x = 35$, another 95% confidence interval were computed when $x = 40$, and yet another one when $x = 45$, what do you think would be the simultaneous confidence level for the three resulting intervals?

e. Return to part **d** and answer the question posed there if the individual confidence level for each interval were 99%.

13.47 By analogy with the discussion in Exercise 13.46, when two different prediction intervals are computed, each at the 95% prediction level, the *simultaneous prediction level* is at least $[100 - 2(5)]\% = 90\%$.

a. Return to Exercise 13.46 and obtain prediction intervals for sunburn index both when distance is 35 cm and when distance is 45 cm, so that the simultaneous prediction level is at least 90%.

b. If three different 99% prediction intervals are calculated for distances (cm) of 35, 40, and 45, respectively, what can be said about the simultaneous prediction level?

13.48 The article "Performance Test Conducted for a Gas Air-Conditioning System" (*Am. Soc. of Heating, Refrigerating, and Air Cond. Engr.* (1969): 54) reported the following data on maximum outdoor temperature (x) and hours of chiller operation per day (y) for a 3-ton residential gas air-conditioning system:

x	72	78	80	86	88	92
y	4.8	7.2	9.5	14.5	15.7	17.9

Suppose that the system is actually a prototype model, and the manufacturer does not wish to produce this model unless the data strongly indicates that when maximum outdoor temperature is 82°F, the true average number of hours of chiller operation is less than 12. The appropriate hypothesis is then

$$H_0: \quad \alpha + \beta(82) = 12 \qquad \text{versus} \qquad H_a: \quad \alpha + \beta(82) < 12$$

Use the statistic

$$t = \frac{a + b(82) - 12}{s_{a+b(82)}}$$

which has a t distribution based on $(n - 2)$ df when H_0 is true, to test the hypotheses at significance level .01.

13.5 Inferences About the Population Correlation Coefficient (Optional)

The sample correlation coefficient r, defined in Chapter 5, measures how strongly the x and y values in a *sample* of pairs are linearly related to one another. There is an analogous measure of how strongly x and y are related in the entire *population* of pairs from which the sample $(x_1, y_1), \ldots, (x_n, y_n)$ was obtained. It is called the **population correlation coefficient** and is denoted by ρ. As with r, ρ must be between

−1 and 1, and it assesses the extent of any *linear* association in the population. To have $\rho = 1$ or -1, all (x, y) pairs in the population must lie exactly on a straight line. The value of ρ is a population characteristic and is generally unknown. The sample correlation coefficient, r, can be used as the basis for making inferences about ρ.

A Test for Independence ($\rho = 0$)

Investigators are often interested in detecting not just linear association but association of *any* kind. When there is no association of any type between x and y values, statisticians say that the two variables are *independent*. In general, $\rho = 0$ is not equivalent to the independence of x and y. However, there is one special, yet frequently occurring, situation in which the two conditions ($\rho = 0$ and independence) are identical. This is when the pairs in the population have what is called a **bivariate normal distribution.** The essential feature of such a distribution is that for *any* fixed x value, the distribution of associated y values is normal, *and* for any fixed y value, the distribution of x values is normal. As an example, suppose that height x and weight y have a bivariate normal distribution in the American adult male population. (There is good empirical evidence for this.) Then when $x = 68$ in, weight y has a normal distribution; when $x = 72$ in, weight is normally distributed; when $y = 160$ lb, height x has a normal distribution; when $y = 175$ lb, height has a normal distribution; and so on. In this example, of course, x and y are not independent, since a large height value tends to be associated with a large weight value and a small height value with a small weight value.

There is no easy way to check the assumption of bivariate normality, especially when the sample size n is small. A partial check can be based on the following property: If (x, y) has a bivariate normal distribution, then x alone has a normal distribution and so does y. This suggests constructing a normal probability plot of $x_1, x_2, \ldots, x_n$ and a separate normal probability plot of $y_1, \ldots, y_n$. If either plot shows a substantial departure from a straight line, bivariate normality is a questionable assumption. If both plots are reasonably straight, bivariate normality is plausible, although no guarantee can be given.

The test of independence (zero correlation) is a t test. The formula for the test statistic essentially involves standardizing the estimate r under the assumption that the null hypothesis H_0: $\rho = 0$ is true.

A Test for Independence in a Bivariate Normal Population

Null hypothesis: H_0: $\rho = 0$

Test statistic: $t = \dfrac{r}{\sqrt{\dfrac{1 - r^2}{n - 2}}}$

The t critical value is based on df $= n - 2$.

Alternative hypothesis:	*P-value*:
H_a: $\rho > 0$ (positive dependence)	Area under the appropriate t curve to the right of the computed t

(continued)

Alternative hypothesis: *P-value*:

$H_a: \rho < 0$ (negative dependence)   Area under the appropriate t curve to the left of the computed t

$H_a: \rho \neq 0$ (dependence)   (i) $2 \cdot$ (area to the right of t) if t is positive

or

(ii) $2 \cdot$ (area to the left of t) if t is negative

Assumption: r is the correlation coefficient for a *random sample* from a *bivariate normal population*.

EXAMPLE 13.13   Is there any relationship between the age of an individual and the age at which that individual plans to retire? The authors of the article "Predictors of Planned Retirement Age" (*Psychology and Aging* (1995): 76–83) hypothesized that younger people would plan to retire earlier than would older people. They selected a random sample of $n = 303$ workers from a wide variety of job positions and recorded $x =$ current age and $y =$ planned retirement age for each individual in the sample. The sample correlation coefficient was $r = .35$. Does this data support the stated hypothesis? Let's carry out a test using a significance level of .01.

1. $\rho =$ the correlation between age and planned retirement age in the population from which the 303 workers were selected

2. $H_0: \rho = 0$

3. $H_a: \rho > 0$ (large values of $y =$ planned retirement age tend to be associated with large values of $x =$ age)

4. $\alpha = .01$

5. *Test statistic*: $t = \dfrac{r}{\sqrt{\dfrac{1 - r^2}{n - 2}}}$

6. *Assumptions*:   Without the actual data values, it is not possible to assess whether the assumption of bivariate normality is reasonable. For purposes of this example, we will assume that it is reasonable and proceed with the test. Had the data been available, we would have looked at normal probability plots of the x values and of the y values.

7. *Calculation*: $t = \dfrac{.35}{\sqrt{\dfrac{1 - (.35)^2}{301}}} = \dfrac{.35}{\sqrt{.0029153}} = 6.48$

8. *P-value*:   The t curve with 301 df is essentially indistinguishable from the z curve, and Appendix Table IV shows that the area under this curve and to the right of 6.48 is approximately zero. That is, P-value ≈ 0.

9. *Conclusion*:   The P-value is smaller than any reasonable significance level; in particular, P-value $\leq .01$. We reject H_0, as did the authors of the article, and confirm their conjecture. Notice, though, that according to the guidelines

described in Chapter 5, $r = .35$ suggests only a weak linear relationship. Since $r^2 = .1225$, fitting the simple linear regression model to the data would result in only about 12% of observed variation in planned retirement age being explained.

In the context of regression analysis, the hypothesis of no linear relationship $(H_0: \beta = 0)$ was tested using the t ratio $t = b/s_b$. Some algebraic manipulation shows that

$$\frac{r}{\sqrt{\dfrac{1 - r^2}{n - 2}}} = \frac{b}{s_b}$$

so the model utility test can also be used to test for independence in a bivariate normal population. The reason for using the formula for t that involves r is that when we are interested only in correlation, the extra effort involved in computing the regression quantities b, a, SSResid, s_e, and s_b need not be expended.

Other inferential procedures for drawing conclusions about ρ—a confidence interval or a test of hypothesis with nonzero hypothesized value—are somewhat complicated. One of the chapter references can be consulted for details.

Exercises 13.49 – 13.57

13.49 Discuss the difference between r and ρ.

13.50 a. If the sample correlation coefficient is equal to 1, is it necessarily true that $\rho = 1$?
b. If $\rho = 1$, is it necessarily true that $r = 1$?

13.51 A sample of $n = 353$ college faculty members was obtained, and the values of x = teaching evaluation index and y = annual raise were determined ("Determination of Faculty Pay: An Agency Theory Perspective," *Academy of Management J.* (1992): 921–955). The resulting value of r was .11. Does there appear to be a linear association between these variables in the population from which the sample was selected? Carry out a test of hypothesis using a significance level of .05. Does the conclusion surprise you? Explain.

13.52 It seems plausible that higher rent for retail space could be justified only by a higher level of sales. A random sample of $n = 53$ specialty stores in a chain was selected, and the values of x = annual dollar rent per square foot and y = annual dollar sales per square foot were determined, resulting in $r = .37$ ("Association of Shopping Center Anchors with Performance of a Nonanchor Specialty

Chain Store," *J. of Retailing* (1985): 61–74). Carry out a test at significance level .05 to see whether there is in fact a positive linear association between x and y in the population of all such stores.

13.53 Television is regarded by many as a prime culprit for the difficulty many students have in performing well in school. The article "The Impact of Athletics, Part-Time Employment, and Other Activities on Academic Achievement" (*J. of College Student Development* (1992): 447–453) reported that for a random sample of $n = 528$ college students, the sample correlation coefficient between time spent watching television (x) and grade point average (y) was $r = -.26$.
a. Does this suggest that there is a negative correlation between these two variables in the population from which the 528 students were selected? Use a test with significance level .01.
b. If y were regressed on x, would the regression explain a substantial percentage of the observed variation in grade point average? Explain your reasoning.

13.54 The accompanying summary quantities for x = particulate pollution ($\mu g/m^3$) and y = luminance (.01 cd/m^2)

were calculated from a representative sample of data that appeared in the article "Luminance and Polarization of the Sky Light at Seville (Spain) Measured in White Light" (*Atmos. Environ.* (1988): 595–599).

$$n = 15 \qquad \Sigma x = 860 \qquad \Sigma y = 348$$
$$\Sigma x^2 = 56,700 \qquad \Sigma y^2 = 8954 \qquad \Sigma xy = 22,265$$

a. Test to see whether there is a positive correlation between particulate pollution and luminance in the population from which the data was selected.
b. What proportion of observed variation in luminance can be attributed to the approximate linear relationship between luminance and particulate pollution?

13.55 In a study of bacterial concentration in surface and subsurface water ("Pb and Bacteria in a Surface Microlayer" *J. of Marine Research* (1982): 1200–1206), the accompanying data was obtained.

Concentration ($\times 10^6$/mL)				
Surface	48.6	24.3	15.9	8.29	5.75
Subsurface	5.46	6.89	3.48	3.72	3.12

(continued)

Concentration ($\times 10^6$/mL)			
Surface	10.8	4.71	8.26	9.41
Subsurface	3.39	4.17	4.06	5.16

Summary quantities are

$$\Sigma x = 136.02 \qquad \Sigma y = 39.35$$
$$\Sigma x^2 = 3602.65 \qquad \Sigma y^2 = 184.27 \qquad \Sigma xy = 673.65$$

Using a significance level of .05, determine whether the data supports the hypothesis of a linear relationship between surface and subsurface concentration.

13.56 A sample of $n = 500$ (x, y) pairs was collected and a test of H_0: $\rho = 0$ versus H_a: $\rho \neq 0$ was carried out. The resulting P-value was computed to be .00032.
a. What conclusion would be appropriate at level of significance .001?
b. Does this small P-value indicate that there is a very strong linear relationship between x and y (a value of ρ that differs considerably from zero)? Explain.

13.57 A sample of $n = 10,000$ (x, y) pairs resulted in $r = .022$. Test H_0: $\rho = 0$ versus H_a: $\rho \neq 0$ at level .05. Is the result statistically significant? Comment on the practical significance of your analysis.

13.6 Interpreting the Results of Statistical Analyses

Although regression analysis can be used as a tool for summarizing bivariate data, more often than not it is also used to enable researchers to make inferences about the way in which two variables are related.

What to Look For in Published Data

Here are some things to consider when you evaluate research that involves fitting a simple linear regression model.

- Which variable is the dependent variable? Is it a numerical (rather than qualitative) variable?

- If sample data has been used to estimate the coefficients in a simple linear regression model, is it reasonable to think that the basic assumptions required for inference are met?

- Does the model appear to be useful? Are the results of a model utility test reported? What is the P-value associated with the test?

- Has the model been used in an appropriate way? Has the regression equation been used to predict y for values of the independent variable that are outside the range of the data?

■ If a correlation coefficient is reported, is it accompanied by a test of significance? Are the results of the test interpreted properly?

The effects of caffeine were examined in the article "Withdrawal Syndrome After the Double-Blind Cessation of Caffeine Consumption" (*New England J. of Medicine* (1992): 1109–1113). The authors found that the dose of caffeine was significantly correlated with a measure of insomnia and also with latency on a test of reaction time. They reported $r = .26$ (*P*-value $= .042$) for insomnia and $r = .31$ (*P*-value $= .014$) for latency. Since both *P*-values are small, the authors concluded that the population correlation coefficients differ from zero. We should also note, however, that the reported correlation coefficients are not particularly large and do not indicate a strong linear relationship.

Regression analysis was used by the authors of the article "On the Generality of the 'Sit and Reach' Test: An Analysis of Flexibility Data for an Aging Population" (*Research Quarterly for Exercise and Sport* (1990): 326–330). A linear regression model was used to describe the relationship between $y = $ head rotation to the left (in degrees) and $x = $ age (in years). The authors report that "regression analysis showed an age effect for leftward head rotation (significant beta weight, $t_{78} = 3.10$, $P < .003$)." The term *beta weight* refers to the β term in the linear regression model. A model utility test was performed, and the value of the test statistic was 3.10. The test was based on 78 degrees of freedom (this is the meaning of the subscript on t_{78}). The associated *P*-value leads to the rejection of $H_0: \beta = 0$ and to the authors's stated conclusion of an "age effect." The reported regression equation is

$$\hat{y} = 87.5 - .31x$$

The coefficient of age in this equation $(-.31)$ indicates that, on average, leftward head rotation decreases by about .31 degrees with each additional year of age. (It is interesting to note that age did not turn out to be an important predictor of rightward motion!)

The article does not provide enough information to determine whether the basic assumptions required for the validity of the test reported are reasonable, and the authors do not address this issue directly. If raw data were available, we could check on this by looking at such things as a standardized residual plot and various normal probability plots.

Summary of Key Concepts and Formulas

Term or Formula	Comment
Simple linear regression model, $y = \alpha + \beta x + e$	This model assumes that there is a line with slope β and y intercept α, called the population (true) regression line, such that an observation deviates from the line by a random amount e. The random deviation is assumed to have a normal distribution with mean zero and standard deviation σ, and random deviation for different observations are assumed to be independent of one another.
Estimated regression line, $\hat{y} = a + bx$	The least squares line introduced in Chapter 5.

$$s_e = \sqrt{\frac{\text{SSResid}}{n-2}}$$

The point estimate of the standard deviation σ, with associated degrees of freedom $n-2$.

$$s_b = \frac{s_e}{\sqrt{S_{xx}}}$$

The estimated standard deviation of the statistic b.

$$b \pm (t \text{ critical value})s_b$$

A confidence interval for the slope β of the population regression line, where the t critical value is based on $(n-2)$ df.

$$t = \frac{b - \text{hyp. val.}}{s_b}$$

The test statistic for testing hypotheses about β. The test is based on $(n-2)$ df.

Model utility test, with test statistic $t = \dfrac{b}{s_b}$

A test of $H_0: \beta = 0$, which asserts that there is no useful linear relationship between x and y, versus $H_a: \beta \neq 0$, the claim that there is a useful linear relationship.

Residual analysis

Methods based on the residuals or standardized residuals for checking the assumptions of a regression model.

Standardized residual

A residual divided by its standard deviation.

Standardized residual plot

A plot of the $(x, \text{standard residual})$ pairs. A pattern in this plot suggests a problem with the simple linear regression model

$$s_{a+bx^*} = s_e \sqrt{\frac{1}{n} + \frac{(x^* - \bar{x})^2}{S_{xx}}}$$

The estimated standard deviation of the statistic $a + bx^*$, where x^* denotes a particular value of x.

$$a + bx^* \pm (t \text{ crit. val.})s_{a+bx^*}$$

A confidence interval for $\alpha + \beta x^*$, the average value of y when $x = x^*$.

$$a + bx^* \pm (t \text{ crit. val.})\sqrt{s_e^2 + s_{a+bx^*}^2}$$

A prediction interval for a single y value to be observed when $x = x^*$.

Population correlation coefficient ρ

A measure of the extent to which the x and y values in an entire population are linearly related.

$$t = \frac{r}{\sqrt{\frac{1-r^2}{n-2}}}$$

The test statistic for testing $H_0: \rho = 0$, according to which (assuming a bivariate normal population distribution) x and y are independent of one another.

Supplementary Exercises 13.58 – 13.78

13.58 The effects of grazing animals on grasslands have been the focus of numerous investigations by ecologists. One such study, reported in "The Ecology of Plants, Large Mammalian Herbivores, and Drought in Yellowstone National Park" (*Ecology* (1992): 2043–2058), proposed using the simple linear regression model to relate y = green biomass concentration (g/cm^3) to x = elapsed time since snowmelt (days).

a. The estimated regression equation was given as $\hat{y} = 106.3 - .640x$. What is the estimate of average change in biomass concentration associated with a 1-day increase in elapsed time?

b. What value of biomass concentration would you predict when elapsed time is 40 days?

c. The sample size was $n = 58$, and the reported value of the coefficient of determination was .470. Does this suggest that there is a useful linear relationship between the two variables? Carry out an appropriate test.

13.59 A random sample of $n = 347$ students was selected, and each one was asked to complete several questionnaires, from which a Coping Humor Scale value x and a Depression Scale value y were determined ("Depression and Sense of Humor" (*Psychological Reports* (1994):

1473–1474). The resulting value of the sample correlation coefficient was −.18.

a. The investigators reported that P-value < .05. Do you agree?

b. Is the sign of r consistent with your intuition? Explain. (Higher scale values correspond to more developed sense of humor and greater extent of depression.)

c. Would the simple linear regression model give accurate predictions? Why or why not?

13.60 Exercise 5.62 gave data on x = bound rubber content (%) and y = tensile modulus (MPa), a measure of coupling effectiveness. A scatter plot shows a substantial linear pattern. Summary quantities are

$$n = 11 \qquad \Sigma x = 292.9 \qquad \Sigma x^2 = 8141.75$$

$$\Sigma y = 69.03 \qquad \Sigma y^2 = 442.1903 \qquad \Sigma xy = 1890.200$$

a. Calculate point estimates for the slope and vertical intercept of the population regression line.

b. Calculate a point estimate for the standard deviation σ.

c. Using a .01 significance level, does the data suggest the existence of a useful linear relationship between x and y?

13.61 Return to the summary quantities of Exercise 13.60.

a. Use a 95% confidence interval to estimate the true mean tensile modulus when the bound rubber content is 20%.

b. Use a 95% prediction interval to predict the value of the tensile modulus resulting from a single observation made when the rubber content is 20%.

c. What aspect of the problem description in part **a** tells you that the requested confidence interval is not for β?

13.62 Data on x = depth of flooding and y = flood damage was given in Exercise 5.63. Summary quantities are

$$n = 13 \qquad \Sigma x = 91 \qquad \Sigma x^2 = 819$$

$$\Sigma y = 470 \qquad \Sigma y^2 = 19,118 \qquad \Sigma xy = 3867$$

a. Does the data suggest the existence of a positive linear relationship (one in which an increase in y tends to be associated with an increase in x)? Test using a .05 significance level.

b. Predict flood damage resulting from a claim made when depth of flooding is 3.5 ft, and do so in a way that conveys information about the precision of the prediction.

13.63 Exercise 13.8 gave data on x = treadmill run time to exhaustion and y = 20-km ski time for a sample of 11 biathletes. Use the accompanying MINITAB output to answer the following questions.

The regression equation is
ski = 88.8 - 2.33 tread

Predictor	Coef	Stdev	t-ratio	p
Constant	88.796	5.750	15.44	0.000
tread	-2.3335	0.5911	-3.95	0.003

s = 2.188   R-sq = 63.4%   R-sq(adj) = 59.3%

Analysis of Variance

SOURCE	DF	SS	MS	F	p
Regression	1	74.630	74.630	15.58	0.003
Error	9	43.097	4.789		
Total	10	117.727			

a. Carry out a test at significance level .01 to decide whether the simple linear regression model is useful.

b. Estimate the average change in ski time associated with a 1-minute increase in treadmill time, and do so in a way that conveys information about the precision of estimation.

c. MINITAB reported that $s_{a+b(10)}$ = .689. Predict ski time for a single biathlete whose treadmill time is 10 min, and do so in a way that conveys information about the precision of prediction.

d. MINITAB also reported that $s_{a+b(11)}$ = 1.029. Why is this larger than $s_{a+b(10)}$?

13.64 Exercise 5.42 presented data on x = squawfish length and y = maximum size of salmonid consumed, both in mm. Use the accompanying MINITAB output along with the values $\bar{x}$ = 343.27 and S_{xx} = 69,112.18 to answer the following questions.

The regression equation is
size = -89.1 + 0.729 length

Predictor	Coef	Stdev	t-ratio	p
Constant	-89.09	16.83	-5.29	0.000
length	0.72907	0.04778	15.26	0.000

s = 12.56   R-sq = 96.3%   R-sq(adj) = 95.9%

Analysis of Variance

SOURCE	DF	SS	MS	F	p
Regression	1	36736	36736	232.87	0.000
Error	9	1420	158		
Total	10	38156			

a. Does there appear to be a useful linear relationship between length and size?

b. Does it appear that the average change in maximum size associated with a 1-mm increase in length is less than .8 mm? State and test the appropriate hypotheses.

c. Estimate average maximum size when length is 325 mm in a way that conveys information about the precision of estimation.

d. How would the estimate when length is 250 mm compare to the estimate of part **c**? Answer without actually calculating the new estimate.

13.65   A sample of $n = 61$ penguin burrows was selected, and values of both $y =$ trail length (m) and $x =$ soil hardness (force required to penetrate the substrate to a depth of 12 cm with a certain gauge, in kg) were determined for each one ("Effects of Substrate on the Distribution of Magellanic Penguin Burrows," *The Auk* (1991): 923–933). The equation of the least squares line was $\hat{y} = 11.607 - 1.4187x$, and $r^2 = .386$.

a. Does the relationship between soil hardness and trail length appear to be linear, with shorter trails associated with harder soil (as the article asserted)? Carry out an appropriate test of hypotheses.

b. Using $s_e = 2.35$, $\bar{x} = 4.5$, and $\Sigma (x - \bar{x})^2 = 250$, predict trail length when soil hardness is 6.0 in a way that conveys information about the reliability and precision of the prediction.

c. Would you use the simple linear regression model to predict trail length when hardness is 10.0? Explain your reasoning.

13.66   The article "Photocharge Effects in Dye Sensitized Ag[Br,I] Emulsions at Millisecond Range Exposures" (*Photographic Science and Engr.* (1981): 138–144) gave the accompanying data on $x =$ % light absorption and $y =$ peak photovoltage.

x	4.0	8.7	12.7	19.1	21.4	24.6	28.9	29.8	30.5
y	.12	.28	.55	.68	.85	1.02	1.15	1.34	1.29

$$\Sigma x = 179.7 \qquad \Sigma x^2 = 4334.41$$
$$\Sigma y = 7.28 \qquad \Sigma y^2 = 7.4028 \qquad \Sigma xy = 178.683$$

a. Construct a scatter plot of the data. What does it suggest?

b. Assuming that the simple linear regression model is appropriate, obtain the equation of the estimated regression line.

c. How much of the observed variation in peak photovoltage can be explained by the model relationship?

d. Predict peak photovoltage when percent absorption is 19.1, and compute the value of the corresponding residual.

e. The authors claimed that there is a useful linear relationship between the two variables. Do you agree? Carry out a formal test.

f. Give an estimate of the average change in peak photovoltage associated with a 1% increase in light absorption. Your estimate should convey information about the precision of estimation.

g. Give an estimate of true average peak photovoltage when % light absorption is 20, and do so in a way that conveys information about precision.

13.67   Reduced visual performance with increasing age has been a much-studied phenomenon in recent years. This decline is due partly to changes in optical properties of the eye itself and partly to neural degeneration throughout the visual system. As one aspect of this problem, the article "Morphometry of Nerve Fiber Bundle Pores in the Optic Nerve Head of the Human" (*Exp. Eye Research* (1988): 559–568) presented the accompanying data on $x =$ age and $y =$ percentage of the cribriform area of the lamina scleralis occupied by pores.

x	22	25	27	39	42	43	44	46	46
y	75	62	50	49	54	49	59	47	54

x	48	50	57	58	63	63	74	74
y	52	58	49	52	49	31	42	41

a. Suppose that the researchers had believed a priori that the average decrease in percentage area associated with a 1-year age increase was .5%. Does the data contradict this prior belief? State and test the appropriate hypotheses using a .10 significance level.

b. Estimate true average percentage area covered by pores for all 50-year-olds in the population in a way that conveys information about the precision of estimation.

13.68   Occasionally an investigator may wish to compute a confidence interval for α, the y intercept of the true regression line, or test hypotheses about α. The estimated y intercept is simply the height of the estimated line when $x = 0$, since $a + b(0) = a$. This implies that s_a, the estimated standard deviation of the statistic a, results from substituting $x^* = 0$ in the formula for s_{a+bx^*}. The desired confidence interval is then

$$a \pm (t \text{ critical value}) s_a$$

and a test statistic is

$$t = \frac{a - \text{hypothesized value}}{s_a}$$

a. The article "Comparison of Winter-Nocturnal Geostationary Satellite Infrared-Surface Temperature with Shelter-Height Temperature in Florida" (*Remote Sensing of the Environ.* (1983): 313–327) used the simple linear regression model to relate surface temperature as measured by a satellite (y) to actual air temperature (x) as determined from a thermocouple placed on a traversing vehicle. Selected data is given (read from a scatter plot in the article).

x	−2	−1	0	1	2	3	4	5	6	7
y	−3.9	−2.1	−2.0	−1.2	0	1.9	.6	2.1	1.2	3.0

Estimate the true regression line.

b. Compute the estimated standard deviation s_a. Carry out a test at level of significance .05 to see whether the y intercept of the true regression line differs from zero.

c. Compute a 95% confidence interval for α. Does the result indicate that $\alpha = 0$ is plausible? Explain.

13.69 Example 13.3 gave data on x = ambient temperature and y = cavity depth. Use the accompanying MINITAB output to estimate the true average depth when temperature = 0°C with a 95% confidence interval. (*Hint:* Refer to the previous exercise.)

The regression equation is
depth = 20.1 - 0.345 temp

Predictor	Coef	Stdev
Constant	20.1251	0.9402
temp	-0.34504	0.06008

S = 2.334   R-SQ = 76.7%

13.70 In some studies, an investigator has n (x, y) pairs sampled from one population and m (x, y) pairs from a second population. Let β and β' denote the slopes of the first and second population lines, respectively, and let b and b' denote the estimated slopes calculated from the first and second samples, respectively. The investigator may then wish to test the null hypothesis $H_0: \beta - \beta' = 0$ (that is, $\beta = \beta'$) against an appropriate alternative hypothesis. Suppose that σ^2, the variance about the population line, is the same for both populations. Then this common variance can be estimated by

$$s^2 = \frac{\text{SSResid} + \text{SSResid}'}{(n-2) + (m-2)}$$

where SSResid and SSResid' are the residual sums of squares for the first and second samples, respectively. With S_{xx} and S'_{xx} denoting the quantity $\Sigma (x - \bar{x})^2$ for the first and second samples, respectively, the test statistic is

$$t = \frac{b - b'}{\sqrt{\dfrac{s^2}{S_{xx}} + \dfrac{s^2}{S'_{xx}}}}$$

When H_0 is true, this statistic has a t distribution based on $(n + m - 4)$ df.

The given data is a subset of the data in the article "Diet and Foraging Model of *Bufa marinus* and *Lepto-*

dactylus ocellatus" (*J. of Herpetology* (1984): 138–146). The independent variable x is body length (cm) and the dependent variable y is mouth width (cm), with $n = 9$ observations for one type of nocturnal frog and $m = 8$ observations for a second type. Test at level .05 to see whether the slopes of the true regression lines for the two different frog populations are identical. (Summary statistics are given in the third table.)

Leptodactylus ocellatus

x	3.8	4.0	4.9	7.1	8.1	8.5	8.9	9.1	9.8
y	1.0	1.2	1.7	2.0	2.7	2.5	2.4	2.9	3.2

Bufa marinus

x	3.8	4.3	6.2	6.3	7.8	8.5	9.0	10.0
y	1.6	1.7	2.3	2.5	3.2	3.0	3.5	3.8

	Leptodactylus	Bufa
Sample size:	9	8
Σx	64.2	55.9
Σx^2	500.78	425.15
Σy	19.6	21.6
Σy^2	47.28	62.92
Σxy	153.36	163.36

13.71 Consider the following four (x, y) data sets: the first three have the same x values, so these values are listed only once (from Frank Anscombe, "Graphs in Statistical Analysis" *Amer. Statistician* (1973): 17–21).

Data Set	1–3	1	2	3	4	4
Variable	x	y	y	y	x	y
	10.0	8.04	9.14	7.46	8.0	6.58
	8.0	6.95	8.14	6.77	8.0	5.76
	13.0	7.58	8.74	12.74	8.0	7.71
	9.0	8.81	8.77	7.11	8.0	8.84
	11.0	8.33	9.26	7.81	8.0	8.47
	14.0	9.96	8.10	8.84	8.0	7.04
	6.0	7.24	6.13	6.08	8.0	5.25
	4.0	4.26	3.10	5.39	19.0	12.50
	12.0	10.84	9.13	8.15	8.0	5.56
	7.0	4.82	7.26	6.42	8.0	7.91
	5.0	5.68	4.74	5.73	8.0	6.89

For each of these data sets, the values of the summary quantities, $\bar{x}, \bar{y}, \Sigma (x - \bar{x})^2$, and $\Sigma (x - \bar{x})(y - \bar{y})$, are identical, so all quantities computed from these will be identical for the four sets: the estimated regression line, SSResid, s_e^2, r^2, and so on. The summary quantities provide no way of distinguishing among the four data sets. Based on a scatter plot for each set, comment on the appropriateness or inappropriateness of fitting the simple linear regression model in each case.

13.72 The accompanying scatter plot, based on 34 sediment samples with x = sediment depth (cm) and y = oil and grease content (mg/kg), appeared in the article "Mined Land Reclamation Using Polluted Urban Navigable Waterway Sediments" (*J. of Environ. Quality* (1984): 415–422). Discuss the effect that the observation (20, 33,000) will have on the estimated regression line. If this point were omitted, what can you say about the slope of the estimated regression line? What do you think will happen to the slope if this observation is included in the computations?

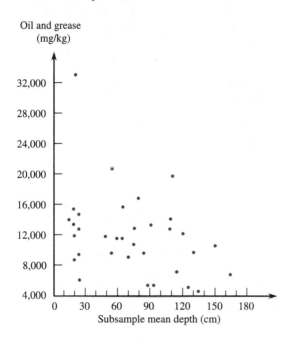

Oil and grease (mg/kg)

Subsample mean depth (cm)

13.73 The article "Improving Fermentation Productivity with Reverse Osmosis" (*Food Tech.* (1984): 92–96) gave the following data (read from a scatter plot) on y = glucose concentration (g/L) and x = fermentation time (days) for a blend of malt liquor.

x	1	2	3	4	5	6	7	8
y	74	54	52	51	52	53	58	71

a. Use the data to calculate the estimated regression line.
b. Does the data indicate a linear relationship between y and x? Test using a .10 significance level.
c. Using the estimated regression line of part **a,** compute the residuals and construct a plot of the residuals versus x (that is, of the (x, residual) pairs).
d. Based on the plot in part **c,** do you think that a lin-

ear model is appropriate for describing the relationship between y and x? Explain.

13.74 The employee relations manager of a large company was concerned that raises given to employees during a recent period might not have been based strictly on objective performance criteria. A sample of $n = 20$ employees was selected, and the values of x, a quantitative measure of productivity, and y, the percentage salary increase, were determined for each one. A computer package was used to fit the simple linear regression model, and the resulting output gave the P-value = .0076 for the model utility test. Does the percentage raise appear to be linearly related to productivity? Explain.

13.75 The article "Statistical Comparison of Heavy Metal Concentrations in Various Louisiana Sediments" (*Environ. Monitoring and Assessment* (1984): 163–170) gave the accompanying data on depth (m), zinc concentration (ppm), and iron concentration (%) for 17 core samples.

Core	Depth	Zinc	Iron
1	.2	86	3.4
2	2.0	77	2.9
3	5.8	91	3.1
4	6.5	86	3.4
5	7.6	81	3.2
6	12.2	87	2.9
7	16.4	94	3.2
8	20.8	92	3.4
9	22.5	90	3.1
10	29.0	108	4.0
11	31.7	112	3.4
12	38.0	101	3.6
13	41.5	88	3.7
14	60.0	99	3.5
15	61.5	90	3.4
16	72.0	98	3.5
17	104.0	70	4.8

a. Using a .05 significance level, test appropriate hypotheses to determine whether a correlation exists between depth and zinc concentration.
b. Using a .05 significance level, does the data strongly suggest a correlation between depth and iron concentration?
c. Calculate the slope and intercept of the estimated regression line relating y = iron concentration and x = depth.
d. Use the estimated regression equation to construct a 95% prediction interval for the iron concentration of a single core sample taken at a depth of 50 m.

e. Compute and interpret a 95% interval estimate for the true average iron concentration of core samples taken at 70 m.

13.76 The accompanying figure is from the article "Root and Shoot Competition Intensity Along a Soil Depth Gradient" (*Ecology* (1995): 673–682). It shows the relationship between above-ground biomass and soil depth within the experimental plots. The relationship is described by the linear equation: biomass = $-9.85 + 25.29$(soil depth) ($r^2 = .65$; $P < 0.001$; $n = 55$). Do you think the simple linear regression model is appropriate here? Explain. What would you expect to see in a plot of the standardized residuals versus x?

13.77 Give a brief answer, comment, or explanation for each of the following.
a. What is the difference between $e_1, e_2, \ldots, e_n$ and the n residuals?
b. The simple linear regression model states that $y = \alpha + \beta x$.
c. Does it make sense to test hypotheses about b?
d. SSResid is always positive.
e. A student reported that a data set consisting of $n = 6$ observations yielded residuals 2, 0, 5, 3, 0, and 1 from the least squares line.
f. A research report included the following summary quantities obtained from a simple linear regression analysis:

$$\Sigma (y - \bar{y})^2 = 615 \qquad \Sigma (y - \hat{y})^2 = 731$$

13.78 Some straightforward but slightly tedious algebra shows that

$$\text{SSResid} = (1 - r^2) \Sigma (y - \bar{y})^2$$

from which it follows that

$$s_e = \sqrt{\frac{n - 1}{n - 2}} \left(\sqrt{1 - r^2} \right) s_y$$

Unless n is quite small, $(n - 1)/(n - 2) \approx 1$, so

$$s_e \approx (\sqrt{1 - r^2}) s_y$$

a. For what value of r is s_e as large as s_y? What is the least squares line in this case?
b. For what values of r will s_e be much smaller than s_y?

References

See the references at the end of Chapter 5.

14

Multiple Regression Analysis

INTRODUCTION

The general objective of regression analysis is to establish a useful relationship between a dependent variable y and one or more independent (i.e., predictor or explanatory) variables. The simple linear regression model $y = \alpha + \beta x + e$, discussed in Chapter 13, has been used successfully by many investigators in a wide variety of disciplines to relate y to a single predictor variable x. In many situations, however, there will not be a strong relationship between y and any single predictor variable, but knowing the values of several independent variables may considerably reduce uncertainty concerning the associated y value. For example, some variation in house prices in a large city can certainly be attributed to house size, but knowledge of size by itself would not usually enable a bank appraiser to accurately assess (predict) a home's value. Price is also determined to some extent by other variables, such as age, lot size, number of bedrooms and bathrooms, distance from schools, and so on. As another example, let y denote a quantitative measure of wrinkle resistance in cotton cellulose fabric. Then the value of y may depend on such variable quantities as curing temperature, curing time, concentration of formaldehyde, and concentration of the catalyst sulfur dioxide used in the production process.

In this chapter, we extend the regression methodology developed in the previous chapter to *multiple regression models,* which include at least two predictor variables. Fortunately, many of the concepts developed in the context of simple linear regression carry over to multiple regression with little or no modification. The calculations required to fit such a model and make further inferences are *much* more tedious than those for simple linear regression, so a computer is an indispensable tool for multiple regression analysis. The computer's ability to perform a huge number of computations in a very short time has spurred the development of new methods for analyzing large data sets with many predictor variables. These include techniques for fitting numerous alternative models and choosing between them, tools for identifying influential observations, and both algebraic and graphical diagnostics designed to reveal potential violations of model assumptions. A single chapter can do little more than scratch the surface of this important subject area.

14.1 Multiple Regression Models

The relationship between a dependent or response variable y and two or more independent or predictor variables is deterministic if the value of y is completely determined, with no uncertainty, once values of the independent variables have been specified. Consider, for example, a school district in which teachers with no prior teaching experience and no college credits beyond a bachelor's degree start at an annual salary of $28,000. Suppose that for each year of teaching experience up to 20 years, a teacher receives an additional $800 per year and that each unit of postcollege coursework up to a limit of 75 results in an extra $60 per year. Define three variables:

y = salary of a teacher who has at most 20 years teaching experience and at most 75 postcollege units

x_1 = number of years teaching experience

x_2 = number of postcollege units

Previously, x_1 and x_2 denoted the first two observations on the single variable x. In the usual notation for multiple regression, however, x_1 and x_2 represent two different variables.

The value of y is entirely determined by values of x_1 and x_2 through the equation

$$y = 28,000 + 800x_1 + 60x_2$$

Thus, if $x_1 = 10$ and $x_2 = 30$,

$$y = 28,000 + (800)(10) + (60)(30)$$
$$= 28,000 + 8000 + 1800$$
$$= 37,800$$

If two different teachers both have the same x_1 values and the same x_2 values, they will also have identical y values.

Only rarely is y deterministically related to predictors $x_1, \ldots, x_k$. A probabilistic model results from adding a random deviation e to a deterministic function of the x_i's.

Definition

A **general additive multiple regression model,** which relates a dependent variable y to k predictor variables $x_1, x_2, \ldots, x_k$, is given by the model equation

$$y = \alpha + \beta_1 x_1 + \beta_2 x_2 + \cdots + \beta_k x_k + e$$

The random deviation e is assumed to be normally distributed with mean value 0 and variance σ^2 for any particular values of $x_1, \ldots, x_k$. This implies that for fixed $x_1, x_2, \ldots, x_k$ values, y has a normal distribution with variance σ^2 and

$$\text{(mean } y \text{ value for fixed } x_1, \ldots, x_k \text{ values)} = \alpha + \beta_1 x_1 + \beta_2 x_2 + \cdots + \beta_k x_k$$

The β_i's are called **population regression coefficients**; each β_i can be interpreted as the true average change in y when the predictor x_i increases by 1 unit *and* the values of all the other predictors remain fixed.

The deterministic portion $\alpha + \beta_1 x_1 + \cdots + \beta_k x_k$ is called the **population regression function.**

As in simple linear regression, if σ^2 is quite close to 0, any particular observed y will tend to be quite near its mean value. When σ^2 is large, many of the y observations may deviate substantially from their mean y values.

EXAMPLE 14.1   Cardiorespiratory fitness is widely recognized as a major component of overall physical well-being. Direct measurement of maximal oxygen uptake (VO_2max) is the single best measure of such fitness, but direct measurement is time-consuming and expensive. It is therefore desirable to have a prediction equation for VO_2max in terms of easily obtained quantities. Consider the variables

$$y = VO_2\text{max (L/min)}$$
$$x_1 = \text{weight (kg)}$$
$$x_2 = \text{age (yr)}$$
$$x_3 = \text{time necessary to walk a mile (min)}$$
$$x_4 = \text{heart rate at the end of the walk (beats/min)}$$

One possible population model for male students that is consistent with information given in the article "Validation of the Rockport Fitness Walking Test in College Males and Females" (*Research Quarterly for Exercise and Sport* (1994): 152–158) is

$$y = 5.0 + .01x_1 - .05x_2 - .13x_3 - .01x_4 + e \qquad \sigma = .4$$

The population regression function is

$$\text{(mean } y \text{ value for fixed } x_1, \ldots, x_4) = 5.0 + .01x_1 - .05x_2 - .13x_3 - .01x_4$$

For individuals whose weight is 76 kg, age is 20 yr, walk time is 12 min, and heart rate is 140 beats/min,

$$\text{(mean value of } VO_2\text{max)} = 5.0 + .01(76) - .05(20) - .13(12) - .01(140) = 1.80$$

With $2\sigma = .80$, it is quite likely that an actual y value will be within .80 of the mean value (i.e., in the interval from 1.00 to 2.60).

The true average change in VO_2max when weight increases by 1 kg and the other predictors remain fixed is $\beta_1 = .01$. Similarly, since $\beta_2 = -.05$, when age increases by 1 year and the other three predictors remain constant, we expect VO_2max to decrease by .05 L/min.

─────

A Special Case: Polynomial Regression

Consider again the case of a single independent variable x, and suppose that a scatter plot of the n sample (x, y) pairs has the appearance of Figure 14.1. The simple linear regression model is clearly not appropriate, but it does look as though a parabola (quadratic function) with equation $y = \alpha + \beta_1 x + \beta_2 x^2$ would provide a very good fit to the data for appropriately chosen values of α, β_1, and β_2. Just as the inclusion of the random deviation e in simple linear regression allowed an observation to deviate from the population regression line by a random amount, adding e to this quadratic function yields a probabilistic model in which an observation is allowed to fall above or below the parabola. The model equation is

$$y = \alpha + \beta_1 x + \beta_2 x^2 + e$$

FIGURE 14.1 A scatter plot that suggests the appropriateness of a quadratic probabilistic model

Let's rewrite the model equation by using x_1 to denote x and x_2 to denote x^2. The model equation then becomes

$$y = \alpha + \beta_1 x_1 + \beta_2 x_2 + e$$

This is a special case of the general multiple regression model with $k = 2$. You may wonder about the legitimacy of allowing one predictor variable to be a mathematical function of another predictor — here, $x_2 = (x_1)^2$. However, there is absolutely nothing in the general multiple regression model that prevents this. *In the model* $y = \alpha + \beta_1 x_1 + \cdots + \beta_k x_k + e$, *it is permissible to have several predictors that are mathematical functions of other predictors.* For example, starting with the two independent variables x_1 and x_2, we could create a model with $k = 4$ predictors in which x_1 and x_2 themselves are the first two predictor variables and $x_3 = (x_1)^2$, $x_4 = x_1 x_2$. (We will soon discuss the consequences of using a predictor such as x_4.) In particular, the general polynomial regression model begins with a single independent variable x and creates predictors $x_1 = x, x_2 = x^2, x_3 = x^3, \ldots, x_k = x^k$ for some specified value of k.

Definition

The **kth-degree polynomial regression model**

$$y = \alpha + \beta_1 x + \beta_2 x^2 + \cdots + \beta_k x^k + e$$

is a special case of the general multiple regression model with $x_1 = x$, $x_2 = x^2$, ..., $x_k = x^k$.

The **population regression function** (mean value of y for fixed values of the predictors) is

$$\alpha + \beta_1 x + \cdots + \beta_k x^k$$

The most important special case other than simple linear regression ($k = 1$) is the **quadratic regression model**

$$y = \alpha + \beta_1 x + \beta_2 x^2 + e$$

This model replaces the line of mean values $\alpha + \beta x$ in simple linear regression with a parabolic curve of mean values $\alpha + \beta_1 x + \beta_2 x^2$. If $\beta_2 > 0$, the curve opens upward, whereas if $\beta_2 < 0$, the curve opens downward (Figure 14.2). A less frequently encountered special case is that of cubic regression, in which $k = 3$.

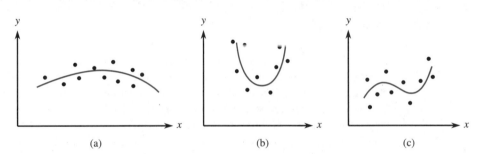

FIGURE 14.2 Polynomial regression: (a) Quadratic regression model with $\beta_2 < 0$; (b) Quadratic regression model with $\beta_2 > 0$; (c) Cubic regression model with $\beta_3 > 0$

EXAMPLE 14.2

Researchers have examined a variety of climatic variables in an attempt to gain an understanding of the mechanisms that govern rainfall runoff. The article "The Applicability of Morton's and Penman's Evapotranspiration Estimates in Rainfall Runoff Modeling" (*Water Resources Bull.* (1991): 611–620) reported on a study in which data on

$$x = \text{cloud cover}$$

and

$$y = \text{daily sunshine (hr)}$$

was gathered from a number of different locations. The authors used a cubic regression model to relate these variables (see Figure 14.2(c)). Suppose that the actual model equation for a particular location is

$$y = 11 - .400x - .250x^2 + .005x^3 + e$$

Then the population regression function is

(mean daily sunshine for given cloud cover x) $= 11 - .400x - .250x^2 + .005x^3$

For example,

(mean daily sunshine when cloud cover is 4) $= 11 - (.400)(4) - (.250)(4)^2 + (.005)(4)^3$
$$= 5.72$$

If $\sigma = 1$, it is quite likely that an observation on daily sunshine made when $x = 4$ would be between 3.72 and 7.72 hr.

The interpretation of β_i previously given for the general multiple regression model cannot be applied in polynomial regression. This is because all predictors are functions of the single variable x, so $x_i = x^i$ cannot be increased by 1 unit without changing the values of all the other predictor variables as well. *In general, the interpretation of regression coefficients requires extra care when some predictor variables are mathematical functions of other variables.*

Interaction Between Variables

Suppose that an industrial chemist is interested in the relationship between product yield (y) from a certain chemical reaction and two independent variables, $x_1 = $ reaction temperature and $x_2 = $ pressure at which the reaction is carried out. The chemist initially suggests that for temperature values between 80 and 110 in combination with pressure values ranging from 50 to 70, the relationship can be well described by the probabilistic model

$$y = 1200 + 15x_1 - 35x_2 + e$$

The regression function, which gives the mean y value for any specified values of x_1 and x_2, is then $1200 + 15x_1 - 35x_2$. Consider this mean y value for three different particular temperature values:

$x_1 = 90$:   mean y value $= 1200 + (15)(90) - 35x_2 = 2550 - 35x_2$

$x_1 = 95$:   mean y value $= 2625 - 35x_2$

$x_1 = 100$:   mean y value $= 2700 - 35x_2$

Graphs of these three mean value functions (each a function only of pressure x_2, since the temperature value has been specified) are shown in Figure 14.3(a). Each graph is a straight line, and the three lines are parallel, each one having slope -35. Because of this, the average change in yield when pressure x_2 is increased by 1 unit is -35, irrespective of the fixed temperature value.

Since chemical theory suggests that the decline in average yield when pressure x_2 increases should be more rapid for a high temperature than for a low temperature, the chemist now has reason to doubt the appropriateness of the proposed model. Rather than the lines being parallel, the line for a temperature of 100 should be steeper than the line for a temperature of 95, and that line in turn should be steeper than the one for $x_1 = 90$. A model that has this property includes, in addi-

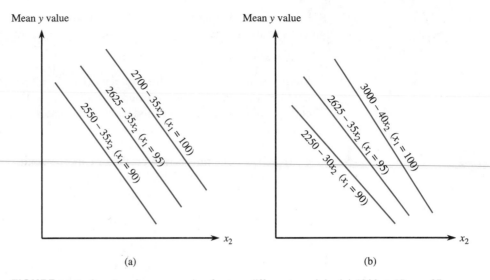

FIGURE 14.3 Graphs of mean y value for two different models: (a) $1200 + 15x_1 - 35x_2$; (b) $-4500 + 75x_1 + 60x_2 - x_1x_2$

tion to predictors x_1 and x_2 separately, a third predictor variable $x_3 = x_1x_2$. One such model is

$$y = -4500 + 75x_1 + 60x_2 - x_1x_2 + e$$

which has regression function $-4500 + 75x_1 + 60x_2 - x_1x_2$. Then

$$\text{(mean } y \text{ value when } x_1 = 100) = -4500 + (75)(100) + 60x_2 - 100x_2$$
$$= 3000 - 40x_2$$

whereas

$$\text{(mean } y \text{ value when } x_1 = 95) = 2625 - 35x_2$$
$$\text{(mean } y \text{ value when } x_1 = 90) = 2250 - 30x_2$$

These are graphed in Figure 14.3(b), where it is clear that the three slopes are different. In fact, each different value of x_1 yields a different slope, so the average change in yield associated with a 1-unit increase in x_2 depends on the value of x_1. When this is the case, the two variables are said to *interact*.

Definition

If the change in the mean y value associated with a 1-unit increase in one independent variable depends on the value of a second independent variable, there is **interaction** between these two variables. When the variables are denoted by x_1 and x_2, such interaction can be modeled by including x_1x_2, the product of the variables that interact, as a predictor variable.

The general equation for a multiple regression model based on two independent variables x_1 and x_2 that also includes an interaction predictor is

$$y = \alpha + \beta_1 x_1 + \beta_2 x_2 + \beta_3 x_1 x_2 + e$$

When x_1 and x_2 do interact, this model will usually give a much better fit to resulting sample data — and thus explain more variation in y — than would the no-interaction model. Failure to consider a model with interaction often leads an investigator to conclude incorrectly that there is no strong relationship between y and a set of independent variables.

More than one interaction predictor can be included in the model when more than two independent variables are available. If, for example, there are three independent variables x_1, x_2, and x_3, one possible model is

$$y = \alpha + \beta_1 x_1 + \beta_2 x_2 + \beta_3 x_3 + \beta_4 x_4 + \beta_5 x_5 + \beta_6 x_6 + e$$

where

$$x_4 = x_1 x_2 \qquad x_5 = x_1 x_3 \qquad x_6 = x_2 x_3$$

One could even include a three-way interaction predictor $x_7 = x_1 x_2 x_3$ (the product of all three independent variables), although in practice this is rarely done.

In applied work, quadratic terms, such as x_1^2 and x_2^2, are often included to model a curved relationship between y and several independent variables. For example, a frequently used model involving just two independent variables x_1 and x_2 but $k = 5$ predictors is the *full quadratic* or **complete second-order model**

$$y = \alpha + \beta_1 x_1 + \beta_2 x_2 + \beta_3 x_1 x_2 + \beta_4 x_1^2 + \beta_5 x_2^2 + e$$

This model replaces the straight lines of Figure 14.3 with parabolas (each one is the graph of the regression function for different values of x_2 when x_1 has a fixed value). With four independent variables, one could examine a model containing four quadratic predictors and six two-way interaction predictor variables. Clearly, with just a few independent variables, one could examine a great many different multiple regression models. In the last section of this chapter, we briefly discuss methods for selecting one model from a number of competing models.

Qualitative Predictor Variables

Up to this point, we have explicitly considered the inclusion only of quantitative (numerical) predictor variables in a multiple regression model. Using a simple numerical coding, qualitative (categorical) variables can also be incorporated into a model. Let's focus first on a dichotomous variable, one with just two possible categories: male or female, U.S. or foreign manufacture, a house with or without a view, and so on. With any such variable, we associate a numerical variable x whose possible values are 0 and 1, where 0 is identified with one category (for example, married) and $x = 1$ with the other possible category (not married). This 0–1 variable is often called a **dummy variable** or **indicator variable.**

EXAMPLE 14.3   The article "Grade Level and Gender Differences in Writing Self-Beliefs of Middle School Students" (*Contemporary Educational Psych.* (1999): 390–405) considered relating writing competence score to a number of predictor variables, including perceived value of writing and gender. Writing competence and perceived value of writing were both represented by a numerically scaled variable, but gender is a qualitative predictor.

Let

$$y = \text{writing competence score}$$

$$x_1 = \begin{cases} 0 & \text{if male} \\ 1 & \text{if female} \end{cases}$$

$$x_2 = \text{perceived value of writing}$$

One possible multiple regression model is

$$y = \alpha + \beta_1 x_1 + \beta_2 x_2 + e$$

Considering the mean y value first when $x_1 = 0$ and then when $x_1 = 1$ yields

$$\text{average score} = \alpha + \beta_2 x_2 \qquad \text{when } x_1 = 0 \text{ (males)}$$
$$\text{average score} = \alpha + \beta_1 + \beta_2 x_2 \qquad \text{when } x_1 = 1 \text{ (females)}$$

The coefficient β_1 is the difference in average writing competence score between males and females when perceived value of writing is held fixed.

A second possibility is a model with an interaction term:

$$y = \alpha + \beta_1 x_1 + \beta_2 x_2 + \beta_3 x_1 x_2 + e$$

The regression function for this model is $\alpha + \beta_1 x_1 + \beta_2 x_2 + \beta_3 x_3$, where $x_3 = x_1 x_2$. Now the two cases $x_1 = 0$ and $x_1 = 1$ give

$$\text{average score} = \alpha + \beta_2 x_2 \qquad \text{when } x_1 = 0$$
$$\text{average score} = \alpha + \beta_1 + (\beta_2 + \beta_3) x_2 \qquad \text{when } x_1 = 1$$

For each model, the graph of the average writing competence score, when regarded as a function of perceived value of writing is a line for either gender (Figure 14.4).

FIGURE 14.4 Regression functions for models with one qualitative variable (x_1) and one quantitative variable (x_2): (a) No interaction; (b) Interaction

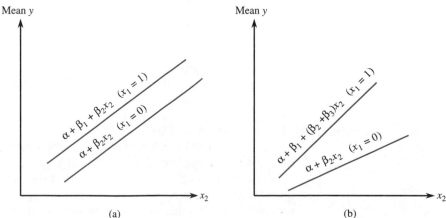

In the no-interaction model, the coefficient on x_2 is β_2 both when $x_1 = 0$ and when $x_1 = 1$, so the two lines are parallel, although their intercepts are different (unless $\beta_1 = 0$). With interaction, the lines not only have different intercepts but also different slopes (unless $\beta_3 = 0$). For this latter model, the change in average writing competence score when perceived value of writing increases by 1 unit depends on gender — the two variables *perceived value* and *gender* interact.

You might think that the way to handle a three-category situation is to define a single numerical variable with coded values such as 0, 1, and 2 corresponding to the three categories. This is incorrect, because it imposes an ordering on the categories that is not necessarily implied by the problem. The correct approach to modeling a categorical variable with three categories is to define *two* different 0–1 variables.

EXAMPLE 14.4

The article "The Effect of Ownership on the Organization Structure in Small Firms" (*Admin. Sci. Quarterly* (1984): 232–237) considers three different management status categories — owner-successors, professional managers, and owner-founders — in relating degree of horizontal differentiation (y) to firm size. Let

$$x_1 = \begin{cases} 1 & \text{if the firm is managed by owner-successors} \\ 0 & \text{otherwise} \end{cases}$$

$$x_2 = \begin{cases} 1 & \text{if the firm is managed by professional managers} \\ 0 & \text{otherwise} \end{cases}$$

x_3 = firm size

Thus, $x_1 = 1$, $x_2 = 0$ indicates owner-successors; $x_1 = 0$, $x_2 = 1$, professional managers; and $x_1 = x_2 = 0$, owner-founders. ($x_1 = x_2 = 1$ is not possible.) The author suggests an interaction model of the form

$$y = \alpha + \beta_1 x_1 + \beta_2 x_2 + \beta_3 x_3 + \beta_4 x_1 x_3 + \beta_5 x_2 x_3 + e$$

This model allows the change in mean differentiation when size increases by 1 to be different for all three management status categories.

In general, incorporating a categorical variable with c possible categories into a regression model requires the use of $c - 1$ indicator variables. Thus, even one such categorical variable can add many predictors to a model.

Nonlinear Multiple Regression Models

Many nonlinear relationships can be put in the form $y = \alpha + \beta_1 x_1 + \cdots + \beta_k x_k + e$ by transforming one or more of the variables. An appropriate transformation could be suggested by theory or by various plots of the data (for example, residual plots after fitting a particular model). There are also relationships that cannot be linearized by transformations, in which case more complicated methods of analysis must be used. A general discussion of nonlinear regression is beyond the scope of this text; you can learn more by consulting one of the sources listed in the Chapter 5 references.

Exercises 14.1 – 14.14

14.1 Explain the difference between a deterministic and a probabilistic model. Give an example of a dependent variable y and two or more independent variables that might be related to y deterministically. Give an example of a dependent variable y and two or more independent variables that might be related to y in a probabilistic fashion.

14.2 A number of recent investigations have focused on the problem of assessing loads that can be manually handled in a safe manner. The article "Anthropometric, Muscle Strength, and Spinal Mobility Characteristics as Predictors in the Rating of Acceptable Loads in Parcel Sorting" (*Ergonomics* (1992): 1033–1044) proposed using a regression model to relate the dependent variable

y = individual's rating of acceptable load (kg)

to $k = 3$ independent (predictor) variables:

x_1 = extent of left lateral bending (cm)

x_2 = dynamic hand grip endurance (sec)

x_3 = trunk extension ratio (N/kg)

Suppose that the model equation is

$y = 30 + .90x_1 + .08x_2 - 4.50x_3 + e$

and that $\sigma = 5$.
  a. What is the population regression function?
  b. What are the values of the population regression coefficients?
  c. Interpret the value of β_1.
  d. Interpret the value of β_3.
  e. What is the mean value of rating of acceptable load when extent of left lateral bending is 25 cm, dynamic hand grip endurance is 200 sec, and trunk extension ratio is 10 N/kg?
  f. If repeated observations on rating are made on different individuals, all of whom have the values of x_1, x_2, and x_3 specified in part **e**, in the long run approximately what percentage of ratings will be between 13.5 kg and 33.5 kg?

14.3 The following statement appeared in the article "Dimensions of Adjustment Among College Women" (*J. College Student Development* (1998): 364):

  Regression analyses indicated that academic adjustment and race made independent contributions to academic achievement, as measured by current GPA.

Suppose

  y = current GPA

  x_1 = academic adjustment score

  x_2 = race (with white = 0, other = 1)

What multiple regression model is suggested by the statement? Did you include an interaction term in the model? Why or why not?

14.4 According to "Assessing the Validity of the Postmaterialism Index" (*American Political Science Review* (1999): 649–664), one may be able to predict an individual's level of support for ecology based on demographic and ideological characteristics. The multiple regression model proposed by the authors was

$$\hat{y} = 3.60 - .01x_1 + .01x_2 - .07x_3 + .12x_4 + .02x_5 - .04x_6 - .01x_7 - .04x_8 - .02x_9 + e$$

where the variables are defined as follows

  y = ecology score (higher values indicate a greater concern for ecology)

  x_1 = age times 10

  x_2 = income (in thousands of dollars)

  x_3 = gender (1 = male, 0 = female)

  x_4 = race (1 = white, 0 = nonwhite)

  x_5 = education (in years)

  x_6 = ideology (4 = conservative, 3 = right of center, 2 = middle of the road, 1 = left of center, and 0 = liberal)

  x_7 = social class (4 = upper, 3 = upper middle, 2 = middle, 1 = lower middle, 0 = lower)

  x_8 = postmaterialist (1 if postmaterialist, 0 otherwise)

  x_9 = materialist (1 if materialist, 0 otherwise)

a. Suppose you knew a person with the following characteristics: a 25-year-old, white female with a college degree (16 years of education), who has a $32,000-per-year job, is from the upper middle class and considers herself left of center, but who is neither a materialist nor a postmaterialist. Predict her ecology score.

b. If the woman described in part **a** were Hispanic rather than white, how would the prediction change?

c. Given that the other variables are the same, what is the estimated mean difference in ecology score for men and women?

d. How would your interpret the coefficient of x_2?

e. Comment on the numerical coding of the ideology and social class variables. Can you suggest a better way of incorporating these two variables into the model?

14.5 The article "The Influence of Temperature and Sunshine on the Alpha-Acid Contents of Hops" (*Ag. Meteorology* (1974): 375–382) used a multiple regression model to relate y = yield of hops to x_1 = mean temperature (°C) between date of coming into hop and date of picking and x_2 = mean percentage of sunshine during the same period. The model equation proposed is

$$y = 415.11 - 6.60x_1 - 4.50x_2 + e$$

a. Suppose that this equation does indeed describe the true relationship. What mean yield corresponds to a temperature of 20 and a sunshine percentage of 40?

b. What is the mean yield when the mean temperature and percentage of sunshine are 18.9 and 43, respectively?

c. Interpret the values of the population regression coefficients.

14.6 The article "Readability of Liquid Crystal Displays: A Response Surface" (*Human Factors* (1983): 185–190) used a multiple regression model with four independent variables, where

y = error percentage for subjects reading a four-digit liquid crystal display

x_1 = level of backlight (from 0 to 122 cd/m²)

x_2 = character subtense (from .025° to 1.34°)

x_3 = viewing angle (from 0° to 60°)

x_4 = level of ambient light (from 20 to 1500 lx)

The model equation suggested in the article is

$$y = 1.52 + .02x_1 - 1.40x_2 + .02x_3 - .0006x_4 + e$$

a. Assume that this is the correct equation. What is the mean value of y when $x_1 = 10$, $x_2 = .5$, $x_3 = 50$, and $x_4 = 100$?

b. What mean error percentage is associated with a backlight level of 20, character subtense of .5, viewing angle of 10, and ambient light level of 30?

c. Interpret the values of β_2 and β_3.

14.7 The article "Pulp Brightness Reversion: Influence of Residual Lignin on the Brightness Reversion of Bleached Sulfite and Kraft Pulps" (*TAPPI* (1964): 653–662) proposed a quadratic regression model to describe the relationship between x = degree of delignification during the processing of wood pulp for paper and y = total chlorine content. Suppose that the actual model is

$$y = 220 + 75x - 4x^2 + e$$

a. Graph the regression function $220 + 75x - 4x^2$ over x values between 2 and 12. (Substitute $x = 2, 4, 6, 8, 10$, and 12 to find points on the graph, and connect them with a smooth curve.)

b. Would mean chlorine content be higher for a degree of delignification value of 8 or 10?

c. What is the change in mean chlorine content when the degree of delignification increases from 8 to 9? From 9 to 10?

14.8 The relationship between yield of maize, date of planting, and planting density was investigated in the article "Development of a Model for Use in Maize Replant Decisions" (*Agronomy J.* (1980): 459–464). Let

y = percent maize yield

x_1 = planting date (days after April 20)

x_2 = planting density (plants/ha)

The regression model with both quadratic terms ($y = \alpha + \beta_1x_1 + \beta_2x_2 + \beta_3x_3 + \beta_44x_4 + e$, where $x_3 = x_1^2$ and $x_4 = x_2^2$) provides a good description of the relationship between y and the independent variables.

a. If $\alpha = 21.09$, $\beta_1 = .653$, $\beta_2 = .0022$, $\beta_3 = -.0206$, and $\beta_4 = .00004$, what is the population regression function?

b. Use the regression function in part **a** to determine the mean yield for a plot planted on May 6 with a density of 41,180 plants/ha.

c. Would the mean yield be higher for a planting date of May 6 or May 22 (for the same density)?

d. Is it legitimate to interpret $\beta_1 = .653$ as the true average change in yield when planting date increases by one day and the values of the other three predictors are held fixed? Why or why not?

14.9 Suppose that the variables y, x_1, and x_2 are related by the regression model

$$y = 1.8 + .1x_1 + .8x_2 + e$$

a. Construct a graph (similar to that of Figure 14.4) showing the relationship between mean y and x_2 for fixed values 10, 20, and 30 of x_1.

b. Construct a graph depicting the relationship between mean y and x_1 for fixed values 50, 55, and 60 of x_2.

c. What aspect of the graphs in parts **a** and **b** can be attributed to the lack of an interaction between x_1 and x_2?

d. Suppose the interaction term $.03x_3$, where $x_3 = x_1x_2$, is added to the regression model equation. Using this new model, construct the graphs described in parts **a** and **b**. How do they differ from those obtained in parts **a** and **b**?

14.10 A manufacturer of wood stoves collected data on y = particulate matter concentration and x_1 = flue temperature for three different air intake settings (low, medium, high).

a. Write a model equation that includes dummy variables to incorporate intake setting, and interpret all the β coefficients.

b. What additional predictors would be needed to incorporate interaction between temperature and intake setting?

14.11 Consider a regression analysis with three independent variables x_1, x_2, and x_3. Give the equation for the following regression models.

a. The model that includes as predictors all independent variables but no quadratic or interaction terms

b. The model that includes as predictors all independent variables and all quadratic terms

c. All models that include as predictors all independent variables, no quadratic terms, and exactly one interaction term

d. The model that includes as predictors all independent variables, all quadratic terms, and all interaction terms (the full quadratic model)

14.12 The article "The Value and the Limitations of High-Speed Turbo-Exhausters for the Removal of Tar-Fog from Carburetted Water-Gas" (*Soc. Chem. Industry*

J. (1946): 166–168) presented data on y = tar content (grains/100 ft^3) of a gas stream as a function of x_1 = rotor speed (rev/min) and x_2 = gas inlet temperature (°F). A regression model using x_1, x_2, $x_3 = x_2^2$, and $x_4 = x_1x_2$ was suggested:

mean y value $= 86.8 - .123x_1 + 5.09x_2 - .0709x_3 + .001x_4$

a. According to this model, what is the mean y value if $x_1 = 3200$ and $x_2 = 57$?

b. For this particular model, does it make sense to interpret the value of any individual β_i (β_1, β_2, β_3, or β_4) in the way we have previously suggested? Explain.

14.13 Consider the dependent variable y = fuel efficiency of a car (mpg).

a. Suppose that you want to incorporate size class of car, with four categories (subcompact, compact, midsize, and large), into a regression model that also includes x_1 = age of car and x_2 = engine size. Define the necessary dummy variables, and write out the complete model equation.

b. Suppose that you want to incorporate interaction between age and size class. What additional predictors would be needed to accomplish this?

14.14 If we knew the width and height of cylindrical tin cans of food, could we predict the volume of these cans with precision and accuracy?

a. Give the equation that would allow us to make such predictions.

b. Is the relationship between volume and its predictors, height and width, a linear one?

c. Should we use an additive multiple regression model to predict a volume of a can from its height and width? Explain.

d. If you were to take logarithms of each side of your equation in part **a**, would the relationship be linear?

14.2 Fitting a Model and Assessing Its Utility

In Section 14.1, we discussed and contrasted multiple regression models containing several different types of predictors. Let's now suppose that a particular set of k predictor variables $x_1, x_2, \ldots, x_k$ has been selected for inclusion in the model

$$y = \alpha + \beta_1x_1 + \beta_2x_2 + \cdots + \beta_kx_k + e$$

It is then necessary to estimate the model coefficients $\alpha, \beta_1, \ldots, \beta_k$ and the regression function $\alpha + \beta_1x_1 + \cdots + \beta_kx_k$ (mean y value for specified values of the predictors), assess the model's utility, and perhaps use the estimated model to make further inferences. All this, of course, requires sample data. As before, n denotes the number of observations in the sample. With just one predictor variable, the sample consisted of n (x, y) pairs. Now each observation consists of $k + 1$ numbers: a value of x_1, a value of $x_2, \ldots$, a value of x_k, and the associated value of y. The n observations are assumed to have been selected independently of one another.

EXAMPLE 14.5

Soil and sediment adsorption, the extent to which chemicals collect in a condensed form on the surface, is an important characteristic because it influences the effectiveness of pesticides and various agricultural chemicals. The article "Adsorption of Phosphates, Arsenate, Methanearsenate, and Calcodylate by Lake and Stream Sediments: Comparisons with Soils" (*J. of Environ. Qual.* (1984): 499–504) presented the accompanying data consisting of $n = 13$ (x_1, x_2, y) triples and proposed the model

$$y = \alpha + \beta_1 x_1 + \beta_2 x_2 + e$$

for relating

y = phosphate adsorption index

x_1 = amount of extractable iron

x_2 = amount of extractable aluminum

Observation	x_1 extractable iron	x_2 extractable aluminum	y adsorption index
1	61	13	4
2	175	21	18
3	111	24	14
4	124	23	18
5	130	64	26
6	173	38	26
7	169	33	21
8	169	61	30
9	160	39	28
10	244	71	36
11	257	112	65
12	333	88	62
13	199	54	40

As in simple linear regression, the principle of least squares is used to estimate the coefficients $\alpha, \beta_1, \ldots, \beta_k$. For specified estimates $a, b_1, \ldots, b_k$,

$$y - (a + b_1 x_1 + b_2 x_2 + \cdots + b_k x_k)$$

is the deviation between the observed y value for a particular observation and the predicted value using the estimated regression function $a + b_1x_1 + \cdots + b_kx_k$. For example, the first observation in the data set of Example 14.5 is $(x_1, x_2, y) = (61, 13, 4)$. The resulting deviation between observed and predicted y values is

$$4 - [a + b_1(61) + b_2(13)]$$

Deviations corresponding to other observations are expressed in a similar manner. The principle of least squares then says to use as estimates of α, β_1, and β_2 the values of a, b_1, and b_2 that minimize the sum of these squared deviations.

Definition

According to the principle of least squares, the fit of a particluar estimated regression function $a + b_1x_1 + \cdots + b_kx_k$ to the observed data is measured by the sum of squared deviations between the observed y values and the y values predicted by the estimated function:

$$\Sigma [y - (a + b_1x_1 + \cdots + b_kx_k)]^2$$

The **least squares estimates** of $\alpha, \beta_1, \ldots, \beta_k$ are those values of a, $b_1, \ldots, b_k$ that make this sum of squared deviations as small as possible.

The least squares estimates for a given data set are obtained by solving a system of $k + 1$ equations in the $k + 1$ unknowns $a, b_1, \ldots, b_k$ (called the *normal equations*). In the case $k = 1$, simple linear regression, there are only two equations, and we gave their general solution — the expressions for b and a — in Chapter 5. For $k \geq 2$, it is not as easy to write general expressions for the estimates without using advanced mathematical notation. Fortunately, the computer saves us! Formulas for the estimates have been programmed into all the commonly used statistical software packages.

EXAMPLE 14.6 Figure 14.5 displays MINITAB output from a regression command requesting that the model $y = \alpha + \beta_1x_1 + \beta_2x_2 + e$ be fit to the phosphate adsorption data of

FIGURE 14.5 MINITAB output for the regression analysis of Example 14.6

THE REGRESSION EQUATION IS
HPO = -7.35 + 0.113 FE + 0.349 AL

Predictor	Coef	Stdev	t-ratio	p
Constant	-7.351	3.485	-2.11	0.061
FE	0.11273	0.02969	3.80	0.004
AL	0.34900	0.07131	4.89	0.000

s = 4.379   R-sq = 94.8%   R-sq(adj) = 93.8%

Coefficient of multiple determination = .948

Analysis of Variance

SOURCE	DF	SS	MS	F	p
Regression	2	3529.9	1765.0	92.03	0.000
Error	10	191.8	19.2		
Total	12	3721.7			

P-value for model utility test

Example 14.5. (We named the dependent variable HPO, an abbreviation for the chlorate H_2PO_4 (dihydrogen phosphate), and the two predictor variables x_1 and x_2 were named FE and AL, the standard abbreviations for iron and aluminum, respectively.) Focus on the column labeled **Coef** (for coefficient) in the table near the top of the figure. The three numbers in this column are the estimated model coefficients:

$a = -7.351$ (the estimate of the constant term α)

$b_1 = .11273$ (the estimate of the coefficient β_1)

$b_2 = .34900$ (the estimate of the coefficient β_2)

Thus, we estimate that the average change in HPO associated with a 1-unit increase in FE while AL remains fixed is .11273. A similar interpretation applies to b_2. The estimated regression function is

(estimated mean value of y for specified x_1 and x_2 values) $= -7.351 + .11273x_1 + .34900x_2$

Substituting $x_1 = 150$ and $x_2 = 60$ gives

$$-7.351 + .11273(150) + .34900(60) = 30.5$$

which can be interpreted either as a point estimate for the mean value of HPO or as a point prediction for a single HPO value.

Is the Model Useful?

The utility of an estimated model can be assessed by examining the extent to which predicted y values based on the estimated regression function are close to the y values actually observed.

Definition

The first predicted value $\hat{y}_1$ is obtained by taking the values of the predictor variables $x_1, x_2, \ldots, x_k$ for the first sample observation and substituting these values into the extimated regression function. Doing this successively for the remaining observations yields the **predicted values** $\hat{y}_2, \ldots, \hat{y}_n$. The **residuals** are then the differences $y_1 - \hat{y}_1, y_2 - \hat{y}_2, \ldots, y_n - \hat{y}_n$, between the observed and predicted y values.

The predicted values and residuals are defined here exactly as they were in simple linear regression, but computation of the $\hat{y}$ values is more tedious because there is more than one predictor. Fortunately, the $\hat{y}$'s and $y - \hat{y}$'s are automatically computed and displayed in the output of all good statistical software packages. Consider again the phosphate adsorption data discussed in Examples 14.5 and 14.6. Since the first y observation, $y_1 = 4$, was made with $x_1 = 61$ and $x_2 = 13$, the first predicted value is

$$\hat{y}_1 = -7.351 + .11273(61) + .34900(13) \approx 4.06$$

The first residual is then

$$y_1 - \hat{y}_1 = 4 - 4.06 = -.06$$

The other predicted values and residuals are computed in a similar fashion. The sum of residuals from a least squares fit should, except for rounding effects, be zero.

As in simple linear regression, the sum of squared residuals is the basis for several important summary quantities that are indicative of a model's utility.

Definition

The **residual (or error) sum of squares, SSResid,** and **total sum of squares, SSTo,** are given by

$$\text{SSResid} = \Sigma\,(y - \hat{y})^2 \qquad \text{SSTo} = \Sigma\,(y - \bar{y})^2$$

where $\bar{y}$ is the mean of the y observations in the sample.

The number of degrees of freedom associated with SSResid is $n - (k + 1)$, because $k + 1$ df are lost in estimating the $k + 1$ coefficients $\alpha, \beta_1, \ldots, \beta_k$.

An estimate of the random deviation variance σ^2 is given by

$$s_e^2 = \frac{\text{SSResid}}{n - (k + 1)}$$

and $s_e = \sqrt{s_e^2}$ is the estimate of σ.

The **coefficient of multiple determination, R^2,** interpreted as the proportion of variation in observed y values that is explained by the fitted model, is

$$R^2 = 1 - \frac{\text{SSResid}}{\text{SSTo}}$$

EXAMPLE 14.7

Looking again at Example 14.6, which contains MINITAB output for the adsorption data fit by a two-predictor model, residual sum of squares is found in the **Error** row and **SS** column of the table headed **Analysis of Variance**: SSResid = 191.8. The associated number of degrees of freedom is $n - (k + 1) = 13 - (2 + 1) = 10$, which appears in the **DF** column just to the left of SSResid. The sample average y value is $\bar{y} = 29.85$, and SSTo $= \Sigma\,(y - 29.85)^2 = 3721.7$ appears in the **Total** row and **SS** column of the **Analysis of Variance** table just under the value of SSResid. The values of s_e^2, s_e, and R^2 are then

$$s_e^2 = \frac{\text{SSResid}}{n - (k + 1)} = \frac{191.8}{10} = 19.18 \approx 19.2$$

(in the **MS** column of the MINITAB output)

$$s_e = \sqrt{s_e^2} = \sqrt{19.18} = 4.379$$

(which appears just above the **Analysis of Variance** table)

$$R^2 = 1 - \frac{\text{SSResid}}{\text{SSTo}} = 1 - \frac{191.8}{3721.7} = 1 - .052 = .948$$

Thus, the percentage of variation explained is $100R^2 = 94.8\%$, which appears on the output as **R-sq** = 94.8%. The values of R^2 and s_e suggest that the chosen model has been very successful in relating y to the predictors.

Generally speaking, a desirable model is one that results in both a large R^2 value and a small s_e value. However, there is a catch. These two conditions can be achieved by fitting a model that contains a large number of predictors. Such a model may be successful in explaining y variation, but it almost always specifies a relationship that is unrealistic and difficult to interpret. What we really want is a simple model — one with relatively few predictors whose roles are easily interpreted and which also does a good job of explaining variation in y.

All statistical software packages include R^2 and s_e in their output, and most give SSResid also. In addition, some packages compute the quantity called **adjusted R^2**:

$$\text{adjusted } R^2 = 1 - \left[\frac{n - 1}{n - (k + 1)} \right] \cdot \frac{\text{SSResid}}{\text{SSTo}}$$

Since the quantity in square brackets exceeds 1, the number subtracted from 1 is larger than SSResid/SSTo, so adjusted R^2 is smaller than R^2. The value of R^2 must be between 0 and 1, but adjusted R^2 can be negative. If a large R^2 has been achieved through using just a few model predictors, adjusted R^2 will differ little from R^2. However, the adjustment can be substantial when a great many predictors (relative to the number of observations) have been used or when R^2 itself is small to moderate (which could happen even when there is no relationship between y and the predictors). In Example 14.6, adjusted $R^2 = .938$, not much less than R^2, since the model included only two predictor variables.

F Distributions

The model utility test in simple linear regression was based on the fact that when H_0: $\beta = 0$ is true, the test statistic $t = (b - 0)/s_b$ has a t distribution. The model utility test for multiple regression uses a type of probability distribution called an *F distribution*. We digress briefly to describe some general properties of F distributions.

An F distribution always arises in connection with a ratio in which the numerator involves one sum of squares and the denominator involves a second sum of squares. Each sum of squares has associated with it a specified number of degrees of freedom, so a particular F distribution is determined by fixing values of df_1 = numerator df and df_2 = denominator df. There is a different F distribution for each different df_1, df_2 combination. For example, there is an F distribution based on 4 numerator df and 12 denominator df, another F distribution based on 3 numerator df and 20 denominator df, and so on. A typical F curve for fixed numerator and denominator df appears in Figure 14.6. All F tests presented in this book are upper-tailed. Recall that for an upper-tailed t test, the P-value is the area under the associated t curve to the right of the calculated t. Similarly, the P-value for an upper-tailed F test is the area under the associated F curve to the right of the calculated F. Figure 14.6 illustrates this for a test based on $\text{df}_1 = 4$ and $\text{df}_2 = 6$.

FIGURE 14.6 A *P*-value for
an upper-tailed *F* test

For example, for a test with $df_1 = 4$ and $df_2 = 6$,

Unfortunately, tabulation of these upper-tail areas is much more cumbersome than for *t* distributions, because here two df's are involved. For each of a number of different *F* distributions, our *F* table (Appendix Table VII) tabulates only four numbers: the values that capture tail areas .10, .05, .01, and .001. Different columns correspond to different values of df_1 (numerator df), and each different group of rows is for a different value of df_2. Figure 14.7 shows how this is used to obtain *P*-value information.

FIGURE 14.7 Obtaining
P-value information from
the *F* table

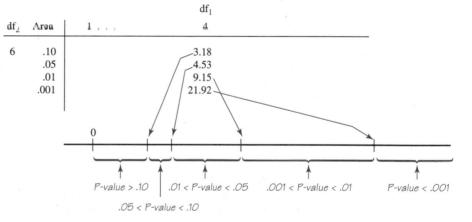

For example, for a test with $df_1 = 4$ and $df_2 = 6$,

calculated $F = 5.70 \;\Rightarrow\; .01 < P\text{-value} < .05$

calculated $F = 2.16 \;\Rightarrow\; P\text{-value} > .10$

calculated $F = 25.03 \Rightarrow P\text{-value} < .001$

Only if calculated *F* equals a tabulated value do we obtain an exact *P*-value (e.g., if calculated $F = 4.53$, then $P\text{-value} = .05$). If $.01 < P\text{-value} < .05$, we should reject H_0 at a significance level of .05 but not at a level of .01. When $P\text{-value} < .001$, H_0 would be rejected at any reasonable significance level.

The *F* Test for Model Utility

In the simple linear model with regression function $\alpha + \beta x$, if $\beta = 0$, there is no useful linear relationship between *y* and the single predictor variable *x*. Similarly, if all k coefficients $\beta_1, \beta_2, \ldots, \beta_k$, are zero in the general k-predictor multiple regression model, there is no useful linear relationship between y and *any* of the predictor variables $x_1, x_2, \ldots, x_k$ included in the model. Before using an estimated model to make further inferences (for example, predictions and estimates of mean values), it is desirable to confirm the model's utility through a formal test procedure.

Recall that SSTo is a measure of total variation in the observed y values and that SSResid measures the amount of total variation that has not been explained by the fitted model. The difference between total and error sums of squares is itself a sum of squares, called **regression sum of squares** and denoted by SSRegr:

$$SSRegr = SSTo - SSResid$$

SSRegr is interpreted as the amount of total variation that *has* been explained by the model. Intuitively, the model should be judged useful if SSRegr is large relative to SSResid, and this is achieved by using a small number of predictors relative to the sample size. The number of degrees of freedom associated with SSRegr is k, the number of model predictors, and df for SSResid is $n - (k + 1)$. The model utility F test is based on the following distributional result.

When all k β_i's are zero in the model $y = \alpha + \beta_1 x_1 + \cdots + \beta_k x_k + e$ and when the distribution of e is normal with mean 0 and variance σ^2 for any particular values of $x_1, x_2, \ldots, x_k$, the statistic

$$F = \frac{\dfrac{SSRegr}{k}}{\dfrac{SSResid}{n - (k + 1)}}$$

has an F probability distribution based on k numerator df and $n - (k + 1)$ denominator df.

The value of F tends to be larger when at least one β_i is not zero than when all the β_i's are zero, since more variation is typically explained by the model in the former case than in the latter. An F statistic value far out in the upper tail of the associated F distribution can be more plausibly attributed to at least one nonzero β_i than to something very unusual having occurred when all β_i's are zero. This is why the F test for model utility is upper-tailed.

The *F* Test for Utility of the Model $y = \alpha + \beta_1 x_1 + \cdots + \beta_k x_k + e$

Null hypothesis: $H_0: \beta_1 = \beta_2 = \cdots = \beta_k = 0$
(There is no useful linear relationship between y and *any* of the predictors.)

Alternative hypothesis: H_a: At least one among $\beta_1, \ldots, \beta_k$ is not zero.
(There is a useful linear relationship between y and *at least one* of the predictors.)

(continued)

Test statistic: $$F = \dfrac{\dfrac{\text{SSRegr}}{k}}{\dfrac{\text{SSResid}}{n - (k + 1)}}$$

where SSRegr = SSTo − SSResid.

An equivalent formula is

$$F = \dfrac{\dfrac{R^2}{k}}{\dfrac{1 - R^2}{n - (k + 1)}}$$

The test is upper-tailed, and the information in Appendix Table VII is used to obtain a bound or bounds on the P-value using numerator df = k and denominator df = $n - (k + 1)$.

Assumptions: For any particular combination of predictor variable values, the distribution of e, the random deviation, is *normal* with mean 0 and *constant variance*.

The null hypothesis is the claim that the model is not useful. Unless H_0 can be rejected at a small level of significance, the model has not demonstrated its utility, in which case the investigator must search further for a model that can be judged useful. The alternative formula for F allows the test to be carried out when only R^2, k, and n are available, as is frequently the case in published articles.

EXAMPLE 14.8   The model fit to the phosphate adsorption data introduced in Example 14.5 involved $k = 2$ predictors. The MINITAB output in Figure 14.5 contains the relevant information for carrying out the model utility test.

1. The model is $y = \alpha + \beta_1 x_1 + \beta_2 x_2 + e$, where y = phosphate adsorption, x_1 = extractable Fe, and x_2 = extractable Al.

2. $H_0: \beta_1 = \beta_2 = 0$

3. H_a: At least one of the two β_i's is not zero.

4. *Significance level*: $\alpha = .05$

5. *Test statistic*: $$F = \dfrac{\dfrac{\text{SSRegr}}{k}}{\dfrac{\text{SSResid}}{n - (k + 1)}}$$

6. *Assumptions*:   The accompanying table gives the residuals and standardized residuals (from MINITAB) for the model under consideration.

AL	FE	HPO	Residual	St Resid
13	61	4.00	-0.06	-0.02
21	175	18.00	-1.71	-0.46
24	111	14.00	0.46	0.11
23	124	18.00	3.34	0.83
64	130	26.00	-3.64	-1.04
38	173	26.00	0.59	0.14
33	169	21.00	-2.22	-0.54
61	169	30.00	-2.99	-0.73
39	160	28.00	3.70	0.89
71	244	36.00	-8.94	-2.22
112	257	65.00	4.29	1.44
88	333	62.00	1.10	0.37
54	199	40.00	6.07	1.45

A normal probability plot of the standardized residuals is shown here. The plot is quite straight, indicating that the assumption of normality of the random deviation distribution is reasonable.

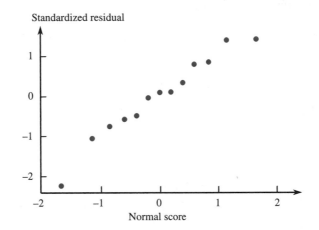

7. Directly from the **Analysis of Variance** table in Figure 14.5, the **SS** column gives SSRegr = 3529.9 and SSResid = 191.8. Thus,

$$F = \frac{\dfrac{3529.9}{2}}{\dfrac{191.8}{10}} = \frac{1764.95}{19.18} = 92.02 \quad (92.03 \text{ in Figure 14.5})$$

8. Appendix Table VII shows that for a test based on $df_1 = k = 2$ and $df_2 = n - (k + 1) = 13 - (2 + 1) = 10$, the value 14.91 captures upper-tail F curve area .001. Since calculated $F = 92.02 > 14.91$, it follows that P-value $< .001$. In fact, Figure 14.5 shows that to three decimal places, P-value $= 0$.

9. Because P-value $< .001 \le .05 = \alpha$, H_0 should be rejected. The conclusion would be the same using $\alpha = .01$ or $\alpha = .001$. The utility of the model is resoundingly confirmed.

EXAMPLE 14.9   A multiple regression analysis presented in the article "The Politics of Bureaucratic Discretion: Educational Access as an Urban Service" (*Amer. J. Political Sci.* (1991): 155–177) considered a model in which the dependent variable was

y = percentage of school board members in a school district who are black

and the predictors were

x_1 = black-to-white income ratio in the district

x_2 = percentage of whites in the district below the poverty line

x_3 = indicator for whether district was in the South

x_4 = percentage of blacks in the district with a high-school education

x_5 = black population percentage in the district

Summary quantities included $n = 140$ and $R^2 = .749$.

1. The fitted model was $y = \alpha + \beta_1 x_1 + \cdots + \beta_5 x_5 + e$.
2. $H_0: \beta_1 = \beta_2 = \beta_3 = \beta_4 = \beta_5 = 0$
3. H_a: At least one among $\beta_1, \ldots, \beta_5$ is not zero.
4. *Significance level*: $\alpha = .01$
5. *Test statistic*: $F = \dfrac{\dfrac{R^2}{k}}{\dfrac{1 - R^2}{n - (k + 1)}}$
6. *Assumptions*:   The raw data was not given in this article, so we are unable to compute standardized residuals or construct a normal probability plot. For this test to be valid, we must be willing to assume that the random deviation distribution is normal.
7. $F = \dfrac{\dfrac{.749}{5}}{\dfrac{.251}{140 - (5 + 1)}} = \dfrac{.1498}{.001873} = 80.0$
8. The test is based on $df_1 = k = 5$ and $df_2 = n - (k + 1) = 134$. This latter df is not included in the F table. However, the .001 cutoff value for $df_2 = 120$ is 4.42, and for $df_2 = 240$ it is 4.25; so for $df_2 = 134$, the cutoff value is roughly 4.4. Clearly, 80.0 greatly exceeds this value, implying that P-value $< .001$.
9. Since P-value $< .001 \leq .01 = \alpha$, H_0 is rejected at significance level .01. There appears to be a useful linear relationship between y and at least one of the five predictors.

In the next section, we presume that a model has been judged useful by the F test and then show how the estimated coefficients and regression function can be used to draw further conclusions. However, you should realize that in many applications, there will be more than one model whose utility could be confirmed by the F test. Suppose, for example, that data has been collected on six independent variables x_1, $x_2, \ldots, x_6$. Then a model with all six of these as predictors might be judged useful, another useful model might have only x_1, x_3, x_5, and x_6 as predictors, and yet another useful model might incorporate the six predictors x_1, x_4, x_6, $x_7 = x_1x_4$, $x_8 = x_1^2$, and $x_9 = x_6^2$. In the last section of this chapter, we briefly consider strategies for selecting a model.

Exercises 14.15 – 14.35

14.15 The article cited in Example 14.1 recommended the following estimated regression equation for relating $y = $ VO$_2$max (L/min) to the predictors $x_1 = $ gender (female = 0, male = 1), $x_2 = $ weight (lb), $x_3 = $ 1-mile walk time (min), and $x_4 = $ heart rate at the end of the walk (beats/min):

$$\hat{y} = 3.5959 + .6566x_1 + .0096x_2 - .0996x_3 - .0080x_4$$

a. How would you interpret the value of $b_3 = -.0996$?
b. How would you interpret the value of $b_1 = .6566$?
c. Suppose that an observation made on a male whose weight was 80 kg, walk time was 11 min, and heart rate was 140 beats/min resulted in VO$_2$max = 3.15. What would you have predicted for VO$_2$max, and what is the corresponding residual?
d. It SSResid = 30.1033 and SSTo = 102.3922, what proportion of observed variation in VO$_2$max can be attributed to the model relationship?
e. The sample size was $n = 196$. Calculate an estimate of σ.

14.16 When coastal power stations take in large quantities of cooling water, it is inevitable that a number of fish are drawn in with the water. Various methods have been designed to screen out the fish. The article "Multiple Regression Analysis for Forecasting Critical Fish Influxes at Power Station Intakes" (*J. Appl. Ecol.* (1983): 33–42) examined intake fish catch at an English power plant and several other variables thought to affect fish intake:

$y = $ fish intake (number of fish)

$x_1 = $ water temperature (°C)

$x_2 = $ number of pumps running

$x_3 = $ sea state (values 0, 1, 2, or 3)

$x_4 = $ speed (knots)

Part of the data given in the article was used to obtain the estimated regression equation

$$\hat{y} = 92 - 2.18x_1 - 19.20x_2 - 9.38x_3 + 2.32x_4$$

(based on $n = 26$). SSRegr = 1486.9 and SSResid = 2230.2 were also calculated.
a. Interpret the values of b_1 and b_4.
b. What proportion of observed variation in fish intake can be explained by the model relationship?
c. Estimate the value of σ.
d. Calculate adjusted R^2. How does it compare to R^2 itself?

14.17 Obtain as much information as you can about the P-value for an upper-tailed F test in each of the following situations.
a. df$_1 = 3$, df$_2 = 15$, calculated $F = 4.23$
b. df$_1 = 4$, df$_2 = 18$, calculated $F = 1.95$
c. df$_1 = 5$, df$_2 = 20$, calculated $F = 4.10$
d. df$_1 = 4$, df$_2 = 35$, calculated $F = 4.58$

14.18 Obtain as much information as you can about the P-value for the F test for model utility in each of the following situations.
a. $k = 2, n = 21$, calculated $F = 2.47$
b. $k = 8, n = 25$, calculated $F = 5.98$
c. $k = 5, n = 26$, calculated $F = 3.00$
d. The full quadratic model based on x_1, x_2 is fit, $n = 20$, and calculated $F = 8.25$.
e. $k = 5, n = 100$, calculated $F = 2.33$

14.19 The ability of ecologists to identify regions of greatest species richness could have an impact on the preservation of genetic diversity, a major objective of the World Conservation Strategy. The article "Prediction of Rarities from Habitat Variables: Coastal Plain Plants on Nova Scotian Lakeshores" (*Ecology* (1992): 1852–1859) used a sample of $n = 37$ lakes to obtain the estimated regression equation

$$\hat{y} = 3.89 + .033x_1 + .024x_2 + .023x_3 - .0080x_4$$
$$- .13x_5 - .72x_6$$

where $y = $ species richness, $x_1 = $ watershed area, $x_2 = $ shore width, $x_3 = $ drainage (%), $x_4 = $ water color (total color units), x_5 = sand (%), and x_6 = alkalinity. The coefficient of multiple determination was reported as R^2 = .83. Use a test with significance level .01 to decide whether the chosen model is useful.

14.20   The article "Impacts of On-Campus and Off-Campus Work on First-Year Cognitive Outcomes" (*J. of College Student Devel.* (1994): 364–370) reported on a study in which y = spring 1992 math comprehension score was regressed against x_1 = fall 1991 test score, x_2 = fall 1991 academic motivation, x_3 = age, x_4 = number of credit hours, x_5 = residence (1 if on campus, 0 otherwise), x_6 = hours worked on campus, and x_7 = hours worked off campus. The sample size was n = 210, and R^2 = .543. Test to see whether there is a useful linear relationship between y and at least one of the predictors.

14.21   Return to the situation described in Exercise 14.15, and carry out the model utility test to decide whether there is a useful linear relationship between y and at least one of the four predictors.

14.22   Is the model fit in Exercise 14.16 useful? Carry out a test using a significance level of .10.

14.23   The accompanying MINITAB output results from fitting the model described in Exercise 14.12 to data.

Predictor	Coef	Stdev	t-ratio
Constant	86.85	85.39	1.02
X1	-0.12297	0.03276	-3.75
X2	5.090	1.969	2.58
X3	-0.07092	0.01799	-3.94
X4	0.0015380	0.0005560	2.77

s = 4.784   R-sq = 90.8%   R-sq(adj) = 89.4%

ANALYSIS OF VARIANCE

	DF	SS	MS
Regression	4	5896.6	1474.2
Error	26	595.1	22.9
Total	30	6491.7	

a. What is the estimated regression equation?
b. Using a .01 significance level, perform the model utility test.
c. Interpret the values of R^2 and s_e given in the output.

14.24   For the multiple regression model in Exercise 14.4, the value of R^2 was .06 and the adjusted R^2 was .06. The model was based on a data set with 1136 observations. Perform a model utility test for this regression.

14.25   *This exercise requires the use of a computer package.* The article "Movement and Habitat Use by Lake Whitefish During Spawning in a Boreal Lake: Integrating Acoustic Telemetry and Geographic Information Systems" (*Transactions of the American Fisheries Society*) 1999: 939–952 included the accompanying data on 17 fish caught in 1995 and 1996.

Year	Fish Number	Weight (g)	Length (mm)	Age (years)
1995	1	776	410	9
	2	580	368	11
	3	539	357	15
	4	648	373	12
	5	538	361	9
	6	891	385	9
	7	673	380	10
	8	783	400	12
1996	9	571	407	12
	10	627	410	13
	11	727	421	12
	12	867	446	19
	13	1042	478	19
	14	804	441	18
	15	832	454	12
	16	764	440	12
	17	727	427	12

a. Fit a multiple regression model to describe the relationship between weight and the predictors *length* and *age*.
b. Carry out the model utility test to determine whether the predictors *length* and *age*, together, are useful for predicting weight.

14.26   *This exercise requires the use of a computer package.* The authors of the article "Absolute Versus per Unit Body Length Speed of Prey as an Estimator of Vulnerability to Predation" (*Animal Behaviour* (1999): 347–352) found that the speed of a prey (twips/s) and the length of a prey (twips × 100) are good predictors of the time (s) required to catch the prey. (A twip is a measure of distance used by programmers.) Data was collected in an experiment where subjects were asked to "catch" an animal of prey moving across his or her computer screen by clicking on it with the mouse. The investigators varied the length of the prey and the speed with which the prey moved across the screen. The following data is consistent with summary values and a graph given in the article. Each value represents the average catch time over all subjects. The order of the various speed–length combinations was randomized for each subject.

Subject	Prey Length	Prey Speed	Catch Time
1	7	20	1.10
2	6	20	1.20
3	5	20	1.23
4	4	20	1.40
5	3	20	1.50
6	3	40	1.40
7	4	40	1.36
8	6	40	1.30
9	7	40	1.28
10	7	80	1.40
11	6	60	1.38
12	5	80	1.40
13	7	100	1.43
14	6	100	1.43
15	7	120	1.70
16	5	80	1.50
17	3	80	1.40
18	6	100	1.50
19	3	120	1.90

a. Fit a multiple regression model for predicting catch time using prey length and speed as predictors.

b. Predict the catch time for an animal of prey whose length is 6 and whose speed is 50.

c. Is the multiple regression model useful for predicting catch time? Test the relevant hypotheses using $\alpha = .05$.

d. The authors of the article suggest that a simple linear regression model with the single predictor

$$x = \frac{\text{length}}{\text{speed}}$$

might be a better model for predicting catch time. Calculate the x values and use them to fit this linear regression model.

e. Which of the two models considered (the multiple regression model from part **a** or the simple linear regression model from part **d**) would you recommend for predicting catch time? Justify your choice.

14.27 *This exercise requires the use of a computer package.* The article "Vital Dimensions in Volume Perception: Can the Eye Fool the Stomach?" (*Journal of Marketing*

Data for Exercise 14.27

Row	Material	Height	Maxwidth	Minwidth	Elongation	Volume
1	glass	7.7	2.50	1.80	1.50	125
2	glass	6.2	2.90	2.70	1.07	135
3	glass	8.5	2.15	2.00	1.98	175
4	glass	10.4	2.90	2.60	1.79	285
5	plastic	8.0	3.20	3.15	1.25	330
6	glass	8.7	2.00	1.80	2.17	90
7	glass	10.2	1.60	1.50	3.19	120
8	plastic	10.5	4.80	3.80	1.09	520
9	plastic	3.4	5.90	5.00	.29	330
10	plastic	6.9	5.80	4.75	.59	570
11	tin	10.9	2.90	2.80	1.88	340
12	plastic	9.7	2.45	2.10	1.98	175
13	glass	10.1	2.60	2.20	1.94	240
14	glass	13.0	2.60	2.60	2.50	240
15	glass	13.0	2.70	2.60	2.41	360
16	glass	11.0	3.10	2.90	1.77	310
17	cardboard	8.7	5.10	5.10	.85	635
18	cardboard	17.1	10.20	10.20	.84	1250
19	glass	16.5	3.50	3.50	2.36	650
20	glass	16.5	2.70	1.20	3.06	305
21	glass	9.7	3.00	1.70	1.62	315
22	glass	17.8	2.70	1.75	3.30	305
23	glass	14.0	2.50	1.70	2.80	245
24	glass	13.6	2.40	1.20	2.83	200
25	plastic	27.9	4.40	1.20	3.17	1205
26	tin	19.5	7.50	7.50	1.30	2330
27	tin	13.8	4.25	4.25	1.62	730

Research (1999): 313–326) gave the accompanying data on dimensions of 27 representative food products.

a. Fit a multiple regression model for predicting the volume (in ml) of a package based on its minimum width, maximum width, and elongation score.

b. Why should we consider adjusted R^2 instead of R^2 when attempting to determine the quality of fit of the data to our model?

c. Perform a model utility test.

14.28 The article "The Caseload Controversy and the Study of Criminal Courts" (*J. Criminal Law and Criminology* (1979): 89–101) used a multiple regression analysis to help assess the impact of judicial caseload on the processing of criminal court cases. Data was collected in the Chicago criminal courts on the following variables:

y = number of indictments

x_1 = number of cases on the docket

x_2 = number of cases pending in criminal court trial system

The estimated regression equation (based on $n = 367$ observations) was

$$\hat{y} = 28 - .05x_1 - .003x_2 + .00002x_3$$

where $x_3 = x_1x_2$.

a. The reported value of R^2 was .16. Conduct the model utility test. Use a .05 significance level.

b. Given the results of the test in part **a**, does it surprise you that the R^2 value is so low? Can you think of a possible explanation for this?

c. How does adjusted R^2 compare to R^2?

14.29 The article "The Undrained Strength of Some Thawed Permafrost Soils" (*Canad. Geotech. J.* (1979): 420–427) contained the accompanying data on y = shear strength of sandy soil (kPa), x_1 = depth (m), and x_2 = water content (%). The predicted values and residuals were computed using the estimated regression equation $\hat{y} = -151.36 - 16.22x_1 + 13.48x_2 + .094x_3 - .253x_4 + .492x_5$, where $x_3 = x_1^2$, $x_4 = x_2^2$, and $x_5 = x_1x_2$.

y	x_1	x_2	Predicted y	Residual
14.7	8.9	31.5	23.35	−8.65
48.0	36.6	27.0	46.38	1.62
25.6	36.8	25.9	27.13	−1.53
10.0	6.1	39.1	10.99	−.99
16.0	6.9	39.2	14.10	1.90
16.8	6.9	38.3	16.54	.26
20.7	7.3	33.9	23.34	−2.64
38.8	8.4	33.8	25.43	13.37

(*continued*)

y	x_1	x_2	Predicted y	Residual
16.9	6.5	27.9	15.63	1.27
27.0	8.0	33.1	24.29	2.71
16.0	4.5	26.3	15.36	.64
24.9	9.9	37.8	29.61	−4.71
7.3	2.9	34.6	15.38	−8.08
12.8	2.0	36.4	7.96	4.84

a. Use the given information to compute SSResid, SSTo, and SSRegr.

b. Calculate R^2 for this regression model. How would you interpret this value?

c. Use the value of R^2 from part **b** and a .05 level of significance to conduct the appropriate model utility test.

14.30 The article "Readability of Liquid Crystal Displays: A Response Surface" (*Human Factors* (1983): 185–190) used the estimated regression equation

$$\hat{y} = 1.52 + .02x_1 - 1.40x_2 + .02x_3 - .0006x_4$$

to describe the relationship between y = error percentage for subjects reading a four-digit liquid crystal display and the independent variables x_1 = level of backlight, x_2 = character subtense, x_3 = viewing angle, and x_4 = level of ambient light. From a table given in the article, SSRegr = 19.2, SSResid = 20.0, and $n = 30$.

a. Does the estimated regression equation specify a useful relationship between y and the independent variables? Use the model utility test with a .05 significance level.

b. Calculate R^2 and s_e for this model. Interpret these values.

c. Do you think that the estimated regression equation would provide reasonably accurate predictions of error rate? Explain.

14.31 The article "Effect of Manual Defoliation on Pole Bean Yield" (*J. Econ. Ent.* (1984): 1019–1023) used a quadratic regression model to describe the relationship between y = yield (kg/plot) and x = defoliation level (a proportion between 0 and 1). The estimated regression equation based on $n = 24$ was $\hat{y} = 12.39 + 6.67x_1 - 15.25x_2$, where $x_1 = x$ and $x_2 = x^2$. The article also reported that R^2 for this model was .902. Does the quadratic model specify a useful relationship between y and x? Carry out the appropriate test using a .01 level of significance.

14.32 Suppose that a multiple regression data set consists of $n = 15$ observations. For what values of k, the number of model predictors, would the corresponding model with $R^2 = .90$ be judged useful at significance level .05? Does such a large R^2 value necessarily imply a useful model? Explain.

14.33 *This exercise requires the use of a computer package.* Use the data given in Exercise 14.29 to verify that the true regression function

$$\text{mean } y \text{ value} = \alpha + \beta_1 x_1 + \beta_2 x_2 + \beta_3 x_3 + \beta_4 x_4 + \beta_5 x_5$$

is estimated by

$$\hat{y} = -151.36 - 16.22x_1 + 13.48x_2 + .094x_3 - .253x_4 + .492x_5$$

14.34 *This exercise requires the use of a computer package.* The accompanying data resulted from a study of the relationship between y = brightness of finished paper and the independent variables x_1 = hydrogen peroxide (% by weight), x_2 = sodium hydroxide (% by weight), x_3 = silicate (% by weight), and x_4 = process temperature ("Advantages of CE-HDP Bleaching for High Brightness Kraft Pulp Production," *TAPPI* (1964): 107A–173A).

x_1	x_2	x_3	x_4	y
.2	.2	1.5	145	83.9
.4	.2	1.5	145	84.9
.2	.4	1.5	145	83.4
.4	.4	1.5	145	84.2
.2	.2	3.5	145	83.8
.4	.2	3.5	145	84.7
.2	.4	3.5	145	84.0
.4	.4	3.5	145	84.8
.2	.2	1.5	175	84.5
.4	.2	1.5	175	86.0
.2	.4	1.5	175	82.6
.4	.4	1.5	175	85.1
.2	.2	3.5	175	84.5
.4	.2	3.5	175	86.0
.2	.4	3.5	175	84.0
.4	.4	3.5	175	85.4
.1	.3	2.5	160	82.9
.5	.3	2.5	160	85.5
.3	.1	2.5	160	85.2
.3	.5	2.5	160	84.5
.3	.3	.5	160	84.7
.3	.3	4.5	160	85.0
.3	.3	2.5	130	84.9
.3	.3	2.5	190	84.0
.3	.3	2.5	160	84.5
.3	.3	2.5	160	84.7
.3	.3	2.5	160	84.6

(continued)

x_1	x_2	x_3	x_4	y
.3	.3	2.5	160	84.9
.3	.3	2.5	160	84.9
.3	.3	2.5	160	84.5
.3	.3	2.5	160	84.6

a. Find the estimated regression equation for the model that includes all independent variables, all quadratic terms, and all interaction terms.
b. Using a .05 significance level, perform the model utility test.
c. Interpret the values of the following quantities: SSResid, R^2, s_e.

14.35 *This exercise requires the use of a computer package.* The cotton aphid poses a threat to cotton crops in Iraq. The accompanying data on

y = infestation rate (aphids/100 leaves)

x_1 = mean temperature (°C)

x_2 = mean relative humidity

appeared in the article "Estimation of the Economic Threshold of Infestation for Cotton Aphid" (*Mesopotamia J. Ag.* (1982): 71–75). Use the data to find the estimated regression equation and assess the utility of the multiple regression model

$$y = \alpha + \beta_1 x_1 + \beta_2 x_2 + e$$

y	x_1	x_2	y	x_1	x_2
61	21.0	57.0	77	24.8	48.0
87	28.3	41.5	93	26.0	56.0
98	27.5	58.0	100	27.1	31.0
104	26.8	36.5	118	29.0	41.0
102	28.3	40.0	74	34.0	25.0
63	30.5	34.0	43	28.3	13.0
27	30.8	37.0	19	31.0	19.0
14	33.6	20.0	23	31.8	17.0
30	31.3	21.0	25	33.5	18.5
67	33.0	24.5	40	34.5	16.0
6	34.3	6.0	21	34.3	26.0
18	33.0	21.0	23	26.5	26.0
42	32.0	28.0	56	27.3	24.5
60	27.8	39.0	59	25.8	29.0
82	25.0	41.0	89	18.5	53.5
77	26.0	51.0	102	19.0	48.0
108	18.0	70.0	97	16.3	79.5

14.3   Inferences Based on an Estimated Model

In the previous section, we discussed estimating the coefficients $\alpha, \beta_1, \ldots, \beta_k$ in the model $y = \alpha + \beta_1 x_1 + \cdots + \beta_k x_k + e$ (using the principle of least squares) and then showed how the usefulness of the model could be confirmed by application of the F test for model utility. If $H_0: \beta_1 = \cdots = \beta_k = 0$ cannot be rejected at a reasonably small level of significance, it must be concluded that the model does not specify a useful relationship between y and any of the predictor variables $x_1, \ldots, x_k$. The investigator must then search further for a model that does describe a useful relationship, perhaps by introducing different predictors or making variable transformations. Only if H_0 can be rejected is it appropriate to proceed further with the chosen model and make inferences based on the estimated coefficients $a, b_1, \ldots, b_k$ and the estimated regression function $y = a + b_1 x_1 + \cdots + b_k x_k$. In this section, we will consider two different types of inferential problems. One type involves drawing a conclusion about an individual regression coefficient β_i— either computing a confidence interval for β_i or testing a hypothesis concerning β_i. The second type of problem involves first fixing values of $x_1, \ldots, x_k$ and then computing either a point estimate or a confidence interval for the corresponding mean y value or predicting a future y value with a point prediction or a prediction interval.

Inferences About a Regression Coefficient

A confidence interval for and hypothesis test concerning the slope coefficient β in simple linear regression were based on facts about the sampling distribution of the statistic b used to obtain a point estimate of β. Similarly, in multiple regression, procedures for making inferences about β_i are derived from properties of the sampling distribution of b_i. Unfortunately, formulas for b_i and its standard deviation σ_{b_i} are quite complicated and cannot be stated concisely except by using some advanced mathematical notation.

The Sampling Distribution of b_i

Let b_i denote the statistic for estimating (via the principle of least squares) the coefficient β_i in the model $y = \alpha + \beta_1 x_1 + \cdots + \beta_k x_k + e$. Assumptions about this model given in Section 14.1 imply the following:

1. b_i has a normal distribution.

2. $\mu_{b_i} = \beta_i$, so b_i is an unbiased statistic for estimating β_i.

3. The standard deviation of b_i, σ_{b_i}, involves σ^2 and a complicated function of all the values of $x_1, x_2, \ldots, x_k$ in the sample. The estimated standard deviation s_{b_i} results from replacing σ^2 with s_e^2 in the formula for σ_{b_i}.

A consequence of the properties of the sampling distribution of b_i is that the standardized variable

$$t = \frac{b_i - \beta_i}{s_{b_i}}$$

has a t distribution with df $= n - (k + 1)$. This leads to a confidence interval for β_i.

A Confidence Interval for β_i

A confidence interval for β_i is

$$b_i \pm (t \text{ critical value}) \cdot s_{b_i}$$

The t critical value is based on df $= n - (k + 1)$.

Any good statistical computer package will provide both the estimated coefficients $a, b_1, \ldots, b_k$ and their estimated standard deviations $s_a, s_{b_1}, \ldots, s_{b_k}$.

EXAMPLE 14.10

Reconsider the regression of phosphate adsorption (y) against extractable iron (x_1) and extractable aluminum (x_2), with the sample data given in Example 14.5 and MINITAB output displayed in Figure 14.5. Suppose that the investigator had required a 95% confidence interval for β_1, the average change in phosphate adsorption when extractable iron increases by 1 unit and extractable aluminum is held fixed. The necessary quantities are

$$b_1 = .11273 \qquad s_{b_1} = .02969 \qquad \text{(from the \textbf{Coef} and \textbf{Stdev} columns in the output)}$$
$$\text{df} = n - (k + 1) = 13 - (2 + 1) = 10$$
$$t \text{ critical value} = 2.23$$

The resulting confidence interval is

$$b_i \pm (t \text{ critical value}) \cdot s_{b_i} = .11273 \pm (2.23)(.02969) = .11273 \pm .06621 = (.047, .179)$$

The standardized variable $t = (b_i - \beta_i)/s_{b_i}$ is also the basis for a test statistic for testing hypotheses about β_i.

Testing Hypotheses About β_i

Null hypothesis: $H_0: \beta_i =$ hypothesized value

Test statistic: $\quad t = \dfrac{b_i - \text{hypothesized value}}{s_{b_i}}$

The test is based on df $= n - (k + 1)$.

(continued)

Alternative hypothesis: *P-value:*

$H_a: \beta_i >$ hypothesized value   Area under the appropriate t curve to the right of the computed t

$H_a: \beta_i <$ hypothesized value   Area under the appropriate t curve to the left of the computed t

$H_a: \beta_i \neq$ hypothesized value   (i) $2 \cdot$ (area to the right of t) if t is positive

                                or

                                (ii) $2 \cdot$ (area to the left of t) if t is negative

Assumptions: For any particular combination of predictor variable values, the distribution of e, the random deviation from the model, is *normal* with mean 0 and *constant variance.*

The most frequently tested null hypothesis in this situation is $H_0: \beta_i = 0$. The interpretation of H_0 is that *as long as the other predictors $x_1, \ldots, x_{i-1}, x_{i+1}, \ldots, x_k$ remain in the model,* the predictor x_i provides no useful information about y, and so it can be eliminated. The test statistic for $H_0: \beta_i = 0$ simplifies to the **t ratio**

$$t = \frac{b_i}{s_{b_i}}$$

EXAMPLE 14.11   Economists are always interested in studying the factors affecting the price paid for a product. The article "Testing for Imperfect Competition at the Fulton Fish Market" (*Rand J. of Econ.* (1995): 75–92) considered a regression of y = price paid for whiting on eight different predictors. (The Fulton Fish Market, located in New York City, is the largest such market in the United States; the many dealers make it highly competitive, and whiting is one of the most frequently purchased types of fish.) There were $n = 54$ observations, and the coefficient of multiple determination was $R^2 = .992$, indicating a highly useful model (model utility $F = 697.5$, P-value $= .000$). One of the predictors used was x_3, an indicator variable for whether a purchaser was Asian. The values $b_3 = -.0463$ and $s_{b_3} = .0191$ were given. Provided that all seven other predictors remain in the model, does x_3 appear to provide useful information about y?

1. β_3 is the average difference in price paid by Asian and non-Asian purchasers when all other predictors are held fixed.

2. $H_0: \beta_3 = 0$

3. $H_a: \beta_3 \neq 0$

4. A significance level of $\alpha = .05$ was suggested in the article.

5. *Test statistic:* $t = \dfrac{b_3}{s_{b_3}}$

6. *Assumptions:*   Without raw data, we cannot assess the reasonableness of the assumptions. If we had the data, a normal probability plot or boxplot of the standardized residuals would be a good place to start. For purposes of this example, we will assume that it is reasonable to proceed with the test.

7. The test statistic value is

$$t = \frac{b_3}{s_{b_3}} = \frac{-.0463}{.0191} = -2.42$$

8. The test is based on $n - (k + 1) = 54 - (8 + 1) = 45$ df. An examination of the 40 and 60 df columns of Appendix Table IV shows that the P-value is roughly $2 \cdot (.010) = .020$.

9. Because P-value $= .020 \leq .05 = \alpha$, H_0 should be rejected. The predictor that indicates whether a purchaser is Asian does appear to provide useful information about price, over and above the information contained in the other predictors. The author of the article indicated that this result is inconsistent with the model of perfect competition.

EXAMPLE 14.12

Our analysis of the phosphate adsorption data introduced in Example 14.5 has so far focused on the model $y = \alpha + \beta_1 x_1 + \beta_2 x_2 + e$ in which x_1 (extractable iron) and x_2 (extractable aluminum) affect the response separately. Suppose that the researcher wishes to investigate the possibility of interaction between x_1 and x_2 through fitting the model with predictors x_1, x_2, and $x_3 = x_1 x_2$. We list a few of the sample values of y, x_1, and x_2, along with the corresponding values of x_3.

Observation	y	x_1	x_2	$x_3 = x_1 x_2$
1	4	61	13	793
2	18	175	21	3675
3	14	111	24	2664
$\vdots$	$\vdots$	$\vdots$	$\vdots$	$\vdots$
13	40	199	54	10,746

In practice, a statistical software package would automatically compute x_3 values upon request once x_1 and x_2 values had been entered, so hand computations would not be necessary. Figure 14.8 displays partial MINITAB output resulting from a request to fit this model. Let's use the output to see whether inclusion of the interaction predictor is justified.

FIGURE 14.8 MINITAB output for model with interaction fit to the phosphate adsorption data (x_1 = FE, x_2 = AL, $x_3 = x_1 x_2$ = FEAL)

Regression Analysis
The regression equation is
HPO = -2.37 + 0.0828 FE + 0.246 AL +0.000528 FEAL

Predictor	Coef	StDev	T	P
Constant	-2.368	7.179	-0.33	0.749
FE	0.08279	0.04818	1.72	0.120
AL	0.2460	0.1481	1.66	0.131
FEAL	0.0005278	0.0006610	0.80	0.445

S = 4.461   R-Sq = 95.2%   R-Sq(adj) = 93.6%

1. The model is $y = \alpha + \beta_1 x_1 + \beta_2 x_2 + \beta_3 x_3 + e$, where $x_3 = x_1 x_2$.
2. $H_0: \beta_3 = 0$
3. $H_a: \beta_3 \neq 0$
4. *Test statistic*: The t ratio for β_3 is

$$t = \frac{b_3}{s_{b_3}}$$

5. *Significance level*: $\alpha = .05$
6. *Assumptions*: The residuals and standardized residuals (from MINITAB) for this model are as follows:

Obs	FE	HPO	Residual	St Resid
1	61	4.00	-2.30	-0.94
2	175	18.00	-1.23	-0.33
3	111	14.00	-0.13	-0.03
4	124	18.00	2.94	0.72
5	130	26.00	-2.53	-0.77
6	173	26.00	1.23	0.30
7	169	21.00	-1.68	-0.41
8	169	30.00	-2.07	-0.52
9	160	28.00	4.24	1.01
10	244	36.00	-8.44	-2.08
11	257	65.00	3.35	1.19
12	333	62.00	-0.31	-0.13
13	199	40.00	6.94	1.68

A normal probability plot of the standardized residuals is shown here. The plot is quite straight, indicating that normality of the random error distribution is plausible.

7. Directly from the t ratio column in Figure 14.8, we find $t = .80$.
8. Figure 14.8 shows that the P-value is .445.

9. Because $.445 > .05$, H_0 cannot be rejected. The interaction predictor does not appear to be useful and can be removed from the model.

An interesting aspect of the computer output for the interaction model in the foregoing example is that the t ratios for β_1, for β_2, and for β_3 (1.72, 1.66, and .80) are all relatively small and the corresponding P-values are large, yet $R^2 = .952$ is quite large. The high R^2 value suggests a useful model (this can be confirmed by the model utility test), yet the size of each t ratio and P-value might tempt us to conclude that all three β_i's are zero. This sounds like a contradiction, but it involves a misinterpretation of the t ratios. For example, the t ratio for β_3, $t = b_3/s_{b_3}$, tests the null hypothesis H_0: $\beta_3 = 0$ *when x_1 and x_2 are included in the model*. The smallness of a given t ratio suggests that the associated predictor can be dropped from the model *as long as the other predictors are retained*. The fact that all t ratios are small in this example does not, therefore, allow us simultaneously to delete all predictors. The data does suggest deleting x_3, because the model that includes x_1 and x_2 has already been found to give a very good fit to the data and is simple to interpret. In Section 14.4, we comment further on why it might happen that all t ratios are small even when the model seems very useful.

The model utility test amounts to testing a simultaneous claim about the values of all β_i's—that they are all zero. There is also an F test for testing a hypothesis involving a specified subset consisting of at least two β_i's. For example, we might fit the model

$$y = \alpha + \beta_1 x_1 + \beta_2 x_2 + \beta_3 x_1 x_2 + \beta_4 x_1^2 + \beta_5 x_2^2 + e$$

and then wish to test H_0: $\beta_3 = \beta_4 = \beta_5 = 0$ (which says that the second-order predictors contribute nothing to the model). Please see one of the chapter references for Chapter 5 for further details.

Inferences Based on the Estimated Regression Function

The estimated regression line $\hat{y} = a + bx$ in simple linear regression was used both to estimate the mean y value when x had a specified value and to predict the associated y value for a single observation made at a particular x value. The estimated regression function for the model $y = \alpha + \beta_1 x_1 + \cdots + \beta_k x_k + e$ can be used in the same two ways. When fixed values of the predictor variables $x_1, x_2, \ldots, x_k$ are substituted into the estimated regression function

$$\hat{y} = a + b_1 x_1 + b_2 x_2 + \cdots + b_k x_k$$

the result can be used either as a point estimate of the corresponding mean y value or as a point prediction of the y value that will result from a single observation when the x_i's have the specified values.

EXAMPLE 14.13   Precise information concerning bus transit times is important when making transportation planning decisions. The article "Factors Affecting Running Time on Transit Routes" (*Transportation Research* (1983): 107–113) reported on an empirical study based on data gathered in Cincinnati, Ohio. The variables of interest were

y = running time per mile during the morning peak period (in seconds)

x_1 = number of passenger boardings per mile

x_2 = number of passenger alightings per mile

x_3 = number of signalized intersections per mile

x_4 = proportion of a route on which parking is allowed

The values of x_1 and x_2 were not necessarily equal, because observations were made over partial segments of routes (so not all passengers entered or exited on the segments). The estimated regression function was

$$\hat{y} = 169.50 + 5.07x_1 + 4.53x_2 + 6.61x_3 + 67.70x_4$$

Consider the predictor variable values $x_1 = 4.5, x_2 = 5.5, x_3 = 5$, and $x_4 = .1$. Then a point estimate for true average running time per mile when the x_i's have these values is

$$\hat{y} = 169.50 + (5.07)(4.5) + (4.53)(5.5) + (6.61)(5) + (67.70)(.1) = 257.05$$

This value 257.05 is also the predicted running time per mile for a single trip when x_1, x_2, x_3, and x_4 have the given values.

━━━━━━━

Remember that before the sample observations $y_1, y_2, \ldots, y_n$ are obtained, a and all b_i's are statistics (because they all involve the y_i's). This implies that for fixed values of $x_1, x_2, \ldots, x_k$, the estimated regression function $a + b_1x_1 + \cdots + b_kx_k$ is a statistic (its value varies from sample to sample). To obtain a confidence interval for the mean y value for specified $x_1, \ldots, x_k$ values, we need some facts about the sampling distribution of this statistic.

Properties of the Sampling Distribution of $\hat{y} = a + b_1x_1 + \cdots + b_kx_k$

Assumptions about the model $y = \alpha + \beta_1x_1 + \cdots + \beta_kx_k + e$ given in Section 14.1 imply that for fixed values of the predictors $x_1, x_2, \ldots, x_k$, the statistic $\hat{y} = a + b_1x_1 + \cdots + b_kx_k$ satisfies the following properties:

1. It has a normal distribution.

2. Its mean value is $\alpha + \beta_1x_1 + \cdots + \beta_kx_k$. That is, the statistic is unbiased for estimating the mean y value when $x_1, \ldots, x_k$ are fixed.

3. The standard deviation of $\hat{y}$ involves σ^2 and a complicated function of all the sample predictor variable values. The estimated standard deviation of $\hat{y}$, denoted by $s_{\hat{y}}$, results from replacing σ^2 with s_e^2 in this function.

The standardized variable

$$t = \frac{\hat{y} - (\alpha + \beta_1x_1 + \cdots + \beta_kx_k)}{s_{\hat{y}}}$$

then has a t distribution with $n - (k + 1)$ df.

The formula for $s_{\hat{y}}$ has been programmed into the most widely used statistical computer packages, and its value for specified $x_1, \ldots, x_k$ is available upon request. Manipulation of the t variable as before gives a confidence interval formula. A prediction interval formula is based on a similar standardized variable.

For fixed values of $x_1, x_2, \ldots, x_k$, a **confidence interval for the mean y value** — that is, for $\alpha + \beta_1 x_1 + \cdots + \beta_k x_k$ — is

$$\hat{y} \pm (t \text{ critical value}) \cdot s_{\hat{y}}$$

A **prediction interval for a single y value** is

$$\hat{y} \pm (t \text{ critical value}) \cdot \sqrt{s_e^2 + s_{\hat{y}}^2}$$

The t critical value in both intervals is based on $n - (k + 1)$ df.

EXAMPLE 14.14

(Example 14.10 continued) Figure 14.5 shows MINITAB output from fitting the model $y = \alpha + \beta_1 x_1 + \beta_2 x_2 + e$ to the phosphate data introduced previously. A request for estimation and prediction information when $x_1 = 150$ and $x_2 = 40$ resulted in the following additional output:

Fit	StDev Fit	95.0% CI	95.0% PI
23.52	1.31	(20.60, 26.44)	(13.33, 33.70)

The t critical value for a 95% confidence level when df = 10 is 2.23, and the corresponding interval is

$$23.52 \pm (2.23)(1.31) = 23.52 \pm 2.92$$
$$= (20.60, 26.44)$$

Using $s_e^2 = 4.379$ along with the given values of $\hat{y}$, $s_{\hat{y}}$, and t critical value in the prediction interval formula results in (13.33, 33.70). Both intervals are centered at $\hat{y}$, but the prediction interval is much wider than the confidence interval.

The danger of extrapolation in simple linear regression is that if the x value of interest is much outside the interval of x values in the sample, the postulated model might no longer be valid, and even if it were, $\alpha + \beta x$ could still be quite poorly estimated (s_{a+bx} could be large). There is a similar danger in multiple regression, but it is not always obvious when the x_i values of interest involve an extrapolation from sample data. As an example, suppose that a single y observation is made for each of the following 13 (x_1, x_2) pairs:

Obs.	1	2	3	4	5	6	7	8	9	10	11	12	13
x_1	0	0	0	0	0	-5	5	5	5	10	-5	-5	-10
x_2	10	5	0	-5	-10	-5	0	5	-5	0	0	5	0

The x_1 values range between -10 and 10, as do the x_2 values. After fitting the model $y = \alpha + \beta_1 x_1 + \beta_2 x_2 + e$, we might then want a confidence interval for the mean y

FIGURE 14.9 The danger of extrapolation: ● denotes an (x_1, x_2) pair for which the sample contains a y observation; ○ denotes an (x_1, x_2) pair well outside the sample region, although the individual values $x_1 = 10$ and $x_2 = 10$ are within x_1 and x_2 sample ranges separately

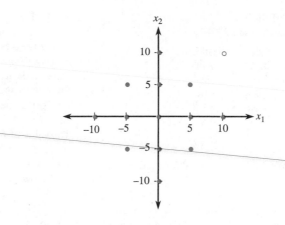

value when $x_1 = 10$ and $x_2 = 10$. However, whereas each of these values separately is within the range of sample x_i values, Figure 14.9 shows that the point $(x_1, x_2) = (10, 10)$ is actually far from (x_1, x_2) pairs in the sample. Thus, drawing a conclusion about y when $x_1 = 10$ and $x_2 = 10$ involves a substantial extrapolation. In particular, the estimated standard deviation of $a + b_1(10) + b_2(10)$ would probably be quite large even if the model were valid near this point.

When more than two predictor variables are included in the model, we cannot tell from a plot like that of Figure 14.9 whether the $x_1, x_2, \ldots, x_k$ values of interest involve an extrapolation. It is then best to compare $s_{\hat{y}}$'s based on $a + b_1x_1 + \cdots + b_kx_k$ for the values of interest with the $s_{\hat{y}}$'s corresponding to $x_1, x_2, \ldots, x_k$ values in the sample (MINITAB gives these on request). Extrapolation is indicated by a value of the former standard deviation (at the x_i values of interest) that is much larger than the standard deviations for sampled values.

Exercises 14.36 – 14.50

14.36 Explain why it is preferable to perform a model utility test before using an estimated regression model to make predictions or to estimate the mean y value for specified values of the independent variables.

14.37 The article "Zoning and Industrial Land Values: The Case of Philadelphia" (*AREUEA J.* (1991): 154–159) considered a regression model to relate the value of a vacant lot in Philadelphia to a number of different predictor variables.

    a. One of the predictors was x_3 = the distance from the city's major east-west thoroughfare, for which $b_3 = -.489$ and $s_{b_3} = .1044$. The model contained seven predictors, and the coefficients were estimated from a sample of 100 vacant lots. Calculate and interpret a

confidence interval for β_3 using a confidence level of 95%.

    b. Another predictor was x_1, an indicator variable for whether the lot was zoned for residential use, for which $b_1 = -.183$ and $s_{b_1} = .3055$. Carry out a test of $H_0: \beta_1 = 0$ versus $H_a: \beta_1 \neq 0$, and interpret the conclusion in the context of the problem.

14.38 Twenty-six observations from the article "Multiple Regression Analysis for Forecasting Critical Fish Influxes at Power Station Intakes" (see Exercise 14.16) were used to fit a multiple regression model relating y = number of fish at intake to the independent variables x_1 = water temperature (°C), x_2 = number of pumps running, x_3 = sea state (taking values 0, 1, 2, or 3), and x_4 = speed (knots). Partial MINITAB output follows.

THE REGRESSION EQUATION is
Y = 92.0 - 2.18X1 - 19.2X2 - 9.38X3 + 2.32X4

Predictor	Coef	Stdev	t-ratio
Constant	91.98	42.07	2.19
X1	-2.179	1.087	-2.00
X2	-19.189	9.215	-2.08
X3	-9.378	4.356	-2.15
X4	2.3205	0.7686	3.02

s = 10.53   R-sq = 39.0%   R-sq(adj) = 27.3%

a. Construct a 95% confidence interval for β_3, the coefficient of x_3 = sea state. Interpret the resulting interval.

b. Construct a 90% confidence interval for the mean change in y associated with a 1° increase in temperature when number of pumps, sea state, and speed remain fixed.

14.39 A study reported in the article "Leakage of Intracellular Substances from Alfalfa Roots at Various Subfreezing Temperatures" (*Crop Sci.* (1991): 1575–1578) considered a quadratic regression model to relate y = MDH activity (a measure of the extent to which cellular membranes suffer extensive damage from freezing) to x = electrical conductivity (which describes the damage in the early stages of freezing). The estimated regression function was

$$\hat{y} = -.1838 + .0272x + .0446x^2$$

with $R^2 = .860$.

a. Supposing that $n = 50$, does the quadratic model appear to be useful? Test the appropriate hypotheses.

b. Using $s_{b_2} = .0103$, carry out a test at significance level .01 to decide whether the quadratic predictor x^2 is important.

c. If the standard deviation of the statistic $\hat{y} = a + b_1(40) + b_2(1600)$ is $s_{\hat{y}} = .120$, calculate a confidence interval with confidence level 90% for true average MDH activity when conductivity is 40.

14.40 The article first introduced in Exercise 14.27 of Section 14.2 gave data on the dimensions of 27 representative food products. Use the multiple regression model fit in Exercise 14.27.

a. Could any of these variables be eliminated from a regression with the purpose of predicting volume?

b. Predict the volume of a package with a minimum width of 2.5 cm, a maximum width of 3.0 cm, and an elongation of 1.55.

c. Calculate a 95% prediction interval for a package with a minimum width of 2.5 cm, a maximum width of 3.0 cm, and an elongation of 1.55.

14.41 Data from a random sample of 107 students taking a managerial accounting course was used to obtain the estimated regression equation $2.178 + .469x_1 + 3.369x_2 + 3.054x_3$, where y = student's exam score, x_1 = student's expected score on the exam, x_2 = time spent studying (hr/week), and x_3 = student's grade point average or GPA ("Effort, Expectation and Academic Performance in Managerial Cost Accounting," *J. Acctg. Educ.* (1989): 57–68). The value of R^2 was .686, and the estimated standard deviations of the statistics b_1, b_2, and b_3 were .090, .456, and 1.457, respectively.

a. How would you interpret the estimated coefficient .469?

b. Does there appear to be a useful linear relationship between exam score and at least one of the three predictors?

c. Calculate a confidence interval for the mean change in exam score associated with a 1-hour increase in study time when expected score and GPA remain fixed.

d. Obtain a point prediction of the exam score for a student who expects a 75, has studied 8 hours per week, and has a GPA of 2.8.

e. If the standard deviation of the statistic on which the prediction of part **d** is based is 1.2 and SSTo = 10,200, calculate a 95% prediction interval for the score of the student described in part **d**.

14.42 Benevolence payments are monies collected by a church to fund activities and ministries beyond those provided by the church to its own members. The article "Optimal Church Size: The Bigger the Better" (*J. for the Scientific Study of Religion* (1993): 231–241) considered a regression of y = benevolence payments on x_1 = number of church members, $x_2 = x_1^2$, and x_3 = an indicator variable for urban versus nonurban churches.

a. The sample size was $n = 300$, and adjusted $R^2 = .774$. Does at least one of the three predictors provide useful information about y?

b. The article reported that $b_3 = 101.1$ and $s_{b_3} = 625.8$. Should the indicator variable be retained in the model? Test the relevant hypotheses.

14.43 The estimated regression equation

$$\hat{y} = 28 - .05x_1 - .003x_2 + .00002x_3$$

where

y = number of indictments disposed of in a given month

x_1 = number of cases on judge's docket

x_2 = number of cases pending in the criminal trial court

$x_3 = x_1 x_2$

appeared in the article "The Caseload Controversy and the Study of Criminal Courts" (*J. Criminal Law and Criminology* (1979): 89–101). This equation was based on $n = 367$ observations. The b_i's and their associated standard deviations are given in the accompanying table.

i	b_i	Estimated Standard Deviation of b_i
1	−.05	.03
2	−.003	.0024
3	.00002	.000009

Is inclusion of the interaction predictor important? Test $H_0: \beta_3 = 0$ using a .05 level of significance.

14.44 The accompanying data was obtained from a study of a certain method for preparing pure alcohol from refinery streams ("Direct Hydration of Olefins" *Indus. and Engr. Chem.* (1961): 209–211). The independent variable x is volume, and the dependent variable y is amount of isobutylene converted.

x	1	1	2	4	4	4	6
y	23.0	24.5	28.0	30.9	32.0	33.6	20.0

MINITAB output — the result of fitting a quadratic regression model where $x_1 = x$ and $x_2 = x^2$ — is given. Would a linear regression have sufficed? That is, is the quadratic predictor important? Use a level .05 test.

THE REGRESSION EQUATION is
Y = 13.6 + 11.4X1 - 1.72X2

Predictor	Coef	Stdev	t-ratio
Constant	13.636	1.896	7.19
X1	11.406	1.356	8.41
X2	-1.7155	0.2036	-8.42

s = 1.428   R-sq = 94.7%   R-sq(adj) = 92.1%

14.45 The article "Bank Full Discharge of Rivers" (*Water Resources J.* (1978): 1141–1154) reported data on $y =$ discharge amount (m²/s), $x_1 =$ flow area (m²), and $x_2 =$ slope of the water surface (m/m) obtained at $n = 10$ flood-plain stations. A multiple regression model using $x_1, x_2,$ and $x_3 = x_1x_2$ was fit to this data, and partial MINITAB output appears here.

THE REGRESSION EQUATION is
Y = -3.14 + 1.70X1 + 96.1X2 + 8.38X3

Predictor	Coef	Stdev	t-ratio
Constant	-3.14	14.54	-0.22
X1	1.697	1.431	1.19
X2	96.1	702.7	0.14
X3	8.38	199.0	0.04

s = 17.58   R-sq = 73.2%   R-sq(adj) = 59.9%

a. Perform the model utility test using a significance level of .05.

b. Is the interaction term important? Test using a .05 significance level.

c. Does it bother you that the model utility test indicates a useful model, but all values in the **t-ratio** column of the output are small? Explain.

14.46 In the article "An Ultracentrifuge Flour Absorption Method" (*Cereal Chem.* (1978): 96–101), the authors discussed the relationship between water absorption for wheat flour and various characteristics of the flour. The model $y = \alpha + \beta_1 x_1 + \beta_2 x_2 + e$ was used to relate $y =$ absorption (%) to $x_1 =$ flour protein (%) and $x_2 =$ starch damage (Farrand units). MINITAB output based on $n = 28$ observations is given. Use a significance level of .05 for all tests requested.

THE REGRESSION EQUATION is
Y = 19.4 + 1.44X1 + .336X2

Predictor	Coef	Stdev	t-ratio	p
Constant	19.440	2.188	8.88	.000
X1	1.4423	0.2076	6.95	.000
X2	0.33563	0.01014	10.51	.000

s = 1.094   R-sq = 96.4%   R-sq(adj) = 96.2%

Analysis of Variance

SOURCE	DF	SS	MS	F	p
Regression	2	812.380	406.190	339.3	.000
Error	25	29.928	1.197		
Total	27	842.307			

a. Does the model appear to be useful? Test the relevant hypotheses.

b. Calculate and interpret a 95% confidence interval for β_2.

c. Conduct tests for each of the following pairs of hypotheses.

  i. $H_0: \beta_1 = 0$ versus $H_a: \beta_1 \neq 0$
  ii. $H_0: \beta_2 = 0$ versus $H_a: \beta_2 \neq 0$

d. Based on the results of part **c**, would you conclude that both independent variables are important? Explain.

e. An estimate of the mean water absorption for wheat with 11.7% protein and a starch damage of 57 is desired. Compute a 90% confidence interval for $\alpha + \beta_1(11.7) + \beta_2(57)$ if the estimated standard deviation of $a + b_1(11.7) + b_2(57)$ is .522. Interpret the resulting interval.

f. A single shipment of wheat is received. For this particular shipment, $x_1 = 11.7$ and $x_2 = 57$. Predict the water absorption for this shipment (a single y value) using a 90% interval.

14.47 Exercise 14.25 gave data on fish weight, length, age, and year caught. A multiple regression model was fit to describe the relationship between weight and the predictors length and age.

a. Could either length or age be eliminated from the model without significantly affecting your ability to make accurate predictions? Why or why not? Give statistical evidence to support your conclusion.

b. Create a dummy (indicator) variable for year caught. Fit a multiple regression model that includes year, length, and age as predictors of weight. Is there evidence that year is a useful predictor given that length and age are included in the model? Test the relevant hypotheses using $\alpha = .05$.

14.48 The article "Predicting Marathon Time from Anaerobic Threshold Measurements" (*The Physician and Sportsmed.* (1984): 95–98) gave data on y = maximum heart rate (beats/min), x_1 = age, and x_2 = weight (kg) for $n = 18$ marathon runners. The estimated regression equation for the model $y = \alpha + \beta_1 x_1 + \beta_2 x_2 + e$ was $\hat{y} = 179 - .8x_1 + .5x_2$ and SSRegr = 649.75, SSResid = 538.03.

a. Is the model useful for predicting maximum heart rate? Use a significance level of .10.

b. Using $s_{b_1} = .280$, calculate and interpret a 95% confidence interval for β_1.

c. Predict the maximum heart rate of a particular runner who is 43 years old and weighs 65 kg, using a 99% interval. The estimated standard deviation of the statistic $a + b_1(43) + b_2(65)$ is 3.52.

d. Use a 90% interval to estimate the average maximum heart rate for all marathon runners who are 30 years old and weigh 77.2 kg. The estimated standard deviation of $a + b_1(30) + b_2(77.2)$ is 2.97.

e. Would a 90% prediction interval for a single 30-year-old runner weighing 77.2 kg be wider or narrower than the interval computed in part **d**? Explain. (You need not compute the interval.)

14.49 The effect of manganese (Mn) on wheat growth is examined in the article "Manganese Deficiency and Toxicity Effects on Growth, Development and Nutrient Composition in Wheat" (*Agronomy J.* (1984): 213–217). A quadratic regression model was used to relate y = plant height (cm) to x = log (added Mn), with μM as the units for added Mn. The accompanying data was read from a scatter plot in the article. Also given is MINITAB output, where $x_1 = x$ and $x_2 = x^2$. Use a .05 significance level for any hypothesis tests needed to answer the questions that follow.

x	−1	−.4	0	.2	1	2	2.8	3.2	3.4	4
y	32	37	44	45	46	42	42	40	37	30

THE REGRESSION EQUATION is
$Y = 41.7 + 6.58X1 - 2.36X2$

Predictor	Coef	Stdev	t-ratio
Constant	41.7422	0.8522	48.98
X1	6.581	1.002	6.57
X2	-2.3621	0.3073	-7.69

$s = 1.963$ R-sq = 89.8% R-sq(adj) = 86.9%

Analysis of Variance

SOURCE	DF	SS	MS
Regression	2	237.520	118.760
Error	7	26.980	3.854
Total	9	264.500	

a. Is the quadratic model useful for describing the relationship between y and x?

b. Are both the linear and quadratic predictors important? Could either one be eliminated from the model? Explain.

c. Give a 95% confidence interval for the mean y value when $x = 2$. The estimated standard deviation of $a + b_1(2) + b_2(4)$ is 1.037. Interpret the resulting interval.

d. Estimate the mean height for wheat treated with 10 μM of Mn using a 90% interval. (*Note:* The estimated standard deviation of $a + b_1(1) + b_2(1)$ is 1.031 and $\log(10) = 1$.)

14.50 *This exercise requires the use of a computer package.* A study on the effect of applying fertilizer in bands is described in the article "Fertilizer Placement Effects on Growth, Yield, and Chemical Composition of Burley Tobacco" (*Agronomy J.* (1984): 183–188). The accompanying data was taken from a scatter plot appearing in the article, with y = plant Mn (μg/g dry weight) and x = distance from the fertilizer band (cm). The authors suggest a quadratic regression model.

x	0	10	20	30	40
y	110	90	76	72	70

a. Use a suitable computer package to find the estimated quadratic regression equation.

b. Perform the model utility test.

c. Interpret the values of R^2 and s_e.

d. Are both the linear and quadratic predictors important? Carry out the necessary hypothesis tests and interpret the results.

e. Find a 90% confidence interval for the mean plant Mn for plants that are 30 cm from the fertilizer band.

14.4 Other Issues in Multiple Regression

Primary objectives in multiple regression include estimating a mean y value, predicting an individual y value, and gaining insight into how changes in predictor variable values affect y. Often an investigator has data on a number of predictor variables that might be incorporated into a model to be used for such purposes. Some of these may actually be unrelated or only very weakly related to y or they may contain information that duplicates information provided by other predictors. If all these predictors are included in the model, many model coefficients have to be estimated. This reduces the number of degrees of freedom associated with SSResid, leading to a deterioration in the degree of precision associated with other inferences (for example, wide confidence and prediction intervals). A model with many predictors can also be cumbersome to use and difficult to interpret.

In this section, we first introduce some guidelines and procedures for selecting a set of useful predictors. In choosing a model, the analyst should examine the data carefully for evidence of unusual observations or potentially troublesome patterns. It is important to identify unusually deviant or influential observations and to look for possible inconsistencies with model assumptions. Our discussion of multiple regression closes with a brief mention of some diagnostic methods designed for these purposes.

Variable Selection

Suppose that an investigator has data on p predictors $x_1, x_2, \ldots, x_p$, which are candidates for use in building a model. Some of these predictors might be specified functions of others, for example, $x_3 = x_1 x_2$, $x_4 = x_1^2$, and so on. The objective is then to select a set of these predictors that in some sense specifies a best model (of the general additive form considered in the two previous sections). Fitting a model that uses a specified k predictors requires that $k + 1$ model coefficients (α and the k corresponding β's) be estimated. Generally speaking, the number of observations, n, should be at least twice the number of predictors in the largest model under consideration to ensure reasonably accurate coefficient estimates and a sufficient number of degrees of freedom associated with SSResid.

If p is not too large, a good statistical computer package can quickly fit a model based on each different subset of the p predictors. Consider the case $p = 4$. There are two possibilities for each predictor — it could be included or not included in a model — so the number of possible models in this case is $2 \cdot 2 \cdot 2 \cdot 2 = 2^4 = 16$ (including the model with all four predictors and the model with only the constant term and none of the four predictors). These 16 possibilities are displayed in the accompanying table.

Predictors included	None	x_1	x_2	x_3	x_4	x_1, x_2	x_1, x_3	x_1, x_4	x_2, x_3	x_2, x_4
Number of predictors in model	0	1	1	1	1	2	2	2	2	2

Predictors included	x_3, x_4	x_1, x_2, x_3	x_1, x_2, x_4	x_1, x_3, x_4	x_2, x_3, x_4	x_1, x_2, x_3, x_4
Number of predictors in model	2	3	3	3	3	4

More generally, when there are p candidate predictors, the number of possible models is 2^p. The number of possible models is, therefore, substantial if p is even moderately large — for example, 1024 possible models when $p = 10$ and 32,768 possibilities when $p = 15$.

Model selection methods can be divided into two types. There are those based on fitting every possible model, computing one or more summary quantities from each fit, and comparing these quantities to identify the most satisfactory models. Several of the most powerful statistical computer packages have an **all-subsets** option, which will give limited output from fitting each possible model. Methods of the second type are appropriate when p is so large that it is not feasible to examine all subsets. These methods are often referred to as **automatic selection,** or **stepwise, procedures.** The general idea is either to begin with the p predictor model and delete predictors one by one until all remaining predictors are judged important, or to begin with no predictors and add predictors until no predictor not in the model seems important. With present-day computing power, the value of p for which examination of all subsets is feasible is surprisingly large, so automatic selection procedures are not as important as they once were.

Suppose then that p is small enough that all subsets can be fit. What characteristic(s) of the estimated models should be examined in the search for a best model? An obvious and appealing candidate is the coefficient of multiple determination, R^2, which measures the proportion of observed y variation explained by the model. Certainly a model with a large R^2 value is preferable to another model that contains the same number of predictors but has a much smaller R^2 value. Thus, if the model with predictors x_1 and x_2 has $R^2 = .765$ and the model with predictors x_1 and x_3 has $R^2 = .626$, the latter model would almost surely be eliminated from further consideration.

However, using R^2 to choose between models containing different numbers of predictors is not so straightforward, because adding a predictor to a model can never decrease the value of R^2. Let

$R^2_{(1)}$ = largest R^2 for any one-predictor model

$R^2_{(2)}$ = largest R^2 for any two-predictor model

$\vdots$

Then $R^2_{(1)} \leq R^2_{(2)} \leq \cdots \leq R^2_{(p-1)} \leq R^2_{(p)}$. When statisticians base model selection on R^2, the objective is not simply to find the model with the largest R^2 value; the model with p predictors does that. Instead, we should look for a model that contains relatively few predictors but has a large R^2 value and is such that no other model containing more predictors gives much of an improvement in R^2. Suppose, for example, that $p = 5$ and that

$$R^2_{(1)} = .427 \qquad R^2_{(2)} = .733 \qquad R^2_{(3)} = .885 \qquad R^2_{(4)} = .898 \qquad R^2_{(5)} = .901$$

Then the best three-predictor model appears to be a good choice, since it substantially improves on the best one- and two-predictor models, whereas very little is gained by using the best four-predictor model or all five predictors.

A small increase in R^2 resulting from the addition of a predictor to a model may be offset by the increased complexity of the new model and the reduction in degrees of freedom associated with SSResid. This has led statisticians to consider an adjusted R^2, which can either decrease or increase when a predictor is added to a model. It follows that adjusted R^2 for the best k-predictor model (the one with coefficient of multiple determination $R^2_{(k)}$) may be larger than adjusted R^2 for the best model based on $k + 1$ predictors. Adjusted R^2 formalizes the notion of diminishing returns as more predictors are added: Small increases in R^2 are outweighed by corresponding decreases in degrees of freedom associated with SSResid. A reasonable strategy in model selection is to identify the model with the largest value of adjusted R^2 (the corresponding number of predictors k is often much smaller than p) and then consider only that model and any others whose adjusted R^2 values are nearly as large.

EXAMPLE 14.15   The article "Anatomical Factors Influencing Wood Specific Gravity of Slash Pines and the Implications for the Development of a High-Quality Pulpwood" (*TAPPI* (1964): 401–404) reported the results of an experiment in which 20 specimens of slash pine wood were analyzed. A primary objective was to relate wood specific gravity (y) to various other wood characteristics. The independent variables on which observations were made were

x_1 = number of fibers/mm^2 in springwood

x_2 = number of fibers/mm^2 in summerwood

x_3 = % springwood

x_4 = % springwood light absorption

x_5 = % summerwood light absorption

The data is displayed in the accompanying table.

x_1	x_2	x_3	x_4	x_5	y
573	1059	46.5	53.8	84.1	.534
651	1356	52.7	54.5	88.7	.535
606	1273	49.4	52.1	92.0	.570
630	1151	48.9	50.3	87.9	.528
547	1135	53.1	51.9	91.5	.548
557	1236	54.9	55.2	91.4	.555
489	1231	56.2	45.5	82.4	.481
685	1564	56.6	44.3	91.3	.516
536	1182	59.2	46.4	85.4	.475
685	1564	63.1	56.4	91.4	.486
664	1588	50.6	48.1	86.7	.554
703	1335	51.9	48.4	81.2	.519
653	1395	62.5	51.9	89.2	.492
586	1114	50.5	56.5	88.9	.517

(*continued*)

x_1	x_2	x_3	x_4	x_5	y
534	1143	52.1	57.0	88.9	.502
523	1320	50.5	61.2	91.9	.508
580	1249	54.6	60.8	95.4	.520
448	1028	52.2	53.4	91.8	.506
476	1057	42.9	53.2	92.9	.595
528	1057	42.4	56.6	90.0	.568

Consider $x_1, x_2, \ldots, x_5$ as the set of potential predictors ($p = 5$, with no derived predictors such as squares or interaction terms as candidates for inclusion). Then there are $2^5 = 32$ possible models, among which 5 consist of a single predictor, 10 involve two predictors, 10 others involve three predictors, and 5 include four predictor variables. We used a statistical computer package to fit each possible model and extracted both R^2 and adjusted R^2 from the output. To save space, results appear for all one- and four-predictor models but only for the five best two- and three-predictor models.

It is immediately clear that the best three-predictor models offer considerable improvement with respect to both R^2 and adjusted R^2 over any model containing one or two predictors and that the model with all five predictors is inferior to the best four-predictor model. The best four-predictor model has the largest value of adjusted R^2 (.709), but the best three-predictor model is not far behind. The five models that seem most appealing to us are shaded in the display of results. The selection of a single model would have to be based on a more detailed comparison of these five models, with special attention given to residuals and other diagnostics (to be mentioned shortly) that bear on model adequacy. In particular, it is dangerous to embrace the model with the largest adjusted R^2 value automatically and reject all other models out of hand.

Models with One Predictor

Predictor	x_3	x_5	x_2	x_4	x_1
R^2	$R^2_{(1)} = .564$	.106	.053	.020	.008
Adjusted R^2	.539	.057	.001	−.034	−.047

Models with Two Predictors

Predictors	x_3, x_5	x_2, x_3	x_1, x_3	x_3, x_4	x_2, x_5
R^2	$R^2_{(2)} = .655$	.621	.603	.564	.158
Adjusted R^2	.614	.576	.556	.513	.059

Models with Three Predictors

Predictors	x_1, x_3, x_5	x_3, x_4, x_5	x_2, x_3, x_5	x_1, x_2, x_3	x_2, x_3, x_4
R^2	$R^2_{(3)} = .723$	.712	.711	.622	.611
Adjusted R^2	.671	.659	.657	.551	.550

Models with Four Predictors

Predictors	x_1, x_3, x_4, x_5	x_2, x_3, x_4, x_5	x_1, x_2, x_3, x_5	x_1, x_2, x_3, x_4	x_1, x_2, x_4, x_5
R^2	$R^2_{(4)} = .770$	.748	.727	.622	.239
Adjusted R^2	.709	.681	.654	.522	.036

The model with all five predictors included has $R^2_{(5)} = .770$, adjusted $R^2 = .689$.

Various other criteria have been proposed and used for model selection after fitting all subsets. A chapter reference can be consulted for more details.

When using particular criteria as a basis for model selection, many of the 2^p possible subset models are not serious candidates because of poor criteria values. For example, if $p = 15$, there are 5005 different models consisting of six predictor variables, many of which typically have small R^2 and adjusted R^2 values. An investigator usually wishes to consider only a few of the best models of each different size (a model whose criteria value is close to the best one may be easier to interpret than the best model or may include a predictor that the investigator thinks should be in the selected model). In recent years, statisticians have developed computer programs to achieve this without actually fitting all possible models. One version of such a program has been implemented in MINITAB and can be used as long as $p \leq 20$. (There are roughly one million possible models when $p = 20$, so fitting them all would be out of the question.) The user specifies a number between 1 and 10 as the number of models of each given size for which output will be provided. In addition to R^2 and adjusted R^2, values of another criterion, called *Mallow's* C_p, are included. A good model according to this criterion is one that has small C_p (for accurate predictions) and $C_p \approx k + 1$ (for unbiasedness in estimating model coefficients). After the choice of models is narrowed, the analyst can request more detail on each finalist.

EXAMPLE 14.16 The accompanying data was taken from the article "Applying Stepwise Multiple Regression Analysis to the Reaction of Formaldehyde with Cotton Cellulose" (*Textile Research J.* (1984): 157–165). The dependent variable

y = durable press rating

is a quantitative measure of wrinkle resistance. The four independent variables used in the model building process are

x_1 = HCHO (formaldehyde) concentration

x_2 = catalyst ratio

x_3 = curing temperature

x_4 = curing time

In addition to these variables, the investigators considered as potential predictors $x_1^2, x_2^2, x_3^2, x_4^2$, and all six interactions $x_1x_2, \ldots, x_3x_4$, a total of $p = 14$ candidates.

Figure 14.10 displays output for the best three subset models of each size from $k = 4$ to $k = 9$ predictor variables and also for the model with all 14 predictors.

Observation	x_1	x_2	x_3	x_4	y	Observation	x_1	x_2	x_3	x_4	y
1	8	4	100	1	1.4	16	4	10	160	5	4.6
2	2	4	180	7	2.2	17	4	13	100	7	4.3
3	7	4	180	1	4.6	18	10	10	120	7	4.9
4	10	7	120	5	4.9	19	5	4	100	1	1.7
5	7	4	180	5	4.6	20	8	13	140	1	4.6
6	7	7	180	1	4.7	21	10	1	180	1	2.6
7	7	13	140	1	4.6	22	2	13	140	1	3.1
8	5	4	160	7	4.5	23	6	13	180	7	4.7
9	4	7	140	3	4.8	24	7	1	120	7	2.5
10	5	1	100	7	1.4	25	5	13	140	1	4.5
11	8	10	140	3	4.7	26	8	1	160	7	2.1
12	2	4	100	3	1.6	27	4	1	180	7	1.8
13	4	10	180	3	4.5	28	6	1	160	1	1.5
14	6	7	120	7	4.7	29	4	1	100	1	1.3
15	10	13	180	3	4.8	30	7	10	100	7	4.6

FIGURE 14.10 MINITAB output for the data of Example 14.16

```
                                                      c  c  c  c  t
                                            t  t  c  o  o  a  a  e
                                      c  c  e  i  o  n  n  *  *  *  m
                                      o  a  m  m  n  *  t  t  t  *
                                t  t  n  t  p  e  *  t  t  t  t  t
                          c  c  e  i  s  s  s  s  c  e  i  e  i  i
               Adj.       o  a  m  m  q  q  q  q  a  m  m  m  m  m
 Vars R-sq  R-sq  C-p    s   n  t  p  e  d  d  d  d  t  p  e  p  e  e
   4  82.2  79.4  13.9  0.63607  X     X        X                 X
   4  82.1  79.2  14.1  0.63843  X              X     X           X
   4  81.7  78.8  14.8  0.64455  X              X                 X              X
   5  86.7  83.9   7.4  0.56196  X        X  X                    X  X
   5  85.5  82.5   9.6  0.58571  X        X  X  X                 X
   5  85.5  82.5   9.6  0.58614  X        X  X        X           X
   6  88.5  85.5   5.9  0.53337  X        X  X                    X  X  X
   6  88.2  85.1   6.5  0.54094  X        X  X  X                 X              X
   6  88.0  84.9   6.8  0.54386  X        X  X                    X  X           X
   7  89.9  86.7   5.2  0.51045  X  X  X  X  X  X                 X
   7  89.9  86.7   5.3  0.51140  X  X     X  X  X  X              X
   7  89.7  86.4   5.7  0.51683  X  X     X  X  X                 X  X
   8  91.5  88.3   4.2  0.47933  X  X  X  X  X  X                 X              X
   8  90.6  87.0   6.0  0.50535  X  X     X  X  X  X              X              X
   8  90.5  86.8   6.1  0.50793  X  X     X  X  X                 X  X  X
   9  91.7  87.9   5.9  0.48650 X X  X  X  X  X  X                 X              X
   9  91.6  87.8   6.0  0.48853   X  X  X  X  X  X              X     X        X  X
   9  91.6  87.8   6.0  0.48860   X  X  X  X  X  X                 X  X           X
  14  92.1  84.8  15.0  0.54639 X X  X  X  X  X  X  X  X  X  X  X  X  X
```

The choice of a best model here, as often happens, is not clear-cut. We certainly don't see the benefit of including more than $k = 8$ predictor variables (after that, adjusted R^2 begins to decrease), nor would we suggest a model with fewer than five predictors (adjusted R^2 is still increasing and C_p is large). Based only on this output, the best six-predictor model is a reasonable choice. The corresponding estimated regression function is

$$-1.218 + .9599x_2 - .0373x_1^2 - .0389x_2^2 + .0037x_1x_3 + .019x_1x_4 - .0013x_2x_3$$

Another good candidate is the best seven-predictor model. Although it includes one more predictor than the model just suggested, only one of the seven predictors is an interaction term (x_1x_3), so model interpretation is somewhat easier. (Notice, though, that none of the best three models with seven predictors results simply from adding a single predictor to the best six-predictor model.) Since every good model includes x_1, x_2, x_3, and x_4 in some predictor, it appears that HCHO concentration, catalyst ratio, curing time, and curing temperature are all important determinants of durable press rating.

The most easily understood and implemented automatic selection procedure is referred to as **backward elimination.** It involves starting with the model that contains all p potential predictors and then deleting them one by one until all remaining predictors seem important. The first step is to specify the value of a positive constant t_{out}, which is used to decide whether deletion should be continued. After fitting the p predictor model, the t ratios $b_1/s_{b_1}, b_2/s_{b_2}, \ldots, b_p/s_{b_p}$ are examined. The predictor variable whose t ratio is closest to zero, whether positive or negative, is the obvious candidate for deletion. The corresponding predictor is eliminated from the model if this t ratio satisfies the inequalities $-t_{out} \leq t$ ratio $\leq t_{out}$. Suppose that this is the case. The model with the remaining $p - 1$ predictors is then fit, and again the predictor with the t ratio closest to zero is eliminated, provided that it satisfies $-t_{out} \leq t$ ratio $\leq t_{out}$. The procedure continues until, at some stage, no t ratio satisfies $-t_{out} \leq t$ ratio $\leq t_{out}$ (all are either greater than t_{out} or less than $-t_{out}$). The chosen model is then the last one fit (though some analysts recommend examining other models of the same size). It is customary to use $t_{out} = 2$, since for many different values of df, this corresponds to a two-tailed test with approximate significance level .05.*

EXAMPLE 14.17   Figure 14.11 (page 600) shows MINITAB output resulting from the application of the backward elimination procedure with $t_{out} = 2$ to the specific gravity data introduced in Example 14.15. The t ratio closest to zero when the model with all five predictors was fit was .12, so the corresponding predictor x_2 was deleted from the model. When the model with the four remaining predictors was fit, the t ratio closest to

---

*Some computer packages base the procedure on the squares of the t ratios, which are F ratios, and continue to delete as long as F ratio $\leq F_{out}$ for at least one predictor. The predictor with the smallest F ratio is eliminated. $F_{out} = 4$ corresponds to $t_{out} = 2$.

FIGURE 14.11 MINITAB output for Example 14.17

STEP	1	2	3	4
CONSTANT	0.4421	0.4384	0.4381	0.5179
X1	0.00011	0.00011	0.00012	
T-RATIO	1.17	1.95	1.98	
X2	0.00001			
T-RATIO	0.12			
X3	-0.00531	-0.00526	-0.00498	-0.00438
T-RATIO	-5.70	-6.56	-5.96	-5.20
X4	-0.0018	-0.0019		
T-RATIO	-1.63	-1.76		
X5	0.0044	0.0044	0.0031	0.0027
T-RATIO	3.01	3.31	2.63	2.12
S	0.0180	0.0174	0.0185	0.0200
R-SQ	77.05	77.03	72.27	65.50

zero was -1.76, which satisfied $-2 \leq -1.76 \leq 2$. Thus, the corresponding predictor, x_4, was eliminated, leaving x_1, x_3, and x_5 still in the model. The next predictor to be dropped was x_1, because its t ratio, 1.98, was the one closest to zero and (barely) satisfied $-2 \leq 1.98 \leq 2$. When the model with predictors x_3 and x_5 was fit, neither t ratio satisfied $-2 \leq t$ ratio ≤ 2, so the procedure terminated. Looking back to Example 14.15, this is actually the best model containing only two predictors. However, x_1 just barely met the elimination criterion, so the model with predictors x_1, x_3, and x_5 should also be given serious consideration.

Unfortunately, the backward elimination method does not always terminate with a model that is the best of its size, and this is also true of other automatic selection procedures. For example, the authors of the article mentioned in Example 14.16 used an automatic procedure to obtain a six-predictor model with $R^2 = .77$, whereas all of the 10 best six-predictor models have R^2 values of at least .87. Because of this, we recommend using a statistical software package that will identify best subsets of different sizes whenever possible.

Checks on Model Adequacy

In Chapter 13, we discussed some informal techniques for checking the adequacy of the simple linear regression model. Most of these were based on plots involving the standardized residuals. The formula for standardizing residuals in multiple regression is quite complicated, but it has been programmed into many statistical computer packages. Once the standardized residuals resulting from the fit of a particular model have been computed, plots similar to those discussed previously are useful in diagnosing model defects. A normal probability plot of the standardized residuals that departs too much from a straight line casts doubt on the assumption that the random deviation e has a normal distribution. Plots of the standardized residuals against each predictor variable in the model — that is, a plot of (x_1, standardized residual) pairs, another of (x_2, standardized residual) pairs, and so on — are analogous to the standardized residual versus x plot discussed and illustrated in the previous chapter. The appearance of any discernible pattern in these plots (for example, curvature or increasing spread from left to right) points to the need for model modification. If observations have been made over time, a periodic pattern when the standardized residuals are plotted in time order suggests that successive observations were not independent. Models that incorporate dependence of successive observations are substantially more complicated than those we have presented here. They are especially important in econometrics, which involves using statistical methodology to model economic data. Please consult one of the references in Chapter 5 for more information.

One other aspect of model adequacy that has received much attention from statisticians in recent years is the identification of any observations in the data set that may have been highly influential in estimating model coefficients. Recall that in simple linear regression, an observation with potentially high influence is one whose x value places it far to the right or left of the other points in the scatter plot or standardized residual plot. If a multiple regression model involves only two predictor variables x_1 and x_2, an observation with potentially large influence can be revealed by examining a plot of (x_1, x_2) pairs. Any point in this plot that is far away from the others corresponds to an observation that, if deleted from the sample, may cause coefficient estimates and other quantities to change considerably. The detection of influential observations when the model contains at least three predictors is more difficult. Recent research has yielded several helpful diagnostic quantities. One of these has been implemented in MINITAB, and a large value of this quantity automatically results in the corresponding observation being identified as one that might have great influence. Deleting the observation and refitting the model will reveal the extent of actual influence (which depends on how consistent the corresponding y observation is with the rest of the data).

Multicollinearity

When the simple linear regression model is fit using sample data in which the x values are all close to one another, small changes in observed y values can cause the values of the estimated coefficients a and b to change considerably. This may well result in standard deviations σ_b and σ_a that are quite large, so that estimates of β and α from any given sample are likely to differ greatly from the true values. There is an analogous condition that leads to this same type of behavior in multiple regression: a configuration of predictor variable values that is likely to result in poorly estimated model coefficients.

When the model to be fit includes k predictors $x_1, x_2, \ldots, x_k$, there is said to be **multicollinearity** if there is a strong linear relationship between values of the predictors. Severe multicollinearity leads to instability of estimated coefficients as well as various other problems. Such a relationship is difficult to visualize when $k > 2$, so statisticians have developed various quantitative indicators to measure the extent of multicollinearity in a data set. The most straightforward approach involves computing R^2 values for regressions in which the dependent variable is taken to be one of the k x's and the predictors are the remaining $(k - 1)$ x's. For example, when $k = 3$, there are three relevant regressions:

1. Dependent variable $= x_1$, predictor variables $= x_2$ and x_3
2. Dependent variable $= x_2$, predictor variables $= x_1$ and x_3
3. Dependent variable $= x_3$, predictor variables $= x_1$ and x_2

Each regression yields an R^2 value. In general, there are k such regressions and, therefore, k resulting R^2 values. If one or more of these R^2 values is large (close to 1), multicollinearity is present. MINITAB will print a message saying that the predictors are highly correlated when at least one of these R^2 values exceeds .99 and will refuse to include a predictor in the model if the corresponding R^2 value is larger than .9999. Other analysts are more conservative and would judge multicollinearity to be a potential problem if any of these R^2 values exceeded .9.

When the values of predictor variables are under the control of the investigator, which often happens in scientific experimentation, a careful choice of values will preclude multicollinearity from arising. Multicollinearity does frequently occur in social science and business applications of regression analysis, where data results simply from observation rather than from intervention by an experimenter. Statisticians have proposed various remedies for the problems associated with multicollinearity in such situations, but a discussion would take us beyond the scope of this book. (After all, we want to leave something for your next statistics course!)

Exercises 14.51 – 14.62

14.51 The article "The Caseload Controversy and the Study of Criminal Courts" (*J. Criminal Law and Criminology* (1979): 89–101) used multiple regression to analyze a data set consisting of observations on the variables

y = length of sentence in trial case (months)

x_1 = seriousness of first offense

x_2 = dummy variable indicating type of trial (bench or jury)

x_3 = number of legal motions

x_4 = measure of delay for confined defendants (0 for those not confined)

x_5 = measure of judge's caseload

The estimated regression equation proposed by the authors is

$$\hat{y} = 12.6 + .59x_1 - 70.8x_2 - 33.6x_3 - 15.5x_5 + .0007x_6 + 3x_7 - 41.5x_8$$

where $x_6 = x_4^2$, $x_7 = x_1 x_2$, and $x_8 = x_3 x_5$. How do you think the authors might have arrived at this particular model?

14.52 The article "Histologic Estimation of Age at Death Using the Anterior Cortex of the Femur" (*Amer. J. Phys. Anthro.* (1991): 171–179) developed multiple regression models to relate y = age at death to a number of different histologic predictor variables. Stepwise regression (an automatic selection procedure favored over the backward elimination method by many statisticians) was used to identify models shown in the accompanying table, for the case of females.

Predictors	R^2	Adjusted R^2
x_6	.60	.60
x_3, x_6	.66	.66
x_3, x_5	.68	.68
x_2, x_3, x_5	.69	.68
x_2, x_3, x_5, x_6	.70	.69
x_2, x_3, x_4, x_5, x_6	.71	.70
$x_1, x_2, x_3, x_4, x_5, x_6$	.71	.70
$x_1, x_2, x_3, x_4, x_5, x_6, x_7$	.71	.70
$x_1, x_2, x_3, x_5, x_6, x_7, x_8$	.72	.71
$x_1, x_2, x_3, x_4, x_5, x_6, x_7, x_8$	.72	.70

Based on the given information, which of these models would you recommend using, and why?

14.53 The article "The Analysis and Selection of Variables in Linear Regression" (*Biometrics* (1976): 1–49) reports on an analysis of data taken from issues of *Motor Trend* magazine. The dependent variable y was gas mileage, there were $n = 32$ observations, and the independent variables were x_1 = engine type (1 = straight, 0 = V), x_2 = number of cylinders, x_3 = transmission type (1 = manual, 0 = automatic), x_4 = number of transmission speeds, x_5 = engine size, x_6 = horsepower, x_7 = number of carburetor barrels, x_8 = final drive ratio, x_9 = weight, and x_{10} = quarter-mile time. The R^2 and adjusted R^2 values are given in the accompanying table for the best model using k predictors for $k = 1, \ldots, 10$. Which model would you select? Explain your choice and the criteria used to reach your decision.

k	Variable Included	R^2	Adjusted R^2
1	x_9	.756	.748
2	x_7, x_9	.833	.821
3	x_3, x_9, x_{10}	.852	.836
4	x_3, x_6, x_9, x_{10}	.860	.839
5	$x_3, x_5, x_6, x_9, x_{10}$	.866	.840
6	$x_3, x_5, x_6, x_8, x_9, x_{10}$	.869	.837
7	$x_3, x_4, x_5, x_6, x_8, x_9, x_{10}$	.870	.832
8	$x_3, x_4, x_5, x_6, x_7, x_8, x_9, x_{10}$	.871	.826
9	$x_1, x_3, x_4, x_5, x_6, x_7, x_8, x_9, x_{10}$	.871	.818
10	All independent variables	.871	.809

14.54 The article "Estimation of the Economic Threshold of Infestation for Cotton Aphid" (*Mesopotamia J. Ag.* (1982): 71–75) gave $n = 34$ observations on

y = infestation rate (number of aphids per 100 leaves)

x_1 = mean temperature (°C)

x_2 = mean relative humidity

Partial SAS computer output resulting from fitting the model $y = \alpha + \beta_1 x_1 + \beta_2 x_2 + e$ to the data given in the article is shown.

		R-SQUARE	0.5008
		ADJ R-SQ	0.4533

VARIABLE	DF	PARAMETER ESTIMATE	STANDARD ERROR	T FOR H0: PARAMETER = 0
INTERCEP	1	15.667014	84.157420	0.186
TEMP	1	-0.360928	2.330835	-0.155
RH	1	1.959715	0.576946	2.877

If the method of backward elimination is to be employed, which variable would be the first candidate for elimina-tion? Using the criterion of eliminating a variable if its t ratio satisfies $-2 \le t$ ratio ≤ 2, can it be eliminated from the model?

14.55 The following statement is from the article "Blood Cadmium Levels in Nonexposed Male Subjects Living in the Rome Area: Relationship to Selected Cardiovascular Risk Factors" (*Microchemical J.* (1998): 173–179):

A multiple regression analyzed ln(blood cadmium level) as a dependent variable, with a model including age, alcohol consumption, daily cigarette consumption, driving habits, body mass index, skinfold thickness, high density lipoprotein cholesterol, non-high density lipoprotein cholesterol, and ln(triglyceride level) as possible predictors. This model explained 30.92% of the total variance in ln(blood cadmium level).

a. A total of $n = 1856$ men participated in this study. Perform a model utility test to determine whether the predictor variables, taken as a group are useful in predicting ln(blood cadmium level).

b. The article went on to state:

Smoking habits, the most important predictor of ln(blood cadmium level), explained 30.26% of the total variation, and alcohol consumption was the only other variable influencing ln(blood cadmium level).

These statements were based on the result of a forward stepwise regression. In forward stepwise regression, variables are added to the model one at a time. At each step, the variable that results in the largest improvement is added to the model. This continues until there is no variable whose addition will result in a significant improvement. Describe what you think happened at each step of the stepwise procedure.

14.56 For the multiple regression model in Exercise 14.4, the estimated standard deviations for each of the coefficients (excluding the constant) are (in order) .01, .01, .03, .06, .01, .01, .03, .04, and .05.

a. If a backward elimination variable selection process were to be used, which of the nine predictors would be the first candidate for elimination? Would it be eliminated?

b. Based on the information given, can you tell what the second candidate for elimination would be? Explain.

14.57 The following table showing the results of two multiple regressions appears in "Does the Composition of the Compensation Committee Influence CEO Compensation Practices?" (*Financial Management* (1999): 41–53):

Independent Variable: Log of Compensation

	Log of 1992 Compensation	
Dependent Variables	**b**	**T**
Intercept	−2.508	4.80
Stock ownership	−.002	−.58
Log of sales	.372	6.56
CEO tenure	.005	.56
Stock returns	.003	2.12
Return on equity	.005	2.79
Insider	.135	1.35

	Log of 1991 Compensation	
Dependent Variables	**b**	**T**
Intercept	−2.098	−3.92
Stock ownership	−.005	−1.73
Log of sales	.286	4.92
CEO tenure	.020	2.16
Stock returns	.006	3.88
Return on equity	.001	.33
Insider	.061	.57

a. Do both regressions show a similar pattern?
b. Calculate the standard error for the coefficient corresponding to the log of sales for the 1992 regression.
c. For the 1991 regression, which variable would be considered first in a backward elimination variable selection procedure? Would it be eliminated?
d. Would the same variable identified in part **c** be the first to be considered in a backward elimination process for the 1992 regression?
e. Assuming the number of observations is 160, determine the P-value for a test of the hypothesis that β_1 in the 1991 model is negative.

14.58 Suppose you were considering a multiple regression analysis with y = house price, x_1 = number of bedrooms, x_2 = number of bathrooms, and x_3 = total number of rooms. Do you think that multicollinearity might be a problem? Explain.

14.59 *This exercise requires use of a computer package.* Using a statistical computer package, compare the best one-, two-, three-, and four-predictor models for the data given in Exercise 14.58. Does this variable-selection procedure lead you to the same choice of model as the backward elimination used in Exercise 14.58?

14.60 The accompanying data is from the article "Breeding Success of the Common Puffin on Different Habitats at Great Island, Newfoundland" (*Ecol. Monographs* (1972): 246–252). The variables considered are y = nesting frequency (burrows per 9 m^2), x_1 = grass cover (%), x_2 = mean soil depth (cm), x_3 = angle of slope (degrees), and x_4 = distance from cliff edge (m).

y	x_1	x_2	x_3	x_4
16	45	39.2	38	3
15	65	47.0	36	12
10	40	24.3	14	18
7	20	30.0	16	21
11	40	47.6	6	27
7	80	47.6	9	36
4	80	45.6	7	39
0	15	27.8	8	45
0	0	41.9	8	54
0	20	36.8	5	60
15	40	34.9	31	3
21	60	45.2	37	12
12	95	32.9	24	18
8	50	26.6	11	24
9	80	32.7	10	30
6	80	38.1	5	36
16	60	37.1	35	6
25	60	47.1	35	12
13	85	34.0	23	18
13	90	43.6	12	21
11	20	30.8	9	27
3	85	34.6	6	33
0	30	37.7	8	42
0	75	45.5	5	48
0	15	51.4	8	54
18	40	32.1	36	6
19	40	35.4	37	9
8	90	30.2	11	18
12	80	33.9	9	24
10	80	40.2	11	30
3	75	33.5	7	36
0	65	40.3	10	42
0	60	31.4	5	39
0	70	32.7	2	48
0	35	38.1	8	51
0	80	40.3	12	45
0	50	43.1	13	51
0	50	42.0	3	57

MINITAB output resulting from application of the backward elimination procedure is also given. Explain what action was taken at each step and why.

STEP	1	2	3
CONSTANT	12.29	11.45	13.96
X_1	-0.019		
T-RATIO	-0.70		
X_2	-0.043	-0.043	
T-RATIO	-1.42	-1.42	
X_3	0.224	0.225	0.176
T-RATIO	2.91	2.94	2.54
X_4	-0.182	-0.203	-0.293
T-RATIO	-2.12	-2.55	-6.01
S	2.83	2.81	2.85
R-SQ	86.20	85.99	85.16

14.61 *This exercise requires use of a computer package.* The accompanying $n = 25$ observations on y = catch at intake (number of fish), x_1 = water temperature (°C), x_2 = minimum tide height (m), x_3 = number of pumps running, x_4 = speed (knots), and x_5 = wind-range of direction (degrees) constitute a subset of the data that appeared in the article "Multiple Regression Analysis for Forecasting Critical Fish Influxes at Power Station Intakes" (*J. Applied Ecol.* (1983): 33–42). Use the variable-selection procedures discussed in this section to formulate a model.

y	x_1	x_2	x_3	x_4	x_5
17	6.7	.5	4	10	50
42	7.8	1.0	4	24	30
1	9.9	1.2	4	17	120

(*continued*)

y	x_1	x_2	x_3	x_4	x_5
11	10.1	.5	4	23	30
8	10.0	.9	4	18	20
30	8.7	.8	4	9	160
2	10.3	1.5	4	13	40
6	10.5	.3	4	10	150
11	11.0	1.2	3	9	50
14	11.2	.6	3	7	100
53	12.9	1.8	3	10	90
9	13.2	.2	3	12	50
4	16.2	.7	3	6	80
3	15.8	1.6	3	7	120
7	16.2	.4	3	10	50
9	15.8	1.2	3	9	60
10	16.0	.8	3	12	90
7	16.2	1.2	3	5	160
12	17.1	.7	3	10	90
12	17.5	.8	3	12	110
26	17.5	1.2	3	18	130
14	17.4	.8	3	9	60
18	17.4	1.1	3	13	30
14	17.8	.5	3	8	160
5	18.0	1.6	3	10	40

14.62 Suppose that $R^2 = .723$ for the model containing predictors x_1, x_4, x_5, and x_8 and $R^2 = .689$ for the model with predictors x_1, x_3, x_5, and x_6.
a. What can you say about R^2 for the model containing predictors x_1, x_3, x_4, x_5, x_6, and x_8? Explain.
b. What can you say about R^2 for the model containing predictors x_1 and x_4? Explain.

Summary of Key Concepts and Formulas

Term or Formula	Comment
Additive multiple regression model, $y = \alpha + \beta_1 x_1 + \cdots + \beta_k x_k + e$	This equation specifies a general probabilistic relationship between y and k predictor variables $x_1, x_2, \ldots, x_k$, where $\beta_1, \ldots, \beta_k$ are population regression coefficients and $\alpha + \beta_1 x_1 + \cdots + \beta_k x_k$ is the population regression function (the mean value of y for fixed values of $x_1, \ldots, x_k$).
Estimated regression function, $\hat{y} = a + b_1 x_1 + \cdots + b_k x_k$	The estimates $a, b_1, \ldots, b_k$ of $\alpha, \beta_1, \ldots, \beta_k$ result from applying the principle of least squares.
Coefficient of multiple determination, $R^2 = 1 - \dfrac{\text{SSResid}}{\text{SSTo}}$	The proportion of observed y variation that can be explained by the model relationship, where SSResid is defined as it is in simple linear regression but is now based on $n - (k + 1)$ degrees of freedom.

Adjusted R^2

A downward adjustment of R^2 that depends on the number of predictors k relative to the sample size n.

F distribution

A type of probability distribution used in many different inferential procedures. A particular F distribution results from specifying both numerator df and denominator df.

$$F = \frac{\dfrac{R^2}{k}}{\dfrac{(1 - R^2)}{n - (k + 1)}}$$

OR

$$F = \frac{\dfrac{\text{SSRegr}}{k}}{\dfrac{\text{SSResid}}{n - (k + 1)}}$$

The test statistic for testing $H_0: \beta_1 = \beta_2 = \cdots = \beta_k = 0$, which asserts that there is no useful linear relationship between y and any of the model predictors. The F test is upper-tailed and is based on numerator df $= k$ and denominator df $= n - (k + 1)$.

$b_i \pm (t \text{ critical values})s_{b_i}$

A confidence interval for the regression coefficient β_i (based on $n - (k + 1)$ df).

$$t = \frac{b_i - \text{hyp. val.}}{s_{b_i}}$$

The test statistic for testing hypotheses about β_i (based on $n - (k + 1)$ df). The most important case is $H_0: \beta_i = 0$, according to which the predictor x_i is not useful as long as all other predictors remain in the model.

$\hat{y} \pm (t \text{ crit. val.})s_{\hat{y}}$
$\hat{y} \pm (t \text{ crit. val.})\sqrt{s_e^2 + s_{\hat{y}}^2}$

A confidence interval for a mean y value and a prediction interval for a single y value when $x_1, \ldots, x_k$ have specified values, where $\hat{y} = a + b_1 x_1 + \cdots + b_k x_k$ and $s_{\hat{y}}$ denotes the estimated standard deviation of $\hat{y}$.

Model selection

An investigator may have data on many predictors that could be included in a model. There are two different approaches to choosing a model: (1) Use an *all-subsets procedure* to identify the best models of each different size (one-predictor models, two-predictor models, etc.) and then compare these according to criteria such as R^2 and adjusted R^2; (2) employ an *automatic selection procedure,* which either successively eliminates predictors until a stopping point is reached (backward elimination) or starts with no predictors and adds them successively until the inclusion of additional predictors cannot be justified.

Supplementary Exercises 14.63 – 14.73

14.63 What factors affect the quality of education in our schools? The article "How Much Is Enough? Applying Regression to a School Finance Case" (*Statistics and the Law,* New York: Wiley, 1986: 257–287) used data from $n = 88$ school districts to carry out a regression analysis based on the following variables:

   y = average language score for fourth-grade students

Background variables:

x_1 = occupational index (% managerial and professional workers in the community)

x_2 = median income

Peer group variables:

   x_3 = % Title I enrollment

   x_4 = Hispanic enrollment ($= 1$ if $> 5\%$ and $= 0$ otherwise)

   x_5 = logarithm of fourth-grade enrollment

   x_6 = prior test score (from 4 years previous to year under study)

School variables:

   x_7 = administrator–teacher ratio

   x_8 = pupil–teacher ratio

x_9 = certificated staff–pupil ratio

x_{10}, x_{11} = indicator variables for average teaching experience (x_{10} = 1 if less than 3 years and 0 otherwise; x_{11} = 1 if more than 6 years and 0 otherwise)

The accompanying table gives estimated coefficients, values of t ratios (b_1/s_{b_1}, b_2/s_{b_2}, and so on), and other relevant information.

Variable	Estimated Coefficient	t ratio
Constant	70.67	6.08
x_1	.458	3.08
x_2	−.000141	−.59
x_3	−58.47	−4.02
x_4	−3.668	−1.73
x_5	−2.942	−2.34
x_6	.200	3.60
x_7	17.93	.42
x_8	.689	.42
x_9	−.403	−.27
x_{10}	−.614	−1.30
x_{11}	−.382	−.58

s_e = 5.57 R^2 = .64

a. Is there a useful linear relationship between y and at least one of the predictors? Test the relevant hypotheses using a .01 significance level.

b. What is the value of adjusted R^2?

c. Calculate and interpret a 95% confidence interval for β_1.

d. Does it appear that one or more predictors could be eliminated from the model without discarding useful information? If so, which one would you eliminate first? Explain your reasoning.

e. Suppose you wanted to decide whether any of the peer group variables provided useful information about y (provided that all other predictors remained in the model). What hypotheses would you test (a single H_0 and H_a)? Could one of the test procedures presented in this chapter be used? Explain.

14.64 The article "Innovation, R&D Productivity, and Global Market Share in the Pharmaceutical Industry" (*Review of Indus. Org.* (1995): 197–207) presented the results of a multiple regression analysis in which the dependent variable was y = the number of patented R&D compounds per R&D employee. The number of observations was n = 78, the model contained six predictors, and SSResid = 1.02, R^2 = .50.

a. Is the chosen model useful? Test the relevant hypotheses.

b. What is the value of adjusted R^2?

c. The predictor x_6 was an indicator variable with value 1 if a firm was headquartered outside the United States. The article reported that b_6 = .001 and the corresponding t ratio was −.92. Provided that the other five predictors remain in the model, is x_6 useful? Test the relevant hypotheses.

14.65 The accompanying data on y = glucose concentration (g/L) and x = fermentation time (days) for a particular blend of malt liquor was read from a scatter plot in the article "Improving Fermentation Productivity with Reverse Osmosis" (*Food Tech.* (1984): 92–96):

x	1	2	3	4	5	6	7	8
y	74	54	52	51	52	53	58	71

a. Construct a scatter plot for this data. Based on the scatter plot, what type of model would you suggest?

b. MINITAB output resulting from fitting a multiple regression model with $x_1 = x$ and $x_2 = x^2$ is shown here. Does this quadratic model specify a useful relationship between y and x?

THE REGRESSION EQUATION is
Y = 84.5 - 15.9X1 + 1.77X2

Predictor	Coef	Stdev	t-ratio
Constant	84.482	4.904	17.23
X1	-15.875	2.500	-6.35
X2	1.7679	0.2712	6.52

s = 3.515   R-sq = 89.5%   R-sq(adj) = 85.3%

c. Could the quadratic term have been eliminated? That is, would a simple linear model have sufficed? Test using a .05 significance level.

14.66 Much interest in management circles has recently focused on how employee compensation is related to various company characteristics. The article "Determinants of R and D Compensation Strategies" (*Personnel Psych.* (1984): 635–650) proposed a quantitative scale for y = base salary for employees of high-tech companies. The following estimated multiple regression equation was then presented:

$$\hat{y} = 2.60 + .125x_1 + .893x_2 + .057x_3 - .014x_4$$

where x_1 = sales volume (in millions of dollars), x_2 = stage in product life cycles (1 = growth, 0 = mature), x_3 = profitability (%), and x_4 = attrition rate (%).

a. There were n = 33 firms in the sample and R^2 = .69. Is the fitted model useful?

b. Predict base compensation for a growth stage firm with sales volume $50 million, profitability 8%, and attrition rate 12%.

c. The estimated standard deviations for the coefficient estimates were .064, .141, .014, and .005 for b_1, b_2, b_3, and b_4, respectively. Should any of the predictors be deleted from the model? Explain.

d. β_2 is the difference between average base compensation for growth stage and mature stage firms when all other predictors are held fixed. Use the information in part **c** to calculate a 95% confidence interval for β_2.

14.67 If $n = 21$ and $k = 10$, for what values of R^2 would adjusted R^2 be negative?

14.68 A study of total body electrical conductivity was described in the article "Measurement of Total Body Electrical Conductivity: A New Method for Estimation of Body Composition" (*Amer. J. Clinical Nutr.* (1983): 735–739). Nineteen observations were given for the variables y = total body electrical conductivity, x_1 = age (years), x_2 = sex (0 = male, 1 = female), x_3 = body mass (kg/m^2), x_4 = body fat (kg), and x_5 = lean body mass (kg).

a. The backward elimination method of variable selection was employed, and MINITAB output is given here. Explain what occurred at each step in the process.

STEPWISE REGRESSION OF Y ON 5
PREDICTORS, WITH N = 19

STEP	1	2	3
CONSTANT	-6.193	-13.285	-15.175
X1	0.31	0.36	0.38
T-RATIO	1.90	2.36	2.96
X2	-7.9	-7.5	-7.0
T-RATIO	-1.93	-1.89	-2.04
X3	-0.43		
T-RATIO	-0.72		
X4	0.22	0.03	
T-RATIO	0.78	0.29	
X5	0.365	0.339	0.378
T-RATIO	2.16	2.09	4.18
S	5.16	5.07	4.91
R-SQ	79.53	78.70	78.57

b. MINITAB output for the multiple regression model relating y to x_1, x_2, and x_5 is shown here. Interpret the values of R^2 and s_e.

THE REGRESSION EQUATION is
Y = -15.2 + 0.377X1 - 6.99X2 + 0.378X5

Predictor	Coef	Stdev	t-ratio
Constant	-15.175	9.620	-1.58
X1	0.3771	0.1273	2.96
X2	-6.988	3.425	-2.04
X5	0.37779	0.09047	4.18

s = 4.914   R-sq = 78.6%   R-sq(adj) = 74.3%

c. Interpret the value of b_2 in the estimated regression equation.

d. If the estimated standard deviation of the statistic $a + b_1(31) + b_2(1) + b_5(52.7)$ is 1.42, give a 95% confidence interval for the true mean total body electrical conductivity of all 31-year-old females whose lean body mass is 52.7 kg.

14.69 The article "Creep and Fatigue Characteristics of Ferrocement Slabs" (*J. Ferrocement* (1984): 309–322) reported data on y = tensile strength (MPa), x_1 = slab thickness (cm), x_2 = load (kg), x_3 = age at loading (days), and x_4 = time under test (days) resulting from stress tests of $n = 9$ reinforced concrete slabs. The backward elimination method of variable selection was applied. Partial MINITAB output follows. Explain what action was taken at each step in the process. MINITAB output for the selected model is also given. Use the estimated regression equation to predict tensile strength for a slab that is 25 cm thick, 150 days old, and is subjected to a load of 200 kg for 50 days.

STEP	1	2	3
CONSTANT	8.496	12.670	12.989
X1	-0.29	-0.42	-0.49
T-RATIO	-1.33	-2.89	-3.14
X2	0.0104	0.0110	0.0116
T-RATIO	6.30	7.40	7.33
X3	0.0059		
T-RATIO	0.83		
X4	-0.023	-0.023	
T-RATIO	-1.48	-1.53	
S	0.533	0.516	0.570
R-SQ	95.81	95.10	92.82

THE REGRESSION EQUATION is
Y = 13.0 - .487X1 + 0.116X2

Predictor	Coef	Stdev	T-ratio
Constant	12.989	3.640	3.57
X1	-0.4867	0.1549	-3.14
X2	0.011569	0.001579	7.33

s = 0.5698   R-sq = 92.8%   R-sq(adj) = 90.4%

14.70 A study of pregnant grey seals involved $n = 25$ observations on the variables y = fetus progesterone level (μg), x_1 = fetus sex (0 = male, 1 = female), x_2 = fetus length (cm), and x_3 = fetus weight (g). MINITAB output for the model using all three independent variables is given ("Gonadotrophin and Progesterone Concentration in Placenta of Grey Seals," *J. Repro. and Fertility* (1984): 521–528).

THE REGRESSION EQUATION is
Y = -1.98 - 1.87X1 + .234X2 + .0001X3

Predictor	Coef	Stdev	t-ratio
Constant	-1.982	4.290	-0.46
X1	-1.871	1.709	-1.09
X2	0.2340	0.1906	1.23
X3	0.000060	0.002020	0.03

s = 4.189   R-sq = 55.2%   R-sq(adj) = 48.8%

Analysis of Variance

SOURCE	DF	SS	MS	F	p
Regression	3	454.63	151.54	8.63	.001
Error	21	368.51	17.55		
Total	24	823.15			

a. Use information from the MINITAB output to test the hypothesis $H_0: \beta_1 = \beta_2 = \beta_3 = 0$.
b. Using an elimination criterion of $-2 \le t$ ratio ≤ 2, should any variable be eliminated? If so, which one?
c. MINITAB output for the regression using only x_1 = sex and x_2 = length is given. Would you recommend keeping both x_1 and x_2 in the model? Explain.

THE REGRESSION EQUATION is
Y = -2.09 - 1.87X1 + .240X2

Predictor	Coef	Stdev	t-ratio
Constant	-2.090	2.212	-0.94
X1	-1.865	1.661	-1.12
X2	0.23952	0.04604	5.20

s = 4.093   R-sq = 55.2%   R-sq(adj) = 51.2%

d. After elimination of both x_3 and x_1, the estimated regression equation is $\hat{y} = -2.61 + .231x_2$. The corresponding values of R^2 and s_e are .527 and 4.116, respectively. Interpret these values.
e. Referring to part **d,** how would you interpret the value of $b_2 = .231$? Does it make sense to interpret the value of a as the estimate of average progesterone level when length is zero? Explain.

14.71 The authors of the article "Influence of Temperature and Salinity on Development of White Perch Eggs" (*Trans. Amer. Fisheries Soc.* (1982): 396–398) used a quadratic regression model to describe the relationship between y = percentage hatch of white perch eggs and x = water temperature (°C). The estimated regression equation was given as $\hat{y} = -41.0 + 14.6x - .55x^2$.
a. Graph the curve corresponding to this equation by plotting the (x, y) pairs using x values of 10, 12, 14, 16, 18, 20, 22, and 24 (these are the temperatures used in the article). Draw a smooth curve through the points in your plot.
b. The authors make the claim that the optimal temperature for hatch is 14°C. Based on your graph in part **a,** does this statement seem reasonable? Explain.

14.72 A sample of $n = 20$ companies was selected, and the values of y = stock price and $k = 15$ predictor variables (such as quarterly dividend, previous year's earnings, debt ratio, and so on) were determined. When the multiple regression model with these 15 predictors was fit to the data, $R^2 = .90$ resulted.
a. Does the model appear to specify a useful relationship between y and the predictor variables? Carry out a test at a significance level of .05. (The value 5.86 captures upper-tail area .05 under the F curve with 15 numerator df and 4 denominator df.)
b. Based on the result of part **a,** does a high R^2 value by itself imply that a model is useful? Under what circumstances might you be suspicious of a model with a high R^2 value?
c. With n and k as given here, how large would R^2 have to be for the model to be judged useful at the .05 level of significance?

14.73 *This exercise requires the use of a computer package.* The article "Entry and Profitability in a Rate-Free Savings and Loan Market" (*Quarterly Review of Econ. and Business* (1978): 87–95) gave the accompanying data on y = profit margin of savings and loan companies in a given year, x_1 = net revenues in that year, and x_2 = number of savings and loan branch offices.

x_1	x_2	y	x_1	x_2	y
3.92	7298	.75	3.78	6672	.84
3.61	6855	.71	3.82	6890	.79
3.32	6636	.66	3.97	7115	.70
3.07	6506	.61	4.07	7327	.68
3.06	6450	.70	4.25	7546	.72
3.11	6402	.72	4.41	7931	.55
3.21	6368	.77	4.49	8097	.63

(*continued*)

x_1	x_2	y	x_1	x_2	y
3.26	6340	.74	4.70	8468	.56
3.42	6349	.90	4.58	8717	.41
3.42	6352	.82	4.69	8991	.51
3.45	6361	.75	4.71	9179	.47
3.58	6369	.77	4.78	9318	.32
3.66	6546	.78			

a. Fit a multiple regression model using both independent variables.

b. Use the F test to determine whether the model provides useful information for predicting profit margin.

c. Interpret the values of R^2 and s_e.

d. Would a regression model using a single independent variable (x_1 alone or x_2 alone) have sufficed? Explain.

e. Plot the (x_1, x_2) pairs. Does the plot indicate any sample observation that may have been highly influential in estimating the model coefficients? Explain. Do you see any evidence of multicollinearity? Explain.

References

Consult the references listed at the end of Chapter 5.

Kerlinger, Fred N. and Elazar J. Pedhazar, *Multiple Regression in Behavioral Research.* Austin, Texas: Holt, Rinehart & Winston, Inc., 1973. (A readable introduction to multiple regression).

15

The Analysis of Variance

Methods for testing $H_0: \mu_1 - \mu_2 = 0$ (that is, $\mu_1 = \mu_2$), where μ_1 and μ_2 are the means of two different populations or the true mean responses when two different treatments are applied, were discussed in Chapter 11. Many investigations involve a comparison of more than two population or treatment means. For example, an investigation carried out to study purchasers of luxury automobiles ("Measuring Values Can Sharpen Segmentation in the Luxury Car Market," *J. of Advertising Research* (1995): 9–22) reported data on a number of different attributes that might affect purchase decisions, including comfort, safety, styling, durability, and reliability. Here is summary information on the level of importance of speed, rated on a seven-point scale.

Type of Car	American	German	Japanese
Sample size	58	38	59
Sample mean rating	3.05	2.87	2.67

Let μ_1, μ_2, and μ_3 denote the true average (i.e., population mean) rating on this attribute for owners of American, German, and Japanese luxury cars, respectively. Does the data support the claim that $\mu_1 = \mu_2 = \mu_3$, or does it appear that at least two of the μ's are different from one another? This is an example of a **single-factor analysis of variance** (**ANOVA**) problem, in which the objective is to decide whether the means for more than two populations or treatments are identical. The first several sections of this chapter discuss various aspects of single-factor ANOVA. In Sections 15.3 and 15.4, we consider more complex ANOVA situations and methods.

15.1   Single-Factor ANOVA and the *F* Test

When two or more populations or treatments are being compared, the characteristic that distinguishes the populations or treatments from one another is called the **factor** under investigation. For example, an experiment might be carried out to compare three different methods for teaching reading (three different treatments), in which case the factor of interest would be *teaching method.* This is a qualitative factor. If the growth of fish raised in waters having different salinity levels — 0%, 10%, 20%, and 30% — is of interest, the factor *salinity level* is quantitative.

A **single-factor analysis of variance** (**ANOVA**) problem involves a comparison of k population or treatment means $\mu_1, \mu_2, \ldots, \mu_k$. The objective is to test

$$H_0: \quad \mu_1 = \mu_2 = \cdots = \mu_k$$

against

$$H_a: \quad \text{At least two of the } \mu\text{'s are different.}$$

The analysis is based on k independently selected samples, one from each population or for each treatment. In the case of populations, a random sample from each population is selected independently of that from any other population. When comparing treatments, the experimental units (subjects or objects) that receive any particular treatment are chosen at random from those available for the experiment. A comparison of treatments based on independently selected experimental units is often referred to as a **completely randomized design.**

The decision as to whether the null hypothesis of single-factor ANOVA should be rejected depends on how substantially the samples from the different populations or treatments differ from one another. Figure 15.1 displays two possible data

FIGURE 15.1 Two possible ANOVA data sets when three populations are under investigation:

• = observation from population 1
x = observation from population 2
○ = observation from population 3

sets that might result when observations are selected from each of three populations under study. Each data set consists of five observations from the first population, four from the second, and six from the third. For both data sets, the three
sample means are located by vertical line segments. The means of the two samples
from population 1 are identical, and a similar statement holds for the two samples
from population 2 and those from population 3.

Almost anyone, after looking at the data set in Figure 15.1(a), would readily
agree that the claim $\mu_1 = \mu_2 = \mu_3$ appears to be false. Not only are the three sample
means different, but there is very clear separation between the samples. In other
words, differences between the three sample means are quite large relative to variability within each sample. (If all data sets gave such obvious messages, statisticians
would not be in such great demand.) The situation pictured in Figure 15.1(b) is
much less clear-cut. The sample means are as different as they were in the first data
set, but there is now considerable overlap among the three samples. The separation
between sample means here can plausibly be attributed to substantial variability in
the populations (and therefore the samples) rather than to differences between μ_1,
μ_2, and μ_3. The phrase *analysis of variance* comes from the idea of analyzing variability in the data to see how much can be attributed to differences in the μ's and
how much is due to variability in the individual populations. In Figure 15.1(a), there
is little within-sample variability relative to the amount of between-sample variability, whereas in Figure 15.1(b), a great deal more of the total variability is due to
variation within each sample. If differences between the sample means can be explained by within-sample variability, there is no compelling reason for rejecting H_0.

Notation and Assumptions

Notation in single-factor ANOVA is a natural extension of the notation used in
Chapter 11 for comparing two population or treatment means.

ANOVA Notation

k = number of populations or treatments being compared

Population or treatment	1	2	. . .	k
Population or treatment mean	μ_1	μ_2	. . .	μ_k
Population or treatment variance	σ_1^2	σ_2^2	. . .	σ_k^2
Sample size	n_1	n_2	. . .	n_k
Sample mean	$\bar{x}_1$	$\bar{x}_2$	. . .	$\bar{x}_k$
Sample variance	s_1^2	s_2^2	. . .	s_k^2

$N = n_1 + n_2 + \cdots + n_k$ (the total number of observations in the data set)

T = grand total = sum of all N observations = $n_1\bar{x}_1 + n_2\bar{x}_2 + \cdots + n_k\bar{x}_k$

$\bar{\bar{x}}$ = grand mean = $\dfrac{T}{N}$

A decision between H_0 and H_a will be based on examining the $\bar{x}$ values to see whether observed discrepancies are small enough to be attributable simply to sampling variability or whether an alternative explanation for the differences is necessary.

EXAMPLE 15.1

The article "Compression of Single-Wall Corrugated Shipping Containers Using Fixed and Floating Text Platens" (*J. Testing and Evaluation* (1992): 318–320) describes an experiment in which several different types of boxes were compared with respect to compression strength (lb). Table 15.1 presents the results of a single-factor experiment involving $k = 4$ types of boxes (the sample means and standard deviations are in close agreement with values given in the paper).

Table 15.1 *Data and summary quantities for Example 15.1*

Type of Box	Compression Strength (lb)						Sample Mean	Sample SD
1	655.5	788.3	734.3	721.4	679.1	699.4	713.00	46.55
2	789.2	772.5	786.9	686.1	732.1	774.8	756.93	40.34
3	737.1	639.0	696.3	671.7	717.2	727.1	698.07	37.20
4	535.1	628.7	542.4	559.0	586.9	520.0	562.02	39.87
							$\bar{\bar{x}} = 682.50$	

With μ_i denoting the true average compression strength for boxes of type i ($i = 1, 2, 3, 4$), the null hypothesis is $H_0: \mu_1 = \mu_2 = \mu_3 = \mu_4$. Figure 15.2(a) shows a comparative boxplot for the four samples. There is a substantial amount of overlap among observations on the first three types of boxes, but compression strengths for the fourth type appear considerably smaller than for the other types. This suggests that H_0 is not true. If the comparative boxplot looked instead like that of Figure 15.2(b), it would not be so obvious whether H_0 were true or false. In situations such as this, we need a formal test procedure.

FIGURE 15.2 Boxplots for Example 15.1: (a) Original data

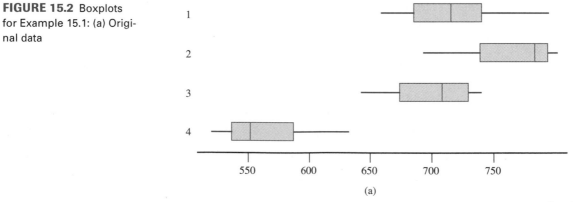

(a)

(*continued*)

FIGURE 15.2 (Continued)
(b) Altered data

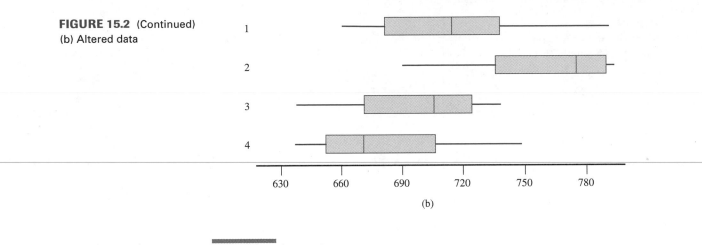

(b)

As with the inferential methods of previous chapters, the validity of the ANOVA test for H_0: $\mu_1 = \mu_2 = \cdots = \mu_k$ requires some assumptions.

Assumptions for ANOVA

1. Each of the k population or treatment response distributions is normal.
2. $\sigma_1 = \sigma_2 = \cdots = \sigma_k$ (The k normal distributions have identical standard deviations.)
3. The observations in the sample from any particular one of the k populations or treatments are independent of one another.
4. When comparing population means, k random samples are selected independently of one another. When comparing treatment means, treatments are assigned at random to subjects or objects (or vice versa).

In practice, the test based on these assumptions will work well as long as the assumptions are not too badly violated. If the sample sizes are reasonably large, normal probability plots or boxplots of the data in each sample are helpful in checking the assumption of normality. Often, however, sample sizes are so small that a separate normal probability plot for each sample is of little value in checking normality. A single combined plot results from first subtracting $\bar{x}_1$ from each observation in the first sample, $\bar{x}_2$ from each value in the second sample, and so on, and then constructing a normal probability plot of all N deviations from their respective means. The plot should be reasonably straight. Figure 15.3 (page 616) shows such a plot for the data of Example 15.1.

There is a formal procedure for testing the equality of population standard deviations. Unfortunately, it is quite sensitive to even a small departure from the normality assumption, so we do not recommend its use. Instead, we suggest that the F test (to be described subsequently) can safely be used if the largest of the sample standard deviations is at most twice the smallest one. The largest standard deviation

FIGURE 15.3 A normal probability plot based on the data of Example 15.1

in Example 15.1 is $s_1 = 46.55$, which is only about 1.25 times the smallest one ($s_3 = 37.20$). The book *Beyond ANOVA: The Basics of Applied Statistics* (see the chapter references) is a good source for alternative methods of analysis if there appears to be a violation of assumptions.

The test procedure is based on the following measures of variation in the data.

Definition

A measure of disparity among the sample means is the **treatment sum of squares,** denoted by **SSTr** and given by

$$\text{SSTr} = n_1(\bar{x}_1 - \bar{\bar{x}})^2 + n_2(\bar{x}_2 - \bar{\bar{x}})^2 + \cdots + n_k(\bar{x}_k - \bar{\bar{x}})^2$$

A measure of variation within the k samples, called **error sum of squares** and denoted by **SSE,** is

$$\text{SSE} = (n_1 - 1)s_1^2 + (n_2 - 1)s_2^2 + \cdots + (n_k - 1)s_k^2$$

Each sum of squares has an associated df:

treatment df $= k - 1$ \qquad error df $= N - k$

A **mean square** is a sum of squares divided by its df. In particular,

$$\textbf{mean square for treatments} = \textbf{MSTr} = \frac{\text{SSTr}}{k - 1}$$

$$\textbf{mean square for error} = \textbf{MSE} = \frac{\text{SSE}}{N - k}$$

The error df comes from adding the df's associated with each of the sample variances:

$$(n_1 - 1) + (n_2 - 1) + \cdots + (n_k - 1) = n_1 + n_2 + \cdots + n_k - 1 - 1 - \cdots - 1 = N - k$$

EXAMPLE 15.2

Let's return to the compression strength data of Example 15.1. With $\bar{x}_1 = 713.00$, $\bar{x}_2 = 756.93, \bar{x}_3 = 698.07, \bar{x}_4 = 562.02, \bar{\bar{x}} = 682.50$, and $n_1 = n_2 = n_3 = n_4 = 6$,

$$SSTr = n_1(\bar{x}_1 - \bar{\bar{x}})^2 + n_2(\bar{x}_2 - \bar{\bar{x}})^2 + \cdots + n_k(\bar{x}_k - \bar{\bar{x}})^2$$
$$= 6(713.00 - 682.50)^2 + 6(756.93 - 682.50)^2 + 6(698.07 - 682.50)^2$$
$$+ 6(562.02 - 682.50)^2$$
$$= 5581.50 + 33{,}238.95 + 1454.55 + 87{,}092.58$$
$$= 127{,}367.58$$

Since $s_1 = 46.55$, $s_2 = 40.34$, $s_3 = 37.20$, and $s_4 = 39.87$,

$$SSE = (n_1 - 1)s_1^2 + (n_2 - 1)s_2^2 + \cdots + (n_k - 1)s_k^2$$
$$= (6 - 1)(46.55)^2 + (6 - 1)(40.34)^2 + (6 - 1)(37.20)^2 + (6 - 1)(39.87)^2$$
$$= 33{,}838.375$$

Degrees of freedom are

treatment df $= k - 1 = 3$ error df $= N - k = 6 + 6 + 6 + 6 - 4 = 20$

from which

$$MSTr = \frac{SSTr}{k - 1} = \frac{127{,}367.58}{3} = 42{,}455.86$$

$$MSE = \frac{SSE}{N - k} = \frac{33{,}838.375}{20} = 1691.92$$

Both MSTr and MSE are quantities whose values can be calculated once sample data is available; that is, they are statistics. Each of these statistics will vary in value from data set to data set. For example, repeating the experiment of Example 15.1 with the same sample sizes might yield

$\bar{x}_1 = 703.24$	$\bar{x}_2 = 769.15$	$\bar{x}_3 = 678.83$	$\bar{x}_4 = 575.50$
$s_1 = 42.69$	$s_2 = 41.35$	$s_3 = 35.02$	$s_4 = 41.20$

from which

MSTr $= 38{,}796.30$ (previously 42,455.86)
MSE $= 1614.02$ (previously 1691.92)

Both MSTr and MSE have sampling distributions and, in particular, mean values. The following box describes the key relationship between μ_{MSTr} and μ_{MSE}, the mean values of the two statistics.

When H_0 is true ($\mu_1 = \mu_2 = \cdots = \mu_k$),

$\mu_{MSTr} = \mu_{MSE}$

However, when H_0 is false,

$\mu_{MSTr} > \mu_{MSE}$

and the greater the differences among the μ's, the larger μ_{MSTr} will be relative to μ_{MSE}.

According to this result, when H_0 is true, we expect the two mean squares to be close to one another, whereas we expect MSTr to substantially exceed MSE when some μ's differ greatly from others. Thus, a calculated MSTr that is much larger than MSE casts doubt on H_0. In Example 15.2, MSTr = 42,455.86 and MSE = 1691.92, so MSTr is about 25 times as large as MSE. Can this be attributed solely to sampling variability, or is the ratio MSTr/MSE of sufficient magnitude to suggest that H_0 is false? Before we can describe a formal test procedure, it is necessary to revisit F distributions first introduced in multiple regression analysis (Chapter 14).

Many ANOVA test procedures are based on probability distributions called F distributions. As explained in Chapter 14, an F distribution always arises in connection with a ratio. A particular F distribution is obtained by specifying both numerator degrees of freedom (df_1) and denominator degrees of freedom (df_2). Figure 15.4 shows an F curve for a particular choice of df_1 and df_2. All F tests in this book are upper-tailed, so the P-value is the area under the F curve to the right of the calculated F.

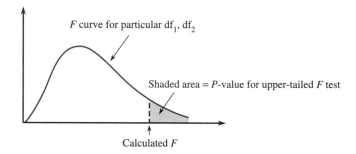

FIGURE 15.4 An F curve and P-value for an upper-tailed test

Tabulation of these upper-tail areas is very cumbersome, because there are two df's rather than just one (as in the case of t distributions). For selected df_1, df_2 pairs, our F table (Appendix Table VII) gives only the four numbers that capture tail areas .10, .05, .01, and .001, respectively. Here are the four numbers for $df_1 = 4$, $df_2 = 10$ along with the statements that can be made about the P-value:

Tail area	.10	.05	.01	.001
Value	2.61	3.48	5.99	11.28
	↑	↑	↑	↑	↑
	a	b	c	d	e

a. $F < 2.61 \rightarrow$ tail area = P-value $> .10$

b. $2.61 < F < 3.48 \rightarrow .05 < P$-value $< .10$

c. $3.48 < F < 5.99 \rightarrow .01 < P$-value $< .05$

d. $5.99 < F < 11.28 \rightarrow .001 < P$-value $< .01$

e. $F > 11.28 \rightarrow P$-value $< .001$

Thus, if $F = 7.12$, $.001 < P$-value $< .01$. If a test with $\alpha = .05$ is used, H_0 should be rejected, since P-value $\leq \alpha$. The most frequently used statistical computer packages will provide exact P-values for F tests.

The Single-Factor ANOVA *F* Test

Null hypothesis: $H_0: \mu_1 = \mu_2 = \cdots = \mu_k$

Test statistic: $F = \dfrac{\text{MSTr}}{\text{MSE}}$

When H_0 is true and the ANOVA assumptions are reasonable, F has an F distribution with $\text{df}_1 = k - 1$ and $\text{df}_2 = N - k$.

Values of F more contradictory to H_0 than what was calculated are values even farther out in the upper tail, so the P-value is the area captured in the upper tail of the corresponding F curve.

EXAMPLE 15.3

The two mean squares for the compression strength data given in Example 15.1 were calculated in Example 15.2 as

$$\text{MSTr} = 42{,}455.86 \qquad \text{MSE} = 1691.92$$

The value of the F statistic is then

$$F = \frac{\text{MSTr}}{\text{MSE}} = \frac{42{,}455.86}{1691.92} = 25.09$$

With $\text{df}_1 = k - 1 = 3$ and $\text{df}_2 = N - k = 24 - 4 = 20$, Appendix Table VII shows that 8.10 captures tail area .001. Since $25.09 > 8.10$, it follows that P-value = captured tail area $< .001$. The P-value is smaller than any reasonable α, so there is compelling evidence for rejecting $H_0: \mu_1 = \mu_2 = \cdots = \mu_k$. True average compression strength appears to depend in some way on the type of box used.

EXAMPLE 15.4

The article "The Soundtrack of Recklessness: Musical Preferences and Reckless Behavior Among Adolescents (*J. Adolescent Research* (1992): 313–331) described a study whose purpose was to determine whether adolescents who preferred certain types of music reported higher rates of reckless behaviors, such as speeding, drug use, shoplifting, and unprotected sex.

Independently chosen random samples were selected from each of four groups of students with different musical preferences at a large high school: (1) acoustic/pop, (2) mainstream rock, (3) hard rock, and (4) heavy metal. Each student in these samples was asked how many times they had engaged in various reckless activities during the last year. The table on page 620 lists data on driving over 80 mph that is consistent with summary quantities given in the article. (The sample sizes in the article were much larger, but for purposes of this example, we use $n_1 = n_2 = n_3 = n_4 = 20$.)

	Musical Preference			
	Acoustic/ Pop	**Mainstream Rock**	**Hard Rock**	**Heavy Metal**
	2	3	3	4
	3	2	4	3
	4	1	3	4
	1	2	1	3
	3	3	2	3
	3	4	1	3
	3	3	4	3
	3	2	2	3
	2	4	2	2
	2	4	2	4
	1	4	3	4
	3	4	3	5
	2	2	4	4
	2	3	3	5
	2	2	3	3
	3	2	2	4
	2	2	3	5
	2	3	4	4
	3	1	2	2
	4	3	4	3
n	20	20	20	20
$\bar{x}$	2.50	2.70	2.75	3.55
s	.827	.979	.967	.887
s^2	.6839	.9584	.9351	.7868

Also, $N = 80$, grand total $= 230.0$, and $\bar{\bar{x}} = 230.0/80 = 2.875$.

Let's carry out an F test to see whether true mean number of times driving over 80 mph varies with musical preference.

1. Let μ_1, μ_2, μ_3, and μ_4 denote the true mean number of times driving over 80 mph for individuals preferring acoustic/pop, mainstream rock, hard rock, and heavy metal, respectively.

2. $H_0: \mu_1 = \mu_2 = \mu_3 = \mu_4$

3. H_a: At least two among μ_1, μ_2, μ_3, and μ_4 are different.

4. *Significance level*: $\alpha = .01$

5. *Test statistic*: $F = \dfrac{\text{MSTr}}{\text{MSE}}$

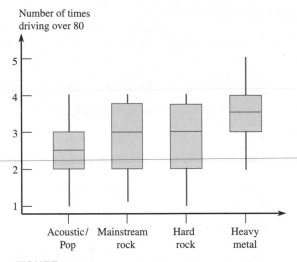

FIGURE 15.5 Boxplots for data of Example 15.4

6. *Assumptions*: Figure 15.5 shows boxplots for the four samples. The boxplots are roughly symmetric, and there are no outliers. The largest standard deviation ($s_2 = .979$) is not more than twice as big as the smallest ($s_1 = .827$). The data consists of independently chosen random samples. The assumptions of ANOVA are reasonable.

7. *Computation*:

$$\text{SSTr} = n_1(\bar{x}_1 - \bar{\bar{x}})^2 + n_2(\bar{x}_2 - \bar{\bar{x}})^2 + \cdots + n_k(\bar{x}_k - \bar{\bar{x}})^2$$
$$= 20(2.50 - 2.875)^2 + 20(2.70 - 2.875)^2$$
$$+ 20(2.75 - 2.875)^2 + 20(3.55 - 2.875)^2$$
$$= 12.850$$

treatment df $= k - 1 = 3$

$$\text{SSE} = (n_1 - 1)s_1^2 + (n_2 - 1)s_2^2 + \cdots + (n_k - 1)s_k^2$$
$$= 19(.6839) + 19(.9584) + 19(.9351) + 19(.7868)$$
$$= 63.9020$$

error df $= N - k = 80 - 4 = 76$

Thus,

$$F = \frac{\text{MSTr}}{\text{MSE}} = \frac{\text{SSTr/df}}{\text{SSE/df}} = \frac{12.850/3}{63.9020/76} = \frac{4.283}{.841} = 5.09$$

8. *P-value*: Appendix Table VII shows that for $df_1 = 3$ and $df_2 = 90$ (the closest tabled df to df = 76), the value 4.01 captures upper-tail area .01 and 5.91 captures upper-tail area .001. Because $4.01 < F = 5.09 < 5.91$, it follows that $.001 < P\text{-value} < .01$.

9. *Conclusion*: Since $P\text{-value} < \alpha$, we reject H_0. The mean number of times driving over 80 mph does not appear to be the same for all four musical preference groups.

Summarizing an ANOVA

Analysis of variance calculations are often summarized in a tabular format called an ANOVA table. To understand such a table, we must define one more sum of squares.

Total sum of squares, denoted by **SSTo,** is given by

$$SSTo = \sum_{\text{all } N \text{ obs.}} (x - \bar{\bar{x}})^2$$

with associated df $N - 1$.

The relationship between the three sums of squares is

$$SSTo = SSTr + SSE$$

which is often called the *fundamental identity for single-factor ANOVA.*

The quantity SSTo, the sum of squared deviations about the grand mean, is a measure of total variability in the data set consisting of all k samples. The quantity SSE results from measuring variability separately within each sample and then combining as indicated in the formula for SSE. Such within-sample variability is present regardless of whether H_0 is true. The magnitude of SSTr, on the other hand, has much to do with the status of H_0 (whether it is true or false). The more the μ's differ from one another, the larger SSTr will tend to be. Thus, SSTr represents variation that can (at least to some extent) be explained by any differences between means. An informal paraphrase of the fundamental identity is

total variation = explained variation + unexplained variation

Once any two of the SS's have been calculated, the remaining one is easily obtained from the fundamental identity. Often SSTo and SSTr are calculated first (using computational formulas given in the chapter appendix), and then SSE is obtained by subtraction: SSE = SSTo − SSTr. All df's, SS's, and MS's are entered in an ANOVA table as displayed in Table 15.2. The P-value will usually appear to the right of F when the analysis is done by a statistical software package.

Table 15.2 *General format for a single-factor ANOVA table*

Source of Variation	df	Sum of Squares	Mean Square	F
Treatments	$k - 1$	SSTr	$MSTr = \dfrac{SSTr}{k - 1}$	$F = \dfrac{MSTr}{MSE}$
Error	$N - k$	SSE	$MSE = \dfrac{SSE}{N - k}$	
Total	$N - 1$	SSTo		

An ANOVA table from MINITAB for the reckless driving data of Example 15.4 is shown in Table 15.3. The *P*-value is .003, consistent with our previous conclusion that $.001 < P\text{-value} < .01$.

Table 15.3 *An ANOVA table from MINITAB for the data of Example 15.4*

One-way Analysis of Variance
Analysis of Variance

Source	DF	SS	MS	F	P
Factor	3	12.850	4.283	5.09	0.003
Error	76	63.900	0.841		
Total	79	76.750			

Exercises 15.1 – 15.18

15.1 Give as much information as you can about the *P*-value for an upper-tailed *F* test in each of the following situations.

a. $df_1 = 4$, $df_2 = 15$, $F = 5.37$
b. $df_1 = 4$, $df_2 = 15$, $F = 1.90$
c. $df_1 = 4$, $df_2 = 15$, $F = 4.89$
d. $df_1 = 3$, $df_2 = 20$, $F = 14.48$
e. $df_1 = 3$, $df_2 = 20$, $F = 2.69$
f. $df_1 = 4$, $df_2 = 50$, $F = 3.24$

15.2 Give as much information as you can about the *P*-value of the single-factor ANOVA *F* test in each of the following situations.

a. $k = 5, n_1 = n_2 = n_3 = n_4 = n_5 = 4, F = 5.37$
b. $k = 5, n_1 = n_2 = n_3 = 5, n_4 = n_5 = 4, F = 2.83$
c. $k = 3, n_1 = 4, n_2 = 5, n_3 = 6, F = 5.02$
d. $k = 3, n_1 = n_2 = 4, n_3 = 6, F = 15.90$
e. $k = 4, n_1 = n_2 = 15, n_3 = 12, n_4 = 10, F = 1.75$

15.3 Employees of a certain state university system can choose from among four different health plans. Each plan differs somewhat from the others in terms of hospitalization coverage. Four samples of recently hospitalized individuals were selected, each sample consisting of people covered by a different health plan. The length of the hospital stay (number of days) was determined for each individual selected.

a. What hypotheses would you test to decide whether average length of stay was related to health plan? (*Note*: Carefully define the population characteristics of interest.)
b. If each sample consisted of eight individuals and the value of the ANOVA *F* statistic was $F = 4.37$, what conclusion would be appropriate for a test with $\alpha = .01$?
c. Answer the question posed in part **b** if the *F* value given there resulted from sample sizes $n_1 = 9, n_2 = 8, n_3 = 7$, and $n_4 = 8$.

15.4 The article "Heavy Drinking and Problems Among Wine Drinkers" (*Journal of Studies on Alcohol* (1999): 467–471) analyzed drinking problems among Canadians. For each of several different groups of drinkers, the mean and standard deviation of "highest number of drinks consumed" were calculated:

	$\bar{x}$	s	n
Beer only	7.52	6.41	1256
Wine only	2.69	2.66	1107
Spirits only	5.51	6.44	759
Beer and wine	5.39	4.07	1334
Beer and spirits	9.16	7.38	1039
Wine and spirits	4.03	3.03	1057
Beer, wine, and spirits	6.75	5.49	2151

Assume that each of the seven samples studied can be viewed as a random sample for the respective group. Is there sufficient evidence to conclude that the mean value of highest number of drinks consumed is not the same for all seven groups?

15.5 Suppose that a random sample of size $n = 5$ was selected from the vineyard properties for sale in Sonoma County, California, in each of 3 years. The following data is consistent with summary information on price per acre (in dollars, rounded to the nearest thousand) for disease-resistant grape vineyards in Sonoma County (*Wines and Vines* (November 1999)).

1996	30,000	34,000	36,000	38,000	40,000
1997	30,000	35,000	37,000	38,000	40,000
1998	40,000	41,000	43,000	44,000	50,000

a. Construct boxplots for each of the 3 years on a common axis, and label each by year. Comment on the similarities and differences.
b. Carry out an ANOVA to determine whether there is evidence to support the claim that the mean price per acre for vineyard land in Sonoma County was not the same for the 3 years considered. Use a significance level of .05 for your test.

15.6 The article "An Analysis of Job Sharing, Full-Time, and Part-Time Arrangements" (*Amer. Business Review* (1989): 34–40) reported on a study of hospital employees from three different groups. Each employee reported a level of satisfaction with his or her work schedule (1 = very dissatisfied to 7 = very satisfied), as shown in the accompanying table.

Group	Sample Size	Sample Mean
1. Job sharers	24	6.60
2. Full-time employees	24	5.37
3. Part-time employees	20	5.20

a. What are numerator and denominator df's for the *F* test?
b. The test statistic value is $F = 6.62$. Use a test with significance level .05 to decide whether it is plausible that true average satisfaction levels are identical for the three groups.
c. What is the value of MSE?

15.7 High productivity and carbohydrate storage ability of the Jerusalem artichoke make it a promising agricultural crop. The article "Leaf Gas Exchange and Tuber Yield in Jerusalem Artichoke Cultivars" (*Field Crops Research* (1991): 241–252) reported on various plant characteristics. Consider the accompanying data on chlorophyll concentration (gm/m^2) for four varieties of Jerusalem artichoke:

Variety	BI	RO	WA	TO
Sample mean	.30	.24	.41	.33

Suppose that the sample sizes were 5, 5, 4, and 6, respectively, and also that MSE = .0130. Does the data suggest that true average chlorophyll concentration depends on the variety? State and test the appropriate hypotheses using a significance level of .05.

15.8 It has been reported that varying work schedules can lead to a variety of health problems for workers. The article "Nutrient Intake in Day Workers and Shift Workers" (*Work and Stress* (1994): 332–342) reported on blood glucose levels (mmol/L) for day-shift workers and workers on two different types of rotating shifts. The sample sizes were $n_1 = 37$ for the day shift, $n_2 = 34$ for the second shift, and $n_3 = 25$ for the third shift. A single-factor ANOVA resulted in $F = 3.834$. At a significance level of .05, does true average blood glucose level appear to depend on the type of shift?

15.9 The chapter introduction discussed a study in which luxury car owners were asked to rate the importance of various attributes on a quantitative scale. Summary information for the importance of speed is as follows:

Type of Car	American	German	Japanese
Sample size	58	38	59
Sample mean	3.05	2.87	2.67

In addition, SSE = 459.04. Carry out a test of hypothesis to decide whether true average importance rating of speed is the same for owners of the three types of cars.

15.10 The article "Utilizing Feedback and Goal Setting to Increase Performance Skills of Managers" (*Academy of Mgmt. J.* (1979): 516–526) reported the results of an experiment to compare three different interviewing techniques for employee evaluations. One method allowed the employee being evaluated to discuss previous evaluations, the second involved setting goals for the employee, and the third did not allow either feedback or goal setting. After the interviews were concluded, the evaluated employee was asked to indicate how satisfied he or she was with the interview. (A numerical scale was used to quantify level of satisfaction.) The authors used ANOVA to compare the three interview techniques. An *F* statistic value of 4.12 was reported.
a. Suppose that a total of 33 subjects were used, with each technique applied to 11 of them. Use this information to conduct a level .05 test of the null hypothesis of no difference in mean satisfaction level for the three interview techniques.
b. The actual number of subjects on which each technique was used was 45. After studying the *F* table, explain why the conclusion in part **a** still holds.

15.11 An investigation carried out to study the toxic effects of mercury was described in the article "Comparative Responses of the Action of Different Mercury Compounds on Barley" (*Intl. J. of Environ. Studies* (1983): 323–327). Ten different concentrations of mercury (0, 1, 5, 10, 50, 100, 200, 300, 400, and 500 mg/L) were compared with respect to their effects on average dry weight (per 100 seven-day-old seedlings). The basic experiment was replicated four times for a total of 40 dry-weight observations (four for each treatment level). The article reported an ANOVA *F* statistic value of 1.895. Using a significance level of .05, test the null hypothesis that the true mean dry weight is the same for all ten concentration levels.

15.12 The accompanying data on calcium content of wheat is consistent with summary quantities that appeared in the article "Mineral Contents of Cereal Grains as Affected by Storage and Insect Infestation" (*J. Stored Prod. Res.* (1992): 147–151). Four different storage times were considered. Partial output from the SAS computer package is shown at the bottom of the page.

Storage Period	Observations					
0 months	58.75	57.94	58.91	56.85	55.21	57.30
1 month	58.87	56.43	56.51	57.67	59.75	58.48
2 months	59.13	60.38	58.01	59.95	59.51	60.34
4 months	62.32	58.76	60.03	59.36	59.61	61.95

a. Verify that the sums of squares and df's are as given in the ANOVA table.
b. Is there sufficient evidence to conclude that the mean calcium content is not the same for the four different storage times? Use the value of *F* from the ANOVA table to test the appropriate hypotheses at significance level .05.

15.13 In an experiment to investigate the performance of four different brands of spark plugs intended for use on a 125-cc motorcycle, five plugs of each brand were tested, and the number of miles (at a constant speed) until failure was observed. A partially completed ANOVA table is given. Fill in the missing entries, and test the relevant hypotheses using a .05 level of significance.

Source of Variation	df	Sum of Squares	Mean Square	F
Brands				
Error		235,419.04		
Total		310,500.76		

15.14 The partially completed ANOVA table given in this problem is taken from the article "Perception of Spatial Incongruity" (*J. of Nervous and Mental Disease* (1961): 222), in which the abilities of three different groups to identify a perceptual incongruity were assessed and compared. All individuals in the experiment had been hospitalized to undergo psychiatric treatment. There were 21 individuals in the depressive group, 32 individuals in the functional "other" group, and 21 individuals in the brain-damaged group. Complete the ANOVA table. Carry out the appropriate test of hypothesis (use $\alpha = .01$), and interpret your results.

Source of Variation	df	Sum of Squares	Mean Square	F
Treatments			76.09	
Error				
Total		1123.14		

15.15 Research carried out to investigate the relationship between smoking status of workers and short-term absenteeism rate (hr/mo) yielded the accompanying summary information ("Work-Related Consequences of Smoking Cessation," *Academy of Mgmt. J.* (1989): 606–621). In addition, $F = 2.56$. Construct an ANOVA table, and then state and test the appropriate hypotheses using a .01 significance level.

Status	Sample Size	Sample Mean
Continuous smoker	96	2.15
Recent ex-smoker	34	2.21
Long-term ex-smoker	86	1.47
Never smoked	206	1.69

15.16 Parents are frequently concerned when their child seems slow to begin walking (although when the child finally walks, the resulting havoc sometimes has the parents wishing they could turn back the clock!). The article "Walking in the Newborn" (*Science,* 176 (1972): 314–315) reported on an experiment in which the effects of several different treatments on the age at which a child first walks were compared. Children in the first group were given

Output for Exercise 15.12   Dependent Variable: CALCIUM

Source	DF	Sum of Squares	Mean Square	F Value	Pr > F
Model	3	32.13815000	10.71271667	6.51	0.0030
Error	20	32.90103333	1.64505167		
Corrected Total	23	65.03918333			

R-Square	C.V.	Root MSE	CALCIUM Mean
0.494135	2.180018	1.282596	58.8341667

special walking exercises for 12 min per day beginning at age 1 week and lasting 7 weeks. The second group of children received daily exercises but not the walking exercises administered to the first group. The third and fourth groups were control groups: They received no special treatment and differed only in that the third group's progress was checked weekly, whereas the fourth group's progress was checked just once at the end of the study. Observations on age (in months) when the children first walked are shown in the accompanying table. Also given is the ANOVA table, obtained from the SPSS computer package.

	Age			n	Total
Treatment 1	9.00	9.50	9.75	6	60.75
	10.00	13.00	9.50		
Treatment 2	11.00	10.00	10.00	6	68.25
	11.75	10.50	15.00		
Treatment 3	11.50	12.00	9.00	6	70.25
	11.50	13.25	13.00		
Treatment 4	13.25	11.50	12.00	5	61.75
	13.50	11.50			

Analysis of Variance

Source	df	Sum of sq.	Mean Sq.	F Ratio	F Prob
Between Groups	3	14.778	4.926	2.142	.129
Within Groups	19	43.690	2.299		
Total	22	58.467			

a. Verify the entries in the ANOVA table.

b. State and test the relevant hypotheses using a significance level of .05.

15.17 The fog index is a measure of reading difficulty based on the average number of words per sentence and the percentage of words with three or more syllables.

High values of the fog index are associated with difficult reading levels. Independent random samples of six advertisements were taken from three different magazines, and fog indices were computed to obtain the data given in the accompanying table ("Readability Levels of Magazine Advertisements," *J. of Ad. Research* (1981): 45–50). Construct an ANOVA table, and then use a significance level of .01 to test the null hypothesis of no difference between the mean fog index levels for advertisements appearing in the three magazines.

Scientific

American	15.75	11.55	11.16	9.92	9.23	8.20
Fortune	12.63	11.46	10.77	9.93	9.87	9.42
New Yorker	9.27	8.28	8.15	6.37	6.37	5.66

15.18 Some investigators think that the concentration (μg/mL) of a particular antigen in supernatant fluids could be related to onset of meningitis in infants. The accompanying data is typical of that given in plots in the article "Type-Specific Capsular Antigen Is Associated with Virulence in Late-Onset Group B Streptococcal Type III Disease" (*Infection and Immunity* (1984): 124–129). Construct an ANOVA table, and use it to test the null hypothesis of no difference in mean antigen concentrations for the three groups.

Asymptomatic infants	1.56	1.06	.87	1.39	.71	.87
Infants with late-onset sepsis	1.51	1.78	1.45	1.13	1.87	1.89
	1.07	1.72				
Infants with late-onset meningitis	1.21	1.34	1.95	2.27	.88	1.67
	2.57					

15.2   Multiple Comparisons

When $H_0: \mu_1 = \mu_2 = \cdots = \mu_k$ is rejected by the F test, we believe that there are differences among the k population or treatment means. A natural question to ask at this point is, Which means differ? For example, with $k = 4$, it might be the case that $\mu_1 = \mu_2 = \mu_4$, with μ_3 different from the other three. Another possibility is that $\mu_1 = \mu_4$ and $\mu_2 = \mu_3$. Still another possibility is that all four means are different from one another. A **multiple comparison procedure** is a method for identifying differences among the μ's once the hypothesis of overall equality has been rejected. We will present one such method, the **Tukey–Kramer** (T–K) multiple comparison procedure.

The T–K procedure is based on computing confidence intervals for the difference between each possible pair of μ's. In the case $k = 3$, there are three differences to consider:

$$\mu_1 - \mu_2 \qquad \mu_1 - \mu_3 \qquad \mu_2 - \mu_3$$

(The difference $\mu_2 - \mu_1$ is not considered, since the interval for $\mu_1 - \mu_2$ provides the same information. Similarly, intervals for $\mu_3 - \mu_1$ and $\mu_3 - \mu_2$ are not necessary.) Once all confidence intervals have been computed, each is examined to determine whether the interval includes zero. If a particular interval does not include zero, the two means are declared to be "significantly different" from one another. An interval that does include zero supports the conclusion that there is no significant difference between the means involved.

Suppose, for example, that $k = 3$ and the three confidence intervals are:

Difference	T–K Interval
$\mu_1 - \mu_2$	$(-.9, 3.5)$
$\mu_1 - \mu_3$	$(2.6, 7.0)$
$\mu_2 - \mu_3$	$(1.2, 5.7)$

Since the interval for $\mu_1 - \mu_2$ includes zero, we judge that μ_1 and μ_2 do not differ significantly. The other two intervals do not include zero, so we conclude that $\mu_1 \neq \mu_3$ and $\mu_2 \neq \mu_3$.

The T–K intervals are based on critical values for a probability distribution called the *Studentized range distribution*. These critical values appear in Appendix Table VIII. Enter the table at the column corresponding to the number of populations or treatments being compared, move down to the rows corresponding to error df, and select either the value for a 95% confidence level or the one for a 99% level.

The Tukey–Kramer Multiple Comparison Procedure

When there are k populations or treatments being compared, $k(k - 1)/2$ confidence intervals must be computed. If we denote the relevant Studentized range critical value by q, the intervals are as follows:

$$\text{For } \mu_i - \mu_j: \quad (\bar{x}_i - \bar{x}_j) \pm q\sqrt{\frac{\text{MSE}}{2}\left(\frac{1}{n_i} + \frac{1}{n_j}\right)}$$

Two means are judged to differ significantly if the corresponding interval does not include zero.

If the sample sizes are all the same, let n denote the common value of $n_1, \ldots, n_k$. In this case, the $\pm$ factor for each interval is the same quantity

$$q\sqrt{\frac{\text{MSE}}{n}}$$

EXAMPLE 15.5   The degree of success at mastering a skill often depends on the method used to learn the skill. The article "Effects of Occluded Vision and Imagery on Putting Golf Balls" (*Perceptual and Motor Skills* (1995): 179–186) reported on a study involving the following four learning methods: (1) visual contact and imagery, (2) nonvisual contact and imagery, (3) visual contact, and (4) control. There were 20 subjects randomly assigned to each method. The accompanying summary data on putting performance was reported.

Method	1	2	3	4
$\bar{x}$	16.30	15.25	12.05	9.30
s	2.03	3.23	2.91	2.85

It is easily verified that MSTr = 202.283, MSE = 7.7861, and F = 25.98. With $df_1 = 3$ and $df_2 = 76$, Appendix Table VII shows that P-value < .001. The authors concluded that the mean performance is not the same for the four methods.

Appendix Table VIII gives the 95% Studentized range critical value $q = 3.74$ (using error df = 60, the closest tabled value to df = 76). The first two T–K intervals are

$$\mu_1 - \mu_2: \quad (16.30 - 15.25) \pm 3.74\sqrt{7.7861\left(\frac{1}{20} + \frac{1}{20}\right)}$$

$$= 1.05 \pm 2.334$$

$$= (-1.284, 3.384) \leftarrow \textit{Includes 0.}$$

$$\mu_1 - \mu_3: \quad (16.30 - 12.05) \pm 3.74\sqrt{7.7861\left(\frac{1}{20} + \frac{1}{20}\right)}$$

$$= 4.25 \pm 2.334$$

$$= (1.916, 6.584) \leftarrow \textit{Does not include 0.}$$

The remaining intervals are

$\mu_1 - \mu_4$	$7.00 \pm 2.334 = (4.666, 9.334)$	$\leftarrow$ *Does not include 0.*
$\mu_2 - \mu_3$	$3.20 \pm 2.334 = (.866, 5.534)$	$\leftarrow$ *Does not include 0.*
$\mu_2 - \mu_4$	$5.95 \pm 2.334 = (3.616, 8.284)$	$\leftarrow$ *Does not include 0.*
$\mu_3 - \mu_4$	$2.75 \pm 2.334 = (.416, 5.084)$	$\leftarrow$ *Does not include 0.*

We would conclude that μ_1 is not significantly different from μ_2, but that all other means differ from one another. That is, there is no significant difference between the visual contact and imagery and the nonvisual contact and imagery treatments. However, the visual contact and the control treatments differ from each other and from treatments 1 and 2.

MINITAB can be used to construct T–K intervals if raw data is available. Typical output (based on Example 15.5) is shown in Figure 15.6. From the output, we see that the confidence interval for $\mu_1 - \mu_2$ is $(-1.284, 3.384)$, that for $\mu_2 - \mu_4$ is $(3.616, 8.284)$, and so on.

FIGURE 15.6 The T–K
intervals for Example 15.5
(from MINITAB)

Tukey's pairwise comparisons
    Family error rate = 0.0500
    Individual error rate = 0.0111
    Critical value = 3.74
    Intervals for (column level mean) - (row level mean)

	1	2	3
2	-1.284		
	3.384		
3	1.916	.866	
	6.584	5.534	
4	4.666	3.616	.416
	9.334	8.284	5.084

Why calculate the Tukey–Kramer intervals rather than use the t confidence interval for a difference between μ's (from Chapter 11)? The answer is that the T–K intervals control the **simultaneous confidence level** at approximately 95% (or 99%). That is, if the procedure is used repeatedly on many different data sets, in the long run only about 5% (or 1%) of the time would at least one of the intervals not include the value of what it is estimating. Consider using separate 95% t intervals, each one having a 5% error rate. Then the chance that at least one interval would make an incorrect statement about a difference in μ's increases dramatically with the number of intervals calculated. The MINITAB output of Figure 15.6 shows that to achieve a simultaneous confidence level of about 95% (experimentwise or "family" error rate of 5%) when $k = 4$ and error df $= 76$, the individual confidence level must be 98.89% (individual error rate 1.11%).

An effective display for summarizing the results of any multiple comparison procedure involves listing the $\bar{x}$'s and underscoring pairs judged to be not significantly different. The process for constructing such a display is described in the accompanying box.

Summarizing the Results of the Tukey–Kramer Procedure

1. List the sample means in increasing order, identifying the corresponding population just above the value of each $\bar{x}$.

2. Use the T–K intervals to determine the group of means that do not differ significantly from the first in the list. Draw a horizontal line extending from the smallest mean to the last mean in the group identified. For example, if there are five means, arranged in order,

Population	3	2	1	4	5
Sample mean	$\bar{x}_3$	$\bar{x}_2$	$\bar{x}_1$	$\bar{x}_4$	$\bar{x}_5$

and μ_3 is judged to be not significantly different from μ_2 or μ_1 but is judged to be significantly different from μ_4 and μ_5, draw the following line:

Population	3	2	1	4	5
Sample mean	$\bar{x}_3$	$\bar{x}_2$	$\bar{x}_1$	$\bar{x}_4$	$\bar{x}_5$

(continued)

3. Use the T–K intervals to determine the group of means that are not significantly different from the second smallest. (You need consider only means that appear to the right of the mean under consideration.) If there is already a line connecting the second smallest mean with all means in the new group identified, no new line need be drawn. If this entire group of means is not underscored with a single line, draw a line extending from the second smallest to the last mean in the new group. Continuing with our example, if μ_2 is not significantly different from μ_1 but is significantly different from μ_4 and μ_5, no new line need be drawn. However, if μ_2 is not significantly different from either μ_1 or μ_4 but is judged to be different from μ_5, a second line is drawn as shown:

Population	3	2	1	4	5
Sample mean	$\bar{x}_3$	$\bar{x}_2$	$\bar{x}_1$	$\bar{x}_4$	$\bar{x}_5$

4. Continue considering the means in the order listed, adding new lines as needed.

To illustrate this summary procedure, suppose that four samples with $\bar{x}_1 = 19$, $\bar{x}_2 = 27$, $\bar{x}_3 = 24$, and $\bar{x}_4 = 10$ are used to test $H_0: \mu_1 = \mu_2 = \mu_3 = \mu_4$, and that this hypothesis is rejected. Suppose the T–K confidence intervals indicate that μ_2 is significantly different from both μ_1 and μ_4, and that there are no other significant differences. The resulting summary display would then be

Population	4	1	3	2
Sample mean	10	19	24	27

EXAMPLE 15.6

A biologist wished to study the effects of ethanol on sleep time. A sample of 20 rats, matched for age and other characteristics, was selected, and each rat was given an oral injection having a particular concentration of ethanol per body weight. The rapid eye movement (REM) sleep time for each rat was then recorded for a 24-hour period, with the results shown in the accompanying table.

Treatment						$\bar{x}$
1. 0 (control)	88.6	73.2	91.4	68.0	75.2	79.28
2. 1 g/kg	63.0	53.9	69.2	50.1	71.5	61.54
3. 2 g/kg	44.9	59.5	40.2	56.3	38.7	47.92
4. 4 g/kg	31.0	39.6	45.3	25.2	22.7	32.76

Table 15.4 (an ANOVA table from SAS) leads to the conclusion that true average REM sleep time depends on the treatment used; the P-value for the F test is .0001.

Table 15.4 *SAS ANOVA table*

Analysis of Variance Procedure
Dependent Variable: TIME

Source	DF	Sum of Squares	Mean Square	F Value	Pr > F
Model	3	5882.35750	1960.78583	21.09	0.0001
Error	16	1487.40000	92.96250		
Corrected Total	19	7369.75750			

The T–K intervals are

Difference	Interval	Includes 0?
$\mu_1 - \mu_2$	17.74 ± 17.446	no
$\mu_1 - \mu_3$	31.36 ± 17.446	no
$\mu_1 - \mu_4$	46.24 ± 17.446	no
$\mu_2 - \mu_3$	13.08 ± 17.446	yes
$\mu_2 - \mu_4$	28.78 ± 17.446	no
$\mu_3 - \mu_4$	15.16 ± 17.446	yes

The only T–K intervals that include zero are those for $\mu_2 - \mu_3$ and $\mu_3 - \mu_4$. The corresponding underscoring pattern is

$\bar{x}_4$	$\bar{x}_3$	$\bar{x}_2$	$\bar{x}_1$
32.76	47.92	61.54	79.28

Figure 15.7 displays SAS output that agrees with our underscoring; letters are used to indicate groupings in place of the underscoring.

FIGURE 15.7 SAS output for Example 15.6

Alpha = 0.05   df = 16   MSE = 92.9625
Critical Value of Studentized Range = 4.046
Minimum Significant Difference = 17.446
Means with the same letter are not significantly different.

Tukey Grouping		Mean	N	TREATMENT
	A	79.280	5	0 (control)
	B	61.540	5	1 gm/kg
C	B	47.920	5	2 gm/kg
C		32.760	5	4 gm/kg

EXAMPLE 15.7   How satisfied are college students with dormitory roommates? The article "Roommate Satisfaction and Ethnic Identity in Mixed-Race and White University Roommate Dyads" (*J. College Student Development* (1998): 194–199) investigated differences among randomly assigned African-American/White, Asian/White, Hispanic/White, and White/White roommate pairs. The researchers used a one-way ANOVA to analyze scores on the Roommate Relationship Inventory to see whether a difference in mean score existed for the four types of roommate pairs. They reported

> significant differences among the means (P < .01). Follow-up Tukey [intervals] . . . indicated differences between White dyads (M = 77.49) and African-American/White dyads (M = 71.27). . . . No other significant differences were found.

Although the mean satisfaction score for the Asian/White and Hispanic/White groups were not given, they must have been between 77.49, the mean for the White/White pairs, and 71.27, the mean for the African-American/White pairs. (If they had been larger than 77.49, they would have been significantly different from the African-American/White pairs mean, and if they had been smaller than 71.27, they would have been significantly different from the White/White pairs mean.) An underscoring consistent with the reported information is

Hispanic/White
and
White/White   Asian/White   African-American/White

Exercises 15.19 – 15.29

15.19   Leaf surface area is an important variable in plant gas-exchange rates. The article "Fluidized Bed Coating of Conifer Needles with Glass Beads for Determination of Leaf Surface Area" (*Forest Sci.* (1980): 29–32) included an analysis of dry matter per unit surface area (mg/cm^2) for trees raised under three different growing conditions. Let $\mu_1, \mu_2,$ and μ_3 represent the true mean dry matter per unit surface area for the growing conditions 1, 2, and 3, respectively. The given 95% simultaneous confidence intervals are based on summary quantities that appear in the article:

Difference	$\mu_1 - \mu_2$	$\mu_1 - \mu_3$	$\mu_2 - \mu_3$
Interval	$(-3.11, -1.11)$	$(-4.06, -2.06)$	$(-1.95, .05)$

Which of the following four statements do you think describes the relationship between $\mu_1, \mu_2,$ and μ_3? Explain your choice.

  i. $\mu_1 = \mu_2$, and μ_3 differs from μ_1 and μ_2.
  ii. $\mu_1 = \mu_3$, and μ_2 differs from μ_1 and μ_3.
  iii. $\mu_2 = \mu_3$, and μ_1 differs from μ_2 and μ_3.
  iv. All three μ's are different from one another.

15.20   The article referenced in Example 15.5 reported on a study involving the following four learning methods: (1) visual contact and imagery, (2) nonvisual contact and imagery, (3) visual contact, and (4) control. There were 20 subjects assigned to each method. The accompanying summary data on putting performance was reported.

Method	1	2	3	4
$\bar{x}$	16.30	15.25	12.05	9.30
s	2.03	3.23	2.91	2.85

These in turn give MSE = 7.7861 and F = 25.98, from which P-value < .001, so H_0 can be rejected at significance level .01. Calculate the 99% T–K intervals, indicate which methods differ significantly from one another, and summarize the results by underscoring. How do the 99% T–K intervals compare to the 95% T–K intervals of Example 15.5?

15.21 The accompanying data resulted from a flammability study in which specimens of five different fabrics were tested to determine burn times.

	1	17.8	16.2	15.9	15.5	
	2	13.2	10.4	11.3		
Fabric	3	11.8	11.0	9.2	10.0	
	4	16.5	15.3	14.1	15.0	13.9
	5	13.9	10.8	12.8	11.7	

MSTr = 23.67

MSE = 1.39

F = 17.08

P-value = .000

The accompanying output gives the T–K intervals as calculated by MINITAB. Identify significant differences and give the underscoring pattern.

Individual error rate = 0.00750
Critical value = 4.37
Intervals for (column level mean) - (row level mean)

	1	2	3	4
	1.038			
2	7.495			
	3.278	-1.645		
3	8.422	3.912		
	-1.050	-5.983	-6.900	
4	3.830	-0.670	-2.020	
	1.478	-3.445	-4.372	0.220
5	6.622	2.112	0.772	5.100

15.22 Exercise 15.6 presented the accompanying summary information on satisfaction levels for employees on three different work schedules:

$n_1 = 24$ $n_2 = 24$ $n_3 = 20$
$\bar{x}_1 = 6.60$ $\bar{x}_2 = 5.37$ $\bar{x}_3 = 5.20$

MSE was computed to be 2.028. Calculate the 95% T–K intervals, and identify any significant differences.

15.23 Sample mean chlorophyll concentrations for the four Jerusalem artichoke varieties introduced in Exercise 15.7 were .30, .24, .41, and .33, with corresponding sample sizes of 5, 5, 4, and 6, respectively. In addition, MSE = .0130. Calculate the 95% T–K intervals, and then use the underscoring procedure described in this section to identify significant differences among the varieties.

15.24 Do lizards play a role in spreading plant seeds? Some research carried out in South Africa would suggest so ("Dispersal of Namaqua Fig (*Ficus cordata cordata*) Seeds by the Augrabies Flat Lizard (*Platysaurus broadleyi*)," *Journal of Herpetology* (1999): 328–330). The re-

searchers collected 400 seeds of this particular type of fig, 100 of which were from each treatment: lizard dung, bird dung, rock hyrax dung, and uneaten figs. They planted these seeds in batches of 5, and for each group of 5 they recorded how many of the seeds germinated. This resulted in 20 observations for each treatment. The treatment means and standard deviations are given in the accompanying table.

Treatment	n	$\bar{x}$	s
Uneaten figs	20	2.40	.30
Lizard dung	20	2.35	.33
Bird dung	20	1.70	.34
Hyrax dung	20	1.45	.28

a. Construct the appropriate ANOVA table, and test the hypothesis that there is no difference between mean number of seeds germinating for the four treatments.
b. Is there evidence that seeds eaten and then excreted by lizards germinate at a higher rate than those eaten and then excreted by birds? Give statistical evidence to support your answer.

15.25 The article "Growth Response in Radish to Sequential and Simultaneous Exposures of NO₂ and SO₂" (*Environ. Pollution* (1984): 303–325) compared a control group (no exposure), a sequential exposure group (plants exposed to one pollutant followed by exposure to the second four weeks later), and a simultaneous-exposure group (plants exposed to both pollutants at the same time). The article states, "Sequential exposure to the two pollutants had no effect on growth compared to the control. Simultaneous exposure to the gases significantly reduced plant growth." Let $\bar{x}_1$, $\bar{x}_2$, and $\bar{x}_3$ represent the sample means for the control, sequential, and simultaneous groups, respectively. Suppose that $\bar{x}_1 > \bar{x}_2 > \bar{x}_3$. Use the given information to construct a table where the sample means are listed in increasing order, with those that are judged not to be significantly different underscored.

15.26 The nutritional quality of shrubs commonly used for feed by rabbits was the focus of a study summarized in the article "Estimation of Browse by Size Classes for Snowshoe Hare" (*J. Wildlife Mgmt.* (1980): 34–40). The energy content (cal/g) of three sizes (4 mm or less, 5–7 mm, and 8–10 mm) of serviceberries was studied. Let μ_1, μ_2, and μ_3 denote the true energy content for the three size classes. Suppose that 95% simultaneous confidence intervals for $\mu_1 - \mu_2$, $\mu_1 - \mu_3$, and $\mu_2 - \mu_3$ are (−10, 290), (150, 450), and (10, 310), respectively. How would you interpret these intervals?

15.27 The accompanying underscoring pattern appeared in the article "Effect of SO₂ on Transpiration, Chlorophyll

Content, Growth and Injury in Young Seedlings of Woody Angiosperms" (*Canadian J. Forest Research* (1980): 78–81). Water loss of plants (*Acer saccharinum*) exposed to 0, 2, 4, 8, and 16 hours of fumigation was recorded, and a multiple comparison procedure was used to detect differences among the mean water losses for the different fumigation durations. How would you interpret this pattern?

Duration of fumigation	16	0	8	2	4
Sample mean water loss	27.57	28.23	30.21	31.16	36.21

15.28 Samples of six different brands of diet or imitation margarine were analyzed to determine the level of physiologically active polyunsaturated fatty acids (PAPUFA, in percent), resulting in the data shown in the accompanying table. (The data is fictitious, but the sample means agree with data reported in *Consumer Reports.*)

Imperial	14.1	13.6	14.4	14.3	
Parkay	12.8	12.5	13.4	13.0	12.3
Blue Bonnet	13.5	13.4	14.1	14.3	
Chiffon	13.2	12.7	12.6	13.9	
Mazola	16.8	17.2	16.4	17.3	18.0
Fleischmann's	18.1	17.2	18.7	18.4	

a. Test for differences among the true average PAPUFA percentages for the different brands. Use $\alpha = .05$.
b. Use the T–K procedure to compute 95% simultaneous confidence intervals for all differences between means and interpret the resulting intervals.

15.29 Consider the accompanying data on plant growth after the application of different types of growth hormone.

	1	13	17	7	14
	2	21	13	20	17
Hormone	**3**	18	14	17	21
	4	7	11	18	10
	5	6	11	15	8

a. Carry out the F test at level $\alpha = .05$.
b. What happens when the T–K procedure is applied? (*Note*: This "contradiction" can occur when H_0 is "barely" rejected. It happens because the test and the multiple comparison method are based on different distributions. Consult your friendly neighborhood statistician for more information.)

15.3 The *F* Test for a Randomized Block Experiment

We saw in Chapter 11 that when two treatments are to be compared, a paired experiment is often more effective than one involving two independent samples. This is because pairing can considerably reduce the extraneous variation in subjects or experimental units. A similar result can be achieved when more than two treatments are to be compared. Suppose that four different pesticides (the treatments) are being considered for application to a particular crop. There are 20 plots of land available for planting. If 5 of these plots are randomly selected to receive pesticide 1, 5 of the remaining 15 randomly selected for pesticide 2, and so on, the result is a *completely randomized experiment,* and the data should be analyzed using single-factor ANOVA. The disadvantage of this experiment is that if there are any substantial differences in characteristics of the plots that could affect yield, a separate assessment of any differences between treatments will not be possible (plot effects are confounded with treatment effects).

Here is an alternative experiment. Consider separating the 20 plots into five groups, each consisting of 4 plots. Within each group, the plots are as much alike as possible with respect to characteristics affecting yield. Then within each group, one plot is randomly selected for pesticide 1, a second plot is randomly chosen to receive pesticide 2, and so on. The homogeneous groups are called *blocks,* and the random allocation of treatments within each block as described results in a *randomized block experiment.*

> **Definition**
>
> Suppose that experimental units (individuals or objects to which the treatments are applied) are first separated into groups consisting of k units in such a way that the units within each group are as similar as possible. Within any particular group, the treatments are then randomly allocated so that each unit in a group receives a different treatment. The groups are often called **blocks,** and the experimental design is referred to as a **randomized block design.**

EXAMPLE 15.8   High energy costs have made consumers and home builders increasingly aware of whether household appliances are energy efficient. A large developer carried out a study to compare electricity usage for four different residential air-conditioning systems being considered for tract homes. Each system was installed in five homes, and the resulting electricity usage (in KWh) was monitored for a 1-month period. Because the developer realized that many characteristics of a home could affect usage (for example, floor space, type of insulation, directional orientation, and type of roof and exterior), care was taken to ensure that extraneous variation in such characteristics did not influence the conclusions. Homes selected for the experiment were grouped into five blocks consisting of four homes each in such a way that the four homes within any given block were as similar as possible. Resulting data is displayed in Table 15.5, in which rows correspond to the different treatments (air-conditioning systems) and columns correspond to the different blocks.

Table 15.5 *Data from the randomized block experiment of Example 15.8*

		Block					
	Treatment	**1**	**2**	**3**	**4**	**5**	**Treatment Average**
	1	116	118	97	101	115	109.40
	2	171	131	105	107	129	128.60
	3	138	131	115	93	110	117.40
	4	144	141	115	93	99	118.40
Block average		142.25	130.25	108.00	98.50	113.25	**Grand mean** 118.45

Later in this section we will analyze this data to see whether electricity usage depends on which system is used.

The hypotheses of interest and assumptions underlying the analysis of a randomized block design are similar to those for a completely randomized design.

Assumptions and Hypotheses

The single observation made on any particular treatment in a given block is assumed to be selected from a normal distribution. The variance of this distribution is σ^2, the same for each block–treatment combination. However, the mean value may depend separately both on the treatment applied and on the block. The hypotheses of interest are as follows:

H_0: The mean value does not depend on which treatment is applied.

H_a: The mean value does depend on which treatment is applied.

The μ notation used previously is no longer appropriate for stating hypotheses, since an observation's mean value may depend on both the treatment applied and the block utilized.

The F Test

The key to analyzing data from a randomized block experiment is to represent SSTo, which measures total variation, as a sum of three pieces: SSTr, SSE, and a block sum of squares SSBl. The latter SS incorporates any variation due to differences between the blocks, which will be substantial if there was great heterogeneity in experimental units (for example, plots) prior to creating the blocks. Once the four sums of squares have been computed, the test statistic is an F ratio MSTr/MSE, but error df is no longer $N - k$ as in single-factor ANOVA.

Summary of the Randomized Block F Test

Notation: Let

k = number of treatments

l = number of blocks

$\bar{x}_i$ = average of all observations for treatment i

$\bar{b}_i$ = average of all observations in block i

$\bar{\bar{x}}$ = average of all kl observations in the experiment (the grand mean)

Sums of squares and associated df's are as follows.

Sum of Squares	Symbol	df	Formula
Treatments	SSTr	$k - 1$	$l[(\bar{x}_1 - \bar{\bar{x}})^2 + (\bar{x}_2 - \bar{\bar{x}})^2 + \cdots + (\bar{x}_k - \bar{\bar{x}})^2]$
Blocks	SSBl	$l - 1$	$k[(\bar{b}_1 - \bar{\bar{x}})^2 + (\bar{b}_2 - \bar{\bar{x}})^2 + \cdots + (\bar{b}_k - \bar{\bar{x}})^2]$
Error	SSE	$(k - 1)(l - 1)$	by subtraction
Total	SSTo	$kl - 1$	$\sum_{\substack{\text{all } kl \\ \text{obs.}}} (x - \bar{\bar{x}})^2$

(continued)

SSE is obtained by subtraction through the use of the fundamental identity

$$SSTo = SSTr + SSBl + SSE$$

Test statistic: $\quad F = \dfrac{MSTr}{MSE}$

where

$$MSTr = \frac{SSTr}{k - 1} \quad \text{and} \quad MSE = \frac{SSE}{(k - 1)(l - 1)}$$

The test is based on $df_1 = k - 1$ and $df_2 = (k - 1)(l - 1)$. *P*-value information comes from Appendix Table VII.

Alternative formulas for the SS's appropriate for efficient hand computation appear in the chapter appendix.

Calculations for this *F* test are usually summarized in an ANOVA table. The table is similar to the one for single-factor ANOVA except that blocks are an extra source of variation, so four rows are included rather than just three.

Table 15.6 shows a mean square for blocks as well as for treatments and error. Sometimes the *F* ratio MSBl/MSE is also computed. A large value of this ratio suggests that blocking was effective in filtering out extraneous variation.

Table 15.6 *The ANOVA table for a randomized block experiment*

Source of Variation	df	Sum of Squares	Mean Square	F
Treatments	$k - 1$	SSTr	$MSTr = \dfrac{SSTr}{k - 1}$	$F = \dfrac{MSTr}{MSE}$
Blocks	$l - 1$	SSBl	$MSBl = \dfrac{SSBl}{l - 1}$	
Error	$(k - 1)(l - 1)$	SSE	$MSE = \dfrac{SSE}{(k - 1)(l - 1)}$	
Total	$kl - 1$	SSTo		

EXAMPLE 15.9

Reconsider the electricity usage data given in Example 15.8.

H_0: The mean electricity usage does not depend on which air conditioning system is used.

H_a: The mean electricity usage does depend on which system is used.

Test statistic: $\quad F = \dfrac{MSTr}{MSE}$

From Example 15.8,

$$\bar{\bar{x}} = 118.45$$

$$\bar{x}_1 = 109.40 \qquad \bar{x}_2 = 128.60 \qquad \bar{x}_3 = 117.40 \qquad \bar{x}_4 = 118.40$$
(these are the four row averages)

$$\bar{b}_1 = 142.25 \qquad \bar{b}_2 = 130.25 \qquad \bar{b}_3 = 108.00 \qquad \bar{b}_4 = 98.50 \qquad \bar{b}_5 = 113.25$$
(the five column averages)

Using the individual observations given previously,

$$\text{SSTo} = \sum_{\substack{\text{all } kl \\ \text{obs.}}} (x - \bar{\bar{x}})^2$$

$$= (116 - 118.45)^2 + (118 - 118.45)^2 + \cdots + (99 - 118.45)^2 = 7594.95$$

The other sums of squares are

$$\text{SSTr} = l[(\bar{x}_1 - \bar{\bar{x}})^2 + (\bar{x}_2 - \bar{\bar{x}})^2 + \cdots + (\bar{x}_k - \bar{\bar{x}})^2]$$
$$= 5[(109.4 - 118.45)^2 + (128.6 - 118.45)^2$$
$$+ (117.4 - 118.45)^2 + (118.4 - 118.45)^2]$$
$$= 930.15$$

$$\text{SSBl} = k[(\bar{b}_1 - \bar{\bar{x}})^2 + (\bar{b}_2 - \bar{\bar{x}})^2 + \cdots + (\bar{b}_k - \bar{\bar{x}})^2]$$
$$= 4[(142.254 - 118.45)^2 + (130.25 - 118.45)^2 + \cdots + (113.25 - 118.45)^2]$$
$$= 4959.70$$

$$\text{SSE} = \text{SSTo} - \text{SSTr} - \text{SSBl}$$
$$= 7594.95 - 930.15 - 4959.70$$
$$= 1705.10$$

The remaining calculations are displayed in the accompanying ANOVA table.

Source of Variation	df	Sum of Squares	Mean Square	F
Treatments	3	930.15	310.05	$\dfrac{310.05}{142.09} = 2.18$
Blocks	4	4959.70	1239.93	
Error	12	1705.10	142.09	
Total	19	7594.95		

In Appendix Table VII with $df_1 = 3$ and $df_2 = 12$, the value 2.61 corresponds to a P-value of .10. Since $2.18 < 2.61$, P-value $> .10$ and H_0 cannot be rejected. Mean electricity usage does not seem to depend on which of the four air-conditioning systems is used.

━━━━━━━━

In many studies, all k of the treatments can be applied to the same experimental unit, so there is no need to group different experimental units to form blocks. For example, an experiment to compare effects of four different gasoline additives on automobile engine efficiency could be carried out by selecting just 5 engines and using all four treatments on each one rather than using 20 engines and blocking them. Each engine by itself then constitutes a block. As another example, a manufacturing company might wish to compare outputs for three different packaging machines. Because output could be affected by which operator is using the machine, a design that controls for the effects of operator variation is desirable. One possibility is to use 15 operators grouped into homogeneous blocks of 5 operators each, but such homogeneity within each block may be difficult to achieve. An alternative approach is to use only 5 operators and have each one operate all three machines. There are then three observations in each block, all three with the same operator.

EXAMPLE 15.10

In the article "The Effects of a Pneumatic Stool and a One-Legged Stool on Lower Limb Joint Load and Muscular Activity During Sitting and Rising" (*Ergonomics* (1993): 519–535), the following data is given on the effort (measured on the Borg Scale) required by a subject to rise from a sitting position for each of four different stools. Because it was suspected that different people could exhibit large differences in effort, even for the same type of stool, a sample of nine people was selected and each tested on all four stools, with the following results:

		Subject								
		1	2	3	4	5	6	7	8	9
	A	12	10	7	7	8	9	8	7	9
Type of	B	15	14	14	11	11	11	12	11	13
stool	C	12	13	13	10	8	11	12	8	10
	D	10	12	9	9	7	10	11	7	8

For each person, the order in which the stools were tested was randomized. This is a randomized block experiment, with subjects playing the role of blocks. The test consists of these hypotheses:

H_0: Mean effort does not depend on type of stool.

H_a: Mean effort does depend on type of stool.

Test statistic: $F = \dfrac{\text{MSTr}}{\text{MSE}}$

Computations are summarized in Table 15.7, an ANOVA table from MINITAB.

Table 15.7 *ANOVA Table for Example 15.10*

Two-way Analysis of Variance
Analysis of Variance for Effort

Source	DF	SS	MS	F	P
Stool	3	81.19	27.06	22.36	0.000
Block	8	66.50	8.31	6.87	0.000
Error	24	29.06	1.21		
Total	35	176.75			

The test statistic value is 22.36, with P-value $= .000$. Since P-value $< \alpha$, we reject H_0. There is sufficient evidence to conclude that the mean effort required is not the same for all four stool types.

Experiments such as the one described in Example 15.10, in which repeated observations are made on the same experimental unit, are sometimes called *repeated measures designs*. Such designs should not be used when application of the first several treatments somehow affects responses to later treatments. This would be the case if treatments were different methods for learning the same skill, so that if all treatments were given to the same subject, the response to the treatment given last would presumably be much better than the response to the treatment initially applied.

Multiple Comparisons

As in single-factor ANOVA, once H_0 has been rejected, further analysis of the data is appropriate to identify significant differences among the treatments. The Tukey–Kramer method is easily adapted for this purpose.

Declare that treatments i and j differ significantly if the interval

$$\bar{x}_i - \bar{x}_j \pm q\sqrt{\frac{\text{MSE}}{l}}$$

does not include zero, where q is based on a comparison of k treatments and error df $= (k - 1)(l - 1)$.

EXAMPLE 15.11   In Example 15.10, we had $k = 4$ and error df $= 24$, from which $q = 4.91$ for a 99% simultaneous confidence level. The $\pm$ factor for each interval is

$$q\sqrt{\frac{\text{MSE}}{l}} = 4.91\sqrt{\frac{1.21}{9}} = 1.80$$

The four treatment means arranged in order are

Treatment	A	D	C	B
Sample mean	8.556	9.222	10.778	12.444

It is easily verified that corresponding underscoring pattern is as follows:

Treatment	A	D	C	B
Sample mean	8.556	9.222	10.778	12.444

Exercises 15.30 – 15.38

15.30 A particular county employs three assessors, who are responsible for determining the value of residential property in the county. To see whether these assessors differ systematically in their appraisals, 5 houses are selected, and each assessor is asked to determine the market value of each house. Explain why a randomized block experiment (with blocks corresponding to the 5 houses) was used rather than a completely randomized experiment involving a total of 15 houses with each assessor asked to appraise 5 different houses (a different group of 5 for each assessor).

15.31 The accompanying display is a partially completed ANOVA table for the experiment described in Exercise 15.30 (with houses representing blocks and assessors representing treatments).

Source of Variation	df	Sum of Squares	Mean Square	F
Treatments		11.7		
Blocks		113.5		
Error				
Total		250.8		

a. Fill in the missing entries in the ANOVA table.
b. Use the ANOVA *F* statistic and a .05 level of significance to test the null hypothesis of no difference between assessors.

15.32 Land-treatment wastewater-processing systems work by removing nutrients and thereby discharging water of better quality. The land used is often planted with a crop such as corn, because plant uptake removes nitrogen from the water and sale of the crop helps reduce the costs of wastewater treatment. The concentration of nitrogen in treated water was observed from 1975 to 1979 under wastewater application rates of none, .05 m/week, and .1 m/week. A randomized block ANOVA was performed, with the 5 years serving as blocks. The accompanying display is a partially completed ANOVA table from the article "Quality of Percolate Water After Treatment of a Municipal Wastewater Effluent by a Crop Irrigation System" (*J. Environ. Quality* (1984): 256–264).

Source of Variation	df	Sum of Squares	Mean Square	F
Treatments		1835.2		
Blocks				
Error		206.1		
Total	14	2134.1		

a. Complete the ANOVA table.
b. Is there sufficient evidence to reject the null hypothesis of no difference between the true mean nitrogen concentrations for the three application rates? Use $\alpha = .05$.

15.33 In a comparison of the energy efficiency of three types of ovens (conventional, biradiant, and convection), the energy used in cooking was measured for eight different foods (one-layer cake, two-layer cake, biscuits, bread, frozen pie, baked potatoes, lasagna, and meat loaf). Since a comparison between the three types of ovens is desired, a randomized block ANOVA (with the eight foods serving as blocks) will be used. Suppose calculations result in the quantities SSTo = 4.57, SSTr = 3.97, and SSBl = .2503. (A similar study is described in the article "Optimizing Oven Radiant Energy Use," *Home Ec. Res. J.* (1980): 242–251.) Construct an ANOVA table and test the null hypothesis of no difference in mean energy use for the three types of ovens. Use a .01 significance level.

15.34 The article "Rate of Stuttering Adaptation Under Two Electro-Shock Conditions" (*Behavior Res. Therapy* (1967): 49–54) gave adaptation scores for three different treatments: no shock (treatment 1), shock following each stuttered word (treatment 2), and shock during each moment of stuttering (treatment 3). These treatments were used on each of 18 stutterers. The 18 subjects were viewed as blocks, and the data were analyzed using a randomized block ANOVA. Summary quantities are SSTr = 28.78, SSBl = 2977.67, and SSE = 469.55. Construct the ANOVA table, and test at significance level .05 to see whether true average adaptation score depends on the treatment given.

15.35 The accompanying table shows average height of cotton plants during 1978–1980 under three different effluent application rates (350, 440, and 515 mm) ("Drip Irrigation of Cotton with Treated Municipal Effluents: Yield Response," *J. Environ. Quality* (1984): 231–238).

	Application Rate		
Year	350	440	515
1978	166	176	177
1979	109	126	136
1980	140	155	156

a. This data was analyzed using a randomized block ANOVA, with years serving as blocks. Explain why this would be better for comparing treatments than a completely randomized ANOVA.

b. With treatments 1, 2, and 3 denoting the application rates 350, 440, and 515, respectively, summary quantities are

$$\Sigma(x - \bar{\bar{x}})^2 = 4266.0 \qquad \bar{\bar{x}} = 149.00$$

$$\bar{x}_1 = 138.33 \qquad \bar{x}_2 = 152.33 \qquad \bar{x}_3 = 156.33$$

$$\bar{b}_1 = 173.00 \qquad \bar{b}_2 = 123.67 \qquad \bar{b}_3 = 150.33$$

Construct an ANOVA table. Using $\alpha = .05$, determine whether the true mean height differs for the three effluent rates.

c. Identify significant differences among the rates. (*Hint*: $q = 5.04$)

15.36 The article "Responsiveness of Food Sales to Shelf Space Changes in Supermarkets" (*J. Mktg. Research* (1964): 63–67) described an experiment to assess the effect of allotted shelf space on product sales. Two of the products studied were baking soda (a staple product) and Tang (considered to be an impulse product). Six stores (blocks) were used in the experiment, and six different shelf-space allotments were tried for 1 week each. Space allotments of 2, 4, 6, 8, 10, and 12 ft were used for baking soda, and 6, 9, 12, 15, 18, and 21 ft were used for Tang. The author speculated that sales of staple goods would not be sensitive to changes in shelf space, whereas sales of impulse products would be affected by changes in shelf space. Data on number of boxes of baking soda and on number of containers of Tang sold during a 1-week period is given in the accompanying tables. Construct ANOVA tables and test the appropriate hypotheses. Use a significance level of .05. Was the author correct in his speculation that sales of the staple product would not be affected by shelf space allocation, whereas sales of the impulse product would be affected? Explain.

Baking Soda

		Shelf Space					
		2	4	6	8	10	12
Store	1	36	42	36	40	30	22
	2	74	61	65	67	83	84
	3	40	58	42	73	69	63
	4	43	65	65	41	43	47
	5	27	33	35	17	40	26
	6	23	31	36	38	42	37

Tang

		Shelf Space					
		6	9	12	15	18	21
Store	1	30	35	25	25	38	31
	2	47	59	43	62	65	48
	3	47	55	48	54	36	54
	4	29	19	41	27	33	39
	5	17	11	25	23	24	26
	6	22	9	19	18	25	22

15.37 The article "Measuring Treatment Effects Through Comparisons Along Plot Boundaries" (*Forest Sci.* (1980): 704–709) reported the results of a randomized block experiment. Five different sources of pine seed were used in each of four blocks. The accompanying table gives data on plant height (m). Does the data provide sufficient evidence to conclude that the true mean height is not the same for all five seed sources? Use a .05 level of significance.

		Block			
		I	II	III	IV
Source	1	7.1	5.8	7.2	6.9
	2	6.2	5.3	7.7	4.7
	3	7.9	5.4	8.6	6.2
	4	9.0	5.9	5.7	7.3
	5	7.0	6.3	4.4	6.1

15.38 The article cited in Exercise 15.37 also gave the accompanying data on survival rate for five different seed sources.

		Block			
		I	II	III	IV
Source	1	62.5	87.5	50.0	70.3
	2	50.0	50.0	54.7	59.4
	3	93.8	92.2	87.5	87.5
	4	96.9	76.6	70.3	65.6
	5	56.3	50.0	45.3	56.3

a. Construct an ANOVA table and test the null hypothesis of no difference in true mean survival rates for the five seed sources. Use $\alpha = .05$.

b. Use multiple comparisons to identify significant differences among the seed sources. (*Hint*: $q = 5.04$)

15.4   Two-Factor ANOVA

An investigator will often be interested in assessing the effects of two different factors on a response variable. Consider the following examples.

1. A physical education researcher wishes to know how body density of football players varies with position played (a categorical factor with categories defensive back, offensive back, defensive lineman, and offensive lineman) and level of play (a second categorical factor with categories professional, college Division I, college Division II, and college Division III).

2. An agricultural scientist is interested in seeing how yield of tomatoes is affected by choice of variety planted (a categorical factor, with each category corresponding to a different variety) and planting density (a quantitative factor, with a level corresponding to each planting density being considered).

3. An applied chemist might wish to investigate how shear strength of a particular adhesive varies with application temperature (a quantitative factor with levels 250°F, 260°F, and 270°F) and application pressure (a quantitative factor with levels 110 lb/in^2, 120 lb/in^2, 130 lb/in^2, and 140 lb/in^2).

Let's label the two factors under study factor A and factor B. Even when a factor is categorical, it simplifies terminology to refer to the categories as **levels.** Thus, in the first example, the categorical factor *position played* has four levels. The number of levels of factor A is denoted by k, and l denotes the number of levels of factor B, as shown in Table 15.8. This rectangular table contains a row corresponding to each level of factor A and a column corresponding to each level of factor B. Each cell in the table corresponds to a particular level of factor A in combination with a particular level of factor B. Because there are l cells in each row and k rows, there are kl cells in the table. The kl different combinations of factor A and factor B levels are often referred to as **treatments.** For example, if there are three tomato varieties and four different planting densities under consideration, the number of treatments is 12.

Table 15.8 *A table of factor combinations for a two-way ANOVA experiment*

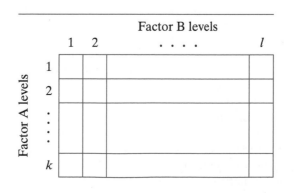

Suppose that an experiment is carried out, resulting in a data set that contains some number of observations for each of the kl treatments. In general, there could be more observations for some treatments than for others, and there may even be a few treatments for which no observations are available. An experimenter may set out to make the same number of observations on each treatment, but occasionally forces beyond the experimenter's control — the death of an experimental subject, malfunctioning equipment, and so on — result in different sample sizes for some treatments. However, such imbalance in sample sizes makes analysis of the data rather difficult. **We will restrict consideration to data sets containing the same number of observations on each treatment and let m denote this number.**

Notation

k = number of levels of factor A

l = number of levels of factor B

kl = number of treatments   (each one a combination of a factor A level and a factor B level)

m = number of observations on each treatment

EXAMPLE 15.12

An experiment was carried out to assess the effects of tomato variety (factor A, with $k = 3$ levels) and planting density (factor B, with l levels — 10, 20, 30, and 40 thousand plants per hectare) on yield. Each of the $kl = 12$ treatments was used on $m = 3$ plots, resulting in the data set consisting of $klm = 36$ observations shown in Table 15.9 (adapted from "Effects of Plant Density on Tomato Yields in Western Nigeria," *Exper. Ag.* (1976): 43–47).

Table 15.9 *Data from the two-factor experiment of Example 15.12*

		Density (B)			
		1	**2**	**3**	**4**
Variety (A)	1	7.9, 9.2, 10.5	11.2, 12.8, 13.3	12.1, 12.6, 14.0	9.1, 10.8, 12.5
	2	8.1, 8.6, 10.1	11.5, 12.7, 13.7	13.7, 14.4, 15.4	11.3, 12.5, 14.5
	3	15.3, 16.1, 17.5	16.6, 18.5, 19.2	18.0, 20.8, 21.0	17.2, 18.4, 18.9

Sample average yields for each treatment, each level of factor A, and each level of factor B are important summary quantities. These can be displayed in a rectangular table (see Table 15.10).

A plot of these sample averages is also quite informative. First, construct horizontal and vertical axes, and scale the vertical axis in units of the response variable (yield). Then mark a point on the horizontal axis for each level of one of the factors (either A or B can be chosen). Now above each such mark, plot a point for the sample average response for each level of the other factor. Finally, connect all points corresponding to the same level of the other factor using straight line segments.

Table 15.10 *Sample means for the 12 treatments*

| | | Factor B (Planting Density) | | | | Sample Average Yield for Each Level of Factor A |
		1	2	3	4	
Factor A	**1**	9.20	12.43	12.90	10.80	11.33
(Variety)	**2**	8.93	12.63	14.50	12.77	12.21
	3	16.30	18.10	19.93	18.17	18.13
Sample Average Yield for Each Level of Factor B		11.48	14.39	15.78	13.91	Grand mean = 13.89

Figure 15.8 displays one such plot for which factor A levels mark the horizontal axis and another plot for which factor B levels mark this axis; usually only one of the two plots is constructed.

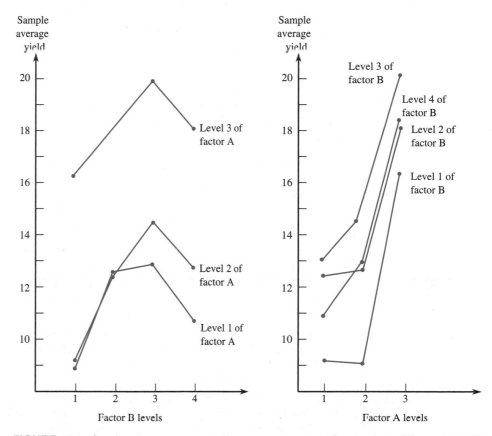

FIGURE 15.8 Graphs of treatment sample average responses for the data of Example 15.12

Interaction

An important aspect of two-factor studies involves assessing how simultaneous changes in the levels of both factors affect the response. As a simple example, suppose that an automobile manufacturer is studying engine efficiency (miles per gallon) for two different engine sizes (factor A, with $k = 2$ levels) in combination with two different carburetor designs (factor B with $l = 2$ levels). Consider the two possible sets of true average responses displayed in Figure 15.9. In Figure 15.9(a), when factor A changes from level 1 to level 2 and factor B remains at level 1 (the change within the first column), the true average response increases by 2. Similarly, when factor B changes from level 1 to level 2 and factor A is fixed at level 1 (the change within the first row), the true average response increases by 3. And when the levels of both factors are changed from 1 to 2, the true average response increases by 5, which is the sum of the two "one-at-a-time" increases. This is because the change in true average response when the level of either factor changes from 1 to 2 is the same for each level of the other factor: The change within either row is 3, and the change within either column is 2. In this case, changes in levels of the two factors affect the true average response separately, or in an additive manner.

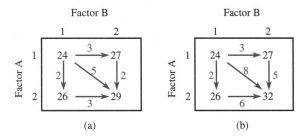

FIGURE 15.9 Two possible sets of true average responses when $k = 2$ and $l = 2$

The changes in true average responses in the first row and in the first column of Figure 15.9(b) are 3 and 2, respectively, exactly as in Figure 15.9(a). However, the change in true average response when the levels of both factors change simultaneously from 1 to 2 is 8, which is much larger than the separate changes suggest. In this case, there is interaction between the two factors, so that the effect of simultaneous changes cannot be determined from the individual effects of separate changes. This is because in Figure 15.9(b), the change in going from the first to the second column is different for the two rows, and the change in going from the first to the second row is different for the two columns. That is, *the change in true average response when the level of one factor changes depends on the level of the other factor.* This is not true in Figure 15.9(a).

When there are more than two levels of either factor, a graph of true average responses, similar to that for sample average responses in Figure 15.8, provides insight into how changes in the level of one factor depend on the level of the other factor. Figure 15.10 shows several possible such graphs when $k = 4$ and $l = 3$. The most general situation is pictured in Figure 15.10(a). There, the change in true av-

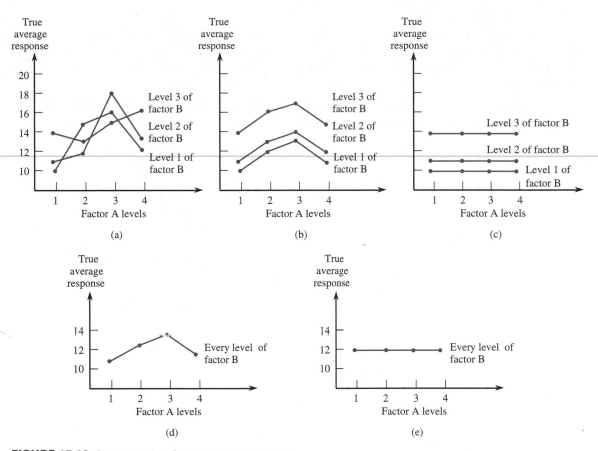

FIGURE 15.10 Some graphs of true average responses

erage response when the level of B is changed (a vertical distance) depends on the level of A. An analogous property would hold if the picture were redrawn so that levels of B were marked on the horizontal axis. This is a prototypical picture suggesting **interaction** between the factors — the change in true average response when the level of one factor changes depends on the level of the other factor.

There is no interaction between the factors when the connected line segments are parallel, as in Figure 15.10(b). Then the change in true average response when the level of one factor changes is the same for each level of the other factor (the vertical distances are the same for each level of factor A). Figure 15.10(c) illustrates an even more restrictive situation — there is no interaction between factors, and, in addition, the true average response does not depend on the level of factor A. Only when the graph looks like this can it be said that factor A has no effect on the responses. Similarly, the graph in Figure 15.10(d) indicates no interaction and no dependence on the level of factor B. A final case, pictured in Figure 15.10(e), shows a single set of four points connected by horizontal line segments, which indicates that the true average response is identical for every level of either factor.

If the graphs of true average responses are connected line segments that are parallel, there is no interaction between the factors. In this case, the change in true average response when the level of one factor is changed is the same for each level of the other factor. Special cases of no interaction are as follows:

1. The true average response is the same for each level of factor A (no factor A main effects).
2. The true average response is the same for each level of factor B (no factor B main effects).

The graphs of Figure 15.10 depict true average responses, quantities whose values are fixed but unknown to an investigator. Figure 15.8 contains graphs of the sample average responses based on data resulting from an experiment. These sample averages are, of course, subject to variability because there is sampling variation in the individual observations. If the experiment discussed in Example 15.12 were repeated, the resulting graphs of sample averages would probably look somewhat different from the graph in Figure 15.8 — perhaps a great deal different if there were substantial underlying variability in responses. Even when there is no interaction among factors, the connected line segments in the sample mean picture will not typically be exactly parallel, and they may deviate quite a bit from parallelism in the presence of substantial underlying variability. Similarly, there might actually be no factor A effects (Figure 15.10(c)), yet the sample graphs would not usually be exactly horizontal. The sample pictures give us insight, but formal inferential procedures are necessary to draw sound conclusions about the nature of the true average responses for different factor levels.

Hypotheses and F Tests

Basic Assumptions for Two-Factor ANOVA

The observations on any particular treatment are independently selected from a normal distribution with variance σ^2 (the same variance for each treatment), and samples from different treatments are independent of one another.

Because of the normality assumption, tests based on F statistics and distributions are appropriate. The necessary sums of squares result from breaking up $\text{SSTo} = \Sigma (x - \bar{\bar{x}})^2$ into four parts, which reflect random variation and variation attributable to various factor effects:

$$\text{SSTo} = \text{SSA} + \text{SSB} + \text{SSAB} + \text{SSE}$$

where

1. SSTo is total sum of squares, with associated df $= klm - 1$.
2. SSA is the factor A main effect sum of squares, with associated df $= k - 1$.

3. SSB is the factor B main effect sum of squares, with associated df $= l - 1$.

4. SSAB is the interaction sum of squares, with associated df $= (k - 1)(l - 1)$.

5. SSE is error sum of squares, with associated df $= kl(m - 1)$.

The formulas for these sums of squares are similar to those given in previous sections, but we will not give them here. The standard statistical computer packages will calculate all sums of squares and other necessary quantities. The magnitude of SSE is related entirely to the amount of underlying variability (as specified by σ^2) in the distributions being sampled. It has nothing to do with values of the various true average responses. SSAB reflects in part underlying variability, but its value is also affected by whether there is interaction between the factors. Generally speaking, the more extensive the amount of interaction (that is, the further the graphs of true average responses are from being parallel), the larger the value of SSAB tends to be. The test statistic for testing the null hypothesis that there is no interaction between factors is the ratio MSAB/MSE. A large value of this statistic suggests that interaction effects are present.

The absence of factor A effects and of factor B effects are both special cases of no-interaction situations. If the data suggests that interaction is present, it does not make sense to investigate effects of one factor without reference to the other factor. Our recommendation is that hypotheses concerning the presence or absence of separate factor effects be tested only if the hypothesis of no interaction is not rejected. Then the factor A main effect sum of squares SSA will reflect random variation and, in addition, any differences between true average responses for different levels of factor A. The same applies to SSB.

Two-Factor ANOVA Hypotheses and Tests

1. H_0:   There is no interaction between factors.

   H_a: There is interaction between factors.

   Test statistic: $F_{AB} = \dfrac{\text{MSAB}}{\text{MSE}}$, based on $df_1 = (k - 1)(l - 1)$ and $df_2 = kl(m - 1)$.

The following two hypotheses should be tested only if the hypothesis of no interaction is not rejected.

2. H_0:   There are no factor A main effects (true average response is the same for each level of factor A).

   H_a: H_0 is not true.

   Test statistic: $F_A = \dfrac{\text{MSA}}{\text{MSE}}$, based on $df_1 = k - 1$ and $df_2 = kl(m - 1)$.

3. H_0:   There are no factor B main effects.

   H_a: H_0 is not true.

   Test statistic: $F_B = \dfrac{\text{MSB}}{\text{MSE}}$, based on $df_1 = l - 1$ and $df_2 = kl(m - 1)$.

Computations are typically summarized in an ANOVA table, as shown in Table 15.11.

Table 15.11

Source of Variation	df	Sum of Squares	Mean Square	F
A main effects	$k - 1$	SSA	$MSA = \dfrac{SSA}{k - 1}$	$F = \dfrac{MSA}{MSE}$
B main effects	$l - 1$	SSB	$MSB = \dfrac{SSB}{l - 1}$	$F = \dfrac{MSB}{MSE}$
AB interaction	$(k - 1)(l - 1)$	SSAB	$MSAB = \dfrac{SSAB}{(k - 1)(l - 1)}$	$F = \dfrac{MSAB}{MSE}$
Error	$kl(m - 1)$	SSE	$MSE = \dfrac{SSE}{kl(m - 1)}$	
Total	$klm - 1$	SSTo		

EXAMPLE 15.13   An ANOVA table for the tomato-yield data of Example 15.12 is given in Table 15.12.

Table 15.12 *Analysis of variance on yield*

Source	df	Sum of Squares	Mean Square	F
Variety	2	327.60	163.80	103.70
Density	3	86.69	28.90	18.30
Interaction	6	8.03	1.34	.85
Error	24	38.04	1.58	
Total	35	460.36		

1. Test of H_0: no interaction between variety and density:

    calculated $F_{AB} = .85$, based on $df_1 = 6$, $df_2 = 24$

    From Appendix Table VII, the smallest value for these df's is 2.04, so P-value > .10. There is no evidence of interaction, so it is appropriate to carry out further tests concerning the presence of main effects.

2. Test of H_0: factor A (variety) main effects are absent:

    $F_A = 103.7$, based on $df_1 = 2$, $df_2 = 24$

    Appendix Table VII shows that P-value < .001. We therefore reject H_0 and conclude that true average yield does depend on variety.

3. Test of H_0: factor B (density) main effects are absent:

    $F_B = 18.3$, based on $df_1 = 3$, $df_2 = 24$

Again, P-value $< .001$, so we reject H_0 and conclude that true average yield does depend on planting density.

After the null hypothesis of no factor A main effects has been rejected, significant differences in factor A levels can be identified by using a multiple comparisons procedure. In particular, the Tukey–Kramer method described previously can be applied. The quantities $\bar{x}_1, \bar{x}_2, \ldots, \bar{x}_k$ are now the sample average responses for levels $1, \ldots, k$ of factor A, and error df is $kl(m - 1)$. A similar comment applies to factor B main effects and significant differences in factor B levels.

The Case $m = 1$

There is a problem with the foregoing analysis when $m = 1$ (one observation on each treatment). Although we did not give the formula, MSE is an estimate of σ^2 obtained by computing a separate sample variance s^2 for the m observations on each treatment and then averaging these kl sample variances. With only one observation on each treatment, there is no way to estimate σ^2 separately from each of the treatments.

One way out of this dilemma is to assume a priori that there is no interaction between factors. This should, of course, be done only when the investigator has sound reasons, based on a thorough understanding of the problem, for believing that the factors contribute separately to the response. Having made this assumption, what would otherwise be interaction sum of squares can then be used for SSE. The fundamental identity becomes

$$\text{SSTo} = \text{SSA} + \text{SSB} + \text{SSE}$$

with the four associated df $kl - 1$, $k - 1$, $l - 1$, and $(k - 1)(l - 1)$.

Table 15.13 gives the corresponding ANOVA table. F_A is the test statistic for testing the null hypothesis that true average responses are identical for all factor A levels. F_B plays a similar role for factor B main effects. The analysis of data from a randomized block experiment in fact assumed no interaction between treatments

Table 15.13 *ANOVA table for two-factor experiment with $m = 1$*

Source of Variation	df	Sum of Squares	Mean Square	F
Factor A	$k - 1$	SSA	$\text{MSA} = \dfrac{\text{SSA}}{k - 1}$	$F = \dfrac{\text{MSA}}{\text{MSE}}$
Factor B	$l - 1$	SSB	$\text{MSB} = \dfrac{\text{SSB}}{l - 1}$	$F = \dfrac{\text{SSB}}{\text{MSE}}$
Error	$(k - 1)(l - 1)$	SSE	$\text{MSE} = \dfrac{\text{SSE}}{(k - 1)(l - 1)}$	
Total	$kl - 1$	SSTo		

and blocks. If SSTr is relabeled SSA and SSBl is relabeled SSB, the formulas for all sums of squares given in Section 15.3 are valid here ($\bar{x}_1, \ldots, \bar{x}_k$ and $\bar{b}_1, \ldots, \bar{b}_l$ are now the sample average responses for factor A levels and factor B levels, respectively).

EXAMPLE 15.14   When metal pipe is buried in soil, it is desirable to apply a coating to retard corrosion. Four different coatings are under consideration for use with pipe that will ultimately be buried in three types of soil. An experiment to investigate the effects of these coatings and soils was carried out by first selecting 12 pipe segments and applying each coating to three segments. The segments were then buried in soil for a specified period in such a way that each soil type received one piece with each coating. The resulting data (depth of corrosion) and ANOVA table are given in Table 15.14. Assuming that there is no interaction between coating type and soil type, let's test at level .05 for the presence of separate factor A (coating) and factor B (soil) effects.

Table 15.14 *Data and ANOVA table for Example 15.14*

		Factor B (Soil)			Sample Average
		1	2	3	
Factor A (Coating)	1	64	49	50	54.33
	2	53	51	48	50.67
	3	47	45	50	47.33
	4	51	43	52	48.67
Sample average		53.75	47.00	50.00	$\bar{\bar{x}} = 50.25$

Source of Variation	df	Sum of Squares	Mean Square	F
Factor A	3	83.5	27.8	$F_A = \dfrac{27.8}{20.6} = 1.3$
Factor B	2	91.5	45.8	$F_B = \dfrac{45.8}{20.6} = 2.2$
Error	6	123.3	20.6	
Total	11	298.3		

Appendix Table VII shows that P-value $> .10$ for both tests. It appears that the true average response (amount of corrosion) depends neither on the coating used nor on the type of soil in which pipe is buried.

Exercises 15.39 – 15.51

15.39 The behavior of undergraduate students when exposed to various odors was examined by the authors of the article "Effects of Environmental Odor and Coping Style on Negative Affect, Anger, Arousal and Escape" (*J. Applied Social Psychology* (1999): 245–260). The following table was constructed using data on reported discomfort level (measured on a scale from 1 to 5). There were 24 students in each odor–gender combination.

	Male	Female
Type of Odor	$\bar{x}$	$\bar{x}$
No odor	1.36	1.68
Rotten egg	1.83	2.33
Skunk	2.42	2.69
Cigarette ash	2.74	3.16

a. Construct a graph (similar to those of Figure 15.8) that shows the mean discomfort level on the vertical axis. Mark the four odor categories on the horizontal axis. Then plot the four means for the males and connect them with line segments. Plot the four means for females and connect them with line segments.
b. Interpret the interaction plot. Do you think that there is an interaction between gender and type of odor?

15.40 Many students report that test anxiety affects their performance on exams. A study of the effect of anxiety and instructional mode (lecture versus independent study) on test performance was described in the article "Interactive Effects of Achievement Anxiety, Academic Achievement, and Instructional Mode on Performance and Course Attitudes" (*Home Ec. Research J.* (1980): 216–227). Students classified as belonging to either high- or low-achievement anxiety groups (factor A) were assigned to one of the two instructional modes (factor B). Mean test scores for the four treatments (factor level combinations) are given in the accompanying table. Use these means to construct a graph (similar to those of Figure 15.8) of the treatment sample averages. Does the picture suggest the existence of an interaction between factors? Explain.

	Instructional Mode	
Anxiety Group	**Lecture**	**Independent Study**
High	145.8	144.3
Low	142.9	144.8

15.41 The accompanying plot appeared in the article "Group Process-Work Outcome Relationships: A Note

on the Moderating Impact of Self-Esteem" (*Academy of Mgmt. J.* (1982): 575–585). The response variable was tension, a measure of job strain. The two factors of interest were peer-group interaction (with two levels — high and low) and self-esteem (also with two levels — high and low).

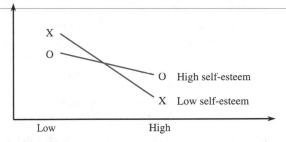

a. Does this plot suggest an interaction between peer-group interaction and self-esteem? Explain.
b. The authors of the article state, "Peer group interaction had a stronger effect on individuals with lower self-esteem than on those with higher self-esteem." Do you agree with this statement? Explain.

15.42 Explain why the individual effects of factor A or factor B cannot be interpreted when an AB interaction is present.

15.43 The article "Experimental Analysis of Prey Selection by Largemouth Bass" (*Trans. Amer. Fisheries Soc.* (1991): 500–508) gave an ANOVA summary in which the response variable was a certain preference index, there were three sizes of bass, and there were two different species of prey. Three observations were made for each size–species combination. Sums of squares for size, species, and interaction were reported as .088, .048, and .048, respectively, and SSTo = .316. Test the relevant hypotheses using a significance level of .01.

15.44 The following partially completed ANOVA table approximately matches summary statistics given in the article "From Here to Equity: The Influence of Status on Student Access to and Understanding of Science" (*Science Education* (1999): 577–602). The study described in this article attempted to quantify the effect of socioeconomic status on learning science. The response variable was "Rate of Talk" (the number of on-task talk speech acts per minute) during group work. Data was also collected on the variable *socioeconomic status* (low, middle, high) and the variable *gender* (female, male). The author allowed for an interaction between gender and status. Assume that there were 12 students at each status–gender level combination, for a total of 72 subjects.

Source	df	SS	MS	F
Status	2			14.49
Gender	1			.15
Interaction	2			.95
Error	66		.0120	
Total	71			

a. Fill in the missing numbers in the ANOVA table.
b. Is there a significant interaction between status and gender?
c. Is there a difference between the mean "Rate of Talk" scores for girls and boys?
d. Is there a difference between the mean "Rate of Talk" scores across the three different status groups?

15.45 Is self-esteem related to year in college or to fraternity membership? The authors of the article "Self-Esteem Among College Men as a Function of Greek Affiliation and Year in College" (*J. College Student Development* (1998): 611–613) interviewed 75 college men who were members of fraternities and 57 who were not. In addition to Greek status (in a fraternity, not in a fraternity), year in college (freshman, sophomore, junior, senior) was also noted. Subjects completed a 10-item, self-esteem inventory, which was used to compute a self-esteem score. The article reported the following *F* statistic values from a two-way ANOVA:

Source	F
Greek status	20.53
Year	2.59
Interaction	.70

a. Is there evidence of a significant interaction between year and Greek status?
b. Is the main effect for Greek status significant?
c. Is the main effect for year significant?

15.46 Three ultrasonic devices (factor A, with levels 20, 30, and 40 kHz) were tested for effectiveness under two test conditions (factor B, with levels plentiful food supply and restricted food supply). Daily food consumption was recorded for three rats under each factor–level combination for a total of 18 observations. Data compatible with summary values given in the article "Variables Affecting Ultrasound Repellency in Philippine Rats" (*J. Wildlife Mgmt.* (1982): 148–155) was used to obtain the sums of squares given in the accompanying ANOVA table. Complete the table, and use it to test the relevant hypotheses.

Source of Variation	df	Sum of Squares	Mean Square	F
A main effects		4206		
B main effects		1782		
AB interaction				
Error		2911		
Total		10,846		

15.47 The article "Learning, Opportunity to Cheat, and Amount of Reward" (*J. Exper. Educ.* (1977): 30–40) described a study to determine the effects of expectations concerning cheating during a test and perceived payoff on test performance. Subjects, students at UCLA, were randomly assigned to a particular factor–level combination. Factor A was expectation of opportunity to cheat, with levels high, medium, and low. Those in the high group were asked to study and then recall a list of words. For the first four lists, they were left alone in a room with the door closed, so they could look at the original list of words if they wanted to. The medium group was asked to study and recall the list while left alone but with the door open. For the low group, the experimenter remained in the room. For study and recall of a fifth list, the experimenter stayed in the room for all three groups, thus precluding any cheating on the fifth list. Score on the fifth test was the response variable. The second factor (B) under study was the perceived payoff, with a high and a low level. The high payoff group was told that if they scored above average on the test, they would receive 2 hours of credit rather than just 1 hour (subjects were fulfilling a course requirement by participating in experiments). The low group was not given any extra incentive for scoring above the average. The article gave the following statistics: $F_A = 4.99$, $F_B = 4.81$, $F_{AB} < 1$, error df ≈ 120. Test the null hypothesis of no interaction between the factors. If appropriate, test the null hypotheses of no factor A and no factor B effects. Use $\alpha = .05$.

15.48 The accompanying (slightly modified) ANOVA table appeared in the article "An Experimental Test of Mate Defense in an Iguanid Lizard" (*Ecology* (1991): 1218–1224). The response variable was territory size.

Source of Variation	df	SS
Age	1	.614
Sex	1	1.754
Interaction	1	.146
Error	80	5.624

a. How many age classes were there?
b. How many observations were made for each age–sex combination?

c. What conclusions can be drawn about how the factors affect the response variable?

15.49 Identification of gender in human skeletons is an important part of many anthropological studies. An experiment conducted to determine whether measurements of the sacrum could be used to determine gender was described in the article "Univariate and Multivariate Methods for Sexing the Sacrum" (*Am. J. Phys. Anthro.* (1978): 103–110). Sacra from skeletons of individuals of known race (factor A, with two levels — Caucasian and black) and gender (factor B, with two levels — male and female) were measured and the lengths recorded. Data compatible with summary quantities given in the article was used to compute the following: SSA = 857, SSB = 291, SSAB = 32, SSE = 5541, and error df = 36.

a. Use a significance level of .01 to test the null hypothesis of no interaction between race and gender.

b. Using a .01 significance level, test to determine whether the true average length differs for the two races.

c. Using a .01 significance level, test to determine whether the true average length differs for males and females.

15.50 The article "Food Consumption and Energy Requirements of Captive Bald Eagles" (*J. Wildlife Mgmt.* (1982): 646–654) investigated mean gross daily energy intake (the response variable) for different diet types (factor A, with three levels — fish, rabbit, and mallard) and temperatures (factor B, with three levels). Summary quantities given in the article were used to generate data, resulting in SSA = 18,138, SSB = 5182, SSAB = 1737, SSE = 11,291, and error df = 36. Construct an ANOVA table and test the relevant hypotheses.

15.51 The effect of three different soil types and three phosphate application rates on total phosphorus uptake (mg) of white clover was examined in the article "A Glasshouse Comparison of Six Phosphate Fertilisers" (*N. Zeal. J. Exp. Ag.* (1984): 131–140). Only one observation was obtained for each factor–level combination. Assuming there is no interaction between soil type and application rate, use the accompanying data to construct an ANOVA table and to test the null hypotheses of no main effects due to soil type and of no main effects due to application rate. Also identify significant differences among soil types.

Application Rate (kgP/ha)	Soil Type		
	Ramiha	**Konini**	**Wainui**
0	1.29	10.42	17.10
75	11.73	21.08	23.69
150	17.63	31.37	32.88

15.5 Interpreting the Results of Statistical Analyses

The analysis of variance procedures introduced in this chapter are used to compare more than two population or treatment means. When a single-factor analysis of variance has been used to test the null hypothesis of equal population or treatment means, the value of the *F* statistic and the associated *P*-value usually are reported. It is also fairly common to see the supporting calculations summarized in an ANOVA table, although this is not always the case.

What to Look For in Published Data

Here are some questions to ask when reading an article that includes a description of a single-factor analysis of variance.

■ Are the assumptions required for the validity of the ANOVA procedure reasonable? Specifically, are the samples independently chosen, or is there random assignment of treatments? Is it reasonable to think that the population or treatment response distributions are normal in shape? Are the reported sample standard deviations consistent with the assumption of equal population or treatment variances?

■ What is the *P*-value associated with the test? Does the *P*-value lead to rejection of the null hypothesis?

- If the ANOVA F test led to rejection of the null hypothesis, was a multiple comparisons procedure used to identify differences in the means? Are the results of the multiple comparisons procedure interpreted properly?
- Are the conclusions drawn consistent with the results of the hypothesis test and the multiple comparisons procedure? If H_0 was rejected, does this indicate practical significance or only statistical significance?

As an example, consider an analysis of variance performed by the authors of "Perceived Age and Attractiveness of Models in Cigarette Advertisements" (*J. of Marketing* (1992): 22–37). The authors hypothesized that certain cigarette brands aimed their advertising at the young and that the average age of readers of magazines in which the cigarette ads appeared was not the same for the 12 brands of cigarettes studied. This hypothesis was tested using a single-factor analysis of variance. The accompanying ANOVA table is from the article.

Source	df	SS	MS	F
Treatments (brands)	11	592.66	53.88	4.13
Error	175	2282.98	13.05	
Total	186	2875.64		

It was reported that the hypothesis of equal mean ages for the 12 brands considered in the study was rejected ($F = 4.13$, P-value $< .001$). This was interpreted as support for the researchers' hypothesis that some brands targeted the young. (Does this conclusion necessarily follow from the result of the ANOVA F test?)

To clarify these results, a multiple comparisons procedure could be used to identify significant differences among brands, although this was not done in the reported research. The article did include sample sizes and sample means for the 12 brands, and this information is reproduced in the accompanying table.

Brand	Sample Size	Average Audience Age for Magazines in Which Ad Appears (Years)
Lucky Strike Lights	3	28.5
Newport Lights	5	31.1
Camel Lights	21	31.3
Kool Milds	24	31.3
Newport	12	31.3
Winston Lights	15	31.3
Winston	8	31.6
Virginia Slims Lights	32	33.9
Marlboro	26	34.3
More	17	34.8
Benson Hedges Light	23	31.9
Carlton	1	41.0

Notice that the sample sizes vary greatly. We might also worry about the validity of the assumptions required for the ANOVA F test. It would be of interest to examine the sample standard deviations and, if the original data was available, to look at various plots of the data.

Summary of Key Concepts and Formulas

Term or Formula	Comment
Single-factor analysis of variance (ANOVA)	A test procedure for determining whether there are significant differences among k population or treatment means. The hypotheses tested are $H_0: \mu_1 = \cdots = \mu_k$ versus H_a: at least two μ's differ.
Treatment sum of squares: $\text{SSTr} = n_1(\bar{x}_1 - \bar{\bar{x}})^2 + \cdots + n_k(\bar{x}_k - \bar{\bar{x}})^2$	A measure of how different the k sample means $\bar{x}_1, \bar{x}_2, \ldots, \bar{x}_k$ are from one another; associated df $= k - 1$.
Error sum of squares: $\text{SSE} = (n_1 - 1)s_1^2 + \cdots + (n_k - 1)s_k^2$	A measure of the amount of variability within the individual samples; associated df $= N - k$, where $N = n_1 + \cdots + n_k$.
Mean square	A sum of squares divided by its df. For single-factor ANOVA, $\text{MSTr} = \text{SSTR}/(k - 1)$ and $\text{MSE} = \text{SSE}/(N - k)$.
$F = \dfrac{\text{MSTr}}{\text{MSE}}$	The test statistic for testing $H_0: \mu_1 = \cdots = \mu_k$ in a single-factor ANOVA. When H_0 is true, F has an F distribution with numerator df $= k - 1$ and denominator df $= N - k$.
$\text{SSTo} = \text{SSTr} + \text{SSE}$	The fundamental identity in single-factor ANOVA, where $\text{SSTo} = $ total sum of squares $= \Sigma (x - \bar{\bar{x}})^2$.
Tukey–Kramer multiple comparison procedure	A procedure for identifying significant differences among the μ's once the hypothesis $H_0: \mu_1 = \cdots = \mu_k$ has been rejected by the ANOVA F test.
Randomized block design	An experimental design that controls for extraneous variation when comparing treatments. The experimental units are grouped into homogeneous *blocks* so that within each block, the units are as similar as possible. Then each treatment is used on exactly one experimental unit in every block (each treatment appears once in every block).
Randomized block F test	The four sums of squares for a randomized block design — SSTo, SSTr, SSBl, and SSE (with df $kl - 1$, $k - 1$, $l - 1$, and $(k - 1)(l - 1)$, respectively) — are related by $\text{SSTo} = \text{SSTr} + \text{SSBl} + \text{SSE}$. Usually SSE is obtained by subtraction once the other three have been calculated using computing formulas. The null hypothesis is that the true average response does not depend on which treatment is applied. With mean squares $\text{MSTr} = \text{SSTr}/(k - 1)$ and $\text{MSE} = \text{SSE}/(k - 1)(l - 1)$, the test statistic is $F = \text{MSTr}/\text{MSE}$, based on $\text{df}_1 = k - 1$ and $\text{df}_2 = (k - 1)(l - 1)$.
Interaction between factors	Two factors are said to interact if the average change in response associated with changing the level of one factor depends on the level of the other factor.
Two-factor ANOVA	When there are k levels of factor A and l levels of factor B, and m (>1) observations made for each combination of A–B levels, total sum of squares SSTo can be decomposed into SSA (sum of squares for A main effects), SSB, SSAB

(interaction sum of squares), and SSE. Associated df are $klm - 1, k - 1$, $l - 1, (k - 1)(l - 1)$, and $kl(m - 1)$, respectively. The null hypothesis of no interaction between the two factors is tested using $F_{AB} = MSAB/MSE$, where $MSAB = SSAB/(k - 1)(l - 1)$ and $MSE = SSE/kl(m - 1)$. If this null hypothesis cannot be rejected, tests for A and B main effects are based on $F_A = MSA/MSE$ and $F_B = MSB/MSE$, respectively.

APPENDIX

ANOVA Computations
Single-Factor ANOVA

Let T_1 denote the sum of the n_1 observations in the sample from the first population or treatment, and let $T_2, \ldots, T_k$ denote the other sample totals. Also let T represent the sum of all N observations — the **grand total** — and

$$CF = \text{correction factor} = \frac{T^2}{N}$$

Then

$$SSTo = \sum_{\substack{\text{all } N \\ \text{obs.}}} x^2 - CF$$

$$SSTr = \frac{T_1^2}{n_1} + \frac{T_2^2}{n_2} + \cdots + \frac{T_k^2}{n_k} - CF$$

$$SSE = SSTo - SSTr$$

EXAMPLE

	1	4.2	3.7	5.0	4.8	$T_1 = 17.7$	$n_1 = 4$
Treatment 2		5.7	6.2	6.4		$T_2 = 18.3$	$n_2 = 3$
	3	4.6	3.2	3.5	3.9	$T_3 = 15.2$	$n_3 = 4$
						$T = 51.2$	$N = 11$

$$CF = \text{correction factor} = \frac{T^2}{N} = \frac{(51.2)^2}{11} = 238.31$$

$$SSTr = \frac{T_1^2}{n_1} + \frac{T_2^2}{n_2} + \cdots + \frac{T_k^2}{n_k} - CF$$

$$= \frac{(17.7)^2}{4} + \frac{(18.3)^2}{3} + \frac{(15.2)^2}{4} - 238.31 = 9.40$$

$$SSTo = \sum_{\substack{\text{all } N \\ \text{obs.}}} x^2 - CF = (4.2)^2 + (3.7)^2 + \cdots + (3.9)^2 - 238.31 = 11.81$$

$$SSE = SSTo - SSTr = 11.81 - 9.40 = 2.41$$

Randomized Block Experiment

Let $T_1, T_2, \ldots, T_k$ denote the treatment totals and $B_1, B_2, \ldots, B_l$ represent the block totals. Also, let T be the grand total of all kl observations and

$$CF = \text{correction factor} = \frac{T^2}{kl}$$

Then

$$SSTo = \sum_{\substack{\text{all } kl \\ \text{obs.}}} x^2 - CF$$

$$SSTr = \frac{1}{l}[T_1^2 + T_2^2 + \cdots + T_k^2] - CF$$

$$SSBl = \frac{1}{k}[B_1^2 + B_2^2 + \cdots + B_l^2] - CF$$

$$SSE = SSTo - SSTr - SSBl$$

EXAMPLE

		Block				
		1	**2**	**3**	**4**	
Treatment	1	4.2	3.7	5.0	4.8	$T_1 = 17.7$
	2	5.2	4.5	6.7	5.4	$T_2 = 21.8$
	3	3.4	3.2	5.1	3.9	$T_3 = 15.6$
		$B_1 = 12.8$	$B_2 = 11.4$	$B_3 = 16.8$	$B_4 = 14.1$	$T = 55.1$

$$CF = \text{correction factor} = \frac{T^2}{kl} = \frac{(55.1)^2}{(3)(4)} = \frac{3036.01}{12} = 253.00$$

$$SSTr = \frac{1}{l}[T_1^2 + T_2^2 + \cdots + T_k^2] - CF$$

$$= \frac{1}{4}[(17.7)^2 + (21.8)^2 + (15.6)^2] - 253.00 = 4.97$$

$$SSBl = \frac{1}{k}[B_1^2 + B_2^2 + \cdots + B_l^2] - CF$$

$$= \frac{1}{3}[(12.8)^2 + (11.4)^2 + (16.8)^2 + (14.1)^2] - 253.00 = 5.28$$

$$SSTo = \sum_{\substack{\text{all } kl \\ \text{obs.}}} x^2 - CF = (4.2)^2 + \cdots + (3.9)^2 - 253.00 = 10.73$$

$$SSE = SSTo - SSTr - SSBl = 10.73 - 4.97 - 5.28 = .48$$

Supplementary Exercises 15.52 – 15.65

15.52 A study was carried out to compare aptitudes and achievements of three different groups of college students ("A Comparison of Three Groups of Academically At-Risk College Students," *J. of College Student Development* (1995): 270–279):

1. Students diagnosed as learning disabled
2. Students who identified themselves as learning disabled
3. Students who were low achievers

The Scholastic Abilities Test for Adults was given to each student. Consider the following summary data on writing composition score:

$$n_1 = 30 \qquad n_2 = 30 \qquad n_3 = 30$$

$$\bar{x}_1 = 9.40 \qquad \bar{x}_2 = 11.63 \qquad \bar{x}_3 = 11.00$$

$$\text{SSE} = 749.85$$

Does it appear that population mean score is not the same for the three types of students? Carry out a test of hypothesis. Does your conclusion depend on whether a significance level of .05 or .01 is used?

15.53 Tobacco companies have denied engaging in any youth-directed marketing efforts, yet critics have observed that adolescents are attracted by the images portrayed in many advertisements. The article "Perceived Age and Attractiveness of Models in Cigarette Advertisements" (*J. of Marketing* (1992): 22–37) reported on the results of a study that focused on certain aspects of this issue. Consider the accompanying data on average median audience ages for readers of magazines in which a sample of cigarette advertisements appeared (obtained from marketing data):

Brand	Sample Size	Average Audience Age
Lucky Strike Lights	3	28.5
Newport Lights	5	31.1
Camel Lights	21	31.3
Kool Milds	24	31.3
Newport	12	31.3
Winston Lights	15	31.3
Winston	8	31.6
Virginia Slims Lights	32	33.9
Marlboro	26	34.3
More	17	34.8
Benson Hedges Lights	23	35.1
Carlton	1	41.0
	187	$\bar{\bar{x}} = 32.96$

Let $\mu_1, \mu_2, \ldots, \mu_{12}$ denote the average audience ages for magazines in which advertisements for the various brands appeared. Test $H_0: \mu_1 = \mu_2 = \cdots = \mu_{12}$ versus H_a: At least two μ's are different, by first filling in the missing entries in the accompanying ANOVA table.

Source	df	SS	MS	F
Treatments (brands)		592.66		
Error				
Total		2875.64		

15.54 Eye inflammation can be induced by the endotoxin lipopolysaccharide (LPS). A random sample of 35 rats was randomly divided into five groups of 7 rats each (a completely randomized design). Rats within each group received the same dose of LPS. Data on vascular permeability was read from plots that appeared in the article "Endotoxin-Induced Uveitis in the Rat: Observations on Altered Vascular Permeability, Clinical Findings, and Histology" (*Exper. Eye Research* (1984): 665–676). Use the accompanying SAS output to test the null hypothesis of no difference between the five treatment (dose) means.

Dependent Variable: VASPERM

Source	DF	Sum of Squares	Mean Square	F Value	Pr > F
Model	4	291.0428571	72.7607143	8.04	0.0002
Error	30	270.5000000	9.0166667		
Corrected Total	34	561.5428571			

15.55 Most large companies have established grievance procedures for their employees. One question of interest to employers is why certain groups within a company have higher grievance rates than others. The study described in the article "Grievance Rates and Technology" (*Academy of Mgmt. J.* (1979): 810–815) distinguished four types of jobs. These types were labeled apathetic, erratic, strategic, and conservative. Suppose that a total of 52 work groups were selected (13 of each type), and a measure of grievance rate was determined for each one. Here are the resulting $\bar{x}$ values:

Group	Apathetic	Erratic	Strategic	Conservative
Sample mean	2.96	5.05	8.74	4.91

In addition, SSTo = 682.10 and SSE = 506.19. Test at significance level .05 to see whether true average grievance rate depends on the type of job. If appropriate, use the T–K method to identify significant differences among job types.

15.56 The results of a study on the effectiveness of line drying on the smoothness and stiffness of fabric was summarized in the article "Line-Dried vs. Machine-Dried Fabrics: Comparison of Appearance, Hand, and Consumer Acceptance" (*Home Ec. Res. J.* (1984): 27–35). Smoothness scores were given for nine different types of fabric and five different drying methods — (1) machine dry, (2) line dry, (3) line dry followed by 15-min tumble, (4) line dry with softener, and (5) line dry with air movement — as given in the accompanying table. Using a .05 significance level, test to see whether there is a difference in the true mean smoothness scores for the drying methods. (There may be "extraneous" variation due to different fabrics.)

	Drying Method				
Fabric	1	2	3	4	5
Crepe	3.3	2.5	2.8	2.5	1.9
Doubleknit	3.6	2.0	3.6	2.4	2.3
Twill	4.2	3.4	3.8	3.1	3.1
Twill mix	3.4	2.4	2.9	1.6	1.7
Terry	3.8	1.3	2.8	2.0	1.6
Broadcloth	2.2	1.5	2.7	1.5	1.9
Sheeting	3.5	2.1	2.8	2.1	2.2
Corduroy	3.6	1.3	2.8	1.7	1.8
Denim	2.6	1.4	2.4	1.3	1.6

15.57 In many countries, grains and cereals are the primary food source. The authors of the article "Mineral Contents of Cereal Grains as Affected by Storage and Insect Infestation" (*J. Stored Prod. Res.* (1992): 147–151) investigated the effects of storage period on the mineral content of maize. Four storage periods were considered: 0 months (no storage), 1 month, 2 months, and 4 months. Twenty-four containers of maize were randomly divided into four groups of six each. The iron content (mg/100 g dry weight) of the first group of six was measured immediately (0 months of storage), the second six were measured after 1 month in storage, etc. The following summary quantities are consistent with information in the article:

Storage Period	$\bar{x}$	s^2
0	4.923	.000107
1	4.923	.000067
2	4.917	.000147
4	4.902	.000057

a. Use a test with $\alpha = .05$ to decide whether true average iron content is the same for all four storage periods.
b. If appropriate, carry out a multiple comparison analysis.

15.58 Controlling a filling operation with multiple fillers requires adjustment of the individual units. Data resulting from a sample of size 5 from each pocket of a 12-pocket filler was given in the article "Evaluating Variability of Filling Operations" (*Food Technology* (1984): 51–55). Data for the first five pockets is given in the accompanying table.

Pocket	Fill (oz)				
1	10.2	10.0	9.8	10.4	10.0
2	9.9	10.0	9.9	10.1	10.0
3	10.1	9.9	9.8	9.9	9.7
4	10.0	9.7	9.9	9.7	9.6
5	10.2	9.8	9.9	9.7	9.8

Use the ANOVA *F* test to determine whether the null hypothesis of no difference in the mean fill weight of the five pockets can be rejected. If so, use an appropriate technique to determine where the differences lie.

15.59 *This problem requires the use of a computer package.* The effect of oxygen concentration on fermentation end products was examined in the article "Effects of Oxygen on Pyruvate Formate Lyase in Situ and Sugar Metabolism of *Streptococcus mutans* and *Streptococcus sanguis*" (*Infection and Immunity* (1985): 129–134). Four oxygen concentrations (0, 46, 92, and 138 μM) and two types of sugar (galactose and glucose) were used. The accompanying table gives two observations on amount of ethanol (μmol/mg) for each sugar–oxygen concentration combination. Construct an ANOVA table and test the relevant hypotheses.

Oxygen Concentration	Galactose	Glucose
0	.59, .30	.25, .03
46	.44, .18	.13, .02
92	.22, .23	.07, .00
138	.12, .13	.00, .01

15.60 The ANOVA table on page 662 is from the article "Bacteriological and Chemical Variations and Their Inter-Relationships in a Slightly Polluted Water-Body" (*Inter. J. Environ. Studies* (1984): 121–129). A water specimen was taken every month for a year at each of 15 designated locations on the Lago di Piediluco in Italy. The ammonia-nitrogen concentration was determined for each specimen and the resulting data analyzed using a two-way ANOVA. The researchers were willing to assume that there was no interaction between the two factors *location* and *month*. Complete the given ANOVA table, and use it to perform the tests required to determine whether the true mean concentration differs by location or by month of year. Use a .05 significance level for both tests.

Source	df	Sum of Squares	Mean Square	F
Location		.6		
Month	11	2.3		
Error				
Total	179	6.4		

15.61 The water absorption of two types of mortar used to repair damaged cement was discussed in the article "Polymer Mortar Composite Matrices for Maintenance-Free, Highly Durable Ferrocement" (*J. Ferrocement* (1984): 337–345). Specimens of ordinary cement mortar (OCM) and polymer cement mortar (PCM) were submerged for varying lengths of time (5, 9, 24, or 48 hr) and water absorption (% by weight) was recorded. With mortar type as factor A (with two levels) and submersion period as factor B (with four levels), three observations were made for each factor–level combination. Data included in the article was used to compute the following sums of squares: SSA = 322.667, SSB = 35.623, SSAB = 8.557, SSTo = 372.113. Use this information to construct an ANOVA table, and then use a .05 significance level to test the appropriate hypotheses.

15.62 Suppose that each observation in a single-factor ANOVA data set is multiplied by a constant c (a change in units; for example, $c = 2.54$ changes observations from inches to centimeters). How does this affect MSTr, MSE, and the test statistic F? Is this reasonable? Explain.

15.63 Three different brands of automobile batteries, each one having a 42-month warranty, were included in a study of battery lifetime. A random sample of batteries of each brand was selected and lifetime (in months) was determined, resulting in the following data:

Brand 1	45	38	52	47	45	42	43
Brand 2	39	44	50	54	48	46	40
Brand 3	50	46	43	48	57	44	48

State and test the appropriate hypotheses using a significance level of .05. Be sure to summarize your calculations in an ANOVA table.

15.64 Let $c_1, c_2, \ldots, c_k$ denote k specified numbers, and consider the quantity θ defined by

$$\theta = c_1\mu_1 + c_2\mu_2 + \cdots + c_k\mu_k$$

A confidence interval for θ is then

$$c_1\bar{x}_1 + \cdots + c_k\bar{x}_k \pm (t \text{ critical val.})\sqrt{\text{MSE}\left(\frac{c_1^2}{n_1} + \cdots + \frac{c_k^2}{n_k}\right)}$$

where the t critical value is based on an error df of $N - k$.

For example, in a study carried out to compare pain relievers with respect to true average time to relief, suppose that brands 1, 2, and 3 are nationally available, whereas brands 4 and 5 are sold only by two large chains of drug stores. An investigator might then wish to consider

$$\theta = \frac{1}{3}\mu_1 + \frac{1}{3}\mu_2 + \frac{1}{3}\mu_3 - \frac{1}{2}\mu_4 - \frac{1}{2}\mu_5$$

which, in essence, compares the average time to relief of the national brands to the average for the house brands.

Refer to Exercise 15.63 and suppose that brand 1 is a store brand and brands 2 and 3 are national brands. Obtain a 95% confidence interval for $\theta = \mu_1 - \frac{1}{2}\mu_2 - \frac{1}{2}\mu_3$.

15.65 One of the assumptions that underlies the validity of the ANOVA F test is that the population or treatment response variances $\sigma_1^2, \sigma_2^2, \ldots, \sigma_k^2$ should be identical regardless of whether H_0 is true: the assumption of constant variance across populations or treatments. In some situations, the x values themselves may not satisfy this assumption, yet a transformation using some specified mathematical function (for example, taking the logarithm or the square root) will give observations that have (approximately) constant variance. The ANOVA F test can then be applied to the transformed data. When observations are made on a counting variable ($x = $ number of something), statisticians have found that taking the square root will frequently "stabilize the variance." In an experiment to compare the quality of four different brands of videotape, cassettes of a specified length were selected, and the number of flaws in each was determined.

Brand 1	10	14	5	12	8
Brand 2	17	14	8	9	12
Brand 3	13	18	15	18	10
Brand 4	14	22	12	16	17

Make a square-root transformation, and analyze the resulting data by using the ANOVA F test at significance level .01.

References

Miller, Rupert. *Beyond ANOVA: The Basics of Applied Statistics*. New York: Wiley, 1986. (This book contains a wealth of information concerning violations of basic assumptions and alternative methods of analysis.)

Neter, John, William Wasserman, and Michael Kutner. *Applied Linear Statistical Models*. New York: McGraw-Hill, 1996. (The latter half of the book contains a readable survey of ANOVA and experimental design.)

Appendix: The Binomial Distribution

This appendix introduces one of the more commonly encountered discrete probability distributions: the binomial distribution. The binomial distribution arises when the experiment of interest consists of making a sequence of dichotomous observations (two possible values for each observation). The process of making a single such observation is called a *trial*. For example, one characteristic of blood type is Rh factor, which can be either positive or negative. We can think of an experiment that consists of noting the Rh factor for each of 25 blood donors as a sequence of 25 dichotomous trials, where each trial consists of observing the Rh factor (positive or negative) of a single donor. Experiments of this type are characteristic of those leading to the binomial probability distribution.

The Binomial Distribution

Suppose we decide to record the gender of each of the next 25 newborn children at a particular hospital. What is the chance that at least 15 are female? What is the chance that between 10 and 15 are female? How many among the 25 can we expect to be female? These and other similar questions can be answered by studying the *binomial probability distribution*. This distribution arises when the experiment of interest is a *binomial experiment*, one having the following characteristics.

Properties of a Binomial Experiment

1. It consists of a fixed number of observations called trials.
2. Each trial can result in one of only two mutually exclusive outcomes labeled success (S) and failure (F).

(continued)

3. Outcomes of different trials are independent.

4. The probability that a trial results in S is the same for each trial.

The binomial random variable x is defined as

x = number of successes observed when experiment is performed

The probability distribution of x is called the *binomial probability distribution*.

The term *success* here does not have any of its usual connotations. Which of the two possible outcomes is labeled "success" will be determined by the random variable of interest. For example, if the variable counts the number of female births among the next 25 births at a particular hospital, a female birth would be labeled success (because this is what the variable counts). This labeling is arbitrary; if male births were counted instead, a male birth would be labeled a success and a female birth a failure.

For example, suppose that each of five randomly selected customers purchasing a hot tub at a certain store chooses either an electric or gas model. Assume that these customers make their choices independently of one another and that 40% of all customers select an electric model. Let's define the variable x = number among the five customers who selected an electric hot tub. This experiment is a binomial experiment with

number of trials = 4 $P(\text{success}) = P(E) = .4$

where success (S) is defined as a customer who purchased an electric model.

The binomial distribution will tell us how much probability is associated with each of the possible x values 0, 1, 2, 3, 4, and 5. There are 32 possible outcomes, and five of them yield $x = 1$:

SFFFF   FSFFF   FFSFF   FFFSF   FFFFS

By independence, the first of these has probability

$$P(SFFFF) = P(S) \cdot P(F) \cdot P(F) \cdot P(F) \cdot P(F)$$
$$= (.4)(.6)(.6)(.6)(.6)$$
$$= (.4)(.6)^4$$
$$= .05184$$

The probability calculation will be the same for any outcome with only one success ($x = 1$)—it does not matter where in the sequence the single success occurs. Thus

$$p(1) = P(x = 1)$$
$$= P(SFFFF \text{ or } FSFFF \text{ or } FFSFF \text{ or } FFFSF \text{ or } FFFFS)$$
$$= .05184 + .05184 + .05184 + .05184 + .05184$$
$$= (5)(.05184)$$
$$= .25920$$

Similarly, there are ten outcomes for which $x = 2$, because there are ten ways to select two from among the five trials to be the S's: *SSFFF, SFSFF, . . . ,* and *FFFSS.*

The probability of each results from multiplying together (.4) two times and (.6) three times. For example,

$$P(SSFFF) = (.4)(.4)(.6)(.6)(.6)$$
$$= (.4)^2(.6)^3$$
$$= .03456$$

and so

$$p(2) = P(x = 2)$$
$$= P(SSFFF) + \cdots + P(FFFSS)$$
$$= (10)(.4)^2(.6)^3$$
$$= .34560$$

The general form of the distribution here is

$$p(x) = P(x \text{ S's among the five trials})$$
$$= (\text{no. of outcomes with } x \text{ S's}) \cdot (\text{probability of any particular outcome with } x \text{ S's})$$
$$= (\text{no. of outcomes with } x \text{ S's}) \cdot (.4)^x \cdot (.6)^{5-x}$$

This form was seen previously where $p(2) = 10(.4)^2(.6)^3$.

Let n denote the number of trials in the experiment. Then the number of outcomes with x S's is the number of ways of selecting x from among the n trials to be the success trials. A simple expression for this quantity is

$$\text{number of outcomes with } x \text{ successes} = \frac{n!}{x!(n-x)!}$$

where, for any positive whole number m, the symbol $m!$ (read "m factorial") is defined by

$$m! = m(m-1)(m-2)\cdots(2)(1)$$

and $0! = 1$.

The Binomial Distribution

Let

n = number of independent trials in a binomial experiment

π = constant probability that any particular trial results in a success*

Then

$$p(x) = P(x \text{ successes among } n \text{ trials})$$
$$= \frac{n!}{x!(n-x)!} \cdot \pi^x (1 - \pi)^{n-x} \qquad x = 0, 1, 2, \ldots, n$$

(*continued*)

---

*Some sources use p rather than π to represent the probability of success. We prefer the use of Greek letters for characteristics of a population or probability distribution, thus the use of π.

The expressions $\binom{n}{x}$ and $_nC_x$ are sometimes used in place of $\dfrac{n!}{x!(n-x)!}$. Both are read as "n choose x" and represent the number of ways of choosing x items from a set of n. The binomial probability function can then be written as

$$p(x) = \binom{n}{x}\pi^x(1-\pi)^{n-x} \qquad x = 0, 1, 2, \ldots, n$$

or

$$_nC_x\pi^x(1-\pi)^{n-x} \qquad x = 0, 1, 2, \ldots, n$$

Notice that the probability distribution is being specified by a formula that allows calculation of the various probabilities rather than by giving a table or probability histogram.

EXAMPLE A.1

Sixty percent of all watches sold by a large discount store have a digital display and 40% have an analog display. The type of watch purchased by each of the next 12 customers will be noted. Define a random variable x by

$x = $ number of watches among these 12 that have a digital display

Since x counts the number of digital watches, we use S to denote the sale of a digital watch. Then x is a binomial random variable with $n = 12$ and $\pi = P(S) = .60$. The probability distribution of x is given by

$$p(x) = \frac{12!}{x!(12-x)!} \cdot (.6)^x(.4)^{12-x} \qquad x = 0, 1, 2, \ldots, 12$$

The probability that exactly four watches are digital is

$$\begin{aligned} p(4) &= P(x = 4) \\ &= \frac{12!}{4!8!} \cdot (.6)^4(.4)^8 \\ &= (495)(.6)^4(.4)^8 \\ &= .042 \end{aligned}$$

If group after group of 12 purchases is examined, the long-run percentage of those with exactly four digital watches will be 4.2%. According to this calculation, 495 of the possible outcomes (there are $2^{12} = 4096$) have $x = 4$.

The probability that between four and seven (inclusive) of these watches are digital is

$$\begin{aligned} P(4 \le x \le 7) &= P(x = 4 \text{ or } x = 5 \text{ or } x = 6 \text{ or } x = 7) \\ &= p(4) + p(5) + p(6) + p(7) \\ &= \frac{12!}{4!8!} \cdot (.6)^4(.4)^8 + \cdots + \frac{12!}{7!5!} \cdot (.6)^7(.4)^5 \\ &= .042 + .101 + .177 + .227 \\ &= .547 \end{aligned}$$

Notice that

$$P(4 < x < 7) = P(x = 5 \text{ or } x = 6)$$
$$= p(5) + p(6)$$
$$= .278$$

so the probability depends on whether $<$ or $\leq$ appears. (This is typical of *discrete random variables*.)

The binomial distribution formula can be tedious to use unless n is very small. Table A at the end of this appendix gives binomial probabilities for selected n in combination with various values of π. This should help you practice using the binomial distribution without getting bogged down in arithmetic.

Using Table A

To find $p(x)$ for any particular value of x,

1. Locate the part of the table corresponding to your value of n (5, 10, 15, 20, or 25).
2. Move down to the row labeled with your value of x.
3. Go across to the columns headed by the specified value of π.

The desired probability is at the intersection of the designated x row and π column. For example, when $n = 20$ and $\pi = .8$,

$$p(15) = P(x = 15) = [\text{entry at intersection of } n = 15 \text{ row and } \pi = .8 \text{ column}] = .175$$

Although $p(x)$ is positive for every possible x value, many probabilities are zero to three decimal places, so they appear as .000 in the table. There are much more extensive binomial tables available. Alternatively, most statistics computer packages and graphing calculators are programmed to calculate these probabilities.

Sampling Without Replacement

Suppose that a population consists of N individuals or objects, each one classified as an S or an F. Usually, sampling is carried out without replacement; that is, once an element has been selected into the sample, it is not a candidate for future selection. If the sampling were accomplished by selecting an element from the population, observing whether it is an S or F, and then returning it to the population before the next selection is made, the variable $x =$ number of successes observed in the sample would fit all of the requirements of a binomial random variable. When sampling is done without replacement, the binomial requirement of a constant probability of success from trial to trial is not met, and the trials (individual selections) are not independent. In this case, the number of successes observed in the sample does not have a binomial distribution, but rather a different type of distribution called a *hypergeometric distribution*. Not only does the name of this distribution sound forbidding, probability calculations for this distribution are even more tedious than for the binomial. Fortunately, when the sample size n is much smaller than N, the population size, probabilities calculated using the binomial distribution and the hypergeometric distribution are very close in value. They are so close, in fact, that statisticians often ignore the difference and use the binomial probabilities in place of the hypergeometric probabilities. Most statisticians recommend the following guideline for determining whether the binomial probability distribution is appropriate when sampling without replacement.

Let x denote the number of S's in a sample of size n from a population consisting of N individuals or objects. If $n/N \leq .05$ (that is, if at most 5% of the population is sampled), then the binomial distribution gives a good approximation to the probability distribution of x.

EXAMPLE A.2

In recent years, homeowners have become increasingly security conscious. A *Los Angeles Times* poll (Nov. 10, 1991) reported that almost 20% of Southern California homeowners questioned had installed a home security system. Suppose that exactly 20% of all such homeowners have a system. Consider a random sample of $n = 20$ homeowners (much less than 5% of the population). Then x, the number of homeowners in the sample who have a security system, has (approximately) a binomial distribution with $n = 20$ and $\pi = .20$. The probability that 5 of those sampled have a system is

$$
\begin{aligned}
p(5) &= P(x = 5) \\
&= \text{entry in } x = 5 \text{ row and } \pi = .20 \text{ column from } n = 20 \text{ part of Table A} \\
&= .175
\end{aligned}
$$

The probability that at least 40% of those in the sample — that is, 8 or more — have a system is

$$
\begin{aligned}
P(x \geq 8) &= P(x = 8, 9, 10, \ldots, 19, \text{ or } 20) \\
&= p(8) + p(9) + \cdots + p(20) \\
&= .022 + .007 + .002 + .000 + \cdots + .000 \\
&= .031
\end{aligned}
$$

If, in fact, $\pi = .20$, only about 3% of all samples of size 20 would result in at least 8 homeowners having a security system. Because $P(x \geq 8)$ is so small when $\pi = .20$, if $x \geq 8$ were actually observed, we would have to wonder whether the reported value of $\pi = .20$ was correct. Although it is possible that we would observe $x \geq 8$ when $\pi = .20$ (this would happen about 3% of the time in the long run), it might also be the case that π is actually greater than .20. In Chapter 10, we show how hypothesis-testing methods can be used to decide which of two contradictory claims about a population (for example, $\pi = .20$ or $\pi > .20$) is more plausible.

The binomial formula can be used to compute each of the 21 probabilities $p(0)$, $p(1), \ldots, p(20)$. Figure A.1 shows the probability histogram for the binomial dis-

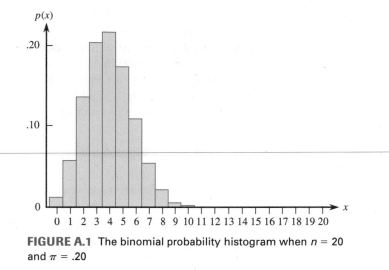

FIGURE A.1 The binomial probability histogram when $n = 20$ and $\pi = .20$

tribution with $n = 20$ and $\pi = .20$. Notice that the distribution is skewed to the right. (The binomial distribution is symmetric only when $\pi = .5$.)

The Mean and Standard Deviation of a Binomial Random Variable

A binomial random variable x based on n trials has possible values $0, 1, 2, \ldots, n$, so the mean value is

$$\mu_x = \Sigma x \cdot p(x) = (0) \cdot p(0) + (1) \cdot p(1) + \cdots + n \cdot p(n)$$

and the variance of x is

$$\sigma^2 = \Sigma (x - \mu)^2 \cdot p(x)$$
$$= (0 - \mu)^2 \cdot p(0) + (1 - \mu)^2 \cdot p(1) + \cdots + (n - \mu)^2 \cdot p(n)$$

These expressions would appear to be very tedious to evaluate for any particular values of n and π. Fortunately, algebraic manipulation results in considerable simplification, making summation unnecessary.

The mean value and the standard deviation of a binomial random variable are, respectively,

$$\mu_x = n\pi \qquad \sigma = \sqrt{n\pi(1 - \pi)}$$

EXAMPLE A.3   It has been reported (*Newsweek*, Dec. 2, 1991) that one-third of all credit card users pay their bills in full each month. This figure is, of course, an average across different cards and issuers. Suppose that 30% of all individuals holding VISA cards issued by a certain bank pay in full each month. A random sample of $n = 25$ cardholders is to be selected. The bank is interested in the variable $x =$ number in the sample who pay in full each month. Even though sampling is done without replacement, the sample size $n = 25$ is most likely very small compared to the total number of credit card holders, so we can approximate the probability distribution of x using a binomial distribution with $n = 25$ and $\pi = .4$. We have defined "paid in full" as a success because this is the outcome counted by the random variable x. The mean value of x is then

$$\mu_x = n\pi = 25(.30) = 7.5$$

and the standard deviation is

$$\sigma = \sqrt{n\pi(1 - \pi)} = \sqrt{25(.30)(.70)} = \sqrt{5.25} = 2.29$$

The probability that x is farther than 1 standard deviation from its mean value is

$$\begin{aligned} P(x < \mu_x - \sigma_x \text{ or } x > \mu_x + \sigma_x) &= P(x < 5.21 \text{ or } x > 9.79) \\ &= P(x \leq 5) + P(x \geq 10) \\ &= p(6) + \cdots + p(5) + p(10) + \cdots + p(25) \\ &= .382 \text{ (using Table A)} \end{aligned}$$

The value of σ_x is zero when $\pi = 0$ or $\pi = 1$. In these two cases, there is no uncertainty in x: We are sure to observe $x = 0$ when $\pi = 0$ and $x = n$ when $\pi = 1$. It is also easily verified that $\pi(1 - \pi)$ is largest when $\pi = .5$. Thus the binomial distribution spreads out the most when sampling from a 50–50 population. The farther π is from .5, the less spread out is the distribution.

Exercises A.1 – A.15

A.1 a. In a binomial experiment consisting of six trials, how many outcomes have exactly one S, and what are these outcomes?

b. In a binomial experiment consisting of 20 trials, how many outcomes have exactly ten S's? Exactly fifteen S's? Exactly five S's?

A.2 Suppose that in a certain metropolitan area, nine out of ten households have a VCR. Let x denote the number among four randomly selected households that have a VCR, so x is a binomial random variable with $n = 4$ and $\pi = .9$.

a. Calculate $p(2) = P(x = 2)$, and interpret this probability.

b. Calculate $p(4)$, the probability that all four selected households have a VCR.

c. Determine $P(x \leq 3)$.

A.3 The *Los Angeles Times* (Dec. 13, 1992) reported that what airline passengers like to do most on long flights is rest or sleep; in a survey of 3697 passengers, almost 80% did so. Suppose that for a particular route, the actual percentage is exactly 80%, and consider randomly selecting six passengers. Then x, the number among the selected six who rested or slept, is a binomial random variable with $n = 6$ and $\pi = .8$.

a. Calculate $p(4)$, and interpret this probability.

b. Calculate $p(6)$, the probability that all six selected passengers rested or slept.

c. Determine $P(x \geq 4)$.

A.4 Refer to Exercise A.3, and suppose that ten rather than six passengers are selected ($n = 10$, $\pi = .8$), so that Table A can be used.

a. What is $p(8)$?

b. Calculate $P(x \le 7)$.

c. Calculate the probability that more than half of the selected passengers rested or slept.

A.5 Twenty-five percent of the customers entering a grocery store between 5 P.M. and 7 P.M. use an express checkout. Consider five randomly selected customers, and let x denote the number among the five who use the express checkout.

a. What is $p(2)$, that is, $P(x = 2)$?

b. What is $P(x \le 1)$?

c. What is $P(2 \le x)$? (*Hint*: Make use of your computation in part **b.**)

d. What is $P(x \ne 2)$?

A.6 A breeder of show dogs is interested in the number of female puppies in a litter. If a birth is equally likely to result in a male or female puppy, give the probability distribution of the variable

x = number of female puppies in a litter of size 5

A.7 Industrial quality control programs often include inspection of incoming materials from suppliers. If parts are purchased in large lots, a typical plan might be to select 20 parts at random from a lot and inspect them. A lot might be judged acceptable if one or fewer defective parts are found among those inspected. Otherwise, the lot is rejected and returned to the supplier. Use Table A to find the probability of accepting lots that have each of the following. (*Hint*: Identify success with a defective part.)

a. 5% defective parts

b. 10% defective parts

c. 20% defective parts

A.8 An experiment was conducted to investigate whether a graphologist (handwriting analyst) could distinguish a normal person's handwriting from that of a psychotic. A well-known expert was given ten files, each containing handwriting samples from a normal person and from a person diagnosed as psychotic. The graphologist was then asked to identify the psychotic's handwriting. The graphologist made correct identifications in six of the ten trials (data taken from *Statistics in the Real World*, Larsen and Stroup, New York: Macmillan, 1976). Does this evidence indicate that the graphologist has an ability to distinguish the handwriting of psychotics? (*Hint*: What is the probability of correctly guessing six or more times out of ten? Your answer should depend on whether this probability is relatively small or relatively large.)

A.9 If the temperature in Florida falls below 32°F during certain periods of the year, there is a chance that the citrus crop will be damaged. Suppose that the probability

is .1 that any given tree will show measurable damage when the temperature falls to 30°F. If the temperature does drop to 30°F, what is the expected number of trees showing damage in orchards of 2000 trees? What is the standard deviation of the number of trees that show damage?

A.10 Thirty percent of all automobiles undergoing a headlight inspection at a certain inspection station fail the inspection.

a. Among 15 randomly selected cars, what is the probability that at most 5 fail the inspection?

b. Among 15 randomly selected cars, what is the probability that between 5 and 10 (inclusive) fail to pass inspection?

c. Among 25 randomly selected cars, what is the mean value of the number that pass inspection, and what is the standard deviation of the number that pass inspection?

d. What is the probability that among 25 randomly selected cars, the number that pass is within one standard deviation of the mean value?

A.11 You are to take a multiple-choice exam consisting of 100 questions with five possible responses to each. Suppose that you have not studied and so must guess (select one of the five answers in a completely random fashion) on each question. Let x represent the number of correct responses on the test.

a. What kind of probability distribution does x have?

b. What is your expected score on the exam? (*Hint*: Your expected score is the mean value of the x distribution.)

c. Compute the variance and standard deviation of x.

d. Based on your answers to parts **b** and **c,** is it likely that you would score over 50 on this exam? Explain the reasoning behind your answer.

A.12 Suppose that 20% of the 10,000 signatures on a certain recall petition are invalid. Would the number of invalid signatures in a sample of size 1000 have (approximately) a binomial distribution? Explain.

A.13 A coin is to be tossed 25 times. Let x = the number of tosses that result in heads (H). Consider the following rule for deciding whether or not the coin is fair:

Judge the coin to be fair if $8 \le x \le 17$.
Judge it to be biased if either $x \le 7$ or $x \ge 18$.

a. What is the probability of judging the coin to be biased when it is actually fair?

b. What is the probability of judging the coin to be fair when $P(H) = .9$, so that there is a substantial bias? Repeat for $P(H) = .1$.

c. What is the probability of judging the coin to be fair when $P(H) = .6$? When $P(H) = .4$? Why are the probabilities so large compared to the probabilities in part **b**?
d. What happens to the "error probabilities" of parts **a** and **b** if the decision rule is changed so that the coin is judged fair if $7 \leq x \leq 19$ and unfair otherwise? Is this a better rule than the one first proposed?

A.14 A city ordinance requires that a smoke detector be installed in all residential housing. There is concern that too many residences are still without detectors, so a costly inspection program is being contemplated. Let π = the proportion of all residences that have a detector. A random sample of 25 residences will be selected. If the sample strongly suggests that $\pi < .80$ (fewer than 80% have detectors), as opposed to $\pi \geq .80$, the program will be implemented. Let x = the number of residences among the 25 that have a detector, and consider the following decision rule:

Reject the claim that $\pi \geq .8$ and implement the program if $x \leq 15$.

a. What is the probability that the program is implemented when $\pi = .80$?

b. What is the probability that the program is not implemented if $\pi = .70$? If $\pi = .60$?
c. How do the "error probabilities" of parts **a** and **b** change if the value 15 in the decision rule is changed to 14?

A.15 Exit polling has been a controversial practice in recent elections, since early release of the resulting information appears to affect whether or not those who have not yet voted will do so. Suppose that 90% of all registered California voters favor banning the release of information from exit polls in presidential elections until after the polls in California close. A random sample of 25 California voters is selected.
a. What is the probability that more than 20 favor the ban?
b. What is the probability that at least 20 favor the ban?
c. What are the mean value and standard deviation of the number who favor the ban?
d. If fewer than 20 in the sample favor the ban, is this at odds with the assertion that (at least) 90% of the populace favors the ban? (*Hint*: Consider $P(x < 20)$ when $\pi = .9$.)

Table A *Binomial probabilities*

$n = 5$

x	π												
	0.05	0.1	0.2	0.25	0.3	0.4	0.5	0.6	0.7	0.75	0.8	0.9	0.95
0	.774	.590	.328	.237	.168	.078	.031	.010	.002	.001	.000	.000	.000
1	.203	.329	.409	.396	.360	.259	.157	.077	.029	.015	.007	.000	.000
2	.022	.072	.205	.263	.309	.346	.312	.230	.132	.088	.051	.009	.001
3	.001	.009	.051	.088	.132	.230	.312	.346	.309	.263	.205	.072	.022
4	.000	.000	.007	.015	.029	.077	.157	.259	.360	.396	.409	.329	.203
5	.000	.000	.000	.001	.002	.010	.031	.078	.168	.237	.328	.590	.774

Table A *Binomial probabilities (continued)*

$n = 10$

							π						
x	0.05	0.1	0.2	0.25	0.3	0.4	0.5	0.6	0.7	0.75	0.8	0.9	0.95
0	.599	.349	.107	.056	.028	.006	.001	.000	.000	.000	.000	.000	.000
1	.315	.387	.268	.188	.121	.040	.010	.002	.000	.000	.000	.000	.000
2	.075	.194	.302	.282	.233	.121	.044	.011	.001	.000	.000	.000	.000
3	.010	.057	.201	.250	.267	.215	.117	.042	.009	.003	.001	.000	.000
4	.001	.011	.088	.146	.200	.251	.205	.111	.037	.016	.006	.000	.000
5	.000	.001	.026	.058	.103	.201	.246	.201	.103	.058	.026	.001	.000
6	.000	.000	.006	.016	.037	.111	.205	.251	.200	.146	.088	.011	.001
7	.000	.000	.001	.003	.009	.042	.117	.215	.267	.250	.201	.057	.010
8	.000	.000	.000	.000	.001	.011	.044	.121	.233	.282	.302	.194	.075
9	.000	.000	.000	.000	.000	.002	.010	.040	.121	.188	.268	.387	.315
10	.000	.000	.000	.000	.000	.000	.001	.006	.028	.056	.107	.349	.599

$n = 15$

							π						
x	0.05	0.1	0.2	0.25	0.3	0.4	0.5	0.6	0.7	0.75	0.8	0.9	0.95
0	.463	.206	.035	.013	.005	.000	.000	.000	.000	.000	.000	.000	.000
1	.366	.343	.132	.067	.030	.005	.000	.000	.000	.000	.000	.000	.000
2	.135	.267	.231	.156	.092	.022	.004	.000	.000	.000	.000	.000	.000
3	.031	.128	.250	.225	.170	.064	.014	.002	.000	.000	.000	.000	.000
4	.004	.043	.188	.225	.218	.126	.041	.007	.001	.000	.000	.000	.000
5	.001	.011	.103	.166	.207	.196	.092	.025	.003	.001	.000	.000	.000
6	.000	.002	.043	.091	.147	.207	.153	.061	.011	.003	.001	.000	.000
7	.000	.000	.014	.040	.081	.177	.196	.118	.035	.013	.003	.000	.000
8	.000	.000	.003	.013	.035	.118	.196	.177	.081	.040	.014	.000	.000
9	.000	.000	.001	.003	.011	.061	.153	.207	.147	.091	.043	.002	.000
10	.000	.000	.000	.001	.003	.025	.092	.196	.207	.166	.103	.011	.001
11	.000	.000	.000	.000	.001	.007	.041	.126	.218	.225	.188	.043	.004
12	.000	.000	.000	.000	.000	.002	.014	.064	.170	.225	.250	.128	.031
13	.000	.000	.000	.000	.000	.000	.004	.022	.092	.156	.231	.267	.135
14	.000	.000	.000	.000	.000	.000	.000	.005	.030	.067	.132	.343	.366
15	.000	.000	.000	.000	.000	.000	.000	.000	.005	.013	.035	.206	.463

(*continued*)

Table A *Binomial probabilities (continued)*

$n = 20$

x	π 0.05	0.1	0.2	0.25	0.3	0.4	0.5	0.6	0.7	0.75	0.8	0.9	0.95
0	.358	.122	.012	.003	.001	.000	.000	.000	.000	.000	.000	.000	.000
1	.377	.270	.058	.021	.007	.000	.000	.000	.000	.000	.000	.000	.000
2	.189	.285	.137	.067	.028	.003	.000	.000	.000	.000	.000	.000	.000
3	.060	.190	.205	.134	.072	.012	.001	.000	.000	.000	.000	.000	.000
4	.013	.090	.218	.190	.130	.035	.005	.000	.000	.000	.000	.000	.000
5	.002	.032	.175	.202	.179	.075	.015	.001	.000	.000	.000	.000	.000
6	.000	.009	.109	.169	.192	.124	.037	.005	.000	.000	.000	.000	.000
7	.000	.002	.055	.112	.164	.166	.074	.015	.001	.000	.000	.000	.000
8	.000	.000	.022	.061	.114	.180	.120	.035	.004	.001	.000	.000	.000
9	.000	.000	.007	.027	.065	.160	.160	.071	.012	.003	.000	.000	.000
10	.000	.000	.002	.010	.031	.117	.176	.117	.031	.010	.002	.000	.000
11	.000	.000	.000	.003	.012	.071	.160	.160	.065	.027	.007	.000	.000
12	.000	.000	.000	.001	.004	.035	.120	.180	.114	.061	.022	.000	.000
13	.000	.000	.000	.000	.001	.015	.074	.166	.164	.112	.055	.002	.000
14	.000	.000	.000	.000	.000	.005	.037	.124	.192	.169	.109	.009	.000
15	.000	.000	.000	.000	.000	.001	.015	.075	.179	.202	.175	.032	.002
16	.000	.000	.000	.000	.000	.000	.005	.035	.130	.190	.218	.090	.013
17	.000	.000	.000	.000	.000	.000	.001	.012	.072	.134	.205	.190	.060
18	.000	.000	.000	.000	.000	.000	.000	.003	.028	.067	.137	.285	.189
19	.000	.000	.000	.000	.000	.000	.000	.000	.007	.021	.058	.270	.377
20	.000	.000	.000	.000	.000	.000	.000	.000	.001	.003	.012	.122	.358

Table A *Binomial probabilities (continued)*

$n = 25$

x	0.05	0.1	0.2	0.25	0.3	0.4	0.5	0.6	0.7	0.75	0.8	0.9	0.95
0	.277	.072	.004	.001	.000	.000	.000	.000	.000	.000	.000	.000	.000
1	.365	.199	.023	.006	.002	.000	.000	.000	.000	.000	.000	.000	.000
2	.231	.266	.071	.025	.007	.000	.000	.000	.000	.000	.000	.000	.000
3	.093	.227	.136	.064	.024	.002	.000	.000	.000	.000	.000	.000	.000
4	.027	.138	.187	.118	.057	.007	.000	.000	.000	.000	.000	.000	.000
5	.006	.065	.196	.164	.103	.020	.002	.000	.000	.000	.000	.000	.000
6	.001	.024	.163	.183	.148	.045	.005	.000	.000	.000	.000	.000	.000
7	.000	.007	.111	.166	.171	.080	.015	.001	.000	.000	.000	.000	.000
8	.000	.002	.062	.124	.165	.120	.032	.003	.000	.000	.000	.000	.000
9	.000	.000	.030	.078	.134	.151	.061	.009	.000	.000	.000	.000	.000
10	.000	.000	.011	.042	.091	.161	.097	.021	.002	.000	.000	.000	.000
11	.000	.000	.004	.019	.054	.146	.133	.044	.004	.001	.000	.000	.000
12	.000	.000	.002	.007	.027	.114	.155	.076	.011	.002	.000	.000	.000
13	.000	.000	.000	.002	.011	.076	.155	.114	.027	.007	.002	.000	.000
14	.000	.000	.000	.001	.004	.044	.133	.146	.054	.019	.004	.000	.000
15	.000	.000	.000	.000	.002	.021	.097	.161	.091	.042	.011	.000	.000
16	.000	.000	.000	.000	.000	.009	.061	.151	.134	.078	.030	.000	.000
17	.000	.000	.000	.000	.000	.003	.032	.120	.165	.124	.062	.002	.000
18	.000	.000	.000	.000	.000	.001	.015	.080	.171	.166	.111	.007	.000
19	.000	.000	.000	.000	.000	.000	.005	.045	.148	.183	.163	.024	.001
20	.000	.000	.000	.000	.000	.000	.002	.020	.103	.164	.196	.065	.006
21	.000	.000	.000	.000	.000	.000	.000	.007	.057	.118	.187	.138	.027
22	.000	.000	.000	.000	.000	.000	.000	.002	.024	.064	.136	.227	.093
23	.000	.000	.000	.000	.000	.000	.000	.000	.007	.025	.071	.266	.231
24	.000	.000	.000	.000	.000	.000	.000	.000	.002	.006	.023	.199	.365
25	.000	.000	.000	.000	.000	.000	.000	.000	.000	.001	.004	.072	.277

Appendix: Statistical Tables

Table I

Random numbers

Row																				
1	4	5	1	8	5	0	3	3	7	1	2	8	4	5	1	1	0	9	5	7
2	4	2	5	5	8	0	4	5	7	0	7	0	3	6	6	1	3	1	3	1
3	8	9	9	3	4	3	5	0	6	3	9	1	1	8	2	6	9	2	0	9
4	8	9	0	7	2	9	9	0	4	7	6	7	4	7	1	3	4	3	5	3
5	5	7	3	1	0	3	7	4	7	8	5	2	0	1	3	7	7	6	3	6
6	0	9	3	8	7	6	7	9	9	5	6	2	5	6	5	8	4	2	6	4
7	4	1	0	1	0	2	2	0	4	7	5	1	1	9	4	7	9	7	5	1
8	6	4	7	3	6	3	4	5	1	2	3	1	1	8	0	0	4	8	2	0
9	8	0	2	8	7	9	3	8	4	0	4	2	0	8	9	1	2	3	3	2
10	9	4	6	0	6	9	7	8	8	2	5	2	9	6	0	1	4	6	0	5
11	6	6	9	5	7	4	4	6	3	2	0	6	0	8	9	1	3	6	1	8
12	0	7	1	7	7	7	2	9	7	8	7	5	8	8	6	9	8	4	1	0
13	6	1	3	0	9	7	3	3	6	6	0	4	1	8	3	2	6	7	6	8
14	2	2	3	6	2	1	3	0	2	2	6	6	9	7	0	2	1	2	5	8
15	0	7	1	7	4	2	0	0	0	1	3	1	2	0	4	7	8	4	1	0
16	6	6	5	1	6	1	8	1	5	5	2	6	2	0	1	1	5	2	3	6
17	9	9	6	2	5	3	5	9	8	3	7	5	0	1	3	9	3	8	0	8
18	9	9	9	6	1	2	9	3	4	6	5	6	4	6	5	8	2	7	4	0
19	2	5	6	3	1	9	8	1	1	0	3	5	6	7	9	1	4	5	2	0
20	5	1	1	9	8	1	2	1	1	6	9	8	1	8	1	9	9	1	2	0
21	1	9	8	0	7	4	6	8	4	0	3	0	8	1	1	0	6	2	3	2
22	9	7	0	9	6	3	8	9	9	7	0	6	5	4	3	6	5	0	3	2
23	1	7	6	4	8	2	0	3	9	6	3	6	2	1	0	7	7	3	1	7
24	6	2	5	8	2	0	7	8	6	4	6	6	8	9	2	0	6	9	0	4
25	1	5	7	1	1	1	9	5	1	4	5	2	8	3	4	3	0	7	3	5
26	1	4	6	6	5	6	0	1	9	4	0	5	2	7	6	4	3	6	8	8
27	1	8	5	0	2	1	6	8	0	7	7	2	6	2	6	7	5	4	8	7
28	7	8	7	4	6	5	4	3	7	9	3	9	2	7	9	5	4	2	3	1
29	1	6	3	2	8	3	7	3	0	7	2	4	8	0	9	9	9	4	7	0
30	2	8	9	0	8	1	6	8	1	7	3	1	3	0	9	7	2	5	7	9
31	0	7	8	8	6	5	7	5	5	4	0	0	3	4	1	2	7	3	7	9
32	8	4	0	1	4	5	1	9	1	1	2	1	5	3	2	8	5	5	7	5
33	7	3	5	9	7	0	4	9	1	2	1	3	2	5	1	9	3	3	8	3
34	4	7	2	6	7	6	9	9	2	7	8	7	5	5	5	2	4	4	3	4
35	9	3	3	7	0	7	0	5	7	5	6	9	5	4	3	1	4	6	6	8
36	0	2	4	9	7	8	1	6	3	8	7	8	0	5	6	7	2	7	5	0
37	7	1	0	1	8	4	7	1	2	9	3	8	0	0	8	7	9	2	8	6
38	9	7	9	4	4	5	3	1	9	3	4	5	0	6	3	5	9	6	9	8
39	0	4	2	5	0	0	9	9	6	4	0	6	9	0	3	8	3	5	7	2
40	0	7	1	2	3	6	1	7	9	3	9	5	4	6	8	4	8	8	0	6
41	3	5	6	6	2	4	4	5	6	3	7	8	7	6	5	2	0	4	3	2
42	6	6	8	5	5	2	9	7	9	3	3	1	6	9	5	9	7	1	1	2
43	9	5	0	4	3	1	1	7	3	9	2	7	7	4	7	0	3	1	2	8
44	5	1	7	8	9	4	7	2	9	2	8	9	9	8	0	6	3	7	2	1
45	1	6	3	9	4	1	3	2	1	1	8	5	6	3	4	1	9	3	1	7
46	4	4	8	6	4	0	3	8	3	8	3	5	9	5	9	4	8	3	9	4
47	7	7	6	6	4	5	4	4	8	4	4	0	0	3	9	8	5	2	0	2
48	2	5	6	6	3	7	0	6	5	6	9	0	1	9	5	2	6	9	1	2
49	9	4	0	4	7	5	3	2	8	7	2	7	4	9	3	9	6	5	5	6
50	7	3	1	5	6	6	5	0	3	5	3	7	2	8	6	2	4	1	8	7

Table I Random Numbers **679**

Table I
*Random numbers
(continued)*

Row																			
51	7	5	8	2	8	8	8	7	6	4	1	1	0	2	3	1	9	3	6	0
52	3	3	6	0	9	1	1	0	3	2	7	8	2	0	5	3	4	8	9	8
53	0	2	9	6	9	8	9	3	8	1	5	3	9	9	7	0	7	7	1	6
54	8	5	9	6	2	9	6	8	2	1	2	4	7	0	6	8	3	4	6	1
55	5	4	7	6	1	0	0	1	0	4	6	1	4	1	5	0	9	6	5	5
56	5	0	3	6	4	1	9	8	4	4	1	2	0	2	5	1	8	1	2	1
57	0	2	6	3	7	5	1	1	6	6	0	5	8	1	2	3	3	6	1	3
58	3	8	1	6	3	8	1	4	5	2	9	4	2	5	7	3	2	3	1	8
59	9	1	5	6	0	6	5	6	6	3	6	2	3	0	0	0	1	8	5	9
60	5	3	5	6	3	9	5	4	7	3	6	6	7	5	0	1	5	6	7	3
61	9	6	6	4	5	7	7	6	1	5	4	4	8	0	6	5	7	6	3	0
62	6	3	0	6	7	9	5	5	4	6	2	2	8	4	4	0	0	9	9	8
63	8	5	8	3	5	2	0	6	6	0	0	6	0	6	3	0	1	7	0	5
64	3	8	2	4	9	0	9	2	6	2	9	5	1	9	1	9	0	8	3	3
65	1	4	4	1	1	7	4	6	3	6	5	6	5	5	7	7	0	3	5	8
66	5	9	9	5	3	7	2	5	1	7	1	1	0	7	1	0	9	2	8	8
67	8	7	1	7	5	2	5	6	8	7	9	9	1	3	9	6	4	9	3	0
68	6	7	2	3	1	4	9	2	1	7	0	8	6	7	8	9	9	4	7	4
69	2	3	2	8	7	0	9	7	1	1	1	2	8	2	9	1	0	6	7	7
70	2	9	5	7	8	4	7	9	0	3	6	9	2	0	6	0	6	2	6	8
71	4	8	9	8	3	2	7	6	9	1	9	8	6	9	5	2	4	9	9	9
72	1	5	6	5	7	7	5	4	3	4	3	8	1	8	9	9	4	4	1	1
73	1	8	1	1	7	2	8	5	5	8	9	9	9	6	2	0	1	6	6	7
74	5	7	7	0	9	5	5	6	8	6	8	2	2	6	0	5	5	1	8	7
75	1	8	6	0	5	4	8	3	4	5	3	5	8	7	7	7	8	5	7	0
76	2	6	6	7	9	4	2	2	8	7	4	3	4	9	6	1	9	4	3	9
77	3	6	6	4	5	7	8	3	0	2	8	4	6	7	2	1	4	5	2	3
78	0	7	8	0	1	2	1	1	3	4	2	1	6	9	3	3	5	4	0	4
79	8	3	6	0	5	7	7	9	1	5	8	8	4	9	5	7	2	2	7	6
80	5	3	6	9	0	6	3	8	7	5	9	5	9	7	4	2	5	6	2	9
81	0	9	3	7	7	2	8	6	4	3	2	9	4	8	2	9	9	6	9	9
82	9	4	7	4	0	0	0	3	5	4	6	6	2	6	2	3	6	1	1	4
83	5	5	4	1	7	8	6	4	2	3	2	9	8	4	6	3	8	3	0	5
84	5	3	0	0	5	4	8	0	7	4	7	6	2	1	1	2	1	2	6	9
85	3	3	0	9	3	2	9	4	0	5	5	4	8	7	5	7	5	3	8	8
86	3	0	5	7	1	9	5	8	0	0	4	5	3	0	3	0	2	7	6	7
87	5	0	8	6	0	8	1	6	2	0	8	6	5	4	0	7	2	9	1	0
88	3	6	4	7	8	2	3	5	7	9	8	5	2	7	6	9	0	2	4	9
89	9	0	4	4	9	1	6	8	5	2	8	9	0	7	5	7	2	5	1	8
90	9	5	2	6	9	3	9	6	5	1	8	8	7	8	2	0	4	4	7	9
91	9	4	5	7	0	3	4	6	4	2	5	4	8	6	1	1	9	1	8	8
92	8	1	1	8	0	5	4	2	8	5	3	3	3	0	1	1	4	4	8	3
93	6	9	4	7	8	3	3	9	1	2	5	0	1	2	3	0	1	1	2	5
94	0	0	6	8	8	7	2	4	4	7	6	6	0	3	4	7	5	6	8	2
95	5	3	3	9	3	8	4	9	1	9	1	7	8	4	5	2	2	5	4	4
96	2	5	6	2	7	6	0	3	8	1	4	4	2	6	8	3	6	3	2	8
97	7	4	3	7	9	6	8	6	2	8	3	8	4	2	2	0	7	0	5	3
98	1	9	0	8	8	0	1	2	2	2	7	5	6	5	5	7	8	7	2	6
99	2	4	8	0	2	5	2	7	0	5	9	6	6	1	5	8	7	9	7	5
100	4	1	7	8	6	7	1	1	5	8	9	4	8	9	8	3	0	9	0	7

Table II

Standard normal probabilities (cumulative z curve areas)

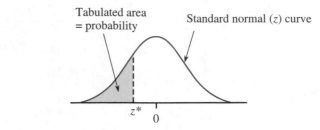

Tabulated area = probability

Standard normal (z) curve

z^* 0

z^*	.00	.01	.02	.03	.04	.05	.06	.07	.08	.09
−3.8	.0001	.0001	.0001	.0001	.0001	.0001	.0001	.0001	.0001	.0000
−3.7	.0001	.0001	.0001	.0001	.0001	.0001	.0001	.0001	.0001	.0001
−3.6	.0002	.0002	.0001	.0001	.0001	.0001	.0001	.0001	.0001	.0001
−3.5	.0002	.0002	.0002	.0002	.0002	.0002	.0002	.0002	.0002	.0002
−3.4	.0003	.0003	.0003	.0003	.0003	.0003	.0003	.0003	.0003	.0002
−3.3	.0005	.0005	.0005	.0004	.0004	.0004	.0004	.0004	.0004	.0003
−3.2	.0007	.0007	.0006	.0006	.0006	.0006	.0006	.0005	.0005	.0005
−3.1	.0010	.0009	.0009	.0009	.0008	.0008	.0008	.0008	.0007	.0007
−3.0	.0013	.0013	.0013	.0012	.0012	.0011	.0011	.0011	.0010	.0010
−2.9	.0019	.0018	.0018	.0017	.0016	.0016	.0015	.0015	.0014	.0014
−2.8	.0026	.0025	.0024	.0023	.0023	.0022	.0021	.0021	.0020	.0019
−2.7	.0035	.0034	.0033	.0032	.0031	.0030	.0029	.0028	.0027	.0026
−2.6	.0047	.0045	.0044	.0043	.0041	.0040	.0039	.0038	.0037	.0036
−2.5	.0062	.0060	.0059	.0057	.0055	.0054	.0052	.0051	.0049	.0048
−2.4	.0082	.0080	.0078	.0075	.0073	.0071	.0069	.0068	.0066	.0064
−2.3	.0107	.0104	.0102	.0099	.0096	.0094	.0091	.0089	.0087	.0084
−2.2	.0139	.0136	.0132	.0129	.0125	.0122	.0119	.0116	.0113	.0110
−2.1	.0179	.0174	.0170	.0166	.0162	.0158	.0154	.0150	.0146	.0143
−2.0	.0228	.0222	.0217	.0212	.0207	.0202	.0197	.0192	.0188	.0183
−1.9	.0287	.0281	.0274	.0268	.0262	.0256	.0250	.0244	.0239	.0233
−1.8	.0359	.0351	.0344	.0336	.0329	.0322	.0314	.0307	.0301	.0294
−1.7	.0446	.0436	.0427	.0418	.0409	.0401	.0392	.0384	.0375	.0367
−1.6	.0548	.0537	.0526	.0516	.0505	.0495	.0485	.0475	.0465	.0455
−1.5	.0668	.0655	.0643	.0630	.0618	.0606	.0594	.0582	.0571	.0559
−1.4	.0808	.0793	.0778	.0764	.0749	.0735	.0721	.0708	.0694	.0681
−1.3	.0968	.0951	.0934	.0918	.0901	.0885	.0869	.0853	.0838	.0823
−1.2	.1151	.1131	.1112	.1093	.1075	.1056	.1038	.1020	.1003	.0985
−1.1	.1357	.1335	.1314	.1292	.1271	.1251	.1230	.1210	.1190	.1170
−1.0	.1587	.1562	.1539	.1515	.1492	.1469	.1446	.1423	.1401	.1379
−0.9	.1841	.1814	.1788	.1762	.1736	.1711	.1685	.1660	.1635	.1611
−0.8	.2119	.2090	.2061	.2033	.2005	.1977	.1949	.1922	.1894	.1867
−0.7	.2420	.2389	.2358	.2327	.2296	.2266	.2236	.2206	.2177	.2148
−0.6	.2743	.2709	.2676	.2643	.2611	.2578	.2546	.2514	.2483	.2451
−0.5	.3085	.3050	.3015	.2981	.2946	.2912	.2877	.2843	.2810	.2776
−0.4	.3446	.3409	.3372	.3336	.3300	.3264	.3228	.3192	.3156	.3121
−0.3	.3821	.3783	.3745	.3707	.3669	.3632	.3594	.3557	.3520	.3483
−0.2	.4207	.4168	.4129	.4090	.4052	.4013	.3974	.3936	.3897	.3859
−0.1	.4602	.4562	.4522	.4483	.4443	.4404	.4364	.4325	.4286	.4247
−0.0	.5000	.4960	.4920	.4880	.4840	.4801	.4761	.4721	.4681	.4641

Table II Standard Normal Probabilities   681

Table II

Standard normal probabilities (continued)

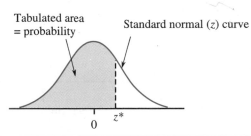

Tabulated area = probability

Standard normal (z) curve

0   z*

z*	.00	.01	.02	.03	.04	.05	.06	.07	.08	.09
0.0	.5000	.5040	.5080	.5120	.5160	.5199	.5239	.5279	.5319	.5359
0.1	.5398	.5438	.5478	.5517	.5557	.5596	.5636	.5675	.5714	.5753
0.2	.5793	.5832	.5871	.5910	.5948	.5987	.6026	.6064	.6103	.6141
0.3	.6179	.6217	.6255	.6293	.6331	.6368	.6406	.6443	.6480	.6517
0.4	.6554	.6591	.6628	.6664	.6700	.6736	.6772	.6808	.6844	.6879
0.5	.6915	.6950	.6985	.7019	.7054	.7088	.7123	.7157	.7190	.7224
0.6	.7257	.7291	.7324	.7357	.7389	.7422	.7454	.7486	.7517	.7549
0.7	.7580	.7611	.7642	.7673	.7704	.7734	.7764	.7794	.7823	.7852
0.8	.7881	.7910	.7939	.7967	.7995	.8023	.8051	.8078	.8106	.8133
0.9	.8159	.8186	.8212	.8238	.8264	.8289	.8315	.8340	.8365	.8389
1.0	.8413	.8438	.8461	.8485	.8508	.8531	.8554	.8577	.8599	.8621
1.1	.8643	.8665	.8686	.8708	.8729	.8749	.8770	.8790	.8810	.8830
1.2	.8849	.8869	.8888	.8907	.8925	.8944	.8962	.8980	.8997	.9015
1.3	.9032	.9049	.9066	.9082	.9099	.9115	.9131	.9147	.9162	.9177
1.4	.9192	.9207	.9222	.9236	.9251	.9265	.9279	.9292	.9306	.9319
1.5	.9332	.9345	.9357	.9370	.9382	.9394	.9406	.9418	.9429	.9441
1.6	.9452	.9463	.9474	.9484	.9495	.9505	.9515	.9525	.9535	.9545
1.7	.9554	.9564	.9573	.9582	.9591	.9599	.9608	.9616	.9625	.9633
1.8	.9641	.9649	.9656	.9664	.9671	.9678	.9686	.9693	.9699	.9706
1.9	.9713	.9719	.9726	.9732	.9738	.9744	.9750	.9756	.9761	.9767
2.0	.9772	.9778	.9783	.9788	.9793	.9798	.9803	.9808	.9812	.9817
2.1	.9821	.9826	.9830	.9834	.9838	.9842	.9846	.9850	.9854	.9857
2.2	.9861	.9864	.9868	.9871	.9875	.9878	.9881	.9884	.9887	.9890
2.3	.9893	.9896	.9898	.9901	.9904	.9906	.9909	.9911	.9913	.9916
2.4	.9918	.9920	.9922	.9925	.9927	.9929	.9931	.9932	.9934	.9936
2.5	.9938	.9940	.9941	.9943	.9945	.9946	.9948	.9949	.9951	.9952
2.6	.9953	.9955	.9956	.9957	.9959	.9960	.9961	.9962	.9963	.9964
2.7	.9965	.9966	.9967	.9968	.9969	.9970	.9971	.9972	.9973	.9974
2.8	.9974	.9975	.9976	.9977	.9977	.9978	.9979	.9979	.9980	.9981
2.9	.9981	.9982	.9982	.9983	.9984	.9984	.9985	.9985	.9986	.9986
3.0	.9987	.9987	.9987	.9988	.9988	.9989	.9989	.9989	.9990	.9990
3.1	.9990	.9991	.9991	.9991	.9992	.9992	.9992	.9992	.9993	.9993
3.2	.9993	.9993	.9994	.9994	.9994	.9994	.9994	.9995	.9995	.9995
3.3	.9995	.9995	.9995	.9996	.9996	.9996	.9996	.9996	.9996	.9997
3.4	.9997	.9997	.9997	.9997	.9997	.9997	.9997	.9997	.9997	.9998
3.5	.9998	.9998	.9998	.9998	.9998	.9998	.9998	.9998	.9998	.9998
3.6	.9998	.9998	.9999	.9999	.9999	.9999	.9999	.9999	.9999	.9999
3.7	.9999	.9999	.9999	.9999	.9999	.9999	.9999	.9999	.9999	.9999
3.8	.9999	.9999	.9999	.9999	.9999	.9999	.9999	.9999	.9999	1.0000

Table III
t critical values

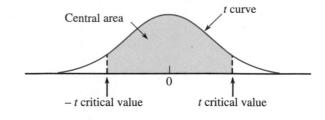

Central area captured:		.80	.90	.95	.98	.99	.998	.999
Confidence level:		80%	90%	95%	98%	99%	99.8%	99.9%
	1	3.08	6.31	12.71	31.82	63.66	318.31	636.62
	2	1.89	2.92	4.30	6.97	9.93	23.33	31.60
	3	1.64	2.35	3.18	4.54	5.84	10.21	12.92
	4	1.53	2.13	2.78	3.75	4.60	7.17	8.61
	5	1.48	2.02	2.57	3.37	4.03	5.89	6.86
	6	1.44	1.94	2.45	3.14	3.71	5.21	5.96
	7	1.42	1.90	2.37	3.00	3.50	4.79	5.41
	8	1.40	1.86	2.31	2.90	3.36	4.50	5.04
	9	1.38	1.83	2.26	2.82	3.25	4.30	4.78
	10	1.37	1.81	2.23	2.76	3.17	4.14	4.59
	11	1.36	1.80	2.20	2.72	3.11	4.03	4.44
	12	1.36	1.78	2.18	2.68	3.06	3.93	4.32
	13	1.35	1.77	2.16	2.65	3.01	3.85	4.22
	14	1.35	1.76	2.15	2.62	2.98	3.79	4.14
	15	1.34	1.75	2.13	2.60	2.95	3.73	4.07
	16	1.34	1.75	2.12	2.58	2.92	3.69	4.02
Degrees of	17	1.33	1.74	2.11	2.57	2.90	3.65	3.97
freedom	18	1.33	1.73	2.10	2.55	2.88	3.61	3.92
	19	1.33	1.73	2.09	2.54	2.86	3.58	3.88
	20	1.33	1.73	2.09	2.53	2.85	3.55	3.85
	21	1.32	1.72	2.08	2.52	2.83	3.53	3.82
	22	1.32	1.72	2.07	2.51	2.82	3.51	3.79
	23	1.32	1.71	2.07	2.50	2.81	3.49	3.77
	24	1.32	1.71	2.06	2.49	2.80	3.47	3.75
	25	1.32	1.71	2.06	2.49	2.79	3.45	3.73
	26	1.32	1.71	2.06	2.48	2.78	3.44	3.71
	27	1.31	1.70	2.05	2.47	2.77	3.42	3.69
	28	1.31	1.70	2.05	2.47	2.76	3.41	3.67
	29	1.31	1.70	2.05	2.46	2.76	3.40	3.66
	30	1.31	1.70	2.04	2.46	2.75	3.39	3.65
	40	1.30	1.68	2.02	2.42	2.70	3.31	3.55
	60	1.30	1.67	2.00	2.39	2.66	3.23	3.46
	120	1.29	1.66	1.98	2.36	2.62	3.16	3.37
z critical values	∞	1.28	1.645	1.96	2.33	2.58	3.09	3.29

Table IV Tail Areas for *t* Curves   683

Table IV
Tail areas for t curves

df	1	2	3	4	5	6	7	8	9	10	11	12
t												
0.0	.500	.500	.500	.500	.500	.500	.500	.500	.500	.500	.500	.500
0.1	.468	.465	.463	.463	.462	.462	.462	.461	.461	.461	.461	.461
0.2	.437	.430	.427	.426	.425	.424	.424	.423	.423	.423	.423	.422
0.3	.407	.396	.392	.390	.388	.387	.386	.386	.386	.385	.385	.385
0.4	.379	.364	.358	.355	.353	.352	.351	.350	.349	.349	.348	.348
0.5	.352	.333	.326	.322	.319	.317	.316	.315	.315	.314	.313	.313
0.6	.328	.305	.295	.290	.287	.285	.284	.283	.282	.281	.280	.280
0.7	.306	.278	.267	.261	.258	.255	.253	.252	.251	.250	.249	.249
0.8	.285	.254	.241	.234	.230	.227	.225	.223	.222	.221	.220	.220
0.9	.267	.232	.217	.210	.205	.201	.199	.197	.196	.195	.194	.193
1.0	.250	.211	.196	.187	.182	.178	.175	.173	.172	.170	.169	.169
1.1	.235	.193	.176	.167	.162	.157	.154	.152	.150	.149	.147	.146
1.2	.221	.177	.158	.148	.142	.138	.135	.132	.130	.129	.128	.127
1.3	.209	.162	.142	.132	.125	.121	.117	.115	.113	.111	.110	.109
1.4	.197	.148	.128	.117	.110	.106	.102	.100	.098	.096	.095	.093
1.5	.187	.136	.115	.104	.097	.092	.089	.086	.084	.082	.081	.080
1.6	.178	.125	.104	.092	.085	.080	.077	.074	.072	.070	.069	.068
1.7	.169	.116	.094	.082	.075	.070	.066	.064	.062	.060	.059	.057
1.8	.161	.107	.085	.073	.066	.061	.057	.055	.053	.051	.050	.049
1.9	.154	.099	.077	.065	.058	.053	.050	.047	.045	.043	.042	.041
2.0	.148	.092	.070	.058	.051	.046	.043	.040	.038	.037	.035	.034
2.1	.141	.085	.063	.052	.045	.040	.037	.034	.033	.031	.030	.029
2.2	.136	.079	.058	.046	.040	.035	.032	.029	.028	.026	.025	.024
2.3	.131	.074	.052	.041	.035	.031	.027	.025	.023	.022	.021	.020
2.4	.126	.069	.048	.037	.031	.027	.024	.022	.020	.019	.018	.017
2.5	.121	.065	.044	.033	.027	.023	.020	.018	.017	.016	.015	.014
2.6	.117	.061	.040	.030	.024	.020	.018	.016	.014	.013	.012	.012
2.7	.113	.057	.037	.027	.021	.018	.015	.014	.012	.011	.010	.010
2.8	.109	.054	.034	.024	.019	.016	.013	.012	.010	.009	.009	.008
2.9	.106	.051	.031	.022	.017	.014	.011	.010	.009	.008	.007	.007
3.0	.102	.048	.029	.020	.015	.012	.010	.009	.007	.007	.006	.006
3.1	.099	.045	.027	.018	.013	.011	.009	.007	.006	.006	.005	.005
3.2	.096	.043	.025	.016	.012	.009	.008	.006	.005	.005	.004	.004
3.3	.094	.040	.023	.015	.011	.008	.007	.005	.005	.004	.004	.003
3.4	.091	.038	.021	.014	.010	.007	.006	.005	.004	.003	.003	.003
3.5	.089	.036	.020	.012	.009	.006	.005	.004	.003	.003	.002	.002
3.6	.086	.035	.018	.011	.008	.006	.004	.004	.003	.002	.002	.002
3.7	.084	.033	.017	.010	.007	.005	.004	.003	.002	.002	.002	.002
3.8	.082	.031	.016	.010	.006	.004	.003	.003	.002	.002	.001	.001
3.9	.080	.030	.015	.009	.006	.004	.003	.002	.002	.001	.001	.001
4.0	.078	.029	.014	.008	.005	.004	.003	.002	.002	.001	.001	.001

(continued)

Table IV

Tail areas for t curves (continued)

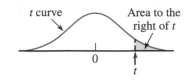

df t	13	14	15	16	17	18	19	20	21	22	23	24
0.0	.500	.500	.500	.500	.500	.500	.500	.500	.500	.500	.500	.500
0.1	.461	.461	.461	.461	.461	.461	.461	.461	.461	.461	.461	.461
0.2	.422	.422	.422	.422	.422	.422	.422	.422	.422	.422	.422	.422
0.3	.384	.384	.384	.384	.384	.384	.384	.384	.384	.383	.383	.383
0.4	.348	.347	.347	.347	.347	.347	.347	.347	.347	.347	.346	.346
0.5	.313	.312	.312	.312	.312	.312	.311	.311	.311	.311	.311	.311
0.6	.279	.279	.279	.278	.278	.278	.278	.278	.278	.277	.277	.277
0.7	.248	.247	.247	.247	.247	.246	.246	.246	.246	.246	.245	.245
0.8	.219	.218	.218	.218	.217	.217	.217	.217	.216	.216	.216	.216
0.9	.192	.191	.191	.191	.190	.190	.190	.189	.189	.189	.189	.189
1.0	.168	.167	.167	.166	.166	.165	.165	.165	.164	.164	.164	.164
1.1	.146	.144	.144	.144	.143	.143	.143	.142	.142	.142	.141	.141
1.2	.126	.124	.124	.124	.123	.123	.122	.122	.122	.121	.121	.121
1.3	.108	.107	.107	.106	.105	.105	.105	.104	.104	.104	.103	.103
1.4	.092	.091	.091	.090	.090	.089	.089	.089	.088	.088	.087	.087
1.5	.079	.077	.077	.077	.076	.075	.075	.075	.074	.074	.074	.073
1.6	.067	.065	.065	.065	.064	.064	.063	.063	.062	.062	.062	.061
1.7	.056	.055	.055	.054	.054	.053	.053	.052	.052	.052	.051	.051
1.8	.048	.046	.046	.045	.045	.044	.044	.043	.043	.043	.042	.042
1.9	.040	.038	.038	.038	.037	.037	.036	.036	.036	.035	.035	.035
2.0	.033	.032	.032	.031	.031	.030	.030	.030	.029	.029	.029	.028
2.1	.028	.027	.027	.026	.025	.025	.025	.024	.024	.024	.023	.023
2.2	.023	.022	.022	.021	.021	.021	.020	.020	.020	.019	.019	.019
2.3	.019	.018	.018	.018	.017	.017	.016	.016	.016	.016	.015	.015
2.4	.016	.015	.015	.014	.014	.014	.013	.013	.013	.013	.012	.012
2.5	.013	.012	.012	.012	.011	.011	.011	.011	.010	.010	.010	.010
2.6	.011	.010	.010	.010	.009	.009	.009	.009	.008	.008	.008	.008
2.7	.009	.008	.008	.008	.008	.007	.007	.007	.007	.007	.006	.006
2.8	.008	.007	.007	.006	.006	.006	.006	.006	.005	.005	.005	.005
2.9	.006	.005	.005	.005	.005	.005	.005	.004	.004	.004	.004	.004
3.0	.005	.004	.004	.004	.004	.004	.004	.004	.003	.003	.003	.003
3.1	.004	.004	.004	.003	.003	.003	.003	.003	.003	.003	.003	.002
3.2	.003	.003	.003	.003	.003	.002	.002	.002	.002	.002	.002	.002
3.3	.003	.002	.002	.002	.002	.002	.002	.002	.002	.002	.002	.001
3.4	.002	.002	.002	.002	.002	.002	.002	.001	.001	.001	.001	.001
3.5	.002	.002	.002	.001	.001	.001	.001	.001	.001	.001	.001	.001
3.6	.002	.001	.001	.001	.001	.001	.001	.001	.001	.001	.001	.001
3.7	.001	.001	.001	.001	.001	.001	.001	.001	.001	.001	.001	.001
3.8	.001	.001	.001	.001	.001	.001	.001	.001	.001	.000	.000	.000
3.9	.001	.001	.001	.001	.001	.001	.000	.000	.000	.000	.000	.000
4.0	.001	.001	.001	.001	.000	.000	.000	.000	.000	.000	.000	.000

Table IV Tail Areas for *t* Curves 685

Table IV

*Tail areas for t curves
(continued)*

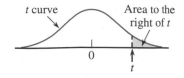

t curve

Area to the
right of *t*

0

t

df *t*	25	26	27	28	29	30	35	40	60	120	∞(=z)
0.0	.500	.500	.500	.500	.500	.500	.500	.500	.500	.500	.500
0.1	.461	.461	.461	.461	.461	.461	.460	.460	.460	.460	.460
0.2	.422	.422	.421	.421	.421	.421	.421	.421	.421	.421	.421
0.3	.383	.383	.383	.383	.383	.383	.383	.383	.383	.382	.382
0.4	.346	.346	.346	.346	.346	.346	.346	.346	.345	.345	.345
0.5	.311	.311	.311	.310	.310	.310	.310	.310	.309	.309	.309
0.6	.277	.277	.277	.277	.277	.277	.276	.276	.275	.275	.274
0.7	.245	.245	.245	.245	.245	.245	.244	.244	.243	.243	.242
0.8	.216	.215	.215	.215	.215	.215	.215	.214	.213	.213	.212
0.9	.188	.188	.188	.188	.188	.188	.187	.187	.186	.185	.184
1.0	.163	.163	.163	.163	.163	.163	.162	.162	.161	.160	.159
1.1	.141	.141	.141	.140	.140	.140	.139	.139	.138	.137	.136
1.2	.121	.120	.120	.120	.120	.120	.119	.119	.117	.116	.115
1.3	.103	.103	.102	.102	.102	.102	.101	.101	.099	.098	.097
1.4	.087	.087	.086	.086	.086	.086	.085	.085	.083	.082	.081
1.5	.073	.073	.073	.072	.072	.072	.071	.071	.069	.068	.067
1.6	.061	.061	.061	.060	.060	.060	.059	.059	.057	.056	.055
1.7	.051	.051	.050	.050	.050	.050	.049	.048	.047	.046	.045
1.8	.042	.042	.042	.041	.041	.041	.040	.040	.038	.037	.036
1.9	.035	.034	.034	.034	.034	.034	.033	.032	.031	.030	.029
2.0	.028	.028	.028	.028	.027	.027	.027	.026	.025	.024	.023
2.1	.023	.023	.023	.022	.022	.022	.022	.021	.020	.019	.018
2.2	.019	.018	.018	.018	.018	.018	.017	.017	.016	.015	.014
2.3	.015	.015	.015	.015	.014	.014	.014	.013	.012	.012	.011
2.4	.012	.012	.012	.012	.012	.011	.011	.011	.010	.009	.008
2.5	.010	.010	.009	.009	.009	.009	.009	.008	.008	.007	.006
2.6	.008	.008	.007	.007	.007	.007	.007	.007	.006	.005	.005
2.7	.006	.006	.006	.006	.006	.006	.005	.005	.004	.004	.003
2.8	.005	.005	.005	.005	.005	.004	.004	.004	.003	.003	.003
2.9	.004	.004	.004	.004	.004	.003	.003	.003	.003	.002	.002
3.0	.003	.003	.003	.003	.003	.003	.002	.002	.002	.002	.001
3.1	.002	.002	.002	.002	.002	.002	.002	.002	.001	.001	.001
3.2	.002	.002	.002	.002	.002	.002	.001	.001	.001	.001	.001
3.3	.001	.001	.001	.001	.001	.001	.001	.001	.001	.001	.000
3.4	.001	.001	.001	.001	.001	.001	.001	.001	.001	.000	.000
3.5	.001	.001	.001	.001	.001	.001	.001	.001	.000	.000	.000
3.6	.001	.001	.001	.001	.001	.001	.000	.000	.000	.000	.000
3.7	.001	.001	.000	.000	.000	.000	.000	.000	.000	.000	.000
3.8	.000	.000	.000	.000	.000	.000	.000	.000	.000	.000	.000
3.9	.000	.000	.000	.000	.000	.000	.000	.000	.000	.000	.000
4.0	.000	.000	.000	.000	.000	.000	.000	.000	.000	.000	.000

Table V *Curves of β = P(type II error) for t tests*

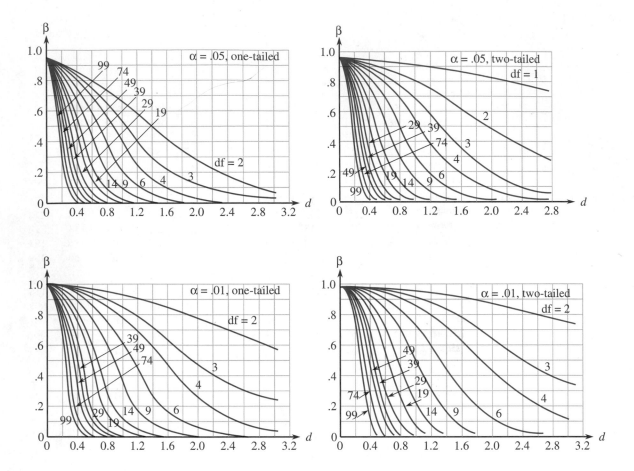

Table VI *P*-value Information for the Rank Sum Test   687

Table VI *P-value information for the rank-sum test*

n_1	n_2	Upper-tailed test		Lower-tailed test		Two-tailed test	
		P-value < .05 if rank-sum is greater than or equal to	*P*-value < .01 if rank-sum is greater than or equal to	*P*-value < .05 if rank-sum is less than or equal to	*P*-value < .01 if rank-sum is less than or equal to	*P*-value < .05 if rank-sum is not between*	*P*-value < .01 if rank-sum is not between
3	3	15	—	6	—	—	—
3	4	17	—	7	—	18,6	—
3	5	20	21	7	6	21,6	—
3	6	22	24	8	6	23,7	—
3	7	24	27	9	6	26,7	27,6
3	8	27	29	9	7	28,8	30,6
4	3	21	—	11	—	—	—
4	4	24	26	12	10	25,11	—
4	5	27	30	13	10	29,11	30,10
4	6	30	33	14	11	32,12	34,10
4	7	33	36	15	12	35,13	37,11
4	8	36	40	16	12	38,14	41,11
5	3	29	30	16	15	30,15	—
5	4	32	35	18	15	34,16	35,15
5	5	36	39	19	16	37,18	39,16
5	6	40	43	20	17	41,19	44,16
5	7	43	47	22	18	45,20	48,17
5	8	47	51	23	19	49,21	52,18
6	3	37	39	23	21	38,22	—
6	4	41	44	25	22	43,23	45,21
6	5	46	49	26	23	47,25	50,22
6	6	50	54	28	24	52,26	55,23
6	7	54	58	30	26	56,28	60,24
6	8	58	63	32	27	61,29	65,25
7	3	46	49	31	28	48,29	49,28
7	4	51	54	33	30	53,31	55,29
7	5	56	60	35	31	58,33	61,30
7	6	61	65	37	33	63,35	67,31
7	7	66	71	39	34	68,37	72,33
7	8	71	76	41	36	73,39	78,34
8	3	57	59	39	37	58,38	60,36
8	4	62	66	42	38	64,40	67,37
8	5	68	72	44	40	70,42	73,39
8	6	73	78	47	42	76,44	80,40
8	7	79	84	49	44	81,47	86,42
8	8	84	90	52	46	87,49	92,44

*Including endpoints. For example, when $n_1 = 3$ and $n_2 = 4$, *P*-value < .05 if $6 \le$ rank-sum ≤ 18.

Table VII *Values that capture specified upper-tail F curve areas*

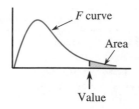

F curve

Area

Value

df₁

df₂	Area	1	2	3	4	5	6	7	8	9	10
1	.10	39.86	49.50	53.59	55.83	57.24	58.20	58.91	59.44	59.86	60.19
	.05	161.4	199.5	215.7	224.6	230.2	234.0	236.8	238.9	240.5	241.9
	.01	4052	5000	5403	5625	5764	5859	5928	5981	6022	6056
2	.10	8.53	9.00	9.16	9.24	9.29	9.33	9.35	9.37	9.38	9.39
	.05	18.51	19.00	19.16	19.25	19.30	19.33	19.35	19.37	19.38	19.40
	.01	98.50	99.00	99.17	99.25	99.30	99.33	99.36	99.37	99.39	99.40
	.001	998.5	999.0	999.2	999.2	999.3	999.3	999.4	999.4	999.4	999.4
3	.10	5.54	5.46	5.39	5.34	5.31	5.28	5.27	5.25	5.24	5.23
	.05	10.13	9.55	9.28	9.12	9.01	8.94	8.89	8.85	8.81	8.79
	.01	34.12	30.82	29.46	28.71	28.24	27.91	27.67	27.49	27.35	27.23
	.001	167.0	148.5	141.1	137.1	134.6	132.8	131.6	130.6	129.9	129.2
4	.10	4.54	4.32	4.19	4.11	4.05	4.01	3.98	3.95	3.94	3.92
	.05	7.71	6.94	6.59	6.39	6.26	6.16	6.09	6.04	6.00	5.96
	.01	21.20	18.00	16.69	15.98	15.52	15.21	14.98	14.80	14.66	14.55
	.001	74.14	61.25	56.18	53.44	51.71	50.53	49.66	49.00	48.47	48.05
5	.10	4.06	3.78	3.62	3.52	3.45	3.40	3.37	3.34	3.32	3.30
	.05	6.61	5.79	5.41	5.19	5.05	4.95	4.88	4.82	4.77	4.74
	.01	16.26	13.27	12.06	11.39	10.97	10.67	10.46	10.29	10.16	10.05
	.001	47.18	37.12	33.20	31.09	29.75	28.83	28.16	27.65	27.24	26.92
6	.10	3.78	3.46	3.29	3.18	3.11	3.05	3.01	2.98	2.96	2.94
	.05	5.99	5.14	4.76	4.53	4.39	4.28	4.21	4.15	4.10	4.06
	.01	13.75	10.92	9.78	9.15	8.75	8.47	8.26	8.10	7.98	7.87
	.001	35.51	27.00	23.70	21.92	20.80	20.03	19.46	19.03	18.69	18.41
7	.10	3.59	3.26	3.07	2.96	2.88	2.83	2.78	2.75	2.72	2.70
	.05	5.59	4.74	4.35	4.12	3.97	3.87	3.79	3.73	3.68	3.64
	.01	12.25	9.55	8.45	7.85	7.46	7.19	6.99	6.84	6.72	6.62
	.001	29.25	21.69	18.77	17.20	16.21	15.52	15.02	14.63	14.33	14.08
8	.10	3.46	3.11	2.92	2.81	2.73	2.67	2.62	2.59	2.56	2.54
	.05	5.32	4.46	4.07	3.84	3.69	3.58	3.50	3.44	3.39	3.35
	.01	11.26	8.65	7.59	7.01	6.63	6.37	6.18	6.03	5.91	5.81
	.001	25.41	18.49	15.83	14.39	13.48	12.86	12.40	12.05	11.77	11.54
9	.10	3.36	3.01	2.81	2.69	2.61	2.55	2.51	2.47	2.44	2.42
	.05	5.12	4.26	3.86	3.63	3.48	3.37	3.29	3.23	3.18	3.14
	.01	10.56	8.02	6.99	6.42	6.06	5.80	5.61	5.47	5.35	5.26
	.001	22.86	16.39	13.90	12.56	11.71	11.13	10.70	10.37	10.11	9.89

Table VII Values That Capture Specified Upper-tail *F* Curve Areas 689

Table VII *Values that capture specified upper-tail F curve areas (continued)*

df$_2$	Area	df$_1$ 1	2	3	4	5	6	7	8	9	10
10	.10	3.29	2.92	2.73	2.61	2.52	2.46	2.41	2.38	2.35	2.32
	.05	4.96	4.10	3.71	3.48	3.33	3.22	3.14	3.07	· 3.02	2.98
	.01	10.04	7.56	6.55	5.99	5.64	5.39	5.20	5.06	4.94	4.85
	.001	21.04	14.91	12.55	11.28	10.48	9.93	9.52	9.20	8.96	8.75
11	.10	3.23	2.86	2.66	2.54	2.45	2.39	2.34	2.30	2.27	2.25
	.05	4.84	3.98	3.59	3.36	3.20	3.09	3.01	2.95	2.90	2.85
	.01	9.65	7.21	6.22	5.67	5.32	5.07	4.89	4.74	4.63	4.54
	.001	19.69	13.81	11.56	10.35	9.58	9.05	8.66	8.35	8.12	7.92
12	.10	3.18	2.81	2.61	2.48	2.39	2.33	2.28	2.24	2.21	2.19
	.05	4.75	3.89	3.49	3.26	3.11	3.00	2.91	2.85	2.80	2.75
	.01	9.33	6.93	5.95	5.41	5.06	4.82	4.64	4.50	4.39	4.30
	.001	18.64	12.97	10.80	9.63	8.89	8.38	8.00	7.71	7.48	7.29
13	.10	3.14	2.76	2.56	2.43	2.35	2.28	2.23	2.20	2.16	2.14
	.05	4.67	3.81	3.41	3.18	3.03	2.92	2.83	2.77	2.71	2.67
	.01	9.07	6.70	5.74	5.21	4.86	4.62	4.44	4.30	4.19	4.10
	.001	17.82	12.31	10.21	9.07	8.35	7.86	7.49	7.21	6.98	6.80
14	.10	3.10	2.73	2.52	2.39	2.31	2.24	2.19	2.15	2.12	2.10
	.05	4.60	3.74	3.34	3.11	2.96	2.85	2.76	2.70	2.65	2.60
	.01	8.86	6.51	5.56	5.04	4.69	4.46	4.28	4.14	4.03	3.94
	.001	17.14	11.78	9.73	8.62	7.92	7.44	7.08	6.80	6.58	6.40
15	.10	3.07	2.70	2.49	2.36	2.27	2.21	2.16	2.12	2.09	2.06
	.05	4.54	3.68	3.29	3.06	2.90	2.79	2.71	2.64	2.59	2.54
	.01	8.68	6.36	5.42	4.89	4.56	4.32	4.14	4.00	3.89	3.80
	.001	16.59	11.34	9.34	8.25	7.57	7.09	6.74	6.47	6.26	6.08
16	.10	3.05	2.67	2.46	2.33	2.24	2.18	2.13	2.09	2.06	2.03
	.05	4.49	3.63	3.24	3.01	2.85	2.74	2.66	2.59	2.54	2.49
	.01	8.53	6.23	5.29	4.77	4.44	4.20	4.03	3.89	3.78	3.69
	.001	16.12	10.97	9.01	7.94	7.27	6.80	6.46	6.19	5.98	5.81
17	.10	3.03	2.64	2.44	2.31	2.22	2.15	2.10	2.06	2.03	2.00
	.05	4.45	3.59	3.20	2.96	2.81	2.70	2.61	2.55	2.49	2.45
	.01	8.40	6.11	5.18	4.67	4.34	4.10	3.93	3.79	3.68	3.59
	.001	15.72	10.66	8.73	7.68	7.02	6.56	6.22	5.96	5.75	5.58
18	.10	3.01	2.62	2.42	2.29	2.20	2.13	2.08	2.04	2.00	1.98
	.05	4.41	3.55	3.16	2.93	2.77	2.66	2.58	2.51	2.46	2.41
	.01	8.29	6.01	5.09	4.58	4.25	4.01	3.84	3.71	3.60	3.51
	.001	15.38	10.39	8.49	7.46	6.81	6.35	6.02	5.76	5.56	5.39
19	.10	2.99	2.61	2.40	2.27	2.18	2.11	2.06	2.02	1.98	1.96
	.05	4.38	3.52	3.13	2.90	2.74	2.63	2.54	2.48	2.42	2.38
	.01	8.18	5.93	5.01	4.50	4.17	3.94	3.77	3.63	3.52	3.43
	.001	15.08	10.16	8.28	7.27	6.62	6.18	5.85	5.59	5.39	5.22

(*continued*)

Table VII *Values that capture specified upper-tail F curve areas (continued)*

df$_2$	Area	1	2	3	4	5	6	7	8	9	10
20	.10	2.97	2.59	2.38	2.25	2.16	2.09	2.04	2.00	1.96	1.94
	.05	4.35	3.49	3.10	2.87	2.71	2.60	2.51	2.45	2.39	2.35
	.01	8.10	5.85	4.94	4.43	4.10	3.87	3.70	3.56	3.46	3.37
	.001	14.82	9.95	8.10	7.10	6.46	6.02	5.69	5.44	5.24	5.08
21	.10	2.96	2.57	2.36	2.23	2.14	2.08	2.02	1.98	1.95	1.92
	.05	4.32	3.47	3.07	2.84	2.68	2.57	2.49	2.42	2.37	2.32
	.01	8.02	5.78	4.87	4.37	4.04	3.81	3.64	3.51	3.40	3.31
	.001	14.59	9.77	7.94	6.95	6.32	5.88	5.56	5.31	5.11	4.95
22	.10	2.95	2.56	2.35	2.22	2.13	2.06	2.01	1.97	1.93	1.90
	.05	4.30	3.44	3.05	2.82	2.66	2.55	2.46	2.40	2.34	2.30
	.01	7.95	5.72	4.82	4.31	3.99	3.76	3.59	3.45	3.35	3.26
	.001	14.38	9.61	7.80	6.81	6.19	5.76	5.44	5.19	4.99	4.83
23	.10	2.94	2.55	2.34	2.21	2.11	2.05	1.99	1.95	1.92	1.89
	.05	4.28	3.42	3.03	2.80	2.64	2.53	2.44	2.37	2.32	2.27
	.01	7.88	5.66	4.76	4.26	3.94	3.71	3.54	3.41	3.30	3.21
	.001	14.20	9.47	7.67	6.70	6.08	5.65	5.33	5.09	4.89	4.73
24	.10	2.93	2.54	2.33	2.19	2.10	2.04	1.98	1.94	1.91	1.88
	.05	4.26	3.40	3.01	2.78	2.62	2.51	2.42	2.36	2.30	2.25
	.01	7.82	5.61	4.72	4.22	3.90	3.67	3.50	3.36	3.26	3.17
	.001	14.03	9.34	7.55	6.59	5.98	5.55	5.23	4.99	4.80	4.64
25	.10	2.92	2.53	2.32	2.18	2.09	2.02	1.97	1.93	1.89	1.87
	.05	4.24	3.39	2.99	2.76	2.60	2.49	2.40	2.34	2.28	2.24
	.01	7.77	5.57	4.68	4.18	3.85	3.63	3.46	3.32	3.22	3.13
	.001	13.88	9.22	7.45	6.49	5.89	5.46	5.15	4.91	4.71	4.56
26	.10	2.91	2.52	2.31	2.17	2.08	2.01	1.96	1.92	1.88	1.86
	.05	4.23	3.37	2.98	2.74	2.59	2.47	2.39	2.32	2.27	2.22
	.01	7.72	5.53	4.64	4.14	3.82	3.59	3.42	3.29	3.18	3.09
	.001	13.74	9.12	7.36	6.41	5.80	5.38	5.07	4.83	4.64	4.48
27	.10	2.90	2.51	2.30	2.17	2.07	2.00	1.95	1.91	1.87	1.85
	.05	4.21	3.35	2.96	2.73	2.57	2.46	2.37	2.31	2.25	2.20
	.01	7.68	5.49	4.60	4.11	3.78	3.56	3.39	3.26	3.15	3.06
	.001	13.61	9.02	7.27	6.33	5.73	5.31	5.00	4.76	4.57	4.41
28	.10	2.89	2.50	2.29	2.16	2.06	2.00	1.94	1.90	1.87	1.84
	.05	4.20	3.34	2.95	2.71	2.56	2.45	2.36	2.29	2.24	2.19
	.01	7.64	5.45	4.57	4.07	3.75	3.53	3.36	3.23	3.12	3.03
	.001	13.50	8.93	7.19	6.25	5.66	5.24	4.93	4.69	4.50	4.35
29	.10	2.89	2.50	2.28	2.15	2.06	1.99	1.93	1.89	1.86	1.83
	.05	4.18	3.33	2.93	2.70	2.55	2.43	2.35	2.28	2.22	2.18
	.01	7.60	5.42	4.54	4.04	3.73	3.50	3.33	3.20	3.09	3.00
	.001	13.39	8.85	7.12	6.19	5.59	5.18	4.87	4.64	4.45	4.29

Table VII Values That Capture Specified Upper-tail *F* Curve Areas   691

Table VII *Values that capture specified upper-tail F curve areas (continued)*

df_2	Area	df_1									
		1	2	3	4	5	6	7	8	9	10
30	.10	2.88	2.49	2.28	2.14	2.05	1.98	1.93	1.88	1.85	1.82
	.05	4.17	3.32	2.92	2.69	2.53	2.42	2.33	2.27	2.21	2.16
	.01	7.56	5.39	4.51	4.02	3.70	3.47	3.30	3.17	3.07	2.98
	.001	13.29	8.77	7.05	6.12	5.53	5.12	4.82	4.58	4.39	4.24
40	.10	2.84	2.44	2.23	2.09	2.00	1.93	1.87	1.83	1.79	1.76
	.05	4.08	3.23	2.84	2.61	2.45	2.34	2.25	2.18	2.12	2.08
	.01	7.31	5.18	4.31	3.83	3.51	3.29	3.12	2.99	2.89	2.80
	.001	12.61	8.25	6.59	5.70	5.13	4.73	4.44	4.21	4.02	3.87
60	.10	2.79	2.39	2.18	2.04	1.95	1.87	1.82	1.77	1.74	1.71
	.05	4.00	3.15	2.76	2.53	2.37	2.25	2.17	2.10	2.04	1.99
	.01	7.08	4.98	4.13	3.65	3.34	3.12	2.95	2.82	2.72	2.63
	.001	11.97	7.77	6.17	5.31	4.76	4.37	4.09	3.86	3.69	3.54
90	.10	2.76	2.36	2.15	2.01	1.91	1.84	1.78	1.74	1.70	1.67
	.05	3.95	3.10	2.71	2.47	2.32	2.20	2.11	2.04	1.99	1.94
	.01	6.93	4.85	4.01	3.53	3.23	3.01	2.84	2.72	2.61	2.52
	.001	11.57	7.47	5.91	5.06	4.53	4.15	3.87	3.65	3.48	3.34
120	.10	2.75	2.35	2.13	1.99	1.90	1.82	1.77	1.72	1.68	1.65
	.05	3.92	3.07	2.68	2.45	2.29	2.18	2.09	2.02	1.96	1.91
	.01	6.85	4.79	3.95	3.48	3.17	2.96	2.79	2.66	2.56	2.47
	.001	11.38	7.32	5.78	4.95	4.42	4.04	3.77	3.55	3.38	3.24
240	.10	2.73	2.32	2.10	1.97	1.87	1.80	1.74	1.70	1.65	1.63
	.05	3.88	3.03	2.64	2.41	2.25	2.14	2.04	1.98	1.92	1.87
	.01	6.74	4.69	3.86	3.40	3.09	2.88	2.71	2.59	2.48	2.40
	.001	11.10	7.11	5.60	4.78	4.25	3.89	3.62	3.41	3.24	3.09
∞	.10	2.71	2.30	2.08	1.94	1.85	1.77	1.72	1.67	1.63	1.60
	.05	3.84	3.00	2.60	2.37	2.21	2.10	2.01	1.94	1.88	1.83
	.01	6.63	4.61	3.78	3.32	3.02	2.80	2.64	2.51	2.41	2.32
	.001	10.83	6.91	5.42	4.62	4.10	3.74	3.47	3.27	3.10	2.96

Table VIII

Critical values q for the Studentized range distribution

Error df	Confidence level	\multicolumn{8}{c}{Number of populations, treatments, or levels being compared}
		3	4	5	6	7	8	9	10
5	95%	4.60	5.22	5.67	6.03	6.33	6.58	6.80	6.99
	99%	6.98	7.80	8.42	8.91	9.32	9.67	9.97	10.24
6	95%	4.34	4.90	5.30	5.63	5.90	6.12	6.32	6.49
	99%	6.33	7.03	7.56	7.97	8.32	8.61	8.87	9.10
7	95%	4.16	4.68	5.06	5.36	5.61	5.82	6.00	6.16
	99%	5.92	6.54	7.01	7.37	7.68	7.94	8.17	8.37
8	95%	4.04	4.53	4.89	5.17	5.40	5.60	5.77	5.92
	99%	5.64	6.20	6.62	6.96	7.24	7.47	7.68	7.86
9	95%	3.95	4.41	4.76	5.02	5.24	5.43	5.59	5.74
	99%	5.43	5.96	6.35	6.66	6.91	7.13	7.33	7.49
10	95%	3.88	4.33	4.65	4.91	5.12	5.30	5.46	5.60
	99%	5.27	5.77	6.14	6.43	6.67	6.87	7.05	7.21
11	95%	3.82	4.26	4.57	4.82	5.03	5.20	5.35	5.49
	99%	5.15	5.62	5.97	6.25	6.48	6.67	6.84	6.99
12	95%	3.77	4.20	4.51	4.75	4.95	5.12	5.27	5.39
	99%	5.05	5.50	5.84	6.10	6.32	6.51	6.67	6.81
13	95%	3.73	4.15	4.45	4.69	4.88	5.05	5.19	5.32
	99%	4.96	5.40	5.73	5.98	6.19	6.37	6.53	6.67
14	95%	3.70	4.11	4.41	4.64	4.83	4.99	5.13	5.25
	99%	4.89	5.32	5.63	5.88	6.08	6.26	6.41	6.54
15	95%	3.67	4.08	4.37	4.59	4.78	4.94	5.08	5.20
	99%	4.84	5.25	5.56	5.80	5.99	6.16	6.31	6.44
16	95%	3.65	4.05	4.33	4.56	4.74	4.90	5.03	5.15
	99%	4.79	5.19	5.49	5.72	5.92	6.08	6.22	6.35
17	95%	3.63	4.02	4.30	4.52	4.70	4.86	4.99	5.11
	99%	4.74	5.14	5.43	5.66	5.85	6.01	6.15	6.27
18	95%	3.61	4.00	4.28	4.49	4.67	4.82	4.96	5.07
	99%	4.70	5.09	5.38	5.60	5.79	5.94	6.08	6.20
19	95%	3.59	3.98	4.25	4.47	4.65	4.79	4.92	5.04
	99%	4.67	5.05	5.33	5.55	5.73	5.89	6.02	6.14
20	95%	3.58	3.96	4.23	4.45	4.62	4.77	4.90	5.01
	99%	4.64	5.02	5.29	5.51	5.69	5.84	5.97	6.09
24	95%	3.53	3.90	4.17	4.37	4.54	4.68	4.81	4.92
	99%	4.55	4.91	5.17	5.37	5.54	5.69	5.81	5.92
30	95%	3.49	3.85	4.10	4.30	4.46	4.60	4.72	4.82
	99%	4.45	4.80	5.05	5.24	5.40	5.54	5.65	5.76
40	95%	3.44	3.79	4.04	4.23	4.39	4.52	4.63	4.73
	99%	4.37	4.70	4.93	5.11	5.26	5.39	5.50	5.60
60	95%	3.40	3.74	3.98	4.16	4.31	4.44	4.55	4.65
	99%	4.28	4.59	4.82	4.99	5.13	5.25	5.36	5.45
120	95%	3.36	3.68	3.92	4.10	4.24	4.36	4.47	4.56
	99%	4.20	4.50	4.71	4.87	5.01	5.12	5.21	5.30
∞	95%	3.31	3.63	3.86	4.03	4.17	4.29	4.39	4.47
	99%	4.12	4.40	4.60	4.76	4.88	4.99	5.08	5.16

Table IX Upper-tail Areas for Chi-squared Distributions   693

Table IX

Upper-tail areas for chi-squared distributions

Right-tail area	df = 1	df = 2	df = 3	df = 4	df = 5
> .100	< 2.70	< 4.60	< 6.25	< 7.77	< 9.23
0.100	2.70	4.60	6.25	7.77	9.23
0.095	2.78	4.70	6.36	7.90	9.37
0.090	2.87	4.81	6.49	8.04	9.52
0.085	2.96	4.93	6.62	8.18	9.67
0.080	3.06	5.05	6.75	8.33	9.83
0.075	3.17	5.18	6.90	8.49	10.00
0.070	3.28	5.31	7.06	8.66	10.19
0.065	3.40	5.46	7.22	8.84	10.38
0.060	3.53	5.62	7.40	9.04	10.59
0.055	3.68	5.80	7.60	9.25	10.82
0.050	3.84	5.99	7.81	9.48	11.07
0.045	4.01	6.20	8.04	9.74	11.34
0.040	4.21	6.43	8.31	10.02	11.64
0.035	4.44	6.70	8.60	10.34	11.98
0.030	4.70	7.01	8.94	10.71	12.37
0.025	5.02	7.37	9.34	11.14	12.83
0.020	5.41	7.82	9.83	11.66	13.38
0.015	5.91	8.39	10.46	12.33	14.09
0.010	6.63	9.21	11.34	13.27	15.08
0.005	7.87	10.59	12.03	14.86	16.74
0.001	10.82	13.81	16.26	18.46	20.51
<0.001	>10.82	>13.81	>16.26	>18.46	>20.51

Right-tail area	df = 6	df = 7	df = 8	df = 9	df = 10
> .100	<10.64	<12.01	<13.36	<14.68	<15.98
0.100	10.64	12.01	13.36	14.68	15.98
0.095	10.79	12.17	13.52	14.85	16.16
0.090	10.94	12.33	13.69	15.03	16.35
0.085	11.11	12.50	13.87	15.22	16.54
0.080	11.28	12.69	14.06	15.42	16.75
0.075	11.46	12.88	14.26	15.63	16.97
0.070	11.65	13.08	14.48	15.85	17.20
0.065	11.86	13.30	14.71	16.09	17.44
0.060	12.08	13.53	14.95	16.34	17.71
0.055	12.33	13.79	15.22	16.62	17.99
0.050	12.59	14.06	15.50	16.91	18.30
0.045	12.87	14.36	15.82	17.24	18.64
0.040	13.19	14.70	16.17	17.60	19.02
0.035	13.55	15.07	16.56	18.01	19.44
0.030	13.96	15.50	17.01	18.47	19.92
0.025	14.44	16.01	17.53	19.02	20.48
0.020	15.03	16.62	18.16	19.67	21.16
0.015	15.77	17.39	18.97	20.51	22.02
0.010	16.81	18.47	20.09	21.66	23.20
0.005	18.54	20.27	21.95	23.58	25.18
0.001	22.45	24.32	26.12	27.87	29.58
<0.001	>22.45	>24.32	>26.12	>27.87	>29.58

(continued)

Table IX

Upper-tail areas for chi-squared distributions (continued)

Right-tail area	df = 11	df = 12	df = 13	df = 14	df = 15
> .100	<17.27	<18.54	<19.81	<21.06	<22.30
0.100	17.27	18.54	19.81	21.06	22.30
0.095	17.45	18.74	20.00	21.26	22.51
0.090	17.65	18.93	20.21	21.47	22.73
0.085	17.85	19.14	20.42	21.69	22.95
0.080	18.06	19.36	20.65	21.93	23.19
0.075	18.29	19.60	20.89	22.17	23.45
0.070	18.53	19.84	21.15	22.44	23.72
0.065	18.78	20.11	21.42	22.71	24.00
0.060	19.06	20.39	21.71	23.01	24.31
0.055	19.35	20.69	22.02	23.33	24.63
0.050	19.67	21.02	22.36	23.68	24.99
0.045	20.02	21.38	22.73	24.06	25.38
0.040	20.41	21.78	23.14	24.48	25.81
0.035	20.84	22.23	23.60	24.95	26.29
0.030	21.34	22.74	24.12	25.49	26.84
0.025	21.92	23.33	24.73	26.11	27.48
0.020	22.61	24.05	25.47	26.87	28.25
0.015	23.50	24.96	26.40	27.82	29.23
0.010	24.72	26.21	27.68	29.14	30.57
0.005	26.75	28.29	29.81	31.31	32.80
0.001	31.26	32.90	34.52	36.12	37.69
<0.001	>31.26	>32.90	>34.52	>36.12	>37.69

Right-tail area	df = 16	df = 17	df = 18	df = 19	df = 20
> .100	<23.54	<24.77	<25.98	<27.20	<28.41
0.100	23.54	24.76	25.98	27.20	28.41
0.095	23.75	24.98	26.21	27.43	28.64
0.090	23.97	25.21	26.44	27.66	28.88
0.085	24.21	25.45	26.68	27.91	29.14
0.080	24.45	25.70	26.94	28.18	29.40
0.075	24.71	25.97	27.21	28.45	29.69
0.070	24.99	26.25	27.50	28.75	29.99
0.065	25.28	26.55	27.81	29.06	30.30
0.060	25.59	26.87	28.13	29.39	30.64
0.055	25.93	27.21	28.48	29.75	31.01
0.050	26.29	27.58	28.86	30.14	31.41
0.045	26.69	27.99	29.28	30.56	31.84
0.040	27.13	28.44	29.74	31.03	32.32
0.035	27.62	28.94	30.25	31.56	32.85
0.030	28.19	29.52	30.84	32.15	33.46
0.025	28.84	30.19	31.52	32.85	34.16
0.020	29.63	30.99	32.34	33.68	35.01
0.015	30.62	32.01	33.38	34.74	36.09
0.010	32.00	33.40	34.80	36.19	37.56
0.005	34.26	35.71	37.15	38.58	39.99
0.001	39.25	40.78	42.31	43.81	45.31
<0.001	>39.25	>40.78	>42.31	>43.81	>45.31

Answers to Selected Odd-Numbered Exercises

CHAPTER 1

1.1 Descriptive statistics is made up of those methods whose purpose is to organize and summarize the values in a data set. Inferential statistics refers to those procedures whose purpose is to allow us to draw a conclusion about a population based on information from a sample.   **1.3** The population is the entire student body (the 15,000) students. The sample consists of the 200 students interviewed.   **1.5** The population consists of all single-family homes in Northridge. The sample consists of the 100 homes selected for inspection.   **1.7** The population consists of all 5000 bricks in the lot. The sample consists of the 100 bricks selected for inspection.

CHAPTER 2

2.1 a. numerical (discrete)   **b.** categorical   **c.** numerical (continuous)   **d.** numerical (continuous)   **e.** categorical   **2.3 a.** discrete   **b.** continuous   **c.** discrete   **d.** discrete   **e.** continuous   **f.** continuous   **g.** continuous   **h.** discrete   **2.5** observational study   **2.7** Cause-and-effect conclusions can't be drawn from this study. Seat belt usage is a possible confounding factor.   **2.9** No, it is an observational study. Cause-and-effect conclusions cannot be made on the basis of an observational study.   **2.13 a.** Stratifying would be worthwhile because cost of books may vary by class standing.   **b.** Stratifying would be worthwhile because cost of books may vary by field of study.   **c.** Stratifying would not be worthwhile because it is unlikely that the alphabetic groups would be any more homogeneous than the population as a whole.   **2.15** Researcher B's plan would result in a simple random sample of trees and would avoid possible confounding factors related to location in the field.   **2.17 a.** The population consists of all 16–24-year-olds who live in New York state, but not in New York City.   **2.19** The sample consisted of volunteers, included only women, included only students from a private university, and included only students attending school in Texas.   **2.21** selection bias   **2.23 a.** strength of binding   **b.** type of glue   **c.** Number of pages in the book and whether the book is paperback or hardback. Other factors might include type of paper (rough or glossy), proportion of paper made with recycled paper, and whether there are any tear-out pages in the book.   **2.25 a.** Age, weight, lean body mass, and capacity to lift weights were all dealt with by direct control.   **b.** Yes. Knowing whether they were receiving creatine might have influenced the effort a subject put into his workout.   **c.** Yes, especially if the trainer is the one taking the measurements. If the trainer knows which men are receiving creatine, it might influence the way in which he works with the subjects.   **2.29** Gender is a useful blocking variable if men and women of the same status tend to differ with respect to "rate of talk." Blocking on gender would make it easier to assess the effect of status on rate of talk.   **2.31** It is unlikely that a person who is described as a moderate drinker would be unable to tell whether they were drinking vodka tonics or virgin tonics.   **2.35** Stratifying by room type would probably be a good strategy.

CHAPTER 3

3.1 b. A bar chart is better in this case because there are 7 categories, which is on the high side for a pie chart.   **3.3** The percent with medical career aspirations has been rising for women, but for men it peaked in 1980 and then declined in 1985 and 1990.   **3.5** The bar chart shows

the percent spent on health care increasing over time at a fairly steady rate.   **3.9 b.** .4759
3.15 a. 2.2   **b.** In the row with the stem of 8. The leaf of 9 would be placed to the right of the
other leaves.   **c.** A large number of flow rates are between 6.0 and 8.0; a typical flow rate
would be 6.9 or 7.0.   **d.** There appears to be a lot of variability in the flow rates.   **e.** The
distribution is not symmetric.   **f.** 18.9 appears to be an outlier.

3.17

1H	8
2L	024
2H	9875697858558776879667585
3L	14
3H	6
4L	
4H	79
5L	4

Stems: Ones
Leaves: Tenths

3.19

64	64, 70, 35, 33
65	26, 83, 06, 27
66	14, 05, 94
67	70, 70, 90, 00, 98, 45, 13
68	50, 73, 70, 90
69	36, 27, 00, 04
70	05, 40, 22, 11, 51, 50
71	31, 69, 68, 05, 65, 13
72	09, 80

Stems: Hundreds
Leaves: Ones

3.21 a. Relative frequencies: .4167, .1792, .1500, .0708, .1000, .0375, .0458   **b.** .7459   **c.** .2541
d. .1833   **e.** The frequencies (and relative frequencies) tend to decrease as the number of
impairments increases.   **3.23 b.** The histogram is positively skewed.   **c.** .016   **d.** between
5 and 10 (inclusive): .636; strictly between 5 and 10: .459   **e.** .033   **3.25 b.** .34, .54   **c.** .60
d. No. There are 8 observations in the interval 40–<50, but we don't know how many of these
are equal to 40.   **3.27 d.** .8652   **e.** .5506   **f.** about 20.46 months   **g.** about 29.21 months
3.29 b. .0603   **c.** .2603   **3.31** Almost all of the differences are positive, indicating that the
runners slow down. The histogram is positively skewed. A typical difference is about 150. About
2% of the runners ran the late distance more quickly than the early distance.   **3.33 a.** .362,
.638   **b.** .894, .830   **3.35 b.** estimated proportion = .34, actual proportion = .3378
c. from density histogram, approximately .09; from frequency distribution, approximately
.1036   **3.37 I:** symmetric;   **II:** positively skewed;   **III:** bimodal and approximately symmetric;   **IV:** bimodal;   **V:** negatively skewed   **3.41** The histogram is positively skewed.
3.43 b. .0908   **c.** .2382   **3.45 c.** Both histograms are positively skewed.

3.49 a and c.

Class Interval	Frequency	Relative Frequency	Cum. Rel. Freq.
0–<.5	5	.1064	.1064
.5–<1.0	9	.1915	.2979
1.0–<1.5	10	.2128	.5107
1.5–<2.0	9	.1915	.7022
2.0–<2.5	3	.0638	.7660
2.5–<3.0	5	.1064	.8724
3.0–<3.5	1	.0213	.8937
3.5–<4.0	3	.0638	.9575
4.0–<4.5	1	.0213	.9788
4.5–<5.0	1	.0213	1.0001

b. The histogram is positively skewed.   **d. i.** .2979   **ii.** .4043   **iii.** .2978
3.51 b. .3648, .9177

CHAPTER 4   **4.1** $\bar{x} = 11.61$, median = 10.05; The mean is larger because of the two large values in the data
set.   **4.3** 122.57

4.5 a.

32	55
33	49
34	
35	6699
36	34469
37	03345
38	9
39	2347
40	23
41	
42	4

Since the distribution is approximately symmetric, the mean and median should be similar in value.   **b.** $\bar{x}$ = 370.69, median = 369.50   **c.** The largest value could be increased without limit without affecting the value of the median. It could be decreased to 370 without affecting the value of the median.   **4.7 a.** Because whether total personal income is judged as high or low depends on how many people are in the area.   **b.** There are not as many people in the area.   **c.** Approximately 1,620,500   **4.9** The statement could be correct if there were a small group of residents with very high wages.   **4.11** Average for diet 1 is larger than that for diet 2.   **4.13** median = 4286, $\bar{x}$ = 3968.67   **4.15** median = 68; 20% trimmed mean = 66.17   **4.17** median = 11; the median is not influenced by the unusually large value of 33.   **4.19** s^2 = 1.70, s = 1.3038   **4.23** The variance and standard deviation are not affected by adding or subtracting a number from each observation.   **4.25** s = 20.86   **4.27** iqr/1.35 is less than the value of s. This suggests that a histogram for this data would be heavy-tailed compared to a normal curve.   **4.29 a.** There are no mild or extreme outliers.   **4.31 a.** lower quartile = 7.82, upper quartile = 8.01, iqr = .19   **b.** The boxplot indicates that the distribution is not symmetric, with a longer tail on the upper end.   **4.35 a.** 40 is one standard deviation above the mean and 30 is one standard deviation below the mean. 45 is two standard deviations above the mean and 25 is two standard deviations below the mean.   **b.** at least 75%   **c.** at most 11%   **d.** approximately 95% between 25 and 45; approximately .3% less than 20 or greater than 50; approximately .15% less than 20   **4.37 a.** at least 75%   **b.** (2.90, 70.94)   **c.** If the distribution of NO_2 values was normal, approximately 2.5% of the values would be less than −9.64 (two standard deviations below the mean). Since NO_2 concentration can't be negative, the distribution shape must not resemble a normal curve.   **4.39** The z score is larger for the second exam, so performance was better on the second exam.   **4.41 a.** approximately 68%   **b.** approximately 5%   **c.** approximately 13.5%   **d.** because the histogram is well approximated by a normal curve   **4.43** The proportion is at most .16.   **4.45** Because the number of answers changed from right to wrong cannot be negative and one standard deviation below the mean is a negative number, the distribution can't be well described by a normal curve. From Chebyshev's Rule, the proportion who changed at least 6 answers from right to wrong is at most .106.   **4.47 b. i.** 13.158   **ii.** 16.25   **iii.** 6.923   **iv.** 21   **v.** 11.842   **4.49 b.** For the cancer group: $\bar{x}$ = 22.81, median = 16; for the no-cancer group: $\bar{x}$ = 19.15, median = 12.   **c.** For the cancer group: s = 31.6553; for the no-cancer group: s = 16.99. There is more variability in the cancer sample values than in the no-cancer sample values.   **4.51** It implies that the median salary is less than $1 million and that the histogram would be positively skewed or that there are outliers with very large values.   **4.53 b.** The mean and median are not the same because the distribution is not symmetric.   **c.** In the interval (0, 45.71). Note: 0 is used for the lower endpoint because score cannot be negative.   **4.55** Various graphical and numerical methods can be used for comparison. In general, they suggest that milk volume for nonsmoking mothers is greater than that for smoking mothers.   **4.59** Since the mean is larger than the median, this suggests that the distribution of values is positively skewed or has some outliers with very large values.   **4.61 a.** $\bar{x}$ = 22.15, s = 11.366   **b.** 10% trimmed mean = 19.4375   **c.** lower quartile = 18, upper quartile = 20.5, iqr = 2.5   **d.** 25 and 28 are mild outliers, and 69 is an extreme outlier   **4.63 a.** If one observation is deleted from each end, the trimming percent is 6.67%. If two observations are deleted from each end, the trimming percent is 13.33%. **b.** 6.67% trimmed mean = 10.66; 13.33% trimmed mean = 10.58   **c.** Averaging the two trimmed means from part **b** gives 10.62. This is a reasonable approach since 10% is halfway between 6.67% and 13.33%.

CHAPTER 5

5.1 a. There is a tendency for y to increase as x does (a positive relationship).   **b.** There are several observations that have identical x values but different y values. Thus, the value of y is not determined solely by x.   **5.3 a.** Both boxplots have two outliers on the high side. Whereas the minimum and lower quartiles are similar for x and y, the median and upper quartile are higher for x.   **b.** The plot shows a linear pattern. The two points that stand out in the plot look like they conform to the linear pattern seen in the rest of the data.   **5.7 a.** The graft weight ratio tends to decrease as recipient body weight increases, but the relationship does not look linear. **5.9 a.** positive   **b.** negative   **c.** positive   **d.** no correlation   **e.** positive correlation **f.** positive   **g.** negative   **h.** no correlation   **5.13 a.** There appears to be a strong positive correlation.   **b.** $r = .9366$ indicates a strong positive linear relationship.   **c.** If x and y had a correlation coefficient of 1, all of the points would lie on a straight line, but the line would not necessarily have slope 1 and intercept 0.   **5.15 a.** $r = .39$ **5.17** No. An r value of $-.085$ indicates at best a weak relationship between support for environmental spending and degree of belief.   **5.19** In this case, r cannot be negative.   **5.21** $r_s = .039$, which is very close to zero.   **5.23** $r_s = .9504$ **5.27 a.** $\hat{y} = .365 + .967x$ **b.** $\hat{y} = .8485$ **5.29 a.** slope = 244.9, intercept = -275.1 **b.** 244.9   **c.** 214.7   **d.** No, the predicted value for height = 1 is negative, which is not a possible value of breaking strength.   **5.31 a.** $\hat{y} = 31.040 - 5.792x$ **b.** -5.792 (a decrease in percent crown dieback)   **c.** 7.872   **d.** No, because 5.6 is outside the range of the data.   **5.33** The relationship observed over the range of the data may not continue to hold outside this range.   **5.37 a.** 76.64% of the variation in clutch size can be explained by the linear relationship with snout-vent length.   **b.** $s_e = 29.25$ **5.39 a.** $\hat{y} = 914.5$, residual = -21.5 **5.41 a.** Predicted values: 40.4048, 42.6245, 49.2837, 53.7231, 54.8330, 56.4978, 58.1626, 58.7175, 62.6020, 68.1513; Residuals: -17.4048, 9.3755, 15.7163, 1.2769, -22.8330, 3.5022, 19.8374, .2825, -1.6020, -8.1513 **b.** SSResid = 1635.6833, $r^2 = .2859$ **5.43 a.** $\hat{y} = 94.33 - 15.388x$ **b.** SSTo = 5534.91667, SSResid = 285.82261   **c.** $r^2 = .94836$ **d.** $s_e = 5.34624$ **e.** Since the slope is negative, $r = -\sqrt{r^2} = -.97384$ **5.45** $r^2 = .9512$. This means that 95.12% of the variability in hardness can be explained by the linear relationship with elapsed time.   **5.47** There is a curved pattern in the plot, suggesting that the linear model may not be appropriate.   **5.51 a.** When $r = 0$, $s_e = s_y$. The least squares line is then a horizontal line with slope = 0 and intercept $\bar{y}$.   **b.** When r is close to 1, s_e will be much smaller than s_y.   **c.** $s_e = 1.5$ **5.53 b.** The plot of $\log(y)$ versus $\log(x)$ looks the straightest. The line for predicting $y' = \log(y)$ from $x' = \log(x)$ is $\hat{y}' = 1.61867 - .31646x'$. When $x = 25$, the predicted y is 15.0064.   **5.55 a.** $r = -.717$ **b.** $r = -.835$ for the transformed data **5.57 a.** The plot does show a positive relationship.   **b.** The plot appears straighter. **c.** The plot also appears straighter, and the points conform more closely to a line.   **d.** The plot shows curvature in the opposite direction as the plot in part **a.**   **5.59** The plot suggests fitting a quadratic curve to the data.   **5.61 a.** The plot does not show a strong linear pattern. **b.** $\hat{y} = 32.254$ **d.** With the outlier deleted, $\hat{y} = 36.4175 - .1978x$, $r^2 = .027$. There is little evidence of a linear relationship.   **5.63 a.** $\hat{y} = 13.9617 + 3.1703x$ **b.** The scatter plot shows some curvature, suggesting it might be possible to do better with a nonlinear model. **c.** 34.5687   **d.** No, because $x = 18$ is outside the range of the data.   **15.65 a.** $r = 0$ **b.** For example, $y = 1$ (Any y value greater than .973 will work.)   **c.** For example, $y = -1$ (Any y value less than $-.973$ will work.)   **15.67 b.** $a = 5.550$, $b = 2.1975$ **c.** $r = .5815$ **d.** $r_s = .625$ **15.69 a.** $r = -.981$. This value of r suggests a strong negative linear relationship. **b.** There is a slight curvature to the plot.

CHAPTER 6

6.1 a. In the long run, 1% of all people who suffer cardiac arrest in New York City survive. **b.** 23 or 24 **6.3** They are dependent. **6.5** They are dependent. **6.7 a.** .001 **b.** .999 **c.** .009 **6.9 a.** .7 **b.** .5 **c.** .714286 **d.** no **e.** They are independent. **6.11 a.** The expert assumed that the positions of the two valves were independent. **b.** 1/12 **6.13 a.** .81 **b.** .19, .19 **c.** .0361, .9639 **d.** .993141 **e.** .926559 **6.15 a.** .46 **b.** the first group **c.** No; for the third priority group, the probability of getting more than 9 units is .09. **6.17 b.** .27 **c.** .43 **d.** not independent **e.** .5263 **f.** .1395 **6.19 a.** .4247 **b.** .3139 **c.** .4375 **d.** .0052 **e.** .2014 **f.** .1962 **g.** .3350 **h.** .1774 **i.** .4876 **j.** .2954 **k.** .5659 **6.21 a.** Results will vary from one simulation to another, but values should be around .25. **6.23** Results will vary from one simulation to another, but values should be around .85. **6.25 a.** .45 **b.** .70 **c.** .75 **6.27 a.** .0119 **b.** .00000238 **c.** .012 **6.29** Results will vary from one simulation to another, but values should be around .94.

CHAPTER 7

7.1 a. discrete **b.** continuous **c.** discrete **d.** discrete **e.** continuous **7.3 b.** .4 **7.5 b.** $x = 0$, since its probability is the largest. **c.** .25 **d.** .55 **7.7 a.** .82 **b.** .18 **c.** .65, .27 **7.9 a.** Supplier 1 **b.** Supplier 2 **c.** Supplier 1, because the bulbs generally last longer and the lifetime is less variable. **d.** about 1000 **e.** about 100 **7.13 b.** .5, .125, .125 **c.** .375 **d.** .4375 **7.15 a.** height = 2 **b.** 1/4 **c.** 7/16 **7.17 a.** .1003 **b.** .1003 **c.** .8185 **d.** .5 **e.** 1 **f.** .9390 **g.** .5910 **7.19 a.** .5398 **b.** .4602 **c.** .1469 **d.** .1469 **e.** .4577 **f.** .8944 **g.** .0730 **7.21 a.** 1.88 **b.** 2.33 **c.** −1.75 **d.** −1.28 **7.23 a.** 1.34 **b.** .74 **c.** 0 **d.** −1.34 **e.** One is the negative of the other. **7.25 a.** .1190, .6969 **b.** .0021 **c.** 1 lb ≈ 453 grams, so P(weight > 7 lb) = P(weight > 3171 g) = .7054 **d.** Those with weights below about 1040 g or above about 5020 g **e.** Weight in pounds = 1/453 (weight in grams), so weight in pounds would have a distribution that is approximately normal with mean 7.576 lb and standard deviation 1.064 lb. **7.27** Recommend machine 2. **7.29** times less than 94.4 seconds **7.31 a.** .5, .5 **b.** .8185 **c.** .0013 **d.** .0252 **e.** below 47.4 wpm **7.33** The plot is quite straight; the normal distribution provides a reasonable description of the steam rate distribution. **7.35** The plot does not look linear; the lifetime distribution is not adequately described by a normal distribution. **7.37** The plot looks linear; a normal distribution provides a reasonable description of the DDT concentration distribution. **7.39** The cube-root transformation results in a more symmetric histogram.

7.41 a.

Class Interval	Frequency
0–< 100	22
100–< 200	32
200–< 300	26
300–< 400	11
400–< 500	4
500–< 600	3
600–< 700	1
700–< 800	0
800–< 900	1

b. The histogram is positively skewed. **c.** The square-root transformation is one transformation that results in a more symmetric distribution. **7.45** .0228, 0 **7.47 a.** No, only about 69.15% are shorter than 5′7″. **b.** about 69% **7.49 a.** .7745 **b.** .1587 **c.** .3085 **d.** The largest 5% are those that exceed 6.1645. **7.51 a.** .8247 **b.** .0516 **c.** .6826 **d.** .0030 **e.** $P(x < 261) = .3783$

CHAPTER 8

8.1 A statistic is computed from the observations in a sample, whereas a population characteristic is a quantity that describes the whole population. **8.3 a.** population characteristic

b. statistic   **c.** population characteristic   **d.** statistic   **e.** statistic

8.7 a.

t value	6	11	15	21	25	30
Probability	1/6	1/6	1/6	1/6	1/6	1/6

b. $\mu = 9, \mu_t = 18$

8.9

Statistic #1:	Value	2.67	3.00	3.33	3.67
	Probability	.1	.4	.3	.2
Statistic #2:	Value	3	4		
	Probability	.7	.3		
Statistic #3:	Value	2.5	3.0	3.5	
	Probability	.1	.5	.4	

8.11 a. 11.8   **8.13** Histograms for samples of size 10 would be centered in the same place but would be less spread out than for samples of size 5.   **8.15** for $n = 36, 50, 100,$ and 400 **8.17 a.** $\mu_{\bar{x}} = 40, \sigma_{\bar{x}} = .625$, approximately normal   **b.** .5762   **c.** .2628   **8.19 a.** $\mu_{\bar{x}} = 2,$ $\sigma_{\bar{x}} = .267$ **b.** for $n = 20, \mu_{\bar{x}} = 2, \sigma_{\bar{x}} = .179$ **c.** for $n = 100, \mu_{\bar{x}} = 2, \sigma_{\bar{x}} = .08$ **8.21 a.** .8185, .0013   **b.** .9772, 0   **8.23** .0026   **8.25** approximately 0   **8.27 a.** .65, .15083   **b.** .65, .10665   **c.** .65, .08708   **d.** .65, .06745   **e.** .65, .04770   **f.** .65, .03373   **8.29 a.** $\mu_p = .005, \sigma_p = .007$ **b.** Since $n\pi < 10$, the sampling distribution of p is not well approximated by a normal curve.   **c.** n would have to be at least 2000   **8.31 a.** for $\pi = .5$: $\mu_p = .5, \sigma_p = .0333$; for $\pi = .6$: $\mu_p = .6, \sigma_p = .0327$; in both cases the sampling distribution of p is approximately normal.   **b.** .0013 (for $\pi = .5$), .5000 (for $\pi = .6$)   **c.** The probability when $\pi = .5$ would decrease and the probability when $\pi = .6$ would remain the same.   **8.33 a.** .9744   **b.** approximately 0   **8.35 a.** The sampling distribution of $\bar{x}$ will be approximately normal with mean 50 and standard deviation .1.   **b.** .9876   **c.** .5   **8.37 a.** $\mu_{\bar{x}} = 52, \sigma_{\bar{x}} = .33$ **b.** approximately 1, approximately 0   **8.39 a.** .0207   **b.** The probability of observing such a sample is approximately 0. It is very unlikely that $\pi = .4$.

CHAPTER 9

9.1 Statistic II would be preferred because it is unbiased and has a smaller standard deviation.   **9.3** .252   **9.5** .262   **9.7 a.** $s = 1.886$ **b.** sample median $= 11.35$ **c.** Trimming one observation from each side gives 8.3% trimmed mean $= 11.73$ **d.** 14.381   **9.9 a.** 120.6   **b.** 1,206,000   **c.** .8   **d.** sample median $= 120$ **9.11 a.** 1.96   **b.** 1.645   **c.** 2.58   **d.** 1.28   **e.** 1.44   **9.13 a.** As the confidence level increases, the width of the interval increases.   **b.** As the sample size increases, the width of the interval decreases.   **c.** As the value of p gets farther from .5, the width of the interval decreases.   **9.15** (.382, .695)   **9.19** (.586, .714), yes   **9.21 a.** (.669, .773)   **b.** (.240, .318)   **c.** narrower   **9.23 a.** (.4140, .4656)   **b.** The entire interval is below .5. It is not plausible that a majority of U.S. adults feel that it makes no difference which party is in control.   **9.25** $n = 2401$ **9.27** $n = 385$ **9.29 a.** 90%   **b.** 95%   **c.** 95%   **d.** 99%   **e.** 1%   **f.** .5%   **g.** 5%   **9.31 a.** $\bar{x} = 115$ **b.** (114.4, 115.6) is the 90% interval and (114.1, 115.9) is the 99% interval   **9.33 a.** narrower, since the z critical value would have been smaller   **b.** The statement is incorrect. The 95% refers to the percentage of all possible samples that would result in an interval that contains μ, not to the chance that any specific interval contains μ.   **c.** Although we would expect 95% of such intervals to include μ *in the long run,* we would not expect to see *exactly* 95 of any specific 100 intervals.   **9.35 a.** (.409, .591)   **b.** No. It does imply that at least some students lie to their mothers, but the mean could be positive even when there are some 0's in the population.   **9.37 a.** LBO firms: $(-.1866, 1.4294)$; non-LBO firms: (.5435, 1.3573)   **b.** the sample size is larger   **9.39** (1.79, 2.61)   **9.41** (19.51, 24.29)   **9.43** (5.77, 28.23)   **9.45** No. The sample size is small and there are two outliers in the data set, indicating that

the assumption of a normal population distribution is not reasonable.   **9.47** $n = 246$
9.51 (9.976, 11.824)   **9.53 a.** (199.407, 216.193)   **b.** Since the sample size is small, the
population distribution must be normal.   **9.55** (.241, .319)

CHAPTER 10   **10.1** not a legitimate hypothesis since $\bar{x}$ is not a *population* characteristic   **10.3** Choose
the first pair of hypotheses, since this places the burden of proof on the welding contractor to
show that the welds meet specifications.   **10.5** $H_0: \pi = .6, H_a: \pi > .6$ **10.7** $H_0: \mu = 170$,
$H_a: \mu < 170$ **10.9** $H_0: \mu = 40, H_a: \mu \neq 40$ **10.11 a.** They failed to reject the null hypothesis because their conclusion of no evidence of increased risk is consistent with H_0.   **b.** Type II,
since a type I error results only when a true null hypothesis is rejected.   **c.** Since the null hypothesis is initially assumed to be true and is rejected only if there is strong evidence against it, if
we fail to reject the null hypothesis we have not "proven" it to be true. We can say only that there
is not strong evidence against it.   **10.13 a.** Pizza Hut's decision is consistent with rejecting the
null hypothesis.   **b.** Rejecting H_0 when it is true is a type I error, so if they incorrectly reject
H_0, they are making a type I error.   **10.15 a.** A type I error is returning to the supplier a shipment that is not of inferior quality. A type II error is accepting a shipment of inferior quality.
b. The calculator manufacturer would most likely consider a type II error more serious, because
they would then end up producing defective calculators.   **c.** From the supplier's point of view, a
type I error is more serious, because the supplier would end up having a good shipment returned.
10.17 a. The manufacturer claims that the percentage defective is 10%. Since we would probably not object if the proportion defective is less than 10%, we would want to determine whether
the proportion defective exceeds the value claimed by the manufacturer.   **b.** A type I error
is concluding that the proportion defective exceeds 10% when, in fact, it does not. The consequence of this decision would be the filing of false advertising charges against a manufacturer
who is not guilty of false advertising. A type II error is concluding that there is no evidence that
the proportion defective is greater than 10% when, in fact, it is. The consequence of this type
of error is that the manufacturer would be permitted to continue with a false advertisement.
10.19 a. $H_0: \pi = .02, H_a: \pi < .02$ **b.** A type I error is changing to robots when in fact they
are not superior to humans. A type II error is not changing to robots when in fact they are superior to humans.   **c.** Since a type I error would result in a substantial monetary loss to the company and also the loss of jobs for former employees, a small α should be used.   **10.21** .001, .021,
and .047   **10.23 a.** .0808   **b.** .1762   **c.** .0250   **d.** .0071   **e.** .5675   **10.25** $z = 4.78$,
P-value ≈ 0, reject H_0 **10.27** $z = -8.24$, P-value ≈ 0, reject H_0 **10.29 a.** $z = -13.91$,
P-value ≈ 0, reject H_0 **b.** A type I error is concluding that there are not enough valid signatures, when in fact there were. If a type I error were to occur, the recall would be tossed out when
it should have been placed on the ballot.   **c.** A type II error would be concluding that there
were enough valid signatures when in fact there were not. If a type II error were to occur, the recall would be placed on the ballot when it should have been tossed out.   **d.** Type I   **e.** Yes,
the test indicates that there is convincing evidence that the number of valid signatures is too small
to qualify for the ballot.   **10.31** $z = 1.78$, P-value $= .0375$, fail to reject H_0 **10.33** $z = .75$,
P-value $= .2266$, fail to reject H_0 **10.35** $z = 3.20$, P-value $= .0007$, reject H_0 **10.37** $z =$
-9.35, P-value ≈ 0, reject H_0 **10.39 a.** $z = 3.00$ **b.** .0014   **c.** reject H_0 **10.41 a.** .040
b. .003   **c.** .019   **d.** 0   **e.** .13   **f.** .13   **g.** 0   **10.43 a.** reject H_0 **b.** reject H_0
c. fail to reject H_0 **10.45 a.** P-value $= .136$, fail to reject H_0 **b.** P-value $= .136$, fail to
reject H_0 **c.** P-value $= .016$, fail to reject H_0 **d.** P-value $= .002$, reject H_0 for any $\alpha > .002$
10.47 $t = -3.89$, P-value $\approx .000$, reject H_0 **10.49** $t = -14.75$, P-value ≈ 0, reject H_0
10.51 $t = -5.05$, P-value ≈ 0, reject H_0 **10.53 a.** Since the boxplot is nearly symmetric
with no outliers and the normal probability plot is reasonably straight, the t test is appropriate.
c. $t = 1.21$, P-value $\approx .256$, fail to reject H_0 **10.55 a.** $t = 1.875$, P-value $\approx .041$, reject H_0
b. yes   **10.57 a.** The sample is randomly selected, the sample size is large, and σ is known.
b. A type I error is concluding that the water discharged is too hot when in fact it is not. A
type II error is concluding that the water is not too hot, when in fact it is too hot.   **c.** .0359

e. .3745   **f.** approximately 0   **g.** fail to reject H_0, type II error   **10.59 a.** $z = 1.71$, P-value $= .0436$, reject H_0, yes   **b.** .3520   **10.61 a. i.** $\beta \approx .85$ **ii.** $\beta \approx .55$ **iii.** $\beta \approx .10$ **iv.** $\beta \approx 0$ **b.** β increases   **10.63 a.** *   **b.** †   **c.** none   **d.** ‡   **10.65** $z = 2.25$, P-value $= .0122$, reject H_0 at $\alpha = .05$, but not at $\alpha = .01$ **10.67 a.** If the distribution were normal, the Empirical Rule implies that about 16% of the values would be less than the value that is one standard deviation below the mean. Since the standard deviation is larger than the mean, this value is negative. Caffeine consumption can't be negative, so it is not plausible that the distribution is normal. However, since the sample size is large ($n = 47$), the t test can still be used.   **b.** $t = .44$, P-value $\approx .346$, fail to reject H_0 **10.69** $z = 4.19$, P-value ≈ 0, reject H_0 **10.71** $t = 2.99$, P-value $\approx .002$, reject H_0 **10.73** $t = -2.87$, P-value $\approx .005$, reject H_0

CHAPTER 11   **11.1** approximately normal with mean 5 and standard deviation .529   **11.3 a.** $H_0: \mu_1 - \mu_2 = 10$; $H_a: \mu_1 - \mu_2 > 10$ **b.** $H_0: \mu_1 - \mu_2 = -10$; $H_a: \mu_1 - \mu_2 < -10$ **11.5** for small prey: $t = 1.27$, df $= 7$, P-value $\approx .23$, fail to reject H_0; for medium prey: $t = 1.83$, df $= 10$, P-value $\approx .102$, fail to reject H_0; for large prey: $t = -18.08$, df $= 12$, P-value ≈ 0, reject H_0 **11.7 a.** yes   **b.** yes   **c.** no, would need to know the sample means and standard deviations   **11.9 a.** $t = -6.56$, df $= 201$, P-value ≈ 0, reject H_0 **b.** $t = 6.25$, df $= 201$, P-value ≈ 0, reject H_0 **c.** $t = .07$, df $= 201$, P-value $\approx .92$, fail to reject H_0 **11.11 a.** $t = 1.77$, df $= 37$, P-value $\approx .08$, fail to reject H_0 **b.** $t = -1.28$, df $= 29$, P-value $\approx .204$, fail to reject H_0 **c.** $t = -7.1$, df $= 332$, P-value ≈ 0, reject H_0 **11.13 a.** $H_0: \mu = 100,000$ would be rejected in favor of $H_a: \mu > 100,000$ only for $\alpha > .212$ **b.** $t = 2.72$, df $= 473$, P-value $\approx .003$, reject H_0 **11.15** $t = 3.1$, df $= 113$, P-value $\approx .001$, reject H_0 **11.17 a.** $t = 2.93$, df $= 54$, P-value $\approx .006$, reject H_0 **b.** $t = .15$, df $= 68$, P-value $\approx .842$, fail to reject H_0 **c.** df $= 65$, (.242, 1.458)   **11.19** $t = 113.2$, df $= 45$, P-value ≈ 0, reject H_0 **11.21** $t = 3.30$, df $= 98$, P-value $\approx .001$, reject H_0 **11.23** $t = 2.97$, df $= 10$, P-value $= .007$, reject H_0 **11.25** $t = 2.94$, df $= 26$, P-value $\approx .004$, reject H_0 **11.27** $t = 2.43$, df $= 32$, P-value $\approx .011$, fail to reject H_0 **11.29** df $= 23$, $(-100.22, 668.22)$ **11.31 a.** $s_p^2 = .00004$, $t = 9.86$, df $= 24$, P-value ≈ 0, reject H_0 **b.** $t = 9.98$, df $= 22$, P-value ≈ 0, conclusion is the same as for the test in part **a**   **11.35 b.** $(-1.03, -.63)$ **11.37** $t = 9.91$, P-value ≈ 0, reject H_0 **11.39** $t = -1.34$, P-value $\approx .206$, fail to reject H_0 **11.41 a.** $t = 3.95$, P-value ≈ 0, reject H_0 **11.43** $t = 0.047$, P-value $\approx .5$, fail to reject H_0 **11.45** $z = -1.67$, P-value $= .048$, reject H_0 **11.47** $z = -4.12$, P-value ≈ 0, reject H_0 **11.49** $z = -4.09$, P-value ≈ 0, reject H_0 **11.51** $z = -1.84$, P-value $= .066$, fail to reject H_0 **11.53** $z = 6.21$, P-value ≈ 0, reject H_0 **11.55** $(-.2053, .0777)$ **11.57** $(-.2743, -.0823)$, the interval does not include 0. The proportion with decayed teeth is lower for children drinking fluoridated water by somewhere between .0823 and .2743.   **11.59** rank sum $= 83$, P-value $> .05$, fail to reject H_0 **11.61** rank sum $= 48$, P-value $> .05$, fail to reject H_0 **11.63** rank sum $= 53$, P-value $> .05$, fail to reject H_0 **11.67** $t = 5.03$, df $= 100$, P-value ≈ 0, reject H_0 **11.69 a.** $t = -1.44$, df $= 108$, P-value $\approx .082$, fail to reject H_0 **b.** $t = -2.85$, df $= 112$, P-value $\approx .002$, reject H_0 **c.** $t = .145$, df $= 96$, P-value $\approx .920$, fail to reject H_0 **d.** $t = -1.72$, df $= 106$, P-value $\approx .092$, fail to reject H_0 **11.71** $t = 2.55$, df $= 77$, P-value $\approx .012$, reject H_0 at $\alpha = .05$, but not at $\alpha = .01$ **11.73** $t = .504$, df $= 288$, P-value $\approx .618$, fail to reject H_0 **11.75 a.** $t = -3.86$, df $= 3$, P-value $\approx .032$, reject H_0 **b.** Since the sample sizes are small, the t test requires that the distribution of number of flashes for both single-peak and multiple-peak storms be normal.   **11.77** $t = 2.13$, df $= 21$, P-value $\approx .024$, reject H_0 **11.79** $t = 3.13$, df $= 35$, P-value $\approx .002$, reject H_0 **11.81 a.** $t = 2.02$, df $= 17$, P-value $\approx .062$, fail to reject H_0 **b.** $t = 1.10$, df $= 22$, P-value $\approx .284$, fail to reject H_0 **c.** (1161.83, 1838.17)   **d.** (1027.19, 1886.81)   **11.83** No, because the large-sample z test for comparing two proportions requires that the samples be independent.   **11.85 a.** $(-.186, .111)$ **b.** It must be reasonable to assume that the distribution of differences is normal.   **11.87** df $= 7$, $(-47.21, 75.01)$; because 0 is in the interval, there may be no difference between the true mean age at death for male and female SIDS victims.   **11.89** $t = 3.59$, df $= 6$, P-value $\approx .006$, reject H_0

CHAPTER 12

12.1 a. $.020 <$ P-value $< .025$ **b.** $.040 <$ P-value $< .045$ **c.** $.035 <$ P-value $< .040$
d. P-value $< .001$ **e.** P-value $> .10$ **12.3 a.** $X^2 = 19.0$, P-value $< .001$, reject H_0
b. If $n = 40$, the chi-squared test should not be used, since one of the expected counts would
be less than 5.   **12.5** $X^2 = 11.242$, $.010 <$ P-value $< .015$, fail to reject H_0 at $\alpha = .01$
12.7 a. $X^2 = 8216.5$, P-value $< .001$, reject H_0 **c.** $X^2 = 10.748$, P-value $> .100$, fail to
reject H_0 **12.9** $X^2 = 253.482$, P-value $< .001$, reject H_0 **12.11** $X^2 = .931$, P-value $> .100$,
fail to reject H_0 **12.13** $X^2 = 1.47$, P-value $> .100$, fail to reject H_0 **12.15 a.** df $= 10$
b. df $= 12$ **c.** df $= 15$ **12.17** $X^2 = 8.6837$, $.065 <$ P-value $< .070$, fail to reject H_0
12.19 a. $X^2 = 6.852$, P-value $> .100$, fail to reject H_0 **b.** yes   **12.21** $X^2 = 73.789$,
P-value $< .001$, reject H_0 **12.23** $X^2 = 6.621$, P-value $\approx .085$ **12.25** $X^2 = 10.976$,
P-value $< .001$, reject H_0 **12.27** $X^2 = 22.855$, P-value $< .001$, reject H_0 **12.29** $X^2 = 1.978$,
P-value $> .100$, fail to reject H_0 **12.31** $X^2 = 22.373$, P-value $< .001$, reject H_0 **12.33** $X^2 =$
9.844, $.005 <$ P-value $< .010$, reject H_0 **12.35** $X^2 = 8.89$, $.001 <$ P-value $< .005$, reject H_0
12.37 $X^2 = 6.54$, $.035 <$ P-value $< .040$, reject H_0 **12.39** $X^2 = 103.87$, P-value $< .001$,
reject H_0 **12.41** $X^2 = 75.35$, P-value $< .001$, reject H_0; note that there are two cells with
expected counts less than 5. If the last two rows of the table are combined, $X^2 = 73.03$,
P-value $< .001$, reject H_0

CHAPTER 13

13.1 a. $y = -5.0 + .017x$ **c.** 30.7 **d.** $.017$ **e.** 1.7 **f.** No, the model should not be
used to predict outside the range of the data.   **13.3 a.** $3.6, 4.3$ **b.** $.1210$ **c.** $.5, .1587$
13.5 a. $47, 4700$ **b.** $.3156, .0643$ **13.7 a.** $r^2 = .6228$ **b.** $s_e = 1.5923$ **c.** $b = 3.4307$
d. 3.4426 **13.9 a.** $r^2 = .883$ **b.** $s_e = 13.682$, df $= 14$ **13.11 b.** $\hat{y} = -.002274 +$
$1.2467x$, predicted value when $x = .09$ is $.1099$ **c.** $r^2 = .436$. This means that 43.6% of the
total variability in market share can be explained by the linear relationship with advertising
share.   **d.** $s_e = .0263$, df $= 8$ **13.13 a.** $.253$ **b.** $.179$, no   **c.** It would require 4 observations at each x value.   **13.15 a.** $s_e = 9.7486$, $s_b = .1537$ **b.** $(2.17, 2.83)$ **c.** Yes, because
the interval is narrow   **13.17 a.** $a = 592.1, b = 97.26$ **b.** $\hat{y} = 786.62$, residual $= -29.62$
c. $(87.76, 106.76)$ **13.19 a.** $t = 2.8302$, P-value $= .008$, reject H_0 and conclude that the model
is useful   **b.** $(4.294, 25.706)$; based on this interval, we estimate that change in mean SAT
score associated with an increase on \$1000 in expenditure per child is between 4.294 and 25.706
13.21 a. $\hat{y} = -96.67 + 1.595x$ **b.** $t = 27.17$, P-value ≈ 0, reject H_0 and conclude that the
model is useful   **c.** The mean response time for individuals with closed-head injury is 1.48 times
as great as for those with no head injury.   **13.23 a.** $t = 6.53$, P-value ≈ 0, reject H_0 and conclude that the model is useful   **b.** $t = 1.56$, P-value $= .079$, fail to reject H_0 **13.25** $t = -17.57$,
P-value ≈ 0, reject H_0 **13.27** The standardized residual plot does not exhibit any unusual features.   **13.29 b.** The plot is reasonably straight. The assumption of normality is plausible.
c. There are two residuals that are unusually large.   **13.31 a.** There are several large residuals and potentially influential observations.   **13.33** The residuals are positive in 1963 and 1964,
and then they are negative from 1965 through 1972. This pattern in the residual plot casts doubt
on the appropriateness of the simple linear regression model.   **13.35** If the request is for a
confidence interval for β, the wording will be something like "estimate the *change* in the average
y value," whereas if the request is for a confidence interval for $\alpha + \beta x$, the wording would be
something like "estimate the *average y value*."   **13.37 a.** $(-.4788, -.2113)$ **b.** $(17.78, 21.78)$
13.39 a. $(6.4722, 6.6300)$ **b.** $(6.4779, 6.6973)$ **c.** Yes, because $x^* = 60$ is farther from $\bar{x}$.
13.41 a. $\hat{y} = -133.02 + 5.919x$ **b.** $s_b = 1.127$ **c.** $t = 5.25$, P-value ≈ 0, reject H_0
d. 251.74 **e.** Shouldn't use regression equation to predict for $x = 105$ because it is outside
the range of the data.   **13.43 a.** $\hat{y} = 2.78551 + .04462x$ **b.** $t = 10.85$, P-value ≈ 0,
reject H_0 and conclude that the model is useful   **c.** $(3.671, 4.577)$ **d.** Since 4.1 is in the
interval, it is plausible that a box that has been on the shelf 30 days will not be acceptable.
13.45 a. $\hat{y} = 30.019 + .1109x$ **b.** $(38.354, 43.864)$ **c.** $(30.311, 51.907)$ **d.** The interval
in part **b** is for the mean blood lead level for all people who work where the air lead level is 100.
The interval in part **c** is for a particular individual who works in a place where the air lead level

is 100. **13.47 a.** prediction interval when $x = 35$: (1.9519, 3.0931); prediction interval when $x = 45$: (1.3879, 2.5271) **b.** The simultaneous confidence level would be at least 97%. **13.51** $t = 2.07$, P-value $\approx .036$, reject H_0 **13.53 a.** $t = -6.175$, P-value ≈ 0, reject H_0 **b.** no, $r^2 = .0676$ **13.55** $r = .574$, $t = 1.85$, P-value $\approx .1$, fail to reject H_0 **13.57** $t = 2.2$, P-value $= .028$, reject H_0 **13.61 a.** (4.903, 5.632) **b.** (4.4078, 6.1272) **13.63 a.** From the MINITAB output, $t = -3.95$, P-value $= .003$, reject H_0 and conclude that the model is useful **b.** $(-3.6694, -.9976)$ **c.** (60.276, 70.646) **d.** because $x = 11$ is farther from $\bar{x}$ than is $x = 10$ **13.65 a.** $t = -6.09$, P-value ≈ 0, reject H_0 **c.** The predicted value when $x = 10$ is negative, and y cannot be negative. $x = 10$ is probably outside of the range of the data, and the model should not be used to predict for $x = 10$. **13.67 a.** $t = .49$, P-value $= .624$, fail to reject H_0 **b.** A 95% confidence interval is (47.083, 54.009). **13.69** (18.0284, 22.2218) **13.71** A linear model is not appropriate for data sets 2, 3, and 4. **13.73 a.** $\hat{y} = 57.964 + .0357x$ **b.** $t = 0.023$, P-value ≈ 1, fail to reject H_0 **d.** The residual plot has a distinct curved pattern. The simple linear regression model is not appropriate. **13.75 a.** $t = -0.06$, P-value $= .922$, fail to reject H_0 **b.** $t = 4.35$, P-value ≈ 0, reject H_0 **c.** $a = 3.0781$, $b = .01161$ **d.** (2.9778, 4.3392) **e.** (3.6197, 4.1619)

CHAPTER 14

14.1 A deterministic model does not have the random error component, e, whereas a probabilistic model does contain such a component. **14.3** $y = \alpha + \beta_1 x_1 + \beta_2 x_2 + e$. An interaction term is not included because the statement indicates that x_1 and x_2 make independent contributions. **14.5 a.** 103.11 **b.** 96.87 **c.** $\beta_1 = -6.6$; this is the expected change in yield associated with a 1-unit increase in mean temperature when mean percentage sunshine remains fixed. $\beta_2 = -4.5$; this is the expected change in yield associated with a 1-unit increase in mean percentage sunshine when mean temperature remains fixed. **14.7 b.** The mean chlorine content is higher for $x = 10$. **c.** When degree of delignification increases from 8 to 9, the mean chlorine content increases by 7. Mean chlorine content decreases by 1 when degree of delignification increases from 9 to 10. **14.9 c.** The parallel lines in each graph are attributable to the lack of interaction between the two independent variables. **d.** Because there is an interaction term, the lines are not parallel. **14.11 a.** $y = \alpha + \beta_1 x_1 + \beta_2 x_2 + \beta_3 x_3 + e$
b. $y = \alpha + \beta_1 x_1 + \beta_2 x_2 + \beta_3 x_3 + \beta_4 x_1^2 + \beta_5 x_2^2 + \beta_6 x_3^2 + e$
c. $y = \alpha + \beta_1 x_1 + \beta_2 x_2 + \beta_3 x_3 + \beta_4 x_1 x_2 + e$; $y = \alpha + \beta_1 x_1 + \beta_2 x_2 + \beta_3 x_3 + \beta_4 x_1 x_3 + e$; $y = \alpha + \beta_1 x_1 + \beta_2 x_2 + \beta_3 x_3 + \beta_4 x_2 x_3 + e$
d. $y = \alpha + \beta_1 x_1 + \beta_2 x_2 + \beta_3 x_3 + \beta_4 x_1^2 + \beta_5 x_2^2 + \beta_6 x_3^2 + \beta_7 x_1 x_2 + \beta_8 x_1 x_3 + \beta_9 x_2 x_3 + e$
14.13 a. Three dummy variables would be needed to incorporate a nonnumerical variable with four categories. **14.15 a.** $b_3 = -.0996$ is the estimated change in mean VO$_2$ max associated with a 1-unit increase in 1 mile walk time when the values of the other predictor variables are fixed. **b.** $b_1 = .6566$ is the estimated difference in mean VO$_2$ max for males and females when the values of the other predictors are fixed. **c.** $\hat{y} = 2.8049$, residual $= .3451$ **d.** $R^2 = .706$ **e.** $s_e = .397$ **14.17 a.** $.01 < P$-value $< .05$ **b.** P-value $> .10$ **c.** P-value $= .01$ **d.** $.001 < P$-value $< .01$ **14.19** $F = 24.41$, P-value $< .001$, reject H_0 and conclude that the model is useful **14.21** P-value $< .001$, reject H_0 and conclude that the model is useful **14.23 a.** $\hat{y} = 86.65 - .12297x_1 + 5.090x_2 - .07092x_3 + .001538x_4$ **b.** $F = 64.4$, P-value $< .001$, reject H_0 and conclude that the model is useful **c.** $R^2 = .908$. This means that 90.8% of the variability in the observed tar content values can be explained by the fitted model. $s_e = 4.784$. This means that the typical distance of an observation from the corresponding mean value is 4.784. **14.25 a.** $\hat{y} = -510.9 + 3.0633length - 1.113age$ **b.** $F = 10.21$, $.001 < P$-value $< .01$, reject H_0 and conclude that the model is useful **14.27 a.** $\hat{y} = -859.2 + 23.72minwidth + 225.81maxwidth + 225.24elongation$ **b.** Because adjusted R^2 takes the number of predictors in the model into account **c.** $F = 16.03$, P-value $< .001$, reject H_0 and conclude that the model is useful **14.29 a.** SSResid $= 390.4347$, SSTo $= 1618.2093$, SSRegr $= 1227.7746$ **b.** $R^2 = .759$. This means that 75.9% of the variability in the observed shear strength values can be explained by the fitted model. **c.** $F = 5.039$, $.01 < P$-value $< .05$, reject H_0 and conclude that the model is useful **14.31** $F = 96.64$, P-value $< .001$, reject H_0 and conclude

that the model is useful   **14.35** $\hat{y} = 35.8 - .68x_1 + 1.28x_2$, $F = 18.95$, P-value $< .001$, reject H_0 and conclude that the model is useful   **14.37 a.** $(-.697, -.281)$; With 95% confidence, we can say that the change in the mean value of a vacant lot associated with a 1-unit increase in distance from the city's major east–west thoroughfare is a decrease of somewhere between .281 and .697, assuming all other predictors remain constant.   **b.** $t = -.599$, P-value $\approx .550$, fail to reject H_0 **14.39 a.** $F = 144.36$, P-value $< .001$, reject H_0 and conclude that the model is useful   **b.** $t = 4.33$, P-value ≈ 0, reject H_0 and conclude that the quadratic term is important   **c.** $(72.0626, 72.4658)$ **14.41 a.** .469 is an estimate of the expected change in mean score associated with a 1-unit increase in the student's expected score, assuming time spent studying and GPA are fixed.   **b.** $F = 75.01$, P-value $< .001$, reject H_0 and conclude that the model is useful   **c.** $(2.466, 4.272)$ **d.** 72.856   **e.** $(61.562, 84.150)$ **14.43** $t = 2.22$, P-value $= .028$, reject H_0 and conclude that the interaction term is important   **14.45 a.** $F = 5.47$, $.01 < P$-value $< .05$, reject H_0 and conclude that the model is useful   **b.** $t = .04$, P-value $\approx .924$, fail to reject H_0 and conclude that the interaction term is not needed in the model   **c.** No. The model utility test looks at the predictors as a group. The t test looks at the predictors one at a time and tests to see whether an individual predictor is useful *given* that the other predictors are included in the model.   **14.49 a.** $F = 30.81$, P-value $< .001$, reject H_0 and conclude that the model is useful   **b.** for β_1: $t = 6.57$, P-value $= 0$, reject H_0; for β_2: $t = -7.69$, P-value $= 0$, reject H_0 **c.** $(43.0, 47.92)$ **d.** $(44.0, 47.92)$ **14.53** The model using the three variables x_3, x_9, and x_{10} is a reasonable choice.   **14.55 a.** $F \approx 86$, P-value $< .001$, reject H_0 and conclude that the model is useful   **b.** The predictor added at the first step was smoking habits. At step 2, alcohol consumption was added. No other variables were added to the model.   **14.57 b.** .0567   **c.** return on equity, yes   **d.** no, CEO tenure would be considered first   **e.** P-value $\approx .04$ **14.59** Reasonable choices would be the model with predictors x_2 and x_4 or possibly using x_2, x_3, and x_4. In either case, the set of predictors is not the same as in Exercise 14.58.   **14.63 a.** $F = 12.28$, P-value $< .001$, reject H_0 and conclude that the model is useful   **b.** .5879   **c.** $(.1606, .7554)$ **d.** x_9 would be considered first, and it would be eliminated.   **e.** H_0: $\beta_3 = \beta_4 = \beta_5 = \beta_6 = 0$. None of the procedures in this chapter can be used to test hypotheses of this form.   **14.65 b.** $F = 21.25$, $.001 < P$-value $< .01$, reject H_0 and conclude that the model is useful   **c.** $t = 6.52$, P-value ≈ 0, reject H_0, the quadratic term should not be eliminated   **14.67** Adjusted R^2 will be negative for values of $R^2 < .5$.   **14.69** The model with all four predictors was fit. The variable *age at loading* was eliminated at step 2, because it had the t ratio closest to 0 and it was between -2 and 2. The variable *time* was deleted at step 3 because it had the t ratio closest to 0 and it was between -2 and 2. No other variables could be eliminated from the model. The final model uses predictors *slab thickness* and *load*.   **14.71 b.** The claim is reasonable because 14 is close to where the curve has its highest value.   **14.73 a.** $\hat{y} = 1.56 + .0237x_1 - .000249x_2$ **b.** $F = 70.66$, P-value $< .001$, reject H_0 and conclude that the model is useful   **c.** $R^2 = .865$. This means that 86.5% of the variability in observed profit margin values can be explained by the fitted model. $s_e = .0533$. This a typical prediction error (distance of a predicted value from the true mean value).   **d.** No. Neither x_1 nor x_2 can be eliminated from the model.

CHAPTER 15   **15.1 a.** $.001 < P$-value $< .01$ **b.** P-value $> .10$ **c.** P-value $= .01$ **d.** P-value $< .001$ **e.** $.05 < P$-value $< .10$ **f.** $.01 < P$-value $< .05$ (Using $df_1 = 4$ and $df_2 = 60$ in F table)   **15.3 a.** H_0: $\mu_1 = \mu_2 = \mu_3 = \mu_4$, H_a: at least two of the μ's are different   **b.** $.01 < P$-value $< .05$, fail to reject H_0 **c.** $.01 < P$-value $< .05$; conclusion would be the same   **15.5 a.** 1996 and 1997 boxplots are similar, but the 1998 boxplot lies entirely to the right of those for 1996 and 1997, indicating higher prices in 1998. The boxplot for 1998 also has a longer tail on the upper end than the other two boxplots.   **b.** $F = 6.83$, P-value $\approx .01$, reject H_0 **15.7** $F = 1.71$, P-value $> .10$, fail to reject H_0 **15.9** $F = 0.70$, P-value $> .10$, fail to reject H_0 **15.11** $F = 1.895$, $.05 < P$-value $< .10$, fail to reject H_0 **15.13** $F = 1.70$, P-value $> .10$, fail to reject H_0 **15.15** $F = 2.56$, $.05 < P$-value $< .10$, fail to reject H_0 **15.17** $F = 6.97$, $.001 < P$-value $< .01$, reject H_0 **15.19** Since the intervals for $\mu_1 - \mu_2$ and $\mu_1 - \mu_3$ do not contain zero, μ_1 is judged to be different from μ_2 and μ_3. Since the interval for $\mu_2 - \mu_3$ contains zero, μ_2 and μ_3 are not significantly different. Statement (**iii**) is the correct choice.

15.21

Fabric	3	2	5	4	1
Mean	10.5	11.63	12.3	14.96	16.35

15.23 No differences are detected. This is in agreement with the results of Exercise 15.7.

15.25

Group	Simultaneous	Sequential	Control
Mean	$\bar{x}_3$	$\bar{x}_2$	$\bar{x}_1$

15.27 Mean water loss for 4 hours of fumigation is significantly different from the other means. The mean water loss for 2 hours of fumigation is different from that for 16 and 0 hours but not from 8 hours. The mean water losses for duration 16, 0, and 8 hours are not significantly different from one another. **15.29 a.** $F = 3.30$, $.01 < P\text{-value} < .05$, reject H_0 **b.** No significant differences are identified by the T–K method.

15.31 a.

Source	df	SS	MS	F
Treatments	2	11.7	5.85	.37
Blocks	4	113.5	28.375	
Error	8	125.6	15.7	
Total	14	250.8		

b. $F = .37$, $P\text{-value} > .10$, fail to reject H_0 **15.33** $F = 79.4$, $P\text{-value} < .001$, reject H_0
15.35 a. Other environmental factors (amount of rainfall, number of days of cloudy weather, average daily temperature, etc.) vary from year to year. Using a randomized block design helps control for variation in these other factors. **b.** $F = 15.03$, $.01 < P\text{-value} < .05$, reject H_0

c.

Application rate	1	2	3
Mean	138.33	152.33	156.33

15.37 $F = .868$, $P\text{-value} > .10$, fail to reject H_0 **15.39 b.** The lines are very close to parallel. The plot does not show evidence of an interaction between gender and type of odor.
15.41 a. The plot does suggest an interaction between peer group and self-esteem. **b.** The change in average response is greater for the low-self-esteem group than it is for the high-self-esteem group when changing from low to high peer group. The authors are correct in their statement. **15.43** test for interaction: $F = 2.18$, $P\text{-value} > .10$, fail to reject H_0; test for main effect of size: $F = 4.00$, $.01 < P\text{-value} < .05$, fail to reject H_0; test for main effect of species: $F = 4.36$, $.05 < P\text{-value} < .10$, fail to reject H_0 **15.45 a.** $F = 0.70$, $P\text{-value} > .10$, fail to reject H_0 **b.** $F = 20.53$, $P\text{-value} < .001$, reject H_0 **c.** $F = 2.59$, $.05 < P\text{-value} < .10$, fail to reject H_0 **15.47** test for interaction: $F < 1$, $P\text{-value} > .10$, fail to reject H_0; test for main effect of A: $F = 4.99$, $.01 < P\text{-value} < .05$, reject H_0; test for main effect of B: $F = 4.81$, $.01 < P\text{-value} < .05$, reject H_0 **15.49 a.** test for interaction: $F = 0.21$, $P\text{-value} > .10$, fail to reject H_0 **b.** test for main effect of race: $F = 5.57$, $.01 < P\text{-value} < .05$, fail to reject H_0 **c.** test for main effect of gender: $F = 1.89$, $P\text{-value} > .10$, fail to reject H_0 **15.51** test for main effect of rate: $F = 76.14$, $P\text{-value} < .001$, reject H_0; test for main effect of soil type: $F = 54.14$, $P\text{-value} < .001$, reject H_0.

Soil type	Ramina	Konini	Wainui
Mean	10.217	20.957	24.557

15.53 $F = 4.13$, $P\text{-value} < .001$, reject H_0
15.55 $F = 5.56$, $.001 < P\text{-value} < .01$, reject H_0

Group	Apathetic	Conservative	Erratic	Strategic
Mean	2.96	4.91	5.05	8.74

15.57 a. $F = 6.24$, $.001 < P$-value $< .01$, reject H_0
b.

Storage period	4	5	2	1
Mean	4.902	4.917	4.923	4.923

15.59 test for interaction: $F = 0.44$, P-value $> .10$, fail to reject H_0; test for main effect of oxygen: $F = 2.76$, P-value $> .10$, fail to reject H_0; test for main effect of sugar: $F = 13.29$, $.001 < P$-value $< .01$, reject H_0 **15.61** test for interaction: $F = 8.67$, $.001 < P$-value $< .01$, reject H_0; significant interaction, so no tests for main effects should be performed
15.63 $F = 0.907$, P-value $> .10$, fail to reject H_0 **15.65** $F = 3.23$, $.01 < P$-value $< .05$, fail to reject H_0

Index

t critical values

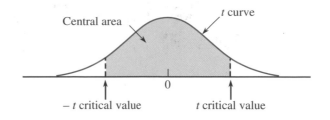

Central area

t curve

−t critical value

0

t critical value

Central area captured:		.80	.90	.95	.98	.99	.998	.999
Confidence level:		**80%**	**90%**	**95%**	**98%**	**99%**	**99.8%**	**99.9%**
	1	3.08	6.31	12.71	31.82	63.66	318.31	636.62
	2	1.89	2.92	4.30	6.97	9.93	23.33	31.60
	3	1.64	2.35	3.18	4.54	5.84	10.21	12.92
	4	1.53	2.13	2.78	3.75	4.60	7.17	8.61
	5	1.48	2.02	2.57	3.37	4.03	5.89	6.86
	6	1.44	1.94	2.45	3.14	3.71	5.21	5.96
	7	1.42	1.90	2.37	3.00	3.50	4.79	5.41
	8	1.40	1.86	2.31	2.90	3.36	4.50	5.04
	9	1.38	1.83	2.26	2.82	3.25	4.30	4.78
	10	1.37	1.81	2.23	2.76	3.17	4.14	4.59
	11	1.36	1.80	2.20	2.72	3.11	4.03	4.44
	12	1.36	1.78	2.18	2.68	3.06	3.93	4.32
	13	1.35	1.77	2.16	2.65	3.01	3.85	4.22
	14	1.35	1.76	2.15	2.62	2.98	3.79	4.14
	15	1.34	1.75	2.13	2.60	2.95	3.73	4.07
	16	1.34	1.75	2.12	2.58	2.92	3.69	4.02
Degrees of	17	1.33	1.74	2.11	2.57	2.90	3.65	3.97
freedom	18	1.33	1.73	2.10	2.55	2.88	3.61	3.92
	19	1.33	1.73	2.09	2.54	2.86	3.58	3.88
	20	1.33	1.73	2.09	2.53	2.85	3.55	3.85
	21	1.32	1.72	2.08	2.52	2.83	3.53	3.82
	22	1.32	1.72	2.07	2.51	2.82	3.51	3.79
	23	1.32	1.71	2.07	2.50	2.81	3.49	3.77
	24	1.32	1.71	2.06	2.49	2.80	3.47	3.75
	25	1.32	1.71	2.06	2.49	2.79	3.45	3.73
	26	1.32	1.71	2.06	2.48	2.78	3.44	3.71
	27	1.31	1.70	2.05	2.47	2.77	3.42	3.69
	28	1.31	1.70	2.05	2.47	2.76	3.41	3.67
	29	1.31	1.70	2.05	2.46	2.76	3.40	3.66
	30	1.31	1.70	2.04	2.46	2.75	3.39	3.65
	40	1.30	1.68	2.02	2.42	2.70	3.31	3.55
	60	1.30	1.67	2.00	2.39	2.66	3.23	3.46
	120	1.29	1.66	1.98	2.36	2.62	3.16	3.37
z critical values	∞	1.28	1.645	1.96	2.33	2.58	3.09	3.29